THE INSIDERS' GUIDE® TO Austin

THE INSIDERS'® GUIDE TO

Austin

by

Cam Rossie

&

Hilary Hylton

The Insiders' Guide®
An imprint of Falcon® Publishing Inc.
A Landmark Communications company
P.O. Box 1718
Helena, MT 59624
(800) 582-2665
www.insiders.com

Sales and Marketing: Falcon Publishing, Inc.
P.O. Box 1718
Helena, MT 59624
(800) 582-2665
www.falconguide.com

Advertising: Falcon Publishing, Inc.
150 W. Brambleton Ave.
Norfolk, VA 23510
(757) 446-2933
rwalsh@infi.net

•

FIRST EDITION
1st printing

•

•

Printed in the United States
of America

•

Publications from *The Insiders' Guide®* series are available at special discounts for bulk purchases for sales promotions, premiums or fundraisings. Special editions, including personalized covers, can be created in large quantities for special needs.
For more information, please contact Falcon Publishing.

ISBN 1-57380-075-9

Preface

Austin!

Just the name evokes so many images. Music. High Tech. Universities. Government. Movies. Research. The Hills. The Lakes. The Springs. Independence! Opportunity! Austin is all those things, and much more, as you'll soon discover.

Riding on nothing more than beauty, its perch on the edge of a wild frontier and on the determination of its citizens, Austin became the capital of the Republic, and then of the state of Texas, a vast territory that reaches from the Mexican border almost halfway to Canada. Like other Texans, Austinites who shaped this region developed a kinship with the land and with one another. To be a Texan is a definite distinction. To add Austinite — now that's the shine on the star.

Like many Austinites, we are not natives. Although Austin is one city that quickly becomes your own, no matter where you've lived before. The familiar bumper sticker "I wasn't born in Texas, but I got here as soon as I could" goes double for Austin. We're speaking from experience when we give these words of caution, especially for you who've come for just a visit: Austin sneaks up on you unexpectedly, like a sudden shower on a hot summer day. It will capture your heart as quickly as a dry field blossoms into wildflowers. Once you've gotten swept up in the energy of this city or given in to our peaceful pastimes, it's hard to leave. Austin is clever that way. It's old, and it's new, and every minute it's got something different to offer you. That's part of the Austin mystique.

Perhaps you've come to see for yourself what it is about Austin that causes people to perk up when they hear the name. We hope you'll find this guide useful in that regard. Within these pages we've shared our ideas about the people and places, the sounds and the scenery that contribute to Austin's unique style. We've sought to give you a deeper understanding of who we are by telling you where Austin has been and where it's headed as this booming region endeavors to define its future and preserve its acclaimed quality of life.

It's hard to argue with the national magazines that have rated Austin among the top cities for living and conducting business. Citing Austin's "emergence as a hotbed for high-tech startup firms," the prestigious *Fortune* magazine listed Austin as "The Best City for Business in North America" in its November 23, 1998 issue. "Austin has always been the sort of town where the '60s never really died, where creativity was encouraged, and free spirits were nurtured," *Fortune* praised. Indeed, Austinites are warmhearted, outgoing people who tolerate about anything but encroachment on our stunning natural environment or challenge to our way of life. Our music scene is so hot that we call ourselves "The Live Music Capital of the World." Our vibrant film industry, which includes local actors and directors who are making it big, is luring more and more internationally known stars and directors to Austin. At any given time there are a dozen or more stage productions to enjoy as well as art museums and galleries to visit and poetry readings to attend. Our countless sports enthusiasts, the bikers, boaters, runners, golfers and swimmers, keep Austin humming with their passion.

The University of Texas contributes much more than character and economic drive. UT, along with our other colleges and universities, draw leading scholars and researchers to Austin and offer our students and the public countless educational opportunities and chances to hear world-renowned speakers. Our bookstores and libraries are abuzz day and night. It's no surprise, then, that Austin is considered a literary capital as well as the center of our massive state government. Along with thousands of jobs, the vigorous high-tech industry adds another dimension to Austin's intellectual community. The reward in living and working in Austin comes in knowing that no matter what challenges the day brings, there is a fascinating, fun, beautiful, easygoing city right outside the door.

Austin's amazing ability to combine that vitality — that feeling that anything is possible here — with a sense of tranquility is among its greatest attributes. There's plenty of space to get away: lying on the beach at Lake Travis, strolling along a wooded trail, flying a kite atop breathtaking Mount Bonnell, taking a cool dip in Barton Springs, picnicking at the park, exploring the natural wonders of the Hill Country, canoeing along Town Lake.

Don't take our word for it, though. Austin is a city that must be experienced firsthand. This book is meant to point you in the right directions. For those of you who've come to live, congratulations, you've chosen well. If you're here as a visitor, enjoy your Austin experience. Like we said, however, beware of its captivating charm.

About the Authors

Cam Rossie

Cam Rossie is a journalist and freelance writer who started her professional career while still a university student, working as a reporter, copy editor and editor for daily and weekly newspapers in the Midwest. A former domestic and foreign correspondent for The Associated Press news service, her news and feature articles have appeared in newspapers throughout the United States and abroad.

Her career with the AP began in Nebraska and later took her to New Mexico, Texas' Rio Grande Valley and New York City. In 1984 she was chosen to open a new AP bureau in Northern Mexico. From her base of operations in Monterrey, Cam covered the U.S.-Mexico border from coast to coast, as well as other regions of Mexico and Central America. She is fluent in Spanish and is an accomplished public speaker who has lectured on journalism issues in the United States and Mexico.

Cam, an Iowa native, realized at an early age that she was born to travel. She has visited more than 25 countries and trekked the United States from coast to coast and border to border. An international journalism scholarship took her to Caracas, Venezuela, where she lived and studied for more than a year.

She met her husband, Cliff Simon, while working in Mexico and decided to stay — for a decade. Their daughter, Quint, was born in Monterrey. Austin and the Texas Hill Country, however, had been calling to Cam since her first trip to nearby Lake Travis on a camping trip in the mid-1980s. She and her family spent many enjoyable vacations exploring the Capital City area, savoring the local music and cultural scenes and hiking the splendid hills before they decided to make Austin their home in 1993. She's amazed that Austin, with its natural beauty and extraordinary people, remained such a well-kept secret for so long.

Hilary Hylton

Hilary Hylton is a freelance writer and author whose work covers a variety of topics including business, social issues, personalities, government, politics, cuisine and travel. Her work has been published in national, international and regional publications.

Hilary has lived in Austin since 1977, watching it grow and change. She has written about many aspects of life in Austin — its food, politics, lifestyles and business for both Texas and national publications. Hilary is a freelance reporter for *TIME* magazine and Reuters, the international news service. In addition, she has written for the Sunday magazines and feature sections of several major daily newspapers, including the *Los Angeles Times*. Her magazine articles also have appeared in major city, business, lifestyle and airline magazines — features on food, travel, business and political personalities.

Prior to freelancing, she worked as a journalist for several Florida and Texas newspapers. Her work was honored with a number of awards, including Texas Star Reporter by the Austin Headliners' Club. Hilary is also the author of a guidebook, *Texas Monthly's Mexico: A Completely Up-to-date Guide to an Extraordinary Country*.

Hilary is married to Peter Silva, an award-winning photographer represented by Zuma Press, an international photo agency based in California. Peter and Hilary moved to Texas in 1974 after meeting while they were both working at *The Palm Beach Post* in Florida. Peter is a native of Manhattan, Kansas, while Hilary was born in Cheshire, England, and moved with her family to the United States as a teenager. They have two dogs, sisters Maddie and Buttons, Australian shepherd/Border collie mix, and a new kitten named Sam who serves as a substitute sheep for Maddie and Buttons.

Hilary's personal interests include reading history, armchair travel, gardening, cooking and collecting cookbooks. Her culinary interests have led to stints in the local media as a food columnist for a magazine and a restaurant reviewer for the *Austin American-Statesman*.

Acknowledgments

Cam Rossie

The finest words a writer and researcher can hear are, "Yes, I have that information for you." In Austin, one might even say it's music to the ears. What a thrill it is, after searching and calling and wading through files, to finally find the person who holds the exact piece of information you are seeking. The people recognized here made my day, time and time again. To all of those fine Austin Insiders who shared their insight and wisdom, I am most grateful. Through their eyes I discovered new dimensions of Austin and grew to appreciate this exciting region even more than before. The information they provided was complete and accurate. Any misinterpretations that appear in this book, however, are mine alone.

I am deeply obliged to Jim Bob McMillan, executive director of the Austin Writers' League, and Sally Baker, the league's associate director, for taking the time to meet with me and for allowing me to share their resources; to Michael Barnes, arts critic for the *Austin American-Statesman*, and Fiona Cherbak, community relations coordinator for Borders Books & Music, for providing outstanding advice and pointing me in the right direction; to John Kunz, owner and resident music expert at Waterloo Records, and Cyndi Hughes, director of the Texas Book Festival, for giving so freely of their time and expertise; and to Jennifer Hill of MEM Hubble Communications, Cathy Osborne of Barnes & Noble Booksellers and David Hutts of Book People for their generous assistance.

Ann Ciccolella, executive director of Austin Circle of Theaters, Sue Fawver, executive director of the Austin Visual Arts Association and Lisa Byrd, managing director of Dance Umbrella, all bestowed pearls of wisdom about their respective artistic arenas. I am eternally grateful to each of them and to their outstanding organizations.

It was such a pleasure to work with Casey Monahan and his incredible staff at the Texas Music Office. They shared their files, their expertise and their enthusiasm for the world of Austin music. I am forever in their debt. Rob Patterson, a freelance writer and columnist for the *Austin American-Statesman*, offered his considerable knowledge of the fast-paced world of Austin radio. Tom Copeland, director of the Texas Film Commission, Gary Bond, film liaison of the Austin Convention and Visitors Bureau, and Ed Crowell, editor of the *Statesman*'s *XL* entertainment section, all took the time to assist with this project. My deepest appreciation to them all.

Art Bussey of the Texas Department of Protective and Regulatory Services, Dwayne Jones of the Texas Historical Commission, Louanne Aponte of Austin Families, Inc., Glen Moorman at Barnes & Noble Booksellers, and Martha Peters, program coordinator for the excellent Art in Public Places program for the City of Austin Parks and Recreation Department, all came through with information just when I needed it.

I would also like to acknowledge the employees of the various media relations offices at The University of Texas for taking the time to respond to my queries. And I must offer a note of appreciation to outstanding Austin photographer Paul Traves, of f-16 Photography, who took my picture for the back of this book.

No work of this magnitude could properly be completed without relying on the wit and wisdom of those writers who paved the way. I am indebted to the authors of the following books whose excellent work provided invaluable information for this project: *Austin: An Illustrated History,* by David C. Humphrey; *Austin: An Historical Portrait*, by Larry Willoughby; *Power, Money & the People: The Making of Modern Austin*, by Anthony M. Orum; *The Raven*, the Pulitzer-prize winning biography of Sam Houston, by Marquis James; *The Improbable Rise of Redneck Rock*, by Jan Reid; *Austin City Limits*, by Clifford Endres; *Texas Music*, by Rick Kostner; *Stevie Ray Vaughan: Caught in the Crossfire,* by Joe Nick Patoski and Bill Crawford; and *Threadgill's: The Cookbook*, by Eddie Wilson. The *Austin American-Statesman* supplement, "Austin 1839-1989," by John Edward Weems, also held nuggets of gold.

I offer particular recognition, also, to all the journalists whose brains I picked while scouring the archives of the *Austin American-Statesman*, *The Austin Chronicle*, *Texas Monthly* magazine and many other fine periodicals around the city. I must acknowledge the consideration of all the employees of the Austin History Center and the Austin Public Library who took the time to answer my queries. Their dedication is exemplary.

I would especially like to thank my coauthor on *The Insiders' Guide® to Austin*, Hilary Hylton. Hilary is a journalist of the first class, whose knowledge of Central Texas and high regard for this region shine through page after page. She is an Insiders' Insider, an esteemed colleague and a true friend. To our editor, Tammy Kennon, a former Austinite who asked the questions and labored behind the scenes to make this book happen. And to Hilary's husband, photographer Peter Silva, for his work in amassing the excellent collection of photographs that bring our stories to life.

This project could never have been completed without the constructive advice and abundant support offered by my close friends and family: Denise Noal, who always kept her eyes and ears open for me, seemed to know intuitively just when I needed a little encouragement and was always there to lend a helping hand; Susana Hayward of the *San Antonio Express-News* offered on-the-spot expertise whenever I called; Patsy and Phillip Christie of Dallas provided insightful information on their hometown; Sara and Eric Simon are much more than Houston experts; they are big supporters — and great in-laws.

My own family in far-off places came through time and time again with suggestions and encouragement. Thanks especially to my brother, Scott Rossi, and sister-in-law, Susannah Hardaway, for providing advice on matters of the arts. My mother, Rose Rossie, and sister, Cindy DeSantiago, were always there when I needed inspiration and support. I am so fortunate to be surrounded by such extraordinary people.

Of all those who contributed immensely to this project, only two were forced to forego living a normal life for the duration. Yet they remained cheerfully optimistic and displayed amazing resilience in the face of deadline pressures and my occasional fits of anxiety. There just aren't enough words to thank them both: my daughter, Quint Simon, a student at Doss Elementary School, and my astute, multi-talented husband, Cliff Simon. Throughout the long months of this endeavor, Quint persevered as my No. 1 assistant, researcher and cheerleader. I am rewarded daily by her patience, understanding and intelligence, and by her radiant smiles. She makes my life such a joy. Cliff's unwavering enthusiasm for this project never failed to dazzle me. He supplied priceless Insider advice, constantly managed to produce just the piece of information I lacked and always mustered the energy to help me explore just one more intriguing spot. His support extends far beyond the pages of this book. For all of the above, and so much more, I thank my lucky stars for them both.

Hilary Hylton

Austin has been home for 21 years now, but working on this book has offered me an opportunity to view the city through a wider perspective. My coauthor, Cam, has made that experience even more stimulating and interesting because of her enthusiasm for her new home. Cam is a true professional whose affability and thoroughness made for smooth sailing on this cooperative effort. I also want to thank Tammy Kennon and the staff at Insiders' Publishing for their professional approach to this project. My husband, Peter A. Silva, who contributed many of the photographs for the book, also was an invaluable fountain of tips and insights on our hometown.

Finally, I want to acknowledge that it was the people of Austin and their unbounded creativity that made this project fun. Austin is a city filled with the unique, and it is always a pleasure to point out the fresh, the singular and the legendary to newcomers and visitors. A tip of the hat to all those who have made Austin special and are working hard to keep it that way.

Table of Contents

Area Overview 1
Politics and Perspectives 11
History 19
Getting Here & Getting Around 33
Hotels and Motels 43
Bed & Breakfasts and Country Inns 67
Restaurants 85
Nightlife 131
The Music Scene 151
Shopping 189
Attractions 221
Kidstuff 255
Annual Events and Festivals 279
The Arts 303
The Literary Scene 331
Parks and Recreation 357
Golf 397
Spectator Sports 405
Daytrips and Weekend Getaways 419
Neighborhoods and Real Estate 453
The Senior Scene 471
Healthcare and Wellness 481
Higher Education 489
Schools and Childcare 501
Media 525
Worship 543
Index of Advertisers 549
Index 550

Directory of Maps

Austin Area Overview xii
Downtown Austin xiii
Greater Austin xiv
University of Texas xv

Austin Area Overview

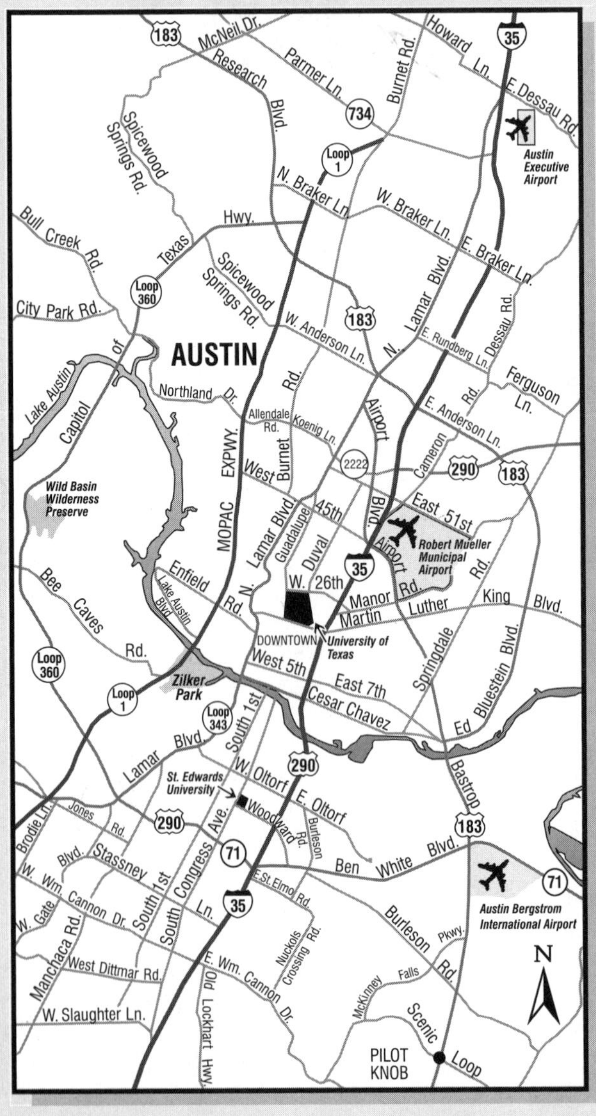

Downtown Austin

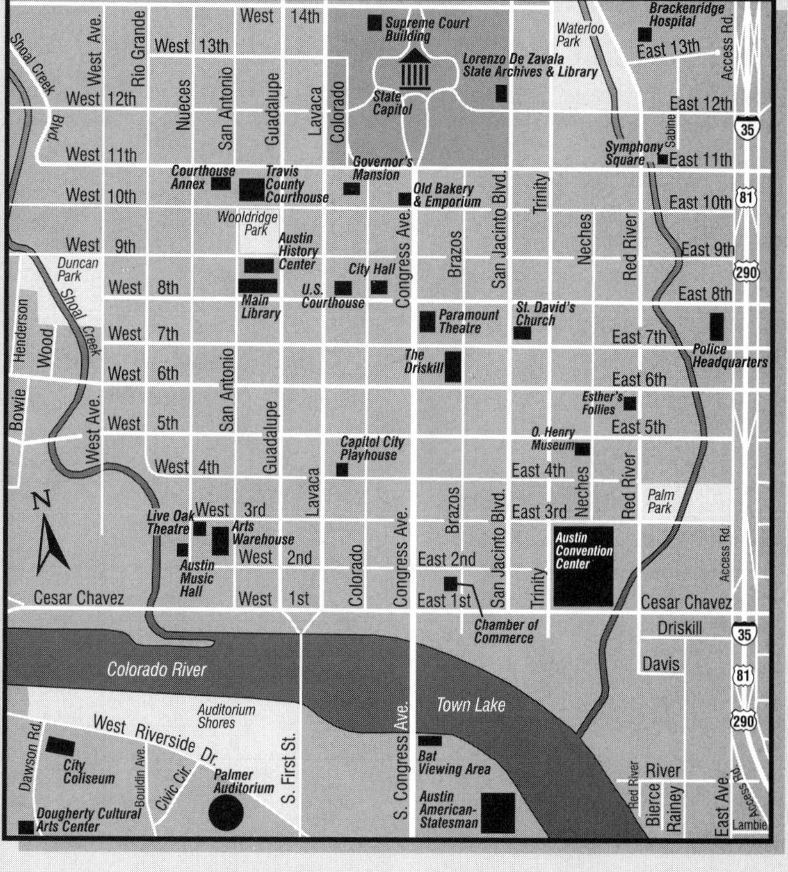

Greater Austin

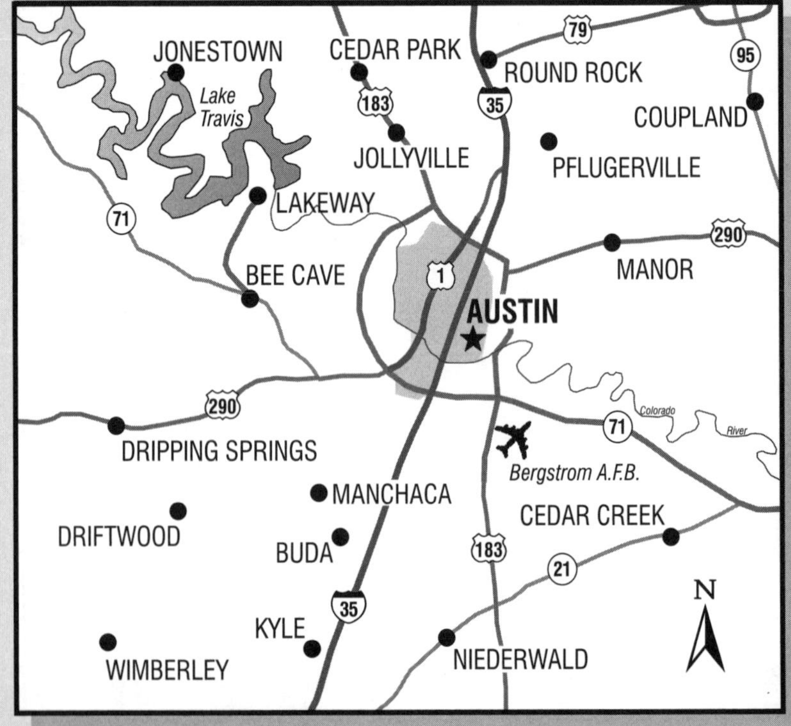

University of Texas

1. Art Building and Gallery
2. College of Business Administration Building
3. Jesse H. Jones Communication Center
4. Disch-Falk Field
5. Frank C. Erwin, Jr., Special Events Center
6. Huntington Art Gallery in the Harry Ransom Center
7. Lyndon B. Johnson Auditorium, Library and Museum
8. Main Building and Tower
9. Bates Recital Hall
10. Performing Arts Center
11. T. S. Painter Hall
12. Perry-Castañeda Library (Main Library)
13. Robert Lee Moore Hall
14. Lyndon B. Johnson School of Public Affairs
15. Darrell K. Royal-Texas Memorial Stadium
16. Joe C. Thompson Conference Center
17. Texas Memorial Museum
18. Texas Union

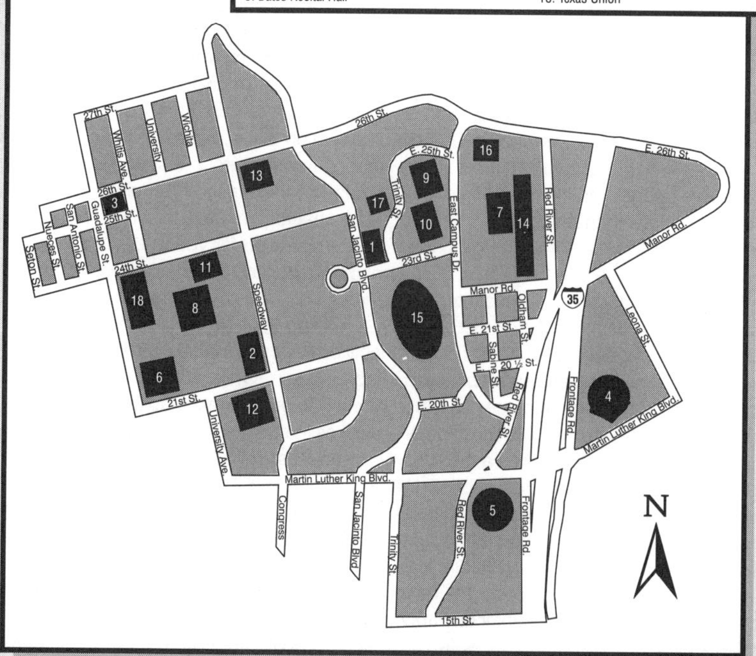

How to Use This Book

Whether you're planning to stay in Austin for a night, a fortnight or the rest of your life, this book will guide you to, and through, the best the Capital City has to offer in more than two dozen areas of interest. *The Insiders' Guide® to Austin* is arranged by categories that appeal to both tourists and newcomers, and can be useful whether you've just arrived or are only contemplating a visit or a move to Austin. Longtime residents may even discover a new thing or two about our city.

Our challenge in writing this book was to provide solid information and arrange it suitably so that you can map out a tour of Austin according to your own interests. It's up to you whether you take in these pages in one big gulp or choose to savor them slowly, chapter by chapter, as you make your way around town. Whatever your style, *The Insiders' Guide® to Austin* is meant to be used and used again as you delve deeper into the treasures of our Capital City. More than anything, we've designed this book to answer that age-old question: Where can I go to find . . . ?

Within these pages you'll encounter detailed descriptions of many of our most popular Restaurants, Attractions, Hotels and Motels, Bed and Breakfasts, and Resorts as well as extensive listings of great places to shop and fun things to do with the kids. The chapter devoted to The Music Scene was a must, as you'll see, and we've dedicated another to Austin Nightlife. We've described our dynamic Literary Scene and given you an introduction to Austin's great Arts community. Nature lovers and outdoor types will discover the best that Austin has to offer in our chapter on Parks and Recreation.

For a wealth of information on our diverse periodicals, and radio and television stations, we've included a chapter on the Media. Newcomers will want to take special note of our chapters on Neighborhoods, The Senior Scene, Worship, and Healthcare and Wellness. Our chapter on Schools and Child Care includes information on private schools and all 10 public school districts in and around Austin, including those in our neighboring communities. Of course, no story of Austin would be complete without an Insider's view of the capital's political personality. Don't miss our Politics and Perspectives chapter to find out what makes Austin tick.

Because much of the subject matter begs to be included in more than one chapter, we've noted where to look in the book for further information on a particular topic. Austin is loaded with resources, and we regret that we could not include every choice available in each chapter. We have, however, provided a solid foundation for you in all our categories and have pointed out additional resource materials that may provide more information.

Finding your way around town will probably be the first challenge you face upon arriving in Austin. While Austin does have some great natural and manufactured boundaries, such as the Colorado River and our main highway arteries, the layout can be confusing due to our unique Hill Country terrain and the fact that Austin isn't too keen on east-west thoroughfares. No two people agree exactly on how to divide Austin into geographic regions, especially now that the city has grown so much. (The area that is still referred to today as West Austin, for example, is now in Central

Austin, while a new West Austin is, well, farther west.)

Start your tour of Austin by reading our chapter on Getting Here and Getting Around. In this chapter we've explained the boundaries we use in this book to divide the city into 10 regions: Central, South Central, North, South, East, West, Northeast, Northwest, Southeast and Southwest. In some chapters we've subdivided these regions even further. In the Hotels and Motels chapter, for instance, you will find an extensive listing for accommodations under the Interstate 35 Corridor heading. Because there are so many Attractions in Central Austin, we've divided that region into Downtown, The University of Texas and Central Austin. Some chapters will also include an additional listing for Lake Travis, and you'll also find some information on Round Rock, Pflugerville and Cedar Park. The boundaries we've described may not be universal boundaries, but they seemed the most realistic for us, and convenient for you. Refer to the maps we've provided to get started on your Austin adventure.

We've made every effort to provide you with the most accurate, up-to-date information in all categories. However, if you discover that your opinion differs from ours or that we've missed an important option, please feel free to send your comments or suggestions to our headquarters. Direct your letters to Insiders' Publishing, P.O. Box 2057, Manteo, NC 27954. Or you can go online to the Insiders' Guide Online website at www.insiders.com. Our website includes a page for comments. We'd love to hear from you.

Anyone who has visited Austin in the spring when the bluebonnets and Indian paintbrushes are in bloom leaves with a much-changed image of Texas.

Area Overview

"Where do you live?" folks on planes sometimes ask us. "Austin, Texas," we say. Nine times out of ten the questioner smiles, sighs and says, "Lucky you."

Austin gets good press. In the last two decades the city has been touted as a top place to live by numerous magazines. Perhaps the most overused adjective in all this positive coverage is "laid-back." But it fits. After all, this is a city where you can get by with one or two pairs of pantyhose a year or keep your tie rack in the back of the closet.

As Mayor Kirk Watson once described Austin to us in an interview, "Austin is a city of boots and suits, hippies and nerds, all in the same boardroom . . . a city that allows almost ironic contradictions — at the same time we boast that we are the Live Music Capital of the World, we also boast we are Silicon Hills."

Laid-back, but on the high-tech cutting edge, cherishing the past, but charting the future. That dichotomy makes Austin an exciting, sometimes challenging place to live. We are embracing the future, yet looking longingly at the past, and, as the mayor told us, so far each new wave of Austinites thinks they got here just in time to enjoy the real Austin.

Austin is a mecca for musicians and movie makers, software engineers and hardware wizards, entrepreneurs and investors, artists and artisans, intellectuals and teachers, political activists and environmentalists, and lots of hardworking, everyday Texans who labor to make this city flourish. More than half a million people call themselves Austinites these days, but there is still a neighborly feel about Austin and a notion that much of what goes on here is authentic.

As Austin has grown in both population and acreage, the pivotal question has been how can Austin stay Austin, yet flourish. The answer, so far, has come from within. Homegrown is the key here — whether it is homegrown businesses such as Dell Computer and Whole Foods Markets or homegrown restaurants such as Threadgill's and Jeffrey's, Austin's creative juices flow from the ground up. Franchise and chain operations, national corporations and international businesses are represented in Austin, and they are growing in number; but, for the most part, they opt to adapt an Austin face, and often are overshadowed when viewed side by side with Austin originals.

This makes Austin a great place to live and to visit. Despite all its attributes, Austin has avoided being labeled a tourist town. Visitors are drawn to Austin not by a single, large attraction, a Disney World or a Fisherman's Wharf, but by the ambiance of Austin. Consequently, we also are relatively free of touristy bric-a-brac, restaurants and other sites that attract only out-of-towners. So whether you're visiting Sixth Street or stopping in for some spicy Tex-Mex food or barbecue, you will find yourself among the locals.

Austin's Many Faces

The population of Austin is diverse and growing more so every year as new residents join the Austin melting pot. According to the U.S. Census Bureau, 12.4 percent of the city's residents are African-American, 23 percent Hispanic, and 3 percent Asian. Approximately 7 percent of the city's residents are older than 65. About 9 percent of Austin's residents are foreign-born, and 23 percent speak a language other than English at home.

The percentage of adults with college degrees stands at 35 percent, fourth place among 77 U.S. cities with a population of 200,000 or more. The median income in Austin in 1996 was $34,000, and only 4.5 percent of households received public assistance, ranking 72nd out of those 77 cities.

One startling statistic is that the Austin labor force increased 44 percent in the decade from 1980 to 1990, and in midsummer 1998, unemployment rates stood at less than 3 percent. Austin residents are predominantly young, diverse, dynamic and hardworking; perhaps that is why the Austin lifestyle is characterized by a love for the outdoors and a lively interest in the latest music and art. But there is also a fondness for old Texas traditions; witness the abundance of annual events dedicated to cultural traditions (see our Annual Events and Festivals chapter).

While the past is celebrated, cultural diversity is unfolding at a furious pace in Austin. Restaurants and shops reflecting diverse cultural origins are growing in number. In a city where 25 years ago the choice of restaurants was relatively limited and dominated by Tex-Mex, barbecue and homestyle cooking, residents and visitors can now choose from a wide variety of cuisines, often presented as "fusion" cuisine by one of the city's hot, young chefs. There is a palpable sense of exploration in the air as the city adopts and absorbs a multitude of influences, translating them into an authentic Austin experience.

The Great Outdoors

No description of Austin would be complete without an ode to the area's physical surroundings. Forget those clichéd Texas movie images you have seen in the Westerns. Austin is a city where trees and plants abound, live oaks and pecans, cedar elms and redbuds shade city streets, and city ordinances make it illegal to cut down trees of a certain diameter. Wildflowers, native plants and grasses provide a year-round palette for both gardeners and Mother Nature as she paints the wild and natural areas of Central Texas.

Anyone who has visited Austin in the spring when the bluebonnets and Indian paintbrushes are in bloom leaves with a much-changed image of Texas. Hill Country pastures cry out for the brush of Monet, while the grassy banks along city freeways and country roads have been painted with a riot of color thanks to the state highway department's wildflower planting program.

The parade of wildflowers continues to bloom through the summer and into the fall. Every visitor and resident should make a pilgrimage to the Lady Bird Johnson Wildflower Center in Southwest Austin to take in the beauty, learn about native plants and pay personal homage to the former First Lady who made saving American wildflowers a personal crusade (see our Attractions chapter).

Other examples of Austin natural wonders include Barton Springs, the spring-fed natural swimming pool that sits in the heart of the city's large downtown greenbelt, Zilker Park (see our Parks and Recreation chapter). Then there are the bats: North America's largest urban colony of Mexican freetail bats lives under the Congress Avenue bridge spring through fall, and their nightly flight in search of bug dinners draws crowds to the shores of Town Lake in downtown Austin (see our Attractions chapter). To the west of the city are the Highland Lakes, a chain of artificial lakes that stretch more than 150 miles, encompass 56,000 acres of water and offer 700 miles of shoreline, making up the greatest concentration of fresh water in Texas. A network of lake and state parks, county and city parks plus nature preserves and greenbelts surround Austin and provide green havens within the city limits (see our Parks and Recreation chapter).

In addition to a beautiful environment, Austinites also enjoy a generally benign climate. There are a few weeks in summer, notably late July and August, when the midday sun can take its toll, but since most buildings and cars in the city are air-conditioned, even those days are bearable. In winter, there can be some brief spells of cold

INSIDERS' TIP

Local weather forecasts are available from a variety of sources, including four local television stations: KTBC-TV, Channel 7; KVUE-TV, Channel 24; KXAN-TV, Channel 36; and KEYE-TV, Channel 42 (see our Media chapter).

Texas Pronunciation Guide

"Texas — It's a whole other country!" Turns out the ad slogan used to promote Texas as a tourist destination is right, at least when it comes to the local lingo. Newcomers and visitors to Austin can be confounded by the local eccentricities in language, so we have developed this handy primer:

Close-up

Balcones (Bal-CONE-niss) — A geological fault line that runs north-south through the city. This is just the first of several Spanish names that are not pronounced the way you were taught in high school Spanish.

Boerne (BURN-nee, rhymes with Bert and Ernie) — A small town southwest of Austin noted for its dude ranches. Just as many local names have their roots in Mexican culture, many also derive from the German settlers who made their homes in the Hill Country in the last century.

Bowie (BOO!-ee) — As in that buoy in the water. A hero of the Alamo Jim Bowie gave his name to both a knife and an Austin high school.

Brazos (BRAA-ziss) — A Texas river that runs through Waco and the name of a downtown Austin street. All seven major Texas rivers give their names to downtown, north-south streets in Austin, memorize their names and their respective east-west position on the Texas map and you will know how to find them in downtown Austin (see our Getting Here and Getting Around chapter).

Buchanan (Buck-ANN-un) — Rhymes with buckin' bronco and is one of the Highland Lakes northwest of Austin. We have no explanation for why this Scottish name lost its "Byew" and became "Buck," except, of course, this is Texas.

Buda (BYEW-dah) — Rhymes with phew! This small town just south of Austin is noted for its small antiques and collectible shops.

Bonnell (Bun-NELL) — That's Mount Bun-nell, a popular spot to take in a view of Austin (see our Attractions chapter).

Burnet (BURN-it) — Rhymes with "durn it" and is a road in Austin and a Hill Country community.

Cameron Road (CAM-run) — Drop the middle syllable here, and you'll sound okay.

Coupland (COPE-land) — As in Aaron Copeland, a musical connection that is appropriate since this is the home of the famous Coupland Dance Hall (see the Insiders' Tips in our Nightlife chapter).

Dessau (DESS-aw) — Dessau Lane is in North Austin.

Del Valle (Dell Valley) — Another Spanish word that has been anglicized, or Texas-ized, Del Valle is a community southeast of Austin near the Austin-Bergstrom International Airport, scheduled to open in 1999.

Elgin (ELL-ghin) — No gin here (it rhymes with "kin"), or vermouth, just sausages. This small town east of Austin makes a famous German-style sausage that some barbecue aficionados regard as a mandatory element in any cookout.

Gruene (Green) — The German word for green and the name of a small town south of Austin known for its antique shops and artists (see our Daytrips chapter).

Govalle (Go Valley) — Another Spanish word corrupted by gringo tongues? Surprise! No, this is derived from a Swedish phrase *go val* meaning "good grazing land," and Swedish settlers gave this name to fertile pasture land east of Austin along the Colorado River. A cabin built there in 1840 by S.M. Swenson, the first Swedish settler in Texas, is now found in the Zilker Park Garden Center (see our Attractions chapter).

Guadalupe (GWA-da-loop) — If you can remember Alley Oop, you will quickly get

— continued on next page

the hang of this street name. The portion of Gwadaloop that runs through the University of Texas campus is known as "The Drag."

Huston (HYOU-stun) — As in Sam Houston, and part of the name of Huston-Tillotson College (see our Higher Education chapter).

Jager (YAY-gahr) — That's Yaeger as in Chuck "The Right Stuff" Yaeger and the name of a lane, now a major roadway, in North Austin.

Koenig (KAY-nig) — Another German name that was given to a lane in North Austin and another of those "lanes" that is now a major thoroughfare.

Kreuz (Cry-tzz) — You don't really have to know how to pronounce this name if you have good sense of smell. Simply start sniffing as you approach Lockhart, and your nose will carry you to the famous barbecue spot (see our Annual Events and Festivals chapter).

Lavaca (La-VAH-cah) — One of the few Spanish names pronounced correctly here, it means "the cow" and is also the name of a famous Spanish explorer, an Austin street and a Texas river.

Llano (LAN-oh) — The name means "plains" in Spanish, but historians believe the county and town of the same name northwest of Austin take their name from the Llano River is rises in the plains west of the Hill Country.

Manchaca (Man-shack) — Not only has this Spanish word been given the Texas treatment, but the spelling has been changed as well. Legend says a spring south of Austin was named for Colonel Jose Antonio Menchaca, the scion of a old San Antonio family. The "e" was changed to an "a" over the years to become Manchaca, the name given the community that grew up around the spring south of Austin. The Manchaca community is now part of the growing Austin, but the elementary school there has been named after Menchaca with the original spelling.

Manor (MAY-ner) — Forget your "to the manor born" accent when pronouncing the name of this community east of Austin and opt for a down-home twang.

Mueller (MILL-er) — As in Lite beer, is the correct pronunciation of Robert Mueller Municipal Airport. It is named for the Austin city councilman who pressed hard for the city's airport, which opened on October 14, 1930.

New Braunfels (New BRAWN-fells) — This is one of several picturesque Hill Country towns that owe much of their character to German settlers (see our Daytrips chapter).

Nueces (New-AY-sez) — The Spanish word means "nuts," but in Austin the Spanish "nway" becomes "new." It is one of those downtown streets named after a Texas river.

Pedernales (PUR-der-nal-liss) — This "purdy" river runs through the LBJ Ranch near Johnson City (see our Daytrips chapter).

Pflugerville (FLEW-ger-ville) — The "p" is silent here, but this small town northeast of is not a quiet backwater anymore. It is a thriving vibrant community (see our Neighborhoods and Real Estate chapter).

Rio Grande (REE-oh Grand) — If it was good enough for John Wayne, then it's good enough for those Austinites who drop the final syllable here. This is another of those downtown river streets.

San Antonio (San An-TONE) — Not everyone opts for this pronunciation, but it does have a Texas ring to it. Again, a downtown street named after this Texas river.

San Jacinto (San Jah-SIN-tow) — In Spanish it would be "San Hah-seen-toh," but locals opt for the hard "J" here when they pronounce the name of this downtown street, another one of those river streets.

San Marcos (San MAR-kiss) — Round vowels are not the preferred Texas pronunciation, especially when they come at the end of a word, like the name of this college town south of Austin.

Texans (TEX-uns) — It is the round vowel syndrome again.

Texas (TEX-us) — And yet again, flat is better than round.

Photo: Peter A. Silva

The Goddess of Liberty, holding a lone star and a sword, stands atop the Texas Capitol building.

weather, but freezes are infrequent and snow is very rare, falling in any measurable amount about once every decade. One local tradition that new residents soon learn is the "plant shuffle" — hauling in all those patio plants that are sensitive to a hard freeze and then hauling them back out again a day or two later, but some winters pass without a single hard freeze.

The so-called "blue norther'" is another Texas phenomenon that quickly becomes part of a newcomer's lexicon. These winter cold fronts often can be seen coming as the wind shifts to the north and the clouds are swept from the sky, allowing temperatures to fall into the 40s and 30s. Visitors often are astounded by how quickly the temperature falls, going from 70-something to 40-something literally in minutes — a good reason to carry a sweater in the winter.

Spring is usually the rainy season, but Austin also enjoys spring days that border on the sublime when residents can keep their windows open night and day. The average yearly rainfall is 32 inches, and there are on average 116 clear days, 114 partly cloudy days, 135 cloudy days and 84 days with measurable rain. While winters are mild, sudden summer thunderstorms can be threatening. The Hill Country is riddled with what appear to be dry creek beds, but after a sudden spring or summer rainfall they quickly become dangerous, as flashfloods rage along their paths. Never try to drive across a flooded creek bed, and be aware of weather warnings about lightning storms and infrequent tornadoes.

For much of the year, the weather is benevolent and beautiful, allowing Austinites to spend their leisure time outdoors enjoying the many parks and recreational facilities in the area, perhaps a cup of coffee at an outdoor cafe, or a walk along Town Lake in the heart of downtown. But when the sun goes down they turn to other activities, enjoying the area's casual dining scene (see our Restaurants chapter) and the abundant nightlife.

The Music Scene

Boasting the hottest live music scene in the country, Austin rocks day and night with just about any style of music imaginable: blues, country, jazz, folk, funk, punk, bluegrass, Tejano, rock 'n' roll, alternative and the savory sounds of our true Texas hybrids. Called a mecca for musical mavericks in 1998 by *Billboard* magazine, Austin is world renowned for its unique brands of original music and for attracting top-notch performers who would rather live and play in Austin than bend to the prevailing winds of musical fashion elsewhere. Home to the world's best-known country music outlaw, Willie Nelson, launching stage for the late blues legend Stevie Ray Vaughan, a haven for scores of world-class artists and up-and-comers, Austin is a paradise of live music. Read more about our music haven in The Music Scene chapter, which includes a close-up on Austin favorites, Willie and Stevie.

The Arts

While they haven't earned equal billing with the Live Music Capital of the World, Austin's dynamic arts and literary scenes lend the cultural dimension that makes this city such an inviting place to live. Long known as a haven for artists and intellectuals; more and more talented artists have found inspiration in Austin over the past few decades. Today, Austin offers more than 250 theater productions a year, including national touring shows and an excellent variety of local productions. Our art museums, galleries and bookstores abound with fresh voices in both the visual and literary arts. The city also is home to the Texas Film Commission, the state agency that has been successful in bringing many movie productions to what is affectionately called The Third Coast. We give complete coverage to the art culture in our chapters on The Literary Scene and The Arts.

The University

Sprawling over 357 acres in the very heart of Central Austin, The University of Texas is an omnipresent force throughout this region. UT's contribution to Austin's economy and to its intellectual, political and artistic development over the past 115 years has helped to make Austin the envy of Texas and one of the coolest places in the land to live, work, study and play. With nearly 49,000 students, UT gives Austin much of its youthful energy while bolstering its reputation as one of the country's hippest small cities. A breeding ground for intellectuals and a renowned research center, UT is one factor driving Austin's knowledge-intensive economy today. What's more, UT rewards Austinites almost daily by offering a rich variety of artistic, educational and sporting events.

Although it's not considered one of the

INSIDERS' TIP

Visitors to Austin are captivated by the flora in Central Texas, particularly the abundant wildflowers. The University of Texas Press publishes a wonderful, full-color guide called *Texas Wildflowers* by Campbell and Lynn Loughmiller. The book has a foreword by Lady Bird Johnson.

country's most beautiful campuses, UT nevertheless is a sight to behold. Towering shade trees, sculptures and fountains by world-class artists, dozens of architectural wonders representing more than a century of development and the 27-story UT Tower that soars as a landmark for all of Austin give the UT campus its unique flair. UT-Austin, the flagship of the system's 15 campuses spread throughout the state, is a source of pride for all Texans. Read about UT in our Attractions, Spectator Sports and Higher Education chapters, and about its libraries in The Literary Scene chapter.

UT's size and importance to the economic development of Central Texas over the past century make UT Austin's most significant institute of higher learning. But our other colleges and universities — St. Edward's University in South Austin, Huston-Tillotson on the east side, Concordia University near UT, Southwestern University north of us in Georgetown, Southwest Texas State University south in San Marcos, and Austin Community College's campuses all over the region — combine to give Central Texas its fame as an educational Eden (see our Higher Education chapter).

Government

The Austin economy rests on three sectors: higher education, government and the high-tech industry. The State of Texas employs approximately 64,000 people in the Austin area. As the state capital, the city is headquarters for many state agencies and, of course, the legislature and high courts.

The Texas legislature is convened on the second Tuesday of January in odd-numbered years for a 120-day regular session. Special sessions are occasionally called at other times by the governor. During the annual session Austin takes on a little different air as hotels and restaurants fill with politicians, their staff and lobbyists. But Austin is also a political city year-round, since many legislative staffers live here, along with those agency heads, judges and state bureaucrats who live, eat and breathe the political air of the city.

Austin is also known for its active local political scene where the environment and the fight to keep Austin true to itself are always center stage (see our Politics and Perspectives chapter).

High Tech

The third major pillar of the Austin economy is a relative newcomer. High tech is now an integral part of the picture, and the three largest private-sector employers in Austin are technology companies — Dell Computer Corp., Motorola Inc. and IBM Corp. The vibrant music industry, a burgeoning film scene and an up-and-coming multimedia sector have added to the diverse economic picture, giving Austin a much wider economic base and ensuring that it is not as subject to the whims of a single economic sector's ups and downs as it was in the past.

Austin's homegrown computer titan, Dell Computer Corp., along with other Fortune 500 companies that established Central Texas branches in the 1980s and 1990s, brought tens of thousands of jobs to become the driving force behind this region's current economic growth. What's more, it didn't take too long for the Texas spirit of adventure to emerge in a big way in the technology field.

Oil wildcatters of earlier decades enhanced Texas' mystique as a hotbed of fiercely independent risk-takers, but a new breed of prospectors is leading Austin today. Armed with computer chips rather than drill bits, Austin's modern wildcatters are gambling on start-up technology companies in computers and especially in software development. And some have hit major gushers (see our Politics and Perspectives chapter).

Growth Issues

Long known as a low-growth region, Austin lived out its unique vision for more than 150 years without much concern for policies in then-far-off Round Rock, Cedar Park, Dripping Springs and other neighboring communities. But as this booming region expands into one big metropolis, Austin now is faced with developing a plan for the future that encompasses all of Central Texas' concerns. Growth has been the No. 1 topic in Austin for the last two decades, and now those once-small, quiet com-

The Littlefield Fountain at the south entrance to the University of Texas campus honors students who died in World War I.

munities like Cedar Park and Dripping Springs are wrestling with the same issue.

Growth has been a two-edged sword for the Austin area. It has brought economic stability and even boom times, but it also has put stress on the environment. It has led to more restaurants, more shops, more donations to the arts and contributions to the cultural scene, but it also has put pressure on infrastructure and public resources. But growth also has led to dynamic, creative solutions, has revitalized old neighborhoods, given downtown a new vibrancy and brought people together in new ways.

INSIDERS' TIP

Looking for a spot to shoot a dramatic picture of the Austin skyline? Head for Loop 360 (Capital of Texas Highway). There are several points along the roadway that offer great views of the city, but just north of Bee Caves Road there is a designated scenic lookout point with parking on the east side of the highway.

Austin Overlook

We called this section Overlook because visitors get many of the grandest views of this city looking down from one of its many hills or from above: the first view of the city from an airplane, a tapestry of lights surrounding two distinctive landmarks, the capitol and the University of Texas tower; a view of the downtown skyline from a scenic lookout point on Capital of Texas Highway west of the city; or the sun shimmering on Lake Travis at sunset, viewed from the deck of a lakeside restaurant; the reflections of the downtown lights in Town Lake viewed from a high-rise hotel; the view of the city from a picnic site on Mount Bonnell.

But Austin is not a city to be experienced only from above — or from afar. To get the most of this city, walk among the people and the places that have made Austin what it is today. So many of the places visitors find enjoyable are places the locals love to visit, also.

By the time you're ready to leave Austin, if you can tear yourself away, you'll really know what it means when the locals bid you farewell with a "Y'all come back." You might even find yourself responding, "Y'all take care!"

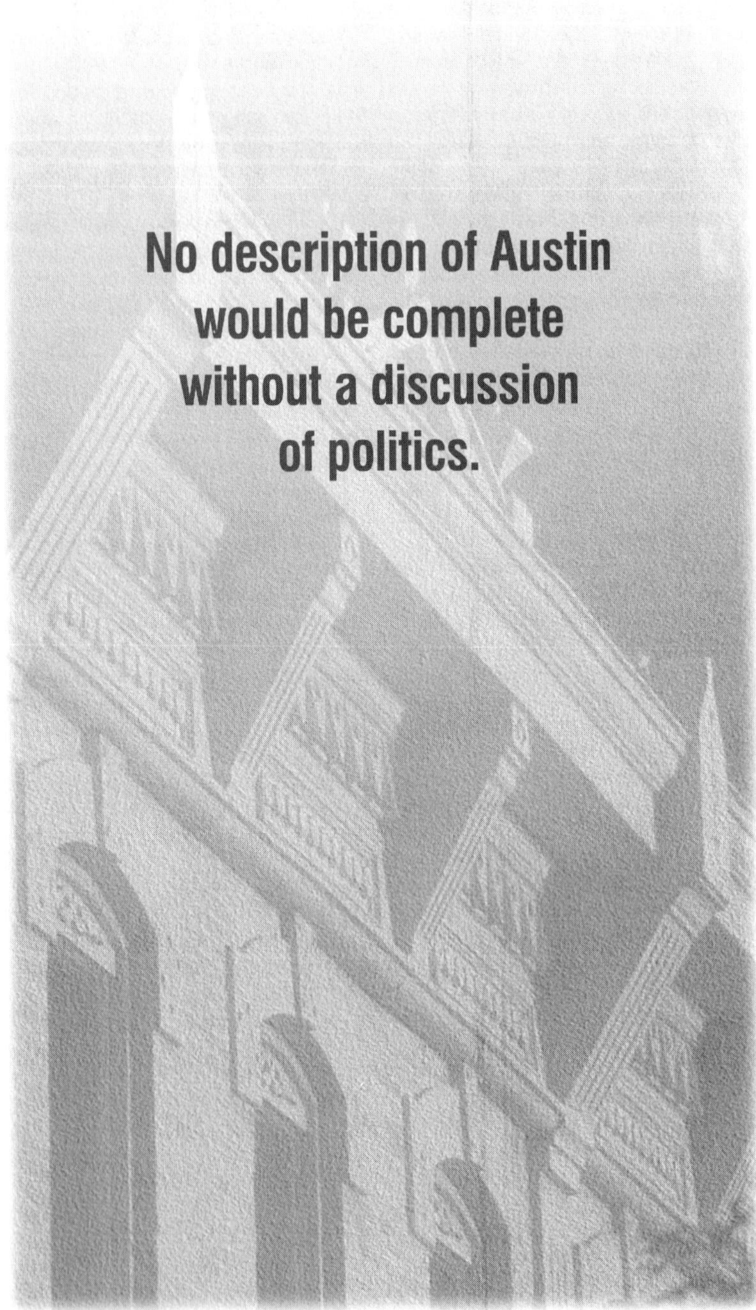

No description of Austin would be complete without a discussion of politics.

Politics and Perspectives

"All politics is local," former U.S. Speaker Tip O'Neill reportedly said, and in no place in Texas is that more true than Austin. Not only are city politics hard fought here, but this is where the state's major parties have their headquarters. Austin is home to political spin doctors and policy wonks, lobbyists of all stripes, political scientists and ardent grassroots volunteers, consultants and imagemakers.

No description of Austin would be complete without a discussion of politics. It is, after all, an Austin industry and one that flourishes year-round, coming into full bloom every other spring during the biennial sessions of the Texas Legislature. Most Texas politicians, no matter their political party, hold to a Texas version of the old saw: "What is good for the country is good for General Motors, and what's good for General Motors is good for the country." Just substitute Texas for country and "bidness" (Texan for "business") for GM, and you'll get the picture.

Economic development, business stimulation and great public works (particularly roads and airports) are viewed as good public policy in Texas by the majority of state legislators. Not all their plans are welcomed by some of the citizens of Austin, and that is at the heart of a long-running love-hate relationship the city has with the legislature. Austin is well-known as a "liberal" city, and the majority of voters within the city limits consistently vote for Democratic candidates, although the voter profile in the fast-growing suburbs is tending to be more Republican. However, Austin remains home to progressives and populists, a town where the most active political segment might be labeled the "Greens," environmentalists, sometimes derided as "no-growthers," who have been sounding a drumbeat of warnings about the need to limit growth, particularly in the Hill Country (see our Close-up on Barton Springs Pool in the Parks and Recreation chapter).

But the political picture is more complicated than that and, in some ways, getting more blurred as Austin's political profile changes. This is also the city that is building the only new international airport in the country, thanks to the clout of powerful Texas politicians such as retired Democratic Congressman J.J. "Jake" Pickle, whose mentor was the biggest Texas politico of them all, President Lyndon B. Johnson. Austin residents can thank Johnson and other Texans with clout in Washington for the Highland Lakes where so many residents and visitors head for recreation.

The Partnership

Government is a major employer in Austin — the State of Texas has 64,000 people on its Austin payroll — and it is also a major partner in the city's economic development. In the 1960s several visionary leaders in business and at the University of Texas began a campaign to bring industry to Austin. Not only did the city provide a pleasant cultural and social climate for new industry, they argued, but the university's engineering and science programs offered a valuable resource to major research operations. In 1966, the efforts paid off with the announcement that IBM was opening a new plant in Austin.

The move was a catalyst that resulted in

Texas Instruments and Motorola opening up plants in the area to link to IBM. The efforts by community leaders had paid off, but they could not know what they had begun.

"IBM was both an end and a beginning — and it was the shape of things to come," Anthony M. Orum wrote in his book *Power, Money & the People: The Making of Modern Austin*.

Fast forward to 1983 when William Norris of Control Data Corporation came up with the notion that U.S. companies needed to form a consortium of private technology companies to design the fifth generation of computers. The consortium, which had to turn to the federal government for exemptions from antitrust laws, was named the Microelectronics and Computer Technology Corporation, or MCC for short, and Norris chose Admiral Bobby Ray Inman, a former deputy director of the Central Intelligence Agency, to head up the effort.

Dozens of U.S. cities joined the chase to bring MCC home. Several cities in Texas made the pitch, and Austin ended up on the short list. The city's business leaders, politicians and the state leadership went into a full court press.

Orum wrote: "By the time MCC officials set foot in Austin, the city's presentation did not include merely local officials, but was an orchestrated effort by major state figures to lure MCC. Governor (Mark) White had been persuaded that the economic future of the state lay with the development of a strong high-technology base of operations and he, in turn, helped to corral a number of other prominent state leaders including computer magnate H. Ross Perot, Houston banker Ben Love, former Governor Allan Shivers, and multibillionaire Perry Bass."

Austin won the prize. The reasons why are disputed, but Orum credits the huge financial package Texas leaders and the university put together: UT committed to $15 million worth of endowed faculty chairs for 30 new positions in computer science and electrical engineering plus $1 million a year for research for each of these areas, grants for graduate students, money for equipment and a lease at the university's Balcones Research Center for a nominal fee. The multimillion dollar package prompted Atlanta Mayor Andrew Young to sniff that Austin had "bought" MCC.

Austin was on the high-tech map. Hadn't *Megatrends* author John Naisbitt predicted it in his bestseller? Suddenly the city was being profiled and touted in national magazines and newspapers. In 1984, Michael Dell began his computer company out of his UT dorm room. Four years later, city and state leaders turned to many of the same team members it had employed in the MCC hunt to lure Sematech, a semiconductor consortium, to town. One key player was Austin lawyer Pike Powers, a member of the powerful Fulbright & Jaworksi law firm and a close friend and former top aide to Gov. White. Powers and the rest of the team brought home the bacon again.

Austin was on a roll. At mid-decade the city's population stood at 436,188, a 26 percent gain since 1980. As the *Austin American-Statesman* noted, the city had gained as many people in five years as it had since World War II. In one of those typical Austin dichotomies, growth had fueled a real estate boom and that had prompted some of the city's most ardent liberals to become lobby-

INSIDERS' TIP

One of the best times to see the state Legislature at work is on the final day of the biennial session — usually dubbed *sine die*, the Latin term meaning the final day. The Texas Legislature is convened on the second Tuesday of January in odd-numbered years for a 120-day regular session. Usually, *sine die* is a hectic day marked with last-minute debate, deal making and parties in the halls and offices of the Capitol.

Photo: Peter A. Silva

The Capitol building stands tall in the center of downtown.

ists and lawyers for development interests. Fortunes were being made, savings and loans were being chartered, and "flipping" real estate — buying it and quickly selling it — became the favorite game in town. At the same time, oil prices were sky-high, and since the oil and gas business still accounted for a third of the state's economy, the banks were flush with money to lend.

Then, the bottom fell out of the oil market, inflated land prices began to fall, and the Texas economy fell into recession. Some of the most well-known names in Austin declared bankruptcy, and a few went to jail. Texas languished and by all outward appearances was stuck in a rut. But behind the scenes, thanks to public policy and private know-how, the high-tech engines were churning and would soon reach a critical mass that would push both the Austin and Texas economy in a whole new direction.

High-Tech Rescue

The Austin economy began to turn around, and it became evident the new Austin was not dependent on real estate speculation and government growth for its economic well-being. In 1993, the *Austin American-Statesman* began to publish "Tech Monday," a business section that appears weekly and gives readers the latest news on the Austin technology scene (see our Media chapter). That also was the year young Michael Dell's company broke the $1 billion mark. By the end of 1997, Dell sales stood at $12 billion and the company was the area's largest private employer, with 12,000 people. Along the way, several Dell employees had gone their own way and established their own businesses plus Dell's success had created hundreds of so-called Dellionaires who were savvy enough to buy Dell stock when it first went public and hang on to it through several stock splits.

In 1994, the daily "Nerd Bird" flights began between Austin and Silicon Valley, California. The city that had called itself the Third Coast in the 1980s now was kicking around the name, Silicon Hills. In 1995, Tivoli Systems issued stock, and Lockheed closed its doors in Austin — software was in, military hardware was out. That same year Austin's first Internet companies were created, including Ichat, Garden Escape, Deja News and others. Within a year, Tivoli, which had raised $34 million in its initial stock offering, was sold to IBM for $743 million.

Samsung broke ground on its memory chip plant in Northeast Austin in 1996. Two years later, the $1.3 billion Samsung plant was in operation. The city had felt some minor bumps on the road as semiconductor prices fell and some ventures failed, but venture capital was being spread around, and new companies were forming weekly. According to the *Austin American-Statesman*, 33 companies raised $164 million in venture capital in 1997, up from $40 million by nine companies in 1995.

The Internet was the hottest new trend in 1998 as the city saw unemployment rates drop to less than 3 percent. The city was enjoying a secure, creative atmosphere for young workers, according to Angelos Angelou, an Austin economist. They flocked to Austin not to sign on for a benefits-loaded package with a traditional employer, but rather to venture forth on their own.

"Internet-related companies being developed in Austin are siphoning off workers from the other technology companies. Multimedia software development — it's fashionable, if you are young and you can roommate with a number of people to cut costs. You can afford to join a start-up company and work for nothing," Angelos said.

Changing Outlook

By the mid-1990s the empty office towers built during the real estate boom were filling up — in some cases government had come to the rescue again with the state and city buying up the unused towers. The state's coffers were filling up as its economy strengthened, boosted in large part by the emerging high-tech sector and the boom in trade with Mexico, prompted by the signing of the North American Free Trade Agreement in 1994.

Support of NAFTA had been a bipartisan affair throughout the late 1980s and early '90s. It was a political sentiment and attitude reflected not only in Texas Gov. George Bush's 1994 campaign for governor, but also in the administration of his predecessors including Democratic Gov. Ann Richards and Republican Gov. William Clements. When some called for a ditch along the Texas-Mexico border during Clements' administration, the gruff, tough-talking governor, an independent oilman, said the United States should be "building bridges with Mexico, not ditches."

That attitude is rooted in both economic realities and cultural predispositions. Texas leads the states in trade with Mexico with more than $30 billion in annual exports, and the state's cultural, political and social history is intertwined with Mexico's. Visitors and newcomers to Texas will not hear the same kind of divisive debate that has occurred in California over issues such as illegal immigration and bilingual education, in part because of the stance taken by leaders in both parties on those issues.

After the peso devaluation in 1994, the number of illegal aliens increased. Federal officials estimated there were 357,000 undocumented workers in Texas — about 2 percent

INSIDERS' TIP

There are five state holidays — Martin Luther King's Birthday on the third Monday in January; Texas Independence Day on March 2; San Jacinto Day, marking the defeat of General Santa Anna, on April 21; Emancipation Day, also called Juneteenth, on June 19; and Lyndon Baines Johnson's Birthday on August 27.

of the population. Texas ranked third in total number of undocumented workers. (California had about 1.4 million, 4.6 percent of its population; New York had 449,000, 2.4 percent of its population.) But while some economists tagged the cost of illegal immigrants to the U.S. economy, others tried to assess their contribution. Texas economist and author M. Ray Perryman estimated their contribution to the Texas economy in 1994 at $5.2 billion in a $471 billion economy.

Undocumented workers build new homes for Texans, baby-sit their children, pick their vegetables and cook for them. When the Immigration and Naturalization Service embarked on a series of raids on workplaces in Austin around July 4th, 1996, public reaction was mixed, but some expressed the view that illegals with jobs should be left alone. Polls show that Texans do not approve of illegal immigration, but most polls also show it is not a major topic of concern for voters. A majority of Texans also support education for the children of illegal immigrants.

Sensitivity to Mexico and Hispanic heritage in Texas is a hallmark of both political parties. Former Gov. Richards and current Gov. Bush both developed diplomatic relations with Mexican leaders and governors south of the border. The political reality is that Hispanic voters have clout in Texas and in Austin. From 1980 to 1990, Texas' Hispanic population grew by 45 percent, and Hispanics make up some 25.6 percent of the state's population and 23 percent in Austin. Overall, by 1990, Texas' minority population was more than 40 percent, compared to the national number, 25 percent. By 2010, Texas is predicted to be a minority majority state, with Hispanics making up the largest sector in that majority.

Demographers predict the Texas population will increase by 99 percent from 1990 to 2030 — Anglo population will increase by 20 percent, African-American by 62 percent, and Hispanic by a whopping 258 percent.

Not only is the Hispanic vote significant in Texas, but also Hispanic leadership. Texas leads the way nationally in the number of Hispanic officeholders. According to the National Association of Latino Elected and Appointed Officials (NALEO), before the 1994 elections, Hispanics held 5,466 seats across the country — 2,215 of them in Texas. California had only 803, and New Mexico was next in line with 716.

The election and appointment of Hispanics in Texas is seen as a significant and necessary move. While the majority of Hispanic officeholders are Democrats, the Texas GOP has a Republican Hispanic Assembly aimed at boosting Republican membership among Hispanics.

Political Changes

In addition to demographic changes, Texas also has undergone significant political realignment, some say because of the influx of new residents, others because of historical changes in the two major political parties. The year 1994 marked a watershed in Texas politics as the Republican Party recorded several landmark achievements. Republican gubernatorial candidate George W. Bush defeated Democratic Gov. Ann Richards, who had achieved national celebrity status. The pundits opined it would

INSIDERS' TIP

In 1907, *The Washington Post* described the Texas Legislature as a place where "money was spent like water, and wine, women and song were integral parts" of the political scene. There is still a little of that, of course, and occasionally legislators can be seen at several local watering holes, perhaps even singing a song or two. There has even been a recent arrest of a state senator for prostitute solicitation. But the overwhelming majority spend their evenings quietly. When they do go out it is likely they will be seen sipping mineral water or a glass of red wine at one of the city's more sophisticated restaurants or bars (see our Nightlife and Restaurants chapters).

be a tight race, but it was not, and Bush recorded the biggest gubernatorial win in 20 years. He continued to get high ratings from voters throughout his first term.

Bush had defeated the woman who once said of his father at the national Democratic Party convention, "Poor George. He can't help it. He was born with a silver foot in his mouth." (The President sent her a silver foot charm.) Richards, who had won the governor's race by attracting moderate Republican women in 1990, won counties in South Texas, several around her hometown of Waco, some rural counties in East and North Texas, and Travis County where the capital city is located. Austin area voters had supported her 59 percent to 41 percent for Bush. Just to the north, in booming Williamson County, home of Round Rock and North Austin suburbs, the numbers were reversed — 58 percent for Bush and 42 percent for Richards.

In the 1996 presidential race the numbers also showed the political differences between what might be called "old Austin" and "new Austin" — Travis County voted 53 percent for President Bill Clinton, 40 percent for U.S. Senator Bob Dole and 6 percent for H. Ross Perot, while Williamson County voted 36 percent for Clinton, 56 percent for Dole and 7 percent for Perot.

The 1994 state election also saw Republicans achieve several significant "firsts," identified by *Dallas Morning News* political writer Carolyn Barta: The state has two Republican senators for the first time in this century; the state has a Republican majority on the highest civil court, the Texas Supreme Court; the Texas Railroad Commission, which regulates the state's oil and gas industries, has an all-Republican membership; and the State Board of Education is dominated by Republicans, including a core group of conservative members aligned with the Christian Coalition.

The Republican Party continued its rise in 1998 as incumbent Gov. George W. Bush led a historic sweep by his party of all the major statewide races. Bush made major inroads into the traditionally Democratic Hispanic vote, winning almost 50 percent of that electorate.

In local politics, the battle between Republicans and Democrats has not reached the critical mass that it has on the state level. Typically, the political map in Austin looks a little like a doughnut with the new, outer suburbs voting Republican and the inner, older neighborhoods voting Democrat.

City elections are, on the surface, nonpartisan, but many of the political consultants who work state races can be found aligned with various factions in city politics — generally Republicans with pro-business candidates and Democrats with pro-environment groups. The world of city politics can be a Byzantine one for newcomers — one of the most frequent questions longtime residents hear is "Why doesn't Austin have single member districts?" (That question ranks first, followed by "Why doesn't Austin have any east-west freeways?" See our Getting Here and Getting Around chapter.)

Unlike many Southern cities where the U.S. Justice Department has required single member districts be drawn to meet the standards in voting rights laws, Austin has managed to avoid federal oversight. For years, there has been what is openly called "a gentlemen's agreement" that called for one seat on the council to be designated the Hispanic seat and another to be the African-American seat. That agreement has generally held, although there have been criticisms over the years. Currently, there is one Hispanic member of the council and one African-American — the latter holds the designated seat under the "gentlemen's agreement," but the Hispanic councilmember holds what was considered an at-large seat and the Hispanic seat is held by an Anglo. Austin city politics may be the ultimate "inside baseball" game, as politicos often call under-the-surface, behind-the-scenes political game.

INSIDERS' TIP

The Texas State Motto is "Friendship," and Texas is said to have been the Spanish pronunciation for a Caddo Indian word meaning "friends" or "allies."

While politics is a full-time business for many in Austin, voter turnout has fallen, as it has across the United States. With a population passing a half-million in Travis County, fewer than 100,000 voted in the 1996 primaries — 40,132 in the Democratic primary and 42,978 in the Republican primary. City and school bond elections attract even fewer voters, but that has not stopped politics from being the talk of the town.

Full Circle

Karma — it's a word heard a lot in Austin, a city where political consultants study yoga and politicians seek psychic renewal from a swim in the city's famed Barton Springs Pool. Karma — consider the story of the Alamo Hotel.

The old brick hotel stood at the corner of Sixth and Guadalupe streets, a few blocks west of Congress Avenue. For decades it had been home to traveling salespeople and visitors on a budget, and the street-level cafe had been a favorite place for breakfast and lunch among downtown workers and business owners. After World War II, the hotel went into a slow decline, but longtime residents, including Sam Houston Johnson, brother to President Lyndon Baines Johnson, continued to call it home. By the early 1980s it was being used as a residence hotel by folks on a budget, and several welfare agencies issued room vouchers for those down and out of luck who needed a place to stay (among the hungry, young artists who stayed here were comedian Harry Anderson and his friend Turk Pipkin, a mime, juggler and writer).

During the real estate boom in the mid-1980s, Lamar Savings bought the property, and in 1984 the S&L announced plans to tear the hotel down and build a office/hotel highrise. Social activist Tony Hearn and others were dismayed since the new plans would not accommodate the needy who had received shelter at the old hotel. Hearn called the local media and announced he would put a blood curse on the property. As television cameras rolled, Hearn circled the old hotel spreading a red liquid on the ground (not blood, but vinegar and red food coloring), murmuring incantations — unless the property was dedicated to meeting the needs of the poor, no one would ever make money from it.

The hotel was torn down, although the demolition crew was plagued by problems and equipment failures. The plans for the high-rise fell apart when the S&L crisis hit. The developer, Lamar chairman Stanley Adams, eventually went to federal prison for bank fraud. The northwest corner of Sixth and Guadalupe streets stood empty.

In the mid-1990s, Sixth Street and the warehouse district brought new life to downtown. All around the old Alamo there were signs of renewal — a '50s era paint shop became a popular bar, and another storefront was turned into a hip bistro. Austin's downtown was turning into a lively place at all hours of the day and night.

But when the U.S. Post Office built a new facility across from where the Alamo had once stood, local critics decried its stern, stark exterior with its large parking lot and drive-through mailboxes — Austin needed a pedestrian-friendly downtown, advocates declared. City planners went on full alert. So when Extended Stay America Inc. announced plans to build a residence hotel on the site of the old Alamo, a city advisory board criticized the design, saying it did not embrace the spirit of downtown Austin.

The battle was just beginning in late summer 1998, but Austin residents were sending signals that what they wanted was what the Alamo had once been — a friendly place where the smells of homecooking had wafted out to the street from the ground-floor cafe and where pedestrians could walk by the lobby and see friends meeting. It promised to be another Austin cause celebre.

The battles between newcomers and oldtimers, the new suburbs and the older parts of the city continue. Changing demographics, economic diversification and shifting political tides are altering the power structure in Austin, but there are some common threads that do bind — preserving the authentic Austin experience is one of them, and that means politics.

In a poignant ceremony held at high noon on February 19, 1846, Texas President Anson Jones declared, "The Republic of Texas is no more."

History

A New Republic and Its Capital

Sam Houston rarely lost a fight. Of all the heroes who struggled for Texas' independence from Mexico, General Houston had been the one to lead the decisive bloody conflict. His troops had captured the ruthless Mexican dictator, General Antonio López de Santa Anna, at the Battle of San Jacinto on April 26, 1836. As commander-in-chief of the Texas Army, he had altered the destiny of a continent.

Houston, a towering figure of a man, was born to lead. As a youth, he had gone off on his own to live among the Indians and had been accepted as a son by a chief of the Cherokees. His Indian name, *Co-lon-neh,* meaning the Raven, would add luster to his legend. Houston had served as governor of Tennessee before striking out for the wilds of Texas. He was among the courageous leaders who had signed the Texas Declaration of Independence at Washington-on-the-Brazos, March 2, 1835. And he had already served a term as the first elected president of the fledgling Republic of Texas. In many ways he was the ultimate prototype of the new Texan: tall, independent, fearless, self-assured, every bit the maverick, a hero among heroes.

And he was furious. The year was 1839, and the new president of the Republic, Mirabeau Lamar, was suggesting that Texas' permanent capital be established in the tiny hamlet of Waterloo. What insanity! The hamlet, on the banks of the Colorado River, sat in the middle of nowhere, perched on the edge of a wild frontier. The U.S. border was 250 arduous miles east at the Sabine River while the disputed Texas-Mexico boundary stood just half that distance away at the Nueces River. Comanche Indians occupied the hills nearby. Mexican marauders could invade at any time. Besides, Houston had already secured a pledge from the Texas government that the capital would remain, at least until 1840, in the town that bore his own name — or so he thought.

Lamar had other ideas. He envisioned a Texas empire that spread far into the west. Moving the capital to the center of the Republic, he believed, would give Texas a launching point from which to carve out its future. Lamar dreamed of the newly adopted Lone Star flag sailing one day over lands still controlled by Mexico and the Indians.

While camping near Waterloo on an excursion with Texas Rangers the year before, Lamar had awakened to shouts that a buffalo herd had been spotted nearby. He rode out and shot the biggest buffalo some had ever seen. As fate would have it, his prey had been standing right on the corner of what would become the heart of downtown Austin at Congress Avenue near Eighth Street. Lamar recalled the beautiful spot when it came time to assign a commission to select Texas' permanent capital.

The new capital was to be named Austin in honor of "The Father of Texas," Stephen F. Austin, who less than 20 years before had brought the first Anglo settlers to the territory. Citizens of Houston, Washington-on-the-Brazos, Matagorda and other Texas towns lobbied hard for the capital. But there was something about Waterloo that drew out the romantic in the roughest of men. According to articles published in the *Austin American*, Indian fighter James Jones described the scene in letters to President Lamar in 1839. "We are marching through a beautiful country — its face presents a scene of grandeur and magnificence rarely, if ever witnessed," Jones wrote. "It is the most beautiful and sublime scene. ... Rome itself with all its famous hills could not surpass the natural scenery of Waterloo."

Equally infatuated, commissioners investigating potential capital sites filed this report: "The imagination of even the romantic will not be disappointed on viewing the valley of the Colorado, and the fertile and gracefully undulating woodlands and luxuriant prairies at a distance from it. The most skeptical will not doubt its healthiness, and the citizen's bosom must swell with honest pride when, standing in the portico of the capitol of this country, he looks abroad upon a region worthy only of being the home of the brave and free."

Waterloo, renamed Austin, got the nod in April of 1839. For the next 33 years Austin would have a precarious grip on the seat of government.

Despite objections from Sam Houston and many others who believed it was madness to venture to the very brink of civilization, Lamar moved quickly to establish the new center of government. He dispatched a veteran of the Texas Revolution, Edwin Waller, to lay out the town and begin construction of its public buildings.

"Convinced that delay would give the opposition an opportunity to crystallize, Waller resolved to have Austin ready when Congress convened in November," Austin historian David C. Humphrey wrote in his book, *Austin: An Illustrated History*. "Despite the frenzied pace, Waller planned his infant city in a manner that has pleased its citizens and visitors ever since."

Waller's popularity soared in the town he designed. In January 1840 he won unanimous election as mayor by the town's 187 voters.

As the capitol and other wooden public buildings took shape along Congress Avenue (the capitol was surrounded by stockades to protect it against Indian attack) more and more souls moved to Austin, many to take jobs as public servants in the fledgling government, some to set up private professions and businesses, still others arriving with their owners as slaves. By 1840, Austin's population grew to 856, according to an informal census taken by a resident, the Reverend Amos Roark. The population, by Roark's count, totaled 711 whites and 145 blacks, included 75 religious people, 35 mechanics, six doctors, four lawyers ... and 20 gamblers.

Sam Houston, still seething over the transfer of power to Austin, made plans to end this wild experiment once and for all. Having been reelected president of the Republic, succeeding Lamar in September of 1841, Houston was provided the perfect excuse when invading Mexicans briefly recaptured San Antonio in 1842 — causing nearly the whole population of Austin to flee. He ordered the official papers be transferred from Austin to Washington-on-the-Brazos, the site Houston had selected for the interim capital. In what has gone down in history as the "Archive War," however, a group of the remaining Austinites fired a cannon at their Texas brethren, then chased them into the night to recover the papers. The following day, December 31, 1842, the victors returned the archives to Austin. Sam Houston, ever the rebel, continued to conduct his presidential business at Washington-on-the-Brazos. Austin, with no reason for existence, slipped into decline as Comanche raids grew more frequent.

This was the darkness before the dawn, as it turned out. A constitutional convention held in Austin on July 4, 1845, voted to approve the United States' offer to annex Texas. Austin was again chosen the interim capital, this time of the State of Texas. In a poignant ceremony held at high noon on February 19, 1846, Texas President Anson Jones declared, "The Republic of Texas is no more." While the decade-long experiment in frontier democracy had come to an end, its legacy would live on in the generations of proud Texans yet to be born.

The 28th State

With Texas representing the 28th star on the flag of the United States, Austin's tensions could ease somewhat. The Mexican-American War, fought largely on Mexican soil, settled the international boundary far south of Austin along the Rio Grande with the 1848 Treaty of Guadalupe Hidalgo. By 1850, when Austin won another 20-year term as the state capital, the city claimed just 629 residents. Ten years later, the number of inhabitants had grown to 3,494,

Photo: Peter A. Silva

The Capitol building is Austin's centerpiece.

nearly a third of them slaves, as the number of government jobs grew and the private sector expanded. While the threat of Indian attack remained strong in the new capital during those years, stalwart Austinites moved ahead to build a lasting city. Texas' first permanent state capitol was open for business by 1853, and the city's master builder, Abner Cook, completed the Governor's Mansion, still in use today, by 1856. The architecturally magnificent Texas Land Office Building, which today is the Capital Complex Visitors Center, was completed by 1857. The future looked bright. Then came the Civil War — and secession.

Sam Houston had envisioned Texas as part of the United States since the early days of the Republic. Now, as the 70-year-old governor of Texas, "Old Sam" denounced the idea of seceding from the Union, despite the incendiary slavery issue and other grievances about states' rights that increasingly angered the South. In the face of growing revolt against the Union, Houston departed the Austin Governor's Mansion and traveled around the state in an attempt to prevent secession. Houston biographer Marquis James reported in *The Raven* that the aging statesman faced an angry mob in Galveston and still would not back down. "Some of you laugh to scorn the idea of bloodshed as the result of secession," Houston told the throng. "But let me tell you what is coming. ... You may, after the sacrifice of countless millions of treasure and hundreds of thousands of lives, as a bare possibility, win Southern independence ... but I doubt it."

In February of 1861, Texas voted overwhelmingly to secede. On March 16, the ever-defiant Houston stepped down as governor rather than take the oath of allegiance to the Confederacy. Despite all his former ill-will toward Austin as the capital, Houston must have taken a small degree of pleasure in learning that Austin and Travis County, as well as neighboring Williamson County, also voted against secession at first. As historian Humphrey reports so well, Austin was a slave city just as Texas was a slave state, but Austinites, like Sam Houston, "opposed efforts to precipitate Texas 'into revolution.'" After war broke out in April, however, most of tolerant Austin accepted the secession while hundreds of local men and boys marched off to battle. Four years later, Houston's dire prediction came true when the South fell.

While Austin had grown by nearly 3,000 people between 1850 and 1860, the war had taken its toll. By 1870, when Union forces (commanded for a time by General George Armstrong Custer) ended a five-year occupation of Austin, the city claimed just 4,428 residents, not even a thousand more than a decade before. A good portion were freed slaves eager to start new lives. Clarksville, still on the west side of town today, became just one of several thriving black communities that grew up during this period (see our Neighborhoods and Real Estate chapter).

Austin was set to take off. But first, it had to battle the city of Houston once again. Austin's 20-year term as interim capital had expired, and the issue again was to be put to a vote. The debate raged across the miles as each side volleyed nasty remarks about its opposition. Houston, according to Austinites, was home to "fetid, green-scum-covered bayous" while Austin was called a "bleak, inhospitable rocky waste," Humphrey reports. In November of 1872 Austin won the vote by nearly a 2-to-1 margin over its longtime nemesis. Four years later, the new state constitution designated Austin the permanent capital. At long last, the issue was settled.

A Thriving Capital

The years following the Civil War became a time of unprecedented growth for Austin, and for Texas as a whole. Despite the enormous suffering brought by the war, the state remained physically undamaged. While much of the South was in shambles, Texas offered huge expanses of open frontier just awaiting settlement. Southern in heritage and yet so Western in character, Texas became the great Southwestern frontier as immigrants poured in. With the coming of the railroad in 1871, Austin surged full steam ahead. The city more than doubled its 1870 population within 10 years, growing to 11,013. The newcomers arrived largely from the South but also from Europe. Germans, more than any other European ethnic group, forged new lives here, but Swedes, English, Irish, Italians and Poles came too. Congress Avenue and Pecan Street (now Sixth Street) became the commercial and political center of this thriving region.

The Texas Constitution, which encouraged immigration, certainly contributed to the state's, and Austin's, open attitude towards diversity as both American and foreign-born newcomers discovered a warm climate of acceptance. Great homes and commercial buildings designed to last the ages appeared on the landscape. Scholz Garten, a restaurant and beer garden built by German immigrant August Scholz in 1866, would become a popular gathering spot for Austin citizens of all nationalities during these years — and remains so to this day. Allen Hall, the first building west of the Mississippi River dedicated to the higher education of blacks, rose up on Austin's east side at Tillotson College, chartered in 1877 and opened to students by 1881. Austin, meanwhile, rallied for its next important phase.

Back in 1839, President Lamar had gained recognition as the Father of Education when, at his urging, the Congress of the Republic set aside land in each existing county to be used for public education. In Austin, a 40-acre site named College Hill had been designated for a university. But Texas in those early days lacked the resources for such a grand scheme, so education had been left to churches and private schools. In 1854 Governor Elisha Pease had signed a bill establishing the Texas Public School System. Now it was time to do something about a university. The Constitution of 1876 called for establishment of "a university of the first class." The location for the University of Texas was to be decided by a vote of the people.

College Hill had been standing by for nearly four decades. But with the location suddenly up for grabs, town leaders throughout the state quickly moved to claim the university as their own. Ten towns, including Waco, Lampasas, Tyler and Matagorda vied with Austin for the honor. But Austin had an ace in the hole in a man by the name of Alexander Penn Woolridge, a New Orleans-born, Yale-educated up-and-comer. As head of the Austin campaign, Woolridge, according to Humphrey, flooded Texas with pro-Austin literature, pointing out the city's beauty, healthfulness, central location and the fact that Austin already had land ready and waiting. East Texas voters went solidly for Tyler, but Austin triumphed. (And Woolridge went on to serve Austin in one capacity or for another four decades. A wonderful downtown city park (see our Parks and Recreation chapter) is named for him.) On September 15, 1883, townspeople gathered for an inaugural ceremony in the unfinished Main Building on College Hill, right on the original 40-acre site. In 1885, St. Edward's opened as a Catholic college on Austin's southern edge.

Three years later, on May 16, 1888, the youngest son of Sam Houston dedicated the magnificent new Texas State Capitol with the words, "Here glitters a structure that shall stand as a sentinel of eternity to gaze upon the ages." Presiding majestically over the hill looking down Congress Avenue, the capitol was, indeed, a site to behold.

Building a Viable Economy

Seat of government. Center of education. The twin economic pillars for Austin's development stood as solidly as the glorious new structures that served as their symbols.

Instead of bringing instant wealth to Austin, however, the University of Texas struggled in its early years.

In fact, all of Austin struggled to define its economic future. Early dreams of a commercial center ushered in by the railroad failed to materialize as rail lines spread and shippers found other cities more convenient. The Colorado River proved unnavigable, dashing hopes for the lucrative barge traffic. Factories were few and far between. Still, Austin remained the seat of political power in Texas. Along with important government jobs came the prestige of catering to the state's most influential men.

Besides, if jobs didn't come from huge factories or meccas of trade, enterprising Austinites would just invent their own. Retailers, lawyers, doctors, journalists, butchers, bakers and brewers as well as operators of boarding houses, brothels and saloons all found work in Austin. Builders certainly didn't lack work. Some of Austin's finest historic buildings today, including the regal hotel built by cattle baron Jesse Driskill, opened in that latter decades of in the 19th century. The distinguished neighborhood of Hyde Park in then far North Austin, which touted electric street car service, got its start during this period and became Austin's first suburb (see our Neighborhoods and Real Estate chapter), while celebrated European sculptor Elizabet Ney set about building her elegant Hyde Park studio. A few blocks west of Congress Avenue, a neighborhood of wealthy merchants and bankers rose up. Churches, hospitals and a courthouse dotted the Austin landscape, along with two grand opera houses that served the growing population's desire for cultural entertainment. Contributing to that scene were locally formed bands as well as The Austin Saengerrunde, a singing society founded by the city's German immigrants in 1879.

By the late 1880s Austin's growing number of professors and students bestowed a scholarly touch on the region, while the presence of the artist Ney and the short-story writer who would later become famous as O. Henry foreshadowed future artistic and literary communities. O. Henry would later give Austin one of its most endearing nicknames, The City of the Violet Crown, in honor of the purplish cast that emerges over the city at dusk. (Some say the color comes from the cedar pollen in the air.)

"Austin's diverse population grew like the town itself during these years," historian John Edward Weems wrote in the 1989 *Austin American-Statesman* supplement "Austin 1839-1989." "The diversity helped give the town a degree of tolerance that, however slight at first and however imperfect still today, broadened into an accommodation of people with a remarkable variety of beliefs and lifestyles."

Through it all, dreams of commerce and manufacturing remained strong among some of Austin's leaders. By 1893, Austinites gathered to celebrate the opening of a new million-dollar dam on the Colorado River and the beautiful lake it created. The dam was aimed at producing enough hydroelectric power for both the city and for the manufacturing plants city officials expected would come along to propel Austin to prosperity. Lake McDonald, named for John McDonald, the building contractor-turned mayor who had championed the dam, quickly became the city's prime recreational center. Accompanied by their dapper escorts, fashionable ladies wearing flower-topped bonnets boarded the great steamers *Ben Hur* and the *Belle of Austin* for relaxing cruises on the lake by day and dances by night. Rowing regattas at the lake attracted sports enthusiasts from around the world. Sunbathers and swimmers relaxed on shore, while the town elite snapped up resort properties along the perimeter.

Despite its increasingly civilized appearance, Austin retained much of its frontier flavor during the last two decades of the 19th century. In 1881 Austinites exhibited a mixture of tolerance and plain common sense by electing Ben Thompson to the job of city marshal. Thompson, considered the best gunfighter in the West by many, was also one of Pecan Street's most notorious gamblers. "During his tenure as marshal, it was claimed that major crime dropped to an all-time low," wrote Larry Willoughby in his book, *Austin: An Historical Portrait*. Unfortunately, the colorful Thompson resigned in 1882 to face murder charges in San Antonio and was killed later in a saloon shoot-out. Well into the 1890s, according to Humphrey, "Cowboys were familiar figures, and horses tied to hitching posts lined dusty Congress Avenue. ... Along the east side of the Avenue the saloons, cowmen, and gamblers were so thick in the evenings that 'ladies' would not think of walking there."

Austin's red-light district grew into a thriving enterprise during these years. Located west of Congress Avenue and called Guy Town, "it was not at all an unpopular part of town for many men — Austin residents, male visitors and legislators," reported Weems. "It was said that additional women were brought in when the state government blossomed into full lawmaking activity."

The 20th Century

Austin's Wild West spirit didn't disappear overnight, but the coming of the 20th century marked the beginning of its decline. By New Year's Day 1900 Austin's eyes were clearly focused on the future — and progress. Only one small item appeared on the front page of the local paper that day to indicate anything might be awry in the land of opportunity. "Saturday and yesterday some alarmists were busy circulating the report that there were great

Photo: Peter A. Silva

Terry's Texas Rangers cavalry unit is remembered on the Capitol grounds.

leaks in the powerhouse, in the dam, in the lake, and everywhere else out at the power and light plant up the river," the article said. "Superintendent Patterson … stated that they were without foundation." Austin got busy with its plans for the new century.

Whether those "alarmist" reports were true at the time mattered little just three months later when the skies unleashed a torrent of rain. On April 7, 1900, dreams of turning Austin into a manufacturing center were literally swept away along with the 7-year-old dam in a devastating flood that cost at least eight lives, destroyed everything in its path and left Austin without power for several months. When Austin overcame the shock enough to take stock of its situation — no big business, no big industry — city leaders determined to make the best of it. Austin's economic future would be built on the twin pillars of education and government the city had fought so hard to win in the past. Besides, they reasoned, Austin was just a beautiful place to live.

Growth and progress were now the name of the game. Wide and stately, yet made of dirt for more than 60 years, Congress Avenue was finally paved with brick in 1905, while a new concrete bridge replaced a rickety iron bridge across the Colorado River at Congress. "By 1910, Austin had its own skyscrapers, the Scarbrough and Littlefield buildings. The horseless carriage was no longer considered an intrusion into the lives of 'civilized' people, and as early as 1910 the automobile was an invaluable part of Austin's lifestyle and economy. When the first airplane landed in Austin in 1911, the 20th century had really arrived," wrote Willoughby.

Color Barriers

While Austinites had always made time for leisure and cultural activities, the coming of the industrial age made those pursuits even easier. Austin's new Majestic Theater (now the Paramount) opened in 1915, hosting major touring acts from around the country. Two years later the Austin Symphony Orchestra presented its first concert. Human habitation at Barton Springs, the jewel in a town endowed by enormous natural beauty, has been traced back several thousand years, but the arrival of the automobile made trips to this glorious swimming hole easier for "modern" Austinites. In 1917, Colonel A.J. Zilker gave the city hundreds of acres around the springs for use as a park. UT football, first played in 1893, became a popular spectator sport in the 1900s, along with the horse races that thrilled the crowds in Hyde Park. Grand balls attended by the city's most fashionable citizens continued at the elegant Driskill Hotel, while the lovely Hyde Park Pavilion hosted other stylish affairs.

Hyde Park, however, was an exclusively Anglo community; its posh gatherings were barred to Austin's minorities, as was Barton Springs, to name just two. Austin's black citizens, who had enjoyed some acceptance during Reconstruction, were now subjected to segregation and discrimination. As far back as 1885 a group of citizens in one ward had formed an "Anti-Colored Movement" to block the reelection of a black city councilmember, Humphrey reported. During the first decade of the 1900s Austin's color barrier became as distinct as in many other cities throughout the South. While the white-robed Ku Klux Klan paraded through Austin streets undeterred, blacks sat in a separate section on streetcars, attended separate schools, drank from separate drinking fountains and used separate public restrooms — when such facilities could be found. They also increasingly congregated on Austin's east side, away from their Anglo oppressors. Austin's many black professionals — doctors, lawyers, dentists and pastors as well as a plenty of business owners — found a racially mixed district to work in, but remained excluded from Austin "society." Not until 1950 would the first black student be admitted to the UT law school — under order from the U.S. Supreme Court.

Austin's small but growing Mexican-American population also faced treatment that would be considered despicable today. Most of the town's Mexicans had been chased out of town during the 1850s, while those that had followed found themselves still considered foreigners, despite their birthright. Even worse, some Austinites counted them as enemies because of the Texas Revolution, forgetting that many Mexicans living in the region during the war had fought — and died — for Texas.

By 1910, Austin claimed not quite 30,000

citizens. Houston, already a railroading and shipping center, witnessed huge industrial development following Texas' first great oil strike in the region in 1901. Its population had surged to nearly 79,000 by 1910. Dallas, enjoying success as a center for insurance, banking, commerce and the cotton trade, had skyrocketed to 92,000 people. Following World War I, Austin's population had increased by just 5,000, while Houston and Dallas soared to 128,000 and 156,000 respectively.

Although not cash rich at the beginning of the Roaring '20s, the University of Texas did own a great deal of land, including 2 million acres in West Texas, some of it leased to oil speculators. On Monday morning, May 28, 1923, the Santa Rita oil well blew in a gusher of black gold. The Big Lake Oil Field out west would continue to pump riches into the Permanent University Fund for nearly seven decades. Wealthy for the first time in its 40-year history, UT went on a building spree.

Now city officials really had something to brag about. Besides the rapidly growing UT, Austin also claimed St. Edward's University on the south side and two black colleges on the east. Austin was indeed becoming the center of culture, learning and politics that leaders had envisioned. They began touting Austin as the "Athens of the West," and citizens responded by earmarking funds to develop the city. Parks and playgrounds, wide boulevards and public buildings rose up. Austin's population more than doubled during the 1920s and '30s, hitting nearly 88,000 by 1940.

UT's spending binge, coupled with an influx of local and federal funds, staved off the worst of the Great Depression for Austin, according to local historians. One of the city's most treasured landmarks today, the 27-story UT Tower, was among many buildings completed on campus during the 1920s and '30s. President Roosevelt's New Deal, solidly backed by Austin's ubiquitous new mayor, Tom Miller, brought millions in construction funds to the area through the Works Progress Administration. Camp Mabry on Austin's west side, home to the Texas Volunteer Guard since 1891, mushroomed with new WPA construction as did other areas of the city. By late 1936, when *Forbes* magazine reported that Austin was one of the "bright spots in the nation," it appeared the worst of the Depression was over. And yet Miller, along with Austin's newly elected U.S. Representative, Lyndon Johnson, won for Austin the country's first federal housing project, completed in 1939 for the city's rapidly expanding Mexican-American population.

Miller, who would remain at the forefront of Austin business and politics throughout the '30s, '40s, and even well into the '50s, was responsible in many ways for fashioning modern Austin. A liberal among liberal Democrats of the era, Miller was a master politician who worked to gain support from all three sectors of Austin's increasingly tri-racial community. Although he did support racial segregation (not unusual even for liberal Southerners of the era), Miller nonetheless promoted equal civil rights for all.

"Miller was one of those fairly numerous anomalies in the South — the good businessman, the deep Southerner, who also stood strong on behalf of much of Roosevelt's New Deal, and Truman's Fair Deal, civil rights, and the like," according to Anthony M. Orum, author of *Power, Money & the People: The Making of Modern Austin*. Low-incoming housing extended to blacks and Mexican Americans under his reign while Miller also saw to it that East Austin's black community received basic city services, and the lovely Rosewood Park that remains today. His broader vision, however, remained on the city's future growth.

Among Miller greatest coups was his success — along with LBJ — in getting federal Depression-era funds to complete the Austin Dam (now named in his honor) by 1940. Two years later, construction of the Mansfield Dam that created Lake Travis wrapped up efforts around these parts to bring the unpredictable Colorado River under control.

Shaping the Future

On December 7, 1941, the United States went to war. While Austin's youth waged battle on far-off fronts, loved ones remained at home, sharing with the rest of the country in the hardships of scarcity and rationing — and the fear that a knock on the door would mean a son, husband or brother, or even a daughter, had paid the ultimate price. In 1943, Congressman Johnson and his wife, University of Texas graduate Lady Bird Johnson, bought small Austin radio station KTBC. Nine years later, on Thanksgiving Day 1952, KTBC became Central Texas' first television station. What more important event could have been chosen as a first broadcast during the heyday of the post-war years? The station aired the football game between arch rivals UT and Texas A&M. UT, of course, prevailed.

According to Humphrey, the seeds of Austin's eventual blossoming as a high-tech mecca were also planted in the 1940s with the creation of The Austin Area Economic Development Foundation. Established in 1948 with C.B. Smith as president, the council "foreshadowed and helped shape what was to come," Humphrey wrote. "Smith's foundation sought to diversify Austin's economy in a manner compatible with its 'way of life.' Research and development laboratories and high technology companies fit the bill."

Austin would also elect its first woman city council member in 1948. Interestingly, Emma Long was not just a female version of the reigning power elite but "an avowed enemy of the city establishment and a champion of the underdog," as Weems described her.

Gaining New Sensibilities

Meanwhile, somewhere during the second half of the 1940s, Austin's population hit 100,000 as the city became one of the fastest growing cities in the Southwest. By 1950 the population had reached 132,459. While nowhere near the size of Houston or Dallas, or even San Antonio, Austin had nevertheless turned into a thriving metropolis.

The time to address some long-ignored social injustices had arrived. Heman Marion Sweatt's victorious Supreme Court battle to gain admission to the UT law school in 1950 cracked UT's doors to other black graduate students. Six years later, by decree of the UT Board of Regents, the university admitted its first black undergraduates, while Austin's public schools began the excruciatingly slow process of integration. In 1954, UT graduate and social activist Ronnie Dugger debuted *The Texas Observer* in Austin. Within months the small biweekly magazine had established itself as the liberal voice in Texas media, reporting on lynchings in East Texas. (*The Observer* continues its mission as a liberal voice in Texas media to this day.) As the tide for racial equality swelled across the United States, students at UT and the city's other colleges spearheaded the Austin movement of the 1950s and 1960s.

The movement, however, reached beyond UT and the city's other campuses to extend deep into the community. As a result, Austin experienced nascent political and social enlightenment as established barriers against minorities slowly cracked. Black and Mexican-American communities began taking places in positions of power by the late '60s and into the '70s.

While UT "radical" politics reached back decades, the university boomed during the 1960s as a haven for serious social activists and the hippies who brought their music and their faith in flower power. Austin's antiwar protesters took to the streets throughout the decade as public opinion against the Vietnam War surged. (In May 1970 students lead Austin's largest protest of the Vietnam era following the deaths of four students during a Kent State University antiwar demonstration.)

UT enrollment had swelled to more than 25,000 by 1966, although only about half remained on campus for the summer session.

The morning of August 1 dawned like any other hot, lazy summer day in the city. A few hours later, Austin became the site of what was then the largest simultaneous mass murder in American history when a heavily armed 25-year-old UT student and ex-Marine climbed the beloved campus Tower and commenced firing. Charles Whitman, who had murdered his mother and his wife the night before, fired round after round at unsuspecting victims below, killing 14 people and wounding 31 more before he was finally shot to death by Austin police. The 19-minute melee would spawn debate across the country over the issue of gun control.

At the epicenter of America's turbulent 1960s stood Lyndon Johnson, the former school teacher who had risen to political power from his boyhood home 50 miles southwest of Austin. A century had passed since Sam Houston stared Southern slave owners in the face — and lost. Now another tall Texan was storming the bastion of bigotry. He had already guided two civil rights acts through the Senate and as president was fighting for passage of a landmark civil rights act. Angry Southerners rebuked Johnson and Lady Bird at every turn, but the Texas leader prevailed. Johnson signed the Civil Rights Act of 1964 and the Voting Rights Act a year later. Johnson, however, would be judged at the time not for his efforts on behalf of human rights nor for the dozens of education bills and social reform measures he championed, but for drawing the United States further into the mire of the Vietnam War. Battered by public opinion against the war, Johnson chose not to seek reelection in 1968. He and Lady Bird returned home to their Central Texas ranch.

The Ups and Downs

While live music concerts had formed part of the Austin lifestyle since its earliest days, the 1960s would see the city boom with musicians of all kinds. Among UT's growing "folkie" music crowd was a shy freshman named Janis Joplin, who performed first on campus and later at a popular beer joint called Threadgill's. Later came the psychedelic sounds, rock 'n' roll, the blues and the country rock that would eventually turn Austin into the Live Music Capital of the World.

The '60s brought much more than music and social change, however. Attracted by UT's excellent reputation for research and development and by the city's attractive surroundings, high-tech manufacturers moved in. By the end of the decade, Austin claimed three major technology plants: IBM, Texas Instruments and Tracor. The high-tech revolution had arrived.

By 1970 Austin's population topped a quarter million. UT had mushroomed to more than 40,000 students. The number of city, county, state and federal government employees reached into the thousands, and high-tech firms had become the city's largest private employers. The Armadillo World Headquarters opened in 1970 and soon earned a nationwide reputation as a hot live music venue. Austin's cultural explosion during this decade extended into the areas of writing, theater and visual art as more and more artists found themselves drawn to the city.

In the summer of 1970, just a couple of months after UT students rallied 25,000 people for a march in protest of the Kent State shootings, a group of UT students gathered to map out a plan for Austin's future, according to Orum. Among the students was Jeffrey Friedman, a law school student who had taken a leadership role in the protest march. Armed with the knowledge that the voting age was about to be lowered to from 21 to 18, and realizing that students could register by proclaiming they intended to remain in Austin after graduation, the group determined to register thousands of university students. That accomplished, Friedman and a slate of other liberal candidates decided to challenge the existing power structure.

Friedman, according to Orum, "wanted things to be better in East Austin for the browns and the blacks. He wanted the poor people to have better jobs and better housing. But he also wanted to bring down the forces of the Establishment. He wanted to bring down the rich and the powerful." For his part, Friedman's conservative opponent, Wick Fowler, ran on a platform "that hippies were unfit to hold public office," Orum states.

While the conservative business sector claimed the majority of seats on the council that year, Friedman won his race to become the first student and youngest council member. Berl Handcox also won election, becoming the first Black to serve on the city council since the 1880s. Five years later Friedman became Austin's youngest mayor in what Orum called "the watershed council election of 1975, in which the majority of those elected were liberals." Among those voted in was John Trevino, Austin's first Mexican-American council member.

Tree Huggers Unite

Apart from the frustration over establishment politics that colored the 1970s, Austin's population explosion became a source of increasing consternation. Longtime residents mourned the good ol' days and expressed fears that Austin's scenic beauty was being bulldozed away to make way for expressways,

Photo: City of Austin

The Driskill Hotel is among the city's oldest and most beautiful buildings.

shopping malls, housing developments and skyscrapers. The slogan, "Keep Austin Austin," became a popular rallying cry during these years, Humphrey reports.

Austin's increasingly powerful environmental protection groups successfully thwarted major development in several environmentally sensitive areas, while helping to keep the protection of Austin's natural endowments on the minds of old-timers and newcomers alike — as well as on the front burner of local politics. Lady Bird Johnson, who divided her time between Austin and her ranch nearby, spearheaded a project to beautify Town Lake, which lead to the planting of thousands of trees as well as construction of a hike and bike trail and gazebos. Austin had indeed changed radically from its days as a small, sleepy town. But of the nearly 94,000 new residents who would move into Austin during the '70s, the majority would still be left breathless by the city's natural appeal — and still are today.

By the mid-1980s nothing appeared to stand in the way of continued growth. The economy boomed as more high-tech industries moved into Central Texas, bringing investment dollars and plenty of jobs. Austinite Michael Dell started his own little computer company in 1984 to add to the high-tech landscape. Housing costs rose, then skyrocketed, as Austin's population continued to expand. Banks made exorbitant loans, with little money down, as real estate speculators and tycoon developers snapped up residential and commercial properties around the region.

Then the bubble burst. Downturns in oil prices — which had already hurt many parts of Texas — contributed to the problem, as did a slump in the technology field, but many economists pointed to the overheated real estate economy as the leading cause of Austin's recession. For awhile during the second half of the decade, it appeared that more people were leaving the city than moving in. Real estate prices plummeted, businesses failed, bankruptcies became common, offices closed. By the end of the decade, according to reports, Austin led the country in the percentage of vacant office space and topped all other Texas cities for amount of indebtedness.

The Beautiful and the Sublime

Austin entered 1990 with a gloomy economic forecast. The United States as a whole was in recession, banks remained in turmoil, and another U.S. President who claimed Texas as home, George Bush, was preparing to declare war on Iraq. Despite earlier indications, however, Austin's population had grown by nearly 120,000 people over the past decade. In 1993, Apple Computer bought 129 acres in neighboring Williamson County for a financial services and customer support site. That same year, Motorola announced plans to build a $1 billion chip plant in Northeast Austin. Austin was on the rebound — big time.

The rest, as they say, is history. By 1998 Austin was riding the crest of another wave in growth and development as Central Texas solidified its reputation as one of the country's leading high-tech hubs. Dell Computer had grown to become the city's largest private employer and the world's third-largest maker of personal computers, with more than $12 billion in annual sales. Samsung built a $1.3 billion Austin plant. But computer manufacturers and chip makers formed just part of scene. Local start-up companies focusing on software development and the Internet also swelled during the '90s.

Along with the economic good times came increasing pressures. Rampant growth became the norm as the city expanded by about 1,500 people each month throughout the decade. The U.S. Census Bureau estimated Austin's population would hit nearly 604,000 by 1999 while the wider Central Texas area would surge well beyond a million inhabitants. Signs of the changing times were clearly visible everywhere as roads jammed, office space diminished, trees were sacrificed to make way for housing and commercial developments, and school districts scrambled to build new facilities to keep up with expanding enrollment.

As a result, a new phrase entered the Austin lexicon in 1998: Smart Growth. Aiming to develop a city that grows "smart" as it grows fast, the Austin City Council and Mayor Kirk Watson presented a series of initiatives designed to protect the environment and to limit sprawl, especially into environmentally sensitive areas, by encouraging development inside city limits. Debate over the plan's merits appeared likely to rage well into 1999. Race relations, often ignored in the past, also climbed on the city agenda as more enlightened leaders sought to bring some sense of community to a city that remained fractured in many respects — despite important strides among Austin's minority racial and ethnic groups over the past 40 years.

Yet somehow the real Austin survives. It's not the city some old-timers remember, but then again, the generations before them most likely said the same. For the thousands of newcomers who are seeing it for the first time, however, Austin remains one of the prettiest, most vibrant spot's on the planet. Austin's once-forlorn downtown has experienced a renaissance over the past couple of decades to become a thriving center for culture and entertainment. Live music pours from clubs all over greater downtown as the Live Music Capital of the World continues to attract the young, the restless and the talented. UT's influence on the arts has helped spawn entire communities of performing and visual artists, writers and filmmakers. Austin's enduring youthful spirit and creative energy add a luster that is as much a hallmark of this city as the State Capitol and the UT Tower.

The Texas pioneers who first laid eyes on this "beautiful and sublime scene" 160 years ago could not possibly have envisioned the Austin of today. And yet, in countless ways, Austin remains ever so sublime.

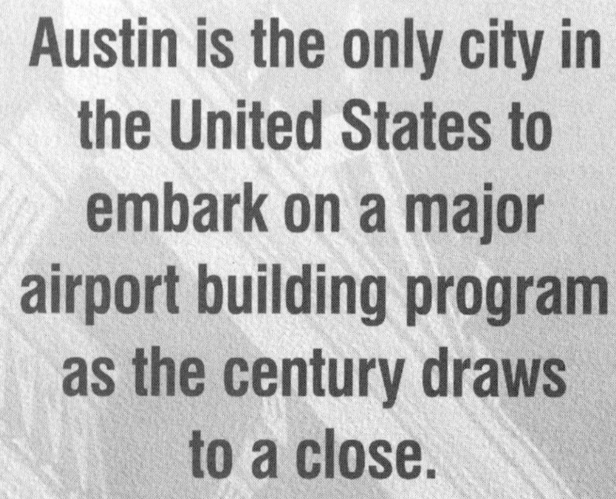

Austin is the only city in the United States to embark on a major airport building program as the century draws to a close.

Getting Here & Getting Around

"X" marks the spot, and smack dab in the middle of Texas is Austin. There is an old saying in the Lone Star State: "The sun has riz and the sun has set, and I ain't outta Texas yit." That says a lot about traversing the state. Austin is about a three-hour drive south of Dallas, a little less than a three-hour drive west of Houston, and a little more than an hour north of San Antonio. It is about a five-hour drive to Nuevo Laredo, Mexico; a five-hour drive to both the Louisiana and Oklahoma borders; and if you are heading west to New Mexico, plan on taking all day for the eight-hours-plus drive.

Interstate 35, often called the Nafta Highway (a reference to the North American Free Trade Agreement), bisects the state from north to south, running from Laredo on the Mexican border up through the middle of the country to the Canadian border. Interstate 10 runs from the Louisiana border through Houston, south of Austin through San Antonio and on to El Paso. U.S. Highway 290 connects Houston to Austin and then joins I-35 for a short stretch, cuts west through the Oak Hill area of Austin and off into the Hill Country.

Austin is literally deep in the heart of Texas. Here are some tips on getting here — and getting around once you have arrived.

Airports/Commercial

Austin is the only city in the United States to embark on a major airport building program as the century draws to a close. In the spring of 1999, the city will shut down the municipal airport near downtown Austin and open a new international facility in the southeast sector of the city to be called Austin Bergstrom International Airport. In 1998 AeroLiteral (AeroMexico's regional carrier) began direct service to and from Monterrey, Mexico, making Austin's airport truly international. Cargo operations have already moved to the new airport, and general aviation will moved there on April 24, 1999.

The same airlines and rental car companies will be serving the new $690 million airport, but the facility will be larger with twice as many gates, two runways (as opposed to one) and a much larger terminal, named in honor of the late Texas Congresswoman Barbara Jordan. Austin Bergstrom also will have a two-level access road (one level for arrivals, the other for departures) and a three-level parking garage.

The designers and builders are hoping to evoke the spirit of Austin at the new facility by including a performance stage in the terminal for live music performances, and landscaping

INSIDERS' TIP

A variety of names were suggested for Austin's new international airport (scheduled to open in 1999), but city officials decided to stick with the name given the Air Force base that occupied the site. It was named in honor of Austin's first World War II casualty, Captain J.A. Bergstrom.

will reflect the Hill Country by using water elements, rocks and native plants. The new terminal will include a business center, 12 restaurants and snack shops (some of them operated by local businesses such as Amy's Ice Cream, Book People and the Salt Lick barbecue), retail shops and bookstores. The restaurants and snack bars promise to sell food at "street prices," rather than the inflated prices often found at airports, plus the retail stores will feature regional items, including music by Austin musicians and works by local artists and crafters.

Robert Mueller Municipal Airport
3600 Manor Rd. • (512) 495-5439, (512) 472-3321 paging, (512) 495-7600 police

Mueller is pronounced "Miller," and Manor Road is pronounced "MAY-ner," but these local eccentricities won't have to puzzle visitors and newcomers after May 1999 when the new airport opens. The municipal airport has served Austin well for more than 60 years. About 3 miles from downtown, this relatively small airport, named after a forward-thinking city councilman in the '30s, has grown to the bursting point as Austin has boomed.

The facility was refurbished and expanded in the '80s, but some believed a new facility was needed. Like all things in Austin, the debate over whether to move the airport was an extended one, requiring several city elections until voters got it right, as the "move it" proponents saw it, and the decision was made to take over the site of the former U.S. Bergstrom Air Force Base near the intersection of U.S. Highway 71 and U.S. Highway 183 southeast of downtown.

Several major airlines service the Austin area, including American, America West, Continental, Delta, Northwest, Southwest, TWA, United and USAir. Southwest, humorously known as the "national" airline of Texas, operates its own gate area at the eastern end of the main building gates 13 through 16, while the other airlines operate gates 1 through 12 from a long, narrow wing running north of the ticket counters. Most flights from Austin connect through Dallas or Houston, although as the city grows, there are a greater number of direct flights to other major cities. One of the most well known is the "Nerd Bird," which shuttles between Austin's Silicon Hills and California's Silicon Valley, carrying the high-tech whiz kids back and forth.

There are snack bar and bar facilities in both gate areas and in the main terminal area where ticket counters are located. Restrooms have baby-changing facilities, but there is no designated play area for children in the airport. Wheelchairs and golf cart shuttles are available for passengers who need them, but there are no long distances to be traversed as in many of the nation's larger airports. The baggage area can be quite congested at busy times.

The Visitor Information desk in the main seating area of the terminal provides information on transportation services. Many Austin hotels operate shuttle buses, and these are listed on signposts in the shuttle-bus pickup area, immediately outside the baggage-claim area exits.

Capital Metro offers bus service from the airport to the downtown area. Bus No. 20 serves that route, and the fare is 50¢ (see the Public Transportation section for information on local bus service). It runs from approximately 4 AM to midnight. Buses run every 20 minutes, and the route runs from the airport, down Red River Street past the LBJ Library to 11th Street and on to Cesar Chavez Boulevard. The route is marked at the bus stop in front of the terminal, and the Visitor Information booth at the main entrance to the terminal also has information about schedules and routes.

Airport Parking

Parking at the municipal airport can be a nightmare on busy travel days and holidays. No parking is allowed in front of the main terminal: A recorded mantra warns drivers picking up and dropping off passengers — over and over and over — not to leave their cars unattended in front of the terminal building. Airport police will ticket unattended cars within minutes. Cars also will be towed if the driver does not return quickly.

Passengers have several parking options at the airport.

Austin's skyline is visible from Interstate 35.

Airport Valet Parking

3511 Manor Rd. • (512) 478-7275

This off-site parking lot offers shuttle buses to the nearby airport plus car-washing services. Rates are $9.95 a day for uncovered parking, $11.95 a day for covered.

AMPCO Parking Inc.

3600 Manor Rd. • (512) 476-7200, (512) 476-4264 valet parking

This company operates the airport's parking facilities. Short-term parking in the lot closest to the terminal is $22 a day, but customers get the first 15 minutes free for picking up and dropping off passengers. All parking is uncovered, and other lots vary in price according to their distance from the main terminal building, from $12 down to $3.75 a day. Shuttle buses serve the far lots. There is a $15-a-day charge for valet parking.

Airports/General Aviation

Austin Aero

1901 E. 51st St. • (512) 479-6666

This fixed base operation (FBO) is at Robert Mueller Airport on the north side of the field. Like other airport operations it will be moving to the new airport in the spring of 1999. Aero can accommodate any size aircraft and offers a fueling station, maintenance and hangar facilities. The company also can arrange for hotel and limo reservations, even restaurant reservations or flower delivery. Hangar space starts at $300 a month. Transient pilots purchasing fuel may park overnight for free.

Cutter Aviation Executive Air Park

811 W. Howard Ln. • (512) 251-2433

Cutter is a fixed base operation (FBO) with a 5,000-foot lighted runway; however, the service company is open only from sunrise to sunset. Cutter offers fueling service from 8 AM to 7 PM, tie down and hanger parking at daily and monthly rates ranging from $5 a day up to $800 a month. The operation also includes two flight schools.

Lakeway

115 Flying Scott Rd. • (512) 261-4385

Operated by Lakeway Airpark Association, a cooperative, this private facility is nonprofit and unattended. There is a 4,000-foot landing strip open from sunrise to sunset plus self-serve gas facilities. Overnight parking is $5, but that is waived with gas purchase. The landing strip is 15.5 statute miles from Austin. The association reminds pilots there is a noise ordinance in place plus pilots should watch for the deer grazing near the landing strip.

Signature Flight Support
East side, Robert Mueller Municipal Airport • (512) 476-5451

Also scheduled to move in the spring of 1999, Signature offers flight support for general and transit aviation. Parking is free with gas purchase, and Signature will coordinate hotels, limos and other travel needs.

Air Charters

Austin Air Taxi Inc.
1901 E. 51st. • (512) 236-1125

Prices for Austin Air Taxi range from $1.30 up to $4 a mile depending on the size of the plane. The planes range from a single passenger plane to a multi-passenger turboprop plane and are available for sightseeing tours and commuter hops.

Capitol Wings
4209 Airport Blvd. • (512) 474-6597

Charter describes itself as an aircraft management company helping the owners of private planes maintain their aircraft, but it also offers charter services for several hundred dollars an hour, depending on the size of the aircraft.

Canales National and International Aircraft Charter Service
1801 E. 51st St • (512) 474-8359

Planning a sightseeing tour? Canales can accommodate your needs with a variety of aircraft. Fees are charged by the hour and begin at $55 for two passengers and a pilot.

Train Stations

There are several recreational trains for sightseeing in the Austin area. (You'll find information on them in our Attractions chapter).

Amtrak
250 N. Lamar Blvd. • (512) 476-5684, (800) 872-7245 reservations

North/south service is available four times a week on the Amtrak *Eagle*. Northbound trains leave on Sunday, Tuesday, Wednesday and Thursday mornings; southbound on Sunday, Wednesday, Friday and Saturday evenings. The north route goes through Dallas to Chicago, the south route goes to San Antonio. Fares to San Antonio range from $9 to $17, depending on how close to departure time reservations are made; fares to Dallas range from $20 to $40. Children 2 to 15 travel for half price with an adult. East-west service is available from San Antonio, that route connects Los Angeles to Miami.

Bus Services

Bus service within the city of Austin is covered in our subsequent Public Transportation section.

Greyhound
816 E. Koenig Ln. • (512) 458-4463, (800) 231-2222

The intercity bus station is near Highland Mall, just west of the intersection of U.S. Highway 290 E. and I-35. Greyhound offers service to more than 2,500 U.S. cities.

Kerrville Bus Co., Inc.
(512) 389-0319, (800) 231-2222

This Texas-grown bus company is also served by the Greyhound station facility (see previous listing). Kerrville serves several Texas cities and small towns.

Roadways

Austin sits at the crossroads of two major highways: Interstate 35 and U.S. Highway 290. That sounds simple, but as visitors and newcomers to Austin quickly discover, the picture gets muddied first by a local propensity for calling highways by names other than the state highway department designations, and second by the absence of any clear east-west routes in the center of the city.

In this section we'll give you a primer on the major roads, their official names and the names they are called by the locals, and then a discussion of Austin traffic and the peculiarities of getting around the city by car.

I-35 runs right through the middle of the city, heading south to San Antonio and on to the Mexican border, heading north to Waco, Dallas-Fort Worth and points north.

U.S. 290 runs from Houston westward to the northeast section of Austin where it is called U.S. 290 E.. It merges with I-35, emerging again in South Austin as U.S. 290 W., where it is called Ben White Boulevard.

Texas Highway 71 merges with U.S. 290 W at I-35 through the southern and southwestern section of the city, separating at what locals call the "Y" in Oak Hill. U.S. 290 W. heads west to Johnson City, while Texas 71 heads northwest to Bee Cave and the Highland Lakes.

U.S. Highway183 runs diagonally through the city from northwest (at Cedar Park) to southeast (near the new Austin Bergstrom International Airport). It has numerous names along its route (see our discussion of east-west roads below).

The MoPac Expressway, called Loop 1 on all the highway signs, runs north-south through the western environs of the city. The locals just call it MoPac as we do throughout this book.

Loop 360, or the Capital of Texas Highway, runs north-south through far West Austin. Businesses along this roadway use Capital of Texas Highway in their addresses, but the locals usually call it 360. We give you both designations in this book.

R.M. 620 is a primarily north-south road that swings around Austin in the Hill Country west of Lake Austin and east of Lake Travis. Usually called just "620." The designation R.M. means Ranch-to-Market road, a leftover from the days when the state built highways so that farmers and ranchers could bring their goods and cattle to town. Some roads are called R.M., while others are F.M. (Farm-to-Market).

One thing you can count on in Austin: Whenever you hear people complaining about the traffic, economic times are good. When times are bad, folks have other things on their minds. In the summer of 1998, as the unemployment rates dropped, and the stock market soared, letters to the editor in the local paper became more and more focused on the state of Austin traffic.

Commute times have become longer as the city has grown, but they pale in comparison to commutes in some of America's larger cities. During morning and evening rush hours (6:30 to around 9 AM and 4:30 to 7 PM) traffic slows to a crawl on the area's major roadways, notably I-35, MoPac and U.S. 183. At other times, driving in Austin is relatively easy.

Perhaps the biggest problem in navigating Austin streets is the fact that there is no major east-west freeway in the heart of the city. In the north, U.S 183 (at intervals called Research Boulevard, Anderson Lane, Ed Bluestein Boulevard and Bastrop Highway) has been widened and improved, while in the southern end of the city U.S. 290 W. (known as Ben White Boulevard for much of its length) has been widened and turned into a freeway from I-35 to Oak Hill. Construction on U.S. 290 through the Oak Hill area is scheduled to be completed in 1999, but until then the western end from Loop 360 to Texas 71 is a bottleneck.

As for a midtown freeway, the issue has been a major political football for years as older central city neighborhoods have fought attempts to widen their streets. Koenig Lane, which becomes R.R. 2222 west of MoPac, has been touted as a possible route, but the idea is opposed by residents in that area. Enfield Road/15th Street, which leads from west of MoPac to the State Capitol, has been considered as another possible route. However, it goes through one of Austin's oldest, wealthiest and most politically influential neighborhoods, so that idea has been a virtual non-starter.

A third option for a midtown thoroughfare is Cesar Chavez Boulevard, which for part of its length is now one-way. Cesar Chavez Boulevard does link I-35 with MoPac, but it also

INSIDERS' TIP

Bicyclists 17 and younger must wear helmets in the city of Austin on all streets, bike trails and in parks. Violation is a Class C misdemeanor punishable with a $20 fine for the first conviction and $40 for each subsequent conviction.

runs along Town Lake, and citizens have been loath to either speeding up traffic adjacent to the city's premier park, or sacrificing any park land just to widen a roadway.

When it comes to north-south streets, Austin does have several freeways that offer nonstop driving. The major roadway, and the one on which most visitors arrive, is I-35, often called the Nafta highway these days because it is a major route between the United States and Mexico. The highway is two-tiered as it passes through downtown Austin; the upper deck has fewer exits, while the bottom deck has entrance and exit ramps to neighborhoods from downtown to just south of U.S. 290 E.

MoPac was built parallel to the Missouri-Pacific Railroad on a north-south axis. There have been battles over the extension of MoPac, primarily at the southern end from Town Lake and beyond. That section passes over the recharge zone for the Edwards Aquifer, the underground water system that feeds Barton Springs (see our Close-up on Barton Springs Pool in the Parks and Recreation chapter). Currently, MoPac runs from Slaughter Lane in far South Austin to Wells Branch in far North Austin. There are stoplights along the north and south portions. Many Austin drivers use MoPac as a way to avoid the I-35 bottlenecks in the center of the city.

There are plans for a north-south toll road east of the city parallel to the Missouri-Kansas railroad, to be named MoKan, which also will divert some traffic away from I-35.

Two major roadways serve the western environs, and with population growth they have become increasingly busy. Loop 360 (Capital of Texas Highway) roughly parallels MoPac but is farther west. Originally intended to be a scenic throughway, the road has been accumulating more and more traffic signals as suburbs and shopping centers spring up along its banks. R.M. 620 sweeps around Austin to the west and serves the Highland Lakes area. Although it is a wide roadway, like Loop 360 it has become busier as the area has grown and development has flourished.

Two scenic west-east roads feed into the city from the west: R.M. 2222 and Bee Caves Road (R.R. 2244). The former spills into Northwest Austin, while the latter winds through West Lake Hills. A wide, four-lane roadway, R.M. 2222 can be dangerous, particularly on weekends when drivers who have been drinking at the lake drive too fast on the curving road. There have been many fatal accidents on R.M. 2222, and drivers should always be alert when driving it. As for Bee Caves Road, it is being widened in several areas, but West Lake Hills residents are concerned that any further widening could turn the roadway through their community into a fast throughway.

Growth and increasing trade with Mexico will continue to have an effect on Austin traffic, ensuring that it will be a hot topic of conversation and political wrangling in the future.

Car Rental

Rental car counters are at the western end of the airport terminal, past the baggage claim area. In addition to airport-based rental car agencies, there are several other companies offering rental car services in the city.

Alamo, at the airport, (512) 474-2922, (800) 327-9633

Avis, at the airport, (512) 476-6137, (800) 831-2847

Advantage Rent-a-Car, 3515 Manor Road and other city locations, (512) 388-3377

Budget, at the airport, (512) 478-9945, (800) 527-0700

Capps Van & Car rental, 4302 Airport Boulevard, (512) 323-0003

Dollar, at the airport, (512) 322-9881

Enterprise, 2131 Theo Drive and several other city locations, (800) RENT-A-CAR

Hertz, at the airport, (512) 478-9321, (800) 654-3131

Montgomery Ward Autorent, Capital Plaza, 5621 I-35 N., (512) 371-0110

INSIDERS' TIP

The pink granite on the outer walls of the new Austin-Bergstrom International Airport comes from Marble Falls, west of the city, and is the same type of granite used at the State Capitol.

National Car Rental, at the airport, (512) 476-6189

RentAWreck, 6820 Guadalupe Street, (512) 454-8621

Parking

Downtown parking can be hard to find — many meters allow only 30-minute parking and two-hour meters are located several blocks away from Congress Avenue.

There are several parking garages in the downtown area, which are a good place to park if the weather is hot (shade is invaluable in the hot Texas summer), or at night when street parking can be hard to find. Other lots have attendants, and some have banks of boxes where patrons must deposit their fees. If you don't, you will be towed.

Parking around the capitol will improve with the opening of a new visitor parking garage on San Jacinto east of the capitol in 1999. Currently, visitors may park for free for two hours in the garage at 15th and San Jacinto streets, longer stays are permitted, but you must get a note from the guard on duty. There is a large parking garage under the capitol extension, but that is for the legislators and their staff. There are also parking spaces for legislators on the capitol grounds, and these are guarded by parking attendants.

Parking meters around the capitol are limited to two-hour stays, which is a hassle for anyone wanting to spend time touring the building or doing business at one of the many state buildings in the area. The idea is to discourage state workers from using street parking.

Taxis

Taxi cabs line up to serve customers at the western end of the airport terminal. Cabs wait in a holding area and are dispatched into the pickup lane. Only at very slow times will a passenger have to call for a cab. Austin's taxi services are regulated by the city, which requires companies to operate both smoking and nonsmoking cabs plus wheelchair-accessible vehicles. The flag-drop charge is $1.50, and each mile is $1.50. The charge from the airport to downtown ranges from $7.50 to $10.50, depending on what part of downtown you need to reach. Taxi service is available 24 hours a day, seven days a week. Taxis cruise downtown, particularly around the capitol area. Reponse time, especially downtown, is very good. Cabbies accept cash and credit cards.

American Yellow-Checker Cab Co., (512) 452-9999, (800) 456-8294, (512) 835-7272 TTY

Austin Cab, (512) 478-2222

Checker Cab Co., (512) 434-7777

Roy's Taxi, (512) 482-0000, (800) 845-ROYS

Taxi companies serving the Round Rock area:

Ace Taxi, (512) 244-1133

Tote-N-Tip, (512) 388-4022

Limousines

There are more than two dozen limousine operators in Austin, and, like taxi cab companies, they are regulated by city ordinances governing safety and business practices. Companies charge hourly rates starting around $55 for four passengers. Most also add service and gratuity charges, usually 15 percent each, and many also charge more during the peak spring prom season and on holidays such as Halloween and New Year's Eve. Sedan limos used for hotel/airport pickups cost around $120 an hour.

The limo business is highly competitive, and there is frequent turnover. Several large chains also operate in Austin. For a complete listing, check the Yellow Pages.

ABC Limo, (512) 371-7722, operates seven days a week, 24 hours a day. ABC offers a Jacuzzi limo (based in Houston, but available in Austin by reservation) that allows passengers to stop the car and soak for awhile, all for $145 an hour.

AusTrans, (512) 326-5466, has several vintage vehicles in its fleet including a 1962 Rolls Royce for $125 (weekday) to $140 (weekend) an hour and a 1964 Cadillac beginning at $45 an hour.

Crown Limo, (512) 250-5466, has limos equipped with televisions and VCRs and smaller luxury sedans for $50 an hour.

Carey, (512) 328-2600, is a national chain operation with outlets in 426 cities and 65 countries. It offers stretch limos, luxury sedans, vans and full-size buses.

Lily White Limos, (512) 842-1431, dubs itself a Christian limo service and caters to nonsmoking, nondrinking customers.

Prime Time, (512) 345-5466, has a popular limo set aside for cigar smokers plus stretch limos to accommodate up to 10 passengers.

Sopha Limos, (512) 499-0225, has the only red limousine in Texas, a 10-passenger 1997 Lincoln that rents for $360 for four hours.

Public Transportation

Capital Metro

106 E. Eighth St. • (512) 474-1200, (512) 385-5872 TDD

One of the easiest ways to navigate the downtown area is to ride the 'Dillo, the free, trolley-style buses that cruise the area from early morning to around 10 PM at night. The 'Dillos are just one service of the Capital Metro public transportation service, a publicly funded agency, that operates buses and shuttle services in the greater Austin area. Most of the major attractions in Austin are located on bus routes, including the museums and live music spots. Capital Metro also operates an airport-to-downtown bus line.

In addition to operating bus routes to many of the city's attractions and shopping centers, Capital Metro also runs the UT Shuttle, a bus service that takes students back and forth to the campus for 50¢ a ride — the same fare it charges on its regular city bus routes. The suburbs are served by flyers, which are nonstop buses that operate from park-and-ride stops in the outlying areas.

The Capital Metro bus system serves a 500-square-mile area that encompasses the cities of Austin, Cedar Park, Leander, Lago Vista, Jonestown, Pflugerville, Manor and San Leanna. Capital Metro offers a comprehensive booklet of its policies and schedules that is available at all area HEB, Fiesta, Randall's and Albertson's grocery stores, Ace Cash Express, major shopping malls and the agency's offices.

Capital Metro's Customer Information Center has operators on duty from 6 AM to 10 PM Monday through Friday, 6 AM to 10 PM on Saturday and 7 AM to 6 PM on Sunday. The agency operates a local toll-free number, (800) 474-1201, that allows customers to dial free from any local pay phone.

There are several methods of payment on Capital Metro buses. Ticket books are available at previously listed grocery stores and at the Capital Metro Customer Information Center. Each ticket book has 20 tickets valued at 50¢ each for $5, a 50 percent savings on the regular ticket price of 50¢. Passengers must have tickets or exact change to board the bus.

Seniors and mobility impaired riders may ride free on city buses by obtaining a free ID at the information center, or, in the case of seniors, by showing an ID with a birth date. There are discounts for individuals who qualify for Special Transit Services, which provides transportation for those who cannot ride public buses. All city buses have bike racks and are equipped with wheelchair lifts.

The agency provides a variety of programs including park-and-ride services, a car-pooling program called Ridefinders, a special van service for seniors called Easyrider, and other programs tailored to the mobility impaired. Capital Metro often provides free public shuttles at major Austin events and festivals, and visitors and downtown workers can avail themselves of the free 'Dillo service, which runs from approximately 6 AM to 10PM. These are modern trolley-like buses that circulate the downtown area. Downtown-area bus stops have 'Dillo route maps.

Bicycling

Austin is trying its best to be a bike-friendly city. The city even employs a Bicycle & Pedestrian Program Coordinator, who is charged with formulating a bicycle and pedestrian-friendly transportation plan. The coordinator may be contacted by calling (512) 499-7032, or by writing to the Department of Public Works and Transportation, City of Austin, P.O. Box 1088, Austin, TX 78767. The city's Bicycle Planning policy is published by the city, and complimentary copies are available at the above address.

The city currently has approximately 62 miles of roadway with marked bicycle lanes. City ordinances also require bicyclists 17 and younger to wear a bicycle helmet. An ordinance to require all bicyclists to wear a helmet was amended after many free-spirited adults complained; however, given the city's busy streets, all riders are advised to wear a helmet in traffic.

We provide more information on recreational biking and cycling in the Austin area in our Parks and Recreation chapter.

There are several organizations in Austin that promote bicycle awareness/commuting/safety. They include:

The Texas Bicycle Coalition, a nonprofit advocacy organization, (512) 476-RIDE;

The Yellow Bike Program, a nonprofit group promoting community free-use bicycles, which are painted yellow and left at various locations, notably around the University of Texas campus, (512) 916-3553;

The Austin Cycling Association, a recreational riding club, P.O. Box 5993, Austin, TX 78763;

Austin/Travis County Super Cyclist Program, a children's bicycle safety and education program, (512) 708-0513;

Austin Ridge Riders, a recreational mountain-biking club, (512) 441-2553;

The City of Austin Bicycle Program, the city's bicycle transportation planning effort, (512) 499-7240;

The University of Texas College Traffic Safety Program, a bicycle safety, education and defensive-cycling course, (512) 475-8252;

Austin Triathletes, a recreational triathlon club, (512) 314-5773.

Walking

There are areas of Austin where walking can be a pleasure, notably Congress Avenue, the Town Lake Hike and Bike Trail, and in some of the neighborhood parks. There are also several popular Historic Walking Tours in the city. For more information on these opportunities, see our Attractions and Parks and Recreation chapters.

Walking in downtown Austin is a wonderful way to see the city. Visitors should, of course, always exercise caution. Street crime is not a problem in downtown Austin, certainly not during daylight hours, but do avoid alleyways after dark. Always exhibit caution when using bank teller machines, and carry purses and wallets in a secure manner. The Austin Police department operates both horseback patrols and bicycle patrols in the city's parks and downtown streets.

Horse-Drawn Carriages

One of the most romantic ways to tour downtown Austin in a horse-drawn carriage. Carriages are not permitted on E. Sixth Street, and its likely the horses would not appreciate the sometimes rowdy atmosphere on that stretch of Sixth between Congress Avenue and I-35, anyway.

Austin Carriage Service
(512) 243-0044

This service has Belgian and Percheron horses to pull the carriages, which take up positions near the capitol, usually around sunset. Fees are $60 an hour or $30 for a half-hour tour of the downtown area. The drivers are equipped with radios so they can be summoned to a restaurant, hotel or nightclub, sometimes for an extra fee if it is far from the capitol. One pleasant ride is a tour of the Bremond Historic District downtown (see our Attractions chapter) or a waterfront tour along Town Lake. Operating hours are Sunday through Thursday from just before sunset to around midnight, and on Friday and Saturday from sunset to around 2 AM.

Die Gelbe Rose Carriage
(512) 477-8824

Headquartered near the Radisson Hotel at Cesar Chavez Street and Congress Avenue, this carriage company uses Clydesdale horses, but also has one Belgian and one Percheron. Rates are $80 an hour or $40 for a half-hour. A popular tour is along Congress Avenue to the capitol and past the Governor's Mansion. If he is in the garden, you may get a wave from Gov. George Bush. Carriages are available from around sunset to midnight during the week and until 2 AM on weekends.

Hotels and Motels

Are you the type of traveler who just wants a comfortable, clean, inexpensive place to fling your bags and rest your body so you can spend all your time getting to know Austin? Or are you looking for a lodging that caters to your every business need? Do you prefer divided space to conduct private meetings or to give you some breathing room from the kids? Perhaps you're looking for accommodations that reflect the history of Austin and transport you back in time. Is luxury the key to your heart? Whether you're looking for a massage and a sauna, a morning jog along Town Lake, a view, shopping or nightlife, you've come to the right place!

While Austin offers plenty of accommodations for the traveler who believes the best surprise is no surprise, there also is an ever-increasing number of rooms for those searching for the unique. If you're wishing to be transported, think of us as "OZ-tin," click your heels, make a reservation and repeat, "There's no place like Texas."

The headline news of the late 1990s regarding Austin's hotel-motel industry is growth and diversity. Austin is in the midst of a building boom, adding hundreds of new rooms around the city. That's a total turnabout from a decade ago, during the real estate bust of the 1980s, when few new lodgings were built. By far, the majority of new rooms are in limited-service or extended-stay facilities. In 1998, however, the grand dame of Austin hotels, the Driskill, underwent a historically accurate restoration estimated at more than $10 million, while another classic Austin landmark, the long-vacant Stephen F. Austin Hotel, was being restored to its early splendor in preparation for the planned 1999 opening. Austin also witnessed tens of millions of dollars invested in additions and upgrades at other hotels around the city. The Driskill and the Stephen F. hotels are Austin through and through, and many of the other major hotels also have created a Texas ambiance. But travelers don't have to shell out big bucks to get a real Austin experience. Some of our locally owned, older motels are truly Austin, and a lot easier on the pocketbook.

Although the hotel industry thrives by catering to convention visitors and corporate travelers, Austin's casual tourists are also reaping the rewards, in the form of more and more lodging options and choices of amenities. Studio and suite hotels are springing up all over the area. They are often called "extended-stay" facilities because they entice long-term visitors by offering fully equipped kitchens and other amenities as well as reduced rates for longer stays. Austin is also seeing an explosion in the number of business express hotels, lower-priced, limited-service versions of some of the luxury chains that cater to the busy executive — and to others.

While Austin may never see a return to the days when the grand hotel was the center of community activity, hotels are giving residents more and more reasons to check in. As a result, out-of-towners aren't the only ones to benefit from Austin's hotel industry. For weddings and other festivities, meetings, dining, socializing or getaway weekends, Austinite's are discovering the pleasures of our local hotels.

Whether you've come to live in Austin, or only wish you could, there are a few things you should know before making your hotel or motel reservation in Austin.

If this is your first visit to Austin, or you haven't had the pleasure of returning for awhile, allow us to orient you to the lay of the land when it comes to accommodations. The majority of Austin's full-service and luxury hotels are clustered around downtown. However, you'll also find several noteworthy full-service hotels along the Interstate 35 corridor. Another luxury lodging, The Renaissance Austin Hotel, is in Northwest Austin in the upscale Arboretum area. Northwest Austin, a beautiful area loaded with live oak trees, has seen tremendous growth in limited-service and suite hotels in the past few years, placing it among Austin's chief lodging locations today. Southeast Austin, anchored by the stately Omni Southpark Hotel, is another area that is experiencing a major boom in the number of hotels and motels.

The highest concentration of hotels and motels in Austin is found along Interstate 35. Because this north-south artery bisects Austin, I-35 hotels and motels can accommodate travelers who want to stay in North, Northeast, East, Central, South and Southeast Austin. For that reason, we've decided to include sections of I-35 to our geographical listings for those who prefer to stay close to this practical thoroughfare.

We've also tried to point out the best of the other hotels and motels scattered around the city. Although there aren't many of them, they can offer some interesting options and are certainly worth checking out. Of course, there are a number of resorts and bed and breakfast establishments in the Lake Travis area. (For information on those see our Resorts Close-up in this chapter and our chapter on Bed and Breakfasts and Country Inns.) Our neighboring communities of Round Rock, Cedar Park and Pflugerville have yet to see construction of a full-service hotel, although they are starting to get some national chain motels and hotels. You'll find some of these properties in the listings of additional addresses we've provided for these chains and in the apartment hotels listings at the end of this chapter.

Austin is bustling, both during the week and often on the weekends, so it's advisable to make advance reservations, especially if you've got a specific hotel in mind. But don't give up the opportunity to stay at the hotel of your choice just because you're late in arriving or making a reservations. There's always a chance. Most often, however, you'll get a better rate with a reservation as many hotels charge more if they're filling up — the old law of supply and demand. Of course, always ask about discounts or weekend packages the hotel may offer. The annual South by Southwest Music Festival (see our Annual Events and Festivals chapter), sessions of the Legislature, University of Texas football weekends and other big UT events all draw crowds to Austin so it's especially important to reserve your room for these times.

Are you arriving by air? Travelers who prefer to stay close to the airport should note that the new Austin Bergstrom International Airport is scheduled to open in 1999 in Southeast Austin (see our Getting Here and Getting Around chapter). This is a tricky issue for many hotels that have borne an "Airport" tag after their name. Fortunately for these hotels, they also are so close to the heart of Austin that they will still easily attract business, especially since most are right on I-35. Also, many of them have established excellent reputations for providing quality and service. South-side hotels, however, are elated by the airport's move. They certainly will see more action and have happily geared up. And the building boom of new lodgings in that area is just getting started. Word came in 1998 that a luxury hotel is in the planning stages at the new airport. The former nerve center of Bergstrom Air Force Base, known locally as "the donut" because of its shape, could become Austin's newest full-service hotel.

The Americans with Disabilities Act led to important changes at hotels throughout the country. These days all but a few lodgings have accommodations for the physically handicapped, and Austin's new Club Hotel by

INSIDERS' TIP

Don't forget to make The Driskill Hotel part of your walking tour of downtown Austin, even if you're lodging elsewhere. Look for "The Driskill, A Walking Tour" brochures in the hotel lobby and learn about this historic site.

DoubleTree offers rooms for the hearing impaired, which feature a special door buzzer and a blinking light in the room. However, there are a limited number of these specially designed rooms at each hotel, so it is crucial to make advance reservations.

Traveling with children, especially small ones, can bring the added concern of finding adequate babysitting so you can enjoy a night on the town or an afternoon of work or play. Several of Austin's better hotels will recommend an in-room babysitting service for you to contact, or they will make the arrangements for you. This is a great option since the hotel can vouch for the quality of service you are getting. If you choose to make babysitting arrangements yourself or need a day-care provider that will accept drop-ins, check out our chapter on Child Care.

If Fido or Fluffy have accompanied you to Austin, it's important to note that some hotels and motels do accept your pet, but many charge a nonrefundable additional fee for the animal. Others require a refundable deposit, while at some accommodations Fluffy stays free. However, this can get complicated also, as your pet may be welcome only on certain floors or in certain rooms. Even if you prefer a top-floor room with a view, for example, your pet (and you) may be relegated to a lower floor. Always check with the hotel before bringing your pet.

Smokers should also check the smoking policy when making a reservation. All but one of the hotels and motels listed below have rooms for smokers, and the policy in many of the full-service hotels is to have smoking floors — many times the lower floors. Bring your smokes if you must, but don't always count on the room with the view.

This chapter includes extensive listings of hotels and motels in Austin. It is not, however, a comprehensive list. Included here are some of Austin's best hotels, some that give you the most for your lodging dollar and, of course, some of our favorites. The listings include a dollar-sign code that will give you an idea of the hotels' rate for a one-night stay for two people in a standard room. Taxes are not included in the rates so when you're calculating the cost of your stay be sure to add 15 percent. The rate information has been provided by the hotels themselves and is subject to change. Unless otherwise noted, all the hotels and motels listed accept major credit cards.

Price Code

The following price code is based on the average room rate for double occupancy during peak business. These prices do not include taxes, which in Austin total 15 percent. Please note that prices may change without notice.

$	**Less than $50**
$$	**$50 to $100**
$$$	**$100 to $150**
$$$$	**$150 to $200**
$$$$$	**$200 or more**

Now that you're armed with the basic facts, read on to learn about some of Austin's great lodgings. Enjoy your stay. We have a feeling you'll be back.

Downtown

The Driskill Hotel

$$$$ • 604 Brazos St. • (512) 474-5911, (800) 252-9367

Cattle baron Jesse Driskill opened his stately hotel in downtown Austin on December 20, 1886, offering guests an architectural wonder and such modern conveniences as steam heat and gas lights. More than a century later, The Driskill adds timeless grandeur to the Sixth Street Historic District, where live music pours from the popular nightclubs and packed restaurants of Austin's most-visited strip. Guests leave all that commotion behind when they step into The Driskill's handsome, marble-floored lobby. In 1997 and 1998, the hotel underwent a historically accurate multimillion-dollar renovation and the results are outstanding. Each of the hotel's 180 rooms and suites is unique, designed to reflect the exceptional beauty of the 1880s Driskill. The hotel's famous Cattle Baron Suite, which features two bedrooms, a dining room and an elegant living area, rents for $2,500 a night — for those who truly want to feel like barons. There's also a sitting room named the Maximilian Room, known for its eight gold-leaf mirrors called the Empress Carlota mirrors. These French mirrors were a wedding gift from Maximilian, briefly emperor of Mexico, to his bride Carlota. The story goes that these mirrors were discovered in crates in San Antonio in the 1930s. The two-story side of the hotel is the original hotel and features spacious, alluring rooms with nearly 14-foot ceilings. The tower side was built in the 1920s and has nine levels, offering guests better views of downtown Austin. Some rooms feature balconies for an even closer perspective on downtown. The ballroom, upper lobby piano bar and the restaurant also have been remodeled to accentuate the beauty of a bygone era. The piano bar, which features live music in the evenings, is also home to portraits of some of Austin's leading historical figures, including Stephen F. Austin, the Father of Texas (see our History chapter for more on Stephen F. Austin). A captivating Western sculpture called "Widow Maker," by the artist Barvo, adorns this lobby — a must see.

A delightful contrast to its subdued charm is the Driskill's growing reputation as Austin's premier murder-mystery dinner theater, held in the Driskill Grill on Saturday nights and on special occasions. The gourmet restaurant is open daily for breakfast, lunch and dinner. The Driskill has no swimming pool or fitness center on the premises, although guests can request free passes to use the World Gym across the street. Neither is there a parking garage on the premises. Guests use valet parking or park at the meters around the hotel.

Four Seasons Hotel

$$$$$ • 98 San Jacinto Blvd. • (512) 478-4500, (800) 332-3442

It doesn't take many steps past the lobby entrance to know you're in one of Austin's premier hotels. Carpeting so thick and plush that your shoes practically disappear leads down the stairs into The Cafe restaurant and terrace, offering a drop-dead gorgeous view of Town Lake and of the hotel's own manicured lawns. The Four Seasons is just an extraordinary lodging. This hotel pampers you, your child AND your pet. Yes, the Four Seasons not only accepts domestic pets of all sizes on certain floors, it even provides treats. Children get cookies and milk or popcorn and sodas the evening of arrival. The hotel and its 292 exceptionally spacious rooms and suites — some offering stunning views of the lake — are designed with a sophisticated Southwestern flair that is both elegant and relaxing. The amenities and services go on and on: 24-hour room service, twice-daily housekeeping service, a heated outdoor pool overlooking Town Lake, a state-of-the-art health club that includes free weights and features a television on every bike, a spa with massage and body treatments offered, complimentary morning newspaper and overnight shoe shine, one-hour pressing service. There's even a dock for sunning, splashing your feet in Town Lake or, if your rowing team is in town, heading out for training. And while you're outside, you can take advantage of the hotel's direct access to Austin's wonderful Hike and Bike Trail. The Four Seasons will even arrange a bicycle if you want.

La Quinta Inn

$$ • 300 E. 11th St. • (512) 476-1166, (800) 531-5900

If you want to stay in downtown Austin, but don't need — or can't afford — all the amenities of Austin's upscale hotels — it's hard to beat the recently renovated La Quinta Inn. For comfort, location and comparative price, La Quinta is an excellent choice. It offers free parking on premises, a real plus for a motel downtown, where finding parking on the street can be a nightmare. The 145 rooms and suites are spotless and comfortably sized. Nice touches have been added to spruce up the outdoor walkways, such as huge potted flowers and plants. Among the motel's many features are free continental breakfasts, in-room coffee makers, Nintendo games, first-run movies, data port telephones, laundry services and an outdoor swimming pool. The Capital Cafe restaurant at La Quinta is leased to a private operator and serves breakfast and lunch Monday through Friday. The motel offers two corner suites with king-size bed, sofa and recliner. Another suite features one bedroom and a living room. All suites have refrigerators. The state capitol is just around the corner, Sixth Street is five blocks

Austin's Resorts

The Texas Hill Country west of Austin is conducive to outdoor recreation and relaxation. The lakes and waterways, the natural beauty of the hills, the hospitable

climate and Texas hospitality have been combined to create several top-quality resorts that offer a variety of experiences. Three of the four listed here are noted golf resorts, and they are detailed in our Golf chapter. The fourth is a Hill Country spa that offers not only outdoors recreational activities, but also all manner of therapies designed to relax both body and spirit.

Barton Creek Conference Resort and Country Club
8212 Barton Club Dr. • (512) 329-4000, (800) 336-6157

A top-flight resort with three beautiful golf courses designed by the top names in the sport, Barton Creek is on some of the most beautiful land just west of Austin. Barton Creek wends its way through the hills here, creating not only a beautiful setting for golf, but also for other activities, including tennis, skeet shooting, jogging on wonderful Hill Country trails, swimming, boating, fishing and horseback riding. The resort also offers sightseeing and shopping tours.

The resort has several top-flight dining facilities, for both casual meals and for special occasions. (It has one of the few restaurants in Austin where a jacket is required.) The resort's spa offers an extensive menu of treatments from facials to salt rubs to aromatic loofah scrubs. There is also a fitness center in the resort complex.

There are 147 guest rooms at the resort with views of the golf course and the surrounding Hill Country. Room rates are on the American Plan (three meals included) and begin in low season (January and December) at $170 per person, double occupancy and rise to $215 in the spring and fall. One-bedroom suite prices range from a low of $370 per person to $450. The presidential suite in high season is $820 per person.

— continued on next page

Photo: Peter A. Silva

Lake resorts offer visitors hours of wet recreation.

Lago Vista Resort & Conference Center

1918 American Dr., Lago Vista
• (800) 288-1882

At the northern end of Lake Travis, about 35 miles northwest of the city, this resort offers a variety of packages for golfers, tennis players, businesses planning retreats and families holding reunions. The lakeside site offers visitors access to watersports, also. In addition to conference facilities, Lago Vista has a spa, boat facilities, tennis courts, swimming pools and can arrange watersport rentals. Rooms at the resort range from guest rooms to two-bedroom suites. Rates are $85 to $125 a day.

Lake Austin Spa Resort

1755 S. Quinlan Park Rd.
• (512) 372-7380, (800) 847-5637

You can ask the concierge to fix you up for a round of golf. Or perhaps a set or two of tennis. A sailboat ride. A little water-skiing. But why would you? Wouldn't you rather just have another massage? This spa on the shores of Lake Austin aims to capture the essence of Austin and rid you of all those uptight urban ills. Lake Austin Spa Resort offers a large variety of spa services by the day or week. A three-night refresher package is a little more than $1,000 and includes two spa treatments of your choice, fitness classes and programs, a 30-minute personal fitness consultation, meals and a deluxe private room. The seven-night, ultimate pampering program costs approximately $3,000 and that includes a monogrammed robe.

Just reading the brochures is enough to make you long for a night or two of pampering. How about a Blue Lagoon massage — a body wrap of blue seaweed. Or a Texas two step — someone rubs your toes while you get an herbal facelift.

The spa also offers special programs throughout the year on diverse topics, including gardening, cooking classes and nutrition. Guest speakers from all walks of life are invited to these presentations. One recent special package was dubbed "A Gathering of Wise Women" and featured experts on women's health issues.

And if you really want to get more active, in addition to golf and tennis, the spa offers a long list of outdoor activities including watersports on adjacent Lake Travis and hiking in the hills.

Lakeway Inn

101 Lakeway Dr. • (512) 261-6600,
(800) LAKEWAY

This resort hotel on Lake Travis, west of the city, has amenities for golfers and tennis players plus provides the facilities and equipment for a variety of watersports. The resort offers a variety of packages ranging in price from approximately $130 a night per person, double occupancy from March 15 to November 15, and $90 per night in value season.

---

down the road and the University of Texas is a mile away. During the week, La Quinta's guests are mostly professionals. Weekends tend to draw a college crowd.

Travelers who prefer staying at a La Quinta Inn will be happy to learn there are six other Austin area locations with more on the way. The toll-free number for other locations is (800) 687-6667.

Omni Austin Hotel Downtown

$$$$ • 700 San Jacinto • (512) 467-3700,
(800) THE-OMNI

Enormous plate-glass windows supported by steel beams rise from the ground to the towering ceiling in this ultramodern hotel, which features huge abstract paintings and polished granite throughout the atrium-style lobby. Sunlight pours through the tremendous wall of glass and illuminates the sprawling lobby, which is home to Ancho's, the hotel restaurant featuring Southwest cuisine. The lobby bar next to Ancho's also has that airy look and is a nice place to relax and have a drink or a bite. The hotel, part of the Austin Centre office complex, has 314 rooms and suites in 14 floors of hotel space. Built in 1986, the hotel was remodeled in 1994. The modern, impeccable rooms offer superior comfort and a cozy capital-city feel, with Texas stars scattered here and there throughout the hotel. Guests are treated to the ultimate in comfort in the hotel's large rooms, meeting and convention spaces and ballroom. The upper floors provide excellent views of downtown Austin and across town. A wide carpeted staircase leads from the lobby to the second-floor assembly rooms. The Austin Centre, whose glass-walled offices overlook the lobby, also provides guests with some features not available on the premises of other hotels, such as an art gallery, custom clothing store and a jewelry store. A hair salon and gift shop are also on-site. The hotel reserves the 13th and 14th floors for its Omni Club patrons. These rooms are more spacious and have higher ceilings and extra amenities in the bathrooms such as robes and bath salts. The Omni Club lounge serves breakfast daily as well as cocktails and hors d'oeuvres in the evening.

Radisson Hotel & Suites on Town Lake

$$$ • 111 Cesar Chavez St. • (512) 478-9611, (800) 333-3333

The tower addition to the Radisson Hotel opened in August of 1998, adding 135 suites to one of Austin's busiest hotels. A fabulous location on Town Lake just off the Congress Avenue bat-viewing bridge (see our Attractions chapter), great service, a lively staff and inviting rooms add up to a great hotel experience. And the Radisson, whose 280 other rooms and suites were remodeled in 1997, is one of the most affordable of the high-quality downtown hotels.

Three huge tropical fish tanks delight guests upon arrival and add a colorful and relaxing touch to the lobby. The outdoor swimming pool, although not heated for winter swimming, is a wonderful place to unwind during Austin's long, hot summers. T.G.I. Friday's restaurant, on the premises, offers breakfast, lunch and dinner starting at 6 AM. Friday's large, outdoor deck is a great, informal place to dine or have drinks while watching the evening bat show during the spring and summer months. The hotel also offers easy access to Austin's Hike and Bike Trail, one of the finest inner-city trails anywhere. One half of the hotel's immaculate, charming rooms offer excellent views of Town Lake, and the view from the upper floors is far-reaching. The recently enlarged fitness center includes a nice selection of equipment for the heart-wise visitor. Radisson has placed a coffee maker, iron and ironing board in every room and delivers *USA Today* to all its guests on weekdays. Radisson is an excellent choice for the business traveler, with modem hookups in all rooms, plenty of fully loaded boardrooms, generous meeting rooms and even an expansive ballroom for the largest of gatherings. The hotel does have a covered parking garage, a plus for a downtown hotel, but charges about $5 per day for its use.

Stephen F. Austin Hotel

$$$$$ • 701 Congress Ave. • (512) 457-8800

"Austin's Dream Comes True With Brilliant Opening of New Hotel."

So read the *Austin American*'s front-page headline on May 20, 1924, the day following the grand opening of the Stephen F. Austin Hotel. Three quarters of a century later, the hotel is set to reopen by early spring of 1999 as Austin's newest luxury hotel. The hotel, vacant for more than a decade, is undergoing a complete renovation aimed at offering guests the latest in comfort and style while retaining the look and feel of the 1920s. A grand staircase of marble and brass will beguile visitors as they enter the lobby and walk up to the Grand Ballroom. The 187 rooms and suites have a truly Texan ambiance, with star emblems on some headboards and lots of wrought iron. Planned facilities include a state-of-the-art fitness center, an indoor swimming pool, a cigar bar, a cafe and a restaurant for fine dining. Additionally, the hotel offers 6,000 square feet of meeting and convention space as well as special services for executive travelers, including a business center.

Modern amenities, however, are just part of the allure of this hotel. Austin and Texas history wafts through the halls and hangs like tapestries from the walls. Lyndon B. Johnson made this grand hotel his congressional campaign headquarters after World War II, and it seems as if everybody who had a hand in shaping modern Texas walked through its doors. In 1984, *The Dallas Morning News* wrote this about the hotel: "To native Austinites and University of Texas exes, she is known simply as 'the Stephen F.' And if walls could talk, they would relate fascinating tales of oil and cattle deals transacted over breakfast and a handshake, of political intrigue involving state legislators, and of romances begun during World War II." Who knows what tales will be told about the Stephen F. in the next century? To ask questions or make reservations at the hotel prior to its opening, call (512) 708-0147.

South Central

Austin Motel

$$ • 1220 S. Congress Ave.
• (512) 444-4966

Location, history, personality and price combine to make the family-owned Austin Motel one of the city's most unique lodgings. As Congress Avenue gentrification spreads south of Town Lake, this motel is in the right spot at the right time, again. The main buildings were built in 1938 on Austin's central thoroughfare and way before the coming of the highway system. With its now classic red and white neon sign, this motel attracted travelers from near and far. When the traffic moved to the highways, so did much of the Austin Motel's business. South Congress, meanwhile, grew into a popular spot for prostitutes and drug dealers. These days South Congress is hip and happening and the bad influences are long gone.

Today's Austin Motel, like many other businesses along this funky stretch, is attracting visitors who want to get a distinct feel for Austin. This is not a place for guests who like modern, cookie-cutter accommodations. Artists, musicians and poets seem especially attracted to the Austin Motel's particular flair as are others who put character before elegance. This motel has 41 rooms for 41 personalities, from small rooms for those who'd rather spend their time out on the town, to spacious executive suites, to rooms overlooking the large, newly renovated pool. A small, shaded garden just off the pool provides a great place for guests to gather. California wicker, New England dark maple, Florida flamingos, Chinese fans, American red, white and blue and Spanish traditional are just a few of the imaginative decor themes that make each visit interesting. Antiques are sprinkled liberally throughout the motel and, while many show their age, all add to the distinctiveness of each room. New owner Dottye Dean, who took over from her mother in 1993, undertook a massive remodeling project that has encompassed every room, including the addition built in the 1960s. Dean and her staff of artists paid special attention to the bathrooms, some that feature original fixtures and tile, others updated to include marble Jacuzzi bathtubs. One room has a cultured marble shower with two shower heads and seating inside — perfect for a couple. El Sol Y La Luna, the Mexican restaurant next door that is leased from the hotel, is a popular spot for

INSIDERS' TIP

A trip to Austin isn't complete without a visit to Amy's Ice Cream. This homegrown ice cream shop, with five locations around the city, draws crowds throughout the year. (They don't take reservations, however, so the wait in summer could be 10 minutes or more — but it's worth it.) The varieties of gourmet ice cream, some with liqueur added, are delicious by themselves. But don't forget to get your personalized "crush 'n": fresh strawberries, Oreo cookies, candies and such folded into the ice cream of your choice at the moment you place your order. Yum!!

travelers and residents alike (see our Restaurants chapter).

Embassy Suites Downtown

$$$$ • 300 S. Congress Ave.
• (512) 469-9000, (800) EMBASSY

Just three blocks south of Town Lake on historic Congress Avenue, this all-suite hotel is perfectly located for the traveler who wants to take advantage of all downtown Austin's attractions — and have room to move around to boot. Each of the 262 suites in the nine-story Embassy features a bedroom with either a king-size bed or two double beds that is separated by a door from the meeting/living area, making each room perfect for a small meeting or gathering-or just a place to put the kids to bed while you relax or watch television. The Presidential Suite, for those who really want space, has two bedrooms and two baths as well as the living area. The suites come fully equipped with refrigerators, microwaves, coffee makers, irons and ironing boards, hair dryers, two television sets and two telephones. The hotel offers an indoor swimming pool and hot tub, an exercise room, a comfortable lobby lounge and the Capital City Bistro restaurant that serves American-style meals beginning at 11 AM. Of course, the Embassy serves its famous complimentary cooked-to-order breakfast daily, just about the best free breakfast in town. And just across the street is Threadgill's World Headquarters (see our Restaurants chapter). For music trivia buffs, this Threadgill's is near the site once occupied by the Armadillo World Headquarters (check out The Music Scene chapter). For social or business gatherings of all kinds, the Embassy offers 2,300 square feet of space in five rooms. You might strain your eyes trying to catch the evening flight of the bats from the hotel, but the Congress Avenue Bridge is just steps away. Don't miss the show in spring and summer (see our Attractions chapter).

Hyatt Regency Austin

$$$$ • 208 Barton Springs Rd.
• (512) 477-1234, (800) 233-1234

From the cowhide seat cushions in the lobby to the bed skirts stamped with a boot motif to the reproductions of historic maps and flags of Texas on the walls, this delightful hotel on the south bank of Town Lake radiates Texas charm. The Branchwater Lounge in the lobby has a stream running through it, with large rocks adorning its "banks," and the bar opens out onto an inviting patio that offers an excellent view of Town Lake. Bat watching is one of the perks for spring and summer guests, although the view of the evening spectacle is not great from the lobby lounge or the lower rooms because the bats take off from the opposite side of the Congress Avenue Bridge (see our Attractions chapter). If you want to catch a glimpse of the bats, be sure to request an appropriate room — perhaps one with a balcony — or take the elevator up to the 17th floor and watch from the huge picture window up there.

For the business traveler, the Hyatt offers the 16th floor, which includes two telephone lines and a fax machine in every room. A business lounge on this floor provides comfortable seating and the use of office equipment. The hotel also offers its Gold Passport floors for guests who want a little extra service while they rack up bonus points for frequent-flyer mileage and free hotel stays. The Hyatt has 23,000 square feet of meeting rooms, boardrooms and ballrooms for every type and size of gathering. The hotel's La Vista restaurant serves breakfast, lunch and dinner starting at 6:30 AM. The Hyatt Regency, one of Austin's largest hotels with 446 rooms and suites, was built in 1982 and remodeled in 1996. The interior atrium, open from the lobby to the rooftop skylights, lends a very spacious look and feel. This hotel is stylish but comfortable and certainly deserving of the Hyatt Regency name. An outdoor swimming pool, fitness center and easy access to Austin's exquisite Hike and Bike Trail along Town Lake provide excellent options for the fitness enthusiast.

Southwest

The Heart of Texas Motel

$$ • 5303 U.S. Hwy. 290 W.
• (512) 892-0644

Owned by the Osbon family since 1981, this 30-room motel draws a steady stream of regular customers and plenty of newcomers. The Osbons live on-site, and the care they take to maintain these rooms and the surrounding premises is obvious. The attractively decorated, good-size rooms all have microwaves, refrigerators and coffee makers. The motel also offers one Jacuzzi-suite room with a king-size, four-poster bed. Other rooms have two double beds or a double bed with a sleeper sofa. Upper-level rooms have ceiling fans, a real plus for Austin's long, hot summers. For those who like to spend their spare time outdoors, The Heart of Texas Motel has a putting green, a horseshoe pit, a basketball hoop and a barbecue grill. For movie buffs, this motel has some interesting local history. Actor Matthew McConaughey shot a music video there before he became famous, and Loni Anderson filmed scenes for a TV movie at the Heart of Texas. On U.S. 290 near the junction with the MoPac Expressway, this motel offers easy access to many parts of town and to the new international airport opening in 1999. For travelers looking for affordable rooms, especially those who have business in this area or just want to stay with someone they can trust, the Heart of Texas Motel is a great choice.

Sands Motel

$ • 4710 U.S. Hwy. 290 W.
• (512) 892-3510

For the traveler on a limited budget who wants to stay in Southwest Austin, the Sands is a clean, functional property. Owned by the Patel family for 20 years, the two-story motel is managed by Mrs. Patel, who makes sure it is well-maintained. Smoking is permitted in all 20 rooms. Each room has a telephone and cable television. Guests can request a refrigerator for an additional charge.

Lake Travis

Mountain Star Lodge

$$ • 3573 R.R. 620 S. • (512) 263-2010, (888) 263-2010

A great location near fabulous Lake Travis and a superb unobstructed view of the Texas Hill Country combine to make the Mountain Star Lodge an excellent choice in accommodations. From its vantage point on Ranch Road 620, the main thoroughfare to an abundance of lakeside recreational spots and restaurants, the lodge offers guests easy access to the community of Lakeway and to fishing, boating, skiing and other outdoor activities. And yet it's just 1 mile north of Texas Highway 71 in Southwest Austin.

Opened in 1997, the two-story Mountain Star Lodge is locally owned and operated. This lovely building of native limestone offers 20 nonsmoking rooms, each with a private patio or balcony overlooking the large outdoor swimming pool and the vast Canyon Lands Nature Preserve. The rooms, which feature outdoor access and parking just outside the rooms, are decorated in an early Texas theme. The wooden headboards, which bear a Lone Star emblem, and the other furnishings were made exclusively for this property by local artisans. Mountain Star offers guest rooms with king-size beds, two queen-size beds and a larger room that features two double beds and a kitchenette. All rooms come with 25-inch cable television sets and telephones with dataport connections. Fresh coffee is provided all day long. Each morning from 7 AM to 9 AM guests are treated to a complimentary continental breakfast in the large inviting lobby, which is designed to reflect the look and feel of a mountain lodge. A large fireplace, a soaring wood-beam ceiling and huge windows that take advantage of that gorgeous view make this a very cozy spot for relaxing, conducting small business conferences or hosting parties or weddings. For those visiting town on business, the lodge offers fax service.

Interstate 35 Corridor — North

Hotels in this area are north of the Interstate 35-U.S. 290 East interchange. Because of the high concentration of hotels and motels along I-35, especially in this area, some of the following hotels are only a few blocks north of those listed under our I-35 Corridor — Central lodgings.

Austin Chariot Inn

$$ • 7300 N. I-35 • (512) 452-9371, (800) 432-9202

Do not let the dated front entrance to this motel fool you. We almost passed it by ourselves. But what a surprise awaited us! The two-acre manicured courtyard of this 157-room motel is one of the loveliest we've seen in Austin, and certainly the best of any in this price range — on the inexpensive end of the scale we've provided. Here, among towering oaks, palm trees and sprawling ivy is a mini oasis with a charming, free-form swimming pool that winds around a gorgeous stone waterfall and under a foot bridge. There's even a separate baby pool. Covered patio tables are scattered here and there among the trees and a spiral staircase leads up to the second-floor rooms. There's a nine-hole putting green and out back is a sand volleyball court. Built around 1960, the Chariot Inn is certainly one of Austin's landmarks — there's even a rumor that Elvis slept here! But the inn was in need of repair when the Kochs family purchased it in 1996. Since then, the family has invested more than $2 million to upgrade the facility and renovate rooms. They've created an attractive, comfortable, inexpensive place to stay in Austin. They haven't gotten around to redoing the front of the inn, however, choosing to invest first in guest facilities. The Chariot offers free continental breakfasts and coffee makers in every room. HBO is included in the cable television package. Deluxe rooms are available for guests requiring more space. A 3,000-square-foot ballroom, other meeting rooms and a large breakfast room complete the facilities. On Interstate 35 at the U.S. 183 intersection, the motel does get traffic noise, but it's also a fine location from which to discover Austin. Unless you're the kind of traveler who prefers to see your car out the window, request a room in the back near the pool. A security guard protects the premises at night.

DoubleTree Hotel

$$$$ • 6505 N. I-35 • (512) 454-3737, (800) 222-TREE

An upscale hotel with a Mediterranean flair, the DoubleTree is designed with imposing archways, lots of stonework and an exquisite multilevel courtyard filled with lush greenery and the gentle sound of flowing water. This palatial Spanish Colonial-style structure with 350 rooms and suites is an attractive Austin landmark along I-35 just one block north of U.S. 290. Minutes from downtown, the University of Texas campus and important high-tech industries, across from major shopping centers, within walking distance of two popular Austin restaurants and close to nearly two dozen more, the DoubleTree is perfectly situated for the traveler who wants to get to know Austin. (The hotel is minutes from Robert Mueller Airport and still a comfortable distance from the new international airport.) Built in 1984, the DoubleTree underwent a $4 million remodeling project in 1998 and today offers the latest in comfort and convenience for the casual and the business traveler. Forget the little candy on the pillow. The DoubleTree offers guests a yummy chocolate-chip cookie upon arrival. For those requiring additional sustenance, the DoubleTree has its own Courtyard Cafe, which overlooks the lovely courtyard and serves continental cuisine with a Texas touch all day long. For the executive traveler there's a full service business center, additional services on the Concierge Floor, dataport jacks for computer access and lots and lots of meeting and convention space — 27,000 square feet to be exact. The hotel's outdoor swimming pool is on a stunning tropical terrace and while the new state-of-the-art fitness center offers the serious health buff plenty of options. There's also a gift shop and the inviting Courtyard Lounge, which features a wide-screen TV, billiards table and a cozy fireplace. This chain also operates the DoubleTree Guest Suites property in Central Austin at 303 W. 15th Street, (512) 478-7000.

Four Points Hotel

$$$ • 7800 N. I-35 • (512) 836-8520, (800) 325-3535

The landscaped 1½ acre courtyard, complete with swimming pool and lighted pavilion, lend an almost bucolic touch to this ITT Sheraton Hotel, even though the Four Points is at one of Austin's busiest junctions. At the interchange of Interstate 35 and U.S. 183, and just north of the U.S. 290, the Four Points serves as a launching point to all parts of the city. The interior guest rooms surrounding the courtyard all have functional balconies or patios, making them a perfect spot to relax in the evening. This is simply a lovely spot, impeccably maintained and well-deserving of the Sheraton name. You wouldn't guess the hotel is about 30 years old. The rooms and suites all come equipped with three telephones, desks and comfortable seating areas. They are totally modern and spacious for fun or work. The elegant suites are huge and include great bathrooms with double-size Jacuzzi tubs. Stringfield's Restaurant serves a complimentary full breakfast buffet daily and is open for lunch and dinner. Stringfield's Club, the hotel lounge, is a great place for drinks and socializing. An exercise facility and indoor hot tub make a great duo for working out and then unwinding. The hotel features 7,000 square feet of space for large and small gatherings.

Habitat Suites Hotel

$$$ • 500 Highland Mall Blvd.
• (512) 467-6000, (800) 535-4663

For the environmentally conscious traveler — or anyone who wants beautiful environs — the Habitat Suites Hotel is a miniature Eden in the heart of a bustling commercial area. This 96-suite, locally owned property in an apartment-like setting received Austin's "Best" award in 1996 as a Business for an Environmentally Sustainable Tomorrow. Everything from breakfast to bedtime is planned to protect and honor the earth's bounty. The complimentary full-course breakfast buffet includes healthy alternatives — soy milk, tofu migas, stone ground tortillas and black beans — as well as an entire range of traditional breakfast dishes. Nontoxic, phosphate-free cleansers are used to maintain the suites and clean the laundry, while the grounds are kept using natural fertilizers and pesticides. Ionizers are used to maintain clean air quality in all the suites, and the hotel uses biodegradable, recycled paper products and returns to the recycling bin all possible items. Habitat is "green" both figuratively and literally. The property is totally surrounded by native foliage and flowering plants that create a lush inviting atmosphere, while they require the least amount of water. The hotel staff even grows a variety of fruits, vegetables and herbs on the property. Habitat's outdoor swimming pool, also enveloped by greenery, uses ionized water and bromine instead of chlorine, better for the environment and for the skin. What's inside is also inviting. The spacious one- and two-bedroom suites, all with fully-equipped kitchens, are tastefully decorated and include, of course, living green plants. The rooms come equipped with irons and ironing boards, telephones with dataport connections, cable televisions that include the premium channels, and most have wood-burning fireplaces. No smoking is allowed in the rooms, but the hotel has plenty of outdoor benches, and provides ashtrays and matches. The upper-level bedrooms in the two-bedroom units have their own private entrances. The hotel offers fax and copying services, express checkout, same-day dry cleaning and laundry service, a do-it-yourself laundry and free newspapers. The 504-square-foot meeting room provides additional space for gatherings of all kinds. The hotel also treats guests to an evening social hour, with free drinks and snacks. While there's no fitness center on the premises, guests are given free passes to use the 24-hour World Gym facilities just down the street. This hotel is within a stone's throw of the Highland Mall shopping center (see our Shopping chapter), 16 movie theaters and several popular restaurants. It's about a 10-minute drive from downtown Austin and offers easy access to all parts of town. This is the only I-35 corridor hotel that's not right on the highway. It's just a few blocks off, but worth the extra effort to locate it.

Hawthorn Suites — Central

$$$ • 935 La Posada Dr.
• (512) 459-3335, (800) 527-1133

Situated just across Interstate 35 from a major shopping mall, with easy access of downtown and many high-tech industries, and nestled between two of Austin's luxury hotels, Hawthorn Suites can claim a great location as one of its major advantages. But there's much more. Hawthorn's 71 spacious one- and two-bedroom suites all have complete kitchens with full-size appliances and they all feature patios or balconies, working fireplaces and telephones equipped with dataports. A collapsible door separates the sleeping area from the living quarters in the one-bedroom studio unit and on the lower level of the two-bedroom lofts. For the business traveler, Hawthorn Suites offers a meeting room that can accommodate up to 50 people. This recently renovated lodging with a Southwestern flair serves a complimentary hot breakfast buffet daily and

free cocktails and hors d'oeuvres Monday through Thursday from 5 to 7 PM. Guests can unwind in the heated outdoor pool or soak in the hot tub. There's even a sports court for playing basketball and a half-size tennis court with rackets and balls available. Guests who really want a workout can pay $5 to use the World Gym facilities less than half a mile away. The Hawthorn has two other facilities in Austin, one northwest and one south. Call the 800 number above for information.

Holiday Inn Express
$$ • 7622 N. I-35 • (512) 467-1701, (800) HOLIDAY

A limited-service hotel that lives up to Holiday Inn standards, the Express offers 125 comfortable guest rooms, including junior and executive suites that come with refrigerators and microwaves. Each room has a coffee maker and one telephone with a dataport hookup. Same day laundry and dry cleaning is offered. The hotel features two meeting rooms that seat up to 35 people each. A free deluxe continental breakfast is served daily in the pleasant lobby cafe. On Wednesday evenings from March through October, weather permitting, the hotels hosts a complimentary cookout on the patio near the swimming pool. Hot dogs and hamburgers are served along with chips and drinks. Monday through Thursday all year long is the evening reception from 5 to 6:30 PM. Bennigan's Restaurant is next door and also provides room service from 2 until 11 PM daily. Located at the Interstate 35 and U.S. 183 interchange, the Holiday Inn Express is 6 miles north of downtown and the capitol complex.

Motel 6 — Austin North
$ • 9420 N. I-35 • (512) 339-6161, (800) 4-MOTEL 6

One of four Motel 6s in Austin for the budget-minded traveler, this North Austin location offers 158 guest rooms on two levels. Guests are treated to free HBO, and the motel's outdoor swimming pool is open from May through September. Complimentary coffee is served in the lobby from 7 to 10 AM. This Motel 6 property, Austin's northernmost, offers easy access to I-35, U.S. 183 and U.S. 290. The capitol, University of Texas and LBJ Library are 6 miles south. Major shopping centers are just a few miles south on Interstate 35. Call the 800 number above for information on other Austin locations.

Interstate 35 Corridor — Central

This area of Interstate 35 is defined in our book as the area south of the Interstate 35-U.S. 290 East junction and north of Town Lake. Hotels in this listing can be found on either side of the interstate, or just a block or two away.

Austin Marriott at the Capitol

$$$$ • 701 E. 11th St. • (512) 478-1111, (800) 228-9290

Guests of this Marriott might wonder why some hallways zig and zag instead of following a straight line as in most hotels. The reason is a "capitol" one. The hotel is designed to give guests on the north side a view of Austin's majestic state capitol. The Marriott, next to Interstate 35 and four blocks from the seat of Texas government, is, after all, very proud of its location and deservedly so. The State Capitol is one of the coolest views in Austin (see our chapter on Attractions). But there's more. Towering windows throughout the lobby and convention rooms also afford glimpses of the imposing pink-granite structure. The use of pink-toned steel and building materials throughout the hotel is a stylish tribute to our capitol. This really is a lovely hotel, with rooms that are ideal for relaxation or for work. All rooms are equipped with two phone lines. The hotel, which has 365 rooms and suites, was built in 1987 and all 16 floor were remodeled in 1998. The Marriott offers 14,000 square feet of meeting and convention space, including two "Capitol View" conference rooms. The hotel even features a separate registration desk for large conventions. This hotel offers something for everyone, from the fully equipped fitness center and two swimming pools for the fitness enthusiast to the "Sports Bar and Grill" — featuring a big-screen TV for those who prefer spectator sports. Allie's American Grille serves up American and Texas specialities for breakfast, lunch and dinner. There's also a business center and a gift shop. And the Marriott's Concierge Lounge for the business traveler is one of the nicest we've seen in the city.

Club Hotel by DoubleTree

$$$ • 1617 N. I-35 • (512) 479-4000, (800) 444-CLUB

DoubleTree's innovative concept has taken the business traveler's hotel to a new level with its Club Hotel. A self-contained business environment — just like the office back home — has been created right off the lobby area for the use of hotel guests. Two private cubicles complete with reference materials and six well-lighted personal work stations create a functional and comfortable work setting. A private conference room in this space would seat three or four people comfortably. And just a step away, guests have access to a copier, a fax machine and a printer for printing from your laptop computer. There is an extra charge for these services. While this area is designed to create an "office-away-from-the-office" setting, the spacious lobby is fashioned to make guests feel as if they are at home. Casual seating arrangements, either at tables or on sofas and chairs around coffee tables, provide a place to relax, watch television, read or conduct business in an informal setting. This is all just steps away from Au Bon Pain — The Bakery Cafe, the hotel's delicatessen-style restaurant serving fresh pastries, soups, sandwiches and more. The limited-service hotel's 152 spacious and immaculate rooms of varying sizes all come equipped with desks, telephones with dataports, and coffee makers. The hotel, which opened in September of 1997, offers many other amenities including an outdoor swimming pool, exercise room, guest laundry facilities and an evening lounge. A larger meeting room on the premises hold ups to 50 people. This hotel is conveniently located just across the interstate from the University of Texas, downtown Austin and the Frank Erwin Center.

Days Inn University

$$ • 3105 N. I-35 • (512) 478-1631, (800) 725-ROOMS

Recently renovated and redecorated, Days Inn University is a reasonable choice for the traveler on a budget who wants to be close to some of Austin's featured attractions. The motel is near the University of Texas and all its sports stadiums. It's also near Robert Mueller Airport, Concordia University, downtown and St. David's Hospital. The motel's 63 rooms feature new, light-wood furniture that gives them a bright, comfortable look. Days Inn features cable television with HBO and ESPN and an outdoor swimming pool. There are many restaurants within easy driving distance and Stars Cafe next door is open for breakfast, lunch and dinner beginning at 6 AM. This motel is right on the interstate, offering easy access to many parts of town. There could be some traffic noise, however. Rates are cheaper during the week. A second facility, Days Inn North, is at 820 E. Anderson Lane, (512) 835-4311 or (800) DAYS INN.

Drury Inn — Highland Mall

$$ • 919 E. Koenig Ln. • (512) 454-1144, (800) 325-8300

A large outdoor patio next to the swimming pool is a splendid place for get-togethers at this practical, well-situated inn. Near the intersection of Interstate 35 and U.S. 290 East, the Drury offers easy access to many parts of town. For shoppers, the hotel is conveniently located half a mile from Highland Mall and the Lincoln Village Shopping Center (see our Shopping chapter). Guests of the Drury Inn are treated to a full continental breakfast daily and evening cocktails, soft drinks and snacks in the Drury's comfortable breakfast room. Coffee is available in the lobby 24 hours a day. The inn's four deluxe rooms are 1½ times the size of a normal room and feature microwave ovens, refrigerators and coffee makers. The Drury also has a conference room that holds 12 people and a meeting room suitable for up to 30 people. The hotel, built in the early 1980s, underwent a major remodeling project inside and out in 1998 and looks terrific. The International House of Pancakes and Carrow's restaurants are adjacent to the Drury Inn and Bombay Bicycle Club is half a block away. Austin's other Drury property is just up the street at 6711 I-35 North, (512) 467-9500.

Embassy Suites Hotel — North

$$$ • 5901 N. I-35 • (512) 454-8004, (800) EMBASSY

Palm trees and tropical plants abound in the Spanish-style indoor atrium of this lovely Embassy Suites. Ducks and fish keep an eye on guests from the delightful waterscape that weaves through the atrium, passing by a cascading waterfall and under a footbridge. And that's just the beginning. The hotel, renovated in 1998, offers 260 spacious guest suites designed for the most comfortable of stays. Guests are treated to the Embassy's complimentary cooked-to-order breakfast daily and to the manager's reception in the evening, which includes soft drinks, cocktails and snacks. The Embassy's classic two-room suites are designed to appeal to both the corporate traveler and to families. Doors divide the bedroom from the living area, freeing up this space for work, conferences or for relaxation. Parents will especially enjoy being able to put the children to sleep in a quiet room. Each suite features a refrigerator, coffee maker, microwave, iron and ironing board, hair dryer, two TVs with a Sony Playstation, and two telephones with modem hookups. All rooms in the 10-floor hotel look out on the atrium and some feature small balconies. The Embassy's Plaza Grill serves lunch and dinner and the cozy Lynx lounge is a great place to unwind over drinks or a game of pool or Foosball. The heated, indoor swimming pool and hot tub are great for year-round enjoyment. We especially like the pool area. It's just brimming with greenery of all kinds and the patio is so spacious that you just don't get that cramped feeling like you do around some indoor pools. Plenty of patio furniture allows guests to just sit and relax. There's even a unisex sauna nearby and a newly remodeled fitness center on the second floor. For those with business to attend, the hotel offers a fax and copy service. About 9,800 square feet of flexible space make the Embassy a great place for gatherings of all sizes. In 1998 Embassy Suites opened its newest hotel in Northwest Austin at 9505 Stonelake Boulevard, (512) 372-8771.

Fairfield Inn — Austin North

$$ • 959 Reinli St. • (512) 302-5550, (800) 228-2800

Comfort and hospitality are the hallmarks of the Fairfield Inn, the Marriott's most affordable lodging in Austin. The Fairfield's 63 attractive

INSIDERS' TIP

Some hotel shuttles, when they're not racing back and forth to the airport, will kindly drop you at other locations around town, and even pick you up. Don't forget to ask in advance and, of course, tip the driver for this courtesy.

guest rooms are ideal for unwinding after a busy day — and the location is great for the traveler on the go. Situated near the junction of Interstate 35 and U.S. 290 East, the Fairfield is close to major shopping centers, and within 3 miles of the University of Texas campus and the LBJ Library and Museum. Carrow's restaurant is adjacent to the hotel, and several other restaurants are within walking distance. The Fairfield offers complimentary continental breakfasts in its charming lobby cafe, while coffee and bowls brimming with fresh fruit are provided all day. The inn features a heated indoor pool and whirlpool, a handy exercise room and guest laundry. All rooms are equipped with irons and ironing boards, Nintendo games and cable TV, including HBO and pay-per-view movies. Marriott standards at an affordable price. What more could you ask? Austin's other Fairfield Inn, Austin South, is at 4525 S. I-35, (512) 707-8899.

Holiday Inn — Town Lake
$$$ • 20 N. I-35 • (512) 472-8211, (800) HOLIDAY

This 320-room property was designed to give guests the best possible view of Town Lake — and what a view it is. On Austin's central waterway, many of the hotel's sleeping quarters, meeting rooms, common areas and the outdoor swimming pool provide stunning views of the lake. Large picture windows in the rooms maximize the view. The 14-floor, round "Capitol Tower" portion of this hotel was built in the 1960s, making it one of Austin's oldest full-service hotels. (The newer "Lake Tower" was built in the mid-1980s.) All the facilities are very well maintained so it's hard to tell when you're in the older part. That, combined with a great location, services and lower prices than some other full-service properties, make the Holiday Inn comfortable in many aspects. All rooms come with phones with modem hookups, hair dryers, irons and ironing boards, coffee makers and makeup mirrors. The larger executive rooms have an extra phone on the desk, bottled water and terry bathrobes. The hotel features a large outdoor deck near the pool. The only problem here, however, is that both the deck and the swimming pool, just off the sixth floor, overlook the interstate and can be a bit noisy. The hotel's restaurant, The Pecan Tree, serves breakfast, lunch and dinner beginning at 6 AM on weekdays and 7 AM on weekends. The Holiday Inn has gone all out on its weekday lunch buffets, offering a different cuisine each day. Room service is also available and for those on the run — or whose appetites peak in the middle of the night — the hotel has a hot vending machine, serving pizza, grilled chicken on sourdough, sandwiches and cheeseburgers at the toss of a few coins. Guests looking for a workout can slip into the exercise room or head on down to the Hike and Bike Trail right outside the door. To relax afterward, there's the indoor hot tub and two saunas with private showers nearby. To catch a game on television, play a game of pool or just to relax, guests can head to Dabber's Bar, named for distinguished UT football recruiter Ken Dabber, who retired in 1995. Because this hotel is right on the lake, there's plenty of room to just enjoy being outdoors — and we saw some picnic tables not too far away. Other Holiday Inn Hotels can be found at 3401 S. I-35, (512) 448-2444, and northwest at 8901 Business Park Drive, (512) 343-0888.

Quality Inn
$$ • 909 E. Koenig Ln. • (512) 452-4200, (800) 228-5151

On the southwest corner of I-35 and U.S. 290, the affordably priced Quality Inn provides quick access to many parts of Austin. This 91-room motel offers free deluxe continental breakfasts to all guests and an evening reception, which includes mixed drinks, sodas, beer and

INSIDERS' TIP

The mall isn't the only place to get your Austin memorabilia or gifts to take home. Many locally owned restaurants sell T-shirts and other gifts with their own logos, and more. At some, you can get locally produced CDs, Austin-made salsas and other treats. When you see a gift shop or gift counter at a restaurant, don't just pass it by. It could have the perfect item for that loved one who didn't get to come to Austin.

snacks from 5 to 7 PM Tuesday through Thursday. Remodeled in 1996, the Quality Inn is exceptionally clean and comfortable. Coffee makers, free HBO and Cinemax and dataport telephones are among the amenities guests can count on at this property. The Quality Inn also features larger executive rooms and a conference room that will accommodate up to 60 people. There are several restaurants within walking distance and, of course, many more Austin attractions within easy driving distance.

Rodeway Inn University

$$ • 2900 N. I-35 • (512) 477-6395, (800) 228-2000

For the budget-minded traveler, Rodeway Inn University is one of the area's best buys, largely due to its proximity to The University of Texas campus, the state capitol and downtown Austin. The 50-room motel is a locally owned franchise and the owner spends a great deal of time on the premises. The rooms are clean and well-maintained. The motel offers free coffee, juice, tea and doughnuts from 6 to 9:30 in the morning. Coffee makers in every room, fax and copying service, an outdoor pool and cable television, including HBO and ESPN complete the amenities. There is no restaurant on the premises, but next door is the Enchiladas y Mas restaurant and there are many choices within walking or easy driving distance. The motel is right next to busy I-35, a plus for many travelers who like easy access, though there could be some traffic noise. Rodeway Inn University was built in 1965 and remodeled in 1997. Another Rodeway is located farther north at 5656 N. I-35, (512) 452-1177.

Interstate 35 Corridor — South

The hotels in this area are on Interstate 35 beginning on the south side of Town Lake and heading south.

Best Western Seville Plaza Inn

$$ • 4323 S. I-35 • (512) 447-5511, (800) 528-1234

One of three independently owned Best Western hotels in Austin and Round Rock, the Seville Plaza Inn offers 95 rooms, most with balconies. Located next to Celebration Station, one of Austin's favorite entertainment centers for children, the hotel is a great location for families although it also attracts Austin visitors of all kinds. A free continental breakfast of pastries, fruit, juice, coffee and tea is served daily in the lobby. The hotel underwent a total renovation in 1997 and looks quite inviting. All rooms have desks, irons and coffee makers and the larger rooms come with love seats or recliners. There's also a self-service guest laundry for those who like to return home with clean clothes. The hotel's restaurant, Saigon Kitchen, serves Vietnamese food for lunch and dinner. A Subway sandwich shop is also on the property. Other Best Western properties are in Round Rock at 1831 N. I-35, (512) 255-3222, and Atrium North at 7928 Gessner Drive, (512) 339-7311.

Excel Inn

$$ • 2711 S. I-35 • (512) 462-9201, (800) 367-3935

For the traveler looking for an affordable room, the Excel Inn is a very nice choice. The inn, remodeled in 1997, features 90 rooms on three floors, including a deluxe room with a whirlpool bath. The rooms, all of which have writing desks with phones, are cute, comfortable and well-maintained. The Excel is close to St. Edward's University and within 3 miles of the state capitol, downtown Austin, Palmer Auditorium and the Convention Center and just 4 miles from the University of Texas. When Austin's new international airport opens in 1999, the Excel Inn will be among the most conveniently located. The outdoor swimming pool, though not heated for use during the cooler months, is perfectly sized for relaxation or for children to play and the new fitness area that opened in 1998 features a variety of exercise equipment. The Excel offers a free continental breakfast daily. A pleasant picnic area with tables is great for travelers who like to enjoy the out of doors.

Homegate Studio and Suites

$$ • 1001 S. I-35 • (512) 326-0100, (800) 456-GATE

Talk about a room with a view! The studios and suites on the north side of Homegate are so close to Town Lake you could almost skip stones off the balconies. This sprawling, ranch-style lodging offers an inviting place to work and relax in quarters that all include kitchen areas. Homegate opened this 149-room hotel in the fall of 1997, completely renovating an existing building, so everything looks like new. By 1998, Homegate had constructed three other slightly smaller Austin studio and suite hotels. The studios are sizable rooms, each of which features a condensed kitchen area that includes a full-size refrigerator, two-burner stove, small microwave, toaster over, coffee maker and dinette table. Each of the larger suites offers a separate bedroom, more spacious kitchen, dishwasher and another television and phone. Each room also comes with an iron and ironing board, desk and a telephone with a personal phone number and dataport hookup. Executive travelers will especially like the Business Center, which features a personal computer with free Internet access, a photocopier, a printer and a fax machine in addition to a work space and free coffee all day. There's also a guest laundry and a small exercise facility. We especially liked the "children's lobby" downstairs close to the snack machines. When we visited, this lobby was decorated with original artwork by school students who benefit from Homegate's aid through the Austin Independent School District's "Adopt-A-School" program. Highlighting the main lobby are huge arched windows framed in red that overlook the lake. Just off the lobby is a lovely balcony with chairs and rockers for enjoying the view over the lake and the outdoor swimming pool. Austin's other Homegate locations are 2700 Gracy Farms Lane, 12424 Research Boulevard and 8221 North I-35. You can reach them at the 800 number listed above.

Omni Austin Southpark

$$$ • 4140 Governors Row
• (512) 448-2222, (800) THE-OMNI

An enticing lobby designed with luxurious dark woods, marble and subdued lighting greets guests upon arrival at the Omni Austin Southpark, Interstate 35's southernmost full-service hotel in Austin. A unique and inviting horseshoe-shaped gourmet coffee and cocktail bar beckons visitors to "come, relax, unwind." The 313 rooms and suites in this 14-story giant are exceptionally large and comfortable, and well-equipped with coffee makers, hair dryers, irons and ironing boards, desks and telephones with dataport connections. The upper-level floors on the north side offer the best views of downtown Austin and St. Edward's University. And for those who prefer the outdoors, the hotel offers 24 rooms with walkout balconies. We especially like the huge heated, outdoor-indoor swimming pool, a wonderfully original concept. The outdoor portion of the pool is surrounded by a large deck and lovely garden area and then wraps around into the fitness center building. The fully equipped fitness center includes a sauna and a hot tub surrounded by tropical foliage. Very relaxing. The Omni's Onion Creek Grille, popular with both travelers and local residents, serves breakfast, lunch and dinner beginning at 6:30 AM. Don't miss the made-to-order pasta bar open for lunch daily. After a full day of work or sightseeing, the Republic of Texas Bar, designed with a Western flair, is a great place to watch a game on television or socialize. For business or social gatherings, the Omni offers 15,000 square feet of space, including a huge ballroom for the large groups. The hotel also features a conference center with tiered seating for 30 people, a gift shop and a full-service business center.

Super 8 Motel

$ • 2525 S. I-35 • (512) 441-0143,
(800) 800-8000

Instead of the standard writing desk, the Super 8 Motel features a table with two chairs in its standard rooms that can work both as a desk and a dining table. This Super 8 was remodeled in 1996 and features 79 functional, exceptionally clean guest rooms, including a huge deluxe room that offers plenty of space in addition to a refrigerator, microwave oven and room seating area. For the budget-minded traveler, the Super 8 is a fine choice, both for quality and location. The motel is just a few minutes drive from downtown Austin and offers easy access to areas both north and south on Interstate 35. Continental breakfast is free and the motel provides irons and ironing boards. Faxing and copying services are also available. Austin has two other Super 8 Motel locations at 6000 Middle Fiskville Road, (512) 467-8163, and 1201 N. I-35, (512) 472-8331.

South

Classic Inn

$, no credit cards • 4702 S. Congress Ave. • (512) 445-2558

Along a strip that can be rough, especially at night, this motel is one of the better choices. For the traveler on a budget who chooses to stay in this area of South Congress Avenue, the Classic Inn offers 24 rooms, including eight bungalows with side doors leading to private parking stalls. The other rooms are more spacious, but guests must park in the lot. The new owner has made a valiant effort to spruce up this old motel — which dates back many decades — and ensures that local prostitutes don't check in. The rooms show wear but are neat, clean and functional. The bungalows have Texas limestone facades and really do remind passersby of another era. Insiders say the Hills Cafe next door was the only place in South Austin to get a steak for eons. Smoking is permitted in all rooms.

Ramada Inn — South

$$ • 1212 W. Ben White Blvd. • (512) 447-0151, (800) 272-6232

Clusters of Austin's famous live oak trees surround this newly remodeled Ramada Inn, providing shade and an inviting atmosphere for travelers from around the country.

Casual comfort is the hallmark of the Ramada, which features 103 guest rooms on six floors. As they say, the cream rises to the top, and the Ramada is no exception. For romantic getaways of all kinds, the Ramada features six Jacuzzi hot tub suites on the top floor. In each room, the double-sized Jacuzzi is up on risers in the center of the sleeping area and next to a picture window that offers a stunning view of downtown Austin's skyline. What a way to get clean!! The hotel also offers six parlor suites in which the living area is divided by a door from the sleeping area. There also are patio rooms that lead directly to the Ramada's outdoor swimming pool. Coachman's Steakhouse serves breakfast lunch and dinner beginning at 6:30 AM and the lounge is open until 'round midnight. Guests staying Sunday through Thursday night get treated to a complete breakfast the following morning. Other amenities include same-day laundry and dry cleaning service, fax and copy service, dataport hookups on the telephones and voice mail. While there's no fitness center on the premises, Ramada guests are offered daily discounted rates at three nearby fitness centers. The Ramada's ballroom seats up to 150 guests banquet style and can be divided to accommodate groups of all sizes. Smaller conference rooms are also available. The hotel, on Ben White Boulevard between MoPac and I-35, is about 3 miles south of downtown and its great entertainment venues. With the coming of Austin's new airport in 1999, this Ramada will have another advantage: location.

Austin has another Ramada Inn and two Ramada Limited hotels. There also is a Ramada Limited on Interstate 35 in Round Rock. They can be reached by calling the 800 number listed above.

INSIDERS' TIP

When packing for a trip to Austin, keep in mind that we're a pretty laid-back city when it comes to dress. Shorts, T-shirts and sandals are the standard Austin uniform for summer, and will get you in just about anywhere. Unless you've come for a gala, casual dress for evening is just perfect. While you can just plan on it being hot during the summer, winter can be trickier. We can have 80-degree days, and we can have weather in the 20s. Mostly, however, Austin's winters are pretty mild, especially compared to up north. It's best to check the forecast.

Northwest

Hampton Inn

$$ • 3908 W. Braker Ln.
• (512) 349-9898, (800) HAMPTON

Efficient and inviting, the Hampton in is one of several newer hotels in this part of town that cater to professionals, including many who work in the high-tech industries. Each of the hotel's 124 rooms is equipped with a small desk and telephone that features a dataport. The comfortably sized rooms feature coffee makers and an iron and ironing board. The hotel also offers one-day valet laundry service and provides a fax service. For those who want to unwind after a busy day, there's an outdoor swimming pool and a small fitness center with a treadmill, stationary bike and stair stepper. The Hampton offers a complimentary continental breakfast daily from 6 to 10 AM and coffee in the lobby throughout the day. The hotel doesn't leave guests feeling left out in the boonies. It is just off the MoPac Expressway and within a couple of minutes drive to more than a dozen restaurants, three large movie theaters, several grocery stores and some of Austin's choicest shops. Hampton Inn has another facility at 4141 Governors Row, (512) 442-4040.

Homewood Suites — Northwest

$$$ • 10925 Stonelake Blvd.
• (512) 349-9966, (800) CALL-HOM

An exceedingly inviting lobby tastefully designed with a Southwest decor greets guests upon arrival at this all-suites hotel fashioned for both the business traveler and for families. Those traveling with children will especially like the solid door that divides the bedroom — or bedrooms — from the living area, so the children can sleep peacefully while the parents relax, entertain guests or watch television. The apartment-style suites are stylish and very comfortable with fully equipped, full-sized kitchens that even include toaster ovens. Homewood offers one- and two-bedroom suites as well as a choice of bed sizes. Each suite has two 25-inch TVs and a video player as well as two dual-line telephones with dataport capabilities. A nice-size outdoor swimming pool is a great place to work out or relax. There's also a sports court and an exercise room. For serious exercisers, Homewood Suites offers free passes to The Q, a great fitness facility a few blocks away. The hotel offers complimentary continental breakfast and an evening social time off the lobby. There's also an executive center with a typewriter, copier and a printer to print from your computer. Guests can use the do-it-yourself laundry facilities or take advantage of the valet laundry service. Homewood opened in 1997 and offers excellent access to Arboretum-area restaurants, shops, movie theaters and grocery stores. Located between MoPac and U.S. 183, the hotel can claim easy access to areas both north and south. Daily rates are lower for extended-stay guests.

In 1998 Homewood Suites opened another hotel in Southeast Austin at 4143 Governors Row, (512) 445-5050.

Renaissance Austin Hotel

$$$$ • 9721 Arboretum Blvd.
• (512) 343-2626, (800) 228-9290

Northwest Austin's luxury hotel, the Renaissance Austin pampers each guest as it caters to nearly every whim and any need. Enter through the lobby into the immense pavilion, the airy indoor courtyard that reaches up 10 stories to the skylight. Here among trees and plants, attractive sculptures and tremendous dangling mobiles, visitors will find the Garden Cafe, which serves breakfast and lunch. Across the pavilion is the hotel delicatessen, open 24 hours a day. Need a sandwich at 3 o'clock in the morning? Stretch your legs for a walk to the pavilion or just dial the phone and the hotel's 24-hour room service will send it up. Feel like dancing? Drop into Tangerine's, the hotel's night club. How about a gourmet Italian meal? The Trattoria Grande delivers excellent dining fare (see our Restaurants chapter). Swim indoors or outdoors, drop in to the fitness center, or walk next door or across the street to some of Austin's finest shops and a great selection of nearby restaurants. The rooms are ample, tasteful and, for those staying on the Hill Country side, afford excellent views of the trees and hillsides. This hotel, owned by Marriott, is the largest of Austin's luxury hotels with 478 rooms and suites. The Renaissance, like many other top-

Photo: Peter A. Silva

The decoration of the Capitol grounds extends to the fence that surrounds the Capitol building.

flight hotels in the area, offers a Club Floor for those guests wanting a little extra space and service. The hotel has an enormous amount of meeting and convention space, including an auditorium with tiered seating for 55 people, an exhibition hall, a 12,000-square-foot ballroom and many other private rooms and halls. The executive traveler can pop downstairs to the Business Center, which offers copying, faxing, shipping, word processing and a notary. The Renaissance is one of the farthest hotels from the airport, but its location near the junction of MoPac and U.S. 183 is great for the discriminating traveler who wants to be on the edge of Austin's beautiful Hill Country and yet have easy access to the high-tech industries in the north and other parts of town.

Courtyard by Marriott — Austin Northwest

$$$ • 9409 Stonelake Blvd.
• (512) 502-8100, (800) 321-2211

A view of the indoor pool and the charming breakfast room, complete with fireplace, greet guests at this modern, efficient hotel designed for business travelers. Each of the hotel's 78 rooms features a coffee maker, iron and ironing board, hair dryer and two telephones, one conveniently located on a desk — a must for travelers using computer modems. Fax service is available at the lobby desk. After a hectic business day, guests can flip on the television and work out in the fitness center, which features treadmills, bicycles and other exercise equipment, or they can take a dip in the pool or a relaxing soak in the hot tub. Courtyard has no outdoor pool on the premises, but guests are allowed to use the pool at Marriott's Residence Inn next door. *USA Today* is delivered free to each room Monday through Friday and other newspapers are available for purchase. A small, do-it-yourself laundry room and a comfortable meeting room that holds about 25 adults complete the amenities. For guests desiring even more, upgraded rooms that include microwave ovens and small refrigerators are available, as are Executive King rooms which are about 1½ times the size of a normal room. Families are also made welcome here, and children will especially appreciate the Nintendo equipment in every room. The hotel opened in May of 1996, and all rooms still look spotless. A continental breakfast or all-you-can-eat buffet is served 6:30 to 10 AM weekdays and 7 to 11 AM on weekends. In the evening, the breakfast room becomes a lounge complete with an honor bar and complimentary snacks. The hotel has no restaurant on premises but it's near restaurants and shopping centers in the area.

Apartment Hotels

While the vast majority of those who visit Austin and our surrounding communities stay less than a week, many people come for reasons that require them to stay much longer — a long-term business contract or the search for suitable housing, for example. While many of the establishments listed above provide reduced rates for long-term stays, some travelers prefer to be in an apartment. For that reason, we're giving you the names of some companies that may be able to fulfill your needs. We have not provided a price code for these apartments as rates can vary greatly. It's best to call for current rates.

INSIDERS' TIP

If you've decided to take a chance on Texas' multimillion-dollar Lotto while you're in town, check the *Austin American-Statesman*'s "Metro & State" section on Thursday and Sunday for results. There's also a toll number to call if you've taken your ticket home: (900) 988-0889. The Texas Lottery also runs other games, Cash 5 and Pick 3, as well as plenty of scratch-off games. Tickets can be purchased at dozens of places around town, mostly at gas stations and convenience stores. We haven't made our fortune this way, but maybe you'll have better luck.

Austin Executive Lodging

11316 Jollyville Rd. • (512) 795-0051, (800) 494-2261

This locally owned company has one-, two- or three-bedroom fully furnished apartments at four locations in the Arboretum area of Northwest Austin. However, they can also provide apartments for temporary residents in other areas. The apartments come with washers and dryers, and the kitchens are complete. Complexes also have tennis courts, swimming pools and fitness centers. Executive Lodging offers daily, weekly and monthly rates.

Balcones Woods Apartments

11215 Research Blvd. • (512) 343-0584

A minimum seven-night stay is required at Balcones Woods Apartments, which offers completely furnished apartments for the temporary resident. The one- and two-bedroom apartments include fully equipped kitchens, washers and dryers. Balcones Woods Apartments feature swimming pools, spas and a fully equipped weight room. Maid service is optional. Rates are by the week or the month.

Corporate Lodging

4815 W. Braker Ln. • (512) 345-8822, (800) 845-6343

Corporate Lodging offers one- and two-bedroom apartment living for temporary lodgers at seven locations, six in the Arboretum area of Northwest Austin and one in South Austin. The apartments are fully furnished, including dishes, washers and dryers, and include membership to The Q Sports Club and guest privileges at two area country clubs. There also are swimming pools and workout facilities on-site. A hostess is available for errands. Daily, weekly and monthly rates are available.

Pinnacle Suites — Round Rock

16601 F.M. 1325 • (512) 218-4050, (800) 586-4050

Located in Round Rock at I-35 and F.M. 1325, Pinnacle suites offers new one-, two- and three-bedroom furnished apartments in a gated community for guests staying a minimum of three nights. The full kitchens are fully equipped and the complex includes two swimming pools, two hot tubs, a sand volleyball court, a tennis court and sport court, two picnic areas, a 1-kilometer jogging trail, a playground, a 24-hour fitness center and a 24-hour business center. Guests can check out videos and sports equipment free of charge.

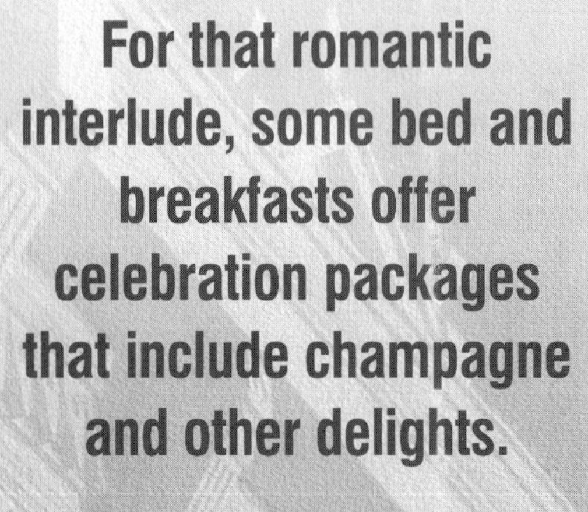

For that romantic interlude, some bed and breakfasts offer celebration packages that include champagne and other delights.

Bed & Breakfasts and Country Inns

For a truly unique Austin experience, spend the night, or the week, in one of our incomparable bed and breakfast establishments. Austin provides an exciting range of possibilities for visitors searching for the unique. Among Austin's many bed and breakfasts today, you'll find some listed as historic landmarks, some wonderful examples of Victorian, Texas Colonial Revival, Mediterranean and Greek Revival styles of architecture as well as some vintage and more modern structures distinctive in their own way. Four of Austin's bed and breakfast establishments have been accepted for membership in the selective organization Historic Accommodations of Texas: Woodburn House, McCallum House, Governor's Inn and Fairview.

Looking for a room with a view? Austin offers several. If you want to get away to a country retreat, Austin can answer that call. And if you're looking to escape to a bed and breakfast and yet remain close to the action of downtown, the UT campus or Austin's other hot spots, there are plenty of inns from which to choose.

For distinctive special events, such as weddings, parties and business gatherings, several of Austin's bed and breakfast establishments can fulfill all your needs by providing an original setting as well as taking care of all your music and catering arrangements. And, for that romantic interlude, some bed and breakfasts offer celebration packages that include champagne and other delights. With all these special services, it's no wonder more and more Austinites are discovering they don't have to leave town to go on vacation.

Though others tried out the bed and breakfast concept before, Austin's present-day bed and breakfast tradition got started in 1983, when the historic McCallum House opened to guests. One of the fastest-growing businesses in the country today, bed and breakfast establishments are becoming a popular alternative for guests seeking the unusual in accommodations and the warm hospitality that only a bed and breakfast can provide. And Austin is blazing that trail.

The special people who operate these lodgings are, in many cases, sharing their own homes, and their lives — not to mention their favorite breakfast recipes. Visitors will also find bed and breakfasts created for the exclusive use of their guests. One common denominator among all our bed and breakfasts, however, is the attention to detail paid to each of these properties. Character, style, charm. There's no better reason to choose a bed and breakfast than simply the desire to stay in a one-of-a-kind lodging.

Bed is just half the equation at these inns. There's also breakfast, of course, and you'll find that Austin's proprietors have put as much effort into the morning fare as they have into their homes. From quick and delightful self-serve continental breakfasts to full-scale seated gourmet meals, the menus are designed to please. What better way to wake up in the morning than to the inviting aroma of a feast someone else has prepared for you. Don't hesitate to tell your host or hostess about any dietary constraints or preferences you may have, as most are willing to accommodate your needs. Some inns serve at specific times of the morning, others are more casual. We've noted where there is a definite seating time.

In this chapter you'll find a wide selection

of the bed and breakfast establishments in Austin. Unless otherwise noted, the inns listed here accept major credit cards. The Americans with Disabilities Act does not require that these lodgings create handicapped-accessible rooms. Southard House in Central Austin does have one room that is wheelchair friendly. Smoking is permitted outdoors only at all these establishments, except Lake Travis Bed & Breakfast, where smoking is totally prohibited. Guests should be aware that check-in times and cancellation policies at bed and breakfast establishments differ from those at hotels and motels, and that some charge a cancellation fee. Please check with the individual establishment regarding the cancellation policy and check-in times when you make your reservation. And if you're planning to stay in Austin for awhile, be sure to ask about extended-stay rates.

Price Code

Our rate categories are based on a one-night stay for two people throughout the year. Because some bed and breakfast offer a wide range of room sizes and amenities, their rates can vary greatly. In that case we have given you two dollar codes and you will expect to find rates within those spectrums. These rates do not include the 15 percent total Austin tax on lodgings. Nor do they take into account the extended-stay rates available at many establishments.

$	**Less than $70**
$$	**$70 to $110**
$$$	**$110 to $150**
$$$$	**$150 or more**

Central

Adams House

$$-$$$ • 4300 Avenue G
• (512) 453-7696

One of Austin's newest bed and breakfasts, Adams House opened for business in 1998. And what a house it is. This 1911 home in historic Hyde Park has been restored from top to bottom by historic-preservation architect Gregory Free. He installed stylish gray slate floors in some areas and added a gray wash to the original hardwood floors in others. White woodwork, high ceilings and wraparound sunrooms on two levels give this home a bright and airy look that adds to its beauty. The current resident owners, Sidney and John Lock, have added their own special touches, which give this old Colonial Revival house the look and feel of a classy modern dwelling — even with the many remarkable antiques throughout.

Adams House originally was built as a one-story bungalow. W.T. Adams and his family purchased the home in 1922 and added another level in 1931. The home, however, fell on hard times during the second half of this century, and was turned into apartments. Free and the Locks have done a wonderful job. Original paintings, a baby grand piano and a designer kitchen with granite counters all contribute to its charm. Adams House offers three rooms, all on the second floor. This inn does not accommodate children. And, sorry, no pets.

The superb King Suite features its own private sun room with shuttered windows on three sides. The king-size, four-poster bed, with a wonderfully high mattress, is draped in custom fabrics from a speciality shop in historic Fredericksburg. This room has a pri-

INSIDERS' TIP

Many of the bed and breakfast establishments we've listed are members of the Greater Austin Bed and Breakfast Association (GABBA), which operates a referral service among members. So, if you find that the bed and breakfast you prefer is booked, ask for the name and phone number of the member contact person that week. That person will be able to help you locate a bed and breakfast that is right for you from among GABBA members.

vate bath with dual sinks and granite counters. The Queen Suite features a four-poster bed, another step-up mattress covered in custom linens, an antique armoire and walnut antique chest. The private bath in this room has a large, walk-in shower and slate floor. Adams House also offers a double-bedroom suite, which can be used for a family or group of friends traveling together. These lovely rooms share a bath, or guests have the option of choosing just one of the rooms, with a private bath just steps away. All the rooms have private telephones. For watching television, socializing or reading from the huge selection of books and magazines, guests are invited to use the comfortable sun room on the main floor. There's also an office area, with the Lock's computer that guests can use to send e-mail if the need arises. Breakfast on weekdays is a serve-it-yourself continental affair, which includes muffins, croissants, fresh fruit, cereals, juice and gourmet coffee. Weekends and special occasions are a treat at Adams House because a local chef often comes to prepare a full, seated breakfast especially for guests. Breakfast tacos, gourmet quiches and other egg dishes, pastries and homemade breads are just some of the delicacies served.

AUSTIN'S WILDFLOWER INN

Bed & Breakfast

1200 West 22½ Street • Austin, Texas 78705
Phone: (512) 477-9639 • (514) 474-4188
E-mail: kjackson@io.com

Austin's Wildflower Inn

$$ • 1200 W. 22½ St. • (512) 477-9639

Lace curtains, handmade quilts and antique furniture contribute country grace to this 1930s colonial-style house. Hostess Kay Jackson adds the Texas charm. The tantalizing aroma of freshly baked breakfast breads and just-brewed coffee wakens guests each morning at the Wildflower Inn. Fresh fruits and a unique specialty breakfast follows give guests a great start on the day. Kay serves a full breakfast daily, usually alternating between a sweet and a savory dish. Her specialities include a vegetable frittata made with eggs, cheese, bell peppers and tomatoes, served with a sour cream salsa and a fresh muffin. She also prepares a yummy baked French toast made with challah bread and blueberries, served with a blueberry sauce laced with Grand Marnier liqueur. She serves breakfast around 8 AM on weekdays and at 9 AM on weekends, but can be flexible.

The Wildflower Inn is a delightful bed and breakfast in a residential neighborhood just minutes from the UT campus and downtown Austin. The inn offers four guest rooms, a cozy living room that's perfect for relaxing in front of a fire or watching television, and plenty of outdoor porches and patios. Behind this charming house is shaded stone patio and a wonderful landscaped garden filled with flowering plants carefully maintained by Kay herself.

The centerpiece of the David G. Burnet Room on the main floor is the antique white iron half-canopy bed. The lace canopy, white wicker desk and antique oak rocker add to the country allure of this room, named in honor of one of the presidents of the Republic of Texas, an ancestor of Kay's. The Carolyn Pearl Walker Room features a four-poster oak bed, antique oak rocker, table and daybed, and soft blue walls stenciled with delicate ivy trim. This room, like the Burnet room, has a private bath. Sharing a bath are the Dawson Schnittker Room and the Texas Country Room.

The Dawson Schnittker is highlighted by a four-poster cherry bed and country jacquard lace curtains. The Texas Country Room features a private upstairs entrance and sitting porch. This room also has cute country stenciling and a white iron bed. This bed and breakfast is owned and operated by Kay and her business partner, Claudean Schultz, two Texans who each worked 24 years in education before they ventured into the bed and breakfast business. They've created a delightful establishment and offer you this wish: "May all your weeds be wildflowers."

Children are invited to stay at Austin's Wildflower Inn, but the hostesses prefer that pets be left at home. A two-night minimum stay is requested on weekends.

Brook House

$$ • 609 W. 33rd St. • (512) 459-0534

Variety is the spice of life at this charming bed and breakfast, which offers six unique rooms from which to choose. Brook House, built in 1922, features three rooms upstairs inside the home as well as more private lodgings in the Carriage House and the Cottage out back across the lawn. The resident owners, Barbara Love and her husband David Wells, have created a cozy country inn with plenty of space both indoors and out for their guests' enjoyment. There's a great covered back porch with large antique tables and ceiling fans where breakfast is served in nice weather. Barbara serves a full, hot breakfast around 8 AM during the week and at 9 AM on the weekends. You'll always find a big bowl of fruit and homemade breads along with a main entree that can be an egg dish, waffles, French toast or other tasty morning fare. Or guests may follow the short path to the gazebo and make themselves at home at one of the patio tables there. Post oaks and elm trees shade this attractive backyard area.

The home itself has high ceilings and lots of windows that bathe the rooms in light. All guest rooms are delightfully adorned with antiques, and feature cable television, telephone and private baths. The stately Green Room, featuring an antique oak queen-size bed, matching armoire and bath stand as well as an extra large bathroom, offers an attached screened sitting porch with wicker chairs. The Blue Room also has a wonderful sitting porch shaded by a 100-year-old Spanish oak. This room is especially light and airy, and features an elevated mahogany queen-size four-poster bed and antique rocking chair. The bathroom is right outside the door. A classic fainting couch highlights the romantic Rose Room. Or guests may choose to "faint" on the antique pine king-size bed or relax in the antique claw-foot tub. The rooms in the Carriage House and the Cottage have private entrances. The spacious Upper Carriage, with high-pitched ceilings, dormer windows, a large walk-in closet and kitchen facilities, is decorated with antique furnishings and a queen-size iron bed. The cozy Lower Carriage features a secluded deck, queen-size brass bed, sofa and desk.

The Cottage is just delightful. This suite has a separate sleeping area with an antique oak queen-size bed. There's also a daybed with trundle in the sitting area for extra guests. Children and pets are welcome to stay in this lovely cottage, which also features kitchen facilities with refrigerator, microwave and coffee maker as well as an antique oak table and chairs. This cottage is perfect for a small family, or anyone who requires a little extra space. Of course, all guests are invited into the cozy living room to watch television, read a book, socialize or just relax. Barbara and David, with their friendly Labrador dog, Ernie, have created something very special here.

Carrington's Bluff

$$-$$$ • 1900 David St.
• (512) 479-0638, (800) 871-8908

A 500-year-old native oak is just one of the many trees that shade the 1-acre bluff where this great bed and breakfast stands. Operated by Lisa and Ed Mugford, this comfy English country house, built in 1877, features five guest rooms decorated with floral fabrics and English and American antiques. All rooms have private bathrooms and come with guest bathrobes, irons and ironing boards, television sets and telephones. Guests are invited to use the refrigerator and microwave in the kitchen. The dining room is decorated with wallpaper stamped with tea cups, which nicely complements Lisa's antique tea cup collection displayed beautifully in an antique cabinet. And, of course, tea service is available for guests all day. The large covered porch is a great place to rock and relax while enjoying the view of the garden and gazebo.

The home, part of an original 22-acre homestead of the Republic of Texas, is just above busy Lamar Boulevard, but it's nestled so well among the lush greenery that it's hard to tell. Here guests feel isolated, even though they're just minutes from The University of Texas and downtown. This bed and breakfast also features a separate cottage, with three bedrooms, three baths and its own kitchen. Although guests are invited to join the others for a hearty breakfast in the main house, they also are free to use the kitchen facilities here. Breakfast, served 7:15 to 8:30 AM on weekdays and 8:30 to 10 AM weekends, includes homemade fresh granola, fresh baked breads, yogurts and a special entree each day during the last hour. House specialties include green-chili cheese casserole, egg blossoms in puff pastry and special quiches. Carrington's Bluff's own special blend of coffee is out of this world.

This cottage is a great place for family retreats or for those who want to feel like they're off on their own, to work or just relax. Many Austin couples have been married near the gazebo in this lovely garden. Lisa, an experienced hotelier who spent nearly 10 years at the Four Seasons, has anticipated her guests' every need. Children of all ages are invited to Carrington's Bluff, and so is the family pet. This is truly a home away from home.

Governor's Inn

$$ • 611 W. 22nd St. • (512) 477-0711, (800) 871-8908

An elegant Neoclassical Victorian home decorated in rich tones and romantic fabrics awaits guests at Governor's Inn, just a short walk from the UT campus. This property is owned by Lisa and Ed Mugford, who also run Carrington's Bluff. Like Carrington's Bluff, Governor's Inn welcomes children and pets. But these are two very distinct properties. Governor's Inn is one of four Austin bed and breakfast establishments listed with Historic Accommodations of Texas (the others are listed in the introduction to this chapter). And this graceful property also was chosen as one of three Texas bed and breakfasts to be featured on The Travel Channel's *Romantic Inns of America*. And no wonder.

Built in 1897 and restored in 1993, this three-story inn features white woodwork and wonderful Laura Ashley and Ralph Lauren fabrics and wall coverings. The dining room, with its high ceiling, wallpaper of white flowers on a bright red background, white damask tablecloths and lace curtains, will transport visitors to another era. Here, guests are offered a full, hot breakfast on elegant china and crystal with silver tableware and serving pieces. Breakfast always includes a wonderful hot entree such as egg blossoms in puff pastry, quiche, French toast or a special casserole. You'll always find homemade granola, fresh baked muffins and breads, fresh fruit and more. Breakfast is served 7:15 to 8:30 AM on weekdays and 8:30 to 10 AM on weekends, with the hot entree served during the last hour. As at Carrington's Bluff, the coffee is a special blend.

The 10 rooms in the Governor's Inn are just gorgeous. Four-poster beds draped in vibrant blue, white iron beds enveloped in delicate flowers with matching draperies, claw-foot bathtubs and an abundance of period antiques are just some of the delights awaiting guests at Governor's Inn. This bed and breakfast has something for every romantic-at-heart.

The home features five rooms with queen beds, four kings and a cozy twin. All rooms come with private baths, cable television, telephones, bathrobes and coffee and tea stations. Lovers and children will delight in the third-floor room, with a large king-size bed and twin daybed, has a pitched ceiling and is filled with lots of cozy nooks and crannies. Victorian rocking chairs and porch swings adorn the two wraparound verandas — a perfect place to unwind or watch the activities of the backpacked bedecked college kids on their way to and from the university. This is a marvelous place to hold a wedding or other special event. Governor's Inn offers a full range of amenities for gatherings of all kinds.

Healthy Quarters

$$ • 1215 Parkway • (512) 476-7484, (800) 392-6566

For guests seeking the ultimate in privacy, a great central location, healthy, do-it-yourself breakfasts and a cheery room, this lovely 1930s cottage may be just right. Healthy Quarters offers two guest rooms, each with a private entrance, bath, telephone and cable television complete with VCRs. And the refrigerators in each are fully stocked with organic produce, milk, coffee and yogurts. The more hearty breakfast eaters will find plenty of eggs, cereal, English muffins, tea and other provisions.

And for guests who want to combine their visit with a rejuvenating New Age Austin experience, Healthy Quarters also offers colon hydrotherapy treatments, electro-lymphatic therapy, ear candling, flower essence therapy and a range of chiropractic treatments. Innkeeper Marilyn Grooms, a registered nurse and alternative therapy professional, works in her own quarters here while chiropractor Kathleen Anderson also offers on-site treatments.

The Ivy Room on the ground level, the smaller of the two rooms, features a double bed, small table and a tantalizing ultramodern Jacuzzi shower and bathtub in the large bathroom. The mini-kitchen in this room includes a coffee maker, toaster, microwave and a special utensil for making eggs in the microwave. The spacious Sun Room upstairs features a pitch ceiling, lots of large windows, a full-size kitchen as well as a queen-size bed, tub and shower. There's also a rollaway bed for an extra person.

For the truly health conscious, there's Austin's own Whole Foods grocery store just a couple of minutes away. And for book lovers, another Austin specialty, Book People (see The Literary Scene chapter), is next to Whole Foods. Within minutes guests can be on popular Sixth Street or on the UT campus. This cottage is right off bustling Lamar Boulevard at 12th Street, but you may as well be in the country. Healthy Quarters accepts well-behaved children. Sorry, no pets are allowed.

The Inn at Pearl Street

$$-$$$ • 809 W. Martin Luther King Blvd. • (512) 477-2233, (800) 494-2261

This gorgeous Greek Revival-style mansion was selected as the 1995 Designer Showhouse by the Austin Symphony League. And it shows. The turn-of-the-century property, completely restored in 1995 and decorated by some of Austin's finest designers, is among the city's most elegant bed and breakfast establishments. Each of the four rooms and the many common areas are luxuriously decorated to reflect Old World radiance. Sumptuous designer fabrics and wallpapers throughout this cozy home add the perfect touch to each room. The French Room, decorated in shades of yellow and gold, features French antique furniture, a stylish four-poster iron bed, a crystal chandelier and a claw-foot bath. The European Room exudes the utmost in Old World charm, with its king-size bed, billowy-topped floral chintz draperies and unique furnishings. The Far East Room, decorated in shades of salmon and featuring a beautiful oriental screen and armoire, offers the perfect escape. Here, guests will discover a lovely private balcony and a fabulous private bathroom.

The grandest of them all is The Gothic Suite. This spacious room, with a separate day room and Jacuzzi bath is perfect for a special occasion, or just a special treat. A glorious cathedral-inspired bed highlights this room, decorated in sage greens, pales reds and coppery metals. The Gothic Suite includes a refrigerator, coffee maker and complimentary toiletries, for those who never want to leave it. The common areas also are a feast for the eyes. The music room is especially attractive, with its ivory lacquered grand piano, mirrored pedestals and antique fireplace. The large outdoor deck, surrounded by oak and pecan trees, is perfect for a wedding or a special gathering of any nature. This is one place that begs to be discovered.

The Inn at Pearl Street offers an elaborate European-style self-serve breakfast during the week from as early as you request it until about 10:30 AM. Cereals, muffins, fruit, bagels and more are presented along with cold cuts and cheeses to give breakfast that European flair. A full-service breakfast is offered on the weekends from 9 to 9:30 AM. While the table service is exquisite every day of the week, the inn pulls out all stops on Sunday with full china and silver service, tantalizing entrees and mimosas. A house speciality is the wonderful egg souffle served with smoked ham and fresh bread. For an extra fee and advance notice, you can request breakfast on your private balcony. There is coffee and tea service on both floors. And for those truly special occasions, the Inn at Pearl offers a celebration package, which includes a bottle of champagne on ar-

Photo: Peter A Silva

The administration building on the University of Texas campus is a familiar Austin sight.

rival and breakfast in bed. For that special occasion, make arrangements in advance for the Inn's Twilight Dinner, an elegant five- or six-course meal served by candlelight for an extra fee. This bed and breakfast is on busy Martin Luther King Boulevard and Pearl Street, just block from the UT campus and close to downtown entertainment of all kinds. Children age 12 and up are invited to stay at this historic inn. And look for the inn's new bed and breakfast to open next door by late 1998.

The McCallum House

$$-$$$ • 613 W. 32nd St.
• (512) 451-6744

Now listed on the National Register of Historic Places, The McCallum House was built in 1907 by A.N. and Jane Y. McCallum. A leader in the Texas Woman Suffrage Movement, Jane McCallum became director of the famous Petticoat Lobby after women achieved the vote in 1920. Twice appointed Texas secretary of state, McCallum is the only person ever to serve two Texas governors in this post — and all while raising five children of her own.

The McCallum House, opened in 1983, is Austin's longest-running bed and breakfast and one of the oldest bed and breakfasts in Texas. Meticulously cared for by Nancy and Roger Danley, who renovated the home and furnished it with lovely antiques, The McCallum House is remarkable in that each room has its own private outdoor porch. The guest rooms are on the second and third floor of the house, while a gorgeous garden apartment is at the back of the grounds in a building constructed in the 1920s. Nancy serves a full hot breakfast every day that concentrates on omitting the fat, not the flavor. House specialties include Southwestern quiche, blueberry gingerbread with a light lemon curd, pumpkin bread with an orange glace and more. Guests can be served in the dining room or can ask for a breakfast tray to be delivered to their room. Breakfast is served about 8 AM weekdays and 9 AM on weekends and holidays.

Each guest room has a private bath and mini-kitchen area with refrigerator, coffee maker, hot plate and microwave. There are televisions and telephones with answering machines in each room as well. And, of course, each room is unique. The Blue Room features a queen-size bed and large private screened porch. The Rose Room, also with a queen-size bed, has a dining table and an open porch. The Green Room has a private entrance from the rear and a covered veranda at the back of the house. For guests requiring more space, The McCallum House offers Jane's Loft on the third floor. This onetime attic has been converted into a bright, airy suite with etched-glass windows. Jane's Loft will accommodate up to four people with a queen bed and two twins.

The Garden Apartment out back is a real work of art. This large apartment, which has a private deck, features a sitting room, bedroom, full kitchen with dining area and a luxurious bathroom with a whirlpool bathtub and private shower. The friendly, outgoing Danleys make a special effort to make guest feel welcome — and the smell of freshly baked cookies adds to the aura of home. And don't forget to ask the Danleys about their special celebration package. A minimum two-night stay is required on weekends and holidays. The McCallum House does not accept pets or children younger than 12. This is one of Austin's classic bed and breakfasts, and it's on the list of Historic Accommodations of Texas.

Southard-House

$$-$$$$ • 908 Blanco St. • (512) 474-4731

Guests at the historic Southard-House can choose from among 15 rooms with private baths in three separate houses, each unique and each truly Texan in its own way. The splendid Greek Revival-style Southard-House, an Austin Historic Landmark, was the Southard family's first property on this residential block. Just a few doors down this residential street, guests will find the Republic and the Lone Star Inn, which has a huge wood deck and swimming pool for all guests to enjoy. But visitors begin their tour of these three Austin dwellings at the Southard, the main location where guests check in, meet their hosts, Regina and daughter Kara, and gather for breakfast.

This home was built in 1880 as a one-story structure. Sometime before World War I the house was raised and an identical first-level was built under it. Restored by the Southards in 1985, the home features original pine floors, 12-foot ceilings and Italian marble fireplaces. Here, guests can choose from among six rooms or suites, all with an Austin or Texas theme. The Treaty Oak Suite, adorned with Belgian antiques, features a parlor with fireplace, a queen-size white iron bed, queen sleeper sofa, television set, refrigerator and desk.

The Governor room has a fireplace in the parlor, an antique piano, refrigerator, and a queen canopy bed and antique armoire. The Moonlight room features a 100-year-old double half-canopy brass bed, an antique oak marble dresser and armoire. The screened claw-foot tub in the bath has a hand-held shower. This home is filled with classic antiques and original crown moldings.

Down the walk is The Republic at 1108 Blanco Street. This home, also built in the 1880s and recently restored, features a great

INSIDERS' TIP

February through June and September through November are the busiest seasons for Austin's bed and breakfasts. We highly recommend making your reservations well in advance, especially if your heart is set on one particular establishment. The limited number of rooms in each inn can fill up quickly, especially during special events in Austin.

bay window, double fireplaces and original art. Here guests will find five guest rooms, including the Sam Houston suite. This suite has a private entrance and features a marble fireplace in the parlor, small kitchenette and Victorian bathroom with French doors and a claw-foot tub and shower. The John C. Hayes is a large one-bedroom apartment with a fully equipped kitchen, marble fireplace and a large skylight over the small Jacuzzi tub. It also has a private entrance. This house is a delight, beautifully decorated throughout.

The Lone Star, built in the 1920s, is a single-story bungalow at 1104 Blanco Street with tall ceilings and original hardwood floors. It has been carefully restored to retain its Texas charm. This home has four rooms, including the Judge Roy Bean, a private-entrance room with a sun porch, queen twig bed, fireplace and claw-foot tub. Guests at the Lone Star and The Republic are invited to join the family and other guests for breakfast in Southard-House, or they may request a continental breakfast basket. Breakfast consists of an expanded continental breakfast during the week, which includes homemade breads, lots of fruit, cereals, yogurts, juices, coffee and tea. More elaborate fare is served on the weekends when a hot quiche, luscious Belgian waffles or other delectable dishes are added to the menu. Breakfast is served weekdays from 8 to 9:30 AM while guests can choose from among three seatings on weekends beginning at 8:30 AM. Weather permitting, breakfast is served in the gazebo outdoors.

Visiting these three homes is like stepping back in time to turn-of-the-century Austin. But guests will have to return many times to Austin to experience all the delights. Children are invited to stay in some of Southard-House rooms. A two-night minimum stay is required on weekends and during special events. Pets are not welcome.

Woodburn House

$$ • 4401 Avenue D • (512) 458-4335

This gracious Austin Landmark features two wonderful wraparound verandas, spacious rooms tastefully adorned with antique quilts and family heirlooms and the allure of historic Hyde Park. (See our Neighborhoods and Attractions chapters). This 1909 two-story bed

and breakfast, one of just four bed and breakfasts in Austin listed as an Historic Accommodation of Texas (see the introduction to this chapter for a list of the others), is named for Bettie Hamilton Woodburn, who bought the house in 1920. Mrs. Woodburn is the daughter of Andrew Jackson Hamilton who was chosen provisional governor of Texas following the Civil War and was a personal friend of Abraham Lincoln.

This great structure narrowly escaped the wrecking ball in the late 1970s, when artist George Boutwell, a former Hyde Park resident, bought the house for $1 and had it moved to its present location. Now beautifully restored, Woodburn House is the home of Herb and Sandra Dickson, who have created a bed and breakfast that exudes Texas charm. This beautifully understated home features original Louisiana long leaf pine woodwork and hardwood floors.

The four guest rooms, all on the second floor, feature private baths, telephones with modem hookups, desks and, of course, rocking chairs in true Texas fashion. The Bettie Hamilton Room features an antique Jenny Lind queen-size bed and a beautiful oriental rug. Our Mother's Room is stylishly decorated with quilts made by Herb's grandmother and also features a queen-size Jenny Lind bed. The H. Dickson Room offers direct access to the wonderful second-floor veranda, where guests can unwind and enjoy the Hyde Park breeze. This room also features a king-size bed and a shower and claw-foot tub. The Frank Woodburn Room can comfortably accommodate three people with a queen-size and twin beds.

Woodburn House guests are treated to a full hot breakfast each morning, cooked up by Herb himself. Guests are treated to a full, hot breakfast each morning, cooked up by Herb himself. The menu is quite varied and exciting here including such delicacies as spinach-feta cheese quiche, migas, German pancakes, blueberry-pecan French toast and sun-dried tomato-basil egg frittata as well as plenty of muffins and fresh ground coffee the Dicksons purchase themselves in Mexico. Seating times are flexible, but breakfast is usually served around 9 AM on weekends. The large table in the dining room is the perfect place to gather, meet other guests and become part of the family. The Dicksons want their guests to feel like they're home — but, please, don't get up to wash the dishes. Guests are invited to use the very comfortable living room to listen to music, watch television or a video. And for those who just want some quiet, there's a formal front parlor. Woodburn House accepts children age 10 and up. Sorry, no pets please. A minimum two-night stay is required on holidays and during special events.

South Central

Citiview

$$$-$$$$ • 1404 E. Riverside Dr. • (512) 441-2606, (800) BST-VIEW

Citiview is unlike any other bed and breakfast you'll find in Austin. This classy property combines a bed and breakfast, a day spa, fully-equipped exercise room and dry sauna, an outdoor swimming pool on a sprawling manicured lawn, an animal sanctuary and a walk-through aviary. Citiview's two houses, built into a 4-acre hillside in 1949 and 1951, are reminiscent of Frank Lloyd Wright designs, and all four guest rooms are exquisitely decorated with European art deco furnishings and modern classics from the '30s, '40s and '50s. Both houses feature wonderful Great Rooms with original hardwood floors and huge wraparound windows that provide stunning views of Town Lake and Austin's downtown skyline.

This is an animal-lover's paradise. That comes as no surprise. Resident proprietor Carol Hayden, well known for her love of animals, founded the Fur Ball in Dallas. The black-tie affair, one of the largest fund-raisers in the state, subsidizes animal causes. The outdoor sanctuary at Citiview features peacocks, Nigerian dwarf goats, two llamas, ducks and rabbits. The indoor aviary is filled with finches, canaries, doves and many more exotic birds. Four enormous, and friendly Great Danes roam the enclave, welcoming guests and vying for top petting honors.

When you step inside the Great Room of Citiview I and hear a friendly "Hello," be prepared to meet Charlie Girl, the best-talking Macaw we've ever heard. She and fellow Macaw, Sky King, are the official greeters for this stylish room, which is designed with art deco and oriental touches and features a black-lacquered baby grand piano. And the 2-acre landscaped lawn here is stunning. A tiered, stone waterfall cascading into a Koi pond and a Zen garden are just two of the attractions out here. A glass-enclosed conservatory sits next to the large outdoor swimming pool. These facilities, both inside and out, are perfect for weddings, receptions, parties or business gatherings.

The guest rooms, two in each house, are equally impressive. The Maple Room features a queen bed, private bathroom, full bathtub and shower and French doors leading to a patio outside. The Walnut Room includes a king-size bed, hardwood floors, small refrigerator and French doors leading to the outside. In the Citiview II house, guests will find The Citiview Room, with access to the semiprivate living room and kitchen area, has a queen-size bed, private bath and features a great view of the Austin skyline through the wraparound windows. The Terrace Room also has wraparound windows and access to the semiprivate living room and kitchen area. The room features a king-size bed and a roomy bathroom with a double-size Jacuzzi bathtub. All rooms have television sets and telephones.

Breakfast is served in the main house around 9:30 AM on weekends, earlier on weekdays if guests choose. It's always a full, hot breakfast that can include such items as waffles, scones, frittatas, migas and breakfast parfaits, alternate layers of yogurt, berries, nuts and granola.

Citiview also offers full spa services by appointment, including massage and body treatments, nail and hair services, waxing and even private meditation and personal training classes. Children are welcome. And, of course, so are animals. A two-night minimum stay is required on weekends during peak season.

Fairview

$$-$$$ • 1304 Newning Ave.
• (512) 444-4746, (800) 310-4746

This beautiful Texas Colonial Revival-style home featuring four towering columns topped with Ionic capitals — like those at the Governor's Mansion — is surrounded by huge live oak trees and a wonderful garden. Built around 1910, Fairview is an Austin Historic Landmark that has been beautifully restored by owners Nancy and Duke Waggoner.

The home is filled with the Waggoner's own family heirlooms, collected over their many years of travels. The piano in the Great Room is dated 1903 and appeared in the 1904 World Fair in St. Louis, Missouri. The dining table where guests enjoy a full breakfast sits in the Great Room and belonged to Nancy's great grandmother and a restored antique half-canopy bed in one of the guest rooms that belonged to Nancy's great grandmother's sister. (Ask Nancy to tell you the story behind that one).

Each of the four large rooms on the second floor has a private bath, television sets and telephones. Some have screened porches or large sunrooms. Guests are welcome to use the refrigerator and microwave in the complimentary kitchen. There's also a collection of "very dull books," Nancy jokes, to help guests fall asleep.

This home, which sits in a quiet residential neighborhood, was once owned by Thomas Gullett and his wife, Lily. Gullett Elementary School is named for Thomas, a prominent Austin educator. In the 1950s, Fairview housed nine apartments. You'd never know it. The work the Waggoners have done to restore the home is apparent in every nook. They've added a huge covered porch to the back of the house, next to the garden. This bed and breakfast also features a carriage house out back.

This house features The Garden Cottage, with a queen-size bed, full kitchen and bath. Take special note of the meadow painted on the bedroom wall. Nancy painted it herself. Upstairs is The Sunday House, a small apartment featuring a sitting room, full kitchen and dining area, bedroom and bath.

Of course, guests are invited to join the family in the main house for a full breakfast. The breakfast specialty of the day can be a cream-cheese-stuffed croissant with strawberries on top, Belgian waffles, French toast with peach sauce, a fresh spinach frittata with mushrooms or other fare designed to get your motor running. Breakfast always includes the designer juice of the day, the Waggoner's own tasty juice concoction. Serving times can vary according to the guests' morning schedule.

The Waggoners have named all their rooms in the main house with political themes, in appreciation of Austin. There's the Back Room, with an iron and brass canopy bed and decorated in white wicker and handpainted ivy. The Texas Heritage Room is just beautiful, with a tall, burled walnut headboard built around 1890. The Governor's Suite is a sumptuous Victorian Renaissance-style room with an ornate headboard and decorated in lace and brocade. A two-night minimum stay is required on weekends. Well-behaved children are welcome in the carriage house only. Pets are not accepted.

Lazy Oak Inn

$$ • 211 W. Live Oak St.
• (512) 447-8873

INSIDERS' TIP

No matter which bed and breakfast you choose in Austin, you'll be staying close to one of our wonderful lakes or parks. Be sure to ask your host about the nearest outdoor oasis and check out our chapter on Parks and Recreation for details.

CARRINGTON'S BLUFF

A great country kitchen, original shiplap walls and turquoise-painted wooden floors in the common areas give this 1911 plantation-style home a very casual and comfy feel. And resident hosts Renee and Kevin Buck were voted "Best Down-Homey Hosts" in a recent *Austin Chronicle* critics poll. This two-story bed and breakfast, for adults and young people age 15 and up, features a wonderful covered porch on the second floor where guests can sit and survey the residential neighborhood, just blocks from the funky South Congress Avenue shopping and dining district and close to downtown Austin. Stairs leading down from this porch allow guests to come and go as they please. The five rooms, each with cable television, telephones and private baths, are detailed with great antiques and original artwork by some of Austin's most interesting artists. And no wonder. The Bucks are great supporters of the city's artists and regularly host shows in their home. There's even a lovely gift shop on the back porch area, where guests can find some small antiques, collectibles and artwork by Central Texas artists.

This house, which the Bucks renovated in 1996, has an open design, with high ceilings and carpeted, nice-size rooms. The large exposed kitchen on the main floor has huge windows adorned with wall-to-wall country shelves, and a fireplace that's just covered in lush potted plants. Renee prepares a breakfast buffet for her guests each morning, with cereals, muffins, fruits, yogurt and luscious gourmet coffee as well as a hot speciality of the day, sometimes an egg souffle or a homemade fruit cobbler. Yum.

The inviting parlor across from the kitchen comes complete with books, collectibles and a guitar for the musically inclined. A wide, carpeted staircase leads to the four second-story rooms, all with the look and feel of a modern country house. Here, guests can choose from among the king and queen rooms, or the room that features two double beds with a private bath just across the hall. The king room features a neat art deco armoire and an especially roomy bathroom. The cozy room on the main floor stands out for its fascinating antique queen bed, with three-dimensional cherubs carved into the foot board. The Lazy Oak Inn has been open since just 1997, but it's rapidly becoming a popular South Austin bed and breakfast.

The Miller-Crockett House

$$-$$$ • 112 Academy Dr.
• (512) 441-1600

Built in 1888, The Miller-Crockett House is a delightful dwelling, filled with Queen Anne and Victorian antiques and bubbling with the delightful personality of owner Kathleen Rikardsen. She and her husband Doug own this superb Victorian home, one of only 12 homes built south of the river during that time period — and one of only five left standing.

The New Orleans-style home features an exquisite wraparound veranda, an inviting parlor with 12-foot-high original pressed-tin ceiling and a spacious tree-filled lawn that is very popular for outdoor weddings and parties. Just south of the Congress Avenue Bridge a few minutes from downtown, the house is distinctive for its excellent views of the downtown skyline. Kathleen and Doug offer three bedrooms in the one-story main house and two more in the bungalows across the lawn. The Harbour Room, whimsically decorated with Kathleen's collection of fish, has a queen-size pine bed, chaise lounge, private balcony and private bath with a 6-foot cleft tub and shower.

Charlotte's Room features a full-size iron-brass bed with a private garden bath and shower and The Lydia Marguerite Room has a queen-size Victorian mahogany bed, also with a private bath and shower. Across the lawn is Bungalow Bill's, a rustic Southwestern-style bungalow with a queen bed, sleeper sofa, kitchen and bath. There's also a lovely patio and garden off this suite. La Casita is decorated with eclectic artwork and Saltillo tile. It, too, features a queen bed and sleeper sofa, kitchen, bath and a garden deck. These two suites include television sets complete with VCRs and cable.

The Miller-Crockett House, which opened in 1997, is one of Austin's newer bed and breakfast establishments. But it already is getting national recognition. The house is featured in a scene in the 1998 movie, *The Newton Boys*, featuring actors Matthew McConaughey, Ethan Hawke, Vincent D'Onofrio and Skeet Ulrich. The Rikardsens request a minimum two-night stay on weekends and holidays. Children are welcome in the bungalows. You can also have pets in the bungalows.

Breakfast is a full, seated gourmet affair on weekends, a delicious hot buffet on weekdays. The menu includes items such as green chili and cheese quiche, French toast with fresh fruit, blueberry pancakes, bacon and sausage, homemade muffins, exotic fresh fruits and fresh-squeezed juice and gourmet coffee.

Ziller House

$$$-$$$$ • 800 Edgecliff Terr.
• (512) 462-0100, (800) 949-5446

A Mediterranean-style villa provides the setting for this upscale bed and breakfast. Town Lake provides the fantastic view! Ziller House is simply a work of art. The 1930s estate, which sits at the end of a quiet lane on a bluff overlooking the lake, combines the ultimate in elegance with all the comforts of a bed and breakfast. Under new ownership and totally renovated in 1997, Ziller House is designed for adults who desire luxury and privacy.

Classic antiques and original works of art adorn the rooms and common areas throughout this two-story villa, and in the separate Cottage Room. The stately living room has a modified German lodge, Ralph Lauren look, with an original stone fireplace, grand piano and featuring a huge slice of lacquered tree trunk as a coffee table.

The breakfast room, with its individual cafe tables, Victrola record player and handpainted "rug" on the hardwood floor, will have guests feeling as if they're on the Continent. The breakfast fare is as impressive as the room. It's a full, hot meal every morning and includes such specialities as ricotta-cheese crepe and fresh fruit served with herbed scrambled egg and maple sausage; a bacon, mushroom and green-chili quesadilla with herbed scrambled eggs; crepes served with the house special bacon, which is baked with chili powder, sugar and pecans until it melts in your mouth. Breakfast is served from 8 to 10 AM all week. There's a complimentary fruit basket in every room.

All five well-appointed guest rooms are designed by professionals for the exclusive use of guests, and each features a private bath, cable television, coffee maker, mini-fridge, microwave and private phone. The Parlor Room, the only room on the main floor, is designed with a British Colonial safari theme and features a posh fainting couch upholstered in leopard-skin fabric. The awning-covered balcony of the appropriately named Balcony Room provides a great view of Town Lake and the downtown skyline and features a modern canopy bed draped in gauzy fabric.

The large Suite Room can accommodate two or three guests with a lovely queen-bed and twin sleigh bed. The sitting room of this suite provides a great view of the manicured lawn. A fireplace with huge wood-carved mantle and a wall of built-in mahogany bookcases adorn the stately Library Room, which

INSIDERS' TIP

Even if business or other activities prevent you from enjoying Austin's great music scene, you can tune in to local bands on any of the great radio stations that program lots of local acts, or catch *Austin City Limits* or *The Austin Music Network* on TV. Check our Media chapter for loads of information on Austin music broadcasts.

opens to a large screened porch. Separate from the main house is the Cottage Room over the garage.

Designed for those seeking rustic elegance, this large room and enormous bath features plaid fabric covered walls and lots of leather and iron — very masculine, yet cozy and inviting. And if that's not enough, the villa features a magnificent stone swimming pool and hot tub overlooking Town Lake and the skyline as well as a cozy oak-paneled billiards room downstairs. The Ziller House is an ideal escape.

Southeast

Carter Lane

$$ • 4706 Carter Ln. • (512) 448-0402

A Texas ranch-style home embellished with artistic touches throughout awaits guests at this charming bed and breakfast. Located in a residential neighborhood surrounded by trees, this bed and breakfast is the perfect getaway — just 10 minutes to downtown and even less to Austin's great McKinney Falls State Park (see our Parks and Recreation chapter). Several of Austin's major high-tech companies are also close by. Proprietor Linda Bennett LeBourgeois offers just two guest rooms in this 1950s home, but has gone all out to make sure no detail is forgotten. Both rooms are attractively decorated with luxurious fabrics and dark woods. The larger room has an exquisite antique armoire, a large queen-size bed and private bath — with a towel warmer! The private bath for the second bedroom, which features a great iron and cherry-stained queen bed, is just a couple of steps down the hall. And both rooms lead out into a very cozy common room that's just brimming with books. Here, guests can relax, listen to music or watch satellite television. The kitchen, which guests are free to use, also features an antique jukebox that has been refitted for CDs. There's a well-equipped fitness room with a television set and a huge selection of videos.

In the backyard guests will find a great wood deck, a lovely swimming pool and hot tub, and even a fishing pond. The 6-year-old boy who caught an 11-pound bass in this pond went home with the fish story of his life! Forgot your pole? Linda can provide one, as well as about anything else you've forgotten. But she's way ahead of you on that. There are terry bathrobes for all her guests, a lovely tea tray in each room stocked with all kinds of goodies. There are bath therapy salts and soaps in each room — and each guest is treated to a lovely welcome basket filled with more delicacies upon arrival. Linda sets out an elaborate serve-it-yourself continental breakfast on weekdays and serves more substantial fare on weekends, including such delights as an artichoke-egg casserole, made-to-order omelets, or simple eggs and pancakes, depending on your tastes. There are always plenty of hot breads, fruit and coffee. She's very flexible and goes out of her way to adjust the morning menu according to her guests wishes. In nice weather, she'll even serve you on the patio by the pool or out by the pond.

She welcomes guests of all ages and even pets who would like to meet her Airedale, Basil Rathbone. Basil is special, too. He's a Therapy Pet Pal who goes to Austin State Hospital to visit the children. Carter Lane accepts cash or checks, unless reservations are made with a credit card through her service, Bed and Breakfast Texas Style at (800) 899-4538.

Gregg House & Gardens

$ • 4201 Gregg Ln. • (512) 928-9777

Just a few houses away from Carter Lane is this quaint bed and breakfast, which will take you back to the 1950s. Avocado-colored kitchen appliances and a real ranch-style abode will have you soon forgetting the personal computer or fax machine ever existed. The large country kitchen and four guest rooms are set up for exclusive use by guests. Owners Jim and Nelda Haynes live nearby and arrive promptly each morning to prepare breakfast for their guests. Some of the produce and herbs come from Nelda's organic garden on the premises. Homegrown strawberries and pecans wind up on the menu as do other delights, like rosemary muffins from homegrown herbs. She'll serve French toast, eggs to order, breakfast tacos made with eggs and Mexican chorizo sausage, homemade biscuits with ham or bacon — whatever her guests request. The serving time is flexible, as is the menu.

Huge live oak, pecan and elm trees cover this 1-acre property, a perfect place for nature walks. The home, which sits on a gentle slope, features a great covered deck out back that overlooks the wooded property and a spring-fed creek. There's also a fish pond just steps away.

Bedroom 1 is just off the living room and features a double bed, three closets and a private bathroom. This room also features a wonderful view of the woods. Highlighting Bedroom 2 is the direct access through sliding glass doors to the covered porch overlooking the woods. This large room has a queen-size bed, two closets and a private bathroom with tiled shower. Bedroom 3 has a double bed and a view in three directions. Bedroom 4 is paneled in knotty pine and features a trundle bed that sleeps two people. Through these windows guests will enjoy a view of the garden and the pond. The two bedrooms share the Gregg House's third bathroom. Guests are welcome to use all the facilities — one family even made Christmas dinner here. Yes, the kitchen is fitted with modern amenities, such as a microwave, ice maker and dishwasher. There's a cozy sitting room for watching television or relaxing and a large living room with its wood-burning stone fireplace is perfectly comfortable and makes you feel as if you've gone to visit grandma, without all the cheek pinching.

Guests are free to use the house phone, but are asked to use a calling card for long-distance calls. The home is named for J.W. Gregg who developed this residential neighborhood in the 1950s. The Haynes first opened this bed and breakfast in the mid-'80s, and later rented it for private use for a number of years. Newly renovated in 1996, the Haynes once again are operating Gregg House as a bed and breakfast. Children are welcome. Reservations made through the service Bed and Breakfast Texas style may be charged to a credit card. That number is (800) 899-4538. Others should plan to pay by cash or check. The Gregg House offers a real country feel just minutes from downtown, McKinney Falls State Park and many of the area's high-tech industries. Pets are not allowed.

Northwest

The Chequered Shade

$$ • 2530 Pearce Rd. • (512) 346-8318

Take a walk down a country lane, enjoy the deer romping among the trees or stroll over to one of Austin's most popular lakeside eateries. The Chequered Shade offers all of these outdoor pleasures, plenty of peace and quiet, plus the many amenities of a well-run bed and breakfast. This 1970s home of white brick sits in a residential neighborhood just across the way from beautiful Lake Austin and near Emma Long Metropolitan Park, a popular Austin spot for boaters and others who love to be outdoors.

Bring your fishing pole, Turkey Creek is nearby. For those who want to escape the city and yet be within 15 minutes of major restaurants, movie theaters and shopping, the Chequered Shade is the perfect location. Proprietor Millie Scott has decorated this Hill Country home with family heirlooms and all the comforts of home. Chequered Shade offers two guest rooms, each with a private bath, hot pot for making coffee or tea, a telephone and cable television. For those traveling with family or friends, another lovely room can be opened with a shared bath. The Master Suite, with a king-size bed, mini-fridge, beamed ceiling and a beautiful handpainted secretary from the 1890s, is especially spacious and inviting.

Millie prepares a full, hot breakfast daily and will serve it anywhere you'd like: in the dining room, on one of the three private patios or porches — you can even request a breakfast tray delivered to your room. Now that's living! Fruit and gourmet breads are always on the morning menu along with delicacies like chili-cheese puff pastry served hot with a baked tomato topped with olive oil and Parmesan cheese, turkey sausage in a puff pastry, and poached pears with a warm berry sauce. On weekdays, Millie serves breakfast before you go off to work, if need be. She offers three seatings on weekends beginning at 8:30 AM.

The home is surrounded by pecan and fig trees and during much of the year visitors will spot many species of birds perching on the branches. While you're staying at the Chequered Shade, don't miss the opportunity to try out Ski Shores restaurant on the lake. This informal, outdoor eatery has been attracting Austin Insiders for decades. Children older than 12 are welcome. And in case you're wondering, this unique name for a bed and breakfast comes from a Milton quote: "To many a youth, and many a maid; Dancing in the chequered shade. And young and old come forth to play; On a sunshine holiday."

Lake Travis

Austin Lake Travis Bed & Breakfast

$$$-$$$$ • 4446 Eck Ln.
• (512) 266-3386, (800) 484-9095 access code 5348

This spectacular bed and breakfast right on Lake Travis is ideal for a romantic getaway, or just a weekend away from the bustle of the city. Proprietors Judy and Vic Dwyer have created a secluded, one-of-a-kind retreat with couples in mind; children are not allowed. This classic Hill Country home of native limestone and redwood features windows and decks galore to take full advantage of the glorious view of Lake Travis.

Each of the four rooms has its own private outdoor deck while the large common deck accommodates a 7-foot-deep swimming pool, a neat in-water table for cooling off while playing cards or having cocktails, and a huge hot tub with 26 jets. (A perfect place for a midnight rendezvous.) And if that's not enough, guests can descend the 130 lighted steps to the covered boat dock below for a chartered boat ride, some sunning on the elevated sun deck, or a private feast. There's a complete kitchen down here.

The Dwyers offer four guest rooms, each with king-size bed, private bath, television, mini-fridge, telephone, binoculars, CD player and sound machine. The Lago Vista Suite, designed in Southwest decor of peach and blue tones and featuring antique accent furniture, is on the ground level and opens onto the main deck with its secluded patio off to the side. The Sunset Suite on the second level has its own deck overlooking the lake and the main deck below. This room, decorated in hues of rose and blue, is a great place to relax while watching the sunset. Above the treetops on the third level is the Eagle's Nest Suite, a tailored room of beiges and blues that offers an awesome view of the lake. And the largest suite, debuted in 1998, is more like a studio hideaway. Here, guests will delight in the enormous pink, heart-shaped tub, three-sided fireplace that's visible from any location in the suite, a lovely sitting area and a kitchenette.

The home, built in 1979 and decorated with a tasteful Southwest theme, conforms perfectly to this type of establishment. There are plenty of parlors and common areas for playing pool, watching television on the big-screen TV or just socializing next to a roaring fire. And the fully-equipped exercise room — massage treatments are available by appointment — offers another great perspective of the lake. Judy, a travel agent for eight years, knows what people want in a bed and breakfast, and has left out no detail. Breakfast is always served in bed — the ultimate in pampering — and includes such creative fare as crescent rolls in the shape of a Longhorn steer, rolls that look like crabs served along with a seafood entree, apples carved in the shape of swans, and other delights. Most times Nancy serves around 8 AM, but she can accommodate late sleepers. She's even got a few surprises for her guests.

Smoking is not permitted anywhere on the premises, and no pets are allowed. Lake Travis requires a two-night minimum.

INSIDERS' TIP

We Austinites take great pride in our clean, natural environment. Find the nearest recycling bin when you need to dispose of trash. Remember: "Don't Mess With Texas," as our award-winning ads warn!

Vintage Villas

$$-$$$$ • 4209 Eck Ln. • (512) 266-9333

Escape to the Hill Country and Lake Travis at these distinctive villas, which combine bed and breakfast hospitality with the space and feel of a hotel. Vintage Villas offers three suites and 40 attractive rooms in three new buildings, each designed with a distinct Texas theme and unique in decor.

This establishment, which opened in 1997 and offers a view of Lake Travis, is fast becoming a popular spot for weddings, social gatherings of all kinds, and business functions. Just next door is the conference and social center leased by Vintage Villas to Sterling Affairs, which can arrange and cater any function. The South Texas Villa, designed in rustic woods and tiles, is the main building on this Hill Country hilltop. Here, guests register and also gather for the breakfast delicacy of their choice, selected from a generous menu that includes egg and crab cake hollandaise, made-to-order omelets, Texas French toast, egg-sausage- and bacon-stuffed tortillas and raspberry lemon zest crepes.

The Central Texas Villa and the East Texas Villa reflect the heritage of those distinct Texas regions. And the living areas of each villa feature original artwork by national and Southwest artists.

The spacious rooms all include a built-in wet bar, microwave, a refrigerator with ice maker and television sets with built-in VCRs. There are even complimentary videos for guests to take back to their rooms. The telephones in each room feature dataport hookups. Guests can choose from among many other in-room amenities at this lovely establishment, including walkout balconies, Jacuzzi tubs or large showers with double heads. There's a lovely gazebo just outside with a view of lake. And just behind Vintage Villas is a winery, which is open for wine tastings and tours. The villas are located about 30 minutes from downtown Austin. Even better, they're just minutes to all kinds of Travis Lake activities. Now this is truly the best of both worlds. Children are welcome; pets are not.

This is a city where
dining is supposed to be
fun, not an exercise in
tailored torture.

Restaurants

If there is one rule on the Austin restaurant scene it likely is: You got a shirt, you got shoes or sandals, you got service! There is not a restaurant in town (maybe a private club or two) where a tie is required. Ties are just targets for bean dribbles and spaghetti spills. This is a city where dining is supposed to be fun, not an exercise in tailored torture.

In the last two decades, the Austin restaurant scene has ridden the same economic roller coaster as the real estate sector, falling in the doldrums in the mid-1980s only to rise from the ashes like the proverbial phoenix. In 1998, the phoenix was soaring with restaurants popping up in converted bungalows in old Austin neighborhoods, sprouting on street corners and slipping into strip shopping centers whenever a storefront became available.

Some of the new restaurants are franchises or outlets for a national chain, but many are homegrown. There has been a dramatic increase in the number of Asian restaurants in the city as immigrants from that continent have found a home here. Several long-established local restaurants have opened up second locations, often in the burgeoning northwest section of the city, but one of the coolest trends has been the emergence of young, dynamic chefs, eager to take advantage of the wide variety of fresh foods in the city and the willingness of Austin diners to try new things.

There is no such thing as "Austin cuisine." But there are certain signature cuisines that do have a connection to Texas culture. Given the fact that Texas once was part of Mexico and Mexican-American life is vibrant and very much a part of the state's cultural weave, it is only natural that Mexico's culinary influence is felt in a number of ways. There's Tex-Mex, Nuevo Tex-Mex, South Texas/Northern Mexico, New Mexican, Interior Mexican and Latin American, even South American.

Tex-Mex is probably the most prevalent and recognizable. Standard fare includes enchiladas, tacos, chalupas and refried beans. An easy way to spot Tex-Mex is whether or not the dish includes yellow cheese instead of the traditional white farmer's-style cheese found in true Mexican cuisine. That's not to put Tex-Mex down. David Garrido, chef at one of Austin's finest restaurants, Jeffrey's, and a native of Mexico, published *Nuevo Tex-Mex* in the spring of 1998, and the book includes an introduction by of one of Texas' top chefs, Stephan Pyles, who remembers that Tex-Mex was everyday fare when he grew up in West Texas.

Pyles notes the processed yellow-cheese phenomenon: "Over the years, processed cheese food and other shortcuts have found their way into many Tex-Mex *cocinas* (kitchens) and compromised the integrity of their cuisine. But in every Texas city, there are still Tex-Mex restaurants that have remained true to their time-honored cooking traditions — traditions rooted firmly in the peasant culture of Texas."

In our listings we have included a variety of Tex-Mex and other Mexican/Latino restaurants in an effort to give readers a good cross section of that multifaceted cuisine. Just as many of us get a hankering for an old-fashioned burger once in a while, yellow-cheese Tex-Mex has its appeal and a loyal following. But readers who want to go beyond that point have a wide variety of restaurants to choose from, including several that celebrate interior Mexican culinary traditions. Those unfamiliar with that territory should not hesitate to explore. Not all Mexican food is spicy hot. The chile pepper is a staple of the Mexican kitchen, but not all peppers are hot, and many are served in rich sauces, called moles, that blend the pepper with herbs, spices, even chocolate to create multi-nuanced tastes.

Most Austinites have their favorite Mexican restaurant, particularly when it comes to weekend brunch. A popular traditional dish is migas, eggs scrambled with tortilla chips, diced chiles and tomatoes. Given the city's late nightlife, weekend breakfast is often served into mid-afternoon. During the week, breakfast tacos are the early morning order of the day, economical and easy to eat — simply flour tortillas stuffed with combinations of eggs, chorizo (sausage), potatoes, bacon and salsa.

A menu staple in Austin and, now, beyond is fajitas. This dish had its origins in South Texas and Northern Mexico when *vaqueros* (Mexican cowboys) would grill skirt steak, a cheap cut taken off the ribs, over coals, perhaps marinating it first in a little beer or simply with salt and pepper. The meat was then cut up or shredded, topped with a salsa cruda, a fiery uncooked mix of tomatoes, onions, serranos or jalapenos and cilantro, and folded into a tortilla. The name comes from the Mexican word *faja,* meaning belt — hence, "little belts," a play on the appearance of the meat and its location on the body of the cow.

Fajitas are now made from the traditional skirt steak or a fancier cut of flank steak, chicken, shrimp, even catfish, and customers are given a choice of corn or flour tortillas (flour tortillas predominate in Northern Mexico and South Texas cuisine, whereas corn are more familiar in the southern parts of Mexico). Sometimes frijoles borrachos, drunken beans, a Northern Mexican favorite concocted from pinto beans, salt, bacon, onions, peppers and beer, are served, but other restaurants serve their fajitas with refried black or pinto beans. (Again, pinto beans are preferred in Northern Mexico and South Texas, while black beans are favored in the southern regions of Mexico.)

Another star in the Texas culinary pantheon is, of course, barbecue. It's a subject, like religion and politics, that should be discussed carefully and with great consideration for individual beliefs — even the spelling of barbecue promotes debate. Generally speaking, Texas barbecue is slow-cooked with indirect heat over wood coals, often mesquite, a quite delicate-looking tree with a gnarled trunk that is the bane of ranchers since it spreads like a weed and sucks up water. Brisket is the most popular cut of meat to be slow cooked, and most cooks "marinate" with a dry rub of spices and sometimes herbs.

(This is treacherous ground, because already some aficionados are saying, "No! No!")

Generally speaking, barbecue is served with pinto beans, potato salad, perhaps cole slaw, certainly sliced raw white onions (or Sweet 1015 Texas Onions), pickles, plain old white bread and barbecue sauce — often the ingredient by which a barbecue joint is judged.

Some of the best barbecue can be found in the small towns of Texas, places like Kreuz Market in Lockhart, 208 S. Commerce Street, (512) 398-2361, open daily from early morning to late afternoon. Saturday is a busy day at this meat market as customers line up, pick their choice of meat, white bread or saltines, and walk to the tables with their "plates" — thick pieces of butcher paper. As you drive through the area towns, follow your nose; sometimes even roadside stands serve up fine barbecue. Our listings include several Austin area barbecue joints, some upscale, some funky.

Almost as revered as barbecue is chicken-fried steak, a staple of the homestyle restaurants and sure to be a blue plate special at most country-cooking restaurants. The chicken fried is usually a salisbury steak, pounded thin to tenderize the meat, then covered with bread crumbs or flour mixed with salt and pepper, then deep fried, just like chicken — hence the name. Some of Austin's upscale restaurants

INSIDERS' TIP

Austin abounds with bakeries where a last-minute picnic can be put together for outdoor (or indoor) munching. Several are listed here in the Restaurants chapter, but also check out the Food/Gourmet/Kitchenware section of our Shopping chapter.

Photo: Austin Tourism and Convention Bureau

Lakeside dining is one way to treat yourself to Austin's many restaurants.

are treating other cuts of meat in this fashion — Z'Tejas (see our Central listings) serves a chicken-fried rib eye.

Another hallmark of Austin cuisine is the emergence of native, homegrown foods. Texas is home to a large variety of foodstuffs, including exotic game, prime beef, fresh seafood, onions, chiles, fruits, handcrafted cheeses and special blends of rice. The Texas Department of Agriculture has an aggressive promotional program, and we have taken a look at this and locally crafted foodstuffs in our Close-up in this chapter, Texas Cuisine: Not Just a Bunch of Beef.

The multitude of cultural influences, the availability of a great variety of ingredients and the innovative abilities of local chefs has led to a wide number of restaurants featuring "fusion" cuisine. Dishes on one menu might exhibit Mexican, Asian, Italian and Mediterranean influences. But there are also a number of restaurants and cafes serving homestyle cooking. In a phrase, there is something for every taste these days in Austin.

A word or two about local customs. As noted above, casual attire is fine at most Austin restaurants, and even the most upscale allow customers to wear jeans and golf shirts, pressed jeans and clean golf shirts, of course. Smoking is a crime in Austin, as the late Timothy Leary, LSD guru, found out when he lit up in the Austin airport. A banner there reminds visitors "Austin is a clean air city." Some restaurants do have a smoking area if they have a bar or outdoor patio, but you will not be asked "Smoking or nonsmoking?" in the Austin city limits when you ask for a table. Outside the city limits, most restaurants do have designated smoking areas.

Many restaurants are open for major holidays, except Christmas. It is wise to call ahead. Most restaurants do not take reservations except for parties of six or more. All restaurants listed accept major credit cards, except where noted. Some take local checks, but that custom is fading as the city grows. More and more restaurants are staying open later to accommodate Austin's penchant for late-night noshing after the movies or theater, but most close at 10 PM during the week and 11 PM on weekends. Some stay open throughout the afternoon to serve late lunch or afternoon snacks since many Austin business people, particularly the city's large self-employed population, utilize favorite local restaurants as a conference room or an office away from their home office. We have noted restaurants that stay open beyond the usual hours.

Our restaurant listings are arranged by area of town and where a local restaurant has more than one location, refer to the first listing for menu information. For the most part, well-known national chains are not listed, although a couple of Texas restaurant groups with a major presence in Dallas or Houston have been included since they are likely not familiar to out-of-state visitors.

Price Code

The price key symbol in each listing gives the range for the cost of a meal for two, an entree and beverage, but not including alcoholic beverages, appetizer or dessert. Since some restaurants serve three meals a day, or a have a wide range of entree prices, the range is noted by the symbols.

$	**Less than $20**
$$	**$20 to $40**
$$$	**$40 to $60**
$$$$	**$60 or more**

One final note: Austin is growing at such a great rate that new restaurants are opening virtually every week, and, given the competitive nature of the business, sometimes others close. Generally those listed here have been open for at least a year, or have achieved such success and popularity that they warrant listing.

Central

Austin Land and Cattle Company

$$$-$$$$ • Enfield Shopping Center, 1205 N. Lamar Blvd. • (512) 472-1813

Steakhouse — the term usually brings to mind leather banquettes, red walls and dark wood paneling — but this locally owned steakhouse in a small, quiet shopping center a few blocks from downtown has a lighter touch. The soft, cool palette acts as a foil to the hearty fare found here. The menu features steak and top-quality seafood, complemented with Southwestern touches, including grilled chile strips. A house specialty is the beer-battered mushrooms made with dark Shiner bock beer from the Central Texas brewery in the town of that name. (See our Annual Events chapter for the annual Shiner picnic.) It is open daily for dinner.

Basil's

$$-$$$ • 900 W. 10th St. • (512) 477-5576

Touted as a romantic dining spot, Basil's is a great date restaurant or a good place to rekindle old flames, celebrate anniversaries or simply fall in love with the food. An old home not far from downtown Austin has been converted into a small, intimate Italian restaurant where candlelight, ceiling fans and hardwood floors suggest another time and place. The food has a light, northern Italian touch, although there are some dishes inspired by other regions. The pastas are handmade here, and the desserts are sinful. Because of its popularity reservations are suggested on weekends. Dinner is served daily.

Bitter End Bistro and Brewery

$$-$$$ • 311 Colorado St. • (512) 478-2337

One name that surfaces with some regularity in any compendium of Austin restaurants is Clemons. Reed and Betsy Clemons are responsible for some of Austin's most popular restaurants including the Bitter End across the street from another Clemons' favorite, Mezzaluna, in the downtown warehouse district. A combination brewpub (read more about Austin's brewpubs in our Nightlife chapter), the Bitter End is the sort of hip bistro favored by Austin's young (and not so young) movers and shakers. The menu is a mix of Italian, Mediterranean, American and French. A wood-fired oven produces a large selection of pizzas and breads, while the salad menu includes a wonderful salade Nicoise with fresh grilled tuna. The wood-roasted trout is popular, and

INSIDERS' TIP

Looking for a picnic site? Two of the easiest to access are Town Lake and the Capitol grounds where you may have to share with the squirrels (look for the famous albino squirrel at the Capitol). For other inspirations check the Parks and Recreation chapter.

the hamburgers are huge and satisfying. Grilled dishes are included on the menu plus several yummy appetizers — calamari, roasted vegetables, steamed mussels. Light dishes are served in the bar, which overlooks the restaurant floor. In addition to a reasonable wine list, the Bitter End serves selections of its made-on-the-premises beers. Next door is the B-side lounge, also owned by the Clemons' restaurant group, where blues and jazz bands play (see our Nightlife chapter). There is also a cigar room on the premises. Lunch, dinner and late-night snacks are served daily in this restored warehouse space.

Brick Oven

$ • 1209 Red River St. • (512) 447-7006
$ • 1608 W. 35th St. • (512) 453-4330

Just east of the capitol on Red River Street is one of Austin's most popular pizza restaurants, noted and named for its wood-fired pies. The menu has a pizza for every taste, thick and thin crust, a variety of toppings, even an all-garlic pizza for those who believe in its efficacy and are not afraid to indulge. In addition to being near the capitol, the Brick Oven is just a few blocks south of the University of Texas Special Events Center so it is popular among concertgoers and basketball fans. Pizza dominates the menu, but there are other offerings, including a vegetarian stromboli. Lunch and dinner are served daily.

The 35th Street restaurant is a relatively new branch of the Brick Oven pizza restaurants. It is in a converted home in the 35th Street shopping district.

Cafe at the Four Seasons

$$$$ • 98 San Jacinto Blvd.
• (512) 478-4500

Elegant is the word most critics apply to this hotel restaurant where the menu is a tribute to the best European traditions touched by Southwestern flair as divined by Chef Elmar Prambs. This is the place for a power lunch, power dinner or divine brunch. The hotel is a favorite among movie stars in town for filming, high-tech wunderkind in town for networking and politicians in town to be taken to dinner by lobbyists. That said, you never can tell who might be grazing on field greens at the next table. The menu is a wondrous combination of elegant dishes, some of them with Texas connections — nachos with smoked lamb, grilled duck salad with black-eyed pea chili — plus bistro fare such as roasted chicken and healthy, low-fat choices, of course all concocted in high style. The cafe, decorated in the same beiges and subdued pastels as the rest of the hotel, features top-flight service and a extensive wine list. One of the best and most affordable ways to experience the cafe is to sample brunch at the Four Seasons. A groaning board of omelets, blintzes, salmon, caviar, desserts and fresh fruits abounds. The restaurant offers a good view of the nightly summer bat flight from under the Congress Avenue bridge, although the tab for your dinner will be considerably more than the bats are going to pay for their bug supper. Lunch and dinner are served daily plus a prix fixe brunch. Reservations are recommended.

Cafe Josie

$$-$$$ • 1200-B W. Sixth St.
• (512) 322-9226

This is one of those Austin cafes that lie hidden behind unassuming storefronts and in back of other businesses where young chefs are exploring the world of fusion cuisine. Here, the emphasis is on Caribbean flavors with dishes like redfish tacos with lime cilantro aioli and mesquite-grilled jerk pork tenderloin. The restaurant is tucked behind the Coffee Exchange in the W. Sixth Street shopping district and has a small indoor dining room plus a comfy outdoor patio. It is open for lunch and dinner daily.

Carmelo's

$$$ • 504 E. Fifth St. • (512) 477-7497

An old favorite just east of downtown and one block south of Sixth Street, Carmelo's serves large portions of rich Italian-American food with flair and drama. Steak Diane is flambeed tableside while lobster-stuffed veal is presented with a flourish and a side order of fettucine alfredo. Another house favorite is pollo Carmelo, cooked with olives, mushrooms, herbs and garlic and served with mashed potatoes flavored with olives. The restaurant is housed in an old limestone building that once served as the Depot Hotel. It serves lunch and dinner daily.

Casita Jorge's

$-$$ • 2203 Hancock Dr.
• (512) 454-1980

For the grownups there are frozen Margaritas topped with a "blast of Cointreau" and for the kids, nachos. Tex-Mex with a tropical flair is the order of the day here, so the Margaritas also come in raspberry, strawberry, peach and banana flavors. The restaurant has an indoor dining room, decorated in bright colors plus a patio lined with banana palms to continue that tropical theme. Entrees include enchiladas, fajitas, tacos — all the standard Tex-Mex fare plus daily specials. The menu includes both crispy tacos and soft tacos, the latter made with flour tortillas. It is open for lunch and dinner daily.

Castle Hill Cafe

$$$ • 1101 W. Fifth St. • (512) 476-0728

Where's the castle? Where's the hill? Old-timers know that this popular cafe began as a tiny, tiny restaurant a few blocks north of its current location near the W. Sixth Street shopping district. (That spot, just off Lamar Boulevard is now occupied by El Rinconcito, listed in this section.)

Just to the west of the original tiny restaurant is a well-known landmark, a home on a hill that looks like a castle — hence the name. Castle Hill outgrew its original location and continues to draw crowds, especially on weekends. The food here is a delightful mix of Southwestern, Asian and Mediterranean with a touch of Caribbean thrown in, perhaps even Indian. There are fixed items on the menu, but new dishes are constantly being introduced. Some of the longtime favorites include Lucinda's basil cheese torta, an appetizer that was inspired by well-known Austin writer and herbal expert, Lucinda Hutson. Another staple on the menu is the spicy sausage and duck gumbo. The restaurant is airy and decorated with Oaxacan folk art, a far cry from the tiny, cramped quarters it once occupied. One thing the larger location does share with the old is the air of culinary excitement. It serves lunch and dinner daily. Reservations recommended on weekends.

Central Market

$ • 4001 N. Lamar Blvd. • (512) 206-1068

Most of us go to the grocery store to shop, not to eat, or not eat substantially, perhaps a munch or two along the way. But Austin's showcase grocery store and top tourist spot (see our Close-up in the Shopping chapter) is a favorite lunch and early dinner spot, particularly among parents and grandparents. The store has added a breakfast/brunch bar and prepares breakfast tacos to go. Central Market Cafe features several "restaurants" — a bistro, an Italian cafe and a bakery — housed in the southern wing of the store and aimed at satisfying a variety of tastes. Mom and Dad can order a roast beef sandwich or a salad, and the kids can peel the cheese off a pizza. The cafe is under the direction of a top chef and the menu reflects Austin's tastes for a mix of traditional, nouvelle and fusion dishes. Dishes are reasonably priced, and customers can either graze or dig into a hearty meal. There is a large indoor dining room, flanked by a wide wooden deck looking out over the greenbelt. Kids can race around outside, dogs can sit in the shade while their owners nosh, and families can enjoy nightly live music concerts featuring a wide variety of musicians. The eateries are open daily for morning breaks, lunch and early dinner.

Chez Nous

$$-$$$ • 510 Neches St.
• (512) 473-2413

Since 1982, Chez Nous has been serving authentic French bistro fare at this cozy restaurant half-block south of Sixth Street. Bistro is a word much bandied about these days, but Chez Nous is as close to the real thing as you can get in Austin with traditional dishes like oven-roasted chicken and homemade pâtés. There is a menu du jour, daily chef's specials plus lighter fare including crepes. The wine list features French wines, of course. The interior evokes the cozy bistros of Paris, and here friends and lovers can enjoy a quiet moment or two, but yet be just a stone's throw from the frenzy of Sixth Street. The bistro is open for lunch and dinner Tuesday through Friday, dinner only on the weekends.

Photo: Courtesy of the Texas Department of Transportation

Don't leave without having a bowl of our tasty Texas chili.

City Grill

$$$ • 401 Sabine St. • (512) 479-0817

One of the first converted warehouses in downtown Austin, City Grill set the tone for the revival of older buildings in the heart of the city. The restaurant is open and airy with wooden floors and sleek, modern fixtures. The menu is just as sleek and modern with grilled seafood dominating plus offerings of grilled chicken and steaks, and several pasta dishes. One signature touch is the choice of special sauces with the grilled dishes. Diners can choose from tomatillo, lemon-herb, aioli, Bearnaise, horseradish cream and Szechwan. Lunch and dinner are served daily, and reservations are recommended on weekends and holidays.

Dan McKluskey's

$$$ • 301 E. Sixth St. • (512) 473-8924

Handcut steaks are the featured item at this restaurant in the heart of the Sixth Street club scene, just three blocks east of Congress Avenue. The menu lists a 20-ounce rib eye, but notes the house butcher will cut a steak to any size. In addition to steaks, fish and chicken dishes are offered, also smoked pork chops, a mixed grill, baby back ribs and all the appropriate side orders — onion rings, sauteed mushrooms, baked potatoes, etc. The restaurant has a traditional steakhouse aura: dark woods, polished brass. It is open for lunch and dinner daily. Given its location, there is a late-night menu on weekends.

Dirty Martin's Place

$ • 2808 Guadalupe St. • (512) 477-3173

In this day of image makers and spin doctors who would ever name a restaurant "Dirty's"? This is a restaurant that has roots back to the '20s, but the story of the name has been lost in time. Some call this campus-area hamburger joint "Martin's Kumback" — and that is what the sign says — but the majority refer to it as "Dirty's." That name has stuck both in the popular imagination and the phone book. The fare is fry-cook simple here: hamburgers off the grill with fries and onions, a cold beer or soda. Dirty's is open daily for lunch and dinner, but the menu doesn't change when the sun goes down.

Dog and Duck Pub

$-$$ • 406 W. 17th St. • (512) 479-0598

Pub grub is the order of the day in this downtown bar and restaurant that has all the comfy, familiar shabbiness of an old British public house. The walls are decorated with a mishmash of souvenirs, trophy cups (there's a dartboard, of course), tankards and ye olde London street signs. The menu is a mix of English pub favorites including fish and chips, shepherd's pie, bangers and mash (the staff will translate — sausage and mashed potatoes) plus dishes the Yanks love such as hamburgers, tacos, chicken-fried steak, even lasagna and macaroni and cheese. The bar serves a wide variety of beers plus has a great selection of British, Irish, Canadian, Australian and American beers and ales on tap. The pub is open daily for lunch and dinner plus late-night snacks.

El Arroyo

$ • 1624 W. Fifth St. • (512) 474-1222

The hallmark of this W. Sixth Street-area restaurant is the large sign out front that offers pithy, scathing and sometimes self-deprecating comments on a daily basis. Commuters making their way downtown off MoPac are entertained by the political humor of the El Arroyo folks every day. The restaurant offers standard Tex-Mex fare, and the owner-humorists have been known to cast aspersions on their own culinary efforts, but that does not stop the crowds from coming. In addition to Tex-Mex, the restaurant serves barbecued chicken. Customers love the funky atmosphere, the cheeky waiters and the lively bar scene featuring "floaters": Margaritas topped with liqueurs. When the restaurant was burned down by an arsonist in early 1998, the faithful customers showed up to help rebuild the structure, including the outdoor deck under the live oaks. El Arroyo is open daily for lunch and dinner.

El Mercado Restaurant & Cantina

$-$$ • 1702 Lavaca St. • (512) 454-2500

One of three El Mercados in the city, this restaurant serves up generous portions of Tex Mex staples — enchiladas, chimichangas and tacos. Some of the dishes have a Texas slant with barbecued meat featured in the brisket tacos and chicken enchiladas. There are lowfat and vegetarian Tex-Mex dishes on the menu, including mushroom and spinach enchiladas. The decor includes huge sombreros and multicolored, stylized parrots. The Mexican background music adds to the fiesta feel. It is open daily for lunch and dinner and on weekends for breakfast.

El Rinconcito

$-$$ • 1014-E N. Lamar Blvd. • (512) 476-5277

Tucked away in the corner of a tiny shopping center behind the Sound Warehouse record store, this must be a lucky location for restaurants. Originally the birthplace of Castle Hill Cafe (see the listing in this chapter), this small jewel of a restaurant now serves interior Mexican and Peruvian food. The name means "little corner," and it reflects not only the size of the place, but also its neighborhood atmosphere. Bright and cheery inside and decorated in primary colors evocative of South America, the dishes here are far from the Tex Mex standard fare. They feature a variety of peppers used in Mexico, included poblanos noted for their complex taste, not so much their heat plus fresh ingredients such as goat cheese and wheat tortillas. Corn and potatoes add a Peruvian touch to the menu. The restaurant is open daily and serves lunch, dinner and a weekend brunch.

Ella's Restaurant

$$-$$$ • 1 Jefferson Sq. • (512) 48-2148

Formerly known as Baby Louie's, this intimate restaurant is part of the Jefferson Square shopping district, off 35th Street (see our Shopping chapter) and, like its neighbors, is housed in a former residence. Despite the name change, which reflected a shuffle in ownership, the menu retains many of the old favorites, including blackened pork tenderloin and linguine alfredo. A mix of pasta dishes, grilled fish and steaks plus creations inspired by Indian, Italian and Southwestern cuisine, mean there is something on the menu here for everyone. The restaurant's soups, salads and vegetable dishes are notable. It is open for lunch and dinner daily.

Frank & Angie's Pizza

$ • 508 West Ave. • (512) 472-3534

Just around the corner from its sister restaurant, Hut's, famed for its hamburgers, this pizzeria pays homage to another American favorite. New York-style pizzas, noted for their thin crusts, are featured here. Everything is homemade, including the house minestrone, the salad dressings and the focaccia used in the sandwiches. In addition to pizza, whole or by the slice, there are sandwiches and calzones and for dessert homemade cannoli, cheesecake and fruit pizzas. This pizza joint, which has a deck overlooking Shoal Creek, opens for breakfast with special early morning pizzas. There is a coffee bar plus wine and beer are served. It is open for breakfast, lunch and dinner daily.

Fresh Planet Cafe

$ • 601 N. Lamar Blvd. • (512) 476-0902

When Whole Foods Market (see our Shopping chapter) moved into its headquarters location to Sixth Street and Lamar Boulevard, the design included a cafe upstairs overlooking the shopping aisles. The menu has gone through several incarnations with the latest being developed by noted Austin chef David Garrido, who now rules the kitchen at one of Austin's premier restaurants, Jeffrey's (see the listing in this section). Garrido has developed a list of moderately priced dishes with Asian and Southwestern touches. Healthy food with flavor is what you'll find, including noodle dishes, spring rolls and masa cakes (masa is the ground corn used to make corn tortillas and tamales), soups and salads, veggie and meat sandwiches and wraps. The build-your-own salads are a popular lunchtime item. Organic wines by the glass are available, as well as beer and a variety of herbal iced teas. It is open for lunch and dinner daily.

Frisco Shop

$ • 5819 Burnet Rd. • (512) 459-6279

There used to be several Night Hawk diners in Austin, but the hometown chain has gone out of the restaurant business, although its frozen dinners are sold in Texas grocery stores — perhaps the most famous being a chopped steak dinner. The Frisco Shop is no longer owned by Night Hawk, but the memories and some of the waitresses remain at this traditional diner on the northern edge of our central district. Breakfasts feature huge homemade biscuits, and the dinner menu retains the famous chopped steak special. For dessert, there are homemade pies. It is typical American diner fare here, served in a Western motif setting. Breakfast, lunch and dinner are served daily.

Gilligans

$$-$$$ • Fourth and Colorado Sts. • (512) 474-7474

There are several culinary influences, including Jamaican, Yucatecan and Cajun, at work in this warehouse district restaurant, a few blocks west of Congress Avenue. Then there are the wild boar potstickers, courtesy of China and South Texas. Wild boar aside, the major emphasis is on seafood here, but the menu also features meat and chicken dishes, pastas and mixed grills. Achiote shrimp takes its inspiration from the annatto seed used in Yucatecan and Caribbean cooking for flavor and color, while mesquite-grilled salmon matches Texas barbecue knowhow with fresh fish from cold northern waters. The lunch menu includes muffeleta sandwiches. The narrow warehouse is divided into several levels, and the north wall has a large mural depicting a sea fantasy complete with mermaids. Live music sparks the atmosphere in the evenings. Gilligans is open daily for lunch and dinner.

Granite Cafe

$$-$$$ • 2905 San Gabriel St. • (512) 472-6483

This was the original restaurant opened by Austin entrepreneurs Reed and Betsy Clemons (see the previous Bitter End listing). The Granite Cafe brought the California-style open-kitchen model featured in several Napa Valley restaurants to Austin, and the Clemons' gave the walls and furniture a Southwestern touch. The menu features that same fortuitous mix of cultures, California, Southwest and a touch of Italy. There are also Basque and Mexican influences seen in dishes emerging from the kitchen. The cafe utilizes local ingredients, notably goat cheese and sausage. Signature dishes include wood-roasted Texas tenderloin and Yukon gold mashed potatoes with crispy onion rings and wild mushroom sauce, sesame-crusted mahimahi on roasted garlic couscous with baby bok choy, daikon sprouts, soba noodles and wasabi aioli. A wood-fired oven also produces a variety of pizzas. The weekend brunch is popular here, especially the cornberry cakes with Virginia ham, served with creme fraiche and fruit. The restaurant is housed in a small, modern brick shopping center not far from the University of Texas cam-

Texas Cuisine: Not Just a Bunch of Beef

Thanks to Hollywood, people around the world know that ranching is big business in Texas, so it comes as no surprise that many unfamiliar with the state's culinary pantheon think a typical Texas meal features a large chunk of beef.

But Texas beef is just one part of the picture as Texas chefs, both professional and amateur, create a wide variety of dishes drawing on several cultural traditions and a multitude of homegrown food products.

Agribusiness is important to the state, making up about 12 percent of the state's gross state product, and behind that number is an incredible diversity of products. Texas farmers produce rice, grains, citrus fruits, nuts, pears, apricots, strawberries and avocados; they raise pigs, dairy cows, goats, chickens and, of course, cattle; and food companies, small and large, are engaged in developing products that tout their Texas origins, everything from axis venison to zucchini flowers.

The Texas Department of Agriculture has developed four programs that give consumers, both home cooks and restaurant chefs, a way to identify and label Texas goods, and the department has launched a "Buy Texas" program that is touted on billboards and in media ads around the state. The program has four components — Taste of Texas, Naturally Texas, Texas Grown and Vintage Texas — and these labels can be found on food and agricultural products.

For example, salsas, barbecue sauces, salad dressings, cheeses, fresh meats, organically produced vegetables, several varieties of rice and hundreds of other goods bear the Taste of Texas label. The Naturally Texas program promotes the state's cotton, wool, mohair and leather production. Texas grows one third of the cotton in the United States, and there are approximately 2 million angora goats in the Hill Country southwest of San Antonio producing about 15 million pounds of mohair. Herbs and garden plants grown in Texas bear the Texas Grown label, while Vintage Texas promotes Texas wine production.

Visitors and newcomers to the Austin area can find Texas food products at local grocery stores and in area farmers markets (see our Shopping chapter), or they can visit one of the local farms to pick their produce, or buy it at a farmhouse or roadside stand. The *Austin American-Statesman* Wednesday food section lists information on seasonal foods and pick-your-own locations. Another excellent way to become familiar with Texas foods, and the chefs who are creating new dishes with them, is to join in the Texas Hill Country Wine & Food Festival, held each April in Austin (see our Annual Events and Festivals chapter).

Within a few miles of Austin, farmers and ranchers are producing apples, peaches (see our Annual Events and Festivals chapter for peach festivals), herbs, organic vegetables, blackberries, pecans, chile peppers, heirloom tomatoes and beans and more. Inside the city, many entrepreneurs have taken home recipes to the marketplace, and their salsas, barbecue sauces, tamales, pestos, salad dressings and sauces now line the shelves of local grocery stores and specialty shops. Others have headed for the countryside to produce gourmet foods such as Texas goat cheese, a mini-industry in Dripping Springs southwest of Austin. Some of these businesses are small, boutique operations, while others are large and well-known such as Blue Bell Ice Cream, made in Brenham east of Austin, a Texas favorite.

Central Texas also has attracted microbreweries (see our Nightlife chapter) and is

— continued on next page

home to two large well-known beer producers, one a Belgian transplant, Celis Brewery (see our Attractions chapter) in Austin, and the other, Shiner Brewery in the town of the same name southeast of Austin, with roots going back 19th-century German settlers. Both breweries are open to the public. Visit Shiner in May during the Annual Catholic Church Picnic (see our Annual Events and Festivals chapter).

Texas beers are not alone in winning kudos. The state also produces several award-winning wines, a fact that draws snickers only among those who have not sampled the wares. Texas is emerging as one of the top-producing wine states in the country, and recent warm summers have led to bumper crops. There are several areas of the state that have microclimates that are very conducive to grape growing, a fact that was not lost on Spanish settlers who planted the first vines in Texas during the 17th century. There are three wineries in the Austin area and they are open to visitors for free tastings and tours.

Fall Creek Vineyards

Tow • (915) 379-5361

Fall Creek has won national awards for its wines and has established a firm reputation as one of the state's leading wineries. The vineyards, some 65 acres, are on the hills above Lake Buchanan, one of the Highland Lakes, about 70 miles northwest of Austin. Founder Ed Auler got the inspiration to start his vineyard while traveling in France 25 years ago when he noticed the wine country terrain matched the land on his Hill Country ranch. The Aulers experienced great success with their wines — President George Bush served them at the White House and took Fall Creek wines with him to Beijing, China, for an official dinner during a state visit.

Tastings, tours and sales are conducted March through October. There are no vineyard tours during the week, but the cellars are open for tastings and sales from 11 AM to 3 PM. Tours, tastings and sales are offered on the weekend, on Saturday from noon to 5 PM and on Sunday from noon to 4 PM. In August Fall Creek hosts a weekend Grape Stomp (see our Annual Events chapter) when the whole family can jump into a grape vat and crush grapes the old-fashioned way. To reach Tow, take Texas Highway

— continued on next page

Photo: Peter A. Silva

Texas beef. Enough said!

1431 from Marble Falls, northwest of Austin, until it dead ends into Texas Highway 261, then take F.M. 2241 to Tow, drive through the community, and the road will end at Fall Creek. The winery also has an Austin office where visitors can inquire about special tours and sales, 1111Guadalupe St., (512) 476-4477. For more information about the vineyard area, see the Highland Lakes section of our Daytrips chapter.

Hill Country Cellars

1700 N. Bell Blvd., Cedar Park
• (512) 259-2000

This Northwest Austin winery, just off U.S. Highway 183, is a short drive from downtown Austin. Those looking for proof of the age of the Texas wine making industry can view the 200-year-old vine that is at the heart of this winery. Winemaker Russell Smith, who learned his trade in California's Napa Valley, produces several varietals, which are available for sampling in the winery's tasting room from noon to 5 PM daily. Winery tours are held Friday through Sunday between 1 and 5 PM on the hour.

Slaughter Leftwich Vineyards

4209 Eck Ln., Austin • (512) 266-3331

Wines from Lubbock? Forget any cliche notions you might have about the Texas High Plains, there are several excellent grape-growing microclimates in West Texas. Slaughter Leftwich has had particular success with Chardonnay grapes there. In order to bring its wines to as many people as possible, the owners decided to grow their grapes in Lubbock and build a winery in Austin. Eck Lane is at the intersection of Hudson Bend Road and R.R. 620, near Lake Travis west of Austin. Tastings are available daily Tuesday through Sunday from 1 to 5 PM, tours on Friday through Sunday at 1:30 and 3:30 PM, except in the busy summer months, June through September, when tours are held Wednesday through Sunday.

---

pus and some of Austin's most prestigious neighborhoods. The second floor dining room is surrounded by a large, airy veranda, which is a great place to enjoy daily lunch, dinner or brunch in spring and fall.

Hang Town Grill

$ • 2828 Rio Grande St.
• (512) 476-TOWN

Hang Town is yet another Clemons' creation (see Bitter End and Granite Cafe listings), which they describe as a "galactic salad/pizza/burger bar for all ages." This is a very popular family dining spot, especially for boomers with toddlers and preteens. The Rowdy Burger comes dressed with jalapenos, grilled onions, hickory sauce and lots of napkins. Another popular sandwich features vegetables grilled in the wood-fired oven, dressed with red onions, pesto, feta cheese and calamata olives. The Thai hacked chicken salad appeals to fans of spicy Asian dishes. The menu also features a variety of pizzas and, for dessert, try one of the house milk shakes. The decor here is lively with a spaceship/cartoon motif. It is open for lunch and dinner daily plus there is take-out service.

Hickory Street Bar & Grille

$ • 800 Congress Ave. • (512) 477-8968

Outdoor dining has become popular in Austin, except on those few days when rain, heat or cold drives folks indoors. While some downtown restaurants had to seek special City Council approval for sidewalk setups, this Congress Avenue restaurant has a large patio set back from the sidewalk and just four blocks from the capitol. A focal point of the menu is a large selection of salads, including a jerk chicken salad, or customers can visit the salad buffet to build their own. There are daily soup specials and chili for colder days. The restaurant opens very early during the week for breakfast, and the weekend brunch features a variety of eggs dishes plus New Orleans touches such as beignets and cafe au lait. It is open daily for breakfast, lunch and dinner.

Hut's Hamburgers

$ • 807 W. Sixth St. • (512) 472-0693

There are 20 types of burgers on the menu here plus chicken-fried steak, fried chicken and meat loaf — in a word all the stuff you want to eat, and you did back when cholesterol was just a gleam in the Surgeon General's eye. The daily blue plate specials attract a faithful crowd. Burgers can be ordered to match your particular tastes, or you can simply pick one off the menu. The Wolfman Jack features sour cream, diced green chilies and jack cheese. The Ritchie Valens has guacamole, grated cheese, jalapeno mayo, chopped tomatoes and mustard. The list of possibilities goes on, including The Beach Boy's favorite with pineapple, Swiss cheese, mayo, lettuce and bell peppers. Don't pass on the onion rings and french fries. The decor here is '50s diner, and the walls are decorated with college sports memorabilia. Hut's is open for lunch and dinner daily.

Hyde Park Bar & Grill

$-$$ • 4206 Duval St. • (512) 458-3168

Look for the two-story giant fork out front and the potato truck parked out back. According to local lore, the grill goes through one and a quarter tons of potatoes a week making its famous spicy, battered fries. They are dipped in buttermilk and rolled in peppered flour before being deep fried (in healthy canola oil) and then served with a mayonnaise flavored with peppers and onions, a Texas take on the European tradition of serving fries with mayo. The restaurant also serves a huge chicken-fried steak plate plus burgers. But not all the fare is hearty — grilled fish and salads are also offered. The restaurant is open daily for lunch and dinner and occupies a large, old home in the Hyde Park neighborhood, the historic heart of Austin just north of the university campus.

Iron Works Barbecue

$$ • 100 Red River St. • (512) 478-4855

Home to the Weigl Iron Works for years, this converted workshop just east of the city's convention center is now a popular barbecue spot. The Weigl family's ironwork can be seen on several buildings around town, including the History Center at 810 Guadalupe Street. Now the walls of the Weigl workshop are decorated with branding irons, an appropriate motif for a restaurant serving all manner of Texas barbecue — chicken, pork ribs, pork loin, beef, brisket and sausage. Side orders of beans, potato salad and baked potatoes are offered. Diners can sit inside or on an outdoor deck. Lunch and dinner are served daily.

Jean-Pierre's Upstairs

$$-$$$ • 3500 Jefferson St., second level • (512) 454-4811

French cuisine with a light Southwestern touch is the fare in this romantic, quiet restaurant on the second level of a modern, brick shopping complex in the 35th Street shopping district. Despite the modern exterior, inside the mood is more traditional with candlelight and fresh flowers at every table. Among the menu favorites are achiote brushed snapper, chicken in a tortilla crust, and bacon-wrapped grilled salmon. After-dinner souffles can be ordered before dinner to ensure a romantic end to supper. It's open for lunch and dinner, and reservations are recommended on weekends. The restaurant is closed Sunday.

Jeffrey's

$$$$ • 1204 W. Lynn St. • (512) 477-5584

This might be the quintessential Austin restaurant. Founded by three University of Texas graduates back in the '60s, Jeffrey's first chef was a self-taught culinary genius, Raymond Tatum. He has moved on to other pastures, but Jeffrey's remains true to its Austin origins. The restaurant's home is a restored house in Clarksville, one of the city's revered central city neighborhoods (see our Neighborhoods and Real Estate chapter). The founders took over a space occupied by a small wine shop, put up an inconspicuous sign outside and the work of local artists inside, and embarked on a culinary journey that draws on the world's cuisines but has Hill Country roots. Dinner items are added and updated regularly, but among recent offerings are a duck and shrimp dish with black bean ravioli and shiitake mushroom sauce, or crispy oysters on yucca root chips with habanero-honey aioli, and grilled sturgeon on champagne mushroom risotto with roquefort and port wine glaze. Chef David Garrido is now in charge of the restaurant's fare. Garrido formerly worked as assistant chef to famed Texas chef Stephan Pyles at the Routh Street Cafe in Dallas. He also coauthored a fun cookbook published by Chronicle Books in 1998, called *Nuevo Tex Mex*, which features "festive" food that can be cooked at home, not the complex, culinary masterpieces served up at Jeffrey's nightly except Sunday.

Katz's

$-$$ • 618 W. Sixth St. • (512) 472-2037

The slogan is "Katz's never Kloses" and it doesn't, making this downtown deli a very popular late-night spot. In the wee hours, customers are likely to look around and think they may have fallen into an intergalactic bar since the clientele is so varied — country music fans, heavy metal types, boomers, Gen-Xers, you name it. All have come for the New York deli fare, corned beef sandwiches, bagels with lox, pickle barrels on every table and blintzes for those who need a late-night sugar rush.

Kerbey Lane Cafe

$-$$ • 3704 Kerbey Ln. • (512) 451-1436

The original Kerbey Lane Cafe now has two sister restaurants, one south and another northwest, testimony to the concept that homemade, healthy food is a necessity 24 hours a day. Many of the cafe's dishes are Tex-Mex in origin, but the emphasis is on fresh local ingredients. The menu also features burgers, sandwiches, omelettes, pancakes and desserts.

Kyoto

$$-$$$ • 315 Congress Ave. • (512) 482-9010

Named after the ancient Japanese imperial city, Kyoto is tucked away in a narrow, stone building on Congress Avenue. There are two dining rooms upstairs: one a sushi bar with counter seating and western-style tables, the second a traditional area with tatami mats and Japanese low tables. In addition to sushi, the restaurant serves yakitori and kushiyaki dishes (tiny grilled shish kebabs of meat, fish and vegetables) plus noodle dishes, tempura and other traditional Japanese offerings. The restaurant offers lunch Tuesday through Saturday and dinner Monday through Saturday.

La Madeleine

$ • 3418 N. Lamar Blvd. • (512) 302-1485

There are three La Madeleine restaurants in Austin, one in a converted bookstore (northwest), another in a new shopping mall (west) and this one in a building that has housed several restaurants over the years. All three share the atmosphere of a French bakery and bistro, so don't be discouraged when you read that service is cafeteria-style. The menu features soups, salads, sandwiches, quiche, pizzas and light dinner entrees that are posted on the blackboard plus an array of breads, desserts, pies, cakes and cookies from the on-site bakery. The restaurants serve breakfast, lunch, dinner, mid-morning and mid-afternoon coffee and snacks daily.

Las Manitas Avenue Cafe

$ • 211 Congress Ave. • (512) 472-9357

The menu features both interior Mexican and South Texas-Mexican dishes plus a healthy dose of Austin art and Austin politics. Breakfast tacos reflect the cuisine of South Texas while other breakfast fare reflects South of the Border traditions. The huevos Motuleños has its roots in the city of Motul, Yucatan — fried eggs atop tortillas dressed with beans, peas, ham and farm cheese. The lunch dishes include carne guisada, a South Texas-Northern Mexico stew, or a tamal vegetariano, traditional corn tamales stuffed with carrots, broccoli and eggplant with a cream cheese sauce and sprinkled with nuts and raisins, an Austin concoction. The enchiladas reflect regional differences in Mexico. The enchiladas Zacatecas are made with poblano peppers and tomatillos, while the enchiladas Morelianos are dressed in an ancho chile sauce. The cafe is housed in a storefront on the lower end of Congress Avenue, next door to Tesoro's folk art shop (see our Shopping chapter.) The window is plastered with posters advertising cultural and political happenings, and inside a bench is loaded with alternative newspapers and news of Latin American political movements. It is open daily for breakfast and lunch only.

Louie's 106

$$$$ • 106 Sixth St. • (512) 476-1997

Housed in the historic Littlefield Building at the busy northwest corner of Sixth Street and Congress Avenue, Louie's has the aura of a grand old restaurant in a European capital. The menu leans towards the classical Spanish with lots of Mediterranean and European touches. Tapas, Spanish noshes, are offered here, and patrons can simply drop in to the bar for a round of snacks or sample some before dinner. Dishes include a traditional Valencian paella plus grilled meats, fish, risottos and bouillabaisse. There is a cigar room plus an extensive wine, single-malt whisky and brandy list. It is open weekdays for lunch and open daily for dinner. Given its busy downtown location, Louie's offers curbside valet parking.

Lucero's

$ • Travis County Farmer's Market, 6701 Burnet Rd. • (512) 450-1006

This is a tiny restaurant that has attracted great praise for its on-the-spot creations made from produce sold at the farmer's market where Lucero's makes it home. There are less than a dozen tables, but they are carefully laid with fresh linen and silverware. The menu leans to Tex-Mex and Mexican favorites, including aguas frescas, the fruit drinks served South of the Border. The staff uses tomatoes and peppers from the vendors to create fresh salsas in the tiny kitchen. Lunch is served daily, and there is a Saturday breakfast menu.

Malaga's Wine and Tapas Bar

$-$$ • 208 W. Fourth St. • (512) 236-8020

A delightful cross between a restaurant and a bar, Malaga's is an Austin version of a Spanish tapas bar, a place to gather and nibble tasty snacks while sipping wine or sherry. Malaga's is next door to a popular jazz and cigar bar, Cedar Street (see our Nightlife chapter), and occupies a narrow, old warehouse space. The floors are hardwood, the walls limestone and lined with wine racks. Among the tapas offerings are traditional Spanish omelettes, called "tortillas" in Spain, stuffed with savory ingredients and served at room temperature, plus ham and sausage, olives and cheese. Malaga's opens at 4 PM during the week for after-work conviviality and closes daily at 2 AM, except Sunday when it closes at midnight. On the weekend, it opens at 6 PM.

Manuel's

$-$$$ • 310 Congress Ave. • (512) 472-7555

The setting is sleek and modern with black booths, neon signs and hip jazz music at this downtown restaurant, but the food is light, saucy and evocative of interior Mexican classics. Chile rellenos are made as they are in Mexico, stuffed with spicy and fruit-studded meat filling then topped with almond sauce. Fish is served Veracruzano-style with tomatoes and peppers, and enchiladas banderas reflect the red, green and white of the Mexican flag. Gorditas, small cakes of corn masa and potato, are topped with a homemade venison chorizo (sausage). Manuel's is open for lunch and dinner and has a jazz brunch on Sundays. There is a late-night snack menu.

Mars

$$-$$$ • 1610 San Antonio St. • (512) 472-3901

Fusion cuisine is a much-used term these days, but it fits the picture at Mars, a place where lovers of spicy food congregate to celebrate a world of flavors. The restaurant was formerly the home of Oat Willie's, the city's famous "head shop," west of the capitol. After several incarnations, it evolved into Mars, where dishes from several cultures have landed. Dishes and techniques are borrowed from the Middle East, Africa, India, Thailand, the Caribbean and Mexico. Tandoori meats are served with pomegranate sauce, while stuffed grape leaves sit alongside potstickers on an appetizer tray. Thai curries and noodle dishes take up another section of the menu, and many patrons return for a house specialty, Thai bouillabaisse. Other popular dishes include grilled salmon in wasabi sauce, or a jerked pork tenderloin. The food is spicy, the walls red, the lights dim and the 2,000-square-foot restaurant crowded. As one critic said, this is not the place to propose marriage unless you want several adjacent diners to accept or decline. But it is a fun place for lively food and conversation so expect a wait on weekends. Mars is open for dinner daily. Reservations are recommended for large parties.

Mezzaluna

$$$ • 310 Colorado St. • (512) 472-6770

One of the nightlife pioneers in the warehouse district west of Congress Avenue, Mezzaluna can be spotted by its large sign shaped like a *mezzaluna*, a half-moon-shaped cutting tool used in Italian cuisine. Yet another restaurant creation by Reed and Betsy Clemons (their Bitter End is across the street), Mezzaluna has been a roaring success since it opened, and on weekend nights it continues to draw crowds, especially the bar where the concrete counters are home to dozens of hip elbows. The menu is nouvelle fare with Italian roots and American knowhow. Antipasti are made from fresh, local ingredients, including sausage served atop polenta. Diners can choose a light supper of salad and antipasti, or sample a pizza, a pasta dish. They can enjoy a grand three-course meal, Italian-style, with antipasti, pasta and an entree or perhaps lasagna with smoked chicken or grilled salmon flavored with chiles and basil. The extensive wine list offers many American and Italian wines by the glass and a selection of grappas, the Italian brandy distilled from the grape pomace that packs a punch. Mezzaluna is open for lunch during the week and dinner nightly. There is late-night service on weekends.

Mongolian Barbecue

$ • 117 San Jacinto Blvd.
• (512) 476-3938

Not far from the city's convention center is a restaurant favored by families and folks on a budget. The menu is simple at this Asian-style buffet, simply head for the cafeteria-style line and pick out the ingredients you want the chef to stir up in the giant wok behind the counter. Vegetarians, meat and fish eaters and finicky kids can all find something to put on their plate. Customers also can select their seasonings and sauce from sweet and sour to spicy Szechwan. It is open for dinner daily and lunch on weekdays.

Mother's Cafe

$-$$ • 4215 Duval St. • (512) 451-3994

Vegetarian food with international inspiration is served at this neighborhood cafe. Tex-Mex dishes are given a vegetarian translation here, while stir fries draw on Asian inspiration. The menu has low fat and vegan options, and local beers and Texas wines are featured. The cafe is in the heart of the Hyde Park neighborhood and features a large outdoor patio. It is open daily for lunch and dinner and serves weekend brunch.

Nau Enfield Drug

$ • 1115 W. Lynn St. • (512) 476-1221

An old-fashioned drugstore in the historic Clarksville neighborhood, Nau's serves up sandwiches, burgers, malts and breakfast dishes daily (see our Attractions chapter). Breakfast is a busy time for Nau's when breakfast tacos, omelettes, and huevos rancheros are on the menu. The atmosphere here is authentic and draws customers from both the neighborhood and downtown to the booths and bar daily for breakfast and lunch.

Ninfa's Mexican Restaurant

$$-$$$ • 612 W. Sixth St.
• (512) 476-0612

Ninfa Lorenzo is a legendary businesswoman in Houston where she took a single, small Mexican restaurant and built it into a food empire. This W. Sixth Street location is next door to Katz's deli, within the ever-expanding shopping and nightlife district west of downtown and is one of two Ninfa's in Austin. The fare is a take on traditional Tex-Mex and Mexican fare with an uptown touch, for example smoked quail marinated in salsa

INSIDERS' TIP

Foodies who want to keep up with the latest trends might want to mark their calendars for the Annual Hill Country Wine and Food Festival (see our Annual Events chapter). The spring event always attracts some of the top chefs in Texas and the nation.

negra, fresh fish tacos, camarones ajillo (shrimp in a garlic sauce) and pollo asado (roasted chicken). Lunch and dinner are served daily.

Old Pecan Street Cafe

$$-$$$ • 310 E. Sixth St. • (512) 478-2491

The changing face of Sixth Street embraces the history of Austin. Back in 1971, this small cafe was one of the first businesses to stir talk of a Sixth Street revival. For almost 30 years, the cafe has withstood the changes and continues to attract faithful customers despite the sometimes rambunctious street life beyond the shutters. The historic building gives the cafe an ambiance reminiscent of an Old World restaurant with its fieldstone walls and wooden floors. It is particularly cozy on a cold winter night when a cup of the house, *kaffe mit schlag*, coffee with cream and kahlua, warms the hands and the heart. The menu features light, cafe-style entrees, crepes, quiche, sandwiches, soups and salads. But it is the cafe's cakes that bring customers back, particularly the Italian cream cake. The cafe is open daily for lunch, dinner and brunch.

Pao's Mandarin House

$$ • One Commodore Plaza, 800 Brazos St. • (512) 482-8100

Inside one of the city's smaller downtown office buildings is this friendly Chinese restaurant where the fare is varied and the choice extensive. There are more than two dozen appetizers and more than 60 entrees on the Pao menu, including house specialties like smoked tea duck and shrimp studded with lotus flower. The restaurant is open for lunch and dinner daily.

Pok-E-Jo's Smokehouse

$-$$ • 1603 W. Fifth St. • (512) 320-1541

There are four Pok-E-Jo's in the Austin area, serving a variety of smoked and barbecued meats, including ribs, pork, beef, ham, pork loin, sausage, turkey and chicken. Meats are mesquite-smoked, and the restaurant serves the usual variety of side orders, beans, potato salad, pickles and onions. The Fifth Street location is housed in small building that looks a little like a country cabin with simple wooden tables. Take-out is a large part of the restaurant's business. It is open daily for lunch and dinner.

Roppolo's

$ • 316 E. Sixth St. • (512) 476-1490

This Austin pizza restaurant with several area locations has been named best pizza in town by readers of *The Austin Chronicle* in several annual surveys. In addition to selling whole pizza pies to eat on the premises or to go, Roppolo's also sells pizza by the slice so strollers along the Sixth Street can munch as they watch the street scene. The menu also includes stromboli, calzone, pasta with meatballs or Sicilian meat sauce, garden vermicelli and meat and veggie lasagna. Roppolo's is open daily for lunch and dinner.

Ruth's Chris

$$$ • 3010 Guadalupe St. • (512) 477-RUTH

When it comes to steakhouses the national Ruth's Chris chain is noted as one of the best. While we don't usually list chain restaurants since they are familiar to our readers, the Austin Ruth's Chris steakhouse is very popular, particularly among the political crowd which gathers every two years in Austin for the legislative session. The historic building, just north of the campus, is where the thick-cut steaks simmered in butter made famous by Ruth Fartel are served up each night for dinner. Chicken and fish dinners are also on the menu. Reservations are recommended, particularly when the legislature is in session — in the odd years from January to May, except for specially called sessions. In January 1999, Ruth's Chris is moving to the Scarbrough Building, one of the city's first downtown "skyscrapers" at Sixth Street and Congress Avenue. The building is undergoing a major renovation, and the restaurant will occupy a large section of the main floor.

Rhythm House

$-$$ • 624 W. 34th St. • (512) 458-4411

There have been several restaurant incarnations at this location, and the latest is part of an interesting new trend in Austin, the emergence of interest in Spanish cuisine. Rhythm House is both a tapas bar and full-service restaurant serving traditional Spanish dishes such as paella. There is also a deck and bar where local musicians play acoustic music. The tapas menu, which is served until late in the evening, features traditional Spanish snacks like ham, sausage, cheese, olives, artichoke dishes and omelettes. Rhythm House is open daily for lunch and dinner, except no lunch is served on Saturday and on Sunday brunch is served with a Spanish flair. The tapas bar is open until midnight during the week and on Sunday and until 2 AM on Friday and Saturday.

Scholz Garten

$ • 1607 San Jacinto St.
• (512) 474-1958

Political junkies regard this old German beer garden as something of shrine, a place that serves as a favorite watering hole and meeting place for political types, their staffers and supporters (particularly Democrats). Hillary and Bill Clinton hung out here during their days as workers for the George McGovern Presidential campaign. The beer garden is also featured in the 1962 novel about Texas politics, *The Gay Place* by Billy Lee Brammer. The beer hall, which dates back to 1866, is east of the capitol and is owned by the Austin Saengerrunde, a German-American fraternal organization. The tree-shaded beer garden is a favorite lunchtime spot for state workers, politicians and pre- and postgame fans of UT football and basketball. The restaurant features German food and typical American down-home fare: burgers, chicken, sandwiches, Tex-Mex specials and beer, of course. Scholz's is open for lunch and dinner, and is closed Sunday.

Serrano's Cafe & Cantina

$$ • Symphony Sq., 1105 Red River St.
• (512) 322-9080

There are six Serrano's cafes in various regions of the city, but this one has the best setting in the small, historic complex saved by the Austin Symphony (see our Attractions chapter). The Jeremiah Hamilton home is original to the site here, east of the capitol. Hamilton was a carpenter and legislative delegate to the Republican convention in 1873 when he built the triangular house in the small complex, which now houses a Tex-Mex restaurant. Hamilton's home has seen lively occupants before, serving as a grocery store, saloon, a barber shop and music club. Now, customers can order fajita nachos, deep-fried jalapenos stuffed with cheese, and a variety of entrees including enchiladas, Tex-Mex plates, grilled meat and chicken plus fajita platters. It is open daily for lunch and dinner.

Shoreline Grill

$$$$ • 98 San Jacinto Blvd.
• (512) 477-3300

Tucked into a prime location on Town Lake, just west of the Four Seasons, the Shoreline is known for its fish and seafood creations and the great view of nightly summer evening exodus of Austin's famous bat colony. The menu changes seasonally, but dishes include semolina-crusted oysters, crab cakes with roasted pepper relish, grilled salmon and a variety of fresh fish from the Gulf of Mexico. The restaurant also serves a variety of meat and pasta dishes plus a good selection of salads. The best bat viewing is on the restaurant's patio, but seating is first come, first served there. Reservations can be made for the indoor rooms. It is open daily for lunch and dinner.

Stubb's Bar-B-Q

$-$$ • 801 Red River St.
• (512) 480-8341

The late C.B. Stubblefield is the soul of this restaurant and his portrait hangs here as an homage to his vision of barbecue and home cooking plus the blues. Barbecue — beef, sausage, brisket, chicken, ribs, turkey — is served with old-fashioned potatoes, beans and greens. (Stubb's barbecue sauce is used in house and can be found in Austin grocery stores.) The menu also includes chicken-fried steak, corn on the cob, okra and squash. This is the kind of food Stubblefield grew up on back in Lubbock, Texas. In addition to serving lunch and dinner and offering live music nightly except Sunday (see The Music Scene chapter), Stubb's also serves a Sunday Gospel Brunch with typical Southern breakfast fare — hash browns, grits, biscuits and gravy plus pancakes and syrup and a live gospel band.

Sullivan's

$$$-$$$$ • 300 Colorado St. • (512) 495-6504

Just when you think you have Austin figured out as a town where the hallmark is natural and laid-back, you walk into Sullivan's where the menu is red meat, red meat, red meat, and the atmosphere reeks of confidence and power. Stand in the lobby during the legislative session and you could get a quorum. Chat with the parking valet, and you will hear tales of movie stars and directors who love to eat here. Sullivan's is in the heart of the downtown warehouse district, but while neighbors offer bistro fare and nouvelle Italian dishes, it touts itself as a "Chicago-style steakhouse." The beef is top-quality here and is served with a variety of side orders, including delicious potatoes au gratin. For dessert, waiters try to entice diners with individual souffles. The atmosphere is clubby and definitely alpha male. Reservations are recommended. Dinner is served daily.

Sweetish Hill Bakery

$ • 1120 W. Sixth St. • (512) 472-1347

The lemon bars are addictive, but since no one can live by sweets alone, Sweetish Hill serves up a popular lunch menu that finds inspiration in several quarters. The eggplant and brie sandwich served on a French baguette is a favorite; the Italian panini brings back memories of Assisi; and the Hero is a fresh take on old favorite. There is also a wide variety of meat and vegetable sandwiches served on the bakery's various grain and herb breads plus daily homemade soups, salads and side orders of fruit and potato salad. The bakery (see our Shopping chapter) is well known for its pastries and breads, so few eat lunch without getting a cookie or loaf to go. Since the bakery is in the middle of the W. Sixth Street district, it is usually busy all morning and into late afternoon as Austinites move to their own internal clocks, eating breakfast and lunch at their own pace. Food can be enjoyed on the premises, inside or on the small sidewalk cafe area, or can be packed for a picnic. The bakery also has a smaller operation on Congress Avenue, just three blocks south of the capitol at 922 Congress Avenue, (512) 477-2441.

Ted's Greek Corner

$ • 417 Congress Ave. • (512) 472-4494

Restaurants and food fashions come and go, but Ted's has survived, serving Greek specialties in this Congress Avenue diner since 1970. Moussaka, gyros (spit-roasted lamb), spanokopeta (phyllo stuffed with spinach and feta), dolmades (stuffed grape leaves), tyrokopita (cheese pastry), souflaki (shish kebabs), pastitsio (pasta and meat casserole) plus Greek salads are standards here. For dessert there is baklava, that wonderful sticky, flaky pastry made from phyllo, honey and walnuts. Ted's is open for lunch and dinner Monday through Saturday.

Texas Chili Parlor

$ • 1409 Lavaca St. • (512) 472-2828

The Texas equivalent of a neighborhood pub, this bar and restaurant attracts a loyal clientele, many of them state workers, attorneys and political types from the nearby capitol. The ambiance is funky bar meets roadhouse. The highlight of the menu is, of course, chili, served at varying degrees of heat and completely without beans (beans are a Yankee aberration). Sandwiches, tacos and burgers are also on the menu plus something called a Frito Pie, a Texas original — the recipe begins, "Take one bag of Fritos . . ." It is open for lunch and dinner daily.

Texas French Bread

$ • 2900 Rio Grande St. • (512) 499-0544
$ • 3213 Red River St. • (512) 478-8796
$ • UT Co-op, 2270 Guadalupe St. • (512) 474-2785
$ • 3112-A Windsor Rd. • (512) 478-8845

This popular Austin bakery chain is expanding quickly in the city. The Rio Grande Street location is just north of the university campus and next door to Breed Hardware (see our Shopping chapter). The bakery serves a variety of sandwiches, including the Nicoise sandwich that reflects Mediterranean flavors — tuna is melded with capers, olives, tomatoes and onions on French bread. Customers can order any sandwich on the bread of their choice, Tuscan, French, cracked rye, white or whole wheat. The menu also features a variety of soups, tortilla soup, cold borscht, Mediterranean vegetable, white bean and pesto. Of course, the bakery also features a large selection of pastries and cookies. Coffee, herbal tea and a pile of free newspapers make this a favorite spot for an early morning stop on the way to work or school. It is open daily for breakfast and lunch.

Thai Passion

$$ • 620 Congress Ave., Ste. 105 • (512) 472-1244

Thai Passion is an elegant, downtown restaurant that features the cuisine of Thailand with its contrasting flavors of spice, heat and herbs. The menu features curries, noodle dishes and traditional pad Thai. Some dishes are vegetarian. It is open daily for lunch and dinner.

The Hoffbrau

$-$$ • 613 W. Sixth St. • (512) 472-0822

Since 1934 they have been serving meat off the grill at this W. Sixth Street simple, no frills restaurant. The decor here has been minimalist before minimalist got a name. The tables are simple orange Formica, and the wall decorations include a print of the Alamo, an old photograph or two and a proclamation from former State Rep. Sarah Weddington (attorney in the *Roe v. Wade* case) praising the joint. In 1934, a T-bone steak was 35¢, and a bottle of beer was a dime. Prices have risen, but the menu has remained the same — steak, or, in a concession to modern times, grilled chicken breast. Salad is extra, but don't expect field greens. On the side there is white bread and saltines. The Hoffbrau is open weekdays for lunch and early dinner and closed on weekends.

Tocai of Austin

$$$ • 601 W. Sixth St. • (512) 457-8880

One exciting aspect of living in Austin is the flourishing restaurant scene. Chain restaurants do abound as the city grows, but Austin is also a fertile city for new, small restaurants that often take hold and become part of the Austin scene. One such place, Tocai, is housed in a former '50s-era storefront along W. Sixth Street and has developed a following among those who enjoy Mediterranean cuisine. The menu features risottos, pastas, hearty Italian fare such as osso buco and delicate dishes combining shrimp and prosciutto in a cream sauce. The small restaurant serves lunch on weekdays and dinner daily except Sunday.

Tres Amigos

$$ • 26 Doors, 1206 W. 38th St. • (512) 453-0026

Many Austin residents have been taking family and friends to the four Tres Amigos restaurants for years, knowing they can be assured of dependable Tex-Mex cooking and friendly service. The restaurant offers tacos, fajitas and all the familiar Tex-Mex fare — don't miss the house specialty, mango ice cream.

This branch in the 26 Doors shopping center evokes Old Mexico in the design and decoration. It is open daily for lunch and dinner.

Upper Crust Bakery

$ • 4508 Burnet Rd. • (512) 467-0102

The city has several neighborhood bakeries that serve as gathering places for friends and a comfy spot to enjoy a breakfast croissant or mid-morning break. In addition to sandwiches, soups and breads, Upper Crust has a selection of croissants, both sweet and savory, that can be enjoyed while perusing the morning papers. It is open daily for breakfast, lunch and afternoon snacks.

Waterloo Ice House

$ • 600 N. Lamar Blvd. • (512) 472-5400
$ • 26 Doors, 1106 W. 38th St. • (512) 451-5245

This hamburger joint serves a variety of American fare. In addition to burgers, customers can order tacos and chicken-fried steaks. The Lamar Boulevard Waterloo is next door to one of the city's most noted record stores, Waterloo Records, in the W. Sixth Street shopping district (see The Music Scene chapter). There are two other Waterloo locations you'll find under our West and North sections, including one at the popular live music venue The Backyard (see The Music Scene chapter).

West Lynn Cafe

$-$$ • 1110 W. Lynn St. • (512) 482-0950

A totally vegetarian restaurant that has a reputation as a chic dining spot? Those who

Photo: Courtesy of the Texas Department of Transportation

Fajitas are an Austin specialty.

think vegetarian means boring have not visited West Lynn Cafe, the Clarksville (see our Neighborhoods and Real Estate chapter) restaurant that won a national architectural design award. The menu draws on influences from Asia, Mexico, India and the Mediterranean for lunch, dinner and brunch daily. Some of the offerings are labelled zero-cholesterol and/or nondairy. Just to prove that not all sybaritic pleasures are verboten, the restaurant has a good wine list.

Z'Tejas Grill

$$-$$$ • 1110 W. Sixth St. • (512) 478-5355

There are two Z'Tejas restaurants in Austin — the original in the W. Sixth Street shopping/restaurant district and a second in Northwest Austin near the Arboretum — and perhaps a visit to both is the best way to get a quick fix on old Austin and new Austin. Both serve much the same menu, but the original Z'Tejas is housed in a converted home where the garage doors can be opened, exposing diners to the elements. (Read about the Northwest location in that section.) The interior of the W. Sixth Street location is decorated in the bright colors of the Southwest, and the outdoor patio serves as lazy-day refuge just a few blocks from downtown, or a place to relax during rush hour and enjoy the restaurant's "appetizer happy hour." The menu is sometimes described as Santa Fe meets Texas with a dash of Louisiana thrown in. The restaurant's gumbo is offered at lunch and dinner; appetizers include oyster "shooters" (fried oysters with chipotle cream), catfish beignets and quesadillas; entrees include Navajo tacos (crisp fried flour tortillas topped with deep-fried spinach, beans, onions and chicken), smoked pork tenderloin, smoked duck enchiladas, and grilled salmon and trout. But don't pass on the restaurant's most famous dessert, Ancho chile fudge pie, which is made with just a touch of ancho chile powder, adding richness to the dish, not spice. Chocolate and chiles are vital components of one of Mexico's most famous dishes, mole poblano, so it is no surprise the chef took inspiration from south of the border. The recipe, by the way, is framed on the wall at the entrance to the restaurant. In addition to lunch and dinner, the downtown location serves breakfast daily.

South Central

Al Capone's

$-$$ • 312 Barton Springs Rd.
• (512) 472-2700

Don't let the name scare you away. It is simply meant to flag the fact that is traditional Italian food, dishes like chicken Parmesan, veal scallopine alla sorrentina or alla marsala. Everything, even the steak dinners, comes with a side order of spaghetti. Given its proximity to downtown, just across the Congress Avenue bridge, Capone's is crowded at lunchtime, but if the weather is fine get there a little early and ask for a table on the patio. Lunch and dinner are served daily.

Artz Rib House

$ • 2230 S. Lamar Blvd. • (512) 442-8283

Live music and Texas barbecue are on the menu at this South Austin restaurant, but just to make sure no one feels left out the menu also offers vegetarian dishes, including a grilled vegetable platter. The barbecue fare includes a combination plate made up of your choice of brisket, chicken, sausage plus baby back ribs, all are served with cole slaw, pinto beans, pickles, bread and spicy potato salad. There is live music seven nights at week at Artz, with regulars playing on certain nights. The Old Time Texas Fiddlers perform on Tuesdays, while Sunday afternoons the Central Texas Bluegrass Club performs. The restaurant has both indoor dining and a screened-in porch with ceiling fans. It is open daily for lunch and dinner.

Aussie's

$-$$ • 306 Barton Springs Rd.
• (512) 474-2255

Part restaurant, part volleyball club and part late-night munchie spot, Aussie's serves everything from hamburgers to shrimp on the barbie. The menu is a mix of sandwiches, snacks, grills and pastas. The restaurant serves lunch, dinner and midnight snacks daily, and since it is just one block south of Town Lake downtown, it is favorite spot for a late-night nosh.

Baby Acapulco

$-$$ • 1628 Barton Springs Rd.
• (512) 474-8774

A favorite with young, downtown workers, this restaurant on the Barton Springs strip is usually packed on weekends, especially when the weather conjures up Margarita fantasies. The menu includes more than a dozen kinds of Margaritas, including banana, pink passion, strawberry, pineapple, etc. and has been named as serving the best Margaritas in town several times in *The Austin Chronicle*'s reader's poll. The Tex-Mex menu offers the usual fare, including 14 types of enchiladas. The outdoor patio is the heart of the action on balmy days, and inside there is a casual, colorful atmosphere. It is open for lunch and dinner daily.

Chuy's

$-$$ • 1728 Barton Springs Rd.
• (512) 474-4452

Chuy's is perhaps the most famous restaurant on the Barton Springs Road strip and

INSIDERS' TIP

Two local writers are indispensable when it comes to understanding vital ingredients in Texas food. Jean Andrews, often called the "Pepper Lady", has written a couple of books of the genus capsicums and her text, recipes and beautiful drawings of peppers are invaluable to food fans and cooks. Another local expert with several books in print is herb and tequila expert Lucinda Hutson.

one of the most colorful in Austin. Where else would you find a shrine to Elvis? Or more than 1,000 wooden fish hanging from the ceiling? The decor is a mixture of fantasy and kitsch with iguanas and lava lamps setting the theme. The food is a mixture of Tex-Mex and New Mexico. When the harvest comes in, New Mexico chiles are grilled out front on a large metal barbecue rig. One house specialty is the Chuychanga, a 12-inch flour tortilla stuffed with cheese, chicken, cilantro and green chiles, then deep-fried and topped with sour cream and a salsa. There are also Chuy's Special Enchiladas made with smoked chicken and blue corn tortillas. The lively atmosphere makes this a popular family spot. Chuy's is open for lunch and dinner daily.

Curra's Grill

$-$$ • 614 E. Oltorf St. • (512) 444-0012

Austin abounds in small, family restaurants that bring the flavors of Mexico home in a variety of ways. Curra's signature is a variety of salsas — borracho, which means "drunken" in Mexico, is made with tomatoes and a touch of beer; pasilla takes its name from the smokey rich taste of the pasilla chile; verde is a green sauce and is made from tomatillos, sometimes called green tomatoes, but really no relation — in fact, tomatillos, which are covered in a papery husk, are actually related to gooseberries. Other sauces include allende in a nutty cream sauce; and chipotle, the name given to smoked jalapenos. The menu features all-day breakfast tacos, enchiladas and carne guisada, a slow-simmered stew. It is open daily for breakfast, lunch and dinner.

El Mercado Restaurant and Cantina

$-$$ • 1302 S. First St. • (512) 447-7445

This South Central location, one of three El Mercados in town (see the others under Central and North), serves up the same generous proportions of Tex-Mex favorites in a lively, colorful setting. The restaurant is open daily for breakfast, lunch and dinner.

El Sol y La Luna

$-$$ • 1224 S. Congress Ave.
• (512) 444-7770

An old motel coffee shop has been revived as a Mexican cantina as part of the changing face of S. Congress Avenue. With so many good Mexican restaurants in town, opening a new venture is not always easy, but El Sol y La Luna (The Sun and the Moon) quickly developed a loyal following, particularly on weekend mornings when a leisurely breakfast of migas (eggs scrambled with peppers and onions) or huevos rancheros is local custom. The outdoor patio with its rustic Mexican furniture is a favorite place to have a late breakfast. The menu also features Latin American and Central American dishes, but for an introduction to classic Mexican cuisine try the house mole poblano, a spicy chocolate sauce with more than two dozen ingredients that is served over meat and enchiladas. The restaurant is open daily for breakfast, lunch and dinner.

Good Eats Cafe

$-$$ • 1530 Barton Springs Rd.
• (512) 476-8141

The name of this cafe tells it all, food that is good to eat and good for you. The emphasis here is on simple, healthy food. Meats and fish are grilled, frying is done in canola oil and vegetables are steamed. The fare is hearty, but the menu offers smaller portions. The atmosphere is evocative of an old diner with big booths, but there is also a full bar. It is open daily for breakfast, lunch and dinner.

Green Mesquite

$-$$ • 1400 Barton Springs Rd.
• (512) 479-0485

Texas barbecue and Louisiana Cajun fare are the specialties here. For avowed meat lovers the barbecue dishes include sausage, turkey, brisket, ribs, but there are also chicken-fried steaks, hamburgers and sandwiches. On the Cajun side, the spicy gumbo and jambalaya are favorites, and there is catfish. The pies are homemade, and there is live music on weekends. Green Mesquite is open daily for lunch and dinner.

Green Pastures

$$$-$$$$ • 811 W. Live Oak Rd.
• (512) 444-4747

In 1945 the Koock family decided to turn their family mansion into a restaurant, and ever since Green Pastures has been a quiet, elegant place to celebrate special events and family gatherings. The mansion was built in 1894 and has been in the Koock family since 1916. Surrounded by a large garden with more than 200 live oak trees, the mansion is hidden away in an everyday South Austin neighborhood. Patrons can begin their dining experience with a glass of milk punch out on the veranda, watch the peacocks stroll on the lawn and listen to music being played on the restaurant's grand piano. The goal at Green Pastures is to re-create the hospitality of the Old South while offering Continental cuisine with touches of Texas. The dinner menu includes duck Texana, duck breasts wrapped in bacon and dressed with blackberry sauce, or snapper Florentine and lobster crepes. The desserts echo the traditions of the past, flaming bananas Foster, bread pudding, and the Texas pecan ball, a take on a traditional hot fudge sundae. The restaurant serves lunch and dinner daily, but one highlight of the week is the Sunday brunch when Green Pastures sets a table that astounds both the eye and the palate. The brunch includes cheese boards, a savory table with bowls of boiled shrimp, huge silver chafing dishes filled with egg dishes and entrees plus a large standing rub roast. A large dessert table is also part of the brunch picture. Reservations are recommended for brunch and for lunch and dinner on the weekends.

Güero's

$-$$ • 1412 S. Congress Ave.
• (512) 447-7688

The stretch of S. Congress Avenue that rises from Town Lake and up the hill to the horizon is undergoing great change as funky shops and restaurants (see our Shopping chapter) convert old buildings to new uses. Architectural ingenuity has turned an old feed store on the avenue into Güero's, where the food reflects both Tex-Mex and Mexican influences. The interior has been decorated with Mexican tiles, old photographs from the Mexican Revolution and a picture of President Bill Clinton, who has eaten here when visiting Austin. A portion of the kitchen is open, and diners can watch tacos and salsas being made. Breakfast tacos are a bargain here and are served all day, although the restaurant is not open for breakfast during the week. Some of the entrees are taken from the Mexican pantheon, dishes like chicken al carbon, a Yucatecan dish that features grilled chicken breasts spiced with chiles and achiote. Steak a la Tampiqueña and snapper a la Veracruzano are on the dinner menu. The steak is grilled and served with grilled vegetables and salsa, while the fish is cooked with tomatoes and green olives. On weekends Güero's opens early for breakfast, featuring tacos, migas, huevos rancheros and other popular Tex-Mex favorites. There is usually live music on Sunday afternoons.

Jalisco Bar

$$ • 414 Barton Springs Rd.
• (512) 476-4838

Traditional Tex-Mex fare, including cabrito, grilled baby goat, is on the menu here at this Mexican-style restaurant just south of Town Lake. Fajitas are featured, including chicken and pork, and grilled steaks with a touch of Mexican flavor. The house special drink is the tequila slammer, which involves banging a shot glass on the table, something the waitress, equipped with a tequila gunbelt contraption, can explain to the uninitiated. A variety of Margaritas is served — strawberry, peach, melon, raspberry, coconut — and Mexican beer is available. Patrons can dine and drink to the sound of live mariachi music. Jalisco is open daily for lunch and dinner.

Kerbey Lane Cafe

$-$$ • 2700 S. Lamar Blvd.
• (512) 445-4451

This is the South Austin location of a very popular local cafe that serves homemade, healthy food 24 hours a day. The menu features sandwiches, salads, Tex-Mex favorites, breakfast specials (available all day and night), omelettes, pancakes and homemade desserts.

La Reyna

$-$$ • 1816 S. First St. • (512) 447-1280

The name means "The Queen," and the reference is to the Virgin Mary, whose image appears on the wall of this family-run bakery and cafe in the heart of one of Austin's predominantly Mexican-American neighborhoods. The cafe is a meeting place for neighbors, local politicians, artists and those who appreciate the homey atmosphere of the long-established South Austin restaurant. The menu is traditional Tex-Mex plus standards from the cooking of South Texas and Northern Mexico, particularly soups and baked goods. La Reyna also serves menudo, a spicy tripe soup that is purported to cure hangovers. Be sure to take home a bag of Mexican pastries and cookies — the conchas, a sweet bread with a whirled shell design in sugar are a favorite. But eat them the same day, Mexican pastries have no preservatives and little salt so they do not stay fresh for long. The cafe is open for lunch and dinner daily and for breakfast on Sunday.

Magnolia Cafe South

$ • 1920 S. Congress Ave.
• (512) 445-0000

There are two Magnolia Cafes, this one in South Austin and the original in West Austin. The cafe is open 24 hours a day, seven days a week and serves a homestyle menu featuring breakfast dishes no matter the hour, sandwiches, fajitas and salads, all in a homey atmosphere.

Matt's Famous El Rancho

$$ • 2613 S. Lamar Blvd.
• (512) 462-9333

In 1998, Matt's celebrated its 46th anniversary. The Martinez family has been in the restaurant business for longer than that, but in 1952 Matt Martinez open up the first El Rancho, now operating in a new, large building south of downtown. President Lyndon B. Johnson ate here before he was president, and lots of other Austin notables have come here for a regular Tex-Mex fix. The guacamole, cheese and meat dip is named for former Texas Land Commissioner Bob Armstrong who went on to serve in the Clinton Administration. The menu includes all the old faithful standbys, enchiladas, fajitas, tacos, chile rellenos and grilled shrimp. The hacienda-style restaurant can seat 500, but there is always a line on weekends at peak dining hours. It is open for lunch and dinner daily except for Tuesdays.

Pizza Nizza

$ • 1600 Barton Springs Rd.
• (512) 474-7470

A fixture on the Barton Springs Road restaurant row, this pizza restaurant forgoes the red and white checkered tablecloths for a livelier decor with yellow walls and primary color accents. The pizza joint was opened by one of the founders of the Whole Food Markets (see our Shopping chapter) and offers a wide variety of pies aimed at matching a diversity of tastes. Diners can design their own pizza, choosing from several sauces, some spicy, others light, and then dress them with the toppings of their choice. It is open daily for lunch and dinner.

Romeo's

$$ • 1500 Barton Springs Rd.
• (512) 476-1090

From the concrete stone swan planters in front to the plastic grapevines inside, the owners of Romeo's have managed to re-create the kitschy atmosphere of a neighborhood Italian-American cafe. This Barton Springs Road restaurant row cafe offers patrons a taste of those old, familiar restaurants as well. Sausage sandwiches, pepperoni pizza, manicotti and eggplant Parmesan are on the menu, but there are a few Texas touches also. Chipotle chicken is a spicy dish served with black beans and fresh cilantro. There are also a few nouvelle Italian dishes that have crept onto the menu — grilled pesto chicken on focaccia, grilled Portobello mushrooms and a pasta salad. The atmosphere and the prices make this a great date restaurant. It is open daily for lunch and dinner plus a Sunday brunch featuring vegetarian and meat fritattas, Italian eggs Benedict and, of course, migas, the Tex-Mex breakfast must.

Schlotzsky's Marketplace/ Bread Alone Bakery

$ • 218 S. Lamar Blvd. • (512) 476-2867

Schlotzsky's is a chain sandwich shop that was founded in Austin and has grown worldwide, including an outpost in Beijing. There are almost two dozen outlets in Austin, but this special branch just south of Town Lake is notable for its breezy atmosphere, airy architecture and its partner on site, Bread Alone Bakery. The famous sandwiches are sold here — the Original is made with special bread (grilled sourdough buns) stuffed with salami, ham, several cheeses, olives, onions, lettuce and tomato — plus soups, salads and small pizzas. The bakery offers whole loafs of specialty bread, cakes, cookies, desserts and coffees. This is a good place to put together lunch or afternoon snacks for an impromptu picnic on the shores of Town Lake. It is open daily for breakfast, lunch and dinner.

Shady Grove

$-$$ • 1624 Barton Springs Rd.
• (512) 474-9991

This Texas roadhouse-style restaurant takes its name from the pecan grove that shades the patio and the parking lot. There is seating inside, but many patrons prefer to sit outside and watch the squirrels race around harvesting pecans or begging for crumbs. The food here is the sort served in roadhouses across America back in the days before interstate highways brought chain food to the crossroads. Hamburgers are a staple, or try a Frito pie (Fritos topped with chili and cheese). For vegetarians there is a variety of salads and a Hippie Sandwich made with grilled eggplant and other vegetables. The Airstream Chili is hot and named for the Airstream trailer that sits in the garden. During the summer, Shady Grove features live music evenings and even movies on the patio. It is open daily for lunch and dinner.

Suzi's Chinese Kitchen

$$ • 1152 S. Lamar Blvd.
• (512) 441-8400

A neighborhood cafe that has a busy takeout kitchen as well as in-house dining, Suzi's offers a long list of well-known favorites in Chinese-American restaurants — duck with ginger, stir-fried noodles, beef with broccoli and mooshu pork — plus daily specials. One item on the menu that has attracted a following is the fried dumplings, and the luncheon specials are a draw for downtown workers. Suzi's is just a few blocks south of Town Lake in a small strip shopping center. The decor is plain, but the service very friendly. It is open daily for lunch and dinner.

Threadgill's World Headquarters Restaurant

$$ • 301 W. Riverside Dr.
• (512) 472-9304

Eddie Wilson founded the Armadillo World Headquarters (see The Music Scene chapter) and now owns Threadgill's, the two Austin restaurants that cherish home-cooking and celebrate the Austin music scene. The original Threadgill's is in North Austin (see North section), but this downtown restaurant has carried the Threadgill's banner back to the block where the legendary Armadillo stood. The restaurant celebrates the past by decorating the walls with Armadillo memorabilia. Much larger than the original Threadgill's, the downtown venue is nevertheless packed, especially at lunchtime. The food here is down-home diner-style with entrees like meat loaf, chicken-fried steak, fried chicken and sandwiches. Side dishes include Cajun eggplant, garlic cheese grits, jalapeno jambalaya and squash casserole, some of which can be found in grocery supermarket freezer cases in Austin. There is live music here, usually on Mondays, and during the week self-described political progressive Jim Hightower, a former editor of the *Texas Observer*, broadcasts his radio talk show from the restaurant. It is open daily for lunch and dinner.

Texas French Bread

$ • 1722 S. Congress Ave.
• (512) 440-1122

One of many branches of a homegrown bakery that consistently ranks among Austin's favorite restaurants, this Westlake Hills branch serves the same wonderful homemade breads, pastries, muffins and cookies daily for breakfast and lunch. There are sandwiches for lunch featuring the various breads that have made Texas French Bread popular, including French and Tuscan varieties.

The Paggi House

$$$ • 200 Lee Barton Dr.
• (512) 478-1121

It is easy to miss the Paggi House, tucked away as it is on a wooded lot just south of Town Lake, but this graceful little restaurant has been a fixture on the Austin restaurant scene for a couple of decades. The restaurant serves a Continental-style menu, dishes such as cannelloni stuffed with chicken, walnuts and peppers and topped with Gorgonzola cream sauce plus grilled meats and fresh fish. The building dates back to the 1840s, the earliest days of Austin's history, and the walls and floors have a patina imparted by history. Reservations are recommended for dinner, which is served Monday through Saturday. Lunch is offered on weekdays.

South

Cherry Creek Catfish Co.

$$ • 5712 Manchaca Rd.
• (512) 440-8810

The decor is designed to re-create a Louisiana wharf, but the menu is both Cajun and Texan with barbecue and seafood holding center stage. On the Cajun side is gumbo, frog legs, blackened catfish, crawfish, shrimp and oysters plus po'boys. You'll also find fried green tomatoes, a dish found throughout the South. Meat lovers can try barbecue ribs, hamburgers or chicken-fried steak. The restaurant also offers family packs of their food to go. It is open daily for lunch and dinner.

La Fuentes Mexican Food Restaurant

$ • 6507 Circle S Rd. • (512) 442-9925

This little neighborhood restaurant comes alive on weekend mornings as nearby residents come in for migas, breakfast tacos or chorizo and eggs. Tex-Mex breakfast is something of an Austin ritual, a time to spend a leisurely hour munching on salsa and chips, sopping up chorizo with a tortilla, sipping fruit juice and reading the paper. La Fuentes is open daily for breakfast, lunch and dinner.

Serrano's Cafe & Cantina

$$ • 321 Ben White Blvd.
• (512) 447-3999

Tex-Mex fare is on the menu here at this, one of six Serrano's in town. Fajita combos, enchiladas and generously sized *antojitos* (appetizers) draw the crowds to this vibrant pink building with a lively decor. The fajita menu even includes a veggie selection made from squash, peppers, onions and mushrooms.

Tres Amigos

$$ • 1807 W. Slaughter Ln. at Manchaca Rd. • (512) 292-1001

This is the South Austin entry in this hometown three-location chain. The menu is classic Tex-Mex and includes tacos, fajitas and enchiladas. Don't pass on the house mango ice cream.

Southwest

Austin Pizza Garden

$-$$ • 6266 U.S. Hwy. 290 W.
• (512) 891-9980

It took 19 years for James Patton to finish the Old Rock Store in Oak Hill, chances are it won't take much more than 19 minutes for you to get your pizza in the restaurant now housed in the historic building. Patton (the local elementary school is named after him) finished the store in 1898, and it has served as home to a variety of businesses over the years. Patton, whose father came to Texas in 1836 and fought in the Texas Revolution, served as postmaster of Oak Hill until the branch closed in 1910. He was known as the "Mayor of Oak Hill" despite the fact the city never incorporated. Now, Oak Hill is a suburb of Austin and a major freeway has wiped out many of the small stores that lined the old highway. But Patton's stone structure is a registered historic building, and so even the highway had to shift south to preserve history. Pizza is the major focus of the restaurant now occupying the site, and there are almost two dozen choices on the menu from quattro formaggio (four cheese) to Texas fajita, a Cajun pizza dubbed Tchoupitoulas with andouille sausage, shrimp, red onions, green and red peppers and garlic, or a Neptune with crab, shrimp and artichoke hearts. The restaurant also offers take-out service and is open daily for lunch and dinner.

Hunan Lion

$$ • Brodie Oaks Shopping Center, 4006 S. Lamar Blvd. • (512) 447-3388

The emphasis is on seafood at this Mandarin Chinese restaurant with dishes such as the seven star platter, a stir fry of Alaskan crab legs, chicken, shrimp, scallops, roasted pork and vegetables. The pescatory theme is also represented in the decor, which features four large tropical fish tanks. A smiling Buddha and flower arrangements

Photo: Courtesy of the Texas Department of Transportation

Some would travel around the world for a traditional meal of Texas barbecue.

plus decorative glass etched with flower designs are just some of the pleasant surprises behind the doors of this shopping center restaurant. In addition to fish specialties, the restaurant also serves classics such as Beijing duck. It is open for lunch and dinner daily.

Serrano's Cafe & Cantina

$$ • 6510 U.S. Hwy. 290 W
• (512) 891-0000

One of six Serrano's in Austin, this one in Oak Hill is housed in what was a steakhouse. The walls are decorated with historic pictures and artifacts from the days when the hill, across the street from the restaurant, was dubbed "Convict Hill." There, convict laborers worked cutting stone for the interior walls of the capitol building. Several are reputed to be buried on the hill, but their graves have been lost. The menu here is typical Tex-Mex and includes fajitas, enchiladas, tacos and generously sized appetizers.

The Salt Lick

$$, no credit cards • R.R. 1826, Camp Ben McCullough Rd., Driftwood
• (512) 858-4959

One of the most atmospheric barbecue restaurants in the area, the Salt Lick occupies a rural site about 12 miles south of U.S. Highway 290 W. on R.R. 1826, known as Camp Ben McCullough Road. Set in a Hill Country pasture, the Salt Lick has garnered a worldwide reputation, thanks to its mail-order food shipments, corporate parties by some of Austin's top employers and coverage in national and international publications. To get there, take F.M. 1826, just past the "Y" in Oak Hill, and head south for 12 miles or until you smell the smoke from the smokehouse. There are picnic tables inside and out, and the place is always busy. In winter a large fireplace inside warms diners. The menu includes brisket, chicken, ribs, sausage, homemade pickles and peach and berry cobblers. It is open daily for lunch and dinner. Reservations are suggested for large groups.

West

Barbara Ellen's Hill Country Restaurant

$-$$ • 13129 U.S. Hwy. 71 W.
• (512) 263-2385

Blue plate daily specials such as chicken and dumplings, or meat loaf and roasted pork plus iced tea served in Mason jars gives this Hill Country restaurant the feel of an old Southern kitchen. The chairs don't match, and the tablecloths are old-fashioned oil cloths, adding to the atmosphere at this cafe not far from Lake Travis. Barbara Ellen's serves breakfast, lunch and dinner daily.

Belgian Restaurant L'Estro Armonico

$$-$$$ • 3520 Bee Caves Rd.
• (512) 328-0580

One of the most romantic places to go for a special evening, this West Lake Hills cozy restaurant features Belgian cuisine and Continental service — female diners are presented with a rose at the end of the meal, and no matter what your gender, you'll get a Belgian chocolate with the bill. The restaurant offers a prix fixe menu plus an array of changing entrees, which might include duck in green peppercorn sauce or with dark cherries or grilled fish topped with sauteed leeks. Given the chef's Belgian roots, desserts featuring chocolates are a specialty — try the chocolate mousse. It is open for lunch and dinner Monday through Friday, dinner only on weekends. Reservations are recommended.

Canyon Cafe

$$ • 701 S. Loop 360 (Capital of Texas Hwy.) • (512) 329-0400

Every effort has been made in this West Lake Hills shopping center restaurant to recreate the feeling of dining in a large mountain lodge somewhere in the Southwest. The menu reflects this same theme with variations on traditional Tex-Mex fare, pastas with a spicy touch, grilled chicken, beef and fish plus house specialties like the chicken-fried tuna. It is open for lunch and dinner daily and Sunday brunch.

Carlos 'N Charlie's

$$ • 5973 Hiline Rd. • (512) 266-1685

Following the floods of 1997, Carlos 'N Charlie's underwent a complete renovation, and the result is a 6,000-square-foot restaurant seating 1,850 and offering a world of fun on the shores of Lake Travis. The restaurant has its own boat dock and a beach volleyball complex. The food is decidedly Tex-Mex with an assortment of enchiladas, fajitas, tacos and burritos. Of course, the bar features a wild variety of drinks, including Margaritas. It is open for lunch and dinner daily, late on weekends. In the past, the restaurant has closed down in December and January, but plans call for the new facility to be open year round.

Chinatown

$$ • 3300 Bee Caves Rd. • (512) 327-6588

Among the most popular items on the menu at this West Lake Hills restaurant are several searing dishes, Thai pepper basil shrimp and jalapeno chicken with black bean sauce, a reflection of the spicy Szechwan-style Chinese cuisine featured at Chinatown. Of course, not all the dishes are spicy, but diners with a taste for the fiery can turn up the heat on request. Chinatown is open daily for lunch and dinner.

County Line on the Hill

$$-$$$ • 6500 Bee Caves Rd. • (512) 327-1742

Upscale barbecue is the order of the day at this hillside restaurant. Over the years, the view from the hilltop patio has changed as Austin has grown and homeowners have headed for the hills. One of the highlights of the menu is the smoked prime rib, served with baked potato, cole slaw and beans. Barbecued ribs, brisket, chicken, sausage, pork and baby back ribs are available by the plate or by the pound. The restaurant is open for lunch during the week and for dinner daily.

Five Star Bar-B-Que

$-$$ • 3638 Bee Caves Rd. • (512) 328-1800

This West Lake Hills barbecue joint has a rustic air and a full menu of barbecue offerings, including smoked ham. A Tex-Mex touch is the brisket fajitas. A variety of homemade pies is offered for dessert, including buttermilk, apple, chocolate, chocolate pecan, Key lime and Toll House. It is open daily for lunch and dinner.

Hang Town Grill

$ • 701 S. Loop 360 (Capital of Texas Hwy.) • (512) 347-1039

This is an Austin favorite among the soccer-mom set because it not only feeds the kids what they want — burgers and pizza — but gives mom a chance to nibble on salads and entrees with an Asian touch. The first Hang Town is in Central Austin (see our listing) and both are the brainchild of Reed and Betsy Clemons, Austin's power restaurant couple.

Hill Country Pasta House

$$-$$$ • 3519 R.R. 620 N. • (512) 266-9445

This Lake Travis-area restaurant offers a variety of pastas and Italian-inspired entrees, for example a salmon fillet stuffed with spinach and pine nuts and topped with a basil cream sauce. The wood-fired oven produces pizza and focaccia, and there are grilled offerings, including steaks. The restaurant is kid-friendly, and crayons come with the menu so the kiddies can be occupied while parents ruminate on the choices. Because it is close to the lake, many patrons come in after a day of boating or swimming so the dress code is relaxed. It is open daily for lunch and dinner.

Hudson's-on-the-Bend

$$$$ • 3509 R.M. 620 • (512) 266-1369

Chef/owner Jeff Blank and Chef Jay Moore have built a wide-ranging reputation as innovators in Texas cuisine from their base near the shores of Lake Travis. The restaurant is housed in and around a small Hill Country cottage. On the grounds are a smokehouse and an herb garden that offers a hint of what Hudson's has to offer. Much of the menu is devoted to showcasing exotic game and ingredients — one of the popular appetizers is Omar's Rattlesnake Cakes with chipotle cream sauce. Other dishes utilize venison, javelina (a South Texas wild boar) and Axis antelope raised on Hill Country ranches. For the less adventurous there are top-quality steaks, veal, seafood and pasta dishes. The restaurant's sauces, both savory and sweet, garnered such a devoted following they are now sold on specialty food store shelves and by mail order. (Look for them at Central Market, and look for Central Market in our Shopping chapter.) The atmosphere at Hudson's is intimate, although the series of small dining rooms when packed with customers can be fashionably noisy. Diners can eat or wait for a table on a balmy evening in the garden decorated with twinkling lights. Weekends are especially busy, so reservations are recommended. The restaurant is open daily for dinner, but closes a little earlier in winter, so it is wise to call ahead. Hudson's also offers cooking classes.

Hula Hut

$$-$$$ • 3825 Lake Austin Blvd. • (512) 476-HULA

Mexican restaurant with a Hawaiian flavor, or a Hawaiian luau with a Mexican touch? One clue, the Huli Huli PuPu Platter includes baby back barbecued ribs, grilled chicken nachos, barbecued chicken tacos, chicken flautas, chopped salad, seasoned red potatoes and chile con queso. This is a lakeside restaurant with multiple personalities, but the crowds indicate the mix seems to work. In addition to traditional Tex-Mex fare plus Asian-style salads, there are "luau dinners" featuring grilled seafood and chicken. Even the fajita menu shows this cross-Pacific flair —choose from six varieties including Shiner Bock (a Texas-brewed beer) grilled chicken fajitas, or Thai barbecue fajitas, perhaps Hawaiian fajitas (beef or chicken glazed with Polynesian plum sauce). The restaurant is on the shores of Lake Austin, just a short ride from downtown along Sixth Street and under MoPac. The outdoor deck is crowded on summer weekends. It is open daily for lunch and dinner.

La Madeleine

$ • 701 S. Loop 360 (Capital of Texas Hwy.) • (512) 306-1998

Unlike the other two Austin locations, which are housed in buildings originally designed for other businesses, this latest addition was built for the French bistro-bakery in a West Austin shopping center. Despite the shopping mall location, the interior is a cozy rendition of a French cafe. See the Central Austin listing for details on the menu.

Las Palomas

$$ • 3201 Bee Caves Rd. • (512) 327-9889

Tucked away in the corner of fairly nondescript strip shopping center, this Mexican restaurant serves interior food in a light, airy setting. Specialities from various Mexican states are featured, including pork pibil, inspired by Yucatecan cuisine, shrimp a la Veracruzana (green olives, tomatoes and capers) and the much-praised mole poblano, a complex sauce made from chiles, chocolate, spice and herbs. The restaurant features live mariachi music on the weekends to add to the ambiance. Las Palomas is open for lunch and dinner daily.

Madame Nadalini's

$$-$$$ • 3663 Bee Caves Rd. • (512) 328-4858

When it first opened, this upscale, smart West Lake Hills Italian restaurant touted its all-vegetarian menu, but that has now been modified, ensuring that Madame Nadalini's is even more popular. The kitchen continues to produce vegetarian dishes such as spinach lasagna and cozze arrabiata, made with tomatoes, basil and sweet onions, but now the pungent sauce finds its way atop fresh mussels. Small and housed in a new building with clean, sleek lines, Madame Nadalini's is good place for a relaxing, intimate dinner or lunch with friends or lovers. It is open daily for lunch and dinner.

Magnolia Cafe

$ • 2304 Lake Austin Blvd. • (512) 478-8645

This is a homey, comfortable diner where gingerbread pancakes rank as comfort food 24 hours a day, seven days a week. The cafe is not far from downtown, just west of MoPac, and serves breakfast dishes, sandwiches, even fajitas whenever you want them, no matter the hour.

Pacific Moon

$$-$$$ • 2712 Bee Caves Rd. • (512) 328-8888

Bee Caves Road, the main artery that runs through West Lake Hills, is blessed with a number of small, exceptional restaurants where diners can enjoy creative cooking in congenial surroundings. One of the latest arrivals is Pacific Moon, where Chef Colin Liu features his nouvelle Asian repertoire, inspired by his teacher Susanna Foo, the Philadelphia cookbook author and chef. Liu takes the best, fresh local ingredients and translates them into his Asian-style dishes, an example is his ancho chile-sauced pan-fried dumplings, utilizing ancho chiles found in local markets. The menu changes frequently, but the surroundings remain tranquil with pale gray walls and small paintings, orchid bud bases and low light. Pacific Moon is open daily for lunch and dinner.

Rosie's Tamale House

$ • 13436 U.S. Hwy. 71, Bee Cave • (512) 263-5245

Willie Nelson ate here so often they named a plate after him — Willie's Plate with a taco, enchilada, guacamole and chile con queso. Willie must have tipped rather well, too, since Rosie's moved from a small building to a big new home a few years ago in the Bee Cave neighborhood. (Careful readers will note it is Bee Caves Road, but Bee Cave neighborhood — not a typographical error, that is what the road is called while the community prefers the singular appellation.) A stop at Rosie's is a regular event for Austinites frolicking at the lake on the weekend. If they don't stop for lunch or dinner, they are sure to drop in for an order or two of tamales to go.

Sam Hill Waterfront Grill

$-$$$$ • 16405 Marina Point Rd. • (512) 266-2811

Where the Sam Hill is Sam Hill? On the shores of Lake Travis, and that explains why the garage door walls can be opened to the elements, giving diners inside a lake breeze. The restaurant also has a series of large decks where patrons can watch the sun go down. The decor and the menu are evocative of a California '50s roadhouse with some Tex-Mex touches — hamburgers, peel 'n' eat shrimp, tacos and taquitos plus a variety of drinks, including a prickly pear pink Margarita (the fruit of the cactus plant). The menu features a variety of dishes ranging from low-cost appetizers and snacks to high dollar entrees, including lobster. The mood is lively here with several bars scattered about the restaurant and the decks. It is open daily for lunch and dinner.

Serrano's Westlake Mesquite Grill

$$ • 3267 Bee Caves Rd. • (512) 327-4100

There are six Serrano's in Austin. This Westlake Hills location features a large deck and a menu emphasizing grilled fajitas and grilled dishes. But there is also a large selection of Tex-Mex staples, including tacos, nachos and enchiladas. It is open daily for lunch and dinner.

Texas French Bread

$ • 3736 Bee Caves Rd. • (512) 306-8010

One of many branches of a homegrown bakery that consistently ranks among Austin's favorite restaurants, this Westlake Hills branch serves the same wonderful homemade breads, pastries, muffins and cookies daily for breakfast and lunch. There are sandwiches for lunch featuring the various breads that have made

INSIDERS' TIP

Want to eat out in? Call EatOutIn, (512) 346-9990, a local delivery company that brings the food of some 20 local restaurants to your door for a fee. The service will fax you a menu, or you can ask them to mail you a brochure or they can brief you on your choices. Another delivery service is Entrees on Trays, (512) 458-MENU.

Texas French Bread popular, including French and Tuscan varieties.

The Emerald Restaurant

$$$-$$$$ • 13614 U.S. Hwy. 71 W. • (512) 263-2147

Step inside this Hill Country cottage and you will think you have crossed the threshold of an Irish country cottage. The walls are decorated with shamrock wallpaper, the tablecloths and curtains are lace, and there are cozy nooks and crannies where diners can enjoy an intimate dinner. The Kinsella family, whose matriarch hails from County Mayo, runs this little Irish gem near Lake Travis. The evening begins here with orders of Irish soda bread and English treacle loaf (made with molasses) served with whipped strawberry butter and goes on from there to embrace roast pork in puff pastry, Chateaubriand for two, roast lamb, grilled salmon inspired by Irish and Continental influences. The desserts are, of course, rich, and Irish coffee is almost an obligatory end to dinner. The Emerald is open daily for dinner.

The Lodge at Lakeview

$$-$$$ • 3825-B Lake Austin Blvd. • (512) 476-7372

Just minutes west of MoPac, The Lodge sits on the site of a former marina on Lake Austin. The design is aimed at creating the atmosphere of a mountain lodge with a stone fireplace and large log beams. Fishing and hunting trophies lining the walls. Perhaps the "wildest" thing on the menu is the Buffalo Burger, a meat that is noted for its low-fat qualities. Other entrees include prime rib and Gulf Coast seafood. For lighter eaters there are pasta dishes and salads. It is open daily for lunch and dinner, plus Sunday brunch.

Tres Amigos

$$ • 1801 S. Loop 360 (Capital of Texas Hwy.) • (512) 327-1776

A longtime fixture on the Westlake Hills scene, Tres Amigos serves familiar Tex-Mex favorites such as enchiladas and tacos, fajitas and Mexican plates. Some of the waitresses have been on the job for years and have watched as families grew up, nourished by the kind of food all Texans hanker for regularly. The setting is a pleasant evocation of Old Mexico. Try the homemade mango ice cream. Tres Amigos is open for lunch and dinner daily.

Waterloo Ice House at The Backyard

$ • 13101 U.S. Hwy. 71 W. • (512) 263-5400

The Backyard, with its natural open-air stage under the live oak trees (see The Music Scene chapter), attracts large crowds on concert nights, but the branch of the Waterloo Ice House that is part of the site here is open for lunch and dinner daily. In addition to Waterloo, which features burgers, sandwiches and chicken-fried steak, there is also a branch of Iron Works barbecue (see our Central listings) where barbecued beef, ribs, chicken, pork and all the fixin's are served.

Zoot American Bistro & Wine Bar

$$$ • 509 Hearn St. • (512) 477-6535

Eclectic — a much overused word — is applicable here at this West Austin restaurant noted for its creativity and innovation. Zoot sits just west of MoPac in an converted 1920s bungalow with wooden floors and small rooms, which now accommodate dining areas and a tiny bar. The menu draws on the best of local ingredients and various culinary styles. The menu changes with the season, but diners can sample dishes such as roasted chicken with corn custard, or shiitake mushroom gnocchi with fresh chanterelles, cedar plank roasted salmon with winter squash melange, pine nut-masa pudding and poblano cream sauce, and grilled beef tenderloin with potato/cheese strudel, sauteed rapini and tangerine demi-glace. The kitchen favors organic vegetables and is not afraid to take traditional dishes to new heights. A good example is the restaurant's version of eggs Benedict — buttermilk biscuits topped with spicy hash, poached eggs and orange hollandaise, just one of the dishes served at the restaurant's Sunday brunch. Zoot is open daily for lunch and dinner; reservations are recommended for lunch and on the weekends for dinner.

Northwest

Azuma Express

$ • 2501 Parmer Ln. • (512) 834-9304

A hip spot that would look at home in Tokyo, Azuma brings Japanese fast food to Austin. The restaurant is just west of MoPac in a strip shopping center, but the interior looks like something out of *The Jetsons* comic strip with red booths and mirrored walls. Japanese comic books are scattered about for diners to browse, but a glimpse is all most customers get since Azuma Express lives up to the latter half of its name. The menu has photographs for those who don't know their way around the Japanese culinary scene. Noodles, sushi, teriyaki and tempura are all featured plus green tea ice cream for dessert. It is open daily for lunch and dinner.

Brick Oven Restaurant

$ • 10710 Research Blvd. • (512) 345-6181

The latest addition to the hometown Brick Oven chain, this Northwest location features pizza baked in a wood-fired oven. Customers can choose from a variety of toppings, thin or thick crust, even an all-garlic pizza. The menu also features other Italian-American staples and salads. It is open daily for lunch and dinner.

Catfish Parlour

$$ • 11910 Research Blvd. • (512) 258-1853

The original Catfish Parlour is in Southeast Austin (see our listing), but its popularity led to a new branch in Northwest Austin. Patrons can enjoy all-you-can-eat catfish and more, including both baked and fried catfish, chicken and shrimp. Cajun touches on the menu include gumbo plus there is a large salad bar. Catfish is open Monday through Saturday for lunch and dinner.

Chez Zee

$$-$$$ • 5406 Balcones Dr. • (512) 454-2666

This stylish bistro with a large outdoor patio, art-studded walls and a baby grand where customers can work a jigsaw puzzle while listening to cafe music is a fixture on the Austin scene. The menu features both American and Continental specialties, including sandwiches, pastas, salads and grilled entrees, but it is the breakfast and weekend brunch menus that get rave reviews, particularly the creme brulee French toast made from challah, soaked with custard, and topped with caramelized sugar. Brunch is served into mid-afternoon on weekends, breakfast begins early during the week, and lunch and dinner are served daily.

Chinatown

$$ • 3407 Greystone Dr. • (512) 343-9307

The original Chinatown opened in Westlake Hills, but this branch in Northwest Austin is equally popular. The restaurant offers many familiar Chinese dishes plus several chef's specialties that cater to Texas tastes for hot and spicy foods. Thai pepper basil shrimp and Szechwan spicy duck are two of the spicy offerings. It is open daily for lunch and dinner.

County Line on the Lake

$$-$$$ • 5204 F.M. 2222 • (512) 346-3664

This Northwest branch of a popular upscale barbecue restaurant (see West Austin) is situated along a creek bed. Diners can wait for a table or enjoy a drink on the outdoor deck under the trees. One word of warning, F.M. 2222 is a wide, winding road that leads to Highland Lakes, making it very busy on weekends. There have been serious accidents here, many involving alcohol; visitors should designate a driver if they plan to drink with dinner. It is open daily for lunch and dinner.

Dan McKluskey's

$$$ • The Arboretum, 10000 Research Blvd. • (512) 346-0780

This steakhouse specializes in hand-cut steaks but also caters to lighter appetites by offering several fish and grilled chicken entrees. The setting is classic steakhouse: dark wood, brass fittings and subdued lighting. The bar stays open late on the weekends for late-night customers who can snack on appetizers and listen to live jazz music. It is open daily for lunch and dinner.

Gateway Mezzaluna

$$$-$$$$ • Gateway Courtyard, 9901 Loop 360 (Capital of Texas Hwy.) • (512) 372-8030

A sister restaurant to Mezzaluna downtown (see the Central Austin listing) and the newest member of the San Gabriel Group, innovative Austin restaurants designed and developed by Betsy and Reed Clemons, Gateway Mezzaluna takes its name from the shopping center where it is located. With the northwest branch of Whole Foods in the neighborhood and shops such as Old Navy and Smith & Hawken nearby, the site is at a nexus of hip action in Northwest Austin. The menu is different from downtown and is described by San Gabriel's Executive Chef Emmett Fox as "contemporary Italian with a rustic flair." That means entrees such as sauteed calf's liver in brown butter and fresh sage, or Tuscan-style prime rib, or rack of lamb with cannellini bean and wine sauce. The restaurant really has two faces, one more casual downstairs where lighter dishes are served, including pizza and focaccia from the wood-burning oven, the other more upscale and upstairs, past a wall mural depicting the Tuscan countryside. In addition to lunch and dinner, Gateway Mezzaluna also serves brunch on the weekends, offering frittato with pancetta, potatoes and spinach; poached eggs with Italian sausage; crepes with raspberries; and grilled steak for hearty eaters.

Hang Town Grill

$ • 9828 Great Hills Tr. • (512) 349-9944

Invent a good idea, and they will come — that is what the creators of Hang Town Grill, Austinites Reed and Betsy Clemons have discovered with this, their third Hang Town location. The menu is both kid friendly and appeals to grownups — burgers and pizza, salads and stir fries. The decor is Flash Gordon comes to Austin. It is open daily for lunch and dinner plus they offer take-out service.

Hudson's Grill

$ • 13376 Research Blvd. • (512) 219-1902

Burger mavens head for Hudson's, where the menu offers over a dozen varieties plus turkey and garden burgers for those who shy away from beef. The fare is all-American here with sandwiches, salads and chicken-fried steak served in a '50s diner atmosphere. Generous portions of French fries and onions plus a slew of desserts round out the menu. It's open daily for lunch and dinner, late nights on Friday and Saturday.

Iguana Grill

$$ • 2900 F.M. 620 • (512) 266-8439

A great view of Lake Travis plus a fresh take on Tex-Mex — dubbed "Lake-Mex" by the restaurant — has made the Iguana Grill a favorite for leisurely dining, particularly on weekends. The fajitas are marinated in pineapple juice and beer, one of the signature touches that makes the food here a little different from the average Tex-Mex fare. A good choice on warm days is the ceviche, marinated fresh fish with peppers and tomatoes, topped with onions and cilantro. The atmosphere is very casual, and no one rushes lunch or dinner here. It is open daily.

Kerbey Lane Cafe

$-$$ • 12602 Research Blvd. • (512) 258-7757

Northwest Austin is where successful longtime Austin institutions break new ground. Kerbey Lane Cafe operates a branch of its popular Central Austin cafe in this fast-growing section of Austin. The same old faithful staples are on the menu including Tex-Mex, burgers, sandwiches, salads and breakfast dishes. The cafe is open seven days a week, 24 hours a day.

La Madeleine

$ • 9828 Great Hills Tr. • (512) 502-2474

You would never guess this French cafe once was a bookstore. The decor has been designed to create the atmosphere of a French neighborhood bakery, and the menu enhances that impression. Soups, salads, quiche, pizzas and light dinner entrees are on the menu with daily specials posted on the blackboard. Save room for dessert. The bakery is open daily for breakfast, lunch and dinner plus mid-morning and mid-afternoon breaks.

Musashino Sushi Dokoro

3407 Greystone Dr. • (512) 795-8593

The extensive menu at this Northwest Austin sushi bar (housed in the same building as Chinatown) features traditional offerings and some hybrid American takes on Japanese classics. The latter are listed under the "Born in The USA" section of the menu and include favorites such as California rolls topped with fresh tuna, shrimp and salmon. Authentic Japanese offerings include seaweed and wild vegetable salads plus an array of sushi and sashimi. The atmosphere is quietly elegant. It is open daily except Monday for dinner only.

Pearl's Oyster Bar

$$-$$$ • 9033 Research Blvd. • (512) 339-7444

Noted as a live music venue, Pearl's also offers Louisiana fare for lunch, dinner and late night on weekends. Both Cajun and Creole dishes are served here with all the staples such as shrimp and crawfish plus a few eye-openers such as fried alligator tail. In addition to seafood, the menu also features sandwiches, pasta and salads. Pearl's is in a shopping center but has the atmosphere of a neighborhood cafe/bar. The restaurant is open daily, but there is a cover charge on weekends.

Pok-E-Jo's Smokehouse

$-$$ • 9828 Great Hills Tr. • (512) 338-1990

One of four Pok-E-Jo's in Austin, this one helps satisfy cravings for Texas barbecue in Northwest Austin. The meats here are mesquite-smoked and include ribs, pork, beef, ham, pork loin, sausage, turkey and chicken. Take-out is popular here. It is open daily for lunch and dinner.

Roppolo's

$ • 8105 Mesa Dr. • (512) 346-9800

The Austin Chronicle's readers' poll helped this Austin restaurant open several locations around town. This Northwest location features the same menu as the other Roppolo's — pizza, stromboli, calzone, pasta with meatballs and veggie lasagna. It is open daily for lunch and dinner.

Rosie's Tamale House No. 2

$ • 13776 Research Blvd. • (512) 219-7793

Associated with Rosie's at Bee Caves (see West Austin), this sister restaurant serves similar Tex-Mex fare.

Rudy's Bar-B-Q

$$ • 11570 Research Blvd. • (512) 418-9898

With so many barbecue restaurants it can be hard to stand out, so Rudy's makes the effort by calling itself "the worst barbecue in Texas," but that belies the packed parking lot. The atmosphere is old country store with gas pumps outside and picnic tables inside, and the menu features all the expected Texas items, including prime rib, smoked pork loin, chicken and chopped beef. Rudy's opens early to serve breakfast tacos and offers lunch and dinner daily. A second Rudy's is now open at 2451 Capital of Texas Highway, (512) 329-5554.

Spiazzo

$$-$$$ • 5416 Parkcrest Dr., Ste. 700 • (512) 459-9960

Never judge a book by its cover or a restaurant by the outside appearance. Spiazzo is tucked away inside a typical neighborhood shopping center just west of MoPac, but inside the atmosphere of a modern Italian cafe has been re-created with lots of vibrant colors. Appetizers are light and include Sicilian caponata, a mix of eggplant, bell peppers, tomatoes, onions, olives and capers plus goat cheese fritti — medallions of breaded, fried cheese topped with roasted tomato-basil sauce. Both the bread and the pizzas are cooked in a wood-fired oven; a variety of salads feature roasted vegetables, pasta and fresh tomatoes and herbs; and the pastas vary from the simple to the rich and creamy. There is a special section of the menu dubbed "Italy SXSW" featuring Italian-style dishes with Southwestern touches — spicy chipotle cappellini, which gets its kick from the chipotle pepper, a smoked jalapeno, and spaghetti with Shiner Bock meatballs. Spiazzo is open daily for lunch and dinner.

Texas French Bread

$ • 10255 Research Blvd.
• (512) 418-1991

As Austin grows, so grows this hometown bakery. There are now almost 10 branches of Texas French Bread, all serving the same wonderful menu of homemade breads, pastries, muffins and cookies daily for breakfast and lunch. There are sandwiches for lunch featuring the various breads that have made Texas French Bread popular, including French and Tuscan varieties.

Z'Tejas Grill

$$-$$$ • 9400 Arboretum Blvd.
• (512) 346-3506

Anyone who wants to get a view of how Austin has evolved in the last two decades should visit both branches of Z'Tejas Grill (see our Central Austin listings for the original restaurant). The original Z is on W. Sixth Street and captures with its menu and atmosphere the much-touted, laid-back Austin lifestyle. The second Z'Tejas is in a new Santa Fe-style building near the Arboretum, and its atmosphere reflects the lively, booming lifestyle of Northwest Austin where many of the newer city residents and high-tech businesses have located. The menu is almost the same with a mix of Southwestern meets European, with a touch of Asian (seared sesame tuna and ancho-rubbed pork tenderloin), but the restaurant does not serve breakfast like the original cafe. It is open daily for lunch and dinner, late night on Friday and Saturday.

North

Chuy's

$-$$ • 10520 N. Lamar Blvd.
• (512) 836-3218

Chuy's is Tex-Mex with attitude. Just like the original down on Barton Springs Road (see our South Central listings), this location is a great mix of good food, lively atmosphere and outrageous decor. Lava lamps and primary colors are the Chuy's hallmarks. The menu features burritos, tacos, enchiladas, fajitas and lots of variations on the nacho theme. Chuy's also offers several sauces, which can be ordered to accompany any entree. Parents like Chuy's because of the great finger food here — a plate of nachos can keep any 4-year-old occupied — and the easygoing atmosphere. Chuy's is open daily for lunch and dinner.

El Mercado Restaurant & Cantina

$-$$ • 7414 Burnet Rd. • (512) 454-2500

One of three El Mercados in town, this North Austin branch serves the same generous proportions of Tex-Mex favorites in a lively, colorful setting. The restaurant is open daily for breakfast, lunch and dinner.

Fonda San Miguel

$$$-$$$$ • 2330 W. North Loop Blvd.
• (512) 459-4121

Some of Austin's finest restaurants are found in unexpected places, such as Green Pastures in South Central Austin. Fonda San Miguel is situated in an everyday neighborhood, but once you step over the threshold it is easy to assume you are in Old Mexico. This is an accurate rendition of both Mexican architectural style and food. Designed to evoke the atmosphere of an old hacienda, the entrance to the restaurant, the bar area, is a small courtyard complete with fountain and plants. Inside, the walls are decorated with antiques and ceramics representative of Colonial Mexico, including Talavera tiles, vases from Guanajuato, clay cooking pots from Puebla, and *ollas* (large water vessels) from Oaxaca.

Until recently, the cuisine of Mexico has been highly underrated and, among those not familiar with its complexities, there are misconceptions that it is simply a version of Tex-Mex. It's not, and this is the place to come to understand why. The menu features regional specialties from throughout the country as interpreted by current Chef Ricardo Muñoz. Former Chef Miguel Ravago hosted cooking classes here with the doyenne of Mexican cooking, Diana Kennedy, and now has gone to other projects, including cookbooks. Muñoz has taken over the kitchen and put his own signature on the dishes. It is a misconception that all Mexican food is hot; many of the chiles and spices used South of the Border are nuanced not fiery. Some dishes are simple fare, steak served a la Tampiqueña, a grilled beef tenderloin, others are more exotic such as quesadillas made with huitlacoche (wheet-laa-koh-chay), the fungus that grows on the ears of corn at certain times of the year and has a mushroom-truffle taste. The menu also features seafood served in Yucatecan and Veracruzano styles, some spicy, others more Spanish in flavor. And there are several moles, the rich, complex sauces usually called by their color — verde (green), negro (black) — or by their geographical origin — poblano (from Puebla). The latter is the most famous made from more than two dozen ingredients, including bitter chocolate, spices, herbs and chiles. A good way to sample a variety of fare is to make a reservation for Sunday brunch. This meal evokes the Sunday custom in Mexico where families sit down for a long, leisurely meal made up of snacks, entrees, desserts, coffee and long conversation. The restaurant is open daily for dinner and on Sunday for brunch. Reservations are recommended.

Hudson's Grill

$ • 8440 Burnet Rd., Ste. 100 • (512) 458-5117

Cousin to the Northwest Hudson's on Research Boulevard, the fare at the 1950s-style diner is an all-American selection of burgers, fries and sandwiches. Leave room for dessert; the menu is packed with pies and ice cream sundaes. It is open daily for lunch and dinner and late on Friday and Saturday.

Kim Phung

$ • 7601 N. Lamar Blvd. • (512) 451-2464

Asian noodle aficionados tout this humble-looking cafe as one of the best places in town to sample a wide variety of the Vietnamese specialty. There are more than 40 varieties of noodle dishes on the menu, including 19 varieties of beef noodle soup plus stir fried and cold noodles. Thai coffee, made with canned evaporated milk, has become part of the coffee craze, and Kim Phung serves this also. The restaurant is in a strip shopping center, and the surroundings are plain and humble. It is open from mid-morning to evening daily.

Korea House

$-$$ • Village Shopping Center, 2700 W. Anderson Ln., No. 501 • (512) 4582477

Garlic, sesame, ginger and peppers are key ingredients in Korean cuisine. Dishes such as Bul Go Ki, a national favorite, is made with beef, chicken or pork, thinly sliced and marinated in a sauce made from onions, soy sauce, garlic, sesame, pepper, sake and grated fruit, then sauteed quickly and served with a variety of garnishes, including Kim Chee, the potent Korean pickle. That is the sort of dish served at Korea House, a restaurant in the Village shopping east of MoPac on Anderson Lane. The small restaurant has a view of an inner courtyard, which adds to the Oriental design. In addition to Korean specialties, the restaurant serves sushi. It is open daily for lunch and dinner.

Laura's Bluebonnet Cafe

$-$$ • 5408 Burnet Rd. • (512) 467-9552

With its proliferation of antique and craft shops (see our Shopping chapter), this section of Burnet Road is developing as new place to explore, particularly among antique and "junque" hunters. This Southern-style cafe is decorated with bric-a-brac including old enamel kitchen ranges and toasters. The cafe's blackboard lists the daily specials for breakfast, lunch and dinner, and the emphasis is on homestyle food.

Ninfa's Mexican Restaurant

$$-$$$ • 214 E. Anderson Ln. • (512) 832-1833

There are two Ninfa's in Austin, one downtown and this second location, both featuring the creations of Houston entrepreneur Ninfa Lorenzo. The food is described as "uptown" Tex-Mex with entrees such as smoked quail in salsa negra, shrimp in garlic sauce and pollo asado (roasted chicken). There are also Mexican dishes on the menu featuring some classics from South of the Border. Expect to pay more than the usual Tex-Mex prices here. Lunch and dinner are served daily.

Pavarotti Italian Restaurant

$$ • 3300 W. Anderson Ln. • (512) 420-0700

Behind the strip shopping center exterior

lies a little piece of Italy, complete with opera music playing softly in the background (hence the name) and candlelight. The menu at this Shoal Creek Plaza restaurant just east of MoPac is familiar, traditional Italian fare — lasagna, ravioli, manicotti and pastas with tomato and alfredo sauces. The kitchen also offers daily specials. The atmosphere is comfortable, relaxed and intimate. It is open on weekdays for lunch and dinner, dinner-only on Saturday. It is closed Sunday.

Pok-E-Jo's Smokehouse

$-$$ • 2121 W. Parmer Ln.
• (512) 491-0434

One of four Pok-E-Jo's in Austin, this one helps satisfy cravings for Texas barbecue in North Austin. The meats here are mesquite-smoked and include ribs, pork, beef, ham, pork loin, sausage, turkey and chicken. Take-out is popular here. It is open daily for lunch and dinner.

Roppolo's

$ • 14200 N. I-35 • (512) 990-2300

The Austin Chronicle's readers have helped this hometown pizza house grow by naming it among their favorites in several annual polls. You'll find the same menu here as at the other Roppolo's — pizza, stromboli, calzone, pasta with meatballs and veggie lasagna. It is open daily for lunch and dinner.

Satay

$$ • Shoal Creek Plaza, 3202 W. Anderson Ln. • (512) 467-6731

The spice trade was a two-way affair, bringing spices from the countries in South Asia to Europe and importing Dutch, British, Spanish and Portuguese customs to the region. Satay celebrates that trade with a menu that reflects Indonesian, Thai, Vietnamese and Malaysian dishes. Dutch traders adopted the Indonesian custom of serving a variety of dishes at one course, dubbing it rijsttafel, or rice table. At Satay it is a great way to share a meal with several friends. Another regional specialty is celebrated in the restaurant's name, satay is a Malaysian shish kebab. The menu also features curries, both Thai and Indian-inspired. Satay is well-known not only for its diverse menu, but also its food products, including a peanut sauce served with satay, which are sold in local food stores. The restaurant is in the Shoal Creek Plaza shopping center, but inside the decor is exotic and features artwork from the South China Seas region. Satay is open daily for lunch and dinner.

Sea Dragon

$-$$ • Grand Central Shopping Center, 8776-B Research Blvd. • (512) 451-5051

This Vietnamese restaurant also offers Chinese dishes on an extensive menu and, given Vietnam's geography, many of the dishes feature fresh seafood. The chef also creates daily specials featuring seasonal foods. Duck is also a house specialty and is prepared in a number of ways, including stir fried with leeks and ginger or tea-smoked. It is open daily for lunch and dinner.

Serrano's Cafe & Cantina

$$ • 3010 W. Anderson Ln.
• (512) 454-7333
$$ • 6406 N. I-35 • (512) 323-2555

There are six Serrano's in Austin, these two North locations offer a large selection of Tex-Mex staples, including tacos, nachos and enchiladas. They are open daily for lunch and dinner. House specials include shrimp flaquitos, flour tortillas stuffed with shrimp and deep fried; carnitas, pork shoulder simmered in spices then grilled; and chile relleno de camarones, a poblano pepper stuffed with shrimp and topped with a cream sauce.

Suzi's China Grill

$$-$$$ • 7858 Shoal Creek Blvd.
• (512) 302-4600

An upscale sister to Suzi's Chinese Kitchen in South Central Austin, (see our listing in that section), the open-air kitchen here gives this Chinese restaurant a different look from others. Much of the menu is familiar Chinese fare, similar to the offerings at Suzi's Chinese Kitchen, and few dishes are grilled, despite the name. The menu caters to both vegetarians and meat eaters. It is open daily for lunch and dinner.

Taj Palace

$$ • 6700 Middle Fiskville Rd.
• (512) 452-9959

Both vegetarians and meat-eaters will find

an abundant selection at this traditional Indian restaurant near Highland Mall. The vegetarian specialties include saag paneer, a homemade cheese and spinach saute, and malai kofta, cheese and vegetable dumplings simmered in a cream and almond sauce, while carnivores can dig into tandoori dishes such as barra kabab, lamb marinated in spiced yogurt, then grilled. The menu also features a variety of curries with varying degrees of heat and the tandoor oven-baked breads are not to be missed — aloo parantha is stuffed with potatoes, green peas and spices. The restaurant is decorated with images of Indian gods and weavings from the subcontinent. There is an all-you-can-eat lunch buffet on Monday night. It is open for dinner daily.

Texas French Bread

$ • 7719 Burnet Rd. • (512) 419-0184

Austinites love their bakeries, and this multi-branched bakery ranks among Austin's favorite restaurants. On the menu for breakfast, muffins, croissants and pastries, while lunch features a variety of sandwiches showcasing the bakery's French, Italian and American breads. It is open daily for breakfast and lunch.

The Oasis

$$ • 6550 Comanche Tr.
• (512) 266-2441

The rap always was a great view and so-so food, but area food critics have credited new chef Stephen Rafferty with improving the offerings at this lakeside restaurant. The view is great, and the restaurant has a series of outdoor decks that hang onto the cliffs, offering diners an especially stunning view of the sunset over Lake Travis. The menu focuses on popular Tex-Mex fare and Margaritas. (Read more about The Oasis in our Attractions chapter.)

Threadgill's Restaurant

$$ • 6416 N. Lamar Blvd.
• (512) 451-5440

Janis Joplin sang here at the legendary (a much overused word, but justified) restaurant and club founded by Kenneth Threadgill on a mundane section of N. Lamar Boulevard. Of course, back when Threadgill got a liquor license for the former Gulf gas station, this was the far northern reaches of Austin, practically a rural outpost. "There's music on the menu" is the boast these days, and the mix of Southern hospitality, music and homestyle cooking packs 'em in. A second Threadgill's has opened near downtown (see our South Central listings), and both locations offer similar food, old-fashioned favorites such as chicken-fried steak, fried chicken, meat loaf, hamburgers and lots of veggies. It is open daily for lunch and dinner and until midnight on Friday and Saturday. (Read more about the Threadgill's legacy in The Music Scene chapter.)

Tien Hong

$$ • 8301 Burnet Rd. • (512) 459-2263

Dim sum is Chinese for brunch, and every Saturday and Sunday this North Austin restaurant is packed as patrons enjoy a variety of what might be called Asian noshes. Waiters roam the dining room with steam carts filled with a variety of dumplings, steamed buns, savory tidbits, deep-fried nuggets of meat and seafood, and tiny sweet creations. Hot tea is the preferred beverage. In addition to the offerings created at the whim of the chef, there is a menu, printed in Chinese, Vietnamese and English. Most patrons, and many hail from Austin's growing Asian community, simply look over the carts and point to their choice, but that can be risky for those unfamiliar with dim sum — one delicacy is fried chicken feet. Tien Hong also serves a familiar Chinese menu at lunch and dinner daily. Dim sum is served usually from mid-morning to mid-afternoon on the weekend.

Waterloo Ice House

$ • 8600 Burnet Rd. • (512) 458-6544

This is another homegrown restaurant chain with four locations in the Austin area. This branch of Waterloo features the same all-American menu of burgers, chicken-fried steak and tacos. It is open daily for lunch and dinner.

Northeast

Tres Amigos

$$ • 7535 U.S. Hwy. 290 E.
• (512) 926-4441

The name means "three friends," and that is appropriate for the three Austin locations of this homegrown restaurant. All are touted by longtime Austin residents as friendly restaurants where both the menu and the staff are familiar. Tex-Mex is the theme here and the surroundings evoke Old Mexico. It is open daily for lunch and dinner.

La Palapa

$-$$ • 6640 U.S. Hwy. 290 E. • (512) 459-8729

The thatched roof is a reminder of La Palapa's roots South of the Border — a palapa is a thatched shelter in Mexico. The restaurant has ties to two La Palapas, one in Laredo, the other in Nuevo Laredo, Mexico. Under the thatch, patrons will find several variations on the fajita theme plus enchiladas and Tex-Mex fare. On Saturday nights the restaurant features an all-you-can-eat fajita bar, and Sunday there is an all-you-can-eat lunch buffet. The restaurant's cantina has live music and karaoke on Wednesday, Friday and Saturday nights. La Palapa is open daily for lunch and dinner.

East

Calabash

$$ • 2015 Manor Rd. • (512) 478-4857

Just east of the university campus and I-35, this neighborhood cafe offers customers a chance to sample Caribbean fare. Dishes include jerk chicken and Jamaican-style patties (turnovers), served with island staples such as fried plantains and pigeon peas. In addition to lunch and dinner, Calabash serves Sunday brunch.

Cisco's

$ • 1511 E. Sixth St. • (512) 478-2420

Rudy "Cisco" Cisneros is no longer with us, but his east-side cafe where the likes of President Lyndon B. Johnson took breakfast is still a fixture. The small bakery and restaurant continues to attract the powerful for breakfast or lunch, and the walls are plastered with photos of both current and former politicos. The menu is not extensive, simple Tex-Mex fare is offered along with sweet rolls and cookies from the bakery. Cisco was something of a humorist so the walls are covered with cartoons, jokes and even a sign hung on an old gasoline pump that says: "Out of gasoline, we sell beans." Cisco's is open for breakfast and lunch only.

Eastside Cafe

$-$$ • 2113 Manor Rd. • (512) 476-5858

Those looking for ways to revive older neighborhoods should visit this cafe east of the interstate in an area of the city that is economically depressed. A small, homey cottage has been turned into a thriving enterprise that includes a large kitchen and herb garden plus a cooking and garden shop. The house has been divided into small cozy dining rooms, while outside there are tables on the patio. Visitors can stroll through the kitchen garden before or after brunch, lunch or dinner. The menu is a variety of pastas, enchiladas, grilled fish and chicken dinners and sandwiches and salads. Brunch begins with mimosas (champagne and orange juice) or poinsettias (champagne and cranberry juice), and then patrons can choose from rich waffle dishes or classics such as eggs Florentine, poached eggs on wilted spinach and topped with hollandaise sauce. After dining here, wander through the on-site store where the house salad dressings are sold plus cookware and garden tools. Eastside is open daily for lunch and dinner, brunch on the weekends.

El Azteca

$-$$ • 2600 E. Seventh St. • (512) 477-4701

Wander the Mexican-American neighborhoods of South Texas and you will find family-owned restaurants like El Azteca, where the menu goes beyond the familiar Tex-Mex as served up by many chain restaurants. Cabrito, spit-roasted baby goat, is a house specialty at this East Austin restaurant, about a mile and a half east of the interstate. Another popular dish is the barbacoa de cabeza (barbecued beef head), but don't wince until you have sampled the meat, the moist and tender cheek meat is touted as the best for folding inside a soft flour tortilla. El Azteca also serves carne guisada, a slow-simmered stew that is served with flour tortillas for a lick-your-fingers meal, and chicken mole enchiladas, dressed in the rich chocolate-chile mole sauce. The walls are hung with portraits honoring Mexican President Benito

Juarez and American Presidents Abraham Lincoln and John F. Kennedy plus the assassinated Robert F. Kennedy. The cafe is open for lunch and dinner every day except Sunday.

Mercado Juarez

$$ • 1121 E. Seventh St.
• (512) 457-8110

There are four Dallas-Fort Worth locations and now an Austin branch of Mercado Juarez. The menu features many Tex-Mex staples, enchiladas, fajitas, flautas and chimichangas, but also what might be called more complex and expensive fare. Cabrito al pastor, roasted baby goat, mesquite-grilled Cornish game hens, and grilled, bacon-wrapped shrimp are among the latter category. The restaurant occupies a hacienda-style building just east of the interstate and not far from the lively scene on Sixth Street. It is open daily for lunch and dinner.

Mexico Tipico

$-$$ • 1707 E. Sixth St. • (512) 472-3222

It doesn't have to be a chilly night to enjoy the house specialty at this family-owned Eastside restaurant, but a bowl of caldo (a rich chicken and vegetable soup) is a favorite winter treat. In summer, patrons enjoy the licuados and aguas frescas, fresh fruit drinks made simply with fruit and water in the case of aguas frescas, or milk for licuados. Try a glass of pina agua fresca (pineapple) with a chile relleno, enchiladas or the fajitas. Another house specialty is menudo, the tripe, hominy and chile soup that is claimed to be a hangover cure, and the menu also features cabrito (roasted baby goat) and tamales. Mexico Tipico is a neighborhood cafe where many of the patrons know each other, but it also has loyal following among Austinites from other sections of the city. The decor is typical of a Texas Mexican family restaurant with warm colors and images of the Virgen de Guadalupe taking a place of honor on the wall. On weekend nights there is live mariachi music. It is closed Monday. Breakfast and lunch are served Tuesday through Thursday; breakfast, lunch and dinner, Friday and Saturday.

Nuevo Leon

$-$$ • 1209 E. Seventh St.
• (512) 479-0097

Nuevo Leon offers pink walls, green booths and a menu that is designed to pay homage to the cooking of Northern Mexico and the state of Nuevo Leon. The dishes make it plain that Texas once was part of Old Mexico, and many of the featured items are found on South Texas Mexican cafe menus — beef and vegetable caldo (soup), fajitas, rib-eye steak with ranchero sauce, and a burrito dressed with chili. Lunch and dinner are served weekdays, breakfast lunch and dinner on weekends.

Sam's Bar-B-Cue

$, no credit cards • 2000 E. 12th St.
• (512) 478-0378

Sam's biggest fan was famed guitarist Stevie Ray Vaughan, and the walls of this authentic barbecue joint are an homage to the late musician with pictures and newspaper clippings. The menu is simple: brisket, chicken, sausage and ribs plus spicy beans and potato salad. Take-out is available at this humble neighborhood cafe. Lunch and dinner are served daily.

Southeast

Catfish Parlour

$$ • 4705 E. Ben White Blvd.
• (512) 443-1698

For more than two decades Catfish Parlour has been pulling in the crowds for all-you-can-eat catfish and more. Both baked and fried catfish are served plus fried shrimp and chicken. The menu has Cajun touches with hush puppies and gumbo plus there is a large salad bar. It is open daily for lunch and dinner.

Marisco's Seafood

$ • 1504 Town Creek Dr.
• (512) 462-9119

In search of an authentic neighborhood restaurant? Marisco's is housed in an A-frame building, east of I-35, on a busy street. The food here is very cheap and simple; seafood entrees are simply prepared, either boiled, fried or broiled, but there are Mexican touches such as the vuelve la vida (back to the good life) seafood cocktail, ceviche and seafood soup. Marisco's is open daily for lunch and dinner.

Round Rock

Antonio's Mexican Restaurant & Cantina

$-$$ • 16912 N. I-35, Round Rock • (512) 238-8969

There's live music at this lively Mexican restaurant where traditional Tex-Mex fare has a few new twists. The restaurant touts its pechugas de pollo (chicken breasts) that are served stuffed with a variety of ingredients. The most requested is the pechugas Antonio, stuffed with Monterey Jack cheese, mushrooms and bacon, breaded and deep fried, then topped with chile con queso. Antonio's has an adjoining bar with big-screen TV and live music on Friday and Saturday. It is open daily for lunch and dinner. Take-out is popular here. It is open daily for lunch and dinner.

Bob's Barbecue

$ • 1601 S. I-35, Exit 251, Round Rock • (512) 255-4840

A family-owned and operated barbecue restaurant, Bob's boasts a house specialty — a plate-sized chicken-fried steak with the special house mashed potatoes. The barbecue menu includes pork loin, ribs, brisket and chicken, all part of the lunch buffet. Don't stop with meat and potatoes, Bob's offers pecan pie, mud pie, peach cobbler and carrot cake for dessert. Bob's is open daily for lunch and dinner.

Chisholms

$$-$$$ • 901 Round Rock Ave., Round Rock • (512) 244-1830

Named after the nearby historic Chisholm Trail, this restaurant is housed in a renovated 1848 stagecoach depot. Patrons can sit on the veranda and imagine the days when cattle were being driven north on the trail, which is just a stone's throw from the restaurant. Top-quality Angus beef, fresh seafood and pasta dishes are on the menu here. Prime rib and smoked baby back pork ribs are two of the favorites. It is open daily for lunch and dinner.

Hunan Lion

$$ • 1208-R I-35, Round Rock • (512) 244-0117

The original Hunan Lion is in Southwest Austin (see our listing), but the success of the original prompted the opening of this second branch in Round Rock, a growing sector of the metropolitan area. The Chinese cuisine focuses on seafood, but there are also classics such as Beijing duck. The same elegant setting created at the Southwest location is duplicated here. It is open for lunch and dinner daily.

Pok-E-Jo's Smokehouse

$-$$ • 1202 N. I-35, Round Rock • (512) 388-7578

The Round Rock branch of a popular Austin barbecue chain, Pok-E-Jo's serves mesquite-smoked meats, including ribs, pork, beef, ham, pork loin, sausage, turkey and chicken. have hailed the pizza here as the closest they have found in Austin to New York-style pizza with its yeasty crust. There are other old faithfuls on the menu, including pasta dishes, and on weekends there can a be wait for a table. Reale's is open for lunch Monday through Saturday.

Serrano's Cafe & Cantina

$$ • 910 Round Rock Ave., Round Rock • (512) 218-8880

Given the proliferation and popularity of Serrano's in Austin, it was inevitable they would open a Round Rock branch. The same Tex-Mex dishes are served here in a lively, colorful atmosphere. House specialties include several kinds of fajitas including, pork, shrimp, beef, chicken and veggie. It is open daily for lunch and dinner.

Taste of Hungary

$ • 900 Palm Valley Rd., Round Rock • (512) 218-1036

Mushroom goulash crepes, chicken paprika, fresh dill homemade cottage cheese pasta with bacon — Hungarian favorites are the order of the day at this cozy restaurant. Original Hungarian seasonings and fresh ingredients are a kitchen mandate. In addition to lunch and dinner, the cafe also offers a picnic menu — hot mushroom sandwich with salad, hot ham sandwich and meat loaf sandwich. If you are a firefighter, senior citizen, police officer or a Dell Computer worker with a badge, you will get a discount. Diners may bring a bottle of wine or beer to enjoy with their meal. It is open for lunch and dinner Tuesday through Saturday.

The Inn at Brushy Creek

$$$$ • 1000 N. I-35, Round Rock • (512) 255-2555

The inn is housed in the oldest house in Round Rock, built in the 1850s and for many years a stagecoach stop on the Chisholm Trail. In 1972, the inn became a restaurant and now serves continental food with touches of the Southwest. Among the favorites are blackened snapper with a white wine and shrimp sauce, Chateaubriand and shrimp and scallops sauteed with garlic, parsley, cilantro, lemon and butter. The inn underwent an ownership change in early 1998, but the new owners insisted they would simply add to the familiar favorites. In the past, the inn had no liquor license and patrons could bring their wine to enjoy with dinner, but the new owners have said they will seek a license. Call ahead for reservations and information on the status of the wine list. The Inn is open for lunch and dinner Tuesday through Saturday.

Pflugerville

Dodge City Steakhouse

$$-$$$ • 111 E. Main St., Pflugerville • (512) 251-3082

A historic building in downtown Pflugerville has been turned into a popular steakhouse, which boasts a "mile-wide salad bar." The fare is all-American with steaks and homestyle accompaniments. It is open for lunch and dinner Thursday through Sunday.

Cedar Park

Brick Oven Restaurant

$ • 11200 Lakeline Mall, Cedar Park • (512) 335-5445

This new location of an old Austin favorite is a popular gathering spot for moviegoers at the nearby Lakeline Mall. The menu features pizza baked in a wood-fired oven. Customers can choose from a variety of toppings, thin or thick crust, even an all-garlic pizza. The menu also features other Italian-American staples and salads. Brick Oven is open daily for lunch and dinner.

China Cafe

$-$$ • 13729 N. U.S. Hwy. 183, Cedar Park • (512) 331-7747

How about a movie and Chinese for dinner? The cafe's location near the Lake Creek cinema complex makes this a popular spot for a pre- or post-movie dinner. The menu features a variety of well-known Chinese dishes with an emphasis on spicy dishes. There are also low-fat and vegetarian entrees, and the cafe offers take-out and delivery within a 3-mile radius. It is open daily for lunch and dinner.

Reale's Pizza & Cafe

$-$$ • 13450 N. U.S. Hwy. 183, Cedar Park • (512) 335-5115

Resident Yankees at *The Austin Chronicle* have hailed the pizza here as the closest they have found in Austin to New York-style pizza with its yeasty crust. There are other old faithfuls on the menu, including pasta dishes, and on weekends there can a be wait for a table. Reale's is open for lunch Monday through Saturday.

Saccone's Pizza

$ • 2701-A U.S. Hwy. 183, Leander • (512) 259-1882

There must be something about the northwest edge of Austin that attracts northerners, specifically pizza makers. Just as Reale's is hailed for its New York-style pizza, Saccone's has been described as "a slice of Hoboken." The small spartan cafe is just beyond Cedar Park on the edge of Leander, but it attracts the faithful from early morning to night. The menu also features hot and cold subs, calzones and stromboli. It is open for breakfast, lunch and dinner daily.

Serrano's Cafe & Cantina

$$ • 12233 F.M. 620, Cedar Park • (512) 918-8181

Another of the popular chain, this Serrano's serves the same Tex-Mex dishes in a lively, colorful atmosphere. House specialties include several kinds of fajitas including, pork, shrimp, beef, chicken and veggie. It is open daily for lunch and dinner.

A Word About Ice Cream

It's hard to beat a cold cup of ice cream on a balmy night as a fitting end to an evening out. There are several Austin small businesses that offer "handmade" ice cream. Perhaps the most famous is Amy's, which began in a single store but now has four outlets and packs ice cream for sale in local shops and restaurants. Patrons pick their flavor and toppings and watch as they are hand beaten to a yummy, creamy, but cold consistency on marble counters.

All four locations are open late, the two downtown at Sixth treet and Guadalupe Street are open until 1 AM on weekends. Look for the big moving cows on the outer wall of Amy's at 1012 W. Sixth Street, (512) 480-0673. Other locations are 3500 Guadalupe Street, (512) 458-6895; 10000 Research Boulevard at the Arboretum in Northwest Austin, (512) 345-1006; and 3300 Bee Caves Road in West Austin, (512) 328-9859.

The Hyde Park neighborhood in Central Austin is home to the Dolce Vita Gelato and Espresso Bar, 4222 Duval Street, (512) 323-2686. This neighborhood coffee shop and Italian-style gelateria opens early for breakfast and stays open late for gelato.

Romina Derra, a native of Milan, Italy, thought Austin needed an authentic gelateria downtown, so he opened Milano's Gelateria at 217 W. Fourth Street, (512) 326-9492. In the heart of the busy warehouse district, this heavenly little piece of Italy serves late into the night. The offerings change as Derra takes the fresh fruit and flavors of the season and creates the kind of ice cream, rich with flavor, that visitors to Italy remember.

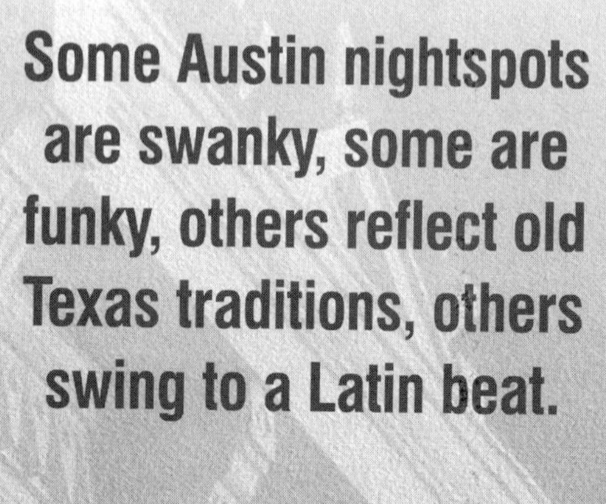

Some Austin nightspots are swanky, some are funky, others reflect old Texas traditions, others swing to a Latin beat.

Nightlife

Austin's nightlife is so vibrant we had to divide it into two chapters: one, The Music Scene is a comprehensive look at the musicians and clubs that have made it possible for Austin to claim the title Live Music Capital of the World; the second, this chapter, also lists a great many music and dance venues, and it takes a look at some of the other spots where residents and visitors gather after the sun goes down.

Some places are swanky, some are funky, others reflect old Texas traditions, and still others swing to a Latin beat. Austin after dark can be a quiet glass of wine in a subdued, sophisticated setting; or a cold brew among friends at a cheery pub; perhaps a shot of tequila and a salsa dance; a glass of sherry with tapas; a beach blanket bingo movie with Coke and pizza; or an evening of satire with Austin's favorite comedy troupe.

One thing that is constant about the Austin Nightlife scene is it is evolving and growing by leaps and bounds. Every month there are new faces on the evening scene as the menu of choices grows. We have divided this chapter into Bars — further subdivided into Sixth Street Bars and Sports Bars — Brewpubs and Pubs; Coffeehouses; Comedy Clubs; Dance Clubs and Nightclubs; The Gay Nightlife Scene; and Movie Houses.

Austin swings every night, and most clubs and bars are open every day, except where we have noted in the listings. Where there is music, either live or electronic, there is likely to be a cover charge of a few dollars, but rarely do those covers top $10. Bars must stop serving alcohol at 2 AM by Texas law and no one younger than 21 can be served, though some clubs do admit them. Driving-while-intoxicated laws are very strict, and bar owners are also held responsible under the state's liquor licensing laws for making sure customers do not overindulge. Taxis cruise the city's major nightlife areas, and patrons who overindulge are wise to take a ride home.

Given the vast and growing number of nightspots in Austin, it is impossible to list them all. Here, we have attempted to give an overview, a wide sampling of the nightspots both residents and visitors enjoy.

Bars

Cedar Door

910 W. Cesar Chavez St.
• (512) 473-3712

When they built the Cedar Door, they should have put wheels on the building. That would have saved this cherished neighborhood-style bar some money. The Door has moved, literally, several times — the original location is now occupied by a high-rise on 12th Street downtown. Originally, a typical Austin cottage-turned-bar, it now sits on stilts on what was a landfill at the corner of Cesar Chavez Street and Lamar Boulevard, just north of Town Lake. A popular watering hole for bureaucrats, politicos and journalists, it has all the hallmarks of an old favorite with mismatched chairs and tables, old prints and posters plus bartenders who know their regulars well. The outdoor deck is a popular late afternoon spot since it affords customers a view of Town Lake.

INSIDERS' TIP

The latest hot dancing trend in Austin is the tango. Austin Tango Connection, (512) 480-9899, is dedicated to spreading the word and has information about classes, practices and dance locations.

Cedar Street Courtyard

208 W. Fourth St. • (512) 495-9669

If you are allergic to cigar smoke, sit out on the patio of this hip bar in the heart of the downtown warehouse district. The renovated buildings here designed by one of Austin's most noted architects, Sinclair Black, who still has his offices on the second floor, and the courtyard still bears the mark of a master designer with restored limestone walls and sculpture. Jazz, martinis and, of course, cigars are on the menu here.

Chambers Bar

700 San Jacinto St. • (512) 476-3700

This is a posh cigar bar in the Omni Hotel, just west of Congress Avenue in the heart of downtown Austin. The sophisticated bar offers whiskey, cognac and other appropriate accompaniments to a grand stogie, all served in a modern, sophisticated, quiet setting.

The Cloak Room

1300 Colorado St. • (512) 478-2622

You will have to look hard for this little bar tucked away in the basement of an old building immediately west of the west door of the capitol. Inside is a cozy piano bar, just the place to gather after a hard day of doing the "people's business," which is why it is so popular with workers at the capitol. It is also a refuge on hot days and a good place to rest after touring the capitol grounds.

Club DeVille

900 Red River St. • (512) 457-0900

Club DeVille is a romantic bar with a homey feel. The guys who founded this warehouse-district club did so because they needed a place to hold their regular weekend cocktail parties. One newspaper critic has described the decor as "hanging out in Grandma's basement while she's in Florida." But instead of turning on Grandma's reading lamps, there are candles on the table and you can actually hear what your table mate is saying. There is also a large outdoor deck equipped with funky furniture and blankets for chilly nights. The bar does get busy on the weekends, but the relaxed atmosphere is constant.

Driskill Hotel Lobby Bar

117 E. Seventh St. • (512) 474-5911

The venerable Driskill Hotel (see our Hotels chapter) is like an island of style amid the cacophony of Sixth Street. The lobby's cool marble floors and pillars, ornate gilt mirrors and chairs a person can sink into make for a plush surrounding for the hotel's piano bar. The half-price-appetizer happy hour draws people in, and they often stay to unwind to the sounds of classic lounge hits played on the grand piano. Later in the evening, folks gather around and even join in as the old romantic hits are played.

Electric Lounge

302 Bowie St. • (512) 476-FUSE

The Electric Lounge is listed in The Music Scene chapter since it is a well-known venue for live music, but this club is also known for its lively happy hour, during which Mariachi Estrella, a Mexican mariachi band, plays plus weekly poetry slams and other eclectic offerings reflecting the diversity of Austin's cultural scene. The bar is a friendly place where many of the customers are regulars.

The Elephant Room

315 Congress Ave. • (512) 473-2279

This smoky, dark basement bar in the heart of downtown is a longtime gathering spot for jazz aficionados. For more information about the jazz scene at the Elephant Room, see The Music Scene chapter.

Four Seasons Lobby Bar

98 San Jacinto Blvd. • (512) 478-4500

The lobby bar of this downtown luxury hotel (see our Hotels chapter) is a great place to people-watch. The patrons here might be top Texas business people, foreign investors, high-tech wizards, top name musicians and movie stars, politicians or media personalities. The color palette is a gentle range of beige and neutral tones, and the furniture is a mix of rustic antiques and luxurious Southwestern pieces, some covered in leather or cowhide. During the biennial legislative session, many of the state's political leaders take advantage of the hotel's extended lease terms and hang their hats here for the duration of the 120-day session. That ensures that a great deal of politicking and lobbying goes on here as folks work the room, passing from table to table. The bar offers an extensive list of single malt whiskey and cognac plus wine and snacks, none of them inexpensive. In the afternoons, tea and sandwiches are available.

Louie's 106

106 E. Sixth St. • (512) 476-2010

Although a Sixth Street bar, we chose to put this in our general Bar category to place it apart from the Sixth Street scene, which it clearly is. Like its neighbor, the Driskill Hotel, Louie's 106 is a classy haven far from the rowdy spirit of Sixth Street. In addition to being a popular, topnotch restaurant (see our Restaurants chapter), Louie's is also home to a cigar bar and a tapas bar. There are several tapas bars in Austin, but Louie's was the first — tapas are those Spanish noshes served after the sun goes down and intended to feed body and spirit until dinnertime (around 11 PM or midnight in Spain). Tapas might include a variety of olives, room-temperature savory omelettes called tortillas in Spain, or a selection of Spanish ham and sausages, all of which can be nibbled along with a glass of sherry or wine. Louie's has a wide selection of wine, whiskey and cognac to go along with either tapas or a fine cigar.

Malaga's Wine and Tapas Bar

208 W. Fourth St. • (512) 236-8020

A recent entry to the warehouse district scene, this wine and tapas bar is inspired by the wonderful Spanish tradition of nibbling on savories while drinking sherry or wine. Malaga's occupies an airy, narrow limestone-walled space next door to Cedar Street Courtyard. There is a full bar, and noshes can be ordered until 2 AM on weekends and midnight during the week and Sunday.

Manuel's

310 Congress Ave. • (512) 472-7555

This Congress Avenue restaurant (see our Restaurants chapter) is also a good place to end a workday with their half-price appetizer happy hour, or wind up an evening with a late night snack at the bar. There is also jazz music, either live or on tape, and an atmosphere that is hip and relaxed.

Rhythm House

624 W. 34th St. • (512) 458-4411

Rhythm House is a Spanish-style restaurant that features an extensive tapas menu. The bar at Rhythm House is open until midnight daily and until 1 AM on Saturday so that patrons can nibble and listen to acoustic music on the patio. The tapas menu includes tortillas (Spanish omelettes served at room temperature), olives, cuts of ham and cheese plus sausage and other Spanish appetizers that go well with wine and sherry.

Star Bar

600 W. Sixth St. • (512) 477-8550

Just beyond the downtown warehouse district, W. Sixth Street is developing into the hottest spot in town for new restaurants and bars. Star Bar once was a paint shop, but the '50s-style building is now a very hip place to be seen and to watch Austin's 20-something set at play. The store's big plate-glass window looks out on a small street-side patio, while inside the low ceiling and retro furnishings give the place an intimate, jazzy sort of feel. Martinis and cocktails are the order of the day, and sipping a gin sling while posed on a bar stool is quite the thing.

Westside Alley

416 Congress Ave. • (512) 708-9477

A new addition to the downtown scene, Westside Alley is for the martini and cigar set. The decor is upscale, and the clientele young urban professionals.

Sixth Street Bars

When Austinites refer to "Sixth Street," they generally are referring to the strip that runs between I-35 and Congress Avenue. The street does have numerous nightspots and restaurants west of Congress, but the original Sixth Street scene, the place that is blocked off to auto traffic on major holidays including Halloween and New Year's Eve, is the section east of Congress.

A word about the bar scene on Sixth: Although some bars and nightclubs have survived the economic ups and downs and the fickle tastes of the public, many are constantly closing and reopening with a new theme or a new look. In the late 1970s and early '80s, Sixth Street was a mix of a few new bars, a new restaurant or two and some longtime tenants, including an African-American blues-barbecue joint, a charity shop, a paint store, a drugstore and a Mexican cantina. Over the years, the old neighborhood spots have been closed, and bars, nightclubs and restaurants now line the street.

Some old-timers miss the diverse flavor of the street and don't like the "Bourbonization" of Sixth Street, but it is a major tourist draw, and it is home to several famed music venues (see The Music Scene chapter). The scene can get rowdy, and visitors should be careful to watch their valuables and avoid dark alleys behind the bars. A special police patrol does monitor Sixth Street activity carefully.

Here is a sampling of some of the Sixth Street bars with an eye to giving you the flavor of the street.

Bob Popular

402 E. Sixth St. • (512) 478-3352

Social scientists wanting to observe *homo fraternitus* at play will head to this Sixth Street lounge where young men enjoy taking to the karaoke stage to relieve themselves of any notion that they will be anything else but lawyers, doctors and businessmen after they graduate. Disco is also popular here, and there is an upstairs pool and game room plus an outdoor patio for quieter moments.

Casino El Camino

517 E. Sixth St. • (512) 469-9330

There is a literally and figuratively a dark feel to this Sixth Street bar — *The Austin Chronicle* describes it as "post-apocalyptic." The dimly lit interior stands in stark contrast to the noise and glare of the street outside, but while you wait for the apocalypse, you can play pool, have a beer and watch the "psychotronic" movies.

Cheers Shot Bar

416 E. Sixth St. • (512) 499-0093

Shot bars are the latest trend on Sixth Street, and this one is just wide enough to allow patrons to tip their tiny glasses of tequila, schnapps or whatever is the fashionable slammer of the moment. This is not the place for a leisurely sip or two of something mellow by anyone of a mellow age.

Hot Shots Bar

500-A E. Sixth St. • (512) 499-0863

Touted as a way to jump-start the evening, Hot Shots offers cheap shots of booze plus beer and mixed drinks. The pace here is lively, and the drinks are served against the background noise of loud television featuring whatever the bartenders find when they flip the dial. A young crowd makes this a regular stop several times a night as they cruise the street.

Iron Cactus

606 Trinity St. • (512) 472-9240

The address says Trinity, but this corner bar and grill has one of the prime people-watching spots on Sixth Street. Its rooftop patio is the place to watch the Sixth Street crowds, especially on special nights like Halloween and New Year's Eve when cover charges and reservations are necessary. The menu of this popular bar at the corner of Trinity and Sixth features an extensive variety of Margaritas.

INSIDERS' TIP

Looking for a unique nightlife experience? The Ceramic Mug, 520 W. Sixth Street, (512) 472-6840, just west of the warehouse district, offers customers a chance to decorate their own ceramic ware while sipping something from the coffee bar. You buy the bisqueware, but the paints, glazing and firing are free. Housed in an old gas station, the studio is open until midnight on Friday, 10 PM during the week and Saturday and until 6 PM on Sunday.

Joe's Generic Bar

315 E. Sixth St. • (512) 480-0171

With all the trendy bars on Sixth, Joe's features a comfy, generic theme. But it also boasts a cast of colorful patrons who enjoy the blues music featured here.

Kenny Luna's Ivory Cat Tavern

300 E. Sixth St. • (512) 478-5287

Singalong piano bars are another popular trend on Sixth Street. This piano bar has the patrons bellying up to the bar to wet their whistles after a round or two of lively singing.

The Library

407 E. Sixth St.• (512) 236-0662

With all the Dellionaires (those lucky Austinites who bought Dell stock at $15 several years ago before it skyrocketed and starting splitting every few months) in town, it was inevitable the Austin night scene would develop a trend towards upscale bars with posh settings, hence the arrival of this new Sixth Street bar with its clubby decor. This has become a popular spot for the university Greek crowd.

Logan's on Sixth

200 E. Sixth St. • (512) 236-0300

Sixth Street goes through periodic evolutions, and in 1998 there was a move to give some of the bars a classy look. Logan's joined the trend sporting a clubby look with wood paneling and brass decorative touches, a Sixth street version of the private downtown business club.

Paradise

401 E. Sixth St. • (512) 476-5667

Back in 1981, Paradise opened up as Sixth Street's first fern bar. While others have come and gone, the Paradise stays on offering drinks and a food menu. Of course, some of the ferns here are older than the customers.

Pete's Piano Bar

421 E. Sixth St. • (512) 472-PETE

If drinking makes your singing better, or makes you think your singing is better, this is the place to go. Dubbed a "Texas-sized singalong bar" Pete's offers peanuts, pianos and plenty of lively music and fun.

Touché

417 E. Sixth St. • (512) 472-9841

One of several skinny shot bars on Sixth Street, this narrow room attracts patrons who want to cruise the district, stopping every few hundred feet or so for a shot or slammer. It is usually packed and popular on weekends.

Wylie's Bar & Grill

400 E. Sixth St. • (512) 472-3712

Even before fern bars came to Sixth Street, there was Wylie's. This bar and grill was one of the first renovations on the street and has been operating for almost two decades. No gimmicks here, just a friendly place where you can sip a beer, order a hamburger and watch the Sixth Street scene from the front bay windows.

Sports Bars

In addition to the sports bars listed here, check the subsequent Brewpub section since many local pubs also turn on the TV when there is a hot sports event.

Aussie's Volleyball and Grill

306 Barton Springs Rd. • (512) 480-0952

Volleyball takes center stage at this South Central Austin bar and grill (see our Restaurants chapter), but sports enthusiasts also gather at the bar to watch sporting events on several television sets. A favorite drink is, of course, Foster's, the national beer of Australia, mate.

BW-3

218 E. Sixth St. • (512) 472-7227

Buffalo wings and football; buffalo wings and baseball; buffalo wings and basketball. You get the picture. (Hence the name BW-3.) This Sixth Street bar is known for its variety of buffalo (chicken) wings and friendly, laid-back atmosphere. There are 18 television sets and three big-screens for sports viewing. In addition to buffalo wings, the bar has other all-American food offerings to go along with the 23-ounce beers. BW-3 is popular at lunch and crowded in the evenings.

Legend's

8901 Business Park Dr. • (512) 343-0888

Housed in the Holiday Inn in Northwest

Austin, Legend's focus is simply sports, cold beer and all-American fare. This is the quintessential sports bar: the 22 televisions are always tuned to sports, and the menu features food like hamburgers and steaks. Occasionally, there is a cover charge when special sports broadcasts are scheduled.

Player's Sports Bar & Billiards

1779 Wells Branch Pkwy. • (512) 252-3056

This North Austin bar caters to sports fans from the nearby Wells Branch neighborhood who enjoy watching games with friends and a cold beer. The bar also has several billiards tables and hosts darts games on Monday night.

Shoal Creek Saloon and Sports Parlor

909 N. Lamar Blvd. • (512) 477-0600

New Orleans Saints fans are drawn to this Central Austin sports bar, perhaps because the pub's menu features Cajun dishes like gumbo and fried catfish. If the Saints are not winning, patrons can eat well.

Texas Sports Palace

9504 N. I-35 • (512) 835-9717

Housed inside Showplace Lanes, a North Austin bowling alley, the Texas Sports Palace offers patrons the next best thing to being at the game. Several big-screen televisions and a state-of-the art sound system add to your experience of the event, be it a regularly scheduled game or a pay-for-view event, all in cool, dark surroundings.

Warehouse Saloon & Billiards

509 E. Ben White Blvd. • (512) 443-8799

This large pool hall is also home to a sports bar where patrons can watch regularly televised events or pay-for-view specials. In addition to 25 tables, the Warehouse also offers video games, pinball and shuffleboard.

Brewpubs and Pubs

In 1993, the Texas Legislature permitted homemade brew products to be sold in public bars, despite the opposition of the big breweries and beer distributors. Microbreweries are as fashionable as coffeehouses these days, and Austin has its share. One prominent local brewer is Celis, where visitors can tour the facility of this Belgian-style brewery and sample the product (see our Attractions chapter).

The Bitter End

311 Colorado St. • (512) 478-2337

A brewpub that has a classy, urban air, The Bitter End is also a popular bistro (see our Restaurants chapter) and offers patrons a opportunity to nibble on some great appetizers, along with a sampler tray of house brews. The bar overlooks the bistro, and the pub's brewing equipment stands in front of the bistro and can be seen through the front window, adding an interesting design element to this converted warehouse. There is a sophisticated but relaxed atmosphere here, attracting crowds on the weekends. The pub brews several English-style beers and two specialty brews, including EZ Wheat, the pub's biggest seller; Aberdeen Amber, a Scottish-style export; Bitter End Bitter; Austin Pale Ale; and Honey Mead Ale. Not all brews are available all the time, but there are always several choices on hand. The snack menu includes calamari, grilled vegetables with French bread and a smoked meat sampler plus wood-fired pizzas.

Copper Tank Brewing Company

504 Trinity St. • (512) 478-8444

This Sixth Street brewpub attracts a diverse crowd, including a large college contingent and sports fan drawn there by the bank of big-screen televisions. Local brewery critics give Copper Tank high marks for its brews like Big Dog Brown Ale and Firehouse Stout. Lighter fare is offered, including White Tail Pale Ale, Copper Lite and River City Raspberry. Happy hour on Wednesdays draws a large crowd, and the bar is popular among downtown workers who want a cold one on hot days.

The Crown & Anchor

2911 San Jacinto Blvd. • (512) 322-9168

This UT campus-area pub is popular among students and perennial campus habitues. The aim here is to re-create an English pub, hence the dartboards and the wide selection of beers. Patrons can play pinball, Foosball and video

Photo: Courtesy of the Texas Department of Transportation

The "Cotton-Eyed Joe" gives you a chance to kick up your heels. Don't worry, we'll teach you.

games and order a burger if they get hungry after a lively game. In balmy weather, patrons can enjoy a beer on the patio.

The Dog & Duck Pub

406 W. 17th St. • (512) 479-0598

This Central Austin bar is as close as Austin gets to an authentic English pub. The food here reflects a mix of English pub grub and popular American dishes (see our Restaurants chapter), and the bar offers, like any English pub, a wide variety of beers on tap and in bottles. The atmosphere here is authentic, also — the dartboard is busy, and the bar is decorated with an assortment of mugs, bottles, knickknacks and souvenirs, and the bartenders are friendly. Many of the patrons are regulars. This is an especially good place to go on a rainy, cold afternoon, sip a Guinness, order some fish and chips and imagine you're back in the Old Country.

The Draught Horse

4112 Medical Pkwy. • (512) 452-MALT

This pub is a neighborhood fixture in Central Austin, just north of the 35th Street medical and shopping district. From the outside it looks like a reproduction of an English country town pub. Inside, the cozy atmosphere attracts a loyal clientele. In addition to stocking 80 different beer brands, the pub has been experimenting with several homemade brews, including a stout produced from an 1850 India Pale Ale recipe from Guinness. Other brews include Old Knucklehead, a traditional-style ale; Midland Cream Ale, a light draft; and Hammerhead Super Stout, a hearty stout that lives up to its name.

Fadó

214 W. Fourth St. • (512) 457-0172

Stepping into this Irish pub in the downtown warehouse district, you almost expect to see John Wayne and Maureen O'Hara at the next table. It's not because the place looks like an old Irish pub, but because it looks more like the Hollywood-set version of an Irish pub. In addition to a menu of Irish-inspired dishes (see our Restaurants chapter), the bar offers a wide selection of beer and whiskey, and the televisions in the bar tune in to satellite transmissions of rugby games, Gaelic football and hurling.

The Ginger Man

303 W. Fourth St. • (512) 473-8801

A favorite pub for those who want a quiet

spot downtown, The Ginger Man has a large selection of beers on tap, which can be quaffed in the cozy, dark interior or out on the patio in back of the bar. Inside, customers can sip their suds while settled on one of the couches, just like home. True to pub tradition, there is a dartboard. Local bands perform on the weekends on the outdoor patio.

Katie Bloom's

419 E. Sixth St. • (512) 472-2528

The building used to be home to the now defunct Armadillo Brewing Company, but now focuses on a wide variety of on tap and bottled beers, all served in an authentic pub setting. It is a popular spot among college students and the younger set making the Sixth Street scene.

Lovejoy's

604 Neches St. • (512) 477-1268

The tables here are created from manhole covers, a coffin serves as a coffee table, and the walls are covered with the work of local artists. The seating ranges from comfy couches to tables and chairs where patrons can enjoy bar food including empanadas, Cornish pasties (meat and potato-filled turnovers), tamales and pretzels. Some of the food items are hearty enough to qualify as lunch. This downtown pub also has two pool tables for a leisurely game. Beer lovers will find an extensive menu of bottled beers plus several homemade brews. A house specialty is Insomnia Coffee Stout, a strong brew made with coffee. Coffee lovers who don't want beer in their brew can avail themselves of espresso drinks. Other crafted brews include Harper Valley IPA (India Pale Ale) and Samson's Best Draft Ale, named after the owner's dog.

Maggie Mae's Long Bar

512 Trinity St. • (512) 478-8541

This well-known Sixth Street bar has grown with the years from a narrow, single-room pub noted for its live-music offerings (see The Music Scene chapter) to a major presence in the downtown nightlife scene. The pub has taken over adjacent buildings and has a rooftop patio for Sixth Street viewing and plans to add a grill. The bar has a pub-like atmosphere and offers a large variety of beers from around the world.

McGillicuddy's Pub and Grill

619 Congress Ave. • (512) 476-4764

Pubs, particularly Irish pubs, are a natural fit for the Austin lifestyle: casual clothes, a cold brew, a snack or two — life doesn't get much better. McGillicuddy's creates the feel of an Irish pub, offering nine drafts and 35 bottled selections plus soups, sandwiches and salads all within a few blocks of the capitol. Darts, pool and TV sports coverage are offered upstairs in the sports lounge.

Old Pecan St. Ale House & Soccer Bar

310 E. Sixth St. • (512) 478-2491

The name says it all here at this cozy Sixth Street alley pub where the emphasis is on soccer. The pub, which is under the same roof as Pecan Street Cafe, is one of the earliest entries in the Sixth Street renaissance. It serves a variety of beers, mixed drinks and snacks in the same surroundings as the cafe — old limestone walls and well-worn floors, cozy seating and dimmed lighting. The pub's television sets feature national and international soccer games.

Waterloo Brewing Company & American Grill

401 Guadalupe St. • (512) 477-1836

Waterloo, named after Austin's original moniker (see our History chapter), became the first brewpub in Texas after the State Legislature gave the go-ahead in 1993. The pub occupies what was a large downtown paint store. The first floor is now a restaurant (see our Restaurants chapter) while the

INSIDERS' TIP

Want to experience a real Texas country dance hall? Head for The Coupland Dance Hall, (512) 856-2226, on Texas Highway 95 between Taylor and Elgin, east of Austin. On weekends this old dance hall is "just a two-step back in time," as it's slogan says.

second-floor [illegible] d rooftop deck are where t[illegible] rs gather. The brewery produ[illegible] lara (Klair-rah's Klaah-rah), a golden ale inspired by Czech beer; Ed's Best Bitter, a traditional English bitter; Sam Houston's Austin Lager, a Vienna-style lager; Waterloo Dunkel Weizen, a German-style wheat beer; O Henry's Porter, a stout; and Guy Town India Pale Ale. The brewery also produces One Ton Stout, which takes, you guessed it, a ton of grain to brew 14 barrels.

Coffeehouses

503 Coffee Bar

503 W. Oltorf St. • (512) 462-0804

There is a relaxed, laid-back feel to this South Austin java joint not far from the St. Edward's University campus. The exterior is decorated with murals; inside, the couches, bookcases and assorted tables give the place a true coffeehouse aura dare we say groovy? Some come here for a quick jolt, others to ponder the Muse, or just to chat and relax with friends. There is a patio out back where customers can enjoy a cup of coffee or a beer. Light snacks are on the menu. Given its location near St. Ed's, it is busy in the morning. The coffeehouse is open daily and closes at midnight Sunday through Thursday, and 1 AM on weekends.

Austin Java Company

1206 Parkway • (512) 476-1829

Austin old-timers and returning visitors may remember the large, revolving bug that twirled on a pole outside an extermination company near 12th Street and Lamar Boulevard. The colorful bug has gone, and now there is a popular coffeehouse occupying the spot. Inside and out Austin Java Company has a relaxed feel with picnic tables on the deck outside for those who enjoy a little sunshine with their coffee. Among the house specialties here are Vietnamese coffee, mocha shakes and mochachinos, little mocha lattes described by an *Austin American-Statesman* critic as tasting like chocolate cream pie. The cafe has expanded its menu from snacks and pastries and now serves sandwiches, salads and pasta dishes. It is open daily for breakfast, lunch and dinner. The coffeehouse offers a late-night menu until 4 AM on weekends.

Captain Quackenbush's

2120 Guadalupe St. • (512) 472-4477

Quack's, as the UT students call it, is a fixture on The Drag. Lively and sometimes noisy at night, Quack's also offers work areas for aspiring poets and playwrights to plug in their laptops. The cafe hosts a weekly poetry workshop under the auspices of Austin Poets At Large (APAL). The work of local artists is featured on the walls, and classical music plays in the background. In addition to work areas, Quack's also has comfy conversation areas where friends can gather for breakfast, lunch and late-night snacks. On the menu are muffins, pastries, soups and sandwiches. Quack's is open until midnight Sunday through Thursday and until 1 AM on Friday and Saturday nights.

Dolce Vita Gelato and Espresso Bar

4222 Duval St. • (512) 323-2686

The name means the sweet life, and there are layers of meaning to that phrase for this Hyde Park-area coffeehouse. The menu is rich with sweets, many with an Italian flavor — gelato, sorbet, granitas, tiramisu, cannoli — and there is also a relaxed, easy-living European atmosphere at this neighborhood cafe. The menu also features Italian sodas, coffees, a full bar, and a variety of cognac, whiskey, liqueur and wine. Dolce Vita opens early for breakfast and stays open late for after-theater snacks.

Ebony Sun Java House

1209 E. 11th St. • (512) 419-7517

This east side coffeehouse is a popular gathering spot for many of the city's minority artists involved in both the musical, literary and visual arts. Evenings are set aside for jazz and poetry. The coffeehouse is run by the ProArts Collective, an arts group that seeks to have an "integrated, cohesive arts community." Hours at the coffeehouse vary depending on planned events. The telephone number listed is for the collective's director.

Flipnotics

1601 Barton Springs Rd. • (512) 322-9750

If the oversized cafe au lait doesn't make you flip for Flipnotics, nothing will. Made from whole milk and condensed milk and served in a cup as big as a soup bowl, this coffee treat is "mmm-mmm good!" The coffeehouse is on the second floor of a building on Barton Springs restaurant row, not far from Zilker Park (see our Parks and Recreation and Attractions chapters). Downstairs is a vintage clothing store while Flipnotics occupies the upstairs space and has a large shaded deck in the back on the hillside. Decorated in a space-theme motif, the cafe offers a light menu of sandwiches, muffins and bagels, wine, beer and coffee, of course. In the evening, local musicians often perform. It is open until midnight every night except Sunday when it closes at 11 PM.

High Life Cafe

407 E. Seventh St. • (512) 474-5338

Not far from the maddening crowd on Sixth Street, the High Life Cafe offers a retreat for the busy hustle of downtown. The old limestone building is a quiet haven on weekday afternoons and early weeknights, but does get livelier on the weekends. The decor is down-home comfy with couches, chairs and tables randomly mixed, and there are stacks of books, magazines and newspapers everywhere. Coffee drinks are limited to espresso-based concoctions, but there's also an extensive wine and beer list. Breakfast fare includes eggs steamed by the espresso machine, while lunch and late-night snacks include soups and sandwiches. The cafe also boasts a large humidor. The cafe is open until midnight during the week and 1 AM Friday, Saturday and Sunday.

Little City

916 Congress Ave. • (512) 476-CITY
3403 Guadalupe St. • (512) 467-BEAN

Just a few blocks from the Capitol, the Congress Avenue coffeehouse helped give new meaning to the word "avenue." The French know an avenue as a place to stroll, sit and watch the world go by. Little City was among the first downtown cafes to promote that idea by putting tables and chairs on the wide sidewalks that line the city's main street. This is a popular meeting place for all manner of people who have business, are visiting or simply want to feel the pulse of the city. The cafe serves coffee, tea, juices, granitas (flavored, shaved ices, sort of Italian snow cones), breakfast items like bagels and muffins and lunch and snack food, including sandwiches and savory pastries. There is a second Little City on The Drag, but here the premises are much smaller. Frappes, a mixture of coffee and fruit juices, are a specialty at this cozy shop. Coffee beans also are offered for sale here. Little City is open at both locations until midnight during the week, until 1 AM on Friday and Saturday, and until 9 PM on Sunday.

Metro

2222 Guadalupe St. • (512) 474-5730

This is the only coffeehouse in Austin that is open all the time, and that means the scene is always changing as the customers come and go. The decor is dark and industrial with an atmosphere that might have existed in a German cafe between the wars. Upstairs is dedicated to smokers who have a hard time finding a place to puff in Austin given the city's public smoking laws. The menu includes a variety of coffees, including the popular House Rocket Shake, made with Amy's chocolate ice cream.

Mojo's Daily Grind

2714 Guadalupe St. • (512) 477-6656

A coffee shop with a bohemian bent, Mojo's is popular with UT students and campus habitues. The 19th-century-home-turned-cafe is open 24 hours daily except Sunday

INSIDERS' TIP

The Southwest Brewing News, (512) 443-3607 or (800) 474-7291, publishes the latest brew news in the Southwest. Features on new pubs, awards and taste tests are included in the paper, which can be found in several Austin pubs.

when it is closed. The purple neon lights and the giant coffee mug sign mark the spot. There is a small outdoor seating area in front, and inside the wooden floors and comfy furniture create a cozy atmosphere. Mojo's prides itself on presenting the work of cutting-edge, and sometimes controversial, artists working in a variety of mediums including photography, painting and collage. There are also poetry events held at the cafe; check the listings section of *The Austin Chronicle*. The popular house drink is the Iced Mojo, a cold, creamy brew. Munchie offerings include coffeehouse-style eggs steamed at the espresso machine, bagels, muffins, oatmeal, pastries and empanadas. Beer is also served at Mojo's.

Mozart's Coffee Roasters

3826 Lake Austin Blvd. • (512) 477-2900

Europe meets Texas at this West Austin cafe, which boasts a large deck overlooking Lake Austin a good spot for a late-afternoon cappuccino or a late-night espresso. On Wednesdays and Saturdays local artists perform contemporary music under the stars on the deck, which seats 350 people. In addition to an extensive coffee bar menu, the cafe also serves iced , herbal, flavored and chai (soy-based) teas, granitas, Italian soda, pastries and snacks. There is a juice bar on the premises as well as a bookstore specializing in arts, travel and literature. Mozart's also roasts and sells a variety of coffee beans. Mozart's is open until 11 PM during the week and on Sunday, 1 AM on Friday and Saturday.

Ruta Maya Coffee Company

218 W. Fourth St. • (512) 472-9637

If there is a single coffeehouse that captures the mood and spirit of Austin, it is Ruta Maya, which occupies an old building in the heart of the warehouse district west of Congress Avenue in downtown Austin. The sidewalks around the building were once loading docks and are elevated above street level offering patrons the opportunity to sit in a sidewalk perch and watch the world go by. The patrons here are a true Austin mix, and on any given night you might see young professionals, aging hippies, Jack Kerouac wannabes, even a spinning yogi chanting mantras on a rotating platform.

Ruta Maya serves coffees produced in Latin America. In 1990 the company was formed to help Latin American farmers sell their products and make a fair return. The guiding principle of the company is "*Oportunidades para Las Americas*" — opportunities for the Americas. Funds from the sale of coffee help support cultural and educational studies of Mayan language and culture. The cafe's coffee is sold on the premises and in local grocery stores.

Ruta Maya Negra Lager Beer, brewed in El Salvador at La Constancia Brewery is sold at the coffeehouse. In addition to coffee, the cafe serves soups and snacks. The large wooden doors of the coffeehouse are open every day, no matter the weather. Inside there are regular music events and poetry readings plus a cigar shop. The walls of the coffeehouse are covered in local artwork and notices on all manner of cultural and political events. Ruta Maya is open until 2 AM on weekends and 1 AM during the week and on Sunday.

Saradora's Coffeehouse & Emporium

101 E. Main St., Round Rock • (512) 310-1200

Not all the coffeehouse action is in Austin. This Round Rock cafe is housed in an old building in the heart of the town's historic district. Local artists sell their jewelry and artwork here, and there is live music several nights a week plus open-mike poetry nights Wednesdays. The vintage coffee grinder churns out beans for a variety of coffee drinks, which patrons can sip in comfortable surroundings decorated with antiques. Saradora's is open until 10 PM during the week and midnight on Friday and Saturday.

Spider House

2908 Fruth St. • (512) 480-9562

This coffeehouse just north of University of Texas campus is packed with old stuff — not really antiques and not really junk, just old stuff like Christmas lights and soft drink machines, old radios and a miscellany of chairs and tables. The large outdoor deck is a stage for local musicians, while inside, an assortment of seating arrangements offers students a chance to sit and ponder life or chat with friends. The low prices attract students — one house speciality is the Spider Bite, a giant cup of coffee with a jolt of espresso. The menu features a variety of coffee drinks, of course plus Italian sodas, smoothies and a large selection of beer. Late-night noshes include tamales and pasta dishes.

Comedy Clubs

Austin is well-known as a funny place — especially when the State Legislature is in session. There is not a session that goes by without some Texas legislator making national headlines for offering one wacky proposal or another. The city also boasts several natural humorists like Austin's answer to Rush Limbaugh, progressive liberal talk show host and former Texas agriculture commissioner Jim Hightower, who broadcasts from Threadgill's restaurant downtown (see our Restaurants chapter). Hightower's signature phrase is, "The only thing in the middle of the road are yellow stripes and dead armadillos."

Visitors will find political humor is high on the agenda at local comedy outposts, notably Esther's Follies, a longtime Austin troupe that takes aim at both local and national politicians. There are only a handful nightclubs dedicated to comedy alone, but a few of the city's live music venues also take a comedy break now and then. That list expands greatly during the annual Big Stinkin' International Improv and Sketch Comedy festival held in April each year, (see our Annual Events and Festivals chapter). The 1998 festival, known in festival shorthand as BS3, featured a wide variety of talent both national and homegrown at over 20 local venues.

Capitol City Comedy Club

8120 Research Blvd. • (512) 467-2333

This Northwest Austin club has pulled in some of the big names in comedy, including Ellen DeGeneres, Jeff Foxworthy and Bobcat Goldthwait. While nationally known comics appear on Friday and Saturday nights, up-and-coming comedians, including local talent, are featured on other nights.

Continental Club

1315 S. Congress Ave. • (512) 441-2444

A well-known music venue detailed in The Music Scene chapter, this South Central Austin nightspot also features half-hour spots of comedy on what is dubbed Blue Tuesday, when there is usually no cover charge.

Esther's Follies/Esther's Pool

525 E. Sixth St. • (512) 320-0553

Like Barton Springs and the old Armadillo World Headquarters, Esther's Follies is part of the fabric of Austin. The comedy troupe performs every Thursday, Friday and Saturday at Esther's Pool on Sixth Street on a stage where the backdrop is three floor-to-ceiling windows looking out on the street. The audience can watch the antics of the troupe and their interactions with the passersby on Sixth Street.

Esther's is named after Esther Williams, the actress and water ballet artist who made all those swimming movies in the 1950s. The group took that name in the 1970s when they performed skits between music sets at another legendary spot, Liberty Lunch (see The Music Scene chapter). Founders Michael Shelton and Shannon Sedwick (he is co-owner of Esther's and the announcer, she is a star of the troupe and co-owner) say they chose the name because the troupe would perform in the Texas heat wearing swimsuits and get cooled by the stage sprinklers.

Satire and outrageous, campy comedy are the troupe's mainstays. National and local politicians are spoofed, caricatured and mimicked. (Before you go you might want to brush up on local and state issues in our Politics and Perspectives chapter.) The show changes routines regularly and puts on special holiday shows, so repeat visitors are never disappointed. There are no reservations taken, and on Friday and Saturday it is wise to arrive early to insure a seat. Performances are at 8 PM on Thursday and 8 PM and 10 PM Friday and Saturday. Tickets are $14, $10 for students.

Ritz Lounge

320 W. Sixth St. • (512) 474-2270

The Ritz Lounge is a nightclub (see listing in the next category), screening room and music venue, but this converted movie theater is also home to a weekly comedy event, the Dark Comedy Hour, on Wednesdays when up-and-coming comedians display their talents.

Velveeta Room

521 E. Sixth St. • (512) 469-9116

If Esther's Follies is the jewel in the crown of the Austin comedy scene, then the Velveeta Room is the jester. Housed on Sixth Street, next door to Esther's Pool, local and visiting comic talent try out some of their more outrageous and irreverent routines here. Sketches and improvisations are performed Thursday, Friday and Saturday nights. There is a $4 admission charge.

Dance Clubs and Nightclubs

Whether it is the Texas two-step, salsa, merengue, swing, even the Lindy hop, there is a club in Austin where dancers can strut their stuff. Even disco, heaven forbid, is alive and well as the 20-something crowd explores retro fashions. Those looking for a Texas experience should consider visiting one of the city's country dance spots, notably The Broken Spoke, which has been described as the best example of a Texas honky-tonk in Austin. But don't miss out on another important cultural experience: dancing to the Latino beat, ranging from tango to Tejano. Austin's Mexican-American residents have supported several Latino clubs over the years, but recently non-Hispanics are discovering the excitement of the salsa music.

Abratto's

318 E. Fifth St. • (512) 477-1641

This is where the young and the beautiful hang out until the wee hours. A dance club where the sounds are a mix of house music and techno, Abratto's stays open until 4 AM for those who want to keep dancing even after the bars close. *The Austin Chronicle* says, "Abratto's seven years on Fifth prove vanity has yet to go out of style."

Atomic Cafe

705 Red River St. • (512) 457-0644

The outside of this downtown nightclub looks as grungy as the inside, but that is part of its charm for the metalhead fans who gather here. The club serves up hard rock nightly, and there are special fetish nights for those who want to show off their chains, piercings and tattoos.

B-Side

311 Colorado St. • (512) 478-2337

The name is a play on the fact that its next-door neighbor and corporate sibling is The Bitter End, an upscale brewpub and restaurant. While The A-side offers topnotch food, wine and beer, the B-side serves up jazz and rock music in a casual atmosphere.

Broken Spoke

3201 S. Lamar Blvd. • (512) 442-6189

An original honky-tonk that merits the description "legendary" (hence its inclusion in The Music Scene chapter), the Spoke is also a great place to dance a little, drink a little and eat a lot (see our Restaurants chapter). There is live music here Tuesday through Saturday, and the cover charges vary. The low ceiling, the tall men in big hats and the wooden dance floor give this place the feel of an authentic Texas roadhouse. No visit to Austin should end without dropping by the Spoke in South Austin for a longneck.

Calle Ocho

706 Congress Ave. • (512) 474-6605

One of the hottest dance trends in Austin — and elsewhere — is salsa. This club evokes the atmosphere of a tropical nightclub, perhaps a club in Old Havana. Dancers can fine-tune their moves by watching themselves in the mirrored wall. Friday and Saturday are set

INSIDERS' TIP

The old Driskill Hotel in downtown Austin on Sixth Street boasts a ghost or two (see our Hotels chapter), so it is appropriate that the hotel also is home to the Driskill Mystery Dinner Theater. Call (512) 474-5911 Ext. 5219 for information.

aside for salsa, and there are salsa dance classes on Wednesday. Other nights, swing dancing is featured. While some Austin salsa venues attract a predominantly Hispanic crowd, the clientele here is diverse. Calle Ocho is open until midnight on Friday and Saturday. Cover charges vary.

Caucus Club

10th and Red River Sts. • (512) 472-CURE

Times they are a-changing, as Bob Dylan once sang, and since the days he sang it, the Caucus Club has undergone several incarnations. Once a political hangout, this downtown club just southeast of the capitol is now a hip, upscale nightclub with a pre-World War II air. Martinis, cigars and cocktails are the fashionable choices here, but some patrons also come to dance, and there are swing and Lindy hop lessons during the week.

Club Carnaval

2237 E. Riverside Dr. • (512) 444-6396

Southeast of downtown, along East Riverside Drive, there are several authentic Hispanic nightclubs that celebrate Mexican-American and Latin dance traditions. Club Carnaval is noted for its *norteño* dances, which originated in Northern Mexico and flourish in South Texas. Male dancers don Western wear, including large belt buckles, tight pressed jeans and white cowboy hats, while the women dance in full skirts or jeans and Western shirts. Some of the top names in *norteño* music play here in a setting that has an Aztec motif. Cover charges vary.

Club Inferno

222 E. Sixth St. • (512) 477-7820

The name sets the mood here, so come in only if you look good when you sweat. Dancers pack three dance floors and literally dance until dawn. The music is DJ-selected and frenetic.

Club Palmeras

217 Congress Ave. • (512) 479-5002

A combination Mexican restaurant and dance club, this Congress Avenue club features a variety of music including merengue, salsa and Mexican rock. Customers dress in stylized salsa fashion with women wearing incredibly high heels and sexy skirts. When not dancing, they are drinking the house bombaritas. On the weekends there is also live mariachi music to set the mood. Happy hour features a free food buffet.

Club Rio

110 E. Riverside Dr. • (512) 462-9222

There are several varieties of Latino music inspired by Mexican and Mexican-American artists — Tejano is the Texas-grown variety. (When Texas was part of Mexico it was called "Tejas." It is stilled called that south of the border, hence the name Tejano.) Like other clubs on the Riverside Drive strip, Club Rio boasts a pre-Colombian decor, but the dancers celebrate *vaquero* (cowboy) roots. Both men and women wear cowboy boots, while the men sport smart cowboy hats and fancy belt buckles. Some of the top Tejano bands play here, but there are also disco nights.

Dallas

7113 Burnet Rd. • (512) 452-2801

Disco meets country at this North Austin nightclub. Much of the music is piped-in country hits with occasional top rock songs. Cheap drinks on Wednesday and Thursday attract a younger crowd, but older couples in their 30s and 40s enjoy the dancing here, also.

Silver Dollar Dance Hall

2201 E. Ben White Blvd. • (512) 441-9101

"I see by your outfit that you are a cowboy ...." So goes the old song about the streets of Laredo. It's a tune you can sing at this South Austin dance hall that claims to have the biggest dance floor in town. It certainly draws a crowd, especially on Wednesday which is ladies night. The music is handpicked by the house DJ and features top country-and-western hits. Most folks know what country sounds like, but they may not be familiar with the customs of the Texas dance hall. First, your outfit is important — urban cowboys tend to wear tight jeans, well-pressed, clean jeans by Wrangler (real cowboys go for loose-fitting, comfortable jeans that get dusty and wrinkled in a day's work), a leather belt with a Western buckle, Western shirts again by Wrangler, boots (see our Shopping chapter) and a cowboy hat. Women wear much the same thing, although urban cowgirls can opt for skirts instead of jeans. The Silver Dollar attracts a college-age crowd and older who follow dance hall customs like sashaying on the floor in a counterclockwise fashion, dipping (that refers to both dancing and snuff — the latter guys only) and heading back to the tables for a longneck or two (guys and gals). The hall also holds Tejano music nights, loosely defined as Mexican C&W, and is open Wednesday through Saturday.

El Borinquen

2728 S. Congress Ave. • (512) 443-4252

This tiny restaurant and bar re-creates the atmosphere of Old San Juan. The food and drinks are Puerto Rican, as are many of the customers, but the dance floor also draws a diverse crowd that enjoys dancing to salsa and merengue sounds on Friday and Saturday nights.

El Coyote

2120 E. Riverside Dr. • (512) 444-7042

Eager to learn about the various Latino music beats? Then drop in on this small, venerable nightclub that is part of the E. Riverside Drive Hispanic club scene in Southeast Austin. For more than two decades, El Coyote has been offering live and recorded music, much of it featuring traditional accordion dance music favored by older generations of Mexican-Americans.

Flamingo Cantina

515 E. Sixth St. • (512) 494-9336

The Flamingo gets consistently good reviews for its music, and the club also offers rock and reggae that keeps the place packed on weekends. The decor and the sounds are designed to evoke the Caribbean with a grass-thatched roof over the stage and pictures of Bob Marley on the walls.

Hang 'Em High

201 E. Sixth St. • (512) 322-9143

OK, the name is a dead giveaway. This is a country-and-western joint. It may seem odd to out-of-towners, but apart from several gay bars downtown, the country-and-western theme does not crop up on the downtown nightlife scene. But this club is Sixth Street's submission in the honky-tonk category. Most nights the country music is spun by a DJ, but there are occasional live music nights featuring well-known stars like Jerry Jeff Walker and Jack Ingram.

The Mercury Lounge

503-A E. Sixth St. • (512) 457-0706

Once the site of The White Rabbit, a venerable hippie club on Sixth Street, The Mercury is now considered one of the grooviest spots in the downtown district, offering hip music described as soulful by critics. There are touring acts on the weekends and local musicians during the week.

Miguel's La Bodega

415 Colorado St. • (512) 472-2369

Miguel's is the hot spot in the downtown warehouse district for the Latino dance scene. Salsa and merengue rule here, and the uninitiated can take midweek lessons on the premises. Live bands on the weekends provide a constant salsa beat, and just to make sure you stay in a south-of-the-border mood, the club serves a Latino menu.

Paradox

311 E. Fifth St. • (512) 469-7615

The Austin Chronicle calls this Sixth Street club the "Wal-Mart of dance clubs," suggesting it is both popular and cheap. It is always packed on the weekends and is popular with the college crowd. Paradox also stays open after the bars close at 2 AM. The Wal-Mart designation aside, there is a dress code here (primarily on Friday and Saturday). Guys may get turned away at the door if their jeans are too ragged or their T-shirts have gaping holes.

Polly Ester's '70s Disco and the Culture Club

404 Colorado St. • (512) 472-1975

Those of us who lived through the '70s (crushed-velvet bell bottoms and white go-go boots!?) just don't get it, but retro is in, and this warehouse district dance club is living proof. Packed on weekends, Polly Ester's is part of a national chain of dance clubs catering to this nostalgia for the decade — the club's ads even feature Pac Man and big daisy graphics. Others are based in Boca Raton, Denver, Washington, New York and Chicago. The club offers Disco Fever Happy Hour on Friday and Saturday, and Thursday is Ladies Night. Polly's is popular with the college crowd.

Ringside at Sullivan's

300 Colorado St. • (512) 474-1870

The limos line up outside Sullivan's, the Chicago-style steakhouse (see our Restaurants chapter) and this adjoining jazz club. The atmosphere is upscale and glamorous with lots of big cigars and cold martinis in view. The adjacent restaurant bar usually is just as crowded and as smoky, especially during the biennial legislative session when The lobbyists are picking up the tab for lawmakers and their staff.

Ritz Lounge

320 E. Sixth St. • (512) 474-2270

You will find several listings for The Ritz in our Nightlife chapter since this important Sixth Street facility operates in a variety of guises. Once a posh downtown movie theater, the Ritz fell on hard times and became a porno palace. In the last two decades it has worn several faces as a music venue, but has emerged as a nightclub/dance club/lounge/ comedy club and movie theater. Inside, you will find a lounge atmosphere in what was the balcony of the movie theater. The atmosphere is swanky, especially on Thursdays when Latin dancing is featured: Tango is big draw here. On other nights the music might be jazz or swing, very hip. It is a favorite late-night spot for some of Austin's young chefs and kitchen wizards who gather here after hours.

Scholz Garten

1607 San Jacinto Blvd. • (512) 474-1958

This old German beer garden is many things to many people. In addition to being a popular restaurant (see our Restaurants chapter), a historical landmark, a favorite postgame gathering spot for University of Texas sports fans and a political watering hole, the old stage in the shaded garden is also a music venue. A variety of live music is offered here. Check local listings in *The Austin Chronicle* and the *Austin American-Statesman*.

Speakeasy

412 Congress Ave. • (512) 476-8017

Listed in The Music Scene chapter, Speakeasy is also a classy spot for a martini or glass of wine. Housed in one of Congress Avenue's older buildings, recently a used appliance store, the renovation has produced one of the fancier nightspots. A mezzanine overlooks the dance floor, and an old elevator has been restored to give the club that '20s feel. There is a screening room upstairs that has been used by some of the hippest young filmmakers, including Richard Rodriguez, to preview films made in Texas. The whole place has a Prohibition theme, hence the emphasis on jazz, cigars and gin.

Tangerine's

9721 Arboretum Blvd. • (512) 343-2626

This upscale disco is on the Renaissance Hotel campus at the Arboretum. The crowd here is upwardly mobile, urban, professional — particularly on weekends. Open nightly except Sunday, Tangerine's plays music until midnight during the week and until 2 AM on weekends.

Tejano Ranch

7601 N. Lamar Blvd. • (512) 453-6616

Tejano music is designed for dancing, and some of the biggest acts in the genre appear at this North Austin nightclub, notably on the weekends. The crowd here is generally older than 30 and familiar with the Tejano scene. The club has a South Texas atmosphere with neon mus-

INSIDERS' TIP

One of the best ways to experience Austin's nightlife and the city's best restaurants at the same time is to spend happy hour downtown. Several restaurants/bars offer half-price appetizer hours. These include 'ZTejas, Gilligan's and Manuel's. Check our Restaurants chapter for more information.

tangs outside and a large Selena mural inside plus the chairs are covered in cowhide.

Top of the Marc

618 W. Sixth St. • (512) 472-8402

This sophisticated nightclub is a noted live music venue (see The Music Scene chapter), but it's also a great place to have an evening nightcap and view the city skyline. The rooftop club, above Katz's Deli (see our Restaurants chapter) is classy and relaxing. Patrons can dance under the stars to great Latin, swing and jazz music.

Gay Nightclub Scene

The gay nightlife scene in Austin seems to divide into two categories — sophisticated downtown clubs where beautiful people gather, and country swing clubs. However, there are also a couple of neighborhood bars that offer relaxing atmosphere after work hours.

1920's Club

918 Congress Ave. • (512) 479-7979

A recent addition to the gay nightlife scene this Congress Avenue club, three blocks south of the capitol, has a '20s theme. Dubbed a "speakeasy," the club features jazz music and martinis, but there is also a food menu.

'Bout Time

9601 N. I-35 • (512) 832-5339

The gay patrons, both men and women, are attracted to this nightclub that aims for a neighborhood tavern theme. Indoors there are pool tables and darts, while outdoors there are sand volleyball courts. The bar also features a big-screen television and video games.

Chain Drive

504 Willow St. • (512) 480-9017

This Central Austin bar is described as Austin's only "leather bar," but this is soft and cuddly leather. Chain Drive is headquarters for a group calling itself The Heart of Texas Bears, a self-described social group for masculine, bearded and/or hairy gay men and their admirers. The bar has pool tables, a small dance floor and is open daily from early afternoon until 2 AM.

Charlie's

1301 Lavaca St. • (512) 474-6481

A longtime fixture on the gay scene, Charlie's is noted for its clubby atmosphere and party mood on weekends. On Sunday nights, the downtown club hosts drag shows, while on Tuesdays the steak and chicken dinners draw regular patrons. There is a dance floor, dartboards, pool tables, two bars plus television sets for special programming. The outdoor patio is a popular gathering spot on mild evenings.

Country Edge

113 San Jacinto Blvd. • (512) 457-8010

The gay and lesbian community comes to this downtown club to kick up its collective heels and dance to the top sounds in country music.

The Edge

213 W. Fourth St. • (512) 480-8686

Like neighbor Oilcan Harry's (see the listing in this section), The Edge attracts a mostly gay clientele, but straights also enjoy the party atmosphere, which is a little less frenzied here than at Harry's. Lots of beautiful people make up the scenery here.

The Forum

408 Congress Ave. • (512) 476-2900

A relatively new addition to the gay nightlife scene in Austin, The Forum attracts an upscale, mature crowd. There is a leather bar, The Cuff, in the back of the club and a second intimate bar with pool tables in another part of the club. A upstairs patio offers respite from the busy dance floor.

Oilcan Harry's

211 W. Fourth St. • (512) 320-8823

Some have dubbed this warehouse district bar a neighborhood bar for Austin's gay, beautiful set. The large bar is a major feature of the club, but the dance floor is the focal point. A patio in the back of the club offers a retreat from the frenzy of the dance floor. Although the majority of the customers are gay, straights also enjoy the atmosphere here — and the dancing.

Rainbow Cattle Co.

305 W. Fifth St. • (512) 472-5288

Photo: Peter A. Silva

One of the best vantage points to view the Austin skyline is from the southern shore of Town Lake.

Country-and-western music is the order of the day at this downtown gay dance club and bar. During the week, patrons can take dance classes. In addition to two bars, there are areas set aside for darts and pool, and on Sundays customers can enjoy a large buffet.

Movies

There are movie complexes in all areas of the city, and several new facilities featuring stadium seating and other state-of-the-art features have been added to the list in 1998. Check the daily *Austin American-Statesman* and the weekly *Austin Chronicle* for featured movies. The following movie houses feature classic, foreign and independent films.

Alamo Draft House

409 Colorado St. • (512) 867-1839

Tired of sitting in movie theatres where the average age of the audience is younger than your family dog? Try the Alamo Draft House, where there is no sticky Coke on the floor and munchie choices go beyond dill pickles and Butterfingers. This warehouse-district movie theater features cult favorites and classics everything from beach movies to horror flicks served in a nightclub setting where you can order beer, wine and food to accompany the evening's celluloid offerings. On the weekends there are midnight flicks and sometimes the movie house puts on special presentation, such as a presentation of the movie *Like Water for Chocolate* featuring dishes mentioned in the book.

Dobie Theatre

2021 Guadalupe St. • (512) 472-FILM

If you're looking for an independent release, foreign film or art movie, check out the listings for this UT campus-area movie complex. The Dobie is housed in the large and ugly tower at the southern end of The Drag that serves as a residence hall and shopping center for students.

Paramount Theatre for the Performing Arts

713 Congress Ave. • (512) 472-5470

The beautifully restored theater on the city's main avenue hosts a summer film festival featuring the great classics of Hollywood. Also, given Austin's emergence as a movie-making venue (see our Close-up in The Arts chapter), premieres are occasionally held at the downtown theater.

Ritz Lounge

320 W. Sixth St. • (512) 472-2270

One of the many facets of the Ritz Lounge on Sixth Street is Funhouse Cinema, the regular showing of old favorites and independent movies. It is only fitting that the Ritz should revive the building's original role as a classy downtown movie theater. The nightclub seating is an extra bonus for movie fans.

Village Cinema Art

2700 Anderson Ln. • (512) 416-3805

If you are a fan of independent movies or so-called art films, it is likely they will be on the bill at this North Austin cinema complex where one screen is set aside for just such movies.

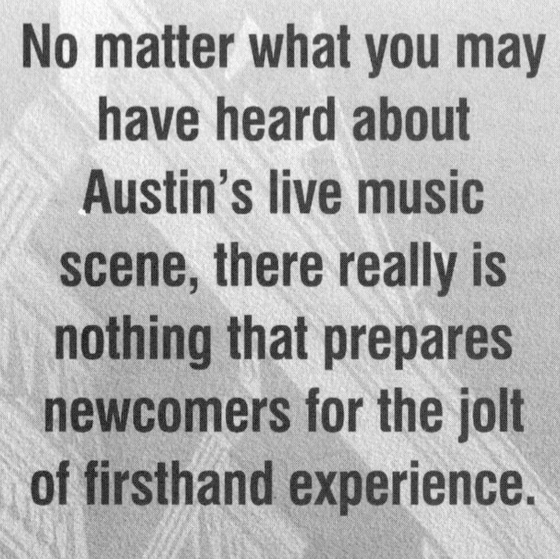

No matter what you may have heard about Austin's live music scene, there really is nothing that prepares newcomers for the jolt of firsthand experience.

The Music Scene

If this chapter were set to the tune of Austin music, the savory sounds of country, blues, folk, funk, punk, pop, jazz, bluegrass, Tejano and rock 'n' roll would waft off these pages and fill the air like a Saturday night on Sixth Street. While we can't reproduce the sounds, we can tell you about some of the artists, the venues, the free concerts and the record stores that constitute The Live Music Capital of the World. So whether you're a music lover eager to explore the sounds of Austin or you've arrived with a guitar on your back and a pocketful of songs, get ready to enter a truly remarkable realm.

No matter what you may have heard about Austin's live music scene, there really is nothing that prepares newcomers for the jolt of firsthand experience. Music is, indeed, here, there and everywhere in Austin. On any given Friday night, music lovers can choose from among as many as 90 venues offering just about any style of music you can imagine, including those exotic strains created by our true Texas hybrids. No weekend-warrior music mentality exists here, however, as our club scene rocks seven nights a week. From national touring shows and top local acts to the most exciting up-and-coming artists and youngsters (some barely past puberty) taking the stage for the very first time, Austin is tuned in to music.

You'll find live music in record stores and bookstores. There's live music to accompany your Sunday brunch and live music to stir your evening coffee. One of our gourmet grocery stores offers live music on its patio (see our Close-up on Central Market in the Shopping chapter). You can listen to live music in our museums and art galleries, and there's live music in our parks and on our sidewalks. Austin's Sixth Street is an entire district dedicated to live music and dance halls, while our own nationally televised music TV show has celebrated Austin music for nearly a quarter of a century. *Austin City Limits*, which has been called the city's cultural calling card to the world, is Austin's top showcase for musical talent. We also have our own 24-hour music channel, the Austin Music Network, which serves up a steady stream of local and national acts on Time Warner Cable channel 15 (see our Media chapter). Our city also hosts one of the most important live music festivals in the country, South by Southwest (see our Close-up in the Annual Events and Festivals chapter).

Though Austin took the motto "The Live Music Capital of the World" in the early 1990s, it gained prominence long before that as a haven for artists seeking to follow their own music and create their own sounds without much interference from the commercial establishment based in L.A., New York and Nashville. In a 1998 feature article, *Billboard* magazine called Austin a "mecca for musical mavericks," saying Austin is known as "a creative oasis, a place that puts music first and career far behind." For local consumption, Austin music critics have a less sympathetic description of this phenomenon, calling it the "Austin Curse," which they define as Austin's seeming inability to translate good music into commercial success. While it's true that many artists are drawn to Austin for its no-strings-attached spirit, so to speak, it is also true that some current and former Austin regulars have found the magic formula that cracks the charts, including Willie Nelson, the late Stevie Ray Vaughan, Lyle Lovett, Jerry Jeff Walker, Christopher Cross, Fastball and others.

In fact, Austin is one of the few cities in the United States where young musicians can go from learning to play to having a garage band to performing in a club to making their own cassettes to getting an independent record contract to earning a major-label deal without ever moving their base of operations. Austin claims several important recording studios as well as almost a hundred independent record labels, including a handful of prestigious names such as Watermelon, Freedom, Antone's and Lazy SOB that actively promote Austin talent — and distribute their music around the country. (While the major label Arista/Austin was established here a couple of years ago, company executives later relocated the offices to Nashville.)

About 10 years ago, the City Council commissioned a survey that showed Austin had a higher number of people involved in the music business per capita than anywhere else in the United States. Our population has grown since then, but so has our music scene. By conservative estimates today, nearly 9,000 people earn a living from Austin's music business, including producers, club staff, recording studios and record companies, music stores and record shops, music teachers, instrument makers and, of course, the artists themselves.

Austin's music scene appears as dynamic today as ever, as more and more young musicians pour into town seeking the freedom to explore their music and the comfort of Austin's appreciative audiences. The constantly changing array of artists on stage — our classic legends and old mainstays combined with young newcomers and emerging talents — renews Austin's status as a musical mecca each and every night. So whether you prefer a lone singer on stage strumming a folk tune on an acoustic guitar or a 10-piece band rocking off the roof, you'll find that Austin has a sound all its own — the sound of originality.

Catch 'em if You Can

With an entire city of musical artists determined to travel to the beat of their own drummers, it's no wonder Austin offers so many choices for the music lover. A city that reestablishes itself as the world's live music capital seven nights a week makes it hard on those of us trying to assemble a list of all the must-see acts. There are just so many talented musicians worthy of mention. The artists listed here are among Austin's favorites, but don't think for a minute that this list is all-inclusive. A little experimentation and willingness to explore the live music scene will bring its own reward.

Among the many artists we've mentioned here, you'll find a number we call Texas hybrids. These artists are the most difficult to categorize because they combine many musical styles. So you'll find artists described as country/folk/rock, bluesy-folk/country, Tex-Mex rock, alternative country and several other such amalgamations. However you describe them, the voices will have you feeling like you've taken a tour across Texas and across the ages during the course of one song.

We've called this section Catch 'em if You Can because Austin's favorite artists are often the most in demand for concerts around the country and around the world. So catch them while they're here. You can't go wrong.

Asleep at the Wheel: Six-time Grammy Award winner Asleep at the Wheel, led by founder/singer/songwriter/guitarist Ray Benson, has perhaps done more to preserve and expand the Western Swing sound popularized by the legendary Bob Wills than any other band. From the group's 1973 debut record *Coming Right at Ya* to the most recent live CD featuring an all-star cast of current and former AATW players, *Back To The Future Now*, Asleep at the Wheel has continued to impress fans with its fiddle- and steel guitar-driven sound. The group's landmark work, *Asleep At The Wheel Tribute to the Music of Bob Wills And The Texas Playboys*, won three Grammys alone. Benson and band came to Austin in 1974 at Willie Nelson's urging and have remained ever since. The group has included dozens of members throughout its nearly 30-year history, including original Wheelers Lucky Oceans and LeRoy Preston, but most recently is made up of Dave Sanger (drums), Cindy Cashdollar (steel guitar/dobro), Michael Francis (sax), Dave Miller (bass), Jason Roberts (fiddle/vocals/electric mandolin) and Chris Booher (piano/fiddle).

Asylum Street Spankers: *Spanks for the Memories* is our favorite CD title by this 10-piece band that eschews the demon electric-

ity in favor of an all-acoustic, string-dominated sound. But with a host of musical voices and a gaggle of instruments among them, who needs a speaker blasting at ya? The Spankers take their name from the original name of Austin's happening Guadalupe Street and the fact that the players "spank" their instruments. They produce original songs on Austin's Watermelon label that include the sounds of blues, bluegrass, country and swing, and they would have been right at home in the '20s, '30s and '40s. They've got ukuleles, kazoos, banjos, mandolins, flatpick and gypsy swing guitars, a washboard, an upright bass, a clarinet and other instruments. The show, often hilarious, sometimes downright rowdy, is always unique and you just know the Spankers are having as much fun as the audience. Current band members are Josh Arnson (vocals/guitar), Leroy Biller (guitar), Pops Bayless (ukulele/tenor banjo/tenor guitar/mandolin/vocals), Wammo (vocals/washboard/harmonica), Stanley Smith (vocals/clarinet), Adam Booker (upright bass), Salty John Salmon (drums), Mysterious John (vocals/kazoo), Eamon McLoughlin (fiddle/violin/mandolin), and Christina Marrs (ukulele/tenor guitar/tenor banjo/musical saw/vocals). Look for the Spankers' new release *Hot Lunch*, expected out on Austin's Cold Springs label by the spring of 1999.

Austin Lounge Lizards: With song titles that include "Jesus Loves Me (But He Can't Stand You)," "Put the Oak Ridge Boys in the Slammer" and "Shallow End of the Gene Pool," it's no wonder this group has earned a reputation for its inventive, and quite entertaining, style of satirical bluegrass, which has won them a number of regional awards as well as national touring dates. Hank Card and Conrad Deisler, former Princeton University and later University of Texas songwriting partners, formed the Lounge Lizards in 1980. Three years later, the Lizards won a Best Band award at the Kerrville Bluegrass Festival. This band, known for its stellar vocal harmonies and lyrical barbs at just about everything, remains an Austin favorite. Deisler, acoustic lead guitarist, is joined by Card on guitar, Tom Pittman on banjo and pedal steel, Boo Resnick on bass and Richard Bowden on fiddle and mandolin. Look for the Lizards' 1998 release, *Employee of the Month*.

Bad Livers: If traditional bluegrass comes to mind when you see a banjo, a fiddle and an upright bass then you haven't heard Bad Livers. "This Austin trio uses instruments associated with traditional music to play a neck-jerking mixture of metal, punk, country and bluegrass with touches of conjunto and Cajun," says the *San Antonio Express-News*. Formed in 1990, the Livers first gained attention, and an impressive network of fans, for playing versions (covers) of songs by Metallica and Motorhead that caused them to be labeled a thrash-bluegrass band. In 1991, the Livers issued a homemade tape of roots-influenced gospel covers called *Dust on the Bible*, which was re-released on Touch & Go Records in 1994. This crisscrossing of genres may be the reason the Livers were named the Austin Music Awards Best None of the Above band three times. It's the Livers' original material, however, that has kept fans enthralled and increased the trio's popularity around the country. With such albums as *Hogs on the Highway* and *Horses in the Mines*, the Livers keep surprising fans with an assortment of musical stylings. Danny Barnes, Mark Rubin and Bob Grant, as Bad Livers, have been featured on the main stage at such events as the Telluride Bluegrass Festival and the Edmonton Folk Festival.

Marcia Ball: *CD Review* called Ball's 1994 release *Blue House* "... another gusto-filled collection of tunes informed by the grit of Texas honky-tonk, the stomp of Louisiana Delta rhythms, and the soul of New Orleans-style blues." This piano-playing dynamo with a full-bodied, earthy voice continues to enchant audiences across the country. Born into a family of musicians in the small southern Louisiana town of Vinton, Ball learned to play the piano at an early age. She moved to Austin in 1970 just as the local music scene was really taking off, played in a progressive country band called Freda and the Firedogs, then hit the road for blues clubs, honky-tonks and blues festivals throughout the South and Southwest. In 1998 Rounder Records released the celebrated *Sing It*, featuring Ball and two other R&B experts, Irma Thomas and Tracy Nelson. Ball's other albums include *Soulful Dress*, *Hot Tamale Baby* and *Gatorhythms*. In 1998 Ball won a Handy Award for Contemporary Blues Female Artist of the Year.

Lou Ann Barton: It's the voice that gets 'em every time. Austin blues luminary Lou Ann Barton's full-throated voice and scorching on-stage performances have been packing clubs in Austin and around the country for years. *Rolling Stone* called her "the most commanding white female belter to erupt out of Texas since Janis Joplin — a singer to whom, in terms of vocal sophistication and emotion, Barton is far, far superior." A native of Fort Worth, Barton performed on stage in R&B clubs before she was 20. Her performance in a New York City club in 1980 so impressed legendary soul/blues producer Jerry Wexler that he signed Barton practically on the spot. *Old Enough* was released in 1982 to rave reviews. Barton's rich musical past includes stints with Stevie Ray Vaughan in the Triple Threat Revue and with The Fabulous Thunderbirds. Her other albums include *Forbidden Tones*, *Read My Lips* and *Dreams Come True*, this last one with musical standouts Marcia Ball and Angela Strehli.

Junior Brown: There are guitar players and then there are GUITAR players. Junior Brown couldn't find an instrument that could produce the sounds his mind was hearing — so he invented one. With his deep voice and trademark double-neck "guit-steel," a combination six-string guitar and steel guitar, Brown produces a sound he calls "free-range country" and his fans call just plain out of sight. His music has been labeled country/rock, alterna-

INSIDERS' TIP

Getting free tickets to a taping of *Austin City Limits* is about as hard as getting in to a David Letterman show in New York. But persistence can pay off. *Austin City Limits* tapes new shows from midsummer through winter. Call the hotline at (512) 475-9077 for dates of upcoming tapings. Then, one to three days prior to a taping, tune in to local radio stations mentioned on the hotline to find out when tickets will be given away. Tickets are distributed at the KLRU-TV studios at Guadalupe and Dean Keeton (formerly 26th Street) streets on the UT campus. Holding a ticket doesn't always guarantee admittance. See our Media chapter for information on ACL as well as information on the great radio stations that regularly present Austin music.

tive country and whatever else label-makers can think of. However you classify it, the sound is a little bit country, a little bit rock 'n' roll with blues, surfer music and Hawaiian threads thrown in. No wonder Austin loves his four-member band, which includes his wife Tanya Rae at rhythm guitar and Steve Layne at the upright bass. Born Jamieson Brown in Cottonwood, Arizona, in 1952, Brown eventually found his way to Austin and the spotlight. His albums include *12 Shades of Brown* and *Guit With It*. Brown's 1998 release is titled *The Long Walk Back (From San Antone)*. Unfortunately for Austin, Brown is spending a great deal of time in Oklahoma these days.

Stephen Bruton: This guy has done it all since his guitar talents were discovered by Kris Kristofferson in Bruton's hometown of Fort Worth. Kristofferson, who called Bruton "one very devil on the guitar," added the young musician to his band back in 1972, while Bruton was still in his 20s. Since then, Bruton has performed two years as lead guitarist for Bonnie Raitt, written a slew of great songs, and spent much of his professional life as a journeyman guitarist and session player. He also has produced a couple of acclaimed albums, Alejandro Escovedo's *Gravity* and Jimmie Dale Gilmore's *After Awhile* (see listings for these artists in this chapter). Bruton's blend of country, soul, rock 'n' roll, R&B and blues makes him a true Texas hybrid, and one of the most original musicians working in Austin today. Look for his talents to shine on his solo debut *What It Is*. Better yet, catch his live show.

Butthole Surfers: This band is one of the reasons that record executives invented the term "alternative" music. There's no easy way to classify it. Punk-industrial-techno-rock-Europop? They call their 1996 major-label release *Electriclarryland*, "a dizzying panorama of power chords, musical pranking, conceptual weirdness and all-out rock 'n' roll hysteria." Okay. Better just to hear it. Whatever you call it, Butthole Surfers, three shock-rockin' avant-garde Texas artists who are veterans of the punk scene, have blasted their way onto the national music stage with a sound that's all their own. Formed in 1981 by two Trinity University students, guitarist Paul Leary and vocalist Gibby Haynes, the two managed to get on the bill with the Dead Kennedys in San Francisco. That led to a record deal on the Alternative Tentacles label. They added drummer King Coffey, released a series of albums, lived on the road and finally settled in Austin. Their deal with Capitol Records was sealed in the early 1990s and Butthole Surfers released *Independent Worm Saloon* in 1993, which produced the alternative rock hit, *Who Was In My Room Last Night*.

W.C. Clark: Few living artists epitomize Austin blues better than W.C. Clark. Born on Austin's East side on November 16, 1939, Clark developed his musical style playing bass and then guitar with the likes of T.B. Bell and Blues Boy Hubbard at the landmark Victory Grill, Charlie's Playhouse and other black blues clubs of the era. Though he seldom toured (a road trip as bassist for soul man Joe Tex nearly 30 years ago took him away for a while) and cut his first nationally distributed record, *Heart of Gold*, just a few years ago, Clark became a mentor for up-and-coming white musicians like Stevie Ray Vaughan and Denny Freeman. In 1976, Clark teamed with Vaughan and Lou Ann Barton in the band Triple Threat Revue. The past few years he's put out an album every other year for Black Top Records, including 1998's *Lover's Plea*. Clark, a member of the Texas Music Hall of Fame, was honored in 1989 with an *Austin City Limits* tribute on his 50th birthday.

Shawn Colvin: With 1996's *A Few Small Repairs*, Austin's gem of the New Folk scene solidified her reputation as an important singer/songwriter. Colvin's first platinum album, *Repairs* produced the single "Sunny Came Home," which won two 1997 Grammys for Record of the Year and Song of the Year and proved to the world what her fans have known all along: this songwriter can play the guitar and owns a set of provocative pipes to boot. Born in 1956 in Vermillion, South Dakota, Colvin started playing the guitar at age 10. She lived in Austin in the mid-1970s and performed with the Dixie Diesels before heading to San Francisco, New York and Boston. Back in Austin since the early 1990s, Colvin's debut album for Columbia Records, *Steady On*, promptly won a Grammy for Best Contemporary Folk Recording. *Fat City*, her 1992 release, includes a wonderful version of her classic song "I Don't Know Why." Colvin's album of holiday music and lullabies was expected in 1998.

Alvin Crow: At home in Carnegie Hall as much as in honky-tonks and clubs around the country and in Europe, this classically trained musician who earned a seat with the Oklahoma City Symphony as its youngest violinist is one of Austin's great fiddlers in the Western Swing tradition of Bob Wills and the Texas Playboys. Western Swing is just one dimension of an Alvin Crow show, however. He tosses in plenty of Cajun music, rockabilly and classic country as well as his own originals. Born in 1950 and raised in Western Oklahoma, Crow has been a fixture on the music scene for nearly 30 years. Alvin Crow and his band, The Pleasant Valley Band, have released eight albums over the years, including 1996's *Texas Classics* on Austin's Broken Spoke record label. *The New York Times* has said Crow represents the "finest flower of Austin's club and concert scene." His other albums include *Pure Country*, *Honky Tonk Trail* and *Long Texas Nights*.

The Derailers: Combining the country sounds of Buck Owens, Merle Haggard and other of the Bakersfield Sound era with influences of rock, R&B and pop, the Derailers are making a major contribution to the music scene in Austin, and now around the country. This four-piece ensemble with slicked-back pompadour hairdos and those '60s-era suits, got together in Austin in the early 1990s. Led by front-men and guitarists Tony Villanueva and Brian Hofeldt, who came to play country music from, of all places, Oregon, the Derailers can always be trusted to provide a dang good, foot-stomping, made-for-dancing good time. Their debut album, *Live Tracks*, was recorded live at Austin's KUT-FM radio station on the local Freedom Records label. They followed up in 1996 with *Jackpot*, on the Watermelon label and, in 1997, got their major-label break when Sire Records teamed up with Watermelon to release *Reverb Deluxe*. The Derailers also include Mark Horn on drums and Ethan Shaw on bass.

Ana Egge: This out-of-New-Mexico singer/songwriter took Austin by storm when she arrived in 1994 at the ripe age of 17. Within a year, she'd won the *Austin American-Statesman*'s Village Voyage Songwriter Search, which led to her New York City debut. In 1998 Egge was named Best Singer-Songwriter in the annual Austin Music Awards, edging out more established Austin musicians such as Trish Murphy, Shawn Colvin and Will Sexton. Her 1997 critically acclaimed debut album *River Under the Road*, released by Austin's Lazy S.O.B. Records, appears to be just the beginning of a long and successful career. It speaks highly of Austin's musical community that so many of our talented and successful musicians contributed to Egge's debut album.

8½ Souvenirs: What is cosmopolitan pop-swing music? Ask 8½ Souvenirs. "Take a little of the legendary French guitarist Django Reinhardt, a little of composers Serge Gainsbourg and Nino Rota, a pint of the classics, a hint of R&B, and swing it in an 8½ style: you have the music of 8½ Souvenirs." That's how this Austin-based quintet, named for the Fellini film *8½*, and the tune "Souvenirs" by Reinhardt, describe themselves in their biography. However you choose to describe them, 8½ Souvenirs is another Austin group that has managed to create a musical amalgamation that goes beyond swing, and works extremely well. This lively group sings in French, Italian and Spanish as well as English. The quintet includes Glover Gill (piano/accordion), Olivier Giraud (guitar/vocals), Adam Berlin (percussion/drums), Kevin Smith (acoustic bass) and Chrysta Bell (vocals). Their 1995 debut disc *Happy Feet,* recorded for Austin's Continental Club record label, was followed in 1997 with *Souvonica*. This unique quintet was discovered in a Manhattan club in 1997. As a result, RCA Victor released a rerecording of *Happy Feet* nationwide, plans to follow up with a new album and a nationwide release of *Souvonica*. Catch them in Austin while you can.

Joe Ely: The flatlands of West Texas have produced some of our state's most inspired musicians. Buddy Holly, Roy Orbison and Waylon Jennings all hail from that sparse outpost of pure Texas. So does Joe Ely. Lucky for us, Ely discovered Austin more than two decades ago and over that time has turned into one of our living musical legends. Not that he was unknown when he arrived. He and fellow Lubbock songwriting sensations

The Music Biz: Cold Beer and Hot Tunes

Austin luminary Eddie Wilson responds matter-of-factly when asked what launched the spectacular music scene we know today. "Cold beer and cheap pot," he says with a laugh. Wilson, however, humbly neglects to mention his own contributions to Austin's rise as a music mecca. As a founder of the renowned Armadillo World Headquarters in 1970, Wilson helped catapult Austin to the big time.

Of course, the collective talent of the hundreds of artists who have illuminated Austin stages over these many years goes without saying. But Wilson points out, too, that the sizable number of sofas offered to musicians during the '60s and '70s allowed brother and sister performers to find, if not a home, at least a place to bed down.

We're getting way ahead of ourselves, though. Austin's music history goes back much further than the 1960s — all the way back to the dance hall pickers, cowboy crooners and black blues belters who were making music around Austin for eons, some as far back as the 1800s, and would continue to fill our city with their own sound of music despite the various musical invasions that followed.

Some say Austin's modern music scene started with Travis County Beer License No. 01, issued to one Kenneth Threadgill on December 6, 1933. Threadgill, a singer and yodeler who sold gasoline from the front side of the Gulf station he operated and bootleg whiskey out the back, stood in line all night to be the first to get a beer license after the county voted to go "wet" following Prohibition. Over the years, this little station evolved into a beer joint and haven for music makers. By the early 1960s the ongoing hootenanny at Threadgill's was attracting University of Texas "folkie" musicians, including a freshman named Janis Joplin, who gathered for the regular Wednesday night jam sessions. "The folkie invasion of Threadgill's was a brave move given the general attitude about hippies, beatniks and long-haired men among the rednecks of the era," Wilson wrote in his book *Threadgill's: The Cookbook*. (As things turned out, however, Threadgill's was just the test kitchen for this bizarre social concoction. A decade later, the Armadillo would perfect the recipe when it became a melting pot of blue-haired grannies, bikers, rednecks and hippies.) Threadgill's proved that the music, not the costume, mattered most.

As the '60s stoked up, Joplin joined up with a few budding UT musicians to form the Waller Creek Boys, a folk group that could play just about any kind of music the Threadgill's crowd demanded: blues, country, bluegrass, whatever. Other musicians soon began arriving in Austin, and finding their way to Threadgill's (now a popular restaurant and music spot — see our Restaurants chapter). Meanwhile, a few joints near UT, including the Jade Room and the New Orleans Club, were making names for themselves by offering Austin's flower children the kind of live music that appealed to them.

UT's hippies may have invaded Austin, but this was still TEXAS as sure as shootin', and no amount of folk, blues or rock 'n' roll could wean this town off good old country-and-western music. In 1964, a young Austinite fresh from service in the Army established a little roadhouse on the southern outskirts of town. The Broken Spoke, as James White would call his restaurant and club, would become a hub for some of the best country bands in Austin and around the country — and remains so to this day.

— continued on next page

By 1965 Joplin had split for San Francisco (being voted the ugliest "male" on campus perhaps hastened the move) and Austin was ripe for a band that could turn on the masses. In the fall of '65 a band called the 13th Floor Elevators burst on the scene at a Jade Room performance. Fronted by a young, good-looking singer/guitarist named Roky Erickson, the Elevators would go on to record two magical albums, break into the top 40, and carve a lasting place for themselves in the collective consciousness of Austin music disciples. (Unfortunately, before the Elevators' genius could spread, Erickson was arrested in 1969 for possession of one joint of marijuana, pleaded insane to avoid prison and was sent to a mental hospital, where he was given shock treatments and heavy-duty drugs. He was never quite the same again, although he did record the 1995 album *All That May Do My Rhyme*.)

Despite Austin's own psychedelic sounds, the blossoming of the counterculture revolution and the drugs that fueled the movement, Austin at that time was still firmly rooted in Bible Belt mores and morality. By the fall of 1967 "there wasn't a hint of the now-bustling music biz in our town," Spencer Perskin, a member of another notable Austin band of the time, Shiva's Headband, wrote in *The Austin Chronicle* in 1993. "To perform only original material was considered almost outrageous by our musician friends, and there was zero tolerance for us at the few bars around town (serving beer-only at the time). Only the opening of the Vulcan Gas Company gave us the foothold we would need."

The Vulcan Gas Company, Austin's first musical haunt for hippies, opened in 1967 at 400 Congress Avenue, just 10 blocks from the State Capitol. "The Vulcan presented a mixed bag of music on its small stage, embellishing the sounds with the first and most creative light show in the state," wrote Joe Nick Patoski and Bill Crawford in the book *Stevie Ray Vaughan: Caught in the Crossfire*. The 13th Floor Elevators, Shiva's Headband and another esteemed Austin band called the Conqueroo all found a home at the Vulcan, while "groundbreaking acts such as the Velvet Underground, Moby Grape and the Fugs would have bypassed the entire state of Texas if not for the Vulcan," according to Patoski and Crawford. The experiment lasted only three years. The Vulcan closed in 1970. As the new decade dawned, however, Austin was set to explode onto the national music stage.

On August 1, 1970, Armadillo World Headquarters opened as a counterculture concert hall. Wilson, a former regular at Threadgill's who was managing Shiva's Headband, says the inspiration for creating the Armadillo came to him one night after an evening at a South Austin honky-tonk called the Cactus Cafe. Responding to the call of nature, Wilson slipped outside to attend to business. That's when he saw it: the big, abandoned National Guard Armory, just sitting there awaiting its future. It took a whole group of people to get the Armadillo to fly, including a graphic artist by the name of Jim Franklin, who created the image of the nine-banded armadillo on ingenious posters that are now collectibles. Wilson took charge as majordomo.

"We wanted to create an entertainment facility that was different from anything Austin had ever seen," Wilson told *The Insiders' Guide®*. Indeed. Despite early wobblings, the Armadillo succeeded in drawing throngs of fans desperate to hear top touring bands and even more of the original music that was by then the "in" thing. As the music grew better and better and the number of fans multiplied, talented musicians from around the country started appearing at the Armadillo. Other entrepreneurs riding the coattails of the Armadillo's success began opening clubs all over town.

"Through the interest of a curious national press and word-of-mouth communication by touring musicians, Austin gained almost overnight a reputation as one of the

— continued on next page

most exciting centers of music activity in the country," Austinite Jan Reid wrote in his book, *The Improbable Rise of Redneck Rock*.

Still, the list of ingredients that went into Austin's magical musical brew was far from complete. Willie Nelson's return to his native Texas led the way for a rising tide of young musicians whose music was labeled progressive country, country rock and redneck rock (see our Close-up on Nelson and Stevie Ray Vaughan in this chapter). A young country rock group led by Marcia Ball called Freda and the Firedogs catered to this new breed of music listeners. San Antonio native Doug Sahm, who'd found musical success on the West Coast, came home to Texas while Jerry Jeff Walker settled in. Michael Murphey released his album *Cosmic Cowboy Souvenirs* in 1973, which unwittingly gave a name to the musical rebels. With the arrival of these and other "Cosmic Cowboys," Austin burst on the national scene as the hub of the redneck rock movement.

Suddenly, hippies and rednecks found themselves bonded by a common sound, rock- and blues-infused country-and-western music. Local radio station KOKE-FM began exalting the new sound, calling it "progressive country." The pickup truck became the preferred mode of transportation, while no self-respecting, long-haired, cowboy-hatted "goat roper" would be caught dead drinking anything but a longneck beer.

"This was a direct reversal of the previous decade's attitudes, when the city's young pacesetters, rebelliously rejecting haircuts while embracing rock, folk and blues, would

— continued on next page

Photo: J. Griffis Smith

Town Lake is a prime venue for outdoor concerts.

have preferred to drink muddy water and sleep in a hollow log rather than betray affinity with their hillbilly cousins," Clifford Endres wrote in his book, *Austin City Limits*.

Before long, however, Willie was on to his next incarnation as a musical outlaw and Austin moved on to new sounds.

The time had come for Austin's music scene to go national. With Willie Nelson as a featured act, Austin's own country music program, *Austin City Limits*, hit the airwaves in the spring of 1975. The program, still aired on Public Broadcasting Stations around the country, features the best-known acts in music today. In its nearly quarter-century of existence, ACL has taken its place among the city's music legends (see our Media chapter).

The cosmic cowboys may have dominated the music scene for a good spell during the 1970s, but theirs wasn't the only sound in town. Down at the Broken Spoke, fans of traditional country music found a refuge away from the city's invading hippies. (Austin lore has it that boys with hair longer than their date's were refused service at the Spoke during these years.)

On other stages, a band that included a young guitarist by the name of Eric Johnson (see the listing in the Catch 'em If You Can section in this chapter) blasted out a radically different tune. The Electromagnets, as the quartet called itself, "generated fan reaction proportional to the volume of its music, gathering an intense, almost worshipful, fan base that seemed to expand with each live date," *Austin American-Statesman* music critic Michael Point wrote in an 1998 article celebrating the reissue of the Electromagnets self-titled album. "Rarely singing and even more rarely acknowledging commercial sensibilities of any sort, the band ... (dazzled) its fans while dazing and confusing the 'cosmic cowboy' contingent who never knew what hit them," Point wrote. As it goes in the music biz, however, the band broke up in 1977, leaving behind just the one album for adoring fans.

A group of West Texas singer/songwriters also migrated to Austin during the 1970s. Joe Ely, Butch Hancock and Jimmie Dale Gilmore (see them in the Catch 'em listings in this chapter), found Austin audiences receptive to the original music they wanted to make — and stayed to make a contribution. So did a teenage Dallas transplant named Jimmie Vaughan. Vaughan's group, Storm, would be just the beginning of the blues tradition Vaughan would help to inspire in his new hometown. Austin's musical tree, it appeared, was destined to produce many different branches.

Yet another Austinite geared up in the '70s to take his place in music history. Clifford Antone, a Port Arthur, Texas, native of Lebanese descent, came to Austin at age 19 to run the family gourmet grocery business. In 1973, the tiny back room of Antone's Imports became the unofficial launching pad for a group of blues artists that included Jimmie Vaughan's little brother, Stevie Ray. Antone opened his first club on Sixth Street July 15, 1975, featuring blues greats such as Muddy Waters, Albert King and Sunnyland Slim — in just its first year. Antone's is credited with helping to develop a blues tradition in Austin where none existed before, at least not in the predominately white area west of Interstate 35.

Antone's has provided a home, and a source of inspiration, for up-and-coming blues artists for almost 25 years. Another of Jimmie Vaughan's bands, The Fabulous Thunderbirds, got its start at Antone's and became the house band when its members were in their 20s. Stevie Ray perfected his talents at Antone's, and went on to be an international superstar. (See our Close-up on Stevie Ray and Willie Nelson in this chapter.)

By the time Armadillo World Headquarters closed in 1980, Austin's status as a "mecca for musical mavericks" had solidified. And there was still more to come.

— continued on next page

Austin's live music scene went ballistic in the '70s, the city's hottest acts continued to record elsewhere, according to Casey Monahan, director of the Texas Music Office. "Most of the artists that had major label money did not record in Austin. Most opted to go to wherever their producer wanted to record, usually L.A. or Nashville," Monahan told *The Insiders' Guide*®. By the mid-1980s, however, Austin was singing a new tune, as more and more artists found they could record albums right here at home. Today, Austin claims more than 130 recording studios, including about two dozen that are competitive with Nashville and Los Angeles, Monahan says. Among the elite is Willie Nelson's Pedernales Studios, the only studio launched by an artist, as well as other topnotch studios operated by entrepreneurs, including Cedar Creek Recording, Austin Recording Studios and Arlyn Studio.

The Sixth Street music scene, which had taken root in the 1970s, fired up in the 1980s and has since become Austin's dominant district for live music and dancing. Well-established Sixth Street hangouts, including Steamboat and Maggie Mae's, have seen the once-tranquil strip turn into a frenzy of clubs turning out live music seven nights a week while the greater downtown area packs in more outstanding live music than anyone could ever experience in a short visit here. Many of Austin's most notable live clubs, including Antone's, La Zona Rosa, Hole in the Wall, Liberty Lunch and the Continental Club can all be found in greater downtown. Wilson himself went on to revive the old Threadgill's saloon, turning it into one of Austin's most illustrious restaurants (featuring live music, of course). Threadgill's now touts two Austin locations, including one near the spot of the former Armadillo and appropriately named Threadgill's World Headquarters (see our Restaurants chapter).

Austin's star on the world stage continues to rise as more and more young artists flock to The Live Musical Capital of the World yearning to make a name for themselves. Many are succeeding as current pop bands, including Fastball, Sister 7 and Sixteen Deluxe, join the ranks of Austin's elite.

As Wilson told us, "There are many more quality musicians and 10 times more music in Austin today than there was during the days of the Armadillo."

Indeed.

Jimmie Dale Gilmore and Butch Hancock (read about them in this listing) had gotten together in 1971 to form the Flatlanders, a short-lived-but-destined-for-the-history-books acoustic band that, according to the *Austin American-Statesman*, "continues to exert an improbable but undeniable hold on the imaginations of Texas music fans and singer-songwriter aficionados on both sides of the Atlantic." Then there was the Joe Ely Band, another Lubbock production, which, like the Flatlanders, mixed country and rock chemicals to form a brand new concoction of musical mastery, and wound up touring across the United States and Europe with, of all things, the punk rock group the Clash. In 1998, Ely released *Twistin' in the Wind*, to both critical and popular acclaim. This work, which includes elements of country, blues, swing, rock, Spanish and more, is destined to be a classic both for the music and for the images this singing storyteller conjures up. Ely has won so many Austin Music Awards it's hard to keep track. If you don't already know Ely's music, check out *Letter to Laredo*, *Live Shots*, *Musta Notta Gotta Lotta* and *Dig All Night* for starters. Ely is also an accomplished visual artist.

Alejandro Escovedo: It's hard to believe a guy who launched his musical career by playing in his own student film about a rock band that couldn't play could have come so far. He has. A founding member of the 1970s landmark San Francisco punk band The Nuns, a member of Texas' influential country-punk band Rank and File and later part of the electrifying rock band True Believers, Escovedo has already left his mark on American music. One of 12 children born in San Antonio into a family of musicians (his dad was a mariachi musician; two of his brothers played with Santana), Escovedo and family left Texas for California in the 1960s. The teenage Escovedo immersed himself in the flourishing music scene and, later, discovered his own unique voice. His songs, according to his bio, "blend lyrical strings and woodwinds with the gritty sound of crunching, sawed-off guitars and pumping pianos." We couldn't have said it better. While Escovedo has only a few records under his own name, *With These Hands*, *Gravity* and *13 Years*, his contribution to the national music scene has been enormous. Look for him, too, on albums by his other musical manifestations, The Setters and Buick MacKane. Escovedo plays with a number of different bands around town.

Fastball: This pop trio had been paying its dues, writing the songs and driving the required hundreds of miles to gigs where a handful of folks, not fans per se, would show up. In Austin, finally, they were getting some notice, despite the fact that their 1996 debut CD for Hollywood Records, *Make Your Mama Proud*, pretty much flopped. (Austin audiences couldn't give a hoot about who's getting air time — they know what they like.) Then in 1998 Fastball became an overnight sensation with the release of the trio's second album *All the Pain Money Can Buy*, which *CMJ New Music Monthly*, in a feature article on the group, called "measurably more ambitious than the punk-inspired, straightforward pop that had made the trio a local favorite in Austin." The album's infectious lead single, "The Way," got plenty of air play, while the album's other songs, including "Warm Fuzzy Feeling," also have a lot to offer. Formed in 1994 as Magento USA, Fastball changed its name shortly before the release of *Mama*. While not too crazy about the "pop" categorization — they insist they're a rock 'n' roll band — Fastball is one band to watch. The trio includes native Austinite Joey Shuffield on drums, and the songwriters Miles Zuniga on guitar and Tony Scalzo on bass.

Davíd Garza: "His future's so bright, he's gotta wear shades." That's what the *Austin American-Statesman* said, quoting Austin group Timbuk3. about this pop singer/songwriter following the release of his 1998 major-label debut *This Euphoria*. Garza, who attended UT on a classical guitar scholarship, has had several musical incarnations. As a member of the now infamous pop trio Twang-Twang-Shock-a-Boom, a group he started when he was just 17, Garza became a favorite on the college circuit and sold thousands of self-released albums from the trunk of his car. His other musical incarnations, Dah-Veed and the Love Beads, went a long way toward establishing this young man as a new voice. His music, rooted in quirky yet alluring rock/pop melodies and lyrics, is sort of early Beatles, but freshened for the '90s. Born one of five children of Mexican-American parents from Texas' Rio Grande Valley, Garza was raised near Dallas. He came to Austin more than a decade ago to launch his musical career. It would seem he's succeeding.

The Geezinslaw Brothers: Though they're not brothers and neither is named Geezinslaw, this musical act nevertheless has become one of Austin's favorite country music attractions. Sammy Allred (also famous in Austin for co-hosting KVET-FM's popular morning radio show) and Dewayne "Son" Smith, the two "brothers" who are supported by a band of four, won a 1993 Austin Music Award for Single of the Year for their rap crossover "Help I'm White and I Can't Get Down," on the hit CD *Feelin' Good, Gettin' Up, Gettin' Down*. With song titles like "Help I'm White," "Daddy Don't Live in Heaven (He's in Houston)" and "Five Dollar Fine for Whining," it's no wonder this group has a reputation for humor. Their musical talents are impressive, too, and have earned them touring dates across the country as well as in Europe and Canada. Sammy and Son, both native Austinites, have been performing together since high school — that would be close to 50 years by our estimate.

Jimmie Dale Gilmore: Three times named *Rolling Stone* magazine's Country Artist of the Year (1991, 1992 and 1993), this songwriting troubadour with a terrific Texas twang is one of those quintessential Austin artists. Born in 1945 in Amarillo, Gilmore moved as a first grader to Lubbock, the West Texas breeding ground for many a great musician. Raised on traditional country and folk, early rock 'n' roll, and the blues, Gilmore turned into a progressive country singer/songwriter with what *Roll-*

ing Stone called "a voice of such rarity and beauty that it's enough to bring one to tears." He's master lyricist, too.

In 1972, Gilmore and fellow Lubbock songwriters Joe Ely and Butch Hancock formed a little acoustic band called the Flatlanders and recorded *One Road More* in Nashville. When the album fizzled, so did the band. (Little did they know the album was to become a collector's item. It was later re-released under the more appropriate title *More a Legend Than a Band*.) Gilmore spent the next decade wandering and wondering. He studied Eastern philosophy, worked as a janitor, became a follower of the teenage Indian guru Maharaj Ji, and finally landed in Austin in 1980 ready to get back to business. During the '80s Gilmore released a couple of solo albums on an independent label. Then came 1991 and Gilmore's major-label debut, the critically acclaimed *After Awhile*. *Spinning Around the Sun* followed in 1993 while *Braver New World* hit the shelves in 1996. Gilmore just keeps getting better and better.

Johnny Gimble: Still one of the greatest living exponents of the Texas fiddle tradition, Gimble was a member of the legendary Country Swing band Bob Wills and the Texas Playboys back in the 1940s and '50s and is featured on Wills' biggest hit, "Faded Love." Gimble moved to Nashville in the late 1960s where he spent many years as a much-in-demand studio musician before returning to Texas in 1978. Since then, the fiddlemeister has recorded *Under the 'X' in Texas*, *Still Fiddling Around* and other albums with his Texas Swing band. Named eight times as the Academy of Country Music Fiddler of the Year and recipient of several other CMA awards, Gimble is a favorite around the country as well as here in Austin. Gimble has played in various reunion bands with other ex-Playboys and also has been featured on many recordings with the likes of Willie Nelson, George Strait and others. Now in his 70s, Gimble appeared on stage at the Austin Music Awards in 1998 with his old buddies Asleep at the Wheel. The venerable fiddler hasn't lost his touch.

The Gourds: Austin's rollickin', good-timin' country/rock band has been compared to The Band more times than anyone can count. This four-member group features Jimmy Smith (bass/guitar/vocals), Kevin Russell (guitar/mandolin/vocals), Claude Bernard (guitar/accordion) and new member Keith Langford (drums). The group's (dare we say the band's) 1996 *Dem's Good Beeble*, and its 1998 calmer follow-up *Stadium Blitzer*, both earned excellent reviews and helped The Gourds establish themselves as a force to be watched on the national, and international, music scene. This band, famous for infectious live performances that also include some great cover songs, will have you singing and dancing along in no time.

Nanci Griffith: Once dubbed "Queen of Folkabilly" by *Rolling Stone* magazine, this three-time Grammy Award-winning artist has produced an impressive body of work that includes 14 solo albums as well as singing and songwriting credits on many, many more. Griffith's 1993 album *Other Voices, Other Rooms* earned her a Grammy for Best Contemporary Folk Performance, while her other two awards were for her performances on albums by Irish artists The Chieftains. *Other Voices Too* was released in 1998. Born in Seguin, Texas, and raised in Austin, Griffith began playing the Austin club circuit when she was just 14, accompanied by her West Texas liberal parents. The guitar-playing Griffith performs today with her band Blue Moon Orchestra, named after Griffith's own album, *Once in a Very Blue Moon*. While she's off

INSIDERS' TIP

For information related to just about any facet of the music business in the state, call the Texas Music Office right here in Austin at (512) 463-6666. The knowledgeable and helpful staff can provide information on all of Austin's live music venues, tell you about the more than 600 annual events centered around music, or answer just about any other question that has to do with The Live Music Capital of the World.

touring quite often, Griffith has found time to work with the Nashville Ballet and the Nashville Symphony on a modern ballet featuring her music. The ballet, *This Heart*, is scheduled to premiere in 1999.

Butch Hancock: Austin's most prolific songwriter is said to have performed six straight nights of original songs at the Cactus Cafe without repeating a single one. It's not hard to imagine he could have gone on for many, many more performances in the same vein, as the body of his work encompasses hundreds of songs. Originally from Lubbock and a member of the 1970s group the Flatlanders along with Joe Ely and Jimmie Dale Gilmore (read about them in this chapter), Hancock is one of those world-class songwriters whose work has been recorded by a bevy of artists including Jerry Jeff Walker, Emmylou Harris, the Texas Tornados, Ely and others. This musical storyteller with the wonderful gravelly voice (hey, it didn't hurt Dylan) has released more than a dozen albums, including 1997s *You Coulda Walked Around the World*, which features Hancock, his guitar and those incredible Hancock stories. Period. Although he's recorded for the prestigious independent label Sugar Hill, Hancock most often releases his work on his own Rainlight Records label. Hancock packed up his stuff, loaded it into his house trailer and headed for Terlingua near Big Bend country in Southeast Texas a few years back, though he still makes it to Austin for performances. While his fame stems more from his talents as a songwriter, it's a rare treat to see him perform.

Sara Hickman: A superb live performer, Hickman is an acoustic rock 'n' roller who mixes folk sweetness with open-eyed humor — and not just a touch of mischievousness. This is another Austin artist who breaks the female singer/songwriter mold, due, perhaps to the fact that she is inspired by all kinds of music. The *Dallas Times-Herald* called her live act "a cross between a stand-up comedy routine and group therapy, with great music as an added bonus." Hickman, who was raised in Houston and graduated from the High School for the Performing and Visual Arts, received her bachelor of arts degree in painting from North Texas State University in Denton. But music was her calling so she headed to Dallas and the music scene there. Her first CD, *Equal Scary People*, released by an independent label, earned her a contract with Elektra Entertainment, which re-released *Scary People* and its follow-up, *Shortstop*. She and Elektra later parted ways and Hickman raised thousands of dollars from loyal fans to buy back an unreleased album, which she later released as *Necessary Angels*, in tribute to the angels who helped her. Hickman's 1998 album, *Two Kinds of Laughter*, is filled with musical marvels. This outstanding performer also has a well-deserved reputation as a humanitarian who spends a good deal of her time performing in hospitals and working for social causes.

Tish Hinojosa: Born the last of 13 first-generation Mexican-American children, Leticia "Tish" Hinojosa grew up in San Antonio listening with one ear to the Spanish-language music her parents played on the radio and with the other ear to the popular American and British recording artists of the '60s. The result was a bilingual singer/songwriter with an remarkable ability to weave both languages into her songs. Her rich-textured music and poetic lyrics have earned her a place in Texas musical history. This guitar-playing songstress has received an Austin Music Award for Best Female Vocalist, Best Folk Artist, Best Latino Record and Best Mexican American Folk, which demonstrates her ability to crisscross genres. All of her albums are gems, but our favorites include *Destiny's Gate*, *Dreaming from the Labyrinth/Soñar del Labertino* and her 1996 children's recording *Cada Niño/Every Child*.

Eric Johnson: Guitar-player extraordinaire and Grammy Award winner Eric Johnson is one of those rare Austin musicians who actually was born here. This tall Texan won his Grammy in 1991 for Best Rock Instrumental Performance for his song "Cliffs of Dover" on the *Ah Via Musicom* album, which proved to the country that lyrics aren't an essential part of rock music. Of course Johnson also sings and writes, but guitar is his forte. In fact, Austin music legend Stevie Ray Vaughan once said Johnson "does incredible things with all kinds of guitars." *Guitar Player* magazine called *Ah Via Musicom* "an artistic triumph, as powerful a statement for Eric Johnson as *Electric*

Ladyland was for Jimi Hendrix." Born in 1954, Johnson developed his style while working Texas' club circuit for years. In the 1970s, he formed part of the Austin supergroup Electromagnets. (See our Close-up on the Music Biz in this chapter). In 1986 Johnson recorded *Tones*, which got national air play and turned into a successful commercial album. He won *Guitar Player* magazine's 1986 award for Best New Guitarist and in 1992 was named the magazine's Best Overall Guitarist. No stranger to the *Austin City Limits* stage, Johnson is a hometown favorite. His latest effort is 1996's *Venus Isle*. Look also for the 1998 rerelease on Rhino Records of the Electromagnets 1975 self-titled album.

Robert Earl Keen: One of Austin's finest country-folk singer/songwriters, Robert Earl Keen won so many Kerrville Music Awards they finally entered him in their Hall of Fame. And still the awards keep coming. This native Texan, whom the *Dallas Morning News* has called a "Lone Star Legend," falls gloriously into the category of lyrical storytellers. "Undone," the lead single on his 1997 release *Picnic* for the short-lived Arista/Austin label, is the story of ruin in a nutshell. "Your soul is junk your brain is dust / All of your memories are eaten up with rust / Your nightmares real, dreams too stark / You love the night but you hate the dark," Keen sings on this highly instrumentalized album. Born in Houston and now living in the Hill Country near Bandera, Keen has been part of Austin's music scene for nearly 20 years, and is a regular on the *Austin City Limits* stage. *Gringo Honeymoon*, Keen and band's 1994 release, received raves from national critics and fans alike. Just in his early 40s, Keen still has a lot of stories to sing.

Jimmy LaFave: *Buffalo Returns to the Plains* is one of the best albums ever released by LaFave, whose talents as a singer, songwriter and guitarist have catapulted him to the top ranks of Austin musicians. The Texas-born LaFave started his musical career in Stillwater, Oklahoma, where he joined a group that labeled its bluesy-folk rock-style "red dirt" music. This poetic lyricist with a wonderfully raspy voice (that *Rolling Stone* magazine compared to a Gasoline Alley-era Rod Stewart) alternates easily between rock numbers and romantic ballads. LaFave discovered Austin in 1985, started out playing acoustic sets around town and later added a band. While he has released four CDs for the Colorado-based Bohemia Beat Records, including 1997's *Road Novel*, it's still much more fun to see him perform live.

Ian Matthews: Gifted with a sweet tenor voice that simply transports anyone fortunate enough to hear him on stage, Matthews is always in command of his musical wizardry. This acoustic folk/rock singer/songwriter, who has called Austin home for many years, is a founding member of Fairport Convention, the influential British folk/rock band of the late 1960s. While he plays the guitar extremely well, the main instrument on stage with Matthews is his voice. In fact, his has been called the "most beautiful voice in acoustic music" and anyone who hears Matthews cover the Joni Mitchell song *Woodstock* in mostly a cappella and two-part harmony — or just about any other song he sings — will agree. Born in Scunthorpe, England, on June 16, 1946, Matthews discovered an early appreciation for British and American traditional music. As a young man he joined a surf band and later became an original member of Fairport Convention. Other groups followed, including Matthews Southern Comfort, Plainsong and Hi-Fi. He has released more than three dozen albums since 1968, including *God Looked Down* and *The Dark Ride* for Austin's Watermelon label. Folk music just doesn't get much better than this.

James McMurtry: If that last name sounds familiar to all you fans of the books *Lonesome Dove*, *Terms of Endearment* and other modern classics, you're on the right track. James is the son of novelist Larry McMurtry. This McMurtry, however, has taken a different writing path. As a singer/songwriter known for his intelligent, narrative-oriented rock 'n' roll songs, McMurtry tells stories his own way. "In Jaws of Life," his song on the 1997 album *It Had to Happen*, McMurtry sings, "I walked in and looked around / You never saw such a burned out crowd / Somebody said boy don't be thinking out loud / You know some of us were once so proud / Just like you we had our days / You'd be amazed how fast they slipped away." Born in Fort Worth in 1962, McMurtry started out performing cover tunes in clubs around the country when he was still in his teens. Later, with a stack of his own songs, McMurtry entered the New Folk songwriting contest in the Kerrville Folk Festival and came away a winner. He recorded three CDs for Columbia Records, *Too Long in the Wasteland*, *Candyland* and *Where'd You Hide the Body*. Now recording for the prestigious independent label Sugar Hill Records, McMurtry is set to follow up *It Had to Happen* with a new release in 1998.

Abra Moore: This reed-thin beauty with the strikingly breathy voice scored a hit with her 1997 major-label debut on Arista/Austin *Strangest Places*, which featured the catchy lead single "Four Leaf Clover." Before that came along, however, Moore had established herself as a voice to be reckoned with on the alternative pop scene. A founding member of the band Poi Dog Pondering, Moore released her critically acclaimed solo debut album *Sing* in 1995. Her passion on that album was described by one critic as that of an "angry young Bob Dylan." Born in 1969 in Mission Bay, California, Moore composed her first song when she was six and living in Hawaii. She studied piano while living in New York City and began playing small clubs while living in Europe. She switches back and forth from piano to guitar as easily as her passionate original songs shift from rock to blues to folk rhythms. Now a distinguished member of the Austin music scene, Moore won a whopping four Austin Music Awards in 1998, including Musician of the Year. She tours quite often, but can still be found playing her favorite Austin venues.

Trish Murphy: A former member with her brother of the Trish & Darin group, one of Houston's successful club bands, Murphy went solo in 1995 and has since become one of Austin's most popular singer/songwriters. In this case, however, singer/songwriter doesn't always translate into folk music. Murphy, whose voice leans potently toward a Bonnie Raitt-style country, produces a fresh pop/rock sound that has managed to gain her an excellent following. Perhaps it's her guitar-playing technique that separates her from the typical female folk singer. "I thrash my guitar, I don't strum," she has said. Today, she's as comfortable playing with a band as without. Born into a family of musicians (her father was a pop songwriter), Murphy learned to play guitar at age 11 by practicing on Bob Dylan and John Prine songs. She earned a psychology degree in Dallas, then turned down a job with the *Wall Street Journal* in Europe to pursue her music. Murphy arrived in Austin in 1996 with an acoustic EP of all new songs and released her first solo CD, *Crooked Mile*, on her own label in 1997. "Running Out of Tomorrows," one of the cuts off *Crooked Mile*, features the line, "I'd rather go hungry than starve my dreams." From the looks of it, starving won't be one of Murphy's concerns. She performed on the prestigious Lilith Fair tour in the summer of 1998 and is aiming to release a new CD in 1999.

Omar & the Howlers: This dynamite rockin' blues band is one of those quintessential Austin groups that just shouldn't be missed. Omar Dykes and the Howlers, bassist Paul Junior and drummer Steve Kilmer, have 10 albums on the shelves (try *World Wide Open*, *Monkey Land* or *Big Leg Beat* for starters), any one of which will serve as a great introduction to this trio, but to see them perform live on stage is to delve delightfully into the Austin music scene. Dykes, a big man with an even bigger gravelly voice that howls, is simply a superb blues guitarist. Together, this trio electrifies the stage. Born in Bo Diddley's hometown of McComb, Mississippi, Dykes absorbed the blues as a youngster hanging out in McComb's black blues clubs. He developed his talents on the road and arrived in Austin in

INSIDERS' TIP

The Austin City Council, the same body that proclaimed Austin the Live Music Capital of the World, has slapped a noise ordinance on Sixth Street clubs. So if you're expecting to be blasted away by the music on Sixth, you may be surprised by the softer tones wafting out of the clubs. Of course that all changes once you open the doors. Did somebody say, "Party"?

1976 ready to wail. Omar & the Howlers soon carved a niche for themselves in the Austin club scene. They started recording in 1980 and haven't stopped yet. *Southern Style*, on Austin's Watermelon label, was released in 1997. Interestingly, this trio has an incredible following overseas, especially in Scandinavia.

Toni Price: Price is a rarity among Austin's divas: she neither writes her own songs nor plays an instrument. But can she sing! This blues/folk/country singer is so popular in Austin that she rarely has to leave to find a gig. She walked away from the Austin Music Awards with Album of the Year and Best Female Vocalist honors three years in a row — and captured yet another Best Female Vocalist award in 1998. Price is a terrific singer who "torches whatever she touches," said *Blues Access*. Price was born in Philadelphia in 1961 and raised in Nashville. But while other musicians were flocking to the Music City hoping to for fame and fortune, Price was heading for Austin. She came for the South by Southwest music festival in 1989, fell in love with Austin and has remained ever since, performing in major venues all over town. Price has been described as a "southern-fried Bonnie Raitt," a comparison we're sure she enjoys since Price has been hooked on Raitt's music since she discovered her nearly 20 years ago. Price released her first CD, *Swim Away*, in 1993. Two more have followed: 1995's *Hey* and *Sol Power*, in 1997, all on the Antone's/Discovery Records label. She most often performs with her own band, Rick "Casper" Rawls and Scrappy Judd Newcomb on guitar and Champ Hood on fiddle and guitar.

Reckless Kelly: "Reckless Kelly, the most promising band to come out of Austin in the past year, could do for alternative-country what Nirvana did for grunge," the *Houston Chronicle* said in 1997. Austin definitely was impressed with this new group, awarding the quintet two Austin Music Awards in 1998 for Best New Band and Best Roots Rock Band, flocking to the group's spirited live shows and snapping up their debut album, *Millican*. Formed in Oregon in 1995 and named for an Australian outlaw, just for fun, the group came to Austin in 1996 to share what it calls its "hick-rock" music. This smashing group is comprised of brothers Willie Braun (singer/songwriter) and Cody Braun (fiddle/mandolin) as well as Casey Pollock (lead guitar), Chris Schelske (bass) and Jay Nazz (drums).

Doug Sahm: As a member of the 1960s band the Sir Douglas Quintet, Sahm scored a couple of national hits, including his song "She's a Mover." This singer/songwriter, who appeared on the cover of *Rolling Stone* magazine in the 1970s, has been called perhaps the last of the "true Texas hippie musicians." Sahm's musical career, which spans more than three decades, has turned him into a veritable legend in his hometown of San Antonio and his adopted home of Austin. Known for multiple music personalities, Sahm is a true Texas hybrid. From the Sir Douglas Quintet to the Texas Tornadoes to The Last Real Texas Blues Band, Sahm has mixed rock 'n' roll, blues, conjunto and country to form a collective sound that is truly unique. His albums, *Doug Sahm and Band*, and *Texas Rock for Country Rollers* by Sir Doug and the Texas Tornados are considered country rock classics.

Sixteen Deluxe: This four-member pop band burst onto the Austin music scene in 1994, headlining shows within months of their club debut. "Sixteen Deluxe has gained a steady following of young people who anticipate the masochistic, pleasurable pain of melodic volume. Primarily through a word-of-mouth campaign based on the strength of its ass-kicking live shows, Sixteen Deluxe is performing some of the most inspirational shows in town." That's what the *Austin American-Statesman* said about this group of native Austinites after their meteoric rise. The band, which includes Carrie Clark (guitars/vocals), Chris Smith (guitars/vocals/"strange noises"), Jeff Copas (bass guitar) and Steven Hall (drums), released its self-produced debut album, *Backfeed Magnetbabe*, in 1995. *Spin* magazine described the work as "noisy pop psychedelia so sweet it could cause cavities." A year later, 16D had a major-label record deal with Warner Bros. Records. The result was *Emits Showers of Sparks*, a 13-track album that Warner Bros. says combines "sonic chaos with classic pop structure." Not bad for a band that just wanted to put on rock shows. "When we first started, we weren't thinking about making albums," bassist Copas says in a news release. "All we wanted was to put on the most over-the-top, classic psychedelic rock show we possible could." Now 16D is thinking about both. Look also for the band's 1996 EP *Pilot Knob*.

Charlie and Will Sexton: These two brothers, both of whom made major-label record deals when they were just teenagers and then spent more than a decade each developing separate musical identities, finally formed a musical family in 1997 when younger brother Will joined the Charlie Sexton Sextet. This melody-driven rock/pop group has recorded a new album for A&M Records and is considering changing its name before the album is released, possibly in late 1998 or early 1999. Guitar star Charlie, a child prodigy who was playing on stage with W.C. Clark when he was just 10 years old, recorded 1985's *Pictures for Pleasure* when he was 16 and then went on to play with David Bowie, Bob Dylan, Keith Richards and Don Henley while barely out of his teens. He is a former member of the highly touted Arc Angels band, a blues-based hard-rocking band. The Charlie Sexton Sextet, which had always been short one member, garnered critical success with its 1995 MCA Records release *Under the Wishing Tree*. Will, who like his brother is a guitar-playing singer/songwriter, formed the group Will & the Cannonballs as a teen and later recorded the album *Will and the Kill* in 1989. Will, whose musical collaborations had kept him hopping back and forth between Austin and Los Angeles, is expected to bring his own songwriting aesthetic to this new group — whatever it chooses to call itself. Other members include drummer J.J. Johnson, Michael Ramos on keyboards and George Reiff on bass.

Sister 7: This funk- and blues-influenced party-rock band, which first gained attention around Austin as Little Sister, was among the original group of bands signed to the Arista/Austin label, which released Sister 7's 1997 CD *This The Trip*. Arista/Austin has since moved on to Nashville while Sister 7 has moved up from its status as a regional band to become a national touring act. Sister 7, three guys and a girl who have no compunctions about using those four-letter words, got its start as an acoustic duo in Dallas featuring vocalist Patrice Pike and guitarist Wayne Sutton. The two, known then as Little Sister, moved to Austin, added Darrell Phillips on bass and Sean Phillips on drums. Little Sister soon had a large and loyal following at The Black Cat on Sixth Street. The group became Sister 7 in 1996 after Arista learned there were several other Little Sister bands around the country. *Free Love & Nickel Beer* and *Sister 7* are this group's other CDs.

Darden Smith: UT alumnus Darden Smith is a singer/songwriter who, like Lyle Lovett, had a hard time finding his niche. Record executives put him for a while on country music labels, as one of those new country artists but Smith's sound was too urbane, the lyrics too complex, to attract a large country following. His music was country in name only. Then in 1989 Smith recorded the collaborative album *Evidence* with English singer/songwriter Boo Hewerdine. The disc earned some excellent critical reviews and helped establish Smith as a pop artist. Recording on pop labels for the past few years, Smith seems to have found his groove. His sound strongly reflects his Austin folk scene roots — more acoustic rock and ballads — in which the story is the heart of it all. Now in his mid-30s, Smith has perfected his on-stage act and possesses an excellent singing voice belting out his own, often bittersweet lyrics like only a songwriter could. *Deep Fantastic Blue* is latest CD, released on Plump Records in 1996. Look also for *Trouble No More* on Columbia Records and others. Smith's first album is called *Native Soil*.

Storyville: One of Austin's favorite performing groups, Storyville combines Texas guitar rock, soul and gospel to form a sound that is all its own. Led by Malford Milligan, who owns, according to the book *Texas Music* by Rick Kostner, perhaps the "finest voice in Texas rock history," and including four other all-star musicians, Storyville has garnered accolades throughout the music industry. The group's 1994 debut album, *The Bluest Eyes*, established Storyville as a musical force. The *New York Post* called it a "pleasure from start to end ... a no-risk disc that will find fans with followers of the blues, R&B, and rock." This is one of those Austin bands that just happened, as the artists all found themselves together on stage one night at Austin's renowned blues club, Antone's (read about Antone's in this chapter). This group includes drummer Chris

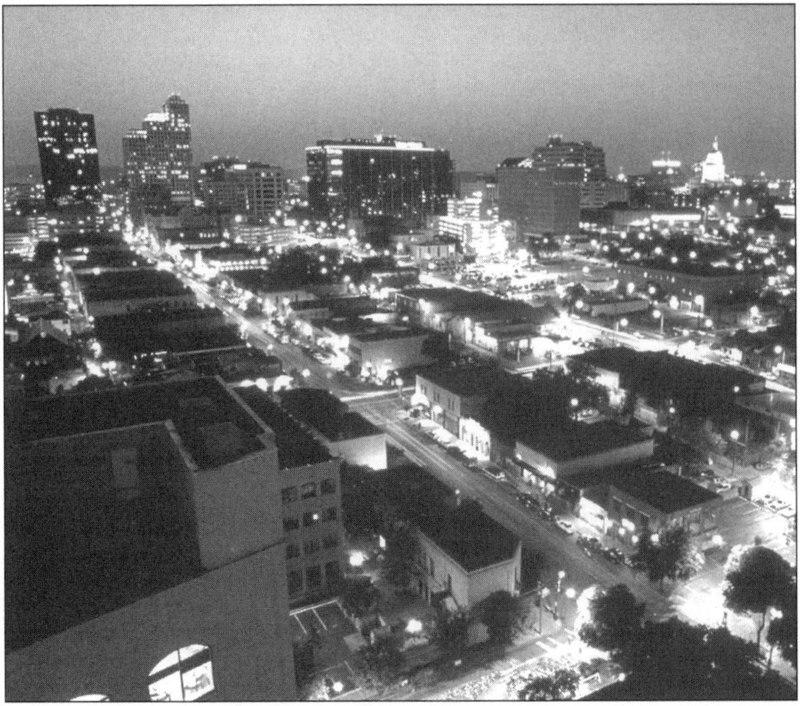

Photo: Courtesy of the Austin Convention and Visitors Bureau

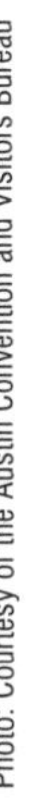

Sixth Street is the heart of Austin's music scene.

Layton and bassist Tommy Shannon, who both played with Stevie Ray Vaughan in Double Trouble. Guitarist David Grissom was formerly with Joe Ely and John Mellencamp, while Dave Holt has played his guitar with the Mavericks, Ely and Carlene Carter. Storyville, named after New Orleans' notorious red-light district, has won at least a dozen Austin Music Awards, including Band of the Year, Best Rock Band and Best Blues Band in a 1997-98 poll. Storyville followed up *Bluest Eyes* with 1996's *A Piece of Your Soul*, the group's Code Blue/ Atlantic debut. *Dog Years*, Storyville's newest CD, hit the stores in 1998. No matter how great their albums are, there's nothing like seeing Storyville perform live. Catch this show if you can. Storyville also tours nationally.

Texas Tornados: The *Houston Chronicle* called the Tornados a "Tejano band contained in a classic rock band masquerading on the charts as a country band." So let's just call it a Texas band. Whatever you call it, this group serves up spicy Tex-Mex on a platter of black-eyed peas. Made up of four eminently talented, and individually successful musicians, the Texas Tornados have been whipping up storms across Texas since the original quartet got together in 1990 to record a self-titled album and play to sold-out crowds around the territory. Their single, "Soy de San Luis," won a 1990 Grammy for Best Mexican-American Performance. (Tex-Mex superstar Freddie Fender, a founding member of this group, has since gone back to his solo career.)

Today's Tornados include distinguished musician Doug Sahm on guitar (read about Sahm in this chapter) and Augie Meyers on keyboards and accordion. These two were members of the 1960s band Sir Douglas Quintet. Roy Head, who replaced Fender, and conjunto accordion wizard Flaco Jimenez round out the foursome. Jimenez's father, Santiago, is in no small part responsible for the development of the accordion techniques that made conjunto music a staple along the border. Flaco has taken that tradition to new heights and is a popular performer and recording artist in his own right. His brother, Santiago, Jr., is also a well-known accordionist. With so many demands made on these individual performers, it isn't easy to get the Tornados together, but they're worth waiting for.

Ugly Americans: This is one of those bands that gets that "Parental Advisory" tag on its disc covers for explicit lyrics. Yes, there's an obscene word or two, or three to be found on *Boom Boom Baby*, the Ugly Americans second Capricorn Records album, for which this pop-rock-funk band grew to a whopping nine members. There's also a new horn section that absolutely shines on several songs and a overall new super groove feel to this one that makes it even more radio friendly than the group's earlier recordings. The Ugly Americans call their first major-label record *Stereophonic Spanish Fly*, released in 1996, an "all-around, smash-'em up rock record." The first single off the album, "Vulcan Death Grip," was a top-10 radio hit while "You Turn Me On" made the top 20. The Uglies, known for the incendiary outrageousness of their live shows, have toured nationally on the H.O.R.D.E. tour and with the Dave Matthews Band and others. The current Uglies include vocalist Bob Schneider, Bruce Hughes (vocals/bass), David "Snizz" Robinson (vocals/drums), David Boyle (keyboards), Adam "Slowpoke" Temple (vocals/guitar), Charles Rieser (vocals/guitar), Carlos Sosa (sax), Fernie "Maddog" Castillo (trumpet) and Rolo (trombone). Their alter-ego band is The Scabs.

Jimmie Vaughan: Vaughan was a teenage rock star in Dallas when the Beatles first ruled the world, opened for Jimi Hendrix in Houston and partied with Janis Joplin just about everywhere else — all before he was 20. Since those days, Vaughan has managed to become a virtual deity — "a living legend with a guitar style so deep that it defies description," according to *Guitar Player* magazine, which featured a Q & A with the Austin blues man in its July 1998 issue. Jimmie, older brother and mentor to the late blues star Stevie Ray (read about Stevie Ray in our Close-up in this chapter), has been devoting himself full time to the blues since he dropped out of his Dallas high school in the mid-1960s and shortly thereafter headed for Austin. He formed the Fabulous Thunderbirds nearly 25 years ago, signed on as the house band for a new Austin blues club called Antone's and headed straight for the history books. Vaughan has toured the world with ZZ Top, the Rolling Stones, B.B. King and Eric Clapton. *Family Style*, an album he recorded with Stevie Ray shortly before the younger Vaughan's death in August 1990, received rave reviews, won a Grammy Award for Best Contemporary Blues Recording, went platinum and continues to be a coveted disc for blues fans everywhere. Vaughan, who quit the Fabulous Thunderbirds in 1990, released *Strange Pleasure* in 1994 and *Out There* in 1998 for Epic Records. If you happen to be in town when Vaughan is performing, your trip is made.

Don Walser: Nicknamed the "Pavarotti of the Plains," Don Walser possesses a talent as big as Texas. This country singer can yodel a cowboy tune like none other. And that's not all. Walser and his Pure Texas Band perform a mesmerizing mix of old-time cowboy music, honky-tonk and Western Swing to audiences from coast to coast. Not bad for a guy who didn't devote himself full time to his career in music until the day he retired from a longtime job with the Texas National Guard just about five years ago. In 1994, Walser's album *Rolling Stone from Texas* earned rave reviews from *Billboard* magazine, *Rolling Stone* and other important music publications when it was released on Austin's Watermelon label. Walser's 1998 release, *Down at the Sky-Vue Drive-In*, is destined to be a classic and, most assuredly, will win him new fans across the country. While national recognition came late in Walser's life, performing has not. This giant of a man — known for wearing double-wide jeans — has been performing since his teens. In fact, Walser once opened for a kid named Buddy Holly in the Texas Panhandle town of Lamesa.

Kelly Willis: Country crooner and darling of the Austin club circuit, Willis is one of those performers who make your jaw drop open the minute she hits her first note. First, that powerful voice of hers comes charging at you like a bull on wings. Then you realize this young woman, who just turned 30 in late 1998, is mixing up some of the best traditional country sounds with a perfect dose of rock 'n' roll. Born in Lawton, Oklahoma, Kelly lived in North Carolina and then Virginia as a youngster. She was barely 18 when she convinced her parents to let her come to Austin with her rockabilly act Kelly and the Fireballs. When that broke up, Kelly went out on her own. She's had some major-label albums but so far no breakthrough successes, probably due to the fact that she's hard to pigeonhole into the nice neat categories that radio stations require. And that's exactly what her listening public most likes about this guitar-playing singer/songwriter. Look for her albums, *Bang, Bang* and *Fading Fast*. Willis is also a budding actress.

The Stages

Janis Joplin overcame her insecurities and launched her singing career in the early 1960s in an Austin beer joint. George Strait was a relative unknown when he first started singing around town. Stevie Ray Vaughan was just another teenager with a used guitar and a dream when he found a stage here. Austin's own Willie Nelson is a regular on our club and music hall scene. While not every artist who performs on an Austin stage goes on to fame and fortune, many of the hottest acts on the nation's club scene today got their start on an Austin stage.

From dark intimate clubs to big concert halls to superb outdoor venues, Austin's club scene swings seven nights a week, bringing a wide array of live music from around Austin and around the country. Few cities in the nation come close to Austin in the number of live acts performed on stage every single night.

If Austin is the Live Music Capital of the World, then Sixth Street is the Live Music Capital of Austin. This lively downtown strip, on East Sixth between Congress Avenue and Interstate 35, packs in more music than any other single part of town. This area, also a national historic district (see our Attractions chapter), is loaded with live music venues, restaurants, comedy clubs, T-shirt shops and tattoo parlors. Because of its national reputation, Sixth Street often gives tourists their first taste of Austin's live music scene. While many of the clubs and restaurants that line East Sixth present some of the hottest acts around today as well as some fascinating up-and-comers, this street also offers plenty of cover bands, DJs and untried acts. So don't miss out on the awesome Sixth Street scene, but check out Austin's other great clubs and music halls as well.

Of course, what would Austin be without music by the side of the lake? Several spots are known for presenting great live bands — some that cover popular songs and old favorites, and others doing original stuff. While the places listed here under The Shore are mainly known as restaurants, we couldn't miss out on telling you about them in this section. Austin music and the lakes are meant to be together like a singer and a guitar.

While there are just too many clubs around Austin to list them all, we've provided you with information about some of Austin's favorites, and some of our own. For information on some of Austin's other hot spots, check the listings in *The Austin Chronicle* and the *Austin American-Statesman*.

We're not providing specific information on cover charges because these can vary greatly, depending on the night of the week, the artist on stage or, it seems, the alignment of the stars in the heavens. Hours vary, too, so check with the club. Some clubs will allow minors in; many don't. Again, check with the club. The drinking age in Texas is 21. Most clubs sell tickets at the door only. We've noted where you can go or call to purchase advance tickets when they're on sale.

INSIDERS' TIP

The *Austin American-Statesman* features a daily "Best Bets" column on the back of the Metro & State section. This points out some of the hottest acts on stage for that evening. Also check out *The Austin Chronicle*, published Thursdays, and the *Statesman*'s XL section on Thursdays for a weekly lineup of live music shows.

Around Town

Antone's

213 W. Fifth St. • (512) 474-5314, (512) 322-0660 tickets

If there's one existing local club practically the whole world has heard of it's Antone's, Austin's home of the blues. Since 1975, this club, now in its fourth Austin location, has featured some of Austin's best blues performers as well as top blues artists from around the country. (See our history of the music scene in this chapter.) This Austin institution swings with live music seven nights a week. Clifford Antone opened his first club on Sixth Street on July 15, 1975. Its fourth Austin location opened at the corner of Fifth and Lavaca Streets downtown in 1997. Despite its renown, Antone's is known for its long history of financial and legal problems. Antone, who served 14 months in prison in 1985-86 on a guilty plea for possession of marijuana, is under indictment on charges of marijuana trafficking and money laundering charges. The trial is expected to take place in late 1998 or early 1999. Antone puts those troubles behind him night after night, however, by offering a continuous lineup of some of the best live music in town. Willie Nelson and Leon Russell packed the house for several sold-out performances here in 1998. And each year Antone's holds an anniversary week that draws some of the top names in blues. Jimmie Vaughan, Lou Ann Barton, Joe Ely, Charlie Sexton and scores of other first class local and national artists have all played this great club. Yet, Antone continues his tradition of presenting some of Austin's most promising up-and-comers. Antone also operates a record store (see our listing in this chapter) as well as a quality record label.

Austin Music Hall

208 Nueces St. • (512) 495-9962, (512) 469-SHOW Box Office

One of Austin's premier venues for national touring shows, the Austin Music Hall's contribution to the local music scene is enormous. Outstanding performing artists from around the country have performed at this 2,400-seat venue, including Bruce Springsteen, the Neville Brothers, Sara McLachlan, John Fogerty and many others. This hall, which is indeed a big hall with folding chairs for seats, also hosts the annual Austin Music Awards and other South by Southwest events, the annual Armadillo Christmas Bazaar as well as a number of benefit events throughout the year. It's also a great place for private parties. The Music Hall, which has gone through a variety of different owners throughout the years, has been operated since 1994 by Austinite Tim O'Connor's Direct Events, Inc., which also operates La Zona Rosa and The Backyard (see listings for them in this chapter). O'Connor's experience in the Austin club scene goes back nearly three decades, and it shows in the way he operates these clubs. O'Connor opened a club called Castle Creek in the early 1970s, which quickly gained a reputation for great touring shows. Later O'Connor opened the Austin Opera House, which often featured partner Willie Nelson as a performer. Direct Events also produces Willie Nelson's wildly popular annual Fourth of July Picnic, most recently in Luckenbach.

The Backyard

13101 W. U.S. Hwy. 71 • (512) 263-4146, (512) 469-SHOW Box Office

This delightful open-air venue surrounded by 500-year-old oak trees has become an Austin favorite since it opened in 1993 on a stretch of highway just west of town. Lyle Lovett, Bonnie Raitt, Gypsy Kings, The Indigo Girls, Willie Nelson, the Allman Brothers and many, many more national touring shows favor The Backyard during its March to mid-October season. For those who want to escape the bustle of booming Austin, the restaurant here, Waterloo Ice House and Ironworks Barbeque, is open year round. The Backyard amphitheater offers both seated concerts for about 2,400 people as well as more laid-back affairs in which people bring blankets to sit on. This venue is also popular for a number of family-oriented musical events, including a Father's Day show, giant Easter egg hunt and the Bee Cave Chili Cookoff. This venue is operated by Tim O'Connor's Direct Events, Inc., which also operates La Zona Rosa and the Austin Music Hall. For really popular shows, get your tickets early, as these events sell out fast. So do the great barbeque sandwiches and wraps on sale along with the drinks during the shows.

Broken Spoke

3201 S. Lamar Blvd. • (512) 442-6189

Willie Nelson calls the Broken Spoke his favorite watering hole. *Texas Highways* magazine has called it the Best Honky-Tonk in Texas while *Entertainment Weekly* has said it's the best country dance hall in the country. The Broken Spoke has appeared in a host of movies, documentaries and commercials (including one for Foster's Beer that made the Spoke a household name in Australia). For 35 years, the Broken Spoke has been dishing up a steady stream of the best country music Austin has to offer — along with a full menu of down-home Texas cookin' (see our Restaurants chapter). Alvin Crow, Asleep at the Wheel, Don Walser, Willie Nelson, the Derailers and The Geezinslaw Brothers are some of the local luminaries that make regular appearances here. Bob Wills and the Texas Playboys, George Strait, Tex Ritter, Ernest Tubb and other country stars have become part of the Spoke's big family.

The hub of this operation is James M. White. Just 25 years old and fresh out of the Army, White spied a patch of land adorned by a big live oak tree on the southern outskirts of Austin, just a couple miles from his boyhood home. On November 10, 1964, he opened the Broken Spoke. The dance hall was added a year later. Since then, White and his wife Annetta have raised two daughters and a whole generation of country music fans. White even wrote his own theme song, *Broken Spoke Legend*. Crow recorded it on his *Pure Country* album on the Broken Spoke's own record label. Whether you come to the Broken Spoke to eat, to dance or just listen to the music, be sure to allow time to visit the two rooms packed with country music memorabilia and mementos from the music stars and film celebrities who've made this an Austin landmark. This ain't no fancy dancer. The low ceiling leaks in places (though White has devised his own intricate system to divert the runoff), and the stage is just a small rise above the dance floor. But, hey, nobody comes to the Spoke because they've seen it in *Architectural Digest*. They come because it's a good-timin', down-home Texas tradition.

Cactus Cafe

Texas Union Building, 24th and Guadalupe Sts. • (512) 475-6515

This excellent club in the Student Union on the University of Texas campus has been serving up live music for 65 years. Opened in 1933 as the Chuck Wagon, the club was among Austin's first hippie hangouts in the 1960s, catering to an emerging group of "folkie" musicians that included a young Janis Joplin. After going through a few names, the club was renamed the Cactus Cafe in 1977, but continues to be one of Austin's prime venues for singer/songwriters presenting acoustic performances. Austin favorites Butch Hancock and Darden Smith perform here along with an assortment of top Austin acts and great national touring acts. You can also find some bluegrass, swing, jazz and an occasional rock act here. Griff Luneburg has managed the Cactus Cafe since 1982. This nonsmoking venue, which opens at 8 AM, is a popular daytime hangout for UT students, faculty and staff. Evening shows draw a healthy mixture of students and members of the Austin general public.

Carousel Lounge

1110 E. 52nd St. • (512) 452-6790

Located just east of Interstate 35, the Carousel Lounge has been serving up drinks and music since 1963 when Cecil and Myrtle Meier opened the place and decorated it with a whimsical circus decor. Now operated by their daughter, Nicki Mebane, the Carousel features live music — usually swing, jazz, big band or lounge acts — on Tuesday, Thursday, Friday and Saturday nights. The place really hops on Wednesday nights, too, when swing dance lessons are offered. The lounge looks much as it did a quarter century ago, with those miniature jukeboxes (not in service) over the tables, an aqua-colored padded bar and a big jukebox that's loaded with lots of old music. Huge circus-theme murals adorn both walls and the backstage area.

The Carousel serves bottled and canned beers only, but features a good list of microbrewed and imported beers. Addition-

Two Voices

The Red Headed Stranger has turned gray before our eyes. The Guitar God will remain forever young in our minds. One became guru of Austin's explosive country rock movement. A decade later, the other put Austin blues on the map. Two Austin music icons. Two international superstars. Two musical styles. Two distinct stories.

Twenty-one years apart in age, Willie Nelson and Stevie Ray Vaughan were both on the run when they discovered Austin in the early 1970s. After a decade of rejection as a performer in Nashville, Willie took it as a sign when his Tennessee home burned to the ground in 1970. The 37-year-old musical outlaw decided to return to his native Texas. Here, at least, he wouldn't be tormented for refusing to bend with the winds of Nashville musical fashion — and certainly no one would bother him if he wanted to grow his hair long or tie a red bandana hippie-style around his forehead. Stevie, a scrawny 17-year-old when he hit town in 1972, was on the lam from the stifling prison of high school and the watchful eye of his parents in their working-class Dallas suburb of Oak Cliff.

Willie and Stevie's timing couldn't have been better. Austin was perched to take the music world by storm (see our Close-up on The Music Biz in this chapter.)

Willie's star would be the first to shine. Born April 30, 1933, in the tiny north central Texas town of Abbott, Willie and his sister Bobbie (now a member of his band) learned music through mail-order courses taught by the grandparents who raised them after their parents divorced. When he wasn't picking cotton, the young Willie spent his childhood glued to the radio, listening to the Grand Ole Opry, New Orleans jazz, black blues from the South, Frank Sinatra, Big Band singers and Western Swing, especially the sound pioneered by the famous Bob Wills. He became a member of a Bohemian polka band at age 10 and as a young man worked selling encyclopedias, Bibles and vacuum cleaners door to door. In an effort to get closer to the music he loved, Willie wheedled his way into his first job as a disc jockey in San Antonio, and later took his talents to Washington State. In 1956, while working as a DJ in Vancouver, Washington, he financed his first recording, "No Place for Me," and sold copies at a dollar each to his radio listeners.

The toddler born Stephen Ray Vaughan on October 3, 1954, meanwhile, was just learning to talk.

Willie returned to Texas in the late 1950s to work as a DJ and musical performer. While in Houston, he wrote some of his most memorable work, including "Night Life" and "Family Bible." He was so broke that he sold both songs for a mere $200, then set out to seek his fortune in Nashville.

In 1961 Pasty Cline recorded Willie's monumental song "Crazy" in Nashville and took it to No. 1 on the charts. Shortly thereafter, Faron Young scored a No. 1 hit with Willie's "Hello Walls." (Stevie, just 7 years old back in Texas, had not yet picked up a guitar.)

While Willie attained extraordinary success as a country songwriter in Nashville and even made his own Grand Ole Opry debut in 1964, Nashville never warmed up to him as a performer. "The hobo funk of Jimmy Rodgers was gone from country music. It was polished, packaged and sold like any other form of commercial music . . ." wrote Austinite Jan Reid in his book, *The Improbable Rise of Redneck Rock*. "All along the real Nashville rebel was Willie Nelson. He made enough money to sit back and be grateful, but he never toed the Nashville line." When his house burned, Willie and family decided to get out of Dodge.

— continued on next page

Photo: E. J. Camp

Willie Nelson. Healing Hands of Time.

Stevie, who by 1971 was a 16-year-old, guitar-playing radical with a blossoming drug habit, had determined that music would be his ticket out of Oak Cliff. His older brother, Jimmie, had proven it could be done when he'd split for Austin a couple of years earlier. Like Willie, Stevie and Jimmie Vaughan were raised on radio. But instead of Bob Wills, the Vaughan boys listened to blues artists such as Muddy Waters, Howlin' Wolf and Bobby "Blue" Bland. When Jimmie broke his collarbone playing football at age 12, a family friend gave him a guitar to help him pass the time. Nine-year-old Stevie heard his big brother playing that guitar like he'd been born with it, and was instantly hooked.

As Stevie later explained, his was the classic, "Wow, me too," reaction of a younger brother. As it turned out, they were both naturals. The older Vaughan had the guitar and enough allowance money to amass a huge record collection that included the likes of B.B. King, Albert King, Lonnie Mack, Otis Rush and Jimi Hendrix. Despite constant threats from his brother, Stevie couldn't keep his hands off either Jimmie's guitar or his record collection.

"I'd come home with a B.B. King album and try to learn all the leads and beginnings and ends, because I was so into the guitar," Jimmie told *Guitar Player* magazine in 1991. "And Stevie was there. He'd play the record over and over, trying to figure out, 'What is he doing here?' . . . I'd put the guitar down and go in the other room, and he'd pick it up . . . We discovered how it worked together."

As the years passed, Jimmie went on to become a blues star in his own right. "Both matured into very distinct blues stylists," according to *Guitar Player*. "In a nutshell, Jimmie became the ultimate minimalist, a master of subtlety, economy, and simplicity; Stevie, three and a half years his junior, played every solo as if it were his last, as though he couldn't rest until he'd said his piece. And he had a lot to say."

Stevie had a lot of dues to pay before he would earn those accolades, however. In 1972, four months shy of graduation, Stevie dropped out of high school and headed for the Austin music oasis with his band Blackbird. He was just 17. "For a Dallas kid bound and determined to play guitar for a living, moving to Austin was better than dying and going to heaven," wrote Joe Nick Patoski and Bill Crawford in their book, *Stevie Ray Vaughan: Caught in the Crossfire*. "Pursuing your art was the name of the game."

Pursuing his art is exactly what Willie had been doing since he had come home to Texas the year before. By August 12, 1972, when Willie first appeared on stage at the Armadillo World Headquarters, it was obvious he had something.

"Who in his right mind could have predicted that the same audience that got turned on by B.B. King and Jerry Garcia would also go nuts for Willie Nelson?" Gary Cartwright wrote in a 1998 *Texas Monthly* article. "This Abbott cotton picker had merged blues, rock and country into something altogether original and evocative." In 1973, the Nashville exile recorded his breakthrough album, *Shotgun Willie*.

Austin, meanwhile, became the epicenter of a trail-blazing movement in country music as other artists battered by the musical establishment found themselves drawn by the city's mounting musical charm. Alternately labeled progressive country, country rock and redneck rock — because radio stations, the music press and others didn't quite know what to make of this country music laced with rock and blues — the style created an enormous new class of country-fried hippies (see our Music Biz Close-up in this chapter).

In 1975, Willie recorded the album that would put him over the top: *The Red Headed Stranger*. Featuring the single, "Blues Eyes Crying in the Rain," the album established Willie as a country music great. The following year RCA Records packaged previously issued material by Willie, Waylon Jennings and others on the album *Wanted: The Outlaws*. It became the first country album to sell a million records, sparked a musical

— continued on next page

revolution and finally branded Willie as a true outlaw. All the while Austin's "ropers and dopers" worshipped their hometown hero.

Stevie, who saw no use for Willie's outlaws, spent his early years in Austin getting high on the drugs that flowed freely and honing his considerable guitar skills at clubs such as the One Knite and the Soap Creek Saloon. The Soap Creek was "the place where he would develop the sophisticated yet hard-driving style that would become the basis of his legacy," wrote Patoski and Crawford.

In 1975, the year Willie accepted the first of his five Grammy Awards, a blues buff by the name of Clifford Antone decided to open a club to draw some of the country's blues greats to town. Austin finally had a home for the blues. At Antone's, Stevie would receive the thrill of his young life when his hero, Albert King, invited him on stage to play.

"Stevie worked the strings with such brute power and brash confidence, King was taken aback. It was like the young boy had just twisted the cap off the bottle that contained the secrets of all blues and poured every guitar lick known to man right out on stage," Patoski and Crawford wrote.

Stevie Ray went on to form Triple Threat Revue and then Double Trouble, the band that would skyrocket him to stardom. In 1983, the year the National Academy of Popular Music honored its first-ever country artist — Willie Nelson, of course — with a Lifetime Achievement Award, Epic Records released Double Trouble's first album *Texas Flood*. An international guitar hero was born. Double Trouble's second album *Couldn't Stand the Weather*, went platinum and was followed by *Soul to Soul*. Double Trouble, fronted by the scrawny young man sporting his trademark flat-brimmed black hat and battered Stratocaster, landed prestigious international touring gigs, an appearance at Carnegie Hall, and legions of worshippers. Through it all, Stevie Ray remained a humble, gentle man who never failed to give credit to his musical mentors or his fellow artists. But Stevie Ray's addiction to drugs and alcohol was literally killing him. He collapsed while on tour in Europe.

Stevie Ray's commitment to beating his addictions and his willingness to share the secrets of his new-found sobriety with others are now legendary within the music industry. He checked himself into a London Clinic in 1986 and emerged from treatment a new man and an even better artist. He moved home to Dallas to renew ties with his mother while he cut a new album with Double Trouble. *In Step*, released in 1988, went platinum and earned the group a Grammy — one of six Stevie would win for his music.

In 1990, Stevie Ray and Jimmie finally got together musically for a Grammy-winning album, *Family Style*. It was released two weeks after Stevie Ray's tragic death. In the early morning hours of August 27, 1990, Stevie Ray Vaughan, blues player extraordinaire, was killed in a helicopter crash while returning to Chicago from an Alpine Valley concert in East Troy, Wisconsin. He was 35 years old.

For Willie, the 1990s brought a mixed bag of professional triumphs and personal hardships. His 33-year-old son, Billy, (one of Willie's seven children) hanged himself in 1991. The tragedy came on the heels of Willie's major clash with the Internal Revenue Service and his arrest on a misdemeanor marijuana possession charge. In 1990, claiming he owed nearly $17 million in back taxes and interest, the IRS seized Nelson's bank accounts and property in Texas and around the country. The crisis brought fans and friends rushing to his rescue — some donating change to a "Where There's a Willie, There's a Way" fund set up in Austin, other wealthier supporters going so far as to buy his ranch outside Austin and his treasured Pedernales Recording Studio, returning one to Willie outright and leasing the other to the artist for, well, a song. Willie himself made light of the calamity by marketing a CD called *Who'll Buy These Memories — The IRS Tapes* and eventually settled with the IRS for $9 million. The marijuana charge, meanwhile, was later dismissed. Nelson, who never has concealed the fact that he

— continued on next page

smokes pot (he once smoked a joint on the roof of President Carter's White House) has always publicly maintained the government has no business regulating an "herb."

Through it all, Willie has remained one of country music's most revered performers. In 1993, Willie broke out of a creative lull and released the exceptional album *Across the Borderline*. *Spirit*, his 1996 album, featured a whole new batch of originals. In 1998 Willie's latest CD, *Teatro*, made its debut. Among Willie's more than 100 albums are many that have gone multi-platinum, including his classics *Red Headed Stranger*, *Stardust* and *Always on My Mind*. Over the years, Willie turned the Fourth of July into one of Texas' greatest musical celebrations with the continuation of the annual concerts he started in 1973.

The Farm Aid concerts Willie stages have raised thousands for farmers and called attention to the plight of family-owned farms across the country while the acting career he launched in 1980 with *Electric Horseman*, is going strong. Just recently Willie launched the Outlaw Music Channel in conjunction with the Kickapoo Indian tribe of Kansas. The cable channel, not yet available in Austin, showcases vintage country music programs, classic performances by Willie and other music greats and includes Indian dance and history programs. Today, his sprawling ranch outside Austin, known as Willie World, includes his home, recording studio, a golf course (for another of his passions) and even a Western movie set.

While Willie tours constantly, he always makes time for his hometown audience, and his Austin concerts invariably wind up as sold-out, standing-room-only events. With only a few chords of "Mamas Don't Let Your Babies Grow Up to Be Cowboys," "Angel Flying to Close to the Ground," "On the Road Again" and countless other classics, his shows turn into a sing-along. After all, every single person in the crowd knows the lyrics by heart.

"When I was a kid working those cotton fields as a kid in Abbott, Texas, I had no idea the ride would be this long or this successful," Willie said in a published 1998 interview. "At that time, success was anywhere except in that cotton patch."

His face may be chiseled by the years, by the whiskey and by a life spent on the road, but his music remains as fresh and as gut-wrenchingly powerful as it was when he started out more than four decades ago. He has definitely kept us satisfied.

Stevie Ray, the man who's been called the soul of Austin, lives on through his music and, as such, remains a beloved icon of this city. His phenomenal guitar talents continue to set the standard by which other Austin musicians are judged. A memorial statue of the late blues rocker, erected in 1993, stands by Town Lake as an eternal reminder of the gentle man and his far-out music. He is always on our minds.

---

ally, this is a brown bag bar, meaning patrons can bring their own hard liquor and then order the soft drink and ice that goes with it. This treasured Austin landmark is now being discovered by a whole new generation of music fans. The bar closes at 8 PM on Mondays but swings late the rest of the week.

Cedar Street Courtyard

208 W. Fourth St. • (512) 495-9669

Jazz under the trees. Since Cedar Street opened in 1994, this lovely outdoor venue that's just loaded with live oak trees has gained a reputation for featuring excellent local jazz musicians as well as acts from around the country. Tucked between two buildings a few steps down from sidewalk level in downtown Austin, this intimate setting is the perfect place for live music. There also are indoor bars along the sides, so the music just moves inside when it rains. Malaga's, a new tapas restaurant and wine bar, opened in 1998 (see our Restaurants chapter).

Continental Club

1315 S. Congress Ave. • (512) 441-2444

Perhaps it's the perennial odor of day-old beer and stale cigarettes that lends this club its primo atmosphere. More likely, it's the long, long list of top Austin acts that have earned their musical wings at the Continental Club over the years that gives it such an excellent reputation among Austin's music lovers. There's generally always somebody worth seeing within these dark walls.

Dessau Music Hall

13422 Dessau Rd. • (512) 252-1123, (512) 703-6994 Information Line

Built about 125 years ago, Dessau Music Hall is without a doubt Austin's oldest existing tradition as a dance hall. This facility, however, has burned down a couple of times, been rebuilt with metal, remodeled and revamped and has had so many different owners that it hasn't retained the flavor of the original 19th-century wooden structure. Yet, for live music and good ol' country and western dances, Dessau is still one popular place to stop. Dessau features regular live music, including both regional and national touring shows, as well as various dance programs such as country-western, ballroom and Tejano.

Elvis Presley played here in 1954, before he became the King, and only a dozen people showed up. Supposedly he came back just a few years later and packed the house. Dessau has packed the house many times over, offering performances by such greats as the Glenn Miller Orchestra and Loretta Lynn. Some of Austin's finest local bands also perform here regularly. While there's almost always live music on Friday and Saturday nights, there also can be shows on other nights of the week too. Call the information hotline, or check the club listings in the *Austin American-Statesman* to find out what's on tap.

Electric Lounge

302 Bowie St. • (512) 476-FUSE

This great space, formerly an abandoned warehouse, is now an inviting club that features live music five to seven nights a week as well as happy hour shows Wednesday through Friday. Mike Henry and partners Mark Shuman and Jay Hughey run this space, which also hosts theater and poetry events. The Electric Lounge offers an eclectic format — just about anything but blues — that includes new local acts and well-established Austin artists as well as national touring shows, sometimes in the same evening. The large paintings that adorn the walls are part of Electric Lounge's ongoing art show and sale. This is one lively club and a great place to see Austin's up-and-comers. Alejandro Escovedo, Fastball, Jimmie Dale Gilmore and other hot Austin acts all have played the Electric Lounge. Lately, Asylum Street Spankers have been presenting a popular Wednesday night show here, which is curious since this band shuns the "demon electricity."

Elephant Room

315 Congress Ave. • (512) 473-2279

Voted Best Jazz Bar in Austin seven years in a row by the Clarksville Jazz Festival, the Elephant Room presents a wide variety of live jazz, including Latin jazz, fusion, traditional and funk. This cozy basement club, opened in 1991 and owned by Jean Pierre Vermaelen, presents an excellent assortment of Austin bands as well as bands from around the country. Audiences are treated to the cool sounds of live jazz seven nights a week. (Yes, some of the artists and members of the audience do don sunglasses — it's that cool.) The Elephant Room also features happy hour shows Tuesday through Thursday. You'll find this club be-

INSIDERS' TIP

With so much live music in town you'd think there would always be plenty of room for one more body to see a show. Think again. Austin audiences swarm to great shows, so be sure to arrive early if you want a good seat. While events in our music halls generally start earlier in the evening, the main act at a club can go on stage at midnight or later. Clubs must pick up drinks at 2 AM. Cover charges vary.

low Kyoto's Restaurant on Congress (see our Restaurants chapter).

Emo's

603 Red River St. • (512) 477-3667

Eric "Emo" Hartman runs this space, which features two indoor stages as well as an outdoor patio. Since 1992, Emo's has developed a solid Austin clientele by presenting both local and national cutting-edge acts five to six nights a week. The big brick hall and main bar holds one stage where live acts perform during the week, as well as pool tables for the afternoon crowd. For other performances music fans move to the space out back. This venue — which actually is a space between two existing structures that has been covered — is the main stage for weekend acts. It can get hot in here, as there's no air conditioning, but with such hot music, who's to complain?

Frank Erwin Center

1701 Red River St. • (512) 471-7744, (512) 477-6060 UTTM Box Office

Austin's largest venue for national touring musicians is also home to University of Texas basketball as well as Disney's On Ice shows, circuses and scores of other events throughout the year. When it comes to music, however, there just isn't any space in Austin as large or as comfortable for the crowds that have turned out to see such top acts as Elton John, Garth Brooks, Kiss, Madonna, Julio Iglesias, Van Halen, Paul Simon, Crosby, Stills and Nash, and many more world-class musical performers, including, of course, many Austin music legends. The Erwin Center also hosts plenty of classical musical performers. Depending on the stage setup, the Erwin Center can hold anywhere from 4,000 to 18,000 fans. Performances are announced well in advance in the local press. The Erwin Center was built in 1977 and named in 1981 for the beloved University of Texas regent and chairman who had been crucial in getting this popular UT facility built.

Hole in the Wall

2538 Guadalupe St. • (512) 472-5599

Hole in the Wall, which celebrated its 25th anniversary in 1998, is an Austin institution. In fact, it's been around so long that it's now run by Douglas Cugini, the son of the original owners. The name says it all. Located near the University of Texas campus, this IS just a hole in the wall. But over its quarter century in business this club and eatery has earned a reputation for presenting excellent up-and-coming and established bands. Fastball used to play here for free on Sunday nights. In fact, Fastball guitarist Miles Zuniga told Jay Leno's Tonight Show viewers in 1998 about how the entire Hole in the Wall crowd went chasing after a thief who'd tried to steal his guitar. Is this family or what? Known mostly for presenting alternative rock bands, Hole in the Wall also presents a wide range of music, including bluegrass, pop, acoustic and country. Mostly regional bands are presented here, although Hole in the Wall also presents an occasional national or international band. In addition to the live music seven nights a week, there's also an additional happy hour show on Tuesdays, Wednesdays and Thursdays.

La Zona Rosa

612 W. Fourth St. • (512) 472-2293

This longtime Austin tradition, formerly a quaint Mexican eatery and music hall, had been going through a series of owners until Direct Events, Inc. purchased it in 1997. Now remodeled and air-conditioned, La Zona Rosa is concentrating on the music and, as such, is high on the list of hot Austin clubs known for providing consistent quality entertainment. La Zona Rosa presents both national touring shows and some of Austin's best up-and-coming artists. Its two rooms can be made into one for shows that seat up to 1,200 people. It's also perfect for catered private parties. Check who's on stage for La Zona Rosa's popular gospel brunch show on Sundays.

Liberty Lunch

405 W. Second St. • (512) 477-0461

Few live music venues have captured Austin's affection like Liberty Lunch. This large airy space (half of it is out under the trees through huge garage-type doors) regularly hosts some of the best music in the city. Lyle Lovett, Blues Traveler, Hootie and the Blowfish as well as Austin's own Willie Nelson, Nanci Griffith and Trish Murphy have played the Lunch. This venue, officially called Liberty

Lunch and Wagon Yard, dates back to the 1800s when it really was the town wagon yard, located next to the Schneider Store, Austin's first grocery store. By the early 1900s, the building sat amidst Guy Town, Austin's red-light district, and then went through a series of incarnations, including a drive-through lumber yard. Austin's famous Esther's Follies (see our Nightlife chapter) turned it into a performance venue in the 1970s. Later it went musical. At one point in the 1980s there was talk of building a City Hall complex with an Italian-style piazza facing Town Lake down here. Liberty Lunch would have been a major feature of the piazza, but its grassroots clientele rebelled, refusing any sort of change to their funky Liberty Lunch. The plan was nixed.

This is not a starter club, but a place to step up to a big stage and a great P.A. system. Often even the warm-up band has produced a CD or two. Under the direction of owner Mark Pratz and his associate J'net Ward, Liberty Lunch hosts established musicians of every style from Austin and around the world. The bar serves just bottled beer, wine, soft drinks, and juices. Totally open air until a few years ago, Liberty Lunch now has a roof to draw larger crowds on chilly nights. Like they say at the Lunch, "We're air conditioned in the winter."

Saxon Pub

1320 S. Lamar Blvd. • (512) 448-2552

Saxon Pub started out as a folk music club when it opened in South Central Austin in 1990. While owner Joe Ables still books acoustic acts, Saxon is now gaining a reputation as a great blues club. Country and rock bands also have found a home here. With great live music seven nights a week, including an occasional early show, it's no wonder this is one place Austin comes to hear live music. Ables books mainly hot Austin acts and some national touring shows. To the delight of music fans, some of the country's most popular musicians also have been known to drop in for a jam session or two. Bonnie Raitt, Kris Kristofferson, Michael Martin Murphey and others make occasional unannounced appearances. This club has had many owners and many names throughout the years, but Saxon Pub is the one that has caught Austin's attention.

South Park Meadows

9600 S. I-35 • (512) 280-8771, (512) 469-SHOW tickets

This great outdoor venue, which features a huge stage, hosts several major shows a year during the spring, summer and fall. South Park garnered a major coup in 1998 with the arrival in Austin of the ultra-hip Lilith Fair tour of female artists that included performances by Sarah McLachlan, Bonnie Raitt and other local and national performers. The grassy amphitheater features scattered shade trees — a perfect place to toss a blanket and enjoy a midsummer concert. South Park, however, doesn't allow coolers on the premises. This Austin hot spot can be found at the corner of Slaughter Lane and Interstate 35 in South Austin. The concerts are always promoted well in advance in local newspapers and on the radio.

Speakeasy

412 Congress Ave. • (512) 476-8017

Opened in 1997, the Speakeasy quickly joined the ranks of Austin's popular night spots. This upscale club — real carpeting on the floors, fresh flowers and cozy booths — features live music six nights a week as well as swing dance lessons Monday through Wednesday. This is the place to play billiards, hear swing bands play some great standards from the '30s and '40s as well as some original music. The Speakeasy also offers plenty of blues, jazz, salsa, lounge music and some country tunes. The rooftop deck, which offers a great view of downtown, features world beat contemporary CDs. This club, run by Austin's Flamingos XCVI Corp., has a happy hour buffet Monday through Friday. While the address for this club is Congress Avenue, the entrance is around back in the alley. It's easy to find.

Stubb's Bar-B-Q

801 Red River St. • (512) 480-8341

It's hard to say which is more enticing at this Austin hangout, the excellent barbeque or the live music acts that perform six days a week on both the indoor and outdoor stages. The building itself is an historical gem. Built in the 1850s of native limestone, the building has been remodeled into a 6,000-square-foot two-level restaurant with mahogany and cherry bars that date to the 1870s. Outdoors are two decks and bars overlooking the stage. In modern times, this was the location of an earlier Austin hotspot, the One Knite. Today, Stubb's presents live music on Tuesday through Saturday nights as well as a Sunday gospel brunch and occasional Sunday night shows. C.B. "Stubb" Stubblefield is the barbeque king behind this operation, having operated barbeque joints in Lubbock and around Texas for more than 40 years. Today, Stubb's showcases both national touring acts and some of Austin's finest musicians. The Ugly Americans, Joe Ely, Storyville, The Derailers and Kelly Willis are just a few of the outstanding Austin artists to grace Stubb's stages. The restaurant is open 11 AM to 11 PM, but the great live music goes on until 2 AM. Stubb's is closed Mondays.

Top of the Marc

618 W. Sixth St. • (512) 472-9849

This classy location above Katz's Deli on West Sixth Street features some of Austin's top bands and performers, as well as occasional touring shows. Top of the Marc gets raves for its lovely rooftop deck, which is perfectly situated so that patrons can still see and hear the live music on stage indoors. This venue has an excellent drink list, which includes a wide selection of martinis as well as cognacs and brandies that appeal to this club's sophisticated crowd. And patrons can order up food from the deli downstairs. W.C. Clark, 8½ Souvenirs and Lou Ann Barton are just three of the great Austin acts who've given Top of the Marc such a fine reputation. Marc Katz, who opened Katz' New York-style deli in 1979 (see our Restaurants chapter), is the man behind this great venue. Live acts go on stage seven nights a week. The entrance is around the corner on Rio Grande Street.

Sixth Street

Babe's

208 E. Sixth St. • (512) 473-2262

Live music seven nights a week, including everything from traditional country to heavy metal, has made Babe's one of Sixth Street's happening clubs. Mostly regional bands perform on Babe's two stages. This has been a favorite of Austin sensations Don Walser and Alvin Crow as well as many other well-established and up-and-coming bands. Babe's serves a steady stream of live music and great food for all to enjoy. Check the listings or call the club for information about Babe's earlier shows during the week. Five nights a week, this historic building rocks with live music on both stages. The restaurant opens at 11 AM.

Bates Motel

317 E. Sixth St. • (512) 480-8121

We thought this gloriously seedy dive was named for Norman Bates of *Psycho* fame but indeed the owner's name is Joe Bates. He offers live music for avant-punk fans five to seven nights a week in a mostly stripped-down joint. (The wild wall murals are worth a look, though.) The mostly local acts present a wide variety of punk music that appeals to both the nerdy art crowd or those who like a super-crusty-punk-drag worm show. The Chumps and F***emo's are two of the most popular bands who perform here. Minors are allowed in, but must have their hand stamped with a "Sucks to Be Me" imprint. Bates also operates Joe's Generic Bar next door.

The Black Cat

309 E. Sixth St. • no phone

It's not the lack of air conditioning that makes this one of Austin's hottest locales for live music. The Black Cat is known for presenting some pretty hot bands during the six nights a week it's open. In operation since 1985 and now operated by Sasha Sessums, the daughter of founders Paul and Roberta, The Black Cat aims to help develop the Austin music scene by presenting unknown local bands and giving them a chance to develop a following by allowing them to play on the same night every week. The system has worked. Many Austin notables, including Sister 7, got their start at this stripped-down venue, which features tiered seating along the side walls. The Black Cat is closed Sundays.

Fat Tuesday

508 E. Sixth St. • (512) 474-0632

This New Orleans-based chain opened in Austin in 1994 and presents a variety of live music seven nights a week in a large and comfortable indoor/outdoor venue. Both original music and cover bands playing top-40 hits, swing, reggae and more are presented on this stage. Fat Tuesday features a full bar as well as an entire wall of 16 frozen daiquiri flavors — if you mix flavors the combinations are endless. The club also has video games and pool tables.

Maggie Mae's

323 E. Sixth St. • (512) 478-8541

With three different stages offering simultaneous music on weekends, an airy rooftop bar upstairs and private courtyard down, Maggie Mae's has no trouble drawing a crowd. Named for a famous London lady of the evening, Maggie Mae's offers live music seven nights a week. One band is featured during the week, but on Fridays and Saturdays this two-story club rocks with different types of music in three different rooms, including at least two live bands. The building, originally a general store built in 1874, predates Sixth Street's historic Driskill Hotel by a dozen years. Owned and operated by the Shea brothers, Bill and Danny, since 1977, Maggie Mae's is one of this strip's longest running and most successful clubs. This club, also acclaimed for its extensive beer selection, hosts beer tastings as well as private, catered parties.

Steamboat

403 E. Sixth St. • (512) 478-2913

After more than two decades in the same spot, Steamboat has earned its enduring status as one of Austin's favorite clubs. This is one place where Christopher Cross got his start before he went on to national fame. Some of Austin's best known performers have started out playing at this inviting space, which owner Danny Crooks says holds about 300 music fans, although he tries not to pack in more than 600. Crooks says any band with the nerve to get up on stage has a shot at Steamboat. "You can get out there and really make a fool out of yourself or maybe impress someone," he says. Singer/songwriter Will Sexton started out playing here when he was just 13, and guitar player Eric Johnson has been a regular. Storyville also started out at Steamboat. Crooks runs the club like a major league farm team system. New bands start out playing on slow nights and, if they can cut it, work themselves up to the prime Friday and Saturday night lineups. Steamboat presents live music seven nights a week.

The 311 Club

311 E. Sixth St. • (512) 477-1630

R&B star Joe Valentine is not just one of The 311 Club's owners, he's also the featured attraction here several nights a week. The New Orleans-born Valentine studied music from the Catholic nuns in his parochial school when he was just a boy and started playing professionally at age 12. By age 16 Valentine was opening for Ray Charles. Since then Valentine has toured the world with his own bands, opened for acts such as Jackie Wilson and Ike and Tina Turner, written songs for James Brown Productions, scored his own hit in 1968 with "I Can't Stand to See You Go" and was the band leader for the Joe Tex Revue. This singer/songwriter/keyboardist is a longtime Austin club owner who formerly ran The Scorpio Club and then Valentine's. Is it any wonder The 311 is one great rhythm and blues club? When Joe Valentine and the Imperials aren't on stage, other blues and R&B bands from around Austin and around the country perform on stage here. There's live music seven nights a week.

The Shores

Music snobs may reckon that venues known primarily as lakeside eateries are unworthy of mention in the same listing with

INSIDERS' TIP

If you've read this chapter, looked through the papers and still can't decide which act to see, check with the staff at some of Austin's record stores. Waterloo Records at the corner of Sixth Street and Lamar Boulevard is particularly helpful. In Northwest Austin try Borders Books & Music or Barnes & Noble's music department.

such Austin classics as Antone's, the Broken Spoke, Liberty Lunch and others here. You might not always hear original music at these restaurants, but sometimes you will. Besides, even the cover bands we've heard at several of these places beat the music many visitors will find at home. And you get to enjoy being out on the lakes at the same time. Water and music — now that's an unbeatable Austin combination. This is just one more dimension of the Live Music Capital of the World. Check the music listings in the local papers to find out which bands are currently playing, then decide for yourself. To find more about most of these eateries, see our Restaurants chapter.

Carlos 'n Charlie's

5793 Hiline Rd. • (512) 266-1683

This popular Tex-Mex eatery was destroyed by rushing flood waters on Lake Travis in the summer of 1997. Now rebuilt — to float — the new, bigger location sacrifices much of the charm of the old place, but makes up for it with a huge dance hall on the lower level. So you can have your dinner upstairs overlooking the lake and then descend the stairs for a night of music and dancing. There's live music Thursday through Sunday.

The Oasis

6550 Comanche Tr. • (512) 266-2441

Situated high above Lake Travis, The Oasis is famous for its fabulous view of the sunset. But the multilayered outdoor decks are also perfect for dining — and for listening to live music Friday, Saturday and Sunday evenings. The bands play all kinds of music, including Motown, top 40, jazz and much more. Austin bands, performing both original hits and popular contemporary music, make this place a must stop for those who want to experience the outdoor music scene in Austin. They've also got a great selection of frozen Margaritas, a full bar and a generous menu.

The Pier

1701 River Hills Dr. • (512) 327-4562

A huge stage shaded by 60-foot elms, a large concrete slab of a dance floor and plenty of picnic tables (though many have seen better days) for dining and drinking make this one great place to hear cover bands play all varieties of music. You can even drive your boat right up to the dock on Lake Austin and listen from there or join the crowds that gather for the show, especially on Wednesday evenings and Sunday afternoons when this place starts to swing. The food is typical lakeside fare: fried foods, sandwiches, salads, grilled food and snacks, but the bar is fully stocked and the frozen Margaritas and rum runner flow. This place also has a lighted sand volleyball court. Check out The Pier for music Wednesday through Sunday.

Sam Hill Waterfront Grill

16405 Marina Pt. • (512) 266-8534

Dance on your boat or come on in for food, fun and, of course live music six nights a week. Sam Hill, on Lake Travis, serves live music Tuesday through Sunday and also offers one of the best beach menus on the lake. Burgers, steaks, prime rib, seafood, pastas, salads and more. You'll pay more here than at some other eateries, but the food is good and so is the atmosphere when the boating crowd gathers round to hear the tunes.

Ski Shores Waterfront Cafe

3101 Pearce St. • (512) 346-5915

Getting raves from Austin crowds since 1954, this is another place where you can just boat right up to the dock and hop in for a meal, a beer or an evening of live music. Ski Shores, on Lake Austin, is one of our favorite outdoor eateries. It raises lakeside eating to a new level with tasty burger and sandwich baskets, salads, fried jalapenos, veggie burgers, chicken strips and gravy and much more. Ski Shores presents live music Wednesday through Sunday. The stage is so close to the water that the wake from the boats going by could almost serve as the rhythm section.

Free Summer Concerts

Auditorium Shores Concert Series

South side of Town Lake near Riverside Dr. and First St. • (512) 442-BAND

Every Wednesday evening from 7 to 9

PM, the Austin Federation of Musicians offers free evening concerts on the outdoor stage. This event, which runs from the end of April through June, has featured some of Austin's top performers over the years. These concerts, a typical Austin mix of music styles, are fun for the whole family and an excellent, and free, way to get acquainted with the Austin music scene.

Blues on the Green

Arboretum Shopping Center, 10000 Research Blvd. • (512) 338-4437

Arboretum merchants have done an excellent job of bringing free live music concerts to Northwest Austin the past few years with the summer Blues on the Green concert series. The blues and jazz shows are presented every other Wednesday at 7 PM in June, July and August in the Arboretum park near the cow statues. Music lovers bring blankets and picnics and enjoy the show while they eat. Merchants (see our Shopping chapter) will have concert schedules early in the season, but tend to run out by early July. Any one of them can tell you when the next concert is scheduled, or call the number above.

Jump on It

Rosewood Park, 2300 Rosewood Ave. • (512) 322-2344

One of the newest additions to the Austin lineup of free summer concerts is Jump on It, held every Wednesday from 6 to 10 PM at this great East Austin park. This series, in its third year in 1999, includes an eclectic array or artists presenting jazz, hip-hop, blues, gospel, rap, R&B, poetry, dance and more. Austin's only performance series to be run by community youth, Jump on It begins each evening with a New Talent Showcase Hour, so come early for a glimpse at Austin's up-and-comers. Local hip-hop artist N.O.O.K. is executive director of this project.

Zilker Hillside Theater

In Zilker Park near Barton Springs Pool • (512) 442-BAND

Another place to hear free live concerts is at Austin's own outdoor amphitheater. On Sunday afternoons from 3 to 5 PM, the Austin Federation of Musicians sponsors live musical entertainment. This series also runs from April to June.

Music Stores

Record stores, both independents and chains, are flourishing throughout Austin these days, some extending into new parts of town as the city grows. These shops, which add yet another dimension to the city's music scene, feature a wide variety of music from jazz to Tejano, hip-hop to blues, classical to funk, and of course, Austin's own local artists. Furthermore, some of these stores go out of their way to promote Austin's music scene by sponsoring live in-store performances, setting aside special sections featuring CDs by local musicians, and offering advice and tips on the Live Music Capital of the World. Stop in any of the shops we've listed here for a taste of Austin.

ABCD's

4631 Airport Blvd., Ste. 110 • (512) 454-1212

Compact discs, both new and used, are stocked at this North Austin store. Customers can sit on couches inside the store and preview tapes. A variety of sounds are featured here, including Texas sounds, industrial, early rock 'n' roll, classical and jazz.

Alien Records

503-B W. 15th St. • (512) 477-3909

This Central Austin store specializes in techno and hip-hop music. The store is a mecca for club DJs, who tout its extensive collection of electronic dance music.

INSIDERS' TIP

Wild About Music offers an impressive assortment of art, collectibles and gifts, all with a music-related theme. Check out the store at 721 Congress Avenue. (See our chapter on The Arts for more about this shop and gallery.)

Antone's Record Shop

2928 Guadalupe St. • (512) 322-0660

Reflecting the music played at the venerable Austin club of the same name (see the listing in this chapter), Antone's focuses on blues music. There is also a large selection of Texas and Cajun music, country sounds, soul, vintage rock 'n' roll, rockabilly and jazz at this Central Austin store. Customers can buy, sell and trade here. This is also the place to buy advance tickets to shows at Antone's club (see our listing in The Stages section of this chapter).

Barnes & Noble Booksellers

10000 Research Blvd. • (512) 418-8985

The name doesn't tout the record store within, but this Barnes & Noble location in the Arboretum Shopping Center in Northwest Austin, and most of the chain's other locations around town, stock an impressive selection of CDs, including the classics, show tunes, pop artists and more. The fine collection of books about music and musicians just outside the music section whet the appetite for the tunes within.

Borders Books & Music

10225 Research Blvd. • (512) 795-9553

Not all of Austin's best record stores are downtown, and not are all homegrown. Those living or visiting up in the 'burbs of Northwest Austin will be pleased to learn that when Borders says it has books AND music, it really means the music part. This national chain offers an enormous selection of CDs and tapes in all categories of music. The store has gone out of its way to prominently display the products of Austin musicians, and includes a good selection of Austin artists among its music samplings. Borders also regularly hosts musical performers in the store.

Cheapo Records

914 N. Lamar Blvd. • (512) 477-4499

Housed in the old Whole Foods store, just north of the West Sixth shopping district, not far from downtown in Central Austin, Cheapo features used CDs, one of the largest selections in Austin. The shop buys used CDs. Technically, Cheapo is part of a small Minnesota-based chain, but it retains the atmosphere of an independent outfit.

Duval Discs

2928 Guadalupe St. • (512) 236-1655

Neighbor to Antone's Record Shop, this small Central Austin record shop touts its collection of hard-to-find current CDs, plus a diverse used CD collection.

Half Price Books Records and Magazines

8868 Research Blvd. • (512) 454-3664
3110 Guadalupe St. • (512) 451-4463
2929 S. Lamar Blvd. • (512) 443-3138

There are three locations of this hometown bookstore/record shop — one in Northwest Austin, the original location in Central Austin, just north of The Drag, and a third in South Austin. The music variety changes, but the stores buy and sell CDs, LPs, vinyl and cassettes.

Local Flavor

305 E. Fifth St. • (512) 472-7773

This downtown record shop features the work of local artists. The owners, two self-described "old hippies," are very knowledgeable and enthusiastic about Austin's musicians. The store sells records and demo tapes by new artists.

Maldonado's

2207 E. Seventh St. • (512) 478-0020

This East Austin record store touts itself as the oldest record shop in Austin. The flavor here is Latin with a large collection of conjunto, norteño (Northern Mexican music), Tejano music and traditional imported Mexican music.

INSIDERS' TIP

For more information about the Austin music scene, look for these books: *Stevie Ray Vaughan: Caught in the Crossfire* by Joe Nick Patoski and Bill Crawford; *Texas Music* by Rick Kostner; *The Improbable Rise of Redneck Rock* by Jan Reid; *Threadgill's: The Cookbook* by Eddie Wilson; and *Austin City Limits* by Clifford Endres.

Musicmania

3909-D N. I-35 • (512) 451-3361

Just east of the interstate in the Fiesta grocery store center, this East Austin record store has a reputation for one of the best R&B and rap music collections in the country. In addition to CDs, the store also has a large collection of vinyl records. Posters, magazines and music-related merchandise are also sold here.

Sound Exchange

2100-A Guadalupe St. • (512) 476-8742

The store, which appeared as a hip hangout on MTV's *Austin Stories*, features a wide variety of records in all formats — mainstream, techno, jazz, punk. The store also sells posters and T-shirts.

Technophilia

2418 Guadalupe St. • (512) 477-1812

The name suggests the musical emphasis at this two-story store on The Drag in Central Austin. The upstairs area is dubbed the Vinyl Attic, while downstairs shoppers can find a large variety of new and used CDs.

33 Degrees

4017 Guadalupe St. • (512) 302-5233

Called the "most unusual record store in Town" by the *Austin American-Statesman*, this music shop features rare discs and CDs in all genres from punk classic to local artists.

Tower Records

2402 Guadalupe St. • (512) 478-5711

If any current UT student can remember when this popular chain store first went in on The Drag near the university, it's definitely time to graduate and join the real world. Its prominent and convenient location in the heart of The Drag has made this store a favorite among the university crowd, and just us regular folk, since it opened in 1990, replacing the old varsity movie theater. Of course, Tower Records offers an outstanding collection of CDs, including world music, local artists, Latin, Cajun and the classics. That could have something to do with its appeal. This huge store also has an excellent book section dedicated to music and musicians, pop culture, erotica, film, cyberculture and more. There's also an extensive magazine rack and plenty of paraphernalia for your sound system.

Turntable 505

507 W. Mary St. • (512) 462-2568

Just west of South Congress Avenue's funky shopping district, this small store sells breakbeat, retro, disco, top 40 and other sounds, including both domestic and imported albums and singles.

Waterloo Records

600-A N. Lamar Blvd. • (512) 474-2500

Consistently voted the "Best Record Store" in town in the annual *Austin Chronicle* Readers' Poll, Waterloo is at the heart of the West Sixth Street shopping district. The shop has a large selection of records and CDs reflecting a wide variety of styles and sounds. In-house performances are held regularly to highlight the work of popular artists, both up and coming and well-known. Waterloo arranges its records by alphabet instead of by music type — making this store extremely user friendly. Trying to decide what band to hear when you're in town — and you can't find any on our "Catch 'em If You Can" list? Stop in Waterloo and ask the advice of owner John Kunz or any other member of the knowledgeable sales staff. Waterloo is also one place to come to get those wristbands or individual tickets for SXSW events (see our Annual Events and Festivals chapter). It's no wonder this store has been going strong since 1982. Kunz also operates the successful independent label, Watermelon Records.

INSIDERS' TIP

Austinite Rosetta Wills has written a new book about her father, the legendary swing artist Bob Wills. Look for *The King of Western Swing: Bob Wills Remembered*.

Local merchants present a dazzling array of arts, crafts, collectibles, folk art, funk, vintage redux and just plain fun items.

Shopping

You can never be too adventuresome or too funky to enjoy shopping in Austin. Sure there are big malls with big parking lots to match, but while they provide Austin shoppers with the opportunity to buy appliances at national discount chain prices, local merchants present a dazzling array of arts, crafts, collectibles, folk art, funk, vintage redux and just plain fun items.

Our aim in this chapter is to give you a feel for what is available in Austin, a sampler tray, if you will. We give you the big, the bold, and the beautiful. First is a look at the city's shopping districts, then a brief overview of the area's major malls, followed by a guide to those temples of savvy shoppers, the outlet shops (even here Austin proves to go beyond the norm, offering several outlet shops that are aimed at target audiences). This is followed by listings, by category and area, of shops in the Austin area. It is impossible to list every noteworthy and intriguing shop in the city, but this list aims to give the reader the flavor of the shopping scene in Austin, plus tips at finding those shops that are unique to the city.

Two significant categories of shops are not included here — bookstores appear in our chapter on The Literary Scene and music stores are featured in The Music Scene chapter.

In recent years, there has been a blossoming of retail in Austin. On the one hand, national giants have emerged from the Austin earth, giants such as Whole Foods Market and Dell Computer; on the other hand, the personal has flourished. Older boulevards and city streets in Austin have seen small, unique shops sprout like cabbages as young Austin goes in search of expression and joy.

Years ago, Texas was like many other states that forced shops to close on Sunday, but the so-called Blue Laws have been revoked, and most shops are open seven days a week. (One exception involves the state's car dealers, who by law must close on Sunday; however, this is being challenged by a national used car mega-dealer so that too may change.) Monday through Saturday most stores open around 9 AM. On Sunday specialty shops and mall stores open around noon and close at 6 PM. Closing hours vary. Smaller shops close at 6 PM, while the malls close at 9 or 10 PM Monday through Saturday. Many stores, particularly discount chains and grocery stores stay open 24 hours a day.

Given Austin's lively night scene, many bookstores and specialty food shops keep late hours. The burgeoning shopping scene along South Congress Avenue is one example of a late-night shopping district — some of the stores stay open until midnight, particularly on weekends. During the Christmas holiday season many stores and malls extend their hours.

Shopping Districts

One of the liveliest shopping districts is on South Congress Avenue, south of Town Lake in south Central Austin. Congress Avenue is wide and magnificent here, but for many years the shops and businesses along the street decayed and stagnated. Now, there is new life on the avenue and resale shops featuring vintage clothing, toy emporiums, funky furnishing stores, and folk art shops flourish — some staying open in the night hours to give the street an after-dark vitality. Mixed in with the new stores are a couple of old standbys that have been revived by the activity.

While South Congress is the funky shopping district, the nexus of West Sixth and North Lamar Boulevard is fast becoming the hippest shopping district in Austin. At its heart is the Whole Foods Market, the natural foods grocery store that is a leitmotif for the Austin economy. Founded more than 20 years ago as a natural foods store by a couple of hippies with a vision, it now serves as the anchor of the country's largest natural foods grocery store empire. Next door is Austin's quintessential bookstore, Book People, a place where incense fills the air, and the titles outnumber any chain store in town.

There are big plans for West Sixth, but even without the proposed new inner city, people-friendly, European-style shopping centers that will replace car lots, this area is packed with small stores and emporiums designed to lead the walking visitor from door to door.

Another area that is a shopping district in the making is along Burnet Road leading from North Austin down into Central Austin. This is a mix of antique shops, ethnic bakeries and grocery stores and crafts stores catering to potters and glassmakers.

One of the city's most enticing shopping corridors lies east of MoPac along 35th Street, flowing into 38th Street and then north on Lamar Boulevard to Central Park, home of the city's second-biggest tourist draw, Central Market (see our Close-up in this chapter) a grocery store that belies the pedestrian name. This corridor is marked by shops dedicated to excellence, be in it gardening or clock repair, pasta making, clothes design or the art of photography. There are no big signs here, but Austin residents know this is where they can find some of the best shops in Austin.

To the northwest, along U.S. Highway 183 is the Arboretum, the Rodeo Drive of Austin. This is where some of the top merchandising names in the country have a foothold. Back in the city is The Drag, the section of Guadalupe Street that runs alongside the University of Texas campus. Here there is a odd mix of hip fashion stores and Vietnamese egg roll stands, old hippie vendors and souvenir shops selling all things Longhorn.

The Austin ethos dictates that nobody shops simply to shop, Austinites shop to find, to discover, to enjoy. If these listings are packed with stores selling folk art, food and plants, it is an indication that Austin residents are sensual folk who love to dip into the unknown, find the new and enjoy the past.

Malls

We have it on good authority that when the Queen of England came to Austin her staff and ladies-in-waiting ventured to a local shopping mall to sample the wares. Austin is booming and strip centers, plus malls at major intersections around the city are blooming. There are some local merchants in the area's malls, but like much of America, the shopping mall is the home of the chain stores, the big-name department stores and the fashionable merchants of the moment.

The malls are open seven days a week, usually from 9 AM to 9 or 10 PM Monday through Saturday, and from noon to 6 PM on Sunday, although hours are extended greatly during the Christmas shopping season and for special promotional sales.

In addition to serving as shopping meccas, many of the malls are a vital resource for seniors who "walk the mall" for exercise during hot or inclement weather. The malls are also a draw for teenagers, most of them well-behaved, but occasionally there will be news stories about negative teen activity at the larger malls.

Shoppers also should be alert when they

INSIDERS' TIP

Bargain hunters can spend Saturday mornings roaming Austin neighborhoods to check out local garage sales. Often, neighbors will band together and have a multifamily sale. Check the classified section of the *Austin American-Statesman* late in the week for ads, and keep your eye on busy intersections or entrances to subdivisions where neighbors post notices of weekend sales.

return to their cars, particularly at night. The malls do provide parking lot security and are well-lighted, but there are occasional purse-snatchings, robberies, even a rare attack of a shopper loaded down with packages, particularly during the busy Christmas season. Always lock your car, check under the vehicle and through the windows into the back seat when you prepare to leave.

And this would not be Austin if there was not at least one political issue involving a local mall. Some Austinites do not shop at Barton Creek Square because it is built within the Barton Creek watershed which feeds Barton Springs. The mall, which opened in the 1980s, was virulently opposed by some of Austin's most vocal environmentalists. That has not appeared to hurt the mall's business, and it is one of the city's largest and busiest shopping centers — in fact this is where the Queen's staff shopped.

The major shopping malls include:

The Arboretum

10000 Research Blvd. • (512) 338-4437

Touted as an open-air mall, the Arboretum design allows shoppers to stroll the sidewalks and landscaped gardens as they window shop. Many exclusive national stores are in this Northwest shopping district including top names such as Ralph Lauren and Koslow's Furs, plus The Pottery Barn, Barnes & Noble, The Gap, Jaeger, Banana Republic and Limited Express. You'll also find some popular local names including Amy's Ice Cream and Higginbottom's (see our Gifts listings in this chapter). In the summertime, there are Blues on the Green concerts held on a green area decorated with large bronzes of longhorn cattle. There are several restaurants in the Arboretum, including a Dan McCluskey's steakhouse (see our Restaurants chapter). The Arbor Movie Theater complex features newly released movies. West of The Arboretum is the Arboretum Market, a smaller shopping center at 9722 Great Hills Trail, which is home to Sak's Fifth Avenue, Talbots and Ann Taylor stores.

Barton Creek Square

2901 Loop 360 (Capital of Texas Hwy.) • (512) 327-7040

Austin's largest indoor mall, located in Southwest Austin, has a terrific view of the city from its northern parking lot. Major anchor shops in the mall include Foley's, JCPenney, Sears, Dillard's and Montgomery Ward. There is a Disney Store here, The Gap, The Limited, Victoria's Secret, Foot Locker, in all a total of 180 stores. The spacious facility is adding a food court, and there are a variety of small vendors scattered about the mall selling various specialty items such as baseball caps, jigsaw puzzles, jewelry, plus arts and crafts.

Brodie Oaks

3940 S. Lamar Blvd.

Not so very long ago, in the early 1980s, this was a ranch site, and drivers heading south on Lamar Boulevard could see sheep grazing here (see our Neighborhoods and Real Estate chapter). In 1984, the sheep moved on, and this Southwest Austin outdoor mall was built. This is home to Neiman Marcus' Last Call (see Outlet listings), a large Mervyn's store, Toys 'R' Us, Sun Harvest Farms food store, several chain restaurants including Lone Star Cafe and Chili's, plus a popular Chinese restaurant, Hunan Lion (see our Restaurants chapter).

Gateway

9901 Loop 360 (Capital of Texas Hwy.)

This new, outdoor mall stands on the northeast corner of the intersection of Research Boulevard and Loop 360, in the middle of what has become a several square mile concentration of shops along Research Boulevard west of MoPac. This is where you will find the northwest branch of Whole Foods Market (see our Food/Gourmet listings later in this chapter), plus Old Navy Clothing Co., CompUSA, a major computer chain, Best Buy, and OfficeMax. Also in the neighborhood is The Container Store and Smith & Hawken (see our Gardening listings in this chapter). One of Austin's most popular Italian restaurants, Mezzaluna, has opened a new branch at the Gateway (see our Restaurants chapter).

Highland Mall

6001 Airport Blvd. • (512) 454-9656

This was Austin's first major mall, built in the 1970s, and it continues to be popular and crowded, particularly during peak shopping seasons. The mall is anchored by major department stores — JCPenney, Dillard's and Foley's — and has a variety of popular shops including Laura Ashley, Banana Republic, Sharper Image, Warner Bros. Studio Store, Pappagallo's, Ann Taylor, The Gap, Express, etc. The food court offers a wide variety of culinary experiences from chocolate chip cookies to stir fry, Philly sandwiches to fried chicken, and it is always packed and noisy.

Lakeline Mall

11200 Lakeline Mall Dr. • (512) 257-7467

This is Austin's newest mall, located in Cedar Park, what is now considered far Northwest Austin. Anchor stores include Foley's, JCPenney, Sears, Montgomery Ward, Dillard's and Mervyn's. The large, airy mall decorated with murals depicting the city has the obligatory movie store, here it is a United Artists Starport store, plus specialty stores, restaurants, a food court, a movie complex and a large interactive video arcade.

Northcross Mall

2525 W. Anderson Ln. • (512) 451-7466

An ice skating rink serves as the heart of this North Austin mall that has undergone considerable change following the growth of larger facilities to the northwest and southwest. More change is ahead, according to new owners, who purchased the mall in mid-1998. The ice rink will remain, plus the movie theater complex and the food court, but there will be new faces in this indoor facility that, unlike some of the newer malls, have a human scale. One of the current clients is Chantal's Antiques (see our Antiques listings in this chapter). The adjacent Oshman's Superstore (see or Travel/Adventure/Outdoors listings in this chapter) attracts shoppers looking for sports equipment and clothing.

Sunset Valley Marketfair

5400 Brodie Ln.

Just as Brodie Oaks once was a sheep farm, this Southwest Austin mall stands on land where cattle grazed not so long ago. It takes its name from the surrounding small

INSIDERS' TIP

Every month the City Coliseum, 101 Dawson Street, just south of Town Lake between Lamar Boulevard and S. First Street, hosts the Citywide Garage Sale and Antique Show, (512) 441-7133. The sale is usually mid-month, and the merchandise varies from kitsch to antiques.

community of Sunset Valley (see our Neighborhoods and Real Estate chapter), a primarily residential community that has tapped into a rich vein of sales taxes with the building of this outdoor shopping mall just south of U.S. Highway 290 W.. Savvy shoppers appreciate the fact that the sales tax is just a smidgen lower in Sunset Valley than in Austin. Shops here include Circuit City, Home Depot, Bed Bath & Beyond, Ross Dress for Less, Petsmart, TJ Maxx and OfficeMax. By late 1998, a new shopping center on the east side of Brodie Lane is scheduled to open featuring an Old Navy store, a new Barnes & Noble, Cost Plus and other well-known national retailers.

Village at Westlake

701 S. Loop 360 (Capital of Texas Hwy.)

There was a battle over the building of this outdoor shopping center at the intersection of Capital of Texas Highway and Bee Caves Road in West Lake Hills, but the developer prevailed and now this large center houses several major national tenants including Old Navy, Barnes & Noble and a large Albertson's grocery store. It is also the site of several Austin restaurants including La Madeleine and Canyon Cafe (see our Restaurants chapter).

Outlet Malls

San Marcos Factory Shops

3939 I-35, San Marcos • (800) 628-9465

Touted as legend among outlet centers, San Marcos Factory Shops is about 45 minutes south of Austin on I-35, Exit 200. With over 100 name-brand outlets, the center attracts over 4 million visitors a year. Among the labels available here are Anne Klein, Ann Taylor, Benetton, Brooks Brothers, Calvin Klein, Donna Karan, Eddie Bauer, Esprit, Gap Outlet, Mikasa, Nike, Sony, Waterford and Wedgwood.

Tanger Factory Outlet Center

I-35, Exit 200 • (512) 396-7444

The shops at this center, 45 minutes south of Austin, include American Eagle, Noritake, Chicago Cutlery, Oneida Factory, Pfaltzgraff, Dansk Factory Outlet, Reebok Factory Direct, Royal Doulton, Fieldcrest Cannon, Florsheim Shoe Factory, Fossil Company Store and Tommy Hilfiger.

The Antique Outlet Center

4200 I-35 • (800) 965-8333

Antique and collectible buffs can combine a trip to the outlet malls in San Marcos with a little antique shopping. The center, next door to the Tanger Factory Outlet Center, features a wide variety of furniture and decorative items, plus collectibles.

Outlet Shops

Fanny's Outlet Fabric Store

1150 S. Lamar Blvd. • (512) 442-8255

The antithesis of an outlet, this small, friendly, south Central Austin neighborhood shop features an assortment of fabrics, samples, plus decorating staples such as wide linen and Egyptian cotton.

Cowgirls and Lace

1111 U.S. Hwy. 290 W., Dripping Springs • (512) 858-4186

A 15-minute drive from the Austin city limits along U.S. 290 W. in Southwest Austin, this outlet store sells designer fabrics at wholesale prices. In addition to over 1,000 bolts of designer fabric at discount fabrics, the store also stocks 100-inch-wide designer sheeting fabric so you can become your own sheetmaker.

Last Call

Brodie Oaks Shopping Center, 4107 S. Loop 360 (Capital of Texas Hwy.) • (512) 447-0701

This is Neiman Marcus without the posh surroundings and posh prices. The famous department store has its discount store at this location in a small mall in Southwest Austin. The store features men's, women's and children's fashions, shoes, some small decorative furniture items and a few household items including sheets, pillows and knickknacks. Savvy shoppers can find last season's designer fashions at greatly reduced prices. Sometimes when you find them, you wonder what all the fuss was about, while sometimes you discover a classic design that will survive both the vagaries of fashion dictates and the demands of your pocketbook. Items are discounted up to 70 percent.

Harold's Outlet Barn
8611 N. MoPac • (512) 794-9036

Harold's is an upscale fashion store specializing in what might be called classic, yuppie clothes. The outlet is in a barn-like structure on the east side of MoPac just south of the Research Boulevard intersection in Northwest Austin.

Antiques/Collectibles/ Folk Art

Central

Whit Hanks Antiques and Decorative Arts
1009 W. Sixth St. • (512) 478-2101

More than 70 antique and arts dealers can be found under one roof at Whit Hanks, an antique showcase on West Sixth Street at the heart of one of Austin's burgeoning shopping districts. From the large, Tuscan-style pottery urns on its lawn to the myriad of collectibles inside, this is one of the most pleasant and amenable antique venues in Austin. The building, located next door to Treaty Oak (see our Attractions chapter), is a popular spot for a weekend outing. The dealers are friendly and ready to educate visitors about their collections, and there is a wide variety of antiques and collectibles — Oriental, European, Southwest, primitive, plus china, antique tile and pottery, household wrought iron, garden decorations and pots. Several Austin artisans display their original iron, ceramic and woodworking pieces here also.

Attal Galleries
3310 Red River St. • (512) 476-3634

Owned by W. C. Attal, a noted Texas appraiser, this store features fine examples of Texana, primitive furniture and antiques, books, prints and maps. The store boasts a great variety of items, most of them high priced and valuable.

Austin Antique Mall
8822 McCann Dr. • (512) 459-5900

There are more than 100 dealers in this 30,000-square-foot facility, including collectors selling pottery, furniture and Victorian jewelry. The management also operates the Antique Mall of Texas in Round Rock.

Bob Larson's Old Timer Clock Shop
1803 W. 35th St. • (512) 451-5016

The Old Timer Shop has been a treasured resource for years for Austin residents. The shop not only sells beautiful old clocks and watches, but also offers a fine repair service.

Dragon's Lair Comics & Fantasy
616 W. 34th St. • (512) 454-2399

Comic books, games, fantasy fiction and videos, particularly those featuring the work of directors John Wu and Jackie Chan, are sold here. Japanese comic books are particularly popular. The Austin Board Game Group meets here every month, and the store also hosts games on site.

Eclectic
700 N. Lamar Blvd. • (512) 477-1816

A longtime Austin shop and gallery that sells crafts from around the world, including Africa, Mexico, Latin America and the Far East. The store lives up to its name and is a veritable bazaar, packed with large and small items, some costly, others bargains. Eclectic sells primitive and Southwest furniture, clothing, decorative items, pottery, textiles, ceramics. The large jewelry section is very popular. Among the rare items are Zuni fetishes and an antique bottle collection, some of the glassware dating back to Roman times.

El Interior
1009 W. Lynn St. • (512) 474-8680

This Clarksville store is one of the best and the oldest folk art stores in Austin. The owners really know where to find the best pottery, jewelry and textiles south of the border. The selection of Oaxacan ceramics is notable, and the store also stocks Guatemalan fabric by the yard.

Kerbey Lane Doll Shoppe

3706 Kerbey Ln. • (512) 452-7086

The store sells both antique dolls aimed at the collectors' market, plus exquisite, new dolls for that special niece or granddaughter. The owners also offer on-site doll repair.

La Cosecha

3703 Kerbey Ln. • (512) 450-0650

The latest addition to the Kerbey Lane shopping scene, part of the 35th through 38th Street corridor, this store features Latin American folk art and clothing, hats, jewelry, plus custom designed fashions and accessories by local Austin artists.

Tesoros Trading Co.

209 Congress Ave. • (512) 479-8377

Tesoros is one of our favorite Austin stores. It features a wide selection of Mexican and Latin American folk art, jewelry, specialty pieces such as doorposts from Peru, African baskets, Day of the Dead tableaux, amulets, loteria art, old Mexican postcards, Moroccan mirrors, jewelry from all over the world, purses made in Vietnam from old Pepsi cans, Mexican grocery store calendars, retablos, Peruvian good luck pigs, etc., etc. The store's Christmas ornaments, particularly those from Latin America, are popular Austin collectibles. Look out for the occasional warehouse sales advertised in the local press. This downtown store is one of those must-see stops for any visitor. Next door is a unique restaurant, Las Manitas (see our Restaurant chapter).

Turquoise Trading Post

6005 Burnet Rd. • (512) 323-5011

In addition to offering a wide selection of contemporary and traditional Native American jewelry, the store also has a collection of Zuni fetishes, Navajo kachinas, plus pottery and sculpture from the Southwest.

Whit Hanks Consignment Shop

1214 W. Sixth St. • (512) 478-2398

After visiting Whit Hanks Antiques, stroll down Sixth Street two blocks to the Whit Hanks Consignment Center. The center offers a variety of furniture, silver and china. Special sales are advertised, but avid collectors and bargain hunters will want to regularly browse the consignment center to keep track of the latest offerings.

Architects & Heroes

1809 W. 35th St. • (512) 467-9393

Architectural elements are a popular decorative tool these days, and this store features stone and wooden decorative pieces that have been rescued from old homes and gardens. The store also sells antique furniture pieces, wrought iron and textiles.

Antigua

1508 S. Congress Ave. • (512) 912-1475

Fossils, dream pillows, tile and tin mirrors, stained glass, suncatchers, decorative items from Thailand and Bali, Mexico and Guatemala are packed into this store in the South Congress shopping district. Two items worth looking for are the *santos*, carved figures of saints used in Southwest and Latin American churches, and *nichos*, household shrines popular in those regions also.

Rue's Antiques

1500 S. Congress Ave. • (512) 442-1775

Rue's has been operating at various locations in Austin for decades. Now housed in the South Congress shopping district, Rue's features antiques, old furniture, and what might be simply called junque items. Finds run the gamut from wonderful old bedroom vanities to chipped china. The store also offers refinishing services, and brass and copper polishing.

The Armadillo

1712 S. Congress Ave. • (512) 443-7552

Handcarved furniture takes center stage here, but the store also sells antique furniture pieces, jewelry, pottery and ceramics that capture the spirit of Texas and the Southwest.

Tinhorn Traders

1608 S. Congress Ave. • (512) 444-3644

The owner likes to call himself a "single dealer with multiple personalities" and the stock shows it — everything from funky to folk art here. Some of the most interesting items

Central Market: Austin's Feeding Frenzy

One surefire way to judge how someone regards their hometown is to ask them where they take out-of-town visitors for an Insider's view of their city. Austin residents are lucky. The list of favorite spots is long and varied, but three spots appear on most short lists — Barton Springs Pool, the State Capitol and Central Market.

Central Market? A grocery store? Yep. This central city grocery store now ranks among the city's most visited landmarks, and it has become a living symbol of the city's lifestyle. Since it opened in January 1994, Central Market has been a popular spot to give visitors a real peek at the Austin approach to living. On any given weekend, when the store is at its busiest, it is possible to see Austinites from all parts of the city, of all ages and backgrounds, speaking a variety of languages. They will be meandering through the store's aisles, tasting this, sampling that, and finding all manner of ingredients, some familiar, others exotic. Many are eagerly showing out-of-town guests or relatives the bounty at hand.

On the eve of holidays such as July Fourth, Thanksgiving and Christmas finding a parking place in the shopping center can be an exercise in patience. What draws the crowds to this Central Austin grocery store? It is a combination of ambiance, incredible variety and the notion that cuisine is an integral part of the Austin lifestyle, particularly on weekends when Austinites light their barbecues, fire up their smokers, pack their picnic baskets and fill up their ice chests.

Central Market is the creation of the H.E.B. grocery store chain, a family-owned South Texas chain now headquartered in restored buildings in the historic King William District in San Antonio (see our Daytrips chapter). In the early '90s, the state legislature gave state agencies the go ahead to lease state lands to private enterprise. One prime piece of state property was in the heart of Austin at 35th Street between Lamar Boulevard and Guadalupe Street. The state leased the property to a developer who then built the shopping center with Central Market as its anchor. Several state buildings still occupy part of the site, and the beautiful roses growing along Lamar Boulevard are a reminder that gardeners employed by the state nurtured this area for many years.

Observers have credited other Austin grocery stores, including Whole Foods Market and the Wheatsville Food Co-op (see our listings in this chapter) with inspiring part of the Central Market concept. Certainly the emphasis on organic products and bulk items such as coffee beans, spices, beans and grains were made popular by Austin's original health food stores. But H.E.B. has developed a grocery-store concept that goes beyond catering to shopper's requests for organic foods or specific ingredients; Central Market is designed to stimulate the imagination, educate the shopper and broaden his or her horizons. In doing so, the store captured the hearts (and pocketbooks) of Austin foodies — although it should be noted that while luxury items do abound here, prices for everyday items are competitive with neighborhood grocery stores.

The operative word here is "market" — Central Market is designed to evoke the spirit of an Old World marketplace. Visitors enter a vegetable and fruit market first, then proceed to a fish and meat market, a wine shop, a specialty food area, a bakery, deli and cheese shop, finally reaching the front of the store where a flower shop stands. The building itself is a blend of local materials and design elements taken from 19th-century Texas buildings with a hint of Italian inspiration. The limestone walls and tin roof reflect

— continued on next page

Photo: Peter A. Silva

The fishmonger's catch lines up for gourmet buyers.

buildings from the Texas frontier while the terra cotta columns evoke Tuscan architecture. A large tile mural by Austin artist Malou Flato at the front of the store depicts Barton Springs pool.

Among Central Market's most crowded spots on the weekend are the butcher shop and fishmonger. The meat market features aged premium choice beef, lamb, veal, big-eye pork and poultry raised on organic grains as well as 48 varieties of custom-made sausage. Special cuts of meat can be ordered, and many Austinites put in their orders for holiday turkeys or rib roasts.

The 75-foot-long seafood counter offers up to 100 varieties of both saltwater and freshwater fish, shellfish and sushi, plus up to six varieties of fresh salmon in season. The market also offers 11 marinades created by local chefs. These can be added to the seafood to marinate on the ride home. Central Market is one of only two retailers in the nation that has been approved by federal government to participate in a voluntary, intensive seafood inspection and safety program known as HACCP — Hazard Analysis of Critical Control Points.

The store's wine and beer shop offers 2,700 domestic and imported wines, and more than 330 varieties of beer produced by American microbreweries and foreign brewers. Many of the wine selections are available for less than $10, and the store's wine shop has been voted Austin's best by *The Austin Chronicle* for four years in a row.

The specialty foods section of the store features more than 175 olive oils, 165 varieties of vinegar, 60 varieties of barbecue sauce, and the list goes on. Freezers hold Indian and Chinese foods, sorbets made from exotic fruits; the dairy case is filled with butter from Europe and milk in glass bottles from Texas cows. The coffee and tea shop has coffee beans from Africa and Brazil, Mexico and Hawaii, teas from the Himalayas, biscotti from Italy. Then there is the bakery where French baguettes are baked daily (along with a large variety of other breads including a personal favorite, southern Burgundy walnut bread) and fresh tortillas roll off the conveyer belt of the tortilla machine.

The deli has prosciuttos from Italy, smoked salmon from Scotland, pâtés and

— continued on next page

organic cold cuts. Then there is the pasta shop where shoppers can match handmade pasta with fresh sauces or pestos, and the cheese shop with cheeses from the best producers in the United States and Europe. Across the way is the salsa, pickle, olive and antipasto bar. One final stop — the flower shop at the front of the market. Here, shoppers can find a wide variety of ready-made bouquets, including Hill Country wildflower bouquets in season, special holiday arrangements and dried-flower creations. You can also get custom-designed bouquets for any occasion.

On the second floor of the store is the Central Market Cooking School where internationally known chefs as well as top Austin chefs have taught, including Paul Prudhomme and Caprial Pence. There are 25 classes each month including classes for kids.

The store also features Central Market Cafe (see our Restaurants and Kidstuff chapters), a popular family gathering spot where patrons can eat inside or listen to a variety of local musicians while eating on the deck.

A gift shop offers a special assembly and packing service. A basket filled with Texas-made goodies is a great souvenir. Out-of-town shoppers can have their purchases packed in ice for the ride home, and dry ice is available for extended chilling.

The popularity of Central Market has made it a top spot on any Austin tour, but it also has prompted H.E.B. to plan a second Central Market to alleviate some of the crush at the original location. The second store is scheduled to open in the spring of 1999 in the Westgate Mall at the southeast corner of Lamar and Ben White boulevards in Southwest Austin. The original location at 4001 N. Lamar Boulevard is open from 9 AM to 9 PM daily, and the cafe is open from 7 AM to 10 PM daily. Call (512) 206-1000 for general information, (512) 206-1013 for the meat market, (512) 206-1012 for the seafood market and (512) 458-3068 for the cooking school.

are planters and architectural elements rescued from old buildings.

Uncommon Objects

1512 S. Congress Ave. • (512) 442-4000

There seems to be a competition in the South Congress shopping district to see which store can qualify for the Best Stuff award. Here, Mexican doors, architectural elements, lamps and clothing all compete for attention.

North

Adobe Pueblo

2117 W. Anderson Ln. • (512) 323-0894

Western, Southwestern and Mexican furniture pieces are sold here, plus Zapotec rugs from Oaxaca, Dhurrie rugs from India and Kilims from Turkey. The store also has a collection of Native American pottery and Hopi kachina dolls.

Austin Antique Mall

8822 McCann Dr. • (512) 459-5900

Housed in a large warehouse, this is the Austin cousin to the Antique Mall of Texas in Round Rock (see listing later in this section). A little smaller than its Round Rock cousin, the large facility still has room for 100 vendors, who sell a wide variety of antiques, collectibles and good stuff. The large building is visible from Research Boulevard but is accessible via Burnet Road.

INSIDERS' TIP

Many of the communities surrounding Austin hold spring and summer festivals celebrating local history and culture. Check out our Annual Events chapter for events such as the Old Gruene Market Days for an opportunity to find arts and crafts.

Antique Marketplace

5350 Burnet Rd. • (512) 452-1000

In 1989, Antique Marketplace opened in a 19,000-square-foot, former grocery store in North Austin. The large space is now a treasure trove of antique, collectible and arts and crafts stalls, featuring a variety of items, some expensive, others at bargain-basement prices. There is a relaxed, down-home atmosphere here, and strolling the aisles can turn into a afternoon adventure.

Chantal's Antique and Design Center

Northcross Mall, 2525 W. Anderson Ln. • (512) 451-5705

Chantal's occupies 8,000 square feet of space in Northcross Mall, home to some 20 antique dealers selling American, Victorian and European furniture, plus accessories and decorative items dating from the late 17th century to modern times. The dealers sell items from more than 450 consigners, including finds from estate sales and European dealers. In addition to furniture, decorative items and jewelry, some of the dealers also sell Texana, Western art and books and religious collectibles.

Courtyard Shops

5453 Burnet Rd. • (512) 451-4203

Several antique dealers and crafters are creating a small shopping and craft center on Burnet Road, all part of the spontaneous revival of this street as a place to roam for special items and bargains. Negrel, one of the tenants, features furniture and household decorative objects from the south of France. Other tenants include Halbert Antiques, L'Elysee Antiques and Austin Brass. The center of the shopping area is a small courtyard decorated by garden artist Bud Twilley. He uses old garden stoneware from Europe and Mexico to create fountains, topiaries and garden art.

Olla Linda

7010 Burnet Rd. • (512) 458-6422

Oaxaca is one of Mexico's richest craft regions and Olla Linda specializes in crafts from that area including Zapotec weavings, pottery and baskets. In addition, there are silver jewelry and hammocks from the Yucatan store, plus a collection of *huipils* — the wonderfully decorated, yet simply cut and shaped blouses worn by indigenous women in Mexico and Guatemala.

West

The Market

The Village Shopping Center at Westlake, Loop 360 (Capital of Texas Hwy.) and Bee Caves Rd. • (512) 327-8866

Decorators working on creating that classic English or French look can find antiques from those two countries here, plus top-quality modern pieces from the Ralph Lauren, Henredon and Hickory Chair Furniture collections.

Round Rock

How Ironic

104 S. Mays St. • (512) 218-1121

If you're looking for the perfect *Leave it to Beaver* formica kitchen set, then check out How Ironic's retro furniture selection. The store describes its inventory of furniture, vintage clothing, books and ceramics as "weird, wild, wacky stuff." Ashtrays are another speciality here, and you can even get your hair trimmed at the on-site hair salon. The store also features works by local artists.

The Antique Mall of Texas

1601 S. I-35 • (512) 218-4290

More than 200 dealers are housed in this mall, selling a wide assortment of collectibles and antiques. The mall is run by the folks who operate the Austin Antique Mall, and it has the same down-home, comfortable atmosphere that engenders leisurely shopping and browsing.

The Apple Barrel

108 E. Main St. • (512) 218-9393

Round Rock's historic city center is home to this old-fashioned antique shop featuring dolls, furniture and other collectibles.

Arts and Crafts

Central

Bydee Arts & Gifts

412 E. Sixth St. • (512) 474-4343

Transplanted from the Caribbean to Austin, Brian "Bydee Man" Joseph has created a friendly new breed — the Bydee people. He describes them as happy, fun-loving and laid back, and they have become an Austin symbol. Bydee stands for "Bringing You Delightful Entertaining Experiences." Joseph, who has a master's degree in urban studies, began painting while recuperating from surgery, and now his Bydee people can be found on posters, T-shirts and note cards. His work is also sold at the airport gift shop.

Clarksville Pottery & Galleries

Central Park, 4001 N. Lamar Blvd., Ste. 200 • (512) 454-9079
9722 Great Hills Tr., Ste. 380 • (512) 794-8580

This pottery shop found life in the old Central Austin neighborhood of Clarksville (hence the name); however, this shop and gallery now has two locations, one in Central Park on North Lamar Boulevard and the other in the Arboretum area. Both stores feature pottery by local artists, including decorative pieces and very practical, sturdy everyday ware; also stone fountains, lamps, beautiful wooden boxes and hummingbird feeders. The store has a large selection of jewelry and wind chimes. (No kid can resist the large outdoor chimes on the deck at the Central Park store.)

Kerbey Lane Dollhouses and Miniatures

3503 Kerbey Ln. • (512) 454-4287

Granddads looking for wallpaper, roof shingles or carpet for that dollhouse project can find it here. The store also has a large collection of dollhouse furniture and tiny household accessories — kitchen soap, flower arrangements, cups and saucers.

Renaissance Market

W. 23rd and Guadalupe Sts.

Some folks joke that Austin is an elephant's graveyard for old hippies, and Renaissance Market may be evidence of that. This small plaza on The Drag is home to a variety of crafters and artists who specialize in Woodstock-era items — tie-dyed shirts and skirts, silver jewelry, suncatchers, leather pouches and purses, etc. The outdoor market also attracts jugglers and mimes. A mural, dubbed "Austintatious" shows the city's life in the hippie heyday. Despite its laissez-faire atmosphere, the market is tightly regulated, and the operation is under the auspices of a special city oversight committee that makes sure only authentic hippie stuff is sold here. No place but Austin!

Silk Road

3910 N. Lamar Blvd. • (512) 302-0844

A plain-looking, small building across from Central Market houses this store that sells natural fabrics from around the world, including cottons, silks and linens.

The Needleworks

26 Doors, 1206 W. 38th St. • (512) 451-6931

A mecca for needlework enthusiasts, this store in the 26 Doors shopping center features all manner of needlework supplies and kits, including traditional yarns, specialty fibers, accessories, books, instruction and finishing.

Feats of Clay

4630 Burnet Rd. • (512) 453-2111

Local potters buy supplies at this Central Austin store, plus the store offers kiln firing

INSIDERS' TIP

It has been described as one of the largest and most diverse outdoor markets in Texas. On the first Saturday of every month from April to December more than 400 vendors gather in Wimberley, at Wimberley Lions Fields, southwest of Austin, for Wimberley Market Days, (512) 847-2201.

for homemade pieces. The store also features in stoneware, earthenware and porcelain by local potters. Pieces include dinnerware, batter bowls, large tureens, teapots and bird feeders.

Mitchie's Fine Black Art Gallery and Bookstore

5312 Airport Blvd. • (512) 323-6901

Mitchie's celebrates African-American, African and Caribbean culture, selling arts, crafts and books that illustrate these regions and the work of the people who live there. The store has a large print collection celebrating the lives of sports figures, cultural and religious heroes, historical figures from the American Civil Rights movement and celebrations of African and African-American life and art.

Renaissance Glass Company

5200 Burnet Rd. • (512) 451-3971

Specializing in stained glass, this arts and crafts store also sells supplies for stained glass artists. It is a good place to find tools for cutting glass and metal foil tapes for picture frames.

North

El Taller Gallery

8015 Shoal Creek Blvd., No. 109 • (512) 302-0100

Amado Peña was an Austin art teacher who sold his paintings and prints on the arts and crafts circuit for years before being discovered. Pena's work features cultural themes reflecting life in the Southwestern United States and Mexico. His stylized figures, notably women in profile with long streaming black hair, large, oval eyes and colorful costumes, are presented in a variety of mediums. Pena's work has been featured on posters advertising annual events in Austin, and his prints and paintings can be seen in Austin homes and businesses. Now his work is featured at this popular gallery, which also sells other noted Southwest artists, including R.C. Gorman. In addition to prints, the gallery also sells Southwest-style jewelry and Mexican textiles. (For more information on Peña and his work, see our listing for Peña Gallery in The Arts chapter.)

East

Fire Island Hot Glass Studio, Inc.

3401 E. Fourth St. • (512) 389-1100

Owners and artists Matthew LaBarbera and Teresa Uelschey create fine art pieces, custom designs and small items for sale at their East Austin studio. The smaller items include perfume bottles and paperweights. The artists also offer demonstrations on Saturday mornings September through January and March through May.

Clothing/Fashion

Sue Patrick

3808 N. Lamar Blvd. • (512) 452-7701
3742 Far West Blvd. • (512) 345-3582

Dressing comfortably and smartly in Austin's climate can be a challenge given the hot summer weather and sudden temperature changes in the winter. Sue Patrick offers a wide variety of casual and dressier fashions well suited to the Austin lifestyle. Some of the casual, but comfortable fashions often have a hint of Texas in their cut or design.

Cowgirls are Forever

12432 F.M. 2244 (Bee Caves Rd.) • (512) 263-7009

The best-dressed cowgirls come here to shop for designers such as Manuel, whose elegant Western-style fashions can be worn to black-tie Longhorn cattle auctions or those big ranch barbecues. The shop also sells what it calls casual Hill Country attire — dreamy, cowgirl-style duds that make you want marry that rancher, or better yet, buy that ranch!.

Capra & Cavelli

3500 Jefferson St., Ste. 110 • (512) 450-1919

This men's boutique features classic looks and design, casual wear or button-down office outfits. The aim is to provide personal service to customers who want to look their best and be comfortable in the Austin climate.

By George

2905 San Gabriel St. • (512) 472-5951
2324 Guadalupe St. • (512) 472-2731
2346 Guadalupe St. • (512) 472-5536

The three By George shops are a favorite among young, hip and well-heeled dressers. The look is simple and very modern; the price tag not so simple. There are three locations — the younger set heads for the stores on The Drag (Guadalupe) where a women's store and men's store stand side by side featuring labels such as Romeo Gigli, Calvin Klein and Massimo. The older Gen-Xers and hip baby boomers head for the San Gabriel location. All three sites also sell personal care items and accessories.

Emeralds

624 Lamar Blvd. • (512) 476-4496

Emeralds is a favorite shopping spot for hip, young women looking for simple, well-designed fashions. The store also has a shoe collection and a variety of modern accessories, plus decorative items for the home.

InStep

3105 Guadalupe St. • (512) 476-5110

This shoe store next door to Wheatsville Co-op features Birkenstock shoes and sandals, a mandatory item for the correctly dressed Austinite — chinos, or khaki shorts, a wrinkled linen shirt or faded T-shirt, Birkenstocks. If your trusty Birkenstocks ever need fixing this is the place; a repair shop is on site.

Scarbrough's

Central Park, 4001 N. Lamar Blvd. • (512) 452-4220

For more than 100 years this family-owned business has operated in Austin. The original downtown location opened in 1894 and, for many years, the Scarbrough building at the southwest corner Sixth and Congress was home for the traditional downtown department store. Now, the family runs this upscale clothing store with a wide variety of evening, day and resort wear in the Central Park Shopping Center.

T. Kennedy

1011 W. Lynn St. • (512) 478-0545

The emphasis is on natural women's clothing here — easy, natural design and natural fabrics including linen, cotton and flax. Batik clothing is a specialty, and the store also features jewelry and accessories.

Tropical Tantrum

Central Park, 4001 N. Lamar Blvd., Ste. 520 • (512) 302-9888

Headed for an island getaway or just a backyard luau? Then check out the clothes at this small Central Park shop. The comfortable wear for both men and women includes handpainted clothing and batiks for tropical nights and days on the Seychelles or Sixth Street.

Josephine

3709 Kerbey Ln. • (512) 452-7575

Cornelia Reich is the owner of this Central Austin boutique and her line of sophisticated, but fun clothes, appropriately named "Cornelia" is in the spotlight here. Cornelia dresses are likely to be free flowing and made of tactile materials such as silk, rayon and crepe. Currently, her inspiration comes from the East with simple lines, bright colors and easy wear.

The Texas Clothier

2905 San Gabriel St. • (512) 478-4956

Owners Dain and LaDonna Higdon have survived the economic roller coaster in 20 years of business in Austin. After working for years in retail, Dain Higdon started his own store in 1976, and ever since Austin's busy, top businessmen have turned to him for fashion advice. Higdon's clients insist on quality and are willing to pay for it. Some of the city's top lawyers and businessmen shop here.

Scott-Wynne Outfitters

Arboretum, 10000 Research Blvd., Ste. 12 • (512) 346-7012

For those whose fashion tastes run to labels such as Patagonia and Woolrich, this is the place. Classic wear with an American flair is the theme of the day here. The store also sells Southwestern-style clothing, Native American jewelry and leather goods.

Round Rock

The Island
105 S. Mays St. • (512) 218-HOOT, (888) 259-7554

Looking for a fashion statement that provokes a "Wow"? The Island creates Hawaiian shirts and tropical wear in unique fabrics. The material is brightly colored fabric printed with tropical birds, fish, lizards, geckos, butterflies and even hundreds of black ants. The store also operates a mail-order business.

Clothing/Kids

Central

Bright Beginnings
38th St. at Lamar Blvd. • (512) 454-KIDS
Loop 360 (Capital of Texas Hwy.) at Bee Caves • (512) 328-8989

Owner Sally Whitehouse keeps the Austin lifestyle in mind when stocking her store. Just like their elders, Austin kids like to play and that means casual clothes, preferably in natural fabrics. Even the dress-up clothes here emphasize easy wearing and easy caring. Jumpers are a big favorite for girls, while boys can often emulate Dad in a vest, but in place of grey worsted the kid's version is emblazoned with dinosaurs.

Picket Fences and Down Cherry Lane
1003 W. 34th St. • (512) 458-2565

More than a kids clothing store, Picket Fences features (hence the name) picket-fence kids beds, plus nursery necessities, baby books, baby bags, decorative accents for the nursery or playroom, fabrics by the yard, window treatments, comfy nursery chairs for Mom or Dad, and maternity clothes. Down Cherry Lane, at the same address, offers handpainted furnishings for nursery or playroom, rocking chairs and vintage armoires. The shop will fill custom orders.

Wild Child and Wild Child Too!
1600 W. 38th St. • (512) 451-0455, (512) 453-4335

Wild Child features "fashion-forward" clothing and shoes for infants and kids through size 6X, Wild Child Too! has the same hip clothing for preteen and junior kids. The store also stocks "preppy" clothes for preteens including madras shirts, twill pants and simple T-shirts.

South Central

Dragonsnaps
1700 S. Congress Ave. • (512) 445-4497

Owned by same folks who own Terra Toys (see our Toys section in this chapter), Dragonsnaps seeks to bring the Terra Toys free spirit to kid's clothing. The clothes are easy to wear, fun and eye-catching.

Simply Divine
1606 S. Congress Ave. • (512) 444-5546

When it gets hot in Austin, no kid wants to be wearing scratchy, sticky polyester. Simply Divine offers original designs made on site. The natural fiber clothes are hand-dyed, and prints are handwoven. Owner Gayle Goff designs and manufactures the kid-friendly outfits.

West

Lambs-e-Divey
Tarrytown Center, 2415 A&B Exposition Blvd. • (512) 479-6619

This West Austin store features both casual wear for kids and outfits for those special occasions, such as Easter, Christmas and family weddings. Owner Wendy Yarbrough says the store specializes in helping moms coordinate the family's wardrobe so that Joe and Jane Jr. can stand out in a crowd. Kids also can find designer togs here, including Ralph Lauren polos and khakis, and there are very traditional pretty girl dresses decorated with lace and smocking just like Grandma likes.

Clothing/Western

The late Texas State Senator Peyton McKnight was an oilman who strode the floor of the Texas Capitol in legendary style, wearing a silver and gold belt buckle the size of a dinner plate and a pair of boots etched with a map of Texas. To mark his hometown of Tyler on the leather map, there was a large diamond smack in the middle of East Texas — one on each boot.

There is an old saying in Texas: "That boy is all hat," meaning, of course, there's too much image and not much substance. If you are going to don Western wear then you have to have the panache and, perhaps, some of the bucks, of Senator McKnight. Good boots, a well-made hat, a sturdy leather belt with a finely made belt buckle do not come cheap.

Not everyone in Texas dresses Western-style, in fact, "cowboys" come in various styles across the state. In Houston and Dallas you are more likely to see a businessman in a Brooks Brothers suit with a finely made pair of cowboy boots. In Amarillo or Midland, you might see a lawyer, a cattleman or oilman dressed for a business meeting in a Western-cut suit, a bolo tie and boots. In the state's smaller towns and on farms and ranches you are sure to see well-worn boots and traditional cowboy hats, while in El Paso and the Rio Grande Valley the influence of Mexico's vaqueros (literally cowboys) can be seen in the design of belt buckles and boots.

In Austin, Western attire is not seen as much as in other parts of the state, although at some Western and Mexican dance clubs (see our Nightlife chapter) you will see both men and women dressed in fine Western wear. While you won't see a lot of Stetsons in Austin (outside the dance halls), you will see boots, particularly well-worn, much loved old boots, usually worn with jeans or a long skirt, in the case of women. Boots with no hat is okay, but a hat and no boots is a social faux pas. Nothing says Yankee like a guy in a cowboy hat and a pair of loafers.

There are several boot outlet stores in Austin, listed below, but the well- heeled will turn to one of the city's master boot makers or specialty shops for a custom-made pair — well-heeled because a good pair of boots can run into several hundreds of dollars. If you can't afford a pair, settle for a kerchief or two. A faded cotton kerchief, dipped in cold water and tied around your neck on a hot day is an authentic cowboy tradition.

Texas Hatters

5003 Overpass Rd., Buda
• (512) 441-4287 Austin, (512) 295-4287 Buda, (800) 421-4287

What does Prince Charles have in common with Willie Nelson? They both own hats made by one of the most famous Western wear artists in the United States, the late Manny Gammage. For decades, country western music stars, politicians, presidents and future kings have worn what are generically called "cowboy hats." The walls of Gammage's workshop and store in the small community of Buda, just south of Austin off I-35, are covered with photos of famous folks. Gammage, like his father before him, blocked his hats by hand rather than by machine. Gammage passed away in 1995, but his family has carried on with the tradition.

Central

Capitol Saddlery

1614 Lavaca St. • (512) 478-9309

Singer Jerry Jeff Walker made this leather shop famous when he sang about the talents of the late master boot maker Charlie Dunn. The store has an old-fashioned air with boots, saddles, tack and assorted leather wear stacked everywhere. Look for the large boot-shaped sign hanging outside the old building.

South Central

Allen Boots

1525 S. Congress Ave. • (512) 447-1413

This Western wear store has been on South Congress for years and now finds itself in the midst of a South Austin shopping revival. This is a great place to find Western wear and boots at reasonable prices. Enjoy the ambience. This is a Western wear shop without the glitz and urban cowboy atmosphere found in some other large Texas cities.

North

Sheplers
6001 Middle Fiskville Rd.
• (512) 454-3000

Looking for a cowboy hat or boots to take home or wear to the office barbecue? Check out this branch of Sheplers, a chain store with a large selection, located near Highland Mall.

Cowtown Boot Company Factory Outlet
6700 Middle Fiskville Rd.
• (512) 467-7117

The best cowboy boots last for years, but strangers to these parts are often taken aback with how much a good pair of boots can cost. This outlet is a good place to search for bargains.

Computers

Austin has more computer stores than Los Angeles has fly-by-night car dealers. Perhaps not factually true, but metaphorically speaking it captures the tech mood in Austin. In addition to several major chain operations including Computer City and CompUSA, there is an ever-growing subculture of small stores and resale outlets in Austin. Judging from the ads in the technology section of the *Austin American-Statesman*, it might appear that there's more money in motherboards than mother's old Buick. However, putting a system together from bits of this and that is easily done in Austin, provided you know your bytes from bits. Keep track of the

Photo: Courtesy of the Austin Convention and Visitors Bureau

Sample a little Texas wine at Fall Creek Vineyard west of Austin.

ads, know who is a fixture on the landscape as opposed to a fly-by-night operation and ask questions. Meanwhile, here are a couple of resources with impeccable reputations.

Goodwill Computer Works
8701 Research Blvd. • (512) 835-8839

Whether you're looking for a cheap PC or an old classic Mac, this may be the place. Given Austin's intense high-tech industry growth and level of computer ownership, the town's closets are filled with old models. So, Goodwill decided to provide a home for the abandoned. Old computers are donated to the shop, fixed up and sold at bargain-basement prices. It's a great place to find a computer for a schoolchild or grandma without spending a fortune.

Dell Outlet
8801 Research Blvd. • (512) 728-5656

Dell computers at discount prices are available at the hometown computer giant's outlet store. The models include demos, discontinued and reconditioned models, plus accessories and software. Discounts vary according to supply, the price of semiconductors, the age of the model, etc., but bargains do abound.

Flea Markets

Central

Austin City-Wide Garage Sales
City Coliseum, 512 E. Riverside Dr. • (512) 441-2828

Every month the City Coliseum on Town Lake is host to a large sale featuring more than 180 vendors selling a variety of flea market merchandise. Dates vary, so check the *Austin American-Statesman* for each monthly sale.

Northeast

Austin Country Flea Market
9500 U.S. Hwy. 290 E. • (512) 928-2795

This is the real thing: an old-fashioned, take-your-chances flea market. A jumble of clothing, rugs, pottery, tools, records, furniture, sporting goods, CDs and videos — all under one roof so you can wander around, rain or shine. Beware, some of the brand-name items may not be the real thing, but nevertheless there are lots of bargains; at least they seem bargains until you get home and wonder, "Why did I buy a set of TV tray tables?" The market's Mexican herb stalls and Latino music stands give the market a south-of-the-border flavor. You also can have your palm or tarot cards read, or enjoy a snow cone and a barbecue sandwich. The market is approximately 5 miles east of I-35 and is open only on weekends.

Southwest

Market Day
Lions Field, Wimberley • (512) 847-2201

On the first Saturday of the month, April through November, flea market mavens flock to Wimberley, southwest of Austin, to comb the multitude of stalls at the famed Wimberley Market Day. Vendors number in the hundreds, and the wise get there early — to get first choice get there by 7:30 AM. Take U.S. Highway 290 west out of Austin to Dripping Springs, then head south on R.R. 12 into Wimberley — about a 45-minute drive. When you reach the fork in the road in the heart of the community, take the right fork about four blocks to Lions Field. The Lions Club sells sausage wraps for breakfast and barbecue later in the day, plus a couple of local churches operate cake and cookie stands.

Farmers Markets

A good resource for keeping track of local farmers market activities and the status of locally produced vegetables and fruits is the *Austin American-Statesman* food section, published each Thursday.

Central

Whole Foods Farmers Market
601 N. Lamar Blvd. • (512) 476-1206

The downtown Whole Foods Market flagship store holds a weekly afternoon farmers market in front of the store. The market is usually held on Wednesday afternoons from spring through the fall, but check with the store for times.

North

Travis County Farmers Market
6701 Burnet Rd. • (512) 454-1002

The Travis County Farmers Market has a permanent home in North Austin that remains open all year, although the peak vegetable and fruit-selling season runs from spring to fall. Throughout the year the market celebrates the seasons and the various harvests with festivals, cookoffs and fiestas. In the spring, Hill Country peaches are featured, followed by the June tomato crop. Fourth of July brings a watermelon patch. In September, the Green Chile Pepper festival is held, and chile roasters, large barbecue-like contraptions, are on hand to roast the end of summer crop of New Mexico-style chiles. In October, the market has a large pumpkin patch. The market also has a Mexican restaurant on the premises (see our Restaurants chapter), a gift shop featuring Texas foods, a coffee-roasting company and, of course, a barbecue joint.

South

South Austin Farmers Market
2910 S. Congress Ave.

Local farmers set up shop in the parking lot of the El Gallo restaurant on Saturday mornings from spring to fall.

West

Westlake Farmers Market
4100 Westbank Dr.

The Westlake market is held year round on Saturday mornings in the parking lot of Westlake High School. In addition to local produce, Bottega della Pasta, a popular local wholesale pasta producer, sets up a stall at the market. Italian gelato is also sold.

Northwest

Whole Foods Farmers Market
Gateway Shopping Center, 9607 Research Blvd. • (512) 345-5003

Whole Foods at Gateway holds a seasonal farmers market spring through fall, usually on Monday afternoons. Check with the store for times.

Georgetown Farmers Market
Town Square, Georgetown

One of the largest farmers markets in Central Texas is held on the town square in historic Georgetown, a 15-minute ride north of Round Rock on I-35. The market is held on Thursday afternoons spring through fall.

Round Rock

Round Rock Farmers Market
221 E. Main St.

Every Saturday from spring to fall, farmers and growers set up stalls in the city hall garage on Saturday morning.

Food/Gourmet/ Kitchenware

Austin is a city that considers food a significant part of life, not in a high falutin' way, although the city's restaurants boast a fair number of topnotch chefs, but in a way that celebrates the mix of food and friends, new tastes and familiar comforts. It is no surprise that when out-of-town visitors arrive, many Austinites take them on a discovery tour of the city's food stores.

Central

Anderson Coffee Company
Jefferson Square • (512) 453-1533

Jefferson Square, just off W. 35th Street near Kerbey Lane, is a collection of small, older homes turned into cozy shops, a fitting setting for Anderson Coffee Company, which sells coffees, teas, mugs and teapots, plus culinary spices — comfort stuff.

Breed & Co.

718 W. 29th St. • (512) 474-6679
3663 Bee Caves Rd. • (512) 328-3960

This is the kind of store that actually can bring couples closer together, even heal marriages. One partner can stroll the nuts and bolts section, while the other daydreams about the days when the entire collection of cooking equipment will find its way to his or her kitchen. Austinites will drive in from the outer reaches of town to shop at this compact, some might say small, hardware store compared to today's megastores. Breed proves the old adage that good things come in small containers. The store stocks hard-to-find and everyday hardware and paint supplies, cleaning solutions for every surface, china and crystal, a perfumery, a specialty food section, garden supplies, picture frames, decorative accessories, throw rugs, coffee beans, bird feeders, knives, cutting boards and all manner of cookware. A second Breed has opened in West Lake Hills on Bee Caves Road.

Central Market

Central Park, 40th St. and Lamar Blvd. • (512) 216-1000

Urban myth says the Central Market grocery store is second only to the capitol in terms of tourists. On a Saturday afternoon as you struggle to bag a few habanero peppers or wait in line for the to-die-for imported prosciutto, it's easy to believe. See our Close-up in this chapter to find out what it's all about.

Dr. Chocolate

Central Park, 4001 N. Lamar Blvd. • (512) 454-0555

Addicted to chocolate? Consult the doctor. The prescription is, of course, chocolate in the form of flowers, hand-dipped chocolates, chocolate ice cream, chocolate pizza, chocolate cakes, chocolate-dipped strawberries, chocolate fudge. . . . The doctor has no shame.

Fabulous Cheesecakes

26 Doors, 1206 W. 38th St. • (512) 453-1228

For 13 years, this speciality store has been cooking up 50 flavors of cheesecake for special occasions, birthdays, anniversaries or just everyday noshing. The shop sells bite-sized and mini-sized cheesecakes for instant gratification. Orders can be placed ahead of time for special events, or customers can pick up a full-sized cheesecake and have it decorated for last-minute celebrations.

India Bazaar

3004 Guadalupe St. • (512) 494-1200

This Indian grocery store is popular among University of Texas students, particularly because in addition to food items it sells henna products for hair dyeing and temporary tattoos. There is also an extensive video and CD collection. Anglophiles may want to browse the food shelves where they can find some British pantry staples, reflecting Anglo-Indian cultural history.

Texas French Bread

2900 Rio Grande St. • (512) 499-0355

A wildly successful Texas bakery that has taken its success citywide, Texas French Bread is headquartered at this central city location, next door to Breed Hardware (see our listing in this chapter). Its breads, which present the best of European and American breadmaking traditions, are now sold to grocery stores and restaurants throughout the city. One of the most popular is a delicious breakfast bread made with pecans. (See our Restaurants chapter for more.)

Pasta & Co.

3502 Kerbey Ln. • (512) 453-0633

Pasta to go is the theme here. The company makes numerous kinds of pasta and sauces, including jalapeno fettucine, wild-mushroom ravioli and ancho-pecan pesto. For

INSIDERS' TIP

Christmas shopping takes on special meaning in Austin because of two popular annual events: the Austin Junior League Christmas Affair in late November and the Armadillo Christmas Bazaar in December. Check our Annual Events chapter for details.

those who can't bring themselves to boil a pot of water, the stores also features ready-cooked pasta dishes that simply need reheating.

Sweetish Hill Bakery

1120 W. Sixth St. • (512) 472-1347
922 Congress Ave. • (512) 477-2441
98 San Jacinto Blvd. • (512) 472-1347

One of Austin's most noted bakeries, Sweetish Hill is famed for its breads, cookies (the lemon bars are addictive) and European-style pastries. This is a great place to order a special birthday cake and many Austinites insist on a chocolate or mocha *buche de noel* (a French cake shaped and decorated like a log, complete with meringue mushrooms) at Christmas time. The bakery is also a popular breakfast and lunch spot (see our Restaurants chapter).

The Coffee Exchange

1200 W. Sixth St. • (512) 474-5300

In addition to coffee beans, this Sixth Street coffee shop also sells tea, wine, cheese, chocolates, plus tea and coffee-making equipment and gift items. (For a complete listing of coffee shops see our Nightlife chapter.)

Upper Crust Bakery

4508 Burnet Rd. • (512) 475-0102

Upper Crust is a neighborhood European-style bakery that serves up a daily feast of fresh breads, croissants, muffins, cookies and tarts. The shop is also a popular neighborhood cafe (see our Restaurants chapter).

Wheatsville Food Co-op

3101 Guadalupe St. • (512) 478-2667

Wheatsville is old-fashioned cooperative grocery store where the customers own the store. Members pay an a $10 annual fee or purchase a share, but anyone can shop here. The co-op specializes in natural foods, and there is a vegetarian deli.

Whole Foods Market

601 N. Lamar Blvd. • (512) 476-1206
9607 Research Blvd. • (512) 345-5003

Take the Austin trivia test: Where was the first Whole Foods Market, and when did Michael Dell graduate from the University of Texas? Answers: 914 N. Lamar Boulevard, and he didn't — the high-tech billionaire dropped out after his computer business could no longer be run from his dorm room. If there are two leitmotifs for Austin's growth and development they are Dell Computers and Whole Foods Markets. Both are now the hottest stocks around, and Austinites who bought both are now zillionaires. Whole Foods Market has expanded from a hippie-dippie, natural foods store to the largest natural foods retailer in the country with $1 billion in sales and a store just a few blocks from L.A.'s Rodeo Drive. It's been a bumpy ride and founders John Mackey (who once drove around in a blue postal van painted with dancing vegetables) and Peter Roy have been criticized by natural foodies and some union activists along the way, but the bottom line is Whole Foods is an unparalleled success.

Whole Foods remains a popular icon on the local landscape, a place where you are just as likely to find a tie-dyed, would-be street mime shopping side by side with a Texas Supreme Court justice. It has always been that kind of place. There's tofu and high-priced Bourdeaux, tabbouleh and hormone-free, top-grade fillet of beef, organic apple juice and high-priced balsamic vinegars. The 38,000-square-foot flagship store, adjacent to the company's corporate offices, opened in 1995 and features both organic and top-grade vegetables and fruit, a wide variety of bulk food, hormone-free beef and chicken, excellent fish, a broad selection of beer, wine, cheese, a deli, an extensive vitamin and supplements department, plus a bakery, sandwich shop and on-site restaurant and masseuse. A second location is in the Gateway shopping center in Northwest Austin.

Ace Mart Restaurant Supply Co.

1025 W. Fifth St. • (512) 482-8700

A little-known secret in cooking circles is that many restaurant supply companies are open to the public. Ace is one that sells both to the trade and the individual customer. Thrifty cooks and hostesses will check out the price of plates, glasses, silverware and party ware here. Good buys are aprons, kitchen towels, oversized cooking pans and stockpots. Ardent cooks are certain to find something they simply must have at this warehouse just west of Lamar Boulevard.

La Victoria Bakery

5425 Burnet Rd. • (512) 458-1898

Owner Anita Becerra creates Mexican specialties at this small bakery on Burnet Road. One seasonal item worth seeking out is her *pan de muerto* or Day of the Dead bread, which celebrates the annual Mexican holiday on All Souls Day. (See our Annual Events chapter for more on All Souls Day.)

Asahi Imports

100 W. North Loop Blvd. • (512) 453-1850

It is easy to miss this store with its unassuming storefront in a strip shopping center, but its selection of everyday Japanese ceramics, sake sets, rice bowls, teapots, plus origami kits and Japanese food items (tea, rice candy, plum wine) is well worth seeking out, both for price and quality.

North

Lamme's Candies

5330 Airport Blvd. • (512) 310-2223, (800) 252-1885

The Lamme family has been making candies in Austin since 1885. Famed for Texas Chewie Pecan Pralines, Lamme's also heralds the early summer with its chocolate-dipped strawberries. The company's headquarters is on Airport Boulevard, but there are other locations around the area: Lamar Village at 38th Street in Central Austin, downtown at Sixth and Congress; Northcross Mall in North Austin, Barton Creek Mall in West Austin, Highland Mall in North Austin, Lakeline Mall in Northwest Austin, R.R. 620 and I-35 in Round Rock, and at San Marcos Factory Outlet stores.

Chef's Tool Box

109-A Denson Dr. • (512) 467-1994

Both the professional and the amateur chef will admire the knives at this North Austin store. You'll find kitchen tools, chef's uniforms, coffee, cigars, gadgets, pastry supplies and, for anyone who loves to cook but hates standing for hours on end, comfortable chef's clogs from Sweden.

Hong Kong Supermarket

8557 Research Blvd. • (512) 339-2068

A stroll around this North Austin supermarket is like a culinary tour of Asia. Formerly a neighborhood grocery store, the owners took over the facility and filled it with Asian foodstuffs, fresh, frozen and canned to meet the needs of Austin's growing Asian population. The meat and fresh fish section features cuts and types of fish and fowl popular among Oriental cooks. There is a cooked meat section with barbecued ducks and meats, plus several aisles featuring kitchen and household goods. It is a good place to buy noodles, tea and rice in bulk.

MGM Indian Foods

9200 N. Lamar Blvd. • (512) 835-6937

This is the city's oldest Indian grocery, stocking herbs, vegetables, dried fruits and nuts and other vital ingredients for Indian cuisine. Recently, the owner, who hails from the state of Kerala in India, has added foods from Ghana and Nigeria to meet customer demands.

My Thanh Oriental Market

7601 N. Lamar Blvd. • (512) 454-4805

This Thai market sells curries, noodles, spices and herbs, Thai peppers, fish sauce, coconut milk — all the necessities for cooking a Thai feast, plus the utensils to do it, including woks and rice cookers, and the serving ware to ring it to the table.

Saigon Oriental Market

8610 N. Lamar Blvd. • (512) 837-6641

This grocery stocks a full line of Vietnamese ingredients and also sells cooking utensils, incense and traditional festival decorations.

East

El Milagro

910 E. Sixth St. • (512) 477-6476

El Milagro — The Miracle — is an authentic tortilla factory that sells both wholesale to Austin grocery stores and restaurants and retail to the walk-in customers. Buying from the source can be fun and it gives you an opportunity to see the inner workings of a authentic culinary tradition both south of the border and in Texas. Ambitious cooks who plan to follow a Texas tradition and make Christmas tamales can buy freshly ground *masa* (cornmeal) from the factory.

Callahan's General Store
501 U.S. Hwy. 183 • (512) 385-3452
220 S. Bell Blvd., Cedar Park
• (512) 335-8585

The closest thing to an old-fashioned general store in Austin, Callahan's sells sausage-stuffing machines, canning equipment and all manner of supplies for cooks. In addition, there is Western wear, boots, saddles and supplies for the farm and ranch.

Fiesta Mart
3909 N. I-35 • (512) 406-3900

A branch of the Houston supermarket chain, Fiesta takes a multicultural approach to the grocery store business. Everything from banana leaves for tamales to British custard mixes can be found on the shelves here. If your Puerto Rican pen pal or your great aunt from Australia is coming to town, check the shelves here for those grocery essentials.

South Central

La Mexicana Bakery
1924 S. First St. • (512) 443-6369

Mexican pastries are intended to be mood-lifters, a little sweet bite to accompany mid-morning coffee, or a late night snack with a cup of hot Mexican chocolate. Many contain no salt or preservatives so they are best eaten the day they are made. La Mexicana offers a variety of cookies and cakes, empanadas stuffed with pumpkin, gingerbread pigs or sugarcoated *conchas* (shell-shaped cakes). Be sure to ask the names of the varieties, often they are a wonderful play on the shape, ingredients or taste of the item. The bakery also sells Mexican sodas.

Phoenicia Bakery & Deli
2912 S. Lamar Blvd. • (512) 447-4444

Phoenicia is a deli specializing in imported foods from those countries and regions that ring the Mediterranean, including Greece, Spain, Italy, North Africa and the Middle East. In addition to olives, olive oils, peppers, spices, sauces, pasta, grains, the store also sells cold cuts such as salami and mortadella, plus cheeses from the region, pickles, stuffed grape leaves, freshly made tahini and hummus. There is a frozen food section where bakers can find phyllo dough. The deli also makes sandwiches (see our Restaurants chapter) and has a small bakery selling pita bread and baklava, plus other regional delights.

Southwest

Piddler & Pro Home and Hardware
7010 Texas Hwy. 71 W. • (512) 288-7223

More than a hardware store, this friendly neighborhood store in Southwest Austin has a wide collection of kitchen and household goods that make great wedding or special occasion gifts. Many of the kitchen and cookware items celebrate Texas and Mexican themes and are suitable for serving Southwestern fare.

West

Great Harvest Bakery
3201 Bee Caves Rd. • (512) 329-9216
4815 W. Braker Ln. • (512) 345-0588

Noted for their crusty, rustic, flavorful European-style breads, Great Harvest has two locations and also sells its breads to local restaurants and grocery stores.

Trianon Coffee Roasters
3201 Bee Caves Rd. • (512) 328-4033
3742 Far West Blvd. • (512) 346-9636
4815 Braker Ln. • (512) 349-7758

This French-style coffee boutique sells freshly roasted beans, pastries, chocolate and candies. The other locations are in Northwest Austin.

Northwest

Williams-Sonoma
Arboretum, 9722 Great Hills Tr.
• (512) 338-4080

Cooking enthusiasts are familiar with the William-Sonoma catalog and many of those items can be found at this Arboretum area store in Northwest Austin. In addition to top-quality small appliances and bakeware, the store stocks imported foods, plus numerous kitchen gadgets, dinner and glassware.

Round Rock

Lone Star Bakery

106 W. Liberty • (512) 255-3629

Lone Star claims to make the best doughnuts in Texas, and there is no harm in testing their claim, even coming back for seconds or thirds to make sure the boast is still true.

Saradora's Coffeehouse & Emporium

101 E. Main St. • (512) 310-1200

In addition to a coffee bar, this store in the historic town center sells roasted beans, fresh breads and pastries to go, plus homemade fudge and Austin's own Amy's ice cream.

Gardening

Central

Gardens

18118 W. 35th St. • (512) 451-5490

The small garden in front of this Central Austin garden shop is living proof that wonderful gardens can be created not only in small spaces, but also in the Austin climate where summer heat and drought can be a challenge. Don't be fooled by the outward appearance of this shop in the 35th Street shopping corridor; it may look small, but inside there is a mother lode of resources for serious gardeners — imported pottery from Italy, Japanese garden elements, English garden tools, books, seeds and an outdoor nursery of herbs and plants, many of them unusual and eye-catching. This is a must-stop for any ardent gardener.

North

Heirloom Gardens

Village Shopping Center, 2700 W. Anderson Ln., No. 904 • (512) 451-0241

Gardeners looking for unusual plants and herbs are attracted to this North Austin garden center. In addition to rare herbs, scented geraniums, old-fashioned flowers such as hollyhocks and poppies, topiaries and day lily bulbs, the store also stocks books on gardening, candles and garden furnishings.

South

It's About Thyme

11726 Manchaca Rd. • (512) 280-1192

Newcomers to Austin who enjoy gardening may be frustrated if they try to grow plants that flourish in cooler, northern climes, but they won't be disappointed if they stick to native plants and those herbs that do well in Mediterranean countries — rosemary, oregano, basil and thymes. This South Austin herb nursery, 2 miles south of Slaughter Lane, has a wide selection of herbs and related items. The shop also sells antique roses, which do well in the Austin climate.

Marbridge Farms Greenhouse

F.M. 1626 and Bliss Spillar Rd. • (512) 282-5504

Marbridge Ranch is a residential facility for mentally handicapped men who earn a living tending the greenhouses that house hundreds of plants. Many Austinites head here for reasonably priced plants for the garden and the vegetable plot. The farm is in far South Austin on the outer edge of the city, but the wide variety and the worthy cause attracts many gardeners.

Southwest

Garden-Ville of Austin

8548 Old Bee Caves Rd. • (512) 288-6113

Owner John Dromgole is a well-known radio personality who preaches the benefits of organic gardening. The nursery, tucked away on a country road in Southwest Austin, is always busy on the weekends as Austin gardeners flock here for plants, flowers, vegetables, seeds and a wonderful variety of tools and garden ornaments. There is an antique rose collection, plus xeriscape plants for low water maintenance gardens. The nursery also sells a line of soils and fertilizers, including Dillo Dirt, a soil enhancer made from recycled Austin sewage wastes. Shoppers can bag their soils or have large amounts delivered.

West

Barton Springs Nursery
3601 Bee Caves Rd. • (512) 328-6655

This West Lake Hills nursery features an extensive collection of native plants. Newcomers soon learn that native is often the best way to go in the Austin climate, and many varieties and species can be found here. The owners and staff have a warehouse of knowledge to help gardeners overcome the challenges of Hill Country gardening. The center also has a collection of wildflower seeds and garden ornaments.

Pots and Plants
5902 Bee Caves Rd. • (512) 327-4564

"That crazy flamingo place" is how you will hear radio ads refer to this West Austin garden center. Austin gardeners know spring is on the way when a few scout pink flamingos show up on the front lawn of Pots and Plants at the intersection of Bee Caves Road and Loop 360. Later, the rest of the pink plastic flock arrives and Austin gardeners know the planting season goes into full swing. A few years ago, some zealous West Lake Hills citizens wanted to ban the flamingos because they thought they were tacky and flew in the face of the community's sign ordinance; but other citizens came to the rescue and the birds are now considered high-class yard art. The garden center has a wide selection of native plants, plus deer resistant varieties.

Northwest

Smith & Hawken Garden
Gateway Courtyard, 9901 Loop 360 (Capital of Texas Hwy.) • (512) 345-8700

Gardening enthusiasts likely are familiar with the Smith & Hawken catalog that features some of the best garden tools, well-designed pottery and gardener's clothing. With the opening of this store, Austin gardeners have the opportunity to browse through the same collection of much-admired garden accoutrements featured in the popular catalog.

Round Rock

Garden Ridge Pottery
F.M. 1325 at I-35 • (512) 310-1130

Pots, pots and more pots — that's what draws avid gardeners to this huge store in Round Rock. In addition to pottery, the 3-acre store is a mecca for crafters who shop here for silk flowers, ribbons, glassware and all manner of crafts items.

Gifts

Central

Atomic City
1700 San Antonio St. • (512) 477-0293

Toys are us — for grownups that is. Atomic City is the place to find Godzillas that spit fire, fighting nuns and other Japanese toys to keep on the desk for those moments when the brain bombs. The store also has a large collection of tin toys, lava lamps, Hawaiian shirts, even boots and shoes to add just the right sartorial touch to a toy player's tropical outfit.

Capitol Complex Visitors Center
112 E. 11th St., Capitol annex • (512) 305-8400

The capitol police report the occasional ardent tourist attempting to remove part of the capitol's wrought-iron fence, a door knob or door hinge as a memento. But law-abiding visitors head to the capitol's gift shop where gifts reflecting these architectural elements can be bought without risking arrest. Replicas of the capitol's door hinges serve as bookends; other architectural elements are reproduced in paperweights. The store has a first-class collection of posters, flags, books about Texas flora, fauna, travel and history. The small shop also sells Texas foods and T-shirts.

Congress Avenue Souvenirs

615 Congress Ave. • (512) 478-1663

Looking for something that says "I went to Texas, and all I bought you was this bluebonnet soap holder"? This is the place. Items, both practical and fanciful, decorated with the Lone Star, the Texas flag, an armadillo or two and the ubiquitous bluebonnet can be found here. Postcards, bumper stickers, stickers for kids and coffee mugs are popular, reasonably priced gift items to send the Texas message.

Cowgirls and Flowers

508 Walsh St. • (512) 478-4626

More than one of the most popular flower shops in the central city, Cowgirls is noted for its jewelry and craft items. If you are looking for a very artsy flower presentation, plus a special gift, check out this Central Austin store.

Morning Star Trading Company

1117 W. Fifth St. • (512) 476-1727

The major trade here is in oils and essences aimed at making folks feel better. The store sells massage, relaxation and bath oils, plus other body-care products all designed to enhance both the skin and the soul. In addition to the personal products, the store also features a jewelry collection.

Necessities and Temptations

1202-A W. Sixth St. • (512) 473-8334

Contemporary Southwestern jewelry and Texas souvenirs are among the items sold at this small gift shop that is part of the Sixth Street strolling strip west of Lamar Boulevard. The store also features Brazilian slate fountains and falling rain chime boxes.

Oat Willie's

617 W. 29th St. • (512) 482-0630

Remember the term "head shop"? A visit to Oat Willie's is a jaunt down memory lane for anyone who grew up in the '60s. Whenever you see an Onward through the Fog bumper sticker, you are a looking at a Austin hallmark — this was Oat Willie's (Yes, Virginia, there was an Oat Willie) slogan. Oat Willie once ran for President and his T-shirts are now collectors' items. T-shirts are still sold at Oat Willie's, along with comic books, videos, toys and clothing. Bongs (pipes for the non-initiated) are no longer sold at Oat Willie's, but street vendors still sell them on The Drag (Guadalupe Street).

Old Bakery and Emporium

1006 Congress Ave. • (512) 477-5961

Austin's senior citizens sell their crafts in this old store just a block south of the capitol (see our Attractions chapter). The seniors also sell homebaked cookies and breads that are a good accompaniment to a stroll down Congress Avenue or a mini-picnic on the capitol grounds.

Pecan Street Emporium

1122 W. Sixth St. • (512) 477-4900

A popular spot for Christmas shoppers — the local merchants decorate this stretch of Sixth Street with luminarias during the season — Pecan Street Emporium is noted for its selection of music boxes, German pottery collectibles and nutcrackers. The shop also has a large collection of tiny boxes, plus jewelry, toys and a great card collection. The back room of the store houses a large collection of Christmas ornaments and villages during the holidays.

The Cadeau

2316 Guadalupe St. • (512) 477-7276
Central Park, 4001 N. Lamar Blvd. • (512) 453-6988

This wonderful shop — in both locations — is more than a gift shop. Since 1952 the Cadeau has been presenting Austin shoppers with a wide variety of gifts, home furnishings, clothes, decorative items, toys, china and crystal. Both the original store on The Drag and the new store in Central Park feature home furnishings by top designers including Versace, Calvin Klein, Baccarat and Kosta Boda. Not all the items are high-priced, and shoppers with a budget can find inexpensive, but unique items. The store also has a good selection of cards and wrapping paper. The location on the Drag also has a selection of kitchenware and cookbooks.

University Co-op

2244 Guadalupe St. • (512) 476-7211

If God isn't a Longhorn why did he paint the sunset burnt orange and then fill this store on The Drag with all that burnt-orange stuff? A philosophical question that needs no answer in Austin. UT fans can find just about anything in their team colors here, from the theological burnt-orange question on a bumper sticker to windsocks. The co-op also has a bookstore (see our chapter Literary Austin), plus a camera shop.

Wild About Music
721 Congress Ave. • (512) 708-1700

If you're looking for a gift that says Texas music, check out this downtown store. All the gifts here have a musical theme, including T-shirts, posters, jewelry, books and knickknacks. The store also sells aquariums made from converted television sets by Austin artist Larry Plitz.

North

Source Menagerie
8015 Shoal Creek Blvd., Ste. 108 • (512) 458-5353

Doggone it, they've got everything under the sun that has a dog motif — from life-size stone statues of labs to fluffy, stuffed Bridget the Border Collie, jigsaw puzzles with a doggy theme, car mats, even a salt and pepper set that has three items — a pepper grinder, a salt shaker and a dog hair shaker. The store also has a catalog business, just call (888) 702-WOOF.

South Central

Off the Wall
1704 S. Congress Ave. • (512) 445-4701

Animal theme gifts are the order of the day here. The store also sells antique clocks, ceramics and occasional pieces of furniture.

The Herb Bar
200 W. Mary St. • (512) 444-6251

Herbs, both culinary and medicinal, can be found here, plus tinctures and body oils designed to soothe what ails you.

Northwest

Higginbottom's
Arboretum, 10000 Research Blvd. • (512) 343-2100

There is a Harrod's feel to this Arboretum gift shop. Perhaps it is because of all the teddy bears, china gifts, imported toys and even Christmas pudding sold during the holidays. The store stocks imported foods, has a large candy department and is a must stop at Christmas.

Round Rock

Paper Dragon Etc.
112 E. Main St. • (512) 255-2227

Only friendly dragons hang out here among the bears, angels, candles and jelly beans. This store in Round Rock's historic center also sells jewelry and other gift items.

Home Furnishings

Central

Fortney's Artful Home Furnishings
1116 W. Sixth St. • (512) 495-6505

Fortney's specializes in custom-made Southwestern and contemporary furniture. The store also sells fountains and sculptures for the garden or patio.

St. Charles
519 E. Sixth St. • (512) 478-5598

A longtime Sixth Street presence, St. Charles is noted for its Art Deco and Art Nouveau furniture and accessories.

North

Cierra
5502 Burnet Rd. • (512) 454-8603

Cierra presents primitive folk art and furnishings from the Southwest and Mexico, including rustic tables, wrought-iron lamps and candleholders, cabinets and chairs evocative of Old Mexico.

East

Frontera
1000 E. Sixth St. • (512) 45-1164

Equipales are the rustic, leather-covered chairs often found on patios and in plazas in Mexico, and Frontera has a large selection in its East Austin warehouse, two blocks east of I-35. Other Frontera specialities include handcrafted furniture, Native American and Mexican artifacts, hammered tin lamps and lamp shades, rustic decorative pieces and handwoven pillows.

Provencal Home and Garden
The Village at Westlake Shopping Center, Loop 360 (Capital of Texas Hwy.) and Bee Caves Rd. • (512) 306-9449

Looking to bring a touch of the South of France to your home? Here is where you can find French china, crystal, linens and custom fabrics. The store also sells rustic furniture for both inside and outside the home.

Jewelry

Central

Gallerie Estate Jewelers
3500 Jefferson St., Ste. 105 • (512) 451-3889

Antique and estate sale jewelry is sold at this Jefferson Square-area jeweler. The store also accepts consignments.

Nomadic Notions
2426 Guadalupe St. • (512) 478-6200
2438 W. Anderson Ln. • (512) 454-0001

With two stores, one in the central area, the other in North Austin, Nomadic Notions sells beads from more than 35 countries, some 5,000 varieties ranging in price from pennies to around $50. The stores also sell jeweler's supplies and offers instruction to those eager to make their own distinctive jewelry. The stores also sell African bead strands and blown Egyptian perfume bottles.

Russell Korman
3806 N. Lamar Blvd. • (512) 451-9292

This is another Austin success story. Back in the '70s, Korman worked on The Drag near the university selling beads; now he is selling custom-made pieces made from precious metals and jewels.

The Turquoise Door
316 Colorado St. • (512) 480-0618

Silver jewelry and Latin American and Southwestern folk art are sold at this downtown store next door to Mezzaluna Restaurant. The sign in the window says Axl Rose and Vanessa Redgrave have shopped here, and it is easy to see why. The turquoise and amber jewelry is particularly beautiful. In addition to top-quality Mexican folk art, the store has a small collection of folk art books.

Photography

Central

Precision Camera and Video
3810 N. Lamar St. • (512) 467-7676

A favorite among Austin's professional and amateur photographers, Precision has grown from a small shop near the university to this large store just north of 35th Street. Services include film processing, camera rental and repair. Check out the store's used-camera department.

South Central

Holland Photo
1221 S. Lamar Blvd. • (512) 442-4274

This is a full-service photographic lab used by many of Austin's professional photographers. It offers a variety of services to both professionals and amateurs alike including two-hour E-6 processing, computer imaging, custom enlargements and film and photo supplies.

Resale Shops/Charity

Recycling is a subject close to Austin's heart, so it is no wonder that resale shops abound. Many are dedicated to raising money for charity; others seek to extend the life of bell-bottoms well beyond their expected life span. Goodwill, the Salvation Army, the MaryLee Foundation, the Junior League, St. Vincent de Paul and other worthy institutions all operate thrift stores in Austin. Donations are encouraged and listings for the stores can be found in the Yellow Pages. Here, we have listed those charity stores with a specific mission, or those with a unique presence in Austin.

Central

Next to New
5308 Burnet Rd. • (512) 459-1288

Next to New Shop is a nonprofit organization sponsored by St. David's Episcopal Church. Staffed by community volunteers, the store's profits go to community outreach programs and to the restoration of historic church buildings.

Top Drawer Thrift
4902 Burnet Rd. • (512) 454-5161

This store supports people living with HIV/AIDS. Proceeds from the sale of donated merchandise benefit Project Transitions, which provides a home-like environment to meet the physical, emotional and spiritual needs of persons experiencing the dying process.

East

Habitat for Humanity Re-Store
310 Comal St. • (512) 478-2165

This large warehouse features donated household fittings such as faucets, miniblinds, bathroom cabinets, stove tops, even the kitchen sink, plus doors, windows and construction lumber. Many of the items are used and have been donated by homeowners and builders upgrading or replacing older items, but some are new. All proceeds benefit Habitat for Humanity, the organization that builds homes in low-income neighborhoods.

Resale/Vintage Clothing and Stuff

Central

Banana Bay Trading Company
2908 San Gabriel St. • (512) 479-8608

Banana Bay is Austin's version of an Army-Navy store. Located on a triangle of land east of Lamar and just north of 29th Street, Banana Bay features a variety of military clothing, including Commie stuff such as ammo boxes, tents and survival kits.

Dressed to Kill
2418 Guadalupe St. • (512) 476-3148

Vintage clothing stores in Austin are a growth industry, and this one capitalizes on the demand for '60s retro, '20s chic and cowboy looks.

Inner Sanctum
504 W. 24th St. • (512) 472-9459

This resale shop near the University of Texas specializes in comics, old records and costume jewelry.

Rethreads
1806 W. 35th St. • (512) 459-3325
8108 Mesa Dr. • (512) 345-5573

Consistently voted one of Austin's top resale shops by the readers of *The Austin Chronicle*, this unassuming (at least on the outside) shop sells top-name designer labels placed here by some of Austin's wealthier residents who live in the western enclaves of the city. The store also sells jewelry on consignment.

South Central

Bohemia Retro-Resale
1714 S. Congress Ave. • (512) 326-1238

Good junk from every era is the boast here. The ever-changing stock includes clothes, furniture and housewares. Like other South Congress stores, Bohemia keeps late hours to encourage after-dinner browsing.

Let's Dish
1102 S. Lamar Blvd. • (512) 444-9801

The vintage clothing at Let's Dish ranges from the turn of the century through the ever-popular '70s disco style. The store also has an extensive vintage jewelry collection and sells pottery, dishware and maps dating from the 1920s to the 1950s.

Electric Ladyland/Lucy in Disguise with Diamonds
1506 S. Congress Ave. • (512) 444-2002

The emphasis here is theatrical with

both gorilla suits and French maid's uniforms in stock. Disco wear also is big, and the store boasts that Bob Dylan shopped here.

North

It's New to Me
7719 Burnet Rd. • (512) 451-0388

A variety of furniture is displayed in the store's 8,000-square-foot showroom, including some good quality pieces from furniture producers such as Henredon. This is a consignment shop where Austin residents sell their good-quality furniture.

Toys

Central

Rootin' Ridge
26 Doors, 1206 W. 38th St.
• (512) 453-2604

Georgean and Paul Kyle have been making toys since 1975, and their store in 26 doors features their own creations, plus handcrafted quality wooden toys, puzzles and musical instruments.

Toy Joy
2900 Guadalupe St. • (512) 320-0090

"You are never too old to play" might be the motto of this store, which boasts of selling toys for kids and grownups. Japanese toys are a speciality, plus there is a large selection of lava lamps, stickers and puppets.

North

World Wind Kite Shop
7208 McNeil Dr. • (512) 250-9454

The store's slogan is "A Hobby to Some. A Way of Life to Us!" Listing it under "toys" may be misleading since this shop sells not only indestructible kid kites, but also high-grade kites for competition. The store also offers repair services and kite-flying lessons.

East

Pinata Party Palace
2023 E. Cesar Chavez Blvd.
• (512) 322-9150

Custom-made pinatas for parties, particularly kid's birthday parties, can be ordered here. Pinatas are papier-mache forms, covered with colorful tissue paper and stuffed with candies and little toys. The pinata is strung up over a tree limb and the birthday boy or girl blindfolded, given a baseball bat to take whacks at the pinata until it breaks open — then there is a mad scramble for the candy and toys. The store also sells ready-to-go pinatas.

South Central

Terra Toys
1708 S. Congress Ave. • (512) 445-4489

A favorite place for shopping for stocking stuffers at Christmas, Terra Toys is hard to wrap up in a small word package. There is a wide selection of toys here including Steiff teddy bears, educational toys, books, miniatures, dolls, tin soldiers, chemistry sets and fingerpaints.

Travel/ Adventure/Outdoors

Central

The Austin Angler
312½ Congress Ave. • (512) 472-4553

Tucked away in an old downtown building, the store offers topnotch advice and sells top-quality equipment. It is so well regarded, it was featured in a national ad campaign for Visa.

McBride's Guns
30th St. and N. Lamar Blvd.
• (512) 472-3532

Popular among hunters, anglers and collectors, McBride's is noted for its extensive collection of antique guns. The store also sells archery equipment and provides gunsmithing services. The store also has a complete line of fishing tackle and lures.

REI

9901 N. Loop 360 (Capital of Texas Hwy.) • (512) 343-5550

This store is a valuable resource for outdoors enthusiasts in Northwest Austin. REI sells and rents outdoor equipment and has an extensive line of clothing and supplies for outdoor activities including camping, hiking, and mountain climbing. The store sponsors nature and outdoor trips, provides information about the outdoor life in Texas and brings in speakers to give their insights on how to enjoy life under the sky.

Rooster Andrews

3901 Guadalupe St. • (512) 454-9631
S. Lamar Blvd. at Ben White Blvd. • (512) 447-5668
Anderson Ln. at Shoal Creek • (512) 458-2103
8650 Spicewood Springs Rd. • (512) 258-3488
5601 Brodie Lane, Sunset Valley • (512) 892-6495

He stands 5 feet tall, but Rooster Andrews is a giant in University of Texas folklore. His real name is William Andrews, but the diminutive man has been called "Rooster" since his World War II days as a manager for the UT Longhorns football team. Andrews owns five sporting goods stores in Austin and continues to be a major organizer and booster of UT sports. His stores (one central, one south, a third north, another northwest and a fifth southwest) sell sports equipment and shoes, offer sports services such as racket restringing and custom T-shirt printing, and stock all the burnt orange Longhorn sportswear any UT fan could want.

Travelfest

1214 W. Sixth St. • (512) 469-7906
9503 Research Blvd. • (512) 418-1515

This is the closest adventurers can come to heading for the safari outfitter. Travelfest sells travel accoutrements from luggage to books, binoculars, buckwheat-stuffed travel pillows and travel gizmos aplenty. The store also offers travel seminars, videos, international newspapers and magazines, a booking and ticket agency and little bags you can tuck away in secret places to hide your money.

Whole Earth Provision Co.

1014 N. Lamar Blvd. • (512) 478-1577

Before Austinites head for the hills, they head for Whole Earth. Not only does the store sell the top labels in camping, hiking, diving, biking and kayaking gear, it also has wonderful rainwear and sweaters, plus imported clothes from Latin America. The shoe shop has everyday, sturdy wear and great hiking boots. Whole Earth also sells tents, backpacks, climbing gear, toys, guidebooks, knives, flashlights, freeze-dried foods, desktop Zen gardens and telescopes. If you are not sure you want to buy a tent, you can rent one here.

North

Golfsmith

11000 N. I-35 • (512) 837-4810

This North Austin outlet is a mecca for golf enthusiasts. The facility boasts that it is has the largest golf inventory in the world where shoppers can buy Golfsmith and Harvey Penick golf clubs. The store has a snack bar, computerized swing analyzer, educational and practice facilities, plus visitors can take a factory tour.

Oshman's Supersports

2525 W. Anderson Ln. • (512) 459-6541

Whether you are looking for a new pair of tennis shoes or a set of skis, Oshman's has it. The store also features several sports arenas where you can try out your new gear before taking it home. Oshman's features a snow ski deck (and ski lessons year round), a children's and an adult's basketball court, a racquetball court, a golf cage with simulated screen, a batting cage with simulated screen, an archery room and a tennis court.

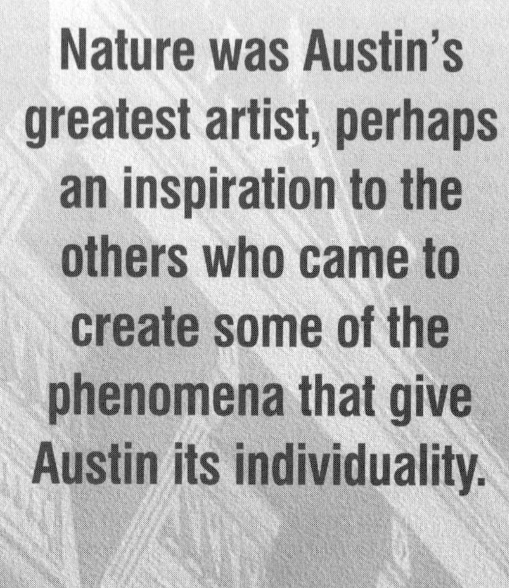

Nature was Austin's greatest artist, perhaps an inspiration to the others who came to create some of the phenomena that give Austin its individuality.

Attractions

First, a word of appreciation to our sponsor: Nature.

It is, after all, our greatest attraction. The bluebonnets in springtime; the sparkle of sunlight on the lakes; the limestone cliffs and green rolling hills; the crisp, rushing creeks; the fresh air; the fauna; the fault and the foliage. Austin's natural beauty and bounty attracted our first visitors, drew our first settlers and continue to entice our newest arrivals. Nature was Austin's greatest artist, perhaps an inspiration to the others who came to create some of the phenomena that give Austin its individuality. So while you're busy enjoying the production that is Austin, take a moment to acknowledge the set design.

While some of the sites below come to us courtesy of nature, we're devoted much of this chapter to giving you a tour of the landscape of invention, the visual sensations contributed by the ingenuity of Austin's own people over the past 150 years or so. Here you'll find attractions to tickle you fancy, tease your brain, touch your heart and, perhaps, stir your own imagination. Among these curiosities, historic treasures and modern marvels you'll discover a provocative portion of Austin's story.

We've pointed out some of our most interesting pieces of public art. Here, you'll receive an introduction to a few of the sculptures, statues, paintings, murals and fountains that are on view for all to appreciate. These artistic creations enhance Austin's natural beauty, and provide a window into the city itself.

Of course, Austin wouldn't be Austin without the many spots dedicated to celebrating our unique natural habitat. So for many more outdoor attractions, don't miss our chapter on Parks and Recreation, where we've introduced you to Lake Travis, Town Lake and many, many other alfresco wonderlands. If you still yearn for more things to see and do, check out our chapters on The Arts, Kidstuff, The Music Scene, Nightlife and Spectator Sports. Come to think of it, much of this book is dedicated to Austin attractions, in one form or another. Note: Because of the high concentration of Attractions in Central Austin, we've divided this section into three smaller parts to make it easier for you: Downtown, The University of Texas and Central.

Downtown

Art at the Austin Convention Center

500 E. Cesar Chavez St. • (512) 476-5461

Even if you're not in town for a convention, stop in here to see artwork installed in 1996 by four Austin artists. One of those artists, Damian Priour, raised some eyebrows with his sculpture *The Waller Creek Shelves*, made of limestone, glass, metal and found objects. Priour used material collected at Waller Creek by homeless people. (Some of Austin's transients were displaced when the Convention Center was built in 1992.) Priour nevertheless proceeded with his plan and the results are fascinating. This large sculpture can be viewed in the center rotunda on Level 1. Also included in the center's collection are 20 oil paintings, called *Texas Botanicals*, by Jill Bedgood. Look for these paintings in the west corridor on Level 3. Austin neon artist Ben M. Livingston created *Confabulating Orbits* for the convention center. His neon and copper sculpture can be found in the palazzo, Level 1. John A. Yancey with Steve Jones created *Riffs and Rhythms*, a broken tile wall mosaic, for the west corridor, Level 1. The convention center is no great work of art on the outside, but these four artists have made a significant contribution to the building and to Austin's Art in Public Places program. The doors are open during the fairly constant events at the center. For access to the building at other times, call the number listed to schedule a visit. For a 24-hour listing of events at the convention center and Palmer Auditorium call the hotline at (512) 404-4404.

The Austin History Center

810 Guadalupe St. • (512) 499-7480

While Austin was among the last major Texas cities to build a public library, the city made up for its delay by constructing a facility that was both inspiring and advanced in its design. This Moderne-influenced, Classical Revival-style building opened in 1933 to replace the city's temporary public library, a wooden structure built in 1926. A showcase for some of Austin's finest crafters in its day, the building features loggia frescoes, a carved mantel and ornamental ironwork balconies. The ironwork was done by a noted family of ironworkers, the Weigl's whose workshop is now a barbecue restaurant, Ironworks Barbecue (see our Restaurants chapter). The History Center building, which served as the city's library for nearly 50 years, now houses of the leading local history collections in the state. Here, visitors will find more than 1 million items documenting the history of Austin from before it was founded to the present day. The center has received national recognition for its collection of more than 600,000 photographic images, which document the people, events, architecture and social customs of this region. The center also has more than 1,000 maps of Austin and Travis County from the mid-1800s to the present as well as 25,500 drawings and documents from local architectural projects. The History Center serves as the official repository for the records of the City of Austin and Travis County. This is also the place to come to find issues of local newspapers dating back more than a century. The center also features regular temporary exhibits of interest to the Austin community. The History Center, part of the Austin Public Library system, is next door to Austin's main public library at the corner of Ninth and Guadalupe Streets in downtown Austin. It is open from 9 AM to 9 PM Monday through Thursday, from 9 AM to 6 PM on Friday and Saturday and from noon to 6 PM on Sunday.

The Bats

Congress Avenue Bridge at Town Lake

Get your cooler and a comfy blanket and head out to Town Lake for a truly unique Austin experience. The largest urban bat colony in North America — as many as 1.5 million Mexican free-tails — resides in the crevices beneath the Congress Avenue Bridge for nearly eight months of the year. When they take off from under the bridge for their evening flight for food, the spectacle is astounding. On their nightly forage the bats devour up to 30,000 pounds of insects. August is the best month for viewing the bats because they often come out before sunset. But they can be seen at other times during their stay here, from about mid-March to early November. You can see the bats from either side of Town Lake under the bridge, or from the top of the bridge. Check out our chapter on Hotels and Motels for the hotels in the area that also provide great bat views. Information kiosks

INSIDERS' TIP

The first and best place to stop for information on Austin attractions is the Visitor Center, 201 E. Second Street, run by the Austin Convention and Visitor Bureau. It features brochures, pamphlets and calling cards. Also look for the quarterly magazine *Experience Austin*, the bureau's official publication, including tourism articles and a seasonal events list. The center is open Monday through Friday from 8:30 AM to 5 PM, Saturday from 9 AM to 5 PM and Sunday from noon to 5 PM. A few free parking places are provided out front.

Photo: Peter A. Silva

The door is always open to visitors at the Texas State Capitol.

are at the *Austin American-Statesman*'s information center on the south shore and on the north bank below the Four Seasons Hotel. The *Statesman* also operates a bat phone, (512) 416-5700, category 3636, with estimated time for the nightly flight. Austin was scandalized when the huge colony first took up residence here in the early 1980s, even going so far as to petition to have the colony eradicated. But when citizens learned that the bats consume so many insects — thus cutting down the need for chemical insecticides — and that the bats pose no danger to the community, Austin changed its mind in a big way. Today, our bat colony is a welcome addition to Austin. Our new hockey team is called the Ice Bats (see our Spectator Sports chapter). Of course, no one should ever try to handle a bat. For more information on these nocturnal creatures, read the information provided at the kiosks, or call Bat Conservation International in Austin at (512) 327-9721.

Capitol Complex Visitor Center
112 E. 11th St. • (512) 305-8400

The Capitol Complex Visitor Center definitely must be added to any list of places to visit while in Austin, both for what it was and what it is today. Built in 1856 and 1857, this is the oldest remaining state office building in Texas and, both for its architectural and historic values, one of the most significant properties owned by the state. Designed by German-born architect Christopher Conrad Stremme for use as the Texas General Land Office, the building is an excellent example of Medieval-inspired architecture and is listed on the National Register of Historic Places. Professor Stremme's design is a unique blending of the German Rundbogenstil (round-arch style) and the Anglo-American Norman style. Today, the two-story "castle" hosts a variety of exhibits relating to the State Capitol and to the history of the Old Land Office itself.

We recommend stopping here before taking a tour of the Capitol. For one thing, the 20-minute film, *Lone Star Legacy: A History of the Capitol*, narrated by Walter Cronkite, will serve as a great initiation to the capitol tour itself. There's also a wonderful exhibit on the massive restoration and extension of the State Capitol and grounds completed in 1997. And don't miss the space next to the "small, dark spiral stairway" dedicated to William Sydney Porter, better known as O. Henry. (See our listing for the O. Henry Museum in this chapter.) The famous short-story writer worked as a draftsman in the Land Office from 1887 to 1891, and two of his stories are set in the Land Office, "Georgia's Ruling" and "Bexar Scrip No. 2692," in which he refers to the spiral stairway.

Upstairs in the wing dedicated to the history of the Land Office, visitors will find two surveyor's transits — those scopes we see surveyors using on the side of the road. Peek through a transit to get a perfect close-up view of the Goddess of Liberty who stands so regally on top of the Capitol Rotunda. (Remember, her features are exaggerated to be seen from afar). The gift shop here is great and so are the people who work as information assistants just inside the front entrance.

The Capitol Complex Visitor Center is open 9 AM to 5 PM Tuesday through Friday and 10 AM to 5 PM on Saturday.

Dewitt C. Greer Building

125 E. 11th St.

What with the splendor of the State Capitol, this building just across the street is easy to miss. But take a moment to enjoy its wonderful Art Deco architecture. Built in 1933, the building features three bronze panels over the main entrance depicting changes in Austin's modes of transportation. The first shows a Native American on horseback, the second is a covered wagon and the third an automobile. There are also two stylized eagles over the entrance and a number of other details from the era that are worth a look. The building houses the administrative offices of the Texas Transportation Commission and was named for Greer, a former state highway engineer and commissioner from 1969 to 1981.

The Driskill Hotel

122 E. Sixth St. • (512) 474-5911

Built in 1886 for cattle baron Jesse Driskill, The Driskill Hotel was restored in 1998 to its original splendor. This Richardsonian Romanesque-style hotel is uniquely Austin and should not be missed. (See our chapter on Hotels and Motels for more details.)

Governor's Mansion

1010 Colorado St. • (512) 463-5516

Home to every Texas governor since 1856, this awesome Greek Revival-style structure is the fourth-oldest continuously used governor's mansion in the United States, and is listed on the National Register of Historic Places. If walls could talk, this stately mansion, reminiscent of a southern plantation home, would tell the tales of the fabulous galas and famous leaders it has hosted, of the turmoil it has witnessed as Texas governors ponder the issues that have shaped Texas for going on 150 years, and of the "ghost" that roamed its halls after the suicide of Gov. Murrah Pendleton's nephew more than 100 hundred years ago. Gov. Sam Houston lived here until he made the monumental decision in 1861 to reject the oath of allegiance to the Confederate States of America. Gov. W. Lee O'Daniel invited all Texans to the mansion to celebrate his second inauguration — and 19,000 people came for lunch. Gov. James Hogg's four children liked to slide down the spiral bannister that graces the entryway, until one fell off. The 100-year-old holes, from the nails that Gov. Hogg pounded into the banister to end the joy rides and prevent further mishaps, call still be seen in the curving wood.

Austin's master builder Abner Cook won the contract to build this home on a small hilltop one block southwest of the State Capitol. The home, facing east to catch prevailing winds during Austin's long hot summers, features six 29-foot fluted columns topped with Greek Ionic capitals below the roof line. Cook selected a simple, square design with four rooms upstairs and four rooms downstairs. In 1914, a conservatory was added and a new kitchen wing was built. Today, the brick, two-story structure, painted white with black trim, stands majestically among the trees and flowers on the one-block lot. Inside, the home is filled with original furnishings and artwork from the era, as well as some more modern Texas treasures, some added during the $4 million restoration led by First Lady Rita Clements in the early 1980s. Visitors are shown only the grounds and the first-floor rooms — two gorgeous parlors rising up 16 feet to the ceiling, the library, the conservatory and the state dining room. The second level is the private home of the current governor. Free guided tours are held every 20 minutes from 10 AM to 11:40 AM. Monday through Friday. Guests are received on a first-come, first-served basis, and it is important to arrive early as the tours are limited to 25 people and do fill up.

Lorenzo de Zavala State Archives and Library Building

1201 Brazos St. • (512) 936-INFO

Make the Lorenzo de Zavala building a stop on your tour of Austin, even if you're in a hurry. Just inside, visitors will find the huge mural, *Texas Moves Toward Statehood*. This epic work, 55 feet long by 18 feet high, depicts 400 years of Lone Star State history. Painted by English artist Peter Rogers and his father-in-law, well known Western artist Peter Hurd, the mural features some of Texas' leading historical figures, including Stephen F. Austin, Sam Houston and Mirabeau B. Lamar, and portrays events in history from the first encounters between Native Americans and European explorers to the emergence of the oil industry. This building, however, offers much more. This is the home of the Texas State Library and Archives Commission. Housed here is the official history of Texas government, including documents dating back to the 18th century. The Genealogy Collection includes most U.S. Census from 1790 to 1920 as well as many other significant holdings. The building, completed in 1961, was named in 1972 in honor of Lorenzo de Zavala, a hero of Texas' struggle for independence and the first vice president of the Republic of Texas. The library is open 8 AM to 5 PM Monday through Friday while the Genealogy Collection is open 8 AM to 5 PM Tuesday through Saturday.

Millet Opera House

110 E. Ninth St.

Now the private Austin Club, tourists can enjoy this edifice from the outside only. But it's definitely worth a walk by when you're visiting downtown. Built in 1878, the opera house became a cultural center for the city. Its large auditorium boasted 800 movable seats. The building, made of Texas limestone, was listed on the National Register of Historic Places in 1978.

Moonlight Towers

Corner of Ninth and Guadalupe Sts.

At this location, which features a historic marker, visitors will find just one of the 17 Moonlight Towers that remain in Austin from 1895 when the towers provided the city's first public electric lights. Austin is the only city in the world to preserve its earliest electric street lamps. And they still work. At 165 feet, they're the city's tallest street lights and a truly unique attraction. The City of Austin contracted the Fort Wayne Electric Company to install 31 towers with carbon arc lamps, believing they would

INSIDERS' TIP

Xeriscaping is environmentally friendly landscaping that requires about 40 percent less water than traditional landscaping, and often less chemical fertilizers and pesticides. In pro-environmental Austin a xeriscaped lawn is a wise choice — and can be beautiful and colorful to boot. Most Austin plant nurseries can recommend appropriate plants, and local bookstores carry a variety of books on the subject (see our Literary Scene chapter for a list of bookstores). The City of Austin Xeriscape Program Planning, Environmental and Conservation Services Department, (512) 499-2199, has produced a booklet and video on the subject. Also visit the xeriscape garden at the Zilker Botanical Garden (listed in this chapter).

be easier to maintain than many small street lamps throughout the city. Some residents of Hyde Park, however, weren't so sure. They feared that the lights, sometimes called Austin moonlight, would trick the vegetables in their gardens into growing day and night. The 17 towers that remain, now with mercury vapor lights, can be found around downtown, in Hyde Park and in Clarksville. The Moonlight Tower in Zilker Park, moved to the park from Congress Avenue in the 1960s, is used every Christmas to support the 3,500 multicolored lights on the Zilker Park Christmas Tree (see our chapter on Annual Events) .

O. Henry Museum

409 E. Fifth St. • (512) 472-1903

William Sydney Porter, who earned international fame as a short story writer under his pen name, O. Henry, lived in this simple Queen Anne-style cottage for three of his nearly 11 years in Austin. Simply Will Porter when he arrived as a bachelor in 1884, Porter would see some of his greatest personal triumphs and his most devastating public humiliation during his era in Austin. It was here where Porter married, had his daughter, sold his first short story to a national publication — and was convicted of embezzlement and sentenced to prison. (A mock court trial conducted at the UT School of Law in 1998, the 100th anniversary of the original trial, exonerated him.) Porter, who lived the dapper bachelor life, singing at parties and serenading girls, worked a variety of odd jobs before he married Austinite Athol Estes when he was 24.

His most stable career before writing took over his life was at the Texas General Land Office, where he worked drawing maps for four years. The Land Office was later to appear in two of O. Henry's short stories. (See our listing on the Capitol Complex Visitors Center.)

When his politically appointed job ended, Porter was finally able to find another job handling accounts at the First National Bank of Austin. During this time, Porter also launched his weekly newspaper, *The Rolling Stone*, which revealed the beginnings of a great talent but lasted only one year. Porter was fired from the bank when the bank discovered shortages in his accounts. He was indicted several months later, fled to Honduras and later returned — due largely to the failing health of his wife in Austin — to face the music. He was sentenced to five years in federal prison in Columbus, Ohio, and never returned to Texas. Porter spent the last eight years of his life drinking, gambling, living the extravagant life, and publishing 381 short stories. He died at age 47 in New York of cirrhosis of the liver, an enlarged heart and complications of diabetes.

The cottage is much as it was during Porters three years in it, from 1893 to 1895. Once slated for demolition, the home was moved twice in the 1930s from its original location at 308 East Fourth Street. Here, visitors will find many furnishings and personal possessions belonging to Porter, his wife and daughter, Margaret. Here also are first editions of O. Henry books, magazines featuring his stories, copies of *The Rolling Stone* newspaper and family photographs. The museum conducts the O. Henry Writing Clubs for Austin school children and hosts several annual programs, including the O. Henry Pun-Off World Championship, a lively and popular event held every May since 1977.

The museum is open from noon to 5 PM Wednesday through Sunday. Admission and parking are free. Guests are asked to wear flat, soft-soled shoes to prevent damage to the original Bastrop pine floors.

The Old Bakery and Emporium

1006 Congress Ave. • (512) 477-5961

When Swedish immigrant Charles Lundberg opened his bakery in 1876, Austinites gathered to buy such delicacies as ladyfingers, sponge cake and glazed kisses. Used as a bakery until 1936, the building then housed a number of different businesses, including a night club. By 1963, the Old Bakery, vacant and deteriorating, was scheduled for demolition. That's when the Austin Heritage Society and the Junior League stepped in to save it, through hard work and donations. Today, the Old Bakery is registered as a national landmark. Owned and operated by the Austin Parks and Recreation Department, the bakery features a sandwich shop where you can still buy cookies, but no ladyfingers or sponge cake. Most interesting, however, is the gift shop. Here visitors will find scores of handicrafts made by hand by Austin's most experienced artists, those age 50 and older. And custom orders are accepted too. The Old Bakery also has a hospitality desk that provides information and brochures about Austin attractions. Just a half block down Congress from the State Capitol, The Old Bakery is a great place to stop on your tour of Austin. It's open Monday through Friday 9 AM to 4 PM but closed on weekends and holidays.

Paramount Theatre

713 Congress Ave. • (512) 472-5411

An Austin jewel, the Paramount Theatre opened in 1915 under the name Majestic Theater. Now, beautifully restored to the most minute detail, the Neoclassic structure is one of the nation's classic theaters. Today, it hosts Broadway shows, local productions, musical events and classic movies. Katharine Hepburn performed here, as did Sara Bernhardt, Helen Hayes and Cab Calloway. The Paramount series for kids is a summer extravaganza. Unfortunately, the Paramount does not offer tours so the only way to see the theater from the inside now is to buy a ticket to an event. We hear they may be considering opening up this historic site for tours. That would be nice. (See our chapter on The Arts.)

Scholz Garten

1607 San Jacinto Blvd. • (512) 474-1958

Built in 1866 by German immigrant August Scholz, the Scholz Garten has been serving up beer and German food ever since. This building is listed as a National Historic Site and as a Texas Landmark. Gen. Armstrong Custer, who was stationed two blocks away during Reconstruction, reportedly ate here and The University of Texas football team celebrated its first undefeated season here in 1893. Photographs from days of old adorn the walls. For more information see our chapters on Restaurants and Politics and Perspectives.

Symphony Square

1101 Red River St. • (512) 476-6064

Four historical limestone buildings and a wonderful 350-seat outdoor amphitheater still used for live performances make up this complex, which serves as the offices of the Austin Symphony Orchestra, the Women's Symphony League and houses Cafe Serranos, a popular Mexican restaurant (see our Restaurants chapter). Located on the banks of historic Waller Creek since the 1970s, Symphony Square represents the efforts of a group of leading citizens, the City of Austin, the Urban Renewal League and the Symphony itself to save and restore these 19th century buildings. The provocative triangular shaped building at the corner of 11th and Red River Streets is believed to be one of just three stone triangular buildings remaining in Texas today. Built in 1871 by Jeremiah Hamilton, one of nine African-American legislators who served in the Texas Legislature, the building today bears his name and is used as the symphony's main office. Symphony Square also contains the Michael Doyle House, considered one of the few remaining examples of a simple, one-story stone cottage in Austin. The Hardeman House, also of native limestone, was moved from its original location to the square and is home to Cafe Serranos, which features a lovely outdoor patio overlooking the amphitheater. During the summer months, Serranos presents outdoor concerts on this stage, to the delight of all. Serranos caters private parties in the fourth building in this complex, the New Orleans Club Mercantile, a beautifully restored 19th century building. On Wednesday mornings in June and July, The Austin Symphony Orchestra hosts Children's Day activities in the square. For information on that and for other children's activities sponsored by the symphony, see our chapter on Kidstuff. Also see our chapter on The Arts for more about the Symphony and its seasonal performances at the Bass Concert Hall.

Texas State Capitol

1100 Congress Ave. • (512) 463-0063

"Here glitters a structure that shall stand as a sentinel of eternity to gaze upon the ages."

Now, more than a century since those words were spoken, visitors from all over the world come to gaze upon this magnificent monument to Texas. Temple Houston, the youngest son of Texas hero Sam Houston, dedicated Texas' new State Capitol, our "sentinel of eternity," on May 16, 1888. This Renaissance Revival-style structure, made of Texas pink granite and native limestone, now stands as gracious and grand as Texas itself on the hilltop overlooking Austin's historic Congress Avenue. Perched atop the soaring Rotunda, which at 311 feet high is taller than our nation's Capitol, is the 15½-foot statue called the Goddess of Liberty, a 1986 aluminum replica of the original zinc goddess. Marble statues of Stephen F. Austin and Sam Houston carved by German-born sculptor Elizabet Ney grace the south foyer as does a portrait of Davy Crockett, martyr of the Alamo, holding his famous coonskin cap. The painting of the *Surrender of Santa Anna* depicts a watershed event in Texas history, while other meaningful works of art can be found throughout the building.

More than a monument, more than a museum, the State Capitol is the seat of Texas government. In this building, among the pioneers of Texas' past, work the leaders of Texas' future. Among many other state government headquarters, the offices of the governor and secretary of state are here, along with the magnificent Senate and House chambers, occupied during the legislative sessions held every two years.

No trip to the Capitol is complete unless you've stood on the Rotunda floor and looked up at the Texas star and the two-foot letters spelling out T-E-X-A-S on the ceiling. From down below, they look about three inches tall. After you've gazed up, be sure to look down. Here are the seals of the six nations whose flags have flown over Texas: France, Spain, Mexico, The United States, the Confederate States of America and, of course, the Republic of Texas. On the Rotunda's circular walls you will find the portraits of every president and governor of Texas beginning with the current chief executive. That means that each time a new governor is elected, every portrait in the Rotunda must be moved back one space.

Visitors can choose to walk through the Capitol themselves or take a free regularly scheduled guided tour. We suggest the tour. Not only are the guides interesting and informative, they also will point out details you might miss and can also take you into areas otherwise locked, such as the Senate and House chambers. And these are definitely worth a look. When the Legislature is in session — every other year on odd years — visitors can watch our lawmakers in action on the third-floor public gallery, open on a first-come, first-served basis. Guided tours are also available of the Capitol grounds. The massive grounds, with their many statues, sculptures, and beautiful old trees are a sight unto themselves. When you're visiting the Capitol, take a moment to enjoy this Austin treasure also. And don't forget to visit the Capitol Complex Visitor Center nearby. See our previous listing for that in this chapter.

A 1983 fire in the Capitol set off such an alarm over the future integrity of the overcrowded, deteriorating building that plans were made to renovate and enlarge the Capitol complex, which sits on 26 acres. By 1997, the massive restoration project, construction of an impressive underground extension, and restitution of the vast Capitol grounds were complete. The project restored our legacy for future generations and the building that Temple Houston had said, "fires the heart" was radiant once again.

The Capitol is open 6 AM to 10 PM weekdays, 9 AM to 8 PM on weekends and holidays. Tours are offered on weekdays from 8:30 AM to 4:15 PM and on weekends from 9:30 AM to 4:15 PM.

The University of Texas

The University of Texas at Austin, founded in 1883 on 40 acres, has grown to 357 acres, and that's just the main campus. Its historical significance, size and allure as one of Texas' most beloved universities, make UT a major tourist attraction. The university is roughly bounded by 26th Street on the north, Martin Luther King Boulevard on the south, Interstate 35 on the east and Guadalupe Street on the west.

Surprisingly — and sadly — UT has not done a great job of late providing visitors with much information on the small treasures scattered around campus. UT closed its wonderful visitor center in the historic Arno Nowotny Building (see below) and hasn't replaced it with much. The best UT has come up with so far is a small visitor center, not always staffed, in Sid Richardson Hall adjacent to the LBJ Library. Here, visitors may find a few pamphlets and basic information about the school.

Lady Bird Johnson: A National Treasure

One of the first display cases visitors encounter at the Lyndon Baines Johnson Library and Museum contains mementos of the whirlwind courtship between the future president of the United States and the woman who would be his bride, Lady Bird Taylor.

Among the documents is a handwritten letter from the 21-year-old recent University of Texas graduate to her suitor.

"Lyndon, please tell me as soon as you can what the deal is," the letter reads. "I am afraid it's politics — Oh, I know I haven't any business — not any "proprietary interest" — but I would hate for you to go into politics . . ."

The year was 1934. Mrs. Johnson, now in her mid-80s, has spent more than six decades in the public eye. During those years she evolved from the shy, nervous girl who deliberately dropped her grade point average in high school to avoid making the speech required of the class valedictorian to become one of the great first ladies in American history. Despite her fragile health by 1998, Lady Bird continued to make public appearances on behalf of her favorite causes. She will forever remain an American treasure, a Texas icon and Austin's most beloved citizen.

On November 22, 1963, an assassin's bullet thrust Mrs. Johnson into the role of first lady of the United States. Asked later what image she hoped to project to the nation, Mrs. Johnson replied, "My image will emerge in actions, not words."

Indeed. A genteel Southern woman whom fate would place at the very center of the turbulent 1960s, Mrs. Johnson's vigorous campaign in the Bible Belt helped the JFK-LBJ ticket take Texas and win the 1960 national election. In 1964, when it was her husband's turn to seek the presidency in his own right, Mrs. Johnson embarked on a massive whistle-stop tour through eight Southern states, often facing hostile crowds because of Johnson's support for civil rights. As First Lady she traveled to some of America's poorest regions to address the crisis of poverty in the country.

The United States had a lot on its mind in 1965. The Vietnam War was beginning to polarize the nation as Johnson's buildup of American troops expanded to 150,000. Mounting racial tension erupted in a five-day riot in the black section of Los Angeles known as Watts. Dr. Martin Luther King, Jr., led marchers from Selma, Alabama, to a rally of more than 25,000 people in Montgomery, and more victims fell along the way. In 1965 President Johnson signed the Medicare Social Security Bill into law and announced the creation of a "Great Society," his plan to help the politically and economically impoverished. Johnson's War on Poverty was in its second year in 1965. Congress passed a bill that year that called for limits on the emission of toxic pollutants in new vehicles. Poet Allen Ginsberg coined the phrase "Flower Power" at an anti-war rally in Berkeley, California, in 1965.

In Washington, the First Lady of the United States was wielding her own brand of flower power. Only old photographs and movies offer proof today of the blitz of billboards that once defiled America's roadsides. Mrs. Johnson changed all that, and became the first First Lady to actively campaign to get a bill made into law. In 1965, despite strong opposition, her noble vision for America paid off with the passage of the Highway Beautification Act, which sought to eliminate the billboards and other eyesores from America's highways.

Her environmental campaign, in those days called "beautification," took her from Washington, where she saw to it that trees and more than a million tulips and daffodils were planted along the Potomac River, to spots across the United States, where she was among the first well-known leaders to champion environmental protection.

— continued on next page

Photo: Cam Rossie

Lady Bird Johnson turned her childhood love of nature into a lifelong mission to beautify America.

She's been honored so many times that the list of her awards fills an entire single-spaced page. In 1977, President Gerald Ford gave her the nation's highest civilian honor, the Presidential Medal of Freedom. President Ronald Reagan added the Congressional Gold Medal in 1988. "She claimed her own place in the hearts and history of the American people. In councils of power or in homes of the poor, she made government human with her unique compassion and her grace, warmth and wisdom. Her leadership transformed the American landscape and preserved its natural beauty as a national treasure," reads her Medal of Freedom certificate, on display along with the medal at the LBJ Library.

As a child growing up in the small East Texas town of Karnack, the girl born Claudia Alta Taylor on December 22, 1912, came to cherish the native flowers that flourished around her home. The daughter of Thomas Jefferson "T.J." Taylor, the wealthy owner of the town's general store, and Minnie Pattillo Taylor, Claudia was just 5 years old when her mother died after falling down a flight of stairs. The role of mothering was left to her maiden Aunt Effie Pattillo, a well-educated, cultured woman who came from Alabama to help raise Claudia and her two older brothers. It was a nursemaid who gave Claudia the name that would remain with her for life, saying she was just "as purty as a lady bird."

Lady Bird was 17 years old when she entered the University of Texas at Austin in 1930. Four years later, she graduated with honors with degrees in journalism and history as well as with a teaching certificate. In Austin she met Lyndon Baines Johnson,

— continued on next page

the up-and-coming assistant to a Washington congressman. Within one day of their meeting Johnson proposed and within two months they were married in San Antonio. He had literally swept her off her feet.

Much more than a Washington political wife, Mrs. Johnson was at her husband's side, providing advice and support, and promoting her own causes, throughout the more than three decades the couple spent in national politics. Johnson's election to Congress in 1937 was just the beginning. In 1949, Texas voters sent him to the Senate where he remained, election after election, despite a near-fatal heart attack in 1955. In 1961 he became vice president of the United States. Less than two years later, Lady Bird was at his side when he took the oath of office aboard Air Force One following the assassination of President Kennedy.

Mrs. Johnson blossomed during her decades in Washington. She took a public speaking course to overcome the fear that had kept her from making the high school valedictory speech. After World War II broke out and LBJ joined the service, Lady Bird ran his congressional office for the half a year Johnson was away. In 1943, the Johnsons, with Lady Bird at the helm, bought a small Austin radio station, KTBC. Mrs. Johnson, who did everything from paint the station walls to sign the checks, proved she was an astute businesswoman. On Thanksgiving Day, 1952, KTBC became Central Texas' first television station, and the cornerstone of the family's multi-million-dollar fortune.

Her two daughters, Lynda Bird and Luci Baines, were born during the Washington years, and both were married in the White House. Luci Baines Turpin is now chairman of the board of the Austin-based LBJ Holding Company, the parent organization of the family's giant business that includes, among other things, five radio stations. Mrs. Johnson, despite all her misgivings about a life in politics, had been the one to urge her husband to seek the offices of vice president and president, although LBJ's attempts to steer the country through the tumultuous '60s were harshly criticized. It was Lady Bird who finally convinced her husband not to seek reelection in 1968, going so far as to strengthen his famous withdrawal speech in which he said, "I will not seek and will not accept the nomination of my party for another term as your president." The Johnsons returned home to their beloved ranch west of Austin in January of 1969. Lyndon Baines Johnson died there on January 22, 1973.

Over the past quarter of a century, Mrs. Johnson has divided her time between Austin and the family ranch in Stonewall, which the Johnsons donated to the American people as a national historic site. Through all these years she has remained at the forefront of the American environmental movement, not as a figurehead but actively involved in the effort to preserve and protect the nation's natural beauty. In Austin, she chaired the Town Lake Beautification Project, a community effort that resulted in the creation of the city's magnificent Town Lake Hike and Bike Trail (see our Parks and Recreation chapter). The city wanted to name Town Lake for Lady Bird, but she demurred. In 1982, on her 70th birthday, Mrs. Johnson founded Austin's National Wildflower Research Center. On a glorious spring day in 1998, the acclaimed center (see the listing in this chapter) was officially renamed the Lady Bird Johnson Wildflower Center in honor of this remarkable woman whom Texas First Lady Laura Bush called "the conductor of the symphony of wildflowers that bloom across Texas."

Mrs. Johnson, wearing a sunflower-bright yellow suit and her trademark radiant smile, received a warm standing ovation as she stood to unveil the new name on the center's logo. "I had great fun campaigning with Lyndon and falling in love with the natural beauty and diversity of this country," she told the audience, speaking in the soft East Texas drawl that has charmed even her staunchest opponents throughout her lifetime.

For prospective students, freshmen and their parents, the Admissions Office in Room 7 of the Main Building below the UT Tower offers regular student-led guided tours of the campus. The public may join in on these tours, which cover some of the sites, but the tours focus on basic information relevant to new students. UT does have copies of *The Perip: A Self-Guided Walking Tour*, perhaps the best information available on campus on university sites, but they don't make them readily available. Those interested in visiting UT should be aware that the streets inside the campus are closed to normal traffic (cars must bear an authorized sticker to enter) during normal school hours. It's okay to enter after 4 PM on weekdays and on weekends. There is public parking in lots, garages and at meters around the perimeter of the university but these can also fill up, especially during UT events. The Dobie parking garage at 21st Street and Whitis Avenue and another garage at 24th and San Jacinto Streets near the Texas Memorial Museum charge a fee. The LBJ Library and Museum has its own free public parking lot.

Below we've provided information on some of the university's most noteworthy attractions.

Battle Oaks

Near 24th St. and Whitis Ave.

In an interesting twist of words, the historic Battle Oaks, three live oak trees at the northwest corner of the campus, are named in honor of the man who saved them, not the battle he waged to do so or the other trees in the grove that were destroyed earlier to build a fortress to protect the capital. The trees are named for Dr. W. J. Battle. His efforts to save the trees, slated for the axe to make room for a new biology building, have now taken on mythic grandeur. Some stories have him perching with a shotgun on one of the largest branches, others say he was on the ground with the shotgun to keep the tree choppers away. Neither version is probably true, but the story is fun anyway.

Of course, way before Battle, and perhaps one of the reasons he saved the trees — the site for the biology building was later moved — was a UT legend about this grouping of trees. According to the story, the largest of the three trees, which existed when Austin was home to Native Americans, learned to speak the native tongue. This tree brought eternal happiness to a young man when he whispered the name of the woman who loved him. When the new settlers came, the trees learned the ways of these people, and provided shelter for them beneath their branches. When the only son of an old man was killed in battle, the oaks brought comfort. And, when northern troops were descending on Austin during the Civil War, all the trees in this grove, but the three remaining, gave their lives for the fortress.

The Drag

Guadalupe St. from Martin Luther King Blvd. to 26th St.

The University of Texas meets Austin on this lively strip filled with restaurants, coffeehouses, bookstores, shops and the outdoor Renaissance Market (see our Shopping chapter), where you can buy tie-dyed clothes and jewelry made by Austin artisans. This is a great place to select UT T-shirts and other memorabilia or just take a break from sightseeing on the UT campus. Captain Quackenbush's Intergalactic Espresso Cafe, known best as Quack's, is along this strip, a small delightfully Austin den that is popular with both students and residents. Check out the University Co-op, Texas Textbooks and Bevo's Bookstore for books and gifts. Nomadic Notions is a top-notch shop for finding unique beads, jewelry-making items and gifts. The Dobie Mall is here, too, along with the Dobie Theater that runs popular movies as well as some great offbeat films (see our Nightlife chapter). The Drag, once made up of mostly locally owned shops, is starting to see more and more national chains move in. You'll find a Gap clothing store, Barnes & Noble Booksellers, a huge Tower Records, Sunglass Hut and Einstein Brothers Bagels.

Jack S. Blanton Museum of Art

23rd and San Jacinto Sts.

• (512) 471-7324

UT's fine arts museum is one of the most-visited galleries in Austin. It features a wonderful permanent collection as well as changing temporary exhibits. For more on this gallery see our description of the Harry Ransom

Center in this chapter as well as more on the Blanton Museum in our chapter on The Arts.

The Lyndon Baines Johnson Library and Museum

2313 Red River St. • (512) 916-5136

While Americans have not gone in for a lot of fanfare about our former presidents, other than the Washington memorials, we do make an exception when it comes to our presidential libraries. And one of the greatest expressions of this American political tradition is the library and museum dedicated to President Lyndon Baines Johnson. Nowhere on earth can visitors see, hear and learn as much about this compelling figure in American history and about the official politics of the turbulent 1960s as in the LBJ Library. This facility is the largest and most-visited presidential library in the country. But one doesn't just visit the LBJ Library; one experiences it. The Vietnam War, The Civil Rights Movement, The War on Poverty and The Great Society all are represented, as well as some aspects of the '60s cultural scene. Here, visitors will learn about Johnson's long and colorful political career, view mementos of the lives of President Johnson and First Lady, Lady Bird Johnson, and visit the replica of the Oval Office as it was during Johnson's time (note, especially the number of television sets and the news wires here. Johnson was a real news hound).

There also are two short video presentations of LBJ himself. A five-minute tape shows how he worked and a seven-minute presentation gives great insight into the humor and personality of this charismatic Texan who was the nation's 36th president. For even better perspective, start your tour by watching the 20-minute movie that traces Johnson's life from his childhood on the banks of the Pedernales River west of Austin (see our Daytrips chapter) to the nation's highest office. The library houses 40 million pages of historical documents. The permanent exhibits are exceptional, and so are the temporary exhibits, a number of which the museum hosts each year. The museum and gift shop are open from 9 AM to 5 PM every day of the year except Christmas. And, because Johnson did not want people to have to pay to see his museum, it's the only presidential library that does not charge an entrance fee. Parking is free, too, in the lot on Red River Street.

Littlefield Building

At the northwest corner of 24th St. and Whitis Ave.

Built in 1894, this ornate red stone and brick Victorian mansion belonged to Maj. George W. Littlefield, an important UT benefactor and member of the Board of Regents. Standing on the edge of the original 40 acres, the mansion was bequeathed to the university in 1939. It was first used as practice rooms for UT music students and in World War II as headquarters for Naval Reserve Officers Training Corps, who set up a firing range in the attic. The first floor, restored to its original splendor, is open for visitors from Monday through Friday 8 AM to 5 PM. Visitors are asked to enter through the east door.

Littlefield Memorial Fountain

21st St. and Whitis Ave.

Visit this fabulous fountain to enjoy its beauty and to mingle with the college students who come here to sit, have lunch and socialize. Dedicated on March 26, 1933, the fountain has become a prominent landmark on the UT campus. Designed by Italian-born sculptor Pompeo Coppini, the fountain is meant to symbolize the revival of American patriotism during World War I, a spirit that Coppini felt had been lost during the Civil War. The large fountain consists of three-tiered pools with water jets spraying the larger-than-life bronze goddess standing on the prow of the battleship *Columbia* as it rushes to aid democracy abroad. The goddess Columbia holds in one hand the torch of freedom and in another the palm of peace. The bronze figures of sea horses bearing tritons represent the surging ocean. On the left side of the grouping stands a young lad representing the army. Over the years this fountain has attracted all kinds of mischief. Soap bubbles and detergent have turned the normally still waters into a foaming spectacle, while an interesting array of reptiles, including alligators, have turned up in the fountain. The memorial, which includes the nearby statues of Texas and national notables, is dedicated both to "the men and women of the Confederacy who fought with valor and suffered with fortitude that states' rights be maintained . . ." and to the "sons and daughters of the University of Texas" who died in World War I.

The fountain is about half a block east of Guadalupe Street at 21st Street.

The Mustangs Sculpture

San Jacinto St. at the base of the Texas Memorial Museum

Dedicated to the "spirited horses that carried the men who made Texas," this gorgeous statue of seven plunging mustangs is a landmark at the University of Texas. Unveiled in 1948, the statue is the work of Phimister Proctor, a famous sculptor of Western subjects. Proctor reportedly spent almost a year observing and measuring the anatomical details of a band of painstakingly chosen *puros españoles*, Spanish mustangs. FYI: It was the Spanish who introduced these powerful and wonderful horses to Texas. The results are marvelous. Proctor created a band of horses that, since 1948, appears as if it could come to life at any moment.

Arno Nowotny Building

709 E. Martin Luther King Blvd.

It's a shame UT did away with the visitor center in this pre-Civil War structure, which is listed on the National Register of Historic Places. Now, visitors no longer have a good excuse to tour the home where Gen. George Armstrong Custer (of Little Big Horn fame) lived briefly during Reconstruction. Designed by Abner Cook, Austin's leading antebellum builder who also did the Governor's Mansion, the Custer House was constructed in 1859 of 2-foot-thick rubble limestone with pine floors. (Today, it's beautifully trimmed in burnt orange, UT's school color.) Acquired by the university in 1925 and restored in 1978, it is UT's oldest building and one of the few pre-Civil War buildings remaining in Austin. This structure is listed on the Civil War Discovery Trail.

Built as an asylum for the blind, which closed during the Civil War, the building was empty until Custer arrived with his wife, brother, father and 4,000 volunteers in December 1865. He departed a few months later and in August of 1966 the building was reestablished as an institute for the blind. It was used as a training center for the U.S. military in both world wars. The building now houses UT's Urban Issues Program. It still contains some displays from its days as a visitor center, and the employees there are very friendly and helpful. This building is on UT's Heman Sweatt Campus (named for UT's first black law student) at the corner of Martin Luther King Boulevard, just off Interstate 35.

Harry Ransom Center

Near Guadalupe and 21st Sts. • (512) 471-7324

Among the exceptional UT properties found at the Harry Ransom Center are a 1456 Gutenberg Bible, one of just 13 complete existing copies of the first book printed with movable type, and the first photograph ever taken, a London cityscape taken in 1826. These priceless treasures as well as selections from the permanent collection of the Jack S. Blanton Museum of Art are on the first two floors of the Ransom Center, which are open to the public. In addition to the Gutenberg Bible, the center houses many more of UT's rare treasures, which are displayed occasionally as part of

INSIDERS' TIP

Ahhhhh. Austin in springtime. The weather is perfect, and the fields and roadsides are filled with miles of bluebonnets. It's an annual tradition to find a field of bluebonnets and take your loved ones' pictures against this stunning backdrop. The Lady Bird Johnson Wildflower Center has tons of bluebonnets, but there are plenty all around the city. And the center also operates a hotline, (512) 832-4059, to provide information on where to find these little beauties. The Highland Lakes west of Austin has a Bluebonnet Trail. For details on this great trail call the Lake Buchanan/Inks Lake Chamber of Commerce at (512) 793-2803.

the gallery's changing exhibitions program. Included in the collection are original manuscripts and compositions by Beethoven, Columbus, Galileo, Hemingway and Shaw. The red velvet gown worn by Vivian Leigh as Scarlet O'Hara in *Gone With the Wind* is part of the center's extensive theater arts collections, along with many other items from the career of film producer David O. Selznick. Costumes worn by Harry Houdini are included in this collection as well as letters and posters that belonged to this great escape artist.

The center's rare book library used by scholars includes 9 million literary manuscripts, 800,000 rare books, 40,000 pieces of literary art works done by or about authors, and about 5 million photographs.

The gallery floors are open from 9 AM to 5 PM Monday, Tuesday, Wednesday and Friday, from 9 AM to 9 PM Thursday, and from 1 to 5 PM on Saturday and Sunday. Admission is free. Museum listings in the *Austin American-Statesman* and *The Austin Chronicle* are the easiest place to find current exhibits or call the number above for recorded information.

Santa Rita Oil Rig

At the corner of Trinity St. and Martin Luther King Blvd.

History buffs will want to search out this rig while touring the University of Texas campus. This little piece of machinery stands as a powerful symbol of the riches UT gained from the legendary Santa Rita oil well in West Texas. On the morning of May 28, 1923, oil gushed forth from the well in Big Lake Oil Field on UT lands. For 19 years, this oil rig worked to draw the black gold to the surface, and help catapult the struggling university to fame as a first-class institution. (UT became one of Austin's economic pillars along the way.) For just short of 67 years, the Santa Rita oil well pumped money into the UT system. The Santa Rita also stands as a symbol of the entire system of oil and gas leases for state-owned land and in state ocean waters. The state bids out the leases to oil and gas companies who pump the resource and then pay the state a royalty on the production, pumping literally millions into state coffers for public schools and higher education. The Santa Rita, by the way, got its name from a group of Catholic investors from New York. Apparently struggling with the decision over whether or not to invest in this unproven field, the investors went to their priest, who suggested they call on the aid of Santa Rita, Patron Saint of the Impossible. Hmmmm!

Texas Memorial Museum

2400 Trinity St. • (512) 471-1604

Opened in 1939 as a permanent memorial of the Texas Centennial celebrations, the Texas Memorial Museum is a showcase for the natural and social sciences. Here, among the bones, rocks, fossils and dinosaur tracks, visitors will discover the distant — and not so distant — past. This museum is a must for anyone interested in the fields of geology, paleontology, zoology, botany, ecology, anthropology or natural history. Life-size dioramas of Texas wildlife, habitat groups of native Texas birds and displays of Texas' poisonous and harmless reptiles are just some of the treasures awaiting visitors in this museum.

Among the museum's many special attractions is the original 16-foot statue of the Goddess of Liberty that stood atop the State Capitol for nearly 100 years until she was replaced with a replica in 1986. The star she holds in her hand, however, is not the original. That can be viewed in the Capitol Complex Visitor Center. There's also the Onion Creek Mosasaur, which has recently been remounted and serves as the centerpiece of the Hall of Geological History. The museum has an outstanding collection of fossil vertebrates. Here, ancient amphibians and reptiles mingle with some of the giant Ice Age mammals, including saber tooth cats and mastodons. There are also fascinating examples of dinosaur troikas. Tracks found in a 105-million-year-old limestone bed near Glen Rose, Texas, record forever the passage of several kinds of dinosaurs.

The Texas Memorial Museum, dedicated to the study and interpretation of the natural and social sciences, also contains internationally known research collections and laboratories. Although the museum focuses on Texas, there's also much to be seen about the Southwest and Latin America. The building itself is a work of art and a true attraction. The museum is open from 9 AM to 5 PM Monday through

Friday, 10 AM to 5 PM Saturday, and 1 to 5 PM on Sunday. There's no entrance fee, but contributions are encouraged. Supporters may wish to consider joining the museum's membership organization.

The Tower

Just look up when you're on the UT campus, and you'll find this 307-foot landmark, the most recognizable symbol of the university, which stands at the very heart of the original 40-acre campus. The Tower of the Main Building was completed in 1937 on the site of the university's first academic building, Old Main. The 27-story tower features a clock whose four faces are more than 12 feet in diameter and the Knicker Carillon with its 56 bells that chime on the quarter hour and hour and are played at other times by the university's carillonneur.

The tower once shared the Austin skies with only one other soaring rival, the State Capitol. Its construction drew the ire of some Austin citizens back then, most notably Austin's master storyteller and UT professor J. Frank Dobie, who suggested the tower be laid on its side. Why, he complained aloud, with all the space in Texas, did a building here have to look like one in New York.

The soaring observation deck, however, afforded an excellent view of the city and quickly became a popular tourist attraction. But a tragic mass murder committed from the tower (see our History chapter) as well as a rash of suicides caused university officials to close the tower to the public in 1975. In late 1998, however, UT regents were expected to approve President Larry Faulkner's request to reopen the observation deck to visitors. Under Faulkner's plan, the deck will undergo a major renovation, and visitors will be required to buy tickets to enter. But what a view!

The Spanish Renaissance-style structure, built of Bedford Indiana Limestone, is lighted orange to commemorate achievements in athletics and academics. At commencement, graduates know the orange glow and sound of the chimes are meant especially for them.

Umlauf Sculptures

Around campus visitors will find 10 sculptures, most of them outdoors, created by Austin artist Charles Umlauf. (See our write-up on the Umlauf Sculpture Garden & Museum in this chapter.) Outside the Jack S. Blanton Museum of Art at the corner of San Jacinto and 23rd Streets is the bronze *Seated Bather II*. Outside the Alumni Center at 2110 San Jacinto is *Mother and Child*. In Centennial Park at Red River Street near 15th Street, across from the Frank Erwin Center, is *Three Muses*. And in front of the Business-Economics Building at West 24th Street is *The Family*, a 15½-foot tall bronze done in 1962. At the Harry Ransom Center near Guadalupe Street and 21st Street, visitors will find two busts. There's a bronze portrait bust of Dr. Ransom in the entrance lobby and a portrait bust of Dr. Merton M. Minter. At the Peter Flawn Academic Center, on the main mall in front of the building, is Umlauf's 1962 bronze sculpture, *Torchbearers*, which is 12½ feet high. The Law School Building at 727 E. Dean Keeton Street features a portrait bust of Gen. Ernest O. Thompson, done in 1953, and the University Catholic Center at 2010 University has Umlauf's *Pieta* done in bronze inside the Newman Chapel.

Central

The Neill-Cochran House Museum

2310 San Gabriel St. • (512) 478-2335

Austin's master builder Abner Cook designed and built this stately home in 1855 following a design plan that is similar to the Governor's Mansion, which Cook also built. Now operated as a museum by The Colonial Dames of America in the State of Texas, the home is a glorious example of Greek Revival architecture. Classic furnishings from the late 18th and early 19th centuries can be viewed throughout this beautifully kept home. The National Trust for Historic Preservation has called this house a "jewel and perfect example of the Texas version of the Greek Revival in the South." The home, originally built for Washington L. Hill, was purchased in 1876 by Col. Andrew Neill. Judge T.B. Cochran bought the house in 1895 and made additions. The museum is open from 2 PM to 5 PM from Wednesday through Sunday. General admission is $2. Children young than 8 are admitted free.

Photo: Peter A. Silva

There is much to see on the Capitol grounds — even at dusk.

Elizabet Ney Museum

304 E. 44th St. • (512) 458-2255

This museum, once the Hyde Park home and studio of celebrated artist Elizabet Ney, features an array of about 50 portrait busts and full-figure statues of European notables, Texas heroes and other figures. An entire section of the museum is dedicated to the life of this amazing sculptor who helped to establish Austin's artistic traditions. This is one museum that should not be missed on any tour of the arts in Austin. For more information about the museum and the home Ney built in the late 1800s, called Formosa, see our chapter on The Arts. The museum is open Wednesday through Saturday from 10 AM to 5 PM, and Sunday from noon to 5 PM. Admission is free.

Treaty Oak

Baylor St. Between W. Fifth and W. Sixth Sts.

The poignant tale of Austin's beautiful and historic Treaty Oak will tug at your heart strings. Estimated to be between 500 and 600 years old, the Treaty Oak once stood more than three stories high and its branches covered more than half an acre. In the Hall of Fame of Forestry, the tree was described as "the most perfect specimen of a tree in North America." Legend has it that the Father of Texas, Stephen F. Austin, and leaders of local Indian tribes signed a treaty under the mighty oak, supposedly dividing the city between them. Although there is no historic evidence that this meeting ever took place, the legend persevered and people came from all over the country just to look at this incredible specimen.

Poisoned in 1989 by a man who was later caught and sentenced to nine years in prison, the majestic Treaty Oak is now about a third its original size, but still definitely worth a visit. Austin's heroic effort to save the Treaty Oak is another chapter in the tree's rich history. Specialists were brought in, sunscreens were erected and people from all over the country prayed and sent letters along with more than $100,000 in donations to help save the tree. Since then, acorns and cuttings from the tree have been planted in Austin and the Treaty Oak was cloned so that identical copies of it are growing in Texas and other parts of the country. It's a story of survival. It's a story of Austin.

South Central

Austin Nature and Science Center

301 Nature Center Dr. • (512) 327-8181

A perfect place to enjoy Austin's great outdoors, the Austin Nature and Science Center in the Zilker Park Nature Preserve features 2 miles of trails with cliffs and a scenic outlook (see our Parks and Recreation chapter). But the facilities here go far beyond trails. Here, in the Visitor Pavilion, guest will learn about the two ecosystems — Hill Country and Caves, and Grasslands — that meet right smack in the middle of Austin. Displays also provide information on two minor ecosystems found throughout Central Texas: Ponds and Creeks, and Woodlands. Wildlife exhibits and a birds of prey exhibit are just a couple of the attractions found at this wonderful spot. Be sure to see our Kidstuff chapter for more information on the Austin Nature and Science Center. The center is open from 9 AM to 5 PM Monday through Saturday, and from noon to 5 PM on Sunday throughout the year. Admission is free.

Philosophers' Rock Sculpture

Entrance to Barton Springs Pool

This exquisite bronze sculpture by artist Glenna Goodacre depicts three of Austin's illustrious figures engaged in animated conversation — just as they were accustomed to doing in life. Life-size images of historian Walter Prescott Webb, naturalist Roy Bedichek and J. Frank Dobie, humorist and folklorist, are presented in this large work, installed November 21, 1994. Webb stands fully clothed next to the rock (he never swam), while Dobie and Bedichek are seated, wearing swimming trunks. As you view this lively sculpture, it's difficult not to wonder what these three great "philosophers" are discussing.

Umlauf Sculpture Garden & Museum

605 Robert E. Lee Rd. • (512) 445-5582

The outdoor setting of this wonderful sculpture garden combines Austin's love for the outdoors and for the arts. Acclaimed artist Charles Umlauf, whose works are on display in museums and public collections across the country, lived in Austin from 1941 until his death and was a University of Texas professor until 1981. The garden is the perfect outdoor setting for 62 of Umlauf's bronze and cast stone pieces. For more on this inspiring Austin museum, see our chapter on The Arts. The museum is open Wednesday through Friday from 10 AM to 4:30 PM, on Saturday and Sunday from September to May from 1 to 4:30 PM, and from 10 AM to 4:30 PM in June, July and August. General admission is $3.

Stevie Ray Vaughan Memorial

Auditorium Shores, south side of Town Lake near Riverside Dr. and First St.

This larger-than-life bronze statue of the late blues/rock legend stands near the site where Vaughan played his last Austin concert on Auditorium Shores. The sculpture by artist Ralph Helmick depicts Vaughan in a relaxed pose wearing his trademark black hat and holding his guitar like a walking stick in his left hand. A long bronze shadow trails behind. When it was dedicated on November 21, 1993, Vaughan fans gathered in tribute to the Austin-based music man who died in a helicopter crash in 1990. The piece continues to draw admirers of both the artist it depicts and the artist who created it. For more on Stevie Ray Vaughan, see our chapter on The Music Scene.

Zilker Botanical Garden

2220 Barton Springs Rd. • (512) 478-6875

The seven theme gardens in this lovely spot are just some of the attractions at this lovely botanical garden, managed jointly by

INSIDERS' TIP

While you're traveling around Austin, see if you can find our official state symbols. Our state bird is the mockingbird. Our flower is the bluebonnet. The pecan is our state tree, and our state fruit is the Texas red grapefruit. The monarch butterfly is Texas' official insect. This may come as no surprise, but our official state dish is chili. We even have a state pepper: the jalapeno. Oh yes, our state name comes from the Native American word Tejas, meaning friendly. That's why our state motto is "Friendship." And, of course, our state nickname is the Lone Star State.

the Austin Area Garden Council and the City of Austin Parks and Recreation Department. Here, visitors stroll among the 22 acres of displays and gardens to learn about different species of plants, get ideas for their own gardens or just to appreciate the beauty of nature. The Rose Garden features over 800 bushes. The butterfly garden and trail has been filled with flowers and plants that attract many species of Texas butterflies, while the xeriscape garden is a showcase of water-tolerant plants and the principles of xeriscaping. In The Oriental garden, visitors will discover a series of waterfalls, lotus ponds and an authentic tea house. There also is a cactus and succulent garden, an herb and fragrance garden and an azalea garden. The Garden Council also sponsors a number of educational and cultural programs on site as well as several popular annual events, including Zilker Garden Festival in May, the Herb Market Festival in September and Yule Fest in December. Flower lovers shouldn't miss the Rose Show in April and the Orchid Shows in March and October. This is the place to come for anyone interested in gardening, as the Garden Center has information on all its member Austin garden clubs.

Here, too, visitors will find two original log structures from the 1800s. The Swedish Log Cabin, built about 1838 on the "Govalle" Ranch — meaning "good grazing land" in Swedish — and moved to the botanical garden in 1966 is fully furnished with such 19th-century necessities as a spinning wheel, loom and baby cradle. The small cabin was built by S.M. Swenson, a settler who encouraged migration of other Swedes to Texas and opened the cabin as a social center for the Swedish community. (Most of the activities must have taken place outdoors, however, as not too many people could have moved about here comfortably.) Right next to the Log Cabin is the Esperanza School Building. Built in 1866, the log building was one of the earliest one-room rural school houses in Travis County. The interior of this school also is furnished as school children would have occupied it in the last century.

The Botanical Garden is open from 7 AM to sunset daily except on Thanksgiving, Christmas and New Year's Day. Admission is free. There is a parking charge on weekends from March through November.

North

The Republic of Texas Museum
510 E. Anderson Ln. • (512) 339-1997

This fascinating space, which is meticulously run and cared for by the Daughters of the Republic of Texas, is packed with Texas history. Here, visitors will learn about the men and women who fought for Texas independence and led The Republic of Texas from 1836 to 1846. The museum features award-winning permanent exhibits and a variety of touring shows. One outstanding section is called Great Grandma's Backyard, where visitors get to see and touch the household implements used by families in the mid-19th century. The museum also features an excellent collection of guns from that period, portraits and statues of Texas leaders, and much, much more. (See also our chapter on Kidstuff.)

South

St. Edward's University
3001 S. Congress Ave. • (512) 448-8400

Don't miss the beautiful Gothic Revival-style Main Building and the other great attributes of this 180-acre campus. The Main Building is one of Austin's most stunning landmarks — a grand structure in the early Southwest when it was built in 1889, and just as grand today. For more information on this historic university, see our chapter on Higher Education.

Southwest

Austin Zoo
10807 Rawhide Trail • (512) 288-1490

Located on the edge of Hill Country about 20 minutes from downtown Austin, the Austin Zoo is a great escape from the hustle and bustle of the city. Here, visitors get a close-up view of domestic and exotic animals as well as a relaxing, enjoyable experience in a natural setting. For more on Austin's young zoo, see our Kidstuff chapter.

Lady Bird Johnson Wildflower Center

4801 La Crosse Ave. • (512) 292-4100

Established in 1982 as the National Wildlife Research Center, this delightful center was renamed in March of 1998 in honor of its founder, Austin's own Lady Bird Johnson. (See our profile of the former First Lady of the United States in this chapter.) This 42-acre Hill Country gem overflows with a brilliant variety of native plants and flowers and has become one of Austin's most visited spots. Here, visitors will see and learn about our own state flower, the bluebonnet, as well as the glorious Indian paintbrush, which is as splendid as its name, and more than 500 other species of native plants. The center's 23 lovely perennial and seasonal gardens display in living color the bounty of Texas' botanical beauties. Much more than a showcase for the magnificent plant life of Texas, however, the center is an ecological sanctuary dedicated to the preservation and reestablishment of native plants — wildflowers, grasses, shrubs and trees. It's the only national nonprofit organization fulfilling that mission and has become the leading national authority on native American plant life. Researchers, staff and volunteers are committed to reversing the threat of extinction to about 3,000 endangered native plant species in North America, nearly 25 percent of the continent's natural plant life. This loss contributes to ecological havoc that goes way beyond vanished beauty. Accolades for the center's original conservation and ecological techniques have come from such prestigious organizations as The Smithsonian Institution and the National Wildlife Federation.

The center, which opened its impressive new facilities in 1995, features stone buildings designed in German Mission and Ranch-style architecture to reflect the region's cultural diversity. There's also a wonderful observation tower offering an excellent view of the surrounding Hill Country, and a central courtyard and stone fountain, a nature trail, ponds and picnic spots. The Wildflower Cafe is a great spot to have a sandwich or refreshment. The gift shop has a good selection of arts, crafts, posters and books.

The center also features North America's largest rooftop rainwater collection system, which provides water for all the gardens. The place to begin the tour of this unique center, however, is at the Visitor Gallery. Here, visitors are introduced to the Wildflower Center and can view interesting displays on the region's plant life. Young children especially will delight in hearing Ralph, the talking lawn mower, just one of the many features designed to appeal to children. Those interested in finding out more about specific plants can browse the research library. Education remains the center's primary goal. To that end, the center sponsors a number of conferences, lectures and workshops on a variety of topics, many in the center's 232-seat auditorium. It also operates a clearinghouse so people from across the country can obtain information about plants native to their region. *The Wildflower Handbook*, a source book on wildflowers and native plant landscaping, with nursery and information directories for all 50 states, is published by the Wildflower Center.

The grounds are open Tuesday through Sunday from 9 AM to 5:30 PM. The Visitors Gallery is open Tuesday through Saturday from 9 AM to 4 PM, and from 1 PM to 4 PM on Sunday. Admission is $3.50 for adults, $2 for seniors and students, and $1 for children 18 months to 5 years. Regular visitors and supporters of the environment may wish to become members — or volunteers.

East

French Legation Museum

802 San Marcos St. • (512) 472-8180

After King Louis Philippe of France officially recognized the fledgling Republic of Texas in 1939, he named Alphonse Dubois de Saligny as *charge d'affaires* and sent him to Austin. De Saligny, a flamboyant character, bought 22 acres of land on a beautiful Austin hilltop and began construction on his luxurious residence and carriage house, which are considered modest by today's standards. De Saligny, who insisted he be called Count, was anything but noble and more like a no-account scoundrel, leaving a trail of debts and angry citizens during his short stay here. While he awaited completion of his residence, de Saligny lived in downtown Austin, where he launched the infamous Pig War. Complaining that his neighbor's pigs were destroying his garden, de Saligny ordered his servant to shoot any pig that even looked like it was going after the garden. The neighbor, Richard Bullock, retaliated by whacking the servant and threatening to come after de Saligny himself. That was about all de Saligny could take of Texas, and vice versa. He headed back to Louisiana and never occupied the home. The home was purchased by Dr. Joseph Robertson in 1848, and it remained in the family's hands for a century. In 1948, the state of Texas bought the property and placed it in custody of the Daughters of the Republic of Texas. They restored the home and opened it to the public in 1956. Today, visitors will find many of the Robertson family furnishings as well as other period pieces. Guided tours include a visit to the original house and the reconstructed French Creole kitchen, which is fully equipped and contains many unique items. The replica of the carriage house contains an 1828 carriage, other exhibits and a gift shop. Tours are conducted Tuesday through Sunday 1 PM to 4:30 PM. The French Legation is also a popular spot for weddings. General admission is $3. Students pay $1.

The French equivalent of our Independence Day, Bastille Day, July 14, is celebrated here with French song, food and dance, and the legation also hosts a popular Christmas event when Pere Noel arrives to celebrate the season with a Gallic flair (see our Annual Events chapter).

George Washington Carver Museum

1165 Angelina St. • (512) 472-4809

This museum is distinguished for being the first African American neighborhood museum in the state of Texas. The building that houses the museum was built in 1926 as Austin's first public library downtown. After a new library was built in 1933, this wood-frame structure was moved to East Austin and served as the city's first branch library. The George Washington Carver Museum opened October 24, 1980 and in the two decades since has evolved into a center of community involvement, enrichment and education. Today, the museum houses a permanent collection of photographs of and memorabilia associated with its namesake, the African American who was born the son of a slave and died a famous scientist. The museum, however, is most known for the constantly changing exhibits that pertain to the history and culture of Austin's African-American community. Its numerous education programs for adults and children include the annual A Smile on My Face workshop, which teaches children from all over the Austin area how to use a camera and darkroom equipment.

Huston-Tillotson College

900 Chicon St. • (512) 505-3025

While the campus has modernized over the past 125 years, two of Huston-Tillotson's historic buildings remain as splendid examples of turn-of-the-century architecture. The Evans Industrial Building, built in 1911-12, was completely renovated in 1984 and designated as a Texas Historical Site. The Old Administration Building, constructed in 1913-14, is one of the few remaining examples of the Modified Prairie Style popularized by Frank Lloyd Wright. This building was entered in the National Register of Historic Places in 1993 and is slowly being restored. For more on this historical African American college, see our chapter on Higher Education.

Oakwood Cemetery

16th and Navasota Sts.

Austin's oldest cemetery is a scene of tranquility and beauty. Created in 1839, the cemetery is the final resting place for many Austin pioneers, prominent Austin families, and community leaders from the past and present. Athol Estes Porter, wife of the short-story writer O. Henry, is interred here as are former Texas Governor James Hogg and his daughter Ima. Mary Baylor, a driving force in the preservation of the Clarksville neighborhood, was buried here in 1997. The cemetery is chock-full of towering trees that provide wonderful shade in the summer. The cemetery was added to the National Register of Historic Places in 1988.

Parque Zaragoza Recreation Center Murals

2608 Gonzales St. • (512) 472-7142

Austin artist Fidencio Duran has captured the essence of the center's Hispanic neighborhood in a series of three immense — and immensely moving — narrative paintings that relate the story of the Hispanic experience in Austin to sweeping historical events in Mexico. *Cinco de Mayo* and *Diez y Seis* are the two 25-foot-tall murals in vivid color and detail that lines the sides of the main entrance hall. Both begin with two infamous dates in Mexican history. *Cinco de Mayo*, or May 5th, depicts the Mexican battle at Puebla that resulted in the defeat of French invaders in 1862, while *Diez y Seis* marks the event on September 16, 1810, when Father Miguel Hidalgo y Costilla uttered the famous *Grito de Dolores*, or cry, for independence from Spanish rule. These two epic paintings include homages to the 1929 *Diez y Seis de Septiembre* celebration in Austin, the neighborhood's first independence day festival. Residents will discover several East Austin landmarks within these works. Another stunning Duran mural, *Comite Patriota* is in the conference room. This series of murals, which visitors saw for the first time when the long-awaited recreation center opened in May 1996, highlight Austin's Hispanic culture and should not be missed. The center is open from 10 AM to 10 PM Monday through Thursday, 10 AM to 8 PM Friday, and 10 AM to 5 PM on Saturday.

Texas State Cemetery

901 Navasota St. • (512) 463-0605

A must-see for anyone who wants to comprehend the scope of Texas history, the 18-acre Texas State Cemetery manages to be both tranquil and exhilarating at the same time. Visitors who walk among the tombs of many of Texas' most noted heroes and legends can't help envisioning the drama of the lives and times of these leaders. Stephen F. Austin, the Father of Texas, is buried here under a bronze statue that shows him standing with his right hand raised and holding a manuscript in his left hand inscribed with the words "Texas 1836." Confederate Gen. Albert Sidney Johnson lies under the recumbent statue of him carved by Elizabet Ney, the German-born sculptor who made Austin her home. Among the other Texas leaders interred here is Barbara Jordan. A beloved scholar, teacher and politician, Jordan was the first African American from Texas elected to the U.S. House of Representatives. Three-term Texas Gov. John B. Connally is buried here along with the bullet fragments left in his body from when he was wounded during the Kennedy Assassination. And there are many more, including 10 other Texas governors, many famous writers and historians, and about 2,200 white marble headstones for veterans of the Confederate Army. Among the graves is that of Gen. Edward Burleson, a vice president of the Republic of Texas and the first person to be buried in the cemetery after its creation in 1851.

A $4.7 million renovation and restoration project at the cemetery was completed in 1997. The project included construction of the Visitor Center made of Texas limestone and inspired by the long barracks of the Alamo. The Visitor Center serves as the main entrance to the cemetery and houses a permanent exhibit on Texas cemeteries. The landscaped grounds, stone recycling pond and the lovely *Plaza de los Recuerdos* (Plaza of Memories) all contribute to the sense of serenity created at this very Texas location, often called the Arlington National Cemetery of Texas. The cemetery is open from 8 AM to 5 PM every day. The Visitor Center is closed Sundays, however. Guests can call ahead to arrange for guided tours, or they be do a self-guided tour with the help of information packets available at the Visitor Center.

West

Laguna Gloria Art Museum

3809 W. 35th St. • (512) 458-8191

One of two facilities of the Austin Museum of Art, Laguna Gloria is important as much for its facilities as for the artworks it exhibits. Constructed in 1915-16 as a private residence, the Mediterranean-style villa covers 4,500 square feet. The outdoor amphitheater hosts a variety of performance artists throughout the year. It's also a great place just to sit by the lake and have a picnic. The sculpture garden is wonderful. For more information on Laguna Gloria, see our chapter on The Arts.

Mount Bonnell
At the top of Mt. Bonnell Rd. off W. 35th St.

This scenic spot overlooking Lake Austin has been attracting nature lovers — and romantic ones — for more than 150 years. At 785 feet above sea level, Mt. Bonnell is one of the highest points in the Austin area and offers a view to end all views. Choose your partner wisely to make that first climb up the steps. According to local lore, two people who make their first climb together will fall in love. Some say Mount Bonnell was named after George W. Bonnell, a newspaperman and mercenary. Others claim it was named for Golden Nell and her "beau" — beau-nell — who leapt off the summit to their deaths in order to avoid capture by Native Americans. Visitors can also reach Mount Bonnell off of Farm-to-Market Road 2222 (Bull Creek). For more information on Mount Bonnell, see our chapter on Parks and Recreation.

Northeast

Celis Brewery
2431 Forbes Dr. • (512) 835-0884

Austin's premier regional brewery, Celis has been in operation since April 27, 1992. Pierre Celis, although not blood kin, was considered a member of a family of Belgian brewers who for four generations brewed an ancient style of "white" beer in the village of Hoegaarden. When the brewery was sold, Celis moved to Austin with his family and established Celis Brewery. Celis says Austin's pure, spring-fed waters and abundant limestone provide important necessities for brewing white beer, a Belgian-style wheat beer brewed with herbs and spices, including orange peel and coriander. Today, Celis White is considered the standard by which other white beers are judged worldwide.

To achieve just the right flavor, Celis imported three 1930s hand-hammered copper kettles from Belgium. Today, Celis also produces Celis Golden, Pale Bock, Raspberry, Grand Cru, Dubble Ale, and a new beer intro-

Photo: Peter A. Silva

The Texas Governor's mansion was built in 1856.

duced to Austin in 1998, Pale Rider Ale, which, according to the label, is "proudly brewed for Clint Eastwood by his friends at Celis Brewery, Austin, Texas." Tours of the Celis Brewery are conducted Tuesday through Saturday at 2 and 4 PM (call to confirm), followed by a sampling of the local product. Group tours also can be arranged. For information on Austin's great brewpubs, see our Nightlife chapter.

Jourdan-Bachman Pioneer Farm
11418 Sprinkle Cut-Off Rd.
• (512) 837-1215

This living history museum, originally part of a 2,000-acre cotton farm, treats visitors to a journey back in time to witness the lifestyle of Central Texas' early settlers. From the dwellings to the farm implements and household items to the guides' dress, everything out here is historically correct. There are plenty of hands-on activities that are fun for the whole family. See our chapter on Kidstuff for more about this enlightening farm.

Lake Travis

The Oasis
6550 Comanche Trail • (512) 266-2442

While a more extensive listing for The Oasis can be found in our Restaurants chapter, we couldn't overlook this spot as one of Austin's most popular attractions. From a vantage point of 450 feet above Lake Travis, the multitudes of terraced outdoor decks and the inside dining room offer breathtaking views of the lake and of the Texas Hill Country. This is one of the best places to see an Austin sunset, with live music included. Margarita anyone?

Of course, Lake Travis offers much, much more. Don't miss our chapter on Parks and Recreation for information about the lake's wonderful outdoor activities and our Restaurants chapter for more lakeside dining opportunities.

National Register Districts

While Austin has numerous residences and commercial buildings listed on the National Register of Historic Places, many of which we've mentioned in this chapter, the city also boasts a number of entire districts listed on this important National Register for historic preservation. Those who don't want to miss one stop on their tour of historic Austin should consider taking a walking tour of some of these uniquely Austin locations. See our listing under Austin Tours in this chapter if you're interested in a guided walking tour of some of the following neighborhoods, or pick up copies of the free series "Historic Walking Tours" at the Austin Visitor Center at 201 E. Second Street. They have brochures for Hyde Park, The Bremond District, and Congress Avenue and E. Sixth Street. These brochures describe each building in more detail and give some interesting tidbits about the buildings' former owners. There's also a brochure available on Camp Mabry.

Barton Springs Archeological and Historic District

This district within Zilker Park in South Central Austin includes our favorite swimming spot, and a most endangered treasure, Barton Springs Swimming Pool. Named to the National Register in 1985, this place is Austin

INSIDERS' TIP

We can't tell you the number of times we've been at the Convention Center and run into lost visitors there who actually wanted to be at Palmer Auditorium. Many people don't realize that a downtown address that includes the word "south" means south of Town Lake. Palmer is that huge, kind of ugly, round building with a dome of green, brown and tan panels at 400 S. First Street. The Convention Center is just about a block *north* of Town Lake at 505 E. Cesar Chavez Street. It's an easy mistake.

through and through and should not be missed on any tour of Austin, prehistoric, historic or otherwise. Barton Springs, made up of four principal springs, is the fifth largest group of springs in the state of Texas. One of the many reasons this site is listed on the National Register of Historic Places is that human habitation has been traced back to approximately 6000 B.C. Archaeologists have found chipped-stone arrowheads, bone fragments and prehistoric ceramics while digging in this area.

The springs are named for one of Austin's earliest modern settlers, William Barton, who moved to the springs in 1837 and built a home. While nothing remains of his homestead, there is evidence (a cistern) of the home built on the property in 1867 by the Rabb family, who had come to Texas as part of Stephen F. Austin's first colony of Anglo settlers (see our History chapter). More modern structures that contributed to the springs' selection for the National Register include the concrete Zilker Amphitheater, built around one of the springs by Austin civic leader and philanthropist Andrew Jackson Zilker in the first decade of the 20th century. And then there's the famous Bath House. Built in 1946, this cool structure has been a source of pride for Austin for more than half a century. During a period when Texas architecture was largely ignored by the national press, the Bath House was the subject of a long article in *Architectural Digest* magazine. The article praised architect Dan Driscoll's ingenuity in designing an imaginative structure that was entirely appropriate for its site. The Bath House, still in use today next to the pool, is practically unchanged from the day it was built. For more information on this 1,000-foot-long spring-fed pool, see our chapter on Parks and Recreation. The pool itself is located at 2201 Barton Springs Road, but the register district is bounded on the north by Barton Springs Road, on the east by Robert E. Lee Road, and on the west by Barton Creek and is situated on both banks of the creek.

Bremond National Register District

For a glimpse into the lifestyles of the rich and prominent from a century ago, include the Bremond Block on your tour of downtown Austin. Here are some of the most elegant and elaborate 19th-century homes still found in the city. Italianate, Greek Revival, Colonial Revival, Queen Anne and Second Empire are just some of the architectural styles borrowed for this collection of 14 homes built between 1854 and 1910. Many of these fabulous homes are historic landmarks. Three of the homes — the Walter Bremond House, the Pierre Bremond House and the stunning John Bremond, Jr., House — were built by Austin builder George Fiegel, who is notable for having planned, constructed or remodeled many of the buildings on historic Congress Avenue.

The histories of those who built and occupied these dwellings are as interesting as the structures themselves. Eugene Bremond and his siblings grew up just a couple of blocks away as the children of wealthy merchant John Bremond, Sr. As it happened, the Bremond homestead was catty-cornered from the homestead of another Austin merchant, John Robinson, Sr. The warm friendship between the patriarchs of these two families must have cast a spell over both houses because Eugene and two of his sisters married Robinsons. Eugene, who parlayed his father's wealth into a fortune first as a lender — it's said he charged 18 percent interest on loans made to early settlers — and then as a banker, bought the north half of the block in 1866 that was to bear his family's name. Over the years, as the families' children grew and married, the block became the Bremond family compound, just as Eugene had envisioned. Not all the homes in this district were owned by the Bremond line, however. Other wealthy Austinites also lived in this compound, including the Harvey North family, the Henry Hirshfelds and William Phillips, one of Austin's first doctors. The district is between Seventh and Eighth streets and Guadalupe and San Antonio Streets.

Camp Mabry National Register District

Established in 1892 as a permanent training ground for the Texas Volunteer Guard, Camp Mabry is the third-oldest active military post in Texas. Today, the West Austin camp is headquarters to the Texas Army National Guard, Texas Air National Guard, the Texas State Guard and the Reserves. Among the many historic buildings on these huge grounds is the Texas Military Forces Museum, built in

1918 as the mess hall for the School of Automobile Mechanics. The mess hall accommodated 4,000 men and had the largest kitchen of its kind in Texas, covering 45,000 square feet. Today, the museum stands alone in presenting the history of the Texas military from the Texas Revolution to the present. Another special attraction on the grounds is the pond and picnic area that has been attracting Austinites for more than 100 years. Here, visitors will find a rustic limestone dam, built in 1892 to create a bathing pool for the Texas Volunteer Guard. The Volunteer Guard, by the way, became the National Guard in 1903. The remaining buildings and grounds also are open to the public for self-guided walking tours, and there's a great cinder track and workout trail that Austinites use for exercise. There are some vintage aircraft on display near the track.

Take special note of the many facilities here that were built by the Works Progress Administration (WPA), the federal program that put people to work during the Depression and wound up providing some of the country's best infrastructure. WPA projects at Camp Mabry include the stone wall and guard post that visitors pass upon entering the camp, the stone arch bridges near the picnic area and a number of workshops and warehouses. The WPA also replaced the dam's original brick with limestone in 1938. Some of these WPA projects were built in the so-called CCC-rustic style, named after the Civilian Conservation Corps. One of the most unique structures at Camp Mabry is the multicolored totem pole, presented to the camp in 1949 by the Royal Canadian Air Force in honor of the Texans who joined the RFAC to fight in World War II. The totem pole represents the Thunderbird family and the figures, from top to bottom, are the son, who makes thunder and wind; the daughter, keeper of hail storms; the mother, maker of lightning, thunder and rain; and Chief Thunderbird, who attempts to subdue a dragon and make huge storms at the same time. The dragon is at the bottom of the totem pole. Camp Mabry was named in honor of Adjutant Gen. Woodford Mabry of the Texas Volunteer Guard, among the first to see the need for a permanent training ground for the Texas military.

The museum is open Wednesday through Sunday from 10 AM to 4 PM. The grounds are open from 6 AM to 10 PM. The camp, listed on the National Register in 1996, is at 2200 W. 35th Street. For more information, call the camp at (512) 465-5001.

Clarksville National Register District

Clarksville is one of four Austin communities founded by African Americans in the years following the end of slavery, on June 19, 1865. Named for Charles Clark, the name taken by freed slave Charles Griffin, the neighborhood started when Clark purchased 2 acres of wilderness land on what was then just west of the Austin city limits. In 1977 Clarksville became the first African American neighborhood in Texas to be listed on the National Register of Historic Places. Many of the homes in this neighborhood were built between the 1870s and the 1930s (see our Neighborhoods and Real Estate chapter). Today, visitors can find the 1930s basilica-style building that houses the Sweet Home Missionary Baptist Church at 1725 W. 11th Street (see our Worship chapter). The church was founded in the 1880s by the freed men and women who built new lives in this district. The neighborhood is in Central Austin and is bounded by MoPac on the west, 10th Street on the south, Waterston Avenue on the north and W. Lynn Street on the east. And don't miss Mary Baylor Clarksville Park at 1811 W. 11th Street. This park was named in 1997 in honor of Mary Baylor, who passed away earlier that year. This dynamic community leader, the great-granddaughter of original Clarksville residents, spent a lifetime fighting to preserve Clarksville's unique character. The annual Clarksville Jazz Festival is held in June just outside this neighborhood in nearby Pease Park and other area venues. Look for more information in our Neighborhoods chapter.

Congress Avenue National Register District

With our grand Texas State Capitol as its crowning glory, Congress Avenue is a showcase for some of the city's finest late-19th century commercial architecture. As you walk this 10-block district from the Capitol south to Cesar Chavez Street, keep in mind that his street was once Austin's main thoroughfare and the nerve center for the capital of a fledgling frontier state. We've introduced you to several of this district's most important structures under the individual listings above, including the State Capitol, the Governor's Mansion, The Old Bakery and the Paramount Theater. We'll point out a few others here. The first is not a structure at all, but a small unassuming park at 11th Street and Congress Avenue. This easy-to-miss parklet actually has significant historical value. There was once a building here, built in 1881, that served as our State Capitol while the grander one you see just across the street was under construction. The University of Texas also held its first classes here in the fall of 1884. But as with an amazing number of Austin's old buildings, this one burned down in 1899. You can still see its foundation and cistern.

Also of note on this street is the Johns-Hamilton Building at 716 Congress Avenue. Built in 1870 with an elegant Gothic Revival store front, the facade has been reconstructed. Just a few doors down are the Walter Tips and Edward Tips Buildings at 708-712 Congress Avenue. These two German-born brothers emigrated to the United States about 1850. Older brother Edward opened his hardware business at 708 Congress Avenue in 1865 and gave his brother a job as clerk. Not to be outdone, Walter built a much more elaborate structure for his business next door, which dealt in heavy machinery. The Walter Tips Building is a three-story structure that features Corinthian architecture on the first floor and Venetian Gothic architecture on the top two floors. Interior columns and girders in this building are made of recast exploded Confederate shells.

At the corner of Sixth Street and Congress Avenue is the Littlefield Building, which we mentioned in our chronicle of the Sixth Street Historic District. Down the block, at 512-520 Congress, is the Littlefield's rival, the Scarbrough Building, which housed the pre-eminent department store in Texas until the early 1980s. Built in 1909 in the Chicago style, the building's exterior was changed to an art deco style in 1931. Next to Scarbrough's, at number 504, is the Robinson-Rosner Building. Built in the mid-1850s, this is the oldest known building on Congress Avenue. We must also point out one of Abner Cook's buildings on this avenue. Cook was Austin's master builder during this era and is responsible for some of the city's most historic landmarks, including the Governor's Mansion and the Neill-Cochran House (see the listings in this chapter). He also built the Sampson-Henricks Building at 620 Congress Avenue in 1859. This, too, is one of Congress' oldest buildings and is distinguished also for its Italianate style and excellent craftsmanship.

Hyde Park National Register District

Hyde Park represents the vision of Monroe Martin Shipe, an entrepreneur who came to Austin from Abilene, Kansas, in 1889. As president of the Missouri, Kansas and Texas Land and Town Company, Shipe had resources as big as his dream. He bought the tract of land that was then in far North Austin, named it Hyde Park, after the distinguished London address, and spent the rest of his life living in and promoting his beloved neighborhood. Elizabet Ney, the sculptor famous for carving the marble statues of heroic Texans found in Austin, was among the first to build her home and studio in this 207-acre suburb, now listed as a National Register District. (See more about Elizabet Ney in this chapter.)

The site of the State Fair of Texas from 1875 to 1884, the area back in Shipe's day still had a prominent horse racing track and those who raced horses there would walk their horses up and down one of the main streets, which became known as The Speedway because of it. Speedway is still one of the major avenues in this Central Austin area.

One of Shipe's first actions to promote development of this suburb was to connect it to the city via his own electric streetcar system. Then he turned the southwest section into a resort that included a dance pavilion and tree-lined walking paths. The middle-class homes, built mostly of wood between 1892 and 1925, reflect a variety of architectural styles and tastes (see our Neighborhoods and Real Estate chapter). The first of Austin's historic Moonlight Towers was built in this neighborhood, and still works. You'll find it at 41st Street and Speedway (see the previous listing in this chapter). A lovely park and playground, now called Shipe Park, was added in 1928 and remains a popular spot for neighborhood families today. The homes are privately owned and not available for tours. The Woodburn House, however, is a bed and breakfast establishment (see our chapter on Bed and Breakfasts). Do take a moment to stop in at the Avenue B. Grocery at 4403 Avenue B. This small neighborhood store will take you back in time. This district is in Central Austin between 39th and 44th Streets, and Avenue B to Avenue H.

Moore's Crossing National Register District

This community just south of the new Austin Bergstrom International Airport in Southeast Austin was added to the National Register of Historic Places in 1996. The community dates to before the turn of the century and reached its peak of prosperity between 1880 and 1920. More than a dozen structures and sites contribute to this historic place, including homes, a hen house, a barn, an abandoned metal-truss bridge and, most significantly, a small country store, known as the Berry & Moore Bros. Store, which dates back to between 1900 and 1914. The store is particularly impressive and important to our historic preservation because these examples of country stores, which were the economic nucleus of rural communities, are becoming harder and harder to find. Moore's Crossing is in the area roughly bounded by Farm-to-Market Road 973, Old Burleson Road and Onion Creek.

Rainey Street National Register District

Located downtown near the Austin Convention Center between Driskill Street and River Street, the Rainey Street district includes 21 Victorian cottages as well as 1930s bungalows and other historic structures. This was a working-class neighborhood during the late-19th and early 20th centuries. None of the structures is open to the public.

Shadow Lawn National Register District

This district includes a couple of blocks of residences within the Hyde Park neighborhood in Central Austin. The Depression-era homes are mostly one-story brick structures, many with Tudor Revival-style touches. The Shadow Lawn district is on Avenue G and Avenue H and includes part of the 3800 block of Duval Street.

Sixth Street National Register District

By night, this strip defends its reputation as Austin's most-visited strip when tourists and residents out for a good time pack its lively, music-filled clubs and restaurants. Don't miss our chapter on The Music Scene for the story of Sixth Street after dark. By day, Sixth Street takes a breather. That's the time to stroll along the uncluttered sidewalks and take in the sites of one of Austin's most historic streets. This section is about East Sixth Street by day, when the sun illuminates the past. Known as Pecan Street in Austin's early days, this district is filled with more than two dozen fascinating examples of Victorian commercial architecture. Many of the buildings here were constructed during the building boom of the 1870s. Others followed in the 1880s and 1890s. Of course, these structures don't disappear at night. They're just a little harder to appreciate. The district encompasses a nine-block street from Lavaca Street on the west to Interstate 35 on the east.

Start your tour at the corner of Sixth and Brazos streets at the famous Driskill Hotel, built in 1886. (See our chapter on Hotels and Motels for more on this landmark.) As you walk east on the north side of Sixth Street, you'll discover many more examples of Victorian architecture. Among the noteworthy structures on Old Pecan Street is the Hannig Building. Built in 1875 at 206 E. Sixth Street, this Renaissance Revival-style structure is considered one of Austin's finest late-19th century, Victorian commercial buildings. The Padgitt-Warmoth Building, built in 1885, is next at number 208. Once a saddlery and leather business, this is one of Old Pecan Street's most interesting buildings, with its fleur-de-lis cutouts and a Star of David cap.

In the next block is the Platt-Simpson Building at 310 E. Sixth Street. This structure, built in 1871, was a livery stable and later a hardware store. St. Charles House, at number 316, was built in 1871 and once was a hotel and restaurant. Among the historic structures in the 400 block is the beautifully restored Dos Banderas at 410 E. Sixth Street. Once a saloon and bawdy house, the building was closed in 1961 for housing "nefarious activities." Next door is the Quast Building, built in 1881 as a residence and later operated as a grocery store. This is one of the oldest stone buildings on the strip. The Risher-Nicholas Building at 422-424 E. Sixth Street is another of the building-boom structures. Built in 1873, it became a drugstore in the early 1900s. Owner J.J. Jennings, a black physician, was once lauded for his work at building up "a trade that would do justice to any drugstore owned by any other race." The *Austin Watchman*, an early African American newspaper, was published here in the early 1900s.

On the south side of Sixth Street, at 421 E. Sixth Street, is the two-story stone and masonry Paggi Carriage Shop, constructed around 1875. Owner Michael Paggi is said to have been the first to bring an ice-making machine from France to Texas. Also on this block, visitors will find two 1875 structures, the J.L. Buass Building at number 407 and the Driskill-Day-Ford Building at number 403. The Cotton Exchange Building next door at 401 E. Sixth also was built about this time. Across the street, at 325 E. Sixth Street, is the Smith-Hage Building. Built in 1873, this building is a good example of commercial Victorian architecture during this time period, with its three arched windows on the second floor and topped by an elaborate metal cornice. One of Austin's few remaining cast-iron-front buildings can be found at 209 E. Sixth Street. This is the Morely-Grove Drug Store, originally built as a two-story structure in 1874. The third floor and a Queen Anne bay window were added about 20 years later. At the corner of Sixth and Congress is the Littlefield Building. Completed in 1912 and built for Maj. George Washington Littlefield (whose opulent home and the fountain named for him are on the UT campus), this elegant structure once was the tallest building between New Orleans and San Francisco. The building originally had eight floors but Littlefield added another floor when the rival Scarbrough Building matched the Littlefield's height.

Swedish Hill National Register District

This district is close to the Oakwood Cemetery just east of Interstate 35 in East Austin. Visitors who walk along E. 14th Street, E. 15th Street, Olander Street and Waller Street will discover 10 architecturally significant residences built from about 1880 to 1938, none open to the public. The neighborhood, now only partially intact, got its name from the area's Swedish immigrants.

Willow-Spence Streets National Register District

This district is in East Austin. Willow Street is a block south of First Street, just east of Interstate 35. Spence Street is another block south of Willow. Along these two streets, visitors will find 38 historically noteworthy buildings constructed from about 1900 to the 1930s. None is open to the public.

Zilker Park National Register District

This great Austin Park, which includes many historic structures and buildings, including a limestone Boy Scout hut, built in 1934, and a Girl Scout lodge built the same year, was added to the National Register of Historic Places in 1997. For more on Austin's favorite

INSIDERS' TIP

It's a good idea to carry a bottle of cool water with you when you're out on the town in Austin, especially in the summer. Drinking fountains are never right there when you need one. Or you could just stop off for a nice cold iced tea at about any restaurant or fast food store around. Don't be surprised if your tea comes in an enormous glass. We Texans love our iced tea.

community park, see our chapter on Parks and Recreation.

Touring Greater Austin . . .

. . . On Foot and On Wheel

Around Austin

(512) 371-9111

To charter a tour of some outstanding Austin sites, Around Austin may be what you're looking for. This company takes groups on van- or motor coach-driven tours through the city of Austin, and stops at spots including the LBJ Library, the State Capitol and the Governor's Mansion. There also are tours of Austin homes, of Mount Bonnell, Zilker Botanical Gardens and the Lady Bird Johnson Wildflower Center. Around Austin can arrange private tours for just a few people, but these are usually pretty expensive. Larger groups and corporations who want to design their own tour, however, may find Around Austin has your ticket.

Austin Convention and Visitors Bureau

(512) 478-0098, (800) 926-2282

The Visitors Bureau offers free, guided walking tours from March through November of the Capitol Grounds, historic Congress Avenue and Sixth Street, and the Bremond District. Tours of the Capitol grounds are conducted on Saturdays at 2 PM, while the walking tour of Congress Avenue begins at 9 AM sharp Thursday through Saturday and at 2 PM on Sunday. The Bremond Historical District tour begins on Saturday and Sunday at 11 AM. These tours leave from the south steps of the Capitol building. While the Visitors Bureau does not run the tours of the State Capitol, it does provide information about the tours, which leave every 15 minutes 8:30 AM to 4 PM Monday through Friday, and beginning at 9:30 AM on Saturday and Sunday. These tours are held year round.

Austin Promenade Tours

(512) 288-4185

For those looking for the decidedly unusual, Austin Promenade Tours offers a variety of van-driven adventures unlike any other tour company. Owner Jeanine Plumer serves as both historian and storyteller — and offers some fascinating tales of old-time Austin. The Ghosts of Austin Tours on weekends take visitors on three-hour visits to some of Austin's most haunted sites. Plumer says there are so many ghosts around town that she decided to offer two separate tours for spirit seekers. There's also the Serial Killings Tour, which takes visitors to see the sites of the 1884-85 murders committed by a person who never was caught. (This was before Jack the Ripper's day in London.) The cemetery tour on Sunday afternoon takes visitors to four of Austin's most interesting graveyards. And new to the tour schedule is The Live Music Capital of the World Tour, which includes visits to the people and places that make music happen here, like production companies, instrument makers and the like. This is not a club tour, but an introduction to Austin's music scene. And for those who want more out of their Capitol tour, Promenade offers an extensive tour that includes the State Capitol, the Texas State Cemetery, the Archives Building and some interesting sites on Austin's historic east side. This is a tour that combines walking with rides on the 'Dillo (see our Getting Here and Getting Around chapter). The regularly scheduled tours meet at Central Austin locations. Call Promenade for a schedule, rates and to make reservations.

Heart of Texas Tours

(512) 345-2043

Groups who desire a personal guide to escort you on a customized tour of Austin

INSIDERS' TIP

For the lastest reviews of restaurants, film, theater as well as a whole bunch more information about happenings around Austin, call the *Austin American-Statesman*'s Inside Line at (512) 416-5700. Look for a listing of extensions in the weekly XL entertainment section.

should check out Heart of Texas Tours. Karen Bluethman can arrange to charter a motor coach for you and will plan your trip from start to finish. Or, if you're a group coming to Austin by motor coach, call Bluethman to be your "step on guide," as it's known in the trade.

Ecotours Texas & Beyond

(512) 794-8096, (888) 640-9500

This company offers van-driven tours of scenic and historic Austin, as well as Lake Travis and the Hill Country. Barbara McMillin is owner and tour guide for this fascinating tour, held Monday through Saturday at 9 AM. The excursion begins with a tour through Austin's natural wonderland and gives people an understanding of the Colorado River, the Balcones Escarpment and the unique Austin landscape. Visitors are driven through the Hill Country to the lake and return to town through interesting Austin neighborhoods. After a stop for lunch at a uniquely Austin restaurant, not included in the price, the tour continues on to Austin's historical treasures: The State Capitol, LBJ Library — depending on the group's wishes. Ecotours has attracted visitors from all over the world who want to learn about Austin's natural attributes and our rich history. McMillin can arrange to pick up guests at most Austin hotels or at the Visitors Center in downtown Austin. Call her for rates and to join in on this Austin adventure. Ecotours also offers a one-day tour to San Antonio.

Star Shuttle & Charter

(512) 928-8893

Star Shuttle offers half-day tours of Central Austin that pack in the sights. The tours begin at the Austin Visitor Center downtown and include a guided, walking tour of the State Capitol and then a drive through downtown, by the Governor's Mansion, through the historic Bremond District, by the Treaty Oak and Zilker Park. The tour makes a stop at Wild About Music, a music store and shop, where guests get an introduction to the Austin music scene and can buy souvenirs. The tour continues through historic Clarksville and The University of Texas, where visitors take a walking tour of the LBJ Library. The daily itinerary can be changed to reflect the wishes of the group. Tours are held from 9 AM to 1 PM Monday through Saturday and from 1 PM to 5 PM on Sunday. Reservations are required at least one day in advance and a minimum of six people is required for the tour to proceed. Star Shuttle will call to confirm that the tour will be held. The company will pick up guests at major hotels or at the Visitor Center. Some hotels will make arrangements for you. Call Star Shuttle for their rates.

The University of Texas

(512) 475-7440

UT students guide these free daily tours of the university. Much of the information is relevant only to new and prospective students, but visitors also will learn a little about the campus. Tours are held Monday through Friday 11 AM and 2 PM and Saturday at 2 PM. The tour lasts about an hour and a half. If you're interested, meet at the Admissions office in Room 7 of the Main Building, under the UT Tower. They also have copies of *The Perip, A Self-Guided Walking Tour*, but you have to ask for them.

. . . On Hoof

Austin Carriage Service

Tours starting and ending at several downtown locations • (512) 243-0044

With Austin's weather so beautiful most of the year, one great way to see the sites of historic downtown and enjoy the outdoors in style is to hop on a *Vis-A-Vis*. That's French for face to face. Indeed. These white, horse-drawn carriages operated by the Austin Carriage Service have seating for up to six people, facing each other, and each features a top that can be raised in case of light rain or harsh sunlight. The carriages, reproductions of a servant-driven carriage from the 18th century, are drawn by draft horses that stand about 6 feet tall and weigh 1,800 to 2,200 pounds. Austin Carriage Service offers a variety of regular tours that take in the sights on Congress Avenue, Sixth Street, the State Capitol and Governor's Mansion, Town Lake and more. Tours depart from several downtown restaurants and hotels, including The Driskill, the Four Seasons, the Hyatt Regency, Embassy Suites and DoubleTree Guest Suites. The service offers

Photo: City of Austin

Austin's architecture can be enjoyed by a simple stroll down Congress Avenue.

day, evening and late-night rides. Call for their schedule. In most cases, there's no need to make a reservation. Just walk up and enjoy the ride. A carriage can also be dispatched to a specific location by making a reservation in advance. Drivers are friendly and also serve as guides on your historic tour. Fees vary according to the length of the tour, from about 20 minutes to 80 minutes.

Die Gelbe Rose Carriage

(512) 477-8824

From its base of operations near the Radisson Hotel & Suites at E. Cesar Chavez Street and Congress Avenue, this carriage company offers horse-drawn carriage tours around downtown's most comely sights. Starting around sunset daily, you can hail a carriage to the State Capitol, head around to the Governor's Mansion or design your own tour. Call ahead if you prefer to have a carriage waiting at a certain time to whisk you away. Magnificent Clydesdales are the most common horses used for this task.

. . . On Rail

The Austin & Texas Central Railroad

116 E. Sixth St., (Driskill Hotel) • (512) 477-8468

All aboard! Like the carriage rides above and the boat rides that follow, the mode of transportation for this tour is a tremendous part of the fun. Take one — or all — of a number of rides on the popular train that runs March through November and on selected holidays. A vintage steam-powered locomotive pulls the day coaches built by the Pennsylvania Railroad in the 1920s. Take a ride on the Hill Country Flyer, a daylong excursion that takes passengers on a 33-mile, two-hour ride over Hill Country plateau to the small town of Burnet, founded in 1852. Here, visitors can enjoy lunch, shops for antiques and collectibles and watch an old-time Western shoot-out staged just for train passengers. Passengers can select coach seats or, for a little higher fare, choose an air-conditioned private compartment or the observation car that features complimentary snacks and has windows on both sides — perfect for viewing the sites on this historic run. This is a fun trip for kids and adults alike. The train leaves on weekends from the station in Cedar Park, about 18 miles northwest of downtown Austin, at 10 AM and returns at 5 PM. During the hot summer months, the Hill Country Flyer makes shorter excursions to historic Liberty Hill, about half the distance between Cedar Park and Burnet.

The Twilight Flyer, boarding at the Cedar Park station, is a romantic two-hour ride that runs on selected Saturday evenings and for special events and includes hors d'oeuvres, beer, wine and soft drinks. Be sure to ask about the New Year's Eve run and murder-mystery trip, two of the Twilight Flyer's most popular special runs.

And for those who want to experience the steam train, but have less time, there's The River City Flyer, which runs on selected Fridays. This is a one-hour train ride around Greater Austin that boards in downtown. The train can also be chartered. The Hill Country Express can accommodate 25 to 400 people for special events or meetings and includes a full-service catering menu. Entertainment can also be arranged.

The nonprofit Texas Steam Train Association that operates the line for the City of Austin is made up of nearly all volunteers who go out of their way to make these trips enjoyable, entertaining and educational. This is the route built in 1881 as the Austin & Northwestern Railroad. The pink granite used to build our State Capitol was hauled over these tracks in the 1880s. Locomotive #786 was retired to an Austin park in 1956 where it sat on display for more than 30 years before being called back to action for this new passenger service.

Call the Austin Steam Train Association to find out the current schedule, rate information and to reserve seats.

. . . On Water

Capital Cruises

At the Hyatt Regency Hotel, 208 Barton Springs Rd. • (512) 480-9264

For private or public cruises of Town Lake, Capital Cruises offers a variety of tour options. Public tours, held March through October, include weekend dinner cruises, and sightseeing tours as well as the popular nightly bat-watching excursions. Capital Cruises also offers private cruises by reservation year round. These include private and group dinner cruises, party boat cruises as well as company outings and picnics. This company also has canoes, kayaks, pedal boats and pontoons for rent. Tickets are required.

Commodore's Pup and Riverboat Commodore

On Lake Austin • (512) 345-5220

These two stern-wheeler riverboats are for chartered cruises of Lake Austin, complete with food and beverage service if you like. Commodore's Pup is for groups of 50 to 100 people, while the Riverboat Commodore is designed for 100 to 300 people. Entertainment can also be arranged for that special party. Call them for rates.

Lone Star Riverboat

On the south shore of Town Lake between the Congress Ave. Bridge and S. First St. Bridge • (512) 327-1388

A double-decked paddle wheel riverboat takes visitors on a 1½-hour cruise of scenic Town Lake from March through October. Lone Star offers a variety of cruise times, including a sunset tour and a close-up view of the evening flight of the bats from the Congress Avenue Bridge (see the previous listing in this chapter). There's also a moonlight cruise on Friday nights during the summer. Group and private charters are also available. The schedule changes according to the time of year. Call for current tours. No reservations are required. Fees vary according to the type of cruise.

Whether yours is a little sprout, a precocious sapling or a young tree whose branches are reaching for the sky, Austin offers plenty of sunshine, water and fertilizer for all.

Kidstuff

"One morning hundreds of years ago, an acorn fell and grew in the earth. And that was me."

So begins *The Tree That Would Not Die*, a wonderful, beautifully illustrated children's book by Ellen Levine and Ted Rand about Austin's legendary Treaty Oak.

It may seem odd to begin a section on children's activities by mentioning a book, or our remarkable tree for that matter. This short, poignant book, available in most area bookstores, however, offers an excellent introduction to Austin for both children and adults. Folklore, history and a somber slice of contemporary life intermingle to deliver a unique perspective on this fascinating city. And don't forget to take your little acorns to visit the real Treaty Oak in Central Austin (see our Attractions chapter).

Did we say little acorns? It seems to us that Austin views its children — both residents and visitors — as if they were wee acorns: little pods of potential that, if nurtured, will grow upright, strong and resilient. So whether yours is a little sprout, a precocious sapling or a young tree whose branches are reaching for the sky, Austin offers plenty of sunshine, water and fertilizer for all.

From the new, wonderfully expanded site of the Austin Children's Museum, to children's theater, the Jourdan-Bachman Pioneer Farm, the Austin Zoo, indoor skating rinks and great outdoor activities, Austinites have put a great deal of energy into providing recreational, educational, cultural and simply fun activities for youth of all ages. The Central Texas area provides even more diversion, including that guaranteed kid-pleaser, the giant amusement park. All the Kidstuff we've included in this chapter can be found within 90 minutes of Austin, but most are right here at home.

When it comes to day camps, Austin is a child's delight. Perhaps because so many parents here work, or maybe because Austin just loves its kids, there's a day camp to tickle nearly every child's fancy. Whether you're looking for camps for the whole summer or just a few days around the holidays or spring break, Austin has a place that's just right for you.

If you want your sprouts to enjoy their visit to Austin, don't miss a few of the places listed here. We've provided six categories designed to direct you to Central Texas' most appealing attractions for "growing" children.

Fertilize Well: While this list includes those attractions designed to stimulate the mind, there's plenty of fun to be found, too.

Just Add Water: What would Central Texas be without diversions designed to get you nice and wet?

Supply Sunshine: These are a few of Austin's outdoor delights that appeal to children.

Let 'em Grow Crazy: For when the kids just need to let loose and have fun.

A Garden of Delights: Check this out for relaxing and entertaining spots that are sure to please.

Don't Eat the Daisies: Sure, Austin has all the fast-food chains that appeal to children, but here's a few local favorites, both homegrown and outside imports. See our Restaurants chapter for even more places to feed yourself and the kids.

At the end of the chapter, you'll find our listings of day camps in Austin. If a camp is what you're after, be sure to check out the other listings in this chapter also, as several also offer summer camps. And don't miss our chapter on Parks and Recreation for information on many more activities that are practically guaranteed to delight kids of all ages. Our chapters on Attractions, Spectator Sports and The Arts offer events and attractions for the young and young at heart. The Literary Scene chapter provides information about our libraries and bookstores, including those that host story times.

Fertilize Well

Aquarena Center

1 Aquarena Springs Dr., San Marcos
• (512) 245-7575, (800) 999-9767

Take a ride on a glass-bottom boat on Spring Lake to view the pristine waters and aquatic life of Aquarena Springs, one of Central Texas' natural wonders. The freshwater springs that created the San Marcos River were formed millions of years ago by a fracture in the earth's crust, known today as the Balcones Fault. The river is home to more than 100 varieties of aquatic life, including several endangered species found nowhere else on earth. Well-informed tour guides take you on a relaxing adventure as you witness, through the bottom of the boat, the springs bubbling up from the Edwards Aquifer. There are also the underwater remains of an archeology dig that unearthed 12,000 years of history, including mastodon bones, Spanish gold coins and arrowheads left by the hunter-gatherers who once lived here. This is a perfect place to spend a couple of hours.

This former theme park was acquired in 1994 by Southwest Texas State University, which changed the focus here from amusement to preservation and education. Aquarena Center features a lovely park next to the lake, a historic village, a gift shop and snack bar as well as a fascinating endangered species exhibit where visitors learn about the Texas Blind Salamander, the San Marcos Salamander and other aquatic life. Admission to the park and exhibits is free, but a fee is charged for a variety of boat tours, including ones focusing on ecology, endangered species, archeology and history. Entrance for those tours range from $3 to $6.50 for adults and $2.25 to $4.50 for children 15 and younger. The center has offered special kids programs in the summer, but check to see if they're still running. Aquarena Center is generally open seven days a week from 9:30 AM to 4:30 PM during the school year and 9:30 AM to 6:30 PM during the summer, but do confirm closing times if you're planning to arrive late. For those planning to stay awhile in San Marcos, The Historic Inn at Aquarena Center is right on the lake. To get to the springs, take Interstate 35 south from Austin, Exit 206 to Aquarena Springs Drive and go about 1.5 miles west.

Austin Children's Museum

Dell Discovery Center, 201 Colorado St.
• (512) 472-2494

Fun AND educational. What better combination is there to please children and parents alike! The new Austin Children's Museum at Dell Discovery Center, which opened in December of 1997, is a 19,000-square-foot playscape filled with galleries and hands-on activities designed to entertain and educate even the youngest visitors. This two-story facility (three if you count the small third-level Time Tower that includes exhibits of Austin history and features a tube slide to the first floor) is just packed with permanent and temporary exhibits — all aimed at encouraging youngsters to explore and use their imaginations.

In the largest permanent exhibit, Global CityWorks, children can pretend they're in charge of the city by role-playing in a doctor's office, a grocery store, a diner, a theater, a "bat" bridge and more. There also is a recording area,

INSIDERS' TIP

The monthly magazine *Austin Family* is an excellent reference for kids activities, especially the February issue, which lists summer camps. It's available free at distribution points around the city. "The Happenings" column in the *Austin American-Statesman*'s XL entertainment section, published on Thursdays, also lists activities of interest to children.

a multimedia center, a teen gathering area and a large space stocked with plenty of recycled materials that children can use to make art. The museum is open Tuesday through Saturday 10 AM to 5 PM and Sunday noon to 5 PM. General admission is $3.50. Children under two are admitted free. Admission is free on Wednesdays from 5 to 8 PM and Sundays from 4 to 5 PM. The museum also offers a wide range of summer camps and special activities for children throughout the year.

Austin Museum of Art at Laguna Gloria

3809 W. 35th St. • (512) 458-8191

Children younger than 12 are admitted free to this great Austin art museum, which also offers art classes for children and sponsors an annual family show that will entice even the smallest budding artist. The 1998 family show included a hands-on area for children to create their own works of art. The museum offers weekly summer art classes for children from ages 4 to 14. Call the art school at (512) 323-6380 for more information.

Austin Nature and Science Center

301 Nature Center Dr. • (512) 327-8181

Children will get a kick out of helping Eco Ernie discover signs of Austin wildlife on the Eco Detective Trail, learn about plants and animals in the Discovery Lab and work in a paleontological dig in the Dino Pit at this great center in the Zilker Park Nature Preserve. Injured owls, hawks and vultures are featured in the Birds of Prey exhibit while the Small Wonders exhibit displays 20 of Austin's small animals. The Nature and Science Center is a perfect introduction to Austin's unique ecosystems, and to the wonders of Austin nature. For more on the center see our chapter on Attractions.

The Center is open 9 AM to 5 PM Monday through Saturday and Sunday noon to 5 PM.

Admission is free. The Austin Nature and Science Center also offers several summer camps for children ages 3 to 13.

The Republic of Texas Museum

510 E. Anderson Ln. • (512) 339-1997

Do you know where and when the Texas Declaration of Independence was signed? How about the year Santa Anna was elected president of Mexico or the reason why washing clothes was dangerous for women in the 1800s? The answer to these questions, and many more, can be found in The Republic of Texas Museum, a compact but fun and educational space for the whole family. Children and adults are given a separate list of scavenger hunt questions, the answers to which can be found by touring the exhibits. The littlest ones get to answer questions such as, where is the chair with the two ears located or find the three chickens in the museum and what are their names? This museum, run by the Daughters of the Republic of Texas, is dedicated to the era of the Texas Republic (1836-1846). Young children especially like Great Grandma's Backyard, a collection of hands-on household items and implements used by families in the mid-19th century. There's something of interest to people of all ages here. The museum is open 10 AM to 4 PM Monday through Friday and 11 AM to 4 PM on Saturday. General admission is $2, 50¢ for kids.

George Washington Carver Museum

1165 Angelina St. • (512) 472-4809

Distinguished for being the first African-American neighborhood museum in the state of Texas, the George Washington Carver Museum hosts a variety of activities for children throughout the year, including the annual A Smile of My Face workshop that teaches children the art of photography. The museum is open 10 AM to 6 PM Tuesday through Thursday, noon to 5 PM Friday and Saturday. (See our Attractions chapter for more information on this museum.)

Inner Space Cavern

I-35, Exit 259, Georgetown • (512) 863-5545

People tend to think that attractions located right beside the interstate are just tourist traps designed to get your money. This one, however, is one of the best and most accessible attractions around for both children and their families. Estimated to be 100 million years old, Inner Space Cavern was discovered in 1963 by workers testing core samples for construction of the interstate. It seems everywhere they drilled, they found air pockets. Now opened for all to appreciate, this living cavern — meaning it continues to grow and develop — features an excellent array of formations beyond the typical stalactites and stalagmites. Guides will lead you on a 75-minute tour and point out such fascinating shapes as the Flowing Stone of Time, The Lake of the Moon and more, including the bones of prehistoric animals who died in here. At a temperature of 72 to 74 degrees, this is the perfect spot to escape the sizzling summer heat, and the winter chill. The cavern has a large gift shop and snack bar. The cavern, located just 24 miles north of downtown Austin, is open 9 AM to 6 PM daily. Admission is $8 for adults and $5 for children ages 4 to 12. Tours depart regularly throughout the day with the last one beginning at 5:50 PM.

Jourdan-Bachman Pioneer Farm

11418 Sprinkle Cut-Off Rd.
• (512) 837-1215

Children will enjoy stepping back in time to share in the lives of Central Texas settlers at this living history museum. The farm, originally part of a 2,000-acre cotton farm, presents the story of rural life in the late 19th century. Here, guides dressed in the styles of the times, will lead visitors on a trip to the past. Historically correct crops, food, clothing, farm implements and dwellings highlight a trip to the farm. On Sunday afternoons, the farm goes all out to involve visitors in the rural lifestyle. Family programs on those days include such interesting topics as dairy day, when visitors get to milk cows and churn butter; bread baking, in which visitors learn the art of making wheat-based bread in a Dutch oven; and blacksmithing, in which the staff blacksmith turns metal into tools and other items used by farmers back then. And don't miss the country store, open most Sundays and featuring locally made craft items, toys, books and more. The farm is open Sunday from 1 to 5 PM and Monday through Wednesday from 9:30 AM to 1 PM. During the summer the farm is also open on Thursday from 9:30 AM to 1 PM. Call the farm or pick up a copy of their regularly updated brochure, which lists special Sunday activities by date. The Austin Visitor Center at 201 E. Second Street will have that brochure.

Natural Bridge Caverns

26496 Natural Bridge Cavern Rd., Natural Bridge Caverns • (210) 651-6101

Located just north of San Antonio and southwest of New Braunfels off Interstate 35 Exit 175, Natural Bridge Caverns boasts more than 10,000 formations, including such wonders as Sherwood Forest, the Castle of the White Giant, and the King's Throne. These living caverns, discovered in 1960, present many spectacular sights, including one underground room that's as big as a football field. The cool caverns (average temperature is 72 degrees) are nestled amid Texas Hill Country terrain and provide plenty of shaded space outside for picnicking or relaxing. There's also a gift shop. The 75-minute tours depart about every 30 minutes beginning at 9 AM daily, except Thanksgiving, Christmas and New Year. Closing time varies depending on the season. Adults pay $9 for admission while children ages 4 through 12 are charged $6.

Splash! into the Edwards Aquifer

2201 Barton Springs Rd.
• (512) 327-8181

This new hands-on educational center, which opened in the fall of 1998 at Barton Springs Pool, is a 1,400-square-foot interactive exhibit on the Barton Springs Edwards Aquifer. Splash! features a continuously running four-minute video, *Carved in Stone*, which shows how the springs were formed. An interactive, three-dimensional relief map that uses animated lights to show the movement of the water lets children push the buttons to make the water flow. There's also a fascinating aquascape model of the aquifer. Aquariums here house specimens of the aquifer's aquatic life. This is a great place to learn about the Barton Springs salamander, an endangered species found only in Austin. Splash! is part of the Beverly Sheffield Education Center run by the Austin Parks and Recreation Department. The various exhibits are designed for use by children in

Photo: Peter A. Silva

Kids will enjoy roaming and climbing around the Capitol grounds.

4th grade and up. Splash is open free to the public, although there may be a charge for guided tours. Hours of operation were not available by press time, so call for information. (For more about Barton Springs, see our Close-up in the Parks and Recreation chapter.)

Star Gazing

T.S. Painter Hall Observatory, near 24th Street and Speedway • (512) 232-4265

No. We're not talking about the kind of star-gazing you'll find in our Close-up on Austin's film industry in The Arts chapter. This is the old-fashioned, out-of-this-world kind. The University of Texas astronomy department offers free star-gazing experiences on the UT campus every Saturday night, weather permitting, during the school year. Families with children seem especially attracted to this kind of educational fun. Astronomy students lead visitors on a tour of the stars, using a cool 10-inch diameter telescope built in 1932. The fun starts around 8:30 PM, but do call ahead to confirm. No reservations are required. Parking is easy at this time of night, except when big UT events, like a Longhorns football game, are scheduled. For further information on other celestial events and other star-gazing activities, call the UT Sky Watchers Report at (512) 471-5007.

Texas State Capitol

1100 Congress Ave. • (512) 463-0063

There's just no better way to introduce your youngsters to the legends and lores of Texas history than taking them on a tour of the Texas State Capitol. We've found the guides to be especially kind and patient with children, making sure to answer all their questions. (For more on this monument to Texas including hours of operation, see our Attractions chapter.)

Umlauf Sculpture Garden & Museum

605 Robert E. Lee Rd. • (512) 445-5582

Ask for the treasure hunt map when you visit the Umlauf Sculpture Garden and your child will be delighted to chase around looking for some of Charles Umlauf's magnificent sculptures. (The diversion will allow you more time to enjoy the sculptures, too.) Because most of the statues are outdoors, this is a great place to introduce children to a museum. They don't have to keep quiet, and they don't have to keep their hands to themselves. (Yes, they can touch the outdoor sculptures!) They'll love you for it. To find out more about this outdoor garden and indoor museum including the hours of operation, see our Attractions chapter.

Wonder World Park

1000 Prospect St., San Marcos • (512) 392-3760

Unlike other caves in Texas that were formed by rushing water, this fascinating underground fissure was formed by a massive earthquake millions of years ago. You can actually see where the earth split, leaving jigsaw-puzzle-like sections of rock that would fit right into each other if pushed back together. And, because it's not growing, kids get to put their hands anywhere they like. Wonder World, said to be the only earthquake-formed cave in the country open for tours, drops more than 160 feet beneath the earth's surface but is accessible for children of all ages. Kid-friendly guides takes visitors on a 45-minute tour of this Texas marvel, pointing out all the prehistoric treasures and naturally glowing rocks. Wonder World also has a 190-foot above-ground observation tower, a deer-petting zoo and an antigravity house. Admission for all four features is $13.95 for adults and $9.95 for children ages 4 to 11. Kids younger than 4 are admitted free. Admission for just the cave is $10 for adults and $7.50 for children. The cave is by far the best feature here. Wonder World is open 8 AM to 8 PM year round.

Just Add Water

Barton Springs

Zilker Park, 2201 Barton Springs Rd. • (512) 928-0014

There's nothing like a cool — and we mean cool — dip in Austin's treasured spring-fed swimming pool to chill out the kids on a hot summer day and make them feel like real Austin Insiders. The water in the pool remains a constant 68 degrees throughout the year. For more on this historic spot and for Austin's other great swimming spots, see our Parks and Recreation chapter.

Deep Eddy Pool's Summer Movies

401 Deep Eddy Ave. • (512) 472-8546

Leave it to Austinites to figure out a way to combine water fun and flicks. West Austin's Deep Eddy Pool, one of our favorite swimming spots, presents family movies right next to the pool on Saturday nights throughout the summer, starting in late May. The schedule includes such winners as *Antz*, *101 Dalmations*, *George of the Jungle*, *Dr. Doolittle* and *Creature from the Black Lagoon*, presented in 3D. Come around 8 PM and bring a picnic basket or buy pizza at the pool. The films begin around sunset, 9:30 PM or so. Admission is $2 for adults and 50¢ for kids. Hint for parents: Bring a babysitter along so you can slip over to the nearby Deep Eddy Cabaret for some music and refreshments while the kiddies enjoy the movie.

Schlitterbahn Waterpark Resort

305 W. Austin St., New Braunfels • (830) 625-2351

Never mind that this waterpark is about 50 miles south of Austin in New Braunfels!

INSIDERS' TIP

The spiral-bound book, *Today's Family Guide*, is an excellent resource for parents. This guide provides information on camps, classes, child-care providers and much more and is available at local bookstores and at the library.

Schlitterbahn is one place many Austin families visit at least once, if not several times, during the summer. Located on the banks of the spring-fed Comal River, Schlitterbahn is 65 acres of high-tech water rides, slides, pools, inner tube floats and kiddie parks. The park has plenty of hair-raising rides sure to please the stoutest thrill-seeker in your group. Schlitterbahn also claims the world's first uphill water coaster. Picnic baskets (no glass or alcohol, please) are welcome here and there are plenty of shaded areas and tables for you to gather. The park is open late April to late September, but on weekends-only during the school year. The fun starts at 10 AM daily and goes until closing time, which varies from 6 to 8 PM. Call the park for specific details. All-day passes cost $23.50 for those ages 12 and older, $19.25 for children ages 3 to 11. Children 3 and younger are admitted free. Midday passes, tickets for the Comal River Rapids only and season tickets also are available. Parking is free. Schlitterbahn also runs two riverside resort hotels (at the same phone number).

Sea World Adventure Park

10500 Sea World Dr., San Antonio • (210) 523-3611

Promise your youngsters a trip to Sea World and you're sure to get at least a day or two of good behavior in exchange. While there are plenty of thrilling water rides, wet playscapes, cool amusement park adventures and shows, kids can actually learn something here too. But keep that part under your hat. This giant park features the only major display of Hammerhead sharks in North America, dozens of penguins, sea lions, whales and, of course, the great Shamu. Sea World says its the world's largest sea life adventure park. While not all the rides are designed to get you wet, there are plenty to keep you cool on a hot summer day. Be sure to pack the swimming suits. Sea World is open March through October, mostly on weekends until school gets out. But all summer long this exciting place is open 10 AM to 10 PM. Admission is $30.95 for adults and $20.95 for children ages 3 to 11. Two-day passes and season tickets also are available. This is definitely worth a trip to San Antonio.

Tubing

City Park, near University and Bobcat Drs., San Marcos • (512) 396-LION

To many Texans, the Hill Country is synonymous with river tubing, in which you ride down the river on big inner tubes. This inexpensive, low-tech pastime is loads of fun, especially on hot summer days. While some tubing areas can be dominated by older kids and young adults, the Lions Club operates a family-oriented tubing, swimming and snorkeling spot on the San Marcos River in nearby San Marcos. They provide rides back to the park once you've gone down river. You can even rent an extra tube, tie it to your own and cart a cooler downstream if you like. This is refreshing and exhilarating fun, and all proceeds go to charity. The all-day rental price is $3 for regular tubes and $5 for tubes with bottoms on weekdays, $4 and $6 on weekends. It's open daily late May to early September from 10 AM to 7 PM. The Lions Club also rents life vests for the little ones and lockers. Take Interstate 35 south to Exit 206 and follow Aquarena Springs Drive to University Drive. Turn left on Bobcat Drive and right just before the railroad tracks. The Lions Club stand is next to the Texas National Guard Armory.

Supply Sunshine

Austin Zoo

10807 Rawhide Tr. • (512) 288-1490, (800) 291-1490

This Hill Country escape about 20 minutes southwest of downtown Austin is a perfect place to bring young children for a close-up look at the animals, a picnic, a pony ride or train ride. Compared to the sprawling super zoos many cities boast, Austin's zoo is small, rustic and very laid back. That makes it easy on young ones and their parents — you don't need to rush madly around the park to see everything. Here, visitors will find Bengal tigers, wallabies, capybaras, African lions, antelope, potbellied pigs and many more exotic and domestic animals. There's a petting corral where you can purchase food to feed the animals. The zoo features a wonderful tortoise barn in which children can get a close-up view of several species. The Austin Zoo is open 10 AM to 6 PM

Photo: Peter A. Silva

Kids love the cool spring-fed waters of Barton Springs Pool.

daily. It's closed on Thanksgiving and Christmas. Admission is $5 for adults, $4 for children ages 2 to 12 and free for children younger than 2. There are discounts for grandparents, seniors and groups. Train and pony rides cost $2.

Butler Pitch & Putt Golf Course

201 Lee Barton Dr. • (512) 477-9025

Tiger Woods would have loved this place when he was just a toddler trying to master the game of golf. This specially designed, nine-hole course in South Central Austin features holes about a third as long as standard ones — 61 to 118 yards long — and also rents short clubs for the kids. Of course, adults who want a quick game of golf enjoy this wonderful course, too, which includes all the fun and frustrations of a regular course, including water hazards and the rough. Run by the Austin Parks and Recreation Department, this golf course is sure to please. It's open 8:30 AM until dark year round. Greens fees are $4 for adults and kids. Club rental is extra.

Children's Day Art Park

Symphony Sq., 1101 Red River St. • (512) 476-6064

Children are encouraged to bang the drums, blow the horns and fiddle the strings at the instrument "petting zoo," just one exciting feature of the Austin Symphony Orchestra's summer art park for children. These delightful outdoor events, held every Wednesday morning in June and July at historic Symphony Square, feature performances by symphony ensembles and by a variety of children's performers, including salsa bands, folk singers and ballet folklórico. There's also an annual Teddy Bear Picnic, in which children bring their bears from home to compete for prizes like the oldest and biggest while musicians perform songs about bears. Symphony musicians are on hand each week to demonstrate the use of various instruments and to provide guidance. When the musical performance ends, children follow the Pied Piper down Waller Creek for more hands-on activities and face painting under a big tent. The Austin Symphony, Austin's oldest performing group, has sponsored these art parks for kids for more than 20 years. They're designed for kids ages 3 to 8, but everyone is invited. Admission is 50¢ for children, free for adults. Check out the art park from 9:30 to 11:30 AM. See our chapter on The Arts for more symphony events for the whole family.

Clear Springs Aviaries and Zoological Gardens

5686 S. I-35, New Braunfels • (830) 606-6029

Central Texas' newest bird and animal kingdom reflects lifelong passion for birds by owner Steve Collins, who has been studying our feathered friends since he was 6. Today, Clear Springs is home to nearly 300 species of birds and animals as well as nearly 2,000 species of tropical and exotic plants. The emphasis is on birds — many migratory birds stop by for visits — but the park also features foxes, llamas, exotic deer, turtles and other animals sure to please the kids. This nicely landscaped park opened in late summer 1998 and includes a duck pond, a 2-acre lake and plenty of places to just relax with the kids and picnic. Bring your own food, as there is no snack bar here. Visitors can walk through 7 acres of the 35-acre park. It's open from 10 AM to 7 PM daily except major holidays. Admission is $4 for adults, $3 for seniors and children 3 to 12. To get there go south from Austin on I-35, take Exit 182 (Engel Road), and travel about ¼ mile.

Peter Pan Mini-Golf

1207 Barton Springs Rd.
• (512) 472-1033

If you've got a hankering to play miniature golf at midnight — or any other time — this is the place for you. Peter Pan offers two 18-hole miniature golf courses and a whole lot of fun for the little ones. What is it about this game that attracts so many kids and adults? It must be the challenge of trying to get that little ball up the hill around the obstacle and into the hole without screaming! Peter Pan is open 9 AM to midnight Sunday through Thursday and 9 AM to 1 AM Friday and Saturday. Admission is $4 for adults and $2.50 for children 5 and younger. You can arrive 20 minutes before opening to get signed up.

Slaughter Creek Metropolitan Park

4103 Slaughter Ln.

Do you have an in-line skating fanatic in the family? This is the outdoor place for those who just couldn't leave home without the skates. The park features a 3-mile veloway (it's nice and smooth) and is popular with skaters and bikers. There are a playground, nature trail, sports courts and picnic facilities here, too. This Southwest Austin park is next to the Lady Bird Johnson Wildflower Center. (See our Parks and Recreation Chapter for more about indoor roller rinks.)

Wild Basin Wilderness Preserve

805 N. Loop 360 (Capital of Texas Hwy.)
• (512) 327-7622

This is a perfect place to educate the kids, and yourself, about Austin's beautiful Hill Country terrain. This 227-acre preserve in West Austin is also great for nature walks as it features a trail system that runs throughout the area. The preserve gives school tours during the week so tour guides know just how to talk to youngsters and are prepared for the guided tours for visitors on weekends. Or you can take a self-guided tour and explore this park yourself. For the budding astronomer in the family, the Austin Astronomical Society holds a family oriented star gazing party here each month. Call them at (512) 252-2966 for details. (See our Parks and Recreation chapter for information about other parks and preserves in the area.)

Zilker Park

2100 Barton Springs Rd.
• (512) 472-4914

If, as they say, Barton Springs is the crown jewel of Austin, then Zilker Park is the crown. This 400-acre park is the city's largest park and definitely one of its most popular. There's a great playscape for kids, miniature train rides, jogging trails and plenty of space to just run, play soccer, throw a Frisbee or toss a ball. Tuck your swimming suits in the trunk when you head for the park, as Barton Springs Pool is right here and you might be tempted. See our Parks and Recreation chapter for more details.

INSIDERS' TIP

If you've just moved to Austin, it's a good idea to get on the mailing list of some of the places listed in this chapter, as many send out flyers advertising special events and camps.

Let 'em Grow Crazy

Celebration Station

4525 S. I-35 • (512) 448-3533

The name says it all. Kids love this place. It features two 18-hole miniature golf courses, go-carts and bumper boats outdoors as well as a whole bunch of interactive arcade-type games inside, including air hockey, pinball, car games and more. This large space is fun for the whole family. There's no charge to enter. Inside games require tokens that cost 25¢ each. Go-cart and bumper boats cost $4 for three minutes; miniature golf is $3.99 for children ages 3 to 12 and $4.99 for adults. Special packages and play packages are available. Celebration Station opens at 10 AM Monday through Saturday and at noon on Sunday. It closes at 11 PM Sunday through Thursday and at midnight on Friday and Saturday. There is a snack bar.

Chaparral Ice Center

14200 N. I-35 • (512) 252-8500
2525 W. Anderson Ln. • (512) 252-8500

Now with two Austin locations, Chaparral Ice is twice the fun! Kids can come daily for skating on their own, or sign up for Learn-to-Skate classes. These well-run, well-maintained skating rinks offer a wonderful variety of year-round activities for children and adults. The Anderson Lane location is in Northcross Mall, so you can shop while the kids skate. Better yet, be bold and lace up some skates for yourself. Classes are for skaters age 3 to adult. There also are classes in ice dance and hockey as well as hockey leagues for children and adults. Chaparral does birthday parties and has a full summer of camps for children. The center usually opens for public skating in the afternoons, but hours at both locations vary as these rinks as they also are used as training centers. Call for the current schedule. Admission is $5. Skate rental is $2.50.

Chuck E Cheese's

8038 Burnet Rd. • (512) 451-0296
502 W. Ben White Blvd. • (512) 441-9681

Ahhhh, the coveted token! There just never seem to be enough of those discs of gold to satisfy even the youngest of competitors. To match wits with a machine and win those esteemed tickets is, at that very moment, the most awesome adventure on the planet. Austin's two Chuck E Cheese's locations in North and South Central Austin are filled with interactive arcade games, playscapes and air hockey tables that are sure to please. The good news for parents is that the food is pretty darn good too. There are pizza and hot dogs, snacks and soft drinks, and even a salad bar. At the end of the day, your youngsters get to go home with the prizes they've won in exchange for the tickets. Chuck E Cheese's does birthday parties too. The stores are open Sunday through Thursday 10 AM to 10 PM, Friday and Saturday 10 AM to 11 PM.

Discovery Zone Fun Center

9503 Research Blvd. • (512) 346-9666

If your child likes to jump around in a pile of brightly colored plastic balls, scamper through tunnels and slide down slides in a giant plastic maze, Discovery Zone could be just the place for the little one. This popular spot also features interactive games, a karaoke stage and an art factory. There's a play area set aside for tots. Discovery Zone offers a full snack bar with pizzas, hot dogs and other kids' delights. It's open Monday through Thursday 10 AM to 8 PM, Friday and Saturday from 10 AM to 9 PM and Sunday 11 AM to 7 PM. All-day admission is $4.99 for children shorter than 38 inches and $7.99 for those 38 inches and taller. The interactive games, in which children earn tickets for prizes, require tokens, purchased separately for 25¢ each. DZ also does birthday parties. Children must remove their shoes at the door and are required to wear socks.

INSIDERS' TIP

Many of Austin's annual events are centered around children or include kid-friendly activities. Be sure to check out our chapter on Annual Events if you're looking for a great family activity.

Gymboree

2121 Parmer Ln. • (512) 335-0038
Oak Acre Shopping Center, 5716 U.S. Hwy. 290 W. • (512) 335-0038

This national learn-as-you-play program helps infants and youngsters develop motor and cognitive skills while building confidence. Gymboree utilizes up to 18 pieces of equipment to provide sensory stimulation for the young. There are singing and storytelling, noncompetitive sports for older children, lots of parent-child interaction and plenty of things to crawl through and climb on. Trained instructors supervise the 45-minute, age-appropriate classes. Classes, for newborns to age 4, are ongoing so children can be enrolled anytime for a one-month minimum commitment. A free introductory class is available.

Laser Quest Austin

523 Highland Mall Blvd., Ste. 100 • (512) 459-5400

Strap on a vest, arm yourself with a laser and enter the 8,000-square-foot maze for a heart-pounding game of laser tag. This giant maze has two levels and three towers to make the game even more exciting as you search for "victims" to blast with your light. The more people you tag, the higher your score. That is, if you don't get tagged too often by others. Both boys and girls, young and old like this game. Music, fog and strobe lights help create the atmosphere here. This is a great location for birthday parties, and corporate team-building gatherings. Yes, adults love to play laser tag, too, so challenge your kids. Laser Quest costs $6.50 per person per game, which lasts about 20 minutes. At the end of the game, you receive a scorecard that tells who you tagged and where you tagged them as well as who tagged you and where. The score card tells you how accurate your shots were and ranks you against the other players. The facility is in the Highland Mall parking lot near Foley's. It's open during the summer Monday through Thursday from 2 to 10 PM, Friday 2 PM to midnight, Saturday noon to midnight and Sunday noon to 10 PM. It opens later on weekdays during the school year.

Pseudo-Rock

200 Trinity St. • (512) 474-4376

Budding rock climbers will adore this huge space, which is filled with 6,000 square feet of sculpted climbing surface. Expert climbers are on hand to introduce kids to the thrill of rock climbing, and adult companions can hold the ropes as children climb higher and higher. One thing, though, this place isn't air conditioned and can get quite hot in the summer, despite the big fans they put here. We go when it's cooler. Pseudo-Rock hasn't offered a special package for children yet, though, so expect to pay the full-day rate of $14 per climber, which includes equipment rental and instruction. Children of any age may climb, but you must be 12 or older to hold the rope for a companion. There's a $2 charge to rent a harness. It's open 10 AM to 10 PM Monday through Friday and 10 AM to 8 PM Saturday and Sunday.

Six Flags Fiesta Texas

17000 I-10 W., San Antonio • (210) 697-5050, (800) 473-4378

You'll need to drive down to San Antonio for this one, but our resident kid advisor for this chapter insists you'll gain major brownie points with your children by letting them know that, yes, Central Texas offers a fantastic amusement park. Fiesta Texas is, indeed, a blast — and not just for the kiddies. Thrilling rides, including the giant purple roller coaster and fun house called The Joker's Revenge, and a huge wooden roller coaster called The Rattler will have your heart in your throat in no time. There also are plenty of exciting rides sure to get you wet — and cool! This giant park offers rides for people of all ages, a special children's area, plenty of shops and restaurants, great shows and, to top it off, a wonderful waterpark — don't forget to bring your swimming suits. This immaculate facility is so fun and so huge that many people purchase two-day or season passes. Fiesta Texas is open 10 AM to 10 PM daily throughout the summer and on weekends with shorter hours in the spring and fall. Call for a schedule. The park is closed November to March. Daily admission is $33 for people 48 inches and taller, $23.50 for children under 48 inches and for those 55 years and older. Children ages 2 and younger are admitted free. Parking is $5 per car. While you're in San Antonio, you might also want to check out Sea World (see the listing in this chapter). (See our Daytrips and Weekend Getaways chapter for more on San Antonio.)

A Garden of Delights

Paramount Theatre Kids' Classics

713 Congress Ave. • (512) 472-5470

Austin's historic Paramount Theatre (see our chapter on The Arts) presents six seasonal productions aimed specifically at children ages 3 through 10. The Paramount brings in some of the country's top children's performers and theater companies for an exciting season of plays, musicals and performing arts. The October through January season has included such productions as *Jack and the Giant Beanstalk*, presented by the acclaimed Dallas Children's Theater, *Swiss Family Robinson*, by Theatreworks/USA, Scholastic's *Magic School Bus* on tour and more. This is fun for the whole family, and a great way to introduce youngsters to live theater. Many people subscribe to the full season, which includes five main series events and one extra production. Tickets may also be purchased individually for about $7 to $11 for children, slightly more for adults.

Sgraffito Studio

809 W. 12th St. • (512) 708-9000

This kid-friendly, paint-it-yourself ceramics studio offers an excellent assortment of pieces from which to create that one-of-a-kind treasure to keep or to give as a gift. Platters, coffee mugs, picture frames, dog dishes, bowls and more are the canvas that artists use to make unique designs. You can even make mosaics here. Sgraffito hosts birthday parties, wedding showers, corporate team-building events and just about any other special event you can imagine. Decorating fees are $7 an hour, $5 for children during the week, and there also are happy hour discounts on Thursday and Friday evenings. The studio is open Tuesday, Wednesday and Saturday 11 AM to 6 PM, Thursday and Friday from 11 AM to 9 PM and Sunday noon to 5 PM. Sgraffito, by the way, is named for a pottery technique in which you scratch through the paint to reveal the original color of the clay,

Hidden Talent

2525 W. Anderson Ln. • (512) 323-2551

This studio in Northcross Shopping Mall features walls and walls of cast plaster of Paris statues and wall ornaments for you and your little ones to paint on the premises. There are plenty of long tables stocked with an assortment of water-based paints and brushes for you to use. When you're finished, the employees with spray on a lacquer coat — and add glitter to your work if you like. Children have a blast here. And you pay only the price of the item. There's no additional cost for the paints. Hidden Talent hosts birthday parties and offers classes, but no experience is really needed for youngsters to paint a treasure to take home. Hidden Talent is open 10 AM to 9 PM Monday through Saturday and noon to 6 PM on Sunday.

Ceramics Bayou

3736 Bee Caves Rd., Ste. 9 • (512) 328-1168

This paint-it-yourself ceramics studio offers a wide range of items — everything from simple tiles and coffee mugs to plates, platters and animals. Children will delight in using their creative powers to design and paint their own piece. At Ceramics Bayou, you pay for the piece plus $6 per studio hour per person and $2 per item for glazing and firing. Finished pieces are fired in the kiln and ready for pick-up in a few days. Hint: These make excellent gifts for parents, friends or for Grandma or Grandpa on their birthday. Speaking of birthdays, Ceramics Bayou hosts those too, as well as private parties. The studio is open Monday, Tuesday, Wednesday and Saturday from 10 AM to 6 PM, Thursday and Friday 10 AM to 9 PM and Sunday noon to 5 PM.

The Bats

Congress Avenue Bridge at Town Lake

Children ogle in wonder when North America's largest urban bat colony sets off en masse on the evening flight for food during the spring and summer. This is a spectacle the whole family can enjoy. For more on these Mexican free-tails, see our Attractions chapter.

Zilker Park Trail of Lights and Christmas Tree

Zilker Park, 2100 Barton Springs Rd. • (512) 472-4914

It only lasts a few weeks once a year, but this is one of THE places to take your kids if you're here around the Christmas holiday. The "tree" is formed using Zilker Park's 165-foot-tall Moonlight Tower as the trunk and strings of multicolored lights — 3,500 of them — to form the tree's cone shape. Children love to stand inside the tree and whirl around until the lights blur. Austin's annual Yule Fest celebration, which features the Trail of Lights, is another tradition that children love. (See our December Annual Events for more on this and on the Lighting of the Zilker Park Christmas Tree.) Admission to the park is free.

Don't Eat the Daisies

Central Market Cafe

4001 N. Lamar Blvd. • (512) 206-1020

The great outdoor patio filled with picnic tables and a playscape that's close enough to keep your eye on the kids are among the attractions for families at Central Market Cafe. This casual restaurant, an extension of Austin's gourmet grocery store, has an extensive menu for people of all ages. Burgers, spaghetti, macaroni, salads, pizzas, gourmet fare and much more, including great desserts. You place your order at the counter and retrieve your meal when your beeper lights up. Central Market also has indoor dining for when it's just too hot outside to breathe. There's live music on the patio several evenings a week. It's a great way to introduce children to the Austin music scene and get them fed, too. (For more about Central Market see our Close-up in the Shopping chapter.)

Güero's Taco Bar

1412 S. Congress Ave. • (512) 447-7688

This Austin institution on funky S. Congress Avenue is a popular family eatery. While Chelsea wasn't with President Clinton when he ate here a few years ago, we're sure she would have been satisfied with the Mexican fare. The kid's menu includes quesadillas, breakfast tacos, chicken breast tacos and enchiladas. All entrees come with rice and beans. The salsa bar is serve-it-yourself so the food isn't too spicy for the kids. You won't have to chide the kids for squirming here. It's just comfy Austin.

Hang Town Grill

9828 Great Hills Tr. • (512) 349-9944
701 N. Loop 360 (Capital of Texas Hwy.) • (512) 347-1039
2828 Rio Grande St. • (512) 476-8696

Pizza, hot dogs, burgers, chicken strips, grilled cheese, corn dogs, quesadillas! Is there anything missing from a child's list of daily requirements? This Austin chain is a surefire kid pleaser — and pretty popular with us older folks, too. They've got a great variety of salads along with some exotic sandwiches that appeal to adults, including a fabulous green-chili chicken burger. Here, you go to the counter to place your order and collect it when they call your name. They also have take-out. This is a totally laid-back, relaxing atmosphere. Hang Town's three locations are in Central, West and Northwest Austin.

Kerbey Lane Cafe

3704 Kerbey Ln. • (512) 451-1436
12602 Research Blvd. • (512) 258-7757
2700 S. Lamar Blvd. • (512) 445-4451

Children just seem to love the huge plate-dwarfing pancakes served round the clock at this popular Austin eatery. But there are many more delicacies sure to please. The children's menu includes enchiladas, tacos, hamburgers, peanut butter and jelly sandwiches, ham and cheese, and other guaranteed kid pleasers. Prices are very reasonable, and with three Austin locations Kerbey Lane is easy to find. All three are open 24 hours a day.

Magnolia Cafe

2304 Lake Austin Blvd. • (512) 478-8645
1920 S. Congress Ave. • (512) 445-0000

Homegrown and down home, Magnolia Cafe serves an excellent assortment of meals for children, including some nutritious items, like steamed broccoli with cheese or a grilled chicken dinner. There are plenty of other kid pleasers as well, including a chicken black bean taco, kid burger with home fries, fish taco, kid French toast and a kid breakfast that includes an egg, pancake and sausage or bacon and is served all day. There's nothing fancy about Magnolia Cafe but the food. Adults will be happy, too, and there's a good selection of vegetarian dishes. Both Magnolia Cafes are open 24 hours a day.

Romano's Macaroni Grill

9828 Great Hills Tr. • (512) 795-0460
701 Loop 360 (Capital of Texas Hwy.) • (512) 329-0000

When you're in the mood for a little more upscale restaurant, but still want to take the kids, try the Macaroni Grill. This Italian restaurant has a kids menu that includes, you guessed it, macaroni and cheese as well as ravioli, grilled cheese sandwiches, corn dogs, chicken tenders, pizzas and more. The tablecloths are covered with sheets of white butcher paper, and crayons are provided. Macaroni Grill's two Austin locations are in the northwest and the west.

T.G.I. Friday's

111 E. Cesar Chavez St. • (512) 478-2991
10000 Research Blvd. • (512) 345-6410

It's a chain, but still one our kid advisor's favorite Austin hangouts. Perhaps those boldly striped red and white tablecloths catch their attention. Kids get a packet of crayons and an activity book to keep them occupied while they wait, and there are always balloons for the little ones. We've even been there to see a magician walk among the tables and do tricks. Kids can choose between hot dogs, fish sticks, chicken fingers, grilled cheese, spaghetti, macaroni and cheese or Friday's own pizzadilla, a pizza-quesadilla combo. The downtown Friday's is in the Radisson Hotel, and the northwest location is in the Arboretum Shopping Center.

Day Camps

You'll never have to hear those dreaded words, "There's nothing to do," if you enroll your child in one, or several, of Austin's amazing day camps. Austin offers something for every child, from the traditional camps that include a little of everything throughout the day to specialized camps in education, the arts, dance and gymnastics, magic, and all kinds of sports. Tuition for a one-week, full-day program generally ranges from about $100 to $190, although specialty camps and University of Texas camps can cost more. Some camps offer financial aid, and some offer discounts if several family members enroll.

Educational

Futurekids of Austin

3818 Far West Blvd. • (512) 346-8020

Start your children off on the road to computer literacy at an early age by enrolling them in a computer camp run by the people who pioneered a method of teaching to the young. Children ages 4 to 14 are offered themed adventures in computer training, including space, robotics, business operation, drama and more. We introduced a youngster to this summer program and discovered at the end of the week that she was hooked on computer technology. These weeklong, half-day camps are held Monday through Thursday throughout the summer for children ages 6 to 14 and end with an open house for parents. Children ages 4 and 5 attend two-hour camps, also with themes, three days a week. Classes are limited in size to allow instructors to give personal attention to each child. During the summer, Futurekids holds camps at two sites: here at the main teaching lab and at another location in West Austin. Classes are offered for both children and adults throughout the school year at the Far West Boulevard location. Austin's Futurekids also is spearheading an excellent program that takes computer learning into the schools.

UT Step Camp

Welch Hall, 24th St. and Speedway • (512) 471-9462

Three separate camps for students entering 7th, 8th, and 9th grades focus on science and technology. The University of Texas Science and Technology Center runs these camps, called Step, Step Up, and Step Beyond, and provides hands-on activities to further the learning process. Students also get a recreational activity each day, visit UT science classrooms, hear guest speakers and take field trips to UT's J.J. Pickle Research Center. Children in Young Scientists classrooms who could be candidates for AISD's science magnet school are given priority, and there are a number of scholarships available. But enrollment is open to other students as well, space provided. Step and Step Up are two-week camps that run from 8:30 AM to 3:45 PM. Step Beyond is a one-week camp.

UTkidz and UTteenz

Thompson Conference Center, near E. Dean Keeton St. and E. Campus Dr. • (512) 471-3125

Designed for motivated, gifted and eager-to-learn students, UTkidz and UTteenz day camps are hands-on educational "exploratories" that cover a variety of topics in the arts, sciences and technology. Campers have been delighted in the past with such themes as A Day in the Life, Playing the Stock Market, Dig it! Archeology, Making a Music Video and other programs designed especially for their age group. Instructors for these programs are primarily UT graduate students, faculty and staff. Students entering 4th, 5th and 6th grades in the fall can sign up for either of UTkidz two-week sessions in July. The camp day runs from 12:30 to 5:30 PM. Group size is limited, and the sign-up deadline for these camps is in late May, so enroll early.

UTteenz has two types of summer camps. Students entering 7th, 8th and 9th grades can choose between two types of summer camps at the university. UTteenz is a two-week camp in which students devote their mornings to investigation of a single major topic area. Past topics have included architecture, TV studio, debate and computers and the Web. This camp, held once during the summer, runs 9 AM to 5:30 PM each weekday. There's also UTteenz Computer Camp, a two-week, full-day adventure dedicated to exploring computers via the World Wide Web and multimedia. This camp, for students entering 9th, 10th and 11th grades, teaches students how to develop Web sites and much, much more. Graduation ceremonies are held at the end of all camp sessions.

Recreational

Camp Doublecreek

Doublecreek Dr., Round Rock • (512) 255-3661

Swimming, archery, arts and crafts, gymnastics, basic horseback riding and more are packed into each week of your child's summer at Camp Doublecreek. This well-established camp for children ages 4 through 12 has been delighting campers for nearly 30 years. A special parents day program is presented every four weeks. Thirteen pickup points are set up around Austin and the camp day begins with camp songs and storytelling just as soon as children board the full-size buses that take them to this large acreage. Counselors are standing by at 7:30 AM to receive your child and buses return at 5 PM, although counselors remain until 5:30 PM. Camp Doublecreek holds an open house every Sunday from 3 to 5 PM for tours. To get to this farm, take Interstate 35 north from Austin to the F.M. 1325 Exit and go east for 2 miles. Take a left on Doublecreek Drive near the water tower and follow the road for 1.25 miles until it dead ends at the farm.

Crowe's Nest Farm, Inc.

9501 Sprinkle Rd. • (512) 926-3311

Children entering Kindergarten through 5th grades will enjoy this 100-acre farm filled with hands-on activities centered around the joys of nature and the care and feeding of farm animals. Campers get to milk cows, make butter, feed the animals, gather eggs and use microscopes to study life in the pond. Youngsters learn about native Texas animals like bobcats, hawks and raccoons, and see in-

INSIDERS' TIP

If you're here in the springtime, when the bluebonnets are in bloom, do what Austinites do and take your child's picture amidst the flowers. Professional photographers will do this for you, too.

jured birds of prey at Crowe's Nest rehab center. There are plenty of other fun-filled activities, including hayrides, crafts and theater arts. This half-day camp runs throughout the summer from 8:30 AM to 12:30 PM. On the final day of camp each week, children put on a show for parents. Crowe's Nest is also open during the school year for two-hour school tours at 9:30 and 11:30 AM weekdays and at 9:30 AM on Saturdays. Families are invited.

Ol' Cactus Jack Summer Day Camp

13433 U.S. Hwy. 71 W. • (512) 263-2388

Children ages 6 to 14 can choose between a half- or full-day schedule at Ol' Cactus Jack for their summer fun. Weekly sessions in June and July include horsemanship skills, riding, swimming, archery, hiking and arts and crafts. Sessions run 9 AM to 2 PM or 8 AM to 6 PM. These camps do sell out so sign up early. Ol' Cactus Jack is also a happening place around Halloween for kids and adults alike. The haunted hayrides held the last three weekends in October starting at dark are lots of fun. There's also a great haunted house out here in Southwest Austin in October, but be sure to know your child's fright level before you go. This one is scary! Ol' Cactus Jack, located on more than 300 acres of scenic Hill Country, offers company parties and guided trail rides throughout the year. Kids must be at least 8 years old but no experience is necessary. Just call for an appointment.

Spicewood Country School Camp

6102 Spicewood Springs Rd. • (512) 346-2992

Established in 1980, Spicewood Country School Camp offers a full day of camp activities for children ages 3 to 10. The two-week sessions include training in horseback riding and swimming as well as hiking, fishing, music, sports, arts and crafts and more. The large shady location provides a perfect setting for your day campers. The camp day is 9 AM to 3 PM with extended hours from 7:30 AM to 5:30 PM available.

Splish-Splash Summer Camp

2517 Enfield Rd. • (512) 477-2100

This camp has it all: sports, gardening, science, swimming, cooking, arts and crafts, nature hikes and overnight field trips. Designed for boys and girls ages 5 through 12, Splish-Splash offer two- and four-week sessions during the summer months. This camp is operated by the well-established Kids Are First daycare school, which has branches in several parts of town and Round Rock. Children can be dropped off at any one of the school's five locations, and they are transported in passenger vans to the Kids Are First location at 13121 Burnet Road in Northwest Austin for camp. Camp activities revolve around a different theme each week. Overnight field trips have included visits to Sea World and Splash Town in San Antonio, the Texas Ranger Museum in Waco and Bastrop State Park.

YMCA Summer Camps

1100 W. Cesar Chavez St. • (512) 476-6705

The YMCA offers an entire summer of an incredible range of activities for children ages 4 to 15. This excellent program, one of the most diverse in the city, includes one-week camps for children ages 5 to 12 at different sites throughout Austin. Camps include amazing artists, lawn sports, space odyssey, super swimmer, leather crafts, rollermania, mad scientist, free wheelin', trail blazers and olympic week. The Y also offers camps in softball,

INSIDERS' TIP

If you're planning to visit a major theme park like Schlitterbahn, Fiesta Texas or Sea World, be sure to check around for discount coupons. Most often you'll find something. See the local newspapers as well as grocery stores, fast food chains and shops. If you go to Schlitterbahn, most locals know to stake a claim on a picnic table early in the day. Put your coolers and towels there and make it your base of operations. Don't leave valuables, of course.

basketball, soccer, flag football, baseball, fishing, roller hockey, golf and cheerleading. Most of these camps run from 7:30 AM to 6 PM. For kids who want even more adventure, the Y offers the two-week Rainbow Ranch Outdoor Adventure day camp for kids ages 9 to 12. This camp at the Rainbow Ranch in nearby Buda, includes hiking, swimming, team sports, swimming, fishing, gardening and arts and crafts. It also includes an overnight camp-out. Transportation is provided daily from the Y's main Town Lake branch. For children ages 11 to 15, the Y offers two-week teen camps that include college tours, swimming, in-line skating, intramural sports, tubing, community service and much more. The Y's new summer program for 4- and 5-year-olds is held in Southwest Austin only and includes a range of indoor and outdoor activities, including swimming, music, computers, dramatic play and more. Enrollment for this program is limited. Many of the other camps do sell out, so sign up early. Call the above number for a complete brochure of summer camp fun.

Dance and Gymnastics

Alisa's Dance Academy

3267 Bee Caves Rd., Ste. 139
• (512) 327-2150

Alisa's summer camps are fun-filled, one-week, full- and half-day sessions for beginning and intermediate dancers ages 3 to 13. Packed into each session are classes in tap, jazz, ballet, theater, voice and choreography as well as in tumbling and arts and crafts. Students put on a great end-of-camp show for parents each week. Children ages 3 to 5 attend half-day sessions from 9 AM to 1 PM while older students attend from 9 AM to 5 PM. The littlest tykes, ages 2 to 4, may wish to sign up for weekly summer combo classes. The academy, which also offers dance classes for children and adults throughout the year

Photo: City of Austin

Zilker Park, in the heart of Austin, is a kids' delight.

and has its own dance company, is in the Westwood Shopping Center in West Austin.

Capital Gymnastics
13900 I-35 N. • (512) 251-2439

This well-established gymnastics program, recognized as a national team training center by the United States Association of Gymnastics, offers a full school year of gymnastics and cheerleading training at several Austin locations as well as a series of wonderful two-week summer camps at the SuperCenter location at the above address. Camp activities include gymnastics, swimming, arts and crafts, games, outside play-time, movies and much more. Children ages 5 to 13 may enroll in full- or half-day camps that run from 8 AM to 5 PM with extended hours available. Four-year-olds attend just half-day sessions. Throughout the school year, Capital Gymnastics, with three other Austin locations in North, Central and Northwest Austin, offers a wide range of classes for school-age boys and girls, parents, tots and preschoolers. There also are competitive teams for boys and girls, and much more. Call them for a complete brochure of classes and activities offered at each location. Capital Gymnastics also does birthday parties and has spring break camps, a moms' day out program and summer classes.

Dancers Workshop
11150 Research Blvd., Ste. 107 • (512) 349-7197

Dancers Workshop offers a full summer of excellent camps for beginning to advanced dancers ages 3 to 13. Experienced professional dancers and drama teachers present a full day of tap, ballet, jazz, voice and drama to 1st graders and older, while preschoolers attend just in the morning from 9 AM to 1 PM. Early morning and after work hours are also available. The weeklong camps end in a Friday evening in-studio performance for parents and friends. You'll be amazed at the dance steps your child can learn in just five days. Dancers Workshop also offers a drill team camp. While it's true, these camps are largely attended by girls, boys are welcome, too. Dancers Workshop also offers classes for both beginners and advanced dancers throughout the school year and has its own outstanding dance company. Call for details.

The Arts

Austin Chamber Music Center
4930 Burnet Rd., Ste. 203 • (512) 454-7562

For intermediate-level musicians and better, the Austin Chamber Music Center offers intensive training and rehearsing in a two-week day camp. The center accepts musicians from age 8 to 18 who play strings, winds and the piano. The center forms groups according to instrument, like string quartets, wind quintets and piano duos, but also mixes instruments. There are also recreation activities and a daily music presentation. This camp concentrates on providing excellent coaching as well as music theory and musicianship classes. Hours are 9 AM to 5:30 PM. This camp usually is held in early June. The Austin Chamber Music Center also offers a music academy throughout the school year.

Dougherty Arts Center
1110 Barton Springs Rd. • (512) 397-1458

This fine, age-specific summer program introduces young children to the visual and performing arts while taking older students to new levels of understanding and appreciation of the arts. Dougherty offers five two-week day camp sessions for children ages 3 to 14. Children ages 3 to 5 attend half-day sessions either in the morning or afternoon while older campers attend full-day sessions from 9 AM to 5 PM, with early and late extended hours available. Preschoolers are introduced to drama, movement, music and the visual arts through a variety of activities. The program for children ages 6 to 8 stresses both the performing and visual arts and focuses on learning the process of creating art, not so much on the product. Beginning at age 9 children may select from programs that specialize in just the visual arts or just the performing arts. There's a camp that teachers computer animation, including cartooning and claymation.

Parents of children starting school in September will be pleased to know that Dougherty also holds one-week camps in August for children ages 6 to 10. Classes in the visual and performing arts are offered throughout the school year for children and adults.

Kids Acting

The Acting Studio, 5811 Burnet Rd. • (512) 452-5989

One of Austin's most popular and well-established studios for young actors throughout the year, Kids Acting also offers a variety of full- and half-day summer camps for children ages 4 to 18. One of the main events here is the presentation of a full-scale musical production, which involves children ages 9 to 18. While the schedule may vary, Kids Acting most recently offered camps in variety show, in which children learn to sing, dance, act and do improvisational comedy; screen acting, which teaches campers to perform for television, film and commercials; play production, which focuses on learning to write, cast, costume, rehearse and perform a play; and combo camp, which combines aspects of all the camps. Kids Acting, established in 1981, presents a variety of musical theatrical shows with casts of young people throughout the year.

Texas Summer Music Academy

13112 Tamayo Dr. • (512) 331-9246

This two-week camp for budding musicians combines piano and vocal training with a variety of excellent activities designed to emphasize the fine arts. Students entering 4th, 5th and 6th grades participate in piano classes, a hand bell ensemble and take classes in music theory, music history and appreciation the first week and spend another week working on the vocal arts. The entire session includes music-related field trips, short concerts, music and dance seminars and performances, and recreational activities. The Texas Summer Music Academy ends in a major performance for family and friends. The academy is designed and operated by piano teacher Martha Buchanan and her partner, Kinley Lange, music and arts director at Austin's First Presbyterian Church. All instructors are professional musicians. And for a different perspective on music, there's the one-week World Music Camp, designed to demonstrate the fine arts as expressed in different countries. Through a variety of hands-on activities and demonstrations, students are introduced to dance and/or music from a different country each day. This camp also includes a daily choir class. Both camps run Monday through Friday from 8 AM to 3 PM, with extended hours available. The Music Academy usually is held in late July, while World Music is held toward the end of June.

Zachary Scott Theatre

1510 Toomey Rd. • (512) 476-6378 Ext. 236

One of Austin's finest professional theaters, Zachary Scott has been providing instruction to budding performers through its Performing Arts School since 1970. Zach's school offers a variety of summer and holiday camps for children ages 5 to 14. Youngsters ages 5 to 7 may enroll in half-day creative drama camps, which include singing, music, creative movement, dance and more. There's a full-day musical theater camp for kids ages 8 to 10 and 11 to 14 who love to sing and dance. Zach also offers a Theatre Variety Camp, also split into age groups, that includes acting basics, singing and vocal expression, comedy and improvisation as well as creative movement. And for those who yearn to do stand-up comedy, there's the comedy camp. This program teaches the ins and outs of modern improvisation. Camp hours are from 9 AM to 5 PM with optional extended hours available.

The Performing Arts School also offers acting, singing and comedy classes throughout the school year for young performers and holds auditions in late September and late January for the school's performance troupes. Yes, parents, Zach also offers classes for adults. By the way, Zach's two adult theater companies present shows specifically for preschool and school age children's groups.

Magic

The Magic Camp

7306 Scenic Brook Dr. • (512) 288-1596

Professional magician Kent Cummins is the wizard behind this exciting day camp for children ages 5 to 18. Campers learn magic tricks, juggling, puppetry and more as they follow a program designed to engage the imagination. Full-day camps are divided between children ages 7 through 9 and 10 through 12. Children ages 5 and 6 attend half-day sessions. And there's also a Performer's Academy for those 5 to 18 in which campers are assisted in developing their own act. The Magic Camp maintains a teacher-to-camper ratio of 1-to-5 or better, which includes adult staff members, teenage counselors and counselors in training. Guest performers and teachers are invited in to share their expertise throughout the sessions. Tuition includes all supplies.

The address listed above is The Magic Camp office. The camp itself is held elsewhere.

Cummins also has held weekend getaway Magic Camps for adults only.

Sports

Austin Yacht Club Junior Sailing Camps

5906 Beacon Dr. • (512) 266-1336

Designed for children 8 to 18, the Austin Yacht Club Junior Sailing Camp concentrates on teaching young sailors the basics of sailing on Sunfish and Optimists. Classes are divided for beginners to advanced so that each child gets the maximum benefit from the learning experience. The four-week camps, held on Lake Travis in June, last from 8 AM to 5 PM, but extended hours for working parents are available. Call the Yacht Club by April or May to sign up as these camps are limited in size and can fill up. And for you adults out there, the Yacht Club also offers a one-time summer learn-to-sail clinic. Call for details.

Bear Creek Stables

13017 Bob Johnson Rd. • (512) 282-0250

Bear Creek offers weekly horseback riding sessions all summer for children 7 to 16. Both boys and girls, beginners to advanced are taught Western pleasure and English horseback styles of riding on this 20-acre facility in Southwest Austin. Instructors, who stress that the emphasis is on the rider, also teach the care, grooming and feeding of horses. A covered arena is perfect for rainy days. There's a riding presentation for parents on the Friday of each session and each Wednesday is trail day. Hours are 8 AM to 4 PM, with extended hours available. Bear Creek also offers English and Western riding lessons.

Blue Star Riding Center

9513 S. U.S. Hwy. 183 • (512) 243-2583

Intermediate-level riders get to test their brain power and their knowledge of horses with a murder-mystery trail ride offered during their two-week session. Students must figure out whodunit by riding around the 50-acre ranch to find clues and interview witnesses. Blue Star, in business since 1985, also offers two-week sessions for beginning and advanced riders ages 8 to 18. Students are introduced to both Western and English styles of riding, and learn about the care and feeding of horses. The center debuted its new covered arena in 1998. Blue Star is in Southeast Austin, but campers are offered pick-up and drop-off service in Northeast, Northwest and Southeast Austin. The riding center is home to the Violet Crown Pony Club, where students learn to participate in Olympic-style riding and jumping events. Blue Star offers riding lessons throughout the year as well as winter holiday and spring break camps.

G.S.I. Scuba Camp

7500 U.S. Hwy. 71 W. • (512) 288-1005

Take your love of swimming to a deeper level in this weeklong camp that teaches participants to snorkel and scuba dive. The camp, taught by experienced, certified divers, is for kids 12 to 17 who know how to swim and want to become certified. Divers practice in a swimming pool and dive in Lake Travis, the San Marcos River and Canyon Lake. The camp is held at the G.S.I. Scuba Center in Southwest Austin, but there is a pick-up point in North Austin. Camp hours are 8 AM to 5 PM. Class space is limited.

Heart of Texas Baseball Camps

6514 McNeil Dr. • (512) 918-0158

Everyone gets to play baseball at these camps, designed for boys and girls 7 to 12. The weeklong, half-day camps include training in every aspect of the game for beginning to advanced players. Athletes receive both individual and team training, and each day ends with a game of baseball. These camps are coached by former UT and Atlanta Braves player Dodd Johnson as well as a team of current college players and ex-professionals. Camps are divided by age groups. There are camps for 7 and 8 year olds and for children 9 to 12. Heart of Texas also offers private and team instruction throughout the school year.

Wolfgang Suhnholz Soccer Academy

10409 Tweedsmuir Dr. • (512) 258-2277

This soccer academy, established in 1988, offers full- and half-day sessions for both beginning and advanced soccer players. Kids 5 to 15 enroll in these camps directed by Suhnholz, assistant coach for the U.S. National Team, Under 20 Division and technical director of both the Lone Stars professional soccer team and the Capital Soccer Club for youth. The program, which stresses the fundamentals of soccer play, is coached by Lone Stars players and Capital Soccer Club coaches. Students are divided by age group and by ability. There are three weeklong sessions offered during the summer as well as a Spring Break camp.

UT Sports Camps

At last count, The University of Texas offered 14 different summer sports camps for kids, representing every major sport. These intensive training programs, which have a stellar reputation in Austin, attract budding athletes from across the state. The camps vary in length and time, some as short as three days and others as long as seven days. Some of the biggest names in coaching today, namely UT's excellent professional coaches, design these programs and most often are on hand daily to provide instruction, and inspiration, to young athletes. Many times, campers are treated to appearances by their favorite UT sports stars. The camps can be attended either as a day camp or a supervised overnight camp in which players stay in a UT dormitory or residence hall. All camps except for golf are held at the appropriate sports facility on the UT campus, usually the ones used by the collegiate athletes themselves. Imagine the delight of a budding football player who gets to take the field at Darrell K Royal-Texas Memorial Stadium for the first time or the swimmer awed by the facilities at the Jamail Texas Swimming Center. Each camp is offered for only a short time during the summer so it's best to sign up early.

Longhorn Baseball Camp

(512) 471-5732

Held at Disch-Falk Field, home to the UT baseball team, and directed by UT's baseball coaching staff, the camp is open to all boys and girls between 7 and 18. There's an instructional and developmental camp, a specialty camp that focuses on key areas of hitting, pitching, defensive and offensive play, and an advanced camp for players between 15 and 18. Instruction covers all areas of the game. With a 1-to-4 coach-to-camper ratio, campers receive individual instruction aimed at helping each student reach his or her full potential.

Boys Basketball Camp

(512) 471-5816

UT head basketball coach Rick Barnes, his staff and some of the best high school and collegiate coaches from across the state provide instruction to campers on shooting, passing, defense, rebounding, ball handling and teamwork. The weeklong camps, for boys 8 to 18, feature individualized instruction, daily league games and tournaments, guest speakers and a report card and discussion of the player's individual skills. Campers are grouped

INSIDERS' TIP

Austin toymakers Georgean and Paul Kyle have been in business nearly a quarter-century. Look for their shop when you want that special something for your child. Austin also has custom-made pinatas — something you don't find everywhere. See the Toys section of our Shopping chapter.

according to age and ability level. The camp is held in the newly renovated Gregory Gym on the UT Campus, but there are also satellite camps held in other Central Texas locations.

Girls Basketball Camp

(512) 471-8822

Conducted by Coach Jody Conradt, the winningest coach in collegiate women's basketball history, these camps offer intense basketball instruction with an emphasis on the fundamentals of dribbling, passing and shooting as well as offensive and defensive positions. The camp, for players age 10 through high school, groups players according to age and skill level. These are challenging, competitive camps filled with plenty of drills and competitions. There's also an elite varsity camp for varsity players who want to improve their games. Current and former Longhorn players and talented coaches from across the state contribute to the coaching staff of this superb camp. Sessions are held at Gregory Gym on the UT campus.

Longhorn Diving Camp

(512) 471-7794

Open to boys and girls 12 to 18 and held at the Jamail Texas Swimming Center, one of the finest swimming facilities in the United States, the summer diving camp draws athletes from around the country. Each seven-day camp offers excellent learning opportunities and a challenging training environment for divers of all abilities. Divers attend lectures about the mechanics of diving, movement and mental focus. They also receive two diving training sessions and an extensive exercise/stretching/spotting session each day. Instruction is provided in all areas of competitive diving, including tower diving.

Longhorn Football Camp

(512) 471-3050

Longhorn head coach Mack Brown directs this program and makes sure each player gets individual attention from the large staff of UT coaches and excellent high school football coaches. Junior Camp is for players entering 4th through 8th grades and is especially designed for the younger players. For older players in grades 9 through 12, there's a skills camp and a lineman camp. Each camp includes lectures, video tape evaluations, daily film study, speed development, weight training instruction, flexibility instruction and more. These camps are held for four, very long days. Camp runs from 9 AM to 7:30 PM.

Longhorn Golf Camp

(512) 471-6169

For boys and girls 11 to 18, the UT golf camp is held at Austin Area golf courses. The one- or two-week, full-day sessions have been held in June. Young golfers receive instruction in all the fundamentals of the game.

Speed Running Day Camp

(512) 471-3931

Not just for future track stars, this camp will help any young athlete, even those who play football, basketball and softball. This three-day camp, for boys and girls 8 to 18, is designed to provide instruction in the mechanics of running mobility and flexibility, weight training and speed development. The camp includes training in elastic strength, lateral speed and backward speed.

Soccer Academy

(512) 471-3624

Young athletes who are serious about playing competitive soccer would do well to check out UT's Soccer Academy. These one-week programs are designed for developing elite or highly competitive soccer players and teams. There's a day camp for boys and girls ages 6 and older in which campers choose between the 3½-hour morning or evening session. Older children ages 12 and older are offered an one-week overnight only camp filled with competi-

INSIDERS' TIP

No matter how much you adore your little ones, sometimes you just want to have an afternoon or an evening to yourself while you're on vacation. See our chapter on Schools and Child Care for some great babysitting options.

tive soccer instruction. This camp is directed by Dang Pibulvech, UT head soccer coach.

Longhorn Softball Camp

(512) 232-2046

Held at UT's new McCombs Field, this softball camp is designed for girls 9 and older and includes training in the fundamentals and strategy. The three camp sessions offered include the four-day all-skills camp that lasts from 9:30 AM to 8 PM, the pitcher/catcher camp, which includes three days of all-day instruction, and the elite varsity camp for players in 10th through 12th grades. Connie Clark, UT head softball coach, directs this great program.

Longhorn Swimming Camp

(512) 475-8652

Designed for male and female competitive swimmers 8 and older, the Longhorn Swimming Camp focuses on intensive long-course conditioning, stroke instruction and analysis. Campers are required to have competitive swimming experience and to be planning to continue competing. This camp is divided into four ability groups. Camp includes swimming-specific dryland exercises, strength training and flexibility exercises. Depending on ability level, long course training lasts from one to two hours daily. Daily training also includes two 1½-hour sessions on technique. This camp is held at UT's fabulous Jamail Texas Swimming Center. The six-day sessions go from 8:30 AM to 8 PM. The camps are directed by Eddie Reese, UT men's swimming coach, and Jill Sterkel, women's head coach.

Longhorn Tennis Camp

(512) 471-4404

The Penick-Allison Tennis Center, one of the finest collegiate tennis facilities in the United States, is home to the annual Longhorn Tennis Camp. This program for boys and girls 10 to 18 offers skills training as well as important motivational and psychological training tools. The sessions are directed by both UT men's and women's head tennis coaches and include an experienced staff of college coaches, high school coaches and men and women collegiate players. The six-day, all-day camp includes private instruction, supervised play, mental training, team competition and more. There's also one session dedicated to elite players. This camp always fills up quickly.

Track and Field/Cross Country Camp

(512) 471-3931

Aimed at boys and girls ages 11 to 17, this camp allows athletes to choose from among several areas of specialization, including distance/cross country, sprints, high jump, pole vault, hurdles, long jump/triple jump, shot/discus and middle-distance running. This camp aims to help junior high and high school athletes improve their athletic performance by increasing their knowledge of the sport and their fitness levels. It is taught by some of the best track and field/cross country coaches in the nation. This four-day session is held from 8 AM to 5 PM.

Texas Volleyball Camp

(512) 471-0804

For girls entering 5th through 12th grades, the Texas Volleyball Camp shows young players how it is that UT women win so many games. This camp, under the leadership of head coach Jim Moore, provides instruction in all areas of the game. Skills camps emphasize the fundamentals, and on-court instruction is provided in serving, serve receiving, forearm passing, setting, attacking, team defense, blocking and more. These camps end in a tournament. The setter/hitter camps are for girls entering 7th through 12th grades. The elite camp is for varsity-level players. The Texas Volleyball Camp, held at the newly renovated Gregory Gym, offers several different sessions.

Springtime is the most
active of all seasons
when it comes to
outdoor fiestas
and festivals.

Annual Events and Festivals

Weekends are the raison d'etre for life in Austin, at least that is what the calendar might lead you to think. The weekday workdays are the equivalent of bench time, as far as many Austinites are concerned.

The generally benign climate affords residents and visitors the opportunity to live life outdoors, and perhaps that is why so many weekend activities are linked to appreciation of sun, sky and landscape. It is significant to note that springtime is the most active of all seasons when it comes to outdoor fiestas and festivals. This, after all, is when the Hill Country blossoms, the sun shines and the sky is generally blue. (It is also the time when hotels are full and few rental cars are available.)

It is impossible to list all the annual events and festivals that take place in Austin and the surrounding Central Texas area. We have chosen our favorites and those that are both widely popular and long standing. Outdoor events tend to outnumber indoor happenings on this list, reflecting not only the climate, but also the local fondness for outdoor celebration. That is not to say there is a lack of indoor weekend activities — theater, music, books, and film are drawing cards for a number of well-established annual events.

Another characteristic of this list is the number of annual events that celebrate local culture, ethnic traditions and historic events. Texans, nonnatives and newcomers will note, are eager to explore their past and have a strong sense of their state's history and culture. Many of the local festivals celebrate that sentiment.

Other events are just sheer expressions of what could be called Texas joy, an embracing of local life and folkways. Whether it is a Woodstock-style romp or an old-fashioned church picnic, the operative word is celebration. So go forth and celebrate!

One note before you do: Admission prices, times and even dates may vary from those listed. Many events are sponsored by nonprofit groups that face the vagaries of economic needs and demands. It is a good idea to check the local media and make a call for additional information before you go; however, should you strike out, don't worry, there is sure to be a weekend event going on somewhere in Central Texas on any given Saturday or Sunday.

January

Citywide Garage Sale and Antique Show

City Coliseum, 101 Dawson St. • (512) 441-7133

This is the first of usually once-a-month sales at the downtown Coliseum, which is located on the southern banks of Town Lake, just west of Palmer Auditorium. Most are scheduled in mid-month and are widely advertised. The merchandise varies from kitschy items to genuine finds. (See the Citywide Garage Sale listing in our Shopping chapter.) Admission is $3.

Austin Boat & Fishing Show

Austin Convention Center, 500 E. Cesar Chavez Blvd. • (512) 404-4404

In a city where water recreation is a major pastime for many residents, this annual show is a popular winter event. The shows runs for four days, usually from noon to 10 PM on Thursday and Friday, 10 AM to 10 PM on Saturday and 10 AM to 6 PM on Sunday. The admission charge is $5 for those 13 and older, $2.50 for children 6 to 12 and seniors, and free for children younger than 6.

FronteraFest

Hyde Park Theatre, 511 W. 43rd St. • (512) 454-TIXS

Local theater critic Michael Barnes has called this "the most exciting fringe festival in the Southwest," and described it as "a Quaker meeting for Austin theater." The annual performance festival runs for five weeks beginning in late January and includes more than 50 productions put on under the auspices of Frontera @ Hyde Park Theatre, the theater company in one of Austin's most popular neighborhoods in Central Austin (see Hyde Park in our Neighborhoods chapter and Frontera Theatre in our Arts chapter). The events afford theater artists an opportunity to explore new territory and, as Barnes says, push the limits. Ticket prices vary and usually begin at around $3. Discount passes are available.

February

Motorola Marathon

(512) 505-8304

The first Motorola-sponsored marathon was run in 1991, but this relative newcomer is becoming more well-known and has been described as the fastest-growing in the country. The number of participants has grown to 2,100 in 1998 competing for a first-place purse of $5,000. Running experts give the sponsors top marks for organization. The course runs from far Northwest Austin towards downtown, ending up on the shores of Town Lake. The race is usually held on the second Sunday of the month. Participation prices range from around $35 to $100, depending on whether participants are running the marathon course, or as a relay team in the 26-mile race. The organizer of the race is RunTex, the running store with two locations in Austin (see the running section in our Parks and Recreation chapter). Registration and prices, even the course, vary each year, so it's a good idea to go by or call RunTex at (512) 472-3254.

Old Gruene Market Days

Gruene • (210) 629-5077

Once a ghost town south of Austin and north of New Braunfels, this revived community is just west of I-35 and the northern banks of the Guadalupe River. The historic community is now a popular home for artists and crafters. Beginning in February, vendors selling Texas crafts and foods gather here for market days, held on the third Saturday and Sunday of each month. In December the market is held on the first weekend of the month. (See our Daytrips chapter for more information on Gruene.)

Carnaval Brasileiro

Austin City Coliseum, 101 Dawson St. • (512) 452-6832

For more than 20 years, Austin has danced to the Brazilian beat of samba in a pre-Lenten festival of conga lines, costumes and cacophony. A couple of thousand or more revelers gather, usually the Saturday before Lent, which can fall in February or March, to emulate Rio's famous Carnival. The costumes are hilarious and sometimes minimalist, which makes this a decidedly grown-up affair. The live music features top names in samba, including some who have performed in Brazil. The music gets under way around 8 PM and doesn't stop until the early hours of the morning. Tickets are $20 and are on sale are various popular record and bookstores in Austin.

March

Riverfest

Along the Colorado River • (888) TEXAS FUN

This is a conglomeration of festivals that takes place along a 500-mile stretch of the Colorado River. The Lower Colorado River Authority (LCRA) has united all these various fes-

Photo: Peter A. Silva

Let your spirits soar at the annual kite-flying contest.

tivals that occur from March through early May under the Riverfest umbrella and coordinates information on them. A complete list can be requested by calling the toll-free telephone number. Events take place in small and large communities, including Austin, from San Saba and Lampasas Counties northwest of the city to the Gulf Coast. They include a spring craft fair in El Campo, the Lometa Diamondback Jubilee (Diamondbacks, as in rattlesnakes) in late March and the River Rendezvous in La Grange for canoeing enthusiasts in late April. There are also nature celebrations and birding events, wildflower festivals and watersports.

Austin/Travis County Livestock Show & Rodeo

Travis County Exposition and Heritage Center, 7311 Decker Ln.
• (512) 467-9811

For two weeks in mid-March country music fans flock to the livestock and rodeo show at the Expo Center in far East Austin. The stars include musicians like Merle Haggard, Kathy Mattea and Rick Trevino. The live music begins after the rodeo performances each night. Rodeo begins at 7:30 PM, and the music usually starts two hours later. In addition to the music, there are livestock shows, a carnival, barbecue and food booths and children's activities. Admission to the grounds is $3, plus $5 for parking. Tickets for the rodeo are $8 to $14. There is extensive coverage of the event in the local media. One note: The show overlaps with SXSW Festival, (see our Close-up in this chapter) and hotel rooms and rental cars are at a premium in March. (See our chapter on Spectator Sports for more information.)

Spring Festival and Texas Craft Exhibition

Winedale, near Round Top
• (409) 278-3530

This tiny village near Round Top, some 90 miles east of Austin, has served as the center for study of Texas culture under the auspices of the University of Texas. The collection of historic buildings was preserved by Ima Hogg, daughter of a Texas governor, who donated the land and buildings to the university. The Round Top area is now a center for cultural events and antique shops, and home to artists and crafters. There are several festivals and events throughout the year that are well worth attending. (See our Daytrips chapter for more information on this historic area.) The third weekend in March, Winedale holds its annual Spring Festival and Texas Crafts Exhibition. This area is an easy drive from Austin but worth an overnight stay at one of the country bed and breakfasts in the area.

Taylor Jaycees National Rattlesnake Sacking Championship

Murphy Park, Lake Dr., Taylor • (512) 365-1988

Not for the faint of heart, this annual event takes place in the small community of Taylor, northeast of Austin. Despite the fast-encroaching suburbs of Round Rock and Georgetown, Taylor is a small town with a rich history and a tradition of spending the first weekend in March sacking snakes. Amateur teams compete for the prize; even young snake handlers test their skills. Professional snake handlers are on hand to show how its done. Visitors can also answer that age-old question — does fried rattlesnake meat taste like chicken? Ticket prices are $6 for those 13 and older, $1 for children 6 to 12, free for children younger than 6.

Zilker Kite Festival

Zilker Park, 2100 Barton Springs Rd. • (512) 499-6700

March winds help more than 200 handmade kites take flight in one of the city's most popular free outdoor events. Usually held on the second Sunday of the month in the city's large downtown park, the festival is sometimes postponed because of spring rains. Anyone can come fly a kite, but there is also an organized competition. Categories includes the smallest kite, the strongest-pulling kite, the highest and the most creative kite, but everyone's favorite is the largest kite. The event begins at 11 AM. Given Austin's growth, parking at Zilker Park events can be headache. In addition to parking in the park, additional space is available under the MoPac overpass to the west.

April

The Annual Austin Rugby Tournament

Zilker Park, 2100 Barton Springs Rd. • (512) 288-3384

Since 1968 this rugby tournament has attracted enthusiasts from across the region. Organizers tout it as the oldest and largest rugby tournament in the Southwest. There are several divisions of play in the two-day tournament and, true to rugby tradition, a post-tournament party on Sixth Street. (See the Rugby section in our Parks and Recreation chapter for more information on the local rugby scene.)

The Texas Relays

The University of Texas Memorial Stadium, San Jacinto St. at Manor Rd. • (512) 471-3333, (800) 982-BEVO

The relays have been run at UT for more than 70 years and feature top high school and collegiate track and field competitors from across the nation. Usually scheduled for the first weekend in April, sessions begin on Friday morning and end Saturday afternoon. The preliminaries are held on Wednesday and Thursday and are free. Ticket prices are $3 for Friday daytime; $5 for adults and $3 for youths Friday evening; $7 and $3 respectively on Saturday. An all-session ticket costs $10. Call the 800 number for additional information and advanced ticket purchase.

Old Settler's Music Festival

Old Settler's Park, Round Rock • (512) 346-1629

This two-day festival, held on the first weekend of the month, celebrates acoustic, bluegrass, jazz and folk music in a park setting. Music lovers can camp out for the event. Tickets are $32 at the gate, a few dollars cheaper if purchased ahead of the festival, for each day's events, or $56 for a weekend pass. Tickets for children younger than 17 are half-price. Camping is free.

The Bob Marley Festival

Auditorium Shores, Riverside Dr. and S. First St. • (512) 447-2382

This laid-back music concert celebrates the life of reggae singer Bob Marley. There's no admission charge, but attendees are asked to bring a donation for the food bank. The event has collected more than 100,000 pounds of food for the needy. The all-day festival features both local and national reggae favorites.

Annual Bluebonnet Festival

Historic Square, Burnet • (512) 756-4297

This is one of several Hill Country events celebrating the wildflower season. Burnet is northwest of Austin on U.S. Highway 281. In addition to an arts and craft show, children's activities, a parade and 5K and 10K runs, the festival also features a golf tournament, a classic car show and special appearances by the Confederate Air Force, an association of vintage airplane owners. The events are scheduled over two weekends in mid-April. The festival is held in conjunction with the Highland Lakes Bluebonnet Trail, a scenic route through the Hill Country where many of the best stands of wildflowers can be viewed. Maps and stories about the best bluebonnet spots are frequently printed in the Austin newspaper.

Big Stinkin' International Improv & Sketch Comedy Festival

Various locations • (512) 912-7837

This comedy festival was launched in 1995 and has grown with each year. National and homegrown comics participate in the five-day festival, and events are held at more than 20 venues throughout the city, including some of the top nightclubs and theatre venues.

Easter Fires Pageant

Gillespie County Fairgrounds, Texas Hwy. 16, Fredericksburg • (830) 997-2359

More than 100 years ago, the story goes, settlers around Fredericksburg met with Native Americans at Eastertime for peace talks. The campfires could be seen burning in the night as talks went on. A pioneer mother and her children looked out over the hills, saw the fires, and the mother attempted to calm the children's fears by telling them a tale: The Easter Rabbit had started the fires to boil the eggs for Easter Sunday. And that's why every year, on the Saturday before Easter, hundreds of people dressed in bunny suits, others dressed as Native Americans and settlers celebrate with a nighttime pageant in this Hill Country town, west of Austin. (See our Daytrips chapter for more on Fredericksburg.) This event blends local folklore with history and religion, and the sight of hundreds of people in bunny suits is not to be missed. Box seats are $9, reserved seating is $7, general admission is $5 for adults and $1.50 for children.

Easter Pageant

Sunken Garden, San Gabriel Park, Georgetown • (512) 930-4649

This popular outdoor pageant is held Easter weekend in a natural setting in Georgetown's major city park, just north of Round Rock, and a short ride north up I-35 from Austin. The pageant, which features a large cast and a variety of live animals, is a musical drama telling the life of Jesus Christ. There are about 300 seats set up at the site, but the crowds are often larger, so many attendees bring lawn chairs and blankets. There are three free performances, Saturday at 4 PM, Sunday at 7 AM and 4 PM. Note: Since the date of Easter is subject to the religious calendar, performance times are subject to change, depending on whether Daylight Savings Time has gone into effect.

Spamarama

Auditorium Shores, Riverside Dr. and S. First St. • (512) 834-1827

Spam sushi? Spam kebobs? Perhaps Spam Jell-O? This annual event, dubbed the "Pandemonious Party of Potted Pork," is a tribute to that World War II staple, Spam, the potted ham that was pulled out of GI knapsacks in the woods of Germany and on the islands of the South Pacific. Cooks, some of them serious professional chefs, compete for prizes, but for those who would rather play with their food there is a Spam Toss, a Spam Relay featuring a Spam baton and, of course, a Spam Jam. The latter does not involving strumming a Spam slice, but it does feature some of Austin's live bands and popular musicians. In recent years Steve Fromholz and the Uranium Savages have been on the menu. The cooking contest judges include celebrities like musician-author Kinky Friedman. Usually held on the second Saturday of April, the location has changed over the years so check the enter-

INSIDERS' TIP

The Austin Convention Center maintains a calendar hotline, (512) 404-4404, for events at three major city facilities, the Convention Center, Palmer Auditorium and the Coliseum.

tainment listings in the local paper. Admission is $5.

Spring Fling

Travis County Farmers' Market, 6701 Burnet Rd. • (512) 454-1002

The market kicks off the growing season with a celebration of local produce, including herbs, vegetables, flowers and fruits. Since this is Austin, the live music capital of the world, there is music to serenade the springtime. Usually held on a Saturday early in the month, the Fling is just one of several annual events at the market, which is located in North Austin. The facility has outdoor stalls, specialty shops and restaurants. (See our Shopping and Restaurants chapters for more information on the market.) Admission is free.

Spring Herb Festival

Fredericksburg Herb Farm, 402 Whitney St., Fredericksburg • (830) 997-8615

Everything you always wanted to know about herbs, from growing them to cooking with them, using them for health, home and body, can be learned at this Hill Country herb farm festival. The Fredericksburg Herb Farm is a working farm that also operates as a spa, restaurant, a bed and breakfast, and tea room. The farm is a favorite shopping and overnight stay spot in Fredericksburg (see our Daytrips chapter) and a very popular destination during the spring wildflower season. Headquarters for the 14-acre farm is a restored historic limestone building six blocks south of Main Street off Milam Street. The farm's owners also operate a shop at 241 E. Main Street. The spring fair held in mid-April, Friday evening, Saturday and Sunday, and features plant sales, demonstrations, tours, food and music. Admission is $3.

Johnson City Market Days

U.S. Hwy. 290, Johnson City • (830) 868-7684

This two-day weekend festival in mid-April takes advantage of the usually glorious spring weather and wildflower scenes in the Hill Country west of Austin. The festival features artists' demonstrations, arts and crafts sales, food and live music. President Lyndon B. Johnson's boyhood home (see our Daytrips chapter) at the nearby Johnson Settlement is the scene for cowboy songs and poetry readings that celebrate the Texas frontier life. There is a small admission to some events.

Paddlefest

Town Lake • (512) 473-2644, (888) TEXAS FUN

This annual event, usually held the third Saturday in April, is part of the Lower Colorado River Authority's Riverfest celebration (see the general listing in March). The downtown Austin event features canoe and kayak racing for all ages and levels of expertise. One popular event is the 25K course that calls for kayak professionals to get out of the water and carry their boats for a stretch of the shoreline — called a portage. These competitors are canoe and kayak professionals who are competing for spots on the national team. Free brochures about Riverfest and Paddlefest can be requested by calling the toll-free number above.

The Real Antique Show

The Gillespie County Fairgrounds, Texas Hwy. 16, Fredericksburg • (830) 995-2884

This annual show, usually held on the third weekend in April, is dubbed the biggest antique show in the Hill Country. Given the popularity of weekend getaways in Fredericksburg and the large number of antique shops and historic homes in the town, this show is extremely popular. Less than a two-hour drive from Austin, it is an easy daytrip (see our Daytrips chapter), but there is so much to see and do in Fredericksburg that many visitors go for a weekend. Make plans for overnight stays ahead of time. Admission to the antique show is $3.50

Wildflower Day in the Spring

Lyndon Baines Johnson State Park, U.S. Hwy. 290, Stonewall • (830) 644-2252

When you stroll through the meadows of President Lyndon B. Johnson's ranch, it is so easy to understand the love of Texas wildflowers that inspired Lady Bird Johnson to embark on a lifetime of work to beautify America. Any spring weekend will afford visitors wonderful views and an opportunity to enhance their understanding of the Johnson family's love for this countryside; however, the park sets aside the third weekend of the month to

South by Southwest

In the dozen years since the first SXSW Music and Media Conference (South by Southwest for the uninitiated) was held it has grown to significant proportions. There is so much energy and growth and creativity associated with this annual festival that it literally takes over the city, as nightclubs, theatres, conference halls, restaurants and hotels get in on the action. The economic impact on Austin is estimated in the millions, perhaps as much as $20 million, and the number of musicians and entertainment professionals is counted in the thousands.

In addition to the SXWS Music festival, there is now a SXSW Film Festival and Conference and a SXSW Interactive Festival. The essence of the festival is to produce a creative critical mass that spills out and energizes all who come into contact with it. Hence, the city of Austin is awash in musicians, filmmakers and high-tech multimedia types for the last two weeks of March. (A word of warning to anyone planning to come to Austin during the festival — make your hotel, air and car rental reservations well in advance.)

In the beginning, the conference was seen as a vehicle to focus attention on the Texas music scene, the so-called Third Coast. The festival is still kicked off at the Austin Music Hall with the Austin Music Awards, a decidedly funky version of the Grammys in which winners are chosen by the public at large — and top names in Austin music perform. The local alternative newspaper, *The Austin Chronicle*, organized the first festival (and remains a primary host), but the conference quickly grew and has expanded at record rates every year. The number of bands participating is approaching the 1,000 mark, performing at more than 50 venues in Austin. The acts include national and international headliners such as Asleep at the Wheel, Johnny Cash, Arlo Guthrie, Doug Sahm, Soul Asylum, Leon Rausch, Johnny Gimble, The Derailers, Kacy Crowley, Trish Murphy, Ana Egee, Lucinda Williams and the list goes on. So extensive is the performance list that SXSW press releases tend to look like the contract you sign to buy a refrigerator at Sears: yards and yards of tiny print. Reading that list of band names can be amusing — 17 Hippies, a 47-piece band from Berlin, Germany, kicked off the 1998 keynote address.

Everyone is on alert during the festival to seek out the next wave. The panelists at the conference count among their numbers major record producers and influential music and film professionals who have come to view SXSW, according to festival sponsors, as "one of the most influential musical events in the world."

While conference participants sign up for the whole shebang of seminars and panel discussions ("Parenting in the Music Business" and "So IS Paul Dead?"), music enthusiasts opt to pay for a wristband that allows them to roam the nightclub scene and hear as many of the bands as possible. Conference fees cost several hundred dollars, but wristbands have been described as affordable. However, grumbling has been heard in recent years as wristband prices approached $100.

Availability of wristbands and their price have caused rumors of rebellion in the Austin ranks, but that has not detracted from the success of SXSW.

The creators of SXSW also launched a SXSW Film Festival, which has been described as "early Sundance" since entrants must be chosen by a panel in order to show their films. The four-day festival includes panels, workshops, meetings, mentor sessions, demo reel sessions and the presentation of more than 150 films at various locations in Austin. Major agents, directors and up-and-coming film producers attend.

Another spin-off festival held in conjunction with the film and music conferences is

— continued on next page

the SXSW Interactive Festival dedicated to discussions and explorations of new media technology. Again, there are panel discussions, star speakers and a trade show featuring local and national high-tech companies. The entertainment events include such things as cyberoperas and intercontinental Internet concerts.

The best way to absorb all the SXSW possibilities is to get on the mailing list. Write to SXSW, P.O. Box 4999, Austin, TX 78765, call (512) 467-7979, or fax at (512) 451-0754.

To learn more about music in Austin, read The Music Scene chapter.

hold special events celebrating the wildflowers. (For more information on the LBJ State Park, see our Daytrips chapter.)

Market Days

Wimberley Lions Field, Wimberley • (512) 847-2201

On the first Saturday of every month from April to December more than 400 vendors gather in Wimberley, southwest of Austin, to sell an assortment of arts, crafts, antiques, collectibles and kitsch. This is one of the most popular flea markets in central Texas. (See our Shopping chapter for more information.)

The Texas Hill Country Wine & Food Festival

Various locations • (512) 329-6431

Texas chefs, vintners, cheesemakers, herb growers and gourmands gather in Austin on the first weekend in April to celebrate Texas wine and foods. The first festival was held in 1985 and was the brainchild of several nationally and internationally recognized chefs, including Dean Fearing, executive chef of Dallas' Mansion on Turtle Creek, and Robert Del Grande, executive chef of Houston's Cafe Annie. The festival is headquartered at Austin's downtown Four Seasons Hotel, but events also take place at restaurants, posh and funky, throughout the city and locations outside the city. Experts in cuisine, wine, cigars, famous chefs and culinary authors from across the country conduct seminars and tastings, create special menus and host field trips. Admission to events varies from $175 a ticket for a celebration dinner to $35 for a Taste of Texas sampler, featuring Texas foods, wine and beer at a country barbecue. Chocolate cigars might be the dessert at a dinner, while bock-beer-battered quail is likely to be on the menu at the outdoor tasting. For a brochure and information write to the festival at 1006 MoPac Circle, Suite 102, Austin, TX 78746.

Liberty Hill Festival

Downtown Liberty Hill • (512) 515-5075

A small community, located in western Williamson County off Texas Highway 29, Liberty Hill is feeling the hot breath of urban growth on its neck, but that has not taken the fun out of the town festival. In fact, it has just made it more popular. This old-fashioned celebration, usually held on the last Saturday of the month, features a pet parade, a cute baby contest, horseshoe and washers tournament, arts and crafts stalls, a carnival and a barbecue at the VFW Hall. On Sunday afternoon there is a gospel sing and covered-dish dinner at Foundation Park. Admission varies for events.

Eeyore's Birthday Party

Pease Park, Parkway St. off W. 12th St. • (512) 448-5160

There is an old line about Austin being an elephant's graveyard for hippies, the place where all the old hippies come to die. Of course, many of them never left, judging from the number of old Hondas and VWs on the road. Some even had new little hippies to add to the population. But you don't have to be a full-time flower child to enjoy Eeyore's Birthday; however, it helps if you have a touch of Woodstock in your heart. (That makes it easier to understand the Summer of Love drumbeat.) Both old and young free spirits meet on the final Saturday of the month at Pease Park in Central Austin to listen to music, dress up (costumes with a pun are favored), paint their faces, dance, watch the jugglers — all for free from mid-morning to sunset. Despite the Winnie the

Pooh connection, Eeyore's Birthday Party might not be suitable for children. Area residents have complained about parking problems and the behavior of a few of the celebrants at this annual event, prompting calls for the party to be moved. So far, those lobbying for a move have been unsuccessful.

Safari

Austin Nature Center, West Zilker Park • (512) 451-3003

This annual family festival on the last weekend of the month is a celebration of nature and a great event for a family outing. There are wildlife and environmental exhibits, games, entertainment, food, hands-on crafts activities and rides. It is learning disguised as fun and a great way for children to become familiar with both their natural surroundings and the resources the nature center offers year round (see our Kidstuff chapter). Admission is $5. The fun begins at 10 AM and ends at 6 PM Saturday and Sunday. Check the newspaper for special parking arrangements and shuttle bus plans.

Yesterfest and the Salinas Art Festival

Bastrop City Park and Main St., Bastrop • (512) 321-6283

Bastrop, the historic, small community just east of Austin on Texas Highway 71, is a town that has worked hard at maintaining its ties to the past. Several historic buildings line Main Street where the art festival takes place on the third Saturday of the month. Out at the city park, the locals celebrate their pioneer past with historical exhibits, re-enactments, craft demonstrations, music and food. Native American dancers perform, cloggers and banjo players entertain, pipes and drum corps members join in Civil War re-enactments, Scottish dancers make note of the town's ties to the Old Country, and it all winds up in a Main Street dance at night and a campfire stew dinner. Admission to the park is $3, $1 for children 13 and younger. Parking is available at the Bastrop High School, and shuttles run to the park. Yesterfest begins at 10 AM and closes at 5 PM.

Austin Auto Show

Austin Convention Center, 505 E. Cesar Chavez St. • (512) 404-4404

This four-day spring show held late in the month features the latest cars, trucks and vans. Hours are Thursday from noon to 10 PM, Friday and Saturday from 10 AM to 10 PM and Sunday from 10 AM to 6 PM. Admission is $5, children younger than 12 are admitted free.

Wildflowers Days Festival

Lady Bird Johnson National Wildflower Research Center, 4801 La Crosse Ave. • (512) 292-4100

The research center celebrates the Hill Country spring wildflower season with a daylong festival featuring native plant experts and authors, an arts and crafts exhibit and live music. Admission is $3.50 for adults, $2 for students and seniors, and $1 for children 5 and younger.

The Capitol 10,000

Downtown, shores of Town Lake • (512) 445-3596

This 10K race is listed among the top 100 road races in the country by *Runner's World* magazine. First held in 1978, it has become a very popular event and attracts approximately 15,000 competitors and hundreds of spectators. The runners — and walkers —

INSIDERS' TIP

One of the charms of life in the Hill Country is the identity many small communities have maintained despite growth and change. These small towns hold annual festivals that offer a glimpse of Texas' past. We've listed several of them, but one local writer, Richard Zelade, has devised driving tours of the Hill Country that include a lot of background information about these Texas towns. His book, *Texas Monthly Guidebook to the Hill Country*, is published by Gulf Publishing.

include famous Texans (Gov. George W. Bush has run), the not so famous, the young and the old. There are many wheelchair athletes also. The course changes every year but always ends on the shores of Town Lake. Entry fees vary. Participants are given a free T-shirt by the major race sponsor, the *Austin American-Statesman*. The shirt features the work of Pulitzer Prize-winning cartoonist Ben Sargent.

Theater Week

Various locations in Austin • (512) 320-7168

This weeklong event, usually held the second week in April, is designed to introduce newcomers and people unfamiliar with the city's theatrical community to the Austin theater scene. The events include special performances and ticket offers, plus behind-the-scenes tours. The offerings run the gamut from musicals, classics, comedies and locally written productions. The Austin Circle of Theaters organizes the event and information on tickets and performance times are available from the theater hotline number above.

The University of Texas Press Book Sale

2100 Comal St. • (512) 471-7233

Usually held in late April or early May, this annual sale is a great place to find book bargains, especially books on subjects like Texana, Latin-American studies, archaeology, Texas and Western history, plus titles that represent doctoral dissertations on subjects of all sorts. The sale is advertised in the local media. Early birds get the best selection.

May

Zilker Garden Festival

Austin Garden Center, Zilker Botanical Gardens, 2200 Barton Springs Rd. • (512) 477-8672

To paraphrase the pitch for a popular local public television show, *Central Texas Gardener*, what flourishes in gardens elsewhere can end up in the compost heap in Austin — too much rain, too much drought, sudden frost, too much heat, too much shade, too much sun. But gardening enthusiasts can find the answers at this, the largest annual garden show in the city. Sponsored by 40 local garden clubs and plant societies, the festival offers plants for sale, advice and garden crafts as well as brochures and books for the gardener's library. Newcomers can roam the gardens at the center and gain insight and inspiration as to what will grow in Central Texas. The show is a two-day event, usually on the first weekend of the month. Admission is $4.

The O. Henry World Championship Pun-Off

O. Henry Museum, Fourth St. at Neches in Brush Park • (512) 397-1465

If you are a pun-lover, and apparently there are hundreds of them in Austin, this is the event for you. Each year, on the first Sunday in May, up to 2,000 people gather at the O. Henry Museum (see our Attractions chapter) to watch and participate in the pun-off. The famous short-story writer William Sydney Porter, who wrote under the nom de plume of O. Henry, was a master punster. The event is free. To join the pun-off, simply show up.

Fiesta

Austin Art Museum at Laguna Gloria, 3809 W. 35th St. • (512) 458-6073

This weekend festival held in mid-May is one of Austin's favorite events and a tradition since 1956. It's always held on the third weekend of May, but keep an eye on the weather. Rain dates are made because May often brings spring showers. Sponsored by the Austin Museum of Art Guild, Fiesta is a top-quality arts and crafts show and more. One of the best facets of the festival is the location, the grounds of Laguna Gloria (see The Arts chapter). Some of the best artists in the Southwest participate in this juried show. Sunday is children's day with special events and entertainment presented for youngsters alongside the adult art auctions and sales. Children younger than 12 get in free on Sunday if they are accompanied by an adult. Admission is $6 for adults, $3 for children 6 to 12 and free for children 5 and younger on both days. The guild also holds a Friday night preview party, reservations required, and tickets are $65.

Mayfair, Artwalk and the Georgetown Fly-in

Various locations in Georgetown
• (512) 930-3535

Georgetown, just north of Round Rock, was a quiet, small town that celebrated a May festival on the courthouse lawn for years. But these days the fast-growing community, just off I-35, expects 30,000 people or more to celebrate Mayfair on first weekend of the month. Three events attract visitors: Mayfair, a large arts and crafts fair and carnival in the city's San Gabriel Park; Artwalk, an art show and performance festival on the town's historic downtown square; and the Georgetown Fly-in and Airshow featuring exhibits of vintage planes and battle re-enactments. Mayfair opens Friday evening at 5 PM and closes at midnight. Weekend hours are 10 AM to midnight on Saturday and noon to 6 PM on Sunday. Admission is $2 and free for children 12 and younger. Artwalk is free and open from 10 AM to 6 PM Saturday and noon to 6 PM Sunday. The air show is at the Georgetown Airport and open from 10 AM to 6 PM Saturday and Sunday. Admission is $6 and free for children 12 and younger.

Old Pecan Street Spring Arts Festival

Sixth St., between Congress Ave. and I-35 • (512) 478-1704

In Austin's early days, many of the downtown east-west streets were named after Texas trees, just as the north-south streets were and still are, for the most part, named after Texas rivers. Many of Austin's famous nightclubs are on Sixth Street, once called Pecan Street. The old name is revived for the spring and fall arts and crafts festivals held there. Several blocks of the street are blocked to vehicular traffic and turned into an outdoor art gallery and live music venue. Food booths sell a variety of carnival fare, including fajitas, cotton candy, hot dogs, funnel cakes, etc. The spring festival is usually held on the first weekend in May.

The Summer Concert Series

Auditorium Shores, Riverside St. and First St., and downtown Austin
• (512) 442-BAND

Organized by the Austin Federation of Musicians, this series of free outdoor summer concerts is held every Wednesday in May at 7 PM on Auditorium Shores, the south shore of Town Lake, just west of S. Congress Avenue. Concerts also are held on Sunday afternoons at the Zilker Hillside Theater at 3 PM. The concert series features a variety of bands and music, including rhythm and blues, Tejano, samba, jazz, etc. Bring a blanket or a lawn chair. Some refreshments are sold at concession stands, but many music lovers bring along a picnic.

Annual Sweet Peach Festival

Travis County Farmers' Market, 6701 Burnet Rd. • (512) 454-1002

This is a celebration of Hill Country peaches. Peaches are for sale, of course, plus there is peach mania at the market with offerings of peach cobbler, peach ice cream, peach preserves and jams. Admission is free.

Chisholm Trail Roundup

City Park, Lockhart • (512) 398-2818

Back in 1840, Lockhart residents fought their way into the history books by defeating the Comanches at the Battle of Plum Creek. Later, this small town southeast of Austin became a staging center for cattle being driven north on the Chisholm Trail to Abilene, Kansas. Lockhart had a reputation as a wild town, famous for its shoot-outs and feuds. The town history is celebrated with a re-enactment of the battle, city tours and a chili cookoff. The weekend-long festival in late May also includes dances, arts and crafts shows and live music. Admission for events varies. If you are visiting, don't leave town without dropping in on a Texas landmark, Kreuz Market. This is where some of the world's most delicious barbecue is served up in simple style, slapped onto butcher paper, not plates, with a side order of white bread or crackers. Some enjoy their barbecue with a bottle of Big Red soda. The restaurant is at 208 S. Commerce and is open daily except Sunday from 7 AM to 6 PM.

Kerrville Folk Festival

Quiet Valley Ranch, Kerrville
• (210) 257-3600, (800) 435-8429 tickets only

This is a legendary 10-day folk festival that is held on a beautiful Hill Country ranch, southwest of Austin near Kerrville. There is a wide variety of bands, reggae, folk, country, etc. The festival usually begins the Thursday before Memorial Day. Quiet Valley Ranch has scenic campgrounds for those who want to stay for several days. Admission fees and campsite prices vary. Call for information. The ranch is 9 miles south of Kerrville on Texas Highway 16. Among the popular performers are Butch Hancock, the Austin Lounge Lizards, Bill and Bonnie Hearne, Lyle Lovett and Russia's Limpopo (The Kit Kat commercial jingle *Gimme a Break* band). The fans, particularly those who camp out for the festival, are known as "Kerrverts." Tom Pittman, a member of the Austin Lounge Lizards told an *Austin American-Statesman* writer: "The typical Kerrvert is a builder, a cellular phone salesman or something like that . . . they just want to get away from ringing telephones for two weeks." Some camp out primitive style, others pack up the fancy RV and head to the hills. The festival is also noted for its campfire gatherings and nightly revelry.

Catholic Church Spring Picnic

American Legion Park, Shiner
• (512) 594-3836

Shiner is a small, central Texas town southeast of Austin well known as the home of Shiner beer. The town retains much of its German-American flavor and one of the best ways to experience that is to visit the annual Catholic church picnic. The event, which dates back to 1897 and is one of the biggest church picnics in the area, is free and features a country store, food, games like horseshoes and dancing all day to polka bands. The fun continues into the evening with more dancing and a church dinner, featuring Shiner Picnic Stew, sausage, fried chicken and all the fixin's. The event is held the Sunday before Labor Day.

Cinco de Mayo

Fiesta Gardens, 2101 Bergman St.
• (512) 499-6270

On May 5, 1862 , Mexican General Ignacio Zaragoza (who was born in Texas) defeated the army of French Emperor Louis Napoleon at Puebla, east of Mexico City. That blow against European imperialism is now a special holiday celebrated in song and dance both in Mexico and Texas. In addition to celebrations at Fiesta Gardens in East Austin, folkloric dancers and mariachi bands often perform at the State Capitol in the rotunda. Most Cinco de Mayo events are free, but some of the evening celebrations at Fiesta Gardens may charge an entrance fee of around $5.

Historic Homes Tour

Various locations in Austin
• (512) 474-5198

On Mother's Day weekend, the Heritage Society of Austin offers history buffs an opportunity to tour some of the city's most historic homes. Each year, the tour has a different theme. One recent tour was dubbed "A Century of Style" and featured homes from the 1850s to the 1950s. The society has played an important role in saving Austin buildings. One of its first projects was to rescue the Driskill Hotel on Sixth Street back in the 1970s. Tickets are available in advance for $12.50 or at the homes on the tour for $15.

June

Festival Institute at Festival Hill

Round Top • (409) 249-3129

In the early 1970s, classical pianist James Dick founded the festival at Round Top, the small German settlement east of Austin in

INSIDERS' TIP

Looking for that Abraham Lincoln letter stuck under the slats of a rocking chair, or a discarded Navajo blanket? Roaming the "junque" and antique markets is a favorite weekend pastime for many of us. We've listed just a few of the country flea markets here that hold regular sales. Look at our Shopping chapter for more, plus a section on holiday shopping.

Fayette County. Round Top has come to represent the best of the Texas cultural scene, combining great music, historical settings and a bucolic atmosphere. There are concerts once a month throughout the year at the institute site, but a special midyear series dubbed Summerfest takes place on each weekend in June and the first two weekends of July. Concerts range from the strictly classical to the popular, for example a concert of George Gershwin favorites. In addition to the concerts, the area offers much to see and do, including historic homes, antiques shops, gardens and herb shops. (See our Daytrips chapter for more on Round Top.) Admission to the concerts is $10, and performances are given Friday at 8 PM, Saturday at 3 and 8 PM. For a concert schedule write to Festival Institute, P.O. Box 89, Round Top, TX 78954.

Cedar Chopper Festival
Leander MHMR State Park, Leander • (512) 258-8007

Cedar Park once was a tiny town settled by cedar choppers, men who made a living chopping down the Hill Country juniper trees called "cedars" and shipping them to be made into fence posts and lumber. These days, Cedar Park is a suburban community on the northwest fringes of the greater Austin area, but the new folks enjoy celebrating its past. On the second weekend in June, there is a community parade, lots of music, a chili cookoff, smoked turkey drumsticks for sale, arts and crafts (including some cedar items) and a street dance. The festival takes place in the state park, just off U.S. Highway 183, 2 miles north of R.M. 620. Admission is $5 at night and $1 during the day.

Clarksville-West End Jazz & Arts Festival
Various locations • (512) 443-3638

This concert salutes jazz greats with a series of club dates around Austin and a free concert in Pease Park, near the old Central Austin where the festival originated. The event is held on the second weekend in June.

Juneteenth
Various locations

Juneteenth is an original Texas celebration and marks the day that Texas slaves learned of the Emancipation Proclamation. On June 19, 1865, Union commander Major General Gordon Granger took Galveston and announced to Texas slaves that they had been freed two years earlier. The day is now marked by festivals of music, barbecues, parades, celebrations of African-American culture and gospel sings. Check the *Austin American-Statesman* and community newspapers for details of this yearly event. Juneteenth is now a state holiday.

Luling Watermelon Thump
Luling • (830) 875-3214

Watermelons and natural gas are the two major "crops" in Luling, a small town southeast of Austin. The last weekend in June is set aside to honor the watermelon. There is a parade, a crowning of the Watermelon Queen, food and music. The highlight of the weekend is the Watermelon Spitting Contest. Children, adults and teams enter in separate categories. The record for spitting a seed is 68 feet, 9.125 inches according to the *Guiness Book of World Records*. Most of the events are free, but tickets to some events are necessary with prices around $5. The town is also home to the Central Texas Oil Patch Museum.

If you go, be sure to drive around the downtown area and take note of the small rocker wells, pumping natural gas from right under the city streets. Each well is decorated like a giant whirligig, one like Uncle Sam, another like a watermelon, of course.

July

Frontier Days
Old Settlers Park, Round Rock • (512) 255-5805

The only shoot-outs these days in Round Rock involve high school basketball tournaments. The only masks being worn are those donned by high-tech workers. But Round Rock, now a booming suburban community, was a typical frontier town back in 1878 when the town's hot and dusty streets were the setting for one of the most famous of Texas shoot-outs between the law and outlaw Sam Bass. "Texas' Beloved Bandit," as Bass was dubbed, rode into town intent on robbing the bank, but he ended the day buried in the local cemetery. Bass likely was dubbed Beloved because, in the grand Texas tradition of Bonnie and Clyde, bank robbers are somehow elevated to folk hero status. On the second weekend of the month the community now celebrates Frontier Days, complete with a re-enactment of the shoot-out, which is the headline event of the two-day festival. There is also a frog-jumping contest, hands-on demonstrations of butter-churning, whittling, soap making and other pioneer skills. Children can try their hand at some of the skills. The grownups can eat fajitas and enjoy the live music, and the whole family can pose for old-style photos complete with a Longhorn steer in the picture. The event is open from 6 PM to midnight on Friday and from 10 AM to 1 AM on Saturday. Admission is $5 on Friday and $7 on Saturday.

Bastille Day

The French Legation, 802 San Marcos St. • (512) 472-8180

The legation was the home and office of Comte Alphonse Dubois de Saligny, charge d'affaires to the Republic of Texas. Francophiles and homesick French citizens gather on the Sunday closest to July 14 to celebrate the French equivalent of July Fourth. The food is French, of course, and very good since it is concocted by local chefs and includes quiche, pâté, brioche, sorbet, pastries and wine. The music is French and the dancers, jugglers and mimes celebrate traditional French culture. Expect to pay about $5 for adults, $3 for kids.

United Confederate Veterans Reunion

Camp Ben McCulloch, F.M. 1826

Descendants of Confederate veterans gather for eight days in July on the banks of Onion Creek, southwest of the Oak Hill area of Austin, just off F.M. 1826 near Driftwood. This extended family gathering has been held every year since 1904. The camp is named after the Texas general who was killed at the Battle of Pea Ridge in Arkansas on March 7, 1862. Visitors are welcome to attend the event and watch a variety of historical programs, including re-enactments of Civil War life, dancing and, of course, barbecues. Admission is free.

Shakespeare at Winedale

Winedale Historic Center, near Round Top • (409) 278-3530

Each summer, University of Texas English literature students gather at historic Winedale (see April events and our Daytrips chapter) to study and perform Shakespeare's plays. The students perform three plays in the theater barn in the historic settlement, beginning the last week of July and continuing through mid-August. The Thursday and Friday performances are at 7:30 PM and on Saturday at 2 and 7:30 PM. Admission is $5. Winedale is about a 90-minute drive east of Austin.

Zilker Summer Musical

Zilker Hillside Theater, Zilker Park • (512) 479-9491

Each summer, for more than 40 years, talented Austin musicians and actors put on a popular Broadway musical in the open-air hillside "arena" adjacent to Barton Springs in the city's major downtown park. The musical is free and performances are at 8:30 PM Thursday through Sunday from mid-July through August.

A Night in Old Fredericksburg

Various locations in Fredericksburg • (830) 997-6523

This Hill Country town west of Austin has preserved its historic buildings, many of which capture the spirit of the German-American pioneers who settled here (see our Daytrips chapter). It is easy to spot the German influence in this town at any time of the year, but on the third weekend in July, the town celebrates with a citywide celebration of its German heritage. In recent years, cultural happenings with a Mexican-American flavor have been added to the festival of food, dance, music and horse racing. Admission prices range from $4 to $10.

Barton Springs Diving Championships

Barton Springs Pool, 2201 Barton Springs Rd. • (512) 476-4521

Elvis is alive and diving at Barton Springs. At least he was in 1997, when he won the "Most Original" prize in this annual contest. The contest includes best splash, best dive and most-original dive categories. Participants

Photo: Peter A. Silva

The Capitol 10,000 attracts thousands of runners.

range in age and their entry fees help fund environmental exhibits. Local musical groups also perform before and after the diving competition, which takes place on the third Sunday of the month. Flyers advertising the event and containing registration forms are widely distributed at Austin's pools, local grocery stores and other outlets. Spectators pay an admission charge of approximately $3 for adults, 50¢ for children. Participants pay a registration fee of approximately $12 for adults, $8 for children. You can save a few dollars by preregistering.

Western Days

Various locations in Elgin • (512) 285-4515

There is hardly a town within Central Texas that does not celebrate its founding or history, or simply its survival, with one festival or another. In Elgin, east of Austin, residents and visitors gather on the third weekend in July for dances, rodeos, arts and crafts exhibitions and food. And it would not be Elgin without generous servings of Elgin sausage. Admission is charged at the dances and rodeos, but most events are free, and many take place in the city's Memorial Park. The festival is held on the fourth weekend of the month.

Austin Symphony Orchestra July Fourth Concert and Fireworks

Auditorium Shores, Riverside Dr. and S. First St. • (512) 476-6064

As Austin grows, the size of the crowd gathering on the shores of Town Lake to watch the July Fourth concert gets larger and larger. The orchestra sets up on the southern shore of Town Lake on Auditorium Shores. The crowds spill over along both banks of the river, and some spectators enjoy the music from small canoes on the lake or on the rooftops of downtown office buildings. No power boats are allowed on Town Lake. The grand finale is, of course, Tchaikovsky's *1812 Overture* complete with cannon and fireworks. The music begins at 8:30 PM, but many families come down earlier and enjoy a family picnic. The fireworks usually start around 9:30 PM. Parking is a major headache, and after the concert the city's major thoroughfares out of the downtown area are jammed, making the trip home a slow one. The concert is free. One tip: If you simply want to enjoy the fireworks, the view from Barton Creek Mall on Loop 360 (Capital of Texas Highway) southwest of downtown is an excellent one.

Fourth of July Festival

San Gabriel Park, Georgetown • (512) 930-3545

Residents of Round Rock, Pflugerville and other communities and neighborhoods in far North Austin find it more convenient to drive to the Williamson County seat, Georgetown, just north of Round Rock on I-35, for July Fourth celebrations. The daylong festival at the park begins at 10 AM and ends at 10 PM with fireworks. The day's activities are free and include a children's carnival, petting zoo, games, live music and a barbecue cookoff.

Lakeway's Fabulous Fourth

Various locations in Lakeway, Lake Travis

The idea here is to emulate the small-town celebrations many of us remember from the past. The parade begins at 8:30 AM at the Live Oak Clubhouse on Lakeway Drive in the Lakeway area on Lake Travis. From 11 AM to 4 PM there is a Picnic in the Park at City Park on Hurst Creek Road. Vendors sell watermelon, fajitas, hot dogs, corn on the cob — all the July Fourth fixin's. There are games for kids and live entertainment. Look for details on shuttle buses in the *Austin American-Statesman*'s roundup on Fourth of July activities. Admission is free.

Willie Nelson's July Fourth Picnic

Luckenbach • (830) 997-3224

Waylon and Willie made Luckenbach a household name, and this tiny town, located on F.M. 1376 off U.S. Highway 290 W., 13 miles from Fredericksburg, has been home for the past couple of years to Willie's legendary Fourth of July Picnic. Nelson is renowned for his concerts, and no one gets shortchanged when he takes to the stage. Over the years, the picnic has changed locations, so it is wise to keep an eye on local music coverage in the media for prices, admission and ticket numbers. Recent prices have been around $25. It is an event that is popular, and concertgoers from all over Texas come to hear Willie sing, so book tickets in advance. The phone number above is the Luckenbach hotline — call and listen to Waylon sing.

August

Texas Folklife Festival

Institute of Texan Cultures, HemisFair Park, San Antonio • (210) 458-2224

In case you had not noticed, Texans are very proud of their heritage and enjoy not only celebrating their own roots, but also dipping into the ethnic melting pot to create truly Texas traditions. To sample the great variety of ethnic folkways that helped form modern Texas, the institute celebrates with this annual festival. The exhibits, demonstrations, music and food are authentic and widen the horizons of both newcomers and visitors to the Lone Star State. The festival usually runs for several days and starts August 1. (See our Daytrips chapter for more information on San Antonio.) This event is well worth the drive to San Antonio since it offers a colorful tapestry of Texas food, traditions, crafts and music without the modern, commercial trappings that spoil so many country fairs. Not only does the festival bring together all the diverse ethnic groups in Texas, it is cross-generational as older Texans demonstrate traditional crafts and skills to the younger folks. This is a great family outing.

Fall Creek Grape Stomp

Fall Creek Vineyards, Llano County • (512) 476-4477

This Hill Country vineyard has established a national reputation for the quality of its wines. Located on the shores of Lake Buchanan, about 70 miles northwest of Austin, Fall Creek is a popular place to visit while touring the Hill Country. But for two days in August, the second and third Saturdays of the month, it is the quality of the fun that counts. The peace and quiet of the winery is broken by the cheers and hollers of barefooted kids and grownups stomping the grapes. The winery opens its doors from 11 AM to 5 PM so that visitors can roll up their jeans, strip off their socks and jump into vats of red grapes. The experience is free.

(See our Close-up on Texas foods in the Restaurants chapter for more about Texas wine and wineries.)

Taylor International Barbeque Cookoff and Rodeo

Murphy Park, Taylor • (512) 352-1988

They take their barbecue very seriously in Taylor, even sleeping with their rigs on the

Friday night before the contest on the third weekend of the month. There are several types of meat cooked at the event, not just beef, and cooks begin to prepare Friday evening. On Saturday the judging begins as contestants compete not for money, but for much-coveted trophies. The winner is designated a Master Cook, while the runner-up is Reserve Master. The whole event is accompanied by live music, and there is also a well-respected rodeo in conjunction with the barbecue. The event is a fund-raiser for the local Jaycees, and admission charges vary for each event from approximately $5 to $10.

September

Kerrville Wine & Music Festival

Quiet Valley Ranch, Kerrville • (210) 257-3600

This Labor day weekend event is a shorter version of the famous spring Kerrville Folk Festival (see our listing in the May section). The events also include wine tastings and a crafts exhibit. The ranch has camping facilities. Admission varies with daily or weekend tickets, plus camping fees.

Oatmeal Festival

Bertram • (512) 335-2197

This tongue-in-cheek Labor Day weekend festival has helped to revive a small community northwest of Round Rock on F.M. 243. The festivities include an oatmeal cookoff and eat-off, an oatmeal sculpture contest and the Miss Bag of Oats (you have to be 55-plus) pageant. For the kids, there is a grasshopper parade where children can parade their pet insects. Most events are free.

Teddy Bear Picnic

Northwest Recreation Center, 2913 Northland Dr. • (512) 472-1305

Toddlers and baby boomers alike can be seen clutching their teddies as they make their way to the annual Teddy Bear Picnic sponsored by the Austin Junior Forum. They are all hoping their bear will win one of the contests at the event — best dressed, silliest, most lovingly worn — which is held on the second weekend of the month. The picnic is a fund-raiser for the Forum, which buys teddy bears for children who are in crisis. Emergency personnel carry the bears for the victims of abuse, accidents or trauma. In addition to contests, there are children's activities, a petting zoo and a teddy bear market. The picnic takes place from 10 AM to 4 PM on Saturday and Sunday. Admission is $3 for adults and $1 for children. Capital Metro runs free shuttle buses to the picnic from the Texas Department of Transportation building at 35th Street and Jackson Avenue in Central Austin.

Diez y Seis de Septiembre

Fiesta Gardens, Fiesta Beach Rd. • (512) 477-4436

This is a major fiesta both north and south of the border, celebrating Mexico's demand for independence from Spain. In 1810, on September 15, Padre Miguel Hidalgo y Costilla, a Mexican priest now hailed as the Father of Mexico, rang the parish church bells in the town of Dolores Hidalgo and summoned the Mexicans to support his call for freedom. That cry, or *grito,* is now a key element in every Diez y Seis fiesta as participants cry out "*Mexico por los Mexicanos*" — "Mexico for the Mexicans." But like the U.S. July Fourth celebration, serious history and fun are combined on Diez y Seis. Mariachi bands perform, folkloric dancers celebrate their heritage, and everyone eats really well. Austin's celebrations center on Fiesta Gardens, on the shores of Town Lake in East Austin. There are ceremonies in Austin on the actual day of the holiday, but the fiesta is usually carried over to the weekend closest to the 16th with events on several consecutive days. Check the local newspaper for details. The number above is for events held at Fiesta Gardens. Admission to the fiesta is usually $5 or $6. In past years free admission has been given to festivalgoers who donate school supplies.

LBJ State Historical Park Wildflower Day

Lyndon B. Johnson State Historical Park, Stonewall • (830) 644-2252

While spring is the season most noted for

wildflowers, fall also offers a palette of flora that can be just as spectacular. One of the best places to enjoy the fall show is at the LBJ park. (See our Daytrips chapter for more information.)

Republic of Texas Chilympiad

Hays County Civic Center, San Marcos • (512) 396-5400

This is one of the top chili-cooking contests in the nation, and more than 400 teams come here on the third weekend in September, hoping to qualify for the international chili cookoff in Terlingua, Texas. Chili cooking involves a great deal of theater and some mystery ingredients. Anyone with a delicate constitution planing on sampling the contestants' offerings should pack some antacid. In addition to the theatrical antics of the cookoff participants, there is a carnival for children, a beauty pageant, a Harley-Davidson show and plenty of country music. The civic center is at Exit 201 on I-35, south of Austin. Admission to the grounds is $2 on Friday, $3 on Saturday. Additional admission is charged for the beauty pageant and the musical shows.

Old Pecan Street Falls Arts Festival

Sixth St., between Congress Ave. and I-35 • (512) 478-1704

This weekend arts and crafts show mirrors the spring festival, which is detailed in our listing in May.

Gillespie County Fair

Fairgrounds, Texas Hwy. 16, Fredericksburg • (830) 997-2359

This is the oldest county fair in the state and is well worth a visit for a glimpse of a time when the county fair was an important date on the local calendar. The fair includes a traditional livestock show, handicrafts and home-baked goods, horse races, a carnival and dances in the evening. The fair takes place on the last weekend of September. Fairground admission is $5, free for children. Additional admission charges may be in place for other events.

Lone Star Weekend Aloft

Harris Branch, 10603 Harris Branch Pkwy. • (800) 788-6642

This annual gathering of hot air balloonists is held on park land surrounding Harris Branch, a suburban development in Northeast Austin, just off U.S. Highway 290 E. In years past, more than 100 balloonists have gathered for the two-day event, which includes balloon races, a balloon glow (the inflated balloons are illuminated at dusk). All the events are very photogenic. Daily tickets are approximately $5 a day; children 12 and younger are admitted free.

October

Halloween on Sixth Street

Sixth St., between Congress Ave. and I-35

Wholesale Halloween madness is one way to describe this event. As many as 60,000 costumed revelers have gathered on the street for the celebration. Several blocks are roped off to vehicular traffic, and participants are urged to walk in a vast oval pattern to avoid gridlock. Since the street is famous for its music clubs and bars, the noise level is high, and some partygoers do become a little rowdy. This is strictly a grown-up celebration and not recommended for children.

Gonzales Come and Take It Days

Town Square, Gonzales • (512) 672-6532

This weekend festival, held on the weekend closest to October 1, commemorates a famous event in the Texas Revolution. Gonzales, a settlement southeast of Austin, was home to a cannon the Texans felt would be targeted by the Mexican Army. In one of the revolution's early skirmishes, they prepared to confront the Army by making a famous revolutionary flag emblazoned with an

INSIDERS' TIP

The Texas Department of Transportation publishes a quarterly Texas events calendar that lists an extensive variety of events around the state. To request a copy write to: Texas Events Calendar, P.O. Box 5064, Austin, TX 78763.

image of the cannon and the words "Come and Take It." Gonzales also is noted as the only Texan settlement to respond to a request by Col. Travis at the Alamo for reinforcements. The town has a rich history, and one of the local tales involves the antics of outlaw John Wesley Hardin who lived around Gonzales for a while. The festival celebrates all this and more with historical re-enactments, an historic homes tour, rodeo, and street dances. Admission is charged for some events, ranging from $5 to $10.

Texas Wildlife Exposition

4200 Smith School Rd. • (512) 389-4472

This large, free two-day fair is a favorite among outdoors enthusiasts. Exhibits focus on fishing and hunting skills, equipment and skill improvement. There are field dog trials, target shooting and archery contests, plus a variety of activities for children. The exposition is held in the Southeast Austin headquarters of the Texas Parks and Wildlife Department. (See our Parks and Recreation chapter for more information on hunting and fishing.)

The Mediterranean Festival

St. Alias Orthodox Church, 408 E. 11th St. • (512) 476-2314

This downtown church holds its annual festival usually on a weekend in mid- or late October. The congregation is made up of families with Lebanese, Greek, Syrian and Mediterranean descent. They celebrate their culture with food, song and exhibits. Many Austin residents mark their calendars so they can buy some of the delicious foods, particularly the pastries, sold at the festival. The church has a beautiful interior graced with traditional icons. Admission is $5 to the fund-raising activities.

Austin Heart of Film Screenwriters Conference and Austin Film Festival

Various locations in the city • (512) 310-FEST

This fall festival, usually held at the beginning of the month, is fast becoming recognized as a significant film and cultural event. The conference offers screenwriters the opportunity to listen to panel discussions by top screenwriters, directors and studio executives. Participants have included director Oliver Stone, actor Dennis Hopper, Mike Judge (creator of *King of the Hill* television show), screenwriter Eric Roth (*Forrest Gump*), Randall Wallace (*Braveheart*), Al Reinart (*Apollo 13*), Buck Henry (*The Graduate*) and many more. The accompanying film festival features movies either scheduled for release or movies that are making the festival circuit. The two festivals vary in admission prices. Tickets to individual films are available on show day. Passes to panel discussions and films also can be purchased for $175, and full registration is $450. The festival also includes a juried competition for screenwriters, and some of the winners have seen their work make it to the big silver screen as a result of the exposure here.

German Oktoberfest

Winedale Historic Center, Round Top • (409) 278-3530

This traditional German celebration is held here amid the historic homes and buildings of this Fayette County settlement (see our Daytrips chapter). The festival is on the first weekend in October. Admission varies.

Halloween at Jourdan-Bachman Pioneer Farm

11418 Sprinkle Cut-Off Rd. • (512) 837-1215

This is a popular place for children's outings (see our Kidstuff chapter), and a week before Halloween the farm offers kids a chance to learn the finer points of pumpkin carving. Other activities include traditional pioneer activities and hands-on exhibits. Admission is $3 for adults, $2 for children 3 to 12.

Oktoberfest

Market Square, Fredericksburg • (830) 997-6523

Fredericksburg has a strong German heritage; in fact, some of the older residents still speak in a form of German heard in the last century in Europe. The traditional festival features beer hall singing, waltz contests and lots of sausage. Admission is $6 for adults, $1 for children 7 to 12, free for those 6 and younger.

November

Dia de los Muertos

Mexic-Arte Museum, Fifth St. and Congress Ave. • (512) 480-9373

It means "Day of the Dead," and this quintessentially Mexican fiesta is celebrated on All Souls Day, November 1. In Mexico, families take food to the local cemetery on that day for a two-day celebration in honor of their ancestors. Families set up altars at the gravesite offering food and drink. Day of the Dead folk art is highly collectible and much of it is humorous, mocking human foibles. Mexic-Arte Museum (see the Arts chapter) sponsors several Day of the Dead events, including the construction of a variety of *ofrendas* by local artists at its downtown museum site. Admission is $2. There is also a parade down East Sixth Street onto Congress Avenue in celebration of Mexican and Chicano culture. Spectators are urged to wear typical Day of the Dead costumes, angels or skeletons, and watch low riders, dancers and musicians parade on the avenue. Check the local paper for additional Dia de los Muertos events.

Powwow and American Indian Heritage Festival

Toney Burger Center, 3200 Jones Rd. • (512) 459-7244

In 1991, the Austin Independent School District and local American Indians joined together to offer this free, one-day insightful festival to Austin residents. The goal was to share Native American culture with neighbors in Central Texas. Attendance has grown to more than 20,000 for the powwow which usually is held on the first Saturday of November. From 10 AM to 10 PM, area residents can sample Native American food, listen to storytellers, stroll through the craft booths and exhibits and listen to American Indian music. The highlight of this free event is a dance competition, which features hundreds of dancers from dozens of tribes. Toney Burger Center is in Southwest Austin near the intersection of U.S. 290 W. and Loop 360 (Capital of Texas Highway).

Wurstfest

Wurstfest Grounds, Land Park, New Braunfels • (830) 625-9167, (800) 221-4369

New Braunfels was founded by Prince Carl von Solms-Braunfels in the 1840s. He was one of several German princes who set out to relieve German overpopulation by organizing immigration settlements in the New World. His settlement flourished, and now New Braunfels, roughly halfway between Austin and San Antonio, just off I-35, is a popular tourist spot (see our Daytrips chapter). Wurstfest is the city's version of Oktoberfest and attracts tens of thousands of visitors who eat sausage, drink beer, sing songs and spend money. Admission is $6 for adults, free for children 12 and younger. Call the toll-free number and order advance tickets for $5 each.

Austin Junior League Christmas Affair

Palmer Auditorium, Auditorium Shores, Riverside Dr. and S. First St. • (512) 467-8982

A sure sign that Christmas is just around the corner is the transformation of Palmer Auditorium into a shopping wonderland. More than 200 specialty merchants offer a variety of Christmas gift ideas, some easily affordable, others high-priced — for those who have been especially good. Not everyone shops at the affair, although the league raises hundreds of thousands of dollars for its community projects at the event, some just stroll, sip some Christmas spiced wine and window shop or gather decorating ideas for their own holiday celebrations. The affair is held the third weekend in November. The four-day event begins on Thursday and winds up on Sunday. Daily admission is $7.

Chuy's Children Giving to Children Parade

Congress Ave. • (512) 473-2783

This is a great way to teach children to give thanks on Thanksgiving weekend. Fast becoming a holiday tradition, this Saturday parade down Austin's main street celebrates two holidays in one. Organizers tout the parade as the Austin equivalent of New York's famous Macy's Christmas parade. Balloons, some up to 80 feet high, depicting popular children's characters lead the parade, followed by marching bands, floats, dancers, clowns and trucks filled with toys donated by children along the route. The donations go to the Austin Police Department's Operation Blue Santa, which gives toys to needy kids at Christmas. The parade is sponsored by Chuy's, the popular local restaurant — popular with kids because of the lively decor, and popular with Mom and Dad because the staff tolerates 2-year-olds (see our Restaurants chapter).

Texas Book Festival

Various locations • (512) 477-4055

A recently conceived, but very successful, celebration of Texas literature, this festival includes book signings, seminars, panel discussions and celebrations of literary history. Every year a "class" photo of the participants is taken in the capitol rotunda, offering a picture of the diversity and extent of Texas literature. Among the panelists in recent years have been Jim Lehrer, Kinky Friedman and Larry McMurtry. The participants also include literary luminaries with cultural or educational ties to Texas, for example the famous Mexican author and scholar Carlos Fuentes has participated. Admission to most events is free, but two fundraising events are held, including a ball and a meet-the-authors reception. (See The Literary Scene chapter for more on this event.)

December

Christmas Lights

Various locations

Some of the most picturesque Christmas light shows can be seen in the small towns around the Austin area. Most of the lights are put up in early December and taken down after New Year's Day. Below are a few locations well worth visiting. The phone numbers are for the local chambers of commerce and visitors bureaus.

Bastrop, to the east, decorates its historic downtown and Old Iron Bridge, (512) 321-2419.

Blanco, southwest of Austin, decorates the old courthouse with thousands of lights, (210) 438-2914.

Johnson City, west of Austin, is ablaze as the local residents cover homes, businesses and the Blanco County Courthouse with lights, (830) 868-7684.

Llano, northwest of Austin, decorates the historic town square and the old courthouse with 10 miles of lights, (915) 556-5172.

Marble Falls, northwest of Austin, boasts it uses 1 million lights to decorate its Walkway of Lights, (800) 759-8178.

In Austin, the local television meteorologists often highlight spectacular Austin neighborhood decorations. One of the best is 37th Street east of Guadalupe Street in Central Austin. Walking through this neighborhood is recommended, rather than driving.

In Round Rock the downtown historic district is decorated for the holidays, and in Cedar Park The Hill Country Flyer (see our Attractions chapter) departs from the train station in mid-afternoon for Burnet, then returns in the evening so that passengers can view the Hill Country homes decorated with lights. Call (512) 477-8468 for information.

Pioneer Farm Christmas Candlelight Tour

Jourdan-Bachman Pioneer Farm, 11418 Sprinkle Cut-Off Rd. • (512) 837-1215

Traditional Christmas activities reflecting the pioneer lifestyle are celebrated each weekend leading up to Christmas, many of them conducted by candlelight just as they would have been done in frontier days. Admission is $6. (See our Kidstuff chapter for information on the farm.)

Candlelight Homes Tour

Fredericksburg • (830) 997-2835

The Historical Society hosts this annual tour on the second Saturday in December. Fredericksburg, west of Austin, is rich in historic landmarks and restored homes, and most of them are decorated for the season. Tickets are on sale at the Pioneer Museum, 309 W. Main, and at Vereins Kirche, 100 W. Main. Ticket prices vary but are usually around $5. (See our Daytrips chapter for information on Fredericksburg.)

Yule Fest

Zilker Park, 2100 Barton Springs Rd. • (512) 478-6875

For the last two weeks of December,

Photo: Peter A. Silva

Every evening from March until October a quarter-million freetail bats fly out from their roost under the Congress Avenue bridge. Don't miss the show.

the southern banks of Town Lake in Zilker Park are the site of Yule Fest and the Trail of Lights. This nighttime Christmas pageant features lighted set pieces decorated according to various Christmas themes. It is a popular family event that has seen lines grow longer and longer, prompting the city in 1998 to eliminate the special nights set aside for drive-through spectators and confine the trail to pedestrian traffic, bicycles and special trams for the disabled.

Armadillo Christmas Bazaar

Austin Music Hall, 208 Nueces St. • (512) 447-1605

This annual arts and crafts fair was originally held at the legendary Armadillo World Headquarters (see The Music Scene chapter) but now is housed in the Austin Music Hall in South Austin. The 'Dillo is long gone, but the spirit of the bazaar lives on as a showplace for local artists and craftspeople, some of them creating fanciful jewelry and whimsical toys. Local musicians also perform nightly at the two-week event, which begins in mid-December and ends Christmas Eve. It is open from 11 AM to 11 PM daily. Admission is $1.75 on weekdays until 7 PM, $3.50 evenings and weekends. Children younger than 12 are admitted free.

Christmas Open House

Winedale Historic Center, near Round Top • (409) 278-3530

Christmas at Winedale is celebrated each year in a different historic home in this wonderful old settlement in Fayette County, east of Austin (see our Daytrips chapter). Usually held the Sunday before Christmas, the celebration features seasonal music and food. The many antique shops offer one-of-a-kind Christmas gifts. Call for hours. There is a small admission charge, usually around $5 or less.

Christmas at the French Legation

French Legation, 802 San Marcos St. • (512) 472-8180

The Daughters of the Texas Republic offer a glimpse of Christmas Past as it might have been celebrated in the mid-19th century. The legation was built for Comte Alphonse Dubois de Saligny, France's charge d'affaires to the Republic of Texas. In addition to Christmas displays, choirs perform Christmas carols and holiday refreshments are offered. Plus, Pére Noel, the French Santa Claus, is on hand. The celebration takes place on the first Sunday of the month from 1 to 5 PM. Admission is $3 for adults and $1 for children younger than 12. Proceeds benefit the legation museum. (See our Attractions chapter.)

Family Christmas Night

Downtown Round Rock • (512) 255-5805

On the first Saturday of the month, the City of Round Rock closes the downtown streets for a family celebration. At the heart of the event is the town's historic town square where Santa appears to assure Round Rock kids that he knows who has been naughty and who has been nice. The festivities begin at 7 PM, and admission is free.

The Lighting of the Zilker Park Christmas Tree

Zilker Park, 2100 Barton Springs Rd.

This annual event on the first Sunday of the month is a true sign that Christmas is nigh. One the city's moonlight towers (see our Attractions chapter) was moved to the park and serves as the main "trunk" of the tree. Thousands of colored Christmas lights are strung from the top of the 165-foot tree to resemble a Christmas tree shape. Tradition calls for children to stand inside the pyramid and whirl around, making the lights blur. Young children are whisked around in their parents' arms. It is one of those simple holiday traditions that children never forget. Admission to the park is free.

Christmas Music and Theater

Various locations

With its rich and talented arts community, Austin offers a large variety of Christmas musical events. There are the long-standing traditions of the holiday, like the annual performances by the Austin Civic Ballet of *The Nutcracker* at Bass Concert Hall, (512) 469-SHOW. Handel's *Messiah* is performed by several musical entities, plus there is the annual "Sing it Yourself *Messiah*" at St. Matthews Episcopal Church, where the audience can join in with the Austin Civic Chorus. Call (512) 454-TIXS for information and tickets. Local theater and comedy troupes offer a variety of performances. Check the listings in the *Austin American-Statesman*.

¡Feliz Navidad!

Various locations

There are a variety of Christmas events with a Mexican flavor held in Austin during the holidays. Plays depicting the nativity, folk music concerts and folk art are popular at this time of year. *La Pastorela*, the traditional Latino nativity play, is performed by several groups. But one of the most interesting and authentic traditions takes place in mid-December as members of Our Lady of Guadalupe Church, 1209 E. Ninth Street, enact La Posada. This is a tradition both in Mexico and Texas as the faithful re-enact Joseph and Mary's search for a place to stay in Bethlehem. The faithful follow members, who are dressed as the Holy Family, as they go from door to door, asking for shelter. When the parade reaches the church there is a mass followed by Christmas treats, tamales and Mexican hot chocolate. Check the arts and events listings in the *Austin American-Statesman* and local community newspapers.

Kwanzaa

Various locations

The Swahili word means "fruits of the harvest," and Kwanzaa, created in 1966, has proved fruitful as millions of African Americans embrace the celebration's principles. From December 26 to January 1, the seven days of Kwanzaa are dedicated to seven principles. In recent years, African-American leaders in Austin have taken Kwanzaa from a family event to a community celebration. During the festival, there are a variety of public events. Check the *Austin American-Statesman* and local community newspapers for details.

New Year's Celebration On Sixth Street

Sixth St., between Congress Ave. and I-35 • (512) 478-1704

New Year's Eve in the heart of Austin's club scene is as wild and crazy as the Halloween celebration (see October listing). Many clubs and downtown restaurants have special performances or menus for the final day of the year. Check the local entertainment press for the particulars. In what is fast becoming a mini-Times Square event, local television and radio stations camp out on Sixth Street rooftops to watch Austin's version of the "big ball" fall. The big ball falls at midnight. But that doesn't end the craziness as the party goes in clubs and on the street itself until the wee hours.

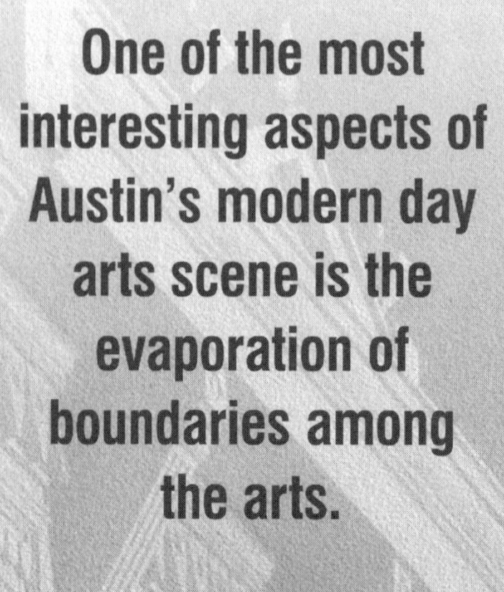

One of the most interesting aspects of Austin's modern day arts scene is the evaporation of boundaries among the arts.

The Arts

What do 20-something slackers, a zany town named Tuna, a statewide high-school competition, a giant university and a celebrated European sculptor have in common? They all have added a few broad brush strokes to the colorful canvas of Austin arts.

Austin attracts artists. While that phenomenon dates back to the 1800s, Austin's status as a hub for artists has developed largely since the 1970s when enough musicians, actors, writers and painters had gathered to form an arts scene. Over the past few decades, more and more talented artists have found inspiration in Austin's artistic communities, and many of those have helped Austin earn a reputation for both appreciating and producing high-quality art. Don't miss our chapters on The Music Scene, The Literary Scene, Nightlife, and Attractions for more about Austin artists. In this chapter we'll tell you about the visual artists and theater troupes, the dancers and filmmakers, the classical performers and the choirs that make Austin sing.

Elizabet Ney, who had sculpted some of the great figures of Europe, was nearly 60 when she moved to Austin in the late 1800s. Back then, Austin had more gambling dens and brothels than galleries and theaters. Ney's celebrity status attracted influential men and women, many who believed, as did she, that art, music and dance rank up there near water and air in importance to life. As Ney's hands transformed crude blocks of marble into glorious statues of Texas heroes, her spirit and her passion shaped a culture that prized the arts. Along the way, she became a pioneer of artistic development in the state of Texas. Her ability to inspire others during a time when the arts weren't exactly on the top of the Texas agenda led to the creation of the Texas Fine Arts Association and later the Texas Commission on the Arts and The University of Texas art department.

The University of Texas gets major billing among the stars of Austin's cultural scene. The university's highly respected film and fine arts schools have turned out some of the most well-prepared graduates in the country. It's impossible to estimate the number of UT alumni, and professors too, who are making significant contributions in Austin and around the country in the fields of dance, film, visual art, theater, literature and music. UT's Performing Art Center is a world-class venue for world-class performers. The University Interscholastic League (UIL), a program started in 1910 to encourage educational development in Texas high schools through competition, began as a sports program. Since the 1920s, the UIL has included an annual theater competition in which high schoolers from across the state vie for top honors. This Texas theater tradition, which produced Broadway's Tommy Tune and others, gets students hooked on theater at an early age.

Speaking of addictions, Austin — and most of the country, it seems — have developed a taste for Tuna. The crazy-quilt of characters that inhabit Tuna, Texas' third-smallest town, come to comic life on stage through actors Joe Sears and Jaston Williams, the Austinites who co-wrote (with Ed Howard) *Greater Tuna* and its two spin-offs. *Greater Tuna*, an Off-Broadway hit in the early 1980s, was followed by *A Tuna Christmas*, which garnered rave reviews on Broadway and earned Sears a Tony nomination. When the latest installment, *Red, White and Tuna*, debuted in Austin in 1998, audience members shot out of their seats to give the pair a standing ovation. Quick-change artists Sears and Williams perform the parts of more than two dozen characters — male and female — in their fictional town of Smut Snatchers and hanging judges. Tuna fanatics know Aunt Pearl Burras and her sister Bertha Bumiller, Didi Snavely, Petey Fisk and Vera Carp as well as they know their own families. *Greater Tuna*, presented in touring versions around the country, in an HBO production, in command performances at the White House and in community theater all over the United States, has placed Austin on the national theatrical map.

What Tuna is to theater, *Slackers* is to film. This 1991 low-budget film by Austinite Richard Linklater made a bundle when it was released nationally and proved to the country that Austin has what it takes to make movies. Since then, Austin filmmaking has jelled into an industry. (See our Close-up on Austin's film culture in this chapter.) Then there's dancer/choreographer Deborah Hay, printmaker Sam Coronado and visual artists Peter Saul and Michael Ray Charles, four nationally proven artists in their fields. We've got Austin Lyric Opera, Zachary Scott Theatre and Austin Musical Theatre, three standouts among many who are taking chances — and succeeding. Austin's experimental theater companies, alternative gallery scene, cutting-edge dancers and performance artists are doing their parts to shake up the arts world, not just locally.

One of the most interesting aspects of Austin's modern day arts scene is the evaporation of boundaries among the arts. When Austin's own Willie Nelson showed up on screen as an actor in the recent film *Wag the Dog*, local filmgoers held their collective breath in homage. Musician Joe Ely is doing well-respected multimedia art. Visual artists who sing, singers who paint, dancers who act, actors who write. It's a reflection on contemporary culture in general. The symbiosis of Austin's artistic scenes also offers Austin audiences incredible choices in venues. You'll find art exhibitions in theaters, dancers at museums, singers at art galleries, film in the clubs.

Austin's rapid artistic development has not come without speed bumps. Today there just isn't enough space for many of Austin's performing and visual artists. Several of Austin's important performing arts venues are booked as much as two years in advance, leaving little room for spontaneity. As Austin heads into the next century, however, the struggle for artistic space could ease. Plans to build a new $26 million community events center on the south bank of Town Lake and to convert Austin's nearby Palmer Auditorium into a multi-theater performing arts center were approved by voters in November 1998. Also approved was a plan to build a long-awaited Mexican-American Cultural Center downtown. Additionally, both of Austin's major museums are set to build state-of-the-art facilities in the early 2000s.

What you'll find in this chapter is an arts scene on the move, a scene that may delight you, inspire you — perhaps even repulse you — as the artists intended.

Performing Arts

Theater

When William Shakespeare wrote that "all the world's a stage," he might have been looking into the future at Austin. With more than 250 different shows a year produced by both national touring companies and the dozens of local troupes that perform at varying intervals, it often seems as if the whole city had been bitten by the bug. Check our local theater listings if you're in doubt. Many times theater patrons have the luxury of choosing from as many as two dozen productions — at once.

INSIDERS' TIP

While you may stumble across any number of film superstars at work in Austin, true stargazers may want to check out the lobby of the Four Seasons Hotel, the bar at the nearby Shoreline Grill or some of our clubs and barbecue joints, like Stubb's. Or you could just go about your normal business. Goldie Hawn was spotted shopping at the Citywide Garage Sale.

Austin does theater in a variety of ways: big Broadway shows like 1998's *The Phantom of the Opera* at The University of Texas Performing Arts Center; the latest installment from the wacky Tuna guys at the Paramount; the ambitiousness of a locally done *Angels in America* at Zachary Scott Theatre; lots of experimental shows at the small Off Broadway-type venues; delightful productions geared toward kids; bilingual comedies and dramas; and performances celebrating the Bard himself on an outdoor stage.

We may all be actors on the stage of life, as Shakespeare suggested, but those who choose the theater as their life make it so much interesting for the rest of us — as we like it.

You know you're in a theater town when you come across currently-out-of-work actors busing tables at local restaurants, serving drinks and driving cabs. While Austin is filled with extremely talented award-winning actors, three especially get pointed to and whispered about when they walk through a room. Singer/actor Joe York, who often appears in musicals, is one such local celeb. Singing sensation Judy Arnold lends much more than her voice to musicals and dramas, while actor/director Boyd Vance has wowed Austin audiences with performances in *Shear Madness* and many others. We doubt these three have had to bus any tables lately, if ever.

Austin also has its own Broadway producer in the likes of Charles Duggan, also of San Francisco. Duggan has produced all the Tuna shows as well as *The Foreigner* and more high-quality productions from coast to coast. Set designers rarely get pointed to and whispered about when they walk into a room, but we couldn't fail to mention Austin's multi-award-winning designer Christopher McCollum. This talented, imaginative artist has created set designs for such diverse companies as Austin Lyric Opera, Austin Musical Theatre and Frontera @ Hyde Park Theatre. If you're impressed by the set at your next show, check the credits for McCollum's name.

While theater can pop up in just about any nook and cranny around the city, we've identified Austin's main performance spaces and theater troupes here. This list will direct you to some of the best and most interesting theater Austin offers. For even more theater, check out the lineup at Austin's colleges and universities. If you prefer to be on stage or behind the scenes rather than sit in the audience, you'll get a feel here for what Austin offers for both theater professionals and budding newcomers. Or you could just form your own troupe. Many have. The Austin Circle of Theaters calculates there are more than 70 theater companies in our city. Some present works occasionally while others, as you'll see here, are busy all the time.

The Presenters

Paramount Theatre for the Performing Arts

713 Congress Ave. • (512) 472-5411, (512) 469-7469 Star Tickets box office

On a stage once graced by the Ziegfeld Follies, Helen Hayes, George M. Cohan, John Philip Sousa, the Marx Brothers and more of history's great performers, the Paramount Theatre presents top artists from Austin and around the country. Built in 1915 as the Majestic Theatre, a vaudeville house that presented variety acts, this elegantly restored venue was designed by one of the most respected theater architects in the United States, John Eberson of Chicago. This is one of the few theaters left in the country that showed the movie *Casablanca* when it was originally released more than half a century ago.

Now listed on the National Register of Historic Places, the Paramount itself is one of the city's main attractions. And the attractions on stage are just as important. This major performing arts venue, which seats nearly 1,300 people, is active almost 300 nights of the year, bringing live theater, dance, music and classic movies to people of all ages. This is where Austin's own blockbuster comedy *Greater Tuna* got its start and where the two Tuna sequels, including 1998's *Red, White and Tuna*, packed the house. *The Foreigner*, another highlight of the Paramount's recent past, starred Tuna creators Jaston Williams and Joe Sears and was co-produced by Charles Duggan.

Excellent touring shows, blockbuster revues like *Beehive* and *Rockin' Christmas Party* produced by Austin's Zachary Scott Theatre, and the success of a homegrown musical theater company, have combined to make the Paramount a must-stop for people all over Central Texas. Today, more than 180,000 people attend events at the theater each year.

Austin Musical Theatre, in residence at the Paramount since 1996, quickly earned a reputation for high-quality work. Under the leadership of Scott Thompson and Richard Byron, Austin Musical Theater has become an important force in local theater and has presented such critical and box office hits as *Peter Pan*, *West Side Story* and *Annie*. The Paramount also presents Kids' Classics, a wonderful series of theatrical events for children, and the Summer Classic Film Series, classic movies from the Golden Age of Hollywood. The annual Broadway Series, presented October through May, includes productions by Austin Musical Theatre as well as midsize touring shows like *Damn Yankees* and *Kiss of the Spiderwoman*, some of which are duplicates of the original Broadway productions. The Paramount also presents Extras, which have included Debbie Reynolds, Maureen McGovern, Spalding Gray and the nationally acclaimed percussion dance troupe Stomp. The Paramount, which almost closed down during the economic bust of the 1980s, is back with bells on. Tickets may be purchased in person at the Paramount box office or over the phone with a credit card through Star Tickets. Tickets may also be purchased at Star Tickets centers in Albertson's grocery stores around town, at Waterloo Records and at other Star outlets.

University of Texas Performing Arts Center

23rd St. and E. Campus Dr.
• (512) 471-2787, (512) 477-6060 UTTM box office

We've said it before, and we'll say it again. Having one of the country's largest universities in our own backyard has its advantages. The UT Performing Arts Center (PAC) is one of the biggies. This huge network of theaters, studios, rehearsal halls and classrooms spreads to several campus locations. At the heart of the PAC system is the complex at 23rd and East Campus Drive.

This immense $44 million structure, which houses two theaters as well as rehearsal halls, offices and massive support facilities, is one of the finest performing arts centers in the United States. Bass Concert Hall, UT's flagship theater, is a 3,000-seat auditorium with an atrium lobby and an orchestra pit that can accommodate even the largest musical group. The Austin Symphony Orchestra, Austin Lyric Opera and Ballet Austin all present their main stage productions here. Once more, some of the finest touring artists and companies in the country perform at Bass Concert Hall. Big Broadway touring shows in the recent past have included *Cats* and *Phantom of the Opera*, which made its long-awaited Austin debut in 1998. Also in this complex is The McCollough Theatre, which seats 400 people and is used by both professional and student performers.

Many people, including local residents, tend to think of the Performing Arts Center as the Bass complex alone. In fact, there's much more. The Performing Arts Center also includes Bates Recital Hall in the Music Building adjacent to Bass. The recital hall is a 700-seat theater designed for acoustic excellence and equipped with a three-story pipe organ. This theater hosts musical performances by some of the best virtuoso performers of the day as well as leading names in jazz, chamber and organ music and more.

Other theaters around campus that contribute to the Performing Arts Center are the B. Iden Payne Theatre, a 500-seat facility used for both professional events and student theatrical productions and Hogg Auditorium, a recently reintroduced theater that's almost as large as the Paramount and is also used for professional and student events. A few smaller theaters and a dance studio complete the Performing Arts Center.

While the PAC is perhaps most known to the public at large for the world-class events it presents, we can't fail to mention the quality and range of many student productions offered at some of these theaters throughout the school year. UT students of theater, dance, film and music present shows that are definitely worthwhile for any fan of the performing arts. University of Texas Ticket Master (UTTM), with locations in H.E.B. grocery stores all over the area, is an easy way to buy tickets to PAC events. Tickets are also on sale directly at the PAC box office and other locations in town.

Zilker Hillside Theater

Near Barton Springs Pool in Zilker Park • (512) 477-5335, (512) 397-1468

Casual outdoor free arts! What better tribute to Austin than this great venue on a natural grassy hillside that hosts some of our city's most anticipated free shows. Start with the annual Zilker Summer Musical, an Austin tradition for more than 40 years. This big splashy show draws more than 2,000 people a night to Zilker Park for some of the best outdoor performances Austin offers all year.

Another outstanding Austin event, the Austin Shakespeare Festival, held each fall for more than 15 years, draws upwards of 15,000 people to the Hillside Theater for a four-week engagement of an excitingly staged and costumed Shakespeare play. Past performances have included *The Winter's Tale*, *Macbeth* and *Twelfth Night*, the last two in association with the National Shakespeare Company. Zilker Hillside Theater also is home to the annual Trail of Lights Festival in December, the event that kicks off Zilker Park's wonderful Trail of Lights. You don't have to wait for an annual event to experience this great Austin theater, however.

Bring a blanket and a picnic basket and enjoy the outdoors while watching any number of dance, music or theatrical events held in this comfy spot, which has room for more than 2,500 people. Officially named the Beverly S. Sheffield Zilker Hillside Theater, the venue is handled by the Dougherty Arts Center. Call the number of DAC's information desk listed above or pick up a program of events at the Arts Center and other places around town.

The Resident Theaters

The Acting Studio

5811 Burnet Rd. • (512) 458-5437, (512) 454-TIXS box office

This small Austin venue is home to both Different Stages Productions and the award-winning KidsActing, which specializes in full-scale musical productions featuring children. Dede Clark operates this space, which seats about 75 people, and is artistic director for the popular KidsActing performances held throughout the year.

Established in 1986, KidsActing presents two big musicals in the fall, two in the spring and one or two during the summer. Past performances have included a contemporary adaptation of *The Velveteen Rabbit*, which won a local award. KidsActing also has summer camps for children.

Started in 1980, Different Stages is a nonprofit organization that produces works by playwrights that are defining forces in theater: Molière, Shakespeare, Shaw and O'Neill, to name a few. The company also has been the first to introduce Austin to new playwrights and has staged four world premieres. Under the artistic directorship of Norman Blumensaadt, the company has presented more than 50 plays, including romantic, neoclassic, realistic and surrealistic. Different Stages also hosts an annual Director's Festival in the spring, which includes four to six one-act plays by selected emerging directors. The company presents a full season of performances from November through August.

Esther's Follies

525 E. Sixth St. • (512) 320-0553

We'll tell you more about this laugh-a-minute riot of a comedy troupe in our chapter on Nightlife. They call themselves Texas's premier musical comedy revue, and we can't argue with them. We've taken more than one out-of-town guest to see Esther's Follies' great show, which combines some classic routines with constantly updated political satire. The follies can be found on Austin's historic and hip E. Sixth Street.

Frontera @ Hyde Park Theatre

511 W. 43rd St. • (512) 302-4933, (512) 454-TIXS box office

"What other experimental groups only aspire to do, Frontera does as a matter of course." That's what the *Austin American-Statesman* said about this exciting theater company that keeps Austin audiences on the cutting edge of new theater. The resident theater company at Hyde Park, Frontera was founded in 1992 by artistic director Vicky Boone and company members Jason Phelps and Annie Suite. Frontera has grown into one of Austin's most popular small troupes, presenting bold works by both Austin artists and others from

Lights! Camera! Austin!

One of the hottest tickets in Hollywood these days is a boarding pass to Austin. Filmmaking is coming of age in Central Texas as many of Hollywood's brightest stars, directors and producers are discovering what Austin-based movie moguls have known all along: These parts offer much more than a great backdrop.

Austin's distinction as a filmmakers' mecca has been shooting upward for a dozen years, but 1998 was the year Hollywood rolled out the red carpet for Austin. The glitzy world premiere of Austinite Richard Linklater's $27 million period film about Texas bank robbers, *The Newton Boys*, was staged at our own Paramount Theatre. The premier for this Austin-made film had it all: the popping flashbulbs, the spotlights, the national media blitz and the droves of fans crushed together to catch a glimpse of stars Matthew McConaughey, Ethan Hawke, Julianna Margulies and Dwight Yoakam step from vintage Model Ts and Studebakers onto — what else? — a red carpet.

Producer Lynda Obst (*Sleepless in Seattle*, *Contact*), who moved to nearby Fredericksburg in 1993, and star Sandra Bullock, who's building a house near Austin, are two Hollywood exiles who came to Texas for the work, and stayed for the freestyle life this region offers. Obst and Bullock spent weeks shooting their 1998 film, *Hope Floats*, also starring Gena Rowlands and Harry Connick, Jr., along the Colorado River just outside Austin in Smithville. Also in 1998, two more of the biggest names in Tinseltown today — Austinites Mike Judge and the husband-wife team of writer/director Robert Rodriguez and producer Elizabeth Avellan — were working simultaneously on major movies on locations around Austin, as were other studios and independent filmmakers.

Our local movie barons aren't the only ones bringing Central Texas to a theater near you. If you've seen John Travolta and Jean Stapleton in *Michael*, Kevin Costner and Clint Eastwood in *A Perfect World*, Johnny Depp in *What's Eating Gilbert Grape*, Denzel Washington and Meg Ryan in *Courage Under Fire* or Tommy Lee Jones and Robert Duvall in the mini-series *Lonesome Dove*, you've seen some part of Austin or our surrounding region. Of course, you may not have recognized it, even if you know Austin. The Chicago skyline that serves as the backdrop for the final scene in *Michael* was shot on our own Sixth Street. Austin's Town Lake doubled as the Arkansas River in *Lonesome Dove*. The mayor's office turned in a fine performance as the Pentagon in *Courage Under Fire*. And there have been many more movies filmed around our picturesque region.

Projects filmed in Austin, including TV shows, mini-series, made-for-TV movies, commercials and feature films, had combined budgets of more than $160 million in 1996 and 1997, at least half spent locally. That's a dramatic increase from the tallies of the mid-1980s, when Austin projects were budgeted at about $10 million a year.

A variety of movie locales draws filmmakers to Central Texas. Want hills? Austin's got plenty of hills. How about a pine forest? There's that nearby too, as are prairies, lakes and ranchland. Need a small town that time has forgotten? Austin is surrounded by towns that will fit that bill, complete with those old courthouses, town squares and general stores that make all of us movie buffs willingly suspend our disbelief. Mild weather and sunny skies almost year round add to Austin's appeal. It doesn't hurt having one of the country's top film schools right in the neighborhood at The University of Texas either.

And there's more. The film term is "crew up." Anyone who sits through the credits that roll on and on at the end of a movie realizes the brain power that goes into making

— continued on next page

a film these days. Austin's film culture abounds with experts in almost every creative facet of filmmaking, from directors, screenwriters and cinematographers to casting directors and film editors, makeup artists and art directors, location managers and production managers, animators and special-effects magicians. Austin even has important entertainment lawyers and animal trainers. In fact, when *Texas Monthly* magazine did a major cover story on the state's film industry in 1998, more than half of the 25 "essential unknowns of the Texas film business" lived in Austin. That says a lot when you consider that Dallas and Houston, the power cities of Texas, have their own thriving film industries.

Photo: Courtesy of Twentieth Century Fox

Sandra Bullock stars as Birdee Calvert, a newly single mother who must start her life all over again.

Austin is also filled with plenty of "knowns," people such as screenwriters Bud Shrake, Academy Award-nominee William Broyles, Jr., (*Apollo 13*), and Bill Wittliff, a dean of the Austin writing and publishing scene whose credits include the landmark 1988 CBS miniseries *Lonesome Dove*, *Legends of the Fall* and *The Black Stallion*. (See our chapter on The Literary Scene for more about Shrake and some of Austin's other notable screenwriters.) Director Terrence Malick (*Badlands*, *Days of Heaven*) is back making films (*The Thin Red Line*) following a 20-year absence. Then there's 20-something Austinite Harry Knowles, who turned his passion for movies into one of the hottest web sites in the country for fellow denizens of dark theaters. Ain't It Cool News, at www.aint-it-cool-news.com, includes his own brand of movie reviews as well as the inside scoop on the filmmaking business around the country, and much more. Knowles is an industry unto himself and has been featured in major magazine articles around the country.

With so many creative talents packed into Austin, it's no wonder our city hosts two nationally known film festivals each year, as well as several other smaller fests that draw plenty a movie buff. The South by Southwest Film Festival and Conference (see our Close-up on SXSW in the Annual Events and Festivals chapter) and the Austin Film Festival, both started in 1994, draw many of the country's biggest films and independent filmmakers to Austin. SXSW, which focuses on filmmaking, already is being called one of the most prestigious events of its kind in the country. SXSW, held in March, has lured Quentin Tarantino, Robert Rodriguez and maverick documentarian Michael Moore as well as other bigwigs in the film business. *The Newton Boys*, a 20th Century Fox production, kicked off the 1998 SXSW festival with a bang. Conference is the word here. These powerhouses come to talk shop before ever-growing crowds of enthusiastic filmmakers and movie fanatics. The Austin Film Festival, which centers on film writing, includes an important screenwriting competition, and some finalists have gone on to see their work produced. The festival, held in October, is on the A-list of major screenwriting contests around the country.

— continued on next page

Of all the major players in Austin today, Linklater is the guru of the city's vibrant film culture. Linklater, whose $23,000 independent film *Slacker*, set in Austin, grossed more than a million dollars in 1991, proved to Hollywood that Austin has what it takes to make lucrative films. Linklater followed up with such favorites as *Dazed and Confused*, starring University of Texas grads McConaughey and Renee Zellweger, and *SubUrbia*. He even established the Austin Film Center, complete with editing suites and a viewing room for dailies, a first for Austin. Before Linklater found major success he helped establish the Austin Film Society in 1985.

The Film Society, one of the driving forces in Austin cinema today, has shown hundreds of free films, mostly experimental, repertory and international films rarely seen in cities the size of Austin. In 1996, the Film Society created the Texas Filmmakers Production Fund, which has given more than $100,000 in grants to budding filmmakers across Texas. The Film Society is credited with developing an audience appreciation for film that is unheard of in many American cities.

The contributions of Rodriguez and Judge to Austin film also are enormous. Rodriguez, whose 1992 flick *El Mariachi* skyrocketed him to the big time, followed up with the sequel *Desperado*. Rodriguez returned to Austin after a stint in Los Angeles and immediately immersed himself in the local film community. Judge, creator of the wildly successful animated television shows *Beavis and Butt-head* and *King of the Hill*, is another who has put his heart and talent behind Austin's film industry.

What does this movie mania mean to those of us who don't know a grip from a gaffer, but are first in line to enjoy the finished product once it hits our local theaters? Plenty.

In addition to the SXSW film festival and the Austin Film Festival, movie buffs can attend any one, or all, of a number of smaller film festivals held throughout the year, including the Austin Gay and Lesbian International Film Festival, which since its founding in 1988 has grown into the biggest regional festival of its kind, and UT's CinemaTexas, which features short films. In 1998, cinephiles launched two *more* festivals, the Festival of New Latin American Cinema and the South by Southwest Alternative Film Festival.

You don't have to wait around for the annual festivals to see outstanding movies in Austin, though. In addition to the chain multiplexes within an easy drive of just about anywhere you're situated in town, Austin offers a few unique theater venues that show more offbeat and experimental films including, yes, documentaries. When you're in the mood for something different, check out the lineup at the Dobie Theatre next to the UT campus, Village Cinema Art in North Austin and the Alamo Drafthouse Theatre downtown (see our Nightlife chapter). This last theater, a major venue for Film Society offerings, features cabaret-style seating and serves beer and snacks along with the standard movie fare. And check out *The Austin Chronicle* and the *Austin American-Statesman* for listings of special screen events going on all the time.

Austin's film industry isn't so out of hand that hawkers need stock up on maps of the stars' home, but serious stargazers can usually stumble across a celeb or two on location around town. (They don't publicize where movies are shooting day by day, but most sets are open and right on the street, so they're fair game for bystanders.) Better yet, answer a casting call and get paid a little something to schmooze with the stars. Who knows? You could be part of the next *Texas Chainsaw Massacre*, shot around our neighboring Round Rock, or *Wings*, the first Academy Award winner for best picture in 1927, filmed just down the road in San Antonio.

Some of the credit for Texas' rise to fame in the film industry goes to the Austin-based Texas Film Commission, and to tax laws that favor filmmakers. Established in 1971, the TFC lures productions of all sizes to the state by offering a complete range of film-related services. The Austin Convention and Visitors Bureau's Film Liaison office scouts locations for prospective clients and can provide information on just about anything a filmmaker needs.

— continued on next page

Experts say the next logical step for Austin, especially if the film industry continues to develop, is construction of a major sound stage and more post-production facilities so rough films don't have to be flown to Hollywood for editing. As it stands now, work requiring indoor sets is done largely in rented warehouses and airplane hangars, both harder and harder to come by as Austin's economy booms.

Musicians, artists and writers have always found a haven in Austin. Some say it's Austin itself that brings out the creative side in people. But most agree that these creative communities feed off each other's enthusiasm, talent and commitment to their work, which in turn is inspiring others. Austin is brimming with lone filmmakers working on little money and even less sleep to produce a film good enough to make it into a festival — and some do. In *Michael*, John Travolta's character tells his friend, "Remember, Sparky, no matter what they tell you, you can never have too much sugar." Filmmakers could say the same about Austin.

---

around the country who are working in theater, dance, film and music. The five-play season, beginning in April, usually includes a few world and regional premieres.

Frontera is also in charge of the largest and most intriguing performance festival in the Southwest: Fronterafest. This annual five-week festival, held in January and February, provides a venue for more than 800 high-caliber local, regional and national artists who present nearly 60 separate productions. Concerts, films, visual arts, performing arts and more are all part of this great award-winning event (see our Annual Events and Festivals chapter). In addition to producing its own shows, Frontera also serves as co-producer, umbrella and performance home to many of Austin's fringe artists and companies. So be sure to look, too, for performances by The Subterranean Theatre Company, which specializes in dark, edgy comedies and has won several local awards for its efforts.

Another fringe group doing work of note here is Root Wy'mn Theatre Company. Nationally recognized writer Sharon Bridgforth, founder and artistic director of Root Wy'mn, also wrote the play and collaborated with Frontera on one of Frontera's 1998 main stage theater productions, *Blood Pudding*. The Hyde Park Theatre also presents works by choreographer Margery Segal's Nerve Dance Company, by filmmaker Susan Provost and by Rude Mechanicals, a theater collective established in 1996 that presents new works by local playwrights as well as original adaptations for the stage. Frontera is outgrowing its 85-seat theater so quickly that it aims to move to a new, larger location by the early 2000s.

Live Oak Theatre at the State
719 Congress Ave. • (512) 472-5143

This professional theater company, operating in Austin since 1982, presents an interesting array of productions during its six-play main stage season that runs from September through June. Live Oak productions, musicals, comedies, dramas and at least one world premiere each season, have delighted an ever-increasing number of subscribers, while theater attendance in general has grown to more than 50,000 a year. The theater's commitment to developing and producing new works has led to the staging of such outstanding works as *A Texas Romance* and *Calvin's Garden* by Ellsworth Schave, and *Bosque County, Texas* by Steven Fromholz and Don Toner, Live Oak's producing artistic director. Live Oak has received acclaim for its productions of *The Dead Presidents' Club* and *The Night Hank Williams Died* by well-known Texas native Larry L. King. Live Oak has also staged perennial favorites, including *A Christmas Carol* and *On Golden Pond*.

After leading a somewhat nomadic life for many years, performing in different theaters around town, Live Oak moved into the State Theatre on historic Congress Avenue in 1995. In June of 1998, Live Oak began an extensive renovation of the old movie house and the adjacent building that will result in another major performing arts center in downtown Austin. (The State is next door to Austin's classic Paramount Theatre.) The new facility, which includes two theaters of 400 and 100 seats each, rehearsal halls, scene and costume shops and offices as well as a restaurant, club and bar, will debut in early 1999. The expanded facility will allow Live Oak to double the size of its School of Acting, which provides professional training to children, teens and adults. The theater also produces the annual Harvest Festival of New American Plays, a three-day event that awards cash prizes to playwrights and includes readings of new plays. Live Oak's public outreach programs include Theatre Discovery, which introduces young audiences to live theater, and the annual Benefit Performance program, which raises about $30,000 per year for Austin human service organizations. For more information about these programs, or for tickets, call the Live Oak Theatre.

Planet Theatre

2307 Manor Rd. • (512) 478-5282, (512) 454-TIXS box office

Home to Austin's Vortex Repertory Company since 1994, Planet Theatre has become the place to go to see original cutting-edge performances that have included such works as *The X & Y Trilogy*, a cybernetic opera by Ethos, *Beirut* by Alan Bowne, a rock musical adaptation of *Faustus* and *Wisdom of the Crone*, conceived and directed by producing artistic director and Vortex founder Bonnie Cullum. Among the leaders of Austin's alternative theater scene, Vortex has produced more than 125 successful works since the semiprofessional company was founded in 1988. World premieres, new plays, Texas premieres and vibrant works by Shakespeare have all been presented on the Planet stage.

This East Austin theater, once an abandoned warehouse that has been converted to an intimate 80-seat venue with comfortable theater seats, is used by other individual performers and theatrical companies for shows of all kinds. Vortex presents four major productions a year as well as a number of smaller performances that showcase the talents of this company. Vortex also has earned a reputation in Austin for presenting shows by nationally known performance artists, including Tim Miller, Annie Sprinkle, Karen Finley and Holly Hughes. Whether it's a simple one-person show with only a chair on stage or a full-scale production with elaborate scenery, lighting and sound, Planet Theatre has done it all. The theater also sponsors Summer Youth Theater, which brings teenagers from around Austin to the theater to create, produce and perform a theatrical show.

The Public Domain

807 Congress Ave. • (512) 474-6202, (512) 454-TIXS box office

Located in a loft theater on historic Congress Avenue, The Public Domain is both the name of the space and the theater company that produces a full season of main stage events here. Established in 1993, Public Domain is a semiprofessional company that presents about four main stage productions as well as a number of smaller-scale shows during its season, which runs from September to May. Additionally, a host of other Austin artists and groups use this black-box venue to present productions of all kinds, including dance, music, visual art, theater and performance art. This versatile space is also used for classes, fund-raisers, workshops and receptions. Gone are the days when patrons sat on metal folding chairs. The Public Domain now features good theater seats that can be configured to hold anywhere from 45 to 90 people.

This company, led by artistic director and cofounder Robi Polgar, is called Public Domain for a reason. Most of the works presented by the company are in the public domain so the company doesn't have to pay for the rights. Public Domain's immensely popular shows have included Arthur Conan Doyle's *Sherlock Holmes*, and *Dracula*, adapted by Steven Dietz. The Public Domain also presents one commissioned work by a local playwright each season. *American Arcana* by Austinite Cyndi Williams was part of the 1997-98 season. This is a great venue for Austin actors, set designers, playwrights and directors.

Zachary Scott Theatre Center

1510 Toomey Rd. • (512) 476-0541

Professional theater in Austin rose to new heights in 1998 with Zachary Scott Theatre's production of Tony Kushner's Pulitzer Prize-winning drama *Angels in America*. The play, about AIDS and modern life, sold out for every performance as Austin audiences turned out in droves to support this substantive production. Zach, as the theater is known locally, has been wowing Austin audiences for years with its broad spectrum of plays and musicals, including some, such as *The Gospel at Colonus*, and *Avenue X,* performed for the first time by a regional theater in the United States. Additionally, Zach has given Austin audiences popular revues such as *Beehive* as well as *Shear Madness*, the longest-running play in Austin history.

Zach, Central Texas's oldest resident theater, began in 1933 when it was incorporated as the Austin Civic Theatre. The theater took a major leap forward in 1972 with construction of its first 200-seat theater at the present location. The theater was renamed that year in honor of Zachary Scott, an Austin-raised actor who went on to a successful Hollywood film career. A second 130-seat theater, costume shop, classroom, rehearsal studio and administrative offices were built in 1990, during the time Zach was moving from community theater to become of one Austin's premier professional theaters. Several of Zach's shows have been so popular that the company has needed to rent Austin's larger Paramount Theatre to accommodate all audiences.

Combined annual attendance has grown to more than 150,000 at all three theaters and season tickets are selling at record levels. Zach presents eight to 10 productions during its yearlong season that runs from September through August on both stages, the main Kleberg Stage and the Whisenhunt Arena Stage. The Zachary Scott Theatre Center also operates a hugely popular Performing Arts School that draws 6,500 children, teens and adults each year. Zach's Project InterAct, a professional company of adult actors, performs children's shows for school students throughout the Southwest, including some outstanding original productions. Theater buffs should include a visit to Zach Scott on any tour of Austin.

The Gypsies

Austin Theatre for Youth
710 E. 41st. • (512) 459-7144,
(512) 459-2289 box office

While Austin offers literally hundreds of theater productions each year for adults, very few are aimed specifically at younger audiences. Austin Theatre for Youth fills that void. And fills it well. Since 1995 Austin Theatre for Youth has been presenting exceptional theater to young people and families. The company performs three to five plays a year using a professional artistic staff led by artistic director Rick Schiller. Each play is relevant to the interests of a specific age group of children and all the acting is done by age-appropriate performers. In other words, kids play kids roles and adults perform the roles of adults. Past performances have included *The Reluctant Dragon*, *The Hardy Boys in the Mystery of the Haunted House*, *The Christmas Schooner*, *Ordinary People* and *Rumplestiltskin*. Austin Theater for Youth performs a couple of shows a year in the Auditorium at Waller Creek at the above address and at other venues around town. The season runs September through May.

Salvage Vanguard Theater
(512) 474-7886

Salvage Vanguard Theater is a young but exciting experimental company that has no permanent home but performs in various locations around town. This company, led by artistic director Jason Neulander, has earned a reputation for presenting hot new writers to Austin in shows that, in the most recent season, were paired with a local band — so mu-

INSIDERS' TIP

Find out about every theater performance currently on stage in Austin by calling the Austin Circle of Theaters Performance Hotline at (512) 320-7168. To find out what's happening in dance, call the Dance Line at (512) 474-1766. Also check the listings in the *Austin American-Statesman* and in *The Austin Chronicle*.

sic fans no longer have to miss out on an interesting theater experience. Catering to Austin's hip crowd, Salvage Vanguard is known for performances that rock the ceiling. The company presents four main stage shows, many of them world premieres, between March and December. Salvage Vanguard also recently started a Second Stage season, a monthly series of quick and dirty events that keeps the actors, and the audience, on their toes. Call Salvage Vanguard for a schedule.

Teatro Humanidad Cansada

2210 S. First St. • (512) 236-1484

Under the artistic directorship of founder Rodney Garza, Austin's only bilingual theater company is becoming a force in Latino theater today. From 1994's *I Don't Have to Show You No Stinkin' Badges!* by California playwright Luis Valdez to the acclaimed production of *Petra's Pecado* by Austinite Rupert Reyes, which highlighted the company's first full season in 1997-98, Teatro Humanidad Cansada continues to impress Austin audiences. This theater company is one of Austin's gypsy troupes that have no real home as of yet, although it has performed at some of Austin's most well-known venues, including the Paramount Theatre, the Hyde Park Theatre and the Dougherty Arts Center. Don't worry if English is your only language. This troupe goes out of its way to reach all members of its audience. The company presents four main stage productions and two Latino Comedy Project productions each year as well as one show through its Summer Youth Program, in which Austin youth involved in the project get paid and share in the profits. This is definitely theater to watch in the coming years. Call them for information about current productions. The season begins in October and runs throughout the year.

In A Class By Itself

The Dougherty Arts Center

1110 Barton Springs Rd.
• (512) 397-1458, (512) 454-TIXS box office

This wonderful facility, an operation of the Austin Parks and Recreation Department, has it all: a comfortable 150-seat theater that's always hosting one show or another, an 1,800-square-foot art gallery, classrooms and plenty of studio-lab spaces. It's impossible to list all the arts-related activities that go on at this center, so we'll give you the highlights.

Among the big winners for Austin audiences of all ages is the spring, summer, and now winter, Playfest, held in the DAC theater. This wonderful series of performing arts shows for children has included productions by Zachary Scott Theatre Center's Project InterAct, The University of Texas Department of Theater and Dance, Express Theater of Houston as well as many shows of all kinds presented during the several-week run each season. Started in 1992, Playfest has become an Austin tradition in the theater arts for children. Call (512) 454-TIXS for information and dates on Playfest. DAC also offers plenty of theater experiences for adults. Teatro Humanidad Cansada (see previous listing) has performed here as has Austin's Ballet East Dance Theater. DAC also has hosted some shows for the Big Stinkin' International Improv and Sketch Festival, an annual event that draws comics from around the world to Austin. The Julia C. Butridge Gallery at DAC hosts art shows of all kinds by Austin area artists and arts organizations. Exhibitions in 1998 were sponsored by Women Printmakers of Austin, the Texas Music Museum, Austin Community College, and La Peña, a nonprofit organization dedicated to promoting Latino art and artists. La Peña's annual Serie Print Project, presented here in the spring, is a great way to see up-and-coming artists.

Austin's only city-run arts complex, DAC provides arts enrichment to citizens of all ages and economic levels. Admission prices to DAC performing arts events are often very reasonable while gallery admission is always free. Many of the Austin's other excellent arts programs are operated out of the Dougherty Arts Center, including Art in Public Places, which commissions artworks for placement in city facilities for all to see and enjoy. Be sure to see our chapter on Attractions for information on some of Austin's easily accessible artworks. DAC runs a wide variety of programs for adults and students, including the nationally recognized Totally Cool, Totally Art program, in which professional artists work with teenagers at local recreation centers. DAC sponsors art classes in many genres and run a wonderful summer camp program. Call them for details about any or all the activities going on a the center. The center is open Monday through Thursday from 9 AM to 9:30 PM, Friday from 9 AM to 5:30 PM and Saturday 10 AM to 2 PM.

Dance and Music

More and more Austin audiences are getting the "pointe" about Austin's rich dance scene, which includes a number of established companies and even more individual dancers and choreographers who bring their unique styles to stages all over the city. So in addition to the dance companies we've listed here, be sure to look for special performances by troupes formed for a specific production. Austin dancers offer a wonderful cross-section of styles, including classical ballet, tap, modern, post-modern and folklorico. The leader among Austin dancer/choreographers is Deborah Hay, nationally recognized as one of the pioneers of post-modern New Dance. If you love dance, be sure to look for occasional performances by the Deborah Hay Dance Company. Andrea Ariel, Toni Bravo and Margery Segal are others of note.

Whether you like a toe-tapping good time, the skirt-swirling grandeur of a Mexican folk dance, the awesome power and grace of a dancer on pointe or the stylized foot- and body-work of modern dance, you'll be inspired by Austin's dance performances. Don't miss the Austin Festival of Dance if you're in town in April. This annual event, started in 1992, brings some of the finest dancers from Austin and around the country to the Paramount Theatre for a pair of AIDS benefit performances. Dance Umbrella, Austin's main dancers organization with about 100 artistic members, also offers a season of performances from October to May. Check with them at (512) 450-0456.

While Texas' mecca for classical music artists is about 70 miles east of Austin in Round Top (see our Daytrips chapter), you'll be pleased to know that you don't have to travel to hear exciting, well-respected ensembles. Austin claims about two dozen classical music groups, about half choral, half instrumental. The two mentioned here are among Austin's leaders, but look, too for outstanding performances by the Austin Choral Union, the Austin Vocal Arts Ensemble, River City Pops, the Austin Lyric Opera Chorus and the Texas Chamber Consort. Those interested in performing will discover that these and many other musical groups, including barbershop and gospel choruses, accept new members by audition. Austin also claims several groups for boys, girls and children.

The classical guitar scene is also alive and well in Austin, and has attracted enough outstanding guitarists to maintain the Austin Classical Guitar Society. The only nationally syndicated classical guitar program is produced right here in Austin and airs out of radio station KMFA. The creme de la creme of Austin's classical guitarists is the world-class player and recording artist Adam Holzman. This virtuoso, who plays recital halls throughout the world, including Carnegie Hall, has won five prestigious international guitar competitions and has created UT's classical guitar program. In a music city dominated by singer/songwriters and rock 'n' rollers blasting chords through amplifiers, Holzman is the artist the *American-Statesman* has called, "the best guitar player in Austin you've never heard of."

Ballet Austin

3002 Guadalupe St. • (512) 476-9051, (512) 476-2163 box office

Under the artistic directorship of Lambros Lambrou, Ballet Austin has become an excellent addition to Austin's cultural scene and the city's premier classical ballet troupe. One of only three professional ballet companies in Texas, Ballet Austin includes 24 dancers from around the world. The 1999-2000 Ballet Austin season will mark the 10th anniversary of Lambrou's artistic directorship. Lambrou, a native of Cyprus, trained at the prestigious Royal Ballet School and worked with major ballet companies around the world before coming to Austin.

Ballet Austin presents five seasonal ballets, including the much anticipated annual performances of *The Nutcracker* in December. Other Austin favorites have included performances of *Firebird*, *Ulysses* and *Cinderella*. This accomplished company traces its roots to 1956, when the company was chartered as the Austin Ballet Society. Over the years, the ballet evolved from a civic, all-volunteer organization to become a professional company.

One major aspect of this company is the Ballet Austin Academy, also established in 1956, which offers classical ballet training as well as jazz, modern dance and fitness classes to dancers from age 3 to adult. The company's regular season performances are held at the Bass Concert Hall on The University of Texas campus. Additionally, Ballet Austin offers full-length and mixed-repertoire performances throughout Texas. This community-based company goes all out to educate school students and adults alike.

Two of Ballet Austin's most popular programs are the Fire House Focus in which the public is invited to the Ballet Austin's historic headquarters in an old firehouse to see part of a live rehearsal and take part in an informal chat and discussion with Lambrou. Another program, Curtain Call, invites matinee-goers to a half-hour pre-performance discussion at the concert hall. For individual or season tickets, call the Ballet Austin box office. The season runs from September to May.

Ballet East

At Dougherty Arts Center
• (512) 478-8717, (512) 454-TIXS box office

Founded by Rodolfo Mendez in 1982, Ballet East is a well-known community dance troupe made up of professional and emerging dancers and choreographers from many ethnic backgrounds, with a strong emphasis on Austin's Latino dancers. The company in residence in East Austin has a solid reputation for developing young dancers and for showcasing the talents of some of Austin's finest dancers and choreographers, including Toni Bravo, Andrea Ariel and Melissa Villarreal, and also works with guest choreographers from nationally known companies, including the Alvin Ailey American Dance School in New York. Ballet East, which most often offers mixed repertoire programs, performs several times a year at various locations in Austin, most often at the Dougherty Arts Center.

Sharir/Bustamante danceworks

3724 Jefferson St., Ste. 201
• (512) 458-8158

The leading modern dance organization in Austin, if not the state of Texas, Sharir/Bustamante danceworks is one of just three arts organization in Austin to have been selected by the National Endowment for the Arts as a participant in the 1994 Advancement Program for "emerging organizations of artistic excellence." Founded in 1982 by choreographer Yacov Sharir, and recently renamed to include the name of artistic co-director Jose Bustamante, the company has built a reputation as an important institution on the forefront of new dance and is known for avant-garde choreography and performances.

Among Sharir's most spellbinding projects are performances that juxtapose live dancers against computer-generated images, just one result of Sharir's experimentation with new technology. The company presents a full season of performances in Austin and regularly tours regionally and nationally. Sharir also has been selected for international festivals in France, Spain, Israel, Canada, Holland and Portugal.

INSIDERS' TIP

You can purchase half-price, day-of-show tickets to some Austin events through Austixs at the Austin Convention and Visitors Bureau at 201 E. Second Street from 11:30 AM to 1:30 PM Thursday through Saturday. Call (512) 454-HALF on Wednesdays around 3 PM for a recording of events offering half-price tickets for the coming weekend. This is a service of the Austin Circle of Theaters, (512) 499-8388. And don't miss ACoT's annual fall giveaway of more than 1,000 tickets to about 100 performing arts venues all over town. Call (512) 454-TIXS to find out the date and location.

As the professional company-in-residence at The University of Texas College of Fine Arts, Sharir has presented and collaborated with many internationally renowned companies, most notably Merce Cunningham. Sharir performs on UT Performing Arts Center stages as well as in other locations around Austin during its Austin season, which runs from November to April or May. Call the Sharir offices or check the local dance listings for information about the company's current performances or to find out where to get tickets.

Tapestry Dance Company

507 B Pressler St. • (512) 474-9846

Founded in 1989 by rhythm tap dancer Acia Gray and ballet/jazz artist Deirdre Strand, Tapestry is a well-established multiform dance company that has delighted audiences all over Austin and in other parts of the country during the company's national performance tour. This professional, nonprofit company presents seasonal multiform concerts from October to June at the Paramount Theatre and is a regular participant in the annual Austin Festival of Dance. The annual Austin Tap Jam, started in 1990, has become an Austin tradition. Tapestry has thrilled Austin audiences by hosting a number of international dance and music artists, including Gregory Hines, Sarah Petronio and James Clouser. The company also operates a downtown dance academy that offers professional classes for children and adults in rhythm tap, jazz and ballet. Tapestry is also known for hosting numerous ethnic and cultural events, including Irish step dancing, clogging and tango. Call Tapestry or the Paramount box office, (512) 472-5411, to find out about performances or to get tickets.

Austin Civic Chorus

(512) 326-1171

Founded in 1965 with just 32 singers, Austin Civic Chorus has as many as 140 members today ranging from high school students to senior citizens. This excellent chorus performs two or three major choral/orchestral masterpieces a year for huge audiences from all over Central Texas and is often a featured chorus with the Austin Symphony Orchestra. Past performances of Austin Civic Chorus have included "Songs of the American People," a concert of spirituals and other American music that featured a guest gospel choir and the singing voice of Austin's accomplished Judy Arnold. The Civic Chorus also has performed *The Passion According to St. John* by Bach and works from many other masters.

Other highlights of the year include the annual *Sing-It-Yourself Messiah* in December, a holiday tradition for hundreds of Austin families. Austin Civic Chorus also produces and performs the annual summer Musical for Children, a fully costumed and choreographed show presented free in eight performances attended by more than 2,000 people. The group works in cooperation with the Austin Vocal Arts Ensemble to present a choral education program in all of Austin Independent School District's middle schools. The Austin Civic Chorus performs mainly in churches around Austin, most often St. Matthews Episcopal Church. Call the chorus at the number listed above, not the church please, for a schedule of events.

Austin Lyric Opera

1111 W. Sixth St. • (512) 472-5927, (512) 472-5992 or (800) 31-OPERA box office

Since its founding in 1986, Austin Lyric Opera has grown dramatically to a seasonal attendance of nearly 35,000 people and has expanded its season to include 12 performances of three operas, most of them sold-out events. That's an outstanding attendance record for a city the size of Austin, and much of the credit goes to Joseph McClain, the opera's general manager since the beginning.

The company is known for presenting both the most popular of the operatic repertoire as well as works that explore the boundaries of opera, including *The Ballad of Baby Doe*, the company's first American work. Central Texas' only professional opera company brings major international and American artists to Austin each season and the results have included many world-class performances. *The Barber of Seville*, *Andrea Chenier* and *La Boheme* are just a few of the performances that have highlighted past seasons.

The season features an opera every other month from November through March and includes a free outdoor performance at the Zilker Hillside Theater each October. All main stage performances are held at the Bass Concert Hall on The University of Texas campus. Opera attendance is on the rise nationwide and one of the reasons is the use of surtitles, the simultaneous translation of the opera on a small screen above the stage. So patrons of Austin Lyric Opera and of operas throughout the country no longer have to speak a foreign language to understand the story. Austin Lyric Opera has its own 65-member orchestra and a 60-member semiprofessional chorus.

The company, known for its commitment to the education of new and young audiences, offers a variety of programs for students in elementary school through high school each year, including a program in which students write, score, direct and perform their own operas. The new Young Artists Program draws students from all over the country for operatic training, and some have gone on to successful opera careers. Austin Lyric Opera is in the process of building a new opera center and community music school, expected to open sometime in 1999. For individual or season tickets, call the box office.

Austin Symphony Orchestra

1101 Red River St. • (512) 476-6064, (888) 4-MAESTRO

Austin's oldest performing arts group, the Austin Symphony Orchestra was founded in 1911. In 1998 American Peter Bay arrived in Austin as the symphony's new conductor and music director following a two-year search for the perfect conductor to lead the orchestra to new artistic challenges and to expand its audience even further in Austin. Bay, especially known for his skill at conducting large contemporary scores and complex pieces, plans to introduce more works of American composers and thematic programs, including music from film scores, to the orchestra's extensive repertoire of classical music. Bay, in his early 40s, has been music director for Pennsylvania's Erie Philharmonic and principal guest conductor for the Rochester Philharmonic Orchestra.

The Austin Symphony Orchestra, which performs its September-through-May concert series at Bass Concert Hall on The University of Texas campus, also presents festive Holiday and Promenade Pops Concerts at Palmer Auditorium, in which the audience brings their own picnic dinners and sits at tables for an evening of lighthearted music. The orchestra offers an assortment of nationally recognized youth programs, including the Young People's Concerts in the spring, which bring more than 28,000 elementary students to Bass Concert Hall for live performances, and the Halloween Children's Concert at the Paramount Theatre.

The symphony also conducts free family concerts throughout the year and is especially known for its popular July 4th concert and fireworks show on the shores of Town Lake, which draws more than 60,000 people a year. Call the box office listed above for tickets or for more information about this Austin institution. And see our chapter on Attractions to learn more about Symphony Square, the complex of historical buildings that houses symphony offices and features an outdoor amphitheater and restaurant.

New Texas Festival

(512) 476-5775

New Texas Festival, an organization dedicated to celebrating the vocal arts, has earned a solid reputation for presenting entertaining, innovative and varied vocal music concerts in Austin and around Texas. Featuring a resident professional chorus and orchestra, the Conspirare Choir and Orchestra, New Texas Festival specializes in music for the human voice. Conspirare has never been known to limit itself to just one genre. Choral, classical, jazz, ethnic, experimental, Broadway, old masterworks and contemporary compositions are all presented by this well-respected group, which performs at various Austin locations. Founded in 1991 by artistic director Craig Hella Johnson, New Texas Festival started out as an annual week-long series of vocal-music performances in the spring. Now the choir performs additional concerts throughout the year, including the annual "Christmas at the Carillon" show performed in an historic chapel in West Austin. Call New Texas Festival for a schedule of performances.

Photo: Courtesy of the Austin Convention and Visitors Bureau

Elizabet Ney's sculptures are featured in her museum in Hyde Park.

The Folk Artists

Aztlan Folklórico Dance Company
Santa Cruz Center, 1805 E. Seventh St. • (512) 478-9717

Both the critics and the public are beginning to rave about this dance company, which presents both traditional Mexican folk dances and original contemporary dances set to the music of popular Latino recording artists. Founded in 1974, this company for many years performed mainly the classic regional folk dances of Mexico. In the past few years, however, choreographer and general director Roén. Salinas has introduced a contemporary format that reflects the folklorico heritage but addresses the Hispanic culture of today's Texas. Instead of the flamboyant costumes typical of some regional dances of Mexico, for example, Aztlan dancers sometimes wear blue jeans and T-shirts while dancing to the music of Los Lobos.

Aztlan still does Mexican folk dances, and does them extremely well, but this new choreography adds an exciting artistic dimension to the troupe. The company of about 16 dancers ranging in age from 13 to 30 debuts all its performances at the popular East Austin performance venue, the Santa Cruz Center. The troupe also has performed at venues all over the city and in Hong Kong and Great Britain. Call them for a current schedule of performances. Academia Aztlan, which aims to promote a greater understanding of the Hispanic cultural arts, offers dance classes, workshops, lectures, art exhibits and more at the Santa Cruz Center and elsewhere in Austin. Call the center at (512) 478-9311 to find out what else in on the calendar there.

Roy Lozano's Ballet Folklórico de Texas

1928-C Gaston Place Dr. • (512) 928-1111

Be sure to check the dance listings for performances by Austin's own Ballet Folklórico de Texas, a company started in 1983 by the late Roy Lozano, a University of Texas alumnus who studied with the world-renowned Amalia Hernandez Ballet Folklórico de Mexico. Now under the artistic directorship of Jesus Chacon, this energetic company presents traditional Mexican folk dances from 19 regions of the country, each with its own dance style and stunning costumes. Ballet Folklórico is a professional troupe that performs all over Texas and has also been asked to perform in Mexico. This company knows Mexican folk dance. The authentic brightly colored costumes Ballet Folklórico is known for only add to the appeal of this fine dance troupe. Ballet Folklórico also operates a youth dance company and a dance school to train young dance talent in the many styles of traditional Mexican dance.

Texas Folklife Resources

1317 S. Congress Ave. • (512) 441-Y'ALL

Modern-day Texas culture is a rich blend of ethnic and regional traditions dating back hundreds of years. There's no better way to discover how well those traditions have survived than by attending events sponsored by Texas Folklife Resources (TFR). This dynamic, nonprofit organization brings the best of those living, breathing cultures to the forefront of public awareness today through a comprehensive calendar of events in Austin and around the state.

TFR works with folk artists all over Texas to document living traditions and present them to the public in many forms, including exhibitions, concerts, radio programs, demonstrations and more. Among TFR's many successful projects is the Texas Culture Bash, an annual Austin festival featuring Texas performers, master crafters and hands-on children's activities that celebrate Texas traditions. Other important past programs have included Hecho Tejano: Four Texas-Mexican Folk Artists, which exhibited 35 sculptural works exemplifying the variety and quality of Texas-Mexican folk art; Austinlore/Dancelore: African American Dance Traditions of Austin; and Accordion Kings, a multi-year performance project celebrating the polka, Cajun, conjunto and zydeco traditions of music in Texas. And there's more: Gospel music, powwow craft traditions, works in wood by folk artists, and songs and ballads of the Texas-Mexico border.

TFR also operates the Apprenticeships in the Folk Arts program, which encourages master folk artists to pass their traditions on to qualified apprentices in their community. The only way to keep fully informed of TFR's extensive list of events is by getting on the mailing list. Better yet, join TFR and become help present, preserve and promote the folk arts and folklife of the Lone Star State.

The Visual Arts

We can think of few better ways to spend an afternoon or a whole day than by visiting some of Austin's exceptional art museums and galleries. In Austin, access to the master artists of the past and present, including celebrated Austin and Texas artists, couldn't be easier. Austin offers two significant museums dedicated to the works of eminent sculptors Elizabet Ney and Charles Umlauf, who both lived and worked in Austin until their deaths.

INSIDERS' TIP

Want to save all kinds of money for on-street parking ($1 an hour) and avoid the hassle of having to run to feed the meter while visiting Austin's uptown theater and museum districts? Park at the Park and Ride lot on Bouldin Street next to Palmer Auditorium between Barton Springs Road and Riverside Drive and catch a free 'Dillo ride to your destination. For more about this wonderful service, see our Getting Here and Getting Around chapter.

The gallery scene offers an excellent opportunity to view works by both established and emerging artists. There's always a chance you'll come face to face with the artists themselves, either working or simply enjoying the company of people like yourself who've come for the experience. You may return home with an art treasure that will delight you for years to come, or perhaps turn out to be a shrewd investment. At the very least, we guarantee you'll be enlightened. Austin seems dominated by so many "alternative" galleries that the term has lost its meaning to a certain extent. Alternative to what? we might ask. Just prepare yourself for the unusual.

Austin still has not achieved the status of Dallas and Houston as a major hub for art buyers, but what it lacks in patrons is more than made up by a dynamic artistic community. Michael Ray Charles and Peter Saul, two internationally recognized artists whose work is occasionally exhibited at museums locally, are perhaps Austin's living masters. Painter Melissa Miller is another Austinite who has captured an audience that extends far and wide. There are many more whose work is recognized, and coveted, beyond our state's borders. And who knows when Austin will produce the next artist to gain national, even international, renown? What better way to become acquainted with these talented artists than by seeing exhibits of their work on their home turf. You'll be astounded by the range of styles and the diverse media on display by the painters, sculptors, photographer and fine crafters working in Austin today.

Austin also is distinguished for producing fine arts prints. Master printmaker Sam Coronado, Flatbed Press and Slugfest are leading the way in that arena. Austin's galleries are not limited to our own artists, however. Among the galleries we've listed below you'll find work by some of the most interesting and well known artists in the country today.

Don't let the idea of visiting a museum or gallery intimidate you, even if you're not an art expert. Austin's showrooms are staffed by knowledgeable, accessible experts, sometimes artists themselves, who are more than willing to offer on-the-spot advice, tips and information about the artists and their works. Artists, always searching for the perfect, cheap space in which to work, are clustering in several areas of the city, some too small yet to be called art colonies. Among these is E. Sixth Street, where Latino and other artists are establishing studios and small galleries. While this area is quite spread out, take a stroll along E. Sixth east of Interstate 35 in the 1100 and 1200 block, and you'll encounter such artistic delicacies as the pottery space called Milagro Del Rio Brazos Studio, the Las Americas fine art gallery and Clayworks Studio and Gallery. This culturally rich area includes several more galleries and studios definitely worth investigating. Try Graphic Glass Studios and Archaic, just southwest of Clayworks on Fifth Street. South Congress Avenue also is starting to see more art development. Those of you who want to extend your study of the visual arts even further may want to check out some of the true art colonies that circle Austin in small towns like Salado, Wimberly and Fredericksburg. These communities are especially known for creating fine art glass and fine art furniture.

Newcomers and visitors who want to get a feel for Austin's visual arts scene, and experience some of our best galleries at the same time, should take a stroll in the 1700 block of Guadalupe and Lavaca Streets. These parallel streets form what is becoming known as the Uptown Cultural District. The eight galleries in this district feature work by some of the best artists working in Austin today as well as work by other high caliber artists. We've also provided information on a developing cultural district along South First Street, which also harbors some remarkable artists, as well as a few of the other leading galleries around town.

Art Museums

Austin Museum of Art — Downtown
823 Congress Ave. • (512) 495-9224

After the Austin Museum of Art outgrew its location at Laguna Gloria, the institution, a public/private partnership between the City of Austin and the Austin Museum of Art, opened this additional 12,000-square-foot space in November of 1996. Like the Laguna Gloria site, the downtown space focuses on presenting temporary exhibits of significant 20th-century American visual art. Works by artists from the United States, Mexico and the Caribbean are presented, including a strong showing of artists from Austin and around Texas.

The museum hosts 10 to 12 exhibitions annually, including those organized in house and by other museums around the country. Past exhibitions have included a collection of photographs by Brian Lanker titled *I Dream a World: Portraits of Black Women Who Changed America*, *Committed to Abstraction: Ten in Texas*, which showcased 10 abstract artists working in Texas. The museum also organized the show *Michael Ray Charles: An American Artist's Work, 1989-1997*, the first major retrospective of the well-known Austin artist whose work satirizes and critiques traditional and contemporary African-American stereotypes. Pieces by Austin's illustrious neo-expressionist, Peter Saul, were featured in another show.

In 1998, the museum presented *American Images: The Southwestern Bell Corporation's Collection of 20th Century American Art,* which included works by Jackson Pollock, Roy Lichtenstein and Marsden Hartley. In 1998 the Austin Museum of Art announced plans to build a new 85,000-square-foot facility expected to open in the early 2000s. The new museum, at the corner of Third and San Jacinto Streets downtown, will include several galleries, a lecture hall, classrooms and other educational facilities as well as a cafe, museum store and outdoor areas. The museum is open Tuesday, Wednesday, Friday and Saturday from 11 AM to 7 PM, Thursday from 11 AM to 9 PM and Sunday from 1 to 5 PM. General admission is $3. Students and seniors pay $2 while members and children are admitted free. Reduced parking rates are available at the 823 Parking Garage on Ninth Street or you can try to park at the always busy meters on the street, for $1 an hour.

Austin Museum of Art at Laguna Gloria

3809 W. 35th St. • (512) 458-8191

Laguna Gloria is a great place to visit, even if you're not a regular museum-goer. This Mediterranean-style villa was built in 1916. The 4,500-square-foot estate and the lush gardens, including a sculpture garden, surrounding the villa are works of art themselves. Opened in 1961, Laguna Gloria was Austin's only city art museum until the downtown facility opened in 1996. This is a fantastic West Austin location. Today, the museum has a national reputation for hosting a wide array of shows by diverse 20th-century artists from Austin and around the world. Performance artists put on regular shows at the outdoor amphitheater near the lake.

The Art School at Laguna Gloria, in a separate facility on site, offers both children's classes and instruction for adults in such things as painting, ceramics, graphic arts, sculpture, jewelry and more. The Art School can be reached at (512) 323-6380. Laguna Gloria hosts AMOA's annual Fiesta, the museum's largest annual fund-raiser and a lively event for the whole family. Put on by the AMOA Art Guild, Fiesta celebrated its 48th year in May 1998 with a juried art show, live auction and activities for the whole family, with plenty of art projects and games for children (see our Annual Events and Festivals chapter for more).

Members receive free admission to the museum, invitations to special events, subscriptions to museum publications and more. At $35 a year for an individual and $50 for a family, membership to this museum is a bargain. Of course, you don't have to be a member to enjoy Laguna Gloria's inspiring exhibits. The daily entrance fee is $2 per person. Students and senior citizens pay just $1 while children under 12 are admitted free. The museum is open Tuesday, Wednesday, Friday and Saturday from 10 AM to 5 PM, Thursday 10 AM to 9 PM and Sunday 1 to 5 PM. Parking is free on site. For recorded information about current exhibits call the number listed above.

Jack S. Blanton Museum of Art

23rd and San Jacinto Sts.
• (512) 471-7324

The University of Texas fine arts museum, one of the leading university art museums in the country, is a key component of Austin's cultural scene as well as an important center of learning and culture for the entire state of Texas. Formerly known as the Archer M. Huntington Art Gallery, the name was changed in 1998 in anticipation of the new state-of-the-art museum that is scheduled to be built on campus by the year 2002.

The museum's collection, now housed at

this site and at the Harry Ransom Humanities Research Center on the opposite side of campus, will be joined when the new museum opens to the public. The Blanton Museum's outstanding permanent collections are the most expansive in Central Texas, especially in the areas of American art, Latin American art, and European prints and drawings. The collection includes more than 12,000 works of art spanning the history of Western civilization from antiquity to the present. This location organizes a constantly changing array of temporary exhibits of works by internationally known artists, major Texas artists, and University of Texas fine arts graduate students. The museum, a strong research-oriented, teaching institution, also hosts an ongoing series of public lectures by museum curators, artists and art historians from UT and around the country. This location houses the Department of Prints and Drawings, the largest and most historically balanced collection in the American South and Southwest. This collection, made up of 12,000 etchings, drawings, engravings and more, includes both university-owned material and objects on long-term loan.

For more information about the museum's outstanding permanent collection, see our listing for the Harry Ransom Humanities Research Center in this chapter. The museum is open from 9 AM to 5 PM Monday, Tuesday, Wednesday and Friday, from 9 AM to 9 PM on Thursday and 1 to 5 PM on Saturday and Sunday. It's closed on university holidays. Admission is free. If you've come by car, park nearby in the garage at 24th and San Jacinto Streets. There is a parking fee.

Mexic-Arte Museum

419 Congress Ave. • (512) 480-9373

Since its founding in 1984 Mexic-Arte Museum has become Austin's leading organization dedicated to the promotion of multicultural contemporary art by both local and internationally known artists from across Latin America. The museum features three galleries that exhibit works from Mexic-Arte's permanent collection as well as from touring and self-curated shows. Among the more memorable shows in recent years, and there have been many, are *The Nearest Edge of the World: Art and Cuba Now*, which featured the work of contemporary young Cuban artists; *Latin American Book Arts*, an exhibition of book art created by Latin American artists from throughout the Americas; *Mario Orozco Rivera*, which featured work by Mexico's master painter. Mexic-Arte works with the Mexican Consulate in Austin to bring exhibitions, and programs from throughout Mexico.

This museum was founded by Sylvia Orozco, Pio Pulido and Sam Coronado, three Austin artists who painted a mural at the former Arts Warehouse in Austin in exchange for exhibit space back in 1983. In its present location since 1988, the museum today also presents musical, theatrical and performing arts events on weekends. More than 100,000 people visit this great Austin museum each year. The museum also houses a gift shop. It's open from 10 AM to 6 PM Monday through Saturday, except during opening receptions when hours are extended. General admission is $2 normally, but can be a bit higher for special events.

Elizabet Ney Museum

304 E. 44th St. • (512) 458-2255

Celebrated sculptor Elizabet Ney put her artistic career back on track when she moved to Austin's Hyde Park in the late 1800s and built Formosa, now an extraordinary museum dedicated to the life and works of this sophisticated woman. Here, visitors will discover a provocative array of about 50 portrait busts and full-figure statues of Texas heroes and of

INSIDERS' TIP

***Austin Arts Downtown* is a small, free monthly arts and culture magazine printed on newsprint and available at several locations around downtown, especially in art galleries. AVAANTI is the journal of the Austin Visual Arts Association published 10 times a year. It's available free at galleries or at AVAA offices in the ArtPlex building at 1705 Guadalupe Street.**

the European notables Ney sculpted as a young artist in Europe. Also here, are the glorious sculptures of Lady Macbeth, Prometheus Bound and *SURSUM*, a delightful sculpture of two young nude boys.

The building itself, which Ney designed as her home and studio, also glorifies Ney's artistic sensibilities. Built in two phases and named Formosa, meaning beautiful in Portuguese, the studio lives up to its name. The first studio section, reminiscent of a Greek temple, was built in 1892, when Ney was 59 years old. Living quarters, which included a Gothic tower study for her husband, philosopher/scientist Edmund Montgomery, were added 10 years later. Today, Formosa is listed on the National Register of Historic Places as well as both the Austin and Texas registers.

The museum includes a wonderful section on the life of Ney herself. Here visitors will find many of the artist's tools as well as a hat, watch, tea cup, glasses and many other items used by the artist. Excellent written accounts of her life are on display here also. Visitors will learn that this great talent came to Texas from Europe with the idea of forsaking her career for, as she put it, the "more important art of molding flesh and blood." In other words, to raise her two boys. Tragically, one son died at age two. Twenty years later, Ney accepted a commission to sculpt the figures of Sam Houston and Stephen F. Austin that stand in the Texas State Capitol today. Her career had resumed.

The museum stands as a monument to Ney's influence on the arts in Texas. Her ability to inspire others during a time when Texas slighted the arts, led to the creation of the Texas Fine Arts Association and later the Texas Commission on the Arts and The University of Texas art department. The Elizabet Ney Museum, one of the oldest museums in Texas, was founded after her death in 1907 by those Ney inspired during her lifetime. Today, the collection is part of UT's Harry Ransom Humanities Research Center. Ney's work can also be seen at the Texas State Cemetery, at UT, at the Smithsonian Institution in Washington, D.C., and in other museums in the United States and Europe.

The museum is open Wednesday through Saturday 10 AM to 5 PM and Sunday from noon to 5 PM. Admission is free as is parking on the residential streets around the building.

Harry Ransom Humanities Research Center

Near Guadalupe and 21st Sts.
• (512) 471-7324

The first two floors of the Ransom Center are established as galleries of the Jack S. Blanton Museum of Art, The University of Texas fine art museum. This location features outstanding selections from the Blanton museum's permanent collection, including the Mari and James A. Michener Collection of 20th Century Art, one of the finest university-held collections of modern American paintings. The collection, started with a huge donation to the university by Pulitzer Prize-winning author James Michener and his wife, is comprised of more than 300 paintings and other objects, including masterpieces by such artists as Thomas Hart Benton, Franz Kline, Adolph Gottlieb and Marsden Hartley. (See our chapter on The Literary Scene for more about Michener.)

Visitors will find selections from the museum's C. R. Smith Collection of Art of the American West and from the Contemporary Latin American Art Collection, the foremost collection of its kind in the United States. Also on view at this location are antiquities from ancient Rome and Greece, medieval art on loan from the Metropolitan Museum of Art in New York, and examples of European painting and sculpture from the Renaissance and Baroque periods.

Samples from the Ransom Center's collection also are on display here, including a 1456 Gutenberg Bible, one of just 13 complete copies of the first book printed with movable type, and a London cityscape, renowned for being the first photograph ever taken. For more information on the Ransom Center's changing exhibits and the research center aspect of this facility, see our chapter on Attractions. See also our listing for the Jack S. Branton Museum of Art in this chapter. The Ransom Center gallery floors are open from 9 AM to 5 PM Monday, Tuesday, Wednesday and Friday, from 9 AM to 9 PM Thursday and from 1 to 5 PM on Saturday and Sunday. Admission is free. Parking for this location is best at the Dobie Parking garage on 21st and Whitis streets, which charges $2.50 per hour.

Umlauf Sculpture Garden & Museum

605 Robert E. Lee Rd. • (512) 445-5582

Directors of the Umlauf Sculpture Garden & Museum like to say this garden epitomizes Austin: it's outdoors, casual and lovely. And they have a great point. Here, in a totally Austin xeriscape garden and pond next to Zilker Park, visitors are treated to the fabulous sculptures of acclaimed artist Charles Umlauf, who came to Austin in 1941 and remained for the rest of his life.

The garden, terrace and surrounding land provide a perfect outdoor setting for 62 of Umlauf's bronze and cast-stone pieces. And there are many more, of exotic woods, marbles and terra cotta, inside the glass-enclosed museum. The pieces, which range from the realistic to the abstract, represent a wide range of subject matter, including children, family groupings, mythological and religious figures, refugees, small animals, and sensuous nudes.

Umlauf, who taught in the University of Texas art department for 40 years and retired in 1981 as professor emeritus, won nearly every professional award offered, including a Guggenheim Fellowship and a Ford Foundation Grant. His works can be seen in museums and public collections across the country, including the Smithsonian Institution in Washington, D.C., and the Metropolitan Museum of Art in New York. Umlauf's pieces can also be found on the UT campus and at a dozen sites around town, including the grounds of the Laguna Gloria Art Museum and the Texas State Cemetery (see our listings in this chapter).

In 1985, Umlauf and his wife, Angeline, donated their longtime home and studio, and more than 200 pieces of his work, to the City of Austin. Mrs. Umlauf, now in her mid-90s, has a life estate in the home next to the garden and remains active in the museum. She also handles the sale of some of Umlauf's work.

The museum, built in 1991, was constructed with private funds. This is a wonderful place to come, and is also popular for weddings and other outdoor events. The city-owned, privately run museum, has gone all out to make this wheelchair accessible and has special programs for the visually and hearing impaired. It's also a great place to bring children (see our Kidstuff chapter). The museum is open Wednesday through Friday from 10 AM to 4:30 PM, on Saturday and Sunday from September to May from 1 to 4:30 PM, and from 10 AM to 4:30 PM in June, July and August. General admission is $3.

Galleries

Uptown Cultural District

ArtPlex

1705 Guadalupe St.
ACA Gallery • (512) 474-7799
Ellos • (512) 457-8104
Pro-Jex Gallery • (512) 472-7707

This great complex is home to three galleries as well as studios for more than three dozen of Austin's working artists. Start on the main floor with the ACA Gallery. This space is operated by the Artists' Coalition of Austin, a nonprofit arts advocacy organization managed by the artists themselves. The 1,600-square-foot exhibition space is filled with members' work in ever-changing exhibits and will introduce you to some of the artists working in our city today. The ACA is also a great community resource for the arts and goes out of its way to promote art awareness in Austin through a series of sponsored events.

INSIDERS' TIP

Michael Barnes, art critic for the *Austin American-Statesman*, provides insightful articles and commentaries about the arts, as does *The Austin Chronicle*. And check out "RSVP" in the *Statesman*'s Sunday Life & Arts section. This calendar of arts events lists the best events for the week.

Also here is Pro-Jex Gallery, perhaps the best known photo gallery in town. All kinds of interesting work is featured in this small space. Upstairs in the ArtPlex is the Ellos gallery, a small space yet well worth the trip upstairs to see its latest exhibitions of Austin artists and others. The Austin Visual Arts Association has offices in this complex and is a great resource for both working artists and members of the general public interested in art. A visit to this complex will start you out well on any tour of the visual arts in Austin, and you may get to see artists at work in any number of their studios.

Galeria Sin Fronteras Sam Coronado Microgallery

1701 Guadalupe St. • (512) 478-9448, (512) 236-8900

Founded in 1986 and at this larger location since 1991, Galeria Sin Fronteras is one of Austin's well-established commercial art galleries. The Gallery Without Borders, as it would be called in English, specializes in contemporary U.S. Latino art as well as art created by selected artists in the United States and elsewhere. Paintings, sculptures, prints and photography are continually exhibited in this spacious gallery, owned and operated by Gilbert Cardenas.

The gallery also sells handicrafts and does custom framing. Among the gallery's best known artists are UT professor Lillian Garcia Riog, a painter; painter Carmen Lomas Garza of San Francisco, Cesar Martinez of San Antonio, a painter and fine art printmaker; and Alejandro Romero of Chicago, who does fine art prints, etchings and paintings. Galeria Sin Fronteras usually shows one artist at a time for about two months and has group shows about twice a year. Call them for details. Also at this location is the marketing and sales office of master printmaker Sam Coronado. There is a very small gallery here, but most of the work is done in Coronado's studio in East Austin.

Lyons Matrix Gallery

1712 Lavaca St. • (512) 479-0068

Arguably the most respected fine arts gallery in Austin today, Lyons Matrix has been in business since 1992. That's a long life span for a privately owned art gallery in Austin, and this one shows no signs of going anywhere. Much of its success is due to the excellent contemporary artists represented here, including many of Austin's most well-known artists as well as a number of distinguished artists from around the country.

This is just a great place for learning more about Austin's art scene. This good-sized, delightful space is perfect for browsing. Renowned painter Melissa Miller is represented by Lyons Matrix as are many other well-known Austin-based artists. Sarah Canright, a University of Texas professor; Judy Jensen, acclaimed reverse glass painter; Damian Priour, who sculpts in glass and limestone; and metal sculptor David Deming are just a few of Lyons Matrix's artists. The owner is Camille Lyons, but any member of the Lyons Matrix's knowledgeable staff can help you. The gallery is open 10 AM to 5 PM Tuesday through Friday, 10 AM to 4 PM on Saturday.

Women & Their Work

1710 Lavaca St. • (512) 477-1064

This nonprofit organization dedicated to promoting women in the arts celebrated its 20th anniversary in 1998. Make no mistake. This is much more than an art gallery. Women & Their Work is the only organization of its kind in Texas that embraces all the arts. The organization promotes women artists in visual art, dance, music, theater, literature and film. As such, it is one of Austin premier resources for the arts.

Gallery exhibitions featuring painting, sculpture, photography, fine crafts and works on paper change regularly. Women & Their Work presents more than 40 diverse events each year, including juried and invitational exhibitions of Texas artists as well as solo and

INSIDERS' TIP

***Paramount Presents* is the publication of the Paramount Theatre for the Performing Arts. It will tell you what's coming up at Austin's premier theater venue. Look for it at the theater or at distribution points around the city.**

group exhibitions. The organization also produces dance, musical and theatrical performances featuring local, regional and national performing artists, often collaborative ventures with other groups. We especially like this organization's motto: "Women & Their Work is dedicated to the belief that women artists should be seen and heard. And paid."

Ask to get on their mailing list and stay up on all the events happening at this site and around town. Better yet, become a volunteer or join the organization. Membership starts at a mere $15 a year. The Gallery is open 10 AM to 5 PM Monday through Friday and 1 to 5 PM Saturday.

Two on South First

Alternate Current Art Space

2209 S. First St. • (512) 443-9674

In the same location as Laughing at the Sun, this studio/gallery has its entrance on the north side of the building. As is the case with many Austin artists, David Lee Pratt and Susan Maynard have opened up a small gallery space in their studio. While the gallery isn't always open, Alternate Current does have an informal core group of Austin artists who exhibit here along with cutting-edge new artists. Pratt, a painter and mixed-media artist, and Maynard, who does painting, sculptures and ceramics, are just two of the Austin artists working in this developing arts district around S. First Street.

While the gallery space is limited, the large parking lot is also used as a performance space for dance, music, movies and performance art. Alternate Current does two to four group shows a year as well as a number of individual shows that emphasize the avant garde focus of this gallery. One of our past favorites was the show Girls and Their Dolls, which featured the work of about two dozen Austin women artists. Call them to find out about show openings, always an event, or to see when you can drop in.

Laughing at the Sun

2209 S. First St. • (512) 326-4410

This inviting space is owned and operated by three Austin artists who are helping to create another arts district in Austin, this one south of Town Lake. Sculptor and jewelry maker Rita Ross, painter Nicole Tarnay and Daryl G. Colburn, a nationally known metal sculptor, opened this space in 1996 and immediately set about establishing it as a comfortable home for artists and patrons alike. Sundays are especially nice here when the gallery sponsors guest artists to discuss and/or demonstrate their work. Many galleries are closed on Sunday so this is a great Sunday outing for those interested in learning more about art. Not only that, this gallery hosts events by musicians, poets and writers.

Adding depth to this up-and-coming cultural district are the artists' studios out back and in the area. Be sure to call Laughing at the Sun to find out their current and upcoming exhibits. We especially enjoyed an exhibit in 1998 featuring the photography of Austinite Blair Pittman, a former *National Geographic* magazine photographer who has gone on to a successful independent career. The gallery is open Monday through Saturday from 11 AM to 6 PM and Sunday from noon to 5 PM.

Around Town

Clarksville Pottery & Galleries

4001 N. Lamar Blvd. • (512) 454-9079
9722 Great Hills Trail, Ste. 380
• (512) 794-8580

Clarksville Pottery & Galleries has grown from a small one-man pottery shop and studio back in the '70s into a major retailer of fine arts and crafts with two prominent Austin locations. The stores in Central and Northwest Austin offer handmade pottery by local and nationally known potters as well as an impressive selection of jewelry, glass, wall art, fine woodcrafts, fountains and more. The stores do a brisk business because, in addition to offering some of the finest crafts available in Austin today, the local owners stock a good supply of items that are affordable. With prices ranging from about $10 to as much as $7,000, Clarksville has become a popular spot for buying gifts as well as wonderful art items for the home.

Started by former art professor Arnie Popinsky and his wife, Syd, in the Clarksville neighborhood of Austin, the business was chosen by *Niche* magazine as a "Top 100 Retailer of American Crafts" in 1995 and 1996. Insiders love to take out-of-town guests to Clarksville Pottery & Galleries. The Lamar store in Austin's Central Market is open Monday through Saturday from 10 AM to 6:30 PM except on Thursday when the store stays open until 8 PM. The Great Hills store in the Arboretum Market is open Monday through Saturday from 10 AM to 6 PM with Thursday hours until 8 PM. Both stores are open noon to 6 PM on Sunday.

Images of Austin and the Southwest

4612 Burnet Rd. • (512) 451-1229

Austin artist Mary Doerr runs this gallery in a small house in Central Austin that showcases Doerr's attractive illustrations and watercolors, often depicting Austin, as well as the work of a number of other selected artists. The gallery features Southwestern sculptures and wall hangings as well as pottery, gourds, jewelry and, of course, prints and paintings. The store also does custom framing. Images of Austin and the Southwest is open 10 AM to 6 PM Monday through Saturday.

Peña Studio/Gallery

227 Congress Ave., #100
• (512) 236-0610

Perhaps the most recognized, and certainly one of the most prolific Southwestern artists of our time, Amado Peña owns a home in Austin and spends a few months out of the year here — when he's not working in Santa Fe or traveling to art shows around the country, that is. Peña, now in his mid-50s, was an Austin art teacher who got his start selling paintings and prints on the arts and craft circuit. He discovered the Southwest in the 1970s and immediately felt a kinship with the land and the people. Since then, he has created highly personal works, often painting people he knows or the pottery and blankets from his own collection. His most universally recognized paintings depict profiles of American Indians, men or women, draped in brightly colored Indian blankets.

But who are we to tell you this? Peña's own niece, Monica Peña, opened this gallery in 1998 and plans to show exclusively Peña works through the first year of operation. Afterward, she will include pieces by other Southwestern artists. This is the largest collection of Peña work in the city and includes paintings, hand-pulled lithographs as well as serigraphs and etchings. Visitors will find work from several of Peña's periods, not just the most recent. Monica can tell you all about each piece. Peña himself works and shows here during his stays in Austin. The gallery handles a line of clothes bearing his signature work as well as posters and gift items. It's open 10 AM to 6 PM Monday through Saturday and noon to 5 PM on Sunday.

Tarrytown Gallery

2414 Exposition Blvd. • (512) 473-2552

This popular gallery in West Austin focuses on Austin artists and handles both established and emerging artists whose work is largely representational. Owner Bill Davis, whose background is in art, opened this business in 1979 as a frame shop and 10 years later moved to this great location in the Tarrytown Shopping Center where he combined the frame shop with a gallery. Among the gallery veterans are artists Glenn Whitehead and Wanda Gamble, who work in pastels, well-known ceramic artist James Tisdale, and Margie Crisp who does prints and charcoals. When we were there recently the gallery was showcasing two excellent new painters. That's one dynamic aspect of this gallery. Tarrytown usually exhibits the work of one or two artists per show but also does long group shows in the summer and winter. Call for dates. The Tarrytown

INSIDERS' TIP

Once a year in the spring, drama critics from the local newspapers get together to announce the "Austin Critics Table Awards." If you're interested in keeping up with the topnotch shows, actors, directors and more, check out the local papers around May for a list of the winners.

Gallery is open 9 AM to 5:30 PM Monday through Friday and Saturday 10 AM to 4 PM.

Wild About Music

721 Congress Ave. • (512) 708-1700

Art with a music theme. What better combination for Austin than an art gallery and gift shop that celebrates music? Guitar-shaped chairs, violin side tables, instrumental wall sculptures, vintage Austin music poster art, accessories with Beatles lyrics, and maps of the world composed entirely of playable music. Those are just a few examples of the art available at this unique galley and store.

Everything in the shop has a music or performing arts motif, including accessories, clothing, jewelry, glass and stationary. Wild About Music, in the heart of downtown Austin, features exceptional work by some nationally known Central Texas artists as well as others from around the country. Acclaimed Austin musician and MCA recording artist Joe Ely is the most prominent of WAM's artists who also are bona fide musicians. And there are other musicians/visual artists as well as dozens of visual artists who are inspired by music.

Larry Piltz, whose whimsical aquariums are made from old TV sets, radios, jukeboxes and more, is just one among many artists represented here. Others include James Plakovic, Robert Hurst, Eddie Myers, Joe Sambataro, Barrett Debusk and Sam Yeates. This gallery also hosts a variety of special events, including visual art demonstrations, touring art shows and, of course, live music performances. Wild About Music is open 11 AM to 7 PM Monday through Saturday and noon to 6 PM on Sunday. Located next to two performing arts centers, The State Theatre and The Paramount Theatre, the store often stays open later on theater nights.

Yard Dog Folk Art

1510 S. Congress Ave. • (512) 912-1613

Fascinating is the word that comes to mind to describe the work of the folk artists, many of them nationally known, represented here. Art dealer Randy Franklin opened this gallery in South Central Austin in 1995 and handles work by artists from the American South. Be sure to ask him about the various artists represented here. They have interesting stories. The outsider art of well-known Austin artist Ike Morgan, a mental patient who has lived many years in the Austin State Hospital, is for sale here as is the work of Sybil Gibson, the Rev. J.L. Hunter and many more. This gallery is definitely worth a visit. It's open from 11 AM to 6 PM Wednesday through Saturday and noon to 5 PM on Sunday. This area of S. Congress Avenue is a fun place to visit even if you're not a folk art buff. The strip is lined with some other funky shops and restaurants that will satisfy any craving for the unusual.

To read Austin writers is to take a joyride on the roller coaster of literary expression.

The Literary Scene

"The tempo of the earth-dwellers to whom I have been listening for many years is the tempo of growing grass, of a solitary buzzard sailing over a valley, of the wind from the south in April, of the lengthening of a tree's shadow on a summer afternoon, of the rise and fall of flames in a fireplace on a winter night. . . ."

With those words, J. Frank Dobie, Texas' first nationally known writer, introduced his book, *Tales of Old-Time Texas*, published in 1928 and still available along with many of his other two dozen collections at bookstores today.

In this chapter, we'll delve into Austin's rich literary history and describe our present status as a writers' mecca. But for those of you in a rush to explore the Austin of letters, we'll get right to the point: If you like books, you'll love Austin.

J. Frank Dobie is one of the reasons. Dobie, a University of Texas professor from 1914 to 1947, with occasional absences, was born in the Texas brush country and lived in and around Austin for most of his adult life, when he was not off wandering around Mexico and the American Southwest in search of someone with a tale to tell.

"Frank Dobie became a hunter of legends and a gatherer of folk tales and the result was one of the most important bodies of literature produced by a Southwesterner," wrote Neil B. Carmony, who edited a collection of Dobie's stories for the book *Afield with J. Frank Dobie*, published in 1992, 28 years after the writer's death.

Names of other luminaries grace Austin's past, including historian Walter Prescott Webb and naturalist Roy Bedichek, who together with Dobie formed a triumvirate of intellectuals that electrified the city's literary ambience. William Sydney Porter, who later was to gain international notoriety as the short-story writer O. Henry, published his first short fiction here in his literary magazine, *Rolling Stone*. A Porter story that appeared in the October 27, 1894, issue of *Rolling Stone* gave Austin one of its most endearing nicknames: City of the Violet Crown. (See our chapter on Attractions for more about O. Henry.) Austinite and LBJ aide Billy Brammer is still known around these parts for his 1962 political novel *The Gay Place*.

John Henry Faulk, for whom our central library is named, was a multi-talented writer, actor, New York radio show host and defender of the First Amendment. As vice president of the American Federation of Television and Radio Artists, Faulk insisted the union take a stand against McCarthy-era blacklistings of entertainers — and was himself blacklisted. Faulk fought back and as a result won the largest libel judgment awarded up to that time. He was one of Dobie's students.

Internationally celebrated short-story writer Katherine Anne Porter (1890-1980) grew up 20 miles down the road from Austin in the small town of Kyle. Her relationship with Texas, however, was a stormy one. It infuriated her, for example, that the Texas Institute of Letters chose to honor Dobie instead of her when it gave its 1939 award for the best book by a Texas writer. (Folklorist Sylvia Ann Grider has written that "Porter's emotional attachment to her home state fell victim to the cowboy mentality that has traditionally proclaimed Texas a fine place for men and horses, but hell on women and oxen.") Of course, her fame eclipsed Dobie's, which probably brought her no small amount of satisfaction. While Porter lived most of her adult life outside of Texas, she nevertheless wrote some of her finest fiction about her home state and chose to be buried in Texas.

Pioneering Texas journalist Bess Whitehead Scott, who broke gender barriers in 1915 as the first woman news reporter in Houston, was a beloved member of the Austin writers community until her death in 1997 at age 107. Noted folklorist and poet J. Mason Brewer, the first African American to become a member of the Texas Institute of Letters and the first African-American vice president of the American Folklore Society, found inspiration among members of his own family in their East Austin home. Dobie called Brewer's work "genuine and delightful." Pulitzer Prize-winning author James Michener is another illustrious writer who found inspiration in Austin — and inspired others. (Find out more about Michener's contributions to Austin's literary scene in our Close-up on him in this chapter.)

Some of these trailblazers not only established Austin's literary traditions, they helped this city earn a reputation as a haven for writers and free thinkers, a distinction that has endured. Austin's literary scene, in fact, is more vibrant today than ever before. Perhaps even Dobie would be amazed at the sheer number of Austin writers and at the contributions many of them have made to the nation's literary wealth. To read Austin writers is to take a joyride on the roller coaster of literary expression: Novels, mysteries, science fiction, cyberpunk, suspense, history, poetry, travel, books for children and young adults, essays, memoirs, how-to books, cookbooks, political satires, biographies, screenplays, short stories. The list goes on. Our city claims bestselling and award-winning writers in a number of genres as well as a host of successful poets, playwrights and screenwriters. Fans of Liz Carpenter, Molly Ivins, Marion Winik, Mary Willis Walker, David Lindsey, Lawrence Wright and the others we list in our Reader's Primer below will be pleased to know these artists live right here in Austin.

It's impossible to pinpoint just one catalyst for Austin's literary explosion. We'd have to include Austin's own magnetism. Once experienced, Austin is hard to abandon. The superlative efforts of The Austin Writers' League to promote and encourage the city's writers has had impressive results. The league, with 1,600 members, has become the largest regional writing organization in Texas and the second largest in the country after Washington Independent Writers in Washington, D.C. The league's annual prizes have also served to spotlight members' works.

Two Austin publications, *Texas Monthly* magazine and *The Texas Observer*, have long and rich traditions of attracting excellent writers to Austin, many of whom have gone on to achieve literary fame. The vibrant music scene and flourishing film industry, illuminated by excellent local songwriters and screenwriters, add further dimension to Austin's literary landscape. (See our chapter on The Music Scene and our Close-up on the film industry in The Arts chapter.) Of course, the presence of outstanding intellectuals at The University of Texas, St. Edward's University and our other colleges and universities have added untold riches to Austin's writing legacy. Adding further dimension to the scene are the university presses and many small- and medium-size publishing houses that are willing to gamble that an author's work will be of interest to others.

The last decade of the 20th century has roused an unprecedented flurry of interest in Austin's literary arts. The major bookstore chains of Barnes & Noble and Borders Books, which opened here in the mid-1990s,

INSIDERS' TIP

For news about writers, books and upcoming literary events, check out the *Austin American-Statesman*'s "Book Events" column on Fridays as well as Anne Morris' column in the Sunday edition. *The Austin Chronicle*, published Thursdays, also lists book-related events around town in its "Litera" column, prints reviews and publishes articles about authors. *The Chronicle* also sponsors a yearly short story contest, for all you budding writers out there. Remember, O. Henry got his start in Austin.

have joined Austin's esteemed Book People in hosting an astounding assortment of readings by national and local authors, as well as book signings and other literary events that, for book lovers, bring the written word to life. Several of Austin's small- and medium-size bookstores, including Resistencia Book Store, Book Woman, Toad Hall and others, have long traditions of providing venues for local and national writers of poetry and prose, as do a number of other venues around town, including the Harry Ransom Humanities Research Center at The University of Texas and St. Edward's University in South Austin. The James Michener Center for Writers, appropriately housed in J. Frank Dobie's home on Waller Creek, sponsors a wonderful series of readings by national and international writers.

Texas Writers Month, first organized in 1994, has become an outstanding statewide celebration of Texas' literary artists. The annual May festival, held in Austin and other major cities around the state, includes book panels, readings, children's events, literacy benefits, signings, musical events and film. Texas Writers Month, originally conceived to convince booksellers to give local authors more prominence in their stores, has become a premier celebration of Texas writers.

The Texas Book Festival, started in 1996, is another major Austin event for writers and readers alike. The November festival, which raises money for Texas public libraries, features readings and panel discussions by more than 100 authors who have been published in the previous year. Texans, Texas natives and those who've written about the Lone Star State are invited to participate. A giant book fair, musical events, children's activities and more highlight this celebration of the state's literary heritage. The Austin International Poetry Festival, held in April since 1993, draws poets and poetry fans from around the globe to venues across Austin. Other venues around town, including Ruta Maya Coffee House, Victory Grill, Mexic-Arte Museum, the Manor Road Coffeehouse and some of the bookstores listed in this chapter, feature poetry readings throughout the year. Look too for the Austin poetry journal, *Borderlands*.

A Readers' Primer of Austin

One of the pleasures of traveling or moving to a new town is the opportunity to discover the writers that contribute to the region's literary landscape. Austin is in no short supply when it comes to outstanding writers, as you'll see here. While there's just too many Austin authors to include all of them, we've introduced you to a selection of some of the best known, and some of our favorites. We promise that you'll be thrilled with their diversity and inspired by their talent. Check with our local libraries and bookstores for more about our city's other literary stars. Of course, it's just not possible to know Texas well unless you've at least read the works of John Graves, Larry McMurtry and John L. King. While not Austinites, their intimate observations embody the heart and soul of Texas, in its multitude of forms.

Some of the information we've provided about the authors comes to us from the Texas Book Festival and the Austin Writers' League. They were most helpful.

Jeff Abbott: "It was really rude of Beta Harcher to argue with me right before she got killed." So begins Abbot's first novel, *Do Unto Others*, which won an Agatha Award for Best First Mystery. Since then he's written a series of fun mysteries set in the small town of Mirabeau, Texas. His hero is librarian Jordan Poteet. Look also for Abbott's books *The Only Good Yankee*, *Promises of Home* and *Distant Blood*.

Neal Barrett, Jr.: *Skinny Annie Blues* was the first in a series of popular Barrett mysteries featuring Wiley Moss. He also wrote *Dead Dog Blues* and *Pink Vodka Blues*. He is also known for his novel *The Hereafter Game*, which *The Washington Post* called "one of the great American novels."

Sarah Bird: Bird's work has been called "nothing short of brilliant" and "falling off the chair hilarious" by prestigious publications around the country. This talented writer of such books as *Virgin of the Rodeo*, *The Mommy Club* and *The Boyfriend School* is also a screenwriter, essayist and magazine writer who has written for *Cosmopolitan*, *Ms.* magazine, *The New York Times Magazine* and *The Texas Ob-*

server. She also writes for TV. *Virgin of the Rodeo*, Bird's last novel published in 1993, received a starred review in *Publisher's Weekly*, which said, "The search for a delinquent father drives this waggish and wonderful novel about the Southwest rodeo circuit out of the chute and into the winner's circle." Fans are anxiously awaiting another book by Bird.

Liz Carpenter: "Austin's answer to Irma Bombeck" is one way bestselling author Liz Carpenter has been described. This Austin treasure spent nearly 20 years as a newspaper correspondent in Washington before she became the first journalist to serve as a First Lady's press secretary, working for sister Texan Lady Bird Johnson. Her books include *Ruffles and Flourishes*, about her days in the Johnson White House, *Getting Better All the Time*, about aging and widowhood, and *Unplanned Parenthood: Confessions of a Seventy-Something Surrogate Mother*, her story of becoming the mother of three teenagers.

Gary Cartwright: A senior editor for *Texas Monthly* magazine, Cartwright is a multi-award-winning author and journalist. His 1998 book is titled *HeartWiseGuy: How to Live the Good Life After a Heart Attack*, a personal account of the author's own recovery after a heart attack and advice on how to care for an aging body. Cartwright's previous books include *Confessions of a Washed-up Sportswriter*, *Dirty Dealing* and *Blood Will Tell*. He has been the recipient of the Dobie-Paisano Fellowship and has won two prestigious Texas Institute of Letters awards. Cartwright also has co-written and co-produced movies. *Blood Will Tell* was filmed by CBS as a four-hour miniseries in 1994. And don't miss *Texas Monthly* for outstanding articles by Cartwright.

Robert Fernea and Elizabeth Warnock Fernea: These two University of Texas professors published *The Arab World: Forty Years of Change* in 1997 and were honored with a Texas Institute of Letters Carr P. Collins Award for nonfiction for their work. Elizabeth, a UT professor of English and Middle Eastern Studies, also has written *Guest of the Sheik*, *A Street in Marrakesh* and *A View of the Nile*. Her latest book is 1998's *In Search of Islamic Feminism: One Woman's Global Journey*. Robert's work includes *Nubians in Egypt: Peaceful People* and *Shaykh & Effendi*. He is a professor of anthropology and Middle Eastern Studies.

Kinky Friedman: A UT graduate, Friedman made a name for himself back in the 1970s as the songwriter and lead singer for the irreverent Kinky Friedman and the Texas Jewboys, which has come out of semi-retirement recently to perform in Austin. Now living on a ranch in the Texas Hill Country, Friedman has turned to writing. And what a writer he is! Molly Ivins (read about her below) said Friedman "spreads more joy than Ross Perot's ears." He has published more than 10 books, including *Road Kill*, *Armadillo & Old Lace*, *Elvis, Jesus & Coca-Cola* and 1998's *Blast From the Past*. These humorous quasi-autobiographical mysteries feature a Jewish Texan country-western music singer turned private detective named, you guessed it, Kinky Friedman.

Stephen Harrigan: A contributing editor to *Texas Monthly* magazine, Harrigan is the multi-talented author of *Water and Light: A Diver's Journey to a Coral Reef*, *Aransas* and the great collection of essays about Texas *A Natural State*, which *The Washington Post* described as "recommended reading not just for Texans but for all who would explore their connections to the natural world." Harrigan also wrote *The Last of His Tribe*, a movie for HBO.

Molly Ivins: *Molly Ivins Can't Say That, Can She?* spent more than a year on the *New York Times* bestseller list. In 1998, Ivins' long-awaited new book was released, *You Got to*

INSIDERS' TIP

If you're planning to stay in the Austin area for awhile, you can apply for a temporary visitors library card at a cost of $15 quarterly or $48 a year. Just fill out an application at any local public library. You will need to show a photo ID, such as your out-of-town or out-of-state driver's license or your passport, and provide the full mailing address of your temporary Austin lodgings. The card will be mailed to you in about a week.

James Michener: A Memorable Character

Pulitzer Prize-winning author James Michener, whose 1991 memoir is titled *The World Is My Home*, chose Austin as his home for many of the last, always prolific, years of his life. Over the course of the Michener Age here, Austin was to become a richer city, not merely because of the millions in art and monetary endowments he gave to the University of Texas, but because of Michener's generosity of spirit.

Close-up

Here was a man whose own life was one of America's great rags-to-riches tales; a man whose appetite for adventure and unquenchable thirst for knowledge were matched only by a gift — he called it a passion — for telling a story; a man who spent his life, and most of his fortune, giving back to the people and communities that had embraced him.

James Michener's legacy lives on in the friends and students he inspired in Austin and around the world during his lifetime. What's more, Michener will continue to enlighten writers for generations to come. The Texas Center for Writers, which he founded at UT, was renamed the James Michener Center for Writers following his death in 1997.

Michener was no stranger to the Capital City when he arrived in 1982 to begin work on his sweeping saga of the Lone Star State. He had known the Austin of the 1940s, when he came as an editor following the publication of his first book, and he'd known the Austin of the 1960s, when he returned to donate his huge 20th-century American Art collection to the University of Texas. By the time the 1980s rolled around, Michener had been decorated with America's highest civilian honor, The Presidential Medal of Freedom. His reputation as America's Storyteller was a solid as his hefty novels — and so was his fame as one of the country's most generous writers. At the time of his death, it was estimated that Michener had given $117 million to museums, libraries, individuals and universities around the country. The largest beneficiary of Michener's generosity was the University of Texas at Austin, which received $44.2 million from the late-in-life Austinite.

Michener's first novel, *Tales of the South Pacific*, published in 1947 when the au-

Photo: Peter A. Silva

James Michener founded The Texas Center for Writers, now named in his honor, at The University of Texas.

— continued on next page

thor was 40 years old, had earned him a Pulitzer Prize. The bestsellers that followed, including *The Fires of Spring*, *The Bridges at Toko-ri*, *Sayonara*, *Caravans*, *The Source*, *Iberia*, *Centennial*, *The Drifters,* and *The Covenant*, earned him millions of loyal readers who found his fictionalized version of history more exciting, more moving, and even more educational, than anything they'd read in nonfiction. It warranted not even a pause when critics called his work too preachy, his characters too one-dimensional or his dialogue too contrived. Readers made Michener famous as they stampeded to the bookstores to get their hands on his latest epic. Perhaps it was his ability to create characters with whom readers could identify that won him such a loyal following.

"I have endeavored to center my writing upon ordinary but memorable characters whose lives shed a kind of radiance, whose behavior, good or bad, illuminated what I was striving to impart, and whose noble, craven, godlike or hellish deportment stood surrogate for the behavior of human beings the reader has known," he wrote in his memoir.

Bill Clements, then governor of Texas, invited Michener to Austin in 1981 to work on a book about Texas for the sesquicentennial. Published in 1985 when Michener was 78, the 1,096-page epic turned out to be his longest work. Like *Hawaii* and *Space* and *Chesapeake* before it, and *Poland*, *Alaska* and *Mexico* that followed, *Texas* required no dramatic title. The image the title conjured in people's imaginations, and the bold name of the author below it, was enough to turn *Texas* into a million-copy blockbuster.

Michener and his wife Mari found a home in Austin during the years the author spent researching and writing his Texas saga. According to the *Austin American-Statesman*, Michener once told a friend as they walked down the West Austin street where he lived, "You know, I think I'm happier living on this street than any street I've lived on in my life." That statement said a great deal about the man who considered the world his home. His memoir features a cover photograph of the author sitting atop Austin's breathtaking Mount Bonnell (see our Attractions chapter).

Born of unknown parents about February 3, 1907, in New York City, Michener was taken as an orphan to a poorhouse in Doylestown, Pennsylvania. Mabel Michener, a Quaker, gave him a name, food and shelter when her finances allowed and, most importantly, a love for learning. "We were very poor," Michener told the *Statesman* on the occasion of his 89th birthday. "As a child I had nothing. I never had a sled. I never had a bicycle. I never had a baseball glove. I never had anything. But I did have people who loved me and looked after my education."

He spent much of his childhood reading books in the public library, excelled in school and sports, and earned a basketball scholarship to Pennsylvania's Swarthmore College, where he went on to graduate with highest honors in 1929. He taught at a prep school for two years then won a two-year scholarship for study and travel in Europe, where he took classes at St. Andrew's University in Scotland. According to published reports, Michener studied art in London and Italy, spent a winter in the Outer Hebrides where he collected folk songs and stories, worked on a Mediterranean cargo vessel and toured northern Spain with a group of bullfighters. Following his return to the United States, Michener earned a master's degree in education from the University of Northern Colorado and then taught at UNC and at Harvard University's School of Education. He was working on a doctorate in education at Harvard when he enlisted in the service in World War II. During his tour of duty with the Navy, Michener served on about 49 different South Pacific islands. The result was *Tales of the South Pacific*. At 41, James Michener turned to writing full time.

Michener followed up his first novel with *The Fires of Spring*, which his closest friends in Austin say reveals more about the author than his official memoir. The book tells the story of a poor Pennsylvania boy who becomes a writer. The books that followed

— continued on next page

championed universal ideals: racial and religious tolerance, self-reliance, hard work and human understanding. His belief in the brotherhood of humanity was, perhaps, one of the strongest undercurrents in his books. A self-described fiery liberal, Michener said in a 1972 interview, "I've never felt in a position to reject anybody. I could be Jewish, part Negro, probably not Oriental, but almost anything else. This has loomed large in my thoughts."

His works represent decades of cultural immersion around the globe. He traveled from Japan to Korea and Hungary, a long stay in Hawaii then on to Afghanistan and Spain, South Africa, Colorado and Israel, Chesapeake Bay and Poland. Texas was Michener's next stop and still the septuagenarian didn't slow down. He was 80 when he published *Alaska* in 1987 and there were 16 books to follow, including *Caribbean* and *Six Days in Havana*, a book he wrote with his Austin friend and associate John Kings. Texas was too big a theme for just one book, albeit his longest, however. *The Eagle and the Raven*, his story of Mexican General Antonio Lopez de Santa Anna and Texas independence hero Sam Houston, was published in 1990. Seven more books followed before Michener published *Recessional* in 1994, which dealt with the right to die with dignity. Mari, his wife of nearly 40 years, died that same year of cancer and is buried next to her husband in Austin. (Michener's two previous marriages had ended in divorce. He never had children.) His last book, *A Century of Sonnets*, was published in 1997.

In his half century of work, Michener wrote nearly 50 books of nonfiction and fiction, many of them as thick as bricks. Along the way, Michener found time to establish The Texas Center for Writers, just one more way he found to give of himself. Center director Jim Magnuson recalled in a *Texas Monthly* tribute following the author's death that Michener's involvement with UT writing students started informally. Michener asked to sit in on Magnuson's graduate fiction workshop as a teaching assistant. "The students were in awe of him, and he took their work seriously," Magnuson wrote. "He was like a Dutch uncle — encouraging, but concerned that no one got too big for his britches."

The university announced in 1988 that Michener was donating $1 million to create an interdisciplinary master of fine arts degree. Under Michener's plan, the program would train students in poetry, prose, screenwriting and playwriting. It would go a step further, however, by requiring students to work in more than one genre. Another $3 million Michener gift to the program came in 1990. Two years later, Michener gave a whopping $15 million to the program. "I was stunned — it was far and away the largest gift ever made to support creative writing anywhere," Magnuson wrote in his article for the December, 1997, issue of *Texas Monthly*, which featured Michener on the cover under the headline, "The Most-Generous Texans."

In the fall of 1993, the Texas Center for Writers admitted the first class of students into its MFA program. Michener, according to Magnuson, offered to read and critique the students' work and was well known for his involvement with them. Each fall he would invite the new class to his home and was a regular guest at the center's annual barbecue, where he would greet each student. Today, the Michener Center for Writers is among the nation's most selective writing programs, admitting just 10 new students each fall and awarding them a $12,000-a-year stipend. Some of the finest writers in the world come to Austin to teach and give seminars at the center. More importantly, graduates of the young program have gone on to find success in a number of writing fields. The public at large also benefits from the center. An impressive series of world-renowned authors have come to Austin, courtesy of the center, to offer readings and host discussions of their work.

Marla Akin, program coordinator for the Michener Center for Writers, says Michener's life is an inspiration to students and to the center itself. "The money that fuels this program is something he worked to earn," she says. "He had such a work ethic and

— continued on next page

such a strong philosophy about sharing the bounty. He gave away 90 percent of what he made, and a good portion of that he to gave to help other people find their voices as writers."

James Michener died of kidney failure on October 16, 1997, within two weeks of voluntarily terminating dialysis. He was 90. In a 1988 interview on *Good Morning America*, Michener talked about his craft. "I think I have a passion for telling a story and then working on it until I think it's coherent," he said. "I'm proud of my profession. I'm a writer. I never say I'm an author, that's somebody else. "I'm a real good writer."

He was also a real good human being.

Dance with Them What Brung You. This hilarious book features such astute Ivins' observations as, "If it weren't for the automatic teller and the self-cleaning garlic press, we'd have no evidence of progress at all — and I know people who think ATMs are part of a plot to prevent people from getting to know one another," and "... there's nothing you can do about being born liberal — fish gotta swim and hearts gotta bleed."

She also has written *Nothing But Good Times Ahead*. This nationally syndicated columnist for the *Fort Worth Star-Telegram*, who can also be read in our own *Austin American-Statesman*, writes with humor and insight about Texas politics and other happenings. Her freelance work has appeared in a number of prestigious magazines, including *Esquire*, *GQ* and *Harper's Bazaar*. Ivins, a former writer for *The Texas Observer*, has won a number of journalism awards and has been a finalist for the Pulitzer Prize three times.

Tina Juarez: Winner of a 1995 Violet Crown Award and the Presidio La Bahia Award from the Sons of the Republic of Texas for her historical novel *Call No Man Master*, Juarez is an Austin educator who also has written for academic journals. She is principal of Stephen F. Austin High School.

David Lindsey: Mystery lovers adore Lindsey's work, which include *An Absence of Light*, *Mercy*, *A Cold Mind* and *Requiem for a Glass Heart*, which was purchased by Universal Studios. He is a bestselling author in Britain and is known for his meticulous research, which has included working with the FBI and detectives in the Houston Police Department. *Publishers Weekly* called *Mercy*, set in Houston, "a lean, gripping, psychological thriller ... Written with masterly skill."

Angela Shelf Medearis: *The Ghost of Sifty-Sifty Sam* is just one of the books written by this distinguished Austin writer of multicultural children's books and cookbooks. *Dancing with the Indians*, *The Singing Man* and *Rum Tum Tum* are among her books for children. Her cookbooks include *A Kwanzaa Celebration* and *Ideas for Entertaining*.

Michael Moorcock: Moorcock, who lives in nearby Bastrop, is the multi-award-winning author of adventure and fantasy novels. He has written more than 100 books, including *Tales from the Texas Woods*, *The War Amongst the Angels*, *Fabulous Harbors* and the Elric series, *Blood*, *Gloriana* and *Mother London*. Michael also edits anthologies, writes short stories, rock songs, screenplays and essays.

Laurence Parent: Parent produces stunningly beautiful books of photographs about the Lone Star State, including *Texas*, *The Texas Hill Country: A Postcard Book*, *Scenic Driving Texas* and *Hiking Big Bend National Park*. He gave up a career in engineering to become a freelance photographer and writer.

Turk Pipkin: Pipkin, a contributing editor to *Texas Monthly* magazine, switches easily from TV to books to journalism. *Fast Greens*, *Born of the River*, *Be a Clown!* and *The Winner's Guide to the Texas Lottery* are among his excellent books. He also coedited *Barton Springs Eternal: The Soul of a City*. Pipkin has written and produced a number of television programs.

Christopher Reich: Reich's debut thriller, *Numbered Account*, hit the bookstores with a bang in 1998 and became a *New York Times* bestseller along the way. Reich, born in Tokyo, drew on his experiences working in a major Swiss bank for three years to provide the basis for this gripping story. This is definitely a name to watch.

Trevor Romain: Romain has written and illustrated more than a dozen books for children, including *Bullies Are a Pain in the Brain* and *How to Do Homework Without Throwing Up*. His is a board member of the Candlelighter's Childhood Cancer Foundation and says his work with sick children has inspired his writing.

Louis Sachar: Middle-graders get a kick out of Sachar's series of books, including *Dogs Don't Tell Jokes*, *There's a Boy in the Girls' Bathroom* and *The Boy Who Lost His Face*. Sachar, who gave up a career in law to become a writer of children's books, titled his first book *Sideways Stories From Wayside School*. The book features a character called Louis the Yard Teacher, coincidentally the nickname schoolchildren had given Sachar when he supervised kids on the playground.

Edwin "Bud" Shrake: Shrake was a sports writer who worked for *The Dallas Morning News* and the *Dallas Times Herald* before becoming a staff writer for *Sports Illustrated*. His 15 books include *Strange Peaches* and *Blood Reckoning* as well as celebrity autobiographies of Willie Nelson and Barry Switzer. Shrake also has written more than a half-dozen screenplays. He coauthored *Harvey Penick's Little Red Book*, the bestselling sports book ever (see our Golf chapter). The University of Texas Press reissued Shrake's classic *Blessed McGill* in 1997.

William Browning Spencer: This science fiction and horror writer's first novel, *Maybe I'll Call Anna*, won a New American Writings Award. *Resume With Monsters*, a satirical novel, won the 1995 Best Novel Award from the International Horror Critics Guild. He also has written *Zod Wallop*. Spencer writes both novels and short stories.

Bruce Sterling: A science-fiction novelist, short-story writer and magazine columnist, Sterling is one of the country's leading voices in science fiction and cyberpunk. His work includes the science fiction novels *The Artificial Kid* and *Heavy Weather*. His nonfiction book, *The Hacker Crackdown: Law and Disorder on the Electronic Frontier*, deals with computer crimes and civil liberties.

Jesse Sublett: For hard-boiled, set-in-Austin mysteries, Sublett's work is unparalleled. Look for his Texas music mysteries, *Rock Critic Murders* as well as *Tough Baby* and *Boiled in Concrete*. Jesse's work also includes more than 25 documentaries. He also has written for television and multimedia.

Mary Willis Walker: *All the Dead Lie Down* is the latest novel from this multi-award-winning Austin mystery writer. Walker's first novel, *Zero at the Bone*, won both the Agatha and Macavity awards. *Red Scream*, her second book, won both an Edgar Award from the Mystery Writers of America and a Violet Crown Award from the Austin Writers' League. *Under the Beetle's Cellar* won the Hammett Award from the International Association of Crime Writers. Her set-in-Austin mysteries are wonderful.

Marion Winik: *The Lunch-Box Chronicles*, published in 1998, is Winik's latest book, which the jacket describes as "part memoir, part survival guide." The book, subtitled *Notes from*

INSIDERS' TIP

If you're reading this book, thank a teacher. Austin offers many opportunities for you to nurture other readers by making donations or volunteering to help a child or adult learn to read. Contact the public library nearest you for details about literacy programs, check with your local public school or call Literacy Austin at (512) 416-7214. Reading is Fundamental of Austin, (512) 472-1791, can always use volunteers or donations. The *Austin American-Statesman* also sponsors a program called Partners in Literacy in which newspapers are donated to Central Texas school districts. To find out more about this program or to sponsor a school, call the *Statesman* at (512) 445-3500.

the Parenting Underground, is filled with humorous and witty observations and lessons about motherhood, based on her own experiences as a single mother of two boys. This popular Austin writer has been a regular commentator on National Public Radio's *All Things Considered* and has written for national magazines, including *Redbook*, *Harper's Bazaar* and *Parenting*. Her first two books were *Telling* and *First Comes Love*.

Lawrence Wright: *"Remembering Satan* catapults Wright to the front rank of American journalists." That's what *Newsweek* said in 1994 about Wright's tragic story of recovered memory. Wright, a staff writer for *The New Yorker*, also has written for *Texas Monthly*, *Rolling Stone* and *The New York Times Magazine*. His wonderful books also include *City Children, Country Summer*, *In the New World*, subtitled *Growing up in America from the Sixties to the Eighties*, *Saints and Sinners*, about religion in America, and *Twins*, published in 1997.

Five Texans

John Erickson: Erickson has written a series of books for children that have reached near-classic status and are wonderful for new or visiting pint-size Texans. *Hank the Cowdog*, who has been described as a "canine Don Knotts," is always solving one mystery or another as he fulfills his duties as Head of Ranch Security. Hank has been featured in more than 30 books by Erickson since the author started writing more than 30 years ago while working as a full-time cowboy, farm hand and ranch manager. Erickson, a UT graduate, now lives on a ranch along the Oklahoma border in Perryton, Texas.

John Graves: One doesn't read John Graves so much as listen while he relates his personal, often poignant, accounts of life and death in Texas. It takes a page, perhaps two, to quiet the modern-day hubbub in your head that anxiously wonders how long he's going to take to describe the fish running in the Brazos River before you realize that you ARE on the river, or sitting around a campfire immersed in the voice of a superlative storyteller. Graves, one of Texas' preeminent authors, has earned a horde of loyal fans who reside far beyond our state's borders. His classic *Goodbye to a River*, published in 1960, is one reason why. His other books, *Hard Scrabble* and *From a Limestone Ledge*, are others. A wonderful anthology of Graves' writing, *A John Graves Reader*, published in 1996 by The University of Texas Press, includes selections from these three books as well as stories first published elsewhere. This collection is a perfect introduction to Graves' work. Don't pass by the introduction to *Reader*. It's written by Edwin "Bud" Shrake (see the previous listing). Graves, who lives in Glen Rose, Texas, also has written for magazines such as *Atlantic Monthly* and *Texas Monthly*.

Larry L. King: You can take Larry L. King out of Texas, but you can't take the Texan out of Larry L. King. This East Texas-born playwright, screenwriter, novelist, essayist and short-story writer may be best known to the outside world as the coauthor of *The Best Little Whorehouse in Texas*, his hit Broadway musical that was later made into a movie. King also conquered Broadway with another play, *The Night Hank Williams Died*. His excellent political novel, *The One-Eyed Man*, was published in 1966. King's work has appeared in periodicals such as *The Texas Observer*, *Texas Monthly*, *The Washingtonian* and *Parade*. He's won an Emmy Award, the Helen Hayes Award, the Stanley Walker Journalism Award and has been nominated for a Tony and a National Book Award. In 1997, The University of Texas Press published King's *True Facts, Tall Tales, Pure Fiction*, a collection of 19 of King's outstanding essays and short stories. That volume, along with the 1984 collection, *Warning: Writer at Work*, will have even you Yankees wishing you'd been born under the Lone Star. King now lives in Washington, D.C.

Larry McMurtry: *Lonesome Dove*, *Terms of Endearment*, *The Last Picture Show*. We probably don't need to say any more about this prolific Texan, but we will. A Pulitzer Prize-winner who now lives in Washington, D.C., McMurtry has published 21 novels, two collections of essays and has written more than 30 screenplays. It doesn't seem too much of a stretch to say most everyone knows of the adventures of Texas Rangers August McCrae and Woodrow F. Call, whose lives are depicted in the epic *Lonesome Dove* and its sequels and prequel, *Streets of Laredo*, *Dead Man's Walk* and *Comanche Moon*. Moviegoers and miniseries watchers have seen McMurtry's stories come to life again and again. It's practically a rule in Texas: Read McMurtry before you get here.

Dan Jenkins: *Baja Oklahoma* is one of the most hilarious books about Texas we've ever read. At times profane and even sexist *Baja* nonetheless will have you falling down with laughter as you follow the trials and tribulations of waitress and aspiring country-western songwriter Juanita (born under the sign of polyester) Hutchins and the other characters who frequent Herb's Cafe. Jenkins, a Fort Worth native who now lives in Manhattan is a former senior writer for *Sports Illustrated* and a monthly columnist for *Playboy Magazine*. He's written other acclaimed books, including *Semi-Tough* and *Dead Solid Perfect*.

Buy The Book

As if in a scene by Kafka, you innocently walk through a door and suddenly you're transformed, into a worm, no less. As you look around you realize the room is crawling with all kinds of worms: big ones, baby ones, curly haired ones, bearded ones, coffee-drinking worms, worms wearing ties, worms taking notes. It's a community, a coterie, a coven of worms. Ahhhh.

You're right at home. Whether it's 10 in the morning or 10 at night, Austin's bookstores are teeming with those literate critters known as bookworms. Austin, the center of state government, home to The University of Texas, and a haven for intellectuals, consistently ranks among the top-10 cities in per capita sales of books, according to nationwide studies done by the book industry. From small specialty stores to giant superstores, Austin's booksellers cater to the complex tastes of our readers. Very few shopping experiences offer the same *esprit de corps* that comes from visiting a bookstore and knowing that you've joined the community of bookworms performing their favorite activities: buying and reading books. Readings and book signings by nationally known and local authors, comfy couches and cafes are just a few of the features some bookstores offer to lure readers — and to add life to Austin's literary scene. For those of you who can't wait to savor the Austin bookstore experience, read below for a listing of some of our outstanding shops.

Central

Adventures in Crime & Space Books

609-A W. Sixth St. • (512) 473-2665

Locally owned and operated since 1994, Adventures in Crime & Space has captured a faithful Austin clientele. The store's 20,000 new and used titles include horror, mystery and science fiction books as well as a number of rare titles and books on art. Art card collectors will find a wide assortment of decks devoted to different artists in the genre. Adventures in Crime & Space also buys used books.

Asylum Books

2906 San Gabriel St. • (512) 479-0015

Asylum Books features about 11,000 titles of used books at reasonable prices. The locally owned and operated store opened in 1993 and specializes in hardbacks that are clean and in good condition. Paperbacks also are sold. The store has an excellent collection of books in a wide range of categories, including modern first editions, mysteries, poetry, books on the military, collectibles and interesting nonfiction works. Asylum is a great place to sell good-condition used books.

Austin Books

5002 N. Lamar Blvd. • (512) 454-4197

For a huge selection of comics and books that celebrate American pop culture, Austin Books is the place to go. This locally owned store, serving Austin since 1978, specializes in science fiction, fantasy and mystery of the American potboiler type. The store stocks about 500 new titles of comic books as well as thousands more classics. The store also has a lot of collectible science fiction as well as out-of-print and hard to find titles. Want to know the names of all the crew members of *Speed Buggy*? These guys have the answer. Some good had to come of their youth spent in front of a television set. Austin Books also has movie posters, vintage toys and sports cards.

Barnes & Noble Booksellers

2246 Guadalupe St. • (512) 457-0581

The newest superstore to hit The Drag across from the University of Texas, this Barnes & Noble is one of four in Austin. While it lacks the great music section of the other stores, this store is well stocked with books of all kinds and also hosts important literary events, some having to do with the university. (For more information on Barnes & Noble, see our write-up in the West Austin listings.)

Bevo's Bookstore

2304 Guadalupe St. • (512) 476-7642

For University of Texas textbooks, school supplies, study aides, gift items and UT souvenirs, Bevo's has been serving the UT community and visitors for two decades at its main location on The Drag across from UT. Bevo's, named for the Longhorn steer that has been UT's mascot since 1916, stocks up to 7,000 titles of UT textbooks and also features a full-service Bank of America. Bevo's also has a store in the Dobie Mall just down the street on Guadalupe. Bevo's two other stores as well as Rother's College Bookstore serve Austin Community College and feature ACC textbooks, school supplies and some logo items. Those stores are in Central Austin at 1202 West Avenue, near the ACC Rio Grande campus, and in North Austin at 11900 Metric Boulevard near the ACC Northridge campus. Rother's, owned by Larry Rother who started Bevo's, is at 801 W. 12th Street near the Rio Grande campus.

Book Market

2025 Guadalupe St. • (512) 499-8707

Located in the Dobie Mall next to the UT campus, Book Market features about 15,000 titles of used books. Book Market specializes in scholarly books and is always on the lookout for books on religion, philosophy, mathematics, military history, literature and poetry, history and more. The store also stocks a good supply of biographies and other nonfiction and fiction works. The store, which opened in 1995, is locally owned.

Book People

603 N. Lamar Blvd. • (512) 472-5050

This Austin institution was the city's first book superstore and continues to be one of Austin's major literary venues. With 200,000 titles, Book People claims to be the largest bookstore in Texas. It definitely is one of Austin's favorite spots to shop for books and to hear authors read from their works. Founded in 1970 by two University of Texas students, the store later became Grok, an alternative bookstore. Book People, still locally owned and operated, has grown to encompass a huge selection of books in all genres and is especially known for an excellent selection of books on alternative healing, computers and cooking. The store features a wonderful children's section and great newsstand as well as books on tape, gift items and computer software for children and adults. Book People's contributions to the Austin literary scene through the years have been enormous. This store goes out of its way to sell books written by local authors, even going so far as to buy books that are self published. The store features a section of books about Texas and another dedicated to Texas authors. Book People sponsors regular book discussion groups and hosts three weekly stratums for children, including one for preschoolers. Check out their monthly calendar for upcoming events. Book People has announced plans to move to a new location nearby.

Bookstop

4001 N. Lamar Blvd. • (512) 452-9541

Started by Austin entrepreneur Gary Hoover, this discount bookstore chain scored an immediate hit with the Austin

INSIDERS' TIP

The Austin Jewish Book Fair has become a literary tradition in the city. Started in 1984, the fair features nationally known speakers, programs for the whole family and hundreds of books, tapes and CDs for sale. The fair, which lasts more than two weeks, is sponsored by the Jewish Community Center, (512) 331-1144, and held in November during Jewish Book Month.

book-buying public, which delighted in the stores' huge selection — and its special prices. Owned since 1989 by Barnes & Noble Booksellers, Bookstop continues its discount tradition. Most books sell normally for 10 percent off list price, and members get an additional 10 percent discount. *New York Times* bestselling hardbacks are 25 percent off list prices every day. Members receive another 15 percent off NYT bestsellers. The reasonable annual fee members pay for a discount card results in immediate savings off the shop's great selection of books in all categories of fiction and nonfiction, including books on tape, magazines and newspapers. The stores all have wonderful children's sections and some stores feature regular story times for children. Special orders are welcome.

Book Woman

918 W. 12th St. • (512) 472-2785

This Austin original will celebrate its 25th anniversary in the year 2000. Book Woman specializes in new books by and about girls and women. But that tells only part of the story. Since 1975, this shop has been a showcase for women writers and musicians. Book Woman, owned by Austinite Susan Post, sponsors a monthly book club for women and hosts readings and books signings by local and national writers. The regular music series held on the third Friday of each month features women singers and songwriters. In addition to its great fiction section, the shop stocks an impressive collection of books on such subjects as self-help, women's health and psychology, girls and teens, memoirs, biographies, spirituality and feminism. It has a wonderful section dedicated to Latina and Chicana books and another section of lesbian fiction and nonfiction works. There's also a small used-book section. The store has a good-sized music section and also sells pride jewelry, bumper stickers, buttons and magnets. Book Woman also has a great selection of T-shirts that laud women artists and feminist politics. The community bulletin board, which displays information on events and services of interest to women, is a popular feature of this store. Book Woman is part of the feminist bookstores network and can do special orders from that catalog.

Congress Avenue Booksellers

716 Congress Ave. • (512) 478-1157

Serving downtown Austin since 1975, Congress Avenue Booksellers is a popular stop for tourists and the downtown community. This general purpose bookstore and newsstand features a wide selection of hardbacks, including *New York Times* bestsellers. The locally owned store also sells paperbacks and has a very good Texana section. The large newsstand offers an extensive selection of magazines and newspapers from around Texas and some from other states. Congress Avenue Booksellers also buys and sells quality used books and has some signed first editions. The store offers books on tape for rent as well as cards, stationary, pens and candy. Congress Avenue Booksellers is experienced in doing searches for out-of-print books.

Folktales

1806 Nueces St. • (512) 472-5657

Folktales focuses on African-American literature for adults and children. This locally owned store, opened in 1993, features about 1,000 titles of new and used books, both fiction and nonfiction. Additionally, Folktales sponsors a number of community-based activities, including children's story time the first Saturday of each month, summer reading camps and teenage reading groups.

Funny Papers

2021 Guadalupe St. • (512) 478-9718

This is one of Austin's one-stop shops for fans of comic books, role-playing games, collectible card games, collectible figurines and more. Funny Papers sells comic-book-related collectibles and many types of players' handbooks that go along with role-playing games. The store, which opened in Dobie Mall near the UT campus in 1990, receives about 100 new titles of comic books each week and also stocks a wide selection of back issues and trade paperbacks. Funny Papers has an assortment of collectible card games as well as magic cards and all the supplies needed for card collectors. Regular comic book subscribers receive a discount.

Half Price Books

3110 Guadalupe St. • (512) 451-4463

One of four locations in Austin, this Half Price Books near the University of Texas sells new and used books at super discount prices. It also buys used books. See our listing for this popular Austin bookstore in our North Austin section.

Kids-N-Cats Book Corner

5808-A Burnet Rd. • (512) 458-6369

This shop that features unique gifts of all kinds also offers used books. Kids-N-Cats stocks all kinds of books for children from babies to preteens as well as adult paperback bestsellers that sell for less than $3. The store also offers a 20 percent discount on the purchase of five or more books. Kids-N-Cats is another Austin-owned shop and has been in business since 1991. The Store is in the HEB shopping center at the corner of Burnet Road and Koenig Lane.

Toad Hall

1206 W. 38th St. • (512) 323-2665

This wonderful bookstore has won *The Austin Chronicle's* award for Best Children's Bookstore a number of times and is one of Austin's most popular spots for kids' books, magazines, music, videos and books on tape. The store, which opened in 1978, has become an Austin institution. Locally owned and operated by Barbara Thomas, Toad Hall features approximately 40,000 titles of new books, including some bilingual books. Toad Hall also features a small section of out-of-print titles. Designed with children in mind, this cute store makes children feel welcome and comfortable. There's also a nice selection of gifts, including book-related characters, science toys and magnets. Toad Hall sponsors a regular story time for children. Thomas just concluded a two-year term as president of the American Booksellers Association.

Travelfest

1214 W. Sixth St. • (512) 469-7906

This Travelfest location opened in 1996. Like the original travel agency on Research Boulevard, it offers a huge selection of travel-related books and much more. See our complete listing under the Northwest heading for more about this locally owned business.

12th Street Books

827 W. 12th St. • (512) 499-8828

Read a book. Have an espresso. 12th Street Books offers thousands of titles of used books as well as a first-rate coffee shop that serves all kinds of coffees, smoothies, bagels and the like. 12th Street specializes in hard-to-find books, first editions and out-of-print books. The store, near Austin Community College's Rio Grande Campus, has several sections dedicated to fiction, biographies, women's books, Western books, religion and philosophy and a full range of books on history, both ancient and modern. And there's much more. This locally owned shop opened in 1994.

University Co-op Bookstore

2244 Guadalupe St. • (512) 476-7211, (800) 255-1896

Founded in 1896, the University Co-op is owned by the students, faculty and staff of The University of Texas at Austin. The bookstore offers UT and Austin Community College textbooks as well as books for UT Extension classes, correspondence courses and informal classes. This is also a great place to shop for UT apparel, gifts and souvenirs as well as greeting cards, art and school supplies. The store has been on The Drag right across the street from the UT campus since 1919, although it moved one door down in 1998 to make room for a new Barnes & Noble. The Co-op East Bookstore at 2902 Medical Arts Street also has some souvenirs but mainly carries textbooks for the UT Law School, the nursing program and other graduate programs.

Whole Life Books

1006 S. Lamar Blvd. • (512) 443-6794

This nonprofit bookstore, music store and gift shop specializes in books on alternative health, metaphysics, spirituality, meditation and New Age topics. Whole Life Books, which opened in 1983, is the only store of its kind in Austin that does not exist for commercial purposes. Austinite Ted Lanier, former UT graduate student in psychology and the former owner of a "hippie bicycle shop," started the operation as a reading room so that people could investigate for themselves the possible approaches to discovering nonmaterial spiritual reality. His patrons, however, wanted to buy the books they found in the reading room — and a business was born. The store stocks about 40,000 titles as well as a wide assortment of CDs and tapes, candles, wind chimes, incense and jewelry.

South Central

Half Price Books

2929 S. Lamar Blvd. • (512) 443-3138

In the Corner Shopping Center, this is one of four Half Price Books locations in Austin. The store sells new and used books at great discount prices. For more on the Dallas-chain's Austin locations see our listing under the North Austin heading.

Resistencia Book Store

2210 S. First St. • (512) 416-8885

Owned by Austin poet raulrsalinas (that's his legal name), Resistencia adds an important dimension to the Austin literary scene. This specialty store, established in Austin in the early 1980s and located in South Central Austin since 1992, is well known for promoting the literary arts through its sponsorship of regular poetry readings, book signings and book readings by local and national authors. The store specializes in Native American, Chicano, Latino, African-American and feminist literature, poetry and history. Resistencia also features CDs and tapes by local and international musicians in its speciality areas. The store offers literary magazines, T-shirts and posters, and features a community bulletin board that announces upcoming literary events. This is one store that Austin relies on for much more than books.

North

Ark Christian Book Store

2438 W. Anderson Ln. • (512) 451-7606

For Bibles as well as books, music and gifts with a Christian theme, Ark Christian Book Store is the place to go. Located in the West Anderson Plaza shopping center, Ark is an Austin-owned shop in business since 1979. The store offers thousands of new hardbacks and paperbacks as well as jewelry, calendars, stationery, cards and blank books. Ark also has Christian CDs, tapes and song books for the music lover.

B. Dalton Bookseller

Highland Mall, 6001 Airport Blvd. • (512) 452-5739

Northcross Mall, 2525 W. Anderson Ln. • (512) 454-5125

This national chain of mall bookstores has been serving Austin for nearly three decades. B. Dalton has two stores in North Austin malls and in late 1998 was set to open Ink, a store dedicated to periodicals and bestsellers, in the Barton Creek Square Mall in West Austin. The stores, part of the Barnes & Noble family, stock a full range of hardbacks, paperbacks, children's books and books on tape as well as national and local magazines. The stores also sponsor occasional book signings and book readings.

Bookstop

9070 Research Blvd. • (512) 451-5798

This location in North Austin is one of two Bookstops in Austin. The stores feature new books at discount prices and offer a membership program for even better discounts. See our listing for Bookstop under Southwest Austin for more on these stores.

Curio Corner Books

7301 Burnet Rd., Ste. 103 • (512) 371-0201

One of Austin's newer used bookstores, Curio Corner opened in 1996. The store stocks about 15,000 titles and specializes in children's books, stories of the Old West, Americana, biographies and some of the 20th century classics, including works by Faulkner, Hemingway and Steinbeck. The locally owned store also has cookbooks, and some soft-cover histories of Texas counties. The large children's section includes Nancy Drew and Hardy Boys books as well as Dr. Seuss books and many, many more. Curio Corner also has some gifts and collectibles, including Ertl car banks, Native American prints and pictures. The store buys used books for cash or store credit.

Emmaus Catholic Books & Gifts Company

6001 Burnet Rd. • (512) 458-2479

Serving Austin since the early 1980s, Emmaus Catholic Books & Gifts offers a wide range of religious books in English and Spanish as well as Bibles, rosaries, gifts and cards. Emmaus also sells music tapes.

Half Price Books

8868 Research Blvd. • (512) 454-3664

With four Austin locations, Half Price Books offers Austinites easy access to its wide selection of used and new books, including rare and out-of-print titles and Texana and Americana titles not easily found elsewhere. The Dallas-based chain opened its first Austin store in 1975 and continues to expand within the city. Half Price Books has a good selection of children's books as well as music in all formats, magazines and videos. New books sell for half price or the current retail price or less. The store buys used books, magazines, videos and music.

East

Ram Bookstore

900 Chicon St. • (512) 236-1140

This is the bookstore for Huston-Tillotson College, and as such deals mainly in textbooks, school supplies and the like. The store does have a selection of clothing and college gifts and souvenirs with Greek and the Huston-Tillotson logos.

West

Barnes & Noble Booksellers

701 Loop 360 (Capital of Texas Hwy.) • (512) 328-3155

This large New York-based chain arrived in Austin in 1994 and has grown to include four superstores around the city. Barnes & Noble has wasted no time in becoming part of, and promoting, Austin's literary, musical and artistic communities. Each store hosts a number of monthly book discussion groups on a variety of areas of interest, including fiction, nonfiction, science fiction and Texana. The stores are a popular place to attend regular book readings and book signings by local, national and international writers and screen writers. Barnes & Noble has also sponsored a number of uniquely Austin events, including *Texas Monthly* magazine's 25th anniversary celebration in 1998. The stores also are extremely active in promoting and hosting events for the annual Texas Writer's Month celebration in May. There's so much going on at Barnes & Noble that each store publishes a monthly calendar of events. This store and the Barnes & Noble in Northwest Austin feature a large music section with headphones for sampling a variety of artists. The children's sections are wonderful and so are the numerous story times the stores host each week. Barnes & Noble also works in conjunction with local and national organizations that promote literacy and is involved with the Austin Independent School District's Adopt-A-School program. In 1998, Barnes & Noble became cosponsor of the Austin Writers' League annual Violet Crown Awards program. The inviting aroma of coffee permeates these stores, thanks to the great cafe and pastry shop inside each one .

Over The Rainbow

2727 Exposition Blvd., Ste. 123 • (512) 477-2954

Primarily a toy store, Over The Rainbow also stocks a large selection of books for children. This locally owned shop has been in the same spot since 1975. Parents will find chapter books, early reading and picture books as well as art books and lots of educational games and toys.

Northeast

Mysteries & More Inc.

11139 N. I-35 • (512) 837-6768

Mysteries & More, started by Austin mystery writer Jan Grape and her husband Elmer, offers a wide selection of new and used books in the categories of British and American mysteries, spy novels, adventure books, horror and Westerns. Serving Austin since 1990, Mysteries & More also is a great place to listen to mystery writers, both national and local, dis-

Photo: Courtesy of the Austin Convention and Visitors Bureau

Writer O. Henry lived in this Austin home.

cuss their craft, sign books and read from their works. The store features first-edition collectibles as well as audio mysteries for sale and rent. The store offers "How to Host a Murder" games, mystery puzzles and *Mystery Scene* and *Mystery News* magazines. The store, on the southeast corner of Braker Lane at Interstate 35, offers a 20 percent discount on all new books. It buys books for store credit.

Northwest

Barnes & Noble Booksellers

10000 Research Blvd. • (512) 418-8985

This Barnes & Noble in the upscale Arboretum Shopping Center opened in 1994 and was the chain's first Austin location. For more on this great book and music store, see our listing for Barnes & Noble in the West Austin listings.

Booksource

13729 Research Blvd. • (512) 258-1313

Booksource carries about 20,000 titles of new and used books and specializes in collectible first editions. The Austin-owned store opened in 1987 also carries comic books and original comic book artwork. Booksource, in the Lake Creek Festival shopping center, has a wide selection of both hardbacks and paperbacks, fiction and some nonfiction.

Borders Books & Music

10225 Research Blvd. • (512) 795-9553

This superstore, which opened in 1995, has earned a great reputation for its support of the Austin literary and music communities. Readers, writers, music lovers and musicians have found a place in this wonderful store. Borders hosts five book discussion groups each month, including one for young adults.

Local and national authors regularly appear at Borders for book readings and/or signings, book discussion panels and other events of interest to the literary community. Borders also is active in sponsoring events for the annual Texas Writers Month celebration in May.

The children's department is always buzzing with activity, and the store hosts two regular story times for children each week. This store has an outstanding selection of computer books and a great Texana section as well as many other well-stocked specialty areas. Borders has a fantastic music department, which includes a huge number of headphones for sampling music selections. It also features live music performances on Fridays and Saturdays. Borders hosts regular events to coincide with new record releases by well-known musicians. The Austin store, one of the Ann Arbor, Michigan-based chain's more than 180 stores nationwide, is a member of the Austin School District's Adopt-A-School program and is active in other community organizations, including the Austin Writers' League. The inviting coffee shop serves a whole range of gourmet coffees as well as pastries and sandwiches. Don't miss the monthly calendar of events to stay abreast of the latest happenings at Borders.

Earful of Books

9607 Research Blvd. • (512) 338-6706

As its name implies, Earful of Books is dedicated exclusively to books on tape. The locally owned store, which opened in 1992, stocks 7,800 titles of audio books for rent and also offers new and used tapes for sale. Book lovers who don't want to miss a word of the original story on tape will be pleased to know that half of the store's titles are unabridged books. Earful of Books has an entire range of both fiction and nonfiction books on tape as well as audio books for children.

Half Price Books

13492 Research Blvd. • (512) 335-5759

One of four Austin locations that specialize in new and used discounted books, this store serves the Northwest Austin community. All four stores are filled with an ever-changing selection of great books. See our description for Half Price Books in the North Austin listings.

Sue's Book Exchange

13450 Research Blvd. • (512) 250-0175

This locally owned store and its branch in Round Rock feature new and used books of all kinds. And Sue's accepts trade-ins for discounts on books — a very popular aspect of this bookstore. About half of the Austin store is dedicated to romance books, and includes both bestsellers and series romances. Romance fans will also find the trade magazine *Romantic Times*. The stores also stock a number of both fiction and nonfiction books of all types. Sue's offers up to a 20 percent discount on new books and sells used paperbacks for half the cover price. With the trade-in of a comparable book, clients can buy used paperbacks for a quarter of the cover price.

Travelfest

9503 Research Blvd. • (512) 418-1515

Established in 1994 by Austinite Gary Hoover, the same entrepreneur who built up a chain of popular discount bookstores called Bookstop, which he later sold to Barnes & Noble, Travelfest is a full-service travel agency and also features just about any kind of travel-related book you need. At Travelfest's two Austin locations (see the other under Central Austin), you'll find travel guides, armchair travel literature, language tapes and books, videos on American and international cities, cookbooks, journals, atlases and maps and good selection of travel books and games to keep the youngsters occupied while you're on the go. The store rents videos of interest to travelers and also stocks plenty of travel-related supplies, including luggage.

Waldenbooks/Waldenkids

Lakeline Mall, 11200 Lakeline Mall Dr. • (512) 257-1950

The largest mall book retailer in the country, Waldenbooks has been in Austin for more than 15 years and at its present location since the Lakeline Mall opened in 1996. This Austin location is one of the chain's large-format stores, which features a larger title selection than most and has a special area with a separate entrance for children's books, called Waldenkids. The store is part of the Borders Group Inc. national chain that includes Borders Books in Austin and Brentanos in other cities in Texas. The store also sells magazines and books on tape. Waldenbooks offers a discount program, which includes all Waldenbooks and Brentano's nationwide. For a $10 annual fee, customers can join the Preferred Reader Program, which offers a 10 percent discount on all purchases except magazines and gift certificates.

Borrow The Book

As centers of learning and for community outreach, Austin's public libraries are among our greatest public assets. Despite the bookstore boom of the 1990s, which brought hundreds of thousands of books to our community, more and more citizens are turning to the public libraries for their reading material. Of course, there's no place like the library for doing research, getting on the Internet free of charge or checking out that vintage recording. Those attractions, and the surge in Austin's population in recent years, has put a strain on our already limited library resources. About 400,000 people hold library cards to Austin's public libraries and nearly a quarter of a million visits are made each month to the city's libraries.

Authorities say the materials collection at the present Central Library is about a third the size it should be to meet Austin's needs. Despite limited resources, however, the library system has won a number of awards for its efforts to make reading and research materials available to everyone, to increase literacy in the city of Austin and to provide after-school tutoring. Our library was named Library of the Year in 1993 by *Library Journal* and Gale Research for its innovative and creative approach to programming in the face of funding shortages. A proposal to build a new Central Library didn't make it on the city's 1998 bond election ballot as a citizen's advisory panel on libraries opted instead to back the expansion and replacement of some existing branch libraries, also a top Austin priority. Austin's existing Central Library, whose 363,000 volumes leave no room for additional books, will remain a substandard facility for at least several years to come. Don't let the statistics prevent you from enjoying our public libraries, however. We couldn't get by a week without seeking out one or another of our libraries — and we always come home with an armload of books.

The Austin public library system is made up of 21 facilities that include the John Henry Faulk Central Library, the Austin History Center and 19 branch libraries located all over the city. The library's collection includes nearly 1.6 million items and almost 3,000 periodical subscriptions. The History Center adds another million items to the collection. Austin's strong neighborhood associations have convinced the City of Austin to construct more and more branch libraries and these same groups have successfully thwarted attempts to close smaller branches. As a result, Austin's branch library system provides easy access to books and to the Internet for citizens all over the city. Some branches are within a mile or two of each other. The hub of the interconnected system continues to be the Central Library, however, which is more than 10 times the size of some of our branches. While branch libraries do not always have the book you want, the library system allows for books to be sent from the Central Library or another branch, usually within a couple of days.

Most of the libraries listed below are open daily. They are generally open Monday through Thursday from 9 AM to 9 PM, and Friday and Saturday from 9 AM to 6 PM. Some have abbreviated hours on Sunday, either 10 AM to 5 PM or noon to 5 PM. Call before you go to verify hours.

Central

John Henry Faulk Central Library
800 Guadalupe St. • (512) 499-7599

Named for revered Austinite John Henry Faulk (see the introduction to this chapter for more in Faulk), Austin's Central Library has more than 335,000 books, manuscripts, periodicals, artistic prints and recordings. It also features eight computers connect to the Internet. The library is open Monday through Thursday from 9 AM to 9 PM, Friday and Saturday from 9 AM to 6 PM and Sunday noon to 6 PM.

Austin History Center

810 Guadalupe St. • (512) 499-7480

This building, which served as Austin's city library for nearly half a century, is now one of the leading local history collections in the state. The History Center houses more than 1 million items documenting the history of Austin to the present day. (See our Attractions chapter for more about this wonderful facility.)

Ralph W. Yarborough Branch, 2200 Hancock Drive, open January 1999

South Central

Twin Oaks Branch, 2301 S. Congress Avenue, #7, (512) 442-4664

North

Little Walnut Creek Branch, 835 W. Rundberg Lane, (512) 836-8975

North Village Branch, 2139 W. Anderson Lane, (512) 458-2239

South

Manchaca Road Branch, 5500 Manchaca Road, (512) 447-6651

Pleasant Hill Branch, 211 E. William Cannon Drive, (512) 441-7993

East

Carver Branch, 1161 Angelina Street, (512) 472-8954

Eustacio Cepeda Branch, 651 N. Pleasant Valley Road, (512) 499-7372

Oak Springs Branch, 3101 Oak Springs Drive, (512) 926-4453

Terrazas Branch, 1105 E. Cesar Chavez Street, (512) 472-7312

University Hills Branch, 4721 Loyola Lane, (512) 929-0551

Windsor Village Branch, 5811 Berkman Drive, #140, (512) 928-0333

West

Howson Branch, 2500 Exposition Boulevard, (512) 472-3584

Northwest

Milwood Branch, 12500 Amherst Drive, (512) 339-2355

Old Quarry Branch, 7051 Village Center Drive, (512) 345-4435

Spicewood Springs Branch, 8637 Spicewood Springs Road, (512) 258-9070

Southeast

Riverside Drive Branch, 2410 E. Riverside Drive, (512) 448-0776

Southeast Austin Community Branch, 5803 Nuckols Crossing Road, (512) 462-1452

Southwest

Will Hampton Branch at Oak Hill, 5125 Convict Hill Road, (512) 892-6680

University of Texas Libraries

It pays to have one of the largest universities in the country right in your own backyard, especially when that university has a great library system, the fifth largest academic library in North America to be exact. The UT library system is made up of 17 facilities, including 14 general libraries — all but the Marine Science Library located in Austin and most open to the public. Visitors who wish to use these UT libraries may ac-

INSIDERS' TIP

Book collectors won't want to miss the twice-yearly Austin Book & Paper Show at Palmer Auditorium. The huge two-day bookfest with about 100 exhibitors is held in January and September and features thousands of rare and used books for children and adults. There is an admission charge, but book lovers can easily wile away the day at this great Austin event.

quire a Courtesy Borrower Card, available for a $40 annual fee at the Courtesy Borrower Desk at the main UT library, the Perry-Castañeda Library, (512) 495-4305. Brochures describing the libraries, their locations and hours of operation, which vary, can also be obtained at the Borrower Desk. On-site use of the other three system libraries, the Center for American History, the Harry Ransom Humanities Research Center and the Tarlton Law Library, is free.

The following information about the UT library system comes from UT's informative booklet, *Guide to General Libraries Resources & Services*, which is also available free at the Borrower Desk. For the latest information or for questions, call the numbers provided below. Vehicular access to the main campus is restricted during normal school hours so if you'd like to visit one of the UT libraries, it's best to park in one of the lots or parking garages located off campus nearby.

Perry-Castañeda Library

21st and Speedway Sts.
• (512) 495-4250

The main library of the UT system contains about 2 million volumes in all subject fields. The PCL, as it is known, emphasizes the humanities, the social sciences, business and education. Subject strengths are American and British history, the South, 20th-century American literature and modern German literature. The PCL also houses the Map Collection, the East Asian Program, South Asian Program and the Middle Eastern Program. U.S. government and United Nations documents can also be found here, along with other collections.

Undergraduate Library

Flawn Academic Center, near 24th and Guadalupe Sts. • (512) 495-4444

The materials in the Undergraduate Library (UGL) are particularly useful to lower-division undergraduates and include a media collection to support classroom instruction and individual research. The Student Microcomputer Facility in the UGL has several hundred workstations and is the largest microcomputer facility on campus but is exclusively for student use. There's also an Audio Visual Library that contains films, musical recordings and spoken recordings. This facility is just west of the UT Tower.

Architecture and Planning Library

Battle Hall, near Guadalupe St. between 21st and 24th Sts. • (512) 495-4620

The collection in this library includes materials on architectural design, history and criticism, building technology, landscape architecture, interior design, and community and regional planning. This library also features the Architectural Drawings Collection that has more than 120,000 drawings and documents.

The Nettie Lee Benson Latin American Collection

Sid Richardson Hall, Manor Rd. between Red River St. and E. Campus Dr.
• (512) 495-4520

Adjacent to the LBJ Library on campus, The Nettie Lee Benson Latin American Collection is an internationally renowned collection containing books and many more materials on subjects relating to Latin America and writings by Latin Americans. The collection includes the Mexican American Library Program, which collects materials relating to all aspects of Spanish-speaking people in the United States, especially Mexican Americans.

The John W. Mallet Chemistry Library

Robert A. Welch Hall, 24th St. and Speedway • (512) 495-4600

This library on campus has more than 70,000 volumes relating to the areas of chemistry, chemical engineering and biochemistry.

Classics Library

Waggener Hall, Speedway between 21st and 24th Sts. • (512) 495-4690

This library has strong holdings in classical philology, Greek and Latin literature, Greek and Roman history, and classical civilization, including art, archeology, epigraphy and numismatics.

The Richard W. McKinney Engineering Library

Ernest Cockrell, Jr. Hall, E. Dean Keeton St. near San Jacinto St. • (512) 495-4500

The McKinney Library maintains a comprehensive collection of books and journals in all fields of engineering. Among other collections, the library features all U.S. patents from 1950 to the present.

Fine Arts Library

Fine Arts Library and Administration Bldg., near 23rd and Trinity Sts. • (512) 495-4680

The library includes materials on art, the performing arts and music, including plenty about Austin's modern music scene. The art collection emphasizes 19th- and 20th-century art of the Americas but includes materials on all art movements and schools, philosophy of art, art education and aesthetics. The music collection provides support for teaching and research in applied music, music education, musicology and more. The performing arts collection is designed to support studies in drama history, performance, play production, playwriting, drama education and dance. The library also houses the Historic Music Recordings Collection with facilities to play selections.

Elizabeth C. and Joseph C. Walter, Jr. Geology Library

Geology Building, near 24th St. between San Jacinto and Speedway • (512) 495-4680

For a wide range of studies relating to the earth sciences, the Walter Library houses many materials, including all U.S. Geological Survey publications and many publications of state geographical surveys. Regional emphasis is on the North American continent, particularly the Southwest, Texas and Mexico.

Life Science Library

Main Building (UT Tower) • (512) 495-4589

The Life Science Library features books and journals relating to the biological sciences and in the pharmacy fields. The Herbarium Collection, adjacent to this library, contains 3,500 volumes on systematic botany.

Marine Science Library

(512) 749-6778

This library is in Port Aransas, Texas, at UT's Marine Science Institute.

John M. Kuehne Library

Robert L. Moore Hall, E. Dean Keeton St. and Speedway • (512) 495-4610

This is UT's Physics-Mathematics-Astronomy Library and houses materials relating to the all three fields of study. Kuehne holdings are mainly upper-division undergraduate, graduate and research materials. There are materials on quantum theory, nuclear physics, atomic physics and more. The mathematics section focuses on the foundations of mathematics, group theory, mathematical analysis, approximation theory, algebra, geometry and topology. The library has a complete collection of star catalogs and atlases as well as space research materials.

Edie and Lew Wasserman Public Affairs Library

Sid Richardson Hall • (512) 495-4400

This library adjacent to the LBJ Library maintains an interdisciplinary collection selected to serve the needs of public administra-

INSIDERS' TIP

For offbeat encounters with Austin's literary scene, don't miss the annual O. Henry Pun-Off in May at the O. Henry Museum (see our chapter on Annual Events and Festivals), or visit a venue that hosts Poetry Slam events, like the Electric Lounge at 302 Bowie Street. Poetry Slam must be experienced to be fully understood, but generally speaking consists of poets giving three-minute performances of their work — usually monologue pieces — which are then judged Olympic style (5.3 is not great, 9.9 is a winner) by a panel of judges picked from the audience. Austin hosted the 1998 National Poetry Slam.

tors and researchers interested in government and public policy.

Special UT Libraries

These libraries are not part of UT's borrower card network, but on-site use is free.

Center for American History

Sid Richardson Hall • (512) 495-4532

More than half the people who use the Center for American History are not associated with the University of Texas. This center, adjacent to the LBJ Library, offers free access to materials after patrons complete an application form and show a photo ID. No materials may be checked out.

The holdings of the Texas Collection Library, the Archives and Manuscripts Unit, the Fleming University Writings Collections, Natchez Trace Collection, Bexar Archives, Congressional History Collection, Sam Rayburn Library and Museum (Bonham, Texas), and the Texas Newspaper and Non-Textural Records Unit form the most extensive collection of Texana in existence and provide a major resource for the study of Southern, Western, and Southwestern history.

Harry Ransom Humanities Research Center

Harry Ransom Center, near 21st and Guadalupe Sts. • (512) 471-7726

Visitors may use the materials here free of charge by filling out an application and showing a photo ID. Materials may not be checked out. The center's collections include more than 800,000 books, about 9 million manuscripts, 4 million photographs and 40,000 pieces of literary iconography. The center offers extensive resources in 20th-century English and American literature and contain important resources for research in English literature from the 17th through 19th centuries. The center also hosts book readings.

Tarlton Law Library

Townes Hall, E. Dean Keeton St. between San Jacinto and E. Campus Dr. • (512) 471-7726

The fifth largest academic law library in the United States and the largest in the Southwest, the Tarlton Law Library contains more than 750,000 volumes of law and law-related materials. Access to the library is free but users who wish to check out materials must obtain a borrower card for a fee. This is separate from the general libraries borrower card.

Southwest Texas State University Collection

Southwestern Writers Collection

Alkek Library, 7th Floor, Southwest Texas State University, San Marcos • (512) 245-3861

It's well worth the trip to San Marcos, about 35 miles south of Austin, to explore Southwest Texas State University's great Southwestern Writers Collection. The collection, which began in 1986 with a major gift of J. Frank Dobie materials from Austinites Bill and Sally Wittliff, has grown into an important archive that records the literary and artistic spirit of the American Southwest. The collection includes books, manuscripts, personal papers and artifacts of Southwestern writers. The Wittliff Gallery of Southwest & Mexican Photography, which opened in 1996, exhibits work of important photographers of the region, included the internationally renowned Texas photographer Keith Carter. Entrance to both collections is free and open to the public. Materials may not be checked out. Patrons must show a photo ID to enter.

Community Libraries

Cedar Park Public Library

550 Discovery Blvd., Cedar Park • (512) 259-5353

Opened in 1981, the Cedar Park Public Library now holds about 35,000 book titles as well as videos, books on tape, music CDs and more than 90 magazine and newspaper titles. The library also has two Internet computers for public use. The library is free for Cedar Park residents. Others may obtain a card for $15 for six months or $30 per year. The library is open Monday through Thursday from 9 AM to 9 PM, and Friday and Saturday from 9 AM to 5 PM.

Lake Travis Community Library

3322 R.R. 620 S. • (512) 263-2885

This library at Lake Travis High School serves Lake Travis community residents as well as all those summer visitors who flock to the lake. In addition to the fiction and nonfiction sections, the library features a good-sized children's section, large print books, newspapers and magazines, audio and video cassettes as well as six Internet computers for public use. This library also features an ongoing bag-of-books sale to raise funds. For $5 visitors can buy repeat books that have been donated to the library. Volunteers who staff this library in the summer say this program is especially popular with out-of-town visitors. The operating hours vary according to season.

Pflugerville Community Library

102 S. Third St., Pflugerville
• (512) 251-9185

This Community Library features more than 12,000 volumes including books on tape and videos. It offers one Internet computer for public use. The library, which opened in 1981, will move to a facility six times as large as the present location in mid-1999. Residents of the Pflugerville School District may obtain free library cards. Out-of-district residents pay $20 per year. The library is open Monday, Tuesday and Thursday from 10 AM to 7 PM, Wednesday from 1 to 7 PM, and Saturday from 10 AM to 4 PM.

Round Rock Public Library

216 E. Main St., Round Rock
• (512) 218-7000

The Round Rock Public Library in the city's historic downtown area houses more than 82,000 items, including books, videos, CDs and books on tape. It offers patrons more than 150 magazine titles and two Internet computers. The library, which opened in the 1960s, is run by the City of Round Rock. Library cards are free for residents. Those living outside the city limits may also obtain a library card for an annual fee of $15 per person or $35 for a family of four. Plans call for the library to be expanded to triple its current size before 2000. The library is open 9 AM to 9 PM Monday through Thursday, 9 AM to 6 PM Friday and Saturday, and 1 to 9 PM on Sunday. Sunday operating hours may vary during the summer.

Writers' Organizations

Writers, like other addicts, need support and there's no better comfort to be found than at the meetings of the groups listed here. We have yet to hear of one that has cured writing fever, however.

Austin Writers' League

1501 W. Fifth St., Ste. E-2
• (512) 499-8914

Established in 1981, the Austin Writers' League has grown from a group of writers gathered in a backyard to include more than 1,600 members, mostly from Austin but including writers from around the state, the country and the world. This fine organization, the largest in Texas, is highly involved in developing the Austin literary scene and providing support for its members. League members host more than a dozen regular informal classes and workshops for writers of many genres. The league also honors members with a number of annual awards and cash prizes. The Violet Crown Awards are given in three categories: fiction, nonfiction and literary nonfiction. The Teddy Book Award goes to a writer of children's books while the Young Texas Writers Scholarship is awarded to students. The nonprofit organization maintains a library and resources center that is chock-full of writing materials and includes two full bookcases of books written by members that can be checked out. The league's monthly newsletter, *Austin Writer*, provides a wealth of information for writers and book lovers. General meetings, open to the public, are held the third Thursday of each month and feature a speaker or panel of experts on topics of interest to writers. Regular membership is $40 a year.

Sisters in Crime — The Heart of Texas Chapter

This group, founded locally in 1994, has about 50 members — females *and* males — who are fans and authors of mystery fiction. Sisters in Crime sponsors a regular book discussion group and a creative writing group. The nonprofit organization holds monthly meetings the first Sunday of every month at 2 PM at the Bank One community room, 3811 Bee Caves Road. The meetings feature a speaker of interest to readers and writers of mystery fiction. Annual dues are $15, although members must also join the national organization. The monthly meetings are open to the public for a $2 donation. The group can be contacted at P.O. Box 160232, Austin, TX 78716.

Society of Childrens' Book Writers and Illustrators — Austin Chapter

10723 Cassia Dr. • no phone

This organization for writers and illustrators of children's books has about 65 members and is affiliated with the national organization. The society holds monthly meetings the second Saturday of each month at the Old Quarry Library in Northwest Austin. The meetings, open to the public, include a featured speaker or writing workshop. Membership is free but subscriptions to the monthly newsletter, *Austintatious Tales*, is $20 per year. The society also host two annual conferences, one featuring authors and illustrators, the other featuring a national book editor. Meredith Davis is the regional advisor.

Romance Writers of America — Austin Chapter

(512) 312-1064

The Austin Chapter of Romance Writers of America is aimed at writers of romance fiction, whether they've been published or are working on a book. The group has about 35 members, mostly female although males are welcome. Founded in 1983, the Austin chapter is affiliated with the national organization, which has about 8,000 members across the country. Local membership is $15 per year. Members, however, must join the national organization separately. The monthly meetings feature speakers, author panel discussions and other events of interest to romance writers. A monthly "Abandoned Bride" trophy is awarded to the member who tells the most humorous, heart-wrenching or horrific story of the evening. Guests are invited to attend one or two monthly meetings free of charge. The Austin chapter also publishes a monthly newsletter, *The Austin Affair*, which is packed with information of interest to romance writers. The chapter can also arrange critique partners or critique groups for those interested in peer discussion of their work. Call or write for information on the meeting site, 107 Lambs Street, Buda, TX 78610.

Texas Institute of Letters

This honorary organization, established in 1936, recognizes practicing writers who have demonstrated substantial literary achievement as well as others who have had a positive influence on the literary arts. Members, who are invited to join, must have a substantial connection to Texas. Most importantly for non-members the TIL, as it is known, determines the winners of about $20,000 in annual writing prizes that are backed by foundations or individuals. The prizes include the prestigious $6,000 Jesse Jones Award for the best book of fiction and the $5,000 Carr P. Collins Award for the best book of nonfiction. Other awards are given for poetry, journalism, short stories, children's books and book design. Additionally, the TIL and The University of Texas determine two annual winners of the Paisano Fellowship, which gives writers a six-month residence at J. Frank Dobie's Paisano ranch and a $7,200 stipend. The goals of the TIL, whose 235 members include more than 50 Austinites, are to stimulate interest in Texas letters, recognize distinctive achievement in the field and promote fellowship among those interested in the literary and cultural development of the state. The organization can be contacted at P.O. Box 298300, Fort Worth, TX 76129.

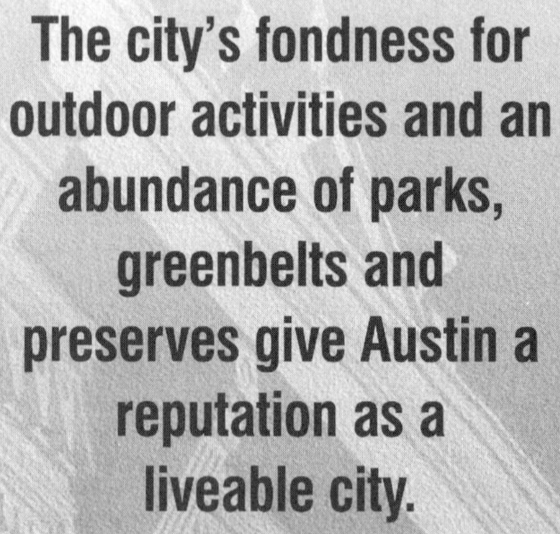

The city's fondness for outdoor activities and an abundance of parks, greenbelts and preserves give Austin a reputation as a liveable city.

Parks and Recreation

No one who has stood on the edge of a Hill Country pasture in springtime could deny the beauty of Central Texas, but even long after the riot of colorful wildflowers is gone there is much to admire in the landscape of the Hill Country. Familiarity breeds admiration and learning about the particulars makes both residents and visitors appreciate the whole.

Central Texas is not only home to some of the world's intriguing and delicate fauna and flora, but is also a land where residents enjoy a generally benign climate. This is a place where Christmas Day may be celebrated with a walk in the sun along Town Lake or a swim in Barton Springs Pool. Life, for much of the year, is lived outdoors in Austin.

Though Austin's nightlife and music scenes are touted, it is also the city's fondness for outdoor activities and an abundance of parks, greenbelts and preserves that give Austin a reputation as a liveable city. Pockets of greenery are fiercely defended against the pressures of urban sprawl. The Highland Lakes, which bring nature into the heart of the city via Town Lake, serve as a natural lifeline between the Hill Country and the city dweller.

The city also rises to the modern challenge to provide its citizens with something to do on the weekends other than mow the lawn. There are 5K runs, 10K runs, marathons, bicycle races, kite-flying contests and rugby games. There are rocks to be climbed and Frisbees to be thrown.

This chapter offers a look at area parks and gives an overview of the many recreational activities popular in Central Texas. It is divided into three general sections: Parks, Recreation and Watersports. The parks section focuses on state, lake, county and city parks. The Recreation section is divided into activities, and the Watersports section offers tips on how to enjoy Austin's lakes, rivers and swimming facilities.

Please note: Wildlife, notably birds and deer, are abundant around Austin, but so are insects and snakes, so pack insect bite treatment and wear sturdy boots when hiking on nature trails. Snakes play a vital role in the ecosystem and are usually shy creatures who avoid human contact. Most snakebites can be treated successfully if aid is sought quickly. If you plan to be outdoors frequently in Austin, familiarize yourself with the snakes found in the Texas countryside; there are several good Texas wildlife guides available at local bookstores (see The Literary Scene chapter).

Parks

State Parks

Forget packing up the family station wagon and driving for hours to reach a campsite or popular natural landmark à la *National Lampoon's Summer Vacation*. There are at least two dozen state parks within an easy two-hour drive of Austin. In total, there are 122 state parks under the management of the Texas Parks & Wildlife Department. Among the 41 historical sites are several national landmarks, including the Admiral Nimitz Museum and Historical Center in Fredericksburg and Lyndon Johnson State Park in Stonewall, both to the west of Austin and easily accessible (see our Daytrips chapter).

Other state parks in Central Texas offer visitors an opportunity to experience Texas natural history. Most offer camping, watersports, nature trails for hiking, walking or mountain biking, plus picnic facilities and perhaps equestrian trails. We have highlighted those near Austin that offer a variety of outdoor activities.

Admission to most state parks is between $1 and $5 per person. There are several state 12-month passports that offer free admission for seniors, discounts or free admissions for veterans and disabled visitors and discounted rates for Texas residents. These Gold and Silver Texas Conservation Passports are available for an annual fee, currently $50 and $25 respectively, and are a real bargain. They entitle the bearer and the occupants of his or her vehicle to unlimited access to certain state areas and parks, depending on the color of the passport. These can be purchased at any state park, regional law enforcement office or at the Austin Parks and Wildlife headquarters listed below.

Most state parks have camping facilities. Advance reservations are advised. Most parks are open for day visitors from 8 AM to 10 PM, but call ahead for hours of operation, particularly on holidays. Those parks that have certain natural attractions, greenbelts, nature trails or swimming holes may have special hours and blackout dates. The Texas Parks & Wildlife Department is at 4200 Smith School Road in Austin, (512) 389-8900.

Bastrop State Park

Bastrop Texas Hwy. 21, 1.5 miles east of Bastrop • (512) 321-2101

This 3,503 acre park is popular, perhaps because its landscape is so different from the surrounding countryside. The park is home to the "Lost Pines," a forest of pine trees (Texans call them "piney woods") that would seem to be more at home in East Texas. During the Depression, the Civilian Conservation Corps built several log cabins at the park, which are now popular for family getaways. There are 12 cabins accommodating from two to eight people. Reservations and a deposit are required. All cabins have bathrooms, kitchen facilities, air conditioning and wood-burning fireplaces. Prices range from $50 to $80. No pets are allowed except for those aiding the physically challenged. Call the park number above for reservations and information.

The park also has camping facilities, a swimming pool open in the summertime, fishing on a 10-acre lake, hiking, golfing on a nine-hole course and hiking trails. Park rangers offer guided nature tours, popular from January to March during the breeding season of the endangered Houston toad.

There is a park road, Scenic Park Road 1, that connects with Buescher State Park, 15 miles east.

Buescher State Park

F.M. 153 off Texas Hwy. 71, Smithville • (512) 237-2241

Pronounced "Bisher" State Park, this 1,016-acre park is a favorite spot for area fishermen. A 30-acre lake is stocked with trout, bass and other fish. There are campsites, screened shelters and picnic areas. Unlike nearby Bastrop State Park, oak trees and Blackland prairie dominate the landscape here. Popular activities at the park include biking, hiking, swimming and boating.

Colorado Bend State Park

F.M. 580, west of Lampasas near Bend • (915) 628-3240

Take U.S. 183 to Lampasas, west on F.M. 580 for about 24 miles, and then follow signs

INSIDERS' TIP

The Texas state parks system celebrated 75 years of stewardship in 1998. One handy guide to the state system is a map of Texas showing all the state park sites. Call (800) 786-8644. The cost is $3.11 to cover postage and handling.

Photo: John S. Petersen

Waterflowers grace the Japanese garden in Zilker Park.

to the park. This 5,328-acre park offers primitive camping, hiking, fishing, swimming, mountain biking, birding, cave tours and nature walks.

Enchanted Rock State Natural Area

R.R. 965, north of Fredericksburg • (915) 247-3903

This popular and legendary park is 18 miles north of Fredericksburg (see our Daytrips chapter). The major feature of this 1,643-acre park is the Enchanted Rock, a 640-acre granite outcropping, a vast stone dome that rises above the Hill Country landscape, similar to its geological cousins Ayers Rock in Australia and Stone Mountain in Georgia. (Enchanted Rock is second only to Stone Mountain in the U.S. rock outcropping category.) Hikers who are in good form can hike to the top (it's easier than Ayers Rock) to enjoy an unparalleled view of Texas.

See our Daytrips chapter to learn more about the Native American origins of the "enchanted" part of the name. It is the "rock" part of the name that beckons the more down-to-earth types who are interested in rock climbing. In addition, there is camping, both tent camping and primitive camping, hiking, nature trails and picnicking. Given its spectacular views and easy access from major population centers, the park reaches its visitor and parking limits early on weekends. Get an early start.

Inks Lake State Park

Texas Hwy. 29 on Park Rd. 4, near Burnet • (512) 793-2223

This 1,201 acre Highland Lakes park 9 miles west of Burnet offers camping, recreational vehicle hookups, backpacking, hiking, golfing, boating, canoeing (canoes and paddleboats for rent), water-skiing, scuba diving and fishing. It is a favorite for boaters and fishermen. The park offers nature trail walks and canoe tours in spring and fall. There is a sunset bat watch, and a grocery store is on-site.

McKinney Falls State Park

Scenic Loop Rd., Austin • (512) 243-1643

Located just 13 miles southeast of downtown Austin off U.S. 183, this 640-acre park encompasses the lands around the confluence of Williamson and Onion Creeks, which flow across southern Hays and Travis Counties. The park is named for Texas pioneer Thomas McKinney, whose home still stands near the confluence of the creeks. He was one of Stephen F. Austin's original 300 colonists.

The pool under the falls is a popular swimming spot, but it is limited to those days when park rangers deem it safe. On some days the bacteria count may be high due to pollution from upstream, non-point sources, so call ahead if you want to swim. The park also has hiking, biking, fishing, picnicking and camping facilities. There are nature study areas, a dirt-bike trail and group picnic facilities.

Pedernales Falls State Park
F.M. 3232, near Johnson City
• (830) 868-7304

The park, 32 miles west of Austin, is reached by taking U.S. 290 West, then heading north for 8 miles on F.M. 3232. The spectacular falls are the highlight of this 5,211-acre park. The falls are even more spectacular after a sudden spring rain when the Pedernales River exhibits all the dangerous beauty of a Hill Country river in flash flood. Newcomers to Central Texas should be aware that even the driest creek bed can become a rushing torrent in literally minutes. The force and power of the water is deceptive and powerful undertows can overturn large trucks and buses in seconds. Do not ignore warnings to keep to the high ground.

With its vast tumble of boulders and Hill Country plants and trees, the falls are beautiful, even on dry, summer days. The park has fishing and nature study facilities, picnic sites, a hike and bike trail, swimming in the lower 3 miles of the river and an equestrian trail.

The Lake Parks

The image of Texas as a land of deserts and vast, treeless wilderness owes a lot more to Hollywood than reality. That is especially true in Central Texas where lakes abound. Most of them are not nature's work, but owe their existence to people with gigantic imaginations who roamed the Texas political landscape in the first half of this century.

Between 1843 and 1938 there were several devastating floods that washed through the Hill Country along the path of the Colorado River. The horror of flooding was contrasted with the blight of drought. Texas leaders looked to the hills and dreamed of damming up the river to stem the floods, defeat droughts and harness the river's power to electrify the wilderness. With the help of engineers and laborers, they succeeded, and now the Highland Lakes climb 646 feet, are over 150 miles long, encompass 56,000 acres of water and 700 miles of shoreline, making up the greatest concentration of fresh water in Texas.

In 1934 the Texas Legislature created the Lower Colorado River Authority (LCRA), a state agency that administers the chain of artificial lakes and dams created to harness the Colorado River. Today, it is one of the most influential state agencies in terms of environmental policy. Though a major power generator, LCRA relies, for the most part, on Wyoming coal and Texas natural gas, not the dams, to light the homes of Texas Hill Country residents.

Hydroelectricity may be a very small part of the function of the Highland Lakes these days, but the lakes are still a vital force in the battle against floods and are a critical water supply for some communities in the area. They also provide water for also rice farms downstream, a major Texas agricultural crop. Lake levels are susceptible to weather vagaries and downstream demand so area residents, particularly those living lakeside, keep a close eye on local weather forecasts, which include lake information. Lake levels and water flows are of interest not only to lake residents; they are of vital importance to the recreation industry, which is now a major economic force in the Highland Lakes area.

There are three major links in the lake chain in the area around and in Austin. The most urban link in the chain is Town Lake, 5 miles long from Tom Miller Dam in West Austin, near Redbud Trail, to Longhorn Dam in East Austin near Pleasant Valley Road.

Lake Austin is 20 miles long, stretching from Mansfield Dam on Lake Travis to Tom Miller Dam. Lake Austin is the oldest of the Highland Lakes. In 1893 it cost a million dollars to build the dam that was later replaced by Tom Miller Dam. In 1900, water poured over the original dam, flooding downtown Austin and causing many drowning deaths. Another million-dollar renovation was undertaken in 1912, but not completed. Finally, with the creation of the LCRA, the work was completed in 1938. The dam, named after former Austin Mayor Tom Miller, has withstood many heavy rains since.

Lake Travis is 64 miles long and was

formed by the construction of the 266-foot-high, 7,089-foot-long Mansfield Dam, which was built in 1941 and named after Texas Congressman J.J. Mansfield. Not only is the lake an increasingly popular recreational spot, but its shores are prized real estate.

With the booming growth, the Highland Lakes are just one focus of the debate among environmentalists and the development community. On the recreation front, there are increasing concerns about crowding on the lakes as Jet Skis, yachts, swimmers, scuba divers, water skiers, windsurfers and cigarette boats vie for space. Jet Skis have been banned from the lakes during the three major summer holiday weekends, Memorial Day, Fourth of July and Labor Day. Following verbal clashes and some accidents between motorized crafts and sailing vessels, there has been some discussion by the LCRA of "zoning" the lakes for various activities.

To the west of Lake Travis is Lake Buchanan, pronounced Buck-ANN-un by the locals (see our Texas Pronunciation guide in the Overview chapter). Created by the Buchanan Dam, the 31-mile-long lake is the highest in the chain and covers the largest surface area, although Lake Travis contains more water. The LCRA operates several parks on the lake as does Burnet County. These parks typically feature little artificial landscaping — hills have not been leveled, and large green spaces are usually Hill Country meadows rather than planted lawns. Picnic and campsites are shaded by oak trees and trails lined with juniper trees.

For more information about all the Highland Lakes, see our Daytrips chapter.

The Lower Colorado River Authority (LCRA)

(512) 473-3200, (800) 776-5272

In addition to a wealth of information on water safety and quality, weather forecasts, utility, energy and conservation issues, the agency also offers newcomers and visitors a park visitor's package, available by calling the local number listed previously and requesting Extension 4083. For detailed information on specific parks, detailed directions and reservations where necessary, call the same extension.

LCRA Primitive Areas

The river authority operates a primitive recreation system along the lake system. These campsites are in natural areas where the typical rugged Hill Country landscape has been minimally disrupted. Most of the sites are in out-of-the-way places, and visitors will need detailed directions or a good area map to find them. Call (512) 473-3200 Ext. 4083 for directions and information.

Camp Creek Primitive Area

Lake Travis, off F.M. 1431

This 600-acre park, east of Marble Falls, 18 miles west of Lago Vista, has nature trails, boat ramps, boating, camping and picnic facilities.

Gloster Bend Primitive Area

Lake Travis, off F.M. 1431

Approximately 6 miles west of Lago Vista, this lakeside site has camping and picnic facilities.

Grelle Primitive Area

Lake Travis, off Texas Hwy. 71 near Spicewood

Grelle is a 400-acre park with woods, trails, camping and access to the lake. The hiking trails are challenging. Next door is the popular Krause Springs swimming hole (see the Swimming section of this chapter).

Muleshoe Bend Primitive Area

Lake Travis, off Texas Hwy. 71 past Bee Caves

A 900-acre facility with trails, lake access, camping and picnicking near the Ridge Harbor subdivision on Burnet County Road 414.

INSIDERS' TIP

There were more than 20 million visits to Texas state parks in 1997 and approximately 262,500 camping reservations made for the 8,000 campsites in the system. Reservations can be made by calling (512) 389-8900 in Austin.

The Narrows Primitive Area
Lake Travis, off Texas Hwy. 71 near Spicewood

This rugged site has a boat ramp, picnic areas and primitive campsites. This is one of the smallest parks in the system encompassing only 250 acres. It is used primarily as boat ramp facility since there are neither potable water nor restrooms on site.

Shaffer Bend Primitive Area
Lake Travis, off F.M. 1431

A 535-acre park with camping, picnicking and lake access about 17 miles west of Lago Vista. The terrain is rough and suitable to trucks and four-wheel drive vehicles.

Turkey Bend (East) Primitive Area
Lake Travis, off F.M. 1431

A 400-acre park with great views of the lake and surrounding countryside. The park has camping and picnic facilities and lake access. The park is about 10 miles west of Lago Vista.

Other Lake Parks

Camp Chautauqua at Lake Travis
R.M. 2322, off Texas Hwy. 71
• (512) 264-1752

This facility is next door to Pace Bend Park (see County Parks) and is run by the Friends of the Colorado River Foundation, a nonprofit group. The site is host to *chautauquas* on the environment — the Native American name that came to signify summer educational programs popular in the late 19th century. The site also has camping (both tent and RV), fishing, boating, swimming and sports facilities. There is an on-site grocery store also. The camp has four covered pavilions for picnics and a large covered, open-sided pavilion for 100 persons, ideal for educational functions. Cabins at the camp cost $25 a night, RV hookups $15, tent sites $7 to $10. Admission to the park is $4, $3 for seniors and free for children 13 and younger.

Travis County Parks

Travis County, home to the capital city, operates 20 parks throughout the county, many of them on the banks of Lake Travis and Lake Austin. Generally, the Lake Austin parks charge no fees, but those on Lake Travis may have vehicle charges and individual entrance fees. We have noted telephone numbers for parks that have them. You can reach Travis County Parks Visitor Information and Reservations at (512) 473-9437.

Arkansas Bend
Sylvester Ford Rd., off R.M. 1431
• (512) 267-4661

This 195-acre park on the shores of Lake Travis is not as primitive as some of the LCRA facilities, but the Hill Country landscape is a backdrop to picnic areas equipped with barbecue pits. The park has hiking trails, swimming facilities, a boat ramp and campsites.

Ben Fisher
F.M. 973 off U.S. Hwy. 290 E.

This park is in eastern Travis County and has picnic and barbecue facilities, hiking trails and sports courts. The landscape east of Austin is called Blackland Prairie and much of it is fertile farmland. Parks in this area have undulating hills, meadows covered with wildflowers, both spring and fall, and large pecan trees. Pecan harvesting is a favorite pastime in the fall.

Bob Wentz Park at Windy Point
On Lake Travis, access from Comanche Trail • (512) 266-2544

This 211-acre lakeside park has barbecue pits, picnic sites, hiking trails, playgrounds, a

INSIDERS' TIP

In 1997 the Texas Legislature authorized $60 million in bonds to upgrade and improve the state's parks system. The state is also calling on citizens to participate by offering volunteer assistance at their nearby state park. A private nonprofit group, Texans for State Parks also is working to improve the parks. Contact the group at P.O. Box 506, Round Rock, TX 78680.

swimming area, showers and a boat ramp for sailboats.

Cypress Creek

On Lake Travis, Anderson Mill Rd. at R.M. 2769

The landscape in this county park on Lake Travis retains its wild character, but there have been some additions including barbecue pits and picnic areas. The park offers access to the lake for swimming and primitive camping.

Dink Pearson Park

On Lake Travis near Lago Vista

Dink Pearson is a lakeside park with picnic and barbecue facilities, access to the lake for swimmers and a boat ramp.

Fritz Hughes

Lake Austin, near Mansfield Dam

This is a good spot for family picnic, but is not suitable for swimming. The park has picnic and barbecue facilities plus a playscape.

Hippie Hollow

Lake Travis, near Comanche Trail off R.M. 620 • (512) 266-1644

This is an Austin landmark. (Its formal name is MacGregor Park, but nobody calls it that.) This clothing-optional park is open to individuals 18 and older, and is particularly popular among gay sun seekers. You can swim in the lake, sunbathe on the park's beach and rocks or hike on the trails (shoes recommended).

Little Webberville

On the Colorado River near F.M. 969

This Colorado River park east of Austin, near the community of Webberville, has picnic and barbecue areas, playscapes and a boat ramp.

Mansfield Dam

R.M. 620

On Lake Travis, just west of Mansfield Dam, this county park offers picnic and barbecue facilities, swimming, a boat ramp and overnight camping facilities. It is a short walk to the dam, which offers a close-up view of engineering feats in Central Texas. The dam is also a favorite place for hawks and other birds of prey to ride the thermal wind currents, which rise off the cliffs and the tall dam.

Pace Bend

2701 F.M. 2322, 4.5 miles off Texas Hwy. 71 • (512) 266-1482

This 1,000-acre-plus park (sometimes called Paleface Park) has equestrian facilities, trails, campsites, picnic and barbecue facilities, plus swimming in the lake.

Richard Moya

Burleson Rd. in eastern Travis County

Named after a popular former county commissioner, this park is a favorite spot for family picnics, particularly on Mexican-American holidays and birthdays when the smell of fajitas cooking and the sound of pinatas being whacked fill the air. Portions of the original downtown Congress Avenue Bridge, c. 1884, now span Onion Creek in the park.

Sandy Creek

On Lake Travis off Lime Creek Rd.

Another rugged hillside park on Lake Travis, this park has hiking trails, offers access to the lake for swimmers and boaters, and has primitive camping facilities.

Selma Hughes Park

Lake Austin off Quinlan Park Rd.

This is the site of a popular boat ramp on busy Lake Austin. There are picnic facilities with barbecue pits.

Tom Hughes Park

Lake Travis on Tom Hughes Park Rd., off R.M. 620

Swimming is the popular attraction in this small county park, which is open in daylight hours only.

Webberville

F.M. 969

This large and popular county park is 3 miles east of Webberville in eastern Travis County on the banks of the Colorado River at the Travis/Bastrop county line. There are picnic and barbecue facilities, hiking trails, playscapes, a boat ramp, ballfields, sports courts and equestrian facilities. The large picnic pavilions can be reserved for gatherings by calling the Travis County parks reservations number at (512) 473-9437.

Windmill Run

U.S. Hwy. 290 W. and Texas Hwy. 71

Windmill Run is a neighborhood park near the Windmill Run subdivision in Oak Hill, with picnic and barbecue facilities, hiking trails and ballfields.

Austin City Parks

The city boasts nearly 200 city parks, hike and bike trails and greenbelts, plus several nature preserves (see our Nature Preserves section in this chapter), all encompassing more than 14,000 acres of urban retreats. The parks are in all areas of the city and vary in size and character. Some are small, urban oases of peace and quiet where the neighborhood kids can toss a ball, couples can walk the dog, or an office worker can pause for a moment or two of lunchtime bird-watching or newspaper-reading. Others are popular gathering spots for annual events — rugby tournaments, summer theater, a Mexican Independence Day celebration, or a whimsical festival in honor of Eeyore, Winnie the Pooh's sidekick.

Given the large number of city parks, we have picked out several of particularly interesting character and detailed them below. The city offers detailed information about all city parks in several brochures, available on request from the Parks and Recreation Department (PARD) listed below. The parks are listed below alphabetically, ending with Zilker Park, the city's major park in the heart of the city and home to Barton Springs Pool, an icon that is perhaps the ultimate natural symbol of Austin life (see our Close-up in this chapter).

Austin has more than 20 miles of surfaced scenic paths in the city's natural greenbelts, plus untold miles of wooded tracks. Bicycles are permitted, but motorized vehicles are not. Pets on leashes are allowed. The city's parks department has been building separate trails for hikers, joggers, walkers and bikers, but there are several popular trails, notably around Town Lake, where the groups must coexist. Rock climbers on the Barton Creek greenbelt also have been at odds with mountain bikers. Peaceful coexistence is encouraged.

The curfew on all trails is 10 PM. They reopen at 5 AM. To access greenbelt head for the address listed with each park. Parking is limited at some greenbelt locations and space is at a premium on weekends, particularly when the weather sends much of Austin outdoors.

Austin Parks and Recreation Department (PARD)

200 S. Lamar Blvd. • (512) 499-6700

Residents and visitors alike should stop by the main office of PARD, as it is called, and pick up a wealth of material on Austin recreational activities and facilities. The office is just south of Town Lake.

Barton Creek Greenbelt

3755-B Loop 360 (Capital of Texas Hwy.)

This is one of the city's most popular, and most crowded, greenbelts, particularly on lazy summer days. The trail follows Barton Creek through the canyon that cuts across Southwest Austin and offers a retreat to the Hill Country without leaving the city limits.

Barton Creek has six official access points, called trailheads, and one very popular unofficial entry. The designated trailheads are at Zilker Park, west of Barton Springs Pool; the intersection of Spyglass Drive and Barton Skyway; 2010 Homedale Drive, behind Barton Hills Elementary School; the Gus Fruh Access at 2642 Barton Hills Drive; the Brodie Oaks office complex, off Loop 360 west of Lamar Boulevard; and the intersection of Camp Craft Road and Scottish Woods Trail. The Gus Fruh and Brodie Oaks access points are wheelchair accessible.

The unofficial access point is easily spotted on a balmy weekend afternoon. The shoulder of the access road leading from Loop 360 (Capital of Texas Highway) onto MoPac south is lined with cars. Just a few yards away, a wide stretch of the creek creates a swimming hole that attracts large crowds on warm days.

Boggy Creek Greenbelt

1114 Nile St.

This East Austin trail runs 3 miles from Rosewood Park to Zaragosa Park. Trails in

Austin's Beloved Waterin' Hole

Barton Springs Pool has been called the soul of Austin and that is really not an exaggeration since this treasured, spring-fed pool stands both as a symbol of Austin's lifestyle, a measure of its commitment to the environment, a political rallying point and even a place of spiritual and psychological renewal. This 1,000-by-125-foot unchlorinated swimming pool, fed by natural spring waters, stands at the heart of Zilker Park and serves as a touchstone for all that was and is Austin. Its symbolic value cannot be underestimated, while its value as a recreational asset is just as highly rated.

The pool is fed by spring waters that bubble up at the rate of 35 million gallons a day through the 354-square-mile Edwards Aquifer, an underground limestone formation that stretches from downtown Austin west through the Hill Country. Rains that fall on the hills west of the city filter down through the limestone, and emerge at temperatures between 67 and 70.

For hundreds of years, before European explorers ventured onto Texas soil, Native Americans gathered around the springs, according to archaeologists. Later, Spanish explorers paused to rest here. In the 19th century among the settlers who came to Austin was William "Uncle Billy" Barton. He set up a homestead near the springs in 1837, and eventually gave his name to both the springs and the creek. City records show that on December 16, 1839, Barton agreed to "give possession of the stream of water from my big spring" for a sawmill. For the next 70 years, the land passed through several owners, eventually being sold to Colonel A.J. Zilker in 1907.

During those years, more and more Austinites began to use the pool. At first, just male residents swam there, but in 1880 a ladies swimming club was formed. While some ethnic minorities swam there in the latter years of the 19th century, by the 1950s the overwhelming majority of African-Americans and Mexican-Americans did not swim at the pool. That changed with the Civil Rights Movement, and now the city pool is a gathering place for all Austinites and visitors.

— continued on next page

Photo: Peter J. Silva

Spring-fed Barton Springs Pool is an unexpected treat in the center of Austin.

In 1917, Zilker deeded the springs and the surrounding 35 acres to the city, and Zilker and his gift are now memorialized in the name of the city park where Barton Springs Pool stands. An additional 330 acres was added to the park in 1932 when Zilker gave the land to Austin schools who then, as part of the agreement, sold the acreage to the city for $200,000. The bathhouse that now stands at the entrance to the pool was built in 1947 and replaced the original bathhouse erected in 1922 by the Chamber of Commerce and the Lions Club. For a time, there was talk of making the springs a city municipal water source, but contamination from fecal coliform was found in some samples and that idea was discouraged. Contamination is still occasionally found in samples, particularly after heavy rains.

The concrete sides of the pool, which mark the current length and breadth, were built in 1929. The pool was by then an Austin fixture. Former Texas Congressman Bob Eckhardt, a well-known environmentalist, remembers swimming there as a 5-year-old boy in 1918. His father, a doctor, would come home from the office and pack the family off for an afternoon swim. In honor of his support for the pool, Eckhardt, who still swims there daily when the air temperature is above 80, was granted a lifetime swimming pass in the summer of 1998 by the Austin City Council. (When it is too cool to swim, he rides his bike, just as he did as a Congress member in Washington.)

Eckhardt's support for Barton Springs had special meaning in 1998 because that was the year he and many others engaged in the Great Salamander Debate. An examination of this confrontation offers a lesson in what Barton Springs is all about:

Since the late '60s, Austin environmentalists, let's dub them the "Greens" have faced off against "The Developers" (see our History and Politics and Perspectives chapters). Barton Springs became a symbol of that fight when the Save Our Springs Alliance (SOS) was formed in the 1980s to do battle against development over the Edwards Aquifer, the watershed that fed the springs. Armed with federal conservation legislation, laws such as the Endangered Species Act (ESA), the Greens lobbied federal regulators and took cases to federal court to fight development.

The Greens saw an opportunity to add another arrow to their quiver in the fight when it was discovered in the early 1990s that the tiny salamander that had been swimming underfoot for years was in fact a rare species found only in the waters of the spring and pool. The inch-long salamander has a pale yellow-cream body, flat snout, long limbs, four toes on its front legs, five on the back, and a short, finned tail marked with a narrow orange-yellow stripe and is unique to the springs. In the early '90s, the Greens pressed for the salamander to be listed as an endangered species.

In 1994, the Clinton Administration announced the salamander would be listed. Then Interior Secretary Bruce Babbitt changed his mind about listing it. Federal and state officials announced a water conservation agreement instead and that was touted as a way to protect the aquifer, the springs and the pool waters. The Greens were very critical of the compromise and went to federal court to force the listing of the salamander. U.S. District Judge Lucius Bunton of Midland, Texas, agreed with them and ordered the Administration to review its decision. In the spring of 1997, the Barton Springs salamander was placed on the ESA list.

In January 1998 an attorney who had, in the past, represented landowners and developers, filed suit on behalf of two scientists against the city, charging that the City of Austin was violating the ESA by killing salamanders during routine pool cleanings when the water level was lowered and the pool bottom scrubbed. The Greens said the lawsuit was aimed at shutting down the pool and claimed that mean-spirited developers were behind the action, but the attorney and his clients insisted they only wanted the city to follow the federal laws and protect the salamander. The local media was filled

— continued on next page

with supporters and detractors, and some observers said the Greens had been hoisted on their petard.

The Greens cried foul and questioned the motives of the plaintiffs. After a great deal of legal maneuvering, U.S. District Judge Sam Sparks of Austin refused to stop the pool cleanings, issuing his ruling in a poem:

Barton Springs is a true Austin shrine,
A hundred years of swimming sublime.
Now the plaintiffs say swimmers must go
'Cause of "stress" to critters, 50 or so.
They want no cleaning 'cause of these bottom feeders,
Saying it's the law from our Congressional leaders.
But really nothing has changed in all these years
Despite federal laws and these plaintiff's fears
Both salamander and swimmer enjoy the springs that are cool.
And cleaning is necessary for both species in the pool.
The City is doing its best with full federal support,
So no temporary injunction shall issue from this Court.
Therefore, today, Austin's citizens get away with a rhyme;
But, the truth is they might not be so lucky the next time.
The Endangered Species Act in its extreme makes no sense.
Only Congress can change it to make this problem past tense.

The city set about developing new cleaning methods with the blessings of the federal regulators. During all this legal wrangling, Barton Springs Pool had been shut down for extended periods for time-consuming cleanings that involved sending biologists to search the pool bottom and scoop up any stranded salamanders and return them to the spring while city workers carefully scrubbed the pool bottom. By late summer 1998, the city was holding hearings hoping to devise an acceptable cleaning program, plus make some modifications to the pool so salamanders and swimmers could peacefully coexist.

The salamanders have now become a popular feature on T-shirts and in paintings that decorate the pool bathhouse. They also have joined the pantheon of Austin-area endangered species, which includes golden-cheeked warblers and black-capped vireos, both songbirds.

Few swimmers claim to have actually seen a Barton Springs salamander, but for those who regard Barton Springs Pool as more than a place to swim, the knowledge that the little creatures also enjoy the waters just adds to the beauty and wonder of the place.

For information about pool hours and admission, see our listing under Swimming in this chapter.

---

the eastern half of the city, roughly defined as east of I-35, have a different flora from those in the western half. The eastern half of the city is built over Blackland Prairie, rich, black soil, compared to the rocky, limestone landscape in the west. The creeks and greenbelts in the east are often shaded by pecan trees and have woodland plants along their banks.

Bull Creek Park and Greenbelt

6701 Lakewood Dr.

This park and greenbelt is a popular spot, particularly in the spring when the rains fill the creek, attracting swimmers and waders. In summer the creek is usually very low or dry. There are picnic facilities and hike and bike trails. The 120-acre greenbelt attracts hikers and mountain bikers. The park is off Loop 360

(Capital of Texas Highway) and south of Spicewood Springs Road.

Emma Long Metropolitan Park (City Park)

1600 City Park Rd. • (512) 346-1831

This large 1,147-acre park with 3 miles of Lake Austin shoreline has boat ramps and picnic sites. It is the oldest city park and is more traditional, showing the human hand in its landscaping and facilities.

Johnson Creek

1715 W. Cesar Chavez Blvd.

This mile-long urban trail runs from Town Lake to Enfield Road, paralleling MoPac. Trail-users can access the greenbelt from the Austin High School parking lot.

Lake Walter E. Long Metropolitan Park

6614 Blue Bluff Rd. • (512) 926-5230

In Northeast Travis County, this 1,300-acre lake is well-known for its fishing and water activities. There are campsites, hike and bike trails, plus park roads that are popular with bicyclists and runners.

Mary Moore Searight Metropolitan Park

907 Slaughter Ln.

This is a new park in far South Austin. The 344 acres contain an 18-hole disc (Frisbee) golf course, a 2-mile hike and bike trail, a 2½-mile equestrian trail and a fishing pier over Slaughter Creek. There are also basketball, tennis and volleyball courts, plus baseball and soccer facilities, barbecue pits and a picnic gazebo for large parties.

Mount Bonnell Park

3800 Mount Bonnell Rd., off Scenic Rd.

For 140 years tourists have been coming to Mount Bonnell and climbing the 99 steps (785 feet) to the peak for a great view of the city. No mountain, but a sturdy climb.

There are several local legends that purport to account for the mount's name. One claims it is named in honor of George W. Bonnell, a New Yorker who came to Texas to fight in the War of Independence against [illegible]co. He fought the Native Americans and was a sometime newspaper editor, but met his death on December 26, 1842, when he was captured and shot by Mexican troops.

Others say the name is a corruption of the names Beau and Nell, two lovers who were married on the peak minutes before a Native American attack. After their first kiss, they leapt to their deaths. Other legends are variations on this theme involving Native American princesses and beautiful Spanish senoritas, all forced to take a dive. On a serious note, visitors should be careful at the peak since an unfortunate few have slipped and fallen down the hillside.

Mount Bonnell is the stuff of romance and a popular spot for young couples who want to watch the stars come out over Austin — a particularly romantic spot for University of Texas students, who can get a clear view of the UT Tower, aglow in orange light when the university's athletic teams win. It is also a great spot for a picnic with a view. The park opens at 5 AM for sunrise viewing and closes at 10 PM.

Pease Park

1100 Kingsbury St.

Along Shoal Creek between 12th and 24th streets, this Central Austin park is popular among lunchtime picnickers and joggers. The land was donated by former Gov. Elisha M. Pease, hence the name. During the Civil War Gen. George Armstrong Custer camped on this site and buried 35 of his men here. There are legends of buried treasure here involving a lost cache of money supposedly stolen by a paymaster in the Mexican Army. Digging, of course, is forbidden.

These days it is known for happier occasions, including Eeyore's Birthday, an annual free-spirit celebration, sort of a mini Woodstock-meets-Mardi Gras event, that includes both the whimsical and the outrageous (see our Annual Events chapter). Street parking on Kingsbury Street and neighboring roads is permitted, but quickly fills up during Eeyore's Birthday. The popularity of this park, particularly the Eeyore's Birthday event, has created tension between park users and the neighborhood. So far, efforts to force the celebration to another location have proved unsuccessful.

Shoal Creek Hike and Bike Trail

Lamar Blvd., from 38th St. to Town Lake

This wide, 3-mile-long greenbelt along the urban pathway of Shoal Creek, roughly paralleling Lamar Boulevard, winds through the heart of Central Austin and can be accessed at many points along the way. This popular trail was heavily damaged by flash floods in 1981. Repairs and flood-control devices have restored the trail, which is always alive with runners, walkers, kids and dogs. Like other urban Austin creek beds, Shoal Creek has an early warning system in place to alert residents and emergency workers of flash floods. These high-tech devices can be seen near bridges and low crossings on city creeks. They look like large traffic signal boxes and are equipped with solar panels and antennas. The warning system does not sound off, but sends alerts to a central point so that emergency workers can monitor rising waters.

Slaughter Creek Metropolitan Park

4103 Slaughter Ln.

Adjacent to the Lady Bird Johnson Wildflower Center in Southwest Austin, this park is at its best in the spring when the Hill Country wildflowers bloom throughout the park. That's not to say the park is not worth a visit during the other seasons. The prime attraction is the 3-mile veloway, which attracts bicyclists and in-line skaters. The park also has a nature trail, picnic facilities, playground, soccer fields, volleyball and basketball courts.

Town Lake Metropolitan Park

Along the Colorado River from Tom Miller Dam in West Austin to the U.S. Hwy. 183 bridge in East Austin, this park graces the Colorado River as it winds through the heart of downtown Austin. There have been suggestions in the past that this stretch of river should be renamed in honor of former First Lady Lady Bird Johnson, who led the beautification effort, but typically she has declined the honor.

There is no other Austin city park, with the exception of nearby Zilker Park, that so captures the Austin spirit. From dawn to beyond dusk, the Hike and Bike Trail is filled with joggers, walkers, bicyclists, nature lovers and dog walkers enjoying the riverside pathways. The spring is an especially beautiful time for a stroll along Town Lake as cherry blossom trees, some of them gifts from Japan, bloom alongside native redbud trees.

The southern shore of Town Lake, just west of South First Street, is known as Auditorium Shores and is the site for outdoor concerts, including the annual July Fourth Pops Concert (see our Annual Events chapter) and various festivals.

In quieter moments, wildlife, particularly turtles, ducks and swans, can be seen swimming and feeding along the banks of Town Lake. Only non-motorized craft are allowed on this stretch of the lake, such as canoes, kayaks and paddleboats, which can be rented in nearby Zilker Park (see our Boating section in this chapter). The Austin Rowing Club has its clubhouse on the north shore near the Four Seasons Hotel, and lone rowers can be seen sculling in the early morning through the light fog rising from the lake. No swimming is allowed in the lake.

On the northern bank of Town Lake and east of I-35 is Fiesta Gardens, a popular community concert and celebration spot. Two notable Mexican-American holidays are celebrated here, Cinco de Mayo and Diez y Seis de Septiembre (see our Annual Events chapter).

Waller Creek Greenbelt

403 E. 15th St.

Stretching from 15th Street to Town Lake, the Waller Street greenbelt is a mixture of urban greenbelt and urban blight. The northern stretch is quite pleasant. City voters recently approved a bond election to improve the southern end of the trail. Supporters touted creating an urban riverwalk, similar to San Antonio's famous riverside trail.

Waterloo Park

403 E. 15th St.

This central city park lies just east of the capitol and is a quiet retreat in the heart of the city. It is also a popular spot for several gatherings during the year, including a Renaissance Festival where participants evoke the spirit of the Middle Ages with jousts and minstrels, country fair-style booths and crafters' stalls (see our Annual Events chapter).

Zilker Botanical Gardens
2200 Barton Springs Rd.
• (512) 477-8672

Just north of Zilker Park (see the subsequent listing) and part of the Zilker experience, the gardens are also home to the Austin Garden Center. There are several gardens within the grounds, including a Rose Garden (a popular site for weddings), a Cactus and Succulent Garden, fragrance and butterfly gardens and woodland trails. There is also a Xeriscape Garden where native plants are shown off to great advantage. Admission to the garden center is free except for certain weekends (see our Annual Events chapter) when garden shows are held on the grounds.

The most beautiful part of the garden center is the Taniguchi Oriental Garden, created by the late Isamu Taniguchi, a native of Osaka, Japan. Taniguchi moved to the United States as a young man, worked as a farmer in California and the Rio Grande Valley and then retired to Austin in the 1960s. Taniguchi, whose son was a noted Austin architect, spent 18 months creating the garden along the hillside site. He worked for free with his own plans and no oversight or interference from city planners. His creation is a symbol of peace, just as Taniguchi wished. He died in 1992 at age 94. The best time to visit the garden is on a quiet weekday since it is a popular attraction on weekends. Many Austin families like to take family portraits in one of the many artfully designed little rooms that are so typical of Japanese garden design.

Zilker Park
2100 Barton Springs Rd.
• (512) 472-4914

This 400-acre downtown park, just south of Town Lake and east of MoPac, is the city's most well-known park and one of its most popular. It became a city park in 1917 when Colonel A.J. Zilker donated the land to the city. The most famous and revered attraction in the park is Barton Springs Pool (see our Close-up in this chapter), but it is also a place of pilgrimage for other reasons. At Christmas one of the city's so-called moonlight towers (see our Attractions chapter) serves as the trunk of the Zilker Park Christmas Tree (see our Annual Events chapter), visible from miles around. The "tree" is created by Christmas lights strung in maypole fashion from the tower to the ground. Tradition calls for children to stand inside the tree and spin around until the lights are blurred and the kids are dizzy. Small children are spun around in a grown-up's arms, making both kid and grown-up enjoy the dizzy spell.

Zilker is home to a miniature train, playscape, picnic grounds, a disc golf course, rugby and soccer fields and a canoe and kayak concession (see our Boating section in this chapter). A grass-covered hillside serves as a natural amphitheater for summer musicals (see our Annual Events and The Arts chapters for more information).

The park is open daily from 6 AM to 10 PM and is free. There is a small parking fee on weekends when the park is very busy.

Round Rock

The city's parks department operates about 30 parks in the city limits, most of them small, neighborhood parks that serve as a play areas for neighborhood children and places to relax, perhaps jog, play tennis or shoot a few baskets for teens and adults. Parks with hike and bike trails, swimming pools or tennis courts are listed in the Recreation and Watersports sections of this chapter under those specific categories. The city's three major parks are described below.

INSIDERS' TIP

Inside the City of Austin, dogs must be leashed, but even Fido can enjoy the city's famous free-spirit lifestyle in certain designated parks. One of the most popular spots is in Zilker Park in an area bounded by Stratford Drive, Barton Springs Road and Lou Neff Drive. For a complete list of places to let Fido feel the wind in his hair, unfettered and free, contact the parks department at (512) 499-6700.

Department (PARD)
605 Palm Valley Blvd. • (512) 218-5540

The city's PARD publishes a program brochure and guides to the city's parks that are available on request. In addition to athletic programs, PARD offers country and ballroom dance classes, Jazzercise, programs for toddlers and seniors, preschool and youth programs, plus Cool Kids Camp, an afternoon recreation program for elementary kids.

Lake Creek Park
800 Deerfoot Dr.

Home to the municipal swimming pool, this 15-acre park also has a playscape area and a pavilion, which can be used for community events. The municipal pool opens a few weeks before Memorial Day and closes around Labor Day. For the first few weeks in May, the pool is open only on the weekends and then is open daily after Memorial Day.

Old Settlers Park
3300 Palm Valley Blvd.

This large, 439-acre park has soccer and softball fields, hike and bike trails, playscapes, a disc golf course and picnic areas. It is also the site of Old Settler Week (see our Annual Events chapter), when Williamson County celebrates its pioneer roots with music, food and carnivals, plus a reenactment of the shootout between outlaw Sam Bass and the law. There is a large pavilion at the park, which is a focal point during community celebrations.

Round Rock Memorial Park
I-35 and R.M. 620

The city's other major park is home to the Legion Field softball complex. In addition to the softball fields, the park features a hike and bike trail and playscape and picnic areas.

Pflugerville

Pflugerville Parks and Recreation Department (PARD)
700 Railroad Ave. • (512) 251-5082

The city of Pflugerville boasts that the city's parks are a "hometown kind of place, where you and your friends and coworkers can celebrate without a lot of big-city fuss and bother." The city's PARD has developed a master plan aimed at helping the city make the transition from a tiny, rural town to a growing suburban community. The city's parks are connected by an integrated trail system, connecting many of the neighborhoods in the city.

PARD also provides swimming, gymnastics, aerobics, soccer, volleyball and basketball programs. There is the Summer Pfun Camp and PARD-organized events such as 5K Pfun Run and Walk, Pfall Pfest and the Pumpkin Pflyer bicycle tour.

Gilleland Creek Park
700 Railroad Ave.

The anchor for the city's integrated trail system, Gilleand also boasts a community swimming pool, picnic areas and volleyball courts.

Pfluger Park
City Park Rd.

This large city park is home to soccer and softball fields, sand volleyball facilities and basketball courts. The park's picnic area has barbecue pits and a playscape, and there are several nature trails running through the park.

Cedar Park

Cedar Park Parks and Recreation (PARD)
600 N. Bell Blvd. • (512) 258-4121

As Cedar Park grows, the number of city parks increases as the city attempts to keep up with the area's booming population. There are 11 neighborhood parks, most of them with picnic facilities and playscapes. Many also have tennis and basketball courts, and some have sand volleyball facilities. The city's parks and recreation department offers information on all city parks and recreation programs.

Elizabeth M. Milburn Community Park
1901 Sun Chase Blvd.

This is the crown jewel of the Cedar Park park system. At the heart of the recently completed park facility is an 8-lane, 25-meter lap pool, with an adjoining recreational pool with a water playscape and a 117-foot water slide. The new park has several soccer fields, plus a large pavilion with picnic tables for reunions and special events. There are also three large gazebos in the park. Scattered throughout the park are picnic tables and barbecue grills, plus tennis courts, a basketball court, a sand volleyball area, playscapes and a hiking path circling the park.

Nature Preserves

Within the Austin city limits are several nature preserves that offer visitors a glimpse of the wild beauty of both the Hill Country and the prairie to the east of Austin. In addition to city preserves, Travis County is also guardian to several nature areas.

Austin Nature Preserves

The city operates 10 nature preserves and a nature center. There are strict rules of behavior within the preserves, designed to protect the ecosystems. Access to some of the preserves is by prearrangement only, and group tours are available. For information call (512) 327-5478.

Motorized vehicles, bicycles, pets, firearms and hunting are prohibited in the nature preserves. Visitors are required to keep noise levels low, stay on trails and may not remove plants or animals from the area.

Austin Nature Center

303 Nature Center Dr. • (512) 327-8180

The center's central exhibit is "The Nature of Austin" illustrating four habitats found in the area, ponds, grasslands, woodlands and a Hill Country cave. The live exhibits feature Texas wildlife — animals that have been rescued and because of permanent injury or human upbringing cannot be returned to their habitat. The center also has a discovery lab and is surrounded by 80 acres of nature preserve with 2 miles of trails.

Barrow Preserve

7715 Long Point Dr.

This 10-acre preserve is on the upper reaches of Bull Creek in Northwest Austin. It has spring-fed canyons and hiking trails.

Blunn Creek Preserve

1101 St. Edwards Dr.

This preserve near the St. Edward's University campus in South Austin boasts two lookout points that offer great views of the city, one of which is atop a 100-million-year-old coral reef. This area of Central Texas once was an inland sea, and now it is surrounded by urban neighborhoods. Within its confines can be seen the remains of volcanic ash deposits spewed out by a dozen active volcanoes that rumbled in this area some 80 million years ago.

The preserve contains three distinct zones, each with its own distinct flora. The Riparian Woodland, along the creek, has cottonwood, pecan and native black willows, while the Rolling Prairie has grasses, wildflowers, cactus and redbud trees. The third zone, the Uplands, has the distinctive live oaks seen throughout the city and delicate Texas persimmon trees that grow underneath the canopies of the large oaks.

Colorado River Preserve

U.S. Hwy. 183 at the Montopolis Bridge

On the banks of the Colorado River, west of the Montopolis Bridge in East Austin, this 43-acre preserve offers views of river life, including turtles, herons and cranes along the sandy banks of the river.

Forest Ridge Preserve

West side of Loop 360 (Capital of Texas Hwy.)

South of Spicewood Springs Road and part of the BCCP property (see the Balcones Canyonlands listing later in this chapter), this 414-acre preserve is the native habitat of the

INSIDERS' TIP

Woolridge Square is a little gem of a park in downtown Austin — squeezed between the Travis County Courthouse and the Austin History Center, 9th and 10th streets on Guadalupe. The park's Victorian bandstand sits in the center of a natural amphitheater and has been the site of weddings, political rallies, small concerts and one murder (according to legend).

golden-cheeked warbler. Bird watchers and environmentalists will know this small migratory songbird is an endangered species that nests in the Spanish oaks and juniper trees of the Hill Country. The trees, grasses and other flora offer visitors a view of what this Hill Country land looked like before the surrounding development occurred.

Indiangrass Wildlife Sanctuary

Walter E. Long Metropolitan Park, U.S. Hwy. 290 E.

The sanctuary is in a 200-acre section of the Walter E. Long Park in Northeast Austin. The sanctuary is designed to protect Blackland Prairie habitat for a variety of flora and fauna, notably a variety of prairie grasses. The wetlands along Lake Long are home to an abundance of wildlife. Access is limited to guided tours only.

Karst Preserve

3900 Deer Ln.

This interesting preserve is off Brodie Lane in Southwest Austin and adjacent to the Maple Run subdivision. Karst is the name scientists have given to the type of honeycombed limestone formations found in several areas of the world, including the Texas Hill Country. This 8-acre site, and this part of Austin, is riddled with sinkholes, caves and honeycombed limestone. Walking over a large expanse of grass, say a soccer field, it is possible to feel the temperature change around your ankles as you pass over trapped pockets of cool air. Some of the caves are off limits, and visitors may want to think twice before stepping off the trail to explore sinkholes since they are home to scorpions, spiders and snakes.

Mayfield Preserve

3505 W. 35th St.

This is a small city enclave that reflects 19th-century Austin. The 22-acre preserve in Central Austin embraces five lily ponds, palm trees, woodlands and several old cottages including one from the late 19th century. A cross between a preserve and a park, this is a quiet spot that is very popular with children who can approach the peacocks (watch out, they have tempers!) and tame deer for close-up viewing. The preserve is next door to Laguna Gloria Art Museum (see our Arts chapter) in West Austin.

Onion Creek Preserve

This secluded preserve is north of Texas Highway 71 along Onion Creek and is open to guided tours by reservation only.

Vireo Preserve

East of the 100 and 200 blocks of Loop 360 north (Capital of Texas Highway), this rugged section of Hill Country is home to the rare black-capped vireo, one of several bird species threatened by development in Central Texas. The preserve is open to guided tours only.

Zilker Nature Preserve

This is a 60-acre preserve at western end of the park (see the listing under Austin Parks in this chapter), which includes 2 miles of trails along cliff edges on the banks of Barton Creek.

Balcones Canyonlands

Following one of those typical Austin political tug-of-wars (see our Politics and Perspectives chapter), city leaders, environmentalists, developers and concerned citizens forged an agreement for a unique wildlife refuge dubbed the Balcones Canyonlands. Under the auspices of the Balcones Canyonlands National Refuge and the Balcones Canyonlands Conservation Plan (BCCP), approximately 76,000 acres are being set aside in the hills west of Austin as a nature preserve.

Some of the tracts are accessible to the public for nature-viewing, others are closed as part of the effort to preserve the ecosystem for endangered species. For information on access call the City of Austin at (512) 263-1410, Travis County Parks Department at (512) 473-9437, or the LCRA at (512) 473-4083.

Travis County Preserves

For additional information call the Travis County Parks Department at (512) 473-9437.

Hamilton Pool Preserve

Hamilton Pool Rd., R.M. 3238 • (512) 264-2740

Located 13 miles south of Texas Highway 71 on R.M. 3238 (Hamilton Pool Road), in western Travis County, this preserve features a nature trail winding through a cypress-lined canyon along Hamilton Creek. There is also a popular natural swimming hole, but it is closed sometimes due to high bacteria count (see the Swimming section in this chapter). Access is limited so call ahead.

Westcave Preserve

Hamilton Pool Rd., R.M. 3238
• (210) 825-3442

On R.M. 3238, west of the Pedernales River, this 35-acre natural area is home to several endangered species including the golden-cheeked warbler. The major feature of the preserve is a collapsed grotto formed 150,000 years ago, creating a giant terrarium covered by towering cypress trees. The sheltered environment created a unique ecosystem where orchids and other semitropical plants flourish. Temperature differences between the grotto floor and the surrounding countryside above can be as much as 25 degrees. The preserve is open only on weekends, and access is limited to guided tours at 10 AM, noon, 2 and 4 PM. Given the fragility of the ecosystem tours are limited to 30 individuals at a time. Call ahead to confirm that the preserve is open.

Wild Basin Wilderness Preserve

805 N. Loop 360 (Capital of Texas Hwy.)
• (512) 327-7622

This popular preserve, a little over one mile north of Bee Caves Road, encompasses 227 acres of pristine Hill Country land along Bee Creek. There are school tours during the week and special guided tours for visitors on the weekend.

Recreation

Looking to play rugby? Climb a rock wall? Join a soccer club? Find the best place to go in-line skating, or view the sunrise from a hot-air balloon? This Recreation section offers a play-by-play breakdown on sports activities in Austin. First, some general information:

Austin Parks and Recreation Department (PARD)

200 S. Lamar Blvd. • (512) 499-6700

The City of Austin Parks and Recreation Department (PARD) operates 17 recreation centers throughout the city, which offer a wide variety of activities, day camps, youth programs, lessons in sports activities and league supervision. PARD is a good place to begin when researching availability of facilities, lessons and league activity.

Cedar Park Parks and Recreation (PARD)

600 N. Bell Blvd. • (512) 258-4121

Cedar Park's parks and recreation department is developing a variety of programs to meet the town's growing population, including league sports, swimming, aerobics and water safety classes.

Pflugerville Parks and Recreation Department (PARD)

700 Railroad Ave. • (512) 251-5082

Pflugerville PARD offers swimming, gymnastics, aerobics, soccer, volleyball and basketball programs. Since Pfun is part of the Pflugerville lifestyle, the PARD also organizes a Summer Pfun Camp and events such as 5K Pfun Run and Walk, Pfall Pfest and the Pumpkin Pflyer bicycle tour.

Round Rock Parks and Recreation Department (PARD)

605 Palm Valley Blvd. • (512) 218-5540

The Round Rock PARD organizes several adult sports leagues, including flag football, basketball and softball and offers a wide variety of adult programs — country dance, ballroom dance and Jazzercise classes — for all age groups. Youth programs include gymnastics, karate, dance and tennis classes. The

INSIDERS' TIP

There are several sports programs for disabled children in Austin. The Austin Parks and Recreation Department offers therapeutic recreation programs, and the YMCA has several programs for special-needs children and adults.

Cool Kids Camp is an afternoon recreation program designed for elementary age children. Program schedules and information are available on request.

University of Texas Recreational Sports Outdoor Program

(512) 471-1093

The university offers noncredit courses in outdoor sports, including canoeing, rock-climbing, windsurfing, cycling and hiking. They are very popular, so sign up early.

YMCA

1100 W. Cesar Chavez Blvd. (Downtown) • (512) 476-6705
6219 Oakclaire Dr., off U.S. Hwy. 290 W. (Southwest) • (512) 891-9622
9616 N. Lamar Blvd. at Rutland Dr. (North) • (512) 973-9622

The Y is always a good place to seek out other athletes with similar interests. The downtown location is just north of the Town Lake Hike and Bike Trail, which makes it a popular fitness club for downtown workers. The Southwest location is in "downtown" Oak Hill in a former privately owned fitness club that was acquired by the Y. Both clubs are popular and have up-to-date fitness equipment, whirlpools, saunas, swimming pools, steam rooms, gyms, indoor running tracks, etc. The Oak Hill branch has a rock-climbing wall and racquetball courts.

Bicycling

Bicycling has taken off in the Hill Country where both road-racing and mountain-biking enthusiasts face some rugged challenges, given the terrain. One of Austin's most famous residents is international racing champion Lance Armstrong, who has raced in several charity events here and who did some of his training in the hills around Austin — one favorite bicycling route for road racers is Loop 360, also known as Capital of Texas Highway.

The 3-mile Veloway in Slaughter Creek Metropolitan Park (see the Austin Parks section of this chapter) is another popular spot for cyclists. Local mountain bikers also enjoy riding the trail in the Barton Creek Greenbelt. Check the Parks section of this chapter for other area venues for road and off-road cycling.

The Bull Creek Greenbelt in Northwest Austin (see our Parks listings above for more details on all these sites) has a hilly bike path in unspoiled, natural surroundings. The Shoal Creek Hike and Bike Trail wends through the center of the city in a more urban parklike setting, while the 2-mile trail in Southwest Austin at the Mary Moore Seabright Metropolitan Park flows through the rolling, wooded hills, typical of the natural landscape in this area.

Another popular route is along the 10-mile Town Lake Hike and Bike Trail, but the popularity and accessibility of this facility has led to some squabbles between joggers and cyclists. There also has been some concern expressed by nature lovers over the impact of mountain bikes on the delicate ecosystem in the area's nature preserves.

Several area parks have extensive mountain trails and park roads that are popular with cyclists. Local cycle shops sell maps of the area showing popular trails. Among the most popular are Colorado Bend State Park (again, see our Parks listings above) and McKinney Falls State Park. The latter has a 3.5-mile trail characterized by woodlands and gently rolling hills. Since McKinney is just 13 miles southeast of Austin, this is easily accessible to local riders.

One popular road route among cyclists is Park Road 1C between Buescher and Bastrop State Parks, about a 40-minute drive east of Austin. This is a very challenging ride as the 13 miles of paved road climbs through steep hills.

The emergence of cycling as a popular sport has brought road racing events to Austin (see our Annual Events and Festivals chapter). Bicyclists are respected in Austin — the city even has a bicycle coordinator on its planning staff (see our Getting Here and Getting Around chapter).

Austin Adventure Co.

(512) 209-6880

This local company offers bicycle rentals and tours, road and off-road tours in Austin and the Hill Country.

Photo: Peter J. Silva

The Hike and Bike Trail route around Town Lake can take you over the Congress Avenue bridge.

Austin Cycling Association

(512) 477-0776

The group publishes a monthly newsletter that previews upcoming events, describes the best places to test your skills and keeps track of the bicycle scene.

Bicycle Sport Shop

1426 Toomey Rd. • (512) 477-3472

Just west of Lamar Boulevard and Riverside Drive, this local shop offers sales, rentals and information on the local scene.

University Cyclery

2901 N. Lamar Blvd. • (512) 474-6696

This University of Texas area store offers rentals, sales, repairs and information on the Austin cycling scene.

Bird-Watching

Texas is the center lane of the migratory pathway of many North American birds, making the state a popular spot for bird-watching. Local environmentalists are working hard to raise the consciousness of newcomers about endangered species in the area and several nature preserves are dedicated to protecting these species. For more information, see the Preserves section of this chapter.

Travis County Audubon Society

(512) 926-8751

There are more than 2,500 members of this local chapter of the society, which meets every month and usually holds at least one field trip a month. From backyard birding to treks into the Hill Country in search of elusive and endangered species such as the golden-cheeked warbler, the society offers practical advice to both members and nonmembers who are eager to protect and conserve the ecosystems so vital to bird life in Central Texas. Every December, the group holds a Christmas bird count, its contribution to the national count. The telephone number above offers information on the group's activities and also serves as a birding hotline, informing callers about recent sightings and migratory patterns.

Vanishing Texas River Cruise

Lake Buchanan • (512) 756-6986

In addition to offering wildflower cruises in the spring, this company also offers winter river cruises up the Colorado River Canyon to view the largest colony of American bald eagles in the state.

Bowling

There are several Austin area bowling facilities. Austin also has hosted professional bowling tournaments, and most lanes offer facilities for disabled bowlers, plus party planning for large groups. The latest craze to hit local lanes is Electric Bowling, known in other parts of the country as Extreme Bowling or Glow-in-the-Dark Bowling. By pumping up the music and bringing down the lights, the bowling facility owners hope to attract a younger crowd and boost interest in the sport.

Two area associations are a good place to obtain information about local bowling activity and league play. The Austin Bowling Association is at 8820 Business Park Drive, (512) 338-6020, and the Austin Women's Bowling Association is at 5700 Grover Avenue, (512) 453-8714.

Highland Lanes

8909 Burnet Rd. • (512) 458-1215

This North Austin bowling facility is home to Electric Bowling three times a week, on Friday and Saturday from 11 PM to 1 AM and Tuesday evenings from 8 to 10 PM. The lights in the 40-lane facility are dimmed and special

INSIDERS' TIP

Austin Metropolitan Trails Council is a coalition of public, private and nonprofit organizations, neighborhood associations and individuals working to "promote a comprehensive system of greenways and trails in the greater Austin area." The council can be contacted through the Austin Parks and Recreation Department at (512) 499-6700.

lighting effects kick in with the music. Highland Lanes also offers bumper bowling for kids, eliminating gutter balls and insuring that kids hit at least some of the pins. There are leagues on site for teens, women, men and seniors. The lanes are open from 9:30 AM to midnight Sunday through Thursday and 9:30 AM to 1 AM Friday and Saturday.

Showplace Lanes

9504 N. I-35 • (512) 834-7733

A large 52-lane facility in North Austin, Showplace is open 24 hours a day. There is a sports bar on site, plus two video game rooms and a nursery. A dart league also holds its events here.

Westgate Lanes

2701 William Cannon Dr. • (512) 441-2695

Home to several popular summer youth leagues, Westgate has 40 lanes and is located in South Austin. The bowling alley is open daily from 10 AM to midnight Sunday through Thursday and 10 AM to 2 AM on Friday and Saturday.

Camping

Camping is not just a recreational activity in Central Texas, it is a way of life for some residents who have chosen to make their homes in the area's private facilities. Perhaps the most famous "campsite" for motor homes is the Shady Grove RV Park smack in the middle of town in an old pecan grove and a few blocks from Zilker Park. Campsites catering to short-term visitors can be found along the I-35 corridor and on the shores of the Highland Lakes.

The Parks section lists area parks with camping facilities, and we have included some of the most popular here in this section, along with privately operated facilities. The Lower Colorado River Authority operates several parks with primitive camping areas (see the LCRA Primitive Areas section). Two guides that are very useful for campers visiting Central Texas are: *The Texas State Travel Guide*, published by the Texas Department of Transportation, (800) 452-9292; and the Lower Colorado River Authority (LCRA) Visitors Package, (800) 776-5272 Ext. 4083, or (512) 473-4083.

Other good resources include:

- Texas Association of Campground Owners, 6900 Oak Leaf Drive, Orange, TX 77630, (409) 886-4082
- Texas KOA Kampgrounds Owners Association, 602 Gembler Road, San Antonio, TX 78219, (210) 547-5201
- Texas Parks & Wildlife Department, 4200 Smith School Road, Austin TX 78744, (512) 389-4800, (800) 792-1112
- Austin Convention & Visitors Bureau, 201 E. Second Street, Austin, TX 78701, (512) 478-0098
- Texas Travel Information Center, Texas State Capitol, 112 E. 11th Street, (512) 305-8400, (800) 452-9292

Austin KOA Campground

7009 S. I-35 • (512) 444-6322, (800) KOA-BOOT

There are 159 RV sites, eight cabins and camping facilities at this South Austin campground. Campsites rent for $21 to $36 a night, and cabins are available for $35 to $49 a night. Access to the site is controlled, and there are facilities for handicapped visitors. The main lodge has a fireplace, a full kitchen, color television and jukebox. There are a small grocery store and laundry facilities on site. Telephone hookups, compatible with modems, and television hookups also are available.

Austin RV Park North

4001 Prairie Ln. • (512) 244-0610

The 20 spaces at this North Austin park, near the intersection of I-35 and F.M. 1325, may be rented on a daily basis for $15, or by the month for $325. The sites all have electricity, water and sewage hookups. There is a pool at the park.

Armadillo RV

4913 Hudson Bend Rd. • (512) 266-9012

This Lake Travis-area RV park has 38 large shaded lots, all with a view of Lake Travis, that rent for $2.50 to $2.75 a day. Cable television and telephone hookups are extra. There is an on-site laundry facility, a grocery store nearby and three marinas within a half mile of the facility. Children and pets are welcome.

Buescher State Park

F.M. 153, off Texas Hwy. 71, Smithville • (512) 237-2241

A popular spot for fisherman, Buescher (pronounced "Bisher") State Park has 34 campsites (20 for tents or pop-ups and 14 for RVs) and four screened shelters. Showers and bathrooms are available for campers. Admission to the park is $3 and free for those 13 and younger. Tent campsites are $7 a night; RV sites with water and electricity are $10 a night.

Camp Chautauqua at Lake Travis

R.M. 2322, off Texas Hwy. 71 • (512) 264-1752

The Friends of the Colorado River Foundation, a nonprofit group, operates this park on the shores of Lake Travis (see our Lake Parks section). The site is host to *chautauquas* on the environment — the Native American name that came to signify summer educational programs popular in the late 19th century — and is open to the public for camping. Cabins at the camp cost $25 a night, RV hookups $15, tents $7 to $10. Admission to the park is $4, $3 for seniors and free for children 13 and younger.

Emma Long Metropolitan Park (City Park)

1600 City Park Rd. • (512) 346-1831

This large 1,147-acre park with 3 miles of Lake Austin shoreline is a popular weekend camping spot (see the Austin City Parks section of this chapter). There are 20 sites with water and electricity, plus 50 tent sites. Campers may stay for up to two weeks. The entry fee to the park is $3 during the week and $5 on weekends. Tent sites are $6 per night and $10 for sites with utilities. The campsites are on an alluvial plain, adjacent to Lake Austin with the hilly park in the background. This is a very popular site so reservations should be made early.

Enchanted Rock State Natural Area

R.R. 965, north of Fredericksburg • (915) 247-3903

This popular and legendary park, detailed above under State Parks, is 18 miles north of Fredericksburg (see our Daytrips chapter). Only walk-in campers and backpackers may pitch their tents in this carefully protected natural area. There are no facilities for RVs or pop-up campers. Campers must call the state's camping reservations number at (512) 389-8900. Walk-in campers pay the park admission fee of $5 for those 13 and older, plus $9 a day camping fee with a maximum of eight people at a walk-in site. Backpackers pay the entrance fee, plus $7 daily camping rate with a maximum of four people at each campsite.

Hudson Bend RV Park

5003 Hudson Bend Rd. • (512) 266-8300

Sites are available at this Lake Travis area facility by the day ($20), week ($80), or month ($245) and all are served with water, electricity and free cable television. There are 29 pads at the site and also six storage sheds available for rent to extended-stay campers.

McKinney Falls State Park

Scenic Loop Rd. • (512) 243-1643

Its location, just 13 miles southeast of downtown Austin off U.S. 183, ensures that this 640-acre state park is usually filled with campers on holidays and weekends. (See our previous State Parks section for a full description of the park.) There are 84 sites in the park for tents, pop-ups or RVs, and these cost $12 a night, including water and electricity. There are 8 walk-in primitive sites for hikers, costing $7 a night. The park entrance fee is $2 per person, free for those 13 and younger. McKinney also rents three screened shelters for $20 a night. The two-room shelters are furnished with eight bunk beds, a cold-water sink, picnic table and barbecue grill.

Lake Travis Inn and RV Park

4511 Doss Rd. • (512) 266-9329, (800) 303-5401

This 8-acre, fenced Lake Travis-area park has 90 shaded sites for RVs that are available for monthly rentals. Rates vary according to amenities, including cable, telephone and other utilities. There are on-site laundry facilities and a small motel.

Pace Bend Park

2701 F.M. 2322, 4.5 miles off Texas Hwy. 71. • (512) 264-1482

This 1,000-plus-acre park (sometimes called Paleface Park) is likely to be packed with campers on weekends and during summer holidays. The park, described in our Travis County Parks section above, has more than 400 sites for tents, pop-ups and RVs. There are also primitive tent sites. Admission to the park is $5 per vehicle, $10 for overnight stays. Sites with water and electricity cost $15 a night. The park has a strict quiet time in effect from 10 PM to 7 AM, and dogs can be allowed to run free if their owners are in control of them. Reservations are critical at this park since it fills up very quickly on major holiday weekends.

Recreation Plantation
County Rd. 198, Dripping Springs
• (512) 894-0567

If you're looking to camp with a crowd, then consider renting this self-described "event facility." For $750 a weekend, you can rent this 40-acre campsite with its own creek frontage and swimming hole. The facility also a two-bedroom cabin on the property and a stage. There are tent sites and RV hookups, also, making this a great place for family reunions and corporate getaways.

Shady Grove RV Park
1600 Barton Springs Rd.
• (512) 499-8432

Shady Grove is just that — a grove of old pecan trees that offers shade and comfort to the 27 sites on this downtown campers' haven east of Zilker Park on Barton Springs Road. Shady Grove has a '50s small-town feel to it, which is probably why rental sites are hard to come by here. The park has many permanent residents who enjoy a laid-back lifestyle in the "shady grove." The park is tucked in between several popular restaurants, including a '50s-style hamburger joint with the same name as the RV park (see our Restaurants chapter). Monthly rental rates are $350 and include electricity, basic cable service, water and sewer, plus trash pickup. There is an on-site laundry facility.

City Leagues

Austin is team player kind of town. Take a weekend tour of the city's parks and recreation areas and you are likely to see a wide variety of sports teams at play. One of the best resources for information on local team sports is the city's parks and recreation department or PARD offices. See the full listing of PARD offices in the previous Recreation introduction.

Another good resource for information on team sports is the YMCA. The Y has three locations in Austin, offering basketball, volleyball, soccer, basketball and T-ball. Listings for the three facilities are also listed in the previous section.

Baseball, basketball, soccer and softball are popular team sports in Austin. The area has an abundance of baseball leagues for all ages. Check with the area PARD for Little League, Optimist and Kiwanis league teams. The Austin PARD supervises several basketball leagues, and the Y offers league and pickup games.

Central Texas is home to soccer Moms and Dads by the thousands, but the sport also attracts Gen-Xers and even older "footballers" from the expatriate crowd in Austin. There are numerous soccer leagues, the vast majority fall under the auspices of two organizations.

The Capital Area Youth Soccer Association at 1029 Reinli Street, Suite 6, (512) 302-4580, has more than 15,000 members. It is an umbrella group that oversees youth league and tournament play in the Central Texas area. The association also offers coaching and referee training sessions and hosts two annual invitational tournaments.

The Austin Municipal Soccer Association, (512) 288-5133, is also an umbrella association that organizes men's, women's and coed league and tournament play in Austin.

One of the best ways to keep track of league play at all levels is to visit one of the Austin area soccer stores. Soccer World has three locations: 5446 U.S. 290 W. (Southwest), (512) 899-1135; 221 S. Lamar Boulevard (Central), (512) 320-8447; and 13376 Research Boulevard (Northwest), (512) 257-8560.

Another center of soccer activity in the Round Rock-Pflugerville area is the Longhorn Soccer Camp, run by Laszlo Merton, a former Hungarian and Austrian professional soccer player. The camp offers top-quality coaching and training for soccer players of all ages. Contact the camp at 1235 Blackthorn Drive, Round Rock, (512) 990-1234.

Softball is an extremely popular sport year round in Austin. The Austin PARD serves as the major clearinghouse for schedules, league and fee information. Call the PARD Athletics Office at (512) 480-3015. Many of the teams play at the Pleasant Valley Sports Complex, 1225 S. Pleasant Valley Road, (512) 445-7595. For softball league information in Round Rock call (512) 218-5540.

Disc (Frisbee) Golf

Pitching a Frisbee at a target is a popular sport in Austin, and many of the area's neighborhood parks feature either 9- or 18-hole disc golf courses. The discs can be found at local sporting goods stores (see our Shopping chapter).

Austin Recreation Center

1301 Shoal Creek Blvd. • (512) 476 5662

The center offers classes to would-be disc masters.

Bartholomew Park

5201 Berkman Dr. • (512) 499-6745

This is a new 18-hole course in Northeast Austin.

Mary Moore Searight Park

907 Slaughter Ln.

This 18-hole course is part of a relatively new park in Austin's growing southern suburbs.

Pease Park

1100 Kingsbury St.

This course is very popular among University of Texas students who live in the neighborhood.

Slaughter Creek Metropolitan Park

5507 Slaughter Ln.

This pleasant, relatively new Southwest Austin park boats a new 9-hole disc golf course.

Wells Branch Greenbelt

Wells Branch Pkwy. at Wells Port Dr. • (512) 251-9814

A new 9-hole course in the Wells Branch subdivision in North Austin, this facility is open to Wells Branch residents only.

Zilker Park

2100 Barton Springs Rd.

You'll find this 9-hole course at the western edge of the city's premier park. It's a popular weekend course.

Old Settlers Park

3300 Palm Valley Rd., Round Rock

This course is in Round Rock's major city park and claims to be the longest disc golf course in America (see our Parks section above).

Fishing

Texans have a reputation for telling tall tales, but when it comes to fishing they have lots to boast about. The state has more than 5,175 square miles of inland freshwater, including lakes, rivers and creeks, plus 624 miles of shoreline. There is a wide variety of fish available for the taking, provided the fish are biting. Native fish include black bass, crappie, bluegill and catfish. Freshwater fishing areas also have been stocked with non-native species including Florida bass, walleye and rainbow trout and saltwater spe-

INSIDERS' TIP

Watch for wildlife when driving in the Hill Country, particularly deer who seem to find the roadside grass — across the road — more delicious than the grass in the pastures and meadows. Also, watch for emus. Emus? Yes, emu ranching was something of a fashionable thing a few years ago (some said it was a pyramid scheme), but the price of emu meat and feathers has fallen, and now some bird ranchers are simply letting them go. There have been several accidents in the Hill Country involving runaway emus.

cies including redfish and striped bass. The Texas Parks & Wildlife Department reports that several Texas lakes are producing striped bass weighing over 30 pounds — some Texas tale!

Texas residents can buy an annual combination fishing-hunting license for $25. Fishing licenses vary in cost and can be purchased on an annual or two-week basis by residents. Nonresident fishermen over the age of 17 must purchase a license, and these can cost $30 for an annual license or $20 for a 5-day license. There are additional charges for stamps for certain fish.

Licenses are sold at sporting goods and tackle stores, some county courthouses, Parks & Wildlife offices and by some local game wardens. The Texas Parks & Wildlife Department also produces several excellent guides to Texas fishing. The department's magazine (see our Media chapter) is also an excellent resource.

Texas Parks & Wildlife Department
4200 Smith School Rd. • (512) 389-4800, (800) 792-1112

The Highland Lakes are popular among anglers (see our Parks listings in this chapter for access and location). Lake Austin record catches include a 43-pound striped bass. Bass fishing is popular in the quieter areas of Lake Austin and Lake Buchanan. Fishing is permitted on Town Lake in Central Austin, but because of urban runoff it is not recommended that you consume your catch.

Bastrop State Park, Bastrop
Texas Hwy. 21, 1.5 miles east of Bastrop • (512) 321-2101

Lake Bastrop boasts a lighted pier. The record catch here is a 43.5-pound catfish. See our State Parks section of this chapter for a description of facilities here.

Buescher State Park, Smithville
F.M. 153, off Texas Hwy. 71 • (512) 237-2241

This state park is considered a fisherman's paradise by some. The park's 30-acre lake is stocked with catfish, bass crappie, perch and rainbow trout.

Fishing Gear

Austin Angler
312½ Congress Ave. • (512) 472-4553

This downtown store is so renowned as an angler's shopping paradise it was featured in a national credit card TV ad. This is the place to go for tips, equipment and even a license.

Git Bit
(512) 280-2861

This fishing guide service offers half-day and full-day bass fishing trips on Lake Travis, a noted hot spot for summertime bass fishing.

Fitness Centers

Fitness centers, gyms, aerobics classes, t'ai chi sessions, health clubs — Austin has them all. Some offer activities priced per session, while others offer membership. There is a wide range of services and amenities, from the basic nuts-and-bolts weight rooms to highly personalized training programs.

Big Steve's Gym and Aerobics Center
1126 S. Lamar Blvd. • (512) 445-2348

A South Austin institution and, consistent with that neighborhood's image, the real thing with real sweat. A favorite among some of Austin's longtime residents including writers Bud Shrake and Gary Cartwright (see our chapter on The Literary Scene), Big Steve also advises clients of all ages and recently developed a program for an 81-year-old health-seeker. You may spot one of the city's cultural or musical well-knowns working out here after a hard day's night in this self-described "old Austin" gym. The basics are practiced here, plus the staff includes a martial arts expert and a boxing coach.

The Hills Fitness Center
4615 Bee Caves Rd. • (512) 327-4881

If Big Steve's is the South Austin gym, this is the West Austin fitness club. Located on a beautiful 12-acre wooded campus, the center features both indoor and outdoor pools; racquetball, squash and basketball courts; a child-care center and cafe among other things.

Hyde Park Gym

4125 Guadalupe St. • (512) 459-9174

"No chrome. No contracts." is the advertising motto of this university-area gym in one of Austin's favorite and most colorful neighborhoods, Hyde Park. The owners describe the place as down-to-earth, and it is, with cement floors, free weights and no fancy contracts to sign. Personal trainers are available.

Premiere Lady

7028 Wood Hollow Dr. • (512) 418-9399

A very popular fitness center in Northwest Austin, this facility caters to women only. In addition to fitness equipment, the center also has a pool, whirlpools and steam and sauna rooms. There are aerobics and fitness classes, plus clients can avail themselves of personal care services such as a hair and nail treatment, facials, massage therapy and tanning. The club has in-house child care available.

Q The Sports Club

10616 Research Blvd. • (512) 794-9151

This large Northwest Austin branch of the fitness club chain is packed with fitness equipment including circuit training, gear, treadmills, step machines, etc. The club offers members a variety of classes — cadio-combo, step aerobics, water exercises, including an arthritis warm-water exercise program. In addition to the swimming pool, there is also an indoor track and facilities for massage and sauna. Members pay a monthly fee and are given a preliminary fitness test with a personal trainer to help them develop an exercise program.

St. David's Health and Fitness Center

900 E. 30th St. • (512) 397-4263

Month-to-month memberships are available at this Central Austin health club, which is affiliated with the St. David's Medical Center. The club has rowing machines, step machines, Cyber weight machines, ski machines, treadmills and stationary bikes. Aerobics classes and individual exercise programs are offered.

World Gym

9101 Research Blvd. (Northwest) • (512) 837-5577
13945 U.S. Hwy. 183 (Northwest) • (512) 219-9338
Lincoln Village, 6406 N. I-35, Ste. 2450 (North) • (512) 467-1900
Littlefield Bldg., 115 E. Sixth St. (Central) • (512) 479-0044
4211 S. Lamar Blvd. (Southwest) • (512) 416-8833
4404 W. William Cannon Dr. (Southwest) • (512) 583-0800
Sky Ridge Plaza, 2000 S. I-35 (Round Rock) • (512) 255-4433

This national chain operates seven gyms in the Austin area. The gym offers dozens of types of aerobic classes, including, disco, kick-boxing and funk aerobics. The facilities also have a variety of training equipment, weights and Cybex, Icarian and Body Master equipment. Several locations are open 24 hours a day during the week.

YMCA

Town Lake Branch, 1100 Cesar Chavez Blvd. (Central) • (512) 476-6705
Southwest Family Branch, 6219 Oakclaire Dr. (Southwest) • (512) 891-9622
North Park Family Branch, 9616 N. Lamar Blvd. • (512) 973-9622

All three facilities offer free weights, treadmills, step machines, Nordic tracks, rowing machines, stationary bikes, aerobics classes, cardio-theater and whirlpools. The Southwest has a Nautilus circuit, Town Lake has a Cybex circuit, and the new North Park branch has a Magnum circuit. Family and individual memberships are available, and guests receive one free visit a year and must be accompanied by a Y member. Out-of-town visitors with a Y membership in another city are welcome — bring along your Y membership card.

Flying

Adventure Aviation

811 W. Howard Ln. • (512) 251-2445

Austin Executive Airport, on the north side of the city's Robert Mueller Municipal Airport, offers aircraft rental, flight instruction and sightseeing flights. Note: Both commercial and private aviation are scheduled to move to the new airport in southeast Austin in late 1999.

Canelas International Aviation Inc.
1801 E. 51st St. • (512) 474-8359

This Cessna Pilot Center offers flight training and aircraft rental and is headquartered at the Robert Mueller Airport.

Hiking

Austin's greenbelts, hike and bike trails in Cedar Park, Pflugerville and Round Rock (see our Parks section above) and hundreds of miles of trails in nearby state parks offer hikers a great variety of terrain, levels of difficulty and scenic views for hiking enthusiasts.

Some of the easiest trails to access are within the Austin Greenbelt network. For more information and brochures showing trails and access points, call Austin PARD at (512) 499-6700. One good way to get started is to join the Sierra Club for its hike around Town Lake every Sunday morning at 8 AM. The group meets by the tennis courts at Austin High School, Cesar Chavez Boulevard and MoPac, and after the walk heads for breakfast. Call (512) 445-6223 for more information.

Popular scenic hikes include the trails at McKinney Falls State Park, in Southeast Austin, and Wolf Mountain Trail in Pedernales Park and Hamilton Pool Park, both west of Austin (see our Parks section in this chapter). A good resource for hikers is the Hill Country Information Service, (512) 478-1337, which sells U.S. Geological Survey maps and other illustrated guides to Hill Country hikes. Other good resources are the outdoor outfitters listed in our Shopping chapter.

The Colorado River Walkers of Austin, (512) 795-0286, organizes scenic hikes. Another Hill Country group that carries on a German tradition of hiking is Volkssporting in Fredericksburg. Call (800) 830-WALK for information on the club's activities. If you need to learn more about backpacking and hiking, consider taking a course at the University of Texas Recreational Sports Division, (512) 471-1093.

Horseback Riding

True to its Texas character, there are several major rodeo and equestrian events in Austin each year. See our Annual Events chapter for details. Several area ranches offer horseback riding — be sure the owner/operator has a Texas Department of Health certificate posted.

Cameron Equestrian Center
13404 Cameron Rd. • (512) 272-4301

This Northeast Austin stable and training center offers English and Western-style lessons and riding opportunities.

Medway Ranch
13500 Pecan Dr. • (512) 263-5151

Off R.R. 620 near Lake Travis, this large ranch offers scenic rides across rocky pastures, along hilly trails lined with juniper trees, cactus and wildflowers and past dry creek beds.

Ol' Cactus Jack
13433 W. Texas Hwy. 71 • (512) 263-2388

Horseback riding, hay rides and moonlight parties in the Hill Country, west of Austin, are the specialties here.

Hot Air Ballooning

The skies over Austin are filled with balloons each September during the annual Lone Star Weekend Aloft (see our Annual Events chapter). During the rest of the year, the following companies offer quiet rides in the sky. Before floating away, check the pilot's FAA certification. Most flights begin in the early morning, and prices per person can range from $150 to $350.

- Central Texas Ballooning Association, (512) 479-9421
- Aeronauts Hot Air Balloons, (512) 440-1492, (800) 444-3257
- Airwolf Adventures, (512) 836-2305
- Balloon Port of Austin, (512) 835-6058
- Hill Country Balloons, (512) 345-1575
- Incredible Journeys, (800) 946-4997
- Skyride Balloons, (512) 310-7944
- Sundance Balloon Adventures, (512) 990-8183
- Sunrise Celebrations, (512) 396-0759

Photo: Peter J. Silva

Austin's mild climate allows runners year-round comfort — unless they don't like the heat!

Hunting

Deer hunting is a popular pastime in the Texas Hill Country where more white-tailed deer live than in any other part of the country. So dense is the population that suburban Austin residents often find their gardens have become a favorite noshing place for the small herds of deer. Driving in the Hill Country at night also can be a challenge since the abundant numbers of deer love to graze on the roadside grasses — usually the grass on the other side of the road.

The Hill Country also is home to several exotic game ranches where, for a hefty fee, hunters can track and hunt wild Corsican rams, African aoudad sheep, Indian blackbuck antelope, axis and sika deer. (Axis deer is a popular item on some area restaurant menus, notably Hudson's-on-the-Bend, one of Austin's leading restaurants. Read about it in our Restaurants chapter.)

Much of the hunting in Texas takes place on private lands where landowners rent out leases or allow hunters to come onto their land for a fee during peak season. The Texas Parks & Wildlife Department, 4200 Smith School Road, Austin, TX 78744, (512) 389-4800 or (800) 792-1112, offers several free comprehensive guides to Texas hunting, including *The Guide to Texas Hunting*.

Ice Sports

Ice sports are becoming more and more popular in Austin, perhaps because of the influx of new residents from colder climates. Youth ice hockey leagues are growing fast.

Austin Hockey Association
(512) 892-3444, (512) 328-6125

This association is open to boys a[illegible] ages 5 to 18. Summer sessions focus[illegible] ing and league competition begins[illegible]

Chaparral Ice Center

14200 N. I-35 • (512) 252-8500
2525 W. Anderson Ln. • (512) 451-5102

Public skating, classes, hockey leagues, birthday parties and broom ball are all offered at these facilities in North Austin. They offer a pro shop and locker facilities. Round Rock PARD offers ice-skating classes at the I-35 location. The I-35 rink is open Monday through Friday from 12:15 to 5 PM, on Tuesday and Thursday from 8:15 to 10:15 PM, Friday from 6:30 to 11 PM, Saturday from 1:15 to 11 PM and Sunday from 1:15 to 4 PM. Skating admission is $5, and skates rent for $2.50 a pair. Chaparral recently purchased the Anderson Lane facility. Call for hours and admission charges.

Rock Climbing

This is a fast growing recreational activity in Austin. A favorite outing for local rock climbers is to Enchanted Rock Park, near Fredericksburg, about 90 miles west of Austin (see above under State Parks).

Pseudo-Rock

200 Trinity St. • (512) 474-4376

Pseudo-Rock offers classes and indoor climbing experiences for individuals or groups on the facility's 6,000 square feet of sculpted climbing surface. Pseudo-Rock also promotes its downtown facilities as a great place to host a kid's party or a group celebration. There is a pro shop on the premises also. The Central Texas Mountaineers meet (upstairs, of course) every first Thursday of the month at Pseudo-Rock. It is open daily.

Texas Mountain Guides

200 Trinity St. • (512) 474-4376

Same place, same number as Pseudo-Rock, but the experienced staff guides offer personalized instruction and take participants ...he field to El Protero Chico, Nuevo Leon, ...Pecos River Cliffs on the Mexican ...co Tanks in West Texas. "Go ... Anything!" is their motto. ...custom trips. Their brochure ...e a wish list? A mountain or ...r imagination?" If you have ...er to that question, call.

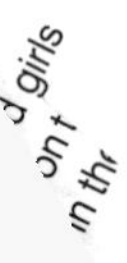

University of Texas Recreational Sports

(512) 471-1093

Information about the classes is detailed in the Recreation section previously in this chapter. Rock climbing classes are included in the curriculum.

YMCA Southwest

6219 Oakclaire Dr., off U.S. Hwy. 290 W. • (512) 891-9622

The southwest branch of the Y has a rock-climbing wall and offers classes. Membership is required to enjoy the Y's facilities; however, guests may pay for one annual visit if they are accompanied by a member.

Rollerskating

These rollerskating facilities are generally open in the evenings until 11 PM. Some offer afternoon sessions, particularly on weekends; however, be forewarned the rinks do close for private parties, so it is wise to call ahead. Admission prices are generally $4 and under; in-line skates cost a couple of dollars more. They also offer a variety of party packages ranging in price from around $5 to $9, depending on whether party favors and snacks are included.

Playland Skating Center

8822 McCann Dr. • (512) 452-1901

The Northeast Austin center offers rollerskating, in-line skating and special adults nights.

Skateworld

9514 Anderson Mill Rd. • (512) 258-8886

Skating lessons and hockey leagues are featured at this Northwest Austin skating rink.

Round Rock Roller Rink

2120 N. Mays St. • (512) 218-0103

This center touts its family activities including skating for families and Christian music on Monday.

Rugby

Rugby can be an exciting game to watch, even if you don't understand the rules — or apparent lack of them. Spectators should remember rugby is a tough sport that often encompasses certain off-pitch lifestyle habits, i.e., revelry. There are two rugby clubs in Austin; several of their players hail from foreign countries where rugby is popular. Both teams have won titles, gone on tour and hosted visits from foreign teams.

The Austin Rugby Football Club
6013 Loyola Ln. • (512) 419-4784 hotline, (512) 926-9017 clubhouse

The Austin Rugby Football Club was founded in the spring of 1967 and was the first club in the Southwestern United States. In 1978, the club became the first rugby club in the United States to purchase its own grounds and then in 1985 the team built a clubhouse — it is one of only two rugby clubs in the United States with its own clubhouse and grounds. Call the clubhouse for directions to the club in East Austin, which can be difficult to find without detailed directions.

The Austin Huns
(512) 459-HUNS

The Austin Huns RFC Pitch is in Zilker Park, and games are usually played on Saturday afternoons. After the game, the Huns head for Nasty's, "Homeland of the Huns," a neighborhood bar at 606 Maiden Lane in Central Austin. The Austin Huns Rugby Football Club was founded in 1972 when the second side of the Austin Rugby Football Club broke away to form their own team.

Running/Walking

There are 5K, 10K and marathon events throughout the year in Austin (see our Annual Events chapter). RunTex is a good source of calendar events; call (512) 472-3254 or (512) 343-1164. The Austin Runner's Club serves as a clearinghouse of information; call (512) 416-5700, punch RACE for all current races.

In addition to the Town Lake Hike and Bike Trail, a popular walking spot is Camp Mabry, headquarters of the Texas Army and Air National Guard, at 35th Street and MoPac in West Austin. The headquarters belies its name and is, in fact, a bucolic park with trees, grass expanses with only the occasional vintage fighter plane on view. There is an oval cinder track for die-hard runners and walkers.

See the previous Austin Parks listings in this chapter for hike and bike trails in the city.

Tennis

In addition to private facilities at some of the area's top resorts (see our Resorts Close-up in the Hotels and Motels chapter) and country clubs, there are 28 first-come, first-served municipal tennis court facilities, some with two courts, others four, located in all sectors of Austin. Tennis players also have access to several school courts during the summer months. For a complete list contact PARD at (512) 480-3020. Courts are concrete, asphalt or laykold and are available free of charge.

Reservations are necessary and fees are charged to play on the courts at the city's four municipal tennis center facilities, which are larger and have lighting. All courts are laykold and lighted. Fees are $3 for adults and $2.50 for children in prime time, which is Monday through Thursday after 6 PM and Saturday and Sunday before 6 PM. Fees are lower at other times.

The Capital Area Tennis Association at 3625 Manchaca Road, (512) 443-1342, is an excellent resource for tennis players. Organized in 1974 and dedicated to promoting amateur tennis competition, the association keeps its members informed of tennis activities in the greater Austin area; conducts educational tennis clinics and seminars; organizes competitive events to fund youth programs and new court construction; and offers consulting services to public officials about the development of tennis facilities. Membership fees are less than $5 a year.

Caswell
24th St. and Lamar Blvd. • (512) 478-6268

This Central Austin tennis center has nir courts and is open from 8 AM to 10 PM M day through Thursday, Friday 8 AM to and Saturday and Sunday from 8 AM A summer tennis league is head here, and lessons are offered.

Pharr

Wilshire Blvd. at Airport Blvd.
• (512) 477-7773

This tennis center in North Austin has eight courts and is open daily from 8:30 AM to 10:30 PM.

Austin High

1715 West St. • (512) 477-7802

This tennis facility is in Central Austin, just east of MoPac at Austin High School. There are eight courts available after school is out during the school year and daily during the summer months.

South Austin

S. 5th St. and Cumberland Rd.
• (512) 442-1466

The city's South Austin facility has 10 courts and is open Monday through Friday from 9 AM to 10 PM and Saturday and Sunday from 9 AM to 6 PM. In the summer, beginning in June, the center opens 30 minutes earlier.

Wells Branch Community Center

2106 Klattenhoff Dr. • (512) 251-9814

The two lighted courts here are open to Wells Branch residents in this North Austin neighborhood.

Round Rock

Several of the city's parks have free courts, including Frontier Park, 1502 Frontier Trail; Greenslopes Park, 1600 Gattis School Road; McNeil Park, 3701 N. I-35; Round Rock West Park, 500 Round Rock West; Stark Park, 1409 Provident Lane; and Stella Park, 803 Nancy Drive. Call Round Rock PARD at (512) 218-5540 for information.

Cedar Park

The city's newest park, Elizabeth M. Milburn Community Park, 1901 Sun Chase ulevard, has tennis facilities. Call the Cedar RD at (512) 258-4121 for information.

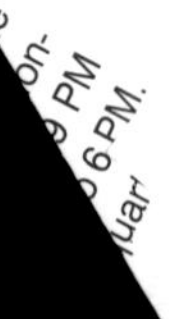

olleyball

Volleyball

al sand volleyball courts in the city's parks, plus a few commercial locations where volleyball enthusiasts gather.

Austin Park facilities

Austin PARD • (512) 499-6700

There are four public sand volleyball courts with nets in Zilker Park, in a green space area north of Barton Springs Road. The three courts at Pease Park lack nets, but you can rent them from PARD.

Aussie's Bar and Grill

306 Barton Springs Rd. • (512) 480-0952, (512) 474-2255 volleyball line

This is a haven for local sand court players. The restaurant operates league play throughout the summer.

Carlos 'N Charlie's

5981 Hiline Rd. • (512) 266-1683

Cousin to those wacky Mexican restaurants south of the border, made popular by spring breakers in Cancun, this Emerald Point restaurant has a well-regarded sand volleyball complex. It is a stop on the women's pro beach tour. The restaurant rents out the volleyball court for $25 a day for private parties.

The Pier

1703 River Hills Rd. • (512) 327-4562

This Lake Austin restaurant has a sand court that attracts lots of players of varying skills, particularly on weekends. According to Miss Volleyball Manners, the way to place your reservation for the court is to tie your shirt to the pole and wait for your turn to come up.

Volente Beach

16107 Wharf Cove • (512) 258-5109

Volente Beach is a private lakeside park that offers volleyball, windsurfing, swimming and other beach/lake activities. It opens at 11 AM daily, closing at 10 PM during the week and 11 PM on weekends. There are three lighted sand volleyball courts on site. Admission is $4.

Indoor Volleyball

The Austin PARD operates two indoor volleyball leagues: one at the Austin Recreation Center, 1301 Shoal Creek Boulevard, (512)

476-5663, and one at the Northwest Recreation Center, 2913 Northland Drive, (512) 458-4107. League play is year round and includes, men's, women's and coed teams.

Watersports

Newcomers to the Texas Hill Country often are taken aback by the abundance of lakes, rivers and creeks in the area. Don't judge Texas by the movies — too often those Hollywood Westerns were filmed in Mexico, Utah or someplace the director thought looked like Texas. Thanks to Mother Nature and Texas politicians, the Austin area abounds in lakes that, in addition to providing electricity for millions of Texans and irrigation for farmers and ranchers, offer opportunities for a wide variety of watersports.

The Highland Lakes, formed by the damming of the Colorado River, are the major water attraction in the area, but Central Texas also has rivers, creeks, natural swimming holes and, of course, the waterhole some have called the "soul of Austin," Barton Springs Pool (see our Close-up in this chapter). This section is divided into several categories encompassing boating (canoeing, rowing and sailing), scuba diving, swimming, water-skiing and windsurfing.

There are several invaluable resources for the watersports enthusiast:

Texas Parks & Wildlife Department
4200 Smith School Rd. • (512) 389-8900

This state agency is not only charged with maintaining the state's parks, but also enforcing water safety laws (see our Boating Safety information in this chapter). Copies of the rules and guidelines on water safety can be obtained from the agency, in addition to information about state facilities, including boat ramps, on Texas lakes and rivers.

The Lower Colorado River Authority (LCRA)
(512) 473-3200

Much of the Highland Lakes area falls under the auspices of the LCRA, a state promulgated agency that is charged with running the utility and overseeing the recreational facilities that are a by-product of the electricity-generating side of the business. In addition to operating parks along the lakes, the LCRA also offers boating safety classes. There are several public boat ramps in the LCRA parks and primitive areas (see our Lake Parks section previously in this chapter).

Travis County Parks
(512) 473-9437

In addition to state parks and wildlife and LCRA wardens, the Travis County Sheriff's Office also has deputies aboard patrol boats on some areas of the lakes. Many of the county parks (see our Travis County Parks section above) include boat ramps.

The Austin Parks and Recreation Department (PARD)
(512) 499-6700

Austin's penchant for the outdoor life means a major focus for PARD in assisting and serving watersports enthusiasts. In addition to operating a network of municipal and neighborhood pools (see our subsequent Swimming section), PARD offers classes in canoeing, kayaking and sailing. The department also operates Emma Long Metropolitan Park (see our Austin City Parks section above), the closest boat ramp to downtown Austin and the only city-run ramp on Lake Austin —

Photo: Peter J. Silva

Rock climbers find lots of spots to climb – even inside the city limits.

Walsh Landing, one block north of the western end of Enfield Drive.

National Aquatic School

University of Texas • (512) 471-3765

The school and the Red Cross hold classes in the spring and summer in sailing, scuba diving and other water skills. These are very popular classes and early reservations are a must.

Boating

Safety

Alarmed by the rising numbers of accidents on Texas waterways, the state legislature passed tougher boating laws in 1997. The highlights include:

- Teenagers 13 to 15 must take a boating education course before they can legally operate a boat of 15 HP or more without adult supervision. By 2001 all 13- to 17-year-olds must complete water safety courses before they can operate a boat or watercraft without adult supervision.
- Children younger than 13 must be accompanied by an adult when operating boats of 10 HP or more or a sailboat longer than 14 feet.
- Jet Skis, also called WaveRunners, cannot be operated except at slow speed within 50 feet of other Jet Skis, stationary objects, the shoreline or other boats.
- And, of course, driving a boat or Jet Ski while intoxicated is against the law.

Boat Rentals and Marinas

Literally dozens of companies rent boats, sailboats, canoes, pontoon boats, and even large party boats in the Austin area. Most also rent Jet Skis, often called WaveRunners. Several of the larger marinas and rental companies are listed below. It is wise to check the Yellow Pages, then call around to check prices and availability. For busy holiday weekends rentals should be made far in advance.

Be aware that there is strict enforcement of state and local boating laws, particularly drunken sailing laws, on area waterways. That enforcement is beefed on the Highland Lakes during holiday weekends. Boat rental agents will brief renters on the laws, local sailing "highway" rules and courtesies, and they will stress safety. Most require a deposit in the form of a credit card, and renters will be held liable for any damage to the craft.

Marinas offer both storage slips for sail and power boats, plus full service for gasoline and marine supplies. Many also rent boats, houseboats and WaveRunners.

Austin Aqua Fun

(512) 459-4FUN

This company rents boats on both Lake Austin and Lake Travis. Their stable includes pontoons, WaveRunners and ski boats. The company also offers ski instruction. Pickups are arranged at various locations on the lakes.

Beach Front Boat Rentals

Volente Beach, 16107 Wharf Cove • (512) 258-5109

The marina at this private lakeside park at the northern end of Lake Travis off R.M. 2769 rents windsurfers, WaveRunners and sail, pontoon, fishing and ski boats. There is a $4 admission to the park, which is a popular spot for windsurfers and volleyball enthusiasts. Sailing and ski lessons are also offered.

Emerald Point Marina

5973 Hiline Rd. • (512) 266-1535

The marina is next door to the popular Carlos 'N Charlie's Bar & Grill on Lake Travis (see our Restaurants chapter). In addition to being a full-service marina with store and gas station, the facility rents houseboats, ski boats and Jet Skis.

Just For Fun Watercraft Rental

5973 Hiline Rd. • (512) 266-9710

This boat rental on Lake Travis at Emerald Point Marina offers a variety of craft, including pontoon boats and party craft for groups up to 150 people.

Lakeway Marina

Lakeway on Lake Travis • (512) 261-7511

One of the larger marinas on the lake, this

business offers boat rentals, lessons, fishing guides and sunset cruises.

Canoeing and Kayaking

Austin Paddling Club
(512) 448-5171

The club is dedicated to promoting canoeing, kayaking and rafting and meets monthly at the LCRA Hancock Building, 3701 Lake Austin Boulevard.

Capital Cruises
Hyatt Hotel Town Lake • (512) 480-9264

Looking for a unique way to view the evening bat flight at the Congress Avenue Bridge? Consider renting a canoe, kayak or electric pedal boat from this Town Lake-based boat company.

Zilker Park Canoe Rentals
**2000 Barton Springs Rd.
• (512) 478-3852**

Since no motorized craft are allowed on Town Lake, one of the best ways to enjoy Town Lake is in a canoe or kayak, and they can be rented at this concession in Zilker Park from 11 AM to dusk daily, March through Labor Day. If you are unfamiliar with the joys of canoeing, try your hand at Paddlefest, the annual April celebration, when a section of Town Lake is roped off, and canoes are rented for short trips across the lake (see our Annual Events chapter).

Cruises

Austin Party Cruises
**Lake Austin • (512) 328-9887
Lake Travis • (512) 266-3788**

Party boats can be rented for sunset cruises, birthday parties, scenic cruises of both lakes and corporate events. The company also offers catering services.

Capital Cruises
Hyatt Hotel Town Lake • (512) 480-9264

In addition to renting electric boats and canoes (see previous listing), Capital also offers dinner cruises on Town Lake, bat-watching parties and sightseeing trips up and down the downtown lake.

Riverboats
6917 Greenshores Dr. • (512) 345-5220

The company's two riverboats, *Commodore Riverboat* and *Commodore's Pup* can accommodate 50 to 500 people as they cruise Lake Austin. The boats can be rented for parties, receptions and corporate outings. Full food and beverage service is available on both boats.

Rowing

Austin Rowing Club
**223-B E. Cesar Chavez Blvd.
• (512) 472-0726**

The advent of rowing on Town Lake has given Austinites the opportunity to view one of the most picturesque of early morning city sights: a lone rower skimming the waters of Town Lake in the morning mist. The rowing club is on the northern bank of Town Lake, near the Four Seasons Hotel. The club serves as headquarters for collegiate team events on Town Lake and serves non-collegiate members of the rowing club. Classes are offered for beginners.

Sailing

The Austin Yacht Club
5906 Beacon Dr. • (512) 266-1336

The club sponsors races every Sunday out on Lake Travis and hosts several regattas and races throughout the year. The club is a good source of information on local sailing opportunities and practices, resources and classes (see our chapters on Spectator Sports and Kidstuff).

Commander's Point Yacht Basin
Lake Travis • (512) 266-2333

One of the few marinas on the lake that rents sailboats and offers training for beginners, Commander's Point is home to a large sailing fleet. The marina also rents captained boats for visitors who want to enjoy a sail on Lake Travis but do not know the ropes.

Sail Aweigh

(512) 250-8141

Sailing lessons with a U.S. Coast Guard-licensed master are offered by this Austin business. The company also offers chartered, captained cruises on Lake Travis.

Texas Sailing Academy

103-B Lakeway Dr., Lake Travis • (512) 261-6193

The academy has been offering sailing lessons on the lake since 1965. Day and weekly charters, captained cruises and sailboat rentals are also available.

Scuba Diving

Aquatic Adventures

12129 R.M. 620 • (512) 219-6990

Saturday morning dives in nearby Lake Travis are a specialty here. The facility also has an on-site swimming pool for lessons and is home to a scuba club.

Pisces Scuba

11401 R.R. 2222 • (512) 258-6646

This scuba school and rental outlet touts the wonders of freshwater diving in Lake Travis, plus organizes trips to other national and international locations. Pisces offers classes and rents and services equipment.

Tom's Dive & Scuba

5909 Burnet Rd. • (512) 451-3425

Offering classes at all levels from beginners to advanced, plus specialties such as underwater archeology, this North Austin diving facility has a 3,000-square-foot, 10-foot-deep pool. The school organizes local fun dives, outings to the Gulf of Mexico and international dive trips to places such as Cozumel in the Yucatan.

Swimming

The Central Texas climate can make swimming a joy or, on a hot day, a necessity. Even on the coldest days of the year, enthusiasts will head for the constant 68 degrees of Barton Springs Pool (see our Close-up in this chapter), which, unlike many municipal and neighborhood pools, is open year round. Of course, the area's lakes and creeks are open throughout the year, but there are dangers there. Diving into creek or riverbeds can be dangerous as water depths can vary with the seasons and rocky bottoms pose hidden dangers. The lakes are really water-filled valleys and rocks, buried tree limbs and duck weed can pose dangers. No swimming is allowed in Town Lake, and it is unlikely you would want to swim there anyway given urban runoff problems.

Instead, head for one of the many neighborhood pools, natural-fed pools or favorite water holes in the area.

Swimming Lessons

American Red Cross

(512) 928-4271

The Red Cross offers a variety of swimming classes for students of all ages and varying degrees of proficiency.

AquaTex Swim Team

St. Edward's University • (512) 255-8633

The program offers training for experienced swimmers, triathletes and also adults who never learned to swim.

Capital Area Rehabilitation Center

919 W. 28½ St. • (512) 478-2581

The center offers classes for adults, children and handicapped students. There are also sessions for persons suffering from chronic disorders such as arthritis.

Seton/Crenshaw Fitness Center

5000 Fairview Dr. • (512) 453-5551

Fitness and water aerobic classes for swimmers with chronic disabilities, or those embarking on a health regimen are offered at this Central Austin fitness center.

YMCA

1110 W. First St. (Downtown) • (512) 476-6705

6219 Oakclaire Dr. (Southwest) • (512) 891-9622

9616 N. Lamar Blvd. (North) • (512) 973-9622

All three Y facilities have indoor pools and a full schedule of swimming classes for all ages.

Austin City Pools

There are two categories of city-run outdoor pools in Austin: municipal pools and neighborhood pools. Municipal pools are large, deep pools and charge small fees for daily use. Multi-visit passes are available from the PARD. All municipal pools have wading areas, lap lanes, diving boards, concessions and sunbathing areas. There are picnic sites adjacent to the pools. Generally neighborhood pools are free, open during summer months and are no deeper than 5 feet. All pools have lifeguards, and all may be rented before and after regular operating hours.

There are 26 neighborhood pools throughout the city. Call the Aquatics hotline below for a list and a map. The neighborhood pools usually open in May and operate on a weekend-only schedule until Memorial Day when they go into daily operation. In mid-August they resume weekend-only operation and then close before Labor Day. Admission and hours of operation vary at each location.

Austin Aquatics Hotline

(512) 476-4521

This city PARD hotline lists class schedules, fee information and status of city pools.

Bartholomew Pool

1800 E. 51st St. • (512) 928-0014

This municipal pool serves the Northeast Austin. Specific times are set aside for recreational swims, lap swimming and lessons.

Barton Springs

Zilker Park, 2201 Barton Springs Rd. • (512) 476-9044

Revered as an icon, the "soul of Austin," this hallowed swimming pool is featured in our Close-up in this chapter.

The pool is open daily, and even during the coldest days of winter you'll see swimmers enjoying the 68-degree water. It is open in the spring and fall, from mid-March to Memorial Day, Labor Day to October 31, from 5 AM to 10 PM. There are no lifeguards on duty from 5 to 9 AM and from 8 to 10 PM. The pool closes on Monday and Thursday at 7:30 PM.

From Memorial Day to Labor Day, the pool is open from 5 AM to 10 PM. There are no lifeguards on duty from 5 to 9 AM and from 9 to 10 PM. The pool closes at 7:30 PM on Monday and Thursday.

From October 31 to mid-March, are 5 AM to 10 PM, and there are no lifeguards on duty from 5 to 9 AM and dusk to 10 PM.

There are no entrance fees during the winter season. Admission during the rest of the year is $2.50 for adults, Monday through Friday, $2.75 on the weekends; 50¢ for juniors (12 to 17); and 25¢ for children 11 and younger.

Call to make sure the pool is open — cleanings and occasional heavy rains do close the pool. There is a gift shop and information booth at the bathhouse, plus a snack bar.

Deep Eddy

401 Deep Eddy Ave. • (512) 472-8546

This West Austin pool is fed by an artesian well, and its fresh water is a major attraction, especially for families who let the little ones wade in the large, shallow end of the pool. Eilers Park at the intersection of MoPac and Lake Austin Boulevard is home to the pool. The early morning hours are set aside for lap swimmers.

Garrison

6001 Manchaca Rd. • (512) 442-4048

Serving South Austin, Garrison opens in early May and closes in mid-August. Lap swimmers have the pool to themselves during early morning and late evening on weekdays. Recreational swimming and swim lessons also have designated hours on weekdays and weekends.

Mabel Davis

3427 Parker Ln. • (512) 441-5257

This Southeast Austin pool opens in mid-May and closes in August. Lap swimmers have the pool to themselves on weekdays from 9 AM to 10 AM. Swim lessons are also offered here during the week.

Northwest Austin Pool

7000 Ardath St. • (512) 453-0194

This Northwest Austin municipal pool opens a little earlier (late April) and closes a little later (mid-September) than some of the other city pools. Lap swimmers enjoy early morning and late evening weekday hours here.

Wells Branch Pool

2106 Klattenhoff Dr. • (512) 251-9932

This facility, in the Wells Branch Municipal District in far North Austin, is dedicated for the use of Wells Branch residents.

Round Rock City Pools

There are two municipal pools in Round Rock. Call the city's Parks Department at (512) 218-5540 for operating hours and information about swimming lessons and summer fun activities at the pools.

Micki Krebsbach Memorial Pool

301 Deepwood Dr. • (512) 218-7090

This city pool opens in early May and operates on a weekends-only schedule until Memorial Day. The pool is open daily through the summer, then shifts to a weekend schedule from mid-August to the end of September. Daily admission to both city pools is $1.25 for those 18 and older and 75¢ for children 17 and younger. Swim passes are also available for multiple visits.

Lake Creek Swimming Pool

Lake Creek Park, 800 Deerfoot Dr. • (512) 218-7030

The pool opens in mid-May on weekends only and then shifts to a daily schedule on Memorial Day for the summer, shutting down in mid-August.

Pflugerville City Pool

Gilleland Creek Park Pool

700 Railroad Ave. • (512) 251-5082

The community pool is located in the city's major park that serves as the focal point of a citywide trail system. Picnic sites are adjacent to the pool, which is open daily throughout the summer. The city's PARD offers swimming and aquatics lessons here.

Cedar Park Pools

Buttercup Creek Pool

407 Twin Oak Trail • (512) 250-9578

The pool opens in early May and operates much of the month on a weekend-only schedule, then switches to a daily schedule following Memorial Day, closing down in mid-August. The pool has a lap swimming area and 1-meter and 3-meter diving boards. The city's PARD offers swimming lessons, water aerobics and family nights at the pool.

Elizabeth M. Milburn Aquatic Facility

1901 Sun Chase Blvd. • (512) 331-9317

This swimming complex includes an eight-lane, 25-meter lap pool and an adjoining recreational pool with a water playscape and a 117-foot water slide. The pool's bathhouse has showers, a concession area, an arcade and aquatics office. The lap pool is heated and remains open year round.

Swimming Holes

There are three natural swimming holes within a 90-minute drive of Austin. Not all are open year round, and some may be closed when high water proves dangerous or park operators limit human traffic to protect delicate ecosystems. It cannot be overemphasized that swimmers must exercise caution when swimming in natural locations. Underwater hazards can prove deadly, and not a summer goes by without area residents mourning the loss of someone killed from diving into a natural hole.

Blue Hole

County Rd. 173, Wimberley • (512) 847-9127

Several years ago there were negotiations by Hays County government to purchase Blue Hole and turn it into a county park, but the talks broke off and Blue Hole remains privately owned. *Texas Monthly* magazine named this swimming hole (featured in several movies) as one of the top ten in Texas. It is along Cypress Creek, near Wimberley, and operates as a club. Members pay by the day, week or month, plus pay a seasonal entrance fee.

Hamilton Pool

Hamilton Pool Rd., F.M. 3238, off Texas Hwy. 71 • (512) 264-2740

The pool and the grotto that serve as the crown jewel of this 232-acre park (see our

Travis County Parks section above) were formed when the dome of an underground river collapsed thousands of years ago. The grotto is now a unique ecosystem. The emphasis is on the environment here, so access to the pool for swimmers is limited, calling ahead is vital. Once the 100-car parking lot is full, the park closes.

Krause Springs
Spur 191, off Texas Hwy. 71
• (830) 693-4181

Devotees of swimming holes tout this natural pool as a great place to take the family since the waters are clear and shallow. The pool is about 7 miles west of the point where the Pedernales River meets Texas Highway 71. Turn north of Spur 191 and follow the signs. The pool is on privately-owned land that is shaded by large cypress trees. There are picnic and camping facilities at the pool. Daily admission is $2.50 for adults and $2 for children ages 4 to 11. There are additional fees for overnight stays.

Windsurfing

Windsurfing is a popular pastime on the Highland Lakes. There are two areas of Lake Travis where windsurfers tend to gather — Mansfield Dam and Windy Point, both near Travis County Parks. Mansfield Dam Park is on R.M. 620 and Windy Point is off Bob Wentz Park (see our Travis County Park section).

Austin Windsurfer Club
(512) 835-2377

The club has adopted Bob Wentz Park as its club project, working to keep the park clean and litter free. In addition to serving as a clearinghouse for windsurfers, the club also meets socially every month, usually at a Lake Travis-area restaurant.

Volente Beach
16107 Wharf Cove • (512) 258-5109

This private lakeside park at the northern end of Lake Travis off R.M. 2769 rents windsurfers. There is a $4 admission to the park.

Water-Skiing

There are two area ski clubs that offer information on classes, tournaments and tips about good ski locations.

Austin Ski Club
(512) 327-1115

The club sponsors two major tournaments each year, the Texas State Championships in mid-July and the Austin Ski Club Novice Slalom in late August.

Capital Area Water Ski Club
(512) 244-9721

The club offers several tournaments throughout the year and touts itself as a "competitive ski club" where members can test their skills against members with similar skill levels. Coaching and clinics are also part of the club's activities.

Riverside Golf Course is where Harvey Penick taught golf luminaries like Ben Crenshaw and Tom Kite.

Golf

Austin is the home of the famous *Little Red Book.*

"Aha!" some might say, at last proof that Austin politics is decidedly more left footed than the rest of Texas. But we are not talking about Chairman Mao's little book here, but Harvey's.

Harvey Penick was the revered golfing pro and teacher who is credited by some of the best players, both amateur and pro, with helping them better their game and reach inner golfing peace. Penick, who lived from 1904 to 1995, is more than an Austin legend. Long known in U.S. golfing circles, Penick became a worldwide legend in the final three years of his life when his small, succinct, plain-talking books of golf wisdom became international bestsellers. In 1992, Austin writer and screenwriter Bud Shrake teamed up with Penick to write the *Little Red Book*. When it became a runaway hit, they followed with a second little book, *And If You Play, You're My Friend*, followed by a third *For All Who Love the Game*. They were working on a fourth when the much-loved Penick died.

Two weeks before he died in an Austin hospital, Penick was visited by one of his longtime students, pro golfer Ben Crenshaw, who was having trouble with his putting game. Penick gave him the advice he needed. Also, just days before he died, Penick saw another of his star pupils score a major breakthrough. Davis Love Jr. won the Freeport McMoran Classic in New Orleans and made the cut for the Masters. Penick died before the Masters ended, but Crenshaw and Love battled it out that year — Crenshaw winning, Love coming in second. Crenshaw said he felt Penick was the 15th club in his bag. Penick's "simple philosophies about golf and life" had helped him win.

Harvey Penick's life spanned almost a century of golf in Austin. He began as a caddy in 1913 and after high school took a job as the pro at the Austin Country Club (ACC). He taught Crenshaw and Tom Kite at the old ACC, now the Riverside Golf Club (see our listing in this chapter), and passed on his quiet knowledge of the game to several generations of golfers. A bronze statue of Penick, shown passing on tips to Tom Kite, stands near the 9th green of the current ACC course in hills of West Austin.

Penick, a religious man, mixed his love of golf with a wonder and praise of nature — easy to do on some of Austin's attractive golf courses. In addition to having some of the most beautiful and challenging golf courses in the country, Austin is also an egalitarian place and the city maintains several excellent municipal courses that can be played at very reasonable rates.

This chapter is divided into four parts — Austin Municipal Courses, Daily-Fee Courses, Private Courses and Driving Ranges.

And for the ultimate pampered golf experience, we've listed several golf resorts.

Austin Municipal Courses

There are five municipal golf courses in the Austin area. Each course offers public league and tournament play, and lessons also are available at each course. Call either the Austin Parks and Recreation Department's golf office at (512) 480-3020, or the office at each course listed below.

Annual cards allow you to play weekdays at any municipal course and seven days a week at the Hancock course. You also pay a surcharge of $1.75 per round for seniors and juniors and $2.50 per round for adults. (Fees, of course, may change as government budgets are scrutinized every year.) Seniors and juniors also get a considerable discount on daily greens fees.

Prices for the annual cards are:

Individual	$525
2-Member Family	$745
Senior	$270
Senior (Husband/Wife)	$370
College Golf Team Member	$205
Junior	$182
Summer Junior	$53

Jimmy Clay Golf Club

5400 Jimmy Clay Dr. • (512) 444-0999

There are two courses at this municipal golf club located in Southeast Austin:

The Roy Kizer Course is 18 holes, 6749 yards, par 71, and has a driving range. The course is described as a "thinking man's golf course" because of its carefully laid out design. The 57 acres of lakes and marshes surrounding the course add to its natural beauty. Tee times for weekdays are taken 3 days in advance; Friday, Saturday and Sunday tee times are taken on Tuesday beginning at 7 AM.

Greens fees are $16 on weekdays, $21 Friday through Sunday. Early bird and evening fees are $13 during the week and $17 Friday through Sunday. Sunset fees are $9. Cart fees are $16.50.

The Jimmy Clay course has 18 holes, 6857 yards, par 72. Tee times for weekdays are taken one day in advance, weekend tee times are taken Friday beginning at 7 AM.

Greens fees are $11.50 on weekdays, $13 Friday through Sunday. Seniors pay $6.50, juniors $5.25 on weekdays only. Evening fees are $10.25, $7 sunset rates, and carts are $16.50.

Hancock Golf Course

811 E. 41st St. • (512) 453-0276

Built in 1899, this is the oldest golf course in the state of Texas. Located in Central Austin, not far from the popular old Hyde Park neighborhood (see our Neighborhoods and Real Estate chapter), this is a pretty course with rolling hills and a small creek that meanders through its heart. The 9-hole course is 2633 yards, par 35.

Reservations are not required, but groups of four or more can make a reservation one day in advance. Sunday group reservations must be made Friday.

Greens fees are $7 for 9 holes, $11.50 for 18 holes on weekdays, $7.50 and $13 on weekends. Seniors pay $6.50; juniors, $5.25. Evening fees are $10.25, and sunset fees are $7. Carts are $15.70.

Lions Municipal Golf Course

2910 Enfield Rd. • (512) 477-6963

In West Austin, south of Enfield and west of MoPac this is the oldest municipal course in Austin, but nevertheless very popular. This is a 6001-yard course, par 71. There is an irons-only driving range, also.

Tee times for weekdays are taken one day in advance, weekend tee times are taken Friday beginning at 7 AM.

Weekday greens fees are $11.50; weekends, $13. The reduced rate for both seniors and juniors is $5.25 is available only on weekdays. Evening fees are $10.25, sunset $7, and carts are $16.50.

Morris-Williams Golf Course

4300 Manor Rd. • (512) 926-1298

This 18-hole municipal course is in East Austin, southeast of Robert Mueller Municipal Airport. The big jets landing and taking off over the greens will be moving on to the new city airport in 1999. The par 72, 6636-yard course is built on an undulating landscape and has a driving range.

Tee times for weekdays are taken one day in advance, weekend tee times are taken Friday beginning at 7 AM.

Greens fees are $11.50 on weekdays and $13 on weekends. Seniors and juniors pay $6.50 and $5.25 on weekdays only. Evening fees are $10.25, sunset fees $7, and carts are $17.

Round Rock

Forest Creek Golf Club

99 Twin Ridge Pkwy. • (512) 388-2874

This municipal golf course has gained a great reputation not only for its challenging design, but also for the quality of the pros who have worked at the club. J.L. Lewis, who went on to the PGA, was the club's first pro. The club is open daily. The par 72 course has 18 holes, 7154 yards.

The club has a golf shop, driving range, putting green, dining facilities and even a stocked fishing lake. Greens fees, including cart, are $40 Monday through Thursday, $45 on Fridays, and $50 on Saturday, Sunday and holidays. Seniors pay $25 on weekdays only.

Daily-Fee Courses

Bluebonnet Hill Golf Course

9100 Decker Ln. • (512) 272-4228

Located in northeast Travis County near Manor, this public course was built to attract beginning golfers and has become very popular. It takes its name from the rolling Hill Country landscape, particularly beautiful in spring when the bluebonnets bloom. Bluebonnet touts itself as being rated one of the top 25 public courses in Texas according to the *Dallas Morning News*.

The course is 18 holes, 6503 yards, par 72. Facilities include a driving range, snack bar, putting green, and chipping green. Greens fees are $15 Monday through Friday, $17 on Friday, and $24 on weekends. Carts are $18, or $9 a person. Seniors pay $10 cart fees. Twilight fees are $11 from 3 to 5 PM, $9 after 5 PM; $15 and $10 respectively on weekends.

Butler Park Pitch and Putt Golf Course

1201 W. Riverside Dr. • (512) 477-9025

For almost 50 years Winston Kinser has been operating this tiny private course on city-owned land just south of Town Lake in the heart of Austin. The par 27, 805-yard course is tucked away just east of Lamar Boulevard and south of Riverside Drive. Each of the 9 holes are par 3, and the longest hole is No. 8, 118 yards. This is a great place to find out if golf is for you. Kinser charges $4 for 9 holes; a second round will cost you $3.50, a third $2.50, and you can play all day for $12. You can rent clubs (you won't need a cart) for 75¢ each. The course opens at 8:30 AM and closes at dusk.

Cedars on Bergstrom Golf Course

Texas Hwy. 71, former site of Bergstrom Air Force Base • (512) 385-4653

The Cedars is the latest addition to the public golf course system in Austin and is in Southeast Austin on land formerly occupied by the U.S. Bergstrom Air Force Base. The course was part of the base and had fallen into disrepair following the defense closures. Now run by a group called Camp Verde, the course has been upgraded and changed to accommodate the plans for the new Austin airport, scheduled to open on the former base in 1999. The cedar trees (actually junipers, but the locals call them cedars) give the club its new name.

The course is 18 holes, 6576 yards, par 71. There is an on-site putting green, a clubhouse and snack bar. Weekday greens fees are $10 for walking, $19 with a cart; weekend fees are $15 for walking and $24 with a cart. Seniors pay $7 to walk the course on weekdays, $16 to ride. Sunset fees are the same as senior rates.

Circle C Golf Cub

7401 Texas Hwy. 45 • (512) 288-4297

This club was designed to give patrons of a daily-fee course a country-club feel. Near the southern end of MoPac in Southwest Austin in the Circle C subdivision, the course apparently succeeded since it was named one of the best new clubs in Texas in 1992 and has remained popular. The course was designed by Jay Morrish to attract new golfers and is regarded as a fun place to play. Circle

INSIDERS' TIP

Want to contribute to the Harvey Penick Memorial Fund? There are three entities who share in the fund's donations: Caritas, 308 E. Seventh Street, (512) 472-4135; The Harvey Penick Scholarship Fund at the University of Texas, P.O. Box 7399, Austin, TX 78713; and Central Christian Church, 110 Guadalupe Street, (512) 476-6941.

C is next door to the Lady Bird Johnson National Wildflower Research Center, and the same rugged beauty preserved at the center is apparent around the golf course.

The 18-hole course is 6859 yards, par 72. Players can avail themselves of the driving range, putting green, dining room, meeting rooms and the 24-hour/10-day advance tee hotline. There is also shuttle service from area hotels.

Greens fees include carts and are $50 on weekdays, $65 Friday through Sunday.

Seniors and juniors pay $25 on weekdays.

River Place Golf Club

4207 River Place Blvd. • (512) 346-6784

On the shores of Lake Austin, west of the city, this course has been a symbol of the economic roller-coaster ride of the last 20 years. Originally planned to be part of a upscale Hill Country development on the shores Lake Austin, it was caught up in the development v. anti-growth wars, then the real estate downturn of the 1980s. Finally, in 1991 it was placed on the auction block by the Resolution Trust Corporation.

Now, after a redesign by professional golfer Tom Kite, the course is described as attractive and sometimes challenging. The 18-hole course is 6611 yards, par 71. Facilities include a driving range, snack bar and putting green.

Greens fees include carts and are $55 on weekdays, $63 on Fridays, and $70 on weekends. Seniors pay $35 Monday through Friday before noon. Juniors pay $35 Monday through Thursday. Twilight fees go into effect after 2 PM and are $35 Monday through Thursday, $40 on Friday, and $44 on weekends.

Riverside Golf Course

1020 Grove Blvd. • (512) 389-1070

This course is a part of golf history. Now a public course in Southeast Austin, this was the home of the Austin Country Club and the place where Harvey Penick taught golf luminaries like Ben Crenshaw and Tom Kite. Penick was the club pro when Austin Community College moved here in 1950. The course is lined with old oak and pecan trees that once stood witness as some of Austin's wealthiest citizens and future national golf champions played. Now, it is owned by Austin Community College and open at very low fees to all comers.

The course is 18 holes, 6500 yards, par 71. There is a snack bar and picnic area on site, plus a putting green, golf shop and chipping green.

Pflugerville

Blackhawk Golf Club

2714 Kelly Ln. • (512) 251-9000

Build it, and they will come! This is true of the Blackhawk Golf Club, which was built in the early '90s by John and Martha Leach in what was then the small country town of Pflugerville, northeast of Austin. These days the club is surrounded by the suburban boom town of Pflugerville. John Leach turned to his sister-in-law for the design of the course — she is Hollis Stacy, three-time U.S. Women's Open Champion, who decided to enter the male-dominated profession of golf course architecture.

Working with local architect Charles Howard, they turned a dairy farm into a highly praised public golf course with abundant water and trees. The course is 18 holes, 6636 yards, par 72. Facilities include a driving range, golf shop and snack bar.

Greens fees include a cart and are $32 Monday through Thursday, $37 on Friday and $42 on weekends; twilight (after 3 PM) fees are $21, Monday through Thursday, and $27 Friday through Sunday. Seniors pay $27 Monday through Thursday.

Private Courses

Austin Country Club

4408 Long Champ Dr. • (512) 328-0030

This is the spiritual home of Harvey Penick who was the club's first pro. A bronze statue of the revered teacher stands near the 9th green. He is shown giving tips to former student Tom Kite, the international golf champion who holds the course record, 64.

This is the third home for the club, which was chartered in 1898, one of the two oldest in the state. The current course in West Austin was designed by Pete Dye, one of the world's top golf course designers. Experts rate this course as one of the toughest in the Central Texas area.

The course is on the shores of Lake Austin — 18 holes, 6822 yards, par 72. Greens fees are $50 Tuesday through Thursday; $65 Friday, Saturday and Sunday. Cart fees are $10 per person.

Balcones Country Club
Balcones Course

8600 Balcones Club Dr. • (512) 258-2775

Spicewood Course

11210 Spicewood Club Dr. • (512) 258-6763

There are two courses at this Northwest Austin club south of U.S. 183, near Spicewood. Each course has its own club and pros, plus members enjoy an additional central clubhouse. The club is one of the largest in the Austin area and has given special emphasis to its junior program.

The rolling hills of the Balcones course is favored by walkers. The course is 18 holes, 6649 yards, par 70. The Spicewood course is 18 holes, 6706 yards, par 72. Spicewood has greater elevation changes, plus more water elements. Greens fees, including cart, for both courses are $25 Monday through Friday, $30 on weekends. Twilight rates, after 4 PM, are half price.

Great Hills Golf Club

5914 Lost Horizon Dr. • (512) 345-0505

This club is known for its wonderful, authentic Hill Country landscape with rolling hills, cliffs and canyons. It is in West Austin but priced in a much more affordable range than its nearby neighbors — Barton Creek Resort and Austin Country Club. Great Hills is regarded as a great bargain and a challenging course.

The course is 18 holes, 6599 yards, par 72. The clubhouse has both casual and formal dining rooms, a swimming pool and tennis courts. Guest fess are $25, $35 on weekends and carts are $18.

Hills of Lakeway Golf Course

26 Club Estates Pkwy. • (512) 261-7272

This Hill Country course west of R.M. 620 near Lake Travis has been ranked among the top five in Texas. It was designed by Jack Nicklaus, one of his first courses in Texas. The course follows a creek and offers wonderful vistas of the surrounding rugged hills.

This is an 18 hole, 6954 yards, par 72 course. There is a marina, tennis courts, swimming pool, driving range and putting green on site. Greens fees are $55 on weekdays, $65 on weekends, and carts are $10 a person.

Lost Creek Country Club

2612 Lost Creek Blvd. • (512) 892-2032

Located just west of Loop 360 (Capital of Texas Highway) in an area of rugged canyonland, this club is not far from Austin's most noted golf resort, Barton Creek. The land around the Lost Creek fairways and greens is rugged, and the precipitous drops along the edges of the course make control even more important than usual. The natural rise and fall of the land, plus the hazards, make the course challenging.

This 18-hole course is 6522 yards, par 72. The clubhouse offers both golf and tennis pro shops, a swimming pool and formal and casual dining areas. There is a driving range, practice bunker and putting green on site. Greens fees are $35 on weekdays, $45 on weekends. Carts are $9.50 per person.

Onion Creek Country Club

2510 Onion Creek Pkwy. • (512) 282-2162

This course was designed by Masters Champion Jimmy Demaret in collaboration with George Fazio. It has been described as a classic golf course and for many years it was the home of the original Legends of Golf tournament on the Senior PGA Tour. The Legends was played here for 12 years, and it proved to be a major building block for the seniors' tour.

INSIDERS' TIP

For a comprehensive brochure detailing Austin's municipal golf courses and programs, contact the Austin Parks and Recreation Golf Office at (512) 480-3020.

Located in far South Austin, the course is the anchor for a country club-style residential development. The clubhouse has all the amenities. The 18-hole course is 6367 yards, par 70. Greens fees are $50 on weekdays, $60 on weekends. Carts are $11 per rider.

Golf Resorts

Barton Creek Conference Resort and Country Club

8212 Barton Club Dr. • (512) 329-4000, (800) 336-6157

This resort with its three highly praised golf courses and beautiful 4,000 acre site is built on one of the most sought after and fought over pieces of land in Austin. Located just a dozen miles from downtown, the resort was created along the banks of Barton Creek, which winds through the hills before feeding the underground spring that, in turn, feeds Barton Springs. Some of Austin's most vocal environmentalists protested its construction, but others have praised the development for its ecological sensitivity — the golf courses are maintained without many of the traditional fertilizers typically used on golf courses, and efforts have been made to embrace the local flora into the resort design. The greens and fairways are planted with drought-resistant grasses to cut down on water usage.

The club has three courses, described below, all designed by leading names in golf course architecture.

Given the resort's popularity as both a country club and conference center, not all three courses are available every day to resort play, with the exception of the Lakeside course. Golf fees, which include cart and range balls, are $100 at Lakeside and $140 at the other two courses. The resort also offers Golf Advantage School packages for $300 a day.

While golf is a great reason to visit the Barton Creek club, the resort also offers other recreational facilities including skeet shooting, tennis and "super sports" for groups — volleyball, tug-of-war and obstacle courses. Jogging, swimming, boating, fishing, horseback riding, sightseeing, even factory outlet mall tours are available.

The resort has several dining facilities, including one of the few restaurants in Austin where a jacket is required. On site there is a fitness center and a spa where you can have everything from facials to salt rubs, marine fango massages to aromatic loofah scrubs.

There are 147 guest rooms at the resort with views of the golf course and the surrounding Hill Country. Room rates are on the American Plan (three meals included) and begin in low season (January and December) at $170 per person double occupancy and rise to $215 in the spring and fall. One-bedroom suite prices range from a low of $370 per person to $450. The presidential suite in high season is $820 per person.

The Crenshaw & Coore Course

This was designed by Austinite Ben Crenshaw and his partner Bill Coore. True to Crenshaw's philosophy, the course is traditional and follows the terrain with broad, rolling fairways. This 18-hole course is 6678 yards, par 71.

The Fazio Course

This is dubbed the resort's signature course, and its dramatic design shows the distinctive signature of Tom Fazio. There are cliff-lined fairways, waterfalls and even caves. *Golf Digest* has rated this Fazio course one of the Best Resort Courses in America, second in Texas and 60th in the ranking of the 100 greatest golf courses in America. The course also has won the USGA's National Environmental Steward Award.

The Arnold Palmer-Lakeside Course

Arnold Palmer designed this course, which opened in 1986 as the Hidden Hills Country Club. Barton Creek now owns and operates the course about 25 miles from the resort on the shores of Lake Travis. The course has been named among the most beautiful in Texas by the *Dallas Morning News*. Golfers enjoy great views from the clubhouse overlooking the lake. The course is 18 holes, 6956 yards, par 72.

Lago Vista Resort & Conference Center

1918 American Dr., Lago Vista • (800) 288-1882

Located at the northern end of Lake Travis, about 35 miles northwest of the city of Austin, this resort has two golf courses and other recreational facilities, including a tennis center. The resort offers golf packages and other promotional packages including weddings and family reunions. The two golf courses are Lago Vista Highland Lakes and Lago Vista.

This Highlands golf course is where most resort guests play. In 1990 it was given a $1.7 million upgrade and now presents golfers with plenty of challenges. The second hole once was featured as *Golf Digest*'s tough hole of the month. The course is 8 holes, 6529 yards, par 72. Greens fees include a cart and are $35 on weekends, $25 on weekdays.

Lago Vista is a popular country club where many local residents and resort guests play. The course has 18 holes, 6576 yards, par 72.

In addition to conference facilities, Lago Vista has a spa, boat facilities, tennis courts, swimming pools and can arrange water sport rentals. Rooms at the resort range from guest rooms to two-bedroom suites. Rates are $85 to $125 a day.

Lakeway Inn

101 Lakeway Dr. • (512) 261-6600, (800) LAKEWAY

This resort hotel on Lake Travis, west of the city, offers golfers and tennis players opportunities to pursue their sports while enjoying the other recreational activities available at the Highland Lakes. There are two golf courses made available to Lakeway Inn guests, and tennis players can enjoy the World of Tennis with its 26 indoor and outdoor courts.

Live Oak Golf Course was created in 1964 by designer Leon Howard. Development restrictions were not in place back then, and Howard was given permission to dredge soil from the lake bottom to spread on the course. Twelve years later, Howard built the Yaupon course at the resort. Both offer dramatic views of the lake — two holes on Live Oak are adjacent to the marina.

Live Oak is 18 holes, 6643 yards, par 72. Yaupon is 18 holes, 6565 yards, par 72. Greens fees are included in the price of packages.

The resort offers a variety of packages. Golf packages are $130 a night per person, double occupancy from March 15 to November 15 (so-called vacation season), and $90 per night in value season.

Driving Ranges

Ben White Golf Center

714 E. Ben White Blvd. • (512) 462-2104

This facility in South Austin has 50 lighted grass tees, a 9-hole putting green and offers chipping green lessons. A small bucket of 80 balls costs $6; a large one with 120 balls is $8.

Eaglequest

10515 N. MoPac • (512) 345-2013

Located in North Austin near Braker Lane, this facility has a driving range, putting green, an indoor learning center, pro shop and offers lessons. Bucket prices for members range from 50 balls for $4 to 400 for $20; nonmembers pay $1 more per bucket.

Golfsmith Practice Facility

11000 N. I-35 • (512) 837-1810

Located next door to the Golfsmith Factory Outlet, the driving range has 70 lighted tees. Golfsmith offers custom golf clubs, clinics, practice greens, computerized swing analysis, factory tours, snack bar and Harvey Penick irons and woods. Bucket prices are $3.50 for 50 balls up to $9 for 180 balls.

Mister Tee

13910 N. R.M. 620 • (512) 335-4444

There are 25 lighted tees at this Northwest Austin driving range. Prices range from $4 for 45 balls to 120 balls for $8.

Oak Hill Driving Range

5243 U.S. Hwy. 290 W. • (512) 892-5634

This Southwest Austin driving range has 65 lighted tees. Buckets cost $2.50 for 35 balls up to $9 for 150 balls.

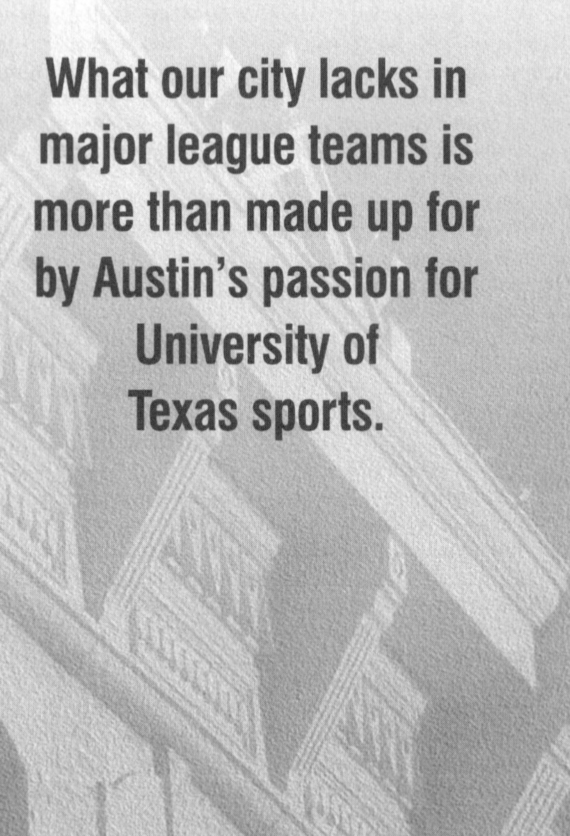
What our city lacks in
major league teams is
more than made up for
by Austin's passion for
University of
Texas sports.

Spectator Sports

Let's face it. When it comes to professional sports, Austin isn't exactly in the big leagues. While the thousands of Austinites who enjoy major league sports find themselves sitting in left field, so to speak, there is still much to celebrate when it comes to sports in Austin. What our city lacks in major league sports is more than made up by Austin's passion for University of Texas sports teams. While UT didn't coin the phrase, "Winning isn't everything, it's the only thing," it has lived by that sentiment for more than a century of athletic achievement and has produced national championship teams in a wide range of sports time and time again. UT's nationally recognized Hook 'em Horns hand signal wasn't voted the best in the country by *Sports Illustrated* magazine in 1997 for nothing.

Austin also claims minor league professional teams in ice hockey and soccer that draw die-hard fans from all over the region. Sports spectators will also discover that Austin boasts an important annual rodeo, a quarter horse track, hugely popular marathons and several spectacular boat races each year.

Another plus for sports fans is Austin's unique location between San Antonio, Dallas and Houston, all within a three-hour drive of our city — and an even shorter flight. San Antonio is 80 miles south on Interstate 35. This quirk of logistical fate affords Austinites incredible choices among major league sports teams in both men's and women's basketball, baseball, soccer, ice hockey and, of course, football — the national pastime of Texas.

The front-page news of 1998 was the announcement by Round Rock officials that our neighboring city will build a $13 million stadium complex to become the home of Nolan Ryan's Double-A baseball team, the Round Rock Express. A group of investors that include Ryan, the former Houston Astros and Texas Rangers pitcher, plans to move the Jackson (Mississippi) Generals to Round Rock by the opening of the 2000 season. Central Texas appears set to lose its title as the largest metropolitan area in the country without a professional baseball team.

Whether your competitive spirit is most roused by a whistle, a buzzer, a starter's pistol or those simple words, "batter up," you're sure to find a Texas sport to call your own.

Minor League Sports

Ice Hockey

Austin Ice Bats
7311 Decker Ln. • (512) 927-PUCK, (512) 469-SHOW Star Tickets box office

The perfect place in Austin for those with a "bat attitude" is in the Travis County Exposition Center on Ice Bats game night. The Expo Center, fondly known as The Bat Cave, has been home to minor league ice hockey since the team was formed in 1996. This exciting team quickly earned a large and loyal following. In its first season, the team led the newly formed Western Professional Hockey League (WPHL) in total attendance, drawing more than 6,200 people per game. The team, one of six charter members of the WPHL, a Southwestern league, finished its second season in 1998 with a 35-23-11 overall record and placed fourth of seven teams in the Eastern Conference. This league is expanding quickly and expects to include at least 16 teams in the 1998-99 season, which runs October through March.

Training camp starts around the first of October, and hockey fans are always invited to watch the team practice. Call them for a schedule. The Ice Bats train at the Expo Center in Southeast Austin or at Chaparral Ice in North Austin. The Expo Center, home to the annual Austin/Travis County Livestock Show

& Rodeo, wasn't exactly designed for ice hockey but has served the team well. Just try to avoid getting seats off in the corners where the visibility isn't great.

Tickets range in price from $6 to $15, with a $1 discount on some seats for children 12 and younger. Season tickets also are available. You can purchase tickets at the Ice Bats Box Office at the Expo Center and at Star Tickets outlets around town, or charge by phone through Star Tickets. Texas' only NHL team is the Dallas Stars. The Ice Bats are affiliated with the Houston Aeros of the International Hockey League.

Soccer

Austin Lone Stars

5446 U.S. Hwy. 290 W., Ste. 105
• (512) 892-7477, (512) 469-SHOW Star Tickets box office

A testament to the rapid growth and popularity of soccer in Austin and across the United States is the number of towns that now claim their own professional soccer teams. Pro soccer came to Austin in 1997 when the Austin Lone Stars moved up from the amateurs into the pro leagues. Home games, held at House Park Stadium at 15th Street and Lamar Boulevard in Central Austin, are fun, family-oriented affairs attended largely by budding soccer stars, both boys and girls, and their parents. (The stadium is an Austin Independent School District facility.) The team is in the South Central Division of the D3 Pro League of the United Systems of Independent Soccer League (USISL), two steps below Major League Soccer. In 1998, the D3 Pro League included 39 teams, making it the largest of the USISL's three outdoor men's leagues. Games are played from April through July, half at home and half on the road.

In 1997, the Lone Stars' first year in the pros, the team finished second in its division and was among eight teams to qualify for the U.S. Open Cup in September, where they lost in the second round in double overtime. The team qualified again for the U.S. Open Cup in 1998. While Lone Stars games don't yet fill half the stadium, this team is beginning to attract attention around Austin and is earning a reputation for high-quality soccer. Other teams in the division include the Houston Hurricanes, Texas Toros, Tulsa Roughnecks, San Antonio Pumas, and Shreveport Lions. Tickets cost $8 for adults and $5 for children ages 3 to 17. Children younger than 3 are admitted free. Season tickets also are available. Purchase tickets before the game starts at the stadium box office and in advance at the Lone Stars office, at Austin's three Soccer World stores, at Star Tickets outlets or charge by phone through Star Tickets. Games are usually played in the evening around 7:30 or 8 PM.

Major Leagues Around Texas

NFL Football

Dallas Cowboys

Texas Stadium, 2401 E. Airport Freeway, Irving • (972) 579-5000, (800) 567-9418

The Dallas Cowboys have competed in the Super Bowl a record eight times and have taken home the trophy in five of those games to tie with San Francisco as the winningest team in Super Bowl history. That's one reason why Texas Stadium, in the Dallas suburb of Irving, draws fans from across the state during football season. Quarterback Troy Aikman and teammates provide the thrills that fill the stands at Texas Stadium, which holds nearly 66,000 fans. Most die-hard fans purchase season tickets, which range in price from about $340 to a whopping $15,000 for seats on the 50-yard line right behind the Cowboys' bench. But those seats can be hard to come by as season ticket holders don't like to give them up. Individual tickets sell for about $35 and are usually available in the upper and lower end zones only because season-ticket holders dominate the stadium.

Photo: Peter A. Silva

The Erwin Center, better known as "The Drum," hosts Longhorn basketball.

A losing 1997 season, which came on the heels of the 1996 Super Bowl victory, led to the resignation under pressure of head coach Barry Switzer, who had coached the team for four years. Chan Gaily, former offensive coordinator for the Pittsburgh Steelers, was named head coach for the Cowboys in 1998. Gaily is just the fourth coach to lead the Cowboys since the team entered the National Football League in 1960. The legendary Tom Landry coached the Cowboys for 29 years, racking up 250 victories and two Super Bowl championships. Jimmy Johnson, who followed Landry, won 44 games and two more Super Bowls in his five years as the Cowboys' head coach.

NBA Basketball

San Antonio Spurs

Alamodome, 100 Montana St., San Antonio • (210) 554-SPUR 7787, (210) 224-9600 Ticketmaster

Austin's closest major league sports venue is about 80 miles down Interstate 35 in San Antonio. This is a popular team for basketball fans throughout Central Texas and the Spurs make a special effort to promote the team in Austin by making appearances at schools and in shopping malls. An average of about 18,000 people attend Spurs home games. The Spurs joined the National Basketball Association in 1976 along with the New York Nets, Denver Nuggets and Indiana Pacers when the former American Basketball Association merged with the NBA. Since then, the Spurs have made it to the NBA playoffs 18 times, including in 1998, but haven't been able to clinch a berth in the finals. The team has played in San Antonio's Alamodome since the $186-million facility opened in 1993. The Alamodome, which is used for many sporting, concert and other events, holds about 20,550 people for normal Spurs games and upwards of 34,000 for special Spurs games. Tickets range in price from about $15 to $160 for regular season games, although tickets can go as low as $5 when upper level seats are opened up. Tickets can be purchased at the Alamodome box office on the southwest corner of the facility or by calling the Spurs box office or Ticketmaster. The regular season runs October through April.

Houston Rockets

Compaq Center, 10 Greenway Plaza, Houston • (713) 627-3865, (713) 629-3700 Ticketmaster

Two-time National Basketball Association champions, the Houston Rockets started in the NBA in 1967 as the San Diego Rockets. The team moved to Houston four seasons later and rewarded supporters with NBA titles in 1994 and 1995. In 1998, the Rockets made it to the playoffs for the sixth straight season but were eliminated by the Utah Jazz, which went on to face the Chicago Bulls for the NBA Championship. The Compaq Center, formerly called The Summit, opened in 1975 and holds nearly 16,300 Rockets fans. This is not an easy team to see at home. The Rockets now have about 1,200 people on the waiting list for season tickets and in the most recent season the team recorded 41 sellouts for 41 games. When you can get them, individual tickets range in price from $12.50 to $475. The regular season runs from October through April. Rudy Tomjanovich coaches the Rockets.

Dallas Mavericks

Reunion Arena, 777 Sports St., Dallas • (972) 988-DUNK, (800) 634-MAVS

Dallas was home to the Chaparrals of the American Basketball Association from 1967 to 1973, but lost its professional basketball team when the Chaparrals moved to San Antonio as the Spurs in 1973. Seven years later pro basketball returned to Big D at the 18,042-seat Reunion Arena when the Dallas Mavericks became an expansion team of the NBA. Three years later the Mavs recorded their first winning season and followed that up with five more winning years that included half a dozen trips to the NBA playoffs. Dallas hasn't fared as well in the 1990s. The team recorded its eighth straight losing season in 1997-98 with a 20-62 record. Maverick fans have remained loyal to coach Don Nelson's team, however. Average attendance hovers around 13,200 for each home game. Individual tickets range in price from about $8 to $42 and can be purchased with a credit card by phone or at the Reunion Arena box office or Dillard's department stores in the Dallas area. The Mavs are soon on the move, planning to debut into a new downtown sports arena by the season opener in the year 2000.

WNBA Basketball

Houston Comets

Compaq Center, 10 Greenway Plaza, Houston • (713) 627-WNBA, (713) 629-3700 Ticketmaster

Two-time NBA champs the Houston Rockets have nothing on this team. In 1998, the dazzling Comets scored their second Women's National Basketball Association national championship in as many years, defeating the Phoenix Mercury. This hot WNBA team also won the leagues inaugural-year national championship in 1997. Coach Van Chancellor was awarded the WNBA Coach of the Year both seasons while standout Cynthia Cooper twice was voted WNBA Most Valuable Player. In 1998, the eight-team league expanded to 10 teams with the addition of Detroit and Washington. Charter members of this summer league also include New York, Los Angeles, Cleveland, Sacramento, Utah, Phoenix and Charlotte. Further expansion of this exciting new league is anticipated. The Comets hold court at the Compaq Center, formerly The Summit, and can easily sell out by game day. Tickets range in price from $8 to $38.50 for regular season games, a little more for post-season games. Call the Comets office or Ticketmaster for tickets. Sea-

INSIDERS' TIP

If you select Upper Arena seats for Ice Bats games at the Travis County Exposition Center, be sure to take along a cushion or blanket to sit on. The metal benches are hard and cold! Can't make it to the game? Tune in to KFON at 1490 on the AM dial. Mark Martello is the voice of the Ice Bats.

On the Ball

She has won more games than any other coach in the history of women's college basketball, and in 1998 she joined the ranks of all-time greats like Wilt Chamberlain, Kareem Abdul-Jabbar and "Pistol" Pete Maravich in the prestigious national Basketball Hall of Fame. When it comes to basketball, men's or women's, Austin's own Jody Conradt is among the elite.

Close-up

"At The University of Texas, Conradt has enjoyed unprecedented success," hailed the Naismith Memorial Basketball Hall of Fame, which selected Conradt for the sport's ultimate honor on her first nomination. "She became head coach in 1976 and quickly established the Longhorns as a national juggernaut and a model program that many other schools have emulated but not duplicated."

Conradt's is a storybook career that started in the small town of Goldthwaite about 100 miles northwest of Austin. Born May 13, 1941, she began playing basketball when girls played six on a side and took the court wearing skirts. At Goldthwaite High School she averaged 40 points a game — when that level of scoring created a stir — and then went on to play for Baylor University in Waco, Texas, where she earned her bachelor's and master's degrees in physical education.

A pioneer for women in the sport, Conradt found role models in the other great women's coaches of the day, all men of course, because they were the only ones coaching women's basketball at the time. She learned well. Conradt racked up winning records as women's basketball coach at Sam Houston State University in Huntsville and then, from 1973 to 1976, at the University of Texas-Arlington.

In the mid-1970s, however, women's basketball flourished in just a few patches of the country — and Texas wasn't one of them. UT-Austin, just coming around to the notion that females could play serious ball, too, named the dynamic Donna Lopiano as head of the new UT women's athletics department, charging her with hiring a coach to direct the fledgling women's basketball program. Lopiano's sights landed on the up-and-coming UT-Arlington coach.

"The coach had to be Texan. Otherwise, I'd always be 'that damned Yankee,'" Lopiano, now executive director of the New York-based Women's Sports Foundation, told the *Austin American-Statesman*. For her part, Conradt sees Lopiano as the sport's visionary. "People didn't think you could build a fan base for women's basketball, but Donna believed it could be done here at Texas," Conradt has told reporters. However, neither Lopiano nor Conradt could have predicted at the time just how far Conradt would take the sport.

Conradt determined early on that her UT teams would need to electrify the courts in order to capture the attention and the imagination of Texas sports fans — and potential players. As a result, hers was the first women's team to institute a full-court-press defense, which she combined with fast-break, thrilling action. To develop winning teams, she believed, UT needed to face tougher competition, so she drafted a schedule to include the country's best. Conradt also was among the first coaches to personally recruit basketball's best and brightest. She traveled throughout the state, meeting with the players, establishing rapport with the coaches, touting her program.

"Her dedication and efforts would prove to be the cornerstone of the powerhouse that she was assembling in the capitol city," UT says of its coach in the sport's media guide.

— continued on next page

Photo: University of Texas

Coach Jody Conradt's basketball teams have captured the attention and imagination of Texas sports fans.

Oh yes, she won games too. Under Conradt's leadership — she began her 23rd season in November of 1998 — the UT Longhorns have won an astounding 80 percent of their games and claimed 10 regular-season Southwest Conference titles and nine post-season championships.

Her 1986 squad became the first women's team in history to go undefeated (34-0) and win the NCAA national championship. The following year, UT made the Final Four. All in all, Conradt's teams have competed in 14 of the past 16 NCAA tournaments. And Conradt led her team's transition from the Southwest Conference to the newly formed Big 12 in 1996. On December 18, 1997, before a crowd of 6,260 screaming home fans, UT defeated Northwestern, 89-86, to clinch Conradt's 700th coaching victory. With that win she

— continued on next page

became the eighth coach — and the first woman — in Division I basketball to hit the 700-win mark. Ironically, while she finished the season with 709 wins, the 1997-98 team wound up with a 12-15 record, only the second losing season in Conradt's UT career.

Along the way, Conradt had made enormous contributions to the evolution of the game, which now claims two professional women's leagues and status as an Olympic sport. She has coached future Olympians and Women's National Basketball Association players as well as 19 All-Americans, six Southwest Conference Players of the Year, a Broderick Award winner and other trophy winners. Throughout her career, Conradt has been known as a patient leader, a team motivator and a coach who rarely gets riled. Her first ejection from a game came during the frustrating 1997-98 season. "She is what sports purists appreciate in a competitor — a combination of grace, wit, intelligence and skill — coupled with a burning intensity to win. She is a great teacher of the game — as well as the ultimate player's coach," praises the UT media guide.

Conradt, who has doubled as director of the UT women's athletic department since 1992, has won numerous distinguished coaching awards. She is a three-time National Coach of the Year and five-time Southwestern Conference Coach of the Year, most recently in 1996. She received the Carol Eckman Award, the highest honor presented by the Women's Basketball Association, and in 1986 was inducted into the Texas Women's Hall of Fame. In 1995, she added induction into the International Women's Sports Hall of Fame to her long list of honors. She also managed, finally, to get the sexist word "Lady" dropped from the Longhorns name — no small feat in a world dominated by male sports writers.

In her 30-year career as a coach, Conradt has written her own book on women's college basketball — and in some ways has become a victim of her own success. Just as Conradt went searching for tough challengers in her early days as UT coach, other coaches later brought their teams to Austin to face the best — and to learn. Today, powerhouse programs now vie with UT for the country's top high school talent — and UT's dominance over the sport has slipped. But you couldn't tell that by Longhorns fans.

Attendance at women's games has skyrocketed from about 1,550 fans per game in 1981-82 to more than 8,000 screaming supporters most recently. Over the past 18 years, the Longhorns have attracted more fans than any other team in women's basketball history.

Now Conradt has the Hall of Fame to add to her list of honors. As is fitting for a great coach of the game, Conradt was elected for enshrinement in the Springfield, Massachusetts, hall along with one of the sport's all-time great players, the former Boston Celtic and current NBA coach Larry Bird.

"When you love the game of basketball the way I do and have had it be such a part of your life, you think of the Hall of Fame as the ultimate," Conradt told reporters. "It's made me reflect back on how all this happened. It's pretty amazing."

INSIDERS' TIP

Bevo, the live Longhorn steer that serves as the UT mascot, made his first appearance at a UT football game on Thanksgiving Day 1916. Bevo, by the way, was the name of a Budweiser near-beer product that was popular around campus during that period.

son tickets also are available. This exciting team has helped prove to the world that an outstanding professional women's basketball league was long overdue. Take your children, especially your girls, to watch the Houston Comets demonstrate what women can do when they take the court.

Major League Baseball

Houston Astros

Astrodome, 8400 Kirby Dr., Houston • (713) 6-ASTROS Ticketmaster

Established in 1962 as the Houston Colt .45s, the team became the Astros in 1965 and moved into the then-new Houston Astrodome, a huge complex that seats more than 54,000 baseball fans. The Astros have won several Central Division pennants, including in 1997 and 1998, but haven't yet made it to the World Series. The team is building a new state-of-the-art facility in downtown Houston and expects to move to the as-yet-unnamed ball park for the season opener in the year 2000. Individual tickets range in price from $4 to $18 and can be purchased through the Ticketmaster number listed above or on game day at the Astrodome box office. Season and group tickets are available by calling (713) 799-9567. The regular season runs April through September.

Texas Rangers

The Ballpark at Arlington, 1000 Ballpark Way, Arlington • (817) 273-5222, (817) 273-5100 ticket office

Formerly the Washington Senators, the team came to Dallas in 1972 as the Texas Rangers. The Rangers, coached by Johnny Oates, have had a large and loyal following over the years and in 1996 and 1998 treated fans to an American League West division championship. The Rangers also hosted the 1995 All-Star Game. Playing since 1994 in a $191 million, state-of-the-art complex, the Rangers claim one of the top stadiums in the country. Even if you're not a baseball fan, The Ballpark is a sight to behold. In addition to the 49,166 seats and boxes, The Ballpark features the Legends of the Game Baseball Museum, which contains some 1,000 artifacts baseball artifacts from the 1800s to the present, including some items on loan from the National Baseball Hall of Fame. The complex also features a children's learning center with interactive exhibits, a youth ballpark and a 12-acre lake.

Tickets can be charged by phone through the number listed above. Individual ticket prices range from $4 to $30. While tickets are sold at the door, it's best to order your tickets early as these games can and do sell out.

University of Texas Sports

Longhorns Football

Darrell K Royal-Memorial Stadium, 23rd St. and Campus Dr. • (512) 477-6060 UTTM box office

No sporting event in Austin comes close to Texas football for the sheer number of burnt-orange-clad fans that turn out to support this team. An average of 74,000 Longhorns fans — students, Texas Exes and just plain football buffs — unite as one big family in Darrell K Royal-Memorial Stadium when the Longhorns play at home. In fact, Texas football is so popular here that many times over the years fans have stood to watch hotly contested games, jamming the stadium to way over capacity.

To attend a UT football game is to become part of a Texas tradition that dates back more than a century. Established in 1893, the Longhorns have left an impressive mark on national collegiate football.

INSIDERS' TIP

If you're interested in attending a professional sporting event in our extended sports region, be sure to check with the team about special discount packages. Many teams offer mini-packages or family packages for certain games.

Over the years, Longhorn loyalists have been rewarded with a number of national and conference titles and more than three dozen NCAA post-season bowl games. They have been treated to performances by Heisman Trophy-winner and future NFL Hall-of-Famer Earl Campbell (1974-1977), now an Austin resident, as well as by dozens of All Americans, future NFL players and other trophy winners. In 1996 the Longhorns defeated Nebraska to win the first-ever Big 12 Conference championship. In 1998 senior halfback Ricky Williams had already broken eight national records by the time this book went to press and was charging toward the national career rushing record held by Tony Dorsett. Needless to say, Williams was on a short list of Heisman Trophy candidates. The list of accolades for this team goes on and on. Mack Brown, former head coach of the North Carolina Tar Heels, became Texas' 28th head football coach in 1998, succeeding John Mackovic, who, despite the 1996 Big 12 championship, presided over a rare losing season for the Longhorns the following season.

Known simply as Memorial Stadium since it was inaugurated in 1924, UT added legendary head football coach Darrell K Royal's name to the stadium in 1996. Royal had led the Longhorns to three national championships and 11 Southwest Conference titles in his 20 seasons at UT (1957-1976). A major renovation and enlargement of the stadium in 1998 raised the seating capacity of the 75,512-seat concrete facility by several thousand and included the addition of a 16-row upper deck on the east side of the stadium and 1,600 field-level seats as well as construction of 52 stadium suites and a club room designed for 1,200 people. The five or six seasonal home games are usually played on Saturday afternoons during the fall football season, which runs from September through November. It's best to get your tickets early as these games can sell out, although the new expanded stadium should make it easier to get tickets for all but the most hotly contested games.

Longhorns Baseball

Disch-Falk Field, I-35 and Martin Luther King Dr. • (512) 471-3333, (800) 982-BEVO

UT baseball fans from across Austin share the blissful moment of striding past the turnstile, ticket in hand, through the stadium tunnel and into the arena that is widely recognized as the best collegiate baseball facility in the country. This team, founded in 1895, has won 64 Southwest Conference titles, appeared in the NCAA College World Series 27 times and taken home the national championship in four of those series, the latest in 1983.

Disch-Falk Field, built in 1975 at a cost of $2.5 million and named for two former Longhorn coaches, holds 5,000 baseball fans in the main chair-back area and can be expanded to hold more. As many as 8,000 fans have packed this facility for important, hotly contested collegiate games. Average attendance in 1997 ran about 4,455 fans, making this one UT sporting event in which tickets can most often be purchased at the gate.

While Round Rock is first breaking ground on a stadium for a Double A franchise, and the Houston Astros and Texas Rangers are just more than three hours away, Longhorns baseball offers fans the enjoyment of precise college ball right here at home.

The Longhorns play an average of 30 home games a year during the January through May season.

Longhorns Softball

McCombs Field, Martin Luther King Dr. and Comal St. • (512) 471-3333, (800) 982-BEVO

Just a home run's distance from home plate at Disch-Falk Field is McCombs Field, a new $4.5-million softball complex that's arguably one of the best in the country. In just its second season at varsity-level play, the UT women's collegiate softball team brought this stadium to life in 1998, winning the NCAA regionals and earning a berth in the College World Series to become perhaps the youngest team ever to make it to the series.

Pitcher Christa Williams, a 1996 Olympic gold medalist on the U.S. women's softball team, was the only player in the NCAA to rank in the top five in four categories: earned run average (0.46), total strike-outs (364), strike-outs per game (11.1) and saves (5 for the season). Williams and Nikki Cockrell (shortstop/ second base) were named First Team All Americans while shortstop Jodi Reeves was named a Second Team All American.

This young team is led by coach Connie Clark, a former All American and winner of the 1987 Broderick Award as the national player of the year. The Longhorns play about 11 home games, most double headers, during the regular season, which runs February through April. These games can and do sell out, so get your tickets early.

Longhorns Basketball

Frank Erwin Center, 1701 Red River St. • (512) 471-3333, (512) 477-6060 UTTM box office

Few teams on the UT campus have captured the attention and admiration of Austin sports fans like our women's basketball team. Over the past 18 years, the team has attracted the most fans in women's basketball history with a total attendance of well over 1.4 million. Success on the court is the reason. Led by Coach Jody Conradt since 1976 (see our Close-up of Conradt in this chapter), the Longhorns have won a stunning 80 percent of their games.

During the 14-year history of the Southwest Conference, the Longhorns took 10 regular-season titles and won nine conference tournaments. In 1986, the Longhorns became the first women's basketball team in the history of the National Collegiate Athletic Association to record a perfect season with a 34-0 record. The Longhorns, who moved to the Big 12 conference for the 1996-97 season, draw an average of more than 5,000 fans to the Frank Erwin Center for the approximately 16 home games played during the regular season, which runs November through February.

Runnin' Horns

Frank Erwin Center, 1701 Red River St. • (512) 471-3333, (512) 477-6060 UTTM box office

With crowds averaging 13,000 fans for each home game, UT's Runnin' Horns men's basketball team is one of the biggest draws in town —and in college basketball anywhere. Founded in 1906, the Horns were members of the Southwest Conference (SWC) from 1915 to 1996. During that time the Horns racked up an impressive 22 SWC titles (12 outright) and a 648-449 total record. In 1997, the Horns along with Southwest Conference members Baylor, Texas A&M and Texas Tech merged with Big Eight teams to form the Big 12. The Runnin' Horns hold court for regular season games at the Erwin Center November through February.

The Best of the Rest

Car Racing

Thunder Hill Raceway, 24601 I-35, Kyle • (512) 262-1352

Located just off Interstate 35 Exit 210 about 25 miles south of Austin, Thunder Hill Raceway presents exciting racing events every Saturday evening from March through September. This is not a sport to watch, it's a sport to experience as the cars speed around a 3/8-mile oval asphalt track, sometimes faster than 120 miles per hour. Thunder Hill, Central Texas' newest and most modern track, opened in 1998 and features a 3,600-seat open-air stadium. The raceway presents hobby stock cars, super stocks, and limited late models regularly and each week also adds a special feature race, such as Texas pro sedans, super late models and American race trucks.

Thunder Hill also sponsors RV shows, car shows, fairs as well as an ongoing live music concert series. Gates open at 5:30 PM. Racing starts at 7 PM. Tickets are on sale at the door. Admission is $10 for adults, $7.50 for

INSIDERS' TIP

Texas law allows ticket brokers to resell tickets at higher than the face value — sometimes much higher. So if you're absolutely dying to see a game that is announced as sold out, or if you just want to get a great seat and are willing to pay the price, check the Yellow Pages under Tickets for any number of local ticket brokers.

Photo: Courtesy of the Austin Convention and Visitors Bureau

The Ice Bats have come to roost in Austin.

children ages six through 12. Children younger than six are admitted free.

Running

Austin Convention and Visitors Bureau, 201 E. Second St. • (512) 478-0098

Two Austin foot races draw lots of spectators each year. The Motorola Marathon, usually held the second Sunday of February, drew more than 2,100 runners in 1998 and is considered one of the fastest-growing events of its kind. Runners start in far Northwest Austin and wind up, hopefully, 26 kilometers later on the shores of Town Lake downtown. The winner gets $5,000. In April, Austin hosts the Capital 10,000, among the top 100 road races in the country. This 10K event draws about 15,000 competitors as well as crowds of spectators. (See our Parks and Recreation chapter for more information on running events and venues.)

Rodeos

Austin/Travis County Exposition and Heritage Center, 7311 Decker Ln. • (512) 467-9811, (512) 477-6060 UTTM box office

Yee haw!! There's nothing like a great rodeo to let you know you've arrived in Texas. Austin's big event is the annual Austin/Travis County Livestock Show & Rodeo held in mid-March. This huge competition, on the official Professional Rodeo Cowboys Association (PRCA) circuit, draws thousands and thousands of people from all over the state for 11 fun-filled days and nights of bull riding, calf roping, team roping, steer wrestling, barrel racing, saddle bronc riding, bareback riding and much, much more. This rodeo ranks 31st out of more than 750 PRCA rodeos in the nation in purse size and in 1996 awarded more than $134,000 in prize money.

Rodeo events aren't the only highlight of this celebration. The livestock show and auction culminates in the award for the Grand Champion Steer, which in 1997 sold for a record $50,000. This is also the Travis County Fair and as such offers fun for people of all ages. There's even a Kid's Town, which features a barnyard and petting zoo, children's shows and many contests, including the biggest bubble contest, the jump rope contest, the whistling contest and the cow-chip toss. To top it all off, the Rodeo features a major concert performance each evening. Brooks & Dunn, Merle Haggard, The Mavericks and many more outstanding musical performers have appeared at this wildly popular event.

There's more to the rodeo than meets the eye, however. Run by a nonprofit organization, the rodeo is also the largest nonprofit fund-raiser for educational programs in Travis County. In 1997 alone, the rodeo raised more than $1 million for educational programs and academic scholarships.

Of course, the largest and most well-known PRCA rodeo in Texas (and one of the largest in the country) is the Houston Livestock Show and Rodeo held toward the end of February in the Astrodome. Like the Austin event, the Houston rodeo offers live music entertainment every night as well as other events for the whole family. Waco, just 90 miles up Interstate 35, holds the annual Dodge Texas Circuit Finals Rodeo. This event, held around the New Year, features the top 15 finalists in all seven rodeo events for the state of Texas. San Antonio, 80 miles south of Austin on Interstate 35, also hosts one of the state's biggest rodeos in early February, while the prestigious Fort Worth rodeo is held in the latter part of January.

Once you've attended the Austin/Travis County Rodeo or any of our state's other outstanding rodeos, you may be hooked on cowboy culture for life. Two publications will keep you up to date on professional and amateur rodeo events around Texas and around the country. The first is the PRCA's official publication, *Prorodeo Sports News*. This magazine contains a calendar of events as well as articles pertaining to the circuit. Call 1-800-RODEO-4U to subscribe. Also of interest is *Cowboy Sports News*. Published in Sealy, Texas, this is the official publication of the Cowboys Professional Rodeo Association (CPRA). The CPRA, while it contains the term "professional" in its title, is an amateur organization. *Cowboy Sports News* lists literally hundreds of events of interest to amateur rodeo fans around Texas and is distributed free at feed and Western stores in Texas and other states. For paid subscriptions call (409) 885-1127.

Sailboat Racing

Austin Yacht Club, 5906 Beacon Dr. • (512) 266-1336

Austin wouldn't be Austin if it didn't have a spectator sport that took advantage of our great waterways. The Austin Yacht Club sponsors three major annual sailboat regattas as well as a number of other races throughout the year. The kickoff event for the summer season is the Turnback Canyon Regatta held over Memorial Day weekend. Lake Travis' oldest and most spectacular sailboat race, the Turnback Canyon event is held over 25 miles of winding river from Mansfield Dam to Lago Vista. This regatta, which began in the 1950s as the Bluebonnet Regatta, offers sailors a choice between competing in the two-day, 50-mile race or taking the same course in a more relaxed "cruising" mode. Nearly 100 boats compete in this great annual spectacle.

The Governor's Cup Regatta, held over

INSIDERS' TIP

While UT football is often just as exciting as any professional game, remember that this is a college game and, as such, no alcoholic beverages are sold or allowed in the stadium. The Texas Ex-Student's Association, fondly known as the Texas Exes, hosts a lively outdoor pregame celebration just across the street from the stadium on San Jacinto Street. They sell food, beer and soft drinks — and will tell you how to join the organization. The event is open to the public.

the Fourth of July and the weekend before, also draws a huge number of sailboats. This race, in which boats follow a course laid out by buoys, is held in the main basin at Lake Travis, the area just below Mansfield Dam. Centerboard boats race one weekend while the larger keel boats race the next.

The Fall Regatta features two races over two days. Racers sail from the Yacht Club to Lakeway and back the first day. A buoy race is held in the main basin on the second day.

Sailors may call the Yacht Club for information on how to participate in these events while those with sailing experience may post information about themselves on the club's bulletin board if they would like to crew these boats.

Spectators will find that the Turnback is best viewed from the Iguana Grill restaurant or Lakeway Inn. The Governor's Cup can best be seen from the Oasis Restaurant on Lake Travis, from Windy Point, an LCRA Lake on Comanche Trail, or from atop Mansfield Dam. The first day of the Fall Regatta is best viewed from the Iguana Grill or Lakeway Inn near the finish line. Always bring your binoculars for these events.

The Austin Yacht Club, founded in 1952, aims to promote the sport of sailboat racing. The club sponsors a summer sailing class for adults and camps for children.

Horse Racing

Manor Downs

U.S. Hwy. 290 E. and Manor Downs Rd., Manor • (512) 272-5581

Established in 1974 as a quarter horse race track for racing enthusiasts, Manor Downs became a parimutuel betting track in 1990 after Texas legalized that form of gambling. The Downs features live horse racing on weekends starting about 1:30 PM during the spring season (from about February to around the end of May). Manor Downs also offers simulcast racing from tracks around the country on screens at other times during the spring meet and throughout the year. While not the fanciest racetrack in Central Texas, Manor Downs is the closest Austinites can get to live horse racing. It's also a wonderful gathering place for the state's horsemen and women who come in from all over to take part in this age-old Texas tradition. The track features covered stadium-type wood seating as well as good old-fashioned picnic tables at track level — all the better for enjoying the barbecue, fajitas and grilled sandwiches served daily. There's also an air-conditioned Turf Club where, for an extra $5, you can sit at the more comfortable tables and chairs while watching the races on TV screens. Admission ranges from $2 to $8, seniors pay just $1 while children 12 and younger are admitted free. This track, just northeast of Austin, is easy to find. Just follow U.S. 290 East from the Interstate 35 junction for about 10 minutes. You can't miss the huge signs pointing the way to the track. Call the number listed for a recorded message of the racing schedule and the simulcast events of the day.

Retama Park

1 Retama Pkwy., Selma • (210) 651-7000

This ultramodern horse racing park features thoroughbred and quarterhorse racing May through June and thoroughbred racing late July to mid-October. Retama also offers simulcast racing year round from top tracks across the country, including the Kentucky Derby, Preakness, Belmont and the Breeders Cup. Retama has a spectacular indoor grandstand and clubhouse as well as a sports bar, and terrace dining. Live racing May to June meet begins at 6:30 PM Thursday through Saturday and 5 PM on Sunday. Races for the thoroughbred meet begin at 6:30 PM Wednesday through Saturday. General admission is $2.50. Simulcast admission is $1. Retama charges $5 extra for a reserved seat in the clubhouse. Selma is about 65 miles south of Austin on Interstate 35. Take the 174-A Exit and follow the signs. Retama is just west of the interstate.

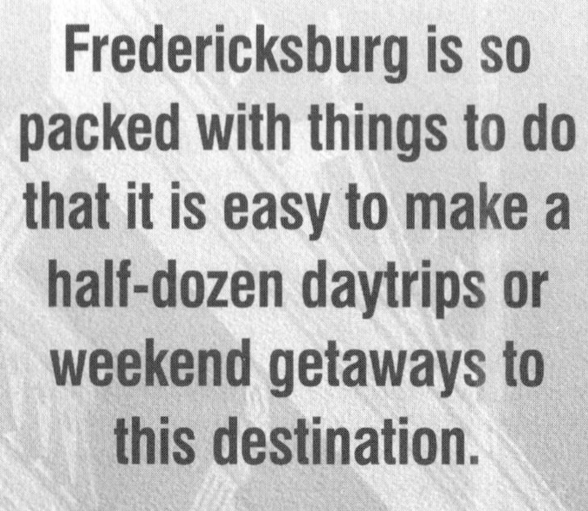

Fredericksburg is so packed with things to do that it is easy to make a half-dozen daytrips or weekend getaways to this destination.

Daytrips and Weekend Getaways

Covering 267,339 square miles, boasting hundreds of miles of seashore, soaring mountains, plunging valleys, vast plains and prairies, pine forests, deserts, islands, lakes of all sizes and shapes, giant metroplexes, small towns and wide open spaces galore, Texas is much more than a state — "It's a Whole Other Country," as our boosters like to say. At the very heart of it all, in spirit if not precise geographic center, lies Austin.

It's no wonder, then, that when Central Texans plan a vacation we often look no farther than our own great big bountiful backyard, so to speak. In fact, for the daytrips and weekend getaways we cover in this chapter, we can't even include all the fascinating sights Texas has to offer. Some are just too far away to make even a weekend trip feasible.

We've limited this section to those regions within a three-hour drive of Austin. That decision has forced us to leave out the Gulf of Mexico seashores at Padre Island, Galveston, Port Aransas and Corpus Christi. We had to bypass the Davis and Guadalupe Mountains and the breathtaking canyonlands of Big Bend National Park. (However, if you want to tour that area look for *The Insiders' Guide® to the Texas Coastal Bend*.) We're missing the Tex-Mex border cities of El Paso, Laredo and Brownsville. We had to skip the Big Thicket, pass over the Little River, shun East Texas and ignore West Texas.

"Could there possibly be anything else left?" the uninitiated among you may ask. You'll soon find out. In this chapter we'll take you on a brief tour of three of America's 10 largest cities: Dallas, Houston and San Antonio, all within a three-hour drive of Austin and each distinct in its own way. For the history buffs among you, we've included an entire section on San Antonio's famous missions, starting of course with the Alamo.

Another historic journey, though of more modern times, takes you to Johnson City, the boyhood home of our country's 36th president. We'll also introduce you to LBJ's beloved ranch, the "Texas White House" during the Johnson Administration, and the place where the elder statesman came home to retire following a lifetime of public service. Both of these areas make up the LBJ National Historic Park.

Not to overlook Texas' other U.S. President, we'll introduce you to Bryan/College Station, home of the new George Bush Presidential Library and Museum, site of the sprawling Texas A&M University and domicile of UT's archrivals, the A&M Aggies. There's plenty to see and do within the environs of these sister cities.

We'll tell you about Gruene, a former ghost town that emerged from ruin to become a thriving city, especially on weekends when the chicken-fried steak disappears faster than the time it takes to pronounce the city's name correctly. This is one place Austinites visit regularly to shop for antiques or to crowd into the historic Gruene Hall for an evening of first-class live music.

We had to include Round Top and Winedale, two communities east of Austin renowned as meccas of classical music and theater. One of the state's oldest communities, Round Top is home to the International Festival Institute, founded by a concert pianist. Winedale hosts the annual Shakespeare at

Winedale festival. Austinites flock to these cities throughout the year to partake of their great annual events and to step back in time.

The little town of Salado, just a stone's throw away from Austin, could have been a contender. An up-and-coming town in the 1880s, Salado was bypassed when the railroad finally came to Central Texas. While railroad towns thrived, Salado slipped into obscurity. Discovered by artists in the second half of the 20th century, Salado is now back on track, so to speak, and a popular daytrip from Austin.

Of course, we couldn't forget Fredericksburg, one of Austin's favorite weekend getaways and a prime example of Hill Country living. This quaint town, founded by German immigrants in 1846, boasts a Main Street that has earned a spot on the National Register of Historic Places. Main Street shops offering antiques, apparel and arts and crafts do a bustling business on weekends as visitors pour in from all over the region. This is one great place to spot a movie star or two, or perhaps just enjoy an authentic German meal.

Considering the important German influences on the culture and development of Central Texas over the past 150 years, it wouldn't do to mention just one German-infused town. New Braunfels, too, retains much of its German flavor, literally. From the great German restaurants to the annual Wurstfest sausage festival, New Braunfels is a delight for the taste buds. We'll give you two other reasons why this town attracts Central Texans year round.

Appropriately, the Highland Lakes come last. After you've spent even a little time trying to see all the sights Central Texas has to offer, you may need to just get away from it all and relax for awhile on a boat or on a beach. Any one of the four lakes we describe in this section will do the trick.

Before you head out, check our Annual Events and Festivals chapter for events in these daytrip destinations. Also, have a look at our Texas Pronunciation Guide in the Area Overview chapter so you'll sound like an Insider when you get there.

Whether you decide to head north, south, east or west to major cities, small towns or a place of quiet solitude, you're sure to find a spot that is Texas through and through.

Up North

Salado

The Village of Salado, 55 miles north of Austin on I-35, is just that — a village and a charming one that owes its existence now to the fact that history passed it by. Founded in 1859 at a low water crossing of Salado Creek, it looked like Salado was destined to become a growing community, especially with the founding of Salado College in 1859. By 1884, the community was on its way to being a town with seven churches, 14 stores, two hotels, two blacksmiths and three cotton gins. But when the railroads were built to the north and east, Salado slipped back to being a village.

Salado's population dwindled from 900 in 1882 to 400 by 1914 and only slightly over 200 in 1950, according to the community's publications. But then artists and artisans began to settle in the area, buying up the old buildings, opening art galleries and antiques shops. Now the village has more than 130 businesses and attracts weekend visitors who come here to relax, browse the stores and soak up the area's history.

One of the best ways to learn about the area is to request a copy of the Driving Tour Tape prepared by the Bell County Historical Commission. Visitors can write to the Bell County Historical Commission, Bell County Courthouse, Belton, TX 76513, or ask at one of Salado's landmarks, like the Stagecoach Inn, 1 Main Street, on the east side of I-35, (254) 947-5111.

The modern, 82-room Stagecoach Inn stands adjacent to what remains of the Shady Villa Hotel where Sam Houston was said to have slept in 1850. Other famous guests include General George Armstrong Custer, and cattlemen Charles Goodnight and Shanghai Pierce, who stopped at this historic spot along the Chisholm Trail.

What remains of the old hotel is part of the inn's restaurant, which also includes an open-air atrium built around a 500-year-old burr oak. Newer dining rooms adjoining the original two-story, clapboard building serve guests at lunch and dinner, but in keeping with tradition the waitresses always recite the menu by heart — prime rib, plate-size steaks, fried chicken, baked ham and lamb, plus desserts such as homemade pie and cobbler.

Salado abounds with historical connections. In the 1830s Sterling C. Robertson, himself of Scottish descent, established a colony here; many of the settlers were Scots. In November, Salado hosts the Annual Gathering of the Clans on the Village Green near the Stagecoach Inn. Hundreds of Texans and Americans of Scottish descent descend on Salado for the weekend festival. Call (254) 947-5232 for information. Another famous Salado native, with Scottish ties of her own, is Liz Carpenter, former press secretary to Lady Bird Johnson and now an Austin writer.

Visitors also flock to Salado for the annual Salado Christmas Stroll & Holiday Home Tour, usually held on the first two weekends of December. Salado is a favorite choice of Central Texans for Christmas shopping and celebrating the season, so the village's hotels and guesthouses are booked in advance. There is also a large July Fourth picnic, a summer art fair in August and a December village artists' sale. Call the Salado Chamber of Commerce, (254) 947-5040, for information on these events. At the Table Rock Amphitheater, (254) 947-9205, an outdoor dinner theater in the community, the Tablerock Theatre group puts on annual performances of a historical pageant, *Salado Legends*, during the summer and dramatizations of Dickens' *Christmas Carol* in December.

There are more than 130 buildings in Salado that are listed on the National Register of Historic Buildings, and several of them serve as guesthouses and bed and breakfast inns. Some are small cottages with cozy fireplaces, while others are large Victorian homes. Some are located in rural settings, others are just a few steps from the shopping district. For a complete listing of hotel facilities, call the Salado Chamber of Commerce at (254) 947-5040. Duffers may want to ask about The Mill Creek Country Club & Guest Houses, (254) 947-5141, which has a Robert Trent Jones II 18-hole golf course as well as swimming and tennis facilities.

The old homes also offer romantic and charming backdrops for dining in Salado. Several serve lunch and afternoon tea, including Browning's Courtyard Cafe on Salado Square, (254) 947-8666; Cathy's Boardwalk Cafe, (254) 947-8162; and the Pink Rose Tea Room on Main Street, (254) 947-9110. Gourmet dinners are served on weekends at the Inn on the Creek, (254) 947-5554, a Victorian bed and breakfast on Center Circle. Reservations are required. Pietro's Italian Restaurant & Pizzeria, 302 N. Main Street, (254) 947-0559, offers a change of pace for lunch and dinner. The Range at the Barton House, Main Street, (254) 947-3828, offers American cuisine with French and Mediterranean touches for lunch and dinner Wednesday through Sunday. No Texas village would be complete without Mexican food, which can be enjoyed at The Salado Mansion, Main Street, (254) 947-5157. Mexican food served in an 1857 mansion — no place but Salado.

Sustenance is necessary in Salado since the village has so many shops it is impossible to list them all here. There are herbalists, antiques dealers, custom furniture stores — Barnhill-Britt sells handcrafted furniture constructed of antique longleaf pine taken from 19th-century Texas buildings; Benton's has custom-order iron beds — Amish quilts, children's fashions, Oriental rugs, Christmas ornaments, folk art, bride's gifts, rare books,

INSIDERS' TIP

Traveling around Texas by car will eventually lead you to a two-lane state highway. When these highways have wide shoulders, it's customary for slower vehicles to drive on the shoulder briefly to allow faster cars to pass. Frankly, we don't know if that's legal, but it's the Texas way.

top women's fashion (Grace Jones, One Royal Street, occupies a building that was the Salado bank and attracts customers from all over the country), native plants, tribal art, gourmet foods, jewelry and rabbits everywhere (Sir Wigglesworth, Rock Creek at Main, a Salado Christmas favorite), paintings and sculpture (The Windberg Gallery, Main Street, features the work of famed Texas artist Dalhart Windberg) and on and on.

Salado is an unincorporated village, but the chamber of commerce estimates the population of permanent residents is about 1,500 — which means there is a shop for about every 10 residents in the area. Most of the shops are open daily, although some do close on Sunday. Most are in the immediate area of Main Street. The chamber has several brochures that list shops, accommodations and attractions in the area. Call them at (254) 947-5040 for information.

From Salado, you could return to Austin or continue up Interstate 35 to the fast-paced world of the Dallas/Fort Worth Metroplex.

Dallas/Fort Worth

While many audacious Austinites make the 400-mile round-trip drive or half-hour flights to and from this sprawling metroplex in one day, there are just too many things to see and do for us to suggest you do the same. This is definitely a weekend getaway destination. The big dilemma if you're driving up is deciding which way to go once you pass Hillsboro where Interstate 35 divides. West will take you to Fort Worth, known fondly as Cowtown. This city proudly proclaims itself as the place "where the West begins." Don't be fooled by the lingo, though, this city is a cultural wonderland. East will take you to sophisticated Dallas, the Big D to those who realize its size translates into grandeur. Both offer an astonishing assortment of things to do, places to go, people to see. We'll point out some of the highlights.

This is an exciting area, encompassing many cities in addition to Fort Worth and Dallas. Arlington and Irving are just two of the larger suburbs. Whatever you choose to visit, you'll find that the metroplex is user friendly and sure to please. Note, also, that this region has perfected a light rail system that Austin has only dreamed about. If you don't want to hassle with parking or trying to find your way around town, check the schedule and routes for the area's DART light rail system, (214) 979-1111. You'll be amazed at how efficiently it operates and how many places it serves.

Home to the annual Texas State Fair in September and October, Dallas' Fair Park attracts tourists throughout the year. This area has been home to Texas state fairs for more than 100 years. New facilities were built here to house the Texas Centennial Exposition of 1936. Now a National Historic Landmark because of its collection of art deco buildings from the period, Fair Park is a 277-acre city park that includes museums, sports venues, entertainment complexes, an aquarium and more. Call the Fair Park administrative offices at (214) 670-8400 or the hotline at (214) 421-9600 to find out about the following venues. Located east of downtown Dallas and bounded by Cullum Boulevard and Fitzhugh, Parry and Washington avenues, Fair Park is a must see. Of course, the Cotton Bowl Stadium is always a big draw. Besides the annual New Year's Day game, the stadium also hosts the annual "Red River War" football game between UT and the University of Oklahoma in the fall as well as a variety of other football games and sporting events. The Coca Cola Starplex Amphitheater, (214) 712-7518, is a 20,000-seat entertainment venue hosting more than three dozen major concerts each year. The Music Hall seats 3,420 people and hosts theater, music and opera events throughout the year. The Coliseum is a great place to see sporting events, including rodeos, polo matches and horse shows.

Fair Park also is home to the African American Museum, (214) 565-9026, at 3536 Grand Avenue. This is the most complete facility in the Southwest dedicated to African-American art, history and culture. The museum also sponsors regular free jazz concerts and other events. It's closed Mondays only, but hours vary. Admission is free. Nearby is the Dallas Museum of Natural History, (214) 421-3466. The Hall of Prehistoric Texas, which includes the nation's largest prehistoric sea turtle, is just one of the many attractions of this facility. Also here is a hands-on discovery center for children, called City Safari. It's open daily, except for major holidays. General admission is

Photo: Peter A. Silva

The splendor of Texas bluebonnets makes for a special trip to Johnson City.

$5. Children of all ages will love The Dallas Aquarium, (214) 670-8443. Located at First Street and Martin Luther King Boulevard the aquarium is easy to spot. It's right in front of Fair Park's giant Ferris wheel. Open daily, the aquarium is home to almost 4,000 sea creatures. Ask about regular times for shark and piranha feedings, which are preceded by a short talk. General admission is $2. The Age of Steam Railroad Museum, (214) 428-0101, at 1105 Washington Street features more than four dozen pieces of historic railroad equipment, including actual railroad cars dating to the early 1900s. The Museum is open Thursday through Sunday only. General admission is $3. The Science Place and TI Founders IMAX Theater, 1318 Second Avenue, (214) 428-5555, is open seven days a week. This hands-on science center is literally packed with exhibits to delight children of all ages. And don't miss out on the opportunity to see an IMAX movie on the giant screen or attend a sky show in the planetarium. General admission is $6; IMAX shows cost extra.

The Dallas Museum of Art, 1717 N. Harwood Street, (214) 922-1200, in the Arts District is among the city's major attractions. Opened at this new location in 1984, the DMA became the centerpiece of this new district on the northern edge of the downtown business district. The DMA owns a significant collection of art dating from prehistoric to modern times. The museum also hosts regular traveling exhibitions. It's open Tuesday through Friday from 11 AM to 4 PM, later on Thursdays, and weekends from 11 AM to 5 PM. General admission is free, although there could be a charge for special exhibits. Another highlight of this district is the Morton H. Meyerson Symphony Center, (214) 629-0202, at 2301 Flora Street. Designed by renowned architect I. M. Pei, the center is home to the Dallas Symphony Orchestra. Call about performances or for tours of this elegant center.

One perennial favorite of visitors from around the world is Dealey Plaza, where President John F. Kennedy was assassinated while passing through in a motorcade on November 22, 1963. Now a National Historic Landmark District, the plaza features a lovely park with a JFK memorial plaque. Of course, the controversial "grassy knoll" is here too. Dealey Plaza is in downtown Dallas near the West End District. Nearby is The Sixth Floor Museum, (214) 747-6660, at 411 Elm Street. Alleged JFK assassin Lee Harvey Oswald is said to have fired the fatal shots from an open window on the sixth floor of what was then the Texas School Book Depository (now the Dallas County Administration Building). While both the Kennedy family and the city of Dallas resisted efforts to memorialize this site, public interest remained so intense through the years that a museum was finally opened. Among the many fascinating exhibits here are hundreds of photographs, documentary films and a large-scale model of Dealey Plaza prepared by the Warren Commission, which investigated the assassination. The museum is open daily. General admission is $5.

If you're one of those Americans who reject the Warren Commission findings that Lee Harvey Oswald was the lone gunman who killed JFK, you might want to check out The Conspiracy Museum, (214) 741-3040, at 110 S. Market Street. In addition to displays furthering the debate over who actually killed Kennedy, visitors will find exhibits dedicated to theories on the assassinations of Robert Kennedy, Martin Luther King, President Lincoln and others. The museum is open daily 10 AM to 6 PM. General admission is $7.

While Austin isn't a paradise of major league sporting events, Dallas is close enough to provide adequate stimulation for sports fans of every variety. The ever-popular Dallas Cowboys, (972) 579-5000, (800) 567-9418, play at Texas Stadium in nearby Irving at 2401 E. Airport Freeway. The Texas Rangers, (817) 273-5100, major league baseball team play at The Ballpark at Arlington, 1000 Ballpark Way. The Ballpark itself is a great tourist destination, featuring the Legends of the Game Baseball Museum, a children's learning center with interactive exhibits, a youth ballpark and a 12-acre lake. For the time being the NBA Dallas Mavericks, (972) 988-DUNK, (800) 634-MAVS, are playing at Reunion Arena at 777 Sports Street. By the season opener in the year 2000, however, the team plans to move to a new stadium.

Another exciting place to visit is Deep Ellum, a revitalized district filled with theaters, restaurants, night clubs, shops and galleries. Centered around Elm Street east of downtown, this district got its name because locals thought of the area as the deep end of Elm Street, and shortened it to Deep Ellum. During its heyday in the 1930s and '40s, Deep Ellum was the principal cultural district of Dallas' African-American community. Clubs here drew some of the most renowned local acts of the time, including Leadbelly and Blind Lemon Jefferson, who went on to national fame. The area deteriorated after World War II, but in recent years it has made a big comeback. While you won't lack for food in this area, you might try one of the nicer, more upscale restaurants, the Green Room, (214) 748-7666, at 2715 Elm Street. It always seems to be crowded, perhaps it's the eclectic menu. It's open daily for dinner.

The sparkling downtown Dallas skyline can best be viewed from the 50-story Reunion Tower at the Hyatt Regency Dallas Hotel, (214) 651-1234 or (800) 233-1234, at 300 Reunion Boulevard. And you don't have to be a guest of this upscale hotel, a downtown landmark, to enjoy the view. The tower, topped by a geodesic dome, features three levels. The Lookout is an indoor-outdoor observation deck that offers a 360-degree view of the city. The next level up is the Antares Restaurant, (214) 712-7145, which slowly rotates to provide a bird's-eye view of the city while you're dining. It's open for lunch, dinner and Sunday brunch. At the very top is The Dome, which also rotates. This is the hotel's cocktail lounge and the perfect place to enjoy a drink before — or after — a night on the town.

The renowned Dallas Zoo, (214) 670-8626, at 650 S. R.L. Thorton Freeway was 110 years old in 1998 — and still growing. This 100-acre park, about 3 miles south of downtown, features more than 2,000 animals. Zoo North allows visitors a close-up view of red pandas, ocelots, wallabies and more and includes the Bird and Reptile Building and the Rainforest Aviary. The 25-acre Wilds of Africa section of the park has been named the best African zoo exhibit in the country. It's open daily. General admission is $5.

Stargazers will want to take a tour of The National Museum of Communications and The Movie Studios at Las Colinas, (972) 869-3456, at 6301 N. O'Connor Road, Building One, in Irving. Touted as the only working movie studio between the two coasts, The Movie Studios at Las Colinas offer visitors a chance to see inside, though not while movies are shooting. The museum includes a massive collection of communications equipment and movie memorabilia. Daily tours cost about $13 for adults.

Who needs to go to Paris or New York to shop when Dallas is right up the road? Dallas, of course, is home to the original Neiman Marcus store, which opened in 1907 and quickly put this city on the national fashion map. Today, Dallas is a retail giant, filled with hundreds of shops offering everything from designer fashions to discount goods. Start your tour of the Dallas shopping scene at the original Neiman Marcus store, (214) 573-5800, at 1618 Main Street. Now the chain's flagship store it features a 5th floor exhibit on its history as well as plenty of upscale items to purchase. The Galleria, (214) 702-7100, at Interstate 635 and Dallas Parkway N. is another Dallas shopping experience. This four-level mall, which includes an ice skating rink, features more than 200 stores. Saks Fifth Avenue, Macy's Marshall Field's and many other shops are here, as are plenty of restaurants. Northpark Center, (214) 363-7441, at Northwest Highway and North Central Expressway is another popular upscale mall. It has a major Neiman Marcus store as well as a Lord & Taylor, Barney New York and many other department stores and specialty shops. For a unique shopping experience, try The Crescent, (214) 871-8500, at 200 Cedar Springs. This crescent-shaped complex includes a small, but well-selected collection of antiques and specialty shops, art galleries and restaurants. Those looking for high-fashion Western wear should check out Henry Jackalope, (214) 692-8928, at 6731 Snider Plaza. This shop features clothing by top designers. The Dallas Farmer's Market, (214) 939-2808, is one of the largest in the country. Open daily year round, the market is filled with stalls offering fresh produce, herbs, flowers and more. The market, at 1010 S. Pearl, spreads over four city blocks.

If you have children along who've grown tired of the shops and the museums, give them a break at Six Flags Over Texas, (817) 640-8900, in Arlington at Interstate 30 and Texas Highway 360. This giant amusement park, featuring more than 100 attractions, brings in visitors from around the world. Hours vary according to the season. Admission is $37.65 for adults, $31.20 for children 48 inches and shorter. Across Interstate 30 is Six Flags Hurricane Harbor, (817) 265-3356, said to be America's largest water park. Admission is $25.85 for adults and $17.19 for children 48 inches and shorter. It's open May through September. Hours vary.

If you are planning to spend the night in Dallas, you're choices are virtually limitless. While you can usually expect to spend about $20 a night more than you would in Austin for a good quality chain motel, the varieties and locations will put you close to about anywhere you want to be in town. Of course, if you're looking for that truly special weekend getaway, and have the money to spend, the Mansion on Turtle Creek, (214) 559-2100 or (800) 527-5432, at 2821 Turtle Creek Boulevard is considered one of the best hotels in the United States. This nine-story Italian Renaissance-style mansion was built in the 1920s by a cattle baron. You'll feel as if you've reached nirvana. The restaurant here is also top of the line. Another historic, and upscale, choice in lodging is The Adolphus Hotel, (214) 742-8200 or (800) 221-9083, at 1321 Commerce Street downtown. Built by brewery magnate Adolphus Busch in 1912, this hotel is the only one to survive the Dallas' downtown grand hotel era. It's a perfect place from which to explore the downtown historic district and pamper yourself at the same time.

Dining can be anything from a quick and casual home-style meal to a full-blown elegant multi-course affair, like you'd find at the Mansion on Turtle Creek. One of Dallas' favorite steakhouses is Del Frisco's, (972) 490-9000, at 5251 Spring Valley. It's expensive, but the beef is out of sight. For a real down home and inexpensive restaurant, try Celebration, (214) 351-5681, at 4503 W. Lovers Lane out near Love Field. It features such items as pot roast, fried catfish, meat loaf — you get the picture. Another nearby casual restaurant is Kathleen's Art Cafe, (214) 691-2355, at 4424 Lovers Lane. This cafe focuses on New American cuisine. For good and inexpensive Italian food, we suggest Campisi's Egyptian Inn, (214) 827-0355, at 5610 Mockingbird Lane, about 4 miles north of downtown. It's open for lunch and dinner daily.

The Dallas Convention & Visitors Bureau, (214) 746-2677 or (800) C-DALLAS, is at 1201 Elm Street, Suite 2000. Check with the bureau for more information about this city or to request an information packet by mail.

If you've decided to take that left branch of Interstate 35 and head toward Fort Worth, you'll find many exciting weekend activities designed to enlighten or entertain.

Among our most favorite Fort Worth gems is the Kimball Art Museum, (817) 654-1034, at 333 Camp Bowie Boulevard in what is known as the Cultural District west of downtown. This area is bounded by Camp Bowie Boulevard, University Drive and Montgomery Street. The museums we've listed in this district are open Tuesday through Sunday with varying hours. Admission is free, except where noted. The Kimball maintains a huge permanent collection, including works by Picasso, Monet, Rembrandt and many other masters, and offers excellent touring shows throughout the year. There is an admission charge for special exhibits only. If you're too immersed in the art to leave for lunch, the buffet here offers some interesting choices. The Modern Art Museum of Fort Worth, (817) 738-9215, at 1309 Montgomery Street is the oldest art museum in the state. It focuses on modern and contemporary American and European art. Also in this district is the Amon Carter Museum, (817) 738-1933, at 3501 Camp Bowie Boulevard, which focuses on American art. Carter, who founded *The Fort Worth Star-Telegram*, bequeathed his collection of Western art to the city along with a foundation to establish a museum. The museum resembles an American Indian lodge.

The Fort Worth Museum of Science and History, (817) 732-1631, at 1501 Montgomery Street is a delightful place to take children because of the many hands-on exhibits. This huge museum includes nine permanent galleries that cover science and history from prehistoric to modern times. There's also a planetarium and OMNI theater. It's open daily. General admission is $5. Admission to the planetarium and the theater is extra. The sprawling Fort Worth Botanic Garden, (817) 871-7689, also is here at 3220 Botanic Garden Drive. This delightful center is chock-full of specialty gardens and features more than 150,000 plants. It's open daily. General admission is free, although there is a small charge to enter the Japanese Garden and the Conservatory. The Will Rogers Memorial Center, (817) 871-8150, is at Amon Carter Square in this district. The center hosts the annual Southwestern Exposition and Livestock Show as well as equestrian events of all kinds. Named for noted cowboy humorist Will Rogers, the center features a statue of Rogers on horseback.

Another area that attracts oodles of tourists is The Stockyards National Historic District north of downtown. This district, along N. Main Street from 23rd to 28th streets encompasses the old stockyards that were once the second largest in the country. The cattle pens here once spread out as far as the eye could see, holding livestock for slaughter by the on-site meat packing plants. Only a fraction of the pens remain today, but they are still put to good use, both as a reminder of days gone by and as useful holding pens for the livestock auctions held here. The Stockyards Collection and Museum, (817) 625-5087, in the Stockyards Livestock Exchange Building at 131 E. Exchange Avenue is a few rooms dedicated to the glory days of the stockyards, the meatpacking industry and the railroads that made it all happen. The museum is open Monday through Saturday 10 AM to 5 PM. Donations are welcome.

You'll also find boutiques, gift shops and saloons in this district as well as many other attractions. Stop in at the Stockyards Visitor Center, (817) 624-4741, at 130 E. Exchange Avenue to pick up information about Stockyards attractions and about attractions and lodgings around the city. The center is open daily. A guided walking tour of this district also starts here. It costs about $7. You can also board the Tarantula Steam Train, (817) 654-0898, here to experience the thrill of passenger train travel. One of the major attractions in this area is Billy Bob's Texas, (817) 624-7117, at 2520 Rodeo Plaza, the world's largest honky-tonk. Seeing is believing. This club features 40 bar stations, two dance floors and still has room for a rodeo arena where, on weekends, you can watch rodeo cowboys ride the bulls. Of course, live music is a major attraction, presented nightly. Admission varies between $1 and $9 depending on the day and time.

One of our favorite Fort Worth Tex-Mex restaurants is near the stockyards at 2201 N. Commerce Street. Joe T. Garcia's, (817) 626-4356, has been called one of America's best grassroots restaurants by the James Beard Foundation. Still, prices are moderate and the food is excellent. It's open for lunch and dinner daily. Last we heard, the restaurant still didn't accept credit cards. On the other hand, while you're at the Stockyards you might want a sample of what made this district famous — steak. Cattlemen's Steakhouse, (817) 624-3945, has been serving up great steaks from its location at 2458 N. Main Street for more than half a century. And the prices are very reasonable. Cattlemen's is open daily for lunch and dinner. Of course, the menu includes non-steak items too.

Don't miss out on Sundance Square district in the beautifully restored area of historic downtown, bounded by Throckmorton, Calhoun, Second and Fifth streets. The Fort Worth Convention and Visitors Bureau, (817) 336-8791 or (800) 433-5747, is at 415 Throckmorton Street. This is a good place to stock up on free maps and pamphlets describing fun things to do throughout Fort Worth. The entertainment district, named for the famous Western outlaw the Sundance Kid, is now filled with specialty shops, art galleries, night clubs, restaurants, theaters and more. One of our favorite restaurants is in this district. Reata, (817) 336-1009, at 500 Throckmorton Street on the 35th floor offers a fantastic view of the city along with modern Tex-Mex and Texas fare. And it's moderately priced. Reata is open daily for lunch and dinner.

Whether you're heading to Dallas/Fort Worth or plan to spend several days exploring the entire metroplex, be sure to check in with the visitors centers or read the local newspapers for a listing of special events. In addition to some wonderful annual events and festivals in the area, you also might happen upon performances by the many outstanding classical performance companies — ballet, opera, symphony, for example — that add to the allure of this region. Of course, there are also plenty of live musical performers around town.

Down South

San Antonio

A perfect daytrip and an even better weekend getaway, the home of the venerable Alamo is one of Texas' largest and most exciting cities — and one of the top tourist destinations in the state. Just 80 miles south of Austin on Interstate 35, this Mexican-American-flavored city pulsates with activity day and night and is a second home to many Austinites who regularly make the trip for professional sporting events, rock concerts, amusement parks, shopping and to see the sights again and again.

Start off your visit downtown at The Alamo, (210) 225-1391, Texas' most famous shrine. Read about the colorful history of this building in our subsequent section on the San Antonio Missions. The Alamo and museum featuring Alamo relics and more are open Monday through Saturday 9 AM to 6:30 PM and Sunday 10 AM to 6:30 PM during the summer, until 5:30 PM the rest of the year. Donations are suggested as admission.

Across the street from The Alamo in The Alamo Plaza, (210) 224-9299, are Ripley's Believe it or Not! gallery and the Plaza Theater of Wax. Ripley's features more than 500 unique oddities from the famous collection of Robert Ripley while the wax museum is filled with more than 225 life-size wax figures, including Elvis Presley and Kevin Costner. The Alamo Plaza is also the place to buy tickets and board classic, early 20th-century-style trolleys for the Lone Star Trolley Tours, (210) 224-9299. These one-hour, narrated tours are designed to introduce visitors to historic downtown San Antonio.

Within walking distance from The Alamo is San Antonio's famous River Walk. Visitors flock here from around the country to stroll along the San Antonio River's Paseo del Rio. The lovely, tree-lined River Walk, a level below the bustling streets of downtown, goes on for several miles and is packed with restaurants featuring outdoor patios, cafes, shops, upscale hotels and clubs. The River Walk boasts both a Hard Rock Cafe *and* a Planet Hollywood for those who want the ultimate in hip as well as a number of homegrown favorites open daily and offering a variety of cuisines. Don't feel like walking the whole distance? Take a half-hour scenic riverboat cruise and let the tour guide point out all the sights. There are several access points to the riverboat cruises along the walk. Nearby is La Villita, the little village. Narrow streets, patios and authentic adobe houses hearken back to an earlier time in this restored Mexican village that features restaurants and shops. The General Cos House in La Villita is a historic structure as well as an excellent example of early San Antonio homes. Market Square or El Mercado, (210) 207-8600, is nearby at 514 W. Commerce Street. This is a Mexican-style shopping district that features fresh produce and lots of local and imported Mexican handicrafts.

One entrance to San Antonio's huge downtown shopping center, the Rivercenter Mall, (210 225-0000, is right on the River Walk too. This giant, modern complex features shops and restaurants. Here visitors can find the IMAX Theatre to view *Alamo ... The Price of Freedom*, a 45-minute docudrama that relates the story of the Alamo martyrs.

While you're downtown, don't miss out on HemisFair Park, site of the 1968 Texas World's Fair. The 750-foot needlelike Tower of the Americas that dominates this park features two dining levels as well as an observation deck offering a panoramic view of the city. The Institute of Texas Cultures, (210) 458-2300, and the Mexican Cultural Institute, (210) 227-0123, can both be found at HemisFair Park. The Institute features a wide variety of exhibits dedicated to Texas' rich ethnic and cultural history as well as a multimedia show presented four times daily in the central dome. The Mexican Cultural Institute is a great place to visit to see works by contemporary Mexican artists. The Institute also hosts the annual Texas Folklife Festival in August (see our Annual Events and Festivals chapter).

The Alamodome, (210) 207-3663, at 100 Montana Street is accessible from the River Walk. It is home to the San Antonio Spurs NBA basketball team and hosts an impressive variety of professional and college sporting events, major concerts and more throughout the year. Even if you're not in town for an event, you can tour this 160,000-square-foot domed stadium Tuesday through Saturday when events are not scheduled. Call for tour times.

Boasting more than a million residents, San Antonio is a large sprawling city with wonderful sights scattered all around. If art museums are your fancy, San Antonio offers the McNay Art Museum, (210) 824-5368, at 6000 New Braunfels Street. This former mansion of Marion Koogler McNay features outstanding works by 19th- and 20th-century painters, including Cezanne, Van Gogh, Gauguin, Diego Rivera and Winslow Homer, to name a few. It's open Tuesday through Saturday 10 AM to 5 PM and Sunday noon to 5 PM. Admission is free. The San Antonio Museum of Art, (210) 978-8169, at 200 W. Jones Avenue is in a historic brewery and includes six buildings housing art works from pre-Colombian to modern times. This excellent museum is open Monday through Saturday 10 AM to 5 PM, later on Tuesday, and Sunday noon to 5 PM. General admission is $4. If you want to learn about Texas' natural history, visit the Witte Museum of History and Science, (210) 357-1990, at 3801 Broadway. This popular tourist spot features numerous exhibits as well as dioramas of Texas wildlife and flora. Four early Texas houses and a furnished log cabin have been rebuilt on the grounds here. The Witte's hours are the same as the museum of art. General admission is $5.95.

To further enjoy Texas flora, visit the Botanical Gardens, (210) 207-3250, at 555 Funston Street. This 33-acre site includes a massive glass-enclosed, below-ground conservatory as well as sprawling outdoor gardens of all kinds. Here, visitors will find the Formal Gardens, a Biblical Garden, a Garden for the Blind, a Japanese Garden, a Children's Garden as well as gardens that celebrate native Texas plants. The gardens are open Monday through Sunday and holidays from 9 AM to 6 PM, 8 AM to 5 PM during the winter. General admission is $4.

For a glimpse at San Antonio's architectural history, tour the elegant King William District. Homes built in the late 19th century by wealthy German merchants line these tree-lined streets. The district begins at the corner of King William and S. St. Mary's streets. While most of these restored old homes are private, The Victorian Steves Homestead is open daily for tours at 509 King William Street. You can also pick up a pamphlet for a walking tour at the Conservation Society office at 107 King William Street.

If you're traveling with children, San Antonio is a perfect getaway. This city features the biggest and best amusement park in Central Texas, Six Flags Fiesta Texas, (210) 697-5050, (800) 473-4378, as well as the wonderful Sea World Adventure Park, (210) 523-3611. (See our Kidstuff chapter for more on these two destinations.) And there's more: Splashtown, (210) 227-1100, is another great water park for children of all ages. The 15-acre park is loaded with children's activities and features water slides, a sandy beach and the world's largest surf-tech pool. It's open April to September. The San Antonio Zoo, (210) 734-7183, boasts the third-largest collection of animals in North America, with more than 3,000 animals. Special exhibits include animals from Australia and Africa as well as huge aquariums housing a variety of marine life. It's open year round near downtown at 3903 N. St. Mary's Street. No city seems complete these days unless it has a children's museum. The San Antonio Children's Museum at 305 E. Houston Street, (210) 212-4453, is packed with hands-on activities for kids. This site, within walking distance of The Alamo, is open Tuesday through Saturday 9 AM to 6 PM and Sunday noon to 5 PM. Admission is $4 per person. Children younger than 2 are admitted free.

If you're planning to spend the weekend in San Antonio, be aware that while the downtown hotels offer the easiest access to The Alamo, the River Walk and all the other downtown tourist destinations, they also are more expensive than those in outlying areas. If you want to splurge, stay at the historic La Mansion del Rio Hotel, (210) 518-1000 or (800) 292-7300. This 337-room luxury hotel, built in 1852 as a private boys' school, is right on the River Walk. Nearby is another historic lodging, The Menger Hotel, (210) 223-4361 or (800) 345-9285. This elegantly restored hotel, built in 1859, has 350 rooms. For less expensive accommodations downtown, try the Days Inn Alamo River Walk, (210) 227-6233 or (800) DAYS-INN.

Many people like to enjoy at least one meal on the trendy River Walk — it's part of the San Antonio experience. But if you're the kind who likes to get out to explore the city and mingle with the locals, try some of our favorites around town. El Mirador, (210) 225-9444, at 722 S. St. Mary's Street in the King William District serves traditional Mexican food as well as contemporary Mexican recipes. It's moderately priced and usually crowded, but the excellent food is worth the wait. Another spot for Mexican fare is Rosario's, (210) 223-1806, at 1014 S. Alamo Street. This casual spot, in an up-and-coming district south of downtown called Southtown, offers a full menu of great south-of-the-border cuisine. It, too, can get quite crowded because this is one place San Antonio comes for Mexican food. In an area known as the St. Mary's District, there's an old two-story building that tilts. This is the Liberty Bar, (210) 227-1187, at 328 E. Josephine Street. The building, now a chic restaurant, survived a San Antonio flood in 1921, which is why it leans a bit. The menu is eclectic.

Check with the San Antonio Visitors Center, (210) 270-8748 or (800) 447-3372, for more information about the Alamo City. It's at 317 Alamo Plaza, just across from the Alamo.

San Antonio Missions

They have been compared to a pearl necklace strung along the banks of the San Antonio River, and it is an apt metaphor for the five Spanish missions that stand inside the city limits of this bustling, modern city whose Spanish name is a daily reminder of the diverse cultural history of Texas.

The San Antonio River has been tamed now and channeled off to wind around cafes

INSIDERS' TIP

Summer is peach season in the Texas Hill Country. If you're heading to Johnson City, Stonewall or Fredericksburg, be sure to stop at any one of a number of businesses along U.S. Highway 290 that sell fresh ripe peaches, homegrown tomatoes and other fruits. Some even have homemade peach ice cream!

and bars, shopping centers and convention halls. The fields that surrounded the Spanish missions are now filled, for the most part, with shops, movie theaters, homes and highways. But within the garden walls of these old Spanish buildings, the past has survived the centuries, providing visitors a glimpse of life in 18th-century Texas. However, they are not just symbols of the past, but a vibrant part of present-day city life — four of the five original missions are parish churches where neighbors can stop for a daily prayer or congregate on feast days for music and celebration.

Touring the five missions, particularly the four that are now part of San Antonio National Missions Park, is a wonderful way for newcomers, visitors and even longtime Texas residents to acquaint themselves with a vital part of Texas history. But a tour of the missions is more than a history lesson. It also offers visitors an opportunity to view some of the most beautiful buildings in Texas, plus experience the ambiance of San Antonio's old neighborhoods and feel the kinship many residents have to their parish churches. It is a great family outing — new interactive media exhibits help bring the Texas frontier to life for young and old alike. Take along a picnic since the grounds and gardens of the missions are ideal for an outdoor meal.

The most famous of the five missions is the Alamo, the monument to Texas independence that is situated just a short walk from the River Walk (see our San Antonio daytrip mentioned previously). The Alamo is no longer a church but is maintained literally as a shrine to the fallen heroes by the Daughters of the Republic of Texas. Given its location in the heart of San Antonio, it is the starting point for our mission tour. The 5.5-mile Mission Trail is clearly marked by brown signs posted around the city. Drivers can pick up the first sign on S. Alamo Street at Market Street. The San Antonio Visitors Center, (210) 270-8748 or (800) 447-3372, at 317 Alamo Street, across from the famous landmark, has information about the missions, plus transportation maps and information. In addition, Bus No. 40 of San Antonio's excellent bus system connects the missions along Mission Trail.

The Alamo was the first Spanish mission built in what is now the city of San Antonio. Named Mission San Antonio de Valero, it was founded in 1718 and then moved to the current site in 1724. The name "Alamo" is believed to have been derived from the Spanish word for cottonwood tree, the species of tree that often grows along riverbeds in the Southwest. Jack Harmon, author of *Texas Missions and Landmarks*, published by The Institute of Texas Cultures (an invaluable resource in researching this daytrip), states that the Alamo was "ill-omened from the beginning." In 1728 an epidemic killed almost all the baptized Native Americans who were living around the mission. It was not the first epidemic to hit the mission, which had other troubles — the first church on the site collapsed, the second was never finished.

By 1793 the mission had been secularized as the brothers focused their religious efforts elsewhere in the area. By 1807 it was being used as a military base, and it continued in that capacity until the famous siege. The Alamo became the "Cradle of Texas Liberty" when a band of 189 Texas volunteers attempted to hold off an invading Mexican army of thousands led by Gen. Santa Anna. The siege lasted 13 days, from February 23 to March 6, 1836, and resulted in the total annihilation of the Alamo defenders, including James Bowie, Davy Crockett and Col. William Barret Travis. Rallying around the battle cry, "Remember The Alamo," a Texas battalion led by Sam Houston defeated the Mexicans and captured Santa Anna a month later at the Battle of San Jacinto near Houston. Texas had gained its independence!

Today, the exterior of the Alamo and the gardens that are contained within its walls are most evocative of a Spanish mission. The interior is quiet and devoid of the ornaments and everyday items that would have filled a Spanish mission in the 18th century. The paintings on the walls, the display cases showing artifacts from the battle, the cold flagstone floors and dim lighting underscore the fact that this was a place where men died in battle.

The bleak history of the Alamo stands in stark contrast to the other four missions within the San Antonio city limits — the only city in the country that can claim five missions within its boundaries. Unlike the Alamo, the four other missions in the city remain under the direction of the Archdiocese of San Antonio, which is responsible for the spiritual functions of the missions while the U.S. Park Service maintains and runs the sites. The federal government took the missions into the federal park system in the early 1990s, collectively dubbing them the San Antonio Missions Historical Park, (210) 229-5701. Admission to the missions is free, although donations are accepted and encouraged. The park facilities and visitor information centers are open daily from 9 AM to 5 PM. They are closed Christmas and New Year's Day, but the churches remain open.

There are four missions in the park, all south of downtown in proximity to the San Antonio River. In their early days, the missions occupied some of the best farmland along the river, thanks to the generosity of the Spanish Crown. The missions served three purposes for the Spanish government, according to Harmon: to convert the Native Americans, to discourage French expansion from Louisiana and to prepare the region for further colonization. Given these goals, the missions were designed to serve both military and religious goals, hence the compound design concept.

The first of the missions on the trail is Mission Nuestra Senora de la Purisma Concepcion (Mission of Our Lady of the Immaculate Conception), usually referred to simply as Mission Concepcion. The mission is at the edge of downtown San Antonio at 807 Mission Road, (210) 229-5732. It is the oldest unrestored church structure in the United States and was dedicated in December 1755. Like the other missions, Concepcion occupied other sites until the current one was chosen in 1731. The ruined walls of the mission compound can be traced from the church to the river bank.

The church walls are 4 feet thick, and the outer walls were originally decorated in vivid colors, patterns and flower designs. This kind of stucco decoration would have been familiar to Native Americans throughout the Americas who also covered their pyramids with colorful designs. The stucco has faded and fallen off the limestone walls now, but inside, visitors can see some original faded designs in the bell tower. Over the years the walls have been marred by graffiti, some dating back into the mid-19th century.

Concepcion was secularized and then abandoned in 1824. It was the site of a battle in the Texas War of Independence, but in 1855 the Brothers of Mary returned and restored the church to the parish.

Mission San José y Miguel de Aguayo has been dubbed the best pearl in the strand of missions, the so-called "Queen of the Missions." Mission San José, 5539 San José Street, (210) 229-4770, is the largest, the most informative and some say the most beautiful of the missions. (The second half of its name is in honor of the Spanish Marquis Miguel de Aguayo who consolidated Spain's control of Texas.) If you only have time for one mission, this is it. In 1996 the park service opened an extensive, interactive information center here in the old granaries that offers a comprehensive look at mission life.

Mission San José was founded by Father Antonio Margil de Jesus, a famous Franciscan, in 1720. It was designed to be a large compound, surrounded by tall walls and four huge gates. Inside were the small homes of the Native Americans — up to 200 lived here in 1749, and by 1786 it was reported 350 people lived here, including 110 Native American warriors converted from various tribes, who helped beat back attacks by Comanches and Apaches. The Native Americans also worked the fields, and at its economic peak, according to Harmon, the San José ranch ran 1,500 cattle and 5,000 sheep and produced 4,000 bushels of corn.

The church itself at Mission San José is famous for one particular architectural element, the Rose Window. Carved by the Spanish master mason Pedro Huizar, who was sent by the king to teach the Native Americans his art, the window has been hailed as one of the most beautiful examples of Spanish Colonial architecture in the United States. There are various legends associated with the window, including one that it is Huizar's tribute to a lost love who drowned on her way from Spain to marry him. Huizar's other handiwork can be seen in various images of the saints that appear in the chapel. A small cemetery nearby contains the bodies of Huizar and some of the early friars who worked at San José.

Every Sunday at noon there is a mariachi mass featuring the lyrical music of Mexico inside the church — come early in order to find a seat — and at Christmas time the parishioners perform *Los Pastores*, a miracle play with Spanish origins. Beyond the mission walls are a major highway, businesses and movie theaters, but inside the 18th century seems alive.

San Juan Capistrano, 9102 Graf Street, (210) 229-5734, is the third mission on the trail. Small, simple and peaceful, San Juan is set in natural surroundings that help the visitor get in touch with the past. Originally located in East Texas, the mission was moved to San Antonio in 1731. The chapel, which now serves as a parish church, was built in 1756. The figures of Christ and the Virgin inside are made of cornstalk pith, a lost art that was practiced by the Native Americans. There is an interpretative trail at the mission, which takes visitors along a third of a mile walk to the river bank.

San Francisco de la Espada is the most southern of the missions and, although surrounded by the city, it retains a pastoral air, perhaps because some of the fields surrounding the mission are still worked and are still irrigated by the Espada Aqueduct. The Espada Acequia, the water system, was built in the 1730s and continues to work.

There is something of a mystery about the name of this mission. St. Francis of the Sword is the literal translation and the peace-loving saint, usually depicted with birds and animals, was originally depicted here bearing a sword. Some historians suggest it is likely *espada* was in honor of a notable person with this name, others suggest it was a gesture of strength, an image the missions were supposed to project.

There is a sense of peace about the place. Inside, the chapel is simple and devoid of a lot of decoration. The Stations of the Cross are simply marked in numerals on the walls. Sitting inside the small chapel is a peaceful way to end a visit to the Mission Trail.

There are two other Spanish Colonial sites that are well worth adding to a tour of old San Antonio. Both are downtown. The Spanish Governor's Palace, 105 Military Plaza, (210) 224-0601, was completed in 1749 and was the home of the captain of the presidio, not the governor, although that name has stuck. Officially called the Commandancia, it is typical of a high-ranking official's home in colonial Spain. Above the doorway is the imperial double eagle, symbol of the Hapsburg emperors and part of the coat-of-arms of Philip V, who was both a Hapsburg and a Bourbon by birth.

The "palace" is far from palatial, but it is a wonderful example of Colonial architecture and the 3-foot-thick walls ensure that even on the hottest days the interior is cool. It stands across the street from San Antonio's current City Hall. Open daily from 9 AM (10 AM on Sunday) until 5 PM, there is a nominal admission charge.

Another noted landmark in the center of the city is San Fernando Cathedral, 115 Main Plaza, (210) 227-1297. The church was begun in 1738 by the original Canary Islanders who settled San Antonio. Completed in 1749, it went on to become famous as the place where Jim Bowie married and allegedly where some of the heroes of the Alamo are buried — but there is much dispute about that. The sanctuary is the oldest part of the building and was part of the original structure, making it the oldest cathedral sanctuary in the United States. The rest of the church was constructed around the sanctuary in 1868 and is Gothic Revival style. There are frequent mariachi masses here; the schedule is posted at the cathedral.

If your visit to San Antonio's missions has you hooked on Spanish Colonial history in Texas, consider visiting the El Paso region where several beautiful missions also stand, or take a weekend getaway from Austin to Goliad, about a three-hour drive southeast of Austin, to visit the Presidio de la Bahia, a Spanish fort and church that stands in one of the most historic regions of Texas. Spring is a great time to visit Goliad since the wildflowers blanket the La Bahia grounds. Plus, Fiesta Zaragoza is held on the weekend closest to May 5, Cinco de Mayo, because native son Gen. Ignacio de la Zaragoza, a Mexican hero, defeated the French at the Battle of Puebla on that date in 1862. For more information about Goliad, call the Chamber of Commerce at (512) 645-3563.

New Braunfels

Only an hour's drive from Austin, or right on your way if you're returning to Austin from San Antonio, New Braunfels attracts visitors for two primary reasons — antiques shopping and watersports. The latter draws thousands of visitors, especially in summer, to a variety of artificial and natural waterways to tube, raft, swim, paddle and plop in the cool, wet stuff.

The two sides of New Braunfels have led to a growth boom, and Comal County has been cited as the fastest growing county in Texas in recent years. Many of the visitors come to enjoy swimming in Landa Park, (830) 608-2165, the downtown home of the state's largest spring-fed pool and also home to a stretch of the Comal River. Another popular destination is Schlitterbahn, the state's biggest water park, which is detailed in our Kidstuff chapter.

Given all the activities available in the area, crowds flock to New Braunfels on weekends in the peak summer season, but thanks to its old German roots the town has maintained its charm. The town is named after Prince Carl of Solms-Braunfels, a member of the Mainzer Adelsverein, or League of Nobles, who encouraged German emigration in the 1840s as an escape from economic hard times in Germany. The young Republic of Texas offered land grants to the nobles as an inducement for European settlers. Prince Carl brought over a large contingent in 1844, many of whom died on the coast of Texas due to an epidemic. The survivors settled in New Braunfels in 1844, and by 1855 the town was the fourth largest in Texas. Meanwhile, Prince Carl had gone home since his fiancee refused to come to Texas.

There are several invocations of the Prince's name in and around the town including Prince Solms Park, where tubers pay a small admission fee to tube in the Comal River, and the Prince Solms Inn, 295 E. San Antonio Street, (830) 625-9169, an upscale bed and

Photo: Texas Department of Transportation

Wildflowers paint the Texas Hill Country in rich hues every spring.

breakfast in a restored Victorian home. Advance reservations are a must at this popular guesthouse and at the on-site cellar restaurant, Wolfgang's Kellar, where elegant German and European cuisine is served. Another hotel with great character is the Faust Hotel, 240 S. Seguin Street, (830) 625-7791, just one block south of the town plaza. The Faust was built in 1928 and has been restored to reflect that period. The rooms here all have character and are decorated individually. Given the reasonable prices (cheaper than some national motel chains), the Faust is a good choice for visitors interested in the historic aspects of New Braunfels.

New Braunfels is of great interest to architecture buffs, particularly for the tiny Sunday houses built by German farmers in the 19th century as weekend town cottages. Many have been restored, but others stand waiting for the deep pocketbooks and eager hands of would-be restorers. Many of the towns antiques shops are housed in old German homes. The New Braunfels Chamber of Commerce, 390 S. Seguin Street, (830) 625-2385, offers an "antique crawl" map.

The chamber also provides a historic walking tour map to guide visitors through the vibrant downtown area where there are more than 30 historic buildings. The heart of the community is the plaza, where the traffic is slowed by a roundabout, and the restored buildings reflect the prosperity enjoyed by the town's forefathers. At 199 Main Plaza is a large modern building that houses The Hummel Museum, (830) 626-5636 or (800) 456-4866, the world's largest collection of drawings and paintings by Sister Maria Innocentia Hummel, whose work inspired the Hummel figurines. The gift shop sells, obviously, Hummel figurines.

Early life in New Braunfels is depicted at the Sophienburg Museum, 401 W. Coll Street, (830) 629-1572. Named after Prince Carl's fiancee who declined to head for the frontier, the museum is built on a small hill where the prince had planned to build his honeymoon castle. The building housed his administrative offices and now has several exhibits showing life on the Texas frontier. The museum is open daily from 10 AM to 5 PM, except Sunday when it is open from 1 to 5 PM, and there is a small admission fee.

Another New Braunfels museum is one of those little gems often tucked away in small towns that receive little attention in these days of theme parks. The Museum of Texas Handmade Furniture, 1370 Church Hill Drive, (830) 629-6504, features more than 75 examples of handcrafted furniture made by German cabinetmakers working in the mid-19th century on the Texas frontier. Housed in the Breustadt House, c. 1858, and listed in the National Register of Historic Places, the museum is open to the public daily during the summer and on weekends the rest of the year.

Nearby, at 1300 Church Hill Drive, the city's Conservation Society has relocated a number of historic buildings in Conservation Plaza. They include several homes, a one-room schoolhouse, a music studio, a barn and a general store. Some have been completely restored; others are awaiting restoration. The society holds a folklife festival here in early May, (830) 625-8766, and the buildings are open at irregular hours during the rest of the year.

Another good way to capture the spirit of 19th-century New Braunfels is to eat at one of the town's German-style restaurants. Krause's Cafe, 148 Castell Street, (830) 625-7581, has been serving German dishes, barbecue and just plain, old-fashioned American cooking since 1938. This is where the courthouse crowd and the business leaders come for breakfast and lunch. The cafe also serves dinner, including chili (William Gebhardt perfected his chili powder formula in downtown New Braunfels a century ago), steaks and burgers. Leave room for pie — Krause's has a wide selection. The cafe is open for breakfast, lunch and dinner daily, closed Sundays and for three weeks in September. No credit cards are taken here.

True to its German roots, New Braunfels is noted for its sausage. The New Braunfels Smokehouse, (830) 625-2416, at the intersection of I-35 and Texas Highway 46 began life as a smokehouse for local farmers and ranchers 50 years ago. Now, it is a restaurant featuring several varieties of sausage and barbecue, plus smoked hams and turkeys. The restaurant is open for breakfast, lunch and dinner daily, and there is a gift shop and mail-order business on the premises.

Sausage is celebrated with relish (and onions) at Wurstfest, the annual 10-day festival that attracts tens of thousands of visitors to New Braunfels every November. The festival centers on sausage-eating, beer drinking and polka dancing (see our Annual Events and Festivals chapter).

Gruene

It is pronounced "Green," and for the savvy developers who revived this ghost town north of New Braunfels, the name proved propitious. These days, old Gruene is anything but a ghost town, particularly on weekends when visitors stroll the narrow streets looking for antiques bargains, visiting craft shops and studios, kicking up a storm at the local dance hall or digging into a chicken-fried steak.

Ernest Gruene originally settled in New Braunfels and then moved his family to this area, about 5 miles north of New Braunfels, in 1872. His son Henry D. Gruene became very influential, and so the town was named after him.

After Henry died in 1920, Gruene suffered two fatal blows — the boll weevil killed the cotton crop and the Depression hit. The city turned into a ghost town, and the old buildings lay empty for years. When investors discovered the community, it looked as if time had stopped back in the '30s. Now, this community on F.M. 306 just north of New Braunfels and about an hour's drive south of Austin on I-35 is listed on the National Register of Historic Places. There is only one intersection in Gruene, and most businesses lie either on Gruene Road or Hunter Road, making a tour of the town easy on the legs.

You will want to save some energy if you plan to spend the evening at Texas' oldest dance hall, Gruene Hall, (830) 606-1281, where some of the top names in country music have played, including Garth Brooks. The first dance was in 1878, and now the bar-cum-dance hall opens daily around midday so visitors can enjoy a longneck or two. The old hall has remained stuck in the years between the two world wars. The posters on the walls are advertisements from the era; there is no air conditioning — the windows and doors are opened wide to catch the breeze — and there are burlap bags hanging from the ceiling. Cover charges for evening performances vary.

During the week, Gruene is quiet unless a popular band is playing, but on the weekends the little town fills up. Tubers are attracted to the Guadalupe River in summertime (Gruene is on the north bank of the river), while antiques hunters and shoppers come to the village to stroll the stores and galleries.

There is one hotel in town, the upscale Gruene Mansion Inn, 1275 Gruene Road, (830) 629-2641, where guests stay in restored 1870 cottages with views of the Guadalupe River. The hotel also operates the Restaurant at Gruene Mansion Inn, (830) 620-0760, which serves lunch and dinner daily inside or out on the deck overlooking the river. The menu features a variety of cuisines, including Cajun, German and continental.

Also overlooking the river is the Grist Mill Restaurant, (830) 625-0684, 1287 Gruene Road, housed, not in a grist mill, but in a converted 100-year-old cotton gin. Lunch and dinner are served daily, and the menu features typical all-American fare, burgers, sandwiches, salads, steaks, plus some Tex-Mex and barbecue dishes.

Most of the businesses in Gruene offer free brochures illustrating walking tours of the community. One popular stop on the tour is the Guadalupe Valley Winery, also housed in an old cotton gin, at 1720 Hunter Road, (830) 629-2351.

Hunter Road has several antiques stores and the old Gruene General Store, built in 1878, that now sells Texana, including cookbooks, cookies and kitchen equipment and offers sodas from the old-style soda fountain. Several artisans, including potters and ironworkers, have studios along Hunter Road, and the Greune Antique Mall is home to several dealers.

Gruene is popular year round, but visitors mark their calendars for the monthly Market Days, held the third weekend of the months February through November, when more than 100 arts and crafts vendors gather in Gruene (see our Annual Events and Festivals chapter).

For more information on Gruene, call the Gruene Information Center at (830) 629-5077.

Out East

Round Top and Winedale

These two tiny communities in Fayette County, about 90 miles east of Austin, have become world-renowned for their cultural events and their celebrations of music and theater that take place in several beautifully restored 19th-century Texas buildings set in landscaped grounds. But even when there are no events scheduled at Round Top or Winedale, a daytrip to the area can be an opportunity for city dwellers to catch a glimpse of small-town Texas.

Round Top is one of the state's oldest communities — the first Fourth of July in Texas was celebrated here in 1828, long before Texas was a republic or a state in the Union. In the mid-19th century several German and Swedish families settled here, but the community never grew beyond a mere handful of homes. Then in the 1960s, artists and wealthy Texans began to be attracted to the area's natural beauty, buying up the old homes and restoring them.

In 1971 concert pianist James Dick chose Round Top as the home for his music institute, designed to offer students an opportunity to study with leading musicians. Dick established the International Festival Institute in historic Round Top. During its first five years, the Festival Institute leased facilities, but a master plan for development of a 200-acre campus was adopted. The first major facility, the Mary Moody Northern Pavilion, was acquired in 1973. It was the largest transportable stage in the world and was used for open-air concerts until 1983. Later it was housed in the 1,200-seat Festival Concert Hall, on which construction began in 1980, until the permanent stage was completed in the Concert Hall in 1993. An abandoned school building and 6 acres of land east of Round Top were acquired in 1973 for the campus, now named Festival Hill. The grounds are open to the public, and they make a great setting for a spring picnic.

Several historic buildings were moved to the festival site. The first historic structure moved to Festival Hill came from nearby LaGrange and was named the William Lockhart Clayton House in honor of the man who created the Marshall Plan. Built in 1885, it was renovated in 1976 for faculty offices, teaching facilities and indoor concerts. The Menke House, built in 1902, was moved to Festival Hill from Hempstead and renovated as a faculty residence and conference center in 1979. Its Gothic Revival ceilings, woodwork and staircases make it a showcase of Texas carpentry.

The historic sanctuary of the former Travis St. United Methodist Church of LaGrange, built in 1883, was moved to Festival Hill in 1994 for restoration as a center for chamber music, organ recitals, lectures and seminars. It was renamed the Edythe Bates Old Chapel to honor one of the great Texan patronesses of the fine arts and houses an 1835 Henry Erben pipe organ. The Festival Institute Museum and Library exhibits art collections in the Festival Concert Hall and the historic house restorations.

There are now seventeen musical programs during June and July each year. The August-to-April Concerts Series, the Early Music Festival and other programs bring the total number of year-round concerts to more than 50. These include orchestral, chamber music,

INSIDERS' TIP

A standard annual membership to the Austin Children's Museum ($45 a family) allows you free admission to the Houston Space Center, the Houston Museum of Natural Science, the Museum of Health and Medical Science in Houston, the Witte Museum in San Antonio, the Dallas Museum of Natural History and the Children's Museum in Houston. And these are just a few of the 210 locations in Texas and around the country that accept your membership card. Be sure to carry it when you travel.

choral, vocal, brass, woodwinds and solo performances. The repertoire extends from ancient to contemporary music.

The campus is also used for conferences, meetings and retreats by businesses and professional organizations. A series of distinguished museum lectures is presented at Festival Hill each year. The campus, famed for its gardens, rare trees, herb collections, cascades, fountains and unusual landscaping is a destination for visitors from all over the world, and the grounds are open daily.

Tickets may be purchased at the Concert Hall beginning one hour prior to each concert, and season tickets are available. For information on the musical season or individual concerts, call (409) 249-3129.

Nearby Winedale has been a center for ethnic studies since Ima Hogg, daughter of a former Texas governor, donated the grounds and several historic buildings to the University of Texas in 1967. Winedale is also home to the Shakespeare at Winedale festival where UT students perform several of Shakespeare's plays in an 1894 barn-turned-theater.

Like Round Top, the grounds are open to the public, and there is a small admission charge. Winedale is open May through October on Saturdays from 10 AM to 6 PM, Sundays from noon to 6 PM, and from November through April from 9 AM to 5 PM on Saturdays and noon to 5 PM on Sundays. Tours of the on-site historic buildings can be arranged, (409) 278-3530, and there is a marked nature trail. There are several annual events that bring visitors to Winedale, including a Christmas Open House, featuring seasonal music and food; a spring festival and Texas Craft Exhibition and a German Oktoberfest, all detailed in our Annual Events and Festivals chapter.

There are several bed and breakfast and guesthouse accommodations in the Round Top/Winedale area. Some Austin residents prefer to stay overnight in the area after a concert or play, turning a night out into a weekend getaway. Guesthouses include Briarfield Bed and Breakfast, (800) 472-1134 or (409) 249-3973; Cedar Tops Cottage, (281) 496-4724; The Heritage Haus, (409) 278-3939; Round Top Inn, (409) 249-5294; Lentz House, (409) 249-3225; Heart of Heart Ranch, (409) 249-3171; and Broomfields, (409) 249-3706. Accommodations range in price. If you plan an overnight stay, book well in advance during those times when concerts and theater presentations are scheduled.

There are several restaurants in the area that feature country cooking, including Klump's restaurant, (409) 249-5696, in Round Top. It's open Wednesday through Saturday for breakfast, lunch and dinner, Sunday and Tuesday for breakfast and lunch only. It's closed Monday. The Madhatter's Table, (409) 249-3331, on the square in Round Top features mesquite-grilled steaks and pastas. It's open for lunch Wednesday through Saturday and dinner Friday and Saturday only. Reservations are suggested. In nearby Ledbetter on U.S. Highway 290, the JRJ Ranch, (409) 249-3066, offers Chuckwagon Cookout, campfire suppers and evening hayrides. The ranch has a Santa's Trail of Lights every Friday and Saturday night from Thanksgiving through December.

The area also has become popular among antiques collectors. In addition to shops in the communities of Round Top, Winedale, Shelby, Warrenton and Carmine, antiques dealers come from across the country for the first weekend in April and October to the Antiques Fair, which is celebrated in each of the small towns.

To reach Round Top or Winedale, take U.S. 290 east towards Houston from Austin. Just beyond Giddings look for Texas Highway 237, head south and follow the signs to Round Top. Winedale is just east of Round Top on F.M. 2714. Many of the merchants in the area have tourist maps showing the locations of the various small communities, lists of accommodations and area attractions, and there is a visitors center on the square in Round Top. Another good place to gather information about local happenings is the Round Top Mercantile Company, on Texas Highway 237, (409) 249-3117, which is open seven days a week. Look for the store's Texaco pumps on the west side of the highway as you drive into Round Top.

Houston

If you've been around Austin long enough to start complaining about the traffic jams and the high-speed lifestyle that are beginning to replace Austin's good ol' laid-back days, it's time to visit Houston, the fourth largest city in the United States. Houston is in every way the giant metropolis that Austin is not — not yet, at least. This racially diverse, multicultural mecca is filled with so many excellent cultural destinations, shopping adventures, institutions of higher education, sporting events, family activities and dining delights that the traffic seems a small price to pay. Nearby is the Johnson Space Center, NASA mission control. A little farther down the road is the beach at Galveston on the Gulf of Mexico.

Texas independence hero Sam Houston tried hard to make his namesake city the capital of Texas (read all about it in our History chapter), but Austin won out. Instead, Houston has become the industrial and financial capital for much of Texas. Located 165 miles southwest of Austin, Houston rests on the Coastal Plains of Texas — so be prepared for humidity. Houstonians, in fact, often joke that the weather forecast is always the same: partly cloudy with a chance of rain.

You can't go wrong by starting your tour of Houston in beautiful Hermann Park, just a few miles southwest of downtown. This large urban park has a golf course, a lake and plenty of room to just stroll or picnic. The Houston Zoo is inside the park at 1513 N. Macgregor Drive, (713) 523-5888. Here you'll find hundreds of exotic animals as well as a tropical birdhouse and aquariums. The Touch Tank allows visitors to touch sea creatures. Also in Hermann Park is the Miller Outdoor Theater. Now this is a find! The amphitheater presents free outdoor performances, including symphony, opera, contemporary musicals and all kinds of dance beginning in April each season. For an even better view, the theater reserves some paid seats up front.

One of the most fascinating aspects of this city is its ever-growing Museum District near Hermann Park. It would take visitors at least a couple of days to appreciate all the wonders in this sprawling district. The Museum of Natural Science, (713) 639-4600, at 1 Hermann Circle Drive is a huge complex that includes the Cockrell Butterfly Center, the Burke Baker Planetarium, the Wortham IMAX Theater and much more. This outstanding facility is definitely worth a visit. Check out the Energy Hall, which guides visitors through the complete process of oil exploration. For a region that refines 50 percent of all U.S. petrochemicals, this exhibit is perfectly located. There also are interactive physical science exhibits and a hall dedicated to archaeology of the western hemisphere. The museum is open Monday through Saturday 9 AM to 6 PM, Sunday 11 AM to 6 PM. General admission is $4 for the main exhibits, but expect to pay more for entrance to the other facilities.

Near the natural science museum is the new Museum of Health & Medical Science, (713) 521-1515, at 1515 Hermann Drive. This new facility boasts a "Texas-size view of the human body" and includes models of giant organs as well as many hands-on exhibits. It's open Tuesday through Saturday 9 AM to 5 PM and Sunday noon to 5 PM. General admission is $4. Two other special interest museums also are in walking distance. The Children's Museum of Houston, (713) 522-1138, is at 1500 Binz Street. This large, delightful space offers a changing assortment of hands-on exhibits for children of all ages. It's open Tuesday through Saturday 9 AM to 5 PM and Sunday noon to 5 PM. General admission is $5. Check, however, for special discount nights and Monday openings. The Holocaust Museum Houston, (713) 942-8000, at 5401 Caroline Street is the first of its kind in the Southwest and serves as an educational center and memorial to the millions of victims of Nazi death camps. The institution, opened in 1996, features a multimedia exhibition space with constantly changing shows as well as a library and a theater where visitors can see a video about Holocaust survivors now living in Houston. The museum is open Monday through Friday 9 AM to 5 PM, Saturday and Sunday noon to 5 PM. Admission is free.

If art is your passion, the vast Museum District will keep you enthralled for hours and hours. The Contemporary Art Museum, or CAM, (713) 284-8250, at 5216 Montrose Boulevard is filled with works by a variety of local, national and international contemporary artists. CAM is open Tuesday through Saturday 10 AM to 5 PM, till 9 PM on Thursday, and Sunday noon to 5 PM. Admission is free. The Museum of Fine Arts, (713) 639-7300, is across the street at 1001 Bissonnet Street. This Houston treasure possesses a collection of more than 35,000 works from around the world and hosts regular special exhibits. The museum is open Tuesday through Saturday 10 AM to 5 PM, until 9 PM on Thursday, and Sunday 12:15 to 6 PM. General admission is $3. Head north on Bissonnet Street a couple of blocks to the Glassel School where you can see the work of the school's art students on display for free Monday through Friday.

If you're looking for a truly unique place to stay in Houston and prefer to be in the Museum District, check out the upscale Park Plaza Warwick Hotel, (713) 526-1991, at 5701 Main Street. Built in 1926 and retaining all the classic elegance of a bygone era, the Warwick is a historic treasure. Even if you're not a guest, however, the Warwick has an excellent Sunday brunch on its top floor. Windows on all sides offer an excellent view of this area of Houston. Call ahead and request a table by the window. If you're traveling with children, or just don't like to wait to be served, try Butera's Restaurant, (713) 523-0722, near the Museum District at 4621 Montrose Street. Casual is the theme here as patrons serve themselves cafeteria style. You'll find a great assortment of deli-style foods, hot and cold sandwiches, hot pastas, desserts and more. Butera's opens daily at 11 AM and serves lunch and dinner.

You'll want to drive from this area to another collection of museums in the northwest corner of the Museum District. Here, art lovers will find a cluster of four impressive facilities. Start at the Menil Collection, (713) 525-9404, at 1515 Sul Ross Street. This museum was established in 1987 to exhibit the significant private collection of Houstonians John and Dominique de Menil and includes more than 15,000 pieces from antiquity to the 20th century. The Menil is open Wednesday through Sunday 11 AM to 7 PM. Admission is free. Nearby at 1519 Branard Street is the Menil's Cy Twombly Gallery, (713) 525-9450, which features about 35 paintings, sculptures and works on paper by the American artist. Also nearby is the Rothko Chapel, (713) 524-9839, at 3900 Yupon Street. Called a chapel because of its meditative environment, the Rothko Chapel houses works by the late abstract painter. It is open 10 AM to 6 PM daily. The Byzantine Chapel Museum, (713) 521-3990, dedicated to Byzantine art, is nearby.

The Houston arts scene wouldn't be complete without the exceptional performing arts for which this city is known. The Theater District in downtown Houston near Texas and Louisiana streets includes performance spaces for many of the city's finest. Call (800) 828-ARTS for a schedule of performances by the city's outstanding classical companies, the Houston Ballet, the Houston Grand Opera and the Houston Symphony. The Alley Theater, (800) 259-ALLE, established in 1947, is one of the oldest resident professional theater companies in the country. This city also claims several multicultural arts centers, including Talento Bilingue de Houston, (713) 222-1213, and Kuumba House, (713) 524-1079.

If sporting events are your style, check out the lineup at the Astrodome, (713) 799-9555, at 8400 Kirby Drive. The Astrodome is home to the Houston Astros major league baseball team during the April to September regular season. The Astrodome is also the site of the largest professional rodeo in Texas (and one of the largest in the country). The Houston Livestock Show and Rodeo is held toward the end of February. Check the schedule, too, at the Compaq Center. This modern arena hosts home games for the two-time NBA champs the Houston Rockets NBA team from fall to spring and WNBA champions, the Houston Comets during the summer. (See our chapter on Spectator Sports for more on all these events). Of course, the Astrodome also presents concerts and other live shows throughout the year. The Astrodome offers daily tours.

Don't forget the kids when you plan your Houston outing. SplashTown Waterpark, (281) 355-3300, just a few minutes north of downtown Houston at 21300 N. Interstate 45 in neighboring Spring, Texas, is another premier attraction for families. This exciting park features more than 40 rides on 50 shaded acres. It's open April through September with varying hours of operation. Admission is about $19 for people taller than 4 feet, $13 for those shorter than 4 feet, while children younger than 3 are admitted free. Six Flags AstroWorld and Six Flags WaterWorld, (713) 799-8404, are near the Astrodome at the 610 S. Loop, Fannin Street Exit. This complex, part of Texas' premier amusement park system, features all the thrill rides you could possibly pack into one day as well as water rides, shows, restaurants and more. Entrance for both parks is about $41 for those taller than 4 feet and $35 for those shorter. Admission is offered for individual parks. Operating hours vary depending on the season.

If you're planning to spend the night in the Astrodome area and don't want to spend an arm and a leg, we recommend the Residence Inn by Marriott, (713) 660-7993, at 7710 S. Main Street or the Holiday Inn Astrodome, (713) 790-1900, at 8111 Kirby Drive. Both are within minutes of The Galleria (read on to find out why you want to be near The Galleria) and the Museum District.

Those with higher education on their minds might want to tour the campus of Rice University near Hermann Park. Call the Office of Admissions at (713) 527-4036 for information about guided walking tours of the campus that are offered Monday through Friday at 11 AM and 3 PM during the school year. You can also check with the office about its summer schedule. Or just stroll around this shady 285-acre campus by yourself, taking in the sights of the elegant Mediterranean-style buildings.

Houston is also a shopper's paradise. People come from all over to shop at The Galleria, (713) 621-1907, Houston's elegant and upscale mall. Located at 5075 Westheimer at Post Oak Road, The Galleria is the focal point of the Uptown Galleria Area. The Galleria features more than 300 world-class stores, including Neiman Marcus, Saks Fifth Avenue, Lord & Taylor, Gianni Versace and Tiffany & Co. There's also a large ice skating rink here, plenty of informal restaurants as well as the posh Westin Galleria Hotel, (800) WESTIN-1. Across the street is the Centre at Post Oak, (713) 866-6905, with more than 25 specialty shops and restaurants, including the great children's toy store F.A.O. Schwarz. Drive north on Post Oak Road from The Galleria and you'll discover a number of other malls and shops, including the Post Oak Shopping Center. The luxury Houstonian Hotel, Club & Spa, (800) 231-2759, is also in the Galleria Area at 111 N. Post Oak Lane. Of course, you don't have to stay in a luxury hotel. For more reasonably priced accommodations, see those listed previously with the Astrodome, or check out La Quinta Inns in the area at (800) NU-ROOMS or the Comfort Suites-Galleria at (713) 787-0004. Within this area is one of Houston's finest restaurants. If you're traveling to Houston for a special event — second honeymoon, birthday, big job promotion — and want to splurge on a gourmet meal, try Cafe Annie, (713) 840-1111, at 1728 Post Oak Boulevard. It's open for lunch and dinner weekdays, dinner only Saturday.

A good excuse to visit the Houston Ship Channel, one of this city's claims to fame, is to head out to Brady Island just a few miles east of downtown for an enormous buffet meal. Brady's Landing, (713) 928-9921, at 8505 Cypress Street and its next door neighbor Shanghai Red, (713) 926-6666, at 8501 Cypress Street feature similar menus, and both offer views of the ship channel. They have excellent Sunday brunch buffets for about $18.95 for adults as well as buffets at other times during the week. Brady's has a prime rib and seafood buffet on Friday and Saturday.

Many people visit Houston from across Texas and across the country specifically for this next attraction. The Johnson Space Center with Space Center Houston, (281) 244-2100, (800) 972-0369, is at 1601 NASA Road 1 off Interstate 45 about midway between Houston and Galveston. When Apollo 13 astronaut Jim Lovell spoke those fateful words, "Houston, we have a problem," back in 1970, he was talking to Mission Control at the Space Center. This exciting and educational complex includes a tram tour of the sprawling NASA complex, featuring Mission Control, the Space Shuttle Training Facility and the Space Environment Simulation Laboratory. Space Center Houston is the stimulating visitors center here and includes all kinds of hands-on activities as well as an IMAX Theater offering thrilling space movies. It's open daily.

If you decide to go on to Galveston, check in at the visitor information centers in Moody Civic Center at Seawall Boulevard and 21st Street or in the Strand Historic District at 2016 Strand for a wealth of information about this great tourist destination.

In Houston, stop in at the Visitor Information Center at 801 Congress Street to pick up the magazine *Official Guide to Houston* published by the Greater Houston Convention and Visitor Bureau for even more things to do and sites to see in this great American city. The center also has maps, brochures and a schedule of upcoming events. Better still, plan ahead and request that literature be mailed to you. The numbers are (713) 227-3100 and (800) 231-7799.

Bryan/College Station

Given the intense sports rivalry between The University of Texas and Texas A&M University, it's practically treason for an Austinite to tout the merits of College Station — home of the Aggies of A&M. This college town and neighboring Bryan (you can't tell where one begins and the other leaves off) offer all kinds of treats for the daytripper or weekend visitor. College Station, 101 miles northeast of Austin, is an easy, stress-free drive along a route now designated as the "Presidential Corridor."

The corridor — U.S. Highway 290 E. and Texas Highway 21 — connects Texas' two presidential libraries, the Lyndon Baines Johnson Library in Austin and College Station's George Bush Presidential Library and Museum, (409) 260-9552, which opened at Texas A&M University in November 1997. It's worth the trip alone to visit this massive facility dedicated to the life and times of the 41st president of the United States. With more than 25,000 square feet of exhibition space, the museum chronicles Bush's life from his youth in Greenwich, Connecticut, to his service as a pilot in the U.S. Navy and through his bold move to the Texas oil fields in the mid-1940s.

In vivid detail, visitors learn abut Bush's career as a congressman, ambassador to the United Nations, director of the C.I.A., then vice president and president of the United States. Here, visitors will find the largest and most complete exhibit in the country dedicated to the 1991 Gulf War. There's also a huge slab of the Berlin Wall, graffiti and all. One section of the museum is dedicated to former First Lady Barbara Bush's efforts on behalf of literacy, volunteerism and AIDS prevention. Of course, the library is also a research institution and, as such, includes 38 million pages of President Bush's official and personal papers. The library, located on the A&M West Campus, is open Monday through Saturday 9:30 AM to 5 PM and Sunday noon to 5 PM. General admission is $3 while children 16 and younger are admitted free.

Just a short distance from the Bush library is the main campus of Texas A&M University, Texas' oldest public college. A&M, the state's land grant college, was founded in 1876 as an all-male military college. On August 23, 1963, the name of the Agricultural and Mechanical College was changed to Texas A&M University. Today, A&M is among the 10 largest universities in the United States, with more than 41,000 students, and ranks among the top three institutions nationally in undergraduate enrollment in agriculture, business administration and architecture.

A&M's nationally known Corps of Cadets program — now open to men and women — has produced more military officers than any other institution in the country except for the service academies. Start your tour of this sprawling campus with a visit to the Aggieland Visitor Center in Rudder Tower on the main campus, (409) 845-5851. Some points of interest include the Academic Building, built in 1912 on the site of Old Main, the first building on campus; the Albritton Bell Tower, a 138-foot tower that contains a 49-bell carillon; the Memorial Student Center, opened in 1950 and dedicated to former students who died in World War II; the Student Recreation Center, the larg-

INSIDERS' TIP

The *Texas State Travel Guide* is an invaluable resource when planning a trip around the state. It is available free by calling (800) 454-9292. *Texas Monthly* magazine, available at newsstands across the state, offers regularly updated restaurant reviews for Texas' major cities as well as a listing of important upcoming events in the state. See our chapter on the Media for more about these two publications.

est student rec center of its kind in the country, completed in 1995; the Cadet Quad, home to those world-famous cadets; and Kyle Field, the impressive 70,210-seat football stadium — home to UT's archrival.

Of course, we're not suggesting you go to cheer for A&M, but if you happen to be in town before a UT-A&M football game here, don't miss the Aggie Bonfire, a massive inferno and pep rally that symbolizes the Aggie's burning desire to beat the hide off the Longhorns. The bonfire is held the night before home games, two days prior to games played in Austin. Check, too, for a listing of events at A&M's Reed Arena, (409) 862-REED. Opened in 1998, the arena features sporting events, concerts, ice shows, circuses and much more. Also in College Station is Wolf Pen Creek Amphitheater, (409) 764-3408. This lovely outdoor arena hosts a wide range of music and entertainment, including some of Austin's finest musical performers.

Bryan is home to the Brazos Valley Museum of Natural History, (409) 776-2195. The museum features a collection of fossils found in the Brazos Valley as well as a constantly changing array of temporary exhibits. Youngsters will find plenty to do in the nature lab and discovery room. The museum is open Tuesday through Saturday 10 AM to 5 PM. And be sure to take your children to the new Children's Museum of the Brazos Valley, (409) 779-5437. Opened in 1997, the museum features all kinds of hands-on learning activities and displays, including the inspiration gallery in which children can perform a puppet show, disassemble a VCR or paint a Volkswagen Beetle. The museum is open Wednesday through Saturday 10 AM to 5 PM and Sunday 1 to 5 PM.

One of our favorite spots in Bryan is the Messina Hof Winery at 4545 Old Reliance Road, (409) 778-9463. Established with the release of its first vintage in 1983, Messina Hof boasts a 200-year heritage with the family traditions of winemaker Paul Bonarrigo going back six generations to Messina, Sicily. Winery tours and tastings, just $3 for adults, attract tourists from all over the region. Messina Hof, the most awarded premium winery in the state, produces a variety of red, white and blush wines as well as ports and champagne. At the inviting Guest Center, visitors can purchase wines as well as a number of other gourmet foods made with the local product, including Riesling raspberry hazelnut fudge. Yum! Recently opened are the Vintage House Trattoria, serving international cuisine at lunchtime Tuesday through Saturday. For those planning a weekend trip to the area, the winery offers the Vinter's Loft bed and breakfast.

Of course, this area offers dozens of hotels and motels — where else would all those Aggie parents and supporters stay? Families like the reasonably priced Vineyard Court Executive Suites, (409) 693-1220, at 216 Dominik Drive. The two-room suites include a small kitchen. For more luxury, there's the College Station Hilton, (409) 693-7500, at 801 University Drive E.

There's no shortage of restaurants in this area either. From the diner-type college hangouts to more elegant surroundings, Bryan and College Station will not fail to provide sustenance. For fine dining with a Texas twist, try The Texan Restaurant, (409) 822-3588, for dinner only Wednesday through Saturday. Seven meals made with ostrich meat are featured on the menu, along with an excellent selection of fish, poultry and beef. The Texan is at 3204 S. College Avenue in Bryan. We've seen many Aggie parents and their college kids at the Oxford Street Restaurant & Pub, (409) 268-0792. Dark wood, low lighting and a Sherlock Holmes motif lend Oxford Street its British flair. The menu includes a full selection of appetizers as well as steaks, chicken, seafood and prime rib. The restaurant, at 1710 Briarcrest Drive in Bryan, is open daily beginning at 11 AM. The Deluxe Diner, (409) 846-7466, at 203 University Drive in College Station, is a great place for a variety of home-style burgers and sandwiches, salads, chicken-fried steak and chicken-fried chicken. The Deluxe is open daily for breakfast, lunch and dinner starting at 6 AM. Save some change for the jukebox.

While you're in the area, you might consider making the drive to Brenham to tour the cool business that put this town on the map. The Blue Bell Creamery, (800) 327-8135, offers tours and samples of its great ice cream Monday through Friday from 10 AM to 3 PM. Reservations are recommended.

For more information about Bryan/College

Station, call the Convention and Visitor Bureau at (800) 777-8292 or (409) 260-9898.

Out West

Johnson City/LBJ Ranch

No, Johnson City was not named after the 36th president of the United States, Lyndon Baines, but one of his ancestors. The young LBJ was raised in the town bearing his family name. Johnson City, 50 miles southwest of Austin, and the LBJ Ranch in Stonewall, about 13 miles farther west, combine to make a perfect daytrip from Austin. As you might expect, attractions in these two locations center around the life of the late President Johnson. The LBJ National Historic Park, in fact, includes both the ranch and LBJ's boyhood home as well as the nearby Johnson Settlement.

Start your visit in Johnson City with a tour of the Visitor Center, (830) 868-7128, on Lady Bird Lane. Turn south off U.S. Highway 290 (Main Street) at Avenue G and drive two blocks to Lady Bird Lane. Here you can pick up a map of the complex, a brochure on the park, and also see the excellent exhibits, including scores of photographs, dedicated to LBJ's life and career. You can also listen to tape recordings of LBJ, Lady Bird Johnson and other state and national leaders speaking on major issues of the 1960s, including poverty, health, civil rights and the environment. This modern, stone facility also includes a gift shop and bookstore. It's open daily, except major holidays, from 8:45 AM to 5 PM.

Across the street is LBJ's Boyhood Home. This simple, but comfortable Folk Victorian style house was LBJ's home from the age of 5 in 1913 until he married Lady Bird in 1926. It was here, on the front porch, that Johnson made his first public speech in 1937, announcing his candidacy for the U.S. House of Representatives. National Park Service guides provide a brief introduction about the restored home and the career of LBJ every half-hour throughout the day beginning at 9 AM. A few items inside the home are original, but many are period pieces. An interesting collection of Johnson family photographs adorn the walls, however. Admission is free.

From here, walk about four blocks along a cinder path through bucolic Hill Country terrain (you cannot drive it) to the Johnson Settlement. This exhibit hall is filled with displays detailing the selection of Johnson City as the site for the town in 1879 and features all kinds of fascinating stories about frontier life, including the cowboys, the cattle drives, the trails and farming. The pleasant covered porch of this stone building is adorned with rocking chairs and has drinking fountains and restrooms. Another block down the path is the Dog-trot Cabin that once belonged to President Johnson's grandfather. The cabin, which has a shaded breezeway — through which a dog could easily trot — is typical of structures built during the 1800s.

This area also includes an authentic Chuck Wagon, used during cattle drives to haul food and supplies for the cowboys. There's also the James Polk Johnson Barn, built by the nephew of LBJ's grandfather in 1975 as well as a windmill, water tank and cooler house. Across the field, in a penned enclosure, you might spy a herd of Longhorn cattle grazing in the field.

If you're in the mood for a bite of lunch before leaving Johnson City, we recommend the Feed Mill Cafe, (830) 868-7771, just down the block off U.S. 290. This restaurant in a converted feed mill is decorated in kitschy beer joint fashion and offers homestyle meals daily beginning at 6:30 AM. The menu includes everything from eggs to burgers and salads to steaks, chicken and seafood. The Feed Mill presents live music Friday and Saturday evenings as well as Sunday afternoons.

While you're in Johnson City, you might also want to check out two attractions not related to LBJ. Take F.M. 2766 about 8 miles to Pedernales Falls State Park. The 4,800-acre park features water falls, fishing, swimming, hiking, camping and great places to picnic. Children will enjoy visiting the Exotic Resort Zoo, (830) 868-4357, on Texas Highway 281, 4 miles north of Johnson City. The zoo's trams take visitors on one-hour guided tours of the 137-acre park that is filled with more than 500 exotic animals from around the world, many that will come right up and eat out of your hand. It's open daily beginning at 9 AM. Closing times vary between 5 and 6 PM depending on the season. This is also a great place to bring a picnic lunch. Admission is $8.95 for adults, $6.95 for children 12 and younger.

Now, it's time to head for Stonewall and the LBJ Ranch, also known as the Texas White House. On your way to Stonewall, however, you might want to take a quick stop at the Hye Post Office, (830) 644-2465, which is right on U.S. 290 about halfway between Johnson City and Stonewall. The future president mailed his first letter here at the age of four and returned as president in 1965 to swear in Lawrence F. O'Brien as Postmaster General. This old post office and general store, built in 1904, is a Texas Historic Landmark.

Follow U.S. 290 west a few more miles until you see the large signs indicating the entrance to the Lyndon B. Johnson National Historic Park, (830) 868-7128. A 75-minute guided bus tour of the LBJ Ranch District is offered from 10 AM to 4 PM daily. There is no set schedule as buses depart depending on demand. National Park Service guides will point out all the areas of interest in this historic spread, including LBJ's reconstructed birthplace, the site where Johnson was born August 27, 1908 (the house was rebuilt by President Johnson in 1964); the Johnson Family Cemetery where generations of Johnsons are buried, including the president; and the show barn, which is the center of present-day ranching operations. You are allowed to get off the bus and look around at these three sites. The bus tour also takes you past the Junction School, where the future president learned to read at age 4, and the Grandparent's Farmhouse, where Johnson's paternal grandparents lived out their lives. The Ranch House, also known as the Texas White House, is on the tour, but visitors cannot go in as this is still the home of Lady Bird Johnson. General admission is $3. Children ages 6 and younger are admitted free.

You can now retrace your path to Austin or head farther west to Fredericksburg.

Fredericksburg

This Hill Country town is so packed with things to do that it is easy to make a half-dozen daytrips or weekend getaways out of this destination. There is something here for history buffs, antiques lovers, foodies, outdoor enthusiasts, architectural historians and military historians.

Fredericksburg, named after Prince Frederick of Prussia, is kin to New Braunfels (see our daytrip under Down South) as both were founded by The Society for the Protection of German Immigrants — New Braunfels in 1845 and Fredericksburg in 1846. The settlers moved into the Comanche territory, and in 1847 their leader, Baron Ottfried Hans von Meusebach, negotiated a peace treaty with the Comanche that is commemorated every year with Easter Fires Pageant, an event that involves hundreds of people in Easter Bunny suits, Comanches and pioneers, Easter eggs and bonfires (read the details in our Annual Events and Festivals chapter).

Fredericksburg has retained its German character in its architecture and cultural traditions. Indeed, many old timers still speak what is called old High German and can be heard talking among themselves on the streets and in stores. Local churches also offer German services and songs. The Vereins Kirche Museum (the People's Church Museum) in Mar-

INSIDERS' TIP

The local newspapers in Houston, Dallas/Fort Worth and San Antonio publish weekly sections devoted to news, reviews and listings of cultural and entertainment events. These cities also have weekly freebie publications highlighting happenings around their cities. Look for the *Houston Chronicle*'s weekend section on Thursday. The *Dallas Morning News*, *Fort Worth Star-Telegram* and *San Antonio Express-News* publish their entertainment pullouts on Fridays. On other days of the week, look for these free weeklies: the *Dallas Observer* and *The Met* in Dallas/Fort Worth, the *San Antonio Current* and the *Houston Press*.

ket Square, at the heart of the city, is a famous landmark. The octagonal building is now a museum of local history that is open Monday through Saturday from 10 AM to 2 PM. There is a small admission charge.

The heart of the town is listed on the National Register of Historic Places. One very wide street cuts through the town, wide enough, it is said, for a team of oxen and a wagon to be turned around. Most of the sights are on Main Street or just a block or two off the thoroughfare. During the Gold Rush of 1849, Fredericksburg merchants made their fortunes as prospectors stocked up at the last Western outpost before embarking into the heart of Indian Territory. These days, there is a similar feel to the town as tourists browse the antiques shops along Main Street, and the locals talk about the latest movie star who has bought a little piece of the picturesque Hill Country. Some Austinites own weekend homes in the town.

One of the first sights the visitor driving in from Austin sees is the Admiral Nimitz State Historical Park, 340 E. Main Street, (830) 997-4379. Chester Nimitz, who commanded the Pacific Fleet in World War II, grew up in landlocked Fredericksburg, and his grandfather once owned the Steamboat Hotel that now serves as the museum; the building looks remarkably nautical. The museum is open daily from 8 AM to 5 PM. Admission is $3, $1.50 for students. Children 6 and younger are admitted free.

A highlight of the museum is an exhibit featuring one of the tiny submarines used in the attack on Pearl Harbor. Other interactive and audiovisual exhibits illustrate the fierce battles in the Pacific. In stark contrast to the exhibits, the museum is also home to a Japanese Garden of Peace, given by the people of Japan to the facility. There is a replica of the study and tea house used by Admiral Togo, Nimitz's counterpart in the Imperial Japanese Navy.

Military buffs also may want to visit nearby Fort Martin Scott, 1606 E. Main Street, (830) 997-9895, a c. 1848 frontier fort that is now being restored. The only original building is the guardhouse, but replicas of original buildings are being constructed. Historical reenactments are periodically held here, and there is ongoing archaeological work at the site. During the summer the fort is open Wednesday through Saturday, and there is a small admission charge. After Labor Day and through March, the fort is open only on weekends.

Many visitors are drawn to Fredericksburg by the architecture and rich pioneer history. The Pioneer Museum, 309 W. Main Street, is made up of several buildings, including a home and general store built in 1849, a barn and smokehouse, a firefighting museum, a pioneer log cabin, an 1855 church and the Weber Sunday House. These tiny houses, sometimes just a single room, can be seen in both Fredericksburg and New Braunfels. They are called Sunday houses because they were built by farmers and ranchers as a place to bring the family on the weekend for Sunday church services. Many of them have been restored and are used as weekend homes by city dwellers. One of the best times of the year to see them is in spring when many of the tiny gardens are filled with wildflowers.

The Fredericksburg Chamber of Commerce, (830) 997-6523, provides walking tour maps and other pamphlets that give detailed information about the Sunday homes and other sights in the city. The maps and brochures also are available at many of the local businesses, including the German-style restaurants that dot Main Street. The Altdorf Restaurant, 301 W. Main Street, has a beer garden and serves lunch and dinner daily, except Tuesday. The Old German Bakery and Restaurant, 225 W. Main Street, (830) 997-9084, serves breakfast, lunch and dinner and sells typical German baked goods, including rye bread, which often runs out early in the day. The bakery is closed on Tuesday and Wednesday.

The Fredericksburg Brewing Co., 245 E. Main Street, (830) 997-1646, sells its own Pedernales Pilsner, a good choice after strolling through some of the 100 shops on Main Street where many artisans and artists, and collectors of antiques and Texana are located. Candle-making and glass blowing are just two of the crafts demonstrated here. One of the specialty shops is an outlet for Fredericksburg Herb Farms (see our Annual Events and Festivals chapter for a description of the local farm and its annual herb festival) where shoppers can buy oils and vinegars flavored with herbs grown in the Hill Country.

In addition to the Easter Fires and the herb festival, there are several other annual events that draw visitors throughout the year. In April there is a large antiques show; A Night in Old Fredericksburg is celebrated in July with food, dance and song; the oldest county fair in Texas takes place in September with a traditional livestock show, horse races, a crafts and home-baked goods competition, plus evening dances; Oktoberfest celebrates the town's German heritage; and at Christmas there is the Candlelight Homes Tour, which offers wonderful views of some of the city's historical homes. All are detailed in our Annual Events and Festivals chapter.

Fredericksburg is 85 miles west of Austin on U.S. 290, so it is an easy daytrip from the city and can be combined with a trip to the LBJ Ranch or Johnson City. (If you're traveling in June or July, be sure to stop along the way at one of the peach stands lining the highway.) But it is also a great weekend getaway location since the town has a wealth of bed and breakfast facilities and guest cottages. The latter are perfect for a romantic weekend since they are very private. Contact the Fredericksburg Chamber of Commerce, (830) 997-6523, for a listing of guesthouses and agencies.

Lovers of the outdoors also head for Fredericksburg to visit Enchanted Rock State Park, just 18 miles north of the city, where a granite dome rises some 325 feet from the earth and offers wide views of the area (see our Parks and Recreation chapter). There are also several vineyards in the countryside around Fredericksburg, including Oberhellmann Vineyards, (830) 685-3297, on Texas Highway 16 about 14 miles north of town. The grapes are grown on the hillside of what is called Bell Mountain. Two other wineries are about 10 miles east of town on U.S. 290: Becker Vineyards, (830) 644-2681, and Grape Creek Vineyards, (830) 644-2710. All offer tastings and tours.

Given the wealth of things to see and do in Fredericksburg, it is an ideal destination for a spur of the moment daytrip.

The Highland Lakes

Perhaps you've already had the pleasure of making a trip out to Austin's beautiful Lake Travis, maybe even taken a swim in the refreshing waters or toured the lake from cove to inviting cove by boat. Possibly you've seen or boated up and down Lake Austin, that lovely stretch of Colorado River that runs between West Austin's Tom Miller Dam and the Mansfield Dam. If so, you've seen two of Central Texas' six Highland Lakes. (Find out more about these two lakes in our chapter on Parks and Recreation.)

Make no mistake, however. Viewing Austin's two Highland Lakes definitely does not mean you've seen them all. Lake Buchanan, Inks Lake, Lake LBJ and Lake Marble Falls all have their own distinct personality, and the only way to discover the wonders is to spend some time visiting them — one by one. Each lake is within 75 miles northwest of Austin, some closer, making visits to them either a perfect daytrip or a wonderful weekend getaway.

The lakes, created by a series of six dams built on the Colorado River during the Depression of the 1930s and 1940s, vary immensely in size, shape and degree of development. The dams were built and are managed by the Lower Colorado River Authority (LCRA), which aimed to control the flood-prone river while providing a dependable source of water and electricity for the Texas Hill Country. For questions about the lakes, dams or any number of the parks and campsites operated by the LCRA, call (800) PRO-LCRA or phone the Park Information Hotline at (512) 473-4083. The common denominator that unites all these lakes is the focus on water activities: swimming, boating, fishing. Camping, either in tents or RVs, is extremely popular around these lakes, although in most cases the campsites are either primitive or just a step above, meaning you'll find restrooms in some but hardly ever showers. In most cases, you'll enjoy the offerings much more by either taking along a boat, renting a pontoon or WaveRunner or taking a guided cruise. We'll tell you where to find some of the best in each of those categories. While there are a few trails, the Highland

Lakes are not renowned for attracting large numbers of hikers or bikers. If you're determined to hike, we'll point out a couple of good spots.

Before heading out on your excursion, you might want to pick up a copy of the map "Highland Lakes North" published by A.I.D. Associates, Inc., or any similar map of the lake area available at retail stores around Austin. Besides helping you chart your trip to the lake, these maps also provide vital information on lake depths and water hazards and also point out landmarks, tourist destinations, places to gas up your boat and accommodations.

Lake Buchanan

Let's start with the granddaddy of them all: Lake Buchanan. While it's the oldest, largest and northernmost (farthest from Austin) of all the Highland Lakes, Lake Buchanan is also one of the most undeveloped, retaining the feel of a laid-back fishing haven. (Although more boating enthusiasts from the "big cities" are beginning to discover the lake.) The eastern shoreline stands out for its rugged, hilly terrain and towering cliffs. (Drivers should take special precaution here.) The western shore is closer to lake level and offers plenty of spots to just stop off and get your feet wet or take a swim.

This immense water basin, which covers 23,060 acres (36 square miles), was created with the completion of the 2.08-mile-long Buchanan Dam in 1937. While the basin itself is dotted by modest lakeside communities, simple bungalow rental units, camping areas and RV parks, the breathtaking region up river is banked by huge privately owned ranches. These landowners thus far have agreed to reject development of the area, choosing to lease some parts out only to hunters. So what you get is a view of the river much as it was in the distant past. This area is especially noted for its three scenic waterfalls — Fall Creek Falls, Deer Creek Falls and Post Oak Falls — as well as for the gorgeous cliffs and rock formations that line the shores. Birds, deer and other wildlife are common sights on this stretch. Only one or two houses can be seen all the way up to Colorado Bend State Park, (915) 628-3240, on the northernmost end of the lake. The park, filled with towering shade trees, is one of the nicest campsites on the lake. It has portable restrooms but no shower facilities or electrical hookups. This campsite, on the western shore, is accessible from the towns of Lampasas or Cherokee by car or by boat. Hikers and mountain bikers will be pleased to know this park also offers excellent choices for both.

Very important to know about boating on Lake Buchanan: This is not a deep lake even in times of abundant rainfall, so be sure to use your map, or better yet talk to the locals, and steer clear of sandbars and other hazards. Also if you're planning to boat up river, please note that the Alexander Boat Dock, (915) 379-2721, on the western side of the lake is the northernmost point to obtain gas. Once past this point, there is absolutely no more gas available, so you must carry plenty on board. Local experts warn that it is unsafe to try to boat upstream from Colorado Bend State Park as you'll run into small but very rocky rapids. You'll find public boat ramps on both sides of the lake at the various parks, including the Burnet County Park (Buchanan Dam), (512) 756-4297, Burnet County Park (White Bluff), same phone number, both on the eastern side of the lake, and Llano County Park, (915) 247-4352, on the southwestern shore, and the Cedar Point Resource Area (LCRA Hotline) in the northwest. Of course, the various rental bungalows and cottages around the lake also feature boat ramps. You don't have to go way upstream to enjoy boating on the lake, however. The huge reservoir is perfect for sailing, speed boating and bopping around on those ever-popular WaveRunners.

If you decide to rent a pontoon, fishing boat or WaveRunner, the following businesses can serve your needs: Lake Point Resort, (512) 793-2918, is just a couple miles west of the dam. The Indian Hills Stop & Go, (512) 793-6438, is on Texas Highway 29 going west from the dam a few blocks before the intersection with State Road 1431. If you're staying in the northwest area of the lake, try Max Alexander's, (915) 379-2721. Each of these businesses offers different types of boats, and each has its own rates. Be aware that you will be asked to leave a deposit or credit card.

This lake also offers excellent scenic drives year round but especially in the springtime when the wildflowers are in bloom. Designated the "Bluebonnet Capital of Texas" by the state legislature, this area and neighboring Inks Lake attract scores of visitors to the Bluebonnet Trail each year during the spectacular wildflower season, which runs March through May depending on rainfall. The Lake Buchanan/Inks Lake Chamber of Commerce, (512) 793-2803, located at Buchanan Dam, offers an annual brochure and operates a hotline of the best viewing locations.

We suggest a stop off at the Buchanan Dam Museum and Visitor Center right off Texas Highway 29 on the southeastern tip of the lake. It is open Monday through Friday 8 AM to 4 PM and 1 to 4 PM weekends and holidays. Here, you'll find a fascinating pictorial history of the construction of the dam, comments from a few of the hundreds of workers who found highly coveted Depression-era jobs building the immense barrier as well as information about the Kingsland Archeological Center on Lake LBJ. The Visitor Center also features an 18-minute documentary about the dam itself. Also, this is where you'd come to take a free guided tour of the huge generating facility. Tours generally run from May to September. And don't miss out on the opportunity to take a stroll along the impressive pedestrian walkway that leads from the Visitor Center all the way out to the spillway. This is the best way to see for yourself what a huge undertaking this project was — and get a great view of Lake Buchanan at the same time. For those not interested in making the trek, there's also an outdoor observation deck right off the parking lot.

From here, you can choose to either head up the eastern side of the lake or follow the western shore. Both have their own attributes and attractions. On the eastern side, visitors will find the Vanishing Texas River Cruise, (512) 756-6986. These year-round, 2½-hour tours offer a great way to see some of the lake and surrounding Hill Country. More importantly, experienced guides will point out the fascinating sites along the way. Tours held November through March are especially interesting because they take visitors on a trip up river to see the winter habitat of the largest colony of American Bald Eagles in the state of Texas. Bring your own picnic, most people do, or request a captain's box lunch and take a cruise aboard the 70-foot vessel, which features an enclosed deck as well as two outdoor decks. Tour days vary depending on the time of year, so call for a current schedule or to find out about the sunset dinner cruises that are also offered. Reservations are recommended. The standard cruises cost $15 for adults, $10 for children ages 6 to 12.

Farther north on the eastern shoreline — and still under development in late summer 1998 — is the Canyon of the Eagles. This vast development in a pristine wonderland is scheduled to include camping facilities for both RVs and tents, as well as restrooms and shower facilities, picnic areas and more. Call the LCRA parks hotline listed previously for more information on this new park. We've also been told that this could one day be the site of the new Central Texas Observatory.

The western side of Lake Buchanan also has some great attractions, most notably the Fall Creek Vineyards and Winery, (915) 379-5351. This winery, 2.2 miles north of the community of Tow (pronounced toe) on the northwest shores of the lake, offers tours, winetastings and sales of its award-winning products. Read about this winery in our Close-up in the Restaurants chapter. To enter the winery, guests drive up a road adorned on both sides by the grapevines that produce some of this winery's product. While tours are held daily during the peak season (March through November) and every day but Sunday the rest of the year, we've found that more extensive tours are given on weekends. But if you just want a brief introduction to the operations and a short tour of the facilities, any time is a good time to visit Fall Creek. Of course, if you happen to be in the area in late August, check with the winery for its annual grape stomp festivities.

Also on this side of the lake is the wonderfully primitive Cedar Point Resource Area (LCRA Hotline) a few miles south of Tow on State Road 2241. This rugged 400-acre waterfront park is dotted with some lovely spots to pitch a tent right near the lake. There's not one modern amenity here, except a boat ramp, but Mother Nature has endowed it with lovely shade trees and plenty of secluded spots.

There's no cost to camp here. Just pitch your tent and enjoy. If you enjoy hiking, this is one very good option.

Fishing is still a major attraction on Lake Buchanan. The Ken Milam Guide Service, (915) 379-2051, at the Alexander Boat Dock in Tow offers year-round fishing excursions for striper bass on the lake and welcomes children and adults. Milam, who has been in business since 1982, offers several fishing packages, including full- and half-day excursions. Also on the lake is the Crawford Guide Service, (915) 388-9187, which also offers full- and half-day all-inclusive excursions on the lake in search of those coveted striper bass, called stripers by the locals. Jim Crawford, who runs this operation, grew up on the lake. For those who just want to drop a pole in the water, the Hi-Line Lake Resort & RV Park, (915) 379-1065 or (888) 379-1065, on the western shore just south of the Tow community features an excellent all-weather fishing marina. The enclosed and lighted marina, which also has an outdoor dock, is a perfect place to fish for crappie, white bass, largemouth bass, catfish and striper bass. And you can fish here day and night. The Hi-Line also can arrange guided service.

If you choose to spend the night on the lake, remember that simple cottages and bungalows are the norm, usually with the added attraction of a kitchenette. Don't come to Lake Buchanan expecting luxury surroundings. The emphasis here is on getting out and enjoying the water. While there are several such locations scattered around the lake, among our favorite is the Hi-Line Lake Resort & RV Park (see telephone numbers listed previously). Jim and Charlotte DeGroat operate the Hi-Line, which features 16 air-conditioned cottages that have new kitchenettes with full-size refrigerators, microwaves and cook tops — a perfect place to fry up that fish you caught. The RV Park offers plenty of spacious sites featuring full hookups. This property also has a lovely sandy beach, perfect for swimming, as well as a boat ramp and outdoor grills. For dining on the water, check out the Rod & Reel Grille, (915) 379-1065, at Hi-Line Resort. This charming spot features an extensive menu that includes everything from burgers to steaks, chicken and seafood. It's open for dinner Monday, Thursday and Friday, lunch and dinner on the weekend. By the way, Jim is also extremely knowledgeable about the lake itself and is a great source of information.

Across the lake on the eastern shore is the well-established Silver Creek Lodge, (512) 756-4854. Silver Creek offers well-maintained air-conditioned cabins with kitchenettes, RV spaces, a swimming pool, a covered fishing dock, covered boat stalls and a boat ramp. Silver Creek also provides fishing guide services and does have a pump to gas up your boat.

Inks Lake

Just a few miles west of the Buchanan Dam off Texas Highway 29 is Inks Lake in what is known as the Central Texas Mineral Region. (Enter at Park Road 4 and travel south.) Only 4.2 miles long and just .6 miles at its widest points, Inks Lake is dwarfed by its gargantuan neighbor. Yet, the lake is surrounded by such rugged natural beauty — highlighted by towering oak trees, wildflowers, scenic bluffs and huge boulders of granite and pink gneiss — that it attracts nature lovers, campers, boaters and fishing enthusiasts year round. This lake was the second created on the Colorado River after the 1,548-foot Roy Inks Dam was completed in 1938.

Inks Lake features one of the most popular state parks in Texas. Inks Lake State Park, (512) 793-2223, is one of the most fully equipped parks in the region, offering both tent and RV sites, a few enclosed shelters, showers and restrooms, picnicking, swimming,

INSIDERS' TIP

When traveling to Houston, choose a hotel or motel closest to your main tourist destinations. It will save you time and prevent the mental anguish that comes from being stuck in traffic. Planning to visit sights all over town? Avoid the main highways at rush hour if you can.

trails, a boat ramp and even a public golf course. The 1,200-acre park extends along the entire eastern shoreline of the lake. Be sure to stop at the scenic overlook along Park Road 4 and check out the Devil's Waterhole, which has a beautiful waterfall. Teenagers just love to climb on the huge granite boulders that adorn this area.

Entrance to the park is $4 a person for those 13 and older. If you're planning to explore several state parks, however, do what most Texans do and buy a one-year vehicle pass for $50 that allows unlimited access to all state parks. You can purchase the passes at any park headquarters, at Wal-Mart stores or any other place that sells hunting and fishing licenses.

From Inks Lake you might want to follow Park Road 4 south about 10 minutes to Longhorn Cavern State Park, (512) 756-4680. While not on a lake, this wonderful 637-acre state park is nevertheless a great place for picnicking and hiking. No overnight camping is permitted. Of course, the major attraction here is the cavern itself. Located in Backbone Ridge, a huge piece of Ellenburge Limestone formed by a shallow sea more than 450 million years ago, the cavern is open for daily tours year round. The 1.25-mile round-trip walking tour takes about 85 minutes.

Lake LBJ

If Buchanan and Inks Lakes are the rugged members of the family, Lake LBJ is the refined cousin. The Colorado River meanders down from Inks Lake and branches out to skirt the town of Kingsland before it widens near the towns of Sunrise Beach on the western shore and Granite Shoals on the east. Once called Granite Shoals Lake, it was renamed in 1965 to recognize President Lyndon Johnson's efforts on behalf of the LCRA. At 6,200 acres, this gorgeous lake is the second largest of these four. Created by the Wirtz Dam, Lake LBJ offers plenty of wide open waters for speed boats, sailboats and Jet Skis. Unlike Inks and Buchanan, however, Lake LBJ stands out for the upscale homes and large manicured lawns that surround the basin. This lake is becoming increasingly developed and includes the new resort community of Horseshoe Bay and others.

Because of its emphasis on residential development, this lake is not stocked with rental units, although there are a few. Our favorite is the secluded Sandyland Resort, (915) 388-4521, at 212 Skyline Drive in the community of Sunrise Beach. This charming two-story lodge features all lakefront rooms, some with kitchenettes, and suites with kitchens. Sandyland also has a lovely, lighted fishing dock, a swimming pool, a boat ramp and a marina that offers both fuel and a small store. Here, guests can rent WaveRunners and pontoon boats or request a guided tour of the lake. This is just a lovely location overlooking a nice wide section of the lake. While this resort does not have a sandy beach, there are two nice beaches nearby. Ask owners Krista and Brad Foster for directions. You can also call ahead and request a brochure. Up river in Kingsland is the River Oaks Lodge, (915) 388-4818, at State Highway 1431 W. This lodge offers eight fully equipped cabins as well as an enclosed fishing house and boat ramps and stalls. The lodge also features a floating gazebo as well as a swimming, picnicking and play areas. Granite Shoals also has a great vacation getaway. The Tropical Hideaway Beach Resort and Marina, (210) 598-9896 or (800) 662-4431, at 604 Highcrest Drive is a lovely condominium complex that offers daily rentals of its one- and two-bedroom suites. All rooms feature living areas, kitchens and private balconies. The grounds here are highlighted by a truly unique Tiki Village that will have you feeling as if you're in the tropics. The outdoor restaurant and bar is shaded by beach-style thatched palapas. You'll also find a swimming pool, sandy beach and tennis courts.

If you're heading south on State Highway 1431 from Kingsland, be sure to take a few moments to stop at Lookout Mountain, just a few miles south of State Highway 2342. This scenic overlook provides an excellent overall view of the Colorado River valley. A few minutes farther south off this highway is the Kingsland Archeological Site, (830) 598-5261, which is open by reservation only. The 10-acre site on the shores of Lake LBJ is a 5,000-year-old prehistoric campsite for hunter-gatherers along the Colorado River. Since it was discovered in 1988, archaeologists have uncovered more than 100,000 artifacts, including projectile points, grinding stones, and animal bone fragments. Photos of this site are on display at the Buchanan Dam Visitor Center.

Lake Marble Falls

Like Lake Austin, Lake Marble Falls is an inner-city lake that appears more like the river it is than a wide open lake. Nevertheless, this 6-mile lake has grown so popular over the years that the community of Marble Falls and the huge Meadow Lake Country Club have grown up around it. The well-shaded 18-acre Johnson Park, (210) 693-3615, on the lake features a public boat ramp, a playscape for children, picnic area, overnight camping and restrooms. Nearby is Lakeside Park (same phone), which also has a boat ramp but is designated for day use only. Entrance to both parks is free. RV campers will want to check out the Riverview RV Park, (830) 693-3910, on the shores of Lake Marble Falls at 200 River Road. This site offers full hookups as well as restrooms, showers and laundry facilities. There really isn't much in the way of lakeside dining in Marble Falls, but if you're ready for a good, inexpensive home-style meal, try the Blue Bonnet Cafe in town at 211 U.S. Highway 281 S., (512) 693-2344. You'll find everything from burgers to chicken-fried steak, pot roast, fried chicken livers and fried catfish. The homemade biscuits melt in your mouth as do the pies. The Blue Bonnet is open for breakfast, lunch and dinner Monday through Saturday, breakfast and lunch on Sunday.

Once you've toured all the Highland Lakes, you'll know for yourself why these are the pride of the Texas Hill Country.

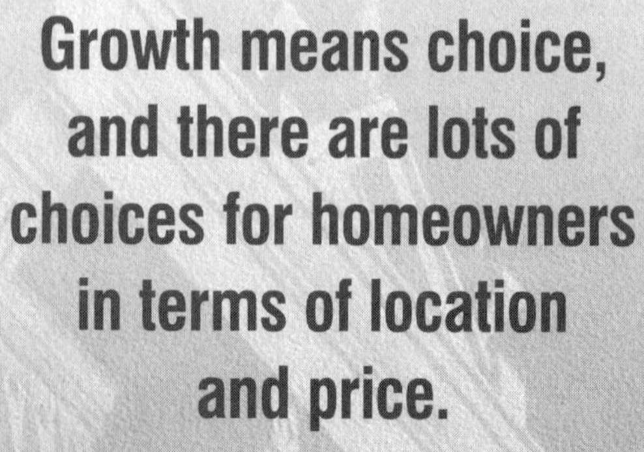

Growth means choice, and there are lots of choices for homeowners in terms of location and price.

Neighborhoods and Real Estate

Growth is many things to Austin area residents. For some it means opportunity, broader horizons and wider dreams, but for others it has come to mean the struggle to maintain the city's identity and quality of life that have been Austin hallmarks. The spirit of Austin is treasured by both longtime residents and newcomers. One key to the preservation of the city's unique character is the vitality of its neighborhoods.

Even the word "neighborhood" is loaded with meaning in Austin. Some neighborhood organizations have wielded considerable political clout at City Hall (see our Politics and Perspectives chapter), while others have created unique identities that act as a draw to both visitors and residents. Even some of the newest neighborhoods have distinct personalities, and have established strong internal bonds as a result of political fights or commitments to community activities.

In Austin, as in some of the smaller rural communities that have been absorbed by the city's growth, maintaining the neighborhood character, the particular sense of place, has been a challenge and a goal. Many of the area's neighborhoods have succeeded; others have not. But with growth has come a dynamism that has revitalized some neighborhoods, created new ones, and, at a minimum, kept the quality-of-life issue on the front burner for every central Texas resident.

The city has been leaping up the population list in record time in recent years. In January 1998, Austin surpassed Seattle as the 22nd-largest city in the United States, and landed in the top 20 by spring as the city annexed several suburban developments on its periphery. Beyond the city limits, the greater Austin metropolitan area has topped the million resident mark, and demographers are predicting the area will surpass 2 million residents in the early years of the next century.

There is a lot of hoopla about the growth in Austin population numbers, but don't be fooled by the numbers. There are approximately 1 million residents in the greater metropolitan area and about half that number within the city limits. Austin, while growing, does not have the sort of metropolitan feel some of the cities it is often compared to in size have. Don't come to Austin expecting to find a dense, intense downtown area, but rather a growing city that still feels, in many ways, like a mid-sized American town.

This booming growth has given both old and new area residents pause. Growth is leaving its mark on central Texas in many ways. On the plus side, growth has given the city a more cosmopolitan air. There is a greater diversity of restaurants, more shops and theaters, and the city's increasingly multicultural population celebrates ethnic traditions and cultural differences. The largest Hindu temple in North America is not far from one of the area's most popular country barbecue joints.

Growth means choice and there are lots of choices for homeowners in terms of location and price. But growth also means traffic jams. Rush-hour commutes are now a factor for homebuyers, in addition to access to city services — police, fire, EMS, parks and libraries.

Several significant trends in Austin's growth offer insight into what makes Austin neighborhoods tick. We begin with a look at some of these trends, followed by a geographic tour of some of the city's neighborhoods.

New Urbanism

It's a phrase that is much discussed in planning circles and in architecture schools across the country. For the uninitiated, "new urbanism" might be simply summed up as a return to the old neighborhoods of fond memory. Advocates, such as Miami architect Andres Duany, considered the grandfather of the movement, see it as a way to create neighborhoods reminiscent of those communities where many Americans lived in the years before suburban sprawl became the norm. A place where residents could shop at the grocery store, drop in for a haircut or pick up a fresh loaf of bread within just minutes of home.

Hal Box, former dean of the University of Texas architecture school, has adopted a litmus test for examples of the "new urbanism" — it is the "five minute Popsicle rule." Every child should be able to walk or ride a bike to the neighborhood store for a Popsicle and be home safely within five minutes. There are several "Popsicle rule" neighborhoods in Austin. Some of them are in upper-income neighborhoods, others in some of the city's older, working-class neighborhoods, but much attention is paid to how they function and what makes them liveable by city planners and neighborhood activists.

Austin has hosted several important conferences on "New Urbanism" and in 1997 launched an effort to draft a building and planning code that would embrace the spirit of the movement. The goal is not to develop a cookie-cutter approach to neighborhood design, but to allow each neighborhood to develop its own identity.

Downtown Discovery

Another important trend in the growth of Austin has been the rediscovery of downtown as a place to live. Thanks to the presence of the Texas Capitol and the city's vibrant music scene, downtown Austin is alive both day and night, and has not suffered the sort of blight some of America's cities have experienced. However, living in the immediate downtown area was limited, until recently, to a couple of condominium towers within a few blocks of the Capitol, occupied primarily by lobbyists and politicians during the legislature's biennial sessions, and a small number of apartment developments. Now, within blocks of the city's main street, Congress Avenue, apartments and lofts offer residents a downtown lifestyle, although not at bargain-basement prices.

Ten blocks to the west of Congress Avenue is the hub of another downtown center that has become a magnet and a model for inner-city growth. Once, the corner of Lamar Boulevard and W. Sixth Street was an area dominated by car lots and automobile showrooms. Now, at the heart of this hub, are the headquarters of two quintessential Austin companies. These local legends — Whole Foods Market, headquarters of a NASDAQ-traded gourmet/health food grocery store chain and GSD&M, an award-winning national advertising agency — were founded by Texas baby boomers.

Whole Foods and GSD&M's "Idea City" headquarters are at the heart of an urban neighborhood of bookstores, ice cream parlors, coffee shops and bakeries, all within a stone's throw of several new loft and apartment developments. The price tags are not cheap — rentals are in the four-digit-a-month range, and condominium-lofts can cost anywhere from $100,000 to a half-million dollars. This is one of those Austin neighborhoods that locals love to visit.

The Austin City Council has encouraged residential development downtown by offering tax abatements for developers. Some Austin residents are leery of the new trend and fearful that they will be unable to afford their "new" neighborhoods. The Rainey Street neighborhood is a small area south of the downtown Austin Convention Center and just west of Interstate 35. Many of the residents here live in small, wooden frame houses and

Photo: Peter A. Silva

The Bremond Mansion, built in 1886, is now home to the Texas Classroom Teachers Association.

rent, rather than own. Lots in the neighborhoods are now selling for as much as $85,000 and are being snapped up by developers with an eye to building condominiums and townhomes.

Gentrification

The downtown development trend is linked to two other Austin market characteristics, the gentrification of older, inner city neighborhoods and what planners call "infilling." Eager to live closer to downtown, or in one of the city's colorful, older neighborhoods, buyers are looking for empty lots, or rundown properties, then either building or moving older homes onto the property.

The gentrification of older central city neighborhoods has been a trend in Austin for several years, but the market pressure to develop housing availability close to downtown has put the trend on the fast track. Homes west of downtown have enjoyed prestige and market value for several decades — a one bedroom bungalow in west Central Austin can cost $250,000. Now, that trend is beginning to occur south of Town Lake in older neighborhoods along South Congress Avenue.

Many of the new residents are young, urban pioneers who are taking on the challenges of moving into older, rundown neighborhoods in areas north of the University of Texas campus and just west of I-35 around the Hancock Center shopping plaza. Generally, neighborhoods close to downtown and west of the capitol have been the first to ride the gentrification boom and are now firmly established as prestigious neighborhoods where a relatively small home can cost $300,000. A home just a mile and a half up MoPac (Loop 1) from downtown in North Loop can cost under $40,000.

Of course, the other side of the

gentrification trend is a growing lack of affordable housing. In early 1998, the Real Estate Center at Texas A&M University named Austin as the second-least affordable market in Texas. The center compares the median household income needed to qualify for a mortgage to the median-priced home in the area.

Nationally, Austin ranks below the midway point for the national median price of a single-family home — $115,400 in 1997. But it is supply that is the challenge for working families. Despite the shortage of affordable housing for low-income residents, Realtors do emphasize the diversity of the market in Austin.

The key for finding a bargain, particularly in an older neighborhood, is knowing which neighborhoods are being revived and which are suffering from the usual urban ills, including problems with crime and vandalism. That can be difficult for a newcomer, but Austin's active neighborhood association infrastructure can be a help. The City of Austin maintains a community registry, a reference guide to the approximately 300 active neighborhood associations in the city. It can be requested by contacting the planning department's neighborhood section at (512) 499-2648.

Suburban Expansion

While some Austin residents are looking to the heart of the city for a home, others are looking to the hills. The major growth trend in the last two decades has been the expansion of the greater Austin area to the west. Back in the 1970s, the Austin City Council adopted a growth plan that called for expansion along the city's north-south corridor defined by I-35. The council was reflecting the concerns of environmentalists who wanted to protect the vast underground Edwards Aquifer, the underground watershed that feeds Austin's icon and symbol of community environmental sensibilities, Barton Springs Pool in downtown Zilker Park (see our Close-up in the Parks and Recreation chapter).

But the lure of the Hill Country with its distinctive flora and scenic views proved more overwhelming. Much of the growth has occurred in the northwest, west and southwest. In fact, the word "west" has something of a cachet in Austin real estate circles. The area's most prestigious neighborhoods are in West Austin; West Lake Hills, the incorporated community west of MoPac (Loop 1); and in western Travis County towards the Highland Lakes.

Austin is built on the border of two distinct geographic areas. The Interstate 35 roughly tracks the break between the Hill Country and the Blackland Prairie. To the west are rolling hills, live oak trees and scrub dominated by so-called cedar trees (actually junipers) growing in the thin soil that barely dusts the limestone ridges. East of the interstate the land is flatter, covered with rich, black soil in which pecan trees flourish.

Both areas are picturesque, but the desire to live west may have more to do with age-old social patterns that have little to do with a modern, integrated Austin. Like so many cities, the interstate highway also serves as a barrier between downtown and Austin's predominantly ethnic neighborhoods. Austin's neighborhoods are well integrated, particularly newer subdivisions, but like most American cities, Austin still has two distinct neighborhoods east of I-35 that have been historically primarily African American and Hispanic. These neighborhoods have strong identities. Neighborhood groups there have fought both to preserve community identity and improve city services in their communities.

INSIDERS' TIP

One of the hottest trends in recent years in the home-building market has been the emergence of publicly held companies. Among the top-10 volume builders in Austin, nine of them are publicly traded. Five years ago, eight of the top 10 were locally owned. *The Austin Home Finder*, a bimonthly publication featuring new homes, showcases 200 new-home neighborhoods where Austin's volume builders are active. Southeast Publishing Ventures, Inc., (512) 451-5777, produces the publication.

The lure of living west has pushed development out beyond the Austin city limits, absorbing once small communities like Cedar Park, northwest of Austin in the next county. Just as the greater Austin area has pushed over the Travis County line into Williamson County in the northwest, in the southwest suburban developments have spilled over into Hays County. The small community of Dripping Springs, on U.S. 290 West about 15 miles from the Austin city limits, is feeling the growth boom as homeowners eager for a spacious home on perhaps an acre or two of land are locating there.

The High Price Boom

One of the hottest commodities in the Austin real estate market has been high-priced homes, those costing $300,000 and up. Realtors attribute this trend to the impact of the city's growing high-tech sector. In 1997, the area had virtually full employment, as the experts define it, with the unemployment rate at 3 percent. The high-tech industry had produced a group of entrepreneurs and a large number of employees with valuable stock options.

Leading the pack, of course, was Michael Dell, founder of Dell Computer, who built a new home in West Lake Hills that has been compared to Bill Gates' mansion in Seattle. Dell's home was appraised by tax authorities at $22.5 million — an appraisal he challenged — which was only half of what Gates' home allegedly cost. However, it did symbolize the high price boom in Austin. Dell's home is not the norm, but in 1997 the number of million dollar homes sold in the area jumped some 15 percent.

These high-priced homes are found in the city's most prestigious neighborhoods, some in close proximity to downtown, others out in the Hills. An old, ivy-clad mansion in the Enfield neighborhood close to downtown might sell for $1.85 million, while a sprawling lakeside home in the hills above Lake Austin might sell for $2 million. Some of the large homes in the hills reflect traditional Hill Country architecture with limestone walls, Mexican tile floors and rustic timbers, others are mock Tudor, or French chateau-style.

The economic boom has made some old Austin hands nervous. They remember the rollercoaster ride of the '80s. First, home prices escalated as the local economy boomed. But the boom was nurtured by a commercial real estate bubble that was being fed by high oil prices and easy loans. Then came the bust as oil prices plummeted and savings and loans closed. A person who bought a home in 1980 in Austin has seen it double in price, then fall by a third or more, then rise again to more than double its original value.

Most economists consider the current boom to be built on much more stable economic ground than the '80s boom. But the increasing number of homes, the number of choices available and the variety of neighborhoods have created a very complex market. Two key factors are price and location. Traffic and commute times were a Houston or Dallas issue five years ago, but now Austin homebuyers must balance affordability with access.

Prices in most neighborhoods rose in 1997, while prices fell in a few. Realtors agree there is no single phrase that describes the Austin real estate market, except perhaps complex.

We'll take a look at the city by geographic area.

Neighborhoods

Central

The geographic center of the City of Austin lies somewhere around Highland Mall at the intersection of I-35 and U.S. 290 E., several miles north of the Capitol. But most Austin area residents consider the center of the city to be the downtown area, along the shores of Town Lake and around the Texas Capitol. Given the city's fast growth, old and new residents often have a different view of where Central Austin becomes North Austin, or where west gives way to northwest, but there is little doubt that the heart of Austin is the downtown area.

For the purposes of this book, we will define Central Austin as the area east of MoPac (Loop 1); south of R.M. 2222, known as Koenig

Lane as it crosses the central section of the city; west of I-35; and north of Town Lake.

The central area embraces some of the city's most prestigious addresses and some of its more rundown, older neighborhoods. It also contains one of the most quintessential neighborhoods, Hyde Park, defined by advocates of new urbanism as a perfect "Popsicle rule" community.

Hyde Park was the city's first planned suburb. In 1889, Col. Monroe Martin Shipe, a businessman from Abilene, Kansas, came to Austin and purchased a 206-acre plot of land, in what was then far north Austin. The new suburb had its own electric streetcar system, dance pavilion and walking paths. Shipe first built large Victorian homes for some of Austin's leading citizens. Later, smaller Craftsman-style bungalows were added to the neighborhood.

Today, Hyde Park is not only a much-sought after address, but also a popular spot for lunch or coffee with friends from across the city. Located north of the University of Texas campus and bounded by Guadalupe Street on the west and 38th Street on the south, the smallest condominium in the neighborhood may sell for close to $100,000, while larger homes are $250,000 and up. It is the ambience of Hyde Park that drives the prices. There are several small restaurants in the neighborhood, a gym, post office and fire station, a couple of neighborhood grocery stores, and a bakery where the neighbors post notices on the bulletin board.

The Hancock Recreation Center is within Hyde Park and the city-owned Hancock Golf Course lies along the eastern edge of the neighborhood. On the northern perimeter, off 45th Street, is the Elisabet Ney Museum, the former studio of the 19th-century sculptor whose work can be seen at the Texas Capitol.

Every year, on Father's Day weekend, the neighborhood opens its doors for a historic homes tour. Visitors stroll the tree-shaded, wide sidewalks and visit some of the restored Victorian homes that give Hyde Park its charm. Hyde Park defines the much-touted Austin quality of life.

Several miles southwest of Hyde Park is the Enfield neighborhood, east of MoPac (Loop 1) and west of Shoal Creek, the creek that wends its way south through Central Austin to Town Lake, running alongside Lamar Boulevard for much of its course. As it crosses Shoal Creek, 15th Street becomes Enfield Road, running west through this affluent, old neighborhood.

You can still find a few small apartments tucked away over old garages and in some of the smaller houses of the area, and even a small circa 1960s apartment complex or two along the major thoroughfare, Enfield Road. But the area is best known for its large homes with hefty price tags, set back on wooded lots lining the area's curving streets. Homes in Enfield can sell for up to $1.5 million or more. Even small, modest homes sell in the $250,000 range. After all, it's just a five-minute drive from the capitol, which can be clearly seen as residents cross over the creek onto 15th Street.

Another central neighborhood with a unique character is Clarksville, just south of Enfield Park. Sometimes described as part of West Austin (a reflection of the days when the city was much smaller), Clarksville is bordered on the west by MoPac, on the south by 10th Street, and north by Waterston Avenue. The property was originally owned by Texas Gov. E.M. Pease, who gave the land to his former slaves in 1863 as an effort to keep them as workers on his plantation.

The neighborhood is named after Charles Griffin, who changed his last name to Clark after he was freed. Clark bought a 2-acre plot on 10th Street in 1871. Some of the current residents are descendants of the founders, but the neighborhood has changed over the years. Originally, according to local historians, Clarksville was home to about 250 African Americans. That number has diminished as the demographics of the neighborhood have changed.

In 1997, one of the keepers of the Clarksville flame, Mary Baylor, died. Baylor's great-grandmother was an original Clarksville resident — the African-American community was then a half-mile outside the city limits. Baylor lived her whole life on W. 10th Street in the home of her ancestors and was very active as a community leader.

The *Austin American-Statesman* lauded her on the day of her funeral for her efforts to save Clarksville for the low- and middle-income families who had called it home for generations.

She personally led the effort to have 18 low-income homes built in the neighborhood. Baylor's funeral was held at the Sweet Home Baptist Church, the church her ancestors built in 1882 in their small neighborhood.

Clarksville remains a mix of comfortable, modest homes and some gentrified houses priced in the $200,000 range. Within the neighborhood are several shops (see our Shopping chapter), bakeries, a pottery store, and restaurants, including one of Austin's top dining spots, Jeffrey's (see our Restaurants chapter). Like Hyde Park, Clarksville is a favorite place for city residents to visit. The neighborhood is also host to the annual Clarksville Jazz Festival (get more information in our Annual Events and Festivals chapter).

Central and South Austinites have an affection for changing the names of streets and rivers as their paths cross the city. In fact, rivers even become lakes — Town Lake, the portion of the Colorado River that runs through the heart of Austin, once represented a dividing line for some in the city. *Austin American-Statesman* humor columnist John Kelso helped engender the myth of North-South differences in the mid-'80s. North Austin, the mythology went, was land of the yuppies while south of the river was occupied by "bubbas," laid-back old hippies, and assorted free spirits. For several years, Kelso helped to hype an annual tug-of-war where north met south on the banks of the river.

Those distinctions have faded somewhat, but South Austin is still viewed by some as a haven for free spirits. The distinctions have faded, perhaps, because the older neighborhoods south of the river are being eyed as fertile territory for downtown living. Prices in neighborhoods south of the river have escalated. One of the most popular neighborhoods is Travis Heights, an area east of South Congress Avenue, south of Riverside Drive and west of I-35.

Homes in Travis Heights vary from 50-year-old bungalows to newer models, restored or relocated in this quiet neighborhood of rolling hills and large oaks, just minutes from downtown. The smallest bungalow in Travis Heights can cost upwards of $150,000, larger homes $250,000 plus.

The popularity of the neighborhood has prompted gentrification and infilling on its southern borders, along streets like W. Mary where small homes now sell for $150,000. The S. Congress Avenue corridor is undergoing rapid change. Once known for its X-rated movie theaters, streetwalkers and even an old feed store, the wide avenue is now alive with restaurants, antique shops, bakeries, boutiques and a software store.

The changes have affected the Bouldin Creek neighborhood, located west of S. Congress Avenue, north of Oltorf Street. Older homes in this area are being snapped up by buyers eager to live near downtown. The neighborhood remains a mix of rundown houses, fixer-uppers and newly renovated homes. In the middle of this diverse neighborhood is one of Austin's most famous restaurants, Green Pastures, an upscale restaurant housed in what was once a Victorian-era family mansion. The southern portion of this area has a distinct Hispanic flavor, with popular Mexican bakeries and restaurants occupying the corner lots. For more information on dining in this neighborhood, see our Restaurants chapter.

The area south of Town Lake, west of Lamar Boulevard and east of MoPac is one of Austin's most popular, older neighborhoods. Zilker Park wraps around the northern end of the area, while the Barton Creek Greenbelt winds around its western perimeter. Older homes in the Zilker neighborhood are much sought after and prices begin at about $150,000. Further south is the Barton Hills neighborhood where homes built 30 years ago are selling in the mid- to upper $100,000s.

INSIDERS' TIP

The City of Austin's Green Building Program, (512) 499-3545, has developed a national reputation. The program has the nation's first environmental rating system for new homes, and it also offers homeowners a database of green remodelers.

The area has two critically acclaimed elementary schools, Zilker and Barton Hills and enjoys quick access to downtown.

South Austin has continued to march southwards, and neighborhoods age much like tree rings as the visitor drives south along the area's three major north-south streets — S. Congress Avenue, S. First Street and Manchaca Road.

Much of the area between Oltorf and U.S. 290 W. is a mixture of older homes in working-class neighborhoods, some of them with a strong Hispanic flavor; others are home to free-spirit Austinites who frequent the area's ethnic restaurants.

South of U.S. 290 W., low- and middle-income homes, many of them built in the 1970s, give way to newer subdivisions. South of William Cannon Drive, neighborhoods like Cherry Creek, Southwest Oaks, Buckingham Estates and Texas Oaks offer low- to mid-priced homes, many of them dubbed "starter homes," that sell in the $80,000 to $115,000 range. These are traditional subdivisions with duplexes or apartments on the outer flanks of the neighborhood, single-family homes on the inner streets and shopping facilities at nearby major intersections. Like most new homes in Austin, yards are enclosed with six-foot privacy fencing, and most homes are constructed with at least the front wall faced in the local limestone or brick.

Southwest

In 1980, the intersection of S. Lamar Boulevard and U.S. 290 W. was bordered by a sheep farm. Now, it is home on all four sides to shopping centers, and a major highway construction project has created a whirligig of flyovers and underpasses to speed traffic in all directions. A Nieman-Marcus outlet store now stands where the sheep once grazed.

Southwest Austin, roughly defined as the area south of U.S. 290 W. and west of Brodie Lane, is one of the fastest-growing areas of the city, despite efforts to slow growth through restrictive city planning ordinances (see our Politics and Perspectives chapter). Much of the area sits above the recharge zone for the southern portion of the Edwards Aquifer, in the Barton Creek watershed. But the area's pleasant topography and easy access to downtown via MoPac has proved too much of a lure.

The Austin city limits do encompass much of this area, but a tiny island of real estate called the City of Sunset Valley marks the entrance to Southwest Austin. This area has few homes, but has fast become a shopping mecca for residents in this part of Austin. Two large farm homesteads occupied much of the small community for years, but now have been sold to retail developers. Since Sunset Valley has a lower sales tax than the City of Austin, the shops here enjoy an advantage over other area merchants.

Brodie Lane flows through Sunset Valley. The road is lined with several large apartment complexes, then an area of smaller, lower priced homes before reaching Shady Hollow and the Estates of Southland Oaks. These two far southwest neighborhoods feature new homes on large 1.5-acre lots that sell in the $150,000 to $250,000 range.

West of Sunset Valley, U.S. 290 W. passes through a community called Oak Hill. This area was settled in the 1840s and has long been a part of Austin, but has clung to its name and some of its identity as a small community in the escarpment above the city. It was known by a variety of names until the locals settled

INSIDERS' TIP

Central Texas enjoys a balmy climate, for the most part, but heavy rainstorms can turn those picturesque Hill Country creeks into deadly torrents within minutes. Creeks, many of them dry creek beds for much of the year, are part of the landscape tapestry in the region. When buying a home near a creek, check its location in relation to the flood plain. And if you are driving in a sudden rainstorm, NEVER try to cross a water-filled creek bed.

on Oak Hill around the turn of the century. The name is appropriate since the land here rises above the city and is shaded by hundreds, if not thousands of live oaks.

The massive U.S. 290 W. construction project, scheduled to be completed around the turn of the century, has stripped the Oak Hill area of some its personality. One wag erected a sign when construction began asking "Will it still be Oak Hill when there are no oaks and no hill anymore?" The old highway was lined with a few small strip centers erected in pseudo Old West style that gave Oak Hill its country character. One symbol of the old Oak Hill remains, the Rock Store, now a pizza restaurant (see our Restaurants chapter), built by pioneer James Patton. It took Patton 19 years to build the store; he finished in 1898. The local elementary school is named in his honor.

Oak Hill is also the site of Convict Hill — a neighborhood is named in its honor. Here, from 1882 to 1886, convict labor was used to quarry limestone for the construction of the Texas Capitol. The stone was used in the capitol's basement. During the operation, eight convicts died and are buried somewhere in the neighborhood on the hill in unmarked graves. The hill stands above the highway just as it splits with U.S. 290 W. heading towards Johnson City and Texas Highway 71 heading northwest to the Highland Lakes. The split is called the "Y" by Austin residents.

Oak Hill is now surrounded by several new neighborhoods and a large Motorola semiconductor plant close to the "Y." The neighborhoods here are popular because of the proliferation of oak trees and the relatively easy commute into town. A nonrush-hour ride from the "Y" to downtown is about 15 minutes, and even a rush hour commute is faster than a ride into the city from northwest suburbs.

Neighborhoods in this area include Westcreek, Maple Run, Legend Oaks, and The Village at Western Oaks. Homes range from $100,000 for a smaller 1,500-square-foot home to $200,000 plus.

Southwest of the "Y" and south of Slaughter Lane is the Circle C Ranch development, named after the ranch that once operated in this area. This development was built under the auspices of a Municipal Utility District, a MUD, a device created by the legislature and much used in the Houston area by developers who sold bonds to support the infrastructure in non-incorporated areas. In early 1998, Circle C was annexed into Austin, but not without protest from some of the homeowners.

Environmentalists had opposed the Circle C construction, but developers and residents boast of its attractive assets, including a large greenbelt, golf course, swim center and community building. The developer, Gary Bradley, also donated Circle C land to house the nearby Lady Bird Johnson National Wildflower Research Center (see our Attractions chapter). Land also was donated for a veloway and nature trail for bicycle riders and walkers. Homes range from $130,000 to $300,000.

Development does not stop at the Austin southwest city limits. There are several rural neighborhoods along F.M. 1826, known as Camp Ben McCullough Road, which runs southwest off U.S. 290 W., just west of the "Y." Other developments can be found further along U.S. 290 W. towards the Hays County line and Dripping Springs. Most of these homes are on larger lots, over an acre or two, and attract homebuyers who want a little rural atmosphere, but a short commute into the city. Some of the homes are quite large and prices range from $150,000 to several hundred thousand dollars.

West

As noted earlier, the area known as Clarksville, just east of MoPac (Loop 1), once was a half-mile outside the city limits. Today, the Austin city limits do not extend much beyond that, but the hills above the city are home to people who consider themselves Austinites. For our purposes, West Austin is the area west of MoPac and north of U.S. 290 W. and south of Lake Austin and R.M. 2222.

Within the city limits, West Austin means two of the city's most prestigious neighborhoods. West of MoPac, between Enfield Road in the south and W. 35th Street in the north are Tarrytown and Brykerwoods.

In the last century, this part of Austin was home to several large estates. After World War II, the landowners began to subdivide the land. The neighborhoods have been built out over a period of 50 years by a variety of builders and homes vary in size and personality. Price is consistent — it's high. The tiniest cottage in this area can cost $150,000, while large homes can sell for several million dollars. But the sheer variety of homes, the old trees and beautifully landscaped gardens make this a favorite location.

The same amount of money can buy a whole lot more house in other parts of the city, but the Tarrytown or Brykerwoods address is still sought after. Many of the city's business and political leaders live in this area. Its proximity to downtown, the two highly rated elementary schools in the area, Casis and Brykerwood, plus the neighborhood's "village" atmosphere attracts homebuyers.

In addition to several small, European-style shopping centers with cafes and shops, there are neighborhood churches, several parks and the nearby Lions Municipal Golf Course. One of the city's popular swimming pools, Deep Eddy, is in this area.

Photo: J. Griffis Smith

Stop to admire the rich detail of the architecture on Congress Avenue.

Another of Austin's prestigious addresses is not in Austin at all. West Lake Hills is an incorporated city that overlooks downtown from the western hills, west of MoPac and east of Loop 360 (Capital of Texas Highway). A major attraction for homeowners in this area is the highly rated Eanes Independent School District, which encompasses West Lake Hills and much of the surrounding area. (See our Schools and Child Care chapter for more information.)

West Lake has its own city government, newspaper, *The West Lake Picayune*, and personality. Many of the homes are on steep, curved roads that have wonderful views of the downtown skyline. Homes in West Lake are varied in price, size and style, but generally are more expensive than most areas in Austin. Few "starter" homes are available in West Lake and even small homes cost $150,000 plus. Prices generally begin in the $250,000 range.

Tucked in between the southeast corner of West Lake Hills and MoPac is the small, incorporated community of Rollingwood. Home prices here are generally upscale and expensive, but some older homes can be found in the $150,000 range. Several large mansions line the cliffs above Town Lake in the Rollingwood area.

The major thoroughfare in West Lake Hills is R.M. 2244, popularly known as Bee Caves Road. This winding, hilly road is lined with several shopping centers that serve the West Lake community. Growth has been a hot issue for West Lake residents, also, particularly the proliferation of large retail centers at the intersection of Bee Caves Road and Loop 360 (Capital of Texas Highway).

The development along Loop 360 is an indication of the boom in the hills west of Austin. The highway was originally planned as a scenic loop with few traffic lights. It has maintained its scenic quality, but there are now several major intersections along the roadway, many leading to new subdivisions. The homebuyer who plans to spend $250,000 and wants more than a two bedroom/one bath Tarrytown cottage has a multitude of choices in the western environs of Travis County.

Just west of Loop 360 and south of Bee Caves Road is Lost Creek, a neighborhood of large family homes on generously sized lots carved out of the hillsides on the eastern edge of Barton Creek. The creek, which feeds Barton Springs Pool, runs through the Lost Creek Country Club. On the western banks of the creek is the Lost Creek Estates development and a little further north is The Estates of Barton Creek, home of the Barton Creek Country Club. The development of the Barton Creek club was hard fought by environmentalists, but the developers have won recognition for their environmentally sensitive golf course design and landscaping methods. Homes in this area begin around $200,000 and go up and up.

The hills south of Lake Austin and north and west of West Lake Hills are home to an ever increasing number of developments of large, comfortable homes priced in the several hundred thousand dollar range, beginning at $200,000 and going up into the half-million-dollar-and-beyond range. Among them are Rob Roy, Davenport Ranch, West Rim and The Preserve. They remain outside the Austin city limits, but some are likely to be targeted for annexation by the City of Austin.

City leaders have defended annexation plans, saying Austin must not become a city where suburban flight threatens the city's viability. Over two-thirds of the homes priced over $300,000 sold in 1997 were outside the city limits. The hottest building areas are also outside Austin and sales taxes show businesses also are moving to the new suburban areas. While West Lake Hills is beyond the city's reach, new subdivisions are not. Davenport Ranch has been placed on the city's annexation list.

East of Lake Austin and south of R.M. 2222 are high-priced developments along the riverbank and in the city limits, including Cat Mountain with homes starting at $300,000.

West of Austin, out towards Lake Travis, are several new developments and one well-known, longtime incorporated resort area called Lakeway. The latter offers a variety of homes and condominiums that vary in price from the $150,000 to a half-million dollars. Popular as a retirement and weekend home area, Lakeway offers a golf course, boating and tennis facilities, even a small airfield. Newer developments "out at the lake," as Austinites call it, are the Steiner Ranch with new homes from $210,000 and St. Andrews at Lakeway, courtyard homes from $130,000.

Northwest

On the north bank of Lake Austin, prices are not quite as steep as those developments west and south of the river. These new, comfortable family neighborhoods feature large homes with prices beginning in the $200,000 range. Shepherd Mountain features homes from $210,000, while Jester Estates has large homes from $240,000 to the $350,000 range.

The neighborhoods east of Loop 360 and west of MoPac feature a variety of homes, some enjoying stratospheric views and prices approaching $500,000. Generally, older homes in this area are closer to MoPac and are priced much lower. Homes in Highland Hills, south of Far West Boulevard and west of MoPac are priced in the $150,000 range.

This pattern holds true for much of the northwest area, older neighborhoods — old is relative in this part of Austin — dating from the early 1980s and on flatter sections of land inside the city limits are priced in $100,000 to $200,000 range. Newer developments, usually outside the city limits on the hillsides and canyons to the west, are more expensive.

Northwest Austin is particularly attractive to employees working for the major high-tech companies, many located along U.S. Hwy. 183 N., dubbed Research Boulevard as it flows through northwest Austin. Once a lonely high-

INSIDERS' TIP

The Austin Convention and Visitors Bureau in cooperation with the Historic Landmark Commission produces an excellent walking tour guide to the Hyde Park neighborhood, one of several historic walking tour brochures available at the bureau. The Visitor Information Center is at 201 E. Second Street, (512) 478-0098.

way that led out of the city, the boulevard is now a major urban roadway, lined with a multitude of shopping centers. Small communities that were once simply a gas station and a house or two along the road, places like Jollyville and Pond Springs, are now busy intersections where the shopping centers boast sushi bars and Korean take-out.

South of Research are several neighborhoods built around the private Balcones Country Club. Homes in this area are in the $200,000-plus range.

The northwest corridor has seen the area's most explosive growth and Austin has spilled over the Travis County line and into Williamson County. Anderson Mill Estates, one of the first northwest Austin subdivisions with mid-sized homes in the $100,000 plus range, is, in reality, in Williamson County and has a different tax rate. Children living in this area attend schools in the Round Rock Independent School District. While Austin has annexed a corridor of land along Research Boulevard, into Williamson County and to the Cedar Park city limits, beyond that strip fire, police and EMS services are the responsibility of Williamson County authorities.

The residential area to the east and west of Research beyond Anderson Mill Road has seen home prices become static as market diversity increased. The growth along the Research Boulevard corridor also has led to long commute times for residents who have jobs in other areas of the city, a factor that may have contributed to static home prices.

North

The area north of R.M. 2222, known as Koenig Lane between MoPac and I-35, is a mixture of older, middle class neighborhoods and some rundown areas. There has been periodic talk of turning Koenig Lane into a major east-west boulevard — the debate over east-west traffic flow is a perennial political topic — but it remains a four-lane, urban road (see our Politics and Perspectives chapter).

Generally to the west of Burnet Road, particularly in the Allandale neighborhood along Shoal Creek, there are many spacious, 1960s-era, ranch-style homes that fetch prices in the $150,000 plus range. The advice of a knowledgeable Realtor is well-advised in shopping North Austin. There are pockets of wonderful, older homes that have survived the urban onslaught of strip shopping centers and suburban flight, but also rundown neighborhoods.

Just as in South Austin, the further a visitor drives towards the city limits the newer the homes become. Many of the northern subdivisions are touted as ripe territory for "starter homes."

Adjacent to the northern city limits is a planned community, Wells Branch, developed as a Municipal Utility District (MUD). Wells Branch has a variety of homes, apartments and condominiums ranging in price from the $80,000 up to $180,000. The MUD is well-designed and landscaped. Shops and gas stations have inconspicuous signs that give the area a well-groomed look.

Northeast

The area east of I-35 and north of U.S. 290 E. has not seen the sort of explosive growth associated with Northwest Austin. Some older, ranch-style homes priced around $90,000 can be found in the North Oaks area. Buyers, particularly working families looking for afford-

INSIDERS' TIP

One of the attractions of living in the hills west of Austin is the beauty of the natural surroundings. In addition to the flora — the wildflowers, the live oaks, redbud trees and cactus flowers — there is the fauna. There are many species of birds, and in the late summer the monarch butterflies pass through on their way to Mexico. And then there are the deer. Some Austinites feed the neighborhood deer, others complain about them. Nurseries sell deer-resistant plants, and neighbors swap stories of how to keep the deer out of their roses (human hair clippings).

able homes, are beginning to take a look at this part of Austin as the nearby Samsung facility gears up.

East

Roughly defined as east of I-35, south of U.S. 290 E. and north of Town Lake, this large area of Austin is destined for change. Just east of the interstate in the northwest quadrant of this section is Robert Mueller Municipal Airport, scheduled to be closed when the city's new airport opens in late 1999.

The city has developed a community discussion process to decide what will be done with the facility. Since it adjoins a municipal golf course in the south, many community leaders have called for the land to be developed as a mixed-use development of housing, shops and recreational facilities.

Immediately to the north of the airport and to the southwest are two older neighborhoods that are beginning to attract the attention of homebuyers who want to live closer to the city center. Again, this is an area where the advice of a real estate agent is invaluable. It is also a good idea to talk to neighbors and check with city planners about the future of the area.

The interstate has served as a dividing line in the city, particularly separating the predominantly older African-American and Hispanic neighborhoods that lie south of the airport. Efforts have been under way, with some success, to bring affordable housing and home ownership to this area of the city.

Austin neighborhoods are integrated, but like most large cities, there are neighborhoods where there is an ethnic concentration. Generally, the area south of Rosewood Avenue and north of Town Lake has a distinctive Hispanic cultural flavor. Many popular Mexican restaurants are located here, also ethnic groceries and tortilla factories. Neighborhood associations in East Austin have fought to maintain their communities' identity and have resisted powerful forces, including and expanding University of Texas, which forged a compromise with area residents over condemnation rights.

Southeast

Just as the northeast has not matched Northwest Austin in growth, so Southeast Austin has not seen the boom experienced by Southwest Austin. There are many apartment complexes east of I-35 along the East Oltorf Street corridor and there have been several entry-level subdivisions built in far Southeast Austin. Homes in this area sell in the $60,000 range.

Since the new airport is scheduled to open in far Southeast Austin on the site of the former Bergstrom Air Force Base, there has not been much residential development in this area.

At the southernmost point of the Austin city limits, on the east side of I-35 is one of Austin's well-known golf communities. Onion Creek was, for many years, home to the Legends of Golf tournament. The secluded country club has a variety of homes and condominiums beginning at around $160,000 for a small home.

Round Rock

For many of their Austin neighbors, Round Rock is viewed as booming bedroom community on their northern border, a place to avoid during rush hour if you are headed north on I-35 to Dallas. But for Round Rock residents their fast-growing town is home, and they are turning to historic preservation and neighborhood planning to keep it that way.

Round Rock gets its name from a round rock. The large rock is located in the middle of Brushy Creek, which flows through what is now a city. Brushy Creek was the name of the village that sprang up here in 1852. Many of the Victorian-era homes in the town center now enjoy protective historic status.

Sam Bass, the infamous Texas outlaw, is buried in the Old Round Rock Cemetery. Until 20 years ago, the shoot-out between Sam Bass and Texas Rangers, sheriff's deputies and local citizens was the liveliest thing that had ever happened in Round Rock. But with the growth boom in Central Texas, things have been humming in Round Rock for the last two decades. (Demographers predict the population of Williamson County could quadruple from 176,000 to 736,000 by 2030.)

Round Rock offers a variety of new homes ranging from small homes suitable for a young family or empty-nest couple in the $90,000 range to large homes with five bedrooms and three living areas for $300,000 and up. Some of the area neighborhoods are west of the city limits — several are in the tree-shaded countryside near Brushy Creek. The city's historic homes also are prized.

Major employers, including Dell Computer have located in Round Rock, but many residents do commute to nearby Austin, making rush-hour traffic on I-35 a headache. There are plans to build a second north-south road along the right-of-way owned by the Missouri Kansas Railroad, east of the interstate. It will be known as Texas Highway 130 or MoKan, just as the major north-south highway in Austin built along the Missouri-Pacific right-of-way is called MoPac by the locals.

Round Rock does have a reputation as a good place to raise a family. The community's conservative values are touted by city boosters, and comparisons are made to the much more liberal politics and lifestyles favored in Austin. These are cliched images, of course, but voting patterns and jury decisions tend to reinforce the two communities' respective images.

Williamson County also touts its lower crime rates compared to the more urban Austin in Travis County.

Pflugerville

Ten years ago, about 4,000 people lived in Pflugerville, the small community southeast of Round Rock and northeast of Austin. In the last three months of 1997 the same number moved into the community. This small, farming community is the latest home hot spot in central Texas, particularly for homeowners who feel priced out of the Austin market.

A four bedroom, two bath, 2,000-square-foot home costs a little over $100,000 in Pflugerville, much less than a comparable home in Austin. Plus, Pflugerville has maintained its small town aura, locally run schools and low crime rate.

The area is experiencing some growing pains and the city council has been forced to raise taxes and annex new areas to support city services. But the city is also putting taxes into city facilities like a recreation center and town library, hoping to add to the city's attractiveness as a good place to find an affordable home in which to raise a family. The new north-south MoKan highway will pass through the area.

Cedar Park

The old-timers in Cedar Park remember how the community got its name. Cedar posts were the town's main business until a few years ago. The small community on U.S. 183, northwest of Austin, was home to several cedar yards where fence posts were stacked before being shipped to ranches all over the west.

Every June, the town's history is celebrated at the Annual Cedar Chopper Festival. Before 1990, most of the festivalgoers came from out of town to enjoy the parade, sample the down-home cooking and take a carnival ride. Now, many of the town's 13,000 new residents join in the community festival.

Cedar Park is trying to hold on to its history, but it is also attempting to attract high-tech companies and other businesses to help boost the local tax rolls, and make Cedar Park something more than a bedroom community by developing a pedestrian-friendly downtown center. Homes in the area, which includes the neighboring community of Leander, offer homebuyers a variety of choices from affordable three bedroom/two bath homes in the $80,000 range to larger homes for around $200,000. Developers are intent on creating neighborhoods, not just suburbs.

The area also features rural homes popularly known as "ranchettes," large country homes on three- or four-acre lots with enough room for a small horse stable or a kennel run.

Apartments

The good news is that Austin has been enjoying a three-year apartment-building boom, but the bad news is that rents are high. A January 1998 study by M/PF Research Inc. found Austin was the third most expensive rental market in the South.

Limited availability was driving the marketplace, according to researchers, making Austin the 15th most expensive nationally. In early 1998, 95 percent of the area's 81,400 apartments were filled, according to Capitol Market Research of Austin.

The average price for a 1,000-square-foot, two bedroom/two bath apartment was $856 — the highest in Texas. In mid-1997, analysts had suggested rents would go down because the city was undergoing a major apartment building boom. Counting projects on the drawing boards at the beginning of 1998, 24,000 units will have been added to the market since 1993.

The area's low unemployment rate is one factor in the tight, expensive market, according to analysts. Another factor is the city's attraction to young college graduates, many of whom are attracted to Austin by the lifestyle and the high salaries paid by high-tech industries. One local marketing firm reported late in 1997 that some young newcomers were coming to the area on spec, without job offers, and finding work readily available.

But the booming economy has put some working Austinites in crisis. The Austin Tenant's Council, (512) 474-1961, a nonprofit social service agency, tries to help apartment renters who cannot afford rent increases.

Those who can afford the rents and are able to find a vacancy do enjoy a lot of amenities. Most new apartment complexes are gated and provide residents with increased security. Many have security cameras in each unit that offer residents a view of the main gate and allow them to buzz visitors through after verifying their identities. Garages are an added feature, plus whole home music systems. Most have recreational facilities, including workout rooms, swimming pools and tennis courts. Others offer business centers.

The extras offered by the newest apartment homes include high-tech gizmos like data outlets for high-speed Internet access, cybercafes and built-in computer desks. Want to get away from the high-tech world? Take a book to the "reading grotto," or stroll through the rose garden. One new development in Austin also offers a potting shed, an organic fruit orchard, and herb and flower-cutting gardens.

Many of the new developments are located along the MoPac corridor, Loop 360 (Capital of Texas Highway), and in Southwest and Northwest Austin, but there also has been some development along south Congress Avenue and north of the University in Central Austin.

Apartments For Rent is a monthly magazine that offers an overview of the area rental market, including some of the newest developments and older apartment facilities. The *TV Guide*-size magazine is available at many local grocery stores and also can be ordered at (512) 326-1133. The guide is published in 24 states and the District of Columbia. Out-of-town residents can order a complimentary copy of the Austin magazine by calling (900) 420-0040. There is a $4 toll charge for the call.

Real Estate Resources

There are more than 4,000 real estate agents and Realtors in the greater Austin area, some operating as individuals, others as members of large, long-established firms.

Given the large number of agents, it is impossible to list them all. The companies listed below are well-known and well-established. Most offer relocation and custom-building services. For a complete list of agencies, contact the Austin Board of Realtors at (512) 454-7636, or consult the Yellow Pages.

INSIDERS' TIP

Driving around the Austin area visitors spot signs saying "Entering the Edwards Aquifer Recharge Zone." What do they mean? They are a polite reminder that Austin's most hallowed spot, the spring-fed Barton Springs pool, is kept pristine and pure because the water flows underground through the limestone formations before it bubbles up in Zilker Park. This huge limestone filter is the underground Edwards Aquifer that lies underground in southwest Travis County.

Austin Board of Realtors

4106 Medical Pkwy. • (512) 454-7636

The Austin Board of Realtors lists over 5,500 area properties using a new computer system dubbed Stellar. This Multiple Listing Service gives potential homebuyers an opportunity to take a tour of central Texas and see what the home market is like in various parts of the area.

Amelia Bullock Realtors

Spicewood/Northwest Office, 8008 Spicewood Ln. • (512) 345-2100
Westlake/Central Office, 950 Westbank Dr., Ste. 100 • (512) 327-4800
Relocation Services, 8008 Spicewood Ln. • (512) 345-7030, (800) 531-5029

The company, co-owned by Amelia Bullock and Barbara Wallace, has been selling homes in Austin since 1969. It is one of the largest locally owned real estate companies. The company offers personalized tours of Austin, a variety of newcomer services and post-relocation support.

Avenue One

2414 Exposition Blvd., Ste. C-100 • (512) 472-3336

Formerly known as Eden Box & Company, this privately owned and locally managed corporation sells properties throughout Austin, but has gained a reputation as an expert company on West Austin sales. The company offices are in the Tarrytown Center, in the heart of one of Austin's most prestigious neighborhoods.

Coldwell Bankers/Richard Smith Realtors

Relocation Services, 3701 Executive Center Dr., Ste. 161 • (512) 343-6278, (800) 531-7667
Northwest Office, 4807 Spicewood Springs Rd. • (512) 343-7500
Westlake Office, 609 Castle Ridge Rd. • (512) 328-8200
Round Rock Office, 2120 N. Mays St. • (512) 255-1060
Southwest Office, 2100 W. William Cannon Dr. • (512) 416-8600

The company operates offices throughout Austin and central Texas and also offers relocation services. Agents offer a wide variety of properties from mansions on Lake Austin to starter homes in new South Austin neighborhoods. The company also publishes a real estate guide available in local grocery stores and on request.

ERA/Capitol Area Realty, Inc.

8320 Bee Caves Rd., Ste. 100 • (512) 328-6684

Jim Jackson acquired this company after retiring from the military. Jackson helps buyers develop a search strategy, a valuable tool in the large Austin marketplace. The company offers property histories, tax records, neighborhood history and comparable sales numbers, plus full MLS for Austin and the Highland Lakes.

J. B. Goodwin Realtors

Relocation Services, 3933 Steck Ave., Ste. 101 • (512) 502-7800
Northwest/North/Central, 3933 Steck Ave., Ste. B110 • (512) 502-7830
Westlake/South/Southeast, 1613 S. Loop 360 (Capital of Texas Hwy) • (512) 502-7600
Round Rock, 402 W. Taylor • (512) 255-4446

This well-known company is a full-service agency providing relocation services and new

INSIDERS' TIP

Most taxpayers in Central Texas pay property taxes to three jurisdictions — the local school district, the city and the county. An Austin city resident pays taxes to Austin Independent School District, the City of Austin, Travis County, and Austin Community College tax district. School taxes are about 60 percent of a property tax bill in Central Texas.

construction programs, working with many of Austin's top builders.

Henry S. Miller Realtors

Relocation Services, 925 Westbank Dr. • (512) 345-9477
Westlake/Southwest Office, 925 Westbank Dr. • (512) 327-9141
Northwest Office, 13376 Research Blvd. • (512) 258-6677
Round Rock Office, 1001 S. Mays St. • (512) 255-2561
Arboretum Office, 11044 Research Blvd. • (512) 343-0270

This well-known company has several offices in key locations around the greater Austin area. The company offers relocation services and valuable information on local builders, government, schools, recreation and sports.

Keller Williams Realty

North Office, 9430 Research Blvd. • (512) 346-3550
South Office, 3755 S. Loop 360 (Capital of Texas Hwy.) • (512) 448-4111
Southwest Office, 3755 S. Loop 360 (Capital of Texas Hwy.) • (512) 327-8848

The company operates throughout the Austin area and in Round Rock. It touts itself as "Austin's Number One Real Estate Company."

Prudential Owens Realty

Central Office, 3303 Northland Dr. • (512) 483-6000
Round Rock, 1717 N. I-35 • (512) 255-3727
Westlake Office, 1000 Westbank Dr. • (512) 328-1110
Relocation Division, 900 Congress Ave. • (512) 478-6400, (800) 866-6125

Owens Realty acquired the Prudential Real Estate franchise for the Austin area in 1991. Principals Diana and Rick Jenkins have over 40 years of combined experience. The company operates a nationwide relocation service and also helps clients with new construction needs. The company publishes a free magazine, *Distinctive Homes,* which is available in many local grocery stores and on request.

Stanberry & Associates Realtors

North Office/Lakeline, 12108 R.R. 620 • (512) 258-9310
South/Westlake, 1101 S. Loop 360 (Capital of Texas Hwy.), Ste. 100-F • (512) 327-9310

The company's relocation department offers a preferred vendor program that offers a package of savings for new Austin residents, including moving discounts.

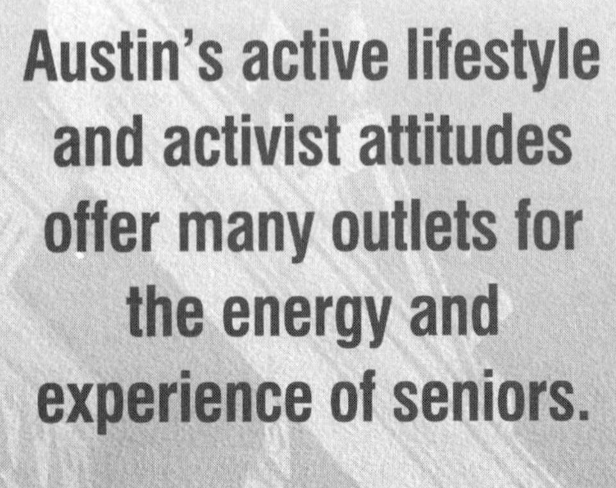

Austin's active lifestyle and activist attitudes offer many outlets for the energy and experience of seniors.

The Senior Scene

What can you say about a city where one of the leading senior citizens is Willie Nelson? The graying ponytail may be one symbol of Austin's senior scene; another may be a subtle shift in attention to senior issues as boomers slip into their 50s.

Of course, not all of Austin's seniors are aging musicians. Among the retired ranks, or semiretired, perhaps, are former Dallas Cowboy football coach Tom Landry, astronaut James Lovell, former First Lady Lady Bird Johnson (see our Close-up in the Attractions chapter) and a host of other notables in science, the arts and public service. Not all are famous, of course, but like so many aging Americans they have a wealth of lifetime experience and energy to offer. Austin's active lifestyle and activist attitudes offer many outlets for that energy and experience.

Austin's population is aging, but the percentage of people over the age of 65 in the Austin area is below the national average — 7 percent in Travis and Williamson Counties, compared to 12 percent in the United States. When it comes to the number of residents 65 or older, among the 77 U.S. cities with populations of over 200,000, Austin ranks 71st.

The 1990 U.S. census revealed some interesting information about demographic trends in Texas. The fastest-growing segment of the state population is 25 to 44, representing 39.6 percent of the Texas population, compared to 28.8 nationally. The percentage of the older-than-65 population in Texas is 25.2 percent, compared to 22.3 percent nationally. The climate may be a factor in that last number since Sunbelt states tend to have a higher percentage of retirees than their northerly cousins.

Some areas of Texas are attractive to retirees, particularly the Rio Grande Valley near the Mexican border, where many retired Midwesterners spend their winters; San Antonio, whose extensive military infrastructure makes it attractive to retired military personnel; and the Hill Country to which many affluent retirees are attracted by the climate and lifestyle. In Central Texas, the small communities of Wimberly, southwest of Austin; Fredericksburg, west of Austin; and San Marcos, particularly along the Guadalupe River south of Austin, are attracting retirees.

In the Austin area, the older-than-65 population is spread out across many neighborhoods. Austin's older neighborhoods, such as Hyde Park, Allandale and Travis Heights, have their longtime residents. Many newcomers are attracted to the Highland Lakes area where the many recreational facilities (see our Parks and Recreation and Golf chapters) offer amenities many seek. Two areas noted for their concentration of senior citizens are Lakeway and Lago Vista, both on Lake Travis, but these communities are by no means restricted to senior citizens.

In Round Rock and the Williamson County area the percentage of persons older than 65 matches Travis County, 7 percent, but the number of residents younger than 18 is higher — 24 percent in Travis, 31 percent in Williamson County.

Developers of retirement homes are finding Williamson County attractive because of its low crime rate, its small-town feel combined with nearby big-city health services, and, perhaps, for some, its more conservative lifestyle. One major development coming is Del Webb's Sun City Georgetown in northern Williamson County.

Sun City is the latest manifestation of a fairly recent trend in central Texas that has seen the development of housing alternatives for retirees. Compared to some regions of the state and other Sunbelt communities, there is not an abundance of retirement communities in the area, but the numbers are growing. However, there already have been some tensions between retired residents and the local tax districts over increasing property taxes to support the booming public school systems in Williamson County.

For those seniors looking for a retirement community or assisted-living facility in the Austin area, one invaluable resource is *Today's Family Guide* published by LCN Inc. This book is one of those homegrown business success stories. Founded over two decades ago by the wives of two local journalists recently transferred from Florida, LCN began life as a resource guide for newly arrived parents in Austin. It then expanded to include resources for seniors. Now, the guide is published in several cities around the country. Its listings are detailed and, while no recommendations are made, it is a valuable tool in finding the right housing option to match an individual's needs.

Senior Resources

In response to the aging of America, local businesses are beginning to recognize a market and, in true American fashion, responding to a need. One local Austin real estate company with longtime experience in the marketplace has created a new service to help people find a new, smaller house or a home in a retirement community.

There are several agencies and organizations that offer information, advice and research on community housing and nursing homes. These are a good starting point before embarking on tours or visits to facilities aimed at attracting and serving seniors. All the experts emphasize that research and careful consideration are vital before making a move to a new home, a residential facility or a nursing home.

The attorney general offers two publications for consumers. They are the *Rights of the Elderly* and *Selecting a Nursing Home*. For copies write to the Texas Attorney General, Attn: Brochure Division, P.O. Box 12548, Austin, TX 78711, or call (512) 936-1300.

Amelia Bullock Relocation Services

8008 Spicewood Ln. • (512) 345-7030, (800) 531-5029

The company has been an Austin presence for almost 30 years. In addition to its services for employees relocating to Austin, the company now offers Timely Solutions, a program to help seniors move to new homes, perhaps smaller homes or homes in communities geared to the senior lifestyle.

American Association of Retired Persons (AARP)

98 San Jacinto Blvd. • (512) 480-9797

This downtown office serves as the state headquarters of the influential national group for 50-plus Americans. Well-known for its advocacy, the AARP also offers information on a variety of topics of interest to seniors. Members receive travel discounts, access to a mail-order pharmacy service, and insurance coverage. Many local chapters hold their meetings at the city's senior activity centers.

Area Agency on Aging of the Capital Area

(512) 916-6062

This is a clearinghouse and ombudsman service agency for the 10 counties of Central Texas. It is a good resource for information on nutrition, transportation, home help, health screening, and legal services.

INSIDERS' TIP

There are perks when you hit 55. Sylvia Spade-Kershaw has written *Discounts & Good Deals for Seniors In Texas*, which wraps them up in one neat package. The book is available at local bookstores.

Austin Groups for the Elderly (AGE)

3710 Cedar St. • (512) 451-4611

Housed in a wonderful Central Austin historic building, c. 1902, AGE is an umbrella agency for more than a dozen nonprofit agencies. It is worth visiting the center both to enjoy the architecture and pick up information on a variety of services — adult day care, respite care, emergency residence for abused and neglected elders, family counseling, information and referral, mental healthcare and adult education.

CEACO Inc.

1715 E. Sixth St. • (512) 472-5575

Located in East Austin, not far from downtown, this community-based organization offers a variety of services and programs aimed at fostering economic, social and self-development. CEACO offers employment and volunteer advice and assistance, wellness classes, including stress reduction, plus transportation for area residents.

Family Eldercare

3710 Cedar St., Ste. 225 • (512) 450-0844

Located in Central Austin, this nonprofit organization offers a wide variety of services for seniors. Eldercare receives some funds from the United Way. Programs include The Gatekeeper, a training program for social service workers and volunteers, plus business owners and members of community groups who interact with the elderly. The program trains them to identify and assist seniors who are suffering from abuse, neglect or who are being exploited.

Another Eldercare program is In Home Care and Respite Services, (512) 467-6168, which provides care for home-bound adults. There is also an Alzheimer's program as part of this service.

Volunteers are trained in the guardianship and money management program and then matched with seniors who need legal guardians, representative payees or money managers.

Eldercare also publishes the *Travis County Guide to Services for Older Adults,* which lists services for seniors. The publication costs $25 and is available by calling (512) 451-0106.

The Retirement Community and Apartment Guide

(512) 476-5335

This guide is produced by Goodwill Industries under the auspices of its Older Worker Program. The information contained in the guide is supplied by the retirement communities and senior housing facilities.

Round Rock Senior Nutrition

(512) 255-4970

Seniors in Williamson County can call this number for information about a variety of recreational, nutritional and assistance programs offered by both government and nonprofit groups in the area.

Texas Department on Aging

4900 N. Lamar Blvd. • (512) 424-6840, (800) 444-2727

This is a state agency designed to assist seniors. The hotline, at the 800 number listed above, offers information and referrals on senior services.

Texas Attorney General

Consumers may request two detailed brochures from the Texas Attorney General, the state's chief law enforcement officer who is empowered to bring suit against offending facilities, including nursing homes, and residential homes for the disabled and the mentally handicapped. Both the current and previous attorneys general have filed suit to close down offending facilities. However, some consumer and advocacy groups have criticized the state legislature for allowing the nursing home industry to influence regulation. In 1997, legislation was passed aimed at responding to those criticisms. Write to: Research and Legal Support Division, Office of the Attorney General, Attn: Brochure Division, P.O. Box 12548, Austin, TX 78711.

Texas Department of Human Services (TDHS)

(800) 458-9858

This state agency can provide consumers with the last two years of compliance history of any facility. The agency says consumers should expect to see some compliance failures on any report, since even the most minor are listed by state inspectors. TDHS can answer four questions: How many complaints have there been in the last year? How many quality-of-care violations have there been in the past two years? When was the last visit by TDHS and why? Has the owner had other facilities recommended for closure?

Texas Department of Insurance (TDI)

(800) 252-3439

The state agency charged with oversight of the insurance industry in Texas provides consumers free of charge and on request with *A Shopper's Guide to Long-term Care*. This brochure is published by the National Association Insurance Commissioners. The agency also offers a great variety of insurance publications on all kinds of policies and state regulations, many of which are helpful to newcomers.

Today's Family Guide

(512) 288-6291, (800) 424-6291

This guide contains detailed information on a wide variety of programs, services and resources for Austin area families, those with young children and those with aging parents. Seniors will find a wealth of information about healthcare and social services, recreation and volunteer opportunities. The guide is regularly updated and is available at local bookstores.

Residential Options

Making a move is a major step at any age, and certainly a step that is not be taken lightly. Experts recommend carefully weighing of needs, both current and future; lifestyle habits and patterns; location; and, of course, cost. Another important part of the process is to visit the community and spend time there. Apply some of the same rules experts recommend in choosing a day-care center for children — visit at different times, talk to the residents, the staff, compare notes with others (important for children helping their parents find a place to live), and read the fine print.

The number of retirement communities and facilities is increasing in Central Texas. We've offered a sampling.

Buckner Villas

11110 Tom Adams Dr. • (512) 836-1515

This is a North Austin nonprofit rental community offering a variety of residential options in a Christian environment. The facility offers the flexibility for residents to change their environment as needs change from independent and assisted living to nursing home care. Apartments have two bedrooms and full kitchens. The facility also has an Alzheimer's program.

The Heritage at Gaines Ranch

4409 Gaines Ranch Loop • (512) 899-8400

This is a new rental community in West Austin scheduled to open in early 1999. The community will have both independent living apartments and an assisted-living program. There will be an on-site health clinic, fitness and exercise programs, dining services and 24-hour concierge, housekeeping and transportation services.

Holiday Corporation

The Clairmont, 12463 Los Indios Trail • (512) 331-7195

The Continental, 4604 S. Lamar Blvd. • (512) 892-5995

Englewood Estates, 2603 Jones Rd. • (512) 892-7226

Renaissance-Austin, 11279 Taylor Draper Ln. • (512) 338-0995

This national company operates four facilities in Austin. Each offers month-to-month rentals, catering of three meals a day, weekly housekeeping, paid utilities, planned activities and on-

INSIDERS' TIP

Several area grocery stores offer nutrition tours where customers can learn how to shop for healthy foods and to meet special dietary needs. Check at the customer service counter for other special perks for seniors. One Texas chain, Randalls, also has initiated Peapod, a computer-based shopping program so that customers can go online, order and expect delivery for a small fee.

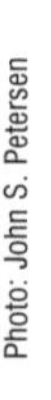

Zilker Park's Japanese garden is popular with nature lovers of all ages.

site resident managers. Some have beauty shop and barber facilities, and transportation services.

The Island on Lake Travis
3404 American Dr. • (512) 267-7107, (800) 422-4753

Literally on an island connected by causeway to the mainland, this independent living community is designed for active seniors. Rental apartments in this Lago Vista-area facility, northwest of Austin, have 24-hour security, indoor parking, an on-site restaurant, weekly housekeeping and recreational facilities.

The Summit at Westlake Hills
1034 Liberty Park Dr. • (512) 328-3775

This retirement community, west of Austin in West Lake Hills, dubs itself as "retirement living for those who aren't the retiring type." The luxury rental community has a variety of apartments, 24-hour security, transportation, catering, an on-site healthcare center and recreational activities. This is an American Retirement Corporation facility.

Westminister Manor Retirement Community
4100 Jackson Ave. • (512) 454-4646

This facility in Central Austin, near Seton Medical center, has what it calls a Life Care Program, which allows residents to buy their apartments and a care program. Up to 90 percent of the entrance fee is returned to the buyer's estate, and a portion of the fee is deductible as a prepaid medical expense.

Advocacy

Gray Panthers of Austin
3710 Cedar St. • (512) 458-3738.

Located in Central Austin in the same facility as Eldercare, this senior citizen advocacy group has a national reputation for its organizational skills and education workshops. The group produces several handy publications, among them *A Caregivers Manual*.

Senior Strategist Group

(512) 458-2517

Senior Strategist Group is a nonprofit speakers bureau that addresses older adult audiences on senior-related topics such as consumer advocacy, legal and financial issues, care-giving and protection from fraud.

Transportation

Austin Capital Metro, the area public transportation service, has several programs designed for seniors. In a city some call an elephant's graveyard for hippies, the free bus pass for seniors is called an EasyRider. These passes are free to citizens 65 and older and can be obtained by showing your Medicare card, driver's license, or Capital Metro senior ID. An ID may be purchased for $3 at the downtown Metro office, 106 E. Eighth Street, which is open from 7:30 AM to 5:30 PM weekdays. It just takes a few minutes to process the ID.

Groups of 20 seniors or more can request free transportation from 10 AM to 2 PM weekdays, 6 AM to 10 PM on weekends. Advanced reservations are required, call (512) 389-7595.

Capital Metro also offers curb-to-curb service and connections to medical services in some areas of the city. There is also a special transit service for the disabled. (See our Getting Here, Getting Around chapter.)

For general schedule information, call (512) 474-1200. Many grocery stores also stock bus schedules at their customer service counters.

Medi Wheels

(512) 476-6325

This service offers rides to medical appointments to people 55 or older. Please call a week in advance of your appointment.

Support Services

(512) 480-3012

This PARD program offers non-emergency medical transportation for seniors 60 and older. Reservations are required, with 24-hour notice.

Lifetime Learning

Austin Community College

5930 Middle Fiskville Rd. • (512) 223-7000

The city's community college has several campuses around the area (see our Higher Education chapter). In addition to a full curriculum of credit courses, ACC offers a variety of enrichment programs, some of them aimed at topics of particular concern to the elderly, including family caregiving, retirement and recreation, and aging classes.

Elderhostel

The University of Texas • (512) 471-3500

The University of Texas offers five-day, non-credit programs in the liberal arts at seven Elderhostel sites. They are at University of Texas in Austin, Big Bend National Park in far southwest Texas, San Antonio, Galveston, El Paso and Fort Worth. Art, music and literature are the themes of the various programs. Lodging, meals, and field trips are included in the $365 tuition fee.

Lifetime Learning Institute

Concordia Lutheran College, 3400 I-35 • (512) 452-7661

In the fall and spring Concordia offers several eight-week courses for people 50 and older on a variety of topics such as art

INSIDERS' TIP

If you are feeling left out in one of America's most wired cities, contact Austin Groups for the Elderly (AGE), (512) 451-4611. AGE offers the Senior Net program for people 55 and older who want to learn to access the Internet and use e-mail.

appreciation, foreign languages, Texas history, financial planning, and social and political history. Tuition is $15 per course, and classes are held at a variety of locations around the city.

Texas Elderhostel

(512) 471-2780

This program is a clearinghouse for information on Elderhostel programs around the state at institutes of higher learning and cultural institutions (the University of Texas programs are listed previously in this chapter). Call for a catalog, which includes information about classes held in state parks, wildlife refuges and research institutes.

University of Texas Continuing Education

The Thompson Conference Center, 26th and Red River Sts. • (512) 471-3121

This facility is near the LBJ Presidential Library on the eastern edge of the campus. Two community outreach programs offer classes for seniors. There is an annual membership program, Learning Activities for Mature People, featuring a series lectures and classes in the fall, winter and spring for $125. Three six-week programs, titled Seminars for Adult Growth and Enrichment, are offered annually in the fall, winter and spring. The cost is $195.

Community Activities

A wide variety of recreational activities are aimed at area seniors and many of them can be found at a network of senior activity centers. These community facilities offer a place to meet for recreation, networking and nutrition. Most city-run centers offer a hot lunch for a nominal fee, around $1.

The centers are operated by the Austin Parks & Recreation Department (PARD), which has numerous brochures and newsletters detailing programs and locations.

Activities at the centers range from arts and crafts to health and fitness classes, line dancing, mah jong, poetry clubs and investment clubs, pool tournaments, stamp collectors' gatherings and outings.

Austin Parks & Recreation Senior Centers

Main Office, 901 W. Riverside Dr. • (512) 480-3000

Just south of Town Lake in South Central Austin, this is the headquarters of the city's senior activity center network. There are senior activities at all of the city's recreation centers and several smaller senior centers at various locations throughout the city. There are also three designated Senior Activity Centers in the city listed below. All have extensive senior programs and support services, and all serve a hot lunch for a small charge. Transportation is provided on request.

Conley-Guerrero Senior Activity Center

808 Nile St. • (512) 478-7695

The daily programs here are designed to enhance the quality of life for seniors in East Austin. Seniors gather here daily to exercise. Domino sessions are a popular pastime, as are the ceramics classes. The center also arranges out-of-town trips for shopping and recreation, and there are popular regular events like Blue Jean Day and Over the Rainbow Social Evenings.

Lamar Senior Activity Center

2874 Shoal Crest Ave. • (512) 474-5921

The seniors at this Central Austin center are avid tripsters, heading off on theatre and museum outings to Houston and Dallas, and visiting historic Texas sites, including the new Bush Presidential Library in College Station. Ballroom dancing is a popular activity and dances are held usually three times a week. There is also an array of classes offered in games, arts and crafts, plus a driving safety class that offers graduates a cut in their insurance premiums.

South Austin Senior Activity Center

3911 Manchaca Rd. • (512) 448-0787

Bridge, dominos and mah jong are popular pastimes at this South Austin center. Students in the ceramics classes can fire their creations in the on-site kiln. Oil painting classes are also offered. The center also organizes daytrips to country music concerts, shopping trips to the outlet malls, and visits to major art exhibits in Dallas and Houston.

Round Rock

Round Rock Senior Center
205 E. Main St. • (512) 255-4970

This senior activity center is open from 8 AM to 3 PM daily and offers a wide variety of senior services and recreational pursuits. The center also serves meals.

Pflugerville

Austin/Travis County Health and Human Services
15803 Windermere Dr. • (512) 251-4168

This is a senior citizen activity center that offers opportunities for recreation and interaction, plus support services and meals.

Nutrition

Maintaining a healthy diet can be difficult for some seniors, particularly those on a tight budget, or those who find themselves suddenly alone or unable to cook and shop for groceries. The programs listed below can lend a helping hand.

Groceries-to-Go
(512) 476-6325

Groceries-to-Go is a program in which volunteers do grocery shopping and delivery for home-bound elderly and disabled people.

Meals on Wheels and More
2222 Rosewood Ave. • (512) 476-6325

This program delivers six meals a week to more than 1,500 home-bound elderly and disabled people in the greater Austin area. The service also offers a grocery shopping and delivery service. A related service is Handi-Wheels, (512) 476-6325, offering minor home safety repairs by volunteers to Meals on Wheels clients.

Senior Support Services
(512) 480-3004

This program provides lunches every weekday to senior citizens at 18 locations in Travis County, including the city's PARD Senior Activity Centers (see previous listing). To be eligible you must be 60 or the spouse of someone enrolled in the meals program. The cost of the hot lunch is minimal, as low as 50¢, a little more in some locations. Free transportation also is provided with 24 hours notice, (512) 480-3012.

Williamson-Burnet County Opportunities Inc.
(512) 930-9011

This two-county service nutrition program offers meals-on-wheels and other nutrition services for seniors in Williamson and Burnet Counties.

Caregivers
Far Northwest Caregivers • (512) 250-5021
Lakeway Service League • (512) 261-3514
N. Central Caregivers • (512) 453-2273
Northeast Austin Caregivers • (512) 459-1122
S. Austin Caregivers • (512) 445-5552
Southeast Austin Caregivers • (512) 472-0997
W. Austin Caregivers • (512) 472-6339
Round Rock Caregivers • (512) 310-1060

Caregivers is a network of volunteers who help those seniors who want to remain in their homes maintain their independence. Volunteers do small, but meaningful tasks for the seniors, including driving

INSIDERS' TIP

***Every Generation's Concern*, a 160-page publication of Gray Panthers of Austin, is a manual to help older adults and their families make choices regarding health and social services. It is available for a $6 donation plus postage and handling at (512) 458-3738.**

them to appointments or grocery shopping for them.

Telephone Reassurance Program

United Austin for the Elderly
• (512) 476-6325

This service offers a daily contact program for seniors who live alone. Volunteers also have Phone-A-Friend, a program aimed at contacting lonely seniors.

Job Opportunities

Austin's unemployment rate has been at record lows in recent years. In fact, some experts have declared Austin is virtually a full employment area as unemployment numbers hover between 3 and 4 percent. This situation has opened up opportunities for employment in several sectors. The high-tech field gets a lot of attention for its youthful work force, but there are opportunities for talented, skilled workers of all ages. The service sector has faced a chronic shortage of workers, and seniors now fill part-time jobs at grocery stores, fast food restaurants and other service-oriented businesses in the area.

Austin Senior Aides

(512) 480-3006

This PARD program matches seniors with nonprofit agencies for part-time work. On-the-job training is offered. To participate, a person must be 55 or older and have a low income.

Experience Unlimited

(512) 480-3013

Another PARD program that encourages individuals 50 or older to register with the program's job referral bank. One of the program's innovative programs offered lifeguard jobs to seniors at the city's swimming pools.

Old Bakery and Emporium

1006 Congress Ave. • (512) 477-5961

A PARD program provides a showcase at the Old Bakery and Emporium for talented seniors to display and sell their crafts at this downtown attraction. (See our Attractions chapter.)

Older Worker Program

Goodwill Industries, 300 N. Lamar Blvd.
• (512) 476-5335

This program for 55 and older residents offers employment counseling, job development training and placement assistance. Goodwill also offers training in areas, including computer skills and nurse's aide classes.

Texas Workforce Commission

Northeast Austin Office, 7517 Cameron Rd. • (512) 452-8850
Southeast Austin Office, 2015 S. I-35, Ste. 100 • (512) 440-7816
Round Rock Office, 206 W. Main, Ste. 111 • (512) 244-3269

Formerly known as the Texas Employment Commission, this is the state agency that offers employment counseling and referrals to Texas residents. The department also has a Mature Worker Services program that conducts seminars to help workers hone their interview and resume-writing skills.

Volunteer Opportunities

Opportunities abound for those with a lifetime of skills to help others in the community. From local museums to the police department, rape-crisis centers to literacy programs, the possibilities for meaningful activity are enormous. We have listed several volunteer clearinghouse organizations and groups who seek out seniors. Each year, around Christmas, the *Austin American-Statesman* publishes a comprehensive wish list from various community groups seeking either volunteers or donations. Following is a list of groups that use volunteers.

- American Red Cross, Central Texas Office, 2218 Pershing Drive, (512)928-4271
- Williamson County Office, 1106 S. Mays Street, Round Rock, (512) 255-9899
- Care Calls, (512) 476-6325
- Court Appointed Special Advocates (CASA), (512) 443-2272
- Foster Grandparents, (512) 371-6098
- Retired and Senior Volunteer Program (RSVP), (512) 473-4130
- United Way, Capital Area's First Call For Help, (512) 323-1899

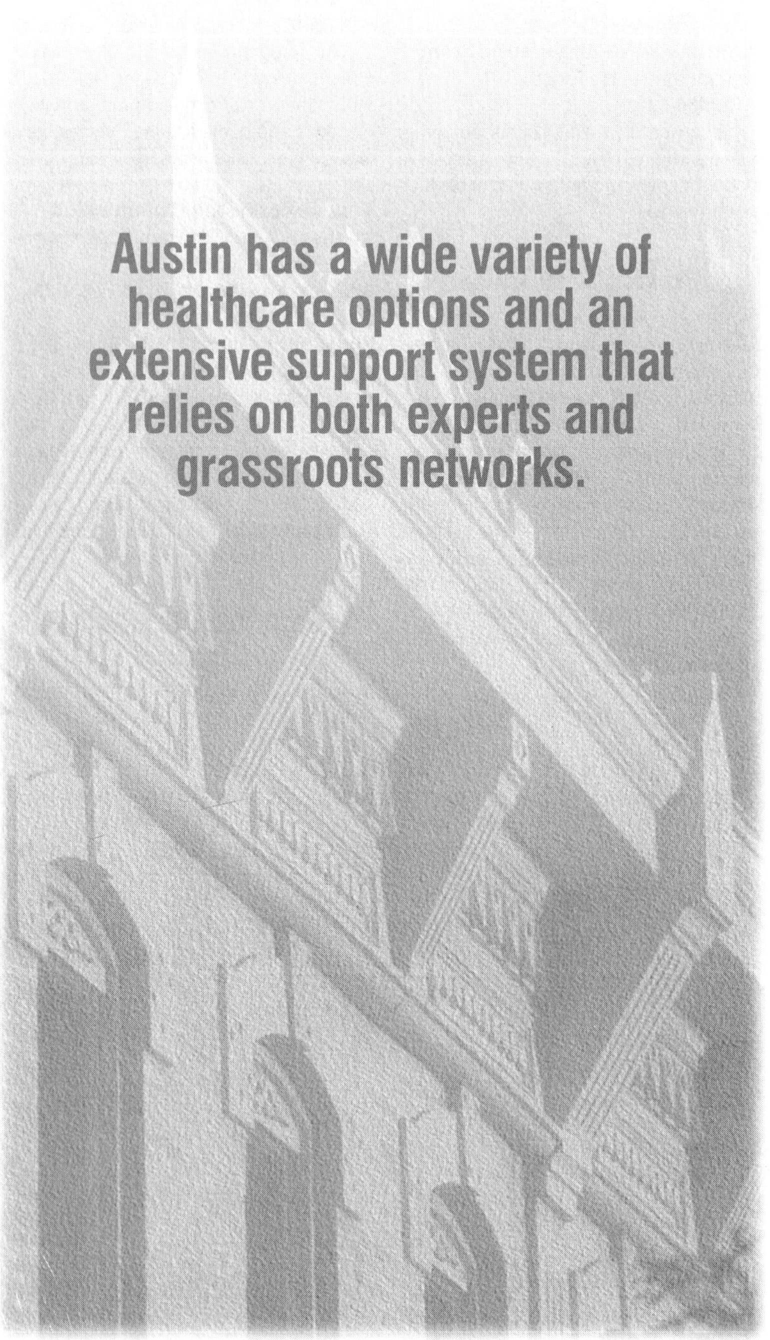

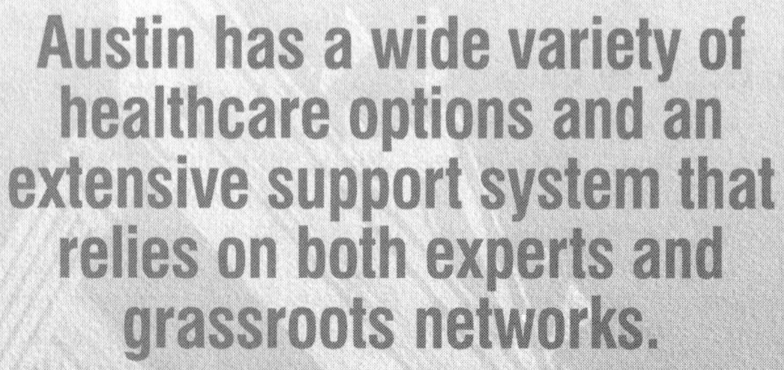

Austin has a wide variety of healthcare options and an extensive support system that relies on both experts and grassroots networks.

Healthcare and Wellness

The first hint that Austin is a city that values wellness is the constant reminder over the airport public address system: Austin is a Clean Air City. Smoking is strictly verboten in most public places, although the rise of cigar bars suggests there is a backlash to political correctness among some Austinites. Perhaps that is an indication of another much-valued community trait — tolerance.

That tolerance combined with a willingness to try new approaches also means Austin is a place where alternative therapies and healthcare options are widely available. Even Austin pets get to choose between traditional and alternative medical care here; one of our pets has been treated with acupuncture and Chinese herbal therapy — at the suggestion, we might add, of our "regular" vet.

Health food stores, including the flagship store of the now national and publicly traded Whole Foods Market chain (see our Shopping chapter), are not only evidence of Austin's concerns about wellness, but also serve as conduits for alternative therapy information. Even the mainstream stores stock organic foods, offer herbal supplements and sometimes have on-site massage.

In addition to concerns about diet and healthcare, Austin residents place a great deal of emphasis on exercise. Running, jogging, walking, swimming and bicycling are important activities, and visitors can see daily evidence of this around Town Lake and at Barton Springs Pool (see our Parks and Recreation chapter).

Austin is consistently included on top-10 lists of great places to live in the United States, and one of the criteria is the quality of healthcare available in a community. There is little doubt that Austin has a wide variety of healthcare options and an extensive support system that relies on both experts and grassroots networks.

There is also little doubt that the city's healthcare system has been evolving and will continue to expand and change in the years ahead. The U.S. healthcare system has been undergoing some radical and profound changes in the last few decades; this combined with Austin's growth has created a fluid picture of the Central Texas healthcare infrastructure.

In the last couple of years, consolidations, expansions and new developments have changed the medical scene. These changes are particularly apparent when reviewing the hospital and clinic scene in Austin and surrounding areas. There are two major players in Austin — the Seton Good Health Network and the Columbia St. David's Healthcare System. A third player, Scott & White, a healthcare provider based in Temple, Texas, is making aggressive moves into Williamson County, notably in Round Rock and Cedar Park, with plans to build an ambulatory care center in Round Rock and clinics in both Round Rock and Cedar Park. Seton has plans to expand in Southwest Austin and is setting up clinic facilities in the Highland Lakes area. All three regularly make business page headlines with their latest plans.

There are several health research facilities in Austin focused on drug and therapy trials. These research facilities frequently advertise in the local media for volunteers (sometimes with pay) to participate in drug trials.

Finding a Physician

This can be a difficult task for newcomers to any city. Both Seton and Columbia/St. David's operate physician referral services. Seton's Physician Referral number is (512) 324-4450. For information about the Columbia/St. David's system and doctors, call (512) 482-4100. Scott & White's health plan information line is (800) 758-3012. The Scott & White Clinic in Round Rock can be reached at (512) 310-3000, or toll free at (888) 883-3676.

There are also several professional organizations that offer referrals to their members. They include the Austin Travis County Chiropractic Society Referral Service, (512) 263-3434; Capital Area Psychological Association, (512) 451-4983; Texas Chiropractic Association, (512) 477-9292; Texas Psychological Association, (512) 454-2449; and the Travis County Medical Society, (512) 458-1121.

Hospitals

Central Brackenridge Hospital

601 E. 15th St. • (512) 476-6461

The city-owned hospital serves as the regional trauma center for the Central Texas area and is served by STARflight medical helicopter services. The hospital also has a children's emergency room facility that offers state-of- the-art crisis care. After grappling with deficits, the city turned operation of the downtown hospital over to the capable hands of the Daughters of Charity, who also run the Seton Healthcare Network, which includes other hospitals and clinics in the Austin area. The 360-year-old Catholic order has gained a reputation for providing quality healthcare for both insured and needy patients while managing to retain profitability in a volatile marketplace.

Brackenridge is an acute-care hospital, which, in addition to the trauma center, provides maternity, critical care, surgery, orthopedics and nephrology services.

Children's Hospital

601 E. 15th St. • (512) 480-1818

Next door to Brackenridge, this Seton Healthcare Network facility is dedicated to the care of children, offering treatment to heart and cancer patients, long-term care for chronically ill children and a pediatric intensive care unit. Next door to the hospital is the Ronald MacDonald House, 403 E. 15th Street, (512) 472-9844, which provides affordable accommodations for the families of children being treated at the hospital.

North Austin Diagnostic Medical Center

12221 MoPac Blvd. N. • (512) 901-1000

Part of the Columbia St. David's Healthcare System, this north Austin hospital has acute-care medical and surgical units, a 24-hour emergency room, an outpatient surgery center, maternity facilities, a women's center, rehabilitation services and oncology programs. The facility also houses the Austin Travel Clinic where would-be world wanderers can receive the necessary shots and health information for travel to any part of the world.

St. David's Medical Center

919 E. 32nd St. • (512) 476-7111

Part of the Columbia St. David's Healthcare System, this downtown hospital is an acute-care facility. Medical services include a rehabilitation center, a psychiatric center for children, maternity and reproductive technology services, and cardiac and urodynamics programs.

Seton Medical Center

1201 W. 38th St. • (512) 323-1000

The home base for the Sisters of Charity network of medical facilities in Austin, Seton Medical Center offers a wide range of medical and surgical services. It is in a "medical arts" area of Austin where many of the city's physicians and medical support services are located. Offerings include a 24-hour emergency room, a neonatal center, a maternity facility and cancer care services. It is also the headquarters for Seton's Good Health program, which focuses on wellness issues. For the families of patients, the hospital operates a nearby accommodations facility, Seton League House at 3207 Wabash Avenue, (512) 323-1999.

Shoal Creek Hospital
3501 Mills Ave. • (512) 452-0361

This private psychiatric hospital serves patients of all ages and is situated along a pleasant stretch of Shoal Creek in the central medical arts area of the city around 35th Street.

South

South Austin Hospital
901 W. Ben White Blvd. • (512) 447-2211

St. David's operates this acute-care facility in south Austin. The hospital has a 24-hour emergency room, a cardiovascular center, maternity services and a neurological center. It also offers lithotripsy for non-invasive kidney stone removal.

West

Renaissance Women's Center Hospital
3003 Bee Caves Rd. • (512) 347-0123

A newcomer to the Austin healthcare scene, this state-of-the art women's center opened in the fall of 1997. The small hospital is associated with doctors in the Women's Renaissance Group and offers both inpatient and outpatient surgery, maternity and OB/GYN services, plus women's health and wellness classes.

Northwest

Seton Northwest Hospital
11113 Research Blvd. • (512) 795-1000

This northwest branch of the Seton network has a minor emergency center, plus 24-hour emergency room, birthing units and maternity services. Seton also offers Good Health School wellness programs on-site, and the facility houses the Seton Northwest Sports Medicine practice. A similar facility is planned for southwest Austin.

Round Rock

Round Rock Hospital
2400 Round Rock Ave. • (512) 255-6066

Undergoing a major $28 million expansion, this acute-care hospital serves the southern Williamson County area. Part of the Columbia St. David's Healthcare Network, the hospital has a 24-hour emergency room, family birthing center, medical-surgical unit, intensive-care unit, cardiopulmonary services center, plus an outpatient surgery facility.

Public Health Services

The Austin/Travis County Health and Human Services Department is a joint city and county tax supported service agency that oversees the operation of 13 community clinics in the city of Austin and the surrounding area. The agency also oversees immunization outreach programs that are held in local shopping malls. The clinics offer maternity care, well-child checkups, dental services at some locations, and tests and treatment for tuberculosis, sexually transmitted diseases and HIV.

INSIDERS' TIP

Hospice Austin, (512) 342-4700, serves both Travis and Williamson counties, covering the Austin and Round Rock metropolitan area. Hospice offers medical, spiritual and bereavement care for terminally ill patients and their families on an outpatient basis. The goal is to take a holistic view of the patient and family. Hospice provides services to patients who have been diagnosed with a terminal illness and have less than six months to live. Payment is on an ability to pay basis.

The Women, Infant and Children's Nutrition program, commonly known as the WIC program, is also administered by the health department. Fees are charged according to the ability of the patient to pay, but the agency says no one is turned away. Call (512) 416-0366 in Austin for locations.

Community Clinics Volunteer Health Care Clinic

4215 Medical Pkwy. • (512) 459-6002

This clinic serves patients who are not eligible for city or county support, Medicare or Medicaid, and do not have their own insurance. The clinic treats only minor illness. Donations are welcome, but no one is turned away.

People's Community Clinic

2909 N. I-35 • (512) 478-8924

Payment is on a sliding scale at this community clinic. No one is refused treatment. The clinic offers adult outpatient and pediatric medical care, free immunizations, family-planning and prenatal services, treatment of sexually transmitted diseases and women's health services.

Seton East Community Health Center

2811 E. Second St. • (512) 323-4930

The Seton network provides medical care and social services for residents in the East Austin area. No one is turned away, and fees are charged on a sliding scale.

Seton South Community Health Center

3706 S. First St. • (512) 323-4940

The center provides similar services to those at the network's East Austin location, listed previously, including medical care and social services on a sliding-fee scale. No one is turned away.

Round Rock

Round Rock Health Clinic

2000 N. Mays St., Ste. 109 • (512) 255-5120

Medicaid and Medicare patients are accepted at this outpatient clinic that offers well-child checkups, prenatal care and family medicine.

Williamson County and Cities Health District Clinic

211 Commerce St. • (512) 248-3257

Williamson County and cities in the area fund local public health clinics that provide medical services on a sliding-fee scale. Screenings for diabetes and blood pressure tests for seniors are among the services provided. The clinics also offer prenatal care, well-child checkups, and testing and counseling for tuberculosis, sexually transmitted diseases and HIV.

Cedar Park

Williamson County and Cities Health Care District Clinic

600 N. Bell, Ste. 200 • (512) 918-1001

The clinic offers medical services on a sliding-fee scale, plus diabetes and blood pressure screenings for seniors and prenatal and well-child services. Counseling for those diagnosed with tuberculosis, sexually transmitted diseases and HIV also is available.

INSIDERS' TIP

Finding a good veterinarian can be as difficult as finding a good family doctor. There is a great variety of vets in the Austin area. Some offer mobile services, others are taking a page out of a popular human medicine trend and turning to alternative healing — acupuncture, homeopathic medicine and massage therapy. Check the Yellow Pages and consult friends and neighbors. The Austin/Travis County Animal Services Department maintains a list of pet clubs and associations, (512) 472-7387.

AIDS Services

The Austin area has an extensive network of services and programs to assist and support people with HIV. For a complete listing of the services, call the AIDS information line, (512) 458-AIDS, or contact AIDS Services of Austin.

AIDS Services of Austin
825 E. 53½ St., Ste. E101 • (512) 458-AIDS

A clearinghouse for AIDS information in Central Texas, this agency serves HIV-positive individuals and their families. The agency also provides information on AIDS network services like the Animal Companions program, a volunteer group that provides, grooming, veterinary care, in-home care and a food bank for the pets of AIDS patients.

Community AIDS Resource & Education (CARE)
1633 E. Second St. • (512) 473-2273

CARE provides legal referrals, counseling, transportation, screening and other services for HIV-positive individuals.

Dental Clinic
3000 Medical Arts St. • (512) 479-6633

Dental care for HIV and AIDS patients is offered on a sliding scale by this Central Austin clinic.

HIV Wellness Center
4301 N. I-35 • (512) 467-0088

The wellness center offers a holistic approach to care for people with HIV and AIDS. Among the therapies are nutritional counseling, acupuncture, massage and other alternative approaches aimed at boosting the immune system.

Informe SIDA
1715 E. Sixth St. • (512) 472-2001

SIDA is the Spanish acronym for AIDS. This program offers bilingual HIV/AIDS outreach and education, plus support groups and emergency assistance.

Support Services

There is an extensive web of support groups in the Austin area for those with medical, psychological or family problems. The Austin Area Mental Health Association, (512) 454-7463, operates a clearinghouse to connect individuals to support groups. The listings maintained by the association are not limited to mental healthcare groups; they include information on medical recovery support groups and substance-abuse groups.

Support group information is also available from local chapters of national associations like the Arthritis Foundation, the American Cancer Society, Overeaters Anonymous, etc. These groups can be found in the Yellow Pages.

Mental Health Services

The Austin area has a wide array of mental health agencies and support services. The Austin area office of the Mental Health Association, (512) 454-7463, offers information and referral services. Following is a sampling of the major agencies and service groups.

The Arc of the Capital Area
(512) 476-7044

The Arc offers support services for families with a mentally retarded member. Those programs include the following: Pilot Parent, providing support groups and other assistance for families of children with disabilities such as spina bifida, autism, cerebral palsy or mental retardation; Project Chance, working with developmentally disabled juveniles and adults who have been involved with the criminal justice program; Community Advocacy Services, matching volunteers one on one with mentally retarded or developmentally disabled adults living in the community or at Austin State School; and Community Living Assistance and Support Services, helping many individuals who might be forced by their disabilities to live in nursing homes or other institutional settings to live in group homes or even on their own.

Austin Child Guidance Center
810 W. 45th St. • (512) 451-2242

Individual, family and group therapy are offered at the center, which also provides counseling and testing services, child-abuse services and parent classes. Fees are charged on a sliding-scale basis.

Austin Recovery Center Inc.
1900 Rio Grande St. • (512) 477-7776

The center operates a detoxification unit, plus outpatient and inpatient care for chemically dependent adults and teens.

Austin State Hospital
4110 Guadalupe St. • (512) 452-0381

The hospital is under the auspices of the Texas Department of Mental Health and Mental Retardation system, which includes seven other state hospitals around Texas. The Austin facility serves the 37-county Central Texas area. Approximately 300 teens and adults receive care at the hospital.

Austin-Travis County Mental Health Mental Retardation Center
1430 Collier St. • (512) 447-4141

The center operates a 24-hour hotline, (512) 472-HELP, in addition to emergency psychiatric services and programs for mental illness, mental retardation and substance abuse. Other services include psychiatric case management, vocational and educational services, diagnosis and evaluation, infant-parent training, child abuse services and homeless services. Fees are determined by the individual's ability to pay.

Austin Women's Addiction Referral and Education Center (AWARE)
1524 S. I-35, Ste. 315 • (512) 326-1222

This YWCA program offers chemical-dependency counseling, assessment, education, information and referral.

Charter Hospital of Austin
8402 Cross Park Dr. • (512) 837-1800

The hospital offers partial hospitalization and outpatient treatment for emotional disorders and chemical dependency.

Columbia St. David's Pavilion
1025 E. 32nd St. • (512) 867-5800

This clinic, part of the Columbia St. David's Healthcare Network, provides both in- and outpatient care for men, women and children. The pavilion has a special program for those with eating disorders.

Immediate-Care Facilities

In the trade they are sometimes called "doc-in-a-box," and immediate-care facilities are springing up in shopping centers and near busy intersections throughout the area. They provide non-emergency, outpatient care for weekend gardeners with battered green thumbs, Sunday jocks, and visitors who slip and fall while getting into the Austin spirit. Call ahead for hours and specific locations, and check your insurance before you check in.

North

Pro Med Medical Care Center, 2000 W. Anderson Lane, (512) 452-0361

St. David's Medicenter, 810 W. Braker Lane, (512) 339-8114

St. David's Medicenter, 6611 U.S. Highway 290 E., (512) 467-2052

South

Pro Med Medical Care Center, 3801 S. Lamar Boulevard, (512) 447-9661

St. David's Medicenter, 1100 S. I-35, (512) 443-5995

Southwest

Seton Southwest Minor Emergency Center, 2100 W. William Cannon Drive, (512) 324-4950

St. David's Medicenter, 6600 S. MoPac, Ste. 2180, (512) 891-0168

Round Rock

First Care Medical Clinic, 900 Round Rock Avenue, (512) 244-2244

Alternative Medicine

Austin is a hotbed of alternative therapies and wellness programs, and some practitioners of traditional medicine also include aspects of holistic healing in their own treatments. The area's hospitals offer wellness programs, plus several fitness centers (see our Parks and Recreation chapter) formulate wellness programs for clients. There are consultants who work with employers to develop wellness and exercise programs for employees or individuals. All manner of therapies are available, including Chinese, homeopathic, ayurvedic and Taoist t'ai chi. Check the Yellow Pages for alternative therapies — the acupuncture listings also include herbal and nutritional therapies.

Another good resource are the bulletin boards at local health food stores. The large outdoor bulletin board at the Whole Foods Market, Sixth Street and Lamar Boulevard, features a variety of alternative therapy providers. (See our Shopping chapter for information on Whole Foods Market.)

Mark Blumenthal runs a nonprofit organization, headquartered in Austin, called the American Botanical Council. The council produces a magazine, *HerbalGram*, that focuses on herbal research and federal regulation of supplements. The council can be contacted at P.O. Box 201660, Austin, TX 78720, or (512) 331-8868.

A Word About Allergies

Allergies. Sooner or later you're gonna get 'em. At least that is what the experts predict for many newcomers to Austin. The abundance of flora has its down side for Central Texas residents. In the winter months, December, January and February, the junipers in the Hill Country produce pollen that sets off the "cedar fever" season — the trees are colloquially known as cedars, but they are in fact junipers. Some opine that the purple haze produced by the pollen prompted Austin to be dubbed the City of the Violet Crown. Most sufferers are too busy sniffling and wiping their watery eyes to notice the violet glow.

In spring, the live oak and elm pollens bring on misery for some, then in summer there are grasses and, of course, year-round attacks by mold spores and animal dander. Not everyone succumbs, but so many do that the local television stations broadcast allergy counts on their daily newscasts. In a classic case of market supply and demand, allergists do a booming business in Austin.

Emergency Numbers

Dial 911 in the Austin area for emergency police, fire and EMS Services.

Poison Center • (800) POISON-1
Crisis Intervention/Suicide Hotline • (512) 472-4357 TTY
Crisis Intervention Hotline • (512) 703-1395
Social Services Referral Hotline operated by United Way, First Call for Help program • (512) 323-1899
Travis County Sheriff's Mental Health Unit • (512) 473-9734
Alcoholics Anonymous • (512) 451-3071
Battered Women Center Crisis Hotline • (512) 928-9070
Williamson County Crisis Center • (512) 255-1212 Round Rock, (800) 460-SAFE

The symbiosis that exists between the Austin community and its various institutes of higher education is one of the defining characteristics of the region.

Higher Education

Back in the 1920s and 1930s, Austin's leaders billed our city as "The Athens of the West," both in tribute to, and promotion of, the element of culture bestowed by the area's colleges and universities. While we dropped that lofty title decades ago, Austin's distinction as an eminent educational center of the South remains. Our institutes of higher education add luster to the jewel that is Austin. For its sheer size and importance in the economic development of Austin, The University of Texas stands in a class by itself. But Austin's other fine colleges and universities are vitally linked to this city in countless ways as well. The symbiosis that exists between the Austin community and its various institutes of higher education is one of the defining characteristics of the region.

One need only walk through the campuses of our institutes to get a feel for Austin's educational traditions. The sprawling UT campus with its giant shade trees, sculptures, fountains, mammoth buildings and the 27-story UT Tower, which has become as much an Austin landmark as a UT symbol, are enough to inspire a certain reverence. The Gothic Revival-style Main Building on the St. Edward's University campus stands as a stately landmark in South Austin, while Huston-Tillotson College's elevated site overlooking downtown from the east is a living legacy to Austin's education of African Americans during Reconstruction and ever since. Austin Community College's many modern campuses around the city serve as a reminder that there's always room for more centers of learning here. Southwest Texas State University south of us in San Marcos and Southwestern University north in Georgetown frame Austin with educational foundations dating back more than a century.

Austin is a thriving intellectual community today, and our area colleges and universities serve to nourish our citizens' appetites for more and more knowledge. About 35 percent of the city's adults have had four years of college or more, and another 27 percent have had some college. More than 100,000 students are enrolled in institutes of higher education in the greater Austin area, nearly half of those at The University of Texas alone. And that doesn't include the many thousands more lifelong learners who attend workshops, seminars or other noncredit continuing education classes every year for the joy of learning and for the benefits advanced learning extend.

Our institutes of higher education are noted also for their involvement in the community. Among UT's many public outreach efforts are programs to encourage youth to stay in school, academic residency camps that attract minority students from across the state, a criminal defense clinic that provides legal advice for those unable to afford a lawyer and a program to help small businesses become more efficient. Huston-Tillotson is an integral force in the enrichment of the East Austin community, while the various programs and services Austin's other schools provide are aimed at the betterment of the city as a whole.

For cultural enrichment, we Austinites often turn to our colleges and universities. Art exhibits, lectures, theater, festivals, fairs, sporting events, symphonies and jazz performances are just some of the many offerings we can enjoy on a regular basis.

The contribution these institutes have made to Austin's bright prospects for the 21st century are enormous. Austin's highly educated population was one of the attributes that attracted the high-tech industry to this area in the 1970s and one of the reasons its numbers continue to grow today. UT's outstanding research facilities act as a huge magnet for these industries, while the city's academic programs, many now aimed at training high-tech workers, continue to turn out qualified graduates.

It's impossible to imagine what life would be like in Austin without our colleges and universities. The University of Texas is not only the flagship of the state university system, it's one of the economic and cultural pillars of Austin. For decades, Austin's economy — and its reputation as an educational and political center — rested on UT and on state government. While UT's burden may be lightened now as new enterprises help drive Austin's economy, its significance to Austin will endure.

Nature endowed Austin with natural beauty — rolling wooded hills and peaceful rivers. Lawmakers, churches and private citizens from all walks of life endowed Austin with its institutes of higher education. The Austin leaders who once envisioned "a university of the first class" could never have foreseen this.

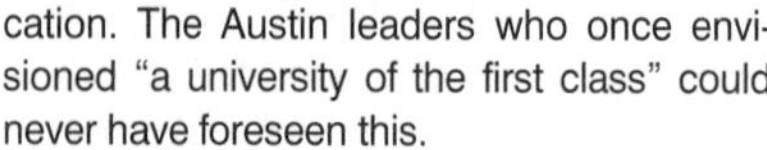

Here, listed by size, are the colleges and universities that enrich our city.

The University of Texas at Austin

24th and Guadalupe Sts.
• (512) 471-3434

The 40 acres! This fond nickname for The University of Texas at Austin dates back to 1839, when city planners set aside a 40-acre plot called College Hill to be used for an institute of higher learning. UT didn't come along for another 44 years — and almost didn't come to Austin at all. The University officially opened on that 40-acre site on September 15, 1883. Today, The University of Texas at Austin's main campus alone sits on more than 350 acres, while the university operates major research facilities on 915 additional acres around the city. UT owns the Marine Science Institute at Port Aransas, the McDonald Observatory near Fort Davis, the Winedale Historical Center near Round Top, the Bee Cave Research Center west of Austin, and writer J. Frank Dobie's ranch in Paisano. To top it off, The University of Texas at Austin is the flagship of the UT System's 15 campuses spread throughout the state. It's the city's largest employer, with 18,000 workers. And, according to fall 1998 enrollment figures, UT is the nation's largest university, with nearly 49,000 students, including full- and part-time scholars.

UT faculty members have won scores of prestigious awards, honors and medals — Nobel Prizes, Pulitzer Prizes, the National Medal of Science and the National Medal of Technology — and have been named to distinguished societies, institutes and academies across the nation. Many alumni have gone on to leave their mark, both on Austin and on the world. Lady Bird Johnson, Walter Cronkite, Bill Moyers, Lloyd Bentsen and Federico Peña are all UT alumni. UT's academic programs and professional schools often rank among the top programs and schools in the country. Seven UT doctoral programs rank in the top 10 in the nation, according to the National Research Council. Civil engineering, computer sciences, aerospace engineering, classics, astrophysics/astronomy, chemical engineering, and the ecology, evolution and behavior program all made the top-10 list.

The university's academic programs, made up of 15 colleges and schools, the Graduate School and the Division of Continuing Education, offer more than 100 undergraduate degree programs and 170 graduate programs. Exceptional facilities abound, including the fifth-largest academic library in North America, with nearly 7 million volumes (see our chapter on The Literary Scene), the Harry Ransom Humanities Research Center, an internationally recognized rare book and manuscript library, as well as state-of-the-art computer facilities.

UT is one of the reasons why so many people around the country get dreamy-eyed just hearing the name Austin. Before the high-tech industry came along to rocket Austin's name into the stratosphere, before the music scene crystallized to give Austin such a hip reputation, before big business discovered us, before the legions of filmmakers and tourists arrived, there was UT. While UT can't take credit for all the excitement surrounding Austin today, its contributions are enormous. Along with state government, The University of Texas has provided the foundation for much of what Austin has become. UT is noted for graduating so many students who've fallen in love

Photo: Peter A. Silva

"The Tower" in the center of the University of Texas campus is visible for miles.

with Austin's natural beauty and tolerant atmosphere that they can't bear to leave.

It's no wonder UT students and the public at large get along so well. Not only do these scholars, some of the nation's brightest, bring a palpable energy to this city (and make valuable contributions to its social consciousness — and conscience), having one of the nation's largest universities at our doorstep gives Austinites incredible opportunities for cultural and educational enhancement, for cutting-edge knowledge in an extraordinary range of professional fields — and for just plain fun. A stroll down "The Drag," the part of Guadalupe Street that runs alongside UT, will have anyone feeling like a college student in minutes. This strip, with its bookstores, restaurants, coffeehouses, shops and markets, is the melting pot of UT and the city.

There are some serious issues facing this university, however. According to fall 1997 enrollment figures, UT's students are 66 percent White, 13 percent Hispanic, 11 percent Asian, 7 percent foreign and 4 percent African American (figures are rounded). UT, however, is grappling with the results of a March 1996 5th Circuit Court of Appeals decision. In the case Hopwood v. Texas, the court ruled that UT's School of Law could no longer consider race or ethnicity in making its admissions decisions. The ruling was interpreted to include all of UT and all of Texas' public institutes of higher learning. The Hopwood decision canceled UT's affirmative action program, leaving UT to devise new methods to draw minority students. More aggressive recruiting efforts coupled with a scholarship program for minorities sponsored by UT's alumni association proved moderately successful in the Law School in 1998. Preliminary figures revealed minority enrollment of African-American and Mexican-American students had climbed somewhat over the previous year but not as high as pre-Hopwood levels. The new freshman class also showed some gains in minority students. UT, meanwhile, announced in 1998 that it would appeal Hopwood.

That's one of the issues facing Larry Faulkner, who took over as UT's 23rd president in the spring of 1998. Faulkner, who received his doctorate in chemistry from UT and then taught at the university, came to Austin from his post as provost and vice chancellor for academic affairs at the University of Illinois at Urbana-Champaign. Faulkner arrived in Austin just a few months after the university launched its largest fund-raising campaign ever.

"We're Texas" is the new slogan for UT-Austin created by UT grads at Austin's mega-advertising agency GSD&M. The slogan was used to kick off UT's $1 billion seven-year fund-raiser, aimed at compensating for dwindling state support of higher education. With the campaign, the university aims to ensure UT remains the system's flagship university in every sense of the word.

Another challenge confronting UT's new leader is overcrowding. A new state law guarantees that students in the top 10 percent of their classes will be admitted to state universities. As the university expands closer toward that 50,000-student figure again (it topped 50,000 in the 1980s), the university faces ever-increasing challenges of dealing with the masses. Just the simple fact of moving students in and out of the downtown campus each day is a major concern, let alone the struggle to ensure students don't end up feeling like Longhorns — the four-legged kind.

One place on campus notorious for overcrowding is Darrel K Royal-Texas Memorial Stadium on a football Saturday. Texas Longhorns games are often the hottest ticket in town as the university and the city turn out to support their beloved team. (See our chapter on Spectator Sports.) Football isn't the only game in town, however. Many other Longhorns teams draw big crowds, including the UT women's basketball team. (See our profile of Longhorns Coach Jody Conradt in the Spectator Sports chapter.) UT puts great emphasis on sports and goes all out to recruit some of the nation's top athletes. As a result, Longhorns teams have won more Southwest Conference championships in all sports than any college or university. In accordance with tradition, the UT Tower glows orange many a night celebrating major UT athletic victories. In addition to intercollegiate sports, which involve less than 500 students, UT's recreational sports program attracts about 80 percent of the student body.

For both students and members of the general public interested in continuing education, culture and entertainment, UT offers an enormous range of options. The Performing Arts Center's public performance spaces and backup facilities, including the Bass Concert Hall and the Bates Recital Hall, rank among the top five on any American campus. The Frank C. Erwin Jr. Special Events Center hosts more than 250 annual events. The Jack S. Blanton Museum of Art has an extensive permanent collection, and The Texas Memorial Museum holds extensive teaching and research collections and an exhibition space that includes the original *Goddess of Liberty* statue from atop the State Capitol. Of course, UT also is home to the Lyndon Baines Johnson Library and Museum (see our chapters on Attractions and The Arts).

UT sponsors two popular programs for the continuing education of Austin's adult com-

INSIDERS' TIP

Students at Southwest Texas State University in San Marcos like to rub their hands over the landmark statue of the fighting stallions to conjure up good luck on a test. *The Fight of the Stallions*, a 17-foot-high sculpture on the campus, depicts two stallions engaged in a fierce battle. A nude rider attempts to subdue one horse while another rider, also nude, cowers below. The sculpture was a 1951 gift from the artist, noted sculptor Anna Hyatt Huntington, and her husband, Archer Huntington, of South Carolina.

munity and for other nontraditional students. The University Extension program allows students to get college credit on a more flexible schedule. This non-degree evening program is aimed at filling students' educational gaps and continuing educational needs. University Extension offers more than 200 courses from anthropology to zoology and awards extension credit that could be applied to a degree program. The extension program also allows students to work toward a Business Foundations Certificate, classes that provide solid basics in business concepts and practices. Students don't have to be accepted to UT to enroll in any of these classes.

Much more casual is UT's Informal Classes program. This efficiently run program provides an amazing variety of workshops, short courses and certificate programs for anyone interested. Here, students can take short classes — from a couple of hours to several sessions — in hundreds of subjects, including such things as country dance, money management, creative writing, computers and how to buy a house. Students can sign up over the phone with a credit card, and the university will mail a receipt and information on where the class is located, most often on the UT campus. (Parking can be a challenge.) UT students, senior citizens and members of the alumni association get discounts on most classes. There are about six sessions per year, and schedules are available at distribution points around the city.

Austin Community College
5930 Middle Fiskville Rd.
• (512) 223-7000

Austin Community College, which celebrates its 27th birthday in 1999, is the baby in the neighborhood when it comes to Austin's institutions of higher learning, most of which were born in the 1800s. Perhaps that's why we call it "junior" college. In fact, this public, two-year undergraduate college is far from junior in size and in importance to the Austin area. ACC's enrollment has grown to more than 26,000 students on six campuses around Austin. Another 15,000 students take noncredit courses at ACC campuses and at various distance learning sites around the region.

The college is the second-largest institute of higher learning in the Austin area, after The University of Texas. That is certainly welcome news to those who fought to establish ACC back in the 1960s when, according to the prevailing conventional wisdom, Austin didn't need another college, what with UT and all the city's other fine colleges and universities. In fact, earlier efforts to establish a community college failed twice. At least some of ACC's success can be attributed to its achievement in taking higher education directly to the people it serves. The college's main campuses dot the Austin map from Oak Hill in the south to Cedar Park in the north, and the new $9.8 million campus in the racially mixed, working class area of East Austin (which will replace an existing facility when it opens for classes in January 1999) demonstrate a strong commitment to provide education to all Austin residents.

Today, ACC offers two-year associate degrees and one-year certificates in 137 majors: 66 in applied sciences, 16 in the arts, 14 in the sciences and 41 in college-credit certificates. Students who graduate with an associate of arts or associate of science degree are prepared to transfer to a four-year college or university. The two-year associate of applied science degree prepares students to enter the local job market or transfer to select universities. For students studying for one-year certificates, ACC is a technical or vocational school, offering courses in such subjects as building construction, automotive technology, financial management, office administration, child development, surgical technology and electronic technology.

As Austin's demand for high-tech workers skyrockets, ACC has established itself as one of the major learning centers focused on filling those jobs. It has invested in both technical infrastructure and in designing programs and courses of study aimed at preparing students for high-tech positions. The semiconductor manufacturing technology program and strong emphasis on classes in the software programming language Java are two of ACC's efforts in this area.

ACC also is gaining a reputation for its role in serving the specific needs of the Austin business community. Two ACC liaisons work with businesses to determine the skills they require for new employees. Then, ACC offers courses to teach those skills. Additionally, The Center for Career and Business Development offers noncredit courses that teach new or updated skills needed by the existing employees of local businesses, industries and governmental agencies. Each year, more than 16,000 employees from 1,500 companies enroll in these specialized courses, some of them designed specifically for the company.

ACC's range of courses embrace wide segments of the Austin population. Students who've dropped out of high school can prepare for their General Educational Development (GED) exam at ACC, or they may study to earn a regular high school diploma. There also are courses for adults who want to improve basic skills in preparation for college, and for students wanting to learn English as a second language. From there, students may choose to pursue courses in job training, with on-the-job apprenticeships leading directly to employment. An important segment of ACC's population takes classes in a wide range of academic courses, including the basics in mathematics, sciences and language arts, that can transfer to a four-year college or university. In that regard, ACC is a strong institution, with some 4,000 of its students co-enrolled each year at The University of Texas. And, for that segment of the population that just can't get enough schooling, ACC offers an enormous variety of classes to audit or for credit.

In all, the 1990s have proven to be an interesting time for ACC. During this decade, the college has moved ahead with the opening of new campuses, developed many new programs to better serve the community, invested in programs and infrastructure, and established a strong presence in this area. It also, however, faced a mild form of sanction by its accrediting board, received a warning from the state auditor's office about its spending practices and was criticized over its large percentage of part-time faculty.

Since arriving in early 1997, ACC President Richard Fonte has made some important changes, including a major reorganization of the college. Under his new "single college structure," Fonte named three college-wide provosts and gave them multi-campus responsibilities. He also eliminated campus deans, division chairpersons and department heads and assigned many of them to full-time teaching positions. Fonte himself teaches a class in government at the college's Riverside Campus. And Fonte has announced a plan to hire 60 more full-time instructors by 2001. At a cost of $3.6 million, the plan would bring the faculty to 42 percent full-time, up from 22 percent.

Southwest Texas State University

601 University Dr., San Marcos
• (512) 245-2111

Southwest Texas State University, about 35 miles south of Austin in San Marcos, is the area's third largest institution of higher education with more than 20,650 students. More than 53 percent of the university's students commute from outside San Marcos, including many from the Austin area. Additionally, Southwest Texas State has a campus in Round Rock at Westwood Community School that offers graduate and undergraduate courses.

This public, four-year university — the alma mater of President Lyndon Johnson — is starting to get national recognition as an affordable, up-and-coming university. Southwest Texas State also has received attention for the important endowments that have come its way recently. In an effort to draw the nation's leading academic talent for the 1998-99 academic year, SWT established five endowed chairs worth $1 million each in semiconductor research, creative writing, cancer research, managed healthcare systems, and entrepreneurship. These endowments were funded by the university's biggest donors, Roy F. and Joann Cole Mitte of Austin.

The university's geography school, a nationally recognized department, was the first to offer a doctoral program in 1996 and today offers two Ph.D. programs in geography. SWT is also known for its teaching and creative writing programs and for its business school, which was accredited in recent years by the American Assembly of Collegiate Schools of Business. In all, Southwest Texas State University offers 105 undergraduate majors in the schools of education, applied arts and technology, business, fine arts and communication, health professions, liberal arts and science. The Graduate School offers 88 master's degree programs covering a wide range of academic disciplines. Among the university's collections is the Southwestern Writers Collection, which includes J. Frank Dobie properties (see our chapter on The Literary Scene) as well as an extensive archive of written material that captures the literary and artistic spirit of the American Southwest. The *Lonesome Dove* archives in this collection include props and memorabilia from the film set of Texan Larry McMurtry's epic story about cattle driving.

Southwest Texas State first opened its doors in 1903 as a teacher training college called Southwest Texas State Normal School. Through the years it became a normal college, teachers college and then college. SWT became a university in 1969. Located on 427 acres and surrounded by magnificent cypress and pecan trees, the campus sits on the banks of the San Marcos River on the edge of the Texas Hill Country. The university offers a vast range of student activities, including more than 50 special-interest organizations, 36 honorary associations and more than 30 professional groups in addition to 20 fraternities and 10 sororities. SWT athletes compete at the NCAA Division I level in eight men's and seven women's sports. The university also offers a wide range of programs for talented students in dance, band, choir, jazz, symphony orchestra, music theater and opera.

St. Edward's University

3001 S. Congress Ave. • (512) 448-8400

A private Roman Catholic liberal arts university, St. Edward's offers undergraduate and graduate degrees to its 3,100 students from 36 states and 50 foreign countries.

Located in South Austin on 180 acres of rolling hills, the university was founded in 1885 as a college but got its start 12 years earlier when it opened as a school with just three farm boys enrolled the first year. As the school grew and began boarding students, Austin residents started referring to St. Edward's as the Catholic Farm due to the fact that it fed its faculty and staff by raising beef, grain, vegetables and fruit on its own land. The Main Building, the imposing Gothic Revival-style building made of Texas white limestone, was dedicated in 1889 — a grand structure for sure in the early Southwest. Rebuilt after a fire destroyed it in 1903, the Main Building was designated a Texas Historic Landmark in 1973.

Today, St. Edward's confers bachelor's degrees in arts, business administration and science. The undergraduate curriculum has been recognized by the Carnegie Foundation as among the most rigorous in the nation. About 400 students are seeking master's degrees in the areas of business administration and human services. Students in the School of Humanities choose from among 11 majors, including art, communications, English literature, religious studies and philosophy. The school of behavioral and social sciences offers undergraduate degrees in such subjects as international studies, social work and criminal justice. For students seeking a degree in education and those working toward teacher certification, St. Edward's offers majors in English, kinesiology, language arts, social studies and Spanish/bilingual education. The School of Business Administration offers majors in accounting, business administration, finance, marketing and management.

In addition to awarding degrees, however, the university is recognized locally for its tradition of producing graduates with strong values, both through required course work in ethics, philosophy or religious studies and through its community outreach programs. Under a program offered by St. Edward's Community Service Institute, small-business owners are offered assistance from the university's business graduate students, many of them older students who already have had up to 20 years of business experience and are returning for their master's degrees. The students analyze financial operations of a business, do market research or offer suggestions on how to im-

INSIDERS' TIP

The annual Red River War is the football game played between arch-rivals Texas and Oklahoma at the Cotton Bowl in Dallas in October.

prove the business. More than 25 years ago, the university created the nationally recognized College Assistance Migrant Program (CAMP). Under the program, the children of migrant farm workers are given freshman scholarships and aid toward finishing their degrees. Many of the students who have taken advantage of this program over the years are first-generation college students in their families.

In the early 1990s, St. Edward's launched its first major fund-raising campaign. Called Second Century, the campaign has brought in more than $20 million in donations, including its largest single gift — $3 million. With these funds, the university has built a $6.2 million campus center and plans to expend another $5.5 million on the CAMP program and other scholarships for students. Additional funds will go to teacher excellence programs, community partnerships, science programs and improvements in information technology.

Athletes at St. Edward's compete in NCAA Division II sports. The university offers basketball, soccer and tennis for men and women, baseball and golf for men and volleyball for women.

Southwestern University

1001 E. University Ave., Georgetown • (512) 836-1200, (800) 252-3166

"Chartered as the state's first university in 1840, until the 1970s it was doing the conventional thing, providing the B.A. union card for its graduates' first jobs. Then with the catalysts of the new president's vision and the generosity of three Texas foundations, it was born again as a place to prepare for the 21st century." So writes Loren Pope in the book, *Colleges That Change Lives*. This book, subtitled, *40 Schools You Should Know About Even If You're Not a Straight-A Student*, is one of several guides to colleges and universities that have taken note of Southwestern University in recent years. Called one of the best sleepers in the nation and one of the buried treasures among the nation's liberal arts colleges, Southwestern University may not remain one of Texas' hidden assets much longer.

Located 28 miles north of Austin in the seat of Williamson County government and even closer to our northern neighbors in Round Rock and Pflugerville, Southwestern University is a private, Methodist, four-year institute of higher learning with a little more than 1,200 undergraduates. Southwestern, chartered in 1840, claims the distinction of being Texas' first institution of higher learning. Under the leadership of President Roy B. Shilling, Southwestern is gaining an even more important distinction as a university of academic excellence and high admission standards. More than 50 percent of the student body entering Southwestern in the fall of 1997 ranked in the top 10 percent of their classes.

The university is on a 100-acre campus filled with trees and dotted with beautiful Texas limestone buildings constructed in the stately Richardsonian Romanesque style of architecture. The university also owns 400 more acres, including a 75-acre golf course. The university, consisting of the Brown College of Arts and Sciences and the School of Fine Arts, offers liberal arts and sciences curriculum as well as pre-professional programs in medicine,

INSIDERS' TIP

For tickets to most UT cultural and athletic events, call the UTTM box office at (512) 477-6060, or stop by any of the UTTM outlets in H.E.B. grocery stores around the region. Note, however, that H.E.B. accepts only cash for tickets. There's also a UTTM outlet at Bass Concert Hall. Tickets may be purchased over the phone with a credit card and picked up the day of the event. Or, with enough time, they will be mailed to you. For athletic events not available through UTTM, call the Athletics Ticket Office at (512) 471-3333 or (800) 982-BEVO. Also, if you're desperate for a good seat, or any seat at all, you should know that scalping is legal in Texas. Several businesses around town may have a ticket for you, but expect to pay much more than the face value.

law, business theology, education and engineering. Southwestern offers 32 majors and bachelor's degrees in arts, science, music and fine arts. The school has an endowment of more than $276 million, making it one of the highest endowments per student in the country.

Southwestern's student body represents 36 states and 14 nations, although the vast majority, 88 percent, of students come from Texas. Nearly 80 percent of students live on campus in Southwestern's residence halls. The university competes in NCAA Division III intercollegiate athletics in basketball, cross country, golf, soccer and tennis for men and women, women's volleyball and men's baseball.

Georgetown itself celebrated its 150th birthday in 1998 with cattle drives through town and many other festivities. Although Georgetown, with about 24,000 inhabitants in 1998, is one of Central Texas' fastest growing communities — increasing population by as much as 10 percent per year over the past few years — it retains its small-town charm and conservative values. In 1993 Georgetown made national news when Williamson County commissioners first rejected, then approved, a tax incentive for Apple Computer, Inc. to build an $80 million plant in the county close to Austin. Apple's policy of providing benefits to domestic partners of its gay and lesbian employees sparked the earlier rejection, but in the end commissioners couldn't deny the economic benefits Apple would bring to the county. As the debate raged, about 200 Southwestern University students signed a petition urging commissioners to support the Apple project.

Concordia University at Austin

3400 N. I-35 • (512) 452-7661

Concordia Lutheran College graduated to university status in 1995 when it became a member of the 10-campus Concordia University System that spans the country. Founded as Concordia Academy in 1926 by pioneers who had Wendish and German ethnic backgrounds, the school originally trained young men for ministry in The Lutheran Church. Women were admitted for the first time in 1955, and in 1979 Concordia implemented a four-year liberal arts program for undergraduates. Concordia in 1998 took its first step toward becoming a graduate-level university when it instituted a master's degree program designed for working teachers. The university, which is owned and maintained by the Lutheran Church-Missouri Synod, has strong ties to the system's nine other universities. Students can transfer easily between schools and take classes offered at other campuses via the Concordia University Education Network, which uses video technology to transmit and receive courses. Concordia offers 16 majors in business, education and liberal arts and sciences. The university also offers pre-professional programs in dentistry, law, medicine and the seminary. The most popular majors at Concordia are in accounting and business administration. Education is another popular career pathway at the university, although students are enrolled in such diverse courses of study as behavioral sciences, church music, computer science, Mexican-American studies and Spanish.

The university set an all-time enrollment record in the fall of 1997 when its enrollment jumped by 8.6 percent to 785. More than 700 of the university's students come from Texas, and about 30 percent of undergraduates live on campus. Lutherans make up less than half the student body at Concordia, which also attracts Roman Catholics, Baptists and students from other Christian and non-Christian denominations.

On a 23-acre campus along Interstate 35 in Central Austin, Concordia has made great strides in serving the educational needs of Austin's working adults by offering evening classes and televised courses under its adult degree program. This centrally located university also opens its doors to the public for an extensive range of cultural and academic events, including art exhibits, lectures, theater and music performances. The University's own OAKWILT Boys gospel group, made up of faculty and staff, perform at the school and other Texas venues. Proceeds from their CD series support the OAKWILT Scholarship Endowment for Concordia students. Concordia sponsors an annual Ethnic Fair to celebrate the city's rich ethnic diversity. The event features live performances by many of the city's ethnic singing and dancing groups as well as the sale of ethnic foods, arts and crafts.

Huston-Tillotson College

900 Chicon St. • (512) 505-3025

Huston-Tillotson College brings much, much more to Austin than merely its distinctions as the city's oldest institution of higher education and its only historically black college.

In East Austin on 23 acres of rolling hills that overlook downtown, Huston-Tillotson is a center of cultural and community involvement for Austin's East-side neighborhoods and one of Austin's largest minority businesses. The college is known locally for its participation in a number of cooperative relationships with the Austin Independent School District, the City of Austin, Austin Community College and local business and community organizations.

This private, four-year undergraduate college, affiliated with the United Methodist Church and the United Church of Christ, offers bachelor's degrees in arts and science to about 650 students from a variety of cultural and ethnic backgrounds. Within the college's five divisions — business, natural sciences, social sciences, humanities and education — students can major in 20 areas of study, including the college's notable programs of chemistry, teacher preparations, sociology and biology.

Huston-Tillotson College dates back to the 1870s, and one of its former buildings, Allen Hall, was, according to the college, the first building in Texas or anywhere west of the Mississippi constructed for the higher education of black students. Tillotson College was established by Congregationalists in 1875 (although it didn't open to students until 1881), and Samuel Huston College was founded by Methodists a year later. The two colleges merged in October 1952 becoming the present-day Huston-Tillotson College.

While the campus has modernized over the past century and a quarter, two of its historic buildings remain as splendid landmarks and fine examples of turn-of-the-century architecture. The Evans Industrial Building, built c. 1912, was completely renovated in 1984 and designated as a Texas Historical Site. The Old Administration Building, completed in 1914, is one of the few remaining examples of the Modified Prairie Style popularized by Frank Lloyd Wright. This building was entered in the National Register of Historic Places in 1993 and is slowly being restored.

Today's campus includes two residence halls, classroom and office space, a student union, a chapel/auditorium, a health center, an athletic field and a library with more than 80,000 volumes.

Austin Presbyterian Seminary

100 E. 27th St. • (512) 472-6736

Known for its excellent preparation of leaders for the church, the Austin Presbyterian Seminary has graduates serving across the country and overseas. More than 300 students are enrolled in its various academic programs. Many live on campus in the seminary's housing units. The seminary opened in 1902 and has been at its present location, on about 12 acres along the wooded banks of Waller Creek, since 1908. Austin Presbyterian Seminary offers master's degrees in arts or divinity and doctor of ministry degrees. Additionally, the seminary offers classes for non-degree students as well as continuing education courses and a yearly series of lectures. An institution of the General Assembly of the Presbyterian Church (U.S.A.) and of the Synod of the Sun, the Austin seminary is one of 10 theological institutions related to the Presbyterian Church. The school is led by President Robert M. Shelton, who heads 20 resident faculty representing a dozen disciplines. The Stitt Library

INSIDERS' TIP

The Texas Tomorrow Fund gives parents and grandparents the opportunity to pay for a future college student's tuition at today's prices. The fund, backed by the State of Texas, allows investors to buy college tuition in one lump sum or make regular payments. Contracts can be obtained for any public or private college or university in Texas.

on campus has more than 150,000 volumes, with a strong representation of material in biblical studies and archeology. The library also houses The Mission Presbyterian Resource Center and the McCoy Presbyterian Historical Research Center. In 1996 the seminary opened the James I. and Hazel McCord Community Center, which houses the Stotts Fellowship Hall and Student Life Area as well as the Continuing Education and Doctor of Ministry offices, additional classrooms and guest facilities. The Austin Presbyterian Seminary opens its doors to the public for worship services, held weekday mornings, except Wednesday. Many Austinites have been married in the chapel.

Photo: J. Griffis Smith

Don't leave Austin without purchasing a little piece of UT spirit as a souvenir.

Some smaller districts have seen their student enrollment more than double over the past few years while other districts are growing by as much as 8 to 10 percent a year.

Schools and Child Care

Schools

Austin is not only moving toward the next century, it's leading the way. As Austin's worldwide reputation as a leader in the field of computer technology skyrockets, more and more high-tech industries are choosing to establish major cutting-edge facilities in the area. And as employment soars, all of the Capital City area's 10 school districts have been affected by growth in student enrollment, whether due directly to industries within the districts, to employees searching for suitable housing nearby or to families fleeing the big city for the more peaceful suburbs. And bulging school districts are passing bond issues to build, enlarge and improve schools at a pace many of us have never witnessed. Some smaller districts have seen their student enrollment more than double over the past few years while other districts are growing by as much as 8 to 10 percent a year.

The question, "Which came first, the chicken or the egg?" as it applies to education and technology, has interesting implications for Austin. While high-tech companies cite Austin's high-education levels as one reason for locating here, these same companies are competing with each other for well-trained, high-quality graduates at both the high school and college level. As a result, many of the area's high-tech industries — and scores of other farsighted businesses and industries — are investing money, time and expertise in local school districts to help propel education levels to new heights.

While Texas as a whole faces considerable challenges in its huge public school system, several districts in the Austin area are among the nation's leaders in providing high quality education and setting high academic standards for both urban and suburban youth. Students in Central Texas consistently beat the nation in Scholastic Aptitude Test (SAT) scores, while statewide results are slightly below the national average. Nearly half — 48 percent — of the state's 3.9 million schoolchildren — are listed as economically disadvantaged and 13 percent have limited English proficiency. Districts in this area vary wildly around those state averages. Gov. George W. Bush has pledged to make improving the state's school system his number one priority.

That's not to say that Texas does not now provide excellent educational opportunities. In fact, Texas high school teams have won the prestigious National Academic Decathlon competition 10 times. That's more top honors than any other state. Additionally, 212 Texas schools, including 26 in this area, have been named U.S. Department of Education Blue Ribbon Schools. This distinction recognizes outstanding schools that satisfy a number of criteria, including a rigorous curriculum, excellent teaching, low dropout rates and documented student achievement. The Texas Education Agency also rates schools and school districts on a four-tier scale of Exemplary, Recognized, Academically Acceptable and Academically Unacceptable. Sixty-four districts, including three in the Austin area, Dripping Springs, Eanes and Lake Travis, have achieved the highest rating. The other seven districts in this area are rated Academically Acceptable, although within those districts some schools are rated Exemplary or Recognized. The ratings are based on schools' performance on the Texas Assessment of Academic Skills (TAAS) tests, annual dropout rates and attendance rates.

Since 1990, students throughout the state have been required to take TAAS tests, which replaced other types of tests and shifted the focus of assessment from minimum skills to academic skills. The tests in reading, math and writing are used in part to measure a district's and individual school's progress in raising education levels. One of the biggest issues facing the state's school system today is funding. In 1993, after nine years of court cases, public debate and failed constitutional amendments, the Texas Legislature passed a school-finance-reform measure that included the so-called Robin Hood tax-sharing provision. Robin Hood requires the state's wealthiest school districts to share their property taxes with poorer districts. The Eanes school district, for example, paid $10 million in 1997-98. Also, as tax revenue increases in a district, the state's contribution decreases until a district achieves a "balanced-budget status" where it neither gives to nor receives money from the state.

School district leaders from Austin, Round Rock, Leander and other growing, property-rich districts contend that in the coming years they, too, will go from getting money from the state to giving it. In fact, according to the *Austin American-Statesman*, the Austin Independent School district is expected to become the largest urban property-rich district in the state by the 1999-2000 school year. At the same time, however, nearly half the district's students themselves are poor. Although they agree that the plan has served poorer districts well, they argue that the state's reliance on local property taxes to pay for public education will not solve the basic problem: not enough state money being dedicated to the Texas school system. It costs taxpayers more than $21 billion a year to educate the state's schoolchildren.

Revenues from the state lottery that go toward public education have not alleviated the pressure on school budgets. The 1997 Legislature saw a return to the old debates of tax reform and school financing. The only relief to come out of the session however was a measure that allowed voters to pass a Constitutional amendment raising the homestead exemption, which will save the average homeowner about $145 a year on school taxes. The state added another $1 billion to the public school coffers as a short-term attempt to make up for the higher exemptions. Several school districts in this area, however, also raised taxes. With Texas riding high on a robust economy preceding the 1998 gubernatorial elections, the issue of school funding became a central focus of the campaign as both Gov. Bush and his opponent outlined plans for steering extra billions into education. School finance reform, meanwhile, is expected to be on the Texas Legislature's agenda in 1999 and perhaps beyond.

Naturally, there is no comparison between the cost of sending a child to a private school versus a public school education. But even in wealthy public school districts, the pressure on local schools to raise money to augment their budgets is intense. Although optional, parents in all the area school districts are urged to participate in fund-raisers. These much-need additional funds go for a wide range of purchases and improvements, including books for the school library, computers and even repairs. Parental involvement, through the area's Parent Teacher Associations or on an individual volunteer basis, provides vital additional

INSIDERS' TIP

Gov. Elisha M. Pease signed the bill setting up the Texas public school system on January 31, 1854. According to a school census that year, there were 65,463 students in the system. The state spent 62¢ per child.

resources in the classrooms, offices and libraries of the area's schools. It is not uncommon to find a dozen or more parents on any given day offering their time and skills to improve their local educational facility. School administrators agree: higher parental involvement results in an improved learning environment. Districts also supplement their budgets through programs that involve the local business community. The Austin and Del Valle districts' Adopt-A-School and the Eanes district's Joint Venture programs, for example, call on businesses to help out by giving money, making in-kind donations or sending volunteers for special events.

All the school districts in the Austin area operate special schools and/or programs for both physically and mentally handicapped students and those with behavioral or emotional problems. Students who require more academic challenge are provided a number of opportunities, including honors programs, advanced-placement classes, programs for talented and gifted youth and, in the Austin school district's case, magnet schools. The region's many Spanish-speaking students are offered bilingual classes or so-called ESL classes, where they study English as a second language.

The school year varies slightly in Central Texas, but generally runs from mid-August to the third week in May for a total of 176 school days. Children entering Austin-area schools must be five years old by September 1 to enroll in kindergarten. Texas also requires that all children receive immunizations to attend school.

School Districts

Austin Independent School District

1111 W. Sixth St. • (512) 414-1700

One of the nation's leading urban school districts, the Austin Independent School District puts great emphasis on providing high quality education for children of all races, economic levels and English-speaking proficiencies. The district offers an excellent core curriculum that stresses math, science, reading and writing as well as special opportunities for a full range of students, from academically superior to those with learning difficulties.

With an annual budget in 1998-99 of $503.5 million, AISD provides educational opportunities for about 77,000 students on 97 campuses, including four for special needs students. The district's commitment to children is evidenced by the number of national honors and rankings it has received in recent years. In 1997, 139 students from AISD's 10 high schools were named National Merit Scholars, and 44 of those were named as finalists. That's six times the average for a district of AISD's size. Austin ISD students taking the Scholastic Aptitude Test (SAT) in 1997 scored 1,055, outperforming their Texas counterpoints by 60 points and beating the national average by 39 points. Eight elementary schools and two high schools have been named Blue Ribbon Schools by the U. S. Department of Education. Brown, Campbell, Highland Park, Hill, Lee, Ortega, Walnut Creek and Zavala elementary schools all have received this important distinction. Bowie and Lanier High Schools also have been awarded national recognition. Additionally, Doss Elementary School has been named a Texas Blue Ribbon School. Fifty percent of the district's students are listed as economically disadvantaged and 15 percent have limited English proficiency. Of course, the student population at individual schools within this huge district reflects the ethnic and economic makeup of the residents themselves. So within AISD, some schools have high concentrations of upper income families while other schools have a higher concentration of economically disadvantaged families. AISD is proud of its record of regularly increasing enrollment of minority and economically disadvantaged students in honors programs and advanced placement classes. But in a district that is growing by as many as 2,000 students per year, the challenge to continue producing top-quality graduates is staggering.

In 1996 voters approved a $369 million school bond program which called for the completion of 11 new schools — eight elementary, two middle and one high school — by the start of school in the year 2000. Two of those elementary schools opened in the fall of 1998. Construction or site preparation is under way on several other new facili-

Photo: Peter A. Silva

Learn more about President Lyndon B. Johnson at his presidential library on the UT campus.

ties. Additionally, bond money has been spent to upgrade aging school facilities, wire classrooms for computers and ease significant overcrowding through the construction of 70 new classrooms in nine existing schools around the district.

Del Valle Independent School District

2407 Shapard Ln., Del Valle
• (512) 389-7334

Once a region primarily of farms and ranches, the Del Valle Independent School District has witnessed major changes of late as more and more high-tech industries, and Austin's new international airport, move into the area. The district, located in the countryside of Southeast Austin and Travis County, serves the urban communities of Montopolis, Frontier Valley, Sunridge Park and Pleasant Valley as well as the rural communities of Garfield, Creedmoor, Mustang Ridge, Elroy, Pilot Knob, Webberville and Hornsby Bend.

Del Valle ISD has about 5,500 students on five elementary campuses, one junior high, one high school and an alternative learning center. In 1997, voters approved a $38.1 million school bond issue to help fund expansion of Del Valle High School and to relocate three elementary schools — Popham, Hillcrest and Baty — that were determined to be in the flight path of the new Austin-Bergstrom International Airport. The new elementary schools, also funded through the sale of the old buildings, are set to open in June of 1999. The new and improved high school will open in June 2000. As a result of the relocations, the district's elementary schools will no longer be clustered in a central location, but spread throughout the area to better serve neighborhoods and encourage parental involvement.

The bond issue also included nearly $11 million to expand and renovate Hornsby-Dunlap and Smith elementary schools and Del Valle Junior High. Del Valle ISD is rated Academically Acceptable by the Texas Education Agency. Smith Elementary School, however, is both an Exemplary school and a U.S. Blue Ribbon School. The high-school class of 1998 taking Scholastic Aptitude Tests scored 919 points, 76 points below the average for Texas.

Sixty-five percent of the district's students are listed as economically disadvantaged and 13 percent have limited English proficiency. Del Valle offers an excellent range of courses from preschool through high school for students of all abilities and talents. Bilingual and English as a Second Language classes are in place throughout the district. Of special note is the district's technology program, which uses computers as an integral component of classroom instruction. Through its Adopt-A-School program, Del Valle enjoys strong support of the area's business and technology community, which provides scholarships, grants and awards.

Dripping Springs Independent School District

311 Old Fitzhugh Rd., Dripping Springs • (512) 858-4905

Located 19 miles west of Austin in Hays County, the Dripping Springs Independent School District has seen explosive growth as a result of the economic boom in the Austin area. This small district of just four schools grew by 51 percent, to 3,082 students between 1993 and 1998. The suburban district is rated Exemplary by the Texas Education Agency. Its students taking Scholastic Aptitude Tests scored 1,086 overall in 1997, among the highest in an area that already beats the national average. The district sets high standards for its students and provides advanced placement and gifted and talented programs to its academically outstanding students. The needs of mentally and physically handicapped students are addressed within the schools themselves, with the assistance and guidance of the Hays County Co-op. To deal with the problem of overcapacity, voters in 1996 passed a $24.7 million bond program to improve and expand existing schools and build a new intermediate school to be completed by the fall of 2000.

Eanes Independent School District

601 Camp Craft Rd. • (512) 329-3600

Considered one of the finest school districts in Texas, the Eanes Independent School District is rated Exemplary by the Texas Education Agency, one of only 64 districts in the state to achieve the highest rating in the 1996-97 school year. In 1997, students taking the Scholastic Aptitude Test scored an impressive average score of 1,157, beating the national average by 141 points. This district has about 7,300 students at six elementary schools, two middle schools and one high school. Six of its nine schools, including Westlake High School, are U.S. Blue Ribbon Schools.

It is one of the wealthiest school districts in Texas, and less than 3 percent of the Eane's students are listed as economically disadvantaged. Less than 1 percent have limited English proficiency. Eanes enjoys the benefits of having strong support from parents and the business community. In addition to its outstanding academic programs, the district is well known for its athletic programs for both boys and girls. In 1996 and 1997 alone, the district racked up an impressive five state championships in golf, football, girls basketball and girls swimming, twice. The Eanes Independent School District encompasses 31.2 square miles in West Austin and in the municipalities of Rollingwood and West Lake Hills. In 1997, voters passed a $41.5 million school bond issue that will result in construction of two new schools in the coming years. In 1998, however, Eanes voters rejected a hotly contested proposal to build a new high school.

Lago Vista Independent School District

8039 Bar-K, Lago Vista • (512) 267-8300

The smallest school district in the Capital City region, the Lago Vista Independent School District has just 850 students in its three schools. The district covers 35 square miles on north Lake Travis and serves the communities of Lago Vista, Point Venture and South Jonestown Hills. Although its communities are known primarily for resort and retirement living, the district is changing as more and more families with children move into the area, many to take advantage of the high quality education the district provides. Lago Vista Middle School and Lago Vista Elementary are both rated Recognized by the Texas Education Agency, while Lago Vista High School received an Academically Acceptable rating.

INSIDERS' TIP

Joe Farley, a 7th-grade Language Arts teacher at Fulmore Middle School in Austin, was named the 1997-98 Texas Teacher of the Year by the Texas Education Agency.

The district emphasizes college preparatory programs and lifelong sports. Schools provide a number of learning opportunities for children of all learning abilities, however, including special education and English as a Second Language. Students needing more challenge and enrichment are offered a Gifted and Talented program as well as a number of advanced placement and honors classes. Fourteen percent of the district's students are economically disadvantaged, compared to 48 percent statewide. Lago Vista ISD, like most in this region, is growing rapidly. School authorities anticipate enrollment will increase by 8 to 10 percent per year over the next few years. As a result, voters passed a $13 million school bond issue in May 1997, which will add 32 school rooms throughout the district, fund construction of a 5,000-square-foot library at the high school, expand computers labs and playgrounds and purchase 100 acres of land for a new high school to be built around the year 2005. The district receives strong community support as evidenced by overwhelming support for the bond issue, which passed by a 2-to-1 margin.

Lake Travis Independent School District

3322 R.R. 620 S. • (512) 263-4400

The Lake Travis Independent School District, one of the smallest in this region with just four schools and about 3,450 students, is rated Exemplary by the Texas Education Agency. Located west/northwest of Austin along Lake Travis' southwest shore, the district serves many nearby communities, including Apache Shores, Bee Cave, Briarcliff, Homestead, Hudson Bend, Lake Pointe, Lakeway, The Hills and Vineyard Bay. Once comprised largely of resorts and retirement communities, the district is seeing its profile change as more families move into the area. The Lake Travis ISD offers excellent educational opportunities at all levels and provides classes and programs for both academically superior students and those requiring special help. Lakeway is proud of its reputation for providing rigorous academic programs for high school students, who are required to earn credits in the four core subjects of math, science, English and social studies, as well as foreign language, technology, find arts, physical education and health. Additionally, students may earn credit in math and science electives, career/technical courses or college preparatory classes.

In addition to its overall district rating of Exemplary, Lake Travis has received Exemplary ratings for Lake Travis Middle School and Lakeway Elementary. Lake Travis High School and Lake Travis Elementary are rated as Recognized. High school students taking the national Scholastic Aptitude Test in 1997 scored 1,076, 60 points higher than the national average. In 1997, the district produced 12 National Merit Scholars. Lake Travis ISD, once a component of the Dripping Springs Independent School District, was formed in 1981 with just 541 students in its kindergarten through 12th grade classes. Today, the district is growing by about 9 percent a year and already is experiencing overcapacity in the high school, the middle school and one of the district's two elementary schools. District voters passed a $41 million bond issue in 1998 to build another elementary school and another middle school as well as expand and improve Lake Travis High school and update technology throughout the district.

Leander Independent School District

401 S. West St., Leander • (512) 434-5000

The Leander Independent School District is northwest of Austin in Williamson and Travis counties and educates students from the com-

INSIDERS' TIP

To report problems at a child-care facility or to get information that may be on record about a particular center, parents should contact the Texas Department of Protective and Regulatory Services at (512) 834-0162.

munities of Leander, Cedar Park and a part of Austin. With nearly 12,000 students, Leander is the fourth-largest district in this 10-district region. This district, which covers 200 square miles, much of it still undeveloped, is in another fast-growing area of Central Texas. And Leander is building schools to keep up with an enrollment increase of nearly 10 percent a year. In fact, half of the district's eight elementary schools have been built since 1994, one of which opened in the fall of 1998. The district's second high school opened in the fall of 1998. Another elementary school will open in 1999 and a third middle school is on the drawing board.

In addition to its traditional schools, Leander operates an alternative learning center, which is designed for students with disciplinary problems as well as for students who work or have themselves become parents and need to study at their own pace. Leander was among the pioneers in the state to develop an educational program aimed at better preparing high school students for college or the work force by requiring them to take classes in a specific discipline. Under the Career Pathways program, students take three and six credit hours in one of six specialty areas: marketing, communications, fine arts, science, technology or community services. District authorities say they launched the program in the early 1990s following talks with business leaders, which revealed that students required more preparation than that provided by core curriculum classes alone. The program also allows students to explore career paths before they get to college. Besides Career Pathways, Leander ISD provides strong core curriculum classes and, for those requiring more challenge, an honors program. Special needs students receive instruction tailored to their requirements within the traditional classrooms. The Leander ISD is rated Academically Acceptable by the Texas Education Agency, although two elementary schools received an Exemplary rating and two were rated as Recognized. The average SAT score in the district was 1,037 in 1977, 42 points above the state average and 21 higher than the national average. Twenty percent of the district's children are listed as economically disadvantaged.

Manor Independent School District

312 Murray Ave. • (512) 278-4000

Ask authorities at Manor Independent School District to name the number one challenge facing the district today and they respond succinctly: growth. This small district in Northeast Austin and Travis County has doubled in enrollment since 1993, to 3,000 students, and is projecting enrollment at close to 7,700 by the year 2002. And amazingly, the district, one of the poorest in the state in 1985, will become one of the richest by 2001. The reason for the meteoric rise: high tech. The Manor school district is home to Applied Materials, the world's largest maker of computer-chip manufacturing equipment. Samsung is opening a $1.3 billion semiconductor factory in stages. Together the companies represent thousands of jobs and major tax revenue. A large industrial park in the district houses, among other businesses, Apple Computers. Sizable housing developments are following as the community moves from one of largely renters and farms to more and more single-family dwellings.

What's happening in Manor demonstrates in microcosm the benefits of having dynamic businesses that lend their support to schools. Not only has the taxable value of the district's property more than tripled, from $491 million in 1995 to $1.6 billion in 1998, the businesses in Manor also are actively helping to improve the schools. Among its many contributions, Applied Materials donated money to develop an up-to-date physics lab at Manor High School. Samsung and Applied Materials are working with Austin Community College to develop a curriculum in the district to begin training students interested in the technology field. That program could bring major opportunities for students in a district traditionally made up of working-class families, farmers and ranchers that lists 50 percent of its students as economically disadvantaged. The Manor school district is rated Academically Acceptable. According to latest scores available on the district's Scholastic Aptitude Test, students averaged 886, below the national and Texas averages. In 1997 voters approved a $20.3 million bond issue that will finance new schools in the future. Meanwhile, a new high school opened in the fall of 1998, and most of the district's other facilities were enlarged. One elementary school, one intermediate school, one junior high and an alternative learning center round out the district's facilities.

Pflugerville Independent School District

1401 W. Pecan, Pflugerville
• (512) 251-4159

Located in Northeast Travis County, close to several of the area's largest high-tech industries, the Pflugerville Independent School District has seen its enrollment more than double over the past decade to about 12,350 students today. That enrollment makes Pflugerville the third-largest district in the region. While the major high-tech companies are not within the jurisdiction of the Pflugerville school system, residential communities are springing up throughout the district to provide homes for families moving into the area to be close to jobs in Round Rock and Austin. The district comprises 17 campuses: two high schools, three middle schools, an alternative learning center, and 11 elementary schools, including two that opened in the fall of 1998. As enrollment continues to climb at a rate of 7 to 8 percent a year, however, the district has called on voters to once again support construction of schools. In response, voters passed a $46 million school bond issue in 1997 to expand Connally High School and build even more schools over the next few years.

The district is rated Academically Acceptable by the Texas Education Agency, although four of its elementary schools have received a Recognized rating. High school students taking the national Scholastic Aptitude Test in 1997 scored an average of 1,030 to beat the national average by 14 points. Sixteen percent of the district's students are listed as economically disadvantaged and 5 percent have limited English proficiency. Pflugerville offers a Spanish bilingual program for kindergarten through 3rd grade. High school students are offered foreign language courses in French, German, Spanish, Latin and Russian in addition to a core curriculum that includes math, science, language arts and science. High school students who desire can choose from among nine vocational programs or they can choose from among eight advanced placement courses and 46 honors classes.

Round Rock Independent School District

1311 Round Rock Ave., Round Rock
• (512) 464-5000

The Round Rock Independent School District, just north of Austin in northern Travis and Williamson counties, is a focal point of community involvement. Like several other districts in this area, Round Rock ISD has a fine reputation for offering excellent educational opportunities. The district has 34 campuses: 23 elementary, seven middle schools, three high schools and one alternative learning center. Students taking the Scholastic Aptitude Test in 1997 scored 1,085, 90 points higher than the average Texas school and 69 points higher than the national average. Additionally, Round Rock has four national Blue Ribbon elementary schools, Laurel Mountain, Live Oak, North Oaks and Pond Springs. Three of its middle schools, Canyon Vista, Chisholm Trail and Grisham, have received this national distinction, along with Westwood High School. Three more schools have been named Texas Blue Ribbon Schools. The district is rated Academically Acceptable by the Texas Education Agency, but within the district nine schools are rated exemplary and seven are Recognized. The district regularly produces a number of National Merit Scholars.

About 20 percent of the district's students are listed as economically disadvantaged compared to 48 percent statewide. Also, 3 percent of Round Rock students are considered to have limited English proficiency, compared to 13 percent statewide.

The Primary Enrichment Program aims to foster creative and productive thinking for youngsters through 3rd grade. The Gifted and Talented program for students from kindergarten through 12th grade offers special enrichments for those students requiring more academic challenges. At the secondary level, students may choose to take honors and/or advanced placement classes or participate in a number of competitions including Texas Future Problem Solving and Academic Decathlon. For students interested in vocational training, the district offers special courses beginning in middle school.

Round Rock is the second-largest school district in this area, with nearly 30,000 students. Only the Austin school district has more students. Like some other districts in this area, Round Rock is experiencing severe growing pains as more and more high-tech industries move into the area. District officials expect enrollment to top 40,000 by the year 2005. A new elementary school opened in the fall of 1998 and a fourth high school is slated to open in the fall of 1999. In March of 1997, voters passed a $99.3 million bond issue to further expand and renovate schools and update technology throughout the district.

Charter Schools

American Institute for Learning

422 Congress Ave. • (512) 472-8220

In 1996, the State Board of Education approved its first applications for charter schools. Among the first six authorized statewide was Austin's American Institute for Learning. The school provides education and job training to students ages 16 to 21 who have dropped out of traditional schools or are considered high risk for staying in school. Students work toward earning a General Educational Development (GED) diploma. The cornerstone of the year-round open-enrollment school is the Certificate of Mastery, which guarantees the student has acquired the skills necessary to succeed in the workplace or in college. Students receive training in computers, business, multimedia and theater arts. Another aspect of the charter school is its involvement with the national AmeriCorps program. For people ages 17 through 25, the Casa Verde Builders program teaches on-the-job construction skills and the Environmental Corps program stresses education in water-quality testing, park maintenance and other environmental areas.

Texas Academy of Excellence

2406 Manor Rd. • (512) 708-1888

Austin's only certified elementary charter school, the Texas Academy of Excellence serves children from pre-kindergarten through 3rd grade and is adding a grade level each year until its 5th-grade class begins in the year 2000. The school in East Austin, a state-funded alternative to traditional elementary schools, integrates music, art, dance and storytelling into its comprehensive educational program. The multicultural, multiracial school introduces children to foreign languages in preschool and continues with a program designed to engage all aspects of a child's development. In addition to the core subjects of math, language arts and science, children are presented a world view through a diversity of subject matter, including history of Texas and the United States, ancient history, multicultural history and the geography of North and South America. The Texas Academy of Excellence received its charter in 1996, but the school itself had been run for two decades under the name Capital Creative Schools, Inc. That nonprofit corporation now runs Texas Academy. About 100 students attend the school and enrollment is limited. The school is open to all children of appropriate age, although the half-day preschool program is limited to economically disadvantaged children.

INSIDERS' TIP

For great, detailed information on a particular public school district, including demographic breakdowns, financial information and student test performance, order *Snapshot* from the Texas Education Agency, Department of Publications Distribution and Sales at (512) 463-9744. This book does not provide information about specific schools. For that, ask the individual school for a copy of the Academic Excellence Indicator System report. These reports are invaluable for parents who want to make informed decisions about where to educate their children.

Private Schools

Whether you're looking for a parochial school, alternative learning, a college-preparatory program or an institute for academically gifted children, Austin probably has a private school that fits the bill. If the city falls short in any category, it would be in the scarcity of high-quality boarding schools similar to those found in larger cities, especially in the East. Only St. Stephen's Episcopal School, an excellent educational institution, provides room and board for high school students. The region also lacks schools just for boys or just for girls. All the private schools in the area are coeducational.

In Austin, many people opt for private schools to round out their children's religious education, although the demand for all types of private schools is growing rapidly. In response, several schools in the Austin area are adding grade levels a year at a time or expanding existing facilities, although the pressure for space keeps mounting. Many schools have extensive waiting lists and require admissions tests and/or interviews. Some schools do not accept students based on a first-come, first-served system, choosing instead to accept students who meet their requirements. Also, some schools offer before- and after-school care and/or extracurricular activities so parents should check with the school if those extras are important.

One of the most important recommendations we can offer, based on our experience in researching the area's private schools, is that it is imperative to visit all the schools under consideration before making a final decision. Surprisingly, a school can sound wonderful over the phone or in writing, but seem unsuitable for any number of reasons once you've seen the campus. The agony of choosing a private school can be lessened by determining your own list of requirements before beginning the search: Religious or nonreligious? Cost? Location? Extracurricular activities? Those are just of few of the factors that must be considered. Parents who do their research, however, should be pleased with the range of educational styles, school sizes and programs available. With few exceptions, they will find administrators who are eager to discuss their educational philosophy and more than willing to offer tours of their facilities. But, again, space is not always available so it's important to plan ahead. In the listing below, we've included most of Austin's largest private schools as well as a representative sampling of all the area's other private schools.

Central

Huntington-Surrey School

308 E. 32nd St. • (512) 478-4743

This college-preparatory senior high school of just 75 students offers an academically stimulating environment for bright students who want to be challenged, like to express themselves and are willing to take on a great deal of responsibility. With a student-teacher ratio of 4-to-1 — and sometimes 1-to-1 — the school has no place for slackers to hide out. Scholastic Aptitude Test results average 1,100 at Huntington-Surrey. The educational focus is on writing, math, history and science. Students sit around a table with the teacher to discuss lessons. The school, in an old house near the University of Texas campus, has a morning session for freshmen and sophomores and an afternoon session for juniors and seniors. All students attend the school at midday to study foreign languages: French, Latin, Spanish and German. The shorter-than-average school day allows students to work, perform volunteer services or pursue outside interests, such as music, dance, karate, swimming and horseback riding, for school credit. Huntington-Surrey is an independent, locally owned school.

Hyde Park Baptist School

3901 Speedway • (512) 465-8331

The largest private school in the Austin area, Hyde Park Baptist School offers a Christ-centered educational program for 900 students on two campuses. The campus on Speedway is for students from kindergarten through high school while the school in Southwest Austin, called the Bannockburn campus, is for K through 6th grades. Hyde Park is a college-preparatory, honors school that stresses educational achievement and a Christ-centered foundation. The school aims to produce Christian individuals who are responsible, productive members of society. Hyde Park, established in 1968, is accredited by the Southern Association of Colleges and Schools. Students taking Scholastic Aptitude Tests averaged 1,182, well above the national average. In addition to daily Bible classes, the teachings of Christ are integrated daily into the basic curriculum. Additionally, students can choose from among three foreign languages: Latin, French and Spanish. All elementary students are included in the schools' Excel program for gifted and talented youth. The school offers state-of-the-art computer labs for all students and has computers with Internet connections in each classroom. Hyde Park offers a wide range of extracurricular sports activities for boys and girls and more than a dozen other after-school activities. The nondenominational school is sponsored by the Hyde Park Baptist Church.

Kirby Hall School

306 W. 29th St. • (512) 474-1770

One of Austin's most academically superior schools, Kirby Hall is an accredited college-preparatory school for students from kindergarten through 12th grade. One hundred percent of Kirby Hall graduates go on to college. Kirby Hall boasts average Scholastic Aptitude Test scores of 1,300 and students rank three to four years above the national average on tests such as the Iowa Test of Basic Skills. In a historic brick building near the University of Texas campus, Kirby Hall is situated to allow students to walk to the university to audit classes and, with testing, achieve college credit. All of the school's core curriculum classes for high school students are advanced placement classes and many students graduate from Kirby Hall with college credit hours. This school is an independent, nondenominational Christian school for bright students who want to excel. It has no facilities for children with learning disabilities or for students with discipline problems. Entrance exams and uniforms are required. About 176 boys and girls attend Kirby Hall in classes that average 16 students in size.

St. Andrew's Episcopal School

1112 W. 31st St. • (512) 452-5779

St. Andrew's was established in 1951, making it one of the area's oldest and best-known parochial schools. St. Andrew's is adding a grade level each year until its 12th grade is completed in 2001. St. Andrew's offers an academically challenging environment that stresses the development of a Christian character. It offers a strong core curriculum along with fine arts, foreign languages and physical education for 440 students. As the school only

Photo: Peter A. Silva

There is an excellent selection of schools ranging from pre-school to universities.

goes to the 9th grade now, SAT scores are not applicable, although the school says its median score on the Stanford Achievement Test is 95 percent. Admission tests and interviews are required. Entrance is determined through an 'applicant pool' instead of by date of application.

St. Austin's School

1911 San Antonio St. • (512) 477-3751

This Catholic parish school was established in 1917 and today educates about 230 students from kindergarten through 8th grade. Daily religious instruction is an integral part of the curriculum at all grades, and students are prepared for the sacraments of Holy Communion, Reconciliation and Confirmation. For students in kindergarten and 1st grade, teachers use a modified Montessori approach designed to encourage students to progress at their own pace stressing basic skills and concepts. The middle school program reinforces basic skills and emphasizes higher-order thinking skills. In addition to a strong core curriculum at all levels, students study Spanish, computers, art, music, health and physical education. The music program for students in kindergarten through 5th grade is integrated with religious instruction through preparation for weekly Masses at St. Austin's Church.

Sri Atmananda Memorial School

4100 Red River St. • (512) 451-7044

The learning approach used at the Sri Atmananda Memorial School was developed in southern India and brought to Austin by the school's director, Patty Henderson. She had placed her 5-year-old son in the India school while the family was there on business and was impressed with the results. Students at Sri Atmananda are not assigned a classroom or a teacher, but instead are allowed to select their own area of interest from among the many labs available to them: math-geography, computer, art, science and others. All subject matter is thoroughly integrated and teachers present material and offer structured activities, especially for older students. Children do not receive grades for their work, although the learning material presented is appropriate for each student's abilities. About 36 students from kindergarten through 5th grade attend the school, although the school is adding a grade level each year. Sri Atmananda is the only school outside India to use this method and several of the school's teachers have received their training in that country.

South Central

Parkside Community School

1701 Toomey Rd. • (512) 472-2559

About 125 students attend this Montessori school for children from three years old through 6th grade. Parkside was established in 1991 and focuses on the teaching methods developed by Dr. Maria Montessori in Italy. The program allows children to express their maximum creativity and to work at their own pace under the guidance of the classroom teacher. The core classes of language arts, math, science and social studies are covered in all classrooms along with art, drama, sewing and others. Preschoolers can attend classes full or half days, depending on the desires of the parents. The school also has an after-school program for students of all ages. There is a waiting list to attend.

St. Ignatius Martyr Catholic School

120 W. Oltorf St. • (512) 442-8547

For students in pre-kindergarten through 8th grade, St. Ignatius educates about 255 students, both members and nonmembers of St. Ignatius Church. The school provides a strong Christian education that includes daily scriptural readings and reflection. Children gather at Liturgy to listen to God's word and to learn to apply it to their daily life. Additionally, St. Ignatius offers a strong core curriculum that includes literature and the language arts, science, math, physical education and the fine arts. Upper-level students are introduced to hands-on learning in the science lab and on computers. The math program includes pre-algebra and algebra for 7th and 8th graders. Students receive instruction in preparation to receive the Sacraments of Holy Eucharist and Confirmation in 2nd grade, and Reconciliation in 4th grade. The school demands parent involvement and requires parents to spend a minimum of 20 hours each year in service to the school, either at the school or at any event sponsored by the Parent Teacher Organization. St. Ignatius is accredited by the Texas Catholic Conference Department of Education.

North

Austin Montessori School — Great Northern

6817 Great Northern Blvd. • (512) 450-1940

Great Northern is for primary students through 3rd grade. About 65 students are enrolled at this school. The classic Montessori classroom design displays all learning materials on shelves and allows students to act on their own initiative in order to maximize independent learning and exploration. The Montessori approach is hands-on. Children work individually, in small groups and participate in whole-class activities. Teachers, known as guides, are trained to recognize a child's particular developmental stage and offer the appropriate learning materials as the child becomes ready to use them. In this way, social studies, math, reading, writing, art and music are presented to students. Ethics, social skills and practical life are emphasized as the school focuses on developing the whole child. The Austin Montessori Schools are considered models for the Montessori approach and the school has hosted observers from all over the world. The school is accredited by Association Montessori Internationale. There is a waiting list.

Austin 7th Day Adventist Junior Academy

301 W. Anderson Ln. • (512) 459-8976

About 30 students from kindergarten through 10th grade attend this Christian school, supported by four 7th Day Adventist churches in the region. Students attend multigrade classes and study from Christian and 7th Day Adventist textbooks. The school stresses academic achievement. It is on the grounds of the Austin First 7th Day Adventist Church and accredited by the 7th Day Adventist School System. Students take classes in language arts, science, social studies and math as well as computer science, physical education. Enrollment is open to anyone.

Brentwood Christian School

11908 N. Lamar Blvd. • (512) 835-5983

About 575 students attend Brentwood Christian School, a kindergarten through 12th grade college-preparatory school that is affiliated with the Brentwood Oaks Church of Christ. The school provides a Christ-centered academic environment that gives high school students a choice of degrees to pursue: standard, advanced or honors advanced. Elementary students are offered a strong basic curriculum that includes daily physical education and music classes and weekly Spanish and library skills classes. Beginning in 5th grade, students may take classes in band, art and choir. Seventh graders and up are offered journalism and drama. Brentwood students score above the 90th percentile compared with students nationwide on national achievement tests such as the Iowa Test of Basic Skills. High school students taking the Scholastic Aptitude Test averaged 1,113, 97 points higher than the national average. Brentwood has an extensive extracurricular sports program for boys and girls that includes baseball, soccer, volleyball, basketball, track and flag football. The school, established in 1963, welcomes students from all religious, ethnic and national origins if they are seeking a solid, Christian education. Brentwood is accredited by the National Christian Schools Association. Entrance exams are required.

Duane Lake Academy

2700 Anderson Ln., Ste. 418 • (512) 454-2260

About 75 students attend this independent alternative school, which offers seven hours of classes on Tuesdays and Thursdays so that students can pursue outside interests and studies. A parent or relative must attend these classes with the student, to fulfill the goal of providing a family-based education, and many parents who are college professors provide instruction. Students are required to submit a log showing they've done 15 hours of independent study each week. Educators say the students use the time to work with mentors, do apprenticeships or research, or to practice artistic or athletic talents. The goal of Duane Lake Academy is to provide flexibility to students who are looking for an opportunity to progress at their own pace. Students are offered a full range of math, from basic math to calculus, and a complete science curriculum that includes physics and astronomy. Duane Lake students can choose from among six foreign languages. The school also has an arrangement with Austin Community College for students to use science labs and other facilities not available at the school, which is in several buildings in a commercial center. Each student's curriculum is designed individually by the student, staff and parents. To try to meet enrollment demand, the school recently tripled its classroom space.

Paragon Prep

2001 West Koenig Ln. • (512) 459-5040

Weekly academic competitions, cooperative projects and an emphasis on technology are just a few of the aspects of this new college-preparatory school for middle school students. Founded in 1997, Paragon Prep seeks bright, motivated students who are aiming for higher education. The independent school for students in 6th, 7th and 8th grades uses renowned educational material, including the Chicago Math Series curriculum and the Junior Great Books program. Paragon calls itself "Internet intensive," and provides regular access to the World Wide Web through Internet classes that emphasize research and multimedia projects. The curriculum is designed so that students returning to public school for senior high will be exceptionally prepared. Paragon expects both student and parental commitments to excellence and offers in exchange a dynamic, fun and stimulating environment. The school aims to produce students who are well-rounded, concerned for others and knowledgeable about democratic and entrepreneurial principals. Admission is selective, based on student testing and interviews with the student and parents. About 120 students attend Paragon.

St. Louis School

2114 St. Joseph Blvd. • (512) 454-0384

This Catholic school, part of St. Louis parish, was established in 1956 and today provides religious and secular education to about 465 students from preschool through 8th grade. The school's well-rounded curriculum includes daily religion classes as well as language arts, math, science, health, computers, social studies, music, physical education, Spanish and the arts. Children attend Mass weekly and are given weekly sacramental preparation to supplement the program at St. Louis parish. The school provides a stimulating and progressive academic program integrated with Catholic values and traditions. Extracurricular activities include liturgical and bell choirs, team sports, cheerleading, student council and altar servers. St. Louis School admits students of all religious, racial and ethnic backgrounds. The school, affiliated with the Catholic schools of the Diocese of Austin, is accredited by the Southern Association of Colleges and Schools.

South

Christ Community Christian School

8210 S. First St. • (512) 282-4263

A college preparatory program combined with a strong emphasis on Bible study at Christ Community Christian School prepares students for higher education. About 200 students from several Christian denominations attend this independent school established in 1982. The school uses ABeka Christian texts for elementary students and Bob Jones texts for upper grades. Bible study is integrated into the curriculum at lower grades and beginning in 7th grade students take a formal Bible class. Because the school is interdenominational, class discussions of the Bible raise diverse points of view, which serves to broaden stu-

INSIDERS' TIP

Mirabeau B. Lamar, the second president of the Republic of Texas, is known as the "Father of Education in Texas." Under his leadership the Republic set aside land for schools. During the Republic, however, most education was provided by private schools and churches.

dents' understanding and challenges them to do research on their own. Guest speakers — priests, pastors, Sunday school teachers — are invited to address students during weekly chapel services. Christ Community is committed to helping all students reach their highest potential academically, but at the same time stresses the development of positive characters traits such as honesty and integrity. Students taking Scholastic Aptitude Tests average 1,090, well above the national average. The school recently opened a computer lab to complement its teaching of core subject material. Students can participate in the schools extracurricular sports programs, which include volleyball, basketball and a coeducational soccer team in the spring.

The Strickland School

7415 Manchaca Rd. • (512) 447-1447

First graders at The Strickland School use the King James Version of the Bible as their basic reader. This religiously independent, nondenominational school was established in 1961 and today provides instruction for 270 students from pre-kindergarten through 8th grade. The school strives to provide academic excellence and a Christian foundation. The school, developed by Texan Corine Strickland, was a leader in teaching children to read phonetically starting in preschool. To this day, the school emphasizes developing strong readers. Its core curriculum also includes writing, spelling and math. Children also take classes in science, social studies and physical education. There is a waiting list to enter.

West

Austin Montessori Middle School

5676 Oak Blvd. • (512) 892-0826

This is the only school in the Montessori system that provides classes for students in 6th through 8th grades. The school extends the Montessori curriculum developed for elementary students by the Italian Maria Montessori. The program stresses individual development and hands-on learning. Teachers act as guides to help lead children along a path of learning appropriate for each. The middle school was established in 1993 and is accredited by Association Montessori Internationale. Thirty students attend the school, and there is a waiting list to enter.

The Children's School

2825 Hancock Dr. • (512) 453-1126

This Montessori school for children 2 to 9, uses a very progressive approach to learning which incorporates the classic Montessori curriculum with training in computer technology. For more than 20 years, computers have been an integral aspect of The Children's School and today's youngsters are introduced to multimedia systems and language development through the use of computers. The technology training only adds to the fundamental teaching methods of the Montessori system, which allows for the physical, emotional and intellectual development of each child. The Montessori curriculum, an extremely individualized approach to education, consists of hands-on learning in all the areas of study, including language arts, music, Spanish, art, science, physical education and math. The Children's School is extremely popular in the Austin area and 90 percent of those who visit the school have been recommended by a parent of a Children's School student. The school puts tremendous effort into nationwide seminars and conferences nationwide in order to remain abreast of the cutting edge of educational technology. In addition to its complete academic program, the school offers a variety of extracurricular activities. The Children's School is accredited by the American Montessori Society. There is a waiting list to enter.

Regents School of Austin

2600 Exposition Blvd. • (512) 472-4060

In the fall of 1998 the Regents School of Austin welcomed its first sophomore class and the school is adding a grade level each year until it opens for seniors in the year 2000. Serving about 300 students beginning in kindergarten, the Regents School is a nondenominational Christian school that integrates a college-preparatory, liberal-arts program with a strong Christian education. The school looks for students who are college bound and want to be challenged. Students begin the study of Latin in 3rd grade, which the school says help them to better understand English, science and history. In addition to Latin, students study the language arts, history, geography, math, science, logic, Spanish and the arts. The Regents School of Austin opened in 1992 and is a founding member of the Association of Christian and Classical Schools. It is on the campus of Terrytown Baptist Church, but directors plan to move upper-level students to a new location once the school is completed. Admissions tests and interviews are required. There is a waiting list for admission. Students wear uniforms.

St. Michael's Academy

3000 Barton Creek Blvd. • (512) 328-2323

St. Michael's Academy offers a rigorous academic environment for about 400 college-bound students. The school, established in 1984, challenges students to reach their full potential and helps them achieve that goal by offering 53 courses, including theology, foreign language, computer science and fine arts. Students desiring more academic challenge can pursue an Advanced Academic Diploma with Honors, which requires the completion of 10 semester hours of honors courses in addition to writing an honors thesis. The school's success in producing top-quality graduates is reflected in the number of students accepted to the nation's leading colleges and universities, in the amount of scholarships and awards seniors receive, in Scholastic Aptitude Test scores that beat the national average by more than 100 points, and in the number of National Merit Scholars the school produces. The admissions process is competitive and selection is based on an application, entrance exam, academic record, teacher recommendations and an interview. The school is dedicated to serving a diverse student body and to that end offers a financial-aid program that allows students of all economic backgrounds the opportunity to attend St. Michael's. The school is on 50 acres in a residential area in Southwest Austin. A new 25,000-square-foot classroom and administrative wing opened in the fall of 1998. The school, which is owned and governed by a board of trustees, is accredited by the Texas Catholic Conference Education Department.

St. Stephen's Episcopal School

2900 Bunny Run • (512) 327-9642

Austin's only boarding school for high school students, St. Stephen's also offers day classes for coed students in 6th through 12th grades. St. Stephen's is one of Austin's most academically superior schools. It regularly produces National Merit Scholars, its most recent Scholastic Aptitude Test scores averaged 1,270 and in 1997 four of its graduates were accepted to Harvard University, from a graduating class of just 72 students. The schools stresses Christian and community values, but welcomes students from all cultures, backgrounds and religions. Its range of academic offerings is outstanding, a factor in its local popularity. St. Stephen's offers classes in theology, Greek, Latin, Spanish, French, Chinese, economics and anthropology as well as the basic core curriculum. Admissions tests and interviews are required. There is a waiting pool for admission. On 428 acres, St. Stephen's has about 580 students. An observatory opened in the fall of 1998. St. Stephen's was established in 1950 and is affiliated with the National Association of Independent Schools and the Southern Association of Episcopal Schools.

St. Theresa's School

4311 Small Dr. • (512) 451-7105

Four-year-olds through 6th graders attend this expanding Catholic school in Northwest Austin. In an attempt to meet the growing demand for education at St. Theresa's, this parish school is adding another class at each grade level per year until all grade levels have two classes. The school expects to have about 460 students when the expansion project is completed. St. Theresa's, on the campus of St. Theresa's Catholic Church, offers a full, academically challenging curriculum designed to allow students to reach their full potential. St. Theresa's students score on average in the 90th percentile on the Comprehensive Test of Basic Skills, a national achievement test. St. Theresa's also provides enrichment opportunities for each course of study, such as the guest artist program, which brings performances of theater and music into the school. In addition to daily religion classes, lessons from the Bible are integrated throughout the basic core subjects. Specially trained instructors provide classes in library skills, physical education and computer training. Students begin using computers in preschool, with a program that reinforces reading skills, and continue their technology training through the 6th grade on the school's classroom computers and in two Internet-connected computer labs. St. Theresa's offers what it calls 'mastery learning,' which couples a well-trained faculty with the utilization of advanced technology and delivery systems.

Northwest

Austin Jewish Community Day School

4300 Bull Creek Rd. • (512) 467-0707

The only Jewish school in the Central Texas area, the Austin Jewish Community Day School opened in the fall of 1997. The school started with kindergarten through 3rd grade and expanded to 5th grade in the fall of 1998. The independent school plans to eventually offer classes through the 8th grade. The approximately 60 students at the school are motivated, creative self-starters who can work within a varying degree of structure. A strong Jewish education is part of the school's curriculum, but the school does not embrace any particular arm of Judaism or require that students be Jewish. Students study Hebrew daily and also take classes in Jewish history, prayer, Bible and the study of Israel. The school also offers a sound core curriculum that includes language arts, math and science as well as social studies, Spanish, art, music, physical education, geography and world cultures. Judaic and secular studies are highly integrated. Strong parental involvement is one of the school's greatest attributes. Although housed in Congregation Agudas Achim, the school is not affiliated with the congregation. It is a member of the National Association for the Education of Young Children and the National Association for Supervision and Curriculum Development. Because of anticipated growth in Austin's Jewish community, many parents have placed their children's names on the list for the kindergarten class of 2000.

Grace Covenant Christian School

9431 Jollyville Rd. • (512) 345-7976

This Christian school for children age one through the 6th grade strives to promote academic excellence and spiritual growth in each student. Founded in 1978, the school is affiliated with Grace Covenant Christian Church and is on the church grounds. Grace Covenant integrates a Bible-based learning environment with a strong core curriculum that includes math, science, language arts and social studies. The school also offers classes in computer science, art, music and physical education. Grace Covenant students rank in the top 25 percentile of students nationwide taking the Stanford Achievement Test. In addition to regular classes, the school offers a Spanish enrichment program after school and in the fall of 1998 added an after-school instrumental music program. The school is a member of the Association of Christian Schools International. Students attending Grace Covenant have a shorter school day than most in this area, attending from 8:40 AM to 2:30 PM. The school says it offers one of the lowest tuition rates among Austin's private schools.

Great Hills Christian School

10500 Jollyville Rd. • 343-6167

An accredited K-12 college-preparatory school, Great Hills Christian School provides an academically challenging environment based on a Christian world view for about 315 students. The school offers a varied but rigorous curriculum designed to develop and encourage the creative, the expressive, the analytical and the critical thinking skills necessary for college admission. Nearly 100 percent of the school's graduates go on to college and a large percentage have received scholarships to prestigious universities, including MIT and Vassar. Students average 1,120 on Scholastic Aptitude Tests, well above the national average. The school starts with kindergartners, stressing a phonics-based approach to spelling and understanding of the language arts. Specially trained teachers introduce elementary students to computer programming skills using classroom computers and the school's computer labs. Middle school students who qualify can enter the advanced math track to begin earning high school credit in 8th grade. The school participates in the Duke University Talent Search, which identifies potential high achievers through SAT and PSAT scores and encourages them to succeed through a variety of programs and scholarships. Great Hills Christian School, at Great Hills Baptist Church, offers a nondenominational Bible program for all students. Bible classes are taught daily and the study of religion is integrated throughout the school's programs. In 1998, the school began selecting a site for a new school.

Hill Country Christian School of Austin

12124 R.R. 620 N. • (512) 331-7036 (K-4)
10713 R.R. 620 N. • (512) 331-1450 (5-11)

The Hill Country Christian School, on two campuses in North Austin, is an expanding school that plans to begin enrolling seniors for classes in the fall of 1999. By 1998, the school provided a Christian and classical education to children from kindergarten through the 11th grade. Students from kindergarten through 4th grade attend one campus and upper-level students attend the other. The nondenominational school, affiliated with Hill Country Bible Church, which employs a phonics-based reading approach and recognizes distinctive learning patterns in each child. Teachings from the Bible are integrated into the school's basic curriculum, which includes language arts, math, science and history, art, music and physical education. The Bible also is taught as a separate lesson or course, depending on the grade level. Students in the upper grades can participate in the school's extracurricular sports program. In the fall of 1998, Hill Country Christian Heritage School merged with the Hill Country Christian School of Austin to form this new school. The school is a member of the Association of Christian Schools International. Nearly 350 students are enrolled.

Redeemer Lutheran School

1500 W. Anderson Ln. • (512) 451-6478

Redeemer Lutheran School is Austin's largest Lutheran school, with about 450 students in its preschool through 8th-grade programs. Founded in 1955, the school aims to share the Christian faith by assisting parents in providing opportunities for spiritual, intellectual, physical, emotional and social growth for children in a Christ-centered environment. The school follows the Texas Essential Knowledge and Skills curriculum program found in most public schools, but incorporates Christ in the daily education process. Although a Lutheran school, children of all faiths attend the school and are welcomed. In addition to the basic core curriculum, Redeemer Lutheran School offers music classes and physical education. Two computers labs give students daily access to computer technology and to the Internet. The school also an active extracurricular sports program and choirs for children of all ages. Preschoolers can attend full or half days. The school is affiliated with the Lutheran Church-Missouri Synod and accredited by the Lutheran School Accreditation Commission.

Southwest

Austin Montessori School — Sunset Trail

5014 Sunset Tr. • (512) 892-0253

Sunset Trail is the Montessori system's largest school in Austin, providing education to about 130 students from age 2½ to 6th grade. The school, founded in 1967, teaches children according to the method developed by Dr. Maria Montessori in Italy, who believed that children possess a natural and intense desire to learn about the world and that they can absorb knowledge effortlessly. The classroom is designed with all the learning material readily available on shelves in order to maxi-

INSIDERS' TIP

Carol Janes Moya has published an informative book on private schools in the Austin area. The book, *A Guide to Austin Private Schools*, lists tuition rates, other costs and admission requirements and provides other basic information. The book is available in area bookstores. You can reach her at the Austin Private School Referral Service, (512) 443-7939.

mize independent learning and exploration. The school does not use textbooks, but chooses to let children explore concrete materials, using their hands and their minds. Teachers, known as guides, are trained to recognize a child's particular developmental stage and offer the appropriate learning materials as the child becomes ready to use them. Children work individually or in small groups in learning science, social studies, math, reading, writing, art and music. Ethics, social skills and practical life are emphasized as the school focuses on developing the whole child. In addition to regular classroom activities, students can choose to learn violin or piano. Austin Montessori uses the Suzuki method of learning, which is based on the concept that children can learn music the same way they learn to speak — by ear. There is a waiting list.

Austin Waldorf School

8702 S. View Rd. • (512) 288-5942

The Austin Waldorf School, the only certified Waldorf program in Texas, is on 11 rural acres in the Oak Hill area of Austin. Waldorf schools, also known worldwide as Steiner schools, are based on the educational philosophy of Dr. Rudolf Steiner, an educator, artist and philosopher who devised a method of instruction based upon the idea that children pass through distinct developmental stages. The independent school, whose program extends from preschool to high school, added a 10th grade in the fall of 1998 and will continue to expand until the high school is completed. The program is designed to engage each child's innate creativity and builds on a strong academic foundation by integrating art, instrumental music, song, stories and crafts into the daily curriculum. The school teaches according to the phases of child development, offering lessons at each stage that are designed to nurture a child's imagination. Mastery of the academic disciplines is of utmost importance at the Waldorf school, where students are introduced to all major fields of human endeavor through the study of mathematics, sciences and language arts. Students are given the opportunity to explore all aspects of a subject matter and, with the guidance of their specially trained teacher, write and illustrate their own textbooks for each lesson. The school, founded in 1980, has grown to 305 students.

Hyde Park Baptist School — Bannockburn

7100 Brodie Ln. • (512) 892-0000

This is the Southwest Austin campus of Austin's largest private school. The Bannockburn campus for students in kindergarten through 6th grade has about 165 of the school's 900 students. Hyde Park's other school in Central Austin is a K-12 school and has more than 700 students. Building on a solid Christian foundation, the school aims to produce educational achievement and offers its elementary students a wide range of opportunities, including introduction to computer technology, foreign languages and a strong core curriculum that integrates Bible study with all areas of course work. All elementary students are included in both schools' Excel program for gifted and talented youth. Students entering the upper grades begin a college preparatory, honors program and most go on to college. The nondenominational school is sponsored by the Hyde Park Baptist Church.

Cedar Park

Hilltop Baptist Academy

1150 S. Bell Blvd., Cedar Park • (512) 258-0080

Hilltop Baptist Academy provides educational and religious training in a Christian environment to about 375 students from kindergarten through high school. On a 40-acre campus in Cedar Park, the school has two instructional buildings, each with its own library, a full-size gymnasium, playgrounds and an athletic field. The school integrates students' Biblical education with strong academic instruction, which has earned the school a reputation for providing high quality education. In addition to a strong basic curriculum, Hilltop Baptist Academy provides a wide range of computer training in the school's two computer labs. One lab is equipped to provide therapy for students and adults with learning difficulties. A well-equipped science lab, home economics lab and a music hall help meet the school's goal of providing students a complete education. Hilltop's extracurricular program includes a variety of athletic, fine arts and academic endeavors. Hilltop Baptist Academy is accredited by the Association of Christian Schools International.

Leander

Cornerstone Christian School

1303 Leander Dr., Leander
• (512) 259-4416

An independent, interdenominational school for 3-year-olds to seniors in high school, the Cornerstone Christian School educates about 275 students. The school is an accredited college-preparatory facility that features a well-rounded basic curriculum enhanced by regular study of the Bible. This evangelical school uses an all-Christian curriculum, including Bob Jones and ABeka texts and incorporates Bible study into all aspects of coursework. A small student-teacher ratio — 16-to-1 in most grades — allows teachers to gain an understanding of their students in order to teach each child to his or her highest potential. A flexible education plan allows students to undertake accelerated programs or take outside coursework, such as teacher-assisted advanced math. The senior class of 1998 averaged 1,067 on SAT tests, more than 50 points above the national average. A solid educational foundation is stressed at the elementary level and includes the study of world geography and world history, much of it from the missionary perspective. Upper grades are introduced to computer technology, the Spanish language, instrumental music and choir. The school offers a full extracurricular athletic program. Cornerstone requires an interview for admission and says it is looking for students with strong character. The school, founded in 1984, draws students from a 50-mile radius of the campus, including children from Round Rock, Pflugerville, Lago Vista and Austin. Students moved into a new school building in 1997.

Round Rock

Cornerstone Connection

1201 Northwest Dr., Round Rock
• (512) 255-8977

About 150 students attend this independent Christian school for children age 3 to 3rd grade. The school offers a Christian environment and stresses teaching children about God and helping to make God important in their lives. The school mostly uses texts found in local public schools, but offers a Christian reading program. Cornerstone incorporates teaching of the Bible throughout the academic curriculum. Older children attend a daily Bible class. Preschoolers start out learning their letters and number and have plenty of time for music and outdoor play. Older children learn basic core material and, importantly, self-respect and control.

Round Rock Christian Academy

301 N. Lake Creek Dr., Round Rock
• (512) 255-4491

Formerly called Central Baptist Academy, this school changed its name in 1998 as it expanded its programs to the 11th grade. The school's first senior class will graduate in the year 2000. Round Rock Christian Academy is a nondenominational school educating about 250 students starting at age 4. The school aims to cultivate a heart for God, develop the mind of Christ and provide a distinctively Christian quality education. The school supports a Christian-based curriculum using primarily the Bob Jones and ABeka text books. Math is taught using the Saxon method. In addition to core curriculum classes of math, history, science and language arts, classes in American sign language, drama, choir, Spanish and logic are offered. The academy's Discovery Program, for students in 1st through 4th grades, is an after-school enrichment program providing more academic challenge to qualified students. Under the Aim program, students with learning disabilities or other special needs work with a staff educational therapist. The school is affiliated with and accredited by the Association of Christian Schools International.

Child Care

For parents, few decisions arouse more angst than determining who will care for their preschool-age child while they're at work. As Austin grows, that concern intensifies as more and more parents compete for existing high quality care. Area child-care referral agencies insist that excellent care can be found, especially since more emphasis is placed these days on professional care, as opposed to just babysitting. Finding high quality child care for infants seems to be the most difficult, according to the referral agencies. As a matter of fact, they say, if people are even thinking about having a child, they need to get on waiting lists at accredited child-care centers. Parents often do not consider planning ahead for infant care, believing that because their infants sleep so often that care shouldn't be difficult to find or cost too much. However, because state regulations require a higher ratio of providers to infants in licensed facilities than any other age group — 4-to-1 — it's often not profitable for a center to provide care for the very young —so they don't.

Finding care for toddlers is not as hard, although in the fastest growing areas, especially in North Austin, Round Rock and Cedar Park, the challenge to locate high quality care increases. Child care in downtown Austin, with its high concentration of state office workers, also seems to be increasingly limited. Although after-school programs are offered at most schools in the Capital area's 10 school districts, waiting lists can be long so it's important to register early.

Another option is to have a child picked up by an after-school care provider. Again, it's important to plan ahead as these also tend to fill up in some areas. For preschoolers, parents can expect to pay between $50 and $200 a week at any one of this area's 506 licensed child-care centers or 568 registered family child-care homes.

While authorities do not consider the Austin area to have a shortage of day-care facilities, they do acknowledge there is a severe shortage of affordable day care, especially for parents required to work under federal welfare reforms. A growing trend among businesses — especially those in the high-tech industry that are competing for well-trained workers — is to provide child-care referral information to employees. That on-the-job resource can help ease the stress parents go through when trying to determine what care is best for their children.

Choosing a day-care provider gets somewhat easier for parents once they know what to look for in a facility. The Texas Department of Protective and Regulatory Services (PRS), which oversees day-care providers, lists three categories of service: licensed, registered and listed. Facilities that care for 13 or more children are considered day-care centers and must be licensed by the state. Registered facilities are home care centers that accept four to 12 children. The standards vary somewhat for these two categories, although they both are subject to unannounced inspections by the PRS. In 1997, the Texas Legislature created the last category: listed. According to new regulations, people who care for one to three children in their home must be listed by PRS and are subject to the same records investigations as other providers. These homes, however, are not inspected unless there is a report of child abuse or neglect. So now, the records of all child-care providers are examined through the PRS's central registry to determine if they have a record of abusing or neglecting a child. Also, all providers must submit to a criminal history check. Anyone convicted of so-called crimes against the family will not be authorized to work in child care.

In addition to receiving state authorization, more and more area child-care centers and home-care facilities are seeking accreditation through national agencies, which certify the standards at their facilities. Although accreditations are not required by the state, an increasing number of parents are seeking out accredited facilities. The accreditation agency for licensed centers is the National Association for the Education of Young Children. For family care providers, the National Association of Family Child Care is the accrediting body. One way for parents to ensure a safe environment for their children is to make sure that the facility is authorized by the state. Authorities at PRS, however, stress that parents are the most important regulators when it comes to child care. Every parent, they say, needs to accept the responsibility of inspecting their children's day-care centers regularly and to insist that any shortcomings be corrected.

Finding reliable and affordable child care, for regular daily care, occasional drop-in care or in-home sitters, can be one of the first tasks a family faces upon arrival in Austin. Some neighborhood associations provide residents with lists of babysitters in their areas, while parents in other areas have formed babysitting co-ops, in which parents take turns at sitting responsibilities. Be sure to check with your neighborhood association for information.

Several referral agencies around town can help by offering experienced guidance in the child-care search and by providing parents with lists of providers from their databases. Also, there's a source book out there for all you parents. For child-care centers by geographical locations and much more, check out *Today's Family Guide to Austin*, published by LCN, Inc. of Austin. Call them at (512) 288-6291 and (800) 424-6291, or look for the book at area libraries and bookstores. Following are some of the sitter services and referral agencies for child care that can help get you off to a good start.

A Mom's Best Friend

4505 Spicewood Springs Rd. • (512) 346-2229

This popular business for the busy parent provides both sitters and nannies. A Mom's Best Friend can arrange for sitters to come to your home, hotel or even your office for the amount of time you need. References and previous employers have been checked for all sitters, and a criminal background check has been conducted on all nannies. Clients looking for a certain age group in a sitter can, with enough advance notice, make a special request from among the staff, which ranges in age from mid-20s to mid-60s. A Mom's Best Friend also offers a service it calls Mother's Helper, which includes light house maintenance as well as child care. Great for the new mom. Separate housekeeping services can also be arranged.

Austin Capital Grannies

1825 Coronado Hills Dr. • (512) 371-3402

A well-established Austin business, Capital Grannies can babysit children for an evening, overnight or for a week if need be. The "grannies" are in their mid-20s to 60s and have all had CPR training and a criminal background check. Most of the sitters have been with the company at least seven years. References can be provided upon request.

Austin Families, Inc.

8000 Centre Park Dr. • (512) 834-0748
3307 Northland Dr. • (512) 454-1194

Austin Families, which has two offices, is a nonprofit organization that has been helping families find child care since 1978. They have an extensive database that includes child-care providers in 10 Central Texas counties and are most helpful when it comes to providing information.

Child Care Management Services

2538 S. Congress Ave. • (512) 326-1881, (800) 825-1914

Managed by the City of Austin, this organization provides child-care subsidies for eligible families in Travis County and nine other Central Texas counties. They also provide technical assistance and resources for child-care providers.

Kidcare Locators

(512) 288-7445

Kim Wittmeyer runs this business to help families locate just the right child-care provider. She is knowledgeable and very informative.

Kids Playhouse

4501 Manchaca Rd. • (512) 443-9246

Kids Playhouse accepts children from 18 months to 12 years for drop-in care both day and night. They have great hours for parents who want to enjoy Austin on a weekend evening. Children can stay until 10 PM Monday through Thursday and until 2:30 AM on Friday and Saturday.

Kid's Space

13376 Research Blvd. • (512) 918-2562

This center in the Galleria Oaks Shopping Center in Northwest Austin accepts children ages 1 to 12 for drop-in child care. Kid's Space offers plenty of entertainment for children of all ages. They're open daily at 8:30 AM and offer service until 12:30 AM on Friday and Saturday nights. It's a good idea to make a reservation, but that can usually be done the day the service is required. Also call to find out about immunization requirements.

Home-Schooling

Home schools might as well been called "underground schools" back in the 1970s and early 1980s because so many parents who chose to educate their own children guarded their secret as if they'd committed a crime — and, indeed, many were prosecuted for failing to apply with compulsory attendance laws. A lot has changed. In an October 1998 cover story on Home Schooling, *Newsweek* magazine, quoting the Home Education Research Institute, reported that about 1.5 million students in the United States are schooled at home, up from about 300,000 in 1990. These days, home-schooling is not only legal in all 50 states, the governor of Texas has recognized the value of home-schooling by proclaiming a Home Education Week. In Austin, parents can attend an annual book fair and convention for home schoolers. The watershed occurred in 1987 when parents won a class-action suit against the state, which stripped the Texas Education Agency of its authority over home schools. The Texas Supreme Court upheld the decision in 1994. Now attitudes toward home schools in Texas are among the most liberal in the country. Here, the state asks only that parents pursue a course of study that includes math, reading, spelling, grammar and a course in good citizenship. The curriculum, however, does not have to be filed with any government agency. An educational approach that was once largely the domain of Christian fundamentalists has spread to families of all kinds, and for many reasons. Certainly, many parents want to emphasize their children's religious education. Some chose to home school because they fear their children will be exposed to violence or the wrong influences in traditional schools. Others opt for home-schooling to give their children more flexibility to pursue outside interests and talents. And many aim to ensure their children achieve academic excellence.

The Texas Home School Coalition, based in Lubbock, is a nonprofit organization that supports parents in their efforts to educate their children at home. The organization operates a database of home school support groups around the state, where parents can go to get information about available curriculums for home schools or about anything else they wish to know about the education their own children. The coalition estimates that more than 150,000 Texas students are educated by their parents. In Austin alone, at least 467 families are involved in home-schooling. For further information on home-schooling, contact the coalition at (806) 797-4927.

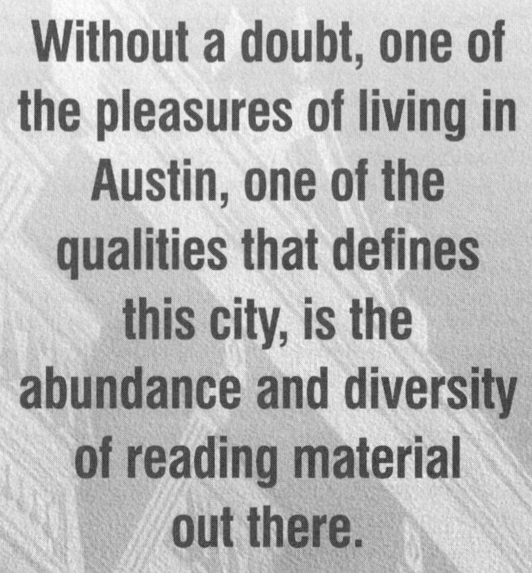

Without a doubt, one of the pleasures of living in Austin, one of the qualities that defines this city, is the abundance and diversity of reading material out there.

Media

Austin's long and rich media history goes almost as far back as the Capital City itself. The *Austin City Gazette*, a four-page weekly, made its debut on October 30, 1839, the same year that Austin became the capital of the Republic of Texas. Published by Samuel Whiting, a journalist from Houston, the *City Gazette* carried local, national and foreign news, letters to the editor, editorials and an occasional work of fiction. By the time the *City Gazette* folded in 1842 (some say due to the threat of invasion from Mexico) the frontier town of Austin had other publications to take its place. Austinites, it seemed, were eager for news. But getting news from the outside to this remote location was never easy, and definitely not quick. During the Civil War, one local publisher debuted his one-page bulletin, the *Texas Almanac Extra*, which he rushed into print three times a week after waiting for pony express riders to hustle in with the latest editions of the Houston and Galveston newspapers.

Decades later, during the Depression of the 1930s, the dean of American television journalism, Walter Cronkite, got his start in Austin.

"My first appearance before a microphone was during the college years at Austin," he writes in his book, *A Reporter's Life*. Cronkite admits his daily sports report on Austin radio station KNOW consisted of scores he memorized from a Western Union sports ticker at a Sixth Street smoke shop while pretending to read the newspaper.

"Once out of sight of the smoke shop, I ran at breakneck speed back to the studio and typed out my daily sports intelligence before it fled my memory," Cronkite reports.

He then moved on to work in print journalism in Austin, covering Texas politics. "It was a vast and diverse state, and the fight for dominance and privilege in Austin was never ending," writes Cronkite.

The Austin media landscape has changed a mite since Cronkite's days here. Today's residents are bombarded with choices over what publications to read, where to land on the radio dial for programming that serves their needs, and which television news program to select. If plans by Austin cable TV giant, Time Warner Cable, are successfully carried out, Austin will have a 24-hour local news channel by the first half of 1999. The fact is, there's a heck of a lot of news and information being disseminated around Austin. The bad news is that it's not all in one spot; you can't just pick up one or two publications or watch the evening news and feel like you've captured the essence of Austin. The good news is that much of it is free! In addition to the radio and television news that's available at the flick of a switch, Austin has about as an eclectic selection of periodicals as one is likely to find in a city the size of Austin.

Without a doubt, one of the pleasures of living in Austin, one of the qualities that defines this city, is the abundance and diversity of reading material out there.

It's not all award-winning stuff, but much of it is — and some of it deserves to be.

Although it often seems these publications appear out of thin air, either resting on our doorsteps or neatly stacked up at nearby newsstands, the journalists out there, both staffers and freelancers, are working their fingertips raw — not to mention their brains — to put out the amount of reading material we Austinites devour regularly. A sizable number publications were started with the sweat, blood and sometimes the rent of writers who saw a need for a particular kind of periodical in the city. As one writer/editor said, "We're writing the kinds of things we want to read."

Some writers have cushy offices and handy editorial staffs. Others are working in cramped spaces using outdated equipment. Several publications are produced in people's homes, and one guy must be putting his stuff together from the seat of a bicycle. While many publications are making a go of it, others are struggling from day to day to survive. But it says a great about the local businesses that advertise, the public contributions some receive and, of course, the readers themselves, that this volume of journals manages to stay afloat. William Sydney Porter, who gained international fame as the short story writer O. Henry, didn't have as much luck. His 1894 Austin weekly newspaper, *The Rolling Stone*, displayed budding talent — but lasted only a year.

The list you'll find below represents a cross section of publications that make up the bedrock of the Austin print media. If your special interests lie elsewhere — in theater, business, technology, religion, public radio or politics — take a look around and you're likely to find some publication that speaks to you.

Newspapers

The Daily

Austin American-Statesman
305 S. Congress Ave. • (512) 445-3500

As Austin's only daily newspaper, the *Austin American-Statesman* is in the unenviable position of trying to satisfy all the news demands of a complex society. In an action that has helped diversify its appeal, the Statesman hired editor Richard Oppel in July of 1995. During Oppel's tenure as editor of *The Charlotte Observer*, the North Carolina paper won three Pulitzer Prizes. The results of his leadership at the *Statesman* have been admirable, especially in the paper's scope of coverage of local and regional news. In the old days one could read the *Statesman* in about the time it takes to get a Jiffy Lube oil change. While there's still a ways to go, articles in the paper today are more substantive and give readers a better understanding of the Capital City's diverse and dynamic communities.

The editorial page also reflects a wider range of opinions of late while readers are seeing more of their views expressed in the expanded "Letters" column.

The Statesman, in fact, seemed so pleased with its improvements that it launched an advertising campaign using the slogan, "It's Not Your Same Old *Statesman*."

Another highlight of today's *Statesman* is the weekly *XL* entertainment section, which made its debut in August of 1994. Published Thursdays — and now available free at area distribution points — this tabloid insert captures the eyes of young-at-heart readers and rivals *The Austin Chronicle* in presenting entertainment news and features. Some media-wise Austinites say *XL* came into being as a result of *The Chronicle*'s success at attracting Generation X readers. Whatever the reason for *XL*, the public now has another well-packaged viable viewpoint for entertainment news and reviews as well as a pleasant source for movie, theater, restaurant and club listings.

In addition to its main section, which features the top stories of the day, editorials, letters to the editor and international news, the *Statesman* prints four other daily news sections: "Metro & State," "Sports," "Business" and "Life & Arts." On Fridays, the "Movies and More" section is included and Sundays deliver the "Travel" section as well as "Insight," which includes comprehensive local, national and international stories, many done by the *Statesman*'s international staff. "Show World," which includes the week's TV lineup, also appears Sundays. Available by request is the Saturday supplement "Weekly Business Review." Of special interest to many in the technology field is the *Statesman*'s Monday business page, called "Tech Monday," which focuses on the high-tech industry. The "Techweek" column in this section lists weekly meetings and events useful for those interested in networking.

In addition to news reported by its own staff and correspondents, the newspaper prints articles of interest from around the country and the world via four international news services, including The Associated Press and *The New York Times*.

Photo: J. Griffis Smith

Austin City Limits is taped at KLRU at the UT campus.

Although many people still feel the need to augment their daily contact with newsprint by receiving national publications such as *The New York Times*, *The Wall Street Journal* and others, the *Statesman* is, indeed, not your same old ....

The newspaper is owned by the Atlanta-based Cox Newspapers Inc, a subsidiary of Cox Enterprises, Inc., which includes 16 daily and 16 weekly newspapers, as well as direct mail marketing firms and a book publishing operation.

The *Statesman* publishes two morning editions; one for outlying areas, the other for Austin. Circulation is about 182,000 daily and 241,000 on Sundays.

The Not-Quite Daily

The Daily Texan

(512) 471-4591

This is the award-winning student newspaper at the University of Texas, published Monday through Friday when school is in session. It covers largely campus news, but when the university is one of the largest in the country, with more than 48,000 students, that's a big ticket. *The Daily Texan* is among the most-recognized student newspapers in the country, and many of its graduates have gone on to win Pulitzer prizes. The newspaper's presence has amplified in recent years since a court decision striking down the UT Law School's affirmative action program put the university squarely in the national spotlight. *The Daily Texan* also provides some interesting state, local and national news. The great thing about *The Daily Texan* is that it serves as a training ground for many journalists who move on to newspapers across the country or stay in Austin after graduation to make a contribution to local professional periodicals. The 30,000 copies are distributed free in bright orange boxes on campus and at various locations around the downtown area.

The Weeklies

Austin Business Journal

111 Congress Ave., Ste. 750
• (512) 494-2500

Published on Fridays, the *Austin Business Journal* is the only newspaper in the area dedicated exclusively to business news and information. Founded locally in 1980, the *Business Journal* was purchased in 1994 by American City Business Journals Inc. Based in Charlotte, North Carolina, American City publishes

37 business journals across the country, including those in San Antonio, Houston and Dallas. The tabloid-format newspaper, with a circulation of about 7,000, covers developments affecting the growth of the region and monitors the progress of new businesses on their way into the area. It also promotes networking by publishing a listing of weekly events and meetings of interest to the business community.

Of special interest to many business people and newcomers are the Journal's annual guides and directories, most notably *The Book of Lists*. This massive volume, issued in December, provides information on more than 1,500 companies of interest to the business community. Other glossy publications printed at different times throughout the year include the "Hi Tech Directory," the "Corporate Relocation Guide" and the "Health Care Directory." These publications are available free with paid subscriptions. If you buy your *Business Journal* at the newsstand, you'll have to purchase the guides separately. The *Journal* is available for delivery or can be picked up at about 65 newsstands around the area.

The Austin Chronicle
4000 N. I-35 • (512) 454-5766

It's hard to plan a weekend out on the town without first picking up a copy of *The Austin Chronicle*. The *Chronicle*, which will celebrate its 20th anniversary in 2001, stresses coverage of music and the arts but also provides a worthwhile alternative voice on local political and environmental issues. The *Chronicle*, a free publication distributed Thursdays around the greater Austin area, was founded as a biweekly by six local entrepreneurs, several of whom had worked on *The Daily Texan*, the student newspaper at the University of Texas. In 1988, the tabloid began weekly publication. Although at times rough around the edges and a bit too caustic, the *Chronicle* disappears 'quicker 'n scat.' Editor Louis Black, one of the original godfathers (as the founders like to call themselves), has become a dynamic voice on the issue of long-range city planning. Take this from one of his past editorials: "I am tired of Austin being treated as a ridiculous environmental community run by crazies. . . . The issues facing Austin are serious issues — how we deal with a growing city and still respect the integrity of the environment. . . ."

But let's not forget the *Chronicle*'s main focus: Entertainment, with a capital E! Movie reviews, book reviews, records reviews, art theater and film listings, cartoons, and some insightful columns on everything from architecture to zydeco (that would be music) cram this hefty 100-page-plus periodical. And, of course, the *Chronicle* knows the Austin club scene. You get the feeling that these writers don't just cover their beats, they live them. Circulation is about 80,000.

The Texas Triangle
611 W. Sixth St. • (512) 476-0576

This publication based in Austin and Dallas provides information for the gay and lesbian community in Texas' major cities. Now published by Angle Media, Inc., of Dallas, the *Triangle* also has bureaus in San Antonio and Houston. It receives the Associated Press news wire and publishes articles from around the

INSIDERS' TIP

To find out Insiders' choices for the best the city has to offer in a variety of categories — including arts and entertainment, shopping, politics, high tech and all kinds of food — check out *The Austin Chronicle*'s annual "Best of Austin" readers poll, published in September. There's also a separate critics poll. Back issues are available at the *Chronicle*. Businesses who win these awards often proclaim their distinction with large banners, so if you see one you'll know what that means. *Chronicle* readers also choose winners for the annual Austin Music Awards, which honors the best of the best in Austin music in its awards ceremony, held in March.

world on issues and events relevant to the gay community. The weekly "Check It Out" column provides listings of selected events around the state of interest to the general population. The *Triangle* is distributed free on Thursdays around the city and is also available by subscription. Averaging about 28 pages today, the periodical made its debut in 1992, but nearly closed down due to financial problems in 1997. Now, with its new owner and investor, the *Triangle* is on more solid ground. Circulation is 23,000.

The Monthlies (and almost monthlies)

Austin Cycling News
1501 W. Fifth St., Ste. 102 • (512) 477-0776

For many, many people in Austin, bicycling is not just a sport or a weekend leisure activity. It's a lifestyle. If you happen to be one of those people, don't miss the *Austin Cycling News*. This neat publication is published 11 times a year by the Austin Cycling Association and is distributed free at nearly 40 distribution points around the area. The *Cycling News*, a tabloid that averages about 16 pages per issue, grew from a small newsletter started in the 1970s called *Austin Cycling Notes*. The *Cycling News* aims to promote bicycle safety, education and access within Austin and includes articles on commuting, recreational cycling, touring, fitness and health. It occasionally takes issue with city officials over bicycling policy decisions. Circulation is about 3,500.

Austin Family
1301 S. I-35, Ste. 206 • (512) 442-7979

Formerly called *Parenting in the '90s*, the editors of this informative monthly journal decided to deal with the name problem before they had to face it in the year 2000. So in January 1997, it became *Austin Family*. This is one Austin publication created out of frustration. As a mother, Sandy J. Kemp searched for information about parenting and ways to keep her child entertained. When she couldn't find one publication that brought all that information together, she decided to start one. That was back in 1992. Since then, *Austin Family* has become an award-winning publication and a great resource for parents looking for information on such things as summer camps, child care, schools, gift ideas, and much more. Look for it at about 550 distribution points around the city, including schools, doctors' offices and children's clothing stores. About 35,000 copies are printed each month.

Austin Monthly
4202 Spicewood Springs Rd., Ste. 209 • (512) 328-7886

Another free publication, *Austin Monthly* focuses on lifestyle and the positive aspects of city life. With regular features on Austin culture and on the movers and shakers around Austin and in Texas state government, *Austin Monthly* provides useful information. Collin Barnes, former owner of an advertising agency, started *Austin Monthly* in 1992 and, as publisher, offers articles on such topics as health, business, cuisine, homes and events. Most of *Austin Monthly*'s readers are working parents, although the magazine appeals to others from their late 20s to 50s. Its regular "Events" section provides listings of support organizations, classes, community happenings and entertainment. Its 20,000 monthly copies can be found at nearly 200 area locations.

The Good Life
(512) 474-1022

Award-winning Austin journalist Ken Martin debuted this monthly magazine in October of 1997, so relatively speaking it's one of the new kids on the block. The magazine itself, however, is aimed at older kids — specifically those 50 and over. Martin researched the Austin market and found more than 112,000 people in Travis County alone who are 50 or older. So, he and his wife Rebecca Melancon, as publisher, decided to put together a monthly periodical that speaks to the large segment of this population that is active, energetic, and yes, hip. The results have been informative and entertaining. Martin writes as if he's still flying high (on life) from the '60s and planning to, as he puts it, "rock on." Another interesting aspect of *The Good Life* is an attempt to build a community around the publication. The magazine, in conjunction with area businesses, has sponsored trips, wine tastings and a book club for older Austinites. Take a look at the people profiled in *The Good Life*. If they're any indication, reaching the big Five-O won't be so bad after all. The magazine, about 24 pages per issue, has a circulation of 15,000 and is available free at area distribution points. Martin also writes a popular weekly newsletter on Austin politics and city government. It is called "In Fact."

New Texas Magazine

1512½ S. Congress Ave.
• (512) 462-1990

Publisher Steve Dodds shies away from the terms "alternative" and "New Age" to describe his monthly magazine, which has been published here since 1979. But in ads promoting the magazine, the term "Socially Conscious Living" appears quite often. In fact, if someone asked us what to read to find out about New Age thinking in Austin, *New Texas Magazine* would be one we'd recommend. *New Texas* readers are accustomed to articles about positive lifestyles, personal growth and improving their quality of life. The magazine, printed 11 times a year on newsprint, focuses on one topic each month. Even the book and music reviews generally pertain to the monthly topic, which has included such subjects as the environment, health, fitness, gardening, alternative technologies, business and travel. About 25,000 copies are circulated free at nearly 400 distribution points around Austin, San Antonio and the Texas Hill Country.

Texas Highways

150 E. Riverside Dr. • (512) 486-5858

Stunning color photographs and in-depth articles that celebrate the glory of Texas abound in this monthly magazine, published in Austin by the Texas Department of Transportation. This is the official travel magazine of Texas and, as such, provides current and accurate information on travel destinations throughout the state. It is a beautiful publication. And with circulation at 330,000, it's obvious that many people agree. *Texas Highways* started as an in-house publication of the Department of Transportation but has been exclusively a travel magazine since May of 1974. The magazine clearly stresses protection of the environment and of the state's cultural heritage and has won awards from such organizations as the San Antonio Conservation Society, the Texas Historical Commission and the International Regional Magazines Association. The December issue includes an index of all the articles written during the year and information about how to obtain back issues. *Texas Highways* can be purchased by subscription or at most major newsstands throughout Austin.

Texas Monthly

(512) 320-6900

Winner of eight National Magazine Awards, *Texas Monthly* is the state's showcase magazine. And it's published in Austin. This full-color, glossy magazine, which celebrated its 25th anniversary in 1998, offers lengthy news and feature articles, and spicy true-crime stories of interest to its affluent, well-educated readers. It also provides frequently updated reviews of selected restaurants in Texas's major cities. Its regular column, "Around The State," is a city-by-city guide to choice entertainment. The annual "Bum Steer Awards," published in the January issue, take an irreverent look at the people and situations in Texas that the editors believe have been particularly weird or foolish over the past year and is perenially one of the magazine's best-selling issues. The "Best and Worst Legislators" is another popular cover feature that comes out

INSIDERS' TIP

On Thanksgiving day 1952, Central Texas got its first television station. KTBC was owned by Texas Broadcasting Company, whose majority stockholder was Ladybird Johnson, future First Lady of the United States. KTBC was a CBS affiliate for years and in July 1995 switched to Fox.

every other July (as the Texas Legislature meets biyearly). Look also for the annual Top Twenty issue, which lists the magazine's choice of the 20 most influential Texans of the year. Publisher Mike Levy, who started the magazine when he was 26 years old, has found a formula that satisfies the majority of *Texas Monthly*'s readers, estimated at 2.5 million people each month.

With Levy as majority shareholder, Mediatex Communications Corp. published *Texas Monthly* until 1998 when the company was sold for a reported $37 million. *Texas Monthly*'s new owner is the Indianapolis-based Emmis Communications Corp., a subsidiary of Emmis Broadcasting Corp., the nation's eighth-largest radio broadcaster. The Emmis publishing venture also includes *Atlanta* magazine, *Indianapolis Monthly* and *Cincinnati* magazine. Levy and staff, including editor Greg Curtis, remain at the helm of this premier Austin production.

Texas Parks & Wildlife
3000 S. I-35, Ste. 120 • (512) 912-7000

This visually enticing, well-written magazine highlights Texas's great outdoors. Published by the Texas Parks and Wildlife Department in Austin and distributed all over the state, *Texas Parks & Wildlife* is a great source of information for newcomers and residents alike who love the open air. The magazine started publishing in 1942 under the name *Texas Game & Fish*. The name was changed in 1967 to reflect a broadening of its editorial scope to include all outdoor recreational activities, including hiking, backpacking, camping, bicycling, rock climbing, kayaking, hunting and fishing. It also includes a great deal of environmental news and is an invaluable source of information on the state park system. In 1998, in fact, the magazine focused on the state park system to commemorate the 75th anniversary of Texas's first state park, Mother Neff State Park, named for the person who donated the land, the mother of former Texas Governor Pat Neff. *Texas Parks & Wildlife*, which has a statewide circulation of 140,000, has won awards for writing and photography from the International Regional Magazines Association, the Association of Conservation Information and others.

The Quarterly, The Bimonthly and The Biweekly

@ Austin
812 San Antonio St., Ste. 505 • (512) 453-0586

A considerable void in the Austin press over the past decade or so has been a viable monthly magazine dedicated to Austin culture. A group of Austin writers led by freelancer Alice Wightman hope to change all that. Their quarterly magazine, *@ Austin*, debuted in 1997. This good-looking, four-color magazine is aimed at readers 35 and older who are interested in reading about Austin culture — books, film, literature, fine arts, music, sports — but want a more sophisticated feel than they get from newsprint. Wightman says the magazine is "geared for people who aren't hanging out in clubs." Only a few issues have been published so far, so it's too soon to say whether *@ Austin* will fulfill its early promise.

Austin Home & Living
12416 Hymeadow Dr. • (512) 926-4663

This bimonthly magazine takes readers inside some of the Austin area's finest and most unique residences. With regular pictorial spreads and articles on Austin homes, this well-designed magazine targets upscale readers. The magazine, a four-color, glossy publication, also includes features on such things as gardening, food and home design. Owned since 1994 by Austin's Publications & Communications, Inc., the magazine was formerly called *Austin Homes & Gardens*. It sells by subscription or at retail locations. Circulation is 28,000.

The Texas Observer
307 W. Seventh St. • (512) 477-0746

Former *Daily Texan* writer Ronnie Dugger debuted *The Texas Observer* in 1954. Within six months the *Observer* established itself as a new voice in Texas media, becoming the first to report on lynchings in East Texas. For nearly half a century this small, biweekly magazine has struggled for survival while breaking the silence on story after story dealing with society's underdogs, the liberal movement and Democratic causes. Dugger, who owned the paper until turning it over to the nonprofit Texas Democracy Foundation in 1994, called his magazine "A Journal of Free Voices," and wrote in *The Observer*'s mission statement, "never will we overlook or misrepresent the truth to serve the interests of the powerful. . . ." Today, the small Austin staff that runs the magazine and the freelance writers from around the state who contribute articles, continue to bring to light liberal/progressive issues not treated in the mainstream media. This 32-page publication, whose small but loyal following keeps it afloat through contributions, fund raisers and subscriptions, accepts advertising but doesn't actively sell space. The result is about 32 pages, just 8¼" by 10½", of nearly solid black-and-white print. *The Observer* is available at selected newsstands around the state and can most easily be found in bookstores in the Austin area. Circulation is 5,000

The Yearly Guides

Austin

111 Congress Ave. • (512) 478-9383

Subtitled "The Chamber of Commerce's Official Guide to Greater Austin," this yearly magazine is written for people moving into the Austin area. The guide gives cost-of-living comparisons for Austin and other major cities in Texas and around the country. Its housing section features comparative information on the cost of buying homes in 10 Austin neighborhoods and in neighboring communities, including Lake Travis, Pflugerville and Round Rock. The guide provides valuable information on public and private schools, healthcare, business, the arts, recreation and retirement. It also lists local elected officials in the city, county, state and federal governments and gives information on such things as getting a driver's license or a business license. The guide is a wonderful source of information for all sorts of important telephone numbers in the area, including libraries, post offices, garbage collectors and voter registration.

Celebrate Austin

7514 N. MoPac, Ste. 200 • (512) 346-6235

This four-color magazine has been giving visitors and newcomers the scoop on Austin for nearly 20 years. *Celebrate Austin*, found in 11,000 hotel rooms around the city, presents features on Austin personalities and places of interest and provides information on a myriad of topics, including homes, government, education, healthcare, recreation, shopping, dining, the arts and the high-tech industry. Journalist Tim Garbutt bought the magazine in 1988 from another local owner and, as publisher, oversees operation of this popular guide. Hardcover versions are placed for permanent use in hotel rooms and visitors can request the softcover version either through the hotel or by mailing in a request card. The publication makes its annual debut each January.

Texas State Travel Guide

150 E. Riverside Dr. • (800) 452-9292

Published in Austin by the Texas Department of Transportation's Travel and Information Division, this hefty guide of nearly 300 pages features highlights of tourist attractions throughout the state. Seven special sections summarize attractions around Texas's major

INSIDERS' TIP

Searching for out-of-town, out-of-state and international periodicals? Austin has them. Book People at 603 N. Lamar Boulevard in Central Austin has received awards as Austin's "Best Periodicals Rack" in *The Austin Chronicle* "Best of Austin" poll. Also check out Borders Books at 10225 Research Boulevard for its great selection of newspapers.

cities, including Austin and the Central Texas area. Information on smaller communities and cities is listed alphabetically. Among the guide's many attributes are listings and descriptions of nearly 150 Texas lakes. The guide also lists national and state forests as well as state parks. Nature lovers can find information on the state's birds and flowers as well. The publication is free and can be requested at the 800 number above. For bulk orders, call (512) 486-5927. The guide, published in late January or February, can also be found at the Capitol Information Center on the grounds of the state capitol building. About 1.5 million copies are printed each year.

The Ethnic Publications

Arriba Art & Business News

1009 E. Cesar Chavez St. • (512) 479-6397

Austin's oldest newspaper for the Mexican-American community, *Arriba* was founded in 1980. This 12- to 16-page tabloid, distributed free biweekly, is written in English and Spanish, highlights community and business news, and goes to great lengths to cover the Latino cultural scene. In addition to regular features on Latino artists, it publishes listings of gallery shows, museum exhibitions and other events of interest to the Latino community. Its music column also regularly features Latino artists, both local and national, and CD reviews of Tejano, salsa, merengue, folk and Latin jazz music. Publisher Romeo Rodriguez started the paper to serve a community not represented in the mainstream press. Circulation is about 6,000.

Asian American Quarterly

(512) 794-0826

This 12-page newsletter is a good source of information for the Asian-American community. Austin's Asian American Alliance publishes the quarterly both as an outreach tool and to serve as a bridge among the Asian cultures and the community at large. It includes information about the Texas Asian Chamber of Commerce and news about the different Asian communities. The newsletter is available free at about 10 distribution points around Austin, including bookstores such as BookPeople, Barnes and Noble and Borders Books. Circulation is about 2,000.

El Norte

504 Sheraton Ave. • (512) 448-1023

Habla Español usted? This Spanish-language monthly newspaper provides information relevant to Austin's Hispanic population, including changes in U.S. immigration policy, news on Hispanic and community leaders, community support organizations and activities within the area's Catholic churches. The 20-page newspaper, with a circulation of 11,000, is distributed free at nearly 400 points throughout the Austin area. Journalist Gloria Montelongo Aguilar, and her husband, Miguel, started *El Norte* in May of 1996 in the back room of their home with two used computers and a printer bought at a pawn shop. *El Norte* provides valuable information to the Spanish-speaking community not found in other publications. Since it debuted, the paper has addressed such issues as college loans, gaining American citizenship, immunization programs for children and the Austin political scene.

Hispanic

98 San Jacinto Blvd. • (512) 476-5599

Another jewel in Austin's media crown is *Hispanic*, a monthly high-gloss magazine aimed at the country's 27 million Hispanics. With a circulation of 250,000 nationwide, *Hispanic* has the second-largest circulation of magazines geared toward Hispanics. And it all started in Austin in 1987. The magazine aims to be the "voice of the Hispanic community" and covers issues and ideas of interest to this market, including politics, business and culture. Started by Fred Estrada, an original investor in the leading national Hispanic magazine *Vista*, and his son Alfredo, a graduate of the University of Texas Law School, the magazine promotes positive Hispanic role models and aims to counteract negative media portrayals of the Latin community. The magazine is published by the Estrada-owned Hispanic Publishing, which in 1996 launched *Moderna*, a bilingual magazine for women.

NOKOA-The Observer

1154-B Angelina St. • (512) 499-8740

Working out of his home, publisher Akwasi

Evans debuted *NOKOA* in 1987 with the goal of creating a newspaper that reflected the interests and views of progressive political activists of all ethnicities. For more than a decade, the free weekly paper has championed the rights of African Americans, Hispanics, Anglos, Asians, Native Americans, Women, Gays, Lesbians and the disabled communities.

Evans calls the publication "a true progressive paper with an unabashed African-American perspective." The paper, published Thursdays, covers Austin city government and the Texas Legislature when it is in session, as well as local, regional, national and international news. *NOKOA*, which aims to be a voice of advocacy, addresses problems of discrimination, exclusion, cultural and political chauvinism and the denial of opportunity. The paper is available at 287 distribution points in Austin and Central Texas. Circulation is 8,000.

Villager Newspaper

1223 Rosewood Ave. • (512) 476-0082

This free weekly newspaper focuses on news of interest to Austin's African-American community. Owner T.L. Wyatt has been publishing the *Villager* since 1973 as a voice of advocacy with a focus on the positive events in the African-American community. Wyatt calls the *Villager*, "the good news newspaper." The paper prints articles not often found in the mainstream press and analyzes news and events that pertain to its readers. Wyatt's weekly editorial column, "Rappin'," appears on the front page.

The 6,000 newspapers published weekly are available at about 125 distribution points in East, South and Central Austin. The paper comes out on Fridays.

The Neighborhoods

Oak Hill Gazette

7200-B U.S. Hwy. 71 W. • (512) 301-0123

A relatively new entry into the community newspaper market, the *Oak Hill Gazette* has been publishing since 1995. Owned by the Oak Hill husband and wife team of Will Atkins and Penny Levers, the paper covers news of general interest to the Oak Hill area, business and political news and provides information on Austin Independent School District schools in Southwest Austin. The *Oak Hill Gazette* also covers news from local neighborhood associations. One of the paper's most popular columns is "Herb Talk" by Oak Hill herbalist Leta Worthington, which focuses on healing herbs. U.S. Rep. Lloyd Doggett contributes a column about twice a month as does Texas Rep. Terry Keel. The paper is published Thursdays and is available by sub-

Photo: Peter A. Silva

The shores of Town Lake are a great vantage point for people watching.

scription or at newsstands in the area. Circulation is 4,000.

West Austin News

3301 Northland Dr., Ste. 408
• (512) 459-5471

Serving the neighborhoods of West Austin, Rollingwood and West Lake Hills, the *West Austin News* focuses on community, society and school news in its communities. The weekly newspaper, published on Thursdays, was started by local owner and publisher Bart Stephens in 1986. The *West Austin News* is available by subscription or at newsstands throughout the West Austin area. The paper does not release circulation figures.

Westlake Picayune

3103 Bee Caves Rd. • (512) 327-2990

This weekly newspaper serving the community of Westlake is a publication of Westward Communications, L.L.C., a Houston-based company that owns four other newspapers in Central Texas and more in Texas, Arkansas, Louisiana and Colorado. The newspaper, founded in 1976, covers community and local government news and the Eanes Independent School District as well as arts and entertainment. While the newspaper is sold by subscription and at newsstands, a monthly special section called "Distinct" is mailed free to 8,100 homes in the area, those with the zip codes 78746 and 78733. "Distinct" is the *Westlake Picayune*'s lifestyle section and regularly features an article on a local resident who has achieved national or international importance. Circulation is about 3,650.

The Outlying Areas

Cedar Post

(512) 258-8850

Every month for more than a quarter of a century, Ben Parham has written, edited and sold the ads for this little newspaper, which features a joke column on the front page and another column by him called "Up and Down the Road by Uncle Ben." Parham says he came to Texas years ago and worked for a company selling equipment to newspapers. "I never found a single newspaper that ever had a single bad person working there," he says. "I thought, well, if they're all so good I'd better join them." So Parham, who never had a day of journalism school in his life, set about establishing his own newspaper. The result was the *Cedar Post*. He was 83 years old when we talked to him and still distributing his 8,000 copies around Williamson and northern Travis counties. They're free.

Hill Country News

103 Woods Ln., Cedar Park
• (512) 259-4449

A weekly newspaper distributed free on Wednesdays, the *Hill Country News* focuses on community news, features and — most importantly of late — the spectacular growth of business in the Cedar Park region. Of special note is its annual Horizon Edition, an information and progress report on businesses in Cedar Park and the Texas Hill Country. Six times a year, the *News* also publishes a 30-page tabloid of upcoming activities in the Leander Independent School District. The *News* was founded in 1967 and is owned by Granite Publications of Marble Falls, which publishes 17 similar newspapers in the Central Texas region.

Lake Travis View

2300 Lohmans Crossing Rd.
• (512) 263-1100

This community newspaper with a circulation of about 3,000 is published Thursdays. Owned by Westward Communications, L.L.C., which owns several other community news-

INSIDERS' TIP

The *Austin American-Statesman* is Austin's oldest surviving newspaper. The newspaper traces its roots back to July 25, 1871, when a newspaper called *The Democratic Statesman* hit the streets for the first time. The name *Austin American-Statesman* first appeared in 1973 on a Sunday edition.

papers in the area, the Lake Travis View focuses on local government, the Lake Travis Independent School District and community news along Lake Travis' south shore. Several local residents write regular columns for the paper, including the popular "Over 50, Going Like 60" by Dot Fowler. The paper is sold by subscription and at newsstands in the area.

Pflugerville Pflag

100 S. Third St., Pflugerville
• (512) 251-5574

Pfinding the *Pflag* isn't too hard in Pflugerville, the pfine community with the pfunny name. The *Pflag* is Pflugerville's weekly newspaper, and Pflugerville is the only news in town. "If it don't happen in Pflugerville, it don't happen," quips Editor-in-Charge Wendell Holloman of the philosophy of the *Pflag*. Indeed, this 16- to 20-page tabloid, published Thursdays, focuses on community news and news of the Pflugerville Independent School District. The *Pflag* is owned by Westward Communications, L.L.C., headquartered near Houston. The company publishes about 55 newspapers in Texas, Louisiana, Arkansas and Colorado. Average circulation is 2,900. The *Pflag* is available by subscription or at newsstands in Pflugerville.

Round Rock Leader

105 S. Blair St., Round Rock
• (512) 255-5827

Established in 1877, just a few years after the community of Round Rock itself was formed, the *Leader* has been providing news and information to this area just north of Austin for more than a century. Today's *Leader*, however, is quite a different paper than it was back in the old days, when its four pages were set by hand and each paper was addressed by hand to subscribers. The Todd family bought the paper in 1972 and since then the *Leader* has grown into a twice-weekly publication averaging 40 pages and reaching 6,700 homes in Round Rock and nearby communities. The paper emphasizes community and school news, covers local and Williamson county politics and also keeps readers informed of the meteoric growth of Round Rock, which had a mere 2,300 residents two decades ago and today claims more than 50,000 residents. Publisher Ken Long, a member of the Todd Family, includes a Bible verse on the editorial page that he says appeals to the conservative, family-oriented community.

Television

Austin's television industry provides a strong and vital link among residents of Central Texas. On weekdays, almost 20 live local news broadcasts relay information and flash the latest images of events and newsmakers around the Texas heartland and the world beyond. In times of tragedy and triumph, no other news medium rivals the awesome power of live television. None but television allows the faces and the voices of the participants themselves to illustrate the immediate events as a story unfolds.

Ranking 63rd among the 210 largest television markets in the United States, Austin claims all four network affiliates: CBS, ABC, NBC and Fox. As a result, Central Texas viewers can catch local news broadcasts in the early morning, at midday and at 5, 6 and 10 PM. While Austin's ABC affiliate, KVUE, had triumphed for years in the ratings wars — longtime anchor Judy Maggio is one of the big draws here — viewers of late have begun surfing channels more. As a result, viewer loyalty may be a thing of the past — or perhaps just in transition as Austin's masses of new residents evaluate each station's merits. KVUE, known nationally for its policy of responsible crime coverage, nevertheless witnessed a slip on its dominance in 1998.

KXAN, the NBC affiliate, now has joined the ranks of popular local news shows and is the only network in the area to simulcast its 6 and 10 PM news in Spanish. KXAN also boasts a fairly regular feature at 10 PM called *On the Porch*, which hearkens back to the days when Austin seemed dominated by laid-back longhairs. Reporter Jim Swift, who does these features, is a welcome blast from the past.

KEYE, the latest arrival on the local news scene and a CBS affiliate, began broadcasting in July of 1995. KEYE boasts veteran Austin newsman and award-winning journalist Neal Spelce at anchor. The efforts of this young station have been recognized of late with several prestigious Associated Press broadcasting awards. Austin's oldest television station, KTBC, is now an affiliate of the young Fox network. Launched in 1952 by Lyndon and Lady Bird Johnson, KTBC was Austin's only news station for 13 years until KXAN appeared in 1965. KTBC, which switched from CBS to Fox in 1995, is putting up a good fight to attract viewers unused to tuning in to Fox for their daily news. Fox's lack of an evening network newscast doesn't help the local team, but KTBC is focusing on pulling in a younger audience familiar with Fox's hip line-up. Only time will tell which of the four will prevail.

In addition to the network affiliates, Austin also claims an independent/Warner Brothers-affiliated station, another independent station and a Public Broadcasting Service station. Dozens of cable channels are available at a price through the area's largest cable provider, Time Warner, or from other cable, microwave and satellite service providers in the area. For Time Warner subscribers, Austin offers no less than 10 local cable television and access channels, where residents can find programming from such institutions as the Austin Independent School District, the City of Austin, Travis County, Austin Community College and the Texas Legislature when it is in session. The three Austin access channels, while not masterful, nevertheless offer a diversity of programs, some in Spanish, on subjects such as religion, the arts, cooking, technology and alternative thinking. Viewers who speak German can find television programs and Deutche Welle news on AISD access Channel 18.

If you're visiting or are new to the Austin area and want to get a taste of the music scene without actually going out, don't miss *Austin City Limits*. The *Austin American-Statesman* has called this program "the city's cultural calling card to the world." And indeed, it is. The program, which debuted in 1975 — six years before MTV — is 100 percent music and showcases local talent as well as nationally and internationally known performers. Taped live on the University of Texas campus in Studio 6-A of the communications complex and featuring the illuminated Austin skyline as a backdrop, *Austin City Limits* can be seen on PBS stations around the country. The weekly one-hour program airs Saturdays at 7 PM and the following Friday at 11 PM on the local PBS station, KLRU. While tapings are supposedly open to the public, tickets can be as hard to come by as a cool day in July (see our tips in The Music Scene chapter).

And where else in the country can you go to watch a locally produced 24-hour music channel? The Austin Music Network on cable channel 15 is another of those wonderful little dividends we Austinites enjoy. AMN features local musicians, presents local music shows and airs music videos from all over the place. According to latest reports, the network also planned to air a live daily show called *What's the Cover* to showcase the artists playing in Austin clubs. Another planned addition to the line-up is a program called *Breakin' In*, which aims to focus on up-and-coming Austin artists. In 1998 the City Council chose producer Rick Melchior to lead the network into the 21st century and turn it into a financially self-sustaining operation. Longtime fans of the network lamented the addition of paid commercials to AMN while others took solace in the fact that the network would perhaps not have to beg for city funds every six months or so in order to survive. Check the TV listings in the Sunday *Austin American-Statesman* supplement "Show World" for AMN's weekly schedule.

Not many residents of a town Austin's size can tune in to a bit of home while they're on the road. Besides *Austin City Limits* our city also claims *King of the Hill*. The Fox-network's popular cartoon sitcom about a family of Tex-

INSIDERS' TIP

When it comes to keeping up with changes in Austin radio, few in town know what's going on as well as Rob Patterson, whose weekly column, "Radio," appears in the *Austin American-Statesman's* XL entertainment section on Thursdays.

ans headed by Hank Hill was created by Texan Mike Judge. Judge, who lives in Austin and commutes to Los Angeles, also created MTV's wildly successful *Beavis and Butt-head*. *King of the Hill* airs Sunday nights at 7:30.

Local Stations

KTBC, FOX , Channel 7 (cable 2)

KVUE, ABC, Channel 24 (cable 3)

KXAN, NBC, Channel 36 (cable 4)

KEYE, CBS, Channel 42 (cable 5)

KNVA, Independent/Warner Brothers affiliated, channel 54 (cable 12)

KLRU, PBS, Channel 18 (cable 9)

KVC-TV, Independent, Channel 13 (cable 13)

Cable Channels

Channel 6, City of Austin Cable (City Council meetings, various commission meetings)

Channel 10, Austin Access

Channel 11, Austin Access

Channel 15, Austin Music Network

Channel 16, Austin Access

Channel 17, Travis County Cable

Channel 18, Austin Independent School District Access

Channel 19, Austin Community College Access

Channel 20, KLRU-2

Channel 22, Austin Independent School District TV

Channel 41, Regional weather

Cable Providers

(Hard Line, Microwave, Direct Broadcast Satellite)

Time Warner Cable, (512) 485-5555

CableVision of Cedar Valley, (512) 288-4980

CableVision of Lake Travis, (512) 263-9194

Circle C Cable TV, (512) 328-3677

Heartland Wireless, (512) 833-6299

Primestar, (512) 873-0318

Radio

In the city that calls itself "The Live Music Capital of the World," one would think that radio would be a hot commodity. And it is. Hot and competitive. While some stations have been around since Marconi, or seemingly so, others last a couple of years at best and then fade quietly into the night. But if recent events are any indication, the Austin radio wars will fascinate listeners for years to come. Take this: In December of 1997, the nation's largest owner of radio stations, the Austin-based Capstar Broadcasting Partners, bought its first local stations. Capstar purchased Austin's top-rated radio station, the country music venue KASE-FM, and its sister AM and FM stations KVET in a sale valued at $90 million. The three stations, which get about 30 percent of Austin's radio listeners, had been owned by former Austin mayor Roy Butler's family partnership. Capstar got Austin's crown jewel and a piece of history. KVET-AM dates back to the post-World War II era and was started by a group of veterans that included John Connally, who was later to become governor of Texas.

In 1998 Capstar, headed by Steve Hicks, was sold to Dallas-based Chancellor Media led by Hicks' brother, Tom. The sale created the largest radio company in existence with nearly 470 stations. The local presence of these stations apparently will remain strong, however, through Steve Hicks' regional company, the Austin-based Gulfstar. Also in the big leagues of Austin airwaves are the New York-based Infinity Broadcasting (formerly CBS Radio Group), which owns four local stations,

INSIDERS' TIP

KUT, Austin's public radio station, began broadcasting on November 10, 1958, a date that marked the beginning of noncommercial public service broadcasting in Central Texas. It was also the first broadcast from the University of Texas at Austin.

the Austin-based LBJ-S Broadcasting and Clear Channel Communications of San Antonio. Of course, this is a dynamic industry to say the least, so radio disciples will want to stay tuned in the local media for further developments.

While Austin listeners can tune in to more country music stations than any other one kind, country isn't the only sound in town, by far. Austin radio serves up a 24-hour feast of music on an impressive number of stations. Rock, blues, folk, soul, Tejano, classical, contemporary and Christian are just some of the music styles catered by the region's two dozen AM stations and 29 FM stations, including the part-time University of Texas student station KVRX, which shares its signal with the community station KOOP at 91.7 on the dial. Not all 29 stations reach the entire Austin market clearly, however, so listeners may find static on some dial positions.

The Austin airwaves thickened in 1998 as two intriguing stations squeezed onto the FM dial. Capstar introduced modern rock station KFMK at 105.9, while Infinity brought in Beat 104.3, station KQBT, offering a contemporary hit format that puts it in direct competition with Austin's young adult favorite KHFI. Austin also has seen a boost of late in the number of stations dedicated to its Spanish-speaking market — and to others who appreciate good Spanish-language music. KQQQ 92.1 FM and KQQA 1530 AM joined the line-up of local station's serving up Spanish/Tejano programming. And the banquet gets even better. Austinites can savor a heaping helping of musical delicacies from our own bands on stations that truly know how to dish it out: KUT, KLBJ-FM, KVET and especially KGSR.

When it comes to the Austin music scene, KGSR is truly in a class by itself. This station, at 107.1 on the FM dial, is a real gem. KGSR plays more local bands than any other station and offers some excellent original programming. Additionally, KGSR releases an annual CD called "Broadcasts." This anniversary series features a wonderful mix of local talent and national acts, most in live performances from the KGSR studio. Proceeds from the project go to charity.

Austin wouldn't be Austin, however, without its extraordinary diversity of stations and local DJs. For Top-40 tunes, KHFI at 96.7 FM, is Austin's station. For news and talk, the station Insiders most listen to is KLBJ-AM. KUT is another decidedly Austin station. This public radio station, which gets great ratings for a noncommercial venue, offers National Public Radio news and a wonderfully eclectic mix of music, local bands and original programming, including such stand-out programs as *Folkways*, *Eklectikos*, *Blue Monday* and *Horizontes*.

For alternative rock, check out KROX at 101.5 on the FM dial. KROX's "All Request Mornings" show hosted by Sara Trexler and sidekick Jenn Garrison has a strong and loyal following. These lively jockeys, whose callers are an integral part of their show, make mornings one part therapy session, one part Bohemian humor, and one very good part music. Of course, you can't discuss morning radio in Austin without mentioning the award-winning "Dudley and Bob with Debra" program on KLBJ-FM. Dale Dudley, along with cohorts Bob Fonseca and Debra Cole, is an institution in local radio, having lasted more than 11 years on the same shift. The show won a *Billboard* magazine award for Local Air Personalities of the Year and it's been named Best Radio Program in the Austin Music Awards. The morning show lineup wouldn't be complete without the gang from Mix 94.7. J.B. Hager and Sandy Rivers, along with Bridget Taylor and "Funky" (producer Mike Raffety) deliver a great mix of fast-paced, lighthearted banter and touching stories that have listeners howling one minute and crying the next.

Last, but definitely not least, are "Sammy and Bob" on KVET-FM. This morning-drive duo has the top-rated show and may well be the most influential radio team in town. Sammy Allred, a longtime Austin personality and half of the Austin-based country music band the Geezinslaw Brothers, and Bob Cole, general manager of KASE and KVET AM and FM, team up to bring listeners a show that has managed to raise the ire of just about everyone in town at some point or another. "Get your butt out of bed and go get a job," Sammy tells one regular caller. But then he adds, "We love you." Their audience loves Sammy and Bob in return.

Photo: City of Austin

Local stations carry music and entertainment from contemporary to jazz and more.

AM and FM Radio Stations

In a Class By Itself

KGSR 107.1 FM (Local bands, blues, jazz, folk, reggae, rock, interviews, live studio performances)

Adult Contemporary

KBAE 104.7 FM (Also broadcasts on 92.5)

Alternative

KAMX 94.7 FM (Alternative hits)
KROX 101.5 FM (New rock alternative)

Christian/Gospel

KIXL 970 AM (Christian information, talk)
KFIT 1060 AM (Gospel)
KNLE 88.1 FM (Contemporary Christian music)
KYCM 104.9 FM (Contemporary Christian music)

Classical/Easy Listening

KKMJ 95.5 FM (Soft Hits)
KMFA 89.5 FM (Classical)
KNCT 91.3 FM (Classical, easy listening)

College Radio

KVRX 91.7 FM (Student operated, eclectic music, 7 PM to 9 PM weekdays, 10 PM to 9 AM weekends)

INSIDERS' TIP

True media buffs will eventually come across a reference to a magazine called *3rd Coast*, which was also spelled *Third Coast*. In its short existence — it lasted only six years and folded in 1987 — the publication gained a reputation for excellence that has yet to be matched in an Austin city magazine. The bust of the Austin economy was blamed for its demise.

Community

KOOP 91.7 FM (Community operated, eclectic music and talk, 9 AM to 7 PM weekdays, 9 AM to 10 PM weekends)

Contemporary Hits

KHFI 96.7 FM

KQBT 104.3 FM

Country

KLNC 93.3 FM (Superstar country)

KASE 100.7 FM (Austin's number one station)

KFAN 107.9 FM (Country, blues, rock)

KHLB 106.9 FM

KRXT 98.5 FM

KVET 98.1 FM

Jazz

KAZI 88.7 FM (Jazz, R&B, blues, gospel, talk)

Spanish/Tejano

KELG 1440 AM (Tejano, international, KXAN-TV local news in Spanish)

KKLB 92.5 FM (Tejano and dance music)

KQQA 1530 AM (Spanish hits)

KQQQ 92.1 FM (Spanish-language comtemporary)

KTXZ 1560 AM (Tejano hits and oldies)

KUOL 1470 AM (Spanish Christian music, talk)

News/Sports/Talk

KFON 1490 AM (Sports)

KJFK 98.9 FM (Talk, sports, Howard Stern)

KLBJ 590 AM (Talk, news, good local news)

KTAE 1260 AM (All-talk Spanish news and sports)

KVET 1300 AM (24-hour sports)

Public Radio

KUT 90.5 FM (Eclectic music, local bands, NPR news)

Rock 'n' Roll/Oldies

KAHK 107.7 FM (Rock from the '60s, '70s and '80s)

KEYI 103.5 FM (Oldies from the '50s and '60s)

KFMK 105.9 FM (Modern rock)

KHLB 1340 AM (Big band; music from the '40s, '50s and '60s)

KLBJ 93.7 FM (Rock and roll)

KPEZ 102.3 FM (Classic rock)

Urban

KJCE 1370 AM (Urban contemporary, soul)

Texas has more
churches than any other
state in the Union.

Worship

When it comes to braggin' rights about whether Texas is God's Country, as many old-timers and newcomers will declare, the facts are clear: Texas has more churches than any other state in the Union. We have approximately 17,000 places of worship, according to the *1997 Texas Almanac*, some 2,500 more than second-ranked California. The state also boasts the largest number of church members, around 5.3 million, according to the almanac.

Roman Catholics make up the largest single group, with 3.8 million adherents. Among Protestants, the largest group belongs to the Southern Baptist Convention — 3.6 million adherents. Survey data compiled by the almanac also suggests church attendance is higher in the rural areas of Texas than it is in the state's larger cities. In many of the state's smaller communities the church or religious meeting place is the center of community activity.

When the Mexican flag flew over Texas, Roman Catholicism was the official state religion, and the parish church was the heart of the community. San Antonio's famous missions (see our Daytrips chapter) were established to bring Christianity to the Native Americans, and some of the mission sites were along creek beds and riverbanks where Native Americans had gathered for centuries to celebrate their own sacred rituals. In the mid-19th century, Protestant preachers accompanied the European settlers, although some groups, notably German, Czech and Polish immigrants were Catholic. No matter the denomination, church picnics and camp meetings were an important part of the social life in 19th-century Texas.

Many of the smaller towns around Austin continue to hold annual church picnics where family members gather, some coming in from their new homes in the city, to renew their ties with their ancestral homes (see our Annual Events and Festivals chapter). A visit to the local church and its accompanying cemetery is a great way to explore Texas history and it offers visitors insight into various ethnic customs that have been preserved by immigrant groups and settlers. For example, some of the small Czech communities east of Austin preserve the custom of decorating gravestones with pictures of their loved ones. (See our Attractions chapter for more on Austin's historic cemeteries.)

Diversity

Religion played an important role in both Austin's early life and its development. The log cabin that served as the first state capitol building also was home to a Presbyterian church, but the Presbyterians were not the only denomination in town. From the beginning, Austin had a diverse religious community. In his book *Power, Money & The People: The Making of Modern Austin*, Anthony M. Orum (see our Politics and Perspectives chapter) cites the city's first census, taken in 1840, showing that of the 900 residents 73 were "professors of religion." There were Methodists, Presbyterians, Episcopalians, Baptists and a large number of Roman Catholics.

INSIDERS' TIP

A rare Gutenberg Bible is on display at the Harry Ransom Humanities Research Center, W. 21st and Guadalupe streets, on the University of Texas campus. One of only 48 copies, the Bible was printed in 1449 (see our Arts chapter for more on the center.)

In the second half of the century the city blossomed as did the variety of religious groups. Several of the city's landmark churches were erected in the central city in the latter half of the 18th century. St. David's Episcopal Church, 304 E. 7th Street, was begun in 1854 and completed 16 years later. The Gothic Revival structure includes several genuine Tiffany stained-glass windows. Legend has it that gamblers helped fund the construction, hence its nickname as the "gamblers' church."

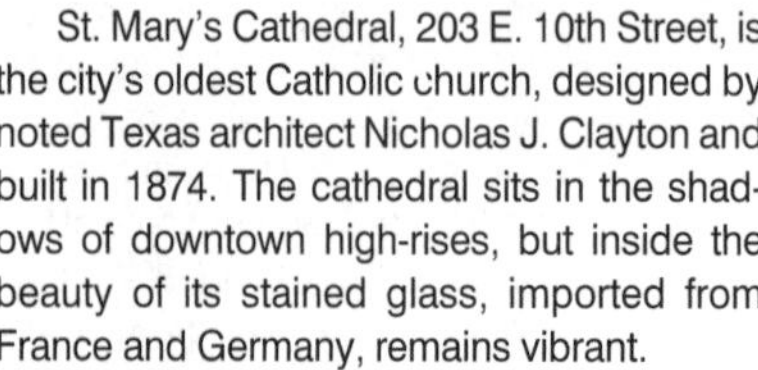

St. Mary's Cathedral, 203 E. 10th Street, is the city's oldest Catholic church, designed by noted Texas architect Nicholas J. Clayton and built in 1874. The cathedral sits in the shadows of downtown high-rises, but inside the beauty of its stained glass, imported from France and Germany, remains vibrant.

Just north of the University of Texas campus in Central Austin is All Saints' Episcopal Chapel, 2629 Whitis Avenue, a Gothic landmark built by Bishop George Herbert Kinsolving in 1899.

The first Swedish Lutheran church in Austin stands at 1510 Congress Avenue. Gethsemane Lutheran Church was built in 1883 in the Gothic Revival style, and builders utilized bricks from the state capitol building that burned down in 1881.

Austin's Jewish Community

Just two years after Gethsemane Lutheran Church was completed, the city's first synagogue opened. Congregation Beth Israel was serving the city's small, but very influential Jewish community. Four of the city's leading businessmen and developers were members — brothers Phineas and Jacob De Cordova, and German immigrants and brothers Henry and Morris Hirschfeld.

That tradition of civic leadership continues in the Jewish community. Austin's most famous business entrepreneur, Michael Dell, chairman of Dell Computer Corp., and his wife Susan have led the way in the development of the Dell Jewish Community Campus, a 40-acre development scheduled to be built over the next few years adjacent to the Northwest Hills neighborhood in Northwest Austin. The campus will be home to both Agudas Achim, a Conservative synagogue, and Beth Israel, the Reform synagogue. The campus also will house the Jewish Community Center and the Jewish federation of Austin, plus cultural, social and educational facilities.

The development of the campus did prompt debate and some opposition from neighbors who feared the complex would be too large and produce heavy traffic. The debate is not a new one in Austin. Several churches have experienced significant growth, prompting some neighbors to voice concerns. There has been a long-running discussion over the growth of Hyde Park Baptist Church and the neighborhood in Central Austin.

On the positive side, the development of the Dell campus is evidence of Austin's flourishing Jewish population, now estimated at 8,000 members. Much of the growth has come as the city's high-tech center brought in professional workers from other locations around the country. Several local supermarkets have begun to offer kosher food handling and food products in response to the growth.

Multicultural Traditions

Another impact of the high-tech boom has been the emergence of eastern religious

INSIDERS' TIP

Each year, usually in June, members of 300 evangelical area churches hold the annual "March for Jesus" up Congress Avenue to the Capitol. The march attracts thousands of participants. For information, call (512) 416-0066.

Photo: J. Griffis Smith

With its gothic style, St. Mary's Cathedral stands out in downtown Austin.

temples in Austin. There are several Buddhist congregations in the city serving Chinese-Americans, Japanese-Americans and other ethnic groups. There is also an Islamic center and mosque in the city. While it is impossible to list every church in the Austin area, several religious organizations are listed at the end of this chapter. The *Austin American-Statesman* has a religion section on Saturday that lists local church and temple activities.

One of the most startling and beautiful sights in the Austin area is the Shree Raseshwari Radaha Rani Temple, a Hindu temple, the largest in North America, located on the outskirts of Southwest Austin. Built by Hindu artisans, this white-walled, Indian-style temple with its colorful, intricate wooden decorations, sits near fields of golden marigolds on what once was a Texas cattle ranch. The temple, part of the Barsana Dham ashram, holds several important celebrations each year that evoke the spirituality of India. The Barsana Dham complex is approximately 5 miles south of U.S. Highway 290 W., on F.M. 1826 (Camp Ben McCullough Road).

Many of the city's diverse religious groups welcome visitors to their celebrations. Chinese and Vietnamese New Year, Hindu festivals, Buddhist observances, Roman Catholic feast days, Greek Orthodox festivals are windows into the multicultural soul of Austin. (See our Annual Events and Festivals chapter for festival days.)

Hispanic Traditions

One popular Catholic festival is held December 12 in honor of Our Lady of Guadalupe, the dark-skinned Virgin who appeared to a poor Mexican peasant on a hill outside of Mexico City. The day is celebrated with dancing and street processions by parishioners of

Our Lady of Guadalupe Church, 1206 E. Ninth Street. Built in 1907, the Catholic church is home to Austin's oldest Hispanic parish.

Several churches in the diocese offer services in Spanish and conduct mariachi masses throughout the year.

Another annual tradition that reflects the rich Hispanic heritage in this region is the Christmas Posada. In the days before Christmas children, dressed as Mary and Joseph, go from door to door seeking a refuge as their namesakes did hundreds of years ago. Named after the Spanish word for "inn," the nightly treks can take place for one night or several, but they always end at the parish church (see our Annual Events chapter).

The Catholic Church is a vital part of Austin's Hispanic traditions, and it also serves as a focal point of community, a central point for social groups and even political grass-roots organizations.

African-American Traditions

Among the first churches in Austin were those serving the city's African-American population. The Metropolitan African Methodist Episcopal Church, 1105 E. 10th Street, in the heart of East Austin, was built in 1923 and is the oldest African-American church in Austin that remains active.

In a time when social inequalities were the norm, the African-American church served a vital role in Austin, as it did throughout the country. One of the first African-American church leaders in Austin was Rev. Jacob Fontaine, who founded the Sweethome Baptist Church in Clarksville (see our Neighborhoods and Real Estate chapter), the historic, once predominantly African-American neighborhood just west of downtown Austin and north of West Sixth Street. The original church is gone, but its name and spirit lives on at the new church, built in 1935 at 1725 W. 11th Street. A historic landmark, it now stands at the heart of a popular gentrified neighborhood.

Rev. Fontaine also was instrumental in founding other historic African-American congregations, according to Orum's *Power, Money & The People*. Fontaine founded the First Baptist Church, which once stood on the site now occupied by the city's downtown library. Another pioneering churchman in the African-American community was Francis Webber, an Anglo priest from Detroit who came to Austin in 1935. Orum credits Webber with reaching out to the African-American community from his parish headquarters, Holy Cross Church, particularly in providing healthcare for the city's Mexican-American and African-American communities.

Throughout the dark days of segregation, into the civil rights era and now in the '90s, the city's African-American churches have been involved in all aspects of the community's growth and survival. Greater Calvary Missionary Baptist Church operates a life training program for African-American male teens called Rites of Passage. Once a week, boys age 6 to 18 gather at the center to participate in the program. The program seeks to boost self-esteem and school grades, and help the participants learn the value of social consciousness, plus learn leadership and decision-making skills. The church members, many of whom are working poor, award small scholarships to the program graduates. The program, now being eyed by other churches in the area, receives no government funding.

Social Activism

Given the city's political life and history, it is natural that social activism has been a hallmark of several Austin churches for decades. Professor Orum cites the impact University of Texas campus church organizations and the Austin YMCA had on bringing students from

INSIDERS' TIP

Several Austin churches celebrate October 4, feast day of St. Francis of Assisi, by holding blessing of the animals gatherings. Check the Religion listings in the Saturday edition of the *Austin American-Statesman*.

diverse backgrounds together in the 1930s and '40s.

Many Austin churches are committed to community causes, such as collecting food for the city's Food Bank, or serving meals to the homeless. One young church member from an affluent and active West Austin church began a book drive for homeless men and women who pass through her church's soup kitchen. From the smallest effort to well-organized, major fund-raising campaigns, Austin's churches are engaged in serving the community. Some have taken their activism into the public-policy arena, representing both conservative and liberal thinking.

One of the most influential organizations, particularly on issues of education, is Austin Interfaith. Its membership is made up of church members from a diversity of congregations, many of them anchored in the city's working class neighborhoods.

Interfaith was organized by Ernesto Cortes Jr., a legendary social activist who heads the Southwest office of a national grass-roots political organization called the Industrial Areas Foundation, a network of mostly church-based coalitions aimed at community activism. The late Saul Alinsky, a community organizer from Chicago, created the foundation in 1940. Like Alinsky, his mentor, Cortes and his followers have been called radical by some, but there is no question the Austin Interfaith group has evolved into a potent force.

Like its sister organizations in Texas, Rio Grande Valley Interfaith and the very powerful Communities Organized for Public Service in San Antonio, the Austin group commands the attention of local politicians.

City council members and school board officials are particularly attentive. Although the group does not endorse candidates it does query them at intense, detailed "accountability sessions." Austin Interfaith also worked recently on a key $80-million school bond issue campaign, and was credited with ensuring strong support for the bond issue in the minority communities where it is particularly active.

Political Clout

Texas is a Bible Belt state. Generally speaking, north of Austin is considered staunch Bible Belt country, home to many of the state's most conservative churches and denominations. South of Austin is generally considered to be less conservative, more likely Catholic than Protestant.

Occasionally, a church in Austin will find itself at odds with a national church body over its stand on issues. Recently, one Baptist church was expelled from the Southern Baptist Convention because of its recognition of gay marriages. The incident is evidence of the city's liberalism, but there are also other Baptist churches in the city that are in step with their national leadership on such issues. Diversity is the keyword in Austin.

In general terms though, conservative religious views do manifest themselves north and east of Austin. In state elections on the lottery, for example, voters north and east of Austin tended to vote against gambling initiatives. Those few dry counties in Texas are located north of Austin, also. In Travis County, home of the capital city, 48.4 percent of the churchgoers are Roman Catholic, according to the *Texas Almanac*, while immediately to the north in Williamson County, home of Round Rock, Southern Baptists make up 46.9 percent of the churchgoing public.

Williamson County politics, both at the school board and city, county and state levels tend to be more conservative. Juries in Williamson County mete out harsher punishments, and the local newspapers are more conservative in tone. That same conservatism is reflected in community religious views.

Places to Worship

There, of course, churches of all persuasions in Austin, some liberal, others conservative, some traditional, others decidedly New Age, some fundamentalist, some experimental.

A resource list of some of the religious organizations follows:

Austin Baptist Association, 1016 E. 38½ Street, (512) 454-2558, is an Austin umbrella group for Southern Baptist churches.

Austin Metropolitan Ministries, 2026 Guadalupe Street, Suite 226, (512) 472-7627, is an interfaith group with 120 churches in its membership and works to coordinate community involvement in social issues.

Hillel Foundation at UT Austin, 2105 San Antonio Street, (512) 476-0125, is a Jewish center for university students that reaches out to convey aspects of Jewish culture to the community.

Church of Jesus Christ of Latter-day Saints, Institute of Religion, 2020 San Antonio Street, (512) 478-8575

Episcopal Diocese of Texas, 606 Rathervue Place, (512) 478-0580

Friends Meeting of Austin, 3014 Washington Square, (512) 452-1841

International Buddhist Progress Society, 8557 Research Boulevard, Suite 118, (512) 836-7459

Islamic Center of Greater Austin, 1906 Nueces Street, (512) 476-2563

Jewish Federation of Austin, 11713 Jollyville Road, (512) 331-1144

Roman Catholic Diocese of Austin, 1600 N. Congress Avenue, (512) 476-4888

Texas District Lutheran Church-Missouri Synod, 7900 U.S. 290 E., (512) 926-4272

Texas Conference of Churches, 6633 U.S. Highway 290 E., Suite 200, (512) 451-0991, represent 51 religious governing bodies and is dedicated to promoting religious unity.

United Methodist Church, Austin district, 3755 S. Loop 360 (Capital of Texas Highway), Suite 150, (512) 444-1983

Index of Advertisers

Club Hotel by Doubletree 42
Mountain Star Lodge 55
Austin's Wildflower Inn 69
Houston House Bed & Breakfast 75
Governors' Inn 78
Texas Hatters Inc. 153
Callahan's General Store 191

Index

Symbols

@ Austin 531
\ 202
12th Street Books 344
1920's Club 147
311 Club 183
33 Degrees 187
503 Coffee Bar 139
8½ Souvenirs 156

A

Abbott, Jeff 333
ABC Limo 39
ABCD's 185
Abratto's 143
ACA Gallery 325
Ace Mart Restaurant Supply Co. 209
Ace Taxi 39
Acting Studio 307
Adams House 68
Admiral Nimitz State Historical Park 445
Adobe Pueblo 198
Adolphus Hotel 425
Advantage Rent-a-Car 38
Adventure Aviation 383
Adventures in Crime & Space Books 341
Aeronauts Hot Air Balloons 384
African American Museum 422
Age of Steam Railroad Museum 423
AIDs Services 485
AIDS Services of Austin 485
Air Charters 36
Airport Parking 34
Airport Valet Parking 35
Airports 33
Airwolf Adventures 384
Al Capone's 106
Alamo (car rental) 38
Alamo Draft House 149
Alamo Hotel 17
Alamo Plaza 427
Alamo, The 427
Alamodome 428
Albertson's 193
Alejandro Escovedo 161
Alexander Boat Dock 447
Alien Records 185
Alisa's Dance Academy 271
All Saints' Episcopal Chapel 544
Allen Boots 204
Allergies 487
Alley Theater 439
Altdorf Restaurant 445
Alternate Current Art Space 327
Alternative Medicine 486
Amelia Bullock Realtors 468
Amelia Bullock Relocation Services 472
American Association of Retired Persons 472
American Eagle 193
American History, Center for 353
American Institute for Learning 509
American Red Cross 392
American Yellow-Checker Cab Co. 39
Amon Carter Museum 426
AMPCO Parking Inc. 35
Amtrak 36
Amy's Ice Cream 129, 191
Ana Egge 156
Anderson Coffee Company 207
Anderson Mill Estates 464
Ann Taylor 191, 192, 193
Anne Klein 193
Annual Events 279
Antares Restaurant 424
Antigua 195
Antique Mall of Texas 199
Antique Marketplace 199
Antique Outlet Center 193
Antiques 194
Antone, Clifford 160, 172
Antone's 172
Antone's Record Shop 186
Antonio's Mexican Restaurant & Cantina 127
Apartments 466
Apple Barrel 199
Apple Computer 30
Aquarena Center 256
AquaTex Swim Team 392
Aquatic Adventures 392
Arbor Movie Theater 191
Arboretum Market 191
Arboretum, The 191
Arc of the Capital Area 485
Archer M. Huntington Art Gallery 232
Architects & Heroes 195
Architecture and Planning Library 351
Area Agency on Aging of the Capital Area 472
Ark Christian Book Store 345
Arkansas Bend 362
Armadillo Christmas Bazaar 300
Armadillo RV 378
Armadillo, The 195
Arno Nowotny Building 234
Arnold Palmer-Lakeside Course 402
Around Austin 250
Arriba Art & Business News 533
Art at the Austin Convention Center 221
Art Museums 321
Art School at Laguna Gloria 322
ArtPlex 325
Arts 303
Arts and Crafts Shops 200
Arts Camps 272
Artwalk 288
Artz Rib House 106
Asahi Imports 210
Asian American Quarterly 533
Asleep at the Wheel 152
Astrodome 439
Asylum Books 341

Asylum Street Spankers 152
At Austin 531
Atomic Cafe 143
Atomic City 213
Attal Galleries 194
Attractions 221
Auditorium Shores Concert Series 184
August-to-April Concerts Series 436
Aussie's 106
Aussie's Bar and Grill 388
Aussie's Volleyball and Grill 135
Austin 532
Austin & Texas Central Railroad 252
Austin 7th Day Adventist Junior Academy 513
Austin Adventure Co. 375
Austin Aero 35
Austin Air Taxi Inc. 36
Austin American-Statesman 526, 546
Austin Angler 218, 382
Austin Antique Mall 194, 198
Austin Aqua Fun 390
Austin Aquatics Hotline 393
Austin Area Economic Development Foundation 27
Austin Area Mental Health Association 485
Austin Auto Show 287
Austin Baptist Association 547
Austin Board Game Group 194
Austin Board of Realtors 468
Austin Boat & Fishing Show 279
Austin Book & Paper Show 350
Austin Books 341
Austin Brass 199
Austin Business Journal 527
Austin Cab 39
Austin Capital Grannies 522
Austin Carriage Service 41, 251
Austin Chamber Music Center 272
Austin Chariot Inn 52
Austin Child Guidance Center 485
Austin Children's Museum 256, 436
Austin Chronicle 528
Austin Circle of Theaters Performance Hotline 313
Austin City Limits 160
Austin City Parks 364
Austin City Pools 393
Austin City-Wide Garage Sales 206
Austin Civic Chorus 317
Austin Community College 476, 493
Austin Convention and Visitors Bureau 250
Austin Country Club 400
Austin Country Flea Market 206
Austin Cycling Association 41, 377
Austin Cycling News 529
Austin Executive Lodging 65
Austin Families, Inc. 522
Austin Family 529
Austin Federation of Musicians 289
Austin Film Festival 297
Austin Gay and Lesbian International Film Festival 310
Austin Groups for the Elderly 476
Austin Heart of Film Screenwriters Conference 297
Austin History Center 222, 350
Austin Hockey Association 385
Austin Home & Living 531
Austin Huns, The 387
Austin Ice Bats 405
Austin Independent School District 503
Austin Interfaith 547
Austin Java Company 139
Austin Jewish Book Fair 342
Austin Jewish Community Day School 517
Austin Junior League Christmas Affair 298
Austin KOA Campground 378
Austin Lake Travis Bed & Breakfast 82
Austin Land and Cattle Company 88
Austin Lone Stars 406
Austin Lounge Lizards 153
Austin Lyric Opera 317
Austin Marriott at the Capitol 56
Austin Metropolitan Ministries 547
Austin Montessori Middle School 515
Austin Montessori School — Great Northern 513
Austin Montessori School — Sunset Trail 518
Austin Monthly 529
Austin Motel 50
Austin Municipal Soccer Association 380
Austin Museum of Art — Downtown 321
Austin Museum of Art at Laguna Gloria 257, 322
Austin Museum of Art Guild 288
Austin Music Hall 172
Austin Nature and Science Center 237, 257
Austin Nature Center 372
Austin Nature Preserves 372
Austin Paddling Club 391
Austin Parks & Recreation Senior Centers 477
Austin Parks and Recreation Department 364, 374, 389
Austin Party Cruises 391
Austin Pizza Garden 111
Austin Presbyterian Seminary 498
Austin Private School Referral Service 518
Austin Promenade Tours 250
Austin Recovery Center Inc. 486
Austin Recreation Center 381
Austin Ridge Riders 41
Austin Rowing Club 391
Austin Rugby Football Club 387
Austin Rugby Tournament 282
Austin Runner's Club 387
Austin RV Park North 378
Austin Saengerrunde 23
Austin Senior Aides 479
Austin Ski Club 395
Austin State Hospital 486
Austin, Stephen F. 19
Austin Symphony Orchestra 25, 318
Austin Symphony Orchestra July Fourth Concert 293
Austin Tango Connection 131
Austin Tenant's Council 467
Austin Theatre for Youth 313
Austin Travis County Chiropractic Society Referral 482
Austin Triathletes 41

Austin Waldorf School 519
Austin Women's Addiction Referral and Education Centre 486
Austin Writers' League 332, 354
Austin Yacht Club 391
Austin Yacht Club Junior Sailing Camps 274
Austin Zoo 239, 261
Austin-Travis County Mental Health Mental Retardation Center 486
Austin/Travis County Health and Human Services 478
Austin/Travis County Livestock Show & PCRA Rodeo 281
Austin/Travis County Livestock Show & Rodeo 415
Austin/Travis County Super Cyclist Program 41
Austin's Wildflower Inn 69
AusTrans 39
Author Profiles 333
Avenue One 468
Avis 38
Aztlan Folklórico Dance Company 319
Azuma Express 118

B

B-Side 143
B. Dalton Bookseller 345
Babe's 182
Baby Acapulco 106
Backyard, The 172
Bad Livers 153
Balcones Canyonlands 373
Balcones Country Club Balcones Course 401
Balcones Woods Apartments 65
Ball, Marcia 154, 159
Ballet Austin 315
Ballet East 316
Balloon Port of Austin 384
Banana Bay Trading Company 217
Banana Republic 191, 192
Barbara Ellen's Hill Country Restaurant 113
Barnes & Noble 191, 193
Barnes & Noble Booksellers 186, 342, 346, 347
Barrett, Neal Jr. 333
Barrow Preserve 372
Bars 131
Bartholomew Park 381
Bartholomew Pool 393
Barton Creek Conference Resort and Country Club 47, 402
Barton Creek Greenbelt 364
Barton Creek Square 191
Barton Hills 459
Barton, Lou Ann 154
Barton Springs 260, 393
Barton Springs Archeological and Historic District 244
Barton Springs Diving Championships 292
Barton Springs Nursery 213
Barton Springs Pool 365
Baseball Museum 424
Basil's 88
Basketball 380
Bastille Day 292
Bastrop State Park 358, 382
Bat Conservation International in Austin 223
Bates Motel 182
Bats 222, 266
Battle Oaks 232
Battle of San Jacinto 430
Beach Front Boat Rentals 390
Bear Creek Stables 274
Becker Vineyards 446
Bed and Breakfasts 67
Bed Bath & Beyond 193
Bedichek, Roy 331
Belgian Restaurant L'Estro Armonico 113
Bell County Historical Commission 420
Ben Fisher 362
Ben White Golf Center 403
Benetton 193
Benson Latin American Collection 351
Best Buy 192
Best Of Austin 528
Best Western Seville Plaza Inn 59
Beth Israel 544
Bevo's Bookstore 342
Bicycle Sport Shop 377
Bicycling 40, 375
Big Lake Oil Field 26
Big Steve's Gym and Aerobics Center 382
Big Stinkin' International Improv & Sketch Comedy 283
Biking 375
Billy Bob's Texas 426
Bird, Sarah 333
Bird Watching 377
Bitter End 136
Bitter End Bistro and Brewery 88
Black Cat 182
Blackhawk Golf Club 400
Blanton Museum of Art 232, 322
Blue Bell Creamery 442
Blue Bonnet Cafe 451
Blue Hole 394
Blue Star Riding Center 274
Bluebonnet Festival 282
Bluebonnet Hill Golf Course 399
Blues on the Green 185
Blunn Creek Preserve 372
Boat Rentals 390
Boater Safety 390
Boating 390
Bob Larson's Old Timer Clock Shop 194
Bob Marley Festival 282
Bob Popular 134
Bob Wentz Park at Windy Point 362
Bob's Barbecue 127
Boggy Creek Greenbelt 364
Bohemia Retro-Resale 217
Book Market 342
Book People 342, 532
Book Woman 343
Booksource 347
Bookstop 342, 345
Bookstores 341
Borders Books & Music 186, 347
Botanical Gardens 428

Bouldin Creek 459
'Bout Time 147
Bowling 377
Boys Basketball Camp 275
Brackenridge Hospital 482
Brady Island 440
Brazos Valley Museum of Natural History 442
Bread Alone Bakery 109
Breed & Co. 208
Bremond National Register District 245
Brentwood Christian School 513
Brewer, J. Mason 331
Brewpubs 136
Briarfield Bed and Breakfast 437
Brick Oven 89
Brick Oven Restaurant 118, 128
Bright Beginnings 203
Brodie Oaks 192
Broken Spoke 143, 157, 173
Brook House 70
Brooks Brothers 193
Broomfields 437
Browning's Courtyard Cafe on Salado Square 421
Bruton, Stephen 155
Bryan 441
Brykerwoods 461
Buchanan Dam Museum and Visitor Center 448
Buckingham Estates 460
Buckner Villas 474
Budget 38
Buescher State Park 358, 379, 382
Bull Creek Park and Greenbelt 367
Burke Baker Planetarium 438
Burnet County Park 447
Bus Services 36
Bush, George 30
Butch Hancock 164
Butera's Restaurant 439
Butler Park Pitch and Putt Golf Course 399
Butler Pitch & Putt Golf Course 262
Buttercup Creek Pool 394
Butthole Surfers 155
BW-3 135
By George 202
Bydee Arts & Gifts 200
Byzantine Chapel Museum 439

C

Cactus Cafe 173
Cadeau, The 214
Cafe Annie 440
Cafe at the Four Seasons 89
Cafe Josie 89
Calabash 125
Callahan's General Store 211
Calle Ocho 143
Calvin Klein 193
Cameron Equestrian Center 384
Camp Chautauqua at Lake Travis 362, 379
Camp Creek Primitive Area 361
Camp Doublecreek 269
Camp Mabry National Register District 245
Camping 378
Campisi's Egyptian Inn 425
Camps 268
Canales National and International Aircraft Charter Service 36
Candlelight Homes Tour 299
Canelas International Aviation Inc. 384
Canoeing 391
Canyon Cafe 113, 193
Capital Area Psychological Association 482
Capital Area Rehabilitation Center 392
Capital Area Tennis Association 387
Capital Area Water Ski Club 395
Capital Area Youth Soccer Association 380
Capital Cruises 253, 391
Capital Gymnastics 272
Capital Metro 40
Capitol 10,000 287
Capitol Area Realty, Inc. 468
Capitol City Comedy Club 142
Capitol Complex Visitor Center 223
Capitol Complex Visitors Center 213
Capitol Saddlery 204
Capitol Wings 36
Capps Van & Car rental 38
Capra & Cavelli 201
Captain Quackenbush's 139
Car Racing 414
Car Rental 38
Caregivers 478
Carey 39
Caritas 399
Carlos 'N Charlie's 114, 388
Carlos 'n Charlie's 184
Carmelo's 89
Carnaval Brasileiro 280
Carousel Lounge 173
Carpenter, Liz 334
Carrington's Bluff 70
Carter Lane 80
Cartwright, Gary 334
Carver Branch Library 350
Casino El Camino 134
Casita Jorge's 90
Castle Hill Cafe 90
Cat Mountain 463
Catfish Parlour 118, 126
Catholic Church Spring Picnic 290
Cathy's Boardwalk Cafe 421
Cattlemen's Steakhouse 427
Caucus Club 144
CEACO Inc. 473
Cedar Chopper Festival 291
Cedar Door 131
Cedar Park 466
Cedar Park Parks and Recreation 371, 374
Cedar Park Public Library 353
Cedar Point Resource Area 447, 448
Cedar Post 535
Cedar Street Courtyard 132, 178
Cedar Tops Cottage 437
Cedars on Bergstrom Golf Course 399
Celebrate Austin 532
Celebration 425
Celebration Station 264

Celis Brewery 243
Central Brackenridge Hospital 482
Central Market 90, 196, 208
Central Market Cafe 267
Central Texas Ballooning Association 384
Centre at Post Oak 440
Ceramic Mug 134
Ceramics Bayou 266
Chain Drive 147
Chambers Bar 132
Chantal's Antique and Design Center 199
Chantal's Antiques 192
Chaparral Ice Center 264, 386
Charlie's 147
Charter Hospital of Austin 486
Charter Schools 509
Cheapo Records 186
Checker Cab Co. 39
Cheers Shot Bar 134
Chef's Tool Box 210
Chemistry Library 351
Chequered Shade 81
Cherry Creek 460
Cherry Creek Catfish Co. 111
Chez Nous 90
Chez Zee 118
Chicago Cutlery 193
Child Care 501, 520
Child Care Management Services 522
Childrens' Book Writers and Illustrators, Society 355
Children's Clothing Stores 203
Children's Day Art Park 262
Children's Hospital 482
Children's Museum of Houston 438
Children's Museum of the Brazos Valley 442
Children's School 515
Chili's 192
China Cafe 128
Chinatown 114, 118
Chisholm Trail Roundup 289
Chisholms 127
Christ Community Christian School 514
Christmas at the French Legation 300
Christmas Lights 299
Christmas Music and Theater 301
Christmas Open House 300
Chuck E Cheese's 264
Chuckwagon Cookout 437
Church of Jesus Christ of Latter-day Saints 548
Chuy's 106, 121
Chuy's "Children Giving to Children" Parade 298
Cierra 215
Cinco de Mayo 290
CinemaTexas 310
Circle C Golf Cub 399
Circle C Ranch 461
Circuit City 193
Cisco's 125
Citiview 76
City Grill 91
City Leagues 380
City of Austin 373
Citywide Garage Sale and Antique Show 279
Clairmont, The 474
Clark, W.C. 155
Clarksville 458
Clarksville National Register District 246
Clarksville Pottery & Galleries 200
Clarksville-West End Jazz & Arts Festival 291
Classic Inn 61
Classics Library 351
Clayworks Studio and Gallery 321
Clear Springs Aviaries and Zoological Gardens 262
Cloak Room 132
Clothing/Fashion Stores 201
Club Carnaval 144
Club DeVille 132
Club Hotel by DoubleTree 56
Club Inferno 144
Club Palmeras 144
Club Rio 144
Clubs 171
Coca Cola Starplex Amphitheater 422
Cockrell Butterfly Center 438
Coffee Exchange 209
Coffeehouses 139
Coldwell Bankers 468
Coliseum, The 422
Collectibles 194
College Station 441
College Station Hilton 442
Colorado Bend State Park 358, 447
Colorado River Preserve 372
Colorado River Walkers of Austin 384
Columbia St. David's Pavilion 486
Colvin, Shawn 155
Comedy Clubs 142
Comfort Suites-Galleria 440
Commander's Point Yacht Basin 391
Commodore's Pup and Riverboat Commodore 253
Community AIDS Resource & Education 485
Community Clinics Volunteer Health Care Clinic 484
Community Libraries 353
CompUSA 192
Computers Stores 205
Concordia University at Austin 497
Congress Avenue Booksellers 343
Congress Avenue National Register District 246
Congress Avenue Souvenirs 214
Conley-Guerrero Senior Activity Center 477
Conradt, Jody 409
Conspiracy Museum 424
Constitution of 1876 22
Container Store 192
Contemporary Art Museum 438
Continental Club 142, 178
Continental, The 474
Convict Hill 461
Cook, Abner 21
Copper Tank Brewing Company 136
Cornerstone Christian School 520
Cornerstone Connection 520
Corporate Lodging 65
Cotton Bowl Stadium 422
Country Edge 147

Country Inns 67
County Line on the Hill 114
County Line on the Lake 118
Coupland Dance Hall 138
Courtyard by Marriott 64
Courtyard Shops 199
Cowgirls and Flowers 214
Cowgirls and Lace 193
Cowgirls are Forever 201
Cowtown Boot Company Factory Outlet 205
Crawford Guide Service 449
Crenshaw & Coore Course 402
Crescent, The 425
Cross Country Camp 277
Crow, Alvin 156
Crowe's Nest Farm, Inc. 269
Crown & Anchor 136
Crown Limo 39
Cruises 391
Culture Club 145
Curio Corner Books 345
Curra's Grill 107
Cutter Aviation Executive Air Park 35
Cy Twombly Gallery 439
Cycling 375
Cypress Creek 363

D

Daily Fee Golf Courses 399
Daily Texan 527
Dallas 144, 422
Dallas Aquarium 423
Dallas Convention & Visitors Bureau 426
Dallas Cowboys 406, 424
Dallas Farmer's Market 425
Dallas Mavericks 408, 424
Dallas Museum of Art 423
Dallas Museum of Natural History 422
Dallas Zoo 424
Dan McCluskey's 191
Dan McKluskey's 91, 118
Dance 315
Dance Camps 271
Dance Clubs 143
Dance Line 313
Dancers Workshop 272
Dansk Factory Outlet 193
Darden Smith 168
Davenport Ranch 463
Davíd Garza 162
Day Camps 268
Days Inn Alamo River Walk 429
Days Inn University 56
Daytrips 419
Dealey Plaza 423
Deep Eddy 393
Deep Eddy Pool's Summer Movies 260
Deep Ellum 424
Deja News 14
Del Frisco's 425
Del Valle Independent School District 504
Dell Computer 30
Dell Jewish Community Campus 544
Dell, Michael 12, 30
Dell Outlet 206
Deluxe Diner 442
Dental Clinic 485
Derailers, The 156
Dessau Music Hall 179
Devil's Waterhole 450
Dewitt C. Greer Building 224
Dia de los Muertos 298
Die Gelbe Rose Carriage 41, 252
Diez y Seis de Septiembre 295
Dillard's 191, 192
Dillo trolley service 40
Dink Pearson Park 363
Dirty Martin's Place 91
Disc (Frisbee) Golf 381
Discounts & Good Deals for Seniors In Texas 472
Discovery Zone Fun Center 264
Disney Store 191
Dobie, J. Frank 331
Dobie Theatre 149
Dodge City Steakhouse 128
Dog & Duck Pub 137
Dog and Duck Pub 91
Dolce Vita Gelato and Espresso Bar 129, 139
Dollar 38
Donna Karan 193
DoubleTree Hotel 53
Dougherty Arts Center 272, 314
Down Cherry Lane 203
Dr. Chocolate 208
Drag, The 232
Dragon's Lair Comics & Fantasy 194
Dragonsnaps 203
Draught Horse 137
Dressed to Kill 217
Dripping Springs Independent School District 505
Driskill Hotel 45, 224
Driskill Hotel Lobby Bar 132
Driskill Mystery Dinner Theater 143
Driving Ranges 403
Drury Inn 57
Duane Lake Academy 513
Dugger, Ronnie 27
Duval Discs 186

E

Eaglequest 403
Eanes Independent School District 505
Earful of Books 348
Early Music Festival 436
Easter Fires Pageant 283
Easter Pageant 283
Eastside Cafe 125
Easyrider 40
EatOutIn 116
Ebony Sun Java House 139
Eclectic 194
Ecotours Texas & Beyond 251
Eddie Bauer 193
Edge, The 147
Educational Children's Camps 268
Eeyore's Birthday Party 286

Egge, Ana 156
Eight-and-a-half Souvenirs 156
El Arroyo 92
El Azteca 125
El Borinquen 145
El Coyote 145
El Interior 194
El Mercado 428
El Mercado Restaurant & Cantina 92, 107, 121
El Milagro 210
El Mirador 429
El Norte 533
El Rinconcito 92
El Sol y La Luna 107
El Taller Gallery 201
Elderhostel 476
Electric Ladyland 217
Electric Lounge 132, 179
Elephant Room 132, 179
Elizabet Ney Museum 237, 323
Elizabeth M. Milburn Aquatic Facility 394
Elizabeth M. Milburn Community Park 371
Ella's Restaurant 92
Ellos 325
Ely, Joe 156
Embassy Suites Downtown 51
Embassy Suites Hotel 57
Emerald Point Marina 390
Emerald Restaurant 117
Emeralds 202
Emma Long Metropolitan Park 368, 379
Emmaus Catholic Books & Gifts Company 346
Emo's 180
Enchanted Rock State Natural Area 359, 379
Enchanted Rock State Park 446
Enfield 458
Engineering Library 351
Englewood Estates 474
Enterprise 38
Entrees on Trays 116
Episcopal Diocese of Texas 548
ERA 468
Eric Johnson 164
Erickson, John 340
Escovedo, Alejandro 161
Esprit 193
Esther's Follies 142, 307
Esther's Pool 142
Eustacio Cepeda Branch Library 350
Every Generation's Concern 478
Excel Inn 59
Exotic Resort Zoo 443
Experience Unlimited 479
Express 192

F

Fabulous Cheesecakes 208
Fabulous Thunderbirds 160
Fadó 137
Fairfield Inn 57
Fairview 77
Fall Creek Grape Stomp 294
Fall Creek Vineyards 95
Fall Creek Vineyards and Winery 448
Family Christmas Night 300
Family Eldercare 473
Fanny's Outlet Fabric Store 193
Far Northwest Caregivers 478
Farmers Markets 206
Fastball 161, 162
Fat Tuesday 182
Faulk, John Henry 331
Faust Hotel 434
Fazio Course 402
Feats of Clay 200
Feed Mill Cafe 443
Feliz Navidad! 301
Fernea, Elizabeth Warnock 334
Fernea, Robert 334
Festival Hill 436
Festival Institute at Festival Hill 290
Festival of New Latin American Cinema 310
Festivals 279
Fieldcrest Cannon 193
Fiesta 288, 322
Fiesta Mart 211
Filmmaking 308
Fine Arts Library 352
Fire Island Hot Glass Studio, Inc. 201
First Baptist Church 546
Fishing 381
Fitness Centers 382
Five Star Bar-B-Que 114
Five-O-Three Coffee Bar 139
Flamingo Cantina 145
Flea Markets 206
Flipnotics 140
Florsheim Shoe Factory 193
Flying 383
Foley's 191, 192
Folk Art 194
Folk Artists 319
Folktales 343
Fonda San Miguel 121
Foot Locker 191
Forest Creek Golf Club 398
Forest Ridge Preserve 372
Fort Martin Scott 445
Fort Worth 422
Fort Worth Botanic Garden 426
Fort Worth Convention and Visitors Bureau 427
Fort Worth Museum of Science and History 426
Fortney's Artful Home Furnishings 215
Forum, The 147
Fossil Company Store 193
Four Points Hotel 53
Four Seasons 132
Four Seasons Hotel 46
Fourth of July Festival 293
Frank & Angie's Pizza 92
Frank Erwin Center 180
Freda and the Firedogs 159
Fredericksburg 444
Fredericksburg Brewing Co. 445
Fredericksburg Chamber of Commerce 445, 446
Fredericksburg Herb Farms 445
French Legation Museum 240
Fresh Planet Cafe 93

Friedman, Jeffrey 28
Friedman, Kinky 334
Friends Meeting of Austin 548
Frisbee Golf 381
Frisco Shop 93
Frontera 215
Frontera @ Hyde Park Theatre 307
FronteraFest 280
Fronterafest 311
Frontier Days 291
Funny Papers 343
Futurekids of Austin 268

G

G.S.I. Scuba Camp 274
Galeria Sin Fronteras 326
Galleria, The 425, 440
Gallerie Estate Jewelers 216
Galleries 325
Gap 191, 192
Gap Outlet 193
Garden Escape 14
Garden Ridge Pottery 213
Garden-Ville of Austin 212
Gardening Shops 212
Gardens 212
Garrison 393
Garza, Davíd 162
Gateway 192
Gateway Mezzaluna 119
Gathering of the Clans on the Village Green 421
Gay and Lesbian International Film Festival 310
Gay Nightclub Scene 147
Geezinslaw Brothers 162
General Cos House 428
Geology Library 352
George Bush Presidential Library and Museum 441
George Washington Carver Museum 241, 257
Georgetown Farmers Market 207
Georgetown Fly-in 288
German Oktoberfest 297
Gethsemane Lutheran Church 544
Gift Shops 213
Gilleland Creek Park 371
Gilleland Creek Park Pool 394
Gillespie County Fair 296
Gilligans 93
Gilmore, Jimmie Dale 162
Gimble, Johnny 163
Ginger Man 137
Girls Basketball Camp 276
Git Bit 382
Glassel School 439
Gloster Bend Primitive Area 361
Golf 397
Golf Resorts 402
Golfsmith 219
Golfsmith Practice Facility 403
Gonzales Come and Take It Days 296
Good Eats Cafe 107
Good Life 529
Goodwill Computer Works 206
Gourds, The 163
Gourmet Shops 207
Governor's Inn 71
Governor's Mansion 224
Grace Covenant Christian School 517
Granite Cafe 93
Grape Creek Vineyards 446
Graphic Glass Studios and Archaic 321
Graves, John 340
Gray Panthers of Austin 475
Great Harvest Bakery 211
Great Hills Christian School 517
Great Hills Golf Club 401
Greater Calvary Missionary Baptist Church 546
Green Mesquite 107
Green Pastures 107
Green Room 424
Gregg House & Gardens 80
Grelle Primitive Area 361
Greyhound 36
Griffith, Nanci 163
Grist Mill Restaurant 435
Groceries-to-Go 478
Gruene 435
Gruene General Store 435
Gruene Hall 435
Gruene Information Center 436
Gruene Mansion Inn 435
Guadalupe Street 232
Guadalupe Valley Winery 435
Güero's 108
Güero's Taco Bar 267
Guy Town 24
Gymboree 265
Gymnastics Camps 271

H

Habitat for Humanity Re-Store 217
Habitat Suites Hotel 54
Halbert Antiques 199
Half Price Books 344, 345, 346, 348
Half Price Books Records and Magazines 186
Halloween at Jourdan-Bachman Pioneer Farm 297
Halloween on Sixth Street 296
Hamilton Pool 394
Hamilton Pool Preserve 373
Hampton Inn 62
Hancock, Butch 164
Hancock Golf Course 398
Handi-Wheels 478
Hang 'Em High 145
Hang Town Grill 96, 114, 119, 267
Harold's Outlet Barn 194
Harrigan, Stephen 334
Harry Ransom Humanities Research Center 234, 324, 353
Harvey Penick Scholarship Fund 399
Hawthorn Suites 54
Healthcare 481
Healthy Quarters 71
Hearn, Tony 17
Heart of Heart Ranch 437
Heart of Texas Baseball Camps 274

Heart of Texas Motel 51
Heart of Texas Tours 250
Heirloom Gardens 212
HemisFair Park 428
Henry Jackalope 425
Henry S. Miller Realtors 469
Herb Bar, The 215
Heritage at Gaines Ranch 474
Hertz 38
Hi-Line Lake Resort & RV Park 449
Hickman, Sara 164
Hickory Street Bar & Grille 96
Hidden Talent 266
Higginbottom's 191, 215
High Life Cafe 140
Higher Education 489
Highland Lakes 446
Highland Lakes Bluebonnet Trail 283
Highland Lanes 377
Highland Mall 192
Hiking 384
Hill Country Balloons 384
Hill Country Cellars 96
Hill Country Christian School of Austin 518
Hill Country Information Service 384
Hillel Foundation at UT Austin 548
Hills Fitness Center 382
Hills of Lakeway Golf Course 401
Hilltop Baptist Academy 519
Hinojosa, Tish 164
Hippie Hollow 363
Hispanic 533
Historic Homes Tour 290
History 19
HIV Wellness Center 485
Hoffbrau, The 104
Hole in the Wall 180
Holiday Corporation 474
Holiday Inn 58
Holiday Inn Astrodome 440
Holiday Inn Express 55
Holland Photo 216
Holocaust Museum Houston 438
Holy Cross Church 546
Home Depot 193
Home Furnishings 215
Home-Schooling 522
Homegate Studio and Suites 59
Homewood Suites 62
Hong Kong Supermarket 210
Horse Racing 417
Horse-drawn Carriages 41
Horseback Riding 384
Hospice Austin 483
Hospitals 482
Hot Air Ballooning 384
Hot Shots Bar 134
Hotels 43
Houston 437
Houston Astros 412, 439
Houston Comets 408
Houston Livestock Show and Rodeo 439
Houston Rockets 408, 439
Houston, Sam 19
Houston Ship Channel 440
Houston Zoo 438
Houstonian Hotel, Club & Spa 440
How Ironic 199
Howson Branch Library 350
Hudson Bend RV Park 379
Hudson's Grill 119, 122
Hudson's-on-the-Bend 114
Hula Hut 115
Humanities Research Center 353
Hummel Museum 434
Hunan Lion 111, 127, 192
Hunting 385
Huntington Art Gallery 232
Huntington-Surrey School 510
Huston-Tillotson College 241, 498
Hut's Hamburgers 97
Hyatt Regency Austin 51
Hyde Park 458
Hyde Park Baptist School 510
Hyde Park Baptist School-Bannockburn 519
Hyde Park Bar & Grill 97
Hyde Park Gym 383
Hyde Park National Register District 247
Hye Post Office 444
Hylton, Hilary 7

I

Ian Matthews 165
IBM 11
Ice Cream 129
Ice Hockey 405
Ice Sports 385
Ichat 14
Iguana Grill 119
Images of Austin and the Southwest 328
IMAX Theater 423, 428
Incredible Journeys 384
India Bazaar 208
Indian Hills Stop & Go 447
Indiangrass Wildlife Sanctuary 373
Industrial Areas Foundation 547
Informe SIDA 485
Ink 345
Inks Lake 449
Inks Lake State Park 359, 449
Inn at Brushy Creek 128
Inn at Pearl Street 72
Inn on the Creek 421
Inner Sanctum 217
Inner Space Cavern 257
InStep 202
Institute of Texas Cultures 428
International Buddhist Progress Society 548
International Festival Institute 436
Iron Cactus 134
Iron Works Barbecue 97
Islamic Center of Greater Austin 548
Island on Lake Travis 475
Island, The 203
It's About Thyme 212
It's New to Me 218
Ivins, Molly 334

J

J. B. Goodwin Realtors 468
Jack S. Blanton Museum of Art 232, 322
Jaeger 191
Jalisco Bar 108
James Michener Center for Writers 335
Japanese Garden of Peace 445
JCPenney 191, 192
Jean-Pierre's Upstairs 97
Jeffrey's 97
Jenkins, Dan 341
Jester Estates 463
Jewelry Stores 216
Jewish Community 544
Jewish Federation of Austin 548
Jimmie Dale Gilmore 162
Jimmie Vaughan 170
Jimmy Clay Golf Club 398
Jody Conradt 409
Joe Ely 156
Joe T. Garcia's 427
Joe's Generic Bar 135
John Henry Faulk Central Library 349
John W. Mallet Chemistry Library 351
Johnson City 443
Johnson City Market Days 284
Johnson Creek 368
Johnson, Eric 164
Johnson, Lyndon 26
Johnson Park 451
Johnson Space Center 440
Jones, Anson 18, 20
Joplin, Janis 28
Josephine 202
Jourdan-Bachman Pioneer Farm 244, 258
Juarez, Tina 338
July Fourth Fireworks 293
Jump on It 185
Juneteenth 291
Junior Brown 154
Just For Fun Watercraft Rental 390

K

Karst Preserve 373
Kathleen's Art Cafe 425
Katie Bloom's 138
Katz's 98
Kayaking 391
Keen, Robert Earl 165
Keller Williams Realty 469
Ken Milam Guide Service 449
Kenny Luna's Ivory Cat Tavern 135
Kerbey Lane Cafe 98, 108, 119, 267
Kerbey Lane Doll Shoppe 195
Kerbey Lane Dollhouses and Miniatures 200
Kerrville Bus Co., Inc. 36
Kerrville Folk Festival 289
Kerrville Wine & Music Festival 295
Kidcare Locators 522
Kids Acting 273
Kids Playhouse 522
Kid's Space 522
Kids-N-Cats Book Corner 344
KidsActing 307
Kidstuff 255
Kim Phung 122
Kimball Art Museum 426
King, Larry L. 340
King William District 428
Kingsland Archeological Site 450
Kirby Hall School 511
Kitchenware 207
Klump's 437
Korea House 122
Koslow's Furs 191
Krause Springs 395
Krause's Cafe 434
Kreuz Market 86
KTBC 27
Kuehne Library 352
Kuumba House 439
Kwanzaa 301
Kyoto 98

L

La Cosecha 195
La Fuentes Mexican Food Restaurant 111
La Madeleine 98, 115, 119, 193
La Mansion del Rio Hotel 429
La Mexicana Bakery 211
La Palapa 125
La Quinta Inn 46
La Quinta Inns 440
La Reyna 108
La Victoria Bakery 210
La Villita 428
La Zona Rosa 180
Lady Bird Johnson 229
Lady Bird Johnson Wildflower Center 240
LaFave, Jimmy 165
Lago Vista Independent School District 505
Lago Vista Resort & Conference Center 48, 402
Laguna Gloria Art Museum 242
Lake Austin Spa Resort 48
Lake Creek Park 371
Lake Creek Swimming Pool 394
Lake LBJ 450
Lake Marble Falls 451
Lake Parks 360
Lake Point Resort 447
Lake Travis Community Library 354
Lake Travis Independent School District 506
Lake Travis Inn and RV Park 379
Lake Travis View 535
Lake Walter E. Long Metropolitan Park 368
Lakeline Mall 192
Lakeside Park 451
Lakeway 35, 463
Lakeway Inn 48, 403
Lakeway Marina 390
Lakeway Service League 478
Lakeway's Fabulous Fourth 294
Lamar, Mirabeau 19
Lamar Senior Activity Center 477
Lambs-e-Divey 203
Lamme's Candies 210

Las Americas 321
Las Manitas Avenue Cafe 98
Las Palomas 115
Laser Quest Austin 265
Last Call 193
Latin American Collection 351
Laughing at the Sun 327
Laura Ashley 192
Laura's Bluebonnet Cafe 122
Lazy Oak Inn 77
LBJ Ranch 443
LBJ State Historical Park Wildflower Day 295
Leander Independent School District 506
Legend Oaks 461
Legend's 135
Legends of the Game Baseball Museum 424
L'Elysee Antiques 199
Lentz House 437
Let's Dish 217
Liberty Bar 429
Liberty Hill Festival 286
Liberty Lunch 180
Libraries 349
Library, The 135
Life Science Library 352
Lifetime Learning Institute 476
Lighting of the Zilker Park Christmas Tree 301
Lily White Limos 40
Limited Express 191
Limited, The 191
Limousines 39
Lindsey, David 338
Lions Municipal Golf Course 398
Literacy Austin 339
Literary Scene 331
Little City 140
Little Walnut Creek Branch Library 350
Little Webberville 363
Littlefield Building 233
Littlefield Memorial Fountain 233
Live Oak Theatre at the State 311
Llano County Park 447
Local Flavor 186
Lodge at Lakeview 117
Logan's on Sixth 135
Lone Star Bakery 212
Lone Star Cafe 192
Lone Star Riverboat 253
Lone Star Trolley Tours 427
Long, Emma 27
Longhorn Baseball Camp 275
Longhorn Cavern State Park 450
Longhorn Diving Camp 276
Longhorn Football Camp 276
Longhorn Golf Camp 276
Longhorn Soccer Camp 380
Longhorn Softball Camp 277
Longhorn Swimming Camp 277
Longhorn Tennis Camp 277
Longhorns Baseball 413
Longhorns Basketball 414
Longhorns Football 412
Longhorns Softball 413
Lorenzo de Zavala State Archives and Library Build 225
Lost Creek 462
Lost Creek Country Club 401
Lou Ann Barton 154
Louie's 106 99, 133
Lovejoy's 138
Lower Colorado River Authority 361, 389, 446
Lucero's 99
Lucy in Disguise with Diamonds 217
Luling Watermelon Thump 291
Lyndon B. Johnson National Historic Park 444
Lyndon Baines Johnson Library and Museum 233
Lyons Matrix Gallery 326

M

Mabel Davis 393
MacGregor Park 363
Madame Nadalini's 115
Madhatter's Table 437
Maggie Mae's 183
Maggie Mae's Long Bar 138
Magic Camp 273
Magic Camps 273
Magnolia Cafe 115, 267
Magnolia Cafe South 109
Majestic Theater 25
Major League Baseball 412
Major League Sports 406
Malaga's Wine and Tapas Bar 99, 133
Maldonado's 186
Mallet Chemistry Library 351
Malls 190
Manchaca Road Branch Library 350
Manor Downs 417
Manor Independent School District 507
Mansfield Dam 363
Mansion on Turtle Creek 425
Manuel's 99, 133
Maple Run 461
Marbridge Farms Greenhouse 212
Marcia Ball 154
Marinas 390
Marine Science Library 352
Marisco's Seafood 126
Market Day 206
Market Days 286
Market, The 199
Mars 99
Mary Moore Searight Park 381
Matthews, Ian 165
Matt's Famous El Rancho 109
Max Alexander's 447
Mayfair, Artwalk and the Georgetown Fly-in 288
Mayfield Preserve 373
McBride's Guns 218
MCC 12
McCallum House 73
McGillicuddy's Pub and Grill 138
McKinney Engineering Library 351
McKinney Falls State Park 359, 379
McMurtry, James 165
McMurtry, Larry 340
McNay Art Museum 428
Meals on Wheels and More 478

Medearis, Angela Shelf 338
Medi Wheels 476
Media 525
Mediterranean Festival 297
Medway Ranch 384
Menger Hotel 429
Menil Collection 439
Mental Health Services 485
Mercado Juarez 126
Mercury Lounge 145
Mervyn's 192
Messina Hof Winery 442
Metro 140
Metropolitan African Methodist Episcopal Church 546
Mexic-Arte Museum 325
Mexican Cultural Institute 428
Mexican-American War 20
Mexico Tipico 126
Mezzaluna 100, 192
MGM Indian Foods 210
Michener, James 332, 335
Micki Krebsbach Memorial Pool 394
Miguel's La Bodega 145
Mikasa 193
Milagro Del Rio Brazos Studio 321
Milano's Gelateria 129
Mill Creek Country Club & Guest Houses 421
Miller Outdoor Theater 438
Miller, Tom 26
Miller-Crockett House 78
Millet Opera House 225
Milwood Branch Library 350
Minor League Sports 405
Mission Nuestra Senora de la Purisma Concepcion 431
Mission San José y Miguel de Aguayo 431
Mister Tee 403
Mitchie's Fine Black Art Gallery and Bookstore 201
Modern Art Museum of Fort Worth 426
Mojo's Daily Grind 140
Mom's Best Friend 522
Mongolian Barbecue 100
Montgomery Ward 191, 192
Montgomery Ward Autorent 38
Moonlight Towers 225
Moorcock, Michael 338
Moore, Abra 166
Moore's Crossing National Register District 248
Morning Star Trading Company 214
Morris-Williams Golf Course 398
Morton H. Meyerson Symphony Center 423
Motel 6 55
Motels 43
Mother's Cafe 100
Motorola 12
Motorola Marathon 280
Mount Bonnell 243
Mount Bonnell Park 368
Mountain Star Lodge 52
Movie Studios at Las Colinas 424
Movies 149
Mozart's Coffee Roasters 141
Muleshoe Bend Primitive Area 361
Municipal Golf Courses 397
Murphey, Michael 159
Murphy, Trish 166
Musashino Sushi Dokoro 120
Museum of Fine Arts 438
Museum of Health & Medical Science 438
Museum of Natural Science 438
Museum of Texas Handmade Furniture 434
Music 315
Music Biz 157
Music Hall 422
Music Scene 151
Music Stores 185
Music Venues 171
Musician Profiles 152
Musicmania 187
Mustangs Sculpture 234
My Thanh Oriental Market 210
Mysteries & More Inc. 346

N

Narrows Primitive Area 362
National Aquatic School 390
National Car Rental 39
National Museum of Communications 424
National Register Districts 244
Natural Bridge Caverns 258
Nature Preserves 372
Nau Enfield Drug 100
NBA Basketball 407
Necessities and Temptations 214
Needleworks, The 200
Negrel 199
Neighborhoods 453
Neill-Cochran House Museum 236
Neiman Marcus 425
Neiman Marcus Last Call 192
Nelson, Willie 159, 174
New Braunfels 433
New Braunfels Chamber of Commerce 434
New Braunfels Smokehouse 434
New Texas Festival 318
New Texas Magazine 530
New Year's Celebration On Sixth Street 301
Newspapers 526
Next to New 217
NFL Football 406
Night in Old Fredericksburg 292
Nightclubs 143
Nightlife 131
Nike 193
Ninfa's Mexican Restaurant 100, 122
NOKOA-The Observer 533
Nomadic Notions 216
Noritake 193
North Austin Diagnostic Medical Center 482
North Central Caregivers 478
North Oaks 464
North Village Branch Library 350
Northcross Mall 192
Northeast Austin Caregivers 478
Northpark Center 425
Nowotny Building 234
Nuevo Leon 126

O

O. Henry 23, 331
O. Henry Museum 226
O. Henry World Championship Pun-Off 288
Oak Hill 460
Oak Hill Driving Range 403
Oak Hill Gazette 534
Oak Springs Branch Library 350
Oakwood Cemetery 241
Oasis, The 124, 184, 244
Oat Willie's 214
Oatmeal Festival 295
Oberhellmann Vineyards 446
O'Connor, Tim 172
Off the Wall 215
OfficeMax 192, 193
Oilcan Harry's 147
Oktoberfest 297
Ol' Cactus Jack 384
Ol' Cactus Jack Summer Day Camp 270
Old Bakery and Emporium 214, 226, 479
Old Fredericksburg 292
Old German Bakery and Restaurant 445
Old Gruene Market Days 280
Old Navy Clothing Co. 192, 193
Old Pecan St. Ale House & Soccer Bar 138
Old Pecan Street Cafe 101
Old Pecan Street Falls Arts Festival 296
Old Pecan Street Spring Arts Festival 289
Old Quarry Branch Library 350
Old Settler's Music Festival 282
Old Settlers Park 371, 381
Older Worker Program 479
Olla Linda 199
Omar & the Howlers 166
Omni Austin Hotel Downtown 48
Omni Austin Southpark 60
Oneida Factory 193
Onion Creek 465
Onion Creek Country Club 401
Onion Creek Preserve 373
Oshman's Supersports 219
Oshman's Superstore 192
Our Lady of Guadalupe Church 546
Outdoors Stores 218
Outlet Malls 193
Outlet Shops 193
Over The Rainbow 346
Overview 1
Oxford Street Restaurant & Pub 442

P

Pace Bend 363
Pace Bend Park 379
Pacific Moon 116
Paddlefest 284
Paggi House 110
Pao's Mandarin House 101
Paper Dragon Etc. 215
Pappagallo's 192
Paradise 135
Paradox 145
Paragon Prep 514
Paramount Theatre 227
Paramount Theatre for the Performing Arts 149, 305
Paramount Theatre Kids' Classics 266
Parent, Laurence 338
Park Plaza Warwick Hotel 439
Parking 39
Parks 357
Parkside Community School 512
Parque Zaragoza Recreation Center Murals 242
Partners in Literacy 339
Pasta & Co. 208
Pavarotti Italian Restaurant 122
Pease, Elisha 22
Pease Park 368, 381
Pecan Street Emporium 214
Pedernales Falls State Park 360, 443
Peña, Amado 201
Peña Studio/Gallery 328
People's Community Clinic 484
Perry-Castañeda Library 351
Peter Pan Mini-Golf 263
Pete's Piano Bar 135
Petsmart 193
Pfaltzgraff 193
Pfluger Park 371
Pflugerville Community Library 354
Pflugerville Independent School District 508
Pflugerville Parks and Recreation Department 371, 374
Pflugerville Pflag 536
Philosophers' Rock Sculpture 238
Phoenicia Bakery & Deli 211
Photography Shops 216
Physician Referral 482
Picket Fences 203
Pickle, J.J. Jake 11
Piddler & Pro Home and Hardware 211
Pier, The 184, 388
Pietro's Italian Restaurant & Pizzeria 421
Pinata Party Palace 218
Pink Rose Tea Room 421
Pinnacle Suites 65
Pioneer Farm Christmas Candlelight Tour 299
Pioneer Museum 445
Pipkin, Turk 338
Pisces Scuba 392
Pizza Nizza 109
Planet Theatre 312
Player's Sports Bar & Billiards 136
Playfest 314
Playland Skating Center 386
Plaza Theater of Wax 427
Pleasant Hill Branch Library 350
Pleasant Valley Sports Complex 381
Pok-E-Jo's Smokehouse 101, 120, 123, 127
Politics 11
Polly Ester's '70s Disco 145
Porter, William Sydney 331
Pots and Plants 213
Pottery Barn 191
Powwow and American Indian Heritage Festival 298
Precision Camera and Video 216

Preface v
Premiere Lady 383
Presbyterian 543
Preserve 463
Price, Toni 167
Prime Time 40
Prince Solms Inn 433
Prince Solms Park 433
Private Golf Courses 400
Private Schools 510
Pro-Jex Gallery 325
Pronunciation Guide 3
Provencal Home and Garden 216
Prudential Owens Realty 469
Pseudo-Rock 265, 386
Public Domain 312
Public Health Services 483
Public Transportation 40
Pubs 136

Q

Q The Sports Club 383
Quality Inn 58

R

Radio 538
Radisson Hotel & Suites on Town Lake 49
Rainbow Cattle Co. 147
Rainey Street National Register District 248
Ralph Lauren 191
Ram Bookstore 346
Ramada Inn 61
Range at the Barton House 421
Rattlesnake Sacking Championship 282
Reading is Fundamental of Austin 339
Real Antique Show 284
Real Estate 453
Reale's Pizza & Cafe 128
Reata 427
Reckless Kelly 167
Recreation 357, 374
Recreation Plantation 380
Recreational Kids' Camps 269
Redeemer Lutheran School 518
Reebok Factory Direct 193
Reed Arena 442
Regents School of Austin 515
REI 219
Reich, Christopher 338
Renaissance Austin Hotel 62
Renaissance Glass Company 201
Renaissance Market 200
Renaissance Women's Center Hospital 483
Renaissance-Austin 474
RentAWreck 39
Republic of Texas Chilympiad 296
Republic of Texas Museum 239, 257
Resale Shops 216, 217
Residence Inn by Marriott 440
Resistencia Book Store 345
Restaurant at Gruene Mansion Inn 435
Restaurants 85
Retama Park 417
Rethreads 217
Retirement Community and Apartment Guide 473
Reunion Arena 424
Reunion Tower 424
Rhythm House 101, 133
Rice University 440
Richard Moya 363
Richard Smith Realtors 468
Ridefinders 40
Ringside at Sullivan's 146
Ripley's Believe it or Not! 427
Ritz Lounge 142, 146, 149
River Oaks Lodge 450
River Place Golf Club 400
Riverboats 391
Rivercenter Mall 428
Riverfest 280
Riverside Drive Branch Library 350
Riverside Golf Course 400
Riverview RV Park 451
Roadways 36
Rob Roy 463
Robert Mueller Municipal Airport 34
Rock Climbing 386
Rod & Reel Grille 449
Rodeos 415
Rodeway Inn University 59
Rollerskating 386
Rollingwood 462
Romain, Trevor 339
Roman Catholic Diocese of Austin 548
Roman Catholicism 543
Romance Writers of America 355
Romano's Macaroni Grill 268
Romeo's 109
Ronald MacDonald House 482
Rooster Andrews 219
Rootin' Ridge 218
Roppolo's 101, 120, 123
Rosario's 429
Rosie's Tamale House 116
Rosie's Tamale House No. 2 120
Ross Dress for Less 193
Rossie, Cam 7
Rothko Chapel 439
Round Rock 465
Round Rock Caregivers 478
Round Rock Christian Academy 520
Round Rock City Pools 394
Round Rock Farmers Market 207
Round Rock Health Clinic 484
Round Rock Hospital 483
Round Rock Independent School District 508
Round Rock Leader 536
Round Rock Memorial Park 371
Round Rock Parks and Recreation Department 370, 374
Round Rock Public Library 354
Round Rock Roller Rink 386
Round Rock Senior Center 478
Round Rock Senior Nutrition 473
Round Top 436
Round Top Inn 437
Round Top Mercantile Company 437

Rowing 391
Roy Kizer Golf Course 398
Roy Lozano's Ballet Folklórico de Texas 320
Royal Doulton 193
Roy's Taxi 39
Rudy's Bar-B-Q 120
Rue's Antiques 195
Rugby 386
Runnin' Horns 414
Running 387, 415
RunTex 387
Russell Korman 216
Ruta Maya Coffee Company 141
Ruth's Chris 101

S

Saccone's Pizza 128
Sachar, Louis 339
Safari 287
Sahm, Doug 159, 167
Saigon Oriental Market 210
Sail Aweigh 392
Sailboat Racing 416
Sailing 391
Sak's Fifth Avenue 191
Salado 420
Salado Chamber of Commerce 421
Salado Christmas Stroll & Holiday Home Tour 421
Salado Mansion 421
Salinas Art Festival 287
Salt Lick 113
Salvage Vanguard Theater 313
Sam Coronado Microgallery 326
Sam Hill Waterfront Grill 116, 184
Sam's Bar-B-Cue 126
San Antonio 427
San Antonio Children's Museum 429
San Antonio Missions 429
San Antonio Missions Historical Park 431
San Antonio Museum of Art 428
San Antonio National Missions Park 430
San Antonio River Walk 427
San Antonio Spurs 407, 428
San Antonio Visitors Center 429
San Antonio Zoo 429
San Fernando Cathedral 432
San Francisco de la Espada 432
San Juan Capistrano 432
San Marcos Factory Shops 193
Sands Motel 52
Sandy Creek 363
Sandyland Resort 450
Santa Rita 26
Santa Rita Oil Rig 235
Saradora's Coffeehouse & Emporium 141, 212
Satay 123
Saxon Pub 181
Scarbrough's 202
Schlitterbahn 433
Schlitterbahn Waterpark Resort 260
Schlotzsky's Marketplace 109
Scholz Garten 102, 146, 227
Schools 501
Science Place 423
Scott & White Clinic in Round Rock 482
Scott, Bess Whitehead 331
Scott-Wynne Outfitters 202
Scuba Diving 392
Sea Dragon 123
Sea World Adventure Park 261, 429
Searight Metropolitan Park 368
Sears 191, 192
Selma Hughes Park 363
Sematech 12
Senior Resources 472
Senior Scene 471
Senior Strategist Group 476
Senior Support Services 478
Serrano's Cafe & Cantina 102, 111, 113, 123, 127, 128
Serrano's Westlake Mesquite Grill 116
Seton East Community Health Center 484
Seton League House 483
Seton Medical Center 482
Seton Northwest Hospital 483
Seton Physician Referral 482
Seton South Community Health Center 484
Seton/Crenshaw Fitness Center 392
Sexton, Charlie and Will 168
Sgraffito Studio 266
Shadow Lawn National Register District 248
Shady Grove 110
Shady Grove RV Park 380
Shady Hollow 460
Shaffer Bend Primitive Area 362
Shakespeare at Winedale 292
Shanghai Red 440
Sharir/Bustamante danceworks 316
Sharper Image 192
Shepherd Mountain 463
Sheplers 205
Shoal Creek Hike and Bike Trail 369
Shoal Creek Hospital 483
Shoal Creek Saloon and Sports Parlor 136
Shopping 189
Shopping Districts 189
Shoreline Grill 102
Showplace Lanes 378
Shrake, Edwin "Bud" 339
Shree Raseshwari Radaha Rani Temple 545
Signature Flight Support 36
Silk Road 200
Silver Creek Lodge 449
Silver Dollar Dance Hall 144
Simply Divine 203
Sister 7 161, 168
Sisters in Crime 354
Six Flags AstroWorld 439
Six Flags Fiesta Texas 265, 429
Six Flags Hurricane Harbor 425
Six Flags Over Texas 425
Six Flags WaterWorld 439
Sixteen Deluxe 161, 167
Sixth Floor Museum 423
Sixth Street 182
Sixth Street Bars 133
Sixth Street National Register District 248
Skateworld 386

Ski Shores Waterfront Cafe 184
Skyride Balloons 384
Slaughter Creek Metropolitan Park 263, 369, 381
Slaughter Leftwich Vineyards 96
Smith & Hawken 192
Smith & Hawken Garden 213
Smith, Darden 168
Soccer 406
Soccer Academy 276
Soccer leagues 380
Soccer World 380
Softball leagues 380
Sony 193
Sopha Limos 40
Sophienburg Museum 434
Sound Exchange 187
Source Menagerie 215
South Austin Caregivers 478
South Austin Farmers Market 207
South Austin Hospital 483
South Austin Senior Activity Center 477
South by Southwest 285
South by Southwest Alternative Film Festival 310
South Park Meadows 181
Southard-House 74
Southeast Austin Caregivers 478
Southeast Austin Community Branch Library 350
Southland Oaks 460
Southwest Brewing News 140
Southwest Oaks 460
Southwest Texas State University 494
Southwest Texas State University Collection 353
Southwestern Exposition and Livestock Show 426
Southwestern University 496
Southwestern Writers Collection 353
Space Center Houston 440
Spamarama 283
Spanish Governor's Palace 432
Speakeasy 146, 181
Spectator Sports 405
Speed Running Day Camp 276
Spencer, William Browning 339
Spiazzo 120
Spicewood Country School Camp 270
Spicewood Course 401
Spicewood Springs Branch Library 350
Spider House 141
Splash! into the Edwards Aquifer 258
Splashtown 429
SplashTown Waterpark 439
Splish-Splash Summer Camp 270
Sports Bars 135
Sports Camps 274
Spring Festival and Texas Craft Exhibition 281
Spring Fling 284
Spring Herb Festival 284
Sri Atmananda Memorial School 512
St. Andrew's Episcopal School 511
St. Austin's School 512
St. Charles 215
St. David's Episcopal Church 544
St. David's Health and Fitness Center 383
St. David's Medical Center 482
St. Edward's 23
St. Edward's University 239, 495
St. Ignatius Martyr Catholic School 512
St. Louis School 514
St. Mary's Cathedral 544
St. Stephen's Episcopal School 516
St. Theresa's School 516
Stagecoach Inn 420
Stanberry & Associates Realtors 469
Star Bar 133
Star Gazing 259
Star Shuttle & Charter 251
State Archives and Library Building 225
State Parks 357
Steamboat 183
Stephen F. Austin Hotel 49
Sterling, Bruce 339
Steves Homestead 428
Stevie Ray Vaughan Memorial 238
Stockyards Collection and Museum 426
Stockyards National Historic District 426
Storyville 168
Strickland School 515
Stubb's Bar-B-Q 102, 181
Sublett, Jesse 339
Sue Patrick 201
Sue's Book Exchange 348
Sullivan's 103
Summer Concert Series 289
Summer Concerts 184
Summerfest 291
Summit at Westlake Hills 475
Sun Harvest Farms 192
Sundance Balloon Adventures 384
Sundance Square 427
Sunrise Celebrations 384
Sunset Valley 460
Sunset Valley Marketfair 192
Super 8 Motel 60
Super Cyclist Program 41
Support Services 476, 485
Suzi's China Grill 123
Suzi's Chinese Kitchen 110
Swedish Hill National Register District 249
Sweet Peach Festival 289
Sweetish Hill Bakery 103, 209
Swimming 392
Swimming Holes 394
Swimming Lessons 392
SXSW 285
SXSW Film Festival 285
SXSW Interactive Festival 285
Symphony Square 227

T

T-ball 380
T.G.I. Friday's 268
Table Rock Amphitheater 421
Taj Palace 123
Talbots 191
Talento Bilingue de Houston 439

Tanger Factory Outlet Center 193
Tangerine's 146
Tapestry Dance Company 317
Tarantula Steam Train 426
Tarlton Law Library 353
Tarrytown 461
Tarrytown Gallery 328
Taste of Hungary 127
Taxis 39
Taylor International Barbeque Cookoff and Rodeo 294
Taylor Jaycees National Rattlesnake Sacking Champi 282
Teatro Humanidad Cansada 314
Technophilia 187
Teddy Bear Picnic 295
Ted's Greek Corner 103
Tejano Ranch 146
Telephone Reassurance Program 479
Television 536
Tennis 387
Terra Toys 218
Terrazas Branch Library 350
Tesoros Trading Co. 195
Texan Restaurant 442
Texas A&M University 441
Texas Academy of Excellence 509
Texas Attorney General 473
Texas Bicycle Coalition 41
Texas Book Festival 299
Texas Chili Parlor 103
Texas Chiropractic Association 482
Texas Clothier 202
Texas Conference of Churches 548
Texas Craft Exhibition 281
Texas Cuisine 94
Texas Department of Human Services (TDHS) 473
Texas Department of Insurance (TDI) 474
Texas Department of Protective and Regulatory Services 506
Texas Department on Aging 473
Texas District Lutheran Church-Missouri Synod 548
Texas Elderhostel 477
Texas Folklife Festival 294
Texas Folklife Resources 320
Texas French Bread 103, 110, 116, 121, 208
Texas Hatters 204
Texas Highways 530
Texas Hill Country Wine & Food Festival 286
Texas Institute of Letters 355
Texas Instruments 12
Texas Land Office Building 21
Texas Memorial Museum 235
Texas Monthly 530
Texas Mountain Guides 386
Texas Music Office 163
Texas Oaks 460
Texas Observer 27, 531
Texas Parks & Wildlife 531
Texas Parks & Wildlife Department 358, 382, 389
Texas Psychological Association 482
Texas Rangers 412, 424
Texas Relays 282
Texas Sailing Academy 392
Texas School Book Depository 424
Texas Sports Palace 136
Texas State Capitol 23, 227, 259
Texas State Cemetery 242
Texas State Fair 422
Texas State Travel Guide 532
Texas Summer Music Academy 273
Texas Tornados 169
Texas Triangle 528
Texas Volleyball Camp 277
Texas Wildlife Exposition 297
Texas Workforce Commission 479
Thai Passion 104
The Heritage Haus 437
The University of Texas 251
Theater 304
Theater Week 288
Thirty-Three Degrees 187
Thompson, Ben 24
Threadgill, Kenneth 157
Threadgill's Restaurant 124
Threadgill's World Headquarters Restaurant 110
Three-Eleven Club 183
Thunder Hill Raceway 414
Tien Hong 124
Tinhorn Traders 195
Tish Hinojosa 164
Tivoli Systems 14
TJ Maxx 193
Toad Hall 344
Tocai of Austin 104
Today's Family Guide 474
Today's Family Guide to Austin 522
Tom Hughes Park 363
Tommy Hilfiger 193
Tom's Dive & Scuba 392
Top Drawer Thrift 217
Top of the Marc 147, 182
Tote-N-Tip 39
Touché 135
Touring 250
Tower Records 187
Tower, The UT 236
Town Lake Metropolitan Park 369
Toy Joy 218
Toys Stores 218
Track and Field Camp 277
Train Stations 36
Travelfest 219, 344, 348
Travis County Audubon Society 377
Travis County Farmers Market 207
Travis County Livestock Show 281
Travis County Medical Society 482
Travis County Parks 362, 389
Travis County Parks Department 373
Travis County Parks Visitor Information and Reserv 362
Travis County Preserves 373
Travis Heights 459
Treaty Oak 237
Treaty of Guadalupe Hidalgo 20
Tres Amigos 104, 111, 117, 124

Trianon Coffee Roasters 211
Trolley service 40
Tropical Hideaway Beach Resort and Marina 450
Tropical Tantrum 202
Tubing 261
Turkey Bend (East) Primitive Area 362
Turntable 505 187
Turquoise Door 216
Turquoise Trading Post 195
Twelfth Street Books 344
Twin Oaks Branch Library 350

U

Ugly Americans 170
Umlauf Sculpture Garden & Museum 238, 260
Umlauf Sculptures 236
Uncommon Objects 198
Undergraduate Library 351
United Artists Starport 192
United Confederate Veterans Reunion 292
United Methodist Church 548
University Co-op 214
University Co-op Bookstore 344
University Cyclery 377
University Hills Branch Library 350
University of Texas 228
University of Texas at Austin 490
University of Texas Continuing Education 477
University of Texas Libraries 350
University of Texas Performing Arts Center 306
University of Texas Press Book Sale 288
University of Texas Recreational Sports 386
University of Texas Recreational Sports Outdoor Program 375
University of Texas Sports 412
Upper Crust Bakery 104, 209
UT Sports Camps 275
UT Step Camp 268
UTkidz and UTteenz 269
UTteenz 269

V

Vanishing Texas River Cruise 377, 448
Vaughan, Jimmie 170
Vaughan, Stevie Ray 160, 174
Velveeta Room 143
Vereins Kirche Museum 444
Veterinarians 484
Victoria's Secret 191
Village at Western Oaks 461
Village at Westlake 193
Village Cinema Art 149
Villager Newspaper 534
Vineyard Court Executive Suites 442
Vineyards 95
Vintage Clothing 217
Vintage House Trattoria 442
Vintage Villas 83
Vireo Preserve 373
Visual Arts 320
Volente Beach 388, 395
Volkssporting 384
Volleyball 388
Volunteer Opportunities 479
Vulcan Gas Company 158

W

Waldenbooks 348
Waldenkids 348
Walker, Jerry Jeff 159
Walker, Mary Willis 339
Walking 41, 387
Waller Creek Greenbelt 369
Waller, Edwin 20
Walser, Don 170
Warehouse Saloon & Billiards 136
Warner Bros. Studio Store 192
Wasserman Public Affairs Library 352
Water-Skiing 395
Waterford 193
Waterloo 20
Waterloo Brewing Company & American Grill 138
Waterloo Ice House 104, 124
Waterloo Ice House at The Backyard 117
Waterloo Park 369
Waterloo Records 187
Watersports 389
Webb, Walter Prescott 331
Webberville 363
Wedgwood 193
Weekend Getaways 419
Wellness 481
Wells Branch 464
Wells Branch Greenbelt 381
Wells Branch Pool 394
West Austin Caregivers 478
West Austin News 535
West End Jazz & Arts Festival 291
West Lake Hills 462
West Lynn Cafe 104
West Rim 463
Westcave Preserve 374
Westcreek 461
Western Days 293
Western Wear 204
Westgate Lanes 378
Westin Galleria Hotel 440
Westlake Farmers Market 207
Westlake Picayune 535
Westminister Manor Retirement Community 475
Westside Alley 133
Wheatsville Food Co-op 209
Whit Hanks Antiques and Decorative Arts 194
Whit Hanks Consignment Shop 195
White, James 157
Whitman, Charles 27
Whole Earth Provision Co. 219
Whole Foods Farmers Market 206, 207
Whole Foods Market 192, 209
Wild About Music 215, 329
Wild Basin Wilderness Preserve 263, 374
Wild Child 203

Wild Child Too 203
Wildflower Center 240
Wildflower Day in the Spring 284
Wildflower Inn 69
Wildflowers Days Festival 287
Will Hampton Branch Library at Oak Hill 350
Will Rogers Memorial Center 426
Williams-Sonoma 211
Williamson County and Cities Health Care District 484
Williamson County and Cities Health District Clini 484
Williamson-Burnet County Opportunities Inc. 478
Willie Nelson 174
Willie Nelson's July Fourth Picnic 294
Willis, Kelly 170
Willow-Spence Streets National Register District 249
Wimberley Market Days 200
Windmill Run 364
Windsor Village Branch Library 350
Windsurfing 395
Winedale 436
Winik, Marion 339
Witte Museum of History and Science 428
WNBA Basketball 408
Wolf Pen Creek Amphitheater 442
Wolfgang Suhnholz Soccer Academy 275
Wolfgang's Kellar 434
Women & Their Work 326
Wonder World Park 260
Woodburn House 75
Woolridge, Alexander Penn 23
World Gym 383
World Wind Kite Shop 218
Worship 543
Wright, Lawrence 340
Writer Profiles 333
Writers' Organizations 354
Wurstfest 435
Wylie's Bar & Grill 135

Y

Yard Dog Folk Art 329
Yellow Bike Program 41
Yesterfest and the Salinas Art Festival 287
YMCA 375, 383, 392
YMCA Southwest 386
YMCA Summer Camps 270
Yule Fest 299

Z

Zachary Scott Theatre 273
Zachary Scott Theatre Center 312
Zilker Botanical Gardens 238, 370
Zilker Garden Festival 288
Zilker Hillside Theater 185, 307
Zilker Kite Festival 282
Zilker Nature Preserve 373
Zilker Park 263, 370, 381, 459
Zilker Park Canoe Rentals 391
Zilker Park Christmas Tree 301
Zilker Park National Register District 249
Zilker Park Trail of Lights and Christmas Tree 267
Zilker Summer Musical 292
Ziller House 79
Zoot American Bistro & Wine Bar 117
Z'Tejas Grill 105, 121

Going Somewhere?

Insiders' Publishing presents these current and upcoming titles to popular destinations all over the country — and we're planning on adding many more. To order a title, go to your local bookstore or call (800) 582-2665 and we'll direct you to one.

Adirondacks

Atlanta, GA

Baltimore, MD

Bend, OR

Bermuda

Boca Raton and the Palm Beaches, FL

Boise, ID

Boulder, CO, and Rocky Mountain National Park

Bradenton/Sarasota, FL

Branson, MO, and the Ozark Mountains

California's Wine Country

Cape Cod, Nantucket and Martha's Vineyard, MA

Charleston, SC

Cincinnati, OH

Civil War Sites in the Eastern Theater

Civil War Sites in the Southern Theater

Colorado's Mountains

Denver, CO

Florida Keys and Key West

Florida's Great Northwest

Golf in the Carolinas

Indianapolis, IN

The Lake Superior Region

Las Vegas, NV

Lexington, KY

Louisville, KY

Madison, WI

Maine's Mid-Coast

Maine's Southern Coast

Michigan's Traverse Bay Region

Minneapolis/St. Paul, MN

Mississippi

Monterey Peninsula

Myrtle Beach, SC

Nashville, TN

New Hampshire

New Orleans, LA

North Carolina's Central Coast and New Bern

North Carolina's Mountains

Outer Banks of North Carolina

Phoenix, AZ

The Pocono Mountains

Relocation

Richmond, VA

Salt Lake City, UT

San Diego, CA

Santa Barbara, CA

Santa Fe, NM

Savannah, GA

Southwestern Utah

Tampa/St. Petersburg, FL

Texas Coastal Bend

Tucson, AZ

Virginia's Blue Ridge

Virginia's Chesapeake Bay

Washington, D.C.

Wichita, KS

Williamsburg, VA

Wilmington, NC

Yellowstone

Insiders' Publishing • P.O. Box 2057 • Manteo, NC 27954
Phone (252) 473-6100 • Fax (252) 473-5869 • *www.insiders.com*

arehouse

Bet 5th + 7th St
1/4 mile E of I 35

Goodwill

Boudro's - San Antonio
Restaurant
on Riverwalk